WILLIAM
CARLOS
WILLIAMS
A New World Naked

WILLIAM
CARLOS
WILLIAMS

Paul Mariani

A New ~ World Naked

W. W. NORTON & COMPANY
New York • *London*

Grateful acknowledgment is made to New Directions
Publishing Company for permission to use excerpts from *White
Mule*, 1937; *Life Along the Passaic River, The Complete
Collected Poems*, 1938; *In the Money*, 1940; *The Broken Span*,
1941; *The Wedge*, 1944; *Paterson 1*, 1946; *Paterson 2, A Dream of
Love*, 1948; *Selected Poems, Paterson 3*, 1949; *Collected Later
Poems, Make Light of It, Collected Short Stories*, 1950; *Paterson 4,
Autobiography, Collected Earlier Poems*, 1951; *The Build-Up*,
1952; *The Desert Music, Selected Essays*, 1954; *Journey to Love*,
1955; *Paterson 5, In the American Grain, I Wanted to Write a
Poem*, 1958; *Many Loves, The Farmers' Daughters*, 1961; *Pictures
from Brueghel*, 1962; *Imaginations*, 1970; *The Embodiment of
Knowledge*, 1974; *A Recognizable Image: William Carlos
Williams on Art and Artists*, 1978.

The material on the following works has been published earlier
in substantially different versions: on *Man Orchid* in
Massachusetts Review, 1973; on *Paterson* in *Denver Quarterly*,
1978; on "Asphodel" in *Contemporary Literature*, 1973.

LIBRARY OF CONGRESS CATALOGING IN PUBLICATION DATA

Mariani, Paul L.
William Carlos Williams : a new world naked.
1. Williams, William Carlos, 1883-1963—Biography.
2. Poets, American—20th century—Biography. I. Title.
PS3545.I544Z626   811'.52 [B]   81-3773

ISBN 0-393-30672-0   AACR2

W. W. Norton & Company, Inc.
500 Fifth Avenue, New York, N.Y. 10110

W. W. Norton & Company, Ltd.
37 Great Russell Street, London WC1B 3NU

1 2 3 4 5 6 7 8 9 0

For Eileen:

the feminine principle,
the radiant gist. Without you
it would all turn back to dust again.

Contents

Preface

Sixteen years ago I walked into a small bookshop near Queens College in New York and spotted a paperback called *Paterson*. Paterson? Hell, I knew Paterson. My mother's family had come from that area of New Jersey: Lodi, Clifton, Passaic. And her cousin and her husband—Minxie and Turk Lacerza—had lived in a ramshackle but clean two-story home three blocks away from the falls. I could remember as a kid back in the late 1940s scrambling under the rusting barrier fence with my younger brother and making my way over the beer cans and garbage to the edge of the falls to stare down trembling at the furious waters boiling below me. I remember hurling cans and rocks over the edge and watching them disappear. Paterson. Who would want to write a poem—and a book-length poem at that—about a sinkhole like Paterson?

When I finally "discovered" Williams I had already been shaped by the universities in the New Criticism. T. S. Eliot's *Waste Land* and James Joyce's *Ulysses* were the key texts to understanding the modern temper. Had not critic after critic in this country said as much? For radical experimentation I had turned to the early Robert Lowell of *Quaker Graveyard in Nantucket*, but for the most part it was the English classics and the time-honored four-hundred-year-old tradition: the Jacobean playwrights, Burke, Gibbon, Keats, Coleridge, Carlyle, Tennyson, Hopkins. Like Lowell twenty years earlier, I tried to pull up to the gas station with a model of poetry looking like a triple-masted schooner sporting gingerbread outriders. In short, I had been a painfully slow learner.

It was really only when I began teaching modern poetry at the University of Massachusetts with my fresh Ph.D. in the fall of '68 that I finally realized what I had been missing in not paying more attention to William Carlos Williams, who by that point had already been dead a full five years. What Williams did for me was to make me seriously reexamine for the first time all of my "classical" assumptions about literature and the Great Tradition. I argued with Williams, fought with him, wrestled, despaired. And in a remarkably short time he became the single most important American poet of the twentieth century for me, with Stevens right behind him. In the early 1970s I spent three years writing what I then saw was a necessary "homework" book: a book-length commentary on everything I could lay my hands on that had been published on Williams up to that point, in an attempt to determine why the critics had for so long either dismissed or tried actually to destroy Williams' poetic reputation. But this man, I soon learned, was tough enough and his poetry so intrinsically good that it would necessarily surface in its own good time. I therefore had the good fortune to witness—and record—not only Williams' acceptance by a wider and wider readership but the rise as well of a truly central poetic presence, more central, finally, than Eliot and Pound and perhaps even Frost. And yet that uphill solo fight of Williams' had not been, even in his lifetime, without its profoundly disturbing costs, including the man's own physical health.

I had thought next to write the biography of the very poem that had by then become an obsession with me: *Paterson.* I wanted to determine its origins, its influences, its development and open-ended processive direction. But as I worked with that poem over several years, I realized that what I was really after was the inner life of Williams himself. Finally, tentatively, my teeth shaking, I realized that what I'd wanted to do from the beginning was to discover the real biography of this extraordinary revolutionary. No day has passed since 1970 that I have not thought about Williams; his life and his achievement have become—as my friends and family will amply testify—an obsession which, hopefully now, I can lay somewhat to rest, having blooded Williams' life with so much of my own.

Mike Weaver in 1971 and Reed Whittemore in 1975 preceded me in attempting to portray something of Williams' life, and I acknowledge with gratitude their prior work here. But even after they had done their work there was still so much that remained to be said, as I think the sheer size of this study will suggest. Williams' life was so much richer and more human than Weaver had depicted and so much more complex than Whittemore had suspected that I knew I would hardly be going over the same ground as they had, each in his own distinctive way. At every turn in the compiling of data for this biography new information kept turning up, revealing new thresholds, new anatomies. From a thousand thousand scattered pieces—conversations, interviews, manuscripts, letters, new readings—a life, a recognizable life, began to take on its idiosyncratic and distinctive coloring. Williams the man began, finally, to walk for me across the pages of my text, revealing himself—as draft gave way to draft—in all his complex tragedy and brilliance.

I have tried to keep in mind many kinds of readers in writing this biography. I want not only the reader particularly interested in Williams himself or more generally in American poetry or American cultural history, but the general reader who might want to see how an American from a small town in New Jersey undertook what his son, William Eric Williams, has so aptly called his father's "colossal, uphill solo battle" to remake American poetry for a wider audience. The proof that Williams won that battle is evident in the central place his poems enjoy today, eighteen years after his death, and in the thousands of young and old poets who know that their poems were significantly shaped by this genial master of the colloquial who preceded them. With Whitman and Stevens he seems to have come to form the familiar literary terrain we call American Poetry in our own time.

21 June 1981
Montague, Massachusetts

Chronology: Life and Works of William Carlos Williams

1883	17 September (Constitution Day). Born in Rutherford, New Jersey. Oldest son of William George and Raquel Hélène Rose Hoheb Williams.
1897–1899	Spends year at Château de Lancy outside Geneva with brother Ed, then to Paris for several months, returning in spring of '99.
1899–1902	Attends Horace Mann School in New York City with brother Ed. Graduates with mediocre record after three years.
1902–1906	School of Dentistry, then switch to School of Medicine at University of Pennsylvania. Meets Pound, H.D., and Charles Demuth.
1906–1908	Interns at the French Hospital, New York City. Meets Viola Baxter.
1908–1909	Interns at Child's Hospital. Resigns on principle.
1909	*Poems* published in Rutherford by Reid Howell, journeyman. Proposes to Florence Herman in July.
1909–1910	Studies pediatrics in Leipzig, September to February. Travels to Netherlands, England, France, Italy, and Spain. Sees Pound and Yeats in London in March.
1910	September. Begins medical practice in Rutherford. Appointed school physician for Rutherford public schools.
1912	December 12. Marries Florence Herman.
1913	*The Tempers* published in London by Pound's publisher, Elkin Mathews. Armory Show. Bill and Floss move to 9 Ridge Road in November.
1914	January 7. Birth of first child, William Eric Williams.
1915–1916	Literary meetings with *Others* group at Grantwood, New Jersey, and New York. Williams meets Alfred Kreymborg, Marianne Moore, Wallace Stevens, Marcel Duchamp, Maxwell Bodenheim.

1916   September 13. Birth of second child, Paul Herman Williams.

1917   *Al Que Quiere!* published in Boston.

1918   December 25. Death of father, William George Williams.

1920   *Kora in Hell: Improvisations* published in Boston. Edits *Contact* 1 with Robert McAlmon. Death of grandmother, Emily Dickinson Wellcome.

1923   *Spring and All* and *The Great American Novel* published in Paris. Summer: Williams begins his sabbatical year. Writes much of *In the American Grain.*

1924   January–June: Bill and Floss in Europe. France, Italy, Austria, Switzerland, and back to Paris. Meets James Joyce, Brancusi, Kassák, and sees Pound. "Rome" improvisation.

1925   *In the American Grain* published, New York.

1926   *Dial* Award for "Paterson" poem. Lawsuit brought against Williams for naming names in short story published in *New Masses.* Out-of-court settlement costs him $5,000.

1927–1928   Floss with William Eric and Paul in Europe. *Voyage to Pagany* and *The Descent of Winter* published. Williams sees Gertrude Stein in Paris in September 1927. Meets Louis Zukofsky in March 1928.

1929   December. Williams sees Hart Crane. Death of Harry Crosby.

1930–1932   Edits *Pagany* with Richard Johns.

1931   February: Zukofsky's Objectivist number of *Poetry,* featuring Williams. August: Bill and Floss take trip down the St. Lawrence to Newfoundland.

1932   *The Knife of the Times* published. Williams edits *Contact* 2 with Nathanael West. Fails after three issues. Death of Hart Crane.

1934   *Collected Poems, 1921–1931* published by Zukofsky's To Publishers in January.

1936   *The First President.* Aborted collaboration with Tibor Serly and Zukofsky. *Adam & Eve & the City.* Cummington Press.

1937   *White Mule* published by James Laughlin. New Directions collaboration begins.

1938   *Life Along the Passaic River* and *The Complete Collected Poems.*

1939   Ford Madox Ford and Les Amis des William Carlos Williams. Pound in the U.S. to talk sense into FDR. Sees Williams.

1940   *In the Money.*

1941   *The Broken Span.* April: Visits Puerto Rico.

1942   Meets Marcia Nardi and David Lyle.

1944   *The Wedge.*

1945   *First Act.*

1946   *Paterson* 1 finally published. *Man Orchid* fragment. LL.D. from University of Buffalo. Two operations for hernia.

1947   July. Salt Lake City Conference. Meets Allen Tate.

1948   February: Heart attack. *Paterson* 2. *A Dream of Love. The Clouds, Aigeltinger, Russia,* and Russell Loines Award. Meets T. S. Eliot.

1949   *Selected Poems. Paterson* 3. *The Pink Church.* Death of mother, Hélène Williams.

1950   *Collected Later Poems* (1940–1950). *Make Light of It: Collected Short Stories.* Yaddo. West Coast trip. Wins National Book Award. Contract with Random House.

1951   March: First stroke. Publishes *Paterson* 4, *Autobiography,* and *Collected Earlier Poems.*

1952   *The Build-Up.* Serious stroke in August. Difficulties with Library of Congress over appointment as Consultant in Poetry.

1953   February–April. Williams hospitalized for severe depression. Forced to relinquish Library of Congress appointment. Shares Bollingen Award with Archibald MacLeish.

1954   *The Desert Music. Selected Essays.*

1955   *Journey to Love.* Reading tour across country.

1957   *Selected Letters.*

1958   *Paterson* 5. *I Wanted to Write a Poem.* October: Third stroke.

1959   *Yes, Mrs. Williams.* Successful off-Broadway run of *Many Loves.*

1961   *The Farmers' Daughters. Many Loves.* November: Williams gives up trying to write following series of strokes.

1962   *Pictures from Brueghel.*

1963   March 4. Death in Rutherford. Pulitzer and Gold Medal for Poetry awarded posthumously.

WILLIAM
CARLOS
WILLIAMS
A New World Naked

ONE

The Beast in the Enchanted Forest: 1883—1902

December 31, 1950: an ending and a beginning. On this particular Sunday morning Williams had driven a friend over to see Paterson from the park road on Garrett Mountain overlooking the city. Just two months earlier he'd finally "finished" his long poem, *Paterson*, and already he'd plunged into another major undertaking: the long-deferred *Autobiography*. Now, coming up momentarily for a breath of fresh air, he'd taken John Husband, up from New Orleans for the holiday, out here to show him the place that for forty years had preoccupied his imagination. From the vantage of his sixty-seven years, Williams could look down from his mountain to survey the decayed, teeming, debased city that he had finally made—with great difficulty—to "flutter into life awhile."

In the back seat of the old Buick his eight-year-old grandson, Paul, was still fidgeting, along for the ride and keeping his eye on the speedometer, hoping to get his grandfather to open up and do eighty along the icy back roads as they drove down to the Great Falls. Annoyed, Williams glanced up into the rearview mirror to fix the boy. "Don't always wish for something dangerous," he warned him. "Some day you might get it when you don't want it." He might have been thinking, just then, of that other Paul, his wife's dead brother, sliding downhill and the loaded shotgun going off point-blank into his groin. Thirty-six years had crashed over the edge since that moment, when Williams had raced his Model-T Ford over the north Jersey roads to do whatever there was to do: console a disconsolate wife and a broken old man. Enough.

Above the Falls Williams parked the car and then the two men, with the boy already in the lead, began moving in a slight descent toward the brink. Icy spray had covered the dead brown edge of the gorge "with a curious formation" of "globes, as big as your head, or larger, of smooth ice, hundreds of them," and the whole isolated scene reminded Williams, appropriately enough, of "a field of hell-cabbages." Paul gave one of the globes a good kick to break it free but then, finding it too heavy to lift, half-demanded, half-pleaded with his grandfather to lift it for him and heave it from the bridge. Husband, unused to the terrain, stood a good ten feet back from the slippery edge of the gorge while the boy, clinging deliriously to his grandfather's topcoat, followed him out onto the middle of the narrow iron bridge. Williams steadied himself and then hurled his grandson's hell-cabbage, watching it rise slightly before it plunged inevitably "downward and disappeared, . . . followed almost at once by an explosive bang as it hit the ice below."

From near this spot a young woman, all words lost, had fallen—or leaped—to her death a century before. From here too in the 1820s a young daredevil had dived (successfully) into the Falls to retrieve a roller when an earlier bridge was being put across the gorge. And there, still dreaming, that hydrocephalic: the old man of the Falls, Williams' secret symbol for himself, a granite outcropping over which the river had crashed for a thousand years. Just how deep was the water, Paul wanted to know, offering him another hell-cabbage and staring bravely over the edge of the bridge. How deep "at the deepest place"?

So the descent could still beckon after all this time: the urge, the need, perhaps, to plunge into the depths and make contact. To make it—life, language—fresh once more. To see it all as it must have been before they'd fouled it, dumping garbage and even excrement into it. To see it, at least in the mind's eye, once more as once it must have been: a new world naked. How deep had it gone? At the deepest place?

*
* *

On the front porch his mother held his hand until he was ready to plunge into the white world he saw everywhere. She had bundled her four-year-old son against the late winter snow that had altered everything overnight, blanketing the steps, the walk, the streets with foot on foot of it. When he was ready, he stepped off into the white, only to find himself disappearing into it, and then he heard himself crying and his mother burrowing down after him to retrieve him. It was, he remembered, his first memory, and it would announce itself with time as the Great Blizzard of '88. But at the time it was a merging with an alien, formless, frozen world: a plunge . . . a short leap . . . and a retrieval.[1]

A new world naked. A new world of bright sunlight and shadows, later to be defined as Passaic Avenue, expanded by degrees to Rutherford. It was a world where he was a center, but a world constantly being washed over and crisscrossed by other presences and other sounds. A mother who spoke French first and then Spanish and—when necessary—a very broken English. A father with a dark beard who was away for long periods of time and silent when he was around, a father who spoke a precise Spanish and an English English. And his father's mother, his English grandmother, who had spent twenty-five years in San Tomas and Santo Domingo. And strange Uncle Godwin who used to stare at him and dapper Uncle Irving, his father's younger half brothers. Uncle Irving it was who used to hit the big drum, twice, BAM! BAM! and then, after a silence, little Billie would answer on his little toy drum: *bam bam.* Oh, the boy had an ear.[2]

*
* *

It was Uncle Godwin who taught him how to suck the insides out of eggs and told him he could catch sparrows by putting a handful of salt on their tails. And once he told Billie that if he put a horsehair into the watertrough and came back next morning the horsehair would be changed into an eel. So that when Billie did come back in the morning to look down into the brown water he did see little black worms squiggling in the golden light at the bottom of the trough. And once, at the Bagellon House, he watched his uncle dig a posthole and saw him crush a garden snake's head. But the tormented body kept lashing and wriggling back on itself, and Uncle Godwin told him that the snake couldn't die until the sun went down.[3] It was Uncle Godwin too who used to save up his nickels and dimes and then go off with his small hoard to the old Clifton racetrack and lose it all there to the sharpsters.

But there was another Godwin too, whose insanity cast a long shadow across the boy's enchanted garden. This Godwin would spy on Billie and little Ed from the bushes or from behind the barn. Like the time they were sitting at the well's edge dangling their bare feet in the water—against Mama's orders—and Godwin swept down on them like a hawk and carried them off, one in each powerful arm, to their mother to be punished. And as Bill got older, Godwin's shadow grew darker. One quiet summer's day when he was about twelve, he was playing in the cellar with his friend, Jim Hyslop, and he looked up to see Godwin's frame looming against the bulkhead, his face white and contorted with rage, those fevered eyes staring at Jim. Godwin was stammering something about what Jim Hyslop and his mother had been saying about him—how he was crazy and all that—and how he had a good mind to kill Jim for saying he was crazy. Now.

The tense, electric shock of it. Bill began to talk rapidly to Godwin, at the same time telling Jim to clear out of there, frozen as both of them were by this terrifying presence, and Godwin blocking the way and Bill beginning to feel that Godwin might, just might, do what he said he would. And then he was telling Godwin that he was going to tell Papa on him if he didn't let them pass. Suddenly Godwin was compressing in on himself, turning and leaving. It was the madness in the family showing itself to young Williams, the fear of which more than any other would shadow him all his life: the fear of ever losing conscious control over his own mind.[4]

It was only later, when Bill Williams was away at the University of

Pennsylvania, in the fall of 1902, that Godwin's psychopathic fears could no longer be covered up or simply dismissed. And—as it turned out—it was Bill's younger brother Edgar rather than Bill who had to take the brunt of the explosion. Godwin had taken an intense dislike to another woman, a Mrs. Dodd, a friend of Elena Williams' who had come up from St. Thomas and was staying with the Williamses at 131 Passaic Avenue. Godwin's anger smoldered, watching this woman watching him in turn, and finally he went after her. "I remember how he looked at Mrs. Dodd," Elena remembered thirty years after the event. "She didn't know it, but such a smile was on his face as he was leaning on the door as much as to say, wait a little bit. He wanted to kill her. He thought she was making the evil spirits come for him."[5] Then Godwin was hurling his weight against the front door, trying to get at her. And there was Ed, not yet eighteen, standing behind the door, shaking with fear and anger and confusion, warning his uncle not to come in, all the while holding a cocked pistol aimed at the place where Godwin kept slamming up against the door. When the local police came to take him away, Godwin—fear in his eyes—kept shouting at them not to touch him because he was after all, as his English mother had so often coached him, a "gentleman."

But for Godwin it was all over. Godwin, whose very name Williams wondered about all his life for the undisclosed dark mystery he believed it might contain. Godwin, ending up, finally, in the insane asylum over in Morris Plains where, in the period just before the Great War, he finally died. Godwin's name—and the mystery it contained—had been bequeathed to him by his enigmatic mother: Emily Dickinson Wellcome. And that mystery was tied up with the secret of Williams' father's paternity. Who was his father's father? Who was this English Williams who had married his English grandmother and had gotten her with child? Try as he might, Carlos Williams could never get his grandmother—that presence who moved through so many of his own primal scenes—to disclose the "mystery" of her past. "The past," she was fond of saying (and that saying haunted Williams till the end), "the past is for those who lived in the past. *Cessa.*"[6] Without sufficient grounding in history, that past became more and more mythologized until it centered on no less than the romantic poetic tradition and Percy Bysshe Shelley's circle of intimates, which had included Mary Wollstonecraft's daughter, the radical philosopher Godwin, and Edward and Jane Williams. It was Edward Williams who had drowned with Shelley off Leghorn in July 1822. He had been Shelley's confidant, a military figure, a retired army lieutenant of the East India Company, whose wife Shelley had addressed in some of his last love poems.

*
**

The pieces, however crazily they fit into the stained glass picture, seemed "there" to Williams. An Emily Dickinson (or Dickenson, orthography being a less exact science then) of Chichester, born when? In the early 1830s? Or could it have been earlier, as early as 1820? Early orphaned and thus brought up by the Godwins of London in wealthy surroundings and easy circumstances, until she was quietly disowned by the family for marrying this mysterious Williams, dark progenitor of the Williams name. And who was this Williams? By one account an Episcopalian minister. By another a common ironworker. In any event, Williams' father, William George Williams, was most certainly born of this mysterious union in 1851, having been conceived in London, though born in Birmingham.[7]

By the time William George was five, his father had "disappeared," and Emily Dickinson's wanderings, begun with the expulsion from the Eden of the Godwins, began again. Now, in 1856, she set out with her son to make her future in the New World, where she hoped to become an actress in New York City. With this journey, then, began the history of the Williamses in America. Presciently, that history began badly enough. Ocean storms drove the Williamses' ship down to the Azores and then back to New York before it finally ran adrift on a shoal off Fire Island on Long Island's southern coast. Williams' father was to remember little of that crossing, except for the fog and a prow looming out of that fog as in a dream and later the crowded hours spent at the Battery. And so, as the fates were to have it, a stranded Emily Dickinson and her son moved into a boardinghouse in Brooklyn, at a moment when Walt Whitman was living nearby and writing his poems.[8]

How long mother and son remained in Brooklyn Williams never learned, but there in that boardinghouse Emily met an itinerant photographer named George Wellcome who had come up from St. Thomas in the Danish West Indies to purchase photographic supplies.[9] Wellcome married Emily and then took his new wife and his stepson back down to St. Thomas, before finally settling in Puerto Plata, Santo Domingo. There Emily had three more children: poor Godwin, then Irving, and finally Rosita, who died early of epilepsy. In fact, when Emily herself finally died of a stroke—a brain hemorrhage—in the fall of 1920 (she was somewhere in her late eighties by then), all of her children had predeceased her. William George was to die on Christmas Day 1918, and Irving in 1919, just a year before her. When she died, therefore, Williams believed that any hope he had of ever learning her secret had finally and forever died with her.

When her photographer husband died in 1874, Emily realized that she would once again have to fend for herself, taking work wherever she could find it, including operating a horse and cab in St. Thomas. But she also made her oldest son aware of his responsibilities not only to her but to his half brothers. So, when William George, who had been a merchant in Puerto Plata, decided to marry and make his fortune in New York City, he arranged for his family to join him along with his wife-to-be. In the summer of 1882 he established himself in Brooklyn, and then sent for his fiancée, Rachel Elena Hoheb of Puerto Rico, and his mother and brothers. When William George and Elena were married on November 29 of that year by a minister at the home of Elena's cousins, the Monsantos, at 66 Hanson Place in Brooklyn, Irving and Godwin served as the official witnesses, as Emily Dickinson Wellcome watched.[10] And when, nine and a half months later, William Carlos Williams was born in Rutherford— one of the first commuter-stop towns for those who worked across the Hudson in New York City—it was Grandma Wellcome who took little "Willie" under her wing. She was about fifty when the boy was born, still full of vigor and independence, and it was she rather than her birdlike, aristocratic, displaced daughter-in-law (who still moped after Paris as Ulysses pined after Ithaka) who became by default the central mythic presence in Williams' young life. It was Emily who taught the boy English, since Elena could barely tolerate the language, learning it only slowly and imperfectly. It was French *she* wanted, French and a serviceable Spanish. Ruther-ford' should have been only a way station, though it proved to be, finally, Elena's permanent exile. From the beginning Emily insisted on taking Willie and then Edgar—born thirteen months after his brother—wherever she went. She would have become the boys' mother if she could have, but Elena—for all of her apparent aloofness—was having none of that. The point came finally when Elena's Latin temper flared up and she slapped her mother-in-law hard across the face to remind the woman of her proper place.

Still, Grandma Wellcome pampered William. He was her baby, so much so that he was still sucking a bottle at five and a half. Williams remembered taking the boat up from New York to New Haven in the summer of '89 and people staring in disbelief at him as he tried to hide behind his grandmother's skirt and drink his bottle in some kind of peace. But those stares cured him at once. He hurled the bottle onto the deck, smashing it, determined there and then never to have anything more to do with it.[11]

Once when he was still quite young he peeked through a keyhole as Grandma Wellcome spongebathed herself out of a porcelain washstand in her upstairs room at 131 West Passaic, and that vision fueled his imagination into making her, as he did, his primary image of the forbidden naked woman, and later his ever virgin Kore. To deepen the mystery surrounding her, Grandma was also a medium, something she—like Elena—had learned down in the islands. Williams recalled those spiritualist gatherings and séances held in his home as a child: strange, haunting, dim-lit experiences which left him and Ed disoriented and terrified. To protect himself from what those séances did to his mind, Williams came to approach such "hallucinations" as tricks of the overwrought or blocked imagination, leaving him guardedly amused and wary of all religionists, and indifferent or even hostile to most clergymen. But that was later. As a boy, he was quite simply terrified and troubled by what those meetings did to his family.[12]

He remembered one meeting in particular when Grandma Wellcome had wanted to contact her dead daughter, Rosita. There in the living room with the small group of believers, including Elena, Grandma Wellcome held her closed fist above her head clenching something and crying out that she wanted to communicate with the person represented by what she held there in her hand. Suddenly young Williams (who could not have been much more than seven or eight at the time) heard his mother groaning and turned to see her shaking her head violently, as though seized by a spirit of some kind. It went on for what seemed forever until some of the others present began praying steadily over her, asking the Lord to let the spirit force leave the woman. Finally Elena stopped shaking and returned to her more normal self. Apparently, as Williams reconstructed that scene years later, his grandmother had hidden a locket of Rosita's hair in her hand and had then called on the girl's spirit to speak through one of those present, the spirit obviously choosing Elena, who had known Rosita in Puerto Rico. Williams never forgot the sight of his mother shaking uncontrollably. He wanted nothing to do with whatever forces there were that could do that kind of thing to his mother.[13]

Later, when Williams' parents became founding members of the Unitarian church in Rutherford, Emily Wellcome herself became a Christian Scientist. As such, she would let no doctor treat her, not even her own grandson, Willie, when he later became one himself. At the end, nearly ninety and nearly blind, she had a disfiguring facial skin cancer which she refused to have treated. Then, at Thanksgiving 1920, she went up to West Haven for a turkey dinner and a visit with her grandson, Irving's boy, Bill Wellcome. That was at her small double cottage fronting an inlet on Long Island Sound at West Haven, when there were still few other houses around. It was there that she had the stroke that killed her. Bill Wellcome wired Bill Williams at once to come up and do what he could to help their grandmother, and Williams raced to get up there. There was of course little he could do, and he had one hell of a time just convincing the woman to let the ambulance take her to the hospital— Grace Hospital in New Haven—where she died a few days later.[14] In one of his strongest poetic understatements, written several years later, Williams recalled the ambulance ride and the way his grandmother kept

staring at the bare elms out there—"fuzzy things" she called them—
before she turned her back on them for the last time in defeat. In the end,
the life she had tried to master and keep somehow intact, simply
dissolved and slipped away:

> *Oh, oh, oh! she cried*
> *as the ambulance men lifted*
> *her to the stretcher—*
> *Is this what you call*
>
> *making me comfortable!*
> *By now her mind was clear—*
> *Oh you think you're smart*
> *you young people,*
>
> *she said, but I'll tell you*
> *you don't know anything.*
> *Then we started.*
> *On the way*
>
> *we passed a long row*
> *of elms. She looked at them*
> *awhile out of*
> *the ambulance window and said,*
>
> *What are all those*
> *fuzzy-looking things out there!*
> *Trees! Well, I'm tired*
> *of them and rolled her head away.*[15]

A resourceful woman, a woman "perfected" in the knowledge of the
world, a wanderer over the face of the earth, repeatedly disappointed and
defeated, a woman who had gone out on her own, swerving from the
Godwins in an irrevocable act of defiance and rebellion for love, she
became—long before her death—Williams' essential muse, identified
with nothing less than the deepest promptings of Williams' poetic
unconscious itself. In 1913, when Williams—at thirty—wrote "The
Wanderer," his early poem of poetic initiation, a journal of his first
successful crossing into the world of the imagination, he made his
grandmother one with the muse who would yank him from his early
Keatsian dream of spiritual release and plunge him roughly into the filthy
pollution-clogged waters of the Passaic to baptize him into the things of
this world. He saw himself in that poem dressed in the woolen shirt and
pale blue necktie his grandmother had once given him, being led down to
Santiago Grove on the Passaic to be immersed in the "river's crystal
beginnings and its black, shrunken present." There—in his mind's
eye—he watched as his earlier self drifted off to be lost forever, a dead,
slack corpse, floating in the element that would henceforth make up his
own fallen world.[16]

The figure of the romanticized grandmother: forever old in the grandson's memory, repeatedly made young again in the alembic of the imagination, a figure of sexual initiation, hag and beloved at once. Demeter and Persephone. Kore in a New World hell. Williams would see his big-mythed grandmother in many women throughout his life, reincarnated in the figure of the Baroness in the 1910s, in Marcia Nardi in the '40s, in his wife, in all those adventurous women pummeled unmercifully by circumstances who somehow managed to survive. Finally, at the end of his own life, Williams would identify his grandmother with no one less than the Virgin Mother herself, the figure of the woman resourceful enough not only to keep the paternity of her son a secret, but able to convince poor Joseph that her pregnancy had been the work of the Spirit. By then, thirty-five years after his grandmother's death, Williams had abandoned the myth of the circle of Shelley for the myth of an Ur-Williams who had been a dashing young English soldier who had probably died in the Crimean War. Thus he became a latter-day parallel to the unknown Roman soldier—in Williams' version of Christ's paternity (perhaps echoed from Hardy and D. H. Lawrence)—who had been the one to impregnate Mary:

> *an old woman to wear a china doorknob*
> *in her vagina to hold her womb up—but*
>
> *she came to that, resourceful, what?*
> *He was the first to turn her up*
>
> *and never left her till he left her*
> *with child, as any soldier would*
>
> *until the camp broke up.*[17]

*
* *

William George Williams was as secretive and private about himself as Emily Wellcome had been. (And in fact Emily had once made her son promise solemnly on her daughter's grave never to disclose to anyone who his father had been, which only piqued William Carlos' curiosity all the more.) Though William George had been taken from England at age five—never to return—he insisted quietly but firmly on remaining a British citizen all his life. He was a quiet man, given to long silences as well as long absences. He was in every respect a solid Victorian gentleman, interested in Wagnerian opera and Kipling, a man of the world who saw that his sons were well read in the classics and thought progressive thoughts and who gave them the best education he could afford, considering, of course, the circumstances of the boys' being brought up in the provinces. When, at age thirty-one, he settled with Elena in Rutherford, he became advertising manager for Lanman and Kemp, a New York City–based company that manufactured a popular cologne called Florida Water, much of it exported to markets in South America and the

Caribbean. For thirty-five years William George remained a faithful employee of the company, commuting each working day he was home on the Erie Railroad from Rutherford to the Jersey City terminal, then under the Hudson to his office in New York's bustling downtown district. For years Williams watched his father with duty-strung regularity (you could have set your watch by the man's habits) leave his home to walk the brisk half mile to the ornate Rutherford station to catch the 8:18.

But there were long periods when his father was simply not at home, when his business called him to take long trips (at least one of which lasted for over a year) to Central and South America, where he was responsible for setting up centers for the manufacturing and distribution of his Florida Water. One senses in Williams' own reminiscences the absence of his father, a vacuum that was naturally—and overwhelmingly —filled by the presence of grandmother and mother. Yet even when his father was at home, there remained the sense of a presence who was more the shadowy figure of the father than anything like a friend or confidant. William George seems to have been there for fatherly advice—when asked—and to direct his sons on the all-important question of their formal educations. Hardly flamboyant, he was a "curiously mild" individual as his son remembered him, a man who lost his temper with Willie only once, when he tried—unsuccessfully—to cram a tomato down the boy's throat.[18]

Williams remained ambivalent about his father until he found himself actually older than his father had been when he died. And then he seems to have somehow resolved whatever it was that was troubling him and moved on to other concerns. He was always deeply attracted to his father's strong sense of duty to family and to those one was supposed to serve, and there are hundreds who have attested to Williams' skill and kindness as a physician, whose sense of obligation to his patients superseded time and time again his own need to write. Like his father, Williams underplayed the element of personal sacrifice, and his real heroes were not the great egoists like Ezra Pound, but rather the nameless figures, the scientists who worked in the field, in the front trenches as it were, like those who finally discovered a cure for malaria by going down to the men working on the Panama Canal and living with the ever-present possibility of contamination in order to discover the source of the disease in the anopheles mosquito. Surely images of his father riding muleback alone across Costa Rica, eating patés of black ants when no other food was available, the double figure of pater familias and emissary of Florida Water, must have merged with Williams' other images of self-effacing, silent, duty-bound heroes. It was one reason Williams was so willing to underestimate his own contributions to the poem, preferring instead to work as part of a larger quasi-anonymous community of poets, all working—as he liked to think—to discover a new kind of poetry. And that communal vision, though it suffered repeatedly from the betrayals and self-interests of others, never did completely die.

William George's refusal ever to adopt the place where he had begotten and raised his sons—that "oedipus complex," as William Carlos himself called it,[19] between an English father and his American son—was to assume macrocosmic implications as the son gradually took on, as he saw it, no less than the entire received English tradition in the figure of T. S. Eliot and the English Departments of every major university both here and in England.

William George was also a late-Victorian socialist, at least in theory, and William Carlos could remember all sorts of forbidding tomes around the house dealing with economic and social theory. "He would have been a socialist if he had lived in England at this time," the son believed, instead of being a relatively successful capitalist and purveyor of cologne. And that interest in social amelioration too was to have a profound effect on Williams' own thinking, particularly from the '30s on. What finally brought socialist theory home to Williams was in fact the economic realities of the working class among whom he labored and who in turn kept Williams from ever becoming an even remotely well-to-do suburban doctor.

It was also left to the father to teach his sons not the language (that was learned from Grandma Wellcome) but rather the values of an English liberal tradition. Williams remembered how his father would read from Shakespeare—the favorite author of both father and son—for hours on those long winter evenings at home in those blessed preradio, pretelevision days. But William George also enjoyed reading Gilbert and Sullivan and the dialect poems of Paul Lawrence Dunbar, who was much in vogue at the turn of the century. Or—more daringly—he would read by kerosene lamp to Elena as she lay in bed more "adult" works like du Maurier's *Trilby*, thinking the boys were asleep in the next room. Young Williams listened of course avidly to the stories of Svengali the Jew and Trilby and Little Billee from his own bed, so delighted with the book that he christened his two pet mice Trilby and Little Billee.[20] There were other forbidden books as well in his father's study, books of anatomy revealing the inner secrets of women, and a book like Dante's *Inferno*, with Gustave Doré's engravings, which Williams pored over in secret, examining Doré's beautiful damned women, hoping to find out what delights lay beneath their splendid clothing. There was too Palgrave's *Golden Treasury of English Verse* to serve as a touchstone of what classical poetry should aspire to, the Ur-text resplendent with the English poetic tradition, where Williams first discovered the poet who would shape his early work so profoundly: Keats, especially the Keats of the *Endymion*.[21]

But for the more difficult books that any enlightened young gentleman should know—serious volumes like Darwin's *On the Origin of Species* and *The Descent of Man*, or Herbert Spencer's *Principles of Philosophy*— Williams senior offered his son a dollar for each he would suffer through. Williams took his father up on that offer and read those books one after the other, until they took root deep within. That liberal education was bolstered too by the "enlightened" minds Williams and his brother were introduced to in their Sunday school classes at the Unitarian church their parents had helped establish in Rutherford. Most of the members of the local Unitarian Society were in fact displaced New England Yankees, Williams remembered, and the stress in classes was less on spiritualism and more on the formation of a well-developed, self-reliant intellectual perspective toward matters spiritual. It was, essentially, the same tradition that seventy years earlier had helped to shape Ralph Waldo Emerson himself.[22]

William George Williams' first love, however (as his attention to Shakespeare would suggest), was theatrics. He became in effect the manager of the local Gilbert and Sullivan Society and went so far as to erect a stage for the performance of their light operas in his cellar, where he supervised productions of *The Mikado* and *H.M.S. Pinafore*, in both of which his sons performed. Amateur theatrics remained a part of Williams' own life up through the 1930s, and it should be no surprise that when William Carlos finally decided on the literary life for good halfway through his medical studies at the University of Pennsylvania, he thought first of becoming an actor and a dramatist before he opted for poetry.

Characteristically, it was important to young Williams that he please his father in his own literary pursuits, even as he unconsciously sought to separate himself out from his father. It was imperative, therefore, that if the boy was going to dabble in poetry, he at least follow the dictates of good taste. Poetry should as a result follow the canons of Victorian sublimity: a poem was to be moral, uplifting, worthy of the time spent in writing it. And it should be formally and grammatically impeccable. When Williams published his first volume of poems in 1909 at the age of twenty-five, William George went through the pamphlet page by page, correcting misspellings and typographical errors, until the pages were birdtracked.[23] As for the poems themselves, Williams had the nagging suspicion that—though they were acceptable for a polite society—they remained failures in the father's eyes.

Since the father was also an impeccable speaker and reader of Spanish, he collaborated with his son (shortly before his death) on a group of translations from the works of several South American writers, including Rafael Arévalo Martínez, José Santos Chocano, Juan Julian Lastra, Leopold Díaz, and José Asunción Silva. Significantly, Williams wrote to his publisher, Edmund Brown, at the time his third book of poems, *Al Que Quiere!*, was published in February 1918, that his father was "furious" at three typographical errors that had crept into the little Spanish piece he had included in the book.[24] By then he also understood that his father did not really care for the unfortunate direction his son's poems were taking: away from the sublimer poetic themes toward the tawdry and the mundane.

Not that William George ever seems to have said so, for by then Williams had learned to read his father's eloquent silences. He could be most entertaining as a storyteller, recalling for his sons' delectation long treks through tropical jungles and the earthquake and tidal wave that devastated St. Thomas in the early 1870s, leaving tall sailing ships high and stranded like so many toys. But that was talk, which was ordered and controlled. What Williams remembered most was the silence. Even when they were together, there were long stretches when only a few perfunctory words passed between them, and those dealing with practical matters. Even on their long walking tours—up the entire western shore of Lake George one summer, or all the way from Rutherford to their summer shack at West Haven on other occasions—walking was a matter of covering distance, as though they were duty-bound to do their thirty miles or more each day. Neither in his letters nor in his *Autobiography* has Williams recorded more than a few short conversations he had with his father. And even the poems written about his father are, in one sense, meditations on the tragic silences between the two.

"Adam," written eighteen years after his father's death, is Williams' attempt to rethink his father, to recover something of the man's uniqueness in a poem. But, for all its words, it is a poem haunted by silence. What fascinated Williams was the tension of opposites he saw both in himself and in his father: a silent northern figure who found himself growing up in the buzzing tropics of the Caribbean and who tried to distance himself from that world by the ordered harmonies of piano and flute until he managed to exile himself even from that earthly paradise to follow the insistent cicada's cry of duty. Roped in all his life by the idea of duty, surrounded by the carnival lushness of the tropics and the beautiful black and Latin women inviting him to dally a while with them, he went about his appointed round of tasks each day, moving inevitably toward his only end:

> *coldly*
> *and with patience—*
> *without a murmur, silently*
> *a desperate, unvarying silence*
> *to the unhurried last.*[25]

In a poem called "Death"—not the later, anthologized version, but an earlier version first published in 1930, before Williams reconsidered and generalized his father's portrait—the dead grotesque is none other than his father, defeated by death, gone beyond recall, beyond anyone's ability to ever touch him by love (or poetry) again:

> *Dead*
> *   his eyes*
> *rolled up out of*
> *the light—*
> *   calabashes—*
>
> *such as he used to bring*
> *home from South*
> *America when he would*
> *go there on business trips—*
> *in the years gone by. . . .* [26]

If Williams ever thought he could reach his father with his poems—his own language constructs—he knew by 1930 that death had forever crushed that hope.

So much did the shadow of his father's judgment on what he was doing disturb him that, for several nights after William George died, Williams himself had a dream of his father that seems to have both devastated and—paradoxically—freed him at last. In the dream he could see his father descending a flight of stairs, preoccupied as he had been in life with his duties. (Those stairs, Williams would later come to realize, were a composite both of the Judgment steps from which Pontius Pilate, in Tadema's painting, *Ecce Homo,* had summoned a condemned Christ to stand before an angry mob, and the broad steps that led down from his father's New York office.) "He was bare-headed and had some business letters in his hand on which he was concentrating as he descended," Williams remembered. "I noticed him and with joy cried out, 'Pop! So, you're *not* dead!' But he only looked up at me over his right shoulder and commented severely, 'You know all that poetry you're writing. Well, it's no good.'" It severed something, that dream, for it was the last time Williams ever remembered dreaming about his father. [27]

*
**

Elena outlasted her husband by another thirty years, the last eighteen of which she lived confined to her bed. From 1924 on, she lived with her older son, and it was only toward the end of her life that Williams could finally bring himself to approach the woman toward whom he felt both deep loyalty and bitter resentment. In the late 1920s he began in earnest to try to get down on paper something of the alien submarine world of the

West Indies which had created his mother like some late, hybrid tropical flower. Williams did not see those islands until the spring of 1941, when he himself was approaching sixty, and by then he had a deep longing to try to understand what his own roots really were. How long his mother's family had been in the islands he never found out. Three generations back, and all records, all memory, ceased. His mother had been christened Raquel Hélène Rose Hoheb in the Catholic cathedral in Mayagüez, Puerto Rico, on Christmas Eve, though she was careful never to confide the year to either of her sons. (It wasn't until 1956, on a visit to Mayagüez, that Williams finally learned the secret of her age.) Elena's mother was a Hurrard (or Jurrard) who had been raised in Martinique: Meline Hurrard, the youngest of three daughters. It was a Basque name, Hurrard, and the family had originally emigrated from Bordeaux. Most of the Hurrards settled in St. Pierre, where they ran a comfortable liqueur business. But when Mt. Pelée blew up in 1902, it wiped out all the New World Hurrards in one horrendous apocalyptic moment.[28]

In the mid-1830s Elena's mother married Solomon Hoheb, a successful merchant in Mayagüez. Hoheb's family ancestors had been Sephardic Jews with roots in Holland; Solomon's own father had died when he was still a boy and his mother had subsequently married an Enriquez, by whom she had a large family. Solomon and Meline in their turn also had a large family, though only the eldest—Carlos—and the youngest—Elena —survived infancy. Carlos, who was ten years older than his sister, always remained Elena's *beau idéal*. He was the only man, she would confide later to her son, who had really ever understood her. As a young girl, Elena had known a modicum of wealth. Her father owned a permanent home in Mayagüez and a summer residence as well. And she remembered her house always being filled with servants. It was also filled with music, for Solomon and Elena played the piano, and Carlos played the piano and flute extremely well. Elena also recalled how the women were always speaking of her father's dancing abilities, how he could dance long and hard and well. She also remembered—she was eight when he died—how he could always make people laugh with his jokes.

He seems to have been a refined and gentle person, a trusting soul, really, but when he died, his business associate, a German merchant named Krug, went to Elena's mother with a story that Solomon still owed him a great sum of money. Mrs. Hoheb did what she could to pay back what Krug said she owed him, even turning over her summer residence to him, and then, when Krug was sure there was no more to be gained, he simply walked out on the family. He had even tried to persuade Mrs. Hoheb to make her eighteen-year-old son return home from the University of Paris, where he was studying to become a physician, so that he might help repay the debts his father had supposedly incurred. But young

Carlos refused to return. Instead he wrote his mother that he would sooner sweep the streets of Paris than return to Puerto Rico without his diploma. When she saw how adamant her son was about staying in Paris, she supported his decision, though it personally cost her a great deal of trouble.

When Elena was sixteen, her mother also passed away, and then Carlos, who had begun practicing medicine in Santo Domingo, assumed full responsibility for his sister. Twelve years later he gave Elena the choice of going to America or to Paris to study art. The decision was simple. Europe was everything, the United States little more than a barbarous colony somewhere to the west of her. So from 1876 until the end of the decade Elena studied art at the School for Industrial Design (*L'Ecole des Arts Industrielles*) in Paris, living with her cousins Alice and Ludovic Monsanto in a small ninth-floor apartment in the rue Notre Dame des Champs. There were, of course, problems. To Elena, Alice seemed mean-spirited, and Ludovic soon began making passes at her. As for her art studies, Elena was out of the mainstream of French painting altogether. She was, after all, a poor woman from the islands, to whom the work of Cézanne, Van Gogh, and Gauguin meant absolutely nothing. Like Ludovic, who painted a portrait of her, she did do some very good academic work—especially portraits and landscapes—and managed to win medals for each of the three years she spent at the academy.[29]

All of that came to an abrupt end for her, however, when her brother—with his own growing family to take care of and economic difficulties to sort out, in part caused by a popular revolution in Santo Domingo from which he barely managed to escape with his life, let alone his property—was finally forced to call his sister home again. When Elena heard the news, she cried for three days, knowing that her cultural interlude was over. There was nothing for it, however, but to obey. She returned to Puerto Plata, and seems to have been considered a popular "catch," for she received an offer of marriage from a certain Frenchman, a de Longueville, which she rejected.[30] There was, however, another young man who lived in a house near the Hohebs who was a very close friend of her brother's. Elena did not meet this gentleman at once, for he was then in the United States having his teeth fixed, but Carlos assured his sister that the man was cultured, responsible, and though he was "no musician," could play the piano. This was William George Williams, who lived with and supported his mother, two half brothers, and a half sister. In the fall of 1881, Williams began courting Elena, visiting her every day for ten months. So enamored, so caught up was William George with this birdlike woman who knew music and art and spoke fluent French that he virtually lived with the Hohebs. Finally, Emily Wellcome, sensing how things stood, ordered the servants to carry her son's trunk over to the Hohebs for all the good it was doing in her home.

In November of 1882, William George and Elena were finally married in Brooklyn, and Elena soon found herself living in a suburban sprawl called Rutherford. It was all so strange to her, even the language, that she kept pretty much to herself or else had her friends come up from the islands to stay with her for extended visits. She had been loosely raised a Catholic in the Caribbean tradition, but she soon saw that there was little sympathy for that sort of thing in a predominantly Protestant community, and she quickly shed whatever vestiges of her childhood faith remained. In the privacy of her own home she practiced her island spiritualism and séances, though she later embraced Unitarianism with her husband. Spanish was the language she used at home, and of course she practiced her beloved French whenever she could find someone who could speak that "civilized" tongue. But for practical reasons it became necessary, living in New Jersey, to learn some English. Especially when her sons came along.

For thirty years there was a steady stream of visitors to the Williamses' home in Rutherford, relatives from Paris and a large number up by steamer from Puerto Rico, St. Thomas, and Puerto Plata who spoke Spanish. "I feel close to Spanish-speaking people," Williams wrote a friend in 1930, "simply because I have heard so much of the language at home and knew so many Spaniards among my parents' friends."[31] And though many of her friends were English, for most of them Spanish came as naturally to them as English. What Williams heard as a young man, then, was Spanish from the lips of the Hazels, the Lambs, the Dodds, and the Forbeses. And English from the Monsantos and Enriquezes of Brooklyn. It was a strange, heady, unorthodox linguistic minestrone Williams tasted growing up. Elena used to point out the language distinctions for him. French and Spanish patois. And an English no Englishman ever spoke. She remembered, for example, how her Brooklyn cousins used to pronounce "birds." It wasn't "bierrds," the way she'd heard it in the islands, but "boids." Imagine that! Another New World language. Boids.[32]

Like Emily Wellcome, Elena too was a spiritualist. It was a condition her husband sometimes tolerated and was always embarrassed by, and it was a condition that quite simply terrified the boys. Williams recalled several instances of his mother's trances from his early years, including one so disturbing that he decided finally not to publish it in his *Autobiography*. What he did publish was an incident that had aspects of mild wonderment and bewilderment. He remembered the family at dinner once and his mother suddenly staring at him in a trance asking him who he and the other young man sitting next to him were. All Williams could see were Ed and himself. But his father seemed to have been through all this before and so quietly asked his wife whom he had the pleasure of addressing now. "Why, I'm Lou Paine," the voice floated back. And then Elena was Elena once again, acting as though nothing had happened. Lou and Jesse Paine had been close neighbors of the Williamses' on Passaic Avenue for years before moving to Los Angeles. But William George was curious. Why should his wife suddenly take on this other woman's identity? That same evening he telegraphed the Paines to find out how Lou was doing.

At first, there was no answer. But two weeks later, Jesse Paine wrote back to Williams senior. When the telegram had come, Paine wrote, his wife was dying and he could not answer the question. But now he was writing to say Lou had recovered. Had Elena's trance and her identification with Lou Paine at the very moment Lou Paine lay dying been merely a coincidence? Better not to think about such things, young Williams early on decided.[33]

The other instance Williams remembered but could not bring himself to publish involved not only his mother but his father, grandmother, and uncles. That time William George was driven to distraction by his mother and his half brothers, crying and moaning in Godwin's bedroom late into the night until William George shouted out through the house that he was sure the whole family was possessed by the devil himself. Those sounds issuing from Godwin especially, sounds like some large beast strangling, deeply upset young Williams. To hell with it all. Better to forget spirit possession and the rest of it altogether. But even in church as she played the organ for the Sunday service, Elena had once begun to shake her head uncontrollably like an epileptic. Willie caught sight of her as he sat singing in the pew and nudged his brother. She was doing it again. He bit his lip and kept hoping no one else had noticed his mother acting like that.

As Williams grew older, his mother's seizures left him not so much terrified as cold and a little ashamed of her and, finally, bemused and aloof. And yet his attachment for her remained what can be described only as passionate. In fact, as he grew into his own difficult manhood, there were times when he even appeared to flirt with her. In 1936, with his mother bedridden and nearly blind with cataracts, Williams—then past fifty—attempted to sum up his feelings about his mother's strange seizures. Shortly before his death eighteen years before, William George had warned William Carlos that his mother would be a difficult person to handle, that she would demand watching and unlimited patience.[34] Now, in "Eve," the poem he wrote to complement the "Adam" poem he had written remembering his dead father, Williams addressed his mother. Here he struck a voice very much like the one his father had used in speaking of his wife after living with her for nearly thirty-five years: patient, but slightly aloof, slightly condescending. "I realize," Williams addressed his mother in his poem,

> *why you wish*
> *to communicate with the dead—*
> *And it is again I*
> *who try to hush you*
> *that you shall not*
> *make a fool of yourself*
> *and have them stare at you*
> *with natural faces—*
> *Trembling, sobbing*
> *and grabbing at the futile hands*
> *till a mind goes sour*
> *watching you—and flies off*
> *sick at the mumbling*
> *from which nothing clearly*
> *is ever spoken. . . .* [35]

Twelve years later, when his mother was nearly a hundred, deaf, blind, and senile, Williams picked up the same subject in a gentler mood, at last reconciled to her strange "visions." They did come, she insisted, and she talked to those ghostly presences in the same familiar way she spoke to her son. Blind, she could see them now more plainly than ever. What else was there for her to do? She could no longer read and she could barely hear the world outside her room. "All I can do," Williams recorded her as saying,

> *is to try to live over again*
> *what I knew when your brother and you*
> *were children—but I can't always succeed.*

One of the things Elena had known when her Willie and Ed were boys—and which she never tired of reiterating to them—was what it had cost her personally to have had to forgo her career as an artist trained in the proper French schools so that she might instead raise her boys in the provinces to which her husband had brought her. Oh, she had made sacrifices, she would confide to them, especially to Willie, who seemed to understand, though there was precious little the boy could do other than try to be an exemplary son and try to be the confidant the father had failed to be. Long years after, Williams remembered the picture of his mother standing out in the fields at the Bagellon House or at Goodale's boardinghouse on Long Island, where the Williamses had gone for a summer vacation in the early 1890s. There she was with her easel board and oil paints and stretched canvas, drenched in sunlight, creating some idyllic landscape.

In time all that disappeared, the half-squeezed tubes of pigment finally relegated to the attic for the boys to eventually discover and play with on a rainy day. Thus the dream of the artist's life was put away with those paints; henceforth Elena would place her thwarted energies and romantic hopes in her two sons. She would live now through them, sons more adapted than she to succeed in a man's world. Her own incredible idealism—an isolated romanticism increasingly out of step with the hurly-burly rough-and-tumble world around her, generating from that humming industrial island just nine miles to the east—would be marshaled now to spur, perversely perhaps, her own sons on to a greatness that had eluded her. For despite the irrelevant fact that she would spend seventy years of her life in Rutherford (except for a few too brief respites and reprieves), her moated world continued to be divided between images of her lost island paradise and those three glorious years she'd spent painting in Paris.

Incredibly, until Williams was in his mid-twenties, he actually tried to mold his life by his mother's impossible idealism: never to do or say the Wrong Thing, never—especially—to tell a Lie. The resultant strain on him, emotionally, intellectually, creatively, even physically, affected him in ways he would spend a lifetime trying to rectify. "It is impossible to recall whether it was in late childhood or early adolescence that I determined to be perfect," Williams wryly recalled in his *Autobiography* as he approached seventy, bemused by his own early scarring:

> The fascination of it still affects me: Never to commit evil in any form, never especially to lie, to falsify, to deceive, but to tell the truth always, come what might of it. The elevation of spirit that accompanies that resolve is a blissful one. It didn't last long, for my perceptions soon convinced me that such resolves would lead, sooner than I wished, to death, definitely and without equivocation. I could see the alternative, sainthood, but had no wish to be a dead saint. But the longing I had to be truthful never quite died. I had to retreat to a more tenable position, as far forward as possible, but I knew it was a retreat. I was a liar and would always be one, sauve qui peut! lay low and raid the enemy when possible, but the heroic gesture of perfection itself was not for me, though I had glimpsed the peaks and should never forget them.[36]

The Peaks! The Alps, which Williams was to see in the late 1890s when he spent a year in Switzerland at a school there, suggest that here in his mother's image of perfection—be ye therefore perfect—was Williams' personal version of the egotistical sublime. And though part of that massive edifice had to crumble into the acid-wasted waters of the Passaic, enough of it remained in the dual roles Williams remained absolutely faithful to all his life: the roles of artist and physician, anxious to attend to the minds and bodies of his people, ministering words of solace and comfort as long as he was able.

*
**

The other side to the sublime—the ideal of perfection—was the rough and tumble of his childhood, where his lifelong sense of loyalty to the group and his strategy of winning through by patiently staying put were first tested. "In retrospect," he wrote in the late '30s, "my writing reveals plenty of allegiances—to the grammar school ideals of my public school bringing up. . . . I was early indoctrinated into the gang spirit of my eight- and ten-year-old pals. I have never forgotten that thrilling world with all its magnificent hopes and determinations."[37] For most of his life Williams was to have recourse to the sense of a community effort, whether as part of a medical team—when he would never hesitate to refer a patient to a specialist, to someone who could better serve a patient than himself—or as part of a community of artists, whether with the *Others* group, with Pound and Stevens and Marianne Moore, or later with the Objectivists, or later still with the younger generation, which included Ginsberg and Lowell and Creeley and Levertov and Tomlinson. Always with Williams it was the ideal of what the pack or the group could effect. Who won through to recognition, who finally managed to put the equation or the poem or the puzzle together, was second to the realization that many had worked to effect that end.

Williams also learned early on that you could win a game like hares and hounds not only by outdistancing your opponents but by learning to stay put in the same place. Once the older boys had come running after him and he had leapt a neighbor's stockade fence to escape, freezing in the underbrush as he landed on the other side. The others had all gone on past him, fanning out, circling, shouting, puzzled at the inexplicable vanishing of their hare. Later, when he thought of the expatriates, of Henry James and Gertrude Stein and Eliot and Pound and Hilda Doolittle, yipping like hounds on the trace of some elusive prey, he would remember back to his boyhood strategy and think how one could also take the prize if one only stayed put long enough.

Williams also remembered idyllic moments frustrated, of swimming bare-assed with the boys at Santiago Grove on the Passaic and the Vreeland girl swimming with them, also nude, under the watchful eye of her big brother, whose look threatened to kill anyone who dared to so much as touch his sister.[38] There were blissful moments, too, as when Willie held hands with a young girl in the privacy of Kipp's Woods and told her he would like to marry her some day.

But it was the long hours spent in Kipp's Woods with his buddy Jim Hyslop that mattered most to him then. Jim would study the trees and Willie the wild flowers, until he could—like Adam—recognize and name them all: the anemone and the blue violet, "stars of bethlehem, spring beauties, wild geranium, hepaticas with three-lobed leaves." But Willie also learned about death and violence in that local Eden: old man Kipp striking a hickory tree until a squirrel, stunned, dropped to the ground only to be torn to pieces by Kipp's mongrel cur. Or a hunter Willie saw there one day holding a freshly killed rabbit. Half fascinated, half terrified, Willie watched the man take his knife, slice it into the animal's privates, and then yank up to disembowel it.[39] Willie nearly fainted when he saw that, as he had once before, at Goodale's boardinghouse, when he happened to look up in time to see a farmer pull back a bleating lamb's head and then, in the same motion, cut the poor animal's throat.

But what was more troubling to Willie was that he'd felt the dark beast stirring in his own breast more than once in those enchanted woods. Once he'd taken his own air rifle with him and killed a robin he'd watched building a nest in an apple tree. Another time he shot a red squirrel. And another time a stray kitten. And what was it welled within him when he brought his nine-year-old girl classmates here with him, what strange urging within? Rites of sacred initiation. So these were his woods finally, more than they were Kipp's, for here, away from home, away from school, among these tall grasses he was lord. And long before he ever thought of becoming a poet or a physician he dreamed of being a forester: a primitive Adam or one of those long-vanished Indian noble savages ranging far and wide in his own primeval world of second-stand woodland growth.

*
* *

The Rutherford and environs of Williams' boyhood were much more rural than a driver racing now down the four and six lane New Jersey Turnpike a few miles from Williams' home would ever suspect. Williams remembered hunters in the meadows looking for duck and muskrat, before sluices from the saline waters of the Hudson were cut into the freshwater swamps in an effort to keep the swarms of summer mosquitoes under some sort of control. He remembered too the old copper mines, already inactive in his youth for well over a century. And the old swamp cedars, massive and eerie in the summer twilight. He remembered wild blueberries and azalea in those swamps and egrets and black ducks and teal, even Canada geese (off course) and an occasional stray deer. And where the driver today sees rough clumps of broken purple-plumed canes stranded among the garbage heaps and dumped concrete and sand, there were once cattails and flowering trees. It was, he would remember, "romantic ground for us boys," and it remained so at least for a while—even for his own small sons. What would change it all forever would be America's coming of age with the Second World War.

When Williams was born, Rutherford was a distinctly rural town of some three thousand, with large farms radiating out from the town in all directions. Ridge Road, at the prow of which sits the home Williams bought in 1913, bravely faces the shops that run up and down Park Avenue, which Ridge Road intersects midway at a sharp angle. Thus

Williams' home serves as a steadily less tenable border between the commercial and residential districts of the town. Like Summit Road and Highland Cross, which skirt or intersect it, Ridge Road occupies the high ground at Rutherford's center. By the mid-1950s, when Williams was nearing seventy-five, those 3,000 had grown to 20,000. By then, too, the staid Victorian residences that had once occupied their places on Park Avenue had yielded those positions to a new wave of chainstores, bakeries, cleaners, small nondescript restaurants, florists, hardware and drugstores, everything but bars, outlawed by Rutherford edict. And where his wife's home with its adjoining woods once stood on Home Avenue, there is now a high-school football field replete with wooden bleachers.

There were still no sewers in Rutherford in the 1890s, Williams recalled in his own autobiography: ". . . no water supply, no gas, no electricity, no telephone, not even a trolley car." Even the sidewalks were rough wooden planks nailed to two-by-fours and laid across the dirt. There were no paved roads then, only mud in spring and dust all summer long. He also remembered cesspools and outhouses and chamber pots under the beds. He remembered pumping rainwater with a kitchen hand pump into a tin-lined wooden storage tank in the attic of his home on Passaic Avenue. The rain would wash off the roof into leaders which in turn funneled down into cisterns for storage before being pumped up again into the attic. And yet there were signs everywhere of progress. Streets were forever being ripped up for water lines, then for sewer lines, and later for gas lines. Then the motorized trolleys came in and ran down Park and all along Ridge Road, jostling noisily with horses and carriages and peddlers' carts, before they in their turn gave way in the 1920s to Buicks and Packards, Dodges and Fords.[40]

Blacks and European immigrants settled on the fringes of the town, but at the center there was still plenty of comfortable old Yankee money and showy opulence around. Large graceful mansions—Victorian and Victorian Gothic both—blossomed along oak- and chestnut-lined streets. There were still the older names around then, names like the Ivesons and Deans and Hollisters and Cummingses. Williams particularly remembered the Iveson mansion across the street from his own far more modest home, remembered its being built, and the wedding there, with the entire house and driveway lit by gas, as the horse-drawn carriages pulled up to the front portico to gently deposit the guests who had arrived from New York and elsewhere by train. But he also remembered fragments of local scandal and rumors of scandal, of acts of passion committed behind the closed doors of those imposing edifices: the gossip that runs through any small town. Once, a man climbing out through the ground-floor window of the Iveson mansion had been shot and killed by a policeman who was walking his night rounds. The officer had ordered the shadowy figure to stop, thinking him a burglar. But when he turned the body over, it turned out to be Mrs. Iveson's neighbor . . . and lover. Such incidents were of course hushed up as well as possible, but they lived on in local memory, on tennis courts and at church picnics: stories of lovers shot or stabbed, of pillars of the community crashing through bay windows, trousers still down around their knees, to make what hasty exit they could. Rutherford, then, at the turn of the century was a town like hundreds of other booming American towns that lie within commuting distance of centers like New York, Boston, Philadelphia, Chicago: respectable, genteel, churchly on the surface, but swarming with another life known mostly to policemen, reporters, physicians, priests, and writers.

Willie and Ed attended the local Rutherford public elementary school on Sylvan Street—the Park School—though there was nothing especially noteworthy about the level of instruction there. Williams was to remain mostly silent about his years there, though he did remember his fourth-grade teacher, Helen Walcott.[41] Dana Ely recalled eighty years after the event how Willie was once suspended by this same Miss Walcott for passing around picture postcards of "Bloomer girls" during recess in the courtyard.[42] But for the most part the eight years Williams spent at the Park School—from 1889 till Christmas 1897—were something to be endured until the parents could find a good high school for their two boys.

Instead, the one instructor Williams did remember from this period for his intelligence was his Unitarian Sunday school teacher, E. J. Luce. Luce was a tough, displaced New Englander, one of the founders—along with Williams' own folks—of Rutherford's Unitarian Society. He'd graduated from Williams College (where Williams would in turn send his own son), played baseball there, and had become a lawyer. It was this man who first taught Williams about the philosophers of light, about Plato and Christ and Kant. Once Luce read a long passage to Williams' class on the nature of love and friendship from Plato's *Symposium* (probably the myth of love that Yeats later used in "Among School Children"). As for Jesus, Luce explained, if he was divine, it was not by any special gift of paternity, but because of the divinely human spirit within him. Here was a democratic concept that Williams could find palpable, and one that as a young man he thought he could emulate by truth telling. Like most American boys, Williams was shaped thus haphazardly by a mixture of second-rate formal education, parental strictures and ignorances, combined with the rough give-and-take of his environment. Imperfect as it was, it would have to serve him as it would serve millions of others.

*
**

The first sharp break with the world of Rutherford came in December 1897, when William George told Elena that he was being sent down to

Buenos Aires to establish a plant for the manufacture of Florida Water there. He would be leaving in a month and would have to be away for at least a year. This was as good a time as any for Elena to return to the beloved Paris she had mourned for the last eighteen years. It would also provide the opportunity for their sons to get a taste of European education and shake off some of their provincialism. Once the parents had formulated their plans, the boys were told the news. They would attend school near Geneva and visit their mother in the city during holiday. A tenant was found for the house and on Thursday, January 13, 1898, Elena and the boys—ages fourteen and thirteen—set sail on the French liner the SS *Bretagne*, from New York Harbor. The winter crossing took fourteen days then, and it was an exciting passage for all of them. As he would each time he made a crossing, Williams made a habit of going up into the foremost part of the ship's prow alone and then of looking down into the dizzy crash of icy whitecaps far below until he felt as though he were crashing, in the advance guard, toward some new and yet undisclosed world.

At Le Havre they entrained for Switzerland and the school the boys would be attending on the outskirts of Geneva: the Château de Lancy, which William George had found for them the previous summer while on business in Switzerland.[43] Elena herself took a modest room at the Pension de Wolff in Geneva, which faced the gardens of the Place Brunswick and the lake only a block away. From here she could take occasional trips by train into Paris to visit her cousins the Truflys in Montmartre. As for the boys, they suddenly found themselves living with sixty-two other young males assembled from all over Europe, Russia, South America, and Asia. Williams heard a polyglot of tongues, though the predominant language at Lancy was not French, as Elena had thought, but English. In fact, the British contingent (as usual) refused to speak anything but English, and the English "colonials"—the Williams boys included—followed suit. The result was that after a year at Lancy neither Bill nor Ed was very fluent in French.[44]

But there were other things the boys had to learn if they were to survive, especially with the public school mentality of the older British boys. So, when Willie dropped a paper-bag water bomb from the third-story window of the Château onto the head of a young Englishman named Potter, he had to make good. That particular bombing had been a mistake. Actually, he liked Potter and had mistaken him for someone else. No matter. Williams would have to be punished for this insult to an Englishman. So, before the entire British contingent, he was held down and his trousers forced down around his knees. Then one of the older boys administered a caning to his bare buttocks in traditional public school fashion. But Williams—half English himself—refused either to struggle or to cry out. "Do you think an American would have turned a hair for an Englishman?" he wrote in his *Autobiography*. "Not likely."

There was an older French boy at the school whom Williams remembered long after. Taciturn, sullen, dark, Jocelin—as he was called—used to ride his bicycle at breakneck speed around the narrow paths of the formal gardens of the school at dusk each day, using an acetylene bike lamp to light his way. Once at dinner sharp words passed between this boy and a Siamese prince named Tum Devis, and then suddenly table knives were being brandished before order could be restored. Williams' own special friend was an Indian from Rajpunta named Leon Pont, who, like Jim Hyslop back in Rutherford, spent long hours with Williams going over every inch of the ground at Lancy, trying to make it give up its secrets. It meant long happy hours with Pont, going through the old barns and sheds, visiting the mountain brooks, and collecting specimens of the native flowers of the area, including the asphodel that Williams would recall again with so much poignancy in his late poem "Of Asphodel, That Greeny Flower."[45]

Williams was growing in sexual awareness as well, though he soon realized he and Ed were still "hundreds of years younger" than the other boys his age at the school. He thought he remembered one of the older boys teaching Ed how to masturbate, though he kept silent about his own initiation.[46] But he did remember how he used to wait for one of the local farm girls (she couldn't have been more than twelve) to pass by the school grounds each day. Begrimed and bedraggled as she was, he used to daydream how he would drag her down to the mountain stream, clean her up, and then carry her off to some spot and rape her. In reality, he couldn't even bring himself to address the girl. He remembered too his first experiences of being followed by older men who had their own strange designs on him. Once, propped into the prow of a river steamer which was taking him and Ed and his mother for a tour of Lake Geneva, he suddenly felt a sharp pressure against his crotch and was stunned to find an elderly, smartly dressed Frenchman resting on a cane and looking off into the distance, while he thrust his right hand up between the boy's legs. Williams got up and pushed past the man, blushing and confused. And though he stared at him, Williams was astonished to see the man looking off into the distance as though nothing in the world had happened. Later, in the winter of '99, living with his mother and Ed at the Truflys, he remembered being followed during Carnival by another elderly French gentleman who made it clear that he too was interested in Williams. Willie told his mother about these disturbing incidents, but Elena would shrug them off, assuring her son that he had merely imagined them and that it would be better simply to forget them. It would take Williams years before he understood what had happened and why. And of course he never forgot.[47]

For a short while in the fall of '98, Bill and Ed were enrolled at the Lycée Condorcet, but their failure to master French while at Lancy put them at a distinct disadvantage and they soon withdrew, M. Trufly, a down-and-out lawyer who knew all the legal angles, demanding that their tuition be returned. The Williamses were staying now with the Truflys— M. Trufly and his wife, Alice, and her spinster sister, Marguerite—all of them living in the same apartment on the rue la Bruyère in Montmartre. The Truflys were churchmouse poor, ever since Trufly had lost everything—practice, an estate in the French countryside, everything— in the collapse of the de Lesseps Company, which had hoped to build the first canal through the Isthmus of Panama until the enormity of the project and the anopheles mosquito ended that scheme. Now the Truflys were glad for the supplemental income Elena's rent provided.

Elena's cousin Alice Monsanto, the one she had lived with back in the '70s, still lived a block and a half away, and now she undertook to teach the boys French. Each day for an hour she did French exercises with them, using the old method of memory learning by making them memorize some of La Fontaine's poems by heart. Williams for one was sure that, had they stayed in Paris long enough, he and Ed would soon have become competent in the language.

Some of Williams' other memories from this period reveal more about Williams than even he may have been aware of in retelling them. He remembered, for example, how "hard up" his spinster cousin Marguerite was for a man, how she used to press up against Ed and him as they leant out the window to watch a newsboy or fishmonger on the streets below. He recalled too how this same cousin had convinced Willie to dress up once in his mother's clothes, high heels and all, and walk over to Aunt Alice Monsanto's apartment. Willie had trouble with his mother's bonnet as he tripped down the street, and he noticed pedestrians beginning to stare at him. But he made it to his aunt's apartment and looked so convincing in his mother's clothes that Aunt Alice embraced him before she realized it was Willie and not Elena. They both laughed then until Alice realized what Willie had done, and then she frightened him by explaining that he could be arrested for impersonating a woman in public. Instead of changing there and then, Willie ran back down the street—still in his mother's clothes—to the Truflys' apartment.

The incident in itself does not seem important—a schoolboy lark, perhaps—but it came at a time when his younger brother—more physically precocious now than he—had begun to surpass him in height and weight. Bad enough that Ed and Willie were in the same classes together, but now Ed began to look like the older brother. To make matters worse, Ed was also to prove the better athlete on the playing field. It was Ed who became the first-string halfback on the Rutherford football team while Bill, slighter in build (like his mother), was relegated to the status of alternate.[48] This reversal of roles would create its own problems in the coming years, but already, at fifteen, Williams understood that in many things important to adolescents, Ed was taking the lead. All that was left in Willie's favor was the illusion of language, of continuing to play big brother to a brother who was in fact bigger than he. But Ed seems to have continued to accept his older brother as the preceptor who could guide him in the truth and the ways of the world, which were not, both came to realize, quite the same thing. These roles of teacher/disciple, of one brother helping the less experienced brother in performing the good and right thing, managed to last for another ten years.

Ed and Bill were given fencing lessons at the Salle d'Armes Bernard, going there several times a week, where they saw men preparing for duels of honor that would actually leave some of them dead. These lessons, too, Williams was to put to good use later when he joined the fencing team at the University of Pennsylvania. Trufly, decked out in his finery, took the boys everywhere about Paris. They saw the Left Bank, climbed the Eiffel Tower, examined the catacombs, visited the old churches, particularly St. Germain-des-Prés, tasted the very fringes of Paris's nightlife in Montmartre, and laughed at the Petoman's ability to play tunes with the gas from his rectum. They heard the old French patriotic songs and remembered the talk then circulating about the notoriously anti-Semitic Dreyfus trial and of Zola's spirited defense of that army officer. And then, in the spring of '99, having been away for nearly a year and a half, Elena's "reprieve" ran out and she and the boys finally sailed back to the provinces and so to Rutherford.[49]

*
* *

When the boys returned, they found themselves together in their first year of high school at the newly established Rutherford Public High. Bill did poorly there. He was restless, bored, vaguely disturbed by the girls, many of them the same girls he had gone through grade school with. He even seems to have felt his father's long absence as a desertion of sorts. It was time, therefore, his parents now decided, to take the boys out of Rutherford (which was still an unknown quantity) and send them to a good private school in New York City. Horace Mann, situated on Morningside Heights at 120th Street (in the shadow of Columbia University), was the school decided on. So, for the next three years that meant Bill and Ed had to get up each morning at six, dress, eat, and run down to the Erie Railroad station half a mile away in time to catch the 7:16 to Jersey City. From there they took the Chambers Street Ferry into downtown New York to streets bustling with immigrant laborers and teamsters and horse-drawn carts. Then the brothers would walk up Chambers or Warren Street to take the newly electrified Ninth or Sixth

Avenue El for the long trip up Manhattan's West Side to 116th or 125th Street, and then take a brisk walk over to Morningside Heights and Horace Mann in time for their nine o'clock class.

"For the first time," he remembered, "I realized what it meant to work, to be pushed, to be in competition with the best."[50] And Horace Mann had a reputation for being one of the best high schools in the East at the turn of the century. He remembered some of his classmates all his life, especially the smart Jewish kids like Fischer and Aegeltinger, the mathematical genius who used to help Williams and the others with their homework on the train ride uptown in the morning, and about whom Williams would later write one of his most moving poems, "Aigeltinger." After an interview with the principal of the school, it was decided—probably by his mother as much as by himself—to enroll in a course of study geared not to the humanities and classics but instead to the sciences, with an eye toward medicine and dentistry. For Elena, with her husband's tacit approval, had already decided that she would give her first son to carry on in the tradition of her own beloved Carlos. It was a practical and professional decision, and of course it went directly counter to Williams' own proclivity for being the romantic solitary who wanted to be free to roam his enchanted forest, perhaps as a tree warden. Instead, he would be thrust into the mainstream of society, to come in daily contact with the sick and the miserable. In time, of course, this relentless, grueling contact with others would help to shape him into a dedicated physician and a great poet, but at the time, he was merely being asked, in some vague and undefined way, to begin living up to his mother's romantic ideal for him.

Williams found himself taking elementary Latin and French (and here the Geneva and Paris experiences helped significantly), some basic scientific German, mathematics, chemistry, physics, classical and English history, and English. He had trouble with math (one reason he was always grateful for having known Aegeltinger), but he pushed on doggedly. And when his math teacher, Mr. Bickford, passed him in quadratics, it wasn't for what he'd achieved (he knew he deserved to fail on that account), but because he had been able to demonstrate to Bickford's satisfaction that he was capable of understanding mathematical processes. "He saw my mind," Williams would later say, "and realized what it was not intended to perform. And he acted accordingly." That, after all, Williams knew, was what it meant to be a teacher.

It was at Horace Mann too that Williams first came into contact with the systematic study of poetry. His teacher here was William Abbott— Uncle Billy as he was fondly called—and he made Williams feel for the first time in his life "the excitement of great books." Abbott taught Williams something of the English tradition: Milton's "Lycidas,"

"Comus," "L'Allegro," and "Il Penseroso," Coleridge's "Christabel" and "The Rime of the Ancient Mariner," Wordsworth's "Intimations" ode. And though the little surviving evidence we have does not demonstrate that Williams' prose was yet very good, Uncle Billy did give him an A— for his prose recounting of Robert Louis Stevenson's travel essay "The Oise in Flood," from his *An Inland Voyage,* about a young man in an upset canoe who refused to let go of his paddle. Williams remembered Uncle Billy all his life as the man who had taken him under his wing and revealed to him the legacy of poetry that could be his. Perhaps Williams was ready for this revelation anyway, and Uncle Billy happened to be there. But half a century later, Williams dedicated his *Selected Essays* to this man's memory, to "the first English teacher who ever gave me an A." It was also, as his records show, one of the few he ever got in his three years at the school, where his overall average was a C.[51]

That first year at Horace Mann Williams went out for, and made, the track team. For if he was small and slight, he was also fast, and he was determined to do as well in track as his brother was doing in football. By his senior year, Williams' event was the 300-yard dash, a difficult distance between sprint and endurance, and the coaches were training him rigorously to take that event in the big Madison Square Garden competitions that fall of 1901. Training for the 300 meant running lap after lap, running distance and then sprinting, as the days got darker and colder. It meant getting home long after dark, bushed, with all his homework still before him. But he wanted that race. Then, one afternoon, just before the Madison Square Garden competitions, he was doing practice laps on the indoor track at the Twenty-second Armory. The trick, he saw, was to increase his speed until the last lap and then sprint as fast as he could. So, as he came into the home stretch, he was already sprinting when someone yelled out to him that he still had another turn to go. It was an old trick, meant to build up stamina, and he knew it, but he still thought he could punish his body into doing it. He did in fact manage to do it, but he collapsed as he went over the finish line. There was a flurry of excitement. Williams assured the coaches that he was all right, and went home, but all the way downtown on the train, and then over to Jersey, he felt nauseous and dizzy, afraid that he was going to pass out at any moment. Dr. Charles Calhoun, the family physician, was called in to examine the boy. It was adolescent heart strain, Calhoun told the family, and Willie was ordered to bed for a week. That diagnosis meant, of course, the end of Williams' running career. He might still continue to exercise by taking long walks as he loved to do, but at eighteen his track days were over.[52]

Williams was shattered. He had fondly hoped that he would at least shine as a track star, and now he went into a black depression. It was, ironically, this touching bottom, this first descent into his private hell, that turned out to yield an unlooked-for gift: the gift of the poem. It was, as far as he could remember, the first poem he had ever written, a short, spontaneous thing, a single sentence containing a symbol of his own despondency. But writing it brought with it a sense of relief, of delight, as though he had done something truly extraordinary:

> *A black, black cloud*
> *flew over the sun*
> *driven by fierce flying*
> *rain.*[53]

And then he began to analyze his flower, to dissect it coldly. It was, he could see, "the most stupid thing" he'd ever said, since, from a scientific point of view, rain did not drive clouds, wind did. Yet, in spite of that, he was pleased at what words had released in him. He'd managed to enjamb them, alliterate them with labials and fricatives, create an image that corresponded with his suicidal despondency and—having articulated his emotion—had helped to lift his dark mood from him. Poetry began, then, for him as a mode of catharsis, as a way of distancing and objectifying his own depressions. "Believe me," he would say a half century afterward, thinking back to this first effort,

> that's the way writing often starts, a disaster or a catastrophe of some sort, as happened to me, and you're a child not knowing where to go or what to think. He's thrown back so much on himself that he's really in distress. . . . And I think that's the basis for my continued interest in writing, because by writing I rescue myself under all sorts of conditions, whatever it may be that has upset me . . . , then I can write and it relieves the feeling of distress. I think quite literally, psychologically, speaking as Freud might think, that writing has meant that to me all the way through.[54]

Sometime after this, perhaps even prompted by Uncle Billy, Williams began to keep a series of notebooks, "ten-cent copybooks" with "stiff board covers of a black and tawny water-wave design and a slightly off-gray cloth binding." How many of them there were and what actually happened to them is a mystery. In one place Williams speaks of having finally accumulated eighteen of them, in another of twenty-three, and in yet another of twenty-eight. They disappeared, finally, their use as commonplace books superseded by other needs, but for years they were "a precious comfort" to him. Here Williams could put down his free-ranging, derivative Whitmanesque thoughts, since it was Whitman of all the poets he had so far read who first made him aware of what was new in American poetry. Using this mode, Williams could purge himself of what he called his "turgid obsessions." But for "real" poetry, for poetry that was recognizably poetry in 1902, he would have to go back to the formal lessons he had gleaned from Palgrave's anthology of English poetry and the examples taught him by Uncle Billy—that is, back to standard verse forms and rhyme schemes, to couplets and sonnets and lilting refrains in the manner of Spenser and Keats and Tennyson as these had been filtered through a late Victorian gauze. Moreover, William George was not all that comfortable with his son's dabbling in poetry. It was an impractical avocation, dangerous, romantic in the worst sense of that much-maligned word. Still, if the boy was going to write the stuff, at least it should conform to the acceptable, the civil, the uplifting. It should be a genteel avocation, like Willie's playing of the violin, while his real energies were focused on more manly pursuits like his studies and his newly found professional ambitions.

But something had already happened to Williams that he wanted to keep a closely guarded secret, at least for the time being. He was beginning to understand that somehow he had already opted for art over science. The choice now was to decide which art. "Music was out," Williams explained long after he'd made his choice:

> I had tried it, and didn't qualify. Besides, I wanted something more articulate. Painting—fine, but messy, cumbersome. Sculpture? I once looked at a stone and preferred it the way it was. I couldn't see myself cutting stone, too much spring in my legs to stand still that long. To dance? Nothing doing, legs too crooked. Words offered themselves and I jumped at them. To write, like Shakespeare![55]

To write, to write the way he wanted to write. But he instinctively understood that there would be no ready-made audience for what he wanted to say. That meant he would have to support himself with a decent job like medicine. And so, quietly, he turned his parents' priorities upside down. He would do Horace Mann in three rather than four years, go to medical school and become a doctor, all that he might write like Shakespeare. Nor did he stop long enough to consider the enormous output in energy and time it would cost him to become both a practicing physician and another Shakespeare. But whatever it cost, no one, neither his father nor his mother, would tell him what he could or could not do. It was a brave vow he made, and it would take another dozen years under his father's roof to begin to fulfill that promise to himself. What he didn't yet realize in his secret rage for artistic independence was that it had been this same father who, on long winter nights in their living room, had read Shakespeare's plays aloud to his sons.

TWO

J'ARRIVERAI:
The Turtle Too Gets There:
1902—1909

*I*f he entered the race early on as an artist, still Williams'
progress was painfully slow. On the other hand, he had
learned the hard way what an all-out effort too early on in the race could
do to one. Better to go slow and steady, like the turtle, which became the
letterhead emblem on his college stationery stepping slowly over the
word *j'arriverai:* I will get there. First, though, he had to find what
direction to move in. With uncanny precision, Ezra Pound chose precisely
this same trait of single-minded tenacity to describe Williams' uniqueness to his readers nearly thirty years later. "There is an anecdote told me
by his mother," Pound wrote in 1928:

> The young William Carlos, aged let us say about seven, arose in the
> morning, dressed and put on his shoes. Both shoes buttoned on the left
> side. He regarded this untoward phenomenon for a few moments and then
> carefully removed the shoes, placed shoe *a*, that had been on his left foot,
> on his right foot, and shoe *b*, that had been on the right foot, on his left
> foot; both sets of buttons again appeared on the left side of the shoes.
> This stumped him. With the shoes so buttoned he went to school,
> but . . . and here is the significant part of the story, he spent the day in
> careful consideration of the matter.[1]

Such an introduction might make some readers wonder if Williams
wasn't somewhat cretinous or at least backward, but actually Pound was
praising his friend, for Williams' "type of sensibility" he found of "almost
unique value in a land teeming with clever people, all capable of
competent and almost instantaneous extroversion." What his tenacity in
doing things his own way did, Pound thought, was distinguish Williams
"from the floral and unconscious minds of the populace and from the
snappy go-getters who'der seen wot wuz rong in er meoment." That
tenacity had, in fact, "prevented our author from grabbing ready-made
conclusions, and from taking too much for granted." It was the key to
Williams' character: a single minded ability to see a thing through his
way, a refusal to be hassled into following the lead of others, including,
finally, even his rabbit-swift friend, Pound himself.

Besides, to the world at large Williams appeared to be moving fast enough. After only three years at Horace Mann, he was able to pass the stiff entrance exam that admitted him directly into the University of Pennsylvania's Medical School. It was still possible in those days to go directly from high school into medical school, and the costs of sending two boys to Horace Mann had dictated the Williamses' decision to get Willie admitted into medical school as early as possible. At nineteen, he was the second youngest in a class of 120. He enrolled initially in a five-year course of study that would lead to a double degree: the MD in medicine and the DDS in dentistry. He would specialize in oral surgery. His decision pleased both his parents, but especially his mother. Willie was a good boy.

The year was 1902, the same year that other things happened to Williams which would eventually loom large in his life. One of these was the destruction of the neighboring city of Paterson by fire that February. The fire began when a pile of paint- and turpentine-soaked rags burst into flame in the city's trolley shed and from there swept over most of the city. Contemporary photos of the charred city remind one of Matthew Brady's photographs of Richmond, Virginia, in the spring of 1865 after Lee had been forced to evacuate, or of Dresden after the Allied bombings of 1943. One of the curious who walked the ice-caked rubble-strewn streets of Paterson that February was Williams himself, amazed at how quickly a raging fire had swallowed up an entire city. And then, as if the poor city hadn't suffered enough, a month later the Passaic River, swollen beyond capacity during the spring thaw, spilled into the city's streets, taking with it whatever homes and stores and sheds had been left unravaged by the fire. Again Williams visited those flooded streets and thought he was watching a city die. And yet, incredibly, almost at once a new Paterson, as vital and as deformed as the old, began to rise from the sodden ashes of the old. It was a lesson in resiliency, this beginning over again, a lesson Williams would never forget.

The second important event of 1902 was Williams' meeting Ezra Pound at Penn. Williams had just come down to the university at the end of September, unpacked his trunk in his room in the freshman dorms— 303 Brooks, a Victorian Gothic affair that looked out over the college triangle—and had entered into his studies at once, as he had promised his parents he would.[2] It was the first time he had been away from the entire family for any length of time, and he was feeling the first bout of a homesickness that would return periodically for the next several years. In fact, he was feeling very sorry for himself and wondering what in the world he was doing at Penn at all.

In his first letter home to his mother, written his first Sunday afternoon there—September 28—Williams wrote dutifully that he'd attended church services that morning at the YMCA there on campus. He'd already met one other college chap, another freshman named Van Winkle, a fellow from Buffalo on scholarship. Van Winkle was, Williams assured his mother, "a gentleman of high morals" and certainly not one of the "fast crowd, which is very easily distinguished by its speech as well as by its looks." He'd also made the acquaintance of an upperclassman, a prominent figure in the YMCA, through whom he was hoping to get into the college's Mask and Wig Society.[3] He would send letters of this domestic banality and high moral tone home frequently to his mother and occasionally to his father over the next four years, always playing the model son on his best behavior, working to capacity to justify his parents' sacrifices in sending him to school. Looking back on the tone and substance of these letters years later, Williams himself was amazed. There was "much that is close to infantile" in them, he told one friend forty years afterward, explaining that he simply "didn't have the courage or the ability" to tell his parents what was really on his mind or "place my most intimate actions and reactions on paper."[4]

It was this Williams, just turned nineteen, earnest, serious, a bit priggish, whom Pound first met the following Tuesday, September 30. Williams was sitting in his room after dinner, he remembered, gazing dreamily out his dorm room window which faced the Botanical Gardens when the sound of someone playing a grand piano in the next room broke his reverie. He'd heard that piano earlier in the day being played by someone who obviously knew what he was doing. Too unsure of himself to simply knock on the door and introduce himself, Williams took his violin from its battered case and began to answer melody for melody. Soon there was a knock on his door and a young man, Morrison Robb Van Cleve, introduced himself and began talking of music. Flustered, Williams had to admit that he was only a passable violin player. His real love, he confided, was poetry. Well, if Williams was interested in poetry, Van Cleve answered, there was a crazy guy in his sophomore class who also wrote the stuff and whom he wanted Williams to meet.

Why not right now, Williams suggested? Van Cleve left and soon returned with the poet he'd been speaking of. It was Ezra Pound, only seventeen, but already the very image of the poet in the cut of his dress and his gesture. What exactly Pound and Williams talked about that first evening Williams could not remember except that they used language to feel each other out. Williams was shy, enthusiastic, unsure of himself, forthright, high-minded. And Pound, though two years younger, was from the start the more self-assured of the two, with a mediocre year at Penn already behind him, the flamboyant sophomore, trying to appear world-weary and worldly wise beyond his years, secretive, oblique, mysterious, and already convinced that he was destined to become an important poet.

Thus began a strange literary friendship that would last—with its violent ups and downs—for sixty years and literally alter the course of modern poetry itself.[5]

But for now there was young Pound, a novice poet from a Philadelphia suburb, trying to act out his version of the Yellow Book Nineties, wickedly suggesting to Bill Williams that the lad close his books and live a little. "My early rekolektn," Pound wrote Williams years later, "is you in a room on the South side of the triangle, and me sayin come on nowt, and you deciding on gawd an righteousness and the pursuit of labour in the form of Dr. Gumbo's treatise on the lesions of the bungbone, or some other therapeutic compilation."[6] For his part Williams was equally uncomplimentary in his early recollections. Pound would come to his room, Williams recalled, and read to him from his manuscript of poems—those derivative exercises collected several years' later in *A Lume Spento*. Having to listen to Pound read his stuff "was a painful experience," Williams confessed:

> For it was often impossible to hear the lines the way he read them, and of all the things in the world the last I should have wanted to do would have been to hurt him—no matter how empty I myself might have felt, and worthless, as a critic. . . . His voice would trail off in the final lines of many of the lyrics until they were inaudible—from his intensity. I seldom let on except, occasionally, to explode with the comment that unless I could *hear* the lines how could he expect me to have an opinion of them. What did he think I was, an apteryx?[7]

Whether or not Williams returned the favor and read Pound some of his own Keatsian imitations Williams does not say, though elsewhere he recalled reading to Pound in Pound's own tower room. In effect it made little difference, since Pound does not mention Williams' poetry from this period. Besides which, Pound was enough of a young cocksure egoist then to be aware of only one voice—his own. That and of course the voices of his Victorian and Edwardian masters, living and dead: Browning, Swinburne, Rossetti, and soon Yeats, whom he heard when Yeats read in Philadelphia during his 1903 tour. Significantly, Williams did not go to hear Yeats then, since for him the tradition was, like Catholic revelation, end-stopped and self-contained and enclosed in his copy of Palgrave's anthology.

In April of that year, however, Williams did go to see Ezra and Van Cleve the musician playing women in the chorus of Euripedes' *Iphigenia in Aulis*, performed in the original language under the auspices of Penn's Department of Greek and directed by Professor Archibald Clark. Williams watched the performance from the balcony of the university theater and was amused to see Pound "dressed in a Grecian robe, . . . a togalike ensemble topped by a great blond wig at which he tore as he waved his arms about and heaved his massive breasts in ecstasies of extreme emotion."[8] One afternoon Pound cajoled Williams into accompanying him down Chestnut Street in the city to help him try and pick up a high-school girl he'd fallen in love with. Williams could see at once how young she was, but he had to admit she was also very good-looking. Like bumbling sheepdogs, the two of them began following on either side of her, Williams silent and Pound doing his best Ronsard imitation to get her to talk. But all this behavior did was to terrify the girl, who pleaded with both of them to please leave her alone. Williams, repulsed, slowed down and then finally stopped, watching Ronsard hurry after the girl for another fifty feet or so until he too gave up the hunt, angry with Williams for having spoiled his fun.[9]

No matter. That was Pound, and though few of his classmates liked the fellow's decadent posturings, Williams knew Pound could be humorous, exciting, intense, blasphemous on any subject except poetry, about which he never joked. Pound could cut you dead, Williams knew, but he could also be exceedingly generous and devoted to his friends. And yet, Williams also had to admit that he "could never take him as a steady diet." For what he found most offensive was Pound's posturing, his constant hiding behind one mask or another. "Any simpleton," Williams wrote later, could see "at once what that came from; the conflict between an aristocracy of birth and that of mind and spirit." On the other hand, his own background, Williams felt, had gone counter to such poetic posturing from the beginning. The study of medicine had "assumed rather the humility and caution of the scientists. One was or one was not there. And if one was there, it behooved one to be at one's superlative best, and, apart from the achievement, a thing in itself, to live inconspicuously, as best it might be possible, and to work single-mindedly for the task. Not so sweet Ezra."[10]

But Williams' assessment of Pound and himself was not quite fair. For Williams' own humility and inconspicuousness was in part a mask, a mask of invisibility from behind which Williams, as he came to know his own strengths, could leap out to take the advantage. It was part of his old hound and hares strategy which had worked so well for him as a boy: let Ezra take the full force of the initial frontal attack, let him take the most outlandish risks. Williams would wait in hiding, assuming his own superiority, until it was time to show himself. In fact Pound would later tell Williams as much. Sure he'd taken some heavy losses early on in the game, he would say, but he'd also won some very important victories for modern poetry from his base in London, while "Bull" Williams was playing it safe back there in the dreary provinces.[11]

*
**

In the fall semester of 1903, Pound transferred from Penn to Hamilton College in upstate New York, near Syracuse. Williams continued to write him and to see him during vacations, and they would be together again for the academic year 1905–06, when Pound, having earned a Bachelor of Philosophy in June 1905, returned to Penn to take an MA in Romanics. Now, however, as Pound was leaving for "exile" in Hamilton, Williams was returning to Penn as a straight medical student, having decided the previous spring that dentistry was not after all for him. In so doing, he had also switched from a five-year to a four-year program.[12] He also down-scaled his self-expectations in other ways and began to breathe a little more easily.

When Williams had first gone away to the university, he'd promised his parents a number of things: that he would not smoke, that, aside from an occasional glass of sherry, he would not drink, that he would not go with the other students when they went down to the barrooms and saloons around Philadelphia. Because he was still trying to be "perfect," he would not go out with girls, except to join in approved and chaperoned dances. But as loneliness and the pressures of his studies mounted, he found himself taking long solitary walks through the working-class sections of Philadelphia looking for a woman who might help alleviate his intense isolation. So the impossible striving after the right thing, expected by his parents but exacerbated by his own idealism, soon became an impossible burden. He would remember these years later with a mixture of self-disgust, disbelief, and astonishment with his own naiveté, resenting deeply what his shyness and isolation had cost him. Moreover, he was without spending money, since his parents were already straining to send one son to Penn and preparing to send another to MIT.[13]

Knowing what it was costing his parents, Williams refused to spend a penny more than he had to, remembering for edification the example of his Uncle Carlos carrying a solitary sou in his pocket during his student days at the University of Paris rather than have to admit to his mother that he didn't have any money. Williams in his turn never forgot the humiliation he felt when, escorting the two daughters of Reverend Ecob, the local Unitarian minister in Philadelphia, he fished in his pockets for trolley fare for himself and them, only to realize that he didn't even have his uncle's solitary sou. There was a moment of awkwardness and a sharp hard glance at him by the ladies, before they paid not only their own fares but his as well. Williams never forgot that incident, nor the look of those young women, as he was forced to accept their charity. What confirmed their disgust was his attempt once to take one of the sisters' arms as she crossed a busy intersection, and her pulling away and screaming at him not to touch her. That incident ended his visits to the local Unitarian church.[14]

Now, however, as he began his second year at Penn, Williams had decided to enjoy himself more than he had thus far allowed himself. He read novels instead of spending every moment with his medical studies, though he still managed to get several near-perfect grades in his courses. And though he refused to join a fraternity—he was too serious for that sort of thing—he did join the university's fencing team. He also tried out a second time for the Mask and Wig, but had to drop pursuing it before he could be voted on. On All Saint's Day, a month into classes, Williams wrote his mother about the Halloween celebrations he'd seen the night before in the city. The celebrations had been, he felt, "a rowdy affair," like those Mardi Gras celebrations he and Ed and Mother had watched in Paris five years before, except that the American version was "less gorgeous." Even as he was writing in his room at 318 Leidy, he could count six horse-drawn fire engines racing down the street toward the western part of the city which seemed "ablaze" following the celebrations.[15]

He'd also met a fine young gentleman over a dish of prunes at Mrs. Chain's boardinghouse on Locust Street, where Williams and a number of the other students took their meals. Charlie Demuth was a young artist taking art courses at Drexel. This was the same Demuth who would become a prominent force in modern American painting in the 1920s, the man who would then paint the proto-pop-art poster called *The Figure Five*, for which the direct inspiration would be a poem by Williams. Until Demuth's death in 1935, the two men would remain close friends, and Williams would come to write one of his most ambitious elegies to this man's memory.

Williams spent the Christmas holidays back home with Ed and his parents and then returned to Penn early in January to begin preparing for the heavy schedule of examinations that were shortly to begin. On Sunday the seventeenth he wrote his mother that, instead of going to church that morning, he'd decided to go down to the west end of Philadelphia to see his grandmother and Uncle Irving's kids.[16] Why Grandma Wellcome had moved to Philadelphia is hinted at neither in the letters nor in the *Autobiography*, but Uncle Godwin's attack on Mrs. Dodd in the fall of 1902 may have had some bearing on the separation of the Wellcomes from the Williamses. Whatever the reason, Willie was still on good terms with the family and used to visit his grandmother frequently, sometimes with Charlie Demuth, especially during the springtime, when they could get to her house after dinner at Mrs. Chain's boardinghouse and before dark.

But now, in midwinter, Williams was preoccupied with only one thing: doing well in his examinations. As a result, his moods, as reflected in his letters home, fluctuated wildly. On the twenty-fourth, just before his finals, he wrote home that he was feeling very "blue." But a week later he was on the upswing, feeling "extremely happy" now with his basic "faith in life." He had recently become convinced that the human spirit never died and that "nothing we love ever ends." All this work he was doing, all these long, tedious hours he was investing in his studies: surely it all tended to some greater end. Surely all this was preparation "for eternal things for we have eternity in which to labor for it." It was only in emptying oneself of oneself, in doing for others, in self-forgetting work that we might find our own happiness. He was filled with this grand theme, and wrote his mother on February 12 again, about true Happiness:

> Last night I went down in the slums of Philadelphia to a settlement club, as they call them, where college fellows devote their spare time to helping the little bums learn something. I went down to fence an exhibition with the captain of last year's fencing team. I pity and admire those poor little kids. Some of them are mighty bright and quick and they know what is good and what isn't. One thing I am convinced more and more is true and that is this: the only way to be truly happy is to make others happy. When you realize that and take advantage of the fact, everything is made perfect.[17]

To make things perfect: thus Williams as philosopher and social ameliorator at age twenty. Besides his studies, he was still going to dances, and was asked in April to stand in with his violin with the university orchestra for a formal university banquet. However, he still refused to join his classmates when they went slumming in the Philadelphia bars to celebrate the end of the winter ordeal of examinations. He began now spending his Sunday afternoons in the second-story Philadelphia studio of his friend John Wilson. Wilson was "a grubby little fellow," Williams remembered, a man already in his mid-fifties, a failed artist who would paint version after version of the same landscape (with cows) there in his studio. Then one Sunday Wilson handed Williams an easel and paints and told him to try his own hand at it, so that for several years then and after he left Penn, Williams would take his oils out into the fields around Rutherford and down to the Passaic to paint impressionistic landscapes and, on at least one occasion, ten years later, render his own self-portrait. He was never really very good at it, certainly not as good as his mother had been, but he enjoyed it immensely and it did help to train his eye to see just what was before it.

*
**

In October 1904, as Williams entered his third year at Penn, he was still writing confidentially to Mama, even as signs of his independence became more noticeable. But Mama could still make her son wince with the broad hints she threw out about her own self-immolation for her family, could still make Willie feel guilty and unworthy of that great sacrifice. Only Carlos, Carlos who had died serving others while at sea and had been buried forever in that vast drear waste, only Carlos had ever understood her. "You said your brother was the only person that ever understood you," a contrite Willie wrote home to Mama on October 10. "Give me a chance, Mama, please do not regret the past so much but think of the future." He wanted her to think of her Willie as "a successful man and Ed also each with a simple loving wife who will love you and be your little daughter." Willie, sexually obtuse as ever, closed his letter by telling his mother to "buck up" and "be a man."[18]

But the signs of Willie's independence at twenty-one were becoming clearer. Three weeks later, for example, he wrote home that he was going out for the Mask and Wig again because he couldn't always be studying in isolated quarters. The world was bigger than 318 Leidy and he needed the company of others.[19] In fact, as those long solitary walks he took looking for girls (which of course he never told Mama about) indicated, Williams was starving for human companionship. But Elena, long out of touch with reality in any case, could not hear what her son was telling her. She wrote back at once that she and Papa had been deeply hurt by the tone of filial rejection in her son's letter, and so once again Willie had to capitulate. He was still their obedient Willie, he reassured them, but he was confused about what was in fact the right thing to do. "You and Papa seem to think that I am always doing just what I shouldn't do. . . . When I am most happy to think I am doing right I am probably doing the worst thing possible." But, he insisted, he had never in all his life yet done "a premeditated bad deed." And, he added, he never would! He had only the purest and highest and best thoughts about his parents, who had sacrificed everything for him. Confused, he answered hurt for hurt: "I try to do right and then I am blamed for doing wrong and really it is hard to be happy then."[20] Mama wrote back at once to say that, if she made Willie sad, he made her feel even sadder by his tone. Nothing for it, then, but for Willie to give in. He was sorry, he told her, sorry and ill about the whole thing. If he had been sharp in his letters, please to forgive him, Mama; her Willie wasn't feeling very well just now. Even his throat was beginning to feel sore again and he was sure he was coming down with a terrible cold. Now surely Mama would forgive him, all anxious about her poor Willie's health.[21] It was Willie's ploy, part conscious, part reflex: a way of forestalling criticism and regaining his mother's love, and Willie used that ploy as long as his mother could effectively use hers.

A few days later, Willie wrote Ed that he had one nasty sore throat for which he was taking daily doses of cod liver oil and Hyperphosphine.[22] Ed was now in his first year at MIT studying architecture, and Willie's tone in his letters to his brother was more relaxed, more down to earth: one brother confiding to another about the pleasures and perils of college life. He wanted very much to make the Mask and Wig this time, to sing and play light spoofs with a bunch of college fellows. He was reading James Whitcomb Riley's Hoosier-dialect poem "Knee-Deep in June" as well as Ulysses S. Grant's *Memoirs*. Old Grant, he confided to Ed, "did just like you and me, but it made me laugh to hear him talk about it." Certainly Williams was not yet ready to make that sort of indiscretion. As for the girls, he was going to give his "little" brother some advice on the subject. When you were twenty or twenty-one, as they were then, it was "perfectly natural and right for a fellow to get after the opposite sex." After all, a fellow wasn't "normal" if he didn't. And those art-school girls up there in Cambridge were "apt to be all to the mustard." In other words: hot stuff.[23]

When Williams went home a few weeks later for Thanksgiving, he made a special trip into New York to look over the French Hospital there, a new building with the latest medical equipment, situated on 34th Street between Ninth and Tenth avenues.[24] Dr. J. Julio Henna, head of residence there, was an old friend of Elena and Carlos', and Willie was interested in interning at the hospital when he graduated from Penn in a year and a half. The French Hospital was, as its name suggested, run by French-speaking Sisters of Charity, and cared for the French- and Spanish-speaking immigrants living on New York's Lower West Side at the turn of the century. Williams knew French and felt he could work up a serviceable Spanish, at least enough to take care of the patients he would be getting. But he also looked into hospitals in the Philadelphia and Boston areas, those choices dictated by his being either close to his university friends and colleagues, several of whom would intern in Philadelphia, or at least close to Ed. Of course there was still time before he had to make his final decision. More important, he resolved now not to dabble for the time being in those poetry notebooks of his, because writing only made him feel "blue to dream." Better, therefore, not to dream at all now.[25] Better to sing, sing Gilbert and Sullivan, sing parodies of Elizabethan song. When he returned to Penn after Thanksgiving, there was good news waiting for him this time. His rendition of "Tit Willow" from *The Mikado*, which he'd performed earlier during the Mask and Wig tryouts, had finally earned him a place with the group he'd wanted to join for three years.

*
**

1905. After the Christmas holidays, Williams once more returned to Penn to prepare for examinations and to pick up his social life—such as it was—once more. On January 12 he wrote Ed that he was supposed to take a young lady, a friend of the painter John Wilson, to a formal dance, but she was such a "regular fart face" that, if he hadn't promised Wilson and his wife, he wouldn't have offered to take the girl at all. As it turned out, he probably did not take her anyway, for this was probably the same girl he mentions in his *Autobiography* for whom he showed up in a tuxedo the day *after* the ball. Even false naiveté has its own strategies.[26] This same month Williams was also called on to deliver his first maternity case in the clinic at Penn. "I have to fool around an old bum's belly," he put it bluntly to Ed, using the tough, matter-of-fact language of the medical student who had to show he'd seen it all. The bum was "a woman of course," and he had to "see which way the kid is coming. Then in about two weeks I will have to yank the thing out." His bravado could not hide the fact that he was nervous about the whole procedure.[27]

Williams was now first alternate (still an alternate) on Penn's fencing team. So, when the team went down by train to Annapolis on Saturday, February 18, minus several of its starters who were out with a variety of illnesses, Williams had to go up against not one but two of Navy's best fencers. He was already at his full height—five nine—and weighed the full 135 pounds he would maintain for the next twenty years. Unlike Ed, who was tall and husky with brave mustaches, Willie had the slender, birdlike build of his mother, "skinny in the legs" but with good shoulders. He was still fast and graceful, with a quick eye and the moves of a dancer, and like his favorite poet, Keats (who'd after all been only five feet tall), Willie wasn't afraid of a fight. He knew he wasn't big enough for football, but fencing, he'd thought, was a game of skill: parry, thrust, touché. So when he went up against his first opponent, who turned out to be the captain of the Annapolis squad, he held his own well enough and put up a good performance, though the other's experience finally bested him. But it was the second match that discouraged him. This time they put a giant up against him. "I'll never forget a big bruiser on the Annapolis team," he remembered a half century later. "My forearm was just tired out. . . . He found he could knock the foil out of my hand by superior strength and get the point." No skill this time, just superior strength. To hell with it. Williams was through. He stayed with the team until the end of the season five weeks later and then quit.[28] (His love of the sport was to continue, however, and when, eighteen years later, he took his first sabbatical to write *In the American Grain* and was living in New York City, he joined the N.Y. Fencing Club to help stay in shape. But that last return to fencing lasted only a few months, and when he returned from Paris in the summer of '24, he put down for good the foils he'd first taken up in Paris in '98.)

Ezra Pound returned home from the wintry province of Hamilton two weeks into spring and was soon shouting up at ol' Bull Williams' window to come on nowt and play . . . now! "Say, Bo," Willie wrote Ed once that human vortex had left, "talk about Phila. being slow, well I can't see it." Ezra had invited Willie out to stay with him at his parents' home at 166

Fernbrook Avenue in Wyncote, a suburb ten miles north of the city, on Monday, April 3, to meet some fellows and—at last—"some dandy ladies." They were "a deuced of an intellectual bunch," Pound's friends, "daughters of professors, doctors, etc." And though the girls weren't particularly good-looking in any conventional way, there were all "pleasant to look upon because they are so nice."[29]

There was one girl there at Pound's place who'd particularly struck him. She was tall, as tall as he was, and rather bony and angular. In fact, she had a habit of getting in her own way. But in spite of that, he thought she too, like those Cambridge girls he'd dreamed of, was "all to the mustard" and he was already half in love with her. She was eighteen and "full of fun" and "bright" and "doesn't care if her hair is a little mussed, and wears good solid shoes. She is frank and loves music and flowers and I got along with her pretty well." She was "the daughter of the professor of astronomy at U. of P. and lives out in the country on the grounds where the [Flower] observatory is."

The girl's name was Hilda Doolittle (a name Pound would later shorten to the more hermetic H.D.). As for Hilda, she liked Billie Williams well enough too, and she invited him to come with Ezra the following Saturday to join a group of other young men and women for an afternoon party. Pound and Williams arrived at the observatory that afternoon to find to their delight that the party was made up of eight men and eight women, and soon all of them were out strolling through the surrounding countryside. At first the group stayed pretty much together, bantering, running, having a generally good time. But soon Hilda was separating herself out from the group to stop the others from trampling on the delicate spring flowers underfoot, and Williams found himself joining her. Before long Pound and the others had had enough and moved on, while Hilda and Billie strayed off into the woods.

"Oh, Ed," he confided to his brother, "but she is a fine girl, no simple nonsense about her, no false modesty and all that, she is absolutely free and innocent. We talked of the finest things: of Shakespeare, of flowers, trees, books & pictures and meanwhile climbed fences and walked through woods and climbed little hills till it began to grow dusky when we arrived at our destination."[30] Years later Williams would more candidly admit that what he'd really been interested in was watching Hilda closely, especially when she was straddling those rickety country fences in her short (ankle-length) skirt. So by the time the sun had begun to sink, Hilda had dubbed herself Rosalind and Williams Celia from *As You Like It*, two friends, though it would take years before Williams caught the full impact of what that change in names and gender might have been intended to convey.[31]

*
**

That fall, Williams began his last year at Penn. And now he understood that his future was fast looming up. He'd seriously considered taking a postgraduate year at the Johns Hopkins Medical School, but he felt guilty asking his father for any more support, especially with Ed still at MIT. Time now to begin making his own way, and so he'd applied to eight hospitals: six in the Philadelphia area, Massachusetts General Hospital in Boston, and the French Hospital in New York. He was also writing again—odes this time—odes in the Keatsian mode for the most part, though he also wrote at least one in a lighter, more whimsical mood addressed to his own voracious appetite.[32]

Now, too, in spite of himself, he was beginning to find himself in love again, not so much with a particular woman, but with the idea of love itself. No sooner was he back at Penn for the last haul than he'd taken Hilda to a full-dress rehearsal of the Mask and Wig. Then, on top of that, he composed a Shakespearean sonnet for her nineteenth birthday (January 13)—the "year's initial ides." The poem's fourteen lines coincided with Hilda's name and Williams wrote each line reinforced with a heavy percussive alliteration to underscore the successive letters in her name:

> Hark Hilda! heptachordian hymns
> Invoke the year's initial ides
> Like liquid lutes' low languishings.
> Dim dawn defeated dusk derides.
> Awake, for at Aurora's advent angel anthemings arise![33]

Those lines were addressed as much to Williams as they were to Hilda, for they signaled a sense of beginning again in poetry. How he'd labored over those lines to give them birth! But Hilda only laughed at him. If those lines had truly been for her, she quipped, then they should have burst spontaneously from Billie's lips like song itself.

Ed, having read his brother's latest collection of derivative Keats, was sure that his brother was indeed a great poet. So he'd collected a batch of them and shown them to his English teacher at MIT, Professor Arlo Bates. First, of course, Ed had written asking Willie if it would be all right to do this, and Willie had in turn written back in his best Parnassian manner assuring Ed that he was fully aware that he was "walking into the danger of even ridicule with a thorough knowledge of what may await me" as this professor scruitinized his poems. Who after all but Williams himself could ever know what those poems had cost him?[34]

A month later Ed reported back that Professor Bates had liked some of the pieces, though he'd thought others a bit too derivative of Keats. No matter, Willie assured Ed. He did appreciate Arlo's criticisms, but after all who knew better than himself what was best for him? Insofar as Arlo liked the poems, the man was "very just and learned." But insofar as he disagreed with what Williams was doing, "why, of course one of us must be wrong and I being right he is 'it,' therefore neither just nor learned."[35]

He was not yet finished with Bates, however, for he would visit him in person two years later, armed then with a massive sheaf of his poeticizings, including a long, serious poem, an epyllion of sorts. And when he saw Bates then, it would be Jacob wrestling with the angel, face to face.

In early March, Willie went out to see Hilda again at Upper Darby, and this time he finally had the opportunity to inspect her father's astronomy laboratory. The sight of Professor Doolittle spending night after night studying and charting the heavens left Williams with a deep impression of awesome respect for the man's single-minded dedication to his life's work. Doolittle was an incredibly remote figure, a silent specter who floated at odd times about the house obsessed, while his poor overworked wife attended to the heavy household duties. At least that was how Williams remembered it. And years later he was to remember Professor Doolittle, gaze fixed, as Pound had once quipped, "on nothing nearer than the moon," spending long years measuring the seasonal oscillations of the earth on its rotational axis, while Mrs. Doolittle would go out to the observatory toward dawn on a January morning with a "kettle of boiling water to thaw the hairs of his whiskers that during his night-long vigil had become frozen to the eyepiece of the machine."[36]

Yet for all the comic aspects of his vignette, Williams was deeply impressed by Doolittle's laboratory and by the quiet devotion of the man to his chosen scientific work. That laboratory with all its complicated instruments brought home to him his own relative ignorance of the whole world of astronomy. Williams was always to hold in awe figures like Doolittle, who did their work quietly and unobtrusively, as he hoped some day to do his own. Here was the necessary quiet needed to pursue beautiful truth. Perhaps a lifetime's solitude for the brief privileged moment of discovery.

But wasn't truth, after all, an act of intuitive faith, something that left poor logic far behind? Truth, he told Ed that same month, was not something reasoned out but something intuitively grasped, something believed in. "Don't reason from feelings or rather don't reason at all," he told his brother. For he saw now that truth was not something arrived at by syllogisms and proofs, but something grasped by a quantum leap of faith. Truth was, after all, an intuitive insight into the essence of a thing, something radiantly perceived in a moment.

And he wasn't talking about a religious experience either. As far as he was concerned, he'd had it with all that "darned rot" about " 'milk and honey blest' heavens as if we were born to live in a pantry." No, truth was an "honest, manly" affair like that he'd discovered in some of the Old Testament psalms, such as the first, twenty-third, and thirty-seventh, all of which stressed that ultimately the good would prosper and the wicked would be defeated. "Remember," he consoled his brother, "you are going to live forever and that's no damned fool poetic figure, it's got to be true for you to be happy and we must therefore do things that will last forever."[37] Doolittle peering into the eternal heavens as though he had all the time in the world: it was an example to cheer Williams on. For Williams knew in his own heart that he might be starting out slowly into art, unlike Ezra, but what after all were a few years in the long run of eternity? And in the long run, he told Ed, "Truth and love will never fail."

He continued in this philosophic vein with Ed a few days afterward. It was not, finally, the rationalists or the philosophers who ever really answered the big questions about life. Had not Hamlet himself chided Horatio's reliance on philosophy to the same effect? Most people committed the serious mistake of separating their practical lives out from their philosophy or religion as though they belonged to separate compartments of one's existence. But the truth was that what a man did with his hands and with his mind had to be part of the same stuff, "one and inseparable." Work, sheer hard work was the answer. How ridiculous to rest from one's labors on Sunday, to divorce oneself from work on that day, to do nothing, when one's very labors could themselves serve as a paean of praise to the divine, when the truly integrated man "might be working at some beautiful secret of nature." What a man worked at—and the weight of Carlyle and Emerson and Ruskin was behind Williams here—what a man worked at was really an extension of himself as a person. And since man himself was divine, since man himself was the truth, so the work he did must also be the truth. And if a man's "works are not divine, if they are not truth in stone, wood or iron, they are nothing." To hell with that "mystic medieval conception of a divine power with frowning brows who swats us one when we get in a dark corner," Williams insisted. As for himself, he was all for the light, for the emanation of the divine energy that people themselves were.[38] Not Calvin, then, but Blake or at least the Unitarian creed. And this Emersonian transcendental mode which Williams argued for so strongly at twenty-two would—transmuted—remain the bedrock of his beliefs for the rest of his life, to rise fully to the surface again in his last years.

What Williams was referring to here in these letters to Ed was a new inner security that he was now experiencing. The clue to this profound conviction of the nature of human experience is given in a letter he wrote Marianne Moore thirty years later. In a review Moore had done of Williams' *Collected Poems (1921–1931)*, she had noticed that what held Williams' poetic world together was a certain "inner security." Williams was astonished at Moore's observation; it was, he said, as though she had looked at what he'd done through his own eyes. And the secret key had been her phrase, "inner security." That inner security, he confessed, had come upon him when he was about twenty (actually he was twenty-two), and it was posited, he said, on nothing less than despair itself. What had happened to him was that he had had to finally and simply resign himself to existence. It was, however, "a despair which made everything a unit and at the same time a part of myself. . . . I decided there was nothing else in life for me but to work." From that point on all schemes and causes and ideologies and philosophies and creeds had simply gone by the wayside. What mattered now was the fact of his own unique existence, his ability to say "I am." Suddenly the entire universe was wiped clean. No longer did names and places carry any special significance, except insofar as he personally invested them with his own meanings. The promise of a heaven, of being rewarded ultimately because one had tried hard to be perfect, had proven a sham and was, frankly, "impossible." Looking out onto the immense universe, he'd known for once his own smallness. He'd plummeted into a new hell and knew he was damned. For the first time in his life he could accept his own ultimate anonymity. But, paradoxically, what had followed this terrifying descent had been a newly found freedom: the freedom of merely being, of being as much a part of things "as trees and stones." All that was left for him while he lived, then, was to work: to work with people, to work with words. To "repair, to rescue, to complete" as he could. In large measure, Williams' life was to be a carrying out of this very sense of the ultimate value of act in a world that was finally, inexplicably, meaningless and paradoxically, therefore, without value, ultimate or otherwise.[39]

The same month Williams underwent his nameless religious experience, Pound invited him out to Wyncote for a weekend. After dinner, the two of them went up to Pound's room to talk about literature and drama and philosophy and the classics, all those subjects, Williams wrote his mother on the thirtieth, "that I love yet have not time to study and which [Pound] is making a life work of." Pound, he added, had an incredibly optimistic outlook and a "castiron faith" in life, and yet Williams also had to note that "not one person in a thousand likes him, and a great many people detest him." Why was this so? Because, Williams ventured, his friend was "so darned full of conceits and affectation." Surely Williams knew how deeply Pound wanted to be liked, but he knew how stubborn the man could be, "too proud to try to please people" or even to trust them. For himself, he said, it was better "to dare all and gain love in the daring." But whose love? Hilda's?[40]

For one can sense in his letter home an undercurrent of tension, and two things especially may have provoked it. One was that Pound, for all his insouciance, his devil-may-care attitude, had his own eye on Hilda (after all, he had introduced Williams to her), and he didn't like the sense of covert rivalry he was smelling.[41] So it may have been on this particular visit, as Williams and Pound entered through the vestibule of Pound's

Victorian home, that Pound—in his best imitation Italian fencing manner—pulled two walking canes from the ornate umbrella stand there, tossed one to Williams, and told him to be on guard. At once the two of them were at it: thrust, parry, counterthrust, the click-click of stick on stick, as Williams, the better swordsman, checked each of Pound's wild lungings. And then Pound was swinging at William's head until, suddenly, he hurled himself at him with all his force, nearly putting Williams' eye out. Williams, feeling the pain under his eye, screamed and put down his sword. Enough was enough. Pound had made his point.

But Williams would never forget that incident. For him it summed up one of Pound's worst characteristics: the need to be an instant expert in whatever he undertook to do, whether it was music (he played execrably and was tone-deaf, Williams always insisted), or politics and economics (both of which were to get Pound in serious trouble years later). Thirty-two years after the offensive stick had struck him, Williams was still smarting. After all these years he still had to defend himself against some of Ezra's verbal "awkward jibes." Ezra, he remembered with some satisfaction, had never been good enough to make the Penn fencing squad—though of course he himself had—and if Williams had wanted to, he "could have shoved the stick through [Pound's] mouth and out at his ass hole if it had been important enough to do so but—holding back, kidding—he damn near put my eye out. Served me damn well right. I should have knocked hell out of him—but didn't."[42]

Perhaps Pound had also meant to teach Williams a lesson about master and disciple, or, more specifically, about which of them had first pickings. But if Pound meant to "tell" Williams that Hilda was in some vague sense his girl, Williams didn't get the message. He was still seeing her, though he was also seeing an old friend from Rutherford, a girl named Dorothy, as well as Hilda's friend Margaret Snively. On Saturday night, April 21—three weeks after his mock duel—he took Hilda to a Mask and Wig performance and then, since it was too late to get a trolley back to campus from Upper Darby, Hilda gave him one of her father's nightgowns and invited him to spend the night on the downstairs sofa. Toward dawn, however, he awoke with a start, realizing he'd had "a wet dream." Frantic that the telltale stain would be discovered by Hilda's father on one of his periodic trips back to earth, Williams pulled the gown off and, standing there naked, began waving it in great circles over his head to dry it as quickly as possible.[43]

That afternoon Margaret Snively rode over from her father's orphanage in a one-seated horse-drawn rig to take Hilda and Willie for a ride through fields blanketed now with spring wild flowers. Then, in the evening, Hilda went up to her room to study for her exams while Willie retired to the library with Hilda's younger brother to read some Kipling before he headed back to his own dorm room. The following Saturday, April 28, Ezra, who had just been appointed a Harrison Fellow in Romanics for 1906–07 by the University of Pennsylvania, set sail for Spain and six months' studying in Madrid. His purpose in going there was to study Spanish literature and to write a thesis on Lope de Vega. But Williams told Ed more simply that Ez was going away "to study some old books there and get a line on the Spanish language." Ezra was, after all, one "bright cuss."[44]

Three days after Ezra sailed for Europe, Williams went to the May Day celebrations at Bryn Mawr to see Hilda. She was dressed as one of Robin Hood's merry band, and Williams was once again taken by her tall form as she marched gaily with the other girls across the campus's lush green fields. He was sure now he was "dead in love with that girl," he confided to his brother: "She isn't good looking and she isn't graceful, she isn't a beautiful dresser and she cannot play any music but by Gee! She is a fine girl and she can have me alright!"[45]

He'd already taken the exams for resident intern at the French Hospital on New York's Lower West Side in mid-April, but how he did in getting placed would depend on how well he performed in his final examinations at Penn, which began on May 20. Time then to grind out the work, to "work and win," as he assured his mother he would do. Yes, he was feeling the attraction of "wine and joy and forgetfulness,"[46] as Keats and thousands before him had, though he meant to reject all those temptations as unworthy. But what he hadn't foreseen was the Great Temptation of Shakespeare in the midst of those finals. That temptation came in the form of the Ben Greet Company of Woodland Players, who set up their portable Shakespearean theater in the old botanical gardens in plain sight of Williams' dorm window. This last temptation proved too much. Four continuous days of Shakespeare, with two different performances each day, in the afternoons and evenings. That was eight—eight! —Shakespearean plays.

To make matters worse, Williams was broke. He had to forgo *A Comedy of Errors* that first afternoon, and immediately regretted his lost chance. By evening, therefore, he was determined to somehow get in to see the second show, *A Midsummer Night's Dream*. This effort included scaling a fence, then jumping to clear a tangle of underbrush, and then, after being turned back once at the admissions gate, pushing his way in with a large party past the ticket taker a second time. Again, the man at the ticket booth spotted him and told him to stop, but this time Williams kept on moving until he'd finally blended in with the others under cover of the gathering dark. Necessity, he was learning, knew no laws.

Shakespeare's example put the neophyte into a philosophical mood. His university years were all but over now and he knew that he was "about to enter the very heart" of life's "rush and tumble." But was not all that bustle, seen through the telescope of philosophical time, a vain and useless thing? Here he was, like thousands of other American boys, about to graduate, only to begin "to fight my way up by pushing others down." And yet for what, especially in the light of what Will Shakespeare had shown us all about the vanity of human wishes? For himself, Williams did not want to be rich and he did not want fame. What he did want, as he'd told Ed earlier, was "to do all I have to do well, and to be left alone to look on people and help them without being myself known."[47] If lack of wealth and a relative lack of fame in his own lifetime were really what he wanted, then the fates were surely listening to Williams.

In mid-June, Bob Lamberton, one of Williams' classmates and a tackle for Penn's varsity football team, invited Williams to a graduation party down at Point Pleasant on the New Jersey seashore. Williams had just been offered the internship at the French Hospital and he would begin work there in July. Now, therefore, he was busier than ever getting his affairs in order. As a result he had a hard time getting away to join the beach party and it was noon before he finally arrived. Hilda he knew would be there, along with Margaret and Ethylwyn Snively and a large group of others. Besides, he knew there wouldn't be much swimming since there'd been a rough storm that morning and the surf was still churning wildly. But Hilda, Williams recalled twenty years later, "seeing the ocean for the first time in several years perhaps, carried to the point of ecstasy by her delight in the waves, rushed into them headlong, not knowing how to swim, not having gauged their force, not waiting for the others. She was crushed, trampled, swept out, drowned." At once Lamberton tore down the beach and dived in after her and, with the help of some of the other men there, dragged Hilda, unconscious, from the ocean.

Williams himself arrived just after Hilda had regained consciousness and had been taken up to the Lamberton house to recuperate. When, in that commotion, Williams learned what had happened, how Hilda had almost died, he was shaken. In fact the image of that tall girl going to meet the ungoverned, unchecked fury of the elements, elements she did not understand, became for Williams a symbol of her subsequent life, when she began to live openly with another woman, Bryher, despite the fact that Bryher was then married to Williams' closest friend Robert McAlmon. Williams would make these remarks in a 1925 review of H.D.'s *Collected Poems*, and he noted there that her poems too had derived their cumulative force from their devastating encounters with the shocks of the war and a difficult marriage and with what had followed after, shocks different in nature but similar to the unchecked fury of Hilda's encounter with the ocean that morning at Point Pleasant.[48]

Ironically, that same afternoon, while Williams chatted and played billiards and drank punch in the crowded pavilion that had been set up against the chance of inclement weather, another electric storm broke over them. At one point he suddenly felt the whip of a lightning bolt slap against the back of his neck at the same moment it sent the woman who'd been standing next to him flying to the ground. A moment later it splintered the flagpole under which both of them were standing. It was a day that nearly changed the subsequent history of American poetry forever. That night, when Williams said good-by and left for home, it was to be the last time he ever saw his college friends as a group together. On top of that he'd almost lost Hilda. And already Pound was gone.

*
* *

But Williams too was walking into his own turbulence as he soon found out. He began interning at the French Hospital on Sunday morning, July 1, and almost at once he found himself knocked under and nearly drowned by the crush of work. When he finally emerged from that pounding, in fact, he would himself have suffered his own sea change. His daily routine had been carefully spelled out for him by Dr. Henna. Rise at 7:00, dress in clean white ducks and be at the breakfast table by 7:30. From 8:00 until 10:00 he had to visit each and every patient in the hospital. Then, when the visiting physician arrived at 10:00, Williams had to go over each case with him, take notes, and then carry out the physician's orders. That took from 10:00 until 1:00, when there was a brief respite for lunch. In the afternoon, he had to write up case histories of patients and then visit the new patients. After dinner, he would have to make his rounds all over again. Then, at 9:00, if no new cases had come in, he could go back to his own room on the fifth floor and rest or read or write until he fell asleep.[49]

It was a hectic and intense time for Williams, that July and August, a time when he was constantly being overworked until his whole body was racked with nervous tension. He kept complaining of feeling poorly, and his telltale sore throats began to return to plague him. Part of the problem was that so much of what he was doing was new for him, but he was also being asked on top of that to fill in for the regular medical staff, who were taking their own well-earned vacations. Still, he did have the moral support of Dr. Henna, who'd been directly responsible for getting Williams into the hospital in the first place, and he soon became very good friends with most of the French-speaking Sisters of Charity who served as the nursing staff. He liked them. They were mostly young, dedicated, vigorous, and interesting, and he was soon half in love with most of them. At first he had some trouble with the superintendent of nurses, an older, tougher nun, but he knew he had the "powers" in his corner, and after she and Williams had crossed swords once too often, Dr. Henna called her down to his office and admonished her to leave Williams alone. She then "promptly went up to her room and had a fit of hysterics," a gleeful Williams wrote his mother, after which she was "very sweet and ashamed of herself."[50]

Finally, at the beginning of September, enough of the regular staff were back to allow Williams a short respite. William George, now fifty-five, had wanted to take an extended walking tour up around Lake George in the Adirondacks with his sons and two of their friends. So, early on Saturday, September 1, they all boarded the train for Albany and then caught a trolley for Watervliet.[51] From there, eager to begin their tour at once, they walked eighteen miles north to the village of Stillwater. Each day Ed would send home postcards to his mother, on which he drew the inns where they were staying, including one picture of Willie and Pop relaxing on the porch of an inn after a good day's walk. They made Lake George on the third, and then were delayed for twenty-four hours by a downpour that turned everything sodden. Then the weather cleared and they were on the road again, averaging twenty-five miles a day, up along the western side of Lake George past Sabbath Day Point (which Ed drew) and on to Fort Ticonderoga and then north again to Port Henry before taking the train back to Rutherford. In six days they'd covered well over a hundred miles on foot, tasted the cool mountain air in their lungs, and seen a good part of the northern forests as these began to turn orange and red. Williams had made Ed write home to Mama to say that Willie was feeling just great again, for she had been shocked to see what hospital work had done to her boy.[52] A snapshot of Williams taken on this trip shows him in knickers, long stockings, comfortable walking shoes, hat, walking jacket and tie, sitting on a rock and holding a walking cane as he stares intently into the camera. The camera seems to have caught him just as he is about to smile, but the eyes still have a tinge of weariness. Williams especially had needed that week in the mountains and the companionship of his father and brother before he dove back into the crushing, lonely work of the hospital.

Despite his work, however, which remained intense, Williams managed to steal time to work on his secret epic, which he'd begun in his last year at Penn. In his hospital quarters late at night or back home on occasional weekends, he worked at his poem with pen and foolscap. That poem was set in a Keatsian fairyland and was about a prince whose entire family had been wiped out by poison administered by the prince's father during the prince's wedding to a young princess. Actually, the father had wanted to kill only his son, but—as in *Hamlet*—he had had to destroy everyone, himself included, in order to get the son to drink the poisoned potion. But the prince had been revived in the end by his haglike grandmother, and when he awoke, he found himself in a strange new world where the inhabitants spoke a strange new tongue. The poem was

written in a Keatsian/Shakespearean blank verse line in a language
redolent of that ersatz medieval which Spenser had invented and which
Keats had early on imitated, and it began (badly) like this:

> Within the lofty hall is gay with flags
> In battle won and many bristling antlers.
> Trophies all, the prowess both in war
> And peace announce of those who dwell herein.
> Ancestral portraits line the smoke stained walls.
> Upon the oaken board a feast is set
> A wedding feast, the guests are gathered round
> The bride leans pensive o'er her heapèd plate
> The jester on his three legged stool is sad.
> Twelve empty glasses stand before the guests
> And sparkle in the full moon's waning light.[53]

Hard to believe, really, that the same man who was performing
emergency appendectomies and treating malaria victims as well as sand-
blast victims from the excavations for the new Pennsylvania Station going
up a block away, that this man who was stitching up ugly knife wounds
and delivering babies of every color and description as the poor mothers
came in off the streets for help, hard to believe that this same man was
spending what free hours he had trying to write his own initiatory epic,
his own version of Keats in this stilted manner. But Williams was
obsessed with that poem, convinced of its importance, and he kept
working at it on and off for three more years. The reason was that what
Williams was really working at here was his own psychodrama, and part
of the problem he was trying to work through was his own reading of how
his businesslike father must have been looking at his oldest son with his
penchant for dreamy poetry. Did Williams see himself as giving "no
heed / To war's account" and as living, like his prince, "a live long
summer's day / A fawning milk-sop by his mother's side"? And did he see
himself as closely allied with his mother as the prince was to his mother,
a woman like Elena who repeatedly reminded her son of

> foreign kingdom's [sic] o'er the sea,
> Of sands that shone like sheeted gold—of waves
> And calm, of auzure [sic] skies so pure and deep
> No clown so low but sang in witless praise
> At magic morn's uncloaking. . . .

Puerto Rico seen through a Keatsian haze. The poem is rambling,
confused, but also revelatory, and it points to Williams' deeply felt need
to erase as effectively as he could his dependence on his parents and to
strike out on his own into a brave new world, as terrifying as that
experience might initially be. If he found himself constantly bested by
language in his talks and in his letters to his parents, at least here in his

long poem he could work out his relationships by a radical beginning again under the aegis of the one relative he could relate to: his renegade Grandma Wellcome. Williams says in his *Autobiography* that he finally destroyed this poem, or at least a version of it, by tossing it into the basement furnace. What probably happened, though, is that he had worked out the problems that were troubling him sufficiently to realize that what was left—a very mediocre and derivative exercise—could now be discarded like an old skin.

In the meantime, there was the sweaty, crass reality of lower New York City, where the hospital was located, with its rank smells and street noises of hawkers and vendors, its Sicilians with fruit carts, its Jewish and Armenian rag merchants, its Irish toughs and black porters, its gas lamps and clanging trolleys and elevated trains shuttling back and forth spitting out sparks from the third rail. And yet none of that seemed to be able to penetrate the Victorian medieval sanctum sanctorum of Williams' world of poesy. Where reality did brush against Williams' imagination, it had first to be transmuted into a fine gold filament of romantic blank verse, where reigned but truth and beauty and a blank space reserved for the initiate in Palgrave's *Golden Treasury*. When Williams did leave the activity of the French Hospital it was usually only for a few hours, a momentary escape to hear a concert at the Aeolian Hall or the Carnegie, for chamber music or a performance of Puccini's *Madama Butterfly* or Wagner's *Parsifal* sung in German.[54] So, even though Pound was back home now, Williams simply could not squeeze in the time to get down to Philadelphia at Halloween for his friend's twenty-first birthday, when— as Pound had told him ironically—he was finally going to become a man.[55] Five months after graduation, Williams was already feeling nostalgic for the cloistral quiet of his university dorm.

By November he was going sixteen-hour days without a break. Election night was especially bad in the city because of the heated electioneering going on between Hughes and Hearst for the mayoralty of New York. One of Williams' emergency calls had been a woman (drunk) who'd been stabbed in the hand by her husband (also drunk). The second had been a "coon" who'd been cornered by a gang of toughs out looking for him. Before they'd let him go, they'd opened his skull with a bottle. But, Williams noted, the guy had been a "good sport" about it all. The third case had been saddest of all: a child had come in with one hand curled in on itself, badly burned, having been pushed into a street bonfire for the hell of it.[56]

Four months in a New York hospital had made of Williams something of a cynic, too. Pushed to it, he had toughened, had opened himself to new explorations. There were fitful interludes, for example, late at night on the tar roof of the French Hospital with the moon coming up from behind tenement chimneys when one of the lay nurses would sit and hold hands with him. And he'd seen enough of the world—of tough streetwalkers and con artists and women patients near term catfighting in the wards because they'd discovered that the same man had made them both pregnant—to have become weary . . . and wary. Girls? As for trying to figure out girls, he advised Ed, well, one might just as soon go and stand on top of that new Times Building and "try to put out the sun by 'peeing' at it as give advice on that subject." Girls, he was learning, were necessary for a guy, "but only girls in general." Better not to get too serious.[57]

Obviously something disturbing had happened to Williams. At some point during his first few months at the hospital—he does not reveal when exactly—he had brushed up against sexual passion and had recoiled from it in order to "preserve" himself. Six days after his cynical remarks to Ed he wrote again to say that he had found it necessary to exert a new and severe discipline over himself. To preserve himself for his higher goals in life, he would have to feel only safe attractions now, such as those for his parents and for Ed himself. Williams had learned the hard way just how passionate he really was in spite of all his repressive energies to the contrary; where women were concerned, he had a real "weakness." Given the right conditions, such as those available in the world of the hospital, an attractive female, perhaps as overworked and as starved for intimacy as himself, might get him to throw over everything he'd worked so hard for. And under such conditions logic and reason meant nothing to him. There would be a trembling, then a shaking of the body, and an irresistible urge—as he would write later—to tear into the woman and possess her. "As a result, in order to preserve myself as I must," he concluded, "girls cannot be my friends."[58]

He had great plans for himself and he was not going to cripple himself at the beginning of an illustrious career. He knew how little a small town like Rutherford had to offer compared to New York, and he wasn't going to be trapped into a life in the sticks if he could help it: "At home the people are in general small; they see their little neighborhood." He'd been raised there, had lived there nearly all his twenty-three years. But he'd also had a taste of places like Geneva, Paris, and now New York. He was after bigger things and so wasn't really much interested "in the people I have known."[59] So when Ed told his big worldly brother that he was feeling depressed because he was finding it so hard to be perfect (as Mama had enjoined on her younger son as well), Williams, having passed through that ordeal already, warned Ed that to be "cast down because we are not perfect" was "vain and priggish."[60] And the following month, in an even more cynical vein, Williams jotted down on the outside of an envelope of a letter from Ed that marriage was "a disease a sickness of the brain. What a crafty thing is it in the Almighty that this love should turn our minds. Else who would marry, who in cold blood would marry if he were honest?"[61] Why marriage, he might have added, when there were lonely nurses enough to flirt with so long as one kept one's head?

*
* *

Williams got home for Christmas and then helped bring in 1907 at the Spanish-American Club in New York as the guest of Dr. Henna. It was a great party and he did not get back to his hospital quarters until five in the morning. Still, despite the intense activity and the nurses, he felt lonely away from home and Philadelphia. Several times he'd wanted to get down to see Hilda in the fall, and he'd finally written her at Thanksgiving that he was feeling out of things. Yet, perversely, when he did get down to Philadelphia two weeks before Chirstmas, he did not go out to see her. So when Hilda's older brother, Eric, bumped into Williams on the street in Philadelphia and mentioned the fact to Hilda, she chided Willie for not coming out to see her, especially if he was as lonely as he said he was.[62] But Williams may not have gone to see her because Pound was back now, and Pound had made it clearer that Hilda was his interest. In return, he was going to fix ol' Bull up with another girl in New York.

On February 6 Pound wrote Williams to say that there was a young woman by the name of Viola Baxter living uptown from the hospital and that he should go and visit her. Viola was the one person, Pound added, who'd made his exile—his "hell"—up in the boondocks of Hamilton "homelike."[63] Five days later he sent Williams Viola's address—143 East 83rd Street—and told him Viola was expecting him. The same day Willie received Viola's address, he wrote Ed that he was finally going to meet "a most excellent New York girl."[64] Then, one night, two weeks later, Willie left the hospital for a late evening visit to meet this girl Pound had told him about. Some of the other interns—his close friend Gaskins no doubt among them—had once told Willie that in New York the "fashionable hour" for calling was nine in the evening, though that seemed inordinately late to him. So, when he got to the apartment house just before the hour, he was so nervous that he almost turned back, prepared to try another time, when he noticed lights on in one of the upstairs rooms. Timidly, he climbed the front stairs and rang the bell. At first—nothing. Then a large, fat German woman—obviously the landlady—answered the door. Was a Miss Viola Baxter in? Go upstairs, she told him, third floor front, the lady was waiting for him. And then she let Willie past to walk up the gas-lighted stairs. As he made the third floor, Williams told his brother, "the door flew open and a big woman started talking to me very familiarly while behind her back I saw a beautiful maiden in decided negligée lying on a sofa." Ah, divine Odalisque, he may have thought. But the reality was different. "It was all over in a moment," he lamented, "the large woman shut the door like a flash all but a crack while the maiden with the 'pootiest' little scream you ever heard disappeared in the folds of a blanket."[65]

Exit Willie, nonplussed, abashed, backing down the stairs and out onto the street toward the el. Back in his room at the hospital next day, he wrote a hurried note apologizing to Miss Baxter for coming to visit her at a most inopportune time, just as she was apparently preparing to go to bed. Would she consider joining him for the Penn-Columbia basketball game uptown that evening? She did join him, and Willie found Viola to be a quiet, young (nineteen), very attractive brunette. He could admire her, he confided to Ed, but he didn't really like her, at least not yet. Thus began a relationship that, over the next eight years, was to prove tortuous, dramatic, and frustrating in the extreme, especially after Willie became engaged to a young girl from Rutherford.

Of course Williams had already made many friends at the hospital. First there were the sisters, a spectrum of dedicated women ranging from Sister Elizabeth, "a pure peasant who was shocked" to learn that a nice young man like Dr. Williams wasn't a Catholic, to fat, cowlike Sister Pelagia, who waddled through the narrow hospital corridors indifferently knocking into trays and patients, to Sister Superior Juliana, a woman Williams admired for her "whiplike intelligence," a woman who was "no prude" and could handle any and all emergencies with a quiet professionalism, and whom Williams came quickly to admire and respect. And then there was, finally, the radiant Kore-like image of Sister Eleanor, dressed in spotless white like some vision, there in the operating room across from him, giving him her quiet strength and comfort, her unattainable beauty haunting him. In old age, Williams would think often of Toulouse-Lautrec, the artist in the Parisian bordello, also surrounded by women who comforted him, but in Williams' imagination those Parisian whores and these New York French virgins were part of the same marvelous spectrum that made up his image of Paradise.

Besides the women, there were five other interns, all part of the tight little world of the hospital: Smith, Maloney (who was fired when he complained to a New York newspaper reporter about the miserable food served in the hospital), Eberhard (who replaced Maloney), and Gaskins, Williams' closest friend and the man who kept Williams laughing in good times and bad. (Gaskins would die fighting the terrible influenza epidemic of 1918 which was to kill so many people, patients and doctors alike.) And then there was Krumweide, the German pathologist, trained in the nineteenth-century German scientific tradition, the man Williams approached with awe and whom he nicknamed "The Wrath of God." Krumweide was the one man on the staff Williams felt he had failed, or at least was made to feel he had failed. This was the story. Krumweide had once given Williams several blood specimens on glass to diagnose—admittedly difficult cases—and Williams had not seen that they might be diagnosed positively for malaria. When Krumweide showed him that he'd misdiagnosed the specimens, Williams knew he was defeated, knew now that Krumweide would never fully trust Williams again since he personally had left Williams in charge of pathological diagnosis. Still, in spite of that irreversible betrayal, the two men got along and often, late at night, when they weren't etherizing the swarms of cockroaches that kept eating Krumweide's all-important blood samples off the glass plates in the darkened lab room, Williams would accompany the German's piano playing on his own battered violin.[66]

There are some snapshots too from this period, showing Williams and his friend Gaskins (with drooping mustache) and a beautiful young nurse's aide outside the hospital. "Why do they call me a 'Gibson man'?" the woman—St. C.—has written in pencil on the back of one photo showing a serious young Williams in white ducks. In another, Gaskins has made Willie laugh, a feat sufficiently noticeable for St. C. to have commented on it on the back of the picture.[67] Willie was loosening up, becoming more human, something nurses and colleagues would help him do all his life.

In early April, Willie, recovering from another of his recurrent sore throats, took a well-earned four-day vacation from the hospital to go down to Philadelphia. Late on Wednesday, the third, he took the train down and stayed with Bob Lamberton (Williams' classmate, the one who'd pulled Hilda from the ocean). Next day he went out to see Charlie Demuth, who would soon be leaving for Paris to study art, and then made a tour of Children's Hospital in Philadelphia, having finally decided that he would specialize in pediatrics and would take another year's internship in the specialty. (He had enough experience by then to see that, though he had the hands and coordination to make a good surgeon, he didn't want to spend the rest of his life dabbling, as he phrased it, in other people's guts.) On Friday he visited some of the other hospitals around Philadelphia and then went out to visit Margaret Snively at her father's orphanage in Upper Darby. Then, on Saturday, he took the trolley out to Wyncote with Bob Lamberton to see Ezra, who was just ending his second year as a graduate student on a sour note, he explained, because of a major difference of opinion with his instructor in literary criticism. Mrs. Pound made lunch for her son and his two friends, and then the men talked about literature until four, when Williams and Lamberton left to visit Hilda at the observatory. But Willie could see that Hilda was not feeling well, that her back was giving her trouble again, and that it was time to leave. Instead, he and Lamberton decided to take a long walk.[68] And though he'd posted a card to his mother earlier in the day showing a drawn-in ink figure of himself walking in front of Hilda's house and had written that the weather was fine and that he was feeling fine, he soon found himself walking into the middle of a gale-force storm in the open fields around Upper Darby.[69] In spite of that, he returned that evening to pick Hilda up and take her to a Mask and Wig performance at his old alma mater. By Sunday afternoon he was back in Rutherford working on a short play of his own, helping his father prepare the lawn and trim their fruit trees, and singing in a local concert that evening. By Monday morning, 7:30, he was back in the corridors of the French Hospital, examining his patients.

So it went. Periods of intense activity interrupted with sudden bursts of devil-may-care activity, like sneaking up in his pajamas with ol' Gaskins to the women's quarters on the sixth floor to dance with the nurses and steal a kiss from them before clearing the hell out of there, afraid to be discovered by one of the staff. Still, he was not as bold as Eberhard, who'd serviced not one but two women over in the women's Brooklyn apartment. Eberhard had tried to save one of them for Willie, but when Willie begged off, Eberhard shrugged and took them both on. If Willie wanted to "preserve" himself, that was his own affair, the fool.[70] By year's end, Willie could sum up his life to his brother in this way: "We both have had a pretty good time in our lives so far, we have seen a little of the world, managed by the grace of God to keep clean, and at last we are at the end of the first stage and in a fair way to earn an honest living soon."[71]

In early August, Willie, Ed, and Pop took another of those walking tours, this one down through the Berkshires of western Massachusetts and Connecticut, and ending at the West Haven cottage.[72] Again, they averaged twenty-five miles a day on foot. William George may well have taken his oldest boy into his confidence on this trip, to ask him to share the burden of caring for Ed and, even more, Elena. "Write to your little brother in Boston," Williams senior had written Willie the year before. "He needs advice. My impression is that he is overdoing himself. . . . You tell him not to drive himself into the ground with overwork, but to give himself rest and long hours of sleep."[73] But now it was Mother he wanted to talk to Willie about. She was becoming more and more erratic in her behavior. She too needed rest, and, since he was going to Central America in six weeks' time for the company, he was anxious that his doctor son take care of her and watch over her, especially since Ed would be back at MIT. William George reiterated his charge again that September in a letter written off Cape Hatteras as he prepared to sail for Panama. He was feeling tired himself and wanted Willie to assume the burden now. Since Mother would need rest, Willie would do well to take her into New York to the Museum and a concert, followed by dinner. That would cost about four dollars and he should take the money out of the household budget. But if Mother's erratic condition persisted, it might be advisable to have her spend three or four weeks at the Jackson Sanatorium at Dansville, New York.[74] That last did not become an eventuality, but it suggests that the old strains were still there, and that William George's long business trips may have served as a welcome escape from an increasingly intolerable situation. For Willie junior, Pop's letter served to reinforce what his mother had already confided to him: that all her married life she had had to struggle in a new world "among an unsympathetic people who were often hostile and perhaps never understood" her, as Willie himself expressed it in a letter to her two years later.[75]

But other people had plans for Willie as well. Once Dr. Henna had come to him with a scheme to make his favorite intern a millionaire overnight. He knew of a very attractive South American widow, in her early thirties, who had over a million dollars in the bank. Her late husband had been a very successful physician and she was looking now for another husband to continue that medical practice. Willie, Henna was convinced, was just the man. But, much to Henna's surprise, Willie turned the offer down. Love wasn't like that. Why, he didn't even know the woman. Henna looked at him, shook his head, and walked away. Then, on December 10, he came to Willie with another scheme to get him some money.[76] One of Henna's patients, a very old Mexican aristocrat named Gonzales, a railroad executive and a sheep raiser, was dying of complications arising from pneumonia. Gonzales knew he was dying and wanted only to end his days in his own country surrounded by his own people. The deal was this: Henna would finagle a week's leave from the hospital for Willie and Willie would have to somehow "keep the old boy alive" long enough to get him back to San Luis Potosí in central Mexico. Henna got Willie a special room at the Belmont Hotel directly across from Grand Central Station with the injunction to be ready to leave at a moment's notice. Next day, a special railroad car had been attached to the end of a New York Central express and, in the middle of a snowstorm, Willie, the old man, the man's son and daughter-in-law, and another woman, left for Mexico.

Williams was worried. He could see that the old man was thankful to have Williams with him and incredibly patient in his last illness. But he could see too that the younger Gonzales did not like him, did not in fact like *gringos* in general. Williams kept thinking about what would happen to him if he failed to get the old man back home alive, seeing in his mind's eye his body dangling from a tree or cactus somewhere in Mexico. For three days, as first the express headed north for Albany then west through Indiana, across the Mississippi to St. Louis, and then south toward Texas and the border, Williams watched over Gonzales. How courteous the man was to him even in his final agony, as Williams massaged his legs to help the circulation and shot him full of caffeine and sodium benzoate. From time to time, as the express raced through Texas, Williams stared out the train window, aware of a whole new world opening up to him even in this wintry descent, a world of "mesquite and palmettos with chollas and barrel cactus scattered here and there" and even a lone Indian patrolling the tracks, "his blanket around his shoulders, head bowed, completely absorbed."[77]

When the train crossed the border at Laredo before dawn on Saturday, December 14, a young Mexican physician who had been dispatched there climbed aboard and took over the care of Gonzales. Finally Williams could relax and take in the Mexican landscape and the figures moving outside the train window, as the express sped south those last four hundred miles. Then, shortly before noon, they were in San Luis Potosí and Gonzales was carried by his distraught servants and the peons of the village into his villa, where he could at last die in his bed. Williams had about an hour then to stroll around the open-air markets and to send his father a postcard with a picture of the Templo de San Agustín and a note that the trip was finally over. Then Señor Gonzales called Williams to his bedside to grasp the young doctor's hand and thank him one last time for getting him home alive. When Willie looked up, it was to see the younger Gonzales motioning him to follow him downstairs, where he gave Williams ten twenty-dollar gold pieces. "You see," the son added, as he swept his hand out in a gesture meant to encompass the paneled walls of the spacious villa, "you see, we live a little better—*un poco mejor que los negros.*" A little better than niggers. Finally, Williams began to understand some of the younger Gonzales' bitterness, something of the condescension Gonzales and his father must have felt all their lives from their neighbors to the north. At three that same afternoon, Williams was on another express heading back to the States. He had just had his first lesson in the vastness and strangeness of *el nuevo mundo*, which was vaster and stranger even than he'd ever suspected.

**

Back in September, two of Williams' closest friends had left Philadelphia to pursue their dreams of leading lives devoted to the arts. Charlie Demuth had sailed for Paris to study painting and, less spectacularly, Ezra had left for Wabash College in Crawfordsville, Indiana, to begin his duties teaching French, Spanish, and Italian literature to undergraduates. Demuth was to remain in Paris for several years, but Ezra would last only four months in Crawfordsville. By then he had alienated too many of his students. His standards were too high and he had a sharp, satirical tongue which he used with devastating effectiveness against his midwestern students at this small, parochial college. What precipitated his dismissal from Wabash, however, was the discovery by Pound's landlady that a woman had spent the night in his room. Pound insisted that he had simply played the good samaritan. He'd been out mailing a letter and had come upon an actress who had been stranded in town during a winter storm. She was cold and hungry and tired and he had offered her some food and his bed to sleep in while he lay down (fully clothed, mind you) wrapped in his overcoat on the floor to sleep.

But there had already been too many complaints lodged against the flamboyant teacher from the big eastern school, and the Presbyterian officials of the college wanted him out. He was known, for example, to have a flask of rum about his person, he smoked eastern cigarettes, he dressed in that smart-aleck European tradition: open collars, bow ties, black velvet jacket, even a malacca cane. This latest scandal on top of everything else was too much, and the young troubador shook the snow from his sandals and left Wabash forever at the end of January 1908 to return to Philadelphia. He had also apparently just ended an engagement of sorts to a Mary Moore of Trenton, New Jersey, a girl he'd seen a great deal of the previous summer, before he'd gone to Wabash. Back home and a free man once again, he began seeing Hilda nearly every day and was soon engaged to her. On February 12, Hilda broke the news of the engagement to Willie, explaining that she was prepared (at twenty-one) to sacrifice herself for one who had been cruelly treated by life. She wanted Willie to know this because she considered him to be one of her closest friends.[78]

But before much could be said, Hilda wrote to say that the engagement was off. Three weeks after announcing it, she told Willie that she and Ezra had reconsidered the whole affair and that Ezra had decided instead to return to Europe via Gibraltar.[79] For his part, Ezra wrote Willie to say that he wanted to come to Rutherford and visit him before he sailed, and that visit took place during the second week of March, just before Ezra boarded ship in New York.[80] Willie and Ezra spoke again about literature, about poetry, about the future, and Ezra showed Willie some of his most recent poems, poems that would be published later that year in Venice under the title *A Lume Spento*. Willie in turn showed Ezra his long *Endymion* poem, and told Ed he even thought Ezra had been impressed with it.[81]

Willie had been working steadily on that poem all through January and into February, because he wanted to get it ready to show to Professor Arlo Bates. When Ed had come home for the Christmas holidays, Willie had told him that he would be willing to take the train up to Boston and talk with Bates about his poetry and so get a professional point of view about his work. A friend of his, a girl from Rutherford named Gussie, had volunteered to type his poems and then he would "be ready for Boston and my first bid for happiness."[82] He'd been working on that epic now for two years and, though he was trembling at what Bates might say, he knew too that he had a profound belief in the worth and goodness of what he was doing. He knew "that faith in truth and beauty inspires me and when a man has that, ultimate failure is impossible." In the light of that certitude, he understood that his mistakes would simply fall away and he could at last "bear witness honestly." For if he could not "sing beautifully of the beautiful," then why sing at all?[83]

Keats still possessed Williams, so much so that Williams was uttering Keats's words as though they'd been his own. "What is beauty by the way but only truth," he explained to Ed. "Beauty is nothing but truth in all its magnificent detail."[84] Forty years later Williams would tell Allen Tate that Keats had been more than just an initial inspiration, he had been his early "delirium." At twenty-four he'd been "soaked, pickled in him [Keats] to the point of (almost) ultimate petrifaction."[85] Now Williams was finally screwing up enough courage to visit Bates in his quarters at MIT in the old Back Bay section of Boston one gray day in late March 1908, carrying with him his epic and some other poems wrapped up in a three-pound packet secured with a broad elastic band.[86] Bates was sitting at a small desk over by his window, Williams remembered, and what he saw was "a tall, middle-aged man with white hair." Williams introduced himself and then handed him the packet and waited while Bates slowly and painstakingly went through the sheaf. "Oh I hope Arlo is patient and kindly," Williams had confessed to his brother three weeks earlier. "And Bo speak to him and tell him about me and ask if he has time to criticize a young man's attempt. . . . Ask him if he would like to see me or if he would mind if I came to talk with him. I never was so happy in my life and I am sure I have at least some slight reason to be so."[87] And now, here he was, watching Bates and waiting nervously for the verdict that would change his whole life. If Bates thought he was as good as he was sure he was, why then he would quit medicine as decisively as Ezra had left Wabash and devote his whole life to his writing. Or, if not, if Bates damned him, why then he was ready to go on doggedly with medicine.

Finally Bates did look up from the poems sprawled out in front of him. It was clear to him that the young man sitting there had imbibed something of the spirit of Keats's work and had even done "some creditable imitations." If he kept after it, he thought Williams might, just might, by the time he was forty-five, attract some modicum of literary attention to himself. In the meantime, better that Williams continue practicing medicine. Then he pulled open a desk drawer and added, "I, too, write poems. And when I have written them I place them here—and —then I close the drawer." At least Bates had cleared the air. Someone who knew literature had examined Williams' poems, a three years' collection of imitation Keats, and told him to go on with medicine.[88]

Williams would continue to dabble with his poem at home, even asking Viola to prepare a clean typed copy of it in May. But a few months later, he must have felt the weight of Bates's strictures, for he suddenly picked up the poem, ran downstairs into the cellar, and chucked it or a draft of it into the furnace. The poem continued to survive in Viola Baxter's version. But the gesture proved cathartic. Now at least Williams could put that obsession behind him and go on to new work, new obsessions.

*
* *

About the same time that Pound and Hilda had become engaged, Williams was writing Ed enthusiastically, extolling the virtues of a beautiful young woman named Charlotte Herman who lived over on Home Avenue. She was the oldest of the three children of a wealthy German-American printer named Paul Herman and already she was a concert pianist with a local reputation who'd spent time abroad studying music at the Leipzig Conservatory. She was stunning, really, and Williams called her "without a doubt the most delightful young lady I have met in a long time," though he realized that he was "inclined to recommend her" to Ed "perhaps too enthusiastically." Ed would see for himself of course when he came home. Still, anyone could see that Charlotte was "calm, intelligent, tactful, musical, of peculiarly attractive feature," and she even had a "decided and most original bump of humor."[89] By late February Willie was playing duets with her over on Home Avenue, she singing at the grand piano and he accompanying on his violin. By mid-March he and Charlotte and another couple had formed "a little musical coterie to meet each week and enjoy some 'musics.' "[90] In time he would read his short plays and his poems to her and her friends. There was also a younger sister around, a quiet, plain-looking sweet sixteen named Florence and a kid brother named Paul, but Willie didn't even think it important enough to mention them.

At the same time, Williams' two-year stint at French Hospital was coming to an end. And now that Bates had told him to go on with medicine, Williams had definitely decided to take another internship in obstetrics and pediatrics, this one at the Nursery and Child's Hospital uptown at 161 West 61st Street, again between Ninth and Tenth avenues. This was another new facility with a small section for pediatrics, only one block west of New York's notorious Hell's Kitchen (or San Juan Hill, as it was also called). His spirits were high, and he wrote in a jovial mood to Viola Baxter (after not have written her in several months) that he was sure the Child's Hospital offer was about to come his way. "Needless to say," he added,

> the definition of "offer" in this case is acceptance. The country [by which he meant setting up a practice back in Rutherford] . . . will but lose me temporarily for they tell me I am an inconstant lover in fundaments, one

being a passion I have for the open air. . . . You remember me perhaps? Well never mind. I read this morning that every two hundred and fifty thousand years the earth dons a glacial period, when perhaps if we're fortunate our graves will not be violated. Things are of such little consequence. However bread and hunger would ever be wedded; therefore I'll spend a hot season in "Hell's Kitchen" ushering the progeny of Caesar perhaps into the world.[91]

It was Willie at his most playful, writing in his best Pierrot-the-clown literary style. After all, he was going to be uptown for at least another year. Why not reacquaint himself with lovely Viola?

He had only a week home in early May between the time he wrapped up his affairs at the French Hospital and his beginning his internship at Child's. It was enough time to read a little, work on one of his plays, and make some notes on the local flora and fauna he observed on his solitary trips around Rutherford and environs.[92]

Then it was back to work. Nursery and Child's Hospital was a non-descript brick affair situated in one of the highest crime areas in New York, and no one—man or woman—ever felt safe out there alone after dark. There were constant muggings, Murphy men, whores, domestic quarrels, gangland-style executions, and therefore victims of knifings and gunshot wounds for Williams and the staff to attend to, despite the fact that Child's was expressly an infant asylum. To make matters worse, Williams soon learned that, though the nursing staff there was excellent, the hospital administration was riddled with corruption. Still, he managed to work very hard in his eight months of service there, delivering over three hundred babies, sometimes at the rate of four or five a day. "I helped four little youngsters into the world yesterday," he wrote Ed on June 22, and had to add—somewhat sardonically—that it was "kind of a mean trick on them" to pull them kicking into the world.[93]

By July, with New York baking under the summer heat, Williams had to take over pediatrics when his superior, Dr. Richardson, went off for his summer vacation, leaving Williams to work with two absolutely green interns. Thank God for the nurses, though, he thought, who helped pull him through. The food too, unlike that at the French Hospital, was really excellent. It was, in fact, as the director in residence had told him, the only way she'd been able to keep resident physicians at the hospital.[94] But in spite of the nurses and the food, Williams found himself in the midst of an outbreak of infant gastroenteritis that began to kill off his babies like so many flies. He worked long and hard both at the hospital and a private mansion uptown that had been donated to the hospital for overflow patients, keeping detailed records and trying to figure what in hell was happening to the poor kids. And still they died. On top of that he had to try and hush up the fact that the kids were dying in the makeshift quarters up at the mansion, for the owner who had loaned them the house had specifically stipulated that she wanted no deaths in her home. At first Williams had even been driven to the extremity of packing one dead infant into a large suitcase to transport it by trolley from the mansion back to Child's, but he'd been so nervous that he'd lose the suitcase or that it would suddenly break open on the trolley that he vowed never to try that again, never mind who knew about the kids dying uptown.[95]

As if that weren't enough, his fitful sleep at Child's was further punctuated by children crying hour after hour throughout the long, hot nights from their city hospital cribs. But this time it was bedbugs, and at least Williams knew how to handle this one. He ordered the children removed, sealed off the nursery—windows, doors, whatever cracks he could find—and then burned a mixture of bar-sulphur and alcohol to fumigate the quarters. When the smoke sufficiently cleared, the staff found mounds of bedbugs all over the place. At least there he had his small victory.

Finally, in early August, he had a few days' rest with his friends the Danielses out at their place on Shelter Island.[96] And then, at the beginning of September, he was able to get away with Ed and Pop for another of those brisk walking tours as the evenings cooled, this time going up through the Catskills, starting from Sloatsburg and then heading north and west.[97] As it turned out, it was to be their last walking tour together, for a year later Ed would be in Rome and Bill in Leipzig. And after that, distance, marriage, and death would intervene.

Williams also got away, though infrequently, to enjoy New York: to hear an opera, visit the new Metropolitan Muscum of Art,[98] and once to see Isadora Duncan. That was on Friday evening, August 21, and Duncan's dancing struck him forcibly (as it would strike another young poet, Hart Crane, a few years later, when he saw her in Cleveland). Really, Williams wrote his brother the day after Duncan's performance, it had been "the most chaste, most perfect, most absolutely inspiring exhibition" he'd ever seen. What had especially impressed him, since he was doing short plays with American themes, was how this woman manifested a national spirit in her movement. Her free forms and graceful, instinctive gestures had had the effect of making Williams determined more than ever "to accomplish my part in our wonderful future." Watching her dance up there on stage like some larger-than-life presence, he'd seen in her a symbol of the true classical tradition. But even more important, she had become the symbol for him of America's as-yet-unrealized future in the arts. So, when he returned to his hospital quarters at Child's he wrote an Italian sonnet (in the Keatsian mode) to this "dear country-maid's" too rare presence:

> *Isadora Duncan when I saw*
> *You dance, the interrupting years fell back,*
> *It seemed, with far intenser leave than lack*

Of your deft step hath e'er conferred. No flaw
However slight lay 'tween me and the raw,
Heatthirsty Scythians craving wrack,
Lithe Bacchanals, or flushed, in roseate track,
Athenian girls completing vict'ry's law.
I breathed their olden virgin purity,
Their guileless clean abandon, in your fling
Those truth's refound which heavenly instinct's bliss
Bare innocence withal, but most to me
I saw, dear country-maid, how soon shall spring
From this our native land great loveliness.[99]

Surely those sentiments were high enough, classical enough, American enough. Arlo Bates had not told Williams to stop moralizing when he wrote poems, and Williams' expectations for art were still only of the highest: that it express only the highest truths in the then-approved high serious tone that somehow got confused with somberness and sententiousness.[100] So it was that when he received a copy of Pound's first book of poems, *A Lume Spento*, published in Venice that summer, Williams felt constrained to remonstrate with what he took to be, not an uplifting quality he was looking for in poetry, but instead a bitterness which pervaded and darkened much of Pound's vision. And what about these strange metrical patterns Ezra was affecting? Certainly they did not derive from the great tradition as embodied in Palgrave's *Treasury*?[101]

That was in early October. On the twenty-first, Pound answered from his tiny rooms in Kensington, London, where he'd settled after Venice. The poems in *A Lume Spento*, he answered, were not all in his own voice by any means. In fact, he had been trying on different voices the way one tried on different *dramatis personae*, different masks. In this he had followed the example of his own master, Robert Browning. And besides, he didn't much care for Willie boy lecturing him in those high-falutin' moral tones of his which had always grated on him anyway. Nor did he give a damn about the scrutinizing "eyes of a too ruthless public." As for his verse music, he was going outside the iamb to try on metrical patterns that derived from the "Spanish, Anglo-Saxon and Greek metric that are not common in the English of Milton's or Miss Austen's day." And then, just to be sure Willie neophyte, Willie provincial, knew his place, Pound added that he really doubted whether his friend was "sufficiently *au courant* to know just what the poets and musicians *and* painters" were doing "with a good deal of convention that has masqueraded as law." Besides, *A Lume Spento* was all early work, behind him now. He was already doing stuff that would surprise Willie. Ah, London! There was the place to be, the center of the vortex. Finally, he was beginning to feel like "a runner in a marathon," who was even now at the quarterpost. But where, then, was poor Willie, that turtle, crawling along back there in the provinces?[102]

Well, Willie was now a member of the Rutherford Dramatic Club, comprised of five young men and five young women. He was singing in local Gilbert and Sullivan productions. He was writing short plays on stirring or comic American themes, such as his *Betty Putnam*, and he was seeing culture about New York. So, while Pound had been walking the streets and bridges of Venice breathing in its Titians and Tiepolos, its Carpaccios and Bellinis, and then London with its Tate Gallery and British Museum, Williams was studying the paintings at the Metropolitan Museum of Art and trying hard to "distinguish a few of the leading characteristics of the principle [sic] schools of painting."[103] Furthermore, he'd enrolled in a course of free lectures on the great masters of music at the Bronx Botanical Gardens. He knew that, while Pound had been studying Spanish, French, Italian and classical literature, he'd had to study anatomy, chemistry, bacteriology, pathology, ophthalmology, gynecology, and that now he had a lot of culture to catch up on. And, though his *Endymion* poem had not, apparently, been the answer to American poetry the world had been waiting for, he still had hopes that someday he could "show the world something more beautiful than it had ever seen before."[104]

Besides, if Ezra could get a volume out, Williams reasoned to himself, and Ezra was two years younger than he, then it was time for him to get busy and gather up his odes and sonnets and songs, find himself a printer, and publish a book of poems of his own. No wonder, then, that two weeks after getting Pound's letter, he was experiencing a new burst of creative energy. And, in spite of his having to give a course in child care to the nursery maids at Child's and having to work up a series of lectures for the nurses at the French Hospital, he was writing and polishing his poems every free moment he could find or steal.[105] He knew that the others —parents, neighbors, friends, nurses, colleagues—were smiling at what they considered an extravagant waste of time until even Williams began to wonder if he wasn't crazy pulling himself like this in two directions. But in spite of everything, in spite of his local conditions, he finally managed to put together a volume by mid-December which he called, simply, *Poems*. Then he took the sheaf to a local Rutherford printer, Reid Howell, a neighbor and friend of Willie's father, for a printing estimate. Howell was simply a job printer, and all he'd ever done up till then were advertisements and announcements and throwaways, not books of verse. But as a favor, he promised to look over the sheaf the kid had shown him and give him an estimate.

A month later, in mid-January 1909, Howell wrote Williams a letter on *New Jersey Printing Company* stationery and sent it to Child's. The booklet, he wrote, would cost $32.45, though that was only an approximate figure.[106] Willie, who still had those ten gold pieces Señor Gonzales' son had given him safely in the bank, told Howell to go ahead and do the job. Actually, Williams' first book was nothing more than a thin paper-covered pamphlet, twenty-two pages long, seven of which were blank. There were twenty-seven poems included, arranged thematically between the first poem, called "Innocence," and the final poem, "Hymn to Perfection." And though he was proud of this first collection at the time, years later he would frankly admit that they were nothing but "bad Keats" and maybe "bad Whitman" as well. In fact, there was nothing "of the slightest value in the whole thin booklet—except the intent."[107]

"Innocence" opened the book this way:

> Innocence can never perish;
> Blooms as fair in looks that cherish
> Dim remembrance of the days
> When life was young, as in the gaze
> Of youth himself all rose-yclad,
> Whom but to see is to be glad. . . .

Thus the stilted octosyllabic couplets and the syntex veering left and right out of control of the author's hand, as rhyme forced him first in one direction and then another. And there was the closing "Hymn" calling in that great immensity, "great ruler / Chief God of all monarchs," perfection itself, for whom Blakean Williams was about to "shatter / The stillness of heaven" to make his own voice heard with the voice of waves scattering "A widening tempest." Perhaps that was Williams' version of his Rutherfordian vortex.

Most of the poems made no attempt to compromise with Williams' own workaday world, the world he himself was living in, the world of hospitals and crowded streets or even quiet, prosperous suburban Rutherford. Instead his poems inhabited some rarefied, Byzantine, gold-laminated stratosphere that sang to secret ladies, unknown ladies, to pale Eros, fraternal love, to his better self, to moralizings on the folly of youth's preoccupations and bewilderments. There were poems too on happiness, on loneliness, rhapsodizings on the passage of the seasons, poems called "June," "July," "September," and "November." There was even a poem in anticipation of spring which he'd written back in March 1907, as he prepared to leave New York's wintry bleakness for sunny Philadelphia. In that poem, an Italian sonnet entitled "On a Proposed Trip South," he had noted how December was a time of ice and snow, a single "weave / Of blanched crystal." But April had meant the fading of winter, a process that could be hastened by an express south, or by flying there on the wings of poesy, where already he could see "lush high grasses" and "gay birds" and hear "the bees making heavy droon."

Even in the one poem that might have been expected to touch on the raw energy of New York (the same New York that had made Henry James shudder as he sailed by the Battery) Williams managed only a pale cameo laquered by his archaic, suffocating language. And yet that poem, "A Street Market, N.Y., 1908," contained within itself clues that Williams himself was growing restless with his Keatsian / Shakespearean mode, even as he failed to pull himself free of that amber-honey language. For years, Williams lamented here in his poem, he'd looked and looked without ever seeing, "Blind to a patent wide reality" that his scientific training, his daily diagnosis of all sorts of human miseries, had taught him to see. Looking down from the fifth-story window of his room at the French Hospital onto the crowded street below, what had he really seen? Well, there was a crowd down there, a bustling crowd of humanity, German Jews and Greeks and Hungarians and Poles all hawking wares and spitting and shouting. A man was trying to maneuver a cart and a team of horses around stands that sprawled over into the street, while others were swearing and trying to bargain for produce and telling jokes with heavy accents or in other languages. It was Whitman's Mannahatta half a century after *Leaves of Grass*, barbaric yawp and all. Well, how sing of it, then? In 1908 this was the best Willie could do:

> Seething below
>   Now with eccentric throe
> The thick souls ebb and flow.
> Far tribes there mingle free,
>   There History
> Welds her gold threads in glittering brilliant show.
>
>   Kaffir and Jew
>   Commerce for bread and brew;
> There die the wars which grew
> When first was quarreling
>   And gaily sing
> Slavs, Teutons, Greeks, sweet songs forever new.[108]

Like Shakespeare, like all those immortalized in Palgrave's *Golden Treasury*, Williams too would offer his best for the world to see at only a quarter a throw, "Dressing Old Words New / Spending Again What Is Already Spent." He would take the debased language he heard about him every day and make it his own, thus spending again what had already been spent on the air a thousand times. Or so he hoped.

It took Reid Howell less than two months to set up the type for Willie's pamphlet and then run off a hundred copies. "The local journey-men must have had a tough time of it," Williams noted wryly many years later. The result was a book "about half errors—like the Passaic River in its relationship to the sewage of that time."[109] Willie sent a few copies out in early March, including one to Ed, who'd designed the cover for the pamphlet, and Ed wrote back how pleased he was to have the poems.

Well, of course there were mistakes in the book, Willie was ready to concede, but he was glad Ed had caught the spirit of the venture. After all, art "should breathe in the common places and inspire us at the moments of decision in our work and play."[110]

But if Ed was satisfied, William George was not. He *should* have liked it. After all, they were all innocent poems on high moral or philosophical themes, written in a high romantic sublime. But the printed text was so atrociously bungled that he was ashamed to let anyone see it. Instead, he went through a copy carefully with pen in hand and marked all the typographical, spelling, and syntactical errors he could find and then gave them to Willie, who then penciled all the changes that would have to be made into his own copy. Then, when that was done, he went back to Howell and had him reprint the entire pamphlet.[111]

The corrected version came off Howell's press in early May in another edition of one hundred copies. Then, with about fifteen copies under his arm, Willie walked over to Mr. Garrison's Stationery Store on Park Avenue and asked him if he could put the book on display there for sale at a quarter apiece. But even with a favorable review in the local *Rutherford American*, Willie managed to interest only four buyers. That came to one dollar. "At odd moments," the reviewer had written, "Dr. Williams, one of the bright young men of whom Rutherford is justly proud, has wooed the muse to good effect, and the result is highly creditable." The reviewer, obviously a friend of Willie's father, added that he hoped the busy young doctor might find "more odd moments in which to record his open-eyed interest in the things of beauty, the mind and the spirit." He also wanted to take this opportunity to remind his Rutherford readers that the father too wielded "a graceful poetic pen" and that this reviewer at least was pleased to see how "gracefully the mantle of good literary expression" fell upon the son.[112]

Willie had also sent a copy on to Pound in Kensington, who replied at once, scribbling across the top of page one of his letter that he hoped to God ol' Bull had no feelings, and that if he did, to burn the letter before he read it. The only value Willie's pamphlet had, Pound told him, was that it confirmed his belief in Williams as one possessing the poetic instinct. Still, if Williams had been in the mainstream of things over here in London instead of over there in the provinces, he wondered how many of these poems Williams would have allowed himself to publish. Pound was willing to admit that maybe he'd printed too much himself, but he'd also "been praised by the greatest living poet," William Butler Yeats himself. Sure, Willie had some fine lines here and there, but nowhere— NOWHERE—had he added anything to Keats or his other literary models.

To remedy all this, Dr. Pound was putting Willie on a diet of Yeats, Browning, Francis Thompson ("The Hound of Heaven"), Swinburne, and

Dante Gabriel Rossetti so that Willie could get a sense of where poetry had gone since Keats. The only real trouble with Willie, after all, was that he was horribly out of touch. Forget the poetry he'd already written, Ezra urged him. After all, what really mattered was the work he still had before him.[113]

Willie got Pound's letter at the beginning of June. By then his *Poems* had been sitting around Garrison's for a month, bleaching in the sun and collecting dust and flies. He went down, picked up all the unsold copies—about eleven—and then passed them around to his family. The others he left to rot (and later burn) in the rafters of Howell's chicken coop. Let it go. So be it. The past was for those who lived in the past, his grandmother had told him. Pound's letter had hurt because Willie knew what Pound had said was true. Well, there was work to do. Good-by Keats. Hello Pound.

THREE

Deaths and Transfigurations:
1909—1914

E ven while Williams was negotiating with Howell about his pamphlet, his hopes for becoming a New York specialist were about to crumble. The trouble began for him at the end of January 1909. By then he had been at Child's Hospital a full six months and had just been given, with the new year, a broader range of responsibilities. Things were definitely beginning to look up for him. Already one member of the senior staff—Dr. Kerley—had suggested that he might come to work with him in his own New York office once Williams' internship at the hospital was finished. But at the end of Williams' first month of new responsibilities, Miss Malzacher, the woman in charge of the hospital's business affairs, a woman Williams was to describe as "a dark, sweaty-looking creature with furtive, bulging eyes," came to him with some forms from the state offices in Albany for him to sign. It was a routine matter, she explained: forms and a slip of paper detailing the numbers of patients the hospital had admitted and discharged in January. Births, deaths, recoveries. Dr. Williams was, she explained, to copy the figures she gave him over again in his own hand, sign the form, and then give figures and form back to her so that the hospital could be reimbursed by the state for services rendered. Sure he would do it, Williams answered. Just show him the outpatient lists so that he could verify her figures, and then he'd sign.

But that, she said, would not be possible. After all, this wasn't some medical matter, just straight business. Besides, none of the other doctors had ever given her any trouble about this before. But Williams refused to sign. So the forms went up to Albany without his signature and were as quickly returned with a letter requesting the proper signature. Now it was the doctors' turn. Sign the damn thing, Williams, they coaxed him. After all, it was only a routine matter that had been going on for years. Sign and be done with it. Then he learned that some big Wall Street names were also involved and that things might get a little hot. Sure, Willie was a man of principles, but this refusal to sign some silly little forms was pig-headed, eccentric. Willie felt himself getting sick to his stomach. He asked one doctor—point-blank—if he would have signed those forms without first being able to verify them and the man said he'd be damned if he would.

But then it wasn't the senior staff but Willie who was on the line. There was a hurried meeting of the hospital's Board of Governors, the treasurer signed the forms, and Williams found himself suspended for two weeks for insubordination. He wanted to resign there and then, but one of the nurses came to him and told him not to quit yet, that she knew something and would bring it forward at the right time. So he spent his two weeks at home and then returned for duty. But at the end of February it began all over again. Williams would have to sign the papers, again without seeing the records.

Then he learned from the nurse who had come to him what lay behind all this. She had gone into the board room one day, she told him, to find out why things were so quiet in there and had discovered Miss Malzacher sitting on the edge of the long table with the president of the board, one of the most powerful men on Wall Street, "facing her . . . in a position" that the nurse refused to describe to Williams. So there it was: petty lust and the petty graft of a payoff from state funds.

Useless to fight the thing when no nurse or doctor on the staff dared come forward and go up against the power of Wall Street and the Board of Governors. Willie found himself now with another of his sore throats and laid up for a week at the hospital while he tried to figure out what his next step was. Finally he wrote a letter to the board, telling them what he thought of them and at the same time offering his resignation. Then he dropped the letter into the mailbox in the hospital's business office. It was just then he remembered that the nurse who had told him about Miss Malzacher had asked him not to resign. But it was already too late. Apparently Malzacher had been watching him, for she picked up the letter at once, took it outside to a U.S. post office box and dropped it in before Williams could do anything about it. As expected, Williams' resignation was accepted at once.[1] On March 18, with the whole affair over, he wrote Ed that the board had promised him "certain things when I went back and when it came time for them to make good they crawled. There was nothing to do but crawl too or get out so I got out."[2] His promising career as a New York specialist with an office on fashionable Park Avenue was over before it had even begun. Now it was back to Rutherford.

But instead of being crushed by the weight of these events, Williams was actually in good spirits. He had not compromised his values and he had free time on his hands in which to write. He made "a deep resolve to finish everything I have ever left undone in these days of otherwise idleness."[3] His *Poems* were about to appear, he was waiting to hear about new job openings from as far away as Colorado, and he was enjoying himself. He revised his play, *Betty Putnam*, about the American Revolution, giving it a new ending, and he was happy when Charlotte and the other local girls told him how impressed they were by his "American" play. And now, he wrote Ed, he was writing "a chorus for angels" for a "mask" he was composing. He'd already been working on it for two days and it was, he added proudly, "about the most absolutely abstract thing" he'd ever done. On the spur of the moment he'd taken it over to show Charlotte and trade it for the pleasure of hearing some more of her music. But Charlotte, as it turned out, was at Eva Hunt's house, and so he'd walked over there to be treated to a double concerto, first one by Mendelssohn and then one by Chopin, played by both Charlotte and Eva on Eva's two baby grand pianos.[4] Two weeks later, in early April, Williams was getting ready to head down to Philadelphia again to see his friends. He was also singing in the local production of *The Mikado* ("Tit Willow" again) and getting ready to put on *Betty Putnam* for the Rutherford Town Tennis Club in early July.

Things were looking up for Ed as well, who had learned in January that he'd been the recipient of the prestigious Prix de Rome to study architecture for three years at the American Academy in Rome. And since William George felt in some sense responsible for Willie's having stuck by his principles and thus for having lost his job at Child's, he had promised him that, if Ed won the Rome prize, he would find a way to finance another year of study in pediatrics abroad to make up for the year his boy had lost.

With time on his hands, Williams also found himself falling in love. He had not seen Viola Baxter since Thanksgiving, when he'd taken her to hear the Knessel Quartet perform in New York, where he'd introduced her to his parents. Mama had been taken by Viola at once. But Willie had not followed that relationship up, for it was becoming clearer and clearer to him that he was in love with Charlotte Herman. Earlier he had taken Charlotte on a tour of Child's to show her the world of the hospital. And now, with the coming of spring, he was seen frequently in her company, listening to her play and sing, and taking her out on the Passaic in a canoe in June to read from his latest poems and his *Betty Putnam*. But what Charlotte remembered most about Willie, filtering through seventy years to do it, was his self-absorption, his preoccupation with himself and his own poems instead of with Charlotte. He had in fact a "very big ego." But his brother Edgar—there was an artist and a gentleman: tall, dark, worldly, gentle. Even at ninety-one, bedridden, shriveled, the shell of her former Venusian beauty, with both Bill and Edgar dead and her own husband long dead, that was how she remembered Willie. And why, she added, why the dickens would anyone want to write a book about Bill Williams? Had she ever been in love with Bill? A glint in her eye meant to conceal as much as reveal, as much as to say: that is my business. And then her answer: "Perhaps. But then one was always 'in love' in those days."[5]

Williams of course had already been in and out of love any number of times, though he did not play Ezra's game of falling in and out of engagements. But this time, Williams was sure, what he felt was something entirely different. Charlotte was his true soul mate. She was beautiful, an artist, accomplished. Oh, he knew there were problems. He knew, for example, that Charlotte's mother, a powerfully built Norwegian woman as tough as they came, didn't take kindly to his sniffing around after her daughter. He didn't seem to have a very promising future and now he didn't even have a job. And besides he was too wild-eyed and eccentric for her tastes with all his poeticizings and his enthusiasms over nothing she could see. Her daughter was going to be trained to sing professionally and had, moreover, already spent three years at the Leipzig Conservatory of Music. Edgar, on the other hand, was different: cooler, more manly, more sure of himself than his older brother. And besides, he had already proven himself by winning that big award.

And for all their closeness, what had never apparently passed between the brothers, either in their letters to one another or in their talks, was what each was feeling about Charlotte. Yes, they both admired her for her accomplishments, her wit, her beauty, her great charm. But neither of them could bear to tell the other what each nevertheless suspected in the letters: that they both wanted the same girl. So when Ed returned home victorious from MIT in June, with a degree and a prize for graduate work, he put it squarely to his brother: would Bill as the older of the two go to Charlotte and ask her to choose between them, granted she was inclined to choose either? Or would Ed go? But Willie could not bring himself to do it, and so, probably on Friday evening, July 2, Edgar went to talk to Charlotte alone.

Willie must have known deep in his own heart what the outcome would be, and so had purposely avoided facing Ed to find out what Charlotte had said until the following morning. Only then did Ed shrug off what had happened as offhandedly as he could. Charlotte had decided on him instead of Willie. Disgracefully, Williams wrote many years later, in a thinly veiled fictionalized account of those events, "he flung his arms about his brother's neck and went mad." Ed was embarrassed and frightened at Willie's behavior and had to pry his brother's fingers from his neck. Then, not knowing what to do, Ed turned and fled. Willie understood of course that Ed had acted every bit the gentleman in the matter, but that only made this new defeat all the more bitter. Now something happened to him that would break off the future irrevocably from the past. Willie had been both rejected and betrayed. All at once the passionate identification he had felt with his brother from his earliest days came forever to an end. "It was," Williams would write more than forty years afterward, the memory of it still raw, "a deeper wound than he should ever thereafter in his life be able to sound. It was bottomless."[6]

For three days Willie stayed up in his room, refusing to come down, refusing even to eat. His mother tried to coax him to take something and on the second day—Sunday—left a bowl of soup for him on his dresser. He would, she tried to tell him, perhaps thinking of her own losses, somehow get over this grief. Then, on the third day he made up his mind. To hell with waiting to be acted upon. The thing was to act, to make the world go your way. He ate the bowl of cold soup, went downstairs, and called up Charlotte's kid sister on the telephone. He had seen her looking at him half furtively and he was sharp enough to know that the girl even had a "crush" on him, though she'd tried, God knows, to hide it as well as she could. Well, if he couldn't have Charlotte, he'd be damned if Mrs. Herman was going to get away with the way she'd treated him, the bitch. He wanted to come over right away and talk to Florence, he explained now over the telephone, without anybody else snooping around. So there, alone, the two of them on the Hermans' porch over on Home Avenue, Willie asked Florence to marry him.[7]

Willie knew Florence was "in love" with him—at least, as she admitted later, in love with his quixotic poet's ways and that big nose of his. And—to give him credit—he realized now how crushed, how rejected she must have felt when he had gone courting after her beautiful and more accomplished sister. But now all that had changed. Now, Willie reasoned, both had experienced rejection and a despair of sorts, and now they might both move beyond the illusion of romantic love to a new kind of love Willie envisioned based on the difficult flower of compassion that could blossom only after the descent into despair. Everything had collapsed for Willie since February: his promise of a New York-based medical profession, his *Poems* dismissed by Pound, and now the double loss of Charlotte . . . and Ed.

He had to explain to Florence now that he did not yet love her, nor would he lie to have her. For he was still the same Willie who had refused to lie to some girl he'd picked up over in Asbury Park when he was fifteen, who'd have been willing to go all the way with him if he'd only tell her first that he loved her. Love her? He didn't even know the girl! That ended that.

He was also the same Willie who the year before had gone down to 23d Street on the West Side to a shabby fourth-floor apartment to visit one of the nurses from Child's. He had held her and kissed her and even tried to coax her over to the bed. And for her part she had been willing, if only he'd tell her he'd marry her. Marry her? For what? Then, too, he'd gotten up and walked away.[8]

And so now. No. He did not love Florence, but he did want to marry her. Marriage first, and then let that difficult flower called love blossom when it would.[9] Florence was only eighteen then, and Willie was almost twenty-six, and there was something perverse and cruel about what he was doing. Was he getting back at Charlotte this way? Was he somehow getting even with her mother for having laughed at him as a serious suitor for Charlotte? (Very well, he would steal this other daughter out from under her eyes.) But could even Willie have given his real motives for what he was doing? He was sure he was no longer in love with Charlotte, he could tell Florence now. That episode was over. But he was tired of being pushed around by others, by fate, by circumstance, by his parents' demands on him, by his brother taking what should have been his, tired of being acted on by Mrs. Herman, by Pound's condescension, by the injustice of the hospital's Board of Governors. Time now to act, to decide his own destiny. He'd hit bottom, descended into his own hell, and now he was struggling for air, for life, for an identity of his own with the help of this young woman he somehow knew instinctively, from the set of her mouth and her chin, could be at least as tough and as resilient as himself. His trained diagnostician's eye—that corrective for his romantic idealism —knew precisely what it was doing.

And just what kind of proposal of marriage was this, Florence for her part thought? Oh, she would need time. Very well, Willie told her, he would give her the rest of the day and then come around to see her later that evening after his performance of *Betty Putnam*, which he and three others were putting on along the embankment of the Rutherford Town Tennis Club. When he did come calling that evening, he managed to get Florence away from the house for a walk around Kipp's Woods. But when he went to hold her hand she pulled away. She was hurt and angry and confused. She was still young, she said, and she didn't know what to make of older men like Willie. But, yes, she said, yes she would marry him someday. Williams made an awkward attempt to hold his fiancée and kissed her half on the lips and half on the nose there in the Rutherford dark. They were unofficially "engaged."

It was Monday, July 5, and it would remain *their* secret day. Florence —Floss—was leaving in the morning with her family for a long summer vacation, and Williams was leaving on the twenty-third for that year in Leipzig his father had promised him. They would not see each other again until the summer of 1910. In the meantime, their engagement was to be kept a secret, especially from Mrs. Herman, who had already caused Williams enough grief. Pound had urged Williams to come on over to

Kensington with him, to London and the hub of the literary world, and catch up on his reading and meet the masters of poetry as he himself had done. Instead, Williams had chosen, perhaps perversely, to follow in the cold tracks of Charlotte by going, as she had earlier, to study in Leipzig. He didn't even know German.[10] No matter, he was going. Now at last he might pursue Charlotte's pale ghost to his heart's exacerbated content.

*
**

Before sailing, Williams spent a few days at the Panther Lodge on Cranberry Lake in northern New Jersey and—in his first note to Florence —confessed that he'd already sat and "spooned" with a girl named Kate under the summer moon. Now he was asking Floss, in what would become a characteristic gesture, for her forgiveness.[11] In his second letter, written on the eleventh, he asked her if she wasn't already beginning to regret the haste with which she'd been pushed to make a decision. Now he wanted to let her know just what kind of man she was getting. "Sometimes I will appear childish," he confessed, "sometimes weak and impotent, often I will come to you for sympathy when I am hurt with what you believe is a foolish thing. I will put all faith in you. Sometimes I will rave you may think and go off in pursuit of vain dreams." After all, he was a poet and poets sometimes did strange things. In fact, he even enclosed a poem he'd recently written which he called, "On Finding a Harebell on a Mountain."[12]

Then, just two days before sailing, he wrote again to tell her that, now he was going away, she might find someone she could love more than him. But poor Florence was not looking for another man. Her difficulty was that for all practical purposes she appeared unattached, and so a number of young bachelors had been pursuing her at the shore, and Williams, when she'd told him that, hadn't liked that at all. Well, he said, if there was someone, then she should go to him, since there was, after all, "only one truth."[13] Cold consolation, that sort of youthful wisdom. On Friday the twenty-third, Willie said good-by to his parents and then set sail from Philadelphia aboard the SS *Marquette*, a second-class liner bound for Antwerp. He was lonely and miserable and—worst of all— perversely spiting himself by leaving behind everyone who meant anything to him to go to a foreign place where even the language was alien. Ironically, the very nightmare he had concocted for himself in his *Endymion* epic—the hero alone in a strange new world—was about to become a reality.

In 1909 the trip across the Atlantic took twelve days, and Willie wrote Ed a long letter in his best Ruskinesque prose, describing the Turner-like skies as he crossed the English Channel.[14] There was a grand military review of British warships anchored at Cowes off his starboard, and all of that armament was truly impressive, despite the summer weather and the holiday atmosphere. On August 4, he landed at Antwerp and went to a cheap hotel that some French cattlemen aboard ship had recommended, a hotel right in the shadow of the Gothic Cathedral of the Holy Virgin. He met some other young Americans there, and over dinner he heard jokes about the pissoirs planted everywhere to accommodate the Dutch intake of beer. Then something happened that struck Williams as the very symbol of the difference between the old hag, Europe, and his own vigorous, brash, and ignorant country. A middle-aged Belgian, a tattered wreck of a man, entered the hotel dining room where Williams and the others were eating and began singing into a battered tin horn, holding out his soiled hat to beg a few coins. "It was a remarkable sight," Williams wrote his brother:

> Here he was, the very essence of the old world spirit, run down, the wreck of the artistic spirit, one might say the refuse of art, failure written all over him and sadness and even desperation in every line of his face, a figure absolutely not to be understood by our Americans and here he had come, Lord knows from where, in the midst of this young, ignorant but enterprising New World spirit full of the strength of abundant resource and opportunity not unmixed with contempt for old forms and the unpractical in art. It was absolutely fascinating for me to watch the play of feelings and forces and to read the contempt on both sides. There stood the old man, dirty, baggy at the knees, with his horn to his mouth and his hat held I don't know how, his eyes staring down sad and far away and singing the old, old songs of the Italian operas with such feeling that sometimes I even thought his color changed. He sang with all the consummacy of an artist, but his voice— Then around the table were the Americans, flunks from colleges, educated bums, football players, at least one famous athlete, three men who are going to teach in Constantinople, and myself.[15]

Williams watched the old man humiliated by the young Americans, one of whom threw an empty matchbox at him, so that the old man muttered something in French about wanting to slit the bastard's throat. But Williams also knew how badly that man needed those few coins tossed his way, and he could also understand better now after his own defeat the defeat this man was experiencing. He tried to thank the derelict as he brushed past him to go out, but it was useless. That image of old Europe singing a tune for young America would stay with Williams for a long time.

It was an experience that only intensified Williams' own sense of alienation. In fact, he felt so homesick now that he aborted his cruise down the Rhine River the first night out, returned to Köln, the starting point of the cruise, and changed his ticket for a sleeper going straight through to Leipzig. He'd planned to take rooms at 431 Promenadinstrasse in Leipzig, but he left almost as soon as he'd arrived when he saw his landlady engaged in "entertaining" her "cousin" on the living room couch. Instead, he left for another rooming house at 221 Munzgasse. He had hoped to find a letter waiting for him from Florence when he reached Leipzig, but there was none and that only intensified the loneliness.[16] Nor did he like the Germans, though for that matter they could have been English, Italians, or Russians. The trouble was that there were too many of them and only one of him. He wrote Ed that the men in Leipzig dressed like hell and the women were even worse. It was a stolid middle-class city with well-built homes but it was poorer than the New York City he knew. To make matters worse, the Leipzig beer gardens reminded him of the beer gardens frequented by the plodding umpah Germans over in Carlstadt, New Jersey. From what he could see, Germany was a tired country, hedged round by enemies, to which the Germans were responding by building up a huge army with which to protect themselves. Before he left Leipzig, he would see German army trucks rumbling down the narrow cobbled streets of the city, following the course of immense Zeppelins which floated silently and ominously across the skies, appearing and disappearing through the low-lying gray mists of early morning. World War I was less than five years away.

But Williams did enjoy Germany's cultural offerings. He saw Ibsen performed at the Altes Theater and Wagner's *Ring* and most of Schiller's plays as well. He enjoyed Wagner's *Götterdämmerung* and Strauss's *Elektra*. He went to hear Bach played at the Thomaskirche, where Bach was buried. He even learned to read Heine and Sudermann in German. And he took a course in modern British drama at the University of Leipzig, taught by an American named Dantzler.[17] For his twenty-sixth birthday that September 17, Williams treated himself to "six sepia photolithographs of paintings by old masters" and stuck them on his dresser, along with photos of Mama (flanked by Pop and Ed), and a blank space for the studio photo he was waiting for Florence to send. There was also a painting of a girl with a bunny and that was his and Florence's joke. "Bunny" was Willie's private name for Florence, since neither cared much for public demonstrations of affection (and of course the secrecy of their engagement precluded such demonstrations), and neither liked terms such as "honey." Willie came up with the substitute, "Bunny," and that stuck.[18]

In spite of Williams' ruse of sending his fiancée a public letter to be read out before the Hermans, full of news about Ed's brother in Leipzig, inside of which Willie would put a private letter for Florence only, Mrs. Herman guessed the truth of what was going on with Williams and her daughter before Thanksgiving. But now that the news was out, Willie insisted, Florence would have to stand by him completely: "Either you give up everything and stand ready to die by me if necessary or else not a word of it ever again."[19] He had come to "hate religious creeds and all dead forms" and he would never again yield to them. But one of the few things he could trust in was a couple's faith in each other. Something was happening to Williams. His hatred of convention had gone so far that he was even experimenting with new forms in his poetry. He was writing a play on Columbus, the brave, isolated figure who had faced west "towards the new world." Williams had even gone bohemian—slightly—and was soon sprouting a mustache and letting his hair grow longer.[20]

He hardly ever mentioned his medical work in his letters. That was a duty, a monotonous duty, which he performed perfunctorily in order to get on with the real business of life, which was art. And, in spite of their strange courtship, Williams found that he missed Florence, or at least what she represented—home, security, a pale memory of another woman —and he told his fiancée that he would have a difficult time expressing his real feelings in the conventional language of love. Marriage was no prison, he reminded her again in mid-January. If she wanted to enjoy herself, she should enjoy herself.[21] Certainly Willie was trying to enjoy himself as well as he could. It was probably at this point, starving for female companionship, that he picked up a little streetwalker in Leipzig and took her into a local restaurant. Everyone, he noticed, was staring at them and he realized quickly that the girl must have quite a reputation. She wanted champagne, but Williams told her he could only afford beer. It was, he later said, "another occasion when poverty was a distinct aid to virtue," for she soon after asked Williams for some coins to go to the ladies' room and then went over to sit with a table of South Americans. Williams felt relieved; once again he had preserved himself.[22] But he couldn't help feeling guilty about his indiscretion. "I have only to confess my errors," he wrote Floss—without actually confessing—"and you have forgiven me." What he did confess to instead was his innocuous staring at a pretty German girl on the Ross Platz, but so intently that she had become flustered and had finally walked off.[23]

But the same day Williams wrote Floss confessing his errors and his wandering eye, he also opened his correspondence with Viola Baxter again. He apologized now to Viola for his "gross ungentlemanliness" when he'd last seen her, and for having argued then so heatedly in favor of Darwin's position on evolution in the *Descent of Man*. Now, he told her, he was in Germany, among a people who had about as much "spontaneity" as a freight train, a people possessed of "a crass, unsympathetic egotism." Viola, on the other hand, was a breath of fresh air, so different, so magical almost, that she was like a fairy. And yet there was something about her "not entirely fairy-like." He was flirting with her again.[24]

He was even—at this distance—flirting with his mother. On December 18, he sent her a letter together with a poem he had written especially for her. He'd visited the convent ruins at Grimma outside Leipzig where Katharina von Bora—who married Luther—had been confined as a nun, "against her will," as Williams noted. Now, as he stood there—like one of the last romantics amidst those Gothic ruins—Williams had thought of his own mother, a prisoner in a world that did not understand her, married to a man who only partly understood her lost greatness, and he began to write a poem which he finished that evening as he waited for his dinner at the nearby inn. The poem was, he told Elena, "a pure love song and all the truer because of the impossibility of passion." Elena, the poem said, was a "priceless nun of holy mind" whom her son was bidding to awaken from the chains and bars of her own self-imposed anguish. She was not too old to live, and he himself would supply the pure, elevated love that she so pined for. What after all, he concluded, was age itself? In the heart it was always spring and always green. Love was calling, her own Willie's love, climbing into the breach left by her husband's spiritual abandon. It was an impossible passion as her son had said, but all the truer as spirit called out across the chasm to kindred spirit.[25]

In February, as his semester of lectures at the university drew to a close, he wrote Floss not about the sciences but about the central importance he believed the arts would have to their future life together. Americans, he could see, were for the most part utterly incapable of understanding what Europe was all about. Germany was a world worn out by age-old customs that had petrified, America still a "rather crude world" caught up in a strict, puritanical moral standard. As far as that went, he'd learned something of how to breathe more freely away from home and he liked his new freedom. He'd learned how to enjoy the local bierfests and had even attended a Katerbrummel as a member of the Philosophische Verein, thanks to Dantzler, his American drama teacher, who'd taken a liking to his student and budding playwright. Such abandon, such marvelous boisterousness as that he'd witnessed in the German beer halls, would have been impossible back home, he saw now. Sure he'd found the Germans to be common, dishonest, and—as for his professors at the university—godlessly scientific. But he'd also found Germans who were "true, kind, homelike, intelligent and clean."[26] Yet his overriding sense of his stay in Germany had been summed up for him by what a Polish university student staying at the same boardinghouse had said one night during a heated political discussion with several other students. What the young Pole saw was "a general European war in the near future" in which Germany would "be crushed and their false, lying underhand system of politics wiped off the face of the earth." In spite of the fact that Floss's father, Pa Herman, was of Prussian stock and a man Williams admired very much, and in spite of the many good Germans

Williams had met, he had to agree with the Pole. Germany was for him "*l'enfer.*" Hell itself.[27]

No wonder, then, that he was eager to leave Leipzig and Germany as soon as he could. He wrote his parents on February 8 that he was waiting for them to wire him the necessary funds so that he could leave by March 4 and get to Pound and London "via the Hook of Holland visiting Hanover, Amsterdam, the Hague and if possible Leiden [sic]. In London I will stay as long as my money allows me to and then go on to Paris via Dover and Calais." He was going to stay with Pound while he was in London if that could be worked out, and he had to admit that it was "mighty nice to have a friend there who I can see but Pound's position in London at present is so unique that it ought to be doubly pleasant and profitable for me to have been acquainted with him."[28]

Williams actually managed to leave Leipzig even earlier than he hoped. For on March 1, after taking care first to shave his mustache and have his long, scraggly hair cut short, he caught the steamer from Bremen. His "bohemian" days, his time spent downing large drafts of good Münchner beer, were over. At Wartburg, Williams stayed at the Hotel Royal Cassel, going on a pilgrimage to the Wartburg castle there, where his hero, Martin Luther, had studied the German Bible in the obscurity of his small, dark study before leaving to marry Katharina von Bora, who was living then in her convent at Grimma.[29] Having spent seven lonely months in his own room in Leipzig with his fiancée waiting back in America for him, Williams, in his best self-pitying manner, thought he could empathize now with what Martin had been through. His trip out to the convent ruins at Grimma in mid-December had evoked a poem to his poor, misunderstood mother in exile in Rutherford. Now, at the beginning of March, the beginning of spring and a new promise, he composed a poem to the promise of new love, using the new twelve-line sonnet form with interlocking rhymes he'd devised in Leipzig. He called his poem, simply, "The Wartburg":

> *Alone today I mounted the steep hill*
> *On which the Wartburg stands. Here Luther dwelt*
> *In a small room a year through, here he spelt*
> *The German Bible out by God's stern will.*
>
> *The birds piped ti-ti-tu, and as I went*
> *I thought how Katherine von Bora knelt*
> *At Grimma, idle she, waiting to melt*
> *Her surpliced heart in folds less straitly meant.*
>
> *As now, it was March then. Lo! he'll fulfill*
> *Today his weighty task! Sing for content*
> *Ye birds! Pipe now! for now 'tis Love's wing's bent.*
> *Work sleeps, Love wakes! Sing and the glad air thrill!*[30]

From Wartburg Williams traveled on to Amsterdam, crossed the rough waters of the English Channel from there, and saw the storied white cliffs of Dover heave into sight. For the first (and only) time in his life, Williams was in England, from which place his Grandmother Wellcome had departed fifty-four years earlier. From Dover he did not go directly to Kensington, but instead traveled up to Olney, some fifty miles north of London, to spend the night with the family of Ivy Peabody, an English girl he'd met in Leipzig who, like Charlotte before her, was studying at the Conservatory of Music there. For the rest of his life Williams would remember that visit with genuine affection. It would in fact become for him the quintessential image of England at its best, with its "church wall, thick with ivy, over a lawn of earth-hugging daisies and primroses."[31] Only then did he go to stay with Ezra at 10 Church Walk in Kensington.

Ezra made no secret of his being miffed that Williams had preferred gawking at sheep (there were sheep enough to gawk at in Hyde Park) to his own company, even if it had been only for one day. Still, he was glad to see his old friend and he meant to show him what the center of the universe looked like. During the week Williams stayed with Pound, he met not only the great man Yeats, but Yeats's intimate, Olivia Shakespeare, and her daughter, Dorothy, who would later marry Pound. Williams saw Yeats twice, both times in Pound's company, first at an intimate gathering of the Abbey Theatre players, when Yeats read Ernest Dowson's "Cynara" in a chanting voice. The second time was at the Adelphi Club, when Yeats lectured on the Celtic Twilight, and then proceeded to get into a heated dispute with Sir Edmund Gosse over what Gosse called the decadent mores of Yeats's so-called tragic generation of poets: Wilde, Lionel Johnson, and Ernest Dowson, all of whom were now dead. Williams had found himself straining in his chair, wanting to jump up and come to Yeats's defense against Gosse and his antiquated views, but he was afraid to take Gosse on and instead merely sank "back once more into anonymity."[32]

Nor was it easy being in close proximity with Ezra for a whole week. Williams especially disliked his friend's posturing. One night, for example, after he and Pound had finished eating at a small Italian restaurant near Pound's apartment, Williams picked up Pound's coat and held it so that Pound could get into it. Instead Pound became furious—or pretended to be—and scolded Willie that in London one didn't do that sort of thing, while the Italian waiter, smiling along with everyone else in the place by that point, eased the coat from Williams and helped Pound on with it. At least the waiter knew his place. The truth was that, though Pound really was at the center of an intense literary vortex, Williams knew he could not have lasted very long in that world. At the end of a week, he left

Pound feeling exhausted, jittery, and relieved to get out of London and back across the Channel to Paris.

After a brief stay with Eliza Anduze, his father's middle-aged English cousin, he took the overnight train to Milan and met Ed, as prearranged, at the Hotel Como. From there the brothers traveled on to Venice and Florence for a tour of the museums and churches.[33] Ed, who'd been over all this earlier, showed his older brother the Uffizi with its Lippo Lippis, its Botticellis and Raphaels and Titians and Cellinis, and then took him through the Boboli Gardens.[34] They also went out to Fiesole, where Ed took a photograph of Willie, dressed in suit, tie, and cravat, looking very aristocratic as he posed on the arena steps of the small ruined Roman amphitheater there. From Fiesole they also caught a glimpse of one of those newfangled heavier-than-air machines trying to lift itself bravely off the ground until it suddenly nosed down and crashed.

In early April Willie and Ed went down to Rome, where, as Williams told Allen Tate many years later, he spent "a bewilderingly happy week at the Villa Mirafiori where the students of the American Academy in Rome lived in 1910; nightingales and all that for it was early spring."[35] In Rome Williams saw all the tourist sights: the Roman Forum, the Temple of the Vestals, the Baths of Caracalla, the Borghese Gardens and the Coliseum, which for him seemed merely "large and dead."[36] Then it was south again to see the Greek temples and Roman ruins at Paestum, Amalfi, Sorrento, Pompeii, Naples, and Capri.[37]

And then it was over. Seven weeks after he'd entered Italy through its northern pass, he was saying good-by to his brother at the dock at Naples. It was May 9 and Williams had been shown a glorious tour of Italy's vast treasures that spring. Ed could speak Italian like a native, and he'd shown his brother an Italy few American tourists had seen. But things had changed between the brothers. The split over Charlotte had of course initiated it, but Italy widened that split. Outwardly, the incident seemed small enough, but the rift it created in Williams was seismic. They'd spent a bad night in Siena, Williams remembered, having been kept awake most of it by voracious bedbugs, so that both men were somewhat cranky. Then, while they were having breakfast in the hotel restaurant, Williams had ladled out some honey and in his impatience had begun to scrape the honey off the ladle with his teaspoon. Suddenly, he was aware of Ed staring at him as Ezra had six weeks earlier. If Willie wanted more honey, then all he had to do was take another ladleful instead of playing with his spoon. Williams knew that, goddamn him. What was this stupid fuss all about anyway? And then it struck him that Ed, like Ez, had bought into the European way of doing things. Two cultures, as much at odds as when he'd been with those Americans in Amsterdam the previous August, sat facing each other across a breakfast table in Siena.

Willie had been made to understand that his little brother had truly arrived.[38]

*
**

When Williams waved good-by to Ed from the stern of the second-class German passenger liner as it pulled out of the Bay of Naples heading south for Palermo, Sicily, he was waving good-by to his youth. Ed was on his way as a successful architect with two more splendid years in Italy and a beautiful girl waiting for him back home in Rutherford. And Willie was on his way back to America to begin a country doctor's practice in the very hometown he'd thought once to escape. But before returning home, he had one more pilgrimage to make, and that was to Spain to pay homage to Columbus, to the man who had faced doggedly toward the west, toward the New World as Williams was about to do.

At least a month earlier, while he was still in Italy, Williams had decided to stop over in Spain, writing Flossie then that he planned to spend a full twelve days (from May 11 till the twenty-third) touring the country there. He made his way from Gibraltar to the small town of Palos de la Frontera on the outskirts of Huelva, the exact place from which Columbus had sailed for the New World, and the place too to which the Genoese had returned in disgrace. It was mostly sand dunes, Palos, with a few shacks dotting the sands here and there and a 112-foot-high statue of Columbus dominating the landscape, a monstrosity that had been raised eighteen years before to commemorate the four hundredth anniversary of Columbus' first voyage out.[39]

Williams was after the primitive, the untouched, the sense of genuine beginnings, as he'd been after when he visited Luther's study and Katharina's convent ruins and all those places meant to him as breakings with the old traditions. So here, what he wanted most were the desolate sands and ocean stretching out to meet an empty horizon, forbidding and at the same time inviting. From there he went to visit the nearby monastery at Santa Maria la Rabida, where Columbus had stayed after the king of Spain had turned a deaf ear to his claim that there really was a way of reaching fabled Cathay across this western ocean. Williams was deeply moved by Palos and the monastery and wrote Floss two days later from the Hotel Continental in Madrid that now, more than ever before, he wanted somehow "to infuse Americans with the strength and purity of their own traditions which are lying all about us unused."[40] And that promise, that green promise of a new world naked, resplendent with its own extraordinary possibilities, had begun here, with Columbus looking west.

After Palos, Williams spent two days at Seville and two more in Madrid, where he saw the impressive Goyas and the Escorial. On the seventeenth he began his loop back down toward Gibraltar, stopping first in Toledo, where he spent the evening in a tiny bar with twelve workmen, all sitting and listening to two blind peasants as they sang to the accompaniment of a guitar. He drank some cheap red wine along with them and wondered if, as the only outsider, he wasn't going to get a knife between his ribs.

It was there too at Toledo that he had his quintessential experience of the truly primitive, the old upon old he'd been searching for since Palos. It happened as he crossed one of the ancient stone bridges that linked the fortress city to the surrounding hills. Suddenly he found himself squeezed against the bridge's parapets by hundreds of bleating sheep being led home by a tall peasant shepherd and his huge dogs. Williams had had to hold on to the stones along the parapet to stop from being hurled down onto the rocks. "It could have been any moment in the past two thousand years as I stood smelling and feeling the animals flood past me among the rocks on all sides," he would remember decades later in his *Autobiography.*[41] And six years after that, in his mid-seventies, he would remember this moment again in his poem "The High Bridge above the Tagus River at Toledo," where the scene would take on the symbolic weight of an old man at the end of his own journey, the threat of that moment defanged now in the lambent glow of his memory:

> The whole flock, the shepherd and the dogs, were covered
>   with dust as if they had been all day long on the road. The
>   pace of the sheep, slow in the mass,
> governed the man and the dogs. They were approaching the
>   city at nightfall, the long journey completed.
>
> In old age they walk in the old man's dreams and still walk
>   in his dreams, peacefully continuing in his verse
>   forever.[42]

In Granada, he finally got to talk to the shadowy figure he knew had been following him at least since Madrid. The man turned out to be a government agent (or so Williams believed) assigned to watch Williams' comings and goings, and when Williams finally spoke to him was probably as relieved as Williams was now to find out that this Americano was nothing more sinister than a tourist.[43] Williams visited the Alhambra and then got himself lost in one of the villages outside the city. He picked up a young Gypsy girl, who showed him how to get back to his hotel and told him that he was a beautiful young man. On his stay in Madrid in 1906, Pound had met a young Spanish girl who became for him the very soul of the land. And so with Williams and this girl, who, grimy and dusty as she was, would remain in his memory as the image of Kore, the radiant gist, leading him unexpectedly down a new path, when he came to write another poem in his old age: "Of Asphodel, That Greeney Flower."

On the twenty-third Williams boarded the North German Lloyd

second-class passenger ship the *Kaiser Friedrich* for the journey home, scheduled to arrive there on June 4. And though his most recent letters to Floss had become distant and cool and matter-of-fact (as a way of letting her know that her own letters were not passionate, not intense enough), he had been sure she would be waiting for him at the dock in Hoboken, New Jersey, with eager, outstretched arms. In the meantime, to while away the loneliness of the ocean passage, he struck up a friendship with a young woman he'd met on board. They got along well, in fact so well that by the time they reached Hoboken the woman had proposed marriage, coupled with the promise of a lucrative medical practice near Pittsburgh. It was all very flattering, but Williams finally had to explain to her that he was already engaged and was returning to his anxious fiancée after an absence of nearly a year.

How surprised he was, then—and disappointed—to find that his beloved fiancée (for whom he'd sacrificed a medical practice and this other woman) was *not* there to greet him when he disembarked at Hoboken.[44] For Floss by then was angry enough to call the whole silly charade off. Willie had criticized her letters with anger and contempt, though they were the best the girl could do. And his reaction to the picture of herself she had sent him to put on his dresser in Leipzig was unforgivable. She had had a photograph taken by a fashionable New York photographer, with her best dress on and her hair done up in the Gibson girl style—like Charlotte's. The photographer had then touched up Floss's shoulders and her neck, but Williams had become so angry with this idealized version of her, with what he considered the image's intrinsic falseness, that he'd scraped away at its surface to try and capture her authentic awkwardnesses, her stooped shoulders and girlish neck. And then, still simmering, he'd sent several caustic letters to her, ridiculing her for sending him such an abomination. Floss of course had only meant to please, to make herself as attractive as possible in the shadow of her more gifted sister, and she had been deeply hurt by Williams' bitter letters until, toward the end of his stay, she had stopped writing to him altogether. Being engaged to Willie was becoming one long painful ordeal. In fact, she seems to have told him that he could have his freedom back if he wanted it. That apparently caught Willie up short. It would take him, by his own admission (Floss being silent about such private things), several weeks of intense wooing to get her interested in him once again.

*
**

Williams spent the rest of the summer of 1910 at home, waiting impatiently for his New Jersey medical license to come so that he might begin practicing medicine officially. In the meantime he helped out his parents as best he could and spent some vacation time up at the summer bungalow in West Haven. In mid-August he was invited to spend a week with Floss and her family at the Mt. Luke Hotel in Cooks Falls, New York, near the Delaware Water Gap. He was writing poetry again and he could tell Floss now that poetry was his greatest happiness. It was his "greatest joy on earth and shares in me with the love of persons such as you and Ed and my mother and my father too in the power it has for creating joy."[45] Now, together with Floss at Cooks Falls, Williams had his first extended chance to get to know his fiancée better. He went fishing with Pa Herman (who, an artist of sorts himself, understood this strange boy and liked him), and he took long walks with Floss and read to her as she sat under a tree and listened. He even wrote several poems about their future life together, including a very good one called "A Coronal." In that poem he said that their life together would be a life of art, of "new books of poetry" and "unheard of manuscripts" delivered by the mailman in "brown paper wrappers." For Flossie, he wrote, was his muse, his green "slender source," his springtime, his inspiration from whom would unfold book after book of poems over the years, "leather-colored / many and many a time." The poem was a coronal for Flossie to wear, but in a deeper sense Williams was still not seeing her as an individual. Instead he was celebrating the mythic woman as generative source, and this young girl sitting with her back against the trunk of a maple was but one important manifestation of that green source.[46] Floss listened to her strange lover but kept her own counsel.

By the end of August and back at 131 West Passaic Avenue, Williams wrote Flossie (who was still on vacation) that he had ordered his doctor's shingle and was waiting for his office telephone to be installed. His first office would be out of his father's house with the front hall serving for the waiting room and the kitchen pantry converted into the consulting room. It meant a flurry of plumbers and carpenters tearing up the downstairs of his parents' home, with dust and noise disrupting everything through the end of August and into September as new sinks and building partitions were added and the room painted and papered green.[47]

And then he began his practice. His license arrived in the mail on September 2, while the office was still being put together. Two weeks later, on the fifteenth, he addressed the assembled grammar-school and high-school children of Rutherford as their new school physician, a position he was to maintain for the next fourteen years. He felt nervous speaking before so many of his own townspeople, and he confessed to Floss that his heart had done "a few fancy Isadora Duncan stunts" of its own before he had calmed down enough to address them.[48] And then, five days later, with his office ready, he began practicing medicine officially in the same town where he would remain until he retired forty years and three thousand babies later. But that first day began with only one patient coming to see him: a little girl with a case of dandruff, which he cured. Still, it was an auspicious enough beginning, a sign to his wait-and-see townspeople that Willie the poet wasn't out to kill them.[49]

After all, Willie was still a young man to be putting out his own shingle. And though he had just turned twenty-seven, he still looked about eighteen. Moreover, he had little confidence in himself as yet, and so could not, as he himself admitted later, have inspired much confidence in potential patients. Nor was his office highly visible, tucked as it was in the middle of a residential street away from Rutherford's business district. But he was a good physician and he'd had excellent training in New York and in Europe, and slowly he began to build up a good practice as the people of Rutherford and Lyndhurst and Garfield and Passaic came to trust him. And yet it could be trying, this practicing medicine out of his father's house in Rutherford, with its farms everywhere to remind him of his provincial status relative to that humming dynamo of a center to the east. "I once pined for the country," he confessed to Viola Baxter (with whom he'd resumed his friendship and correspondence the same month he'd begun practicing medicine). "But my blood is freezing here. Nothing but the intellectually unborn from before breakfast till after supper." He missed her, he had to admit, as he missed now the excitement of New York and all Viola had represented for him: a world that had seemed within his grasp, but which had slipped through his fingers at last. Nothing for it, then, but to keep the mind as active as he could devouring Ibsen (Viola became his "Hedda" now) and writing and staging several of his one-act plays for the local Rutherford Theatre.[50]

In the meantime there was still a long courtship ahead for Willie and Floss. He still had no money to speak of and he would have to work hard to make his practice pay. In his first year, he made a total of $750, and that sum included the $500 he was offered annually as school physician. Moreover, Floss at nineteen was still, as he knew, "little more than a kid," and he for his part was still a wild-eyed artist intent on being a successful dramatist. More and more Viola became a substitute for all he'd lost in losing Charlotte (though he must have known Viola could not fill that role very adequately). And yet she was the closest of anyone he knew to the figure of the sophisticated, urbane woman, the artist of consummate sensitivity, and his letters to her were accordingly more "worldly," charged with a knowingness and an affected world-weariness absent from the more idealistic letters he was writing to his fiancée. "You are quite right, Viola," he wrote in one letter in January 1911. "Men are not strong enough to 'bat air' with women. That forever proves to me I am not a man; they, men, disgust me and if I must say it fill me with awe and admiration. I am too much a woman."[51] And in another letter to her he complained that he had a new play "charging and recharging across the field of my brain" and "pomes" to be reworked, simplified and clarified. And then there was his medical practice and caring for "men folks who smoke too much and women folks who don't smoke enough to take care of."[52]

Pound had come back to the States via England aboard the RMS *Slavonia* in June 1910, the same month Williams had returned. His reason for coming back to Murica, or Murka, as he disdainfully termed it, was to get treatment for a case of jaundice. He spent his first few weeks in New York and then returned to Philadelphia, apparently spending the summer at Swarthmore, working on his translation of Guido Cavalcanti. Then he returned to New York, this time to an apartment at 164 Waverly Place in Greenwich Village. In October Hilda Doolittle had come up to New York to visit him and together they went out to Rutherford to visit Williams and meet the girl he was engaged to. It may have been on this visit that Flossie's parents extended an invitation to have Willie and his poet friends over for dinner and some excellent Rudesheimer 1905. Certainly Pound lived up to Mrs. Herman's suspicions about Willie's friends, for at one point he "stood on his chair at table to kill a mosquito on the ceiling." Flossie especially was not impressed.[53]

Pound came again, alone this time, to spend Thanksgiving Day with Williams at 131 West Passaic Avenue. And it was probably during this visit, as Ezra and Willie and Pop sat around in the living room drinking Pop's Goldwasser that the question of Pound's poetry came up. Pound had been reading some of his most recent stuff and had included a sequence called "Und Drang," already published in magazine form and to be included in his next book of poems, *Canzoni* (1911). In one of the poems from that sequence, "The House of Splendour," Pound had written of a lady with "six great sapphires hung along the wall," and though Pound later insisted to Williams that those sapphires were nothing *but* sapphires, Williams was just as sure that Pound had explained those precious stones to William George as being the backs of books ranged along book shelves, jewels because they were rare and treasured artifacts.

Eight years later, in his "Prologue" to *Kora in Hell*, he recalled with relish how his father had questioned young, flamboyant Pound and how glad he was that his father had decided to turn his displeasure on his friend instead of himself:

> My parent had been holding forth in downright sentences upon my own "idle nonsense" when he turned and became equally vehement concerning something Ezra had written: what in heaven's name Ezra meant by "jewels" in a verse that had come between them. These jewels,—rubies, sapphires, amethysts and whatnot, Pound went on to explain with great determination and care, were the backs of books as they stood on a man's

shelf. "But why in heaven's name don't you say so then?" was my father's triumphant and crushing rejoinder.[54]

Whether it was a "crushing rejoinder" or no—Pound recalling the event thought otherwise[55]—it is clear that Williams himself had fared little better with his father when it came to poetry.[56]

It was probably on this visit too that Pound and Williams went for a walk around Kipp's Woods, and Williams had pointed to the winter wheat, three or four inches high, which he said was rising up to greet Pound. Pound quipped that if that was so, then it was the first intelligent wheat he'd ever met. And he meant it. As for wheat, Pound had one for Williams. He, Pound, had opted for caviar, but his friend had merely settled for bread. Williams agreed wholeheartedly, but not in a way Pound had foreseen. Yes, bread, bread for the people.

Was it really impossible to get Willie back over to Europe again? For all its incredible energy and potential, Pound felt that New York was no place to live (and he was spelling out his own relationship to that city in a series of essays he was writing then and which he would publish back in London in a book entitled, with a mixture of irony and regret, *Patria Mia*). Pound had a scheme for getting Willie out of Rutherford, and Williams remembered it this way in his *Autobiography*: Ezra and he would "get a big supply of '606,' the new anti-syphilitic arsenical which Ehrlich had just announced to the world, and go at once with it to the north coast of Africa and there set up shop." Between them, with Williams' medical license and experience and Pound's "social proclivities," they might be able to "clean up a million treating all the wealthy old nabobs there— presumably rotten with the disease—and retire to our literary enjoy- ments within, at most, a year." When Williams' father heard that one, though, he merely shook his head in disbelief. Willie dropped the subject.[57]

When Pound came out again on February 13, it was to say good-by before he left on the twenty-second for London. It would be the last time he would see Williams for thirteen years and the last time he would ever see Williams' father. When he left, he left behind a copy of Metastasio's *Varie Poesie* (Venice 1795), which, seven years later, as Williams' father lay dying of cancer, Williams would use as a model for putting together the prose experiments he'd gathered in *Kora in Hell*. The choice of that particular book may have been Williams' way of paying homage to those early sessions he and Ez and Pop had spent together in Rutherford in 1910 and 1911 and which by 1918 must have seemed part of a lost world.

In July, the Hermans moved once again up to Monroe, New York, for the summer. Monroe was forty miles north of Rutherford and still very much in the country and the Hermans were seriously looking in that area for a second home. Since Monroe was close to the railroad line going directly into New York, Pa Herman could commute to his printing business in the city and then come back to enjoy his country retreat. Williams himself spent the Fourth of July weekend up at West Haven and from there wrote Floss the news that Ed and Charlotte were breaking their engagement of two years' standing.[58] Apparently, since Charlotte felt three years was a very long time to wait for Ed, Ed had given her back her "freedom." Willie felt perversely protective toward his brother now and wanted to blame the breakup on Charlotte. But he knew it was better to let the matter drop. After all, what Ed and Charlotte did was their business. But if Williams saw several lessons in irony in the whole proceeding, he never let on. It had been two years too, almost to the day, that he and Floss had also been engaged.[59]

He made several overnight trips up to see Floss in Monroe, and he casually mentioned to her in one letter that he'd recently been into New York to visit his old friend, Viola, only to learn that she'd moved without leaving a forwarding address.[60] He wrote too that practice was becoming much more active, at his home office as well as over at Passaic General Hospital.[61] That hospital was right across the Passaic River in the next county, and it was the one he would work out of for the next forty years, until his retirement. In another letter he told Floss that Holeman's Store House in Rutherford had been struck by lightning and he'd been part of the crowd who had watched it burn to the ground.[62] The conflagration itself had been a "wonderful sight" to see, and he would remember it again thirty years later when he imaginatively reconstructed the fire in *Paterson*, the roof of a warehouse lifted

> *like a*
> *skirt, held by the fire—to rise at last,*
> *almost with a sigh, rise and float, float*
> *upon the flames as upon a sweet breeze*

floating over "the frizzled elms" and the railroad tracks "to fall / upon the roofs beyond."[63]

On Saturday, July 22d, he took the train into New York to see Hilda Doolittle off for England from the pier at the Twenty-third Street Ferry Terminal.[64] She was going to England, ostensibly to complete her education, but Williams knew that she was really going there to meet Ezra in London, and he was sure Professor Doolittle, who'd come to see her off, knew that that was how things really stood. But there it was. She was twenty-four now and old enough (as Charlotte had been) to know her own mind. There were only the two of them—Willie and Hilda's father—in all that crowd to see her off, and Professor Doolittle was as abstract now as Williams had remembered him at Upper Darby six years before. He just sat "on a trunk," Williams remembered, "completely silent. No word to me or to anyone."[65] When Hilda sailed from New York, Williams was not to see her for another nine years, by which time a war would have intervened, Williams would have two sons, and Hilda would be the mother of a daughter and the intimate companion of another woman.

Williams also worked on his poems through the summer of 1911, did some translations from the Spanish in conjunction with his father, and continued to work on his American play, *Betty Putnam*, which he described as his "near-bloody" colonial piece. By August he'd heard of Viola's whereabouts and when he wrote her he enclosed a poem and a note that told her that her beauty had become for him that summer a very torture. New York City without her, the poem said, became merely a hodgepodge of streets and buildings and empty rooms. But with her, the entire city took on order and meaning. That was to Viola.[66] Six days later he wrote a more pastoral piece for his country lass. It was a pastel-sad lyric and it was intended to convey to Floss how much he was missing her:

> I will sing a joyous song
>   To you, my Lady!
> On a hill the wind is blowing!
> Lady, Lady, we have stood upon the hill
>   But now I'm far
> And you are far from me
> And yet the wind is all between us blowing.[67]

He went into New York's Chinatown with Jack Kavanaugh, a friend of his, on one occasion that summer, and then went down to the Italian Settlement over by the old copper mines in Fort Lee to take in the feast of San Rocco put on by the Italian Catholic church there. He would remember the Church of San Rocco in *Paterson* too, particularly the wax replicas of arms and legs hung inside the church in thanksgiving by the faithful as signs that they'd been cured by heavenly intercession. And those replicas would then stand for his own need to make of his life a replica in words approximating his own deepest understanding of himself:

> Not until I have made of it a replica
> will my sins be forgiven and my
> disease cured—in wax: la capella di S. Rocco
> on the sandstone crest above the old
>
> copper mines—where I used to see
> the images of arms and knees
> hung on nails . . . [68]

But what impressed Williams most in 1911 about the feast was not the faith of these people but rather the polyglot of English dialects he heard spoken there—the way the Irish and Poles and Italians each spoke their own version of the one common language: American English.[69] He was listening hard to those rhythms and he was beginning to incorporate them into his own poems. He could still hear in his mind's ear Italians speaking in Milan and Rome and Naples, and he remembered Sicilians in the streets of Palermo. And now here were these transplanted Sicilians speaking their fresh, vibrant, broken English and he tried—falteringly— to capture something of their music in a poem he wrote now called "Sicilian Emigrant's Song":

> O—eh—lee! La—la!
>   *Donna! Donna!*
> *Blue is the sky of Palermo;*
> *Blue is the little bay;*
> *And dost thou remember the orange and fig,*
> *The lively sun and the sea-breeze at evening?*
>   *Hey—la!*
> *Donna! Donna! Donna!*[70]

He was still learning, mostly from reading Pound's poems. There were also concerts of Beethoven to attend in the city and something Pound did not have: the New York Giants. That was Willie's team, all his life, in good seasons and in bad.[71]

That September Willie went to talk to Floss's father and make his intentions clear.[72] He wanted to make his engagement to Floss "official," though he still didn't know for sure when he would be making enough of an income to support Pa Herman's favorite daughter. Pa Herman understood. He liked Willie. On October 15, Williams wrote Viola to tell her where he thought their relationship stood now that he was officially engaged. "Certainly I will never be anything but truthful to myself," he waffled, "and certainly to be truthful I dearly love a lady near me at home" (by whom he meant Floss). But he also told Viola that he still felt deeply about her and "two other ladies both now in Europe," by whom he may have meant Hilda and Ivy Peabody. Why he should feel so strongly about not one but four women and what the outcome of that division of affections might augur he didn't know for sure, but "for the practical conduct of affairs which is life" he felt constrained now "to confine my resources of passion." Still, he wanted Viola to understand that she had "a splendid physical makeup," and he added that he still intended to be a successful dramatic artist some day.[73] He was sure she would understand.

Then, five days later, he sent Viola a poem about the conflict he was being tortured by of being tempted by a false love (eros, presumably) and the need he felt to rise above any love less than the highest and noblest. But the poem was as confusing in its intention as Williams' own feelings at the time seem to have been.[74] The truth was that he didn't like this being engaged at all and didn't really care for this institution called marriage toward which he had steered himself. But he didn't dare confess that to himself, and certainly not to Flossie, especially after all this time. Only years later could he admit that the whole courtship scene had had about as much reality for him as one of those Mask and Wig performances he'd acted in while he was at Penn.[75]

But by month's end he was laughing at himself and his own pretensions of still trying to ignore his own sexual nature. The result was that his male friends were sure he was trying to "do" them, that is, fool them, with his talk of purity. And as for the ladies: well, he could see that they were being "patient" with him, waiting for Willie to finally say what was really on his mind. From now on, he promised, he was going to "strive to be satisfied with gargoyles on my greek temple," though he did not promise that the resulting compromise with his own (damaged) sense of perfection would leave him with an "equanimity of temper."[76] No wonder he would remember himself at this age as something of a wild-eyed young man. By December of that year he could finally tell Viola that virginity was nothing more than a "myth," as any child of three might have told him. Love, he had discovered (apparently without Freud's help), would have its own way. "Be willful in spite of Him and you are met as by a hawk, swiftly!"[77] From now on he would have to acknowledge the presence of goat-footed Pan in his reckonings. Yes, he had so much wanted to have his soul free and virginal, but he was also learning that even the scented, white lily-of-the-valley had its roots mired deeply "in the mud."[78]

*
* *

By the spring of 1912 Williams was busy making house calls and visiting the Rutherford schools and going out via Union Avenue over the Passaic to the hospital, riding everywhere in a buggy driven by a little mare named Astrid. That March he gave a lecture to a club in the west end of Rutherford on the importance of physical education for children, and bluntly told his audience that the sanest way of thinking of their bodies was not as perpetually clothed but rather as naked and free to move. Clothes were to help the body, not torture it.[79] He got into New York as often as he could, whether to see Viola or the Metropolitan Museum of Art or, more and more now, to visit the art gallery exhibits along Fifth Avenue. He was particularly interested in the painting being done by young Americans working in and around New York, and he told Floss about the work of one such painter named Brown which had particularly impressed him. That man, he said, was for him "a modern Giotto," and the best hope he'd so far found in contemporary America who might "free our art from its byzantine, that is its quasi mystic-symbolic, modern influences." It was realism and not symbolism Williams was looking for.[80] He was working then on yet another play and reading Ibsen more intently than ever, having just seen a performance of his *Gho*̀*sts* done in Russian at the Garrick Theater in New York. Now, he said, he was willing to place the Norwegian playwright—the realist of realists—on the same level with his beloved Shakespeare.[81]

At the same time he was heading into conflict with his father. "My father tells me," he wrote Viola, "being asked directly whether or not in his estimation I was a simple jussack [i.e., jackass], that I am tardy in development, that is all." Williams was impressed at how delicately his father had phrased it, and then explained that after all the man was a "distinguished linguist" who had learned the niceties of language "by writing advertisements for perfumery and liver pills."[82] Beneath the acerbic lightness of this note may have been some of the residual anger he was feeling as he came now to pit his own will against his father's equally fierce will. At twenty-eight, Willie was still not in a position to begin his own family, and yet it was clear that the sexual limbo of his engagement had already gone on longer than it should have. He had talked to his father, asking him if, in addition to keeping his office downstairs, he might not also bring Floss to live there when they got married. This would mean Pop and Mama moving their things upstairs and turning over the whole first floor, except for the kitchen, to the young couple. His father said he would talk it over with Mama and let him know. The answer was yes, yes, they could manage that, though it would mean some adjustments in living.

But when, on top of that, Willie began talking about how he was going to do over the downstairs for himself and his bride, his father suddenly went stone cold. There would be no such changes as Willie was envisioning in his house as long as he was living there. Willie shouted, raged—it was the young buck up against the older—and then stormed out of the house and into the spring night. It was after ten when he left the house and he just kept walking and walking out on the highway toward Hackensack, mulling over his options, until two in the morning. Then, his head clearer, he turned around and walked back home. Neither father nor son ever brought the subject up again. But when the time came, Willie made arrangements with his next-door neighbors the Ackers to rent two small upstairs rooms from them. He and Floss would live there but take their meals with Willie's parents. The office would remain where it was. And Bill and Flossie would be married at year's end. It was a first tentative step toward an independence of sorts[83]

In the summer of 1912, Floss went back up to Monroe with her family and Williams continued with his practice in Rutherford. He wrote her about the news, about the incredible sinking of the *Titanic* in June, about his reappointment to the Rutherford school physician's post, about a biography of Martin Luther he was reading and of his intense interest in the events that had led up to Luther's marrying Katharina. He'd already written a poem on that topic and now he was contemplating a play which he was thinking of calling *Luther at Wittenberg—1526.* He was also wondering how he could get enough cash together to get himself a car so that he could move around more easily.[84] And he was writing poems, including one unlike anything he'd done before, a poem he called "Hic Jacet" (Here Lies), about the gaiety of the coroner's little children who could afford to be merry because a kind Providence had provided for them. It was a gaiety, Williams suggested, that came from the final deprivations of others in death, for the children's little paunches were kept filled precisely because there was always business for their father.

"Hic Jacet" was unlike most of the abstract and derivative pieces Williams still managed to write, and, despite several archaisms in the poem, it pointed toward the kind of thing Williams would be writing five years later:

> The coroner's merry little children
>   Have such twinkling brown eyes.
> Their father is not of gay men
>   And their mother jocular in no wise,
> Yet the coroner's merry little children
>   laugh so easily.
>
> They laugh because they prosper.
>   Fruit for them is upon all branches.
> Lo! how they jibe at loss, for
>   Kind heaven fills their little paunches!
> It's the coroner's merry, merry children
>   Who laugh so easily.

It was this poem with its new, sardonic tone that Pound was to single out a year later as the one piece that had revived Elkin Mathews, Williams' (and Pound's) English publisher, after the man had "whiffed" one of Willie's "worst and more pseudo philosophic pieces."[85]

When Williams went up to Monroe in July of that year to visit Floss, he also met the Hermans' new neighbors, the Earles. Ferdinand Earle was even at first glance a dashing, handsome, wealthy, and self-assured figure, and it soon became obvious that, though already married to his second wife, he was much taken by Charlotte's beauty. Among other talents he possessed, Earle was a decent portrait painter, and he had undertaken to do a portrait of Flossie's brother, Paul, who was then twelve years old. Earle's generosity allowed him to see the Hermans—and especially Charlotte—nearly every day, and Willie smelled trouble almost from the beginning. Here in the flesh was Charlotte's soulmate at last, the one who was finally to win the prize.

Earle was also editor of *The Lyric Year,* an annual anthology of the best recent verse America had produced (at least by blighted contemporary standards). Earle let Willie know he liked him in a paternalistic sort of way (after all, he was thirty-seven, Willie twenty-eight), and he promised

Willie that he was going to try and get some of Willie's poems published in *The Lyric Year.* A month later, however, Earl had to tell him the bad news: that though he personally liked Willie's stuff, he hadn't been able to get the other editors to see it his way, and they'd rejected his poems.[86] This, *this,* from the man who was making his surreptitious moves around his own wife and the Hermans for the very woman whom just three years before Willie had wanted so badly he'd almost gone mad. Flossie could sense what was up. Her own wedding to Willie was only four months away and here her beau was pining after her sister again. The tension became so great that Williams had to write Floss at the end of August that, though he still did not like the idea of marriage, he was still willing to marry her. "Perhaps I loved Charlotte," he tried to explain to her, to himself. "I'm not sure but I never thought of marrying her. I rejected the very idea of a proposal of marriage when Ed asked me to go to her. My first thought concerning you was marriage, I wanted you yourself."[87] True, he had rejected the notion of proposing to Charlotte, but what he couldn't bear to dwell on in his explanation to Floss was his fear that he hadn't even been seriously in the running. And asking Floss to marry him three days after Charlotte had accepted Ed had had its own complex am- bivalances to say the least. Ed's proposal had been one thing. In a sense, that would still have been family, a partial victory of sorts. But to see this other interloper, handsome and cocksure in his ways, who had rubbed salt in the wound by rejecting Willie's poems, was too much to ask anyone to accept. Very early on, Willie came to hate the man with a stone-cold intensity.

The upshot of the *Lyric Year* business was that, when the anthology was published in the spring of 1913, Williams sent a poem enclosed in a letter to Harriet Monroe, editor of *Poetry Magazine,* where the poem, entitled (after Keats) "On First Opening *The Lyric Year,*" appeared in the "Letters to the Editor." It was a twelve-line effort in couplets and Williams employed the clever image of well-ordered graves, row on row exact, and spoke of how he too had once wanted to join all those others who made it into anthologies until he realized that acceptance meant that one was already dead from a poetic point of view.[88] He also let Floss know how he felt about Earle after he'd learned about his being rejected from the anthology, telling her he was sick and tired of the "worn out 'coney island' stuff in a gospel tent that we see every day in the magazines." But the truth was he felt heartsick at his failure to appear, miserable that he could find absolutely no outlet, no forum, for his verse in America as he approached his thirtieth birthday.

*
**

It was Pound now who came to Williams' rescue by telling him in late August that *The Poetry Review* (London) was going to publish seven of

Williams' poems as a selection from his projected second book of poems, to be called *The Tempers*. Pound had urged his own publisher, Elkin Mathews, to publish Williams in England (something he was doing for another poet ten years older than Williams—and equally unknown—an American named Robert Frost). The deal with Williams was that Williams would guarantee to buy 250 copies of the book for ten pounds (about fifty dollars) to help defray printing costs and that the book would appear in the fall of 1913. In the meantime, there were seven poems and an introductory note by Pound himself to whet the appetites of the hundred or so English readers of *The Poetry Review* and show them what was in store for them from Williams. The poems and Pound's note appeared in October, and Pound wrote there that, though he certainly hadn't intended to introduce "Mr. Williams as a cosmic force" (in fact the poems themselves would show how very difficult a time Williams had had writing poems), certainly they would show that the man was determined to win through. At least, Pound added, the poems were "not overcrowded with false ornament" like so much stuff coming off the presses in 1912. He had chosen to present some of Willie's lighter, less philosophical effusions, including several "Songs" and closing with the one piece he could stomach, "Hic Jacet."[89]

"Surely there is a big part of me clings upon your destructive savor," Williams had written Viola in mid-July. "But Pluto be blessed Orpheus did turn to look behind—how else would he ever have possessed her [Persephone, Kore] to this day."[90] With preparations for his wedding going forward, Williams was already looking back on his earlier freedom, toward the gaiety Viola could—at least from a distance—offer him. In short, he did not want to give her up. We do not have Viola's response to this turn of events in writing—Williams having finally destroyed most of his letters from her—but she assumed a wait-and-see posture, knowing her man better than he knew himself. By way of light banter he sent her a poem addressed to his Lady's teeth:

> Oh beloved when you brush your teeth
> Both over—top and underneath
> My heart grows overbold
> For I'd hate to see them funny,
>   hollow, empty when
> You're old.[91]

And in another poem he assured Viola that "No herring from Norway / Can touch you for flavor," and that her "Piquancy" was far greater than pimento. He was tortured by Viola's worldliness and experience, the artist living daringly in the Great City, something that would appeal to Williams' sense of the erotic and adventurous until World War II had changed the face of the city he had known so intimately. Viola must love him very desperately, he'd written her months earlier, for why else would she torture herself to take away his own "poor happiness."[92] But he also told Floss just ten weeks before their wedding that he was keeping "virtuous" not for virtue's empty sake, but because she wanted it that way.[93]

Finally, the day came. On Thursday, December 12, 1912—12/12/12 —William Carlos Williams and Florence Herman were married in Rutherford's Presbyterian church—Floss's church—in the presence of both a Presbyterian and a Unitarian minister, the latter a woman who had been momentarily overlooked in the hurly-burly of the last-minute preparations, but who had had enough presence of mind to get over to the church on her own in time for the wedding ceremony. Elena and William George were there, and Paul and Nannie Herman and young Paul. Ed, who'd come back from Italy that summer and had been teaching at Boston Tech, served as Willie's best man. But Floss had chosen her best friend, Clara Ely, and not Charlotte, to be maid of honor.[94] And though Willie didn't want him there, Ferdinand Earle had come as Charlotte's guest. Unfortunately, Mrs. Earle herself hadn't been able to get away for the ceremony.

Willie himself felt aloof from the proceedings, as though he were backstage at the performance of some ornate masque instead of at his own wedding. But when Pa Herman finally began walking down the church aisle holding his favorite daughter by the arm, Williams was astonished. Ed was standing there next to him, and he could see his mother and father in the front pew, and now the organ music rose higher and higher. And there was Flossie, approaching him in her white gown, virginal, "pale as a ghost," coming to this young wild poet, and his heart went out to her. That image of her would stay with him all the rest of his life, in spite of the vicissitudes of their fifty years of married life together, growing dearer as he grew older. In his seventies, his face and right side crippled by strokes, an old man, desperate, he would cling to the young promise of this moment:

> At the altar
>   so intent was I
> before my vows,
>   so moved by your presence
>   a girl so pale
> and ready to faint
>   that I pitied
>   and wanted to protect you.
> As I think of it now,
>   after a lifetime,
>   it is as if
> a sweet-scented flower
>   were poised
>   and for me did open.[95]

After the wedding and the rice throwing, there was a grand reception for the newlyweds at the Hermans' home, the whole house transformed with gas lamps and candles and champagne and champagne punch and dancing and drunken giddiness. And then it was time for the couple to head for New York. Now it was more confetti and streamers and artificial rose petals and the couple dashing for the door and their getaway . . . only to find the front doors roped shut together. That had been Ferdinand Earle's idea of a practical joke, and Charlotte had gone along with it.[96] There was a moment of confusion and a pileup at the doors, before Bill's friends cut the ropes and the couple was on their way at last, tin cans and streamers dangling from the open touring car as they held each other closely against the wintry night air, both of them intent and serious about their new roles, beginning only now to relax with each other a little after three and a half years of interminable waiting.

What those first few weeks of marriage were like, however, we do not know. Floss kept her silence and Williams, for all his words, never directly wrote about this initiation into marriage. It is likely that, unlike his bride, he was no longer a virgin, though that must as of now remain a surmise. Floss would soon find herself pregnant with her first child and Williams, after apparently promising to remain the faithful husband at least, soon after his marriage was seeing Viola once again. This time it was—apparently—without coyness on either of their parts.

The wedding had been planned so that Bill and Floss could spend their first night together at a hotel in New York before boarding a liner next day for a leisurely cruise down to Bermuda. But that trip had been delayed five days because of winter storms, and so Bill and Floss had decided to drive up to Boston in Bill's new car, a 1913 Ford he'd finally found the down payment for in October. When they reached Boston, they took rooms at the Hotel Victoria so that they could see Ed, and Bill took Floss around to see some American history and culture. One place he took her to was Concord to see the sites associated with Hawthorne and particularly Emerson and to see where the American Revolution had begun. At the old colonial graveyard there, overlooking the tavern and the road down which the British had marched that April morning, Floss suddenly became sick and puked on one of the graves. So much for history. The couple was back in New York on the eighteenth, in time to catch their boat for Bermuda. And though the seas were still running high and they had a rough trip down, the tropics, alive with color at that season, made the journey worth it all.[97]

When Bill and Floss returned to Rutherford and winter at the beginning of January, they moved into their crammed rooms at the Ackers', taking their meals as planned at Elena's table next door. That meant a diet of beans, rice, potatoes, and meat, all cooked through and through, the way Williams senior, that inveterate Englishman, had always liked them. Such fare was not easy for Floss, but she bore with it for Bill's sake. As for Bill himself, he had his patients to look after out of his small office, or around Rutherford, or up at the hospital. And he was painting now, whenever he had the time, driving down Union Avenue that spring to the place where the road passed over the Passaic, to paint an impressionistic landscape of the river and trees he could see north from the bridge. He was also collecting the poems Mathews would publish that fall. Moreover, armed now with Pound's introduction, he submitted his first sheaf of poems to *Poetry* (Chicago) the rallying point for the new poetry in 1913. If Pound had a special liking for one poem of Williams' other than "Hic Jacet," it was for his "Postlude," a poem studded with classical allusions and bearing the mark of a new rhythm, closer to Pound's own advanced metrical experiments, and Pound sent it on to Harriet Monroe in February with directions to be sure and print it. Monroe too liked the poem and wrote Williams that she planned to publish four of his pieces in her June number.

Startled by her unexpected courtesy, Williams wrote back at once to say how pleased he was to be getting published in *Poetry*. But he also wanted to get something straight with her from the beginning. There was, as they both knew, a profound revolution going on at that very moment in American poetry. Sandburg was there, and Lindsay and Pound. And modern verse—such as his own—would have to manifest that revolution in the very "irregularities" of its form. These so-called irregularities were, he knew, nothing more than refusals to be dominated by the traditional meters, the old rhythms. The same revolution was also going on in painting, in the work of the French impressionists, for example, who, despite the fact that many of them would have received low marks from the official Academy for bad drawing, had had to be accepted by the world "for the sake of art's very life."[98]

Harriet Monroe too had a place in the new revolution, he went on, and he only hoped she was enough of a true revolutionary not to tamper with the revolutionary nature of his lines or change his lower-case line beginnings back to the old orthodox standard capitals. For God's sake, what true revolutionary would abide by such outmoded typographical strictures? Until now, he had felt terribly isolated by the state of poetry in America, and he was relieved to have found one magazine into which he could pour himself. But Monroe would have to be damn careful about what she printed. For it was, he insisted, "the new seed, the one little new seed that counts in the end—that will ultimately cover fields with vigorous growth." He knew she didn't put Bill Williams in the same class with the divine Ezra who sent his missives and poems from the vortex beyond the sea, but Williams had enough faith in himself to know that it was only a matter of time before he became a great poet. And he didn't mind saying so.[99]

What was behind this letter, behind its sense of a bright new dawn for American poetry, was the fact of the New York Armory Show, which first revealed to America the radical new directions European and especially French painting had been taking for over four decades already. By 1913 Williams had made the Metropolitan Museum of Art and New York's private art galleries regular stops on his frequent trips into the great city. So he was sure years later he'd seen the Armory Show sometime after its grand opening on February 17 at the old brick Sixty-ninth Regiment building on 25th Street. But Floss was just as certain and just as adamant that he'd missed it and was confusing the Armory Show with the Exhibition held by the Society of American Artists in the spring of 1917. (This was the one in which Marcel Duchamp submitted a ready-made, a urinal signed R. Mutt, which the society rejected, in spite of the fact that Duchamp was then vice-president of the society.) In his *Autobiography* Williams did conflate the two shows, and he did attend the 1917 Exhibition, where he read his futurist poem, "Overture to a Dance of Locomotives," even using that exhibition as a symbolic event in his "Prologue" to his *Kora in Hell*.

Still, it is difficult to believe that Williams missed the Armory Show, in spite of Floss's usually excellent memory about such things, since he was frequently in New York then and because even by 1913 he was so intensely interested in what was happening in the world of art.[100] The truth is that he may have driven into the city alone to spend a few hours walking through the crowded makeshift rooms or he may have gone in with someone besides Floss. But in another sense, even if he did miss walking about the floors of the enormous buildings, looking at some of the two thousand European and American paintings and sculptures massed there on display like an assault against middle-class American taste, he could not have missed reading about the show in the newspapers. For there was something about the Armory in the papers almost every day during the winter and early spring of 1913: editorials, articles, and reviews that defended or attacked the work of the impressionists, cubists, fauvists, expressionists, and the Americans. It was the gathering place, the vortex, where Europeans like Matisse and Kandinsky and Cézanne and Braque and Picabia and Americans like Sheeler and Sloan and Bellows and Glackens first became known to the American public.

So when Williams lectured Harriet Monroe in March about the lesson she as editor and conservator of the modern could learn from the example of the impressionists, he was undoubtedly thinking of the Armory Show itself. Those artists had been like a breath of fresh air to him and other young writers, so much so that within a few years Williams' artist heroes would become Cézanne among the impressionists, Picasso, Braque, and especially Juan Gris among the cubists, Kandinsky among the expressionists, and Sheeler, Marsden Hartley, and Demuth among the Americans. Duchamp, grudgingly, remained centrally important for Williams as an exponent of radical experimentation in the arts and would become for Williams the modernist *par excellence* as well as the main aesthetic impetus behind Williams' *Improvisations* (1917–18).

"There had been a break somewhere," Williams remembered, looking back on this period in his *Autobiography*. "We were steaming through, each thinking his own thoughts, driving his own designs toward his self's objectives. Whether the Armory Show in painting did it or whether that was also no more than a facet—the poetic line, the way the image was to lie on the page was our immediate concern."[101] The Armory Show of course could be only a facet—the growth of any artist being too complex to ascribe to one cause only—but looking at what the French had done with their world and the Americans with theirs in the paintings assembled together at the Armory, Williams could feel justified in asserting that the local culture, the flower with roots in his own environment, could be made to bloom in New York as it had bloomed in Paris. After all, there was nothing intrinsically different, except for the long cultural layering, between Cézanne's Provence and Williams' Passaic River. What mattered was the freshness of the eye that beheld and, beholding, could then recreate a world on canvas or on paper.

*
* *

That summer, with Marconi's radio waves and the abstract world of mathematical formulae fresh in his mind (thanks to Pound), Williams wrote down his ideas on what he thought the components of his craft were. These he collected into an essay he called "Speech Rhythm" which he had written for *Poetry* (though it was not published there or anywhere until after his death).[102] The essay is crucial because it shows how early Williams began thinking systematically about the idea of time and measure in poetry. A poem, he said, was not a series of metric lines repeated over and over with unfailing regularity, but rather like the sea, "an assembly of tides, waves, ripples," a matter of regular rhythmic particles that were repeated as part of a greater pattern. A rhythmic unit did not consist of longs and shorts but was, finally and simply, "any repeated sequence of lengths and heights," like a wave, which carried water but was not itself that water. Words *conveyed* a rhythm, but the rhythm itself was antecedent and independent of those words.

Rhythm, then, was a motion unfolding in time, with a forward thrust combined with a simultaneous rising and falling. That, of course, was what Whitman had learned looking out at the breakers coming in along the New Jersey shore in an attitude Williams would himself later call the single most important moment for the history of American poetry.[103] Williams too could hear it—the slap and sigh of all that marine polyphony—before he finally fell asleep at his West Haven cottage just yards from the Sound on summer weekends.

By 1913, then, Williams had already rejected *vers libre* even as other American and English poets were on the point of discovering it. After all, he saw, *vers libre* was really a contradiction in terms, for no verse could be free and still remain verse. In the hands of Whitman *vers libre* had been a good tool: "In his bag of chunks even lie some of the pieces of rhythm life of which we must build."[104] But Whitman had not put the new prosody, the new measure—as Williams would come to call it—on a scientific enough basis to be of much use to younger American poets like himself. On the other hand, metrical forms, with "their rigid stress and counted syllables," had come to seem, after ten painful years working with them, little more than primitive counters. It was time itself, then, and not a mechanical counting of syllables, that was important: that flexibility of hollow, crest, and hollow, of swift and slow, all following the abstract contours of the music.

Lacking any other forum, Williams continued to draw Harriet Monroe into an exchange. He wanted her to be more of a revolutionary than she was capable of being. "To me," he wrote her in October, "what is woefully lacking in our verse and in our criticism is not hammered out stuff but stuff to be hammered out." What was needed was a little magazine that would serve as a free forum to ask only one important question: was the poem under discussion really new, really interesting? "I should think, even," he added by way of challenge, "that at times you would be concerned lest you get nothing but that which is hammered and worked out—except when the divine Ezra bludgeons you into it."[105] What irked Williams into saying this had been Monroe's letter to him saying she hadn't liked one of his poems and so was sending it to Pound for his opinion. Look, Williams tried to tell her, wouldn't she "rather have anticipated a Lincoln then acclaimed a McMahon?" Williams, of course, was to figure as the Lincoln.[106]

But Monroe couldn't be budged. She wanted Pound to see Williams' poem first. By the gods of exchange, then, Williams shot back perturbed, let the "divine" Ezra be "greeted and the words presented to him for the acid test." But he wanted her to know anyway that the poem he'd written and allowed to get away from him was always "mighty worth while and that nobody else has ever come as near as I have to the thing I have intimated if not expressed."[107] Already Williams was beginning to establish himself as the wild young rebel of American poetry, Don Quixote tilting at windmills. This shouting, of course, owed as much to his own surface insecurities as it did to his deeper inner security in his own demonic ego.

Still, little of all this stirring of the new got into *The Tempers*, Williams' second book of verse, which Mathews published in London in mid-September, in time for Williams' thirtieth birthday. The book itself was a tiny thing—only four inches by five—and it was only thirty-one pages long. There were eighteen poems in it and four translations from the Spanish *El Romancero*, and Williams dedicated it to the memory of his Uncle Carlos. What *was* new in these poems was the ironic and even sardonic tone, and the sense especially that this poet was capable of better things to come. In "Peace on Earth," for example, the traditional Christmas wish, the poet looks into the heavens to see them not at peace but rather alive with passion and anger. In another, a love poem for Floss called "First Praise," he calls his lady the one of "dusk-wood fastnesses" (Keats still present even here), the lady he'd sat with at Cooks Falls and Monroe "on the brown forest floor," and with whom he'd searched for hidden brooks, "Clear-skinned, wild from seclusion," jostling "white-armed" now down summer's "tent-bordered thoroughfare."

He was being tempered in these early pieces he'd written since the fiasco of *Poems* four years before, tempered like the fire salamander, that phoenix symbol, which appeared as a motif in several of the poems in this volume. But it was the last poem, "To Wish Myself Courage," which pointed bravely ahead. He knew now that his own youth was behind him and that he hadn't even approached Keats' mastery, though that master had died at twenty-five. For himself, Williams knew his own song would have to be "long in the making," and that he would achieve it, if at all, only after "the stress of youth" had been left behind. For him—as with so many American poets of his generation—he would be "long at the birth." Only in middle age would he learn how to sing the song his whole youth had desired to sing. The trick, then, would be to stretch springtime into summer, and Williams, by dint of hard work and some good fortune, managed to experience a late spring not once but twice: first in his late thirties and again in his sixties and seventies.

Like the friend he was, Pound tried to arouse some interest in *The Tempers* in England, not because he liked the volume (he didn't particularly, except for two pieces), but because he still had hopes that Williams could do better than he so far had. "Mr. Williams' poems," he wrote for the December 1 number of the London weekly *The New Freewoman*, were distinguished "by the vigour of their emotional colouring." He saw now that, while literary allusions and the example of others (including his own) was generally a good practice for young poets to follow, these pointers had in Williams' case turned out to be snares rather than helps. For Williams' most characteristic pieces were those in which he expressed himself directly in his own voice rather than through the medium, presumably, of other personae like Keats or even Pound.[108]

Ezra also wrote to tell Williams that the Great Man Yeats himself had "liked one or two things" in this "new born book." On December 19, he dispatched a newsy letter from Coleman's Hatch in Sussex where he was happily living and working as Yeats's secretary. Pound had been going through all the old Ernest Fenollosa manuscripts that Fenollosa's widow had given him and which would have such a profound effect upon both Pound and Yeats in opening up the world of Japanese and Chinese literature to England and America. He also passed on the news that a young Englishman named Richard Aldington was about to marry H.D. and that Aldington was taking over the job of editing *The New Free-woman*. Soon it would be called *The Egoist,* and Pound had seen to it that Williams would be featured in its pages with a selection of fifteen poems. There was also a young and very promising sculptor in London named Gaudier-Brzeska. Finally, Pound told Williams to look up an Alfred Kreymborg, poet and editor, who published a magazine called *The Glebe* out of New York City. Pound had met Kreymborg in England recently and thought he might be someone Williams would find worth talking to. He ended his letter by saying what he'd said to Williams before, that in the end his friend's work *would* hold and that he still had a lifetime in front of him to perfect his craft. He was even willing to admit that Williams might, just might, get something "slogging away" by himself there in Rutherford that he would have missed "in the Vortex" of London.[109]

"A letter from Ezra," Williams wrote Viola on New Year's Day, 1914. "He tells me of a sojourn in Sussex with W. B. Yeats—praises me—tells me I am a Catullus . . . says he has discovered *the* coming sculptor, a Russian, Gaudier-Brzeska. It is a male." Williams also mentioned that there might be an American publisher for *The Tempers* and the new work he was doing: Albert and Charles Boni, who were going to publish Pound's anthology, *Des Imagistes,* in the spring. Williams' own "Post-lude" was going to be among the selections. He ended his letter to Viola by noting that the baby had not yet appeared. "Flossie is more or less disgusted and more than less uncomfortable. It really is quite hard on her, poor kid."[110]

For other things were stirring for the Williamses in 1913. By late April Williams knew Floss was pregnant, especially when she began becoming nauseous with morning sickness. That would mean finding a larger place for Floss and the baby, and Williams jumped when Dr. Wood, his dentist and a fellow Penn alumnus, offered him his house at 9 Ridge Road just across from Park Avenue. It was an ideal home for a young physician, on the border between Rutherford's residential and business districts. Williams still had no money of his own to speak of, and this time he could not go to his own father, who simply did not have the necessary capital. So, after he'd talked it over with Floss, he went to his father-in-law for a loan. Dr. Wood had asked $8,000 for the house, a good but firm price. No wrangling, no deals. With the $2,000 that Pa Herman had given them for a wedding gift, they had the down payment. Now Williams' father-in-law paid out the remaining $6,000. The agreement was that twice a year Bill and Floss would make payments to Pa Herman on the principal, together with five percent interest. But Pa Herman always turned around and made his daughter generous gifts for the same amount he'd received from them: half at Christmas, and half each April 18 on Floss's birthday. In effect, Pa Herman bought the house at 9 Ridge Road for the Williamses where they would live the rest of their lives. Both their sons would be born there, and eventually both Bill and Floss would die in that house.[111]

When the couple moved into that late-Victorian three-story house with its mustard-yellow clapboard and gingerbread finish in November, Floss was already in her seventh month. They had no furniture of their own as yet with which to fill those eight rooms, except, as Williams remembered, a hogshead of majolica Ed had given them for a wedding gift and which rattled now as they danced around it in their empty living room. No matter. Finally they were on their own.

In *The Build-Up* (1952), Williams described the birth of his firstborn, and though nearly forty years had elapsed by then, he could remember that event with absolute clarity. "All during the latter days of December they waited for the pains to begin. On Christmas Day they started." Then, on New Year's, they began again. That was the day he'd written Viola to say the baby had failed to put in an appearance. And he remembered telling Floss the same day that the kid was "an accommodating little bastard" who "didn't want to interfere with the festivities." Then, on the early morning of January 7, with the year's first snowfall— as Floss had predicted—the pains began in earnest.[112] It was 2:00 AM, an unpublished note of Williams' tells us, and Floss sat upright in bed holding her stomach until 4:00, when she could no longer take the discomfort.[113] Then Bill called their physician, Dr. Ogden. Next, he took his own bed apart and moved it into the northwest room, where he reassembled it with the headboard resting up against the wall opposite the headboard of Floss's bed in the next room.

When Dr. Ogden arrived, he and Williams discovered that between them they had only half a bottle of chloroform, and there were no drugstores open. Floss muttered something between clenched teeth about the doctor's wife always getting the worst of it, but she was in too much pain to joke much about it. While Ogden prepared Floss for the delivery, Williams began administering the precious chloroform drop by drop until it was gone. By this time he was almost beside himself, but Floss he remembered was superb: "not an unnecessary cry, not shirking, no weeping, she gritted her teeth" and did her best. And then a cry! Williams began to weep himself, caressing his wife cautiously and tentatively. It was 6:45 AM and he was looking at a son: "a great long clean looking pink fellow with generous balls." Together the two doctors cleaned the baby and then placed him in the cradle in the corner of the room that had been prepared against his arrival. Later that day Williams would dash off an ecstatic note to Viola: "It's a bear, it's a boy, it's a bear! Yes, William Eric Williams is here! Blond, seven pound, bald, pink, lusty lunged, big-handed—perfect!" Floss was doing fine and he was back slaving away at a translation he was doing of Lope de Vega's *Nuevo Mundo*. Oh yes indeed, it was a brave new world![114]

*
* *

In the spring of 1914 Charlotte finally convinced her father to give her a year abroad—in Berlin—to study at the conservatory there. She was already twenty-five, and if she was ever going to be a serious concert pianist she would have to act now. Reluctantly Pa Herman agreed, and at the end of March Charlotte sailed aboard the *Kaiser Wilhelm der Grosse*. In Berlin, in spite of what she'd told her father, Earle, now separated from his wife, was waiting for Charlotte, and a short time later they were married. But the story hit the sensational New York papers, and Pa Herman felt so humiliated that he publicly branded Earle, in Williams' remembrance, a "moral leper." Moreover, he was so hurt by Charlotte that he publicly disowned her now, telling the papers that in fact Charlotte wasn't even his real daughter and that he'd adopted her when she was still an infant.[115] Williams and Floss both supported Pa Herman in the affair, Floss because of her allegiance to her father and because she'd never really felt close to her older sister, and Williams for even more complex reasons.

By 1914 Ed had also married—a Swedish girl named Hulda whom Flossie had befriended during her year at the New York finishing school. Hulda was bright, vivacious, extraverted, and Ed must have seen her as the kind of wife he would need in Rutherford society. He first met Hulda, apparently, at the Herman farm up in Monroe, and he married very shortly after his brother. In 1914 the first of his four daughters was born. This was Ingrid, to be followed in due course by Palamona, Edith, and finally Christine. The two Williams families would grow up side by side in Rutherford: Ed in his parents' home at 131 West Passaic, and Bill at 9 Ridge Road. The cousins would go to school together, celebrate each others' birthdays and share the holidays together. But really the two families belonged to different worlds with different values. Floss and Hulda saw each other socially, but they were on different tracks, like their husbands, and anything like a shared intimacy beyond the schoolgirl level was out of the question. It was more a matter of a mutual toleration, as much for the brothers' sake as anything else. As for Bill and Ed, some cleavage too deep to sound had taken place. The earlier intimacy was gone and gone forever, and Bill at least understood what that had cost.

In the spring of 1914 Viola Baxter also married: one Virgil Jordan, a successful businessman whom Williams initially tried to like before he gave up even trying. And Ezra Pound married Dorothy Shakespeare, the daughter of Yeats's longtime intimate. "Yes, Ezrazukovitch is marriedskie," Williams wrote Viola on April 29. He described Dorothy to Viola as a beautiful English girl he'd met briefly when he'd been with Pound in London four years before.[116] This same spring, too, Williams' long poem "The Wanderer: A Rococo Study," appeared in the pages of *The Egoist*.[117]

This was Williams' poem of initiation, his early crossing, his coming to some sort of terms at last with his own imperfect, vibrant world. Finally, here, Keats was submerged in order that Whitman's presence might surface. How, Williams asked here, could he "be a mirror to this modernity" everywhere rife about him? Behind him were Rutherford and Paterson, with its history-making terrible mill strike which had lasted through much of 1913. And before him, as he crossed on the Hudson Ferry, standing at the prow again as the gray waters slapped and churned, watching the seagulls dipping and rising, was New York, Whitman's Mannahatta. Except for the "great towers" of the city, those primitive skyscrapers rising vertically into the gray sky, this young poet was seeing exactly what Whitman had seen sixty years earlier crossing the East River on the Brooklyn Ferry. For years Willie had tried on the old Romantic Sublime, had sung his pastel hymns to something called Perfection. Now it was time to give himself over to the old hag, whorelike, vital, "Forgiveless" and "unreconcilable." Time now to pay homage to an old queen in beggar's clothes who looked suspiciously like his aging English grandmother. Time finally to celebrate what he had failed to celebrate before: the teeming millions flooding up and down New York's Broadway.

This was no ideal humanity he was after, no dukes and duchesses and peasant clowns. Instead, this was more recognizably his world, "Old men with red cheeks" (a sign of vigor, or a sign of alcoholism?) and "Young men in gay suits" (suitors, dandies, or con men?). These were real human beings just as he'd seen them, "Dogged, quivering, impassive." Finally, the romantic prince was about to awaken from his dream, to be led by the benevolent old witch of his earlier, aborted *Endymion* poem. Now he would pray. Pray to the hag muse, the old bitch gone in the teeth for an inverted Sublime, for the power to capture this teeming world he'd walked through as in a dream now for thirty years. Pray for the power to catch in words "something of this day's / Air and sun" in the muse's service. And though he knew it was late in the poetic tradition, though his muse had been whored and whored again by generation after generation of young lovers promising her the world, he was still asking her to let him be some small part of that visionary company, if only as "a burr" that might cling tenaciously to the ancient muse's "streaming tatters."

But first he would have to be made to realize what it was he was asking for. Did he really want to be a mirror to this modernity? Very well. Let him first go out to Paterson to walk its deserted streets and climb its mountain, and then from that height let him look down to observe its people standing shivering in the cold wind on public bread lines. Did he want to feel the tense electric energy of these people he would sing, the great masses? Very well, let him taste their brutality, their sullenness, let him witness mounted policemen charge into those crowds to keep "order." Let him see the paid goons, the pathetic idealism of the Wobblies, Billy Sunday—paid by the banks and businesses—preaching obedience and a return to the mills for God and country. These, when he could manage them, would be the poet's subject. Call it Hyperion's scream, a new birth into reality, where finally the poet might come into relentless contact with

> the low, sloping foreheads
> The flat skulls with the unkempt black or blond hair,
> The ugly legs of the young girls, pistons
> Too powerful for delicacy!
> The women's wrists, the men's arms red
> Used to heat and cold, to toss quartered beeves
> And barrels, the milk-cans, and crates of fruit!

He was still very uneasy, very tentative, about this world into which, with that resignation he had first experienced at twenty-two, he was about to enter. These people, these great crowds of dagos, Polacks, Irish, blacks, and Dutchmen, with their ugly, venomous, gigantic energy that both terrified and attracted him, were like some great father tossing his infant son above his head until the baby, disoriented and terrified, should "shriek with ectasy / And its eyes roll and its tongue" hang out. How he wanted to sing to these people, to those millions living in American cities like New York and Paterson, and tell them of the green world about them that was theirs. How he wanted to waken them to "the boughs green / With ripening fruit," to "the myriad cinquefoil / In the waving grass," to the "silent phoebe nest / Under the eaves of your spirit." Now at last he would renew his world through his words, renew the great towers of New York rising in the east, renew

> the little creeks, the mallows
> That I picked as a boy, the Hackensack
> So quiet that seemed so broad formerly:

> *The crawling trains, the cedar swamp on the one side—*
> *All so old, so familiar—so new now*
> *To my marveling eyes . . .*

Now he saw himself in the vigor of youth, a new Atlas, holding up the world he would create with his own words. He would be a force as strong as the wind itself, a Blakean giant, "Linking all lions, all twitterings / To make them nothing!" But first would have to come the initiation into his river, the filthy, sewage-clogged Passaic, accompanied by the muse who was so much like his English grandmother, her face disfigured now by cancer, her body beginning to stink, who had wandered from place to place—London, Brooklyn, St. Thomas, Rutherford, Philadelphia—like the mythic Wandering Jew, cursed to walk forever over the face of the earth.

Now it was down to St. James' Grove on the river, with its "Deep foliage, the thickest beeches— / Though elsewhere they are dying," to the "most secluded spaces / For miles around, hallowed by a stench," where as a boy of fifteen he'd watched the Vreeland girl go bathing naked with the boys—himself among them (that was before the girl, like the river, like the language, had been whored). And now to plunge into the river, to merge with that alien element and feel it begin to enter him even as he entered it, to feel first the "crystal beginning of its days" and then, muddy, "black and shrunken," to feel the river's death, the "vile breadth of its degradation" and understand his own mortality. Now he could watch all that he had been, all his earlier self, all his early dreams of the Sublime, begin drifting off into the river's depths like some sloughed skin turning in the water. Time, now, to say good-by to all that and be off on his own ambiguous "new wandering."

FOUR

Smashing Windows in Paper Houses:
1914—1921

On April 10, Williams sent Viola a postcard with some lines from a poem he would later publish as "The Gulls":

I saw an eagle once circling against the clouds
Over one of our principal churches—
It was Easter—a beautiful day.
Three gulls rose from above the river
And crossed slowly seaward![1]

He of course was the eagle, spreading his independent, solitary wings aloft, but what Viola remarked was that Willie was beginning to sound like Whitman. That was too close to the truth, and it evoked the sharp retort, "Where I am Whitman God damn me."[2] But he *was* assuming the posture of Whitman in several important poems he was writing in late 1913 and '14 and '15, especially in the poems he was addressing now to his "townspeople," poems like "The Gulls," and "Invitation" and "Tract":

I will teach you my townspeople
how to perform a funeral
for you have it over a troop
of artists—
unless one should scour the world—
you have the ground sense necessary.[3]

It was time now, as he wrote in "Rendezvous," one of the group of poems published as "Invocations" in *The Egoist* that August of 1914, time finally to stop pointing and gawking at what others like the Europeans had done and open the windows to let the cold wind "come whistling in, blowing the curtains."[4] Let the American artist embrace the female wind who rode her wild blind horse and who called to him to come out into the wide world beyond his local surroundings. Williams could hear the wind "whistling, waiting / Impatiently to receive" him and his new songs.[5] He could see her out there mixed with the elements: the beautiful woman draped in robes that fell from her shoulders. This was what he'd been waiting for, he confessed now, for just such a woman, "some small passer." He was ready now—as Walt Whitman had been ready before him—to "spring up beside her well at ease" and marry this figure of a new concrete reality.[6]

That woman would take a hundred shapes and forms over his lifetime, and Floss, troubled, confused, angry, amazed, would have to chide her husband for falling in love with every two- and four-legged female he met. He painted them continually now in his poems, as though he were painting portraits. First would come the setting, some part of his boring, tired locale, seen perhaps from his office window or while out driving around Rutherford:

> *An oblique cloud of purple smoke*
> *Across a milky silhouette*
> *Of house sides and tiny trees*
> *That ends in a saw edge*
> *Of mist-covered trees*
> *On a sheet of grey sky.*
> *To the left, a single tree;*
> *To the right, jutting in,*
> *A dark crimson corner of roof.*
> *God knows I'm tired of it all.*

And into this familiar landscape would come, then, the woman. Like a blessing she would come, this idealized version of some real woman he knew, like the woman who brought fresh eggs to the back door every few days:

> *Powerful woman,*
> *Coming with swinging haunches,*
> *Breasts straight forward,*
> *Supple shoulders, full arms*
> *And strong, soft hands (I've felt them)*
> *Carrying the heavy basket.*
> *I might well see you oftener!*[7]

Or there were the high-school girls he saw as school physician or about town who tortured him with their beauty. "I dreamt of a beautiful young high school graduate last night," he wrote Viola in early July, "she leaned on the door of my Ford car—silently and surreptitiously stroking my hand—and her soul came up out of her eyes! I awoke exquisitely unhappy."[8] That dream became the source of "The Revelation," published six weeks later in *The Egoist*:

> *A girl*
> *One whom I knew well*
> *Leaned on the door of my car*
> *And stroked my hand—*

> *I shall pass her on the street*
> *We shall say trivial things*
> *To each other*
> *But I shall never cease*
> *To search her eyes*
> *For that quiet look.*[9]

The fires of eros were burning within him now in spite of whatever constraints he felt as husband, father, physician, or as citizen of Rutherford. "Do you think I like to practice medicine here in Rutherford?" he complained to Viola, who had chided him about Pound's greater freedom in England. "And see others skipping over the face of the globe from the two poles to London, New York, Hoboken and Pekin?" He was here in this town with these townspeople of his for one reason only: that he did not "see how I can be anywhere else and do what I have determined to do." If Rutherford was a kind of hell, at least he'd avoided other hells, like his grandmother's "Christian Science" trap with her face rotting like that. He'd avoided drugs too like morphine and whiskey, and even "church going, medicine, laziness," and sex. The reward for all this self-abnegation would have to be found over the rough road he'd chosen for himself: heaven at the end of "a bridge of cobble stones."[10] Tentatively, he was also beginning to receive the encouragement he needed from others if he was to go on as an artist. In late May, for example, he thanked Harriet Monroe for accepting a group of his poems (though it would be a year before they appeared).[11] "Certainly I can work for any imaginable period at the work I choose without the encouragement of recognition," but to think that he was making a real contribution to *Poetry* was important to him and doubled all his "brilliances."[12] For the first time in his life he felt like a new man in touch with the electric vortex that he, with his eyes and ears open to such things, could see around him on all sides. "If I talk to things," he told his audience,

> *Do not flatter yourself*
> *That I am mad*
> *Rather realize yourself*
> *To be deaf and that*
> *Of two evils, the plants*
> *Being deaf likewise,*
> *I choose that*
> *Which proves by other*
> *Attributes worthier*
> *Of the distinction.*[13]

And he did talk to the things around him: to the blue moss and the "black earth / In the twisted roots / Of the white tree" and the "Long red-grass / Matted down / And standing in the wind." He praised the lightning storm

on a summer's night, "the blinding white / That was saffron / Change to
steel blue / Behind shaking trees," glad to be safe in bed while his young
wife came and tucked him in and then brought him the baby—little
Billie—to play with:

> *I move over*
> *Into the cold sheets*
> *To make room for him*
> *And thinking*
> *Of the freezing poor*
> *I consider myself*
> *Happy—*
> *Then we kiss.*[14]

It was an idyllic time, all in all, a time for pastorals and self-portraits
in poems and paint (it was during this summer that he probably painted
his self-portrait, looking boyish and slightly satyrlike with those pointed
faun's ears of his.) But there were rumblings of war that summer too, of a
war no one really wanted but which would happen anyway. And just as
the guns of August 1914 made themselves heard in Europe, the Hermans
and the Williamses experienced their own tragedy. Young Paul—who was
fourteen then—had returned from summer camp and had gone directly to
his parents' home in Monroe for the few weeks remaining before school
began again. He'd been out hunting rabbits and woodchucks in the woods
around the Herman property when he tripped over a piece of barbed wire
and slid down the embankment, his loaded shotgun following after him.
Suddenly it went off, exploding at point-blank range into the boy's crotch.

Williams had received a telephone call at the office from his mother-
in-law that Paul had been hurt and to please come up to the farm at once.
He and Floss dropped off the baby at a neighbor's and then Williams drove
as fast as he could the forty miles up to the Hermans' place. He was
almost there when he saw his mother-in-law in her own car driving in the
opposite direction and waving him to turn around and follow her. The boy
had been operated on at the hospital in Tuxedo, and Williams was told to
drive down to the railroad station to look for Pa Herman, who had been
notified at his printing office in New York to come home at once.
Williams remembered boarding the afternoon coach at the station in
Tuxedo and going through the cars looking in each one for his father-in-
law. He found him, finally, hunched over and dazed with disbelief, in the
last car. Then Williams took him to the hospital, just in time to see his
son before he died. From that time on, Williams says, his father-in-law
was a broken man. He had just disowned a daughter, and now he was
seeing his only son, the hope of his old age, wither before him. A world
had been wiped out like that. Williams would be haunted by that loss, so
much so that he would write his own American tragedy, the ultimate

failure of the American Success Story that the Hermans represented for him, in his Stecher trilogy, but especially in *The Build-Up*. Even as he was beginning an auspicious career as poet and doctor, he witnessed his wife's father's life come to its irrevocable close in the death of this boy.[15]

There remained one final chapter in Pa Herman's tragedy, and it was World War I itself that brought the tragedy to its focus. When he returned to Rutherford in the fall of the year, after his son's burial in the family plot in Rutherford, Pa Herman found himself the new president of the prestigious Fortnightly Reading Club. (The organization still meets regularly in the town, and still requires its members to wear formal dress at its monthly meetings.) And in the fall of 1914 and with increasing intensity up through American entry into that war, the question of which side America should join was very much on everyone's mind. Pa Herman, whose family had come from Bavaria, felt that the German cause had fallen victim to an Anglo-American press, and stories of German massacres, the destruction of the library at Louvain, and the devastation created by German submarines attacking so-called neutral ships were all creating a psychological situation favorable to England. German-Americans in Rutherford were watched closely; the German-American ex-mayor himself was accused of keeping a portrait of the Kaiser in his living room until, getting wind of these rumors, he invited the press into his home to view the picture. It turned out to be a portrait of himself in hunting clothes. Even Paul Herman caught a glimpse of one of his best friends spying on him from the cover of the rhododendrons on his property.[16]

Williams, always a fighter, came to his father-in-law's defense. When rumors grew that the German-Americans who had joined a Bund in the neighboring town of Carlstadt were in fact organizing a machine-gun crew to attack other Americans, Williams reacted by joining the Carlstadt Turnverein there. That was nothing more dangerous than a gymnastics club, but his own mother was furious that her son, who was half English and half French (to oversimplify), had elected to side with the Germans in spite of what those "barbarians" were doing to her beloved France. Even more than that, another Rutherford doctor wrote to the *Rutherford American* in 1916 condemning a certain young doctor in town who was openly supporting the Kaiser. Williams was incensed when he read that. He was defending German-Americans from witch hunters, he insisted, not supporting the Kaiser. And, moreover, America was supposed to be neutral, not pro-British. Nor were his sympathies naturally with the Germans. He had foreseen the inevitability of a war with Germany as the enemy back in 1910 when he was in Leipzig, and he even wrote a letter to the local paper blasting the Germans the same month America entered the war, because he had by then become "so god-damned sick and tired of a pro-German atmosphere" and because he was afraid finally of "the inevitability of a triumph for the German idea of brute force in the world."[17] In fact, Williams had seriously considered joining the American Red Cross as a first lieutenant and serving in Europe when war was declared in April 1917. But Ed, who had spent three years in Italy, volunteered first, leaving Williams to take care of two aging parents and his own family, as well as watching after Ed's wife, Hulda and their two small daughters, all living in Rutherford. In any case, Williams was very much needed in Rutherford to care for the sick.

Perhaps his real feelings about the war are best expressed in a short story—an anecdote really—he published in 1939, with the lights going out all over Europe for a second time. It was called "The Drill Sergeant" and in it Williams remembered with distaste that he had had to give physical examinations to hundreds of draftees, many of them just a few years younger than himself, in the spring of 1917. He hated the job, especially when it came to passing young German-American draftees from Carlstadt and West Lyndhurst. For all the talk about fighting for Uncle Sam, he could see that these boys did not want to fight and would make any excuse to keep from going. He was glad, then, when the heavy part of the examinations was over and he could get back to regular practice. But when all those who had worked in the recruiting station were invited down to Fort Dix, New Jersey, that summer to see how the boys were doing, he went too. When he got there they took the group out on the fields to watch the boys at bayonet practice, with a short, baldheaded drill instructor shouting orders, one two, come on fellows, chests out, one two. Williams noticed one of the boys he'd passed there in the front row drilling with the rest, not enthusiastically, just going through the motions with the bayonet: one two. It was the instructor, though, that he never forgot, teaching the young men how to kill, how to bayonet the enemy:

> I'll never forget him—especially when I remember what Fred March told me, how when the Marines met the Prussians in the middle of the road at Belleau Woods and he jammed his bayonet up behind the jaw of the boy facing him till it came out of the top of his head, he had to put his foot down on his face so he could pull it out again.
>
> I wasn't brought up to do that, he told me. I saw that boy every night for ten years afterward. He would come and sit on the foot of my bed every night and look at me. I almost went crazy.[18]

Paul Herman was in a sense one more casualty of the war. For when the Fortnightly Club voted in 1916 to support the British cause should America go to war, Herman cast the only negative vote. His friends asked him to reconsider and make the vote unanimous when they sent it on to President Wilson. But he refused. And so, from that point on, many of his closest friends refused to have anything more to do with him. For his part,

Paul Herman was an American first in the old sense, and when Congress declared war on Germany in April 1917, he supported his country unequivocally, even buying $5,000 worth of American War Bonds (though he did draw the line by refusing to allow his printing presses to be used for overt British propaganda directed against the Germans). But it was useless: the Hermans were ostracized from the community for all practical purposes, and they soon left Rutherford for Monroe. In 1922 they would move into their new, quite substantial stone house, Alverheim, which Ed Williams, on his return from ambulance duty in Italy, would design for them. There Floss's parents lived until the 1930s, when Paul Herman died on his own property of a shotgun wound—self-inflicted but apparently accidental—just as his only boy had died.

*
**

When Viola read Williams' poems in *The Egoist* in late December 1914, she noticed now that it was Pound's presence which was very much there. Pound's 1911 imagist haiku, "In a Station of the Metro," for example, with its "apparition of these faces in the crowd; / Petals on a wet, black bough," found its response now in Williams' "Aux Imagistes," where the poet addressed the blossoms and advised them to "make much of the sunshine," for even they, like the imagists, would "not endure for ever."[19] Nor, Williams insisted, would Pound's influence be foremost in his own development. That influence, he was prematurely ready to assert by the beginning of 1915, was already behind him. "I thank God that someone has at last found that I approach the Poundesque—I can now put that aside." Still, if he did not wish to be Pound's disciple any longer, he did want to acknowledge that his friend's lead had given him the courage to go his own way. After all, Williams was, as Floss had pointed out to him, "terribly sentimental" about his friends.[20] Art, like baseball and medicine, was for Williams very much a team effort.

Pound's newer work Williams found superb. His translations from the Chinese in *Cathay* were, Williams was willing to admit, "perhaps a few of the greatest poems ever written." And the "first part of the Anglo Saxon thing," by which he meant *The Seafarer*, made a splendid contrast with the "oriental stuff."[21] Still, Pound was in England, separated by an ocean and now by a war, and what Williams needed was a forum for himself on this side of the Atlantic, which he had hoped *Poetry* would provide but had not. Williams' answer came finally in the form of *Others*, based right there in New York, a magazine founded by the New York art patron Walter Arensberg and Alfred Kreymborg in the spring of 1915, though Arensberg soon retired from any active participation in the little magazine. In New York that spring, Williams would write a year later, "one was feeling a strange quickening of artistic life."[22] The city was already filled with French artists and painters who had fled military conscription and the nightmare of trench warfare, and Williams would soon meet some of them: figures like Marcel Duchamp and Albert Gleizes and Jean Crotti. There were important art exhibits to see in New York, in the spirit of the Armory Show, some featuring the French impressionists or cubists or fauvists, and others the younger Americans.

But the real hero in all of this "quickening of life" in New York was the man Pound had told Williams to get in touch with two years earlier: Alfred Kreymborg. By 1915 Kreymborg had given up his work on *The Glebe*, left his New York garret, married, "and in a little hut" in the summer artists' colony in Grantwood on the New Jersey Palisades started his magazine, *Others*. The hut had no running water (water had to be gathered from an outdoor pump), and the shack was suitable only for the summer season. But in 1915 that and the surrounding shacks became the meeting place for the younger New York artists every Sunday afternoon during the warm weather. There would be a business meeting, a picnic-style lunch, a game of ball in the yard, attempts at conversation, some reading of one's own or others' poems, embarrassing silences, bad jokes, contacts. It was here in this most inauspicious of places that Williams first met some of the leading poets, painters, and critics of the day: Orrick Johns, Alanson Hartpence, Man Ray, Malcolm Cowley, Walter Arensberg, Mina Loy, Marcel Duchamp, Robert Sanborn, and young Maxwell Bodenheim.

The first issue of *Others* came out in July and featured the work of Orrick Johns (who had beaten out Edna St. Vincent Millay for the first *Lyric Year* prize two years before), Mina Loy, intimate of the smart New York set who were being published in the *Rogue*—a group that also included Wallace Stevens and Walter Arensberg—and finally Alfred Kreymborg himself. *Others* was an unprepossessing-looking magazine which usually ran to sixteen pages and had light yellow paper covers and abstract modernist drawings by a young graphic artist named William Zorach. It cost twenty-five dollars to print five hundred copies, because the printer, an old-time New York radical, refused to make any profit on the venture, so intent was he on doing something for the cause of avant-garde letters in America. Moreover, contributors were expected to give their work to the magazine for nothing.

The idea behind *Others* was to get copies of the magazine spread around New York (and Chicago), each issue featuring two or three poets, as many as possible of these to be from the New York ambience. This was meant to let the *Poetry* Chicago group know that artistic life was stirring up out of the ashes of New York as well. But other poets also appeared in *Others*, among them two young Harvard graduates, Conrad Aiken and Tom Eliot. Eliot, living in London, was Pound's discovery, and Pound had written Kreymborg telling him to be sure and print what he was sending from his man, who was the hottest thing around in modernism. *Others* even published a special Chicago number which featured many of the poems that Harriet Monroe had rejected. It wasn't long, given that sort of tactic, before there was a quiet feud going on between the two magazines, a feud that generated more heat than light.

Exactly when Williams first met Kreymborg is hazy; little remains on either side of what must have once been a generous and important correspondence. But Williams quickly assumed an important editorial role and Kreymborg just as quickly came to depend on this wild-eyed poet from Rutherford, this Don Quixote charging into Grantwood on Sunday afternoons in his already battered Ford flivver. Two years earlier, Pound had sent the package of materials to Kreymborg that would be printed as *Des Imagistes*, telling him that unless he was just another American ass, he'd set up the anthology of imagists just as he had sent it to him, adding that Bill Williams (whose "Postlude" Pound had included) was his "one remaining pal in America" and that he should get in touch with this fellow who lived "in a hole called Rutherford, New Jersey."[23] And though it was not until 1915 that Kreymborg did get in touch with Williams, the friendship soon became close and intense, Williams sending his candid comments on the manuscripts Kreymborg sent him back to Kreymborg interspersed with a handful of damns and exclamations and the rest of it. For the first time, Williams had his American forum, not one that was going to doctor up his manuscripts as Harriet had done because they had lower-case letters at the beginning of their lines. The *Others* connection would be a serious, free-wheeling affair, and Williams spent every Sunday afternoon he could get during the summer and fall of 1915 driving down to those unheated shacks on the lower Palisades, with their outhouses and outdoor water pumps, reading his poems aloud with evident embarrassment and trying to get to know this splendid crowd of New York literati.[24]

Here, among these people, Williams hoped to find his own vortex to counter Pound's. So, when that summer he read Gaudier-Brzeska's posthumous vorticist manifesto in Wyndham Lewis' London *Blast* (Brzeska having been killed in the trenches in July), Williams tried, haltingly, stumblingly, to defend his own New York–centered vortex. He would take "whatever character my environment has presented" and turn it, twist it if need be, to his own ends, and thus express his ultimate independence even from his own world.[25] He would express the uniqueness of his emotions as they were colored and shaped by the world of New York and Paterson in which he just happened to find himself. And he would not leave his place because he refused to admit that he was dependent on *any* place. He did not need Pound's London to write poetry.

Rutherford and Grantwood and New York, believed in hard enough, could become vortices of their own. And when, in the fall of 1918, he was working on the "Prologue" to his *Improvisations*, he remembered the bravado of this early manifesto: "I wish that I might here set down my 'Vortex' after the fashion of London, stating how little it means to me whether I live here, there or elsewhere or succeed in this, that or the other so long as I can keep free from the trammels of literature, beating down every attack of its *retiarii* [the London vorticists] with my *mirmillones*."[26]

Kreymborg and his wife, Gertrude, got four issues assembled and printed in the summer and fall before they returned to New York City for the cold weather, setting up their new headquarters on Bank Street downtown. Williams himself had four poems in the second issue in August, where he appeared with Wallace Stevens, Skipwith Cannell, Alanson Hartpence, and Robert Carlton Brown (Grantwood's own plutocrat, as Williams styled him, a man who'd made his hundred thousand and could now afford to write at his leisure). In September it was T. S. Eliot's "Portrait of a Lady" (submitted with high praise by Pound), John Gould Fletcher and Maxwell Bodenheim, the oldest, saddest twenty-two-year-old Kreymborg and Williams had ever met. In October *Others* was given over to something called the Choric School, with an introduction by Pound himself.

For the first fourteen numbers, the magazine appeared each month with surprising regularity, though Kreymborg's other projects meant turning the business of selecting manuscripts and getting the thing published over to his friends, like Williams himself, who edited a competitive number in July 1916. But by the fall of that year, funds for keeping the magazine going had all but disappeared. There had been a slight stir in the New York papers when *Others* first appeared, and editors and reviewers had had their fun quoting lines out of context and taking pokes at that strange crowd of aesthetes gathered on the Palisades. But all that was soon over and New York went about its business. For Williams, the initial revolutionary seriousness of the undertaking of an avant-garde magazine had soon been washed under with business talk of a stock company and a clubhouse and social meetings in the classier part of New York above 42d Street. (That sort of thing Williams was sure his plump, groomed, fastidious friend, Stevens, who refused to take the long barbarous trip out to Grantwood, would appreciate.) What had started out with some semblance of a united front, as a revolutionary confraternity of sorts, had deteriorated within a year. Almost at once, the French expatriates and some of the New York poets had gone for each other's throats. Hadn't Marcel Duchamp himself snubbed Williams in Walter Arensberg's studio apartment on West 67th Street when all Williams had meant to do was pay the Frenchman a compliment? Williams had been admiring Duchamp's *The Sisters* displayed on one of Arensberg's walls and had tried to tell Duchamp just that. He'd finally screwed up enough courage to tap Duchamp on the shoulder and point to the picture to say, in his broken French, how much he liked it. But the Frenchman had simply looked at him, shrugged, and then cut him short with the patronizing reply, "Oh, do you?"

Williams was sharp enough to know Duchamp had nailed him there and then, and he never forgot his lesson. He felt insecure enough as it was, knowing he was just another young American from the sticks confronting these French expatriates in the houses of the Great City sophisticates, and that sense of inferiority would dog him for years until he could learn to make a virtue of a disadvantage. But his only defense now, he saw, would be to withdraw and keep his own counsel, refuse to allow himself to be trapped again, and in the meantime—like any good revolutionary who meant to win through—he would work like hell, cost what it might, until he too could achieve in his own sphere what Duchamp and his confrères had achieved in theirs.[27]

But if there was this kind of divisiveness among the *Others* group, how could anything like a united front in modernism be achieved? Williams needed the pack and could be counted on to give generously for the revolution. But he could also see that these artists and poets were too much concerned with their own names and with their own precious reputations. Perhaps, then, *Others* had already served its purpose. After all, two of the group—Wallace Stevens and Maxwell Bodenheim—had already been selected to appear in Stanley Braithwaite's popular anthology of contemporary American poets. The real *Others* movement, then, was already finished by mid-1916. But at least in passing it had advanced Alfred Kreymborg's little book of poems, *Mushrooms*, and that was important. What had been achieved might seem small, but the living seed had been there, and there were far-reaching implications for the advancement of modern poetry. Hadn't Kreymborg, for example, demonstrated how small words could be made to carry an enormous weight in the new poetry, the artistic effect not "depending on the meaning or connotative values of words but rather on their ability to help create an overall musical design"? In doing that, in restructuring the values inherent in the way language might be employed, Williams concluded with exacerbated irony, America had indeed triumphed.[28]

But *Others* was not over then, and Williams would have to wait another three years for its actual demise, when he really did sound the death knell for the magazine. The truth was that in the four years of *Others'* existence Williams himself found a forum for his poems and for his own manifestos in an age rank with competing manifestos. From the vantage of *Others* he could attack *Poetry* for what he considered its early intellectual sclerosis. "Whatever intellectual significance *Poetry* ever had has long since departed,"[29] he told Harriet in January 1916, when the magazine was still only three years old, and he added six weeks later that the magazine was not only intellectually dead, it was also "a little too epicurean."[30] He didn't like Monroe's interference with his poems and he didn't mind telling her that *Poetry* was already "closed to rugged beginnings." *Poetry* would have to get tougher or stop publishing. And the fact that *Poetry* insisted on paying its contributors (unlike *Others*) could only hurt. "Verse don't pay," he told her, "and no boosting by *Poetry* will ever make it pay." One wrote because one had something to say, and not for money.[31]

But Williams could also act as mediator between the two magazines, in a way Kreymborg himself could not. So, when a *Poetry* reviewer attacked the first *Others* anthology in April 1916, Alfred Kreymborg as its editor was so incensed he demanded that Harriet Monroe return at once the poem he'd offered to *Poetry*. It was Williams, then, who wrote Monroe to smooth things over. "For the sake of humor give him the ha, ha!" Williams wrote her. "Take a chance on it please for it means a lot to me. . . . If you allow him to take back his things, back come mine too and that would break me all up." After all, he added, if *Others* had its faults, at least it was "a free running sewer" and for the reviewer in *Poetry* "to ignore its positive qualities for the mere accident of its contents" had been a lost opportunity.[32] Forget it. There was still important work to do.

It was either up or down between Williams and *Poetry* since, as Williams phrased it in a letter to Monroe in late October, he kept addressing her with outbursts of either "extravagant love" or extravagant "indignation." If he interceded for Kreymborg in April, it was Bodenheim in December. "I do not know that he will accept my mediation," Williams wrote Monroe, "but should I be able to get him to reconsider his withdrawal of the verse and play you had accepted would you print them for him?" Yes, Bodenheim could put people off with his mask of the misanthropic aesthete, Williams knew, but he was only a young man and, being "wilfully" unattractive and physically (though not spiritually) unfortunate, in short, being the artist he was, much should be forgiven him.[33] A month later, when Monroe still hadn't changed her mind, Williams tried a more philosophical approach. *Poetry* should print Bodenheim's work regardless of how Bodenheim and she felt about each other. Personal reasons should not interfere with the magazine's publishing him. But when Monroe wrote back saying how Bodenheim had personally treated her, Williams backed off. Personalities did, after all, enter the world of poetry, even revolutionary poetry, like everything else.

Williams' own difficulties with Monroe persisted. He never got used to her tampering with his poems, as she tampered with other poets as well, including Wallace Stevens, whose "Sunday Morning" she reordered before she would print it. Williams himself could not understand why an editor would want "to change and rearrange according to some yard-stick which has not the slightest application in the matter the work of some person who has spent time and attention and even more important substances to bring that piece of work into the exact mould in which it is presented."[34] But if Stevens resigned himself to Monroe's tampering with his texts, Williams hated her old-fashioned, "vicious" editorial methods, and asked her to figure out what her own theory of the poetic line was before she tried to touch his lines. He did not endear himself to her.

So, when Kreymborg asked Williams to take over the editing and selection of poems for the July 1916 number of *Others*, Williams had a chance to put his own ideas about what he wanted in a poem into practice. The difference between Monroe and Williams, finally, was Williams' through and through commitment to modernism. And he knew how to select. So, for example, he went after Marianne Moore, whose work he admired, writing her on May 9 that he wanted to put "some one thing, something new," by each of the persons he'd selected, something "that he or she is willing to stand to."[35] What he wanted as his first stint as editor was a competitive number, a hard jostling of good talents side by side, the poems refracting their hard edges one against the other, as in a cubist painting by Braque or Picasso. So Moore sent Williams her "Critics and Connoisseurs," which Williams admired, pleading as it did for careful thought and execution in one's work.

At the same time he wrote Wallace Stevens asking for new work, and then had to reject what Stevens sent because the material he had wanted for *Others* had already been published. He told Stevens he liked the last section of "For an Old Woman in a Wig" because fastidious Stevens had allowed himself "to become fervent for a moment."[36] In turn, Stevens tried again, sending Williams "The Worms at Heaven's Gate," the ending of which Williams changed (having suffered momentary amnesia with regard to his own feelings about editorial interference) and sent back to Stevens with the note, "For Christ's sake yield to me and become great and famous."[37] Which Stevens did. Williams also asked Pound to contribute, but Pound shot back that he needed to get paid for his work now and *Others* wasn't paying. Instead, he sent the work of one of his young protegées, Iris Barry, with the comment that *Others* wasn't half bad "for a dung continent that keeps Wilson as president."[38] (At the same time Pound wrote Iris Barry telling her to contribute, and that *Others* was "a harum scarum vers libre American product, chiefly useful because it keeps 'Arriet [Monroe] from relapsing into the Nineties."[39])

Williams also wrote Amy Lowell, though by 1916 he felt extremely ambivalent toward her, especially for the way she had taken over, as he saw it, Pound's imagist movement with her money and connections. He wanted her to send him something for his issue of *Others*, and at the same time wanted to know why she and her friend John Gould Fletcher had withdrawn their support and influence from the magazine. Amy Lowell wrote explaining that while she liked Williams' own work, even admired him exceedingly, she disliked the kind of thing that woman Mina Loy had contributed. She was referring to Loy's "Pig Cupid," whose image of a pig with its erotic snout digging in the rank garbage for food had caused a small fuss in the papers when it first appeared in *Others*. As a result, Lowell and Fletcher had decided not to send anything to *Others*, but now that Williams had written her directly, she'd have to write to Fletcher over in England to see what he thought about contributing.[40] Williams wrote back to tell her it had just so happened that Fletcher had already sent along a poem,[41] at which Lowell, a bit flustered, mumbled something about that pact being therefore at an end, and that she was therefore sending along one of her fresh new "Chinoiseries."

If Mina Loy's work troubled Amy Lowell, though, what must she have thought of Williams himself, who chose as his own offering a brash new poem called "Drink," which ended by saying that his own drink was "the feel of good legs / and a broad pelvis / under the gold hair ornaments of skyscrapers."[42] In fact, a number of his newer poems published in *Others* in 1915 and 1916 were dark confessionals about what he as a physician felt toward women, including very young girls. After all, he had once told Viola that any three-year-old could tell that virginity was a myth, and in poems like "The Ogre" and "Touché," he addressed this subject with extraordinary honesty. "Sweet child," he wrote in "The Ogre,"

> *little girl with well-shaped legs*
> *you cannot touch the thoughts*
> *I put over and under and around you.*
> *This is fortunate for they would*
> *burn you to an ash otherwise.*
> *Your petals would be quite curled up.*[43]

And in "Touché," he wrote of the "murderer's little daughter," a ten-year-old he was sure had been flirting with him, jerking "her shoulders / right and left / so as to catch a glimpse of me / without turning round" and touching him with "the knife / that darts along her smile."[44]

This was daring stuff he was writing now, and it was the New York crowd that had given him the audience he needed for this kind of statement, the kind of audience Rutherford and MIT and Penn had not offered. There was a constant erotic energy that Williams could feed off in New York, an energy Williams could tap into and then retreat from to the more stable domesticity of Rutherford. Greenwich Village was there—14th Street and below—forty-five minutes away by Ford flivver or Dodge Roadster and so on through eleven different automobiles. The Village would always be there as a kind of feverish oasis, a little false, as Williams acknowledged, but a splendid counterbalance to his life as busy physician and husband and father, that other world he was also committed to.[45]

In New York Williams was just another figure, another artist among artists, whose particular comings and goings were hardly noticed. But when the Village descended on Rutherford, that was another story. As happened, for example, in April 1916, when Williams decided to throw a big bash for the *Others* crowd. It was still early spring, as the two photographs of the crowd taken that Sunday—one of the men and the other of the women—show.[46] Alanson Hartpence was there, and Alfred Kreymborg in hat and wild bow tie, and of course Williams with Mother Kitty (the stray cat who spent twelve years living in the Williams home), and Skip Cannell, Jean Crotti, Marcel Duchamp, Walter Arensberg, Man Ray, J. A. Sanborn and—off by himself holding a volume of verse (his own, presumably)—Maxwell Bodenheim. And the women, in ankle-length dresses: Helen Slade and Mary Davis and Yvonne Crotti and Floss in the center, trying to smile but ill at ease with Bill's friends, and Kitty Cannell and her mother, and Arensberg's wife (getting ready to leave early to get somewhere else) and Gertrude Kreymborg, who would soon leave Alfred to return to her first husband. It was up to Floss to get the food out and get the house ready even though she was already four months pregnant with her second son.

There were others not in the photographs who showed up during that morning and afternoon and evening as the party got under way and the Williamses wined and dined the crowd into the next morning. Williams remembered Skip Cannell jumping half drunkenly onto the running board of his car as he drove over to Ed's house to get some more ice. And he remembered Duchamp—the same who had snubbed him—twitting Bodenheim in his living room for his "tragic posturing." He wondered too what the neighbors would say as his party guests swarmed over the lawn and in and out of the house all through the afternoon and evening, but they seemed to accept it and to go about their own business. It was a scene—Bill's wild friends carousing in Rutherford—that would be repeated many times over the next thirty years.

The same month that he had the *Others* gang out to Rutherford, Williams was trying to sum up where he had arrived at in relation to his friend Pound. He'd been looking over all of Pound's early volumes, he wrote his mother on the twenty-seventh: *A Lume Spento, A Quinzaine for This Yule, Personae, Exultations, Canzoni, Ripostes, Lustra, Cathay* —at least eight volumes—and he was trying to make a selection from all

his prolific friend had accomplished over the past decade. His mother—
eternal idealist that she was—had sent Willie a letter describing the three
kinds of love. Now Williams tried to talk of these types in relation to
himself and Pound. The first kind of love was "the primitive" kind, a
furious passion such as Pound most often manifested and which Williams
felt he by contrast showed least often. It was a "mysterious, mystic
attraction of one person for another" and Pound had celebrated it
effectively in his own poems. But being the most intense, "the hottest,
the most brilliant," it was also the soonest to go "and woe to the man
who has nothing to take its place." Unless the resultant vacuum was
filled, a man could be forced to suicide. So with Pound, whose first
exclusive intensity had left him, and who had not yet learned how to open
himself to "the democracy of love that would bring him happiness." The
result was that Pound was now "in a desperate fix" in terms of his own
marriage. And though he lamented Pound's condition, he also wished he
himself could have lived more freely and uninhibitedly as a younger man.
Oh, he knew he had patience, he knew he had a love of life, "of men and
women and children and trees," he knew he had the nurturing instinct
and could watch over something for years. But he still secretly yearned
after the thing he had yearned after for so long: perfection. Only now he
knew it was no "heavenly perfection" he wanted but rather "a full
blooded earthly perfection," sweet and fragile as life itself.[47] This was
vague enough, but what he was after finally was contact with life, with
art, with women.

He still yearned to accomplish something, though he didn't know
what it was for sure. When his mother complained to him in the fall of
1915 that her whole life had been a failure, that she would never be the
great artist she had thought she might have been—as all those canvases
in the attic attested—Williams told her what was on his own mind. He
too, he'd said, had wanted to do something great, "to write great good
poems" and "to help the poor and the unhappy." He wanted to be as
happy in life as anyone, but who could guarantee that happiness for him?
He knew that his whole life might still turn out to be a failure, but that
did not worry him in the least. What mattered really was living up to
something like the Paterian aesthetic (though he did not name it that): to
live life passionately, "full of striving, full of eager attempts to the whole
extent of the power that is in me." In that way he would make himself
worthy, really worthy of her. She was still perhaps his dearest possession,
he told her, in spite of the fact that by then he'd been married nearly three
years to Floss.[48]

Six months later he was still speaking to his mother of performing
"some deed of great love for humanity," perhaps "some venture for the
sake of poetry, the art I love." Buying the house at 9 Ridge Road had

seemed to be a step in the right direction, but that had happened two years ago and it was losing some of the force it had had. It was, after all, only the fire—that salamander—which a person put into his life that mattered: the fire of the imagination, the fire of love itself. He had given up dentistry for medicine at Penn, and in turn he had given up medicine for poetry. And then he had given up "a personal disappointment and its bitterness for dearest Flossie's love and the care of it," that disappointment being the loss of Charlotte to his brother. So now he felt on the brink of some new, undefined change in his life. It was difficult to say just what that change would bring, but clearly his voice as a poet had already been transformed in a few short years.[49] By 1916 he was writing or was capable of writing the kind of poem that would become his signature for the rest of his life in spite of inevitable and welcome changes over the next forty years. Somehow he had already crossed the threshold that had given him a distinctive American voice.

At home there were the usual domestic satisfactions and difficulties of any young married couple. Williams made sure he spent some time each summer on vacation with his wife and family. In late August 1915, he and Floss and little Billy had gone up to Monroe to the Herman farm and pitched a tent near the house for a mixture of privacy and companionship. It had been raining three days when he wrote his mother on the twenty-sixth that he enjoyed hearing the rain spattering down above them "almost upon our noses." Little Billy was nineteen months old then and could already say a dozen words. Williams loved him, and like any doting father had to enlarge on his baby son's every action. Even as he wrote his mother, he was watching the baby trying to get into the icebox there in the tent or trying to feed their dog Mac from an empty beer bottle. The kid was hard and active and smart! "I like the way he looks at me when I tell him to do anything he stops what he is doing, turns round and looks at me carefully and seriously as if gathering his thoughts together then he instantly obeys—first however he looks and thinks." He'd have to be careful what he said in front of that boy. Kathleen McBride, their baby's nurse, was there, and Nana Herman and some others, and except for "a few futile arguments about the war" in France they were all getting along fine and they still had two weeks of vacation to go. He and Floss were both reading Turgenev's *Virgin Soil* and enjoying it.[50]

Two months later, on October 28, Ferdinand Earle, who was back in the U.S. and living in Seabright, New Jersey, with Charlotte and their infant son, Ferdinand, Jr., wrote to Willie to ask him to act as a mediator between the Hermans and him and his wife. What was done was done, he argued, and behind them. But the estrangement had been particularly hard on Charlotte. Surely Williams could talk to the Hermans? After all,

Earle had always liked Bill Williams, had even liked his poetry, though he admitted he found this new Poundesque stuff of his too impressionistic or cubist for his own liking, and he was still sorry about that old *Lyric Year* business.[51] But if Williams did do anything, it was probably to side with his father-in-law, a man he deeply loved. And that Earle had run off with the prize he had wanted could not have helped matters. In any event, Charlotte would not see her parents again until 1924, when she left her husband in Hollywood, California, to return to Monroe for a visit. By then young Ferdinand had died (at age ten) of bulbar polio. She took her younger son, Eyvind, who was eight at the time, with her when she went to visit her parents, and when she and her son returned to California at year's end it was not to return to Earle. That marriage was over.

When Bill and Floss's second son was born on September 13, 1916— four days before Bill's thirty-third birthday—he was named Paul Herman Williams, in memory of the brother Floss had lost two years earlier. Nothing has surfaced to recall the event; there are no letters for this period that touch on Paul's birth, and *The Build-Up*, which had spoken in detail of William Eric's birth, ends just before Paul Williams was born. But Williams must have celebrated that event as he had the birth of his first son. And that baby would find his way into his father's experimental improvisations six months later as that "waking baby whose arms have been lying curled back" in its crib.[52]

Two months before his second son was born, Williams was trying to give birth to his third volume of poems. He wrote to Edmund Brown of the Four Seas Company in Boston—one of several potential American publishers that he approached—on July 18 that he would have to have another book soon or start destroying "nearly all I have written." He found he could only "tolerate 50 or 60 of my things at a time," and that as he wrote "the new, the old dies off at the other end of the string."[53] To make publishing matters more imperative, he still did not have a book he could really say was representative of himself. He refused to even admit to the 1909 *Poems*, did not mention it among his publications, and refused during his lifetime to let any of those poor things be reprinted. *The Tempers* had been published in London (where no one had bought it), and—except for what he'd distributed gratis—the copies were sitting in a box up in his attic. It was time for a new book to let America see what he was capable of doing.

Brown was willing to do the book for fifty bucks, which disappointed Williams, who had hoped that by now at least he wouldn't have to pay to get himself printed. "At the present moment I am so utterly exhausted," he told Brown that July, "from battling the heat, death, in the person of a young man and my own heaped fatigues, accumulated since last summer that I can scarcely turn a sheet into a typewriter much less invent a good name for a volume of verse or choose the pieces to be left off." But he liked Brown and thought he would work with him, even though Brown's request for money had reminded him of that old New England love of cruelty he'd sensed in his new publisher's letters.[54] As for a title, he added in a letter a few days later, he thought he might go with *Pagan Promises*.[55]

That ended the discussion for three months, when Brown wrote to say that he was going to offer free subscriptions to *Others* with every subscription to his own Boston-based journal. Williams thanked him for his "strange spirit of co-operation," and then brought up the question of a book again, only this one a volume featuring his work along with Kreymborg's and Bodenheim's. The book would be called *Three Others* and would be evenly divided among the three poets.[56] But Bodenheim balked at that suggestion, and on Halloween Williams told Brown that Kreymborg had told him to forget that idea and to have Brown publish a book of Williams' own poems.[57]

In early November Kreymborg wrote to Williams with the suggestion that he and Williams and Bodenheim appear together instead in a special *Others* booklet. Williams agreed, and this issue of *Others* appeared that December, with Williams sandwiched between Kreymborg and Bodenheim. There were sixteen poems by Williams in this issue, the first time Williams had been featured in America, and his poems dealt with a multitude of subjects: a young man's guilty lovemaking, the turbulence of marriage, praise for the old men in New York who had "studied / every leg show / in the city," a young housewife in negligee seen on the streets of Rutherford, a woman down and out on her luck who wanted only to be left alone to die, his black Persian, Mother Kitty, pregnant yet again, and the poet dancing naked in the north room of his house in the best style of a Nijinsky. He wrote too of water in his kitchen sink splashing down to transform for a moment his quotidian world into a memory of three girls out of Degas in crimson satin dancing before a large crowd, and another poem, a pastoral, on the values to be found in working—as he did—among the very poor, whose decaying shacks could reveal the most delicate patina of bluish green he'd ever seen anywhere. Together these poems managed to generate a sense of Williams' locality, a vortex with its own center at 9 Ridge Road.

In the fall of 1916 Williams continued his work as an editor of *Others*, even as he wrote to *The Egoist* that the real importance of *Others* as a vortex was past and the movement it had stirred already dead. That August he had edited a Spanish-American number, with his father's translations of R. Arévalo Martinez making up the entire issue. Then, in September, Helen Hoyt had put together a women's number. But Kreymborg was busy with other projects, including writing political speeches for the leader of the Hungarian Americans in New York. By that time the new financial backer of *Others*, a Canadian named John Marshall, who had replaced Arensberg and who had had great ideas for the magazine, had had to tell Kreymborg finally that he could no longer underwrite the project and had gone back to Canada. *Others* was beginning to list.

On October 4, Williams took matters into his own hands. Despite his feelings for Amy Lowell, he wrote to tell her that he liked one of her poems and wanted her to accept his homage, "much as I dislike you."[58] He also told her at the same time he needed money so that he could get on with the work of keeping *Others* afloat. Amy Lowell wrote back a few days later to thank Williams for his "love letter," telling him straightforwardly at the same time not to expect any money for his magazine.[59] She also asked him which movement he had meant was dead in that letter he'd sent to *The Egoist*. Certainly not the Imagistes? Why, their 1915 *Anthology*, minus that nuisance Pound, had just gone into its third edition. Anyway, she was going to be in New York the following month and wanted to talk to Williams.

Williams was furious with Lowell's response. Yes, he wrote her, Amy had done well with her money. She'd "gathered together a few rather well advertised people from both sides of the Atlantic" and together with her "own unquestioned prestige and a little stolen notoriety from the omission of Pound" had put together a financially successful book. And, yes, damn it, it was the *Others* movement and not imagism which was finished. But, he added, facing one of the most influential American writers of the time, still fiercely loyal to his friend Pound, "aside from what you stole from Pound, your venture is worthless." Moreover, aside from the fact that it had failed, the *Others* movement had "held the future of such a man as Bodenheim in its palms, even if only for a short while." As for seeing Lowell, he had absolutely nothing to say to her. She had, he said, a "lamentable stinginess of spirit" toward young, unknown American writers who were trying to break through the crust and into the sunlight where she herself was basking.[60]

But matters did not end there. Williams did not really believe that a whole movement in poetry could be snuffed out simply by the failure of one little magazine like *Others*, did he? Lowell taunted him. Why, the thing had been fumbled from the very start. There had been a little newspaper notoriety in the summer of 1915 and the *Others* crowd had been fooled into thinking their magazine's future had been thereby secured. But Lowell and others like her had withdrawn their support as soon as they saw the poor stuff Kreymborg and his followers had allowed to get into the magazine. She'd only contributed to Williams' July number because of Pound's old fondness for his friend and because she'd liked Williams the one time she'd met him at Arensberg's studio in the fall of 1915.

Then Williams had betrayed her by printing people in his issue whom she didn't like, right there next to her. Why, she could have bought up a poor little thing like *Others* any number of times had she wanted, but having refused Pound's help in putting her imagist anthology together, it was silly of Bill Williams to expect that she would now "try to purchase" the support of one of Pound's henchmen. Surely Willie was naive to think that the United States was teeming with new poetic talent. Conrad Aiken had been closer to the mark when he'd quipped that if there were as many excellent poets as people like Stanley Braithwaite the anthologist and Williams were claiming, then the country would now be passing through "one of the most remarkable eras in the history of the world." That of course was silly. Maybe when they saw each other, she could explain all this to her young friend.[61]

Williams thanked Lowell for her "very reserved letter in which you make all the conventional and obvious mistakes in attempting to apprehend my feelings concerning the demise of *Others*." To her, Bodenheim—whom she'd called "pathetic"—was a hopelessly unhappy man, and if he himself, who thoroughly believed in Pound, was therefore Pound's "henchman," then so be it. But how could she understand what *Others* had meant to him? As for the politics of prize poems and mutual backscratching, he asked Lowell to explain how Stanley Braithwaite could really have chosen as the best poem of the year "that piece of yours which I quite sincerely believe to be twaddle and which I have never yet heard anyone admire." As for seeing her: since everything she represented was opposed to everything important to him, he simply wasn't interested. That cooled the correspondence on both sides for a while.[62]

But in spite of Williams' bravado, the truth was that he and Kreymborg couldn't find a market even for the five hundred copies of the magazine they were already publishing. They couldn't sell it. They couldn't even give the thing away, he complained to Brown in early November. He knew that the magazine, for all its innocuous appearance, remained a force, "a threat to conventional mediocrity."[63] In fact, the magazine was still needed, though not as much as it had been needed in the beginning. The truth was, even more than Williams could then know, that the magazine had fostered several poetic reputations, not only figures like Kreymborg and Bodenheim and Mina Loy—the ones being singled out at the time—but others too whose reputations were to survive the weathering that all poetic reputations must take, others like Stevens and Marianne Moore and Williams himself.

The magazine did continue to function by gasps and spurts. So when Williams wrote to Elijah Hay, the pseudonym of Marjorie Allen Seiffert, on Columbus Day 1916, that *Others* was dead as a result of "anaemia of the liver,"[64] and that he wouldn't be able to print her work, she took the initiative and asked if she might finance an issue of the magazine to show off the work of her own "Spectric School," consisting of herself, Morgan, and the ubiquitous Kreymborg. Williams told her to go ahead and take over the January number: *Others* was still breathing and he could still act as editor. The magazine was to be a magic name "for any poet who is an artist and can earn, borrow or steal a few dollars." And even that necessity would be dispensed with "whenever it was possible." *Others* was broke, "but not in spirit."[65]

Another poet who introduced himself by letter to Williams in the fall of 1916 was a seventeen-year-old from Ohio who'd recently come east to settle in Brooklyn. His name was Hart Crane and Williams took some of his pieces for a future issue of *Others*, calling the poems "damned good stuff."[66] But the poems were never published. When Crane wrote Williams five months later to ask about the fate of the poems and whether it might not be possible to actually meet Williams—whose work he very much admired—Williams put him off by saying he was sure he'd see Crane "sooner or later" somewhere around the city.[67] As it turned out, it would be ten years before they would meet, largely because that was the way Williams wanted things, especially as Crane's New York reputation began its meteoric rise among the younger New York poets and critics, threatening to eclipse Williams' own.

*
**

With his rejection by the Fortnightly Club in the spring of 1916 for having refused to sign the letter backing England and condemning Germany, Paul Herman had had no choice but to resign as president. It was therefore no accident that Williams was instrumental in founding another Rutherford social club modeled in part on the Fortnightly but set up in part in opposition to it. It would meet to discuss whatever was of contemporary interest and it was called the Polytopics Club. Like its parent, it was composed of about a dozen couples, younger than the Fortnightly group and somewhat more avant-garde and freer, though it too required tuxedos and evening gowns at its monthly meetings. It would meet eight times a year, each month at a different home, on the last Saturday of the month. The meetings would begin in October and end in May for the summer. Meetings were instructed to begin at eight and to adjourn at midnight, and each host couple would be responsible for the topic of the month and for refreshments, which were generally quite lavish. Usually an outside speaker was invited to address the group on a topic on which the speaker was an expert. So, for example, Williams invited Libby Burke, Kenneth Burke's wife, to address the group on one occasion, and on another occasion asked Gorham Munson to talk about Social Credit.

Williams himself addressed the group several times on the topic of modern and improvisational verse, though he left most of them sitting there with their mouths open or smirking that their friend was daffy.

To keep the evenings light, there was music and singing. As for the topics themselves, they covered everything a well-to-do middle-class American suburb could be expected to be interested in: Mah-Jongg, Tiger Hunting in China, Epilepsy, the High Cost of Living, but also George Bernard Shaw, James Whitcomb Riley, Dante, Modern Poetry, and—in March 1921—a reading by Bill Williams from his recently published *Kora in Hell*, followed by an informal lecture on the topic, "What Is Art and Why Is Poetry?" He stunned his Rutherford audience on that occasion by propounding the theory that poetry was not a matter of high seriousness, but rather a kind of spontaneous combustion. Now that kind of talk might be all right for those poet types over there in New York, but this was, after all, Rutherford, stronghold of American standards and the guardian of the (Presbyterian) faith. It was one of the few times that the secretary of the Polytopics Club noted that the discussion following a talk had actually become animated to the point of becoming heated.[68]

For her part, Floss had warned her husband that Rutherford was not New York, and that these businessmen and lawyers and doctors wouldn't know *what* he was talking about. Why, they'd even laughed in the wrong places when he'd read his poems and improvisations to them and she had to make him promise not to read his poems to them anymore.[69] Madeline Spence, who joined the club in 1924, was another who remembered how Bill's poetry had been received by the group, and she too had taken him aside and told him to forget trying to make his "townspeople" understand what it was he was doing.[70] It was only after he won the *Dial* Award in 1926 that his Rutherford friends began to take him at all seriously, and that was because he'd won $2,000 for his poems. That was big money then and so he must have been a real poet, even if they still didn't know what the hell he was talking about.

But Williams thoroughly enjoyed the people who made up the Polytopics Club, which came to include his brother and Hulda, as well as Madeline and Andrew Spence. Williams' own name was to appear frequently in the minutes for the club over the next thirty-five years. He was generous with his time, and he was generous in contributing to worthwhile liberal causes. He could poke fun at the Rutherford middle class—of which he was one—and they poked fun at this artsy doctor, as when they did a biblical exegesis of some of his modernist poems in early 1931, using the Polytopic Puppets for the demonstration. During the 1930 Christmas festivities held at his home, Williams himself wrote and acted in several short light plays (in the old Kreymborg mode) for what he called the Tyro Theatre Group. One of these was called—significantly —"Intimate Strangers," and featured Williams himself, face full of shaving cream, as the "Husband," while Floss—her face masked in a mud pack—played opposite him as the "Wife." It was a wry, sad comment—beneath the bantering—on modern American marriages, its deeper significances and plagencies probably drifting off to be lost in the recesses of the crowded room or out into the small kitchen, where Lucy the black maid waited to serve drinks and dainties.

Williams put on another play that same evening, this one called "Parisian Café Klotch," with Floss and Hulda playing the parts of two rich American women sitting in a Parisian café in the 1920s and ordering something called *hommes* as though they were appetizers.[71] Ed had made two life-size posters for the café scene in that one: a monkish figure called *le Père Tranquil* and a mother superior called *la Mère Prudente*, and Bill was so taken with those posters that he absconded with them after the play and kept them in his attic study framing the west windows, where for the next twenty years he might enjoy their company as he prepared his own aesthetic meditations.[72]

During the Christmas 1933 meeting—at his home again—Williams did a dark cabaret piece, dressing up like that German upstart Herr Adolf Hitler, his hair wet-brushed down and sporting a small black mustache, and sang some Nazi parodies. At Halloween 1936, he held a Gothick Shakespeare evening, acting out the witches' scene from *Macbeth* and then Othello's murder of "Mrs. Desdemona," which Williams' darker side executed with terrifying effectiveness, as the gasps from the members of the club testified. And though he no longer read his poems to the group, he did read them the libretto for *The First President* in 1937, shortly after he'd completed it.

In another vein, Williams also lectured during the depression on the need for more effective birth control measures, citing the work of Margaret Sanger done in this regard, and he also strongly supported the East Rutherford Day Nursery for making it possible for women with small children, who wanted or needed to, to hold down jobs. And when a motion was made to donate fifty cents a couple to support the nursery's work, Williams moved to raise that amount to five dollars a couple, a motion that was carried. With his peers in Rutherford he showed himself to be the good guy, congenial, more than willing to do his part for the community. He could be many things to many people.

From the mid-1920s on, Bill and Floss socialized with three other couples from the Polytopics Club. These were the Spences (whose daughter, Daphne, would marry their Bill Jr. in 1949), Dr. Alison Dugdale and his wife, Helen, and Earl and Louise Wagner. They all enjoyed a good laugh and they all got along well with each other. Alison Dugdale in particular was a character, Madeline Spence (at eighty-seven) remembered, and he was always telling some new joke—usually off-color—that would send Bill Williams into paroxysms of laughter. On the other hand, because poetry used to make Dugdale feel "creepy," Williams stayed away from the subject.[73] He tried to diagnose his audience quickly and accommodate himself to them. Poetry was out, then, though everything else, of course, was still fair game. The Polytopics group, in short, made up their closest friends in and around Rutherford.

*
* *

Williams of course had never lost his love for the stage, and in November and early December 1916, he had a chance to act in his first legitimate New York play, a one-acter by Kreymborg called *Lima Beans*. Kreymborg had wanted Eugene O'Neill's Provincetown Players on MacDougal Street in the Village to sponsor the piece, a light fantastic, but O'Neill wasn't particularly interested in doing dada stuff when he was preoccupied with the dark realism of his own plays. But Kreymborg had connections, had some clout in New York circles, and a compromise was reached. If Kreymborg could come up with his own actors—he would need two men and a woman—and would wait until O'Neill's own rehearsals for *After Breakfast* and *Fog* were done with, then Kreymborg's actors could use the stage, and the Provincetown Players would bill Kreymborg's one-acter along with two of their own for three nights running.

Kreymborg agreed. He got Bill Zorach, who'd designed the covers for *Others*, to put together a black and white cubist pastiche to represent a middle-class American kitchen, and then used bright colorful plates and utensils to offset the stark backdrop. Then Kreymborg got Mina Loy—a very beautiful woman—to play the American wife-as-soubrette, with Bill Williams playing opposite her as her husband. Finally, Zorach dressed up in Harpo Marx fashion to play the street vendor/huckster who kept chanting out the list of vegetables he had for sale, lima beans included.

It was a frail piece, really, a modern comedy of manners, the characters more puppetlike than real, and Williams understood at once how the piece would have to be played if it was to succeed. He and Mina and Zorach should be life-sized mannequins, manipulated by some mad director intent on making his comment on the American bourgeoisie; their movements would have to be jerky, wooden, exaggerated, their lines delivered in staccato fashion. It was hard work really, especially for Williams, who would have to get into New York each night after office hours, when he would call for Mina Loy at her apartment on 57th Street next to Carnegie Hall, and then escort her downtown to the Village. Kreymborg wrote him a note to apologize that for the next three weeks Williams' evenings wouldn't be his own. But he also added that Williams would be rewarded with all those kisses from Mina, lovely, lovely Mina.[74]

There was in fact one moment in *Lima Beans* when Williams did have to kiss Mina Loy, but he had chosen to do that for the sake of the play much as an automaton might kiss a china doll, and he had to ignore the shouts that arose from the darkened theater where some of O'Neill's actors were watching him and telling him to stop pussyfooting around and kiss the woman like a man. No doubt about it: Mina Loy was an extremely attractive single woman, as Williams admitted on more than one occasion, and he liked being in her company. She was young, sophisticated, very English, and very cosmopolitan. Besides which, she had written some very fine, very startling modern poems for *Rogue* and *Others* and *Poetry*. But Williams also knew Loy was too smart to get herself involved with any of the *Others* group, himself included. He probably tried to find out at least once in the relative privacy of her apartment, but apparently got nowhere with her. The play itself fared better. It went off as planned, the little theater was filled, and when the thing was over the audience signaled its approval by demanding sixteen curtain calls on opening night, as Kreymborg himself remembered. For Williams, however, *Lima Beans* was at best a "qualified success," though he may have been thinking of Mina rather than the play.[75]

Kreymborg made a halfhearted attempt after this to get some of the other poet-playwrights' work on the stage—Orrick Johns, Bodenheim, Wallace Stevens and Williams himself. Williams wrote at least one verse play for the Provincetown Playhouse called *The Apple Tree* and sent it to Kreymborg, who held onto it for a while before he lost it.[76] That was too bad, since Williams had no other copy of the thing, though he remembered years later that it called for "an improvised curtain made of newspaper with a flagpole sticking through the center of it," and that it had players designated "Bright Young Men." Stevens' artificial flower, *Bowl, Cat and Broomstick*, performed a year later at the Neighborhood Playhouse in the Village, is probably a close cousin to the kind of thing Williams wrote.[77]

*
**

In 1917 the women's movement was very much in the air and in the news, with women—and men—demonstrating for women's suffrage. Williams was concerned with the issue, though his wryness could be at times condescending and even exacerbating. In a reply to a letter from Marjorie Allen Seiffert in April 1917, Williams told this independent woman that, yes, he did espouse the suffrage cause, but that he also tickled Floss "into hysteria every election day." Whatever he meant by that last remark, it is clear he took the whole issue of women's political rights lightly. The truth was that he refused to take such questions as feminism and women's rights very seriously. In large part this was simply because he could not give himself to any cause other than art. So, he went on in his letter to Seiffert, he also loved music, but was bored with his violin, had studied in Germany but also in Palos (where he'd actually spent one day), sometimes enjoyed his meals, sometimes forgot to eat, and wrote "for the fun I get out of that reminder which writing is of what I am not & can never be." In short, he couldn't see what all the fuss the suffragettes were making was about.[78]

The same month he wrote Seiffert, he also wrote a long letter to *The Egoist* which had to be printed in two installments—in April and August—criticizing Dora Marsden's "Lingual Psychology," which had been appearing serially in that magazine. Williams had read Otto Weininger's text, *Sex and Character,* published in 1906, and wanted to discuss Marsden's attack on agnosticism for what he thought it really was: not an attack on agnosticism at all but an attack rather on male philosophy, or male psychology, which amounted to the same thing. But since Marsden's central attack—covert though it was—was against the creative process itself, Williams felt called upon to respond. There was, he said, an important revolution even then occurring, which would give rise to nothing less than the eventual domination of female over male psychology. There were two elements involved in this reappraisal of modern psychology: an engendering (male) force and a specific point of action (female). In other words, in embryo: a wandering sperm (ideas) and a receptive ovum (the mind), and the interpenetration of these loci.

Reality and the perception of reality were necessarily different for men and for women, so that a man could no more get inside a woman's head than a woman could get inside a man's. This difference in perception was as fundamental a difference as a person's biological traits. Men were rarely connected with reality; in effect it was a man's function to fertilize the egg and then get back to his essential idleness and stargazing or philosophizing. But the woman was linked by her gestation and nurturing functions with the reality principle itself. Now in *Sex and Character,* Williams remembered, Weininger had claimed souls for men but not for women. But here, Williams asserted, Weininger was wrong. Both had souls—whatever *they* were—the difference being that man was the vague generalizer, *homo ludens,* playing word games and idea games, while woman was the concrete thinker. Weininger, seeing the disparity between the two sexes, had tried to create or discover a third gender, a unisex figure moving toward some eventual convergence, but there he had failed. There were men and there were women, and, moreover, Williams was willing to concede—without getting anxious over the discovery—it was woman—with her genetic grasp of reality—who was inevitably the superior of the two sexes.[79]

Williams was surely having some fun in his critique of Dora Marsden, but beneath all the joking, his own deepest sympathies and leanings were with women rather than with men. In fact, as he got older, he came to enjoy their company more and more. And he learned to learn from them, learned patience, long suffering, wisdom, love, among other things. If they wanted the vote, he wrote in a short story written at this time—a piece called "The Buffalos"—let them have it, so long as it did not interfere with the real business of life. He remembered long fruitless arguments with a woman he called Francie in the story, but who was probably none other than Viola Baxter, how during Teddy Roosevelt's administration she would "waste" his time by drawing him into the suffrage question. Exasperated finally, he had told her that as far as he was concerned, women could have all the votes in the world, since they were "the ones who biologically" and economically needed the votes and the power and the property that went with it. Men would live like Indians, hunting, fishing, and fighting. And then, once a year, the women could pick the "most able, most vigorous, most desirable" of the males for breeding purposes. It was hardly a sufficient answer to the problem of women's rights.[80] In fact, it was an exacerbated response to a question that was to dog Williams all his life: the relationship between men and women. Williams often did better than this in trying to understand women, those who were all that he was not, and he still had half a lifetime to learn. But even after a lifetime married to the same woman, he had to admit in his old age that much that Floss was had remained a private affair of her own.

Part of the problem—as the *Improvisations* and other pieces Williams published in 1918 that clearly grew out of the *Improvisations* make clear—was that Williams and Floss were going through an intense period of trying to understand each other. In his "Prose About Love," which appeared in *The Little Review* in June 1918, and again in "The Ideal Quarrel," published in the same magazine that December, Williams looked hard at the institution called marriage. So many writers had written of love, erotic love, spiritual love, modern love, of illicit love affairs after marriage. But what of the sheer power of love, as Boccaccio had dealt with it in *The Decameron* or Sudermann in his *Johannisfeuer*? What did love mean, after all? Love, which laid "everything flat before it" and scattered "its own roses and palm branches." Or consider, Williams proffered, the example of his beloved Wagner, whose "brave burst of passion" had lasted his entire life. Or the example of Lope de Vega, horribly bowdlerized for public consumption in James Maurice-Kelly's biography. Or Shaw, whose *Candida* might have ended, as its own logic insisted, in favor of a love freely given and freely accepted. Instead, Shaw had lost his nerve for some "childish democracy of thought."

What was needed to make a modern marriage work, Williams insisted, was violence: "Anger spitting through a mush of lumpy stuff—mouldy words" and "lie-clots" which neither party any longer believed. There was a place in marriage for "righteous wrath," for realigning priorities, for scaling off the dead shells of words, telling it straight on both sides "in bed at night, the children, dirt under the piano, systematic, get up earlier, the dishes, smell of cooking, sweetheart, darling, dearest, pimples on your back, your breath smells, your thighs are not . . . I thought I was marrying a . . . I demand a God." Thus, breaking through the crust of the intervening years back again to the beginning that a new life might begin again, a new life with new possibilities.[81]

*
**

At the end of January 1917 Williams told Ed Brown that he'd just about made up his new book of poems. It would have thirty-three poems and "The Wanderer" as an appendix or final section.[82] That would make one poem for each year of Williams' life. Ten days later he explained to Brown that he wanted his volume to follow the format of Richard Hovey and Bliss Carman's enormously popular *Songs from Vagabondia,* in the ninth edition of 1907. He wanted the same "Bourgeoise type"; only the cover design would be different. For the past few weeks Kreymborg had been going over Williams' poems with him. Now that selection process was nearly complete and Williams would be sending the manuscript shortly, along with a money order for fifty dollars to help defray the cost of the printing. Some of the poems, he realized, might be censorable, but he had not "wantonly" tempted the censor. He wanted the book out and behind him so that he could get on to other things.[83] In mid-February he finally mailed the manuscript, enlarged now to fifty-two poems, which he was sending to Brown's office in Boston "with its hands on its balls —fearfully."[84] There was a little problem with the wording of the contract, Williams added, since he didn't see how he could be held "responsible" for "personal and scandalous remarks," but Williams signed anyway.[85]

Then there was the question of the title for his new book, and Williams sent off a letter to Marianne Moore for her advice. He had called it *Pagan Promises* half a year before. Now he was thinking of calling it *Al Que Quiere!,* since foreign titles for books of poems were in just then, but he was troubled with his choice. "You see," he explained to her, "I am a mixture of two bloods, neither of them particularly pure." Part of him was therefore always "harking back to some sort of an aristocracy —probably of the gallows, or worse," which always seemed to interfere with his "democratic impulses." On the other hand, he was also something of a Roundhead with "a certain broad-fingered strain in me that will always be handling an axe for budding King Charles Firsts." The Spanish title, he felt, was like some "Chinese image cut out of stone," undemocratic in its impulse, so that he had added *The Pleasures of Democracy* to his title to appease his Roundhead impulses. He asked her to help him with his dilemma, since she was, after all, the "leading light of the Sex of the Future."[86]

But he unraveled the problem himself. On the twenty-third, he wrote Brown to get rid of the second half of the title—*or the Pleasures of Democracy*—and to have the title read: *A Book of Poems / Al Que Quiere!* That way it would read, as Williams spelled it out: "a book of poems to him who wants it. Get me?"[87] But there was a pun there as well, and Alfred Kreymborg—Al K—applauded when he caught it, realizing that Williams had dedicated the book to him. Williams had proofs for the book by the end of May, but it was not until late November—six more months—that the first copy of the book was actually printed and sent on to him. "Of all the devilish torment that I have ever passed through this that I am now suffering in waiting for my book is not perhaps the strongest but it is by far the most subtle." As a result he was finding himself "paralyzed in pen and in thought."[88] By November he was almost beside himself.

It was Williams' first representative volume, this third book of poems. It was a strong book with no waste, and it showed a clear and distinctively poetic American voice dealing with a variety of subjects in a characteristic mode. Fifty-two poems: perhaps for the weeks of the year, like that other great democrat, Walt Whitman, in his *Song of Myself.* The book opened with "Sub Terra," and a call for a band of "grotesque fellows" to come with him,

> *poking into negro houses*
> *with their gloom and smell!*
> *in among children*
> *leaping around a dead dog!*[89]

He called for others to come into the sunlight with him, to see the world around them that had always been there but which had been ignored or obfuscated by symbol or decorum.[90] "When I was younger," he wrote in one of his "Pastorals," thinking of his own long struggle to find a voice, "it was plain to me / I must make something of myself." But he had learned, had given up those pretensions, had instead immersed himself in the flux of life, as inconstant and shifting and eternally fresh as the wind itself:

> *Older now*
> *I walk back streets*
> *admiring the houses*
> *of the very poor:*
> *roof out of line with sides*
> *the yards cluttered*
> *with old chicken wire, ashes,*

> *furniture gone wrong;*
> *the fences and outhouses*
> *built of barrel-staves*
> *and parts of boxes, all,*
> *if I am fortunate,*
> *smeared a bluish green*
> *that properly weathered*
> *pleases me best*
> *of all colors.*[91]

He caught his older boy, "Sonny," in these poems, walking down the road with his father, whose thoughts were already on his next poem as he showed his son how to "throw pebbles into / this water-trickle," and then how to make a coronal of broken leaves and fern plumes and flowers . . . "a red clover, one / blue heal-all, a sprig of / bone-set, one primrose, / a head of Indian tobacco, this / magenta speck and this / little lavender," all for Floss.[92] He caught his young wife too in these poems, telling her to put on a new dress and to walk outdoors with him while the "elm is scattering its little loaves / of sweet smells / from a white sky." He had a poem to the indomitable spirit of his grandmother, "Dedication for a Plot of Ground," another to Kathleen McBride, the young girl who helped Floss with the boys and with the house, and even one to Maxwell Bodenheim in his "borrowed room" in Alfred Kreymborg's flat on Bank Street in the Village, disdaining the world outside his window and "even the sun / walking outside / in spangled slippers," that he might live in a world of poetry and heavy tobacco incense. There were poems about his patients, especially the women he loved so much: the little girls awakening to their own sexuality and the young housewife imprisoned by her middle-class circumstances, and the down-and-out women, beaten by life, afraid even to get out of bed anymore, squatters in abandoned houses, anemic, alcoholic, rasping with pneumonia:

> *This house is empty*
> *isn't it?*
> *Then it's mine*
> *because I need it.*
> *Oh, I won't starve*
> *while there's the bible*
> *to make them feed me.*
>
> *Try to help me*
> *if you want trouble*
> *or leave me alone—*
> *that ends trouble.*[93]

And, finally, there was a poem like "Danse Russe," a lighthearted lyric Williams wrote after seeing the Russian ballet perform in New York.

With Floss and the baby and Kathleen asleep and the sun already shining,
Williams caught himself dancing

> *naked, grotesquely*
> *before my mirror*
> *waving my shirt round my head*
> *and singing softly to myself*
> *"I am lonely, lonely.*
> *I was born to be lonely,*
> *I am best so!"*[94]

Dionysios / Pan, admiring every part of his comic body after making sure
the shades were drawn. Given this moment of realization, who could
say—since everyone else was asleep anyway—that he was "not / the
happy genius of my household"? Though Williams ended the volume
with his "Wanderer" poem, his long poem of initiation and of setting out,
he thought of that piece more as an appendix, as a verification of his
crossing into the fallen world for his songs. So the volume ended, really,
with his "Love Song," addressed not specifically to Floss but to the Muse
as perfect woman, with the stain of love smearing his entire world and all
his poems with honey yellow, thus "spoiling the colors / of the whole
world" with the color of love itself.

Brown sent out review copies of *Al Que Quiere!* in January and
February of 1918, and Williams waited for the critical response. He didn't
want Pound seeing the book yet until he had some sense of how it was
going to sit with the reviewers. At the same time the critical silence that
greeted the book actually made Williams feel happy, "happy as I'd be in a
wood, a true forest, some August noon."[95] Brown had gotten wind of a
rumor that Aiken might review the book for *The Dial,* and he warned
Williams in mid-February to watch out for "torpedo ripples."[96] Three
months earlier, Williams himself had told Brown that he didn't trust
what Aiken or Carl Sandburg might say about his book, because he was
sure they would simply not understand what it was he was trying to do.
And if Aiken did decide to review the thing, he was sure he'd get hell.[97] As
it turned out, however, Aiken—*and* Sandburg—simply ignored it. By
March 15, Brown could at least report on the reviews in the various
newspapers that had noticed the book: "a very good one in the *Richmond
Journal,* and a very bad one in the *Baltimore News,* and an editorial in last
week's *Minneapolis Bellman* giving me hell for what I said on the
jacket."[98]

The jacket comments—written by Brown—had indeed stirred up a
small hornet's nest because of their iconoclastic tone. In fact the tone was
so close to Williams' own smashing of windows, Roundhead style, that
some reviewers—and friends—were sure Williams himself had been the
one snubbing his nose at the potential bourgeois reader. The gentle

reader, so went Brown's blurb, probably wouldn't like these poems because they were "brutally powerful and scornfully rude." (They were neither, but it helped perpetuate the myth of Williams as wild man.) "The author has done his work, and if you *do* read the book you will agree that he doesn't give a damn for your opinion." And the publishers didn't give a damn either whether or not readers read the thing. But let the reader be aware that at least the publishers knew they had an important book here, one in which "poets of the future will dig for material as the poets of today dig in Whitman's *Leaves of Grass.*"⁹⁹

*
**

The important reviews, finally, were rather in the form of letters written to Williams by other poets like Marianne Moore and Wallace Stevens and Pound and H.D. Besides, the book was behind Williams now, and he was already deeply involved in something altogether different from the lyrics in *Al Que Quiere!* For by the summer of 1917, he had begun writing his *Improvisations,* prose poems culled from the day's experiences, something written each and every day for a year, regardless of how tired he felt or how flat the day had been. They were unlike anything he had tried before, and they owed something to the prose pieces Rimbaud had done nearly a half century before in his *Improvisations.* It was a kind of automatic writing, Williams' attempt to "loosen the attention" and descend deeper than ever into his poetic unconsciousness to tap energies so far left dormant. Later, the conscious mind could be called upon to select and order and even comment on what had been achieved. Having succeeded in the short, imagist lyric, Williams found it necessary to do the very thing Stevens had warned him not to do: make a new beginning into another kind of poetry.

"I decided that I would write something every day, without missing one day, for a year," Williams wrote in his *Autobiography* thirty-three years later. "I'd write nothing planned but take up a pencil, put the paper before me, and write anything that came into my head. Be it nine in the evening or three in the morning, returning from some delivery on Guinea Hill, I'd write it down."¹⁰⁰ It is difficult to pin down the exact beginning and end of the "year" Williams talks about, since he has purposely scrambled the diurnal turn of the seasons, preferring, as he says at the close of the improvisations, the seasons of the imagination, which keep their own elastic times. But a guess from internal evidence points to sometime late in the spring of 1917 and ending in September 1918, when Williams composed a twenty-page "Prologue" to his *Improvisations.*¹⁰¹ One finds here—as always with Williams—scenes extrapolated, heightened, transformed, from his own life during his thirty-fifth year (*nel mezzo del cammin di nostra vita* as Dante has it). There are glimpses of

Williams as husband and as father, of Floss cleaning house or chasing after Sonny, of Williams looking down at his infant son, Paul, or examining the corpse of some drifter found amid the goldenrod up by the Rutherford cemetery. There is a glimpse of Williams squinting at the cheap prints seen in the houses of the poor, who made up the bulk of his patients,[102] and another of him at an inquest with the Bergen County district attorney, Peter Valuzzi, a bullet-riddled corpse laid out before them on the stone table on a summer's night. There is even an apotheosis of Floss, made to "pass up into a cloud and look back at me," where then she will "not count the scribbling foolish that puts wings to your heels, at your knees."

Some of the improvisations are purposely obscure, obfuscated beyond reconstruction, but these are the exception. The derangement of the senses here is finally only partial, a way of making the reader slow down and engage the writer in the act of seeing what we call the "common" freshly, as if we were to discover it for the first time. Everywhere Williams leaves traces of the kind of thing he is attempting. This is his world and he is the Emersonian cosmic voice, transcending his place and time, his mind floating up through the slate roof, but remembering to maintain certain self-imposed limits, like an airplane, Williams says, that cannot allow itself to lose all contact with the world from which it has taken off and to which it must return. For if "all sense of direction and every intelligible perception of the world were lost there would be nothing left to do but come down to that point at which eyes regained their power."[103]

Joyce's *Ulysses*, appearing in installments in *The Little Review* at the same time that Williams was publishing his improvisations in the same magazine, also had a profound effect upon Williams, particularly in helping him shake loose his old rigidities and let logical meaning go, in order to work with language as language. But he also made it clear in the *Improvisations* themselves that he would use Joyce as he would any other plundered resource. "Reproduction lets death in, says Joyce. Rot, say I. To Phyllis this song is!"[104] If there were giants in the dirt in Joyce's Dublin, if Joyce could find analogues for Ulysses and Penelope and the Sirens and the Cyclops and even Circe in his provincial world, then why couldn't Williams do the same thing in his?

> The gods, the Greek gods, smothered in filth and ignorance. The race is scattered over the world. Where is its home? Find it if you've the genius. Here Hebe with a sick jaw and a cruel husband,—her mother left no place for a brain to grow. Herakles rowing boats on Berry's Creek! Zeus is a country doctor without a taste for coin jingling. . . . The ground lifts and out sally the heroes of Sophokles, of Aeschylus. They go seeping down into our hearts, they rain upon us and in the bog they sink down through the white roots, down—to a saloon back of the railroad switch where they

have that girl, you know, the one that should have been Venus by the lust
that's in her. . . . They are the same men they always were—but fallen.
Do they dance now, they that danced beside Helicon? They dance much
as they did then, only, few have an eye for it, through the dance and
fumes.[105]

Williams was also testing the limits of the imagination against the
countercurrents of reality, including the fact of death. What does the
imagination do, for example, when confronted with the fact of a corpse on
the inquest table, even as one knows—as Williams knew—that his own
father was slowly dying of an inoperable cancer of the lower colon? No
time for symbols here, of symbols of the "beautiful white corpse of
night." Here before him was the actual thing, death itself in the shape of a
young man murdered by his wife in a rage of passion. And what had
remorse to do with the scene now? Useless, Williams noted, "to accept it
as a criticism of conduct." What had motiviated this death was not
remorse, not the afterthought of the consequences of this death, but the
phosphorescent flare of violence itself. And what could the imagination
cling to now, staring down on this corpse with the three bullet holes in it?

All the troubled stars are put to bed now: three bullets from wife's hand
none kindlier: in the crown, in the nape and one lower: three starlike
holes among a million pocky pores and the moon of your mouth.[106]

In his imagination Williams could watch the corpse before him
transformed into a Ptolemaic map of the cosmos, a solarcentric universe
with all the stars of the corpse of night itself melted now "into this one
good white light over the inquest table." He could watch too "the
traditional moth," sign of the soul escaping heavenward, except that
there were two moths here fluttering against the lamp. Even Valuzzi, the
prosecuting attorney, and the county physician and the police officers
could defeat death and become for a moment pastoral maples waving
their green arms "to the tinkling of the earliest ragpicker's bells" as a new
day began to dawn. And the voices of the men, whispering question after
question, all as Williams noted, "infinitely beside the question" now the
man was dead, but still "restfully babbling of how, where, why and night
is done and the green edge of yesterday has said all it could."

Looking at his year's work in experimental prose in the summer of
1918, Williams knew at once that something would have to be done to
attempt to make the improvisations more accessible, without however,
reworking their unique if idiosyncratic surfaces. He added interpretations, some of them as obscure as the *Improvisations* themselves, as if to
say—as they did—that the "meaning" inhered in the words themselves
as written, and that to rewrite would be to alter whatever "meaning"
they had. Then, looking through one of the books Pound had left with

Williams when he left for England, the *Varie Poesie* of the Abbot Pietro Metastasio, Venice, 1795, Williams found his answer: "I took the method used by the Abbot of drawing a line to separate my material. First came the Improvisations, those more or less incomprehensible statements, then the dividing line and, in italics, my interpretations of the Improvisations. The book was broken into chapters, headed by Roman numerals; each Improvisation numbered in Arabic."[107]

And then he wrote his "Prologue" while on vacation at Floss's aunt's farm in Wilmington, Vermont. It was here that he undertook to explain what it was he'd done and why he'd done it, placing the *Improvisations* against the electric moment in American literature out of which they'd been generated. He used the example of his mother, with her knack of continually getting lost—as she had managed to do when she'd visited Ed in Rome in 1911—before she could extricate herself "from the strangeness of every new vista" to find a recognizable landmark. The *Improvisations* were like that, Williams suggested now. For like his mother he too lived in an Eden of the imagination. It might be "an impoverished, ravished Eden," but it was finally as "indestructible as the imagination itself." Like his mother, Williams too had learned the important lesson that whatever was before him, in all its concrete strangeness and newness, was "sufficient to itself and so to be valued."[108] It could be a brave new world anywhere.

The trick was to see whatever was before one's eyes "without forethought or afterthought but with great intensity of perception." Once he had been talking with Walter Arensberg at a restaurant on 63d Street and he'd asked him about the new work the cubists were doing, what its value was. Arensberg's answer had been that what really mattered in art was "the truly new," the new creation. As an example of the kind of thing he meant, he pointed to Duchamp's full-sized photograph of his own painting, *Nude Descending a Staircase*, which Duchamp had retouched to create—as simply as that—a second work of art distinct from the first. Everywhere around one, Williams insisted, there was this buzzing of the new. The new escaped time, remained eternally fresh. Like the recently discovered six-thousand-year-old cave paintings at Altamira, with their "galloping bison and stags, the hind feet of which have been caught in such a position that from that time until the invention of the camera obscura . . . no one on earth had again depicted the most delicate and expressive posture of running."[109]

And in his own poems too, in "March" and "History," for example, Williams had celebrated the indestructibility of the imagination, as in the faience work uncovered from the Egyptian mummies at the Metropolitan Museum of Art, or in the marvelous woman and androgynous angels of Fra Angelico he remembered seeing in Florence:

> *an angel*
> *with colored wings*
> *half kneeling before her—*
> *and smiling—the angel's eyes*
> *holding the eyes of Mary*
> *as a snake's hold a bird's.*
> *On the ground there are flowers,*
> *trees are in leaf.*[110]

He had seen time obliterated in these masterpieces, had felt love itself rekindled from the very dust of the sarcophagi along which he'd run his fingers one Sunday morning at the Metroplitan Museum. But love was not there only. It was to be found in those amateur paintings hanging on the walls of houses he had visited on his appointed rounds, paintings with their "untold gaiety of flowers and sobriety of design." So, in "Effie Deans," written in the mid-1930s, he would catalog some of those pictures he'd seen over the years: signs of a delicate, nascent American flower different in impulse from and at odds with the mass-produced imitations of the old masters. It was a frail thing, this American primitive impulse for amateur landscapes and portraits and the rest of it, beyond flowering perhaps, but for all that important and something to be cherished.[111]

He argued in his "Prologue" with Stevens, who hoped Williams would settle on "a single manner or mood" and let that position become "thoroughly matured and exploited," rather than keep going after his incessant new beginnings.[112] He also argued with H.D. for trying to make of poetry and tradition too solemn an affair, telling her that he'd "write whatever I damn please, whenever I damn please and as I damn please," provided only that he tried to keep not a deadening classical stasis, but rather "the authentic spirit of change."[113] He hit—obliquely —at Pound as well, telling his "mentor" that he intended to avoid "the spell of a certain mode," whether of his classical "Postlude" or even of his more ironic "Hic Jacet," because he'd learned that old modes, old musics too had their own traps, especially where a mode's origins were obscured by time, "leaving thus certain of its members essential to a reconstruction of its significance permanently lost," as Williams felt was true of Provençal and more especially of classical Chinese poetry.[114] He used the analogue of his marriage to Flossie, to whom he'd been married for nearly six years when he wrote that it was "in the continual and violent refreshing of the idea that love and good writing have their security." Writing, like marriage, inevitably went through cycles, ascents, descents, ascents. It was absolutely necessary to recognize these changes, to break the old molds when they no longer served, so that "a new growth of passionate attachment" to a woman or to the imagination might follow.[115] It was for these reasons that he now praised Marianne Moore and

Alfred Kreymborg, especially as "innovators of the musical phrase," a sign of the new growth Williams demanded in poetry.

And then, in the midst of writing his "Prologue," Williams' eye had caught an article by one Edgar Jepson, a British reviewer, in the September issue of *The Little Review*. The piece was called "The Western School," and it was an attack on American prizes given for decidedly inferior work. In the main Williams had to agree that Jepson's attack had been well aimed. (After all, hadn't he himself served as one of the judges, along with Helen Hoyt and Eunice Tietjens, for *The Little Review*'s Vers Libre Contest the year before? And hadn't most of the poems been rank as dishwater?[116]) But what Williams didn't like was the tone this Englishman assumed, with his "slipshod" epithets and phrases, "rank bad workmanship of a man who has shirked his job" in a prose that Williams found as "rancid as *Ben Hur*."[117]

What really rankled him, however, what really stuck in his craw —though he couldn't bring himself to admit it—was Pound's support of Jepson's position, especially Jepson's holding up of T. S. Eliot and his "Love Song of J. Alfred Prufrock" as the only American poetry even worth considering! Williams' attack in the "Prologue" would be only the first of many such waged over the next thirty-five years against Eliot in print: in his letters, in his poems, in his interviews. Here, for starters, Williams attacked Eliot's "attenuated intellectuality." Eliot was, after all, nothing more than "rehash, repetition in another way of Verlaine, Baudelaire, Maeterlinck."[118] But Williams also lashed out at what he read as Pound's betrayal of all he himself had tried to accomplish by staying in America. Pound had clearly given the laurel now to Eliot, and so Williams, hurt, lashed out at his friend as well. Pound too was finally like Eliot, Williams wrote, a man "content with the connotations" of his masters: Yeats and the Renaissance and Provence and the modern French writers. Alas, there would always be "some everlasting Polonius of Kensington forever to rate highly his eternal Eliot."[119]

But J. Alfred Prufrock as the type of the American? That was pure nonsense, Williams insisted. After all, Jepson himself might have served as the model for that "nibbler at sophistication." Look rather to Montezuma or Gautemozin than to a failed butler for the New World type! And was Eliot's "La Figlia che Piange" really the "summit of United States achievement"? Jepson had chosen that poem only because it conformed to existing norms of British taste, without noticing how Eliot—that "fumbling conjurer" of words—had had to distort speech itself to achieve the rhymes he was after. And yet Williams knew Eliot was good and respected him for his craftsmanship. He even saw the man had not been able to completely submerge the fact that he was an American whose language was not, first of all, British. In short, Williams was ambivalent toward Pound and this new upstart. He praised them for their ability to see that London had already achieved a set of cultural guideposts while New York and Chicago were still struggling to formulate their own, but he also damned them "for their paretic assumption that there is no alternative but their own groove." Williams had chosen to make his stand with Kreymborg and Bodenheim and to rise or fall with them. As it turned out, within a short time of writing his "Prologue," he would find himself alienated from both of them as well, and would be looking for a new band of American grotesques, even as Eliot was writing and Pound editing *The Waste Land.*

Within a week of writing his "Prologue," Williams let Harriet Monroe know that *Kora in Hell* was ready to be published, though he was also sure that the commercial presses would have nothing to do with it. He knew he would have to help pay for this book as he had all his others, and so had set himself the task, as he put it, "of earning enough money by my writing in the next six months to get my book out."[120] That December he wrote Edmund Brown that he wanted to publish "this spring [1919] a volume of poems—so to speak—short pieces, paragraph length which I have named *Improvisations.*" The manuscript would go to him after the first of the year.[121]

But other events were crowding in on Williams that fall. First, there was the end of the war in November, and the ticker tape parades and celebrations that followed. Soon Ed would return from Italy, perhaps in time to see his father die. *Others* was still alive, but moving by desperate fits and starts. One number had come out in February, and then nothing. But now Kreymborg was preparing to get another issue out by December. Again, it had been Marjorie Seiffert who had provided Kreymborg with the necessary funds, and Williams told Harriet Monroe in early October that the stuff he'd given Kreymborg six months before—a long poem called "Romance Moderne" which had been moldering in Kreymborg's attic—would fill three pages of a new issue.[122] Obviously Kreymborg was preoccupied with other matters besides *Others* and Williams. And when Williams ran into Kreymborg in mid-November in New York City and asked him what he was going to do about getting Williams' play put on by the Provincetown Players as he had promised, Kreymborg had to tell him, rather sheepishly, that he'd decided to go ahead and work with Edna St. Vincent Millay in putting on her *Da Capo* instead. Kreymborg added that he hoped Williams wouldn't mind. After all, it was a tough world out there, and everyone had to look out for himself first.[123] But Williams was furious. A few days later he wrote to Monroe to tell her he'd just broken with Kreymborg and that Kreymborg had given Williams his manuscripts back so that he might turn them over to *Poetry.* Frankly, Williams added, he wanted to get paid now for his poems; he was "sick of standing at the

Paying Teller's window."[124] And when *Poetry* published Williams' sheaf in March 1919, it was called, significantly, "Broken Windows."

In spite of the rupture, Williams and Kreymborg managed to patch things up. Kreymborg for his part did publish several additional things of Williams', including—ironically—a play, and Williams went to see Millay's *Da Capo*, which he enjoyed and even borrowed from when he came to write *Paterson* 4 thirty years later. He even dedicated his next book of poems, *Sour Grapes*, to Kreymborg in 1921, though with a title like that even Kreymborg had to catch the irony. But the closeness that Williams had felt toward Kreymborg was gone. For three and a half years the two men had worked closely together, and Williams' allegiance to Kreymborg would seem to have been total. But circumstances and interests had intervened, and other vortices were soon to take the place of *Others*.[125]

*
**

"You who had the sense / to choose me such a mother," Williams had written to his father in 1916,

> *you who had the indifference*
> *to create me,*
> *you who went to some pains*
> *to leave hands off me*
> *in the formative stages*
> *(I thank you most for that, perhaps) . . .* [126]

He had reached a truce with his father by then, had reached the age where he could afford to take himself less seriously and laugh and walk next to his father. And now, throughout 1918, he had to watch as his father began to lose weight dramatically, to shrivel in on himself, as cancer took its toll. "I can clearly remember the last months seeing that figure," he would recall years later, "slightly stooped, wearing a sort of dark combination mackintosh and overcoat, the squarish derby, going down Park Avenue before my own house every morning for the 8:18. I would still be dressing, perhaps, in the front room. All I could do was shake my head and feel my heart drop to my very shoes at the sight of him."[127] And then the trips to the city stopped altogether, and Williams senior spent what time he had in his own room, trying to get his papers in order. By December, William George was confined to his bed.

Then, on Christmas Eve, Williams went to 131 Passaic to see his father and to try to give his wasted colon some relief by giving him an enema. He had to force the nub in and it frightened him to do it, but his father was as stoic and as silent as ever. Still, he knew he'd hurt him. That night, with his own children in bed, he went up to his room and wrote to Brown that he'd be sending along the *Improvisations* shortly, but was too busy to do much of anything at the moment. Then he wrote to Wallace Stevens:

> Three Amens! It might be three blackbirds, or three bluejays in the snow [Stevens would catch the allusion]—but it is three Amens! Well, all I can answer is—I feel restless tonight, no place to sit down, no place to write in,—rain and warmth outside—my wife downstairs trimming the tree—the children asleep behind me, on the other side of the wall. It is the spirit of Santa Claus—it has me in the crotch—Amen, Amen, Amen!
> What in God's name can a man say to Christ these days. I'd not know what he wanted to hear me talk about if I met him—on a corner somewhere. Ice, sharp edges, a lust for the chase of the ever changing world—Proteus—but not Amen![128]

He had written Stevens, he said, to thank him for his criticism in the December *Little Review*. This was "Nuances of a Theme by Williams," which Stevens had written in direct response to Williams' own "El Hombre." Then, late on Christmas Day, before mailing the letter to Stevens, he added: "My poor father died on Christmas day. Who can say what this may do."[129]

At seven that morning, his mother had called him to come as quickly as he could; his father was dying. It was a cerebral accident, and Williams knew that the enema forcing of the previous evening was the probable cause of the hemorrhage. Now he looked down at his father and then whispered to his mother: "He's gone." But his father began to shake his head slowly back and forth. He had heard his son pronounce him dead. And then the phone rang. It was a maternity case and no one else was available. He had to leave. When he got back, his father really was dead.

A few nights after his father's death, Williams had the dream about his father coming down a flight of stairs, looking over his shoulder and saying, "You know all that poetry you're writing. Well, it's no good." Williams awoke, speechless and trembling.

On the way to the Rutherford cemetery, all Williams could think of was the description of the funeral ride to Glasnevin Cemetery he'd read of in Joyce's *Ulysses*. At that point, he would write, "Joyce's technique seemed to me childish—Victrola." The funeral had been decently done, he wrote a week afterward. "I was affected by the burial service. I felt warm toward my mother. I felt grateful to my wife and others for their solicitous behavior. I was touched by the letters of sympathy. There was not a cruel or bitter thought in my body." But the fact remained, that his father was gone. And no matter how difficult he found it to believe, it was true: his father really was gone this time, not to Costa Rica or Buenos Aires or Geneva. Just gone.

It was a time for reevaluating his life. Why, he asked, did he continue to write? Why did he serve his neighbors? For nothing, because he was simply damned otherwise. "I go in one house and out of another practicing my illicit trade of smelling, hearing, touching, tasting, weighing," he noted candidly:

> I do not always get on well in this town. I am more than likely to turn out a bankrupt any day. I will move away then. I see no other reason for moving. I especially cannot compete with other doctors. I refuse to join church, Elks, Royal Arcanum club, Masons. . . . I do not see the sense of operating on people myself when they can get a better man to do it cheaper in New York. I know I cannot safely lance every bulging eardrum. . . . I find a doctor in this community to have a special function. He is primarily an outpost. I am interested in babies because their processes are not yet affected by calcification and because diagnosis rests almost wholly upon a perception of the objective signs. Courage seems singularly out of place in my life.[130]

And yet, that wasn't quite fair to himself. All during the great influenza epidemic of 1918, which had decimated the world's population and—closer to home—had killed one of the younger doctors in Rutherford as well as some of Williams' strongest patients, Williams had worked day after day and night after night, making, he tells us, as many as sixty house calls in a day. Everyone in Williams' family group, except his father and himself, had caught the flu, which in some cases—as with Floss —had been dangerously compounded with pneumonia. There it was. Death was no tragedy for Williams, since for him the tragic was frankly out of the question for human beings. No, death was merely a biological matter. When it looked like he might contract the flu, his own primary concern had been to get through his list of patients and then lie down to see what would follow. If he died, he died. The human organism would have failed to respond adequately to an invasion by foreign microbes into its system. It was all as simple and as stark, finally, as that.

"I have been driven to the wall by sheer inhuman work for the past four months," Williams explained to Brown at the end of January 1919, "and whereas I looked for a brief respite about the first of the year it did not materialize."[131] He sent the *Improvisations* on to Boston on the twenty-seventh, though he still wanted to make some changes. In the meantime, he wanted Brown to look over the manuscript and set it up to follow the type and format of *The Little Review*, where a number of the prose poems had already appeared.[132]

By imitating *The Little Review* in this way, Williams would pay homage to the little magazine that by 1917 had replaced *Others* for him as the cutting edge of the avant-garde. It had given him, as he twitted Harriet Monroe, the "entré" he needed which neither her magazine nor *Others* could any longer provide. He didn't much care for the English adulation *The Little Review*'s editor, Margaret Anderson, was getting, but he watched with admiration the care Jane Heap was giving to the

Americans in the magazine. *The Little Review* had provided at least a narrow opening for him when all the other magazines had proven dead-ended. And he had said as much to Jane Heap in a letter printed in the January 1919 issue of the magazine: "You have your foot in the jamb of the door and your services are flamingo-winged compared to those of the builders of the Cathedral of St. John the Divine." In fact *The Little Review* was rendering a service far more important than the U.S. Senate itself, which at that point was doing nothing better than blocking the treaty work of "Wilson the-Sedately-Impetuous."[133]

When Brown looked over the *Improvisations*, he saw the economic risks he would be taking bringing out a book that few would take the trouble to read. But he was willing to do the book if Williams would agree to buy two hundred dollars' worth of stock in the Four Seas Company. Williams balked. That was asking too much. But Floss told her husband that if two hundred dollars would get the book published to go ahead.[134] It was not easy for Williams to part with that much money. Early on in his writing career he'd made it a cardinal rule to pay for getting his books published out of the money he made selling his writing to the little magazines. He'd even found it necessary to tell Brown that the fact that he was writing him on Hotel Chalfonte stationery from Atlantic City was not to be construed to mean that he had money. He had merely been invited down there for some convention, all expenses paid.[135]

But he wanted the book done and there was no one else to do it. So, on March 3, he wrote Brown that "after quarreling vainly with my wife this morning over the proper schedule for starting the day's activities," he had finally decided to sign the contracts and send along the check. Still, he couldn't help adding that parting with that much money in hopes of seeing his book published made him feel like "one of those Mexicans who crawl a mile or two on their bare knees whipping their backs to get up their potential ardor."[136]

A few days later Williams was on an express bound for Chicago. He had been signed up by Mitchell Dawson of the *Others* Lecture Bureau to read and lecture before a Chicago audience. He would be gone a full week, without his practice to worry about, leaving Floss behind with their two sons, five and two-and-a-half. Suddenly, he found himself a free man, lionized, in the presence of Dawson and Ben Hecht and Carl Sandburg, whose early poems he had so admired. And then there was Marion Strobel, Harriet Monroe's assistant at *Poetry* and a poet herself. It was a strange interlude for Williams, this week in March in Chicago, with spring in the air and a terrific storm over wind-whipped Lake Michigan, whose waters he could see crashing onto the wall retainers from his hotel window. He was here, he suddenly realized, as a recognized poet, and he gave his wild side as free a reign as he'd ever allowed himself.

He gave a talk on the *Others* platform about the role of the poet, who went "up and down continually empty-handed." It was the poet's task, he insisted, "to tear down, to destroy life's lies, to keep the senses bare, to attack." The sign of the poet's "unforgiving seriousness," he added as he warmed to his task, was "his rebellious laughter, which he guards with immaculate craft." That craft, he added, was constantly in need of being sharpened. Once a formal perfection had been achieved, it had then to be broken down to the bare dregs again so that the poet might escape self-parody, self-entrapment. It meant a constant beginning again. The poet was the true democrat who had a quarrel with no one, especially the common man, the regular fellow (this last directed as much to Sandburg as to anyone). He remembered the guys, the tough ones, from his own youth, he added, diving from trains, plunging deep into the swamps to escape the "hounds": Fred Sempken and Dago Shenck and Vincent Stephenson. And poets, he said, were like that: rebels who took calculated chances.

There were only the emotions, strong and free, not etiolated and reserved as in that sickly Prufrock figure. The poet was the true revolutionist, he added, like the scientists who had discovered new laws and new energies with passionate attachment far deeper than most people suspected. Madame Curie had been one and H.D.'s father at his telescope night after night watching the planets swim into ken had been another. These scientists had strained after an emotion of stability, fixity, truth, which, once discovered, they could then let pass on to go after other truths. Triumphs themselves were necessarily fleeting, almost accidental to the process of discovery, like Curie's discovery of radium (or Columbus' discovery of a New World, he might have added). So with poetry: it too was a language of the emotions and modern poetry meant discovering a fresh language. Down with the rigidities of rhyme and fixed forms, Williams the New World Jacobin shouted, and on with the search for a new language and new forms in which to couch the contours of one's own emotions![137]

Williams decided to live what he had preached that night in Chicago. He apparently had a brief, passionate interlude with Marion Strobel that week, and he wrote a poem for her:

> Go to sleep—though of course you will not—
> to tideless waves thundering slantwise against
> strong embankments, rattle and swish of spray
> dashed thirty feet high, caught by the lake wind,
> scattered and strewn broadcast in over the steady
> car rails![138]

There was a sense of the *carpe diem* in this poem, with the inevitable night of death coming on:

A black fungus springs out about lonely church doors—
sleep, sleep. The night, coming down upon
the wet boulevard, would start you awake with his
message, to have in at your window. Pay no
heed to him. He storms at your sill with
cooings, with gesticulations, curses!
You will not let him in. He would keep you from sleeping.

And then, before he fully realized what had happened, Williams was heading back home on an eastbound express, talking with some young woman and still feeling romantic and free. It was only when he got to the back door, he remembered, and saw his sons running toward him and Floss relieved to have him back home that it suddenly dawned on him once again that he was indeed married.[139]

When he wrote to Harriet Monroe at the end of April, enclosing the talk he'd given in Chicago, he apologized. He had been ungracious to her, had not even kept his appointments with her. The truth was, he admitted, that he'd acted "insane" in Chicago, the way he remembered Lake Michigan itself:

> *I flung myself about like a silly wave. . . . I cannot say that I shall ever recover from that rain sodden but vicariously sunshiney week! It was as if, or rather it was actually—I had never in my life before had an opportunity to be just a poet, the one thing I want to be. I was, to the vulgar eye at least, a poet! I was at least as near to being a poet as I had ever been and it was as if new bones had been put into me.*

But he had come away refreshed, enlivened and, unless death intervened, he would "see some work done in the next five years that will be unrivaled anywhere at any time." Finally, he was convinced, there was about to dawn "the opening of a golden age of poetry HERE."[140] Twenty years later he would still be looking back at that miraculous week, convinced that something had happened, that marvelous energies had flared up, the very memory of which still had the power to shake him.[141]

*
* *

Another woman he met this spring—probably in April—was the Baroness Elsa von Freytag-Loringhoven, already a celebrated phenomenon in and around the Village. Once, when Williams had gone into the city to see Jane Heap and Margaret Anderson at their rooms over the *Little Review* offices on West 16th Street, Williams had noticed a sculpture under glass that looked like chicken guts. It was, they explained to him, a dadaist sculpture by the Baroness, who, it turned out, wanted very much to meet the doctor from Rutherford whose improvisations in *The Little Review* she had so much enjoyed. He'd heard strange things about this woman, stories of how she dressed in purple and yellow clothes with a coal scuttle on her head or a tam-o'-shanter complete with feathers and ice cream spoons, or black vest and kilts, with brass teaballs suspended from her nipples. Once she'd even shaved her head and painted her face two colors divided down the center so that seen from either profile she offered two distinct faces.

And once Wallace Stevens had seen her parading through the streets of the Village and had applauded her latest costume. She had turned and run after him, enamored by the portly poet in suit and vest. It was years, Williams remembered, before Stevens could bring himself to venture again below 14th Street.[142] Hart Crane too had had a run-in with the Baroness when he was living above the *Little Review* offices in 1919. She had borrowed his typewriter and he, after a few days, wanting it back, went down with a friend to ask for it. They spent several hours talking with her, trying to work up enough nerve to ask for the typewriter —which was sitting there in full view on the table—but they left without it, and several days later Crane's friend went out and bought him another. Yes, Williams wrote Jane Heap, he wanted to meet this fascinating woman.

That would be fine, the answer came back. But at the moment the Baroness was confined in the Women's House of Detention (down in the Village) on a charge of petty larceny—some shoplifting she'd been arrested for. The Baroness wrote Williams a note and asked him to come on down and bail her out, which he promptly did, and then took her to a small restaurant nearby on Sixth Avenue and 8th Street for breakfast. He was struck by her. She was, it turned out, an authentic baroness, stranded in New York when her husband, rather than serve in the German Army when World War I started, had decided instead to blow his brains out. She was extraordinary, this woman, with her black lipstick and teats akimbo with empty sardine cans sitting across from him, speaking to him with a strong guttural German accent of everything in the world, exactly as it came into her head, as she wolfed down her food. Williams was thirty-five then and she was ten years older, though Williams was sure from the way life had treated her that she was at least fifty. But what struck him most forcefully was that here, in front of him, in the flesh, was the mythic Old Woman he had portrayed in "The Wanderer" five years before, "Ominous, old, painted— / With bright lips, and lewd Jew's eyes / Her might strapped in by a corset / To give her age youth." She was, moreover, the very incarnation of dadaism itself.

"He looked into her eyes and she into his across the Atlantic Ocean–white porcelain table," Williams wrote two years after the immense event, remembering that "she talked and he listened till their heads melted together and went up in a vermillion balloon through the ceiling drawing Europe and America after them." Here was the hag-ridden soul of a potentially decadent America in the flesh, living in a filthy and disgusting cold-water flat in the city. He remembered when he went to see her, climbing the wooden stairs and walking down the musty hall-way, seeing her there in the gray, sodden light of a rainy spring day with her three mongrels, two of them copulating there on the bedcovers. He had written to her that she had excited his imagination with her uninhibited manners, and that he loved her. For she was the soul of his wandering grandmother, the woman too who had refused his help in his "Portrait of a Woman in Bed." And when he had gone to kiss her in greeting, she had taken his lips between her broken, jagged teeth and bit-ten down hard, holding him like that until he had tasted her—it was like the taste of poi. Then they had sat and talked, while Williams had kept his distance. The Baroness, he claimed, had offered him a covenant: make love with her, let her give him the flowering gift of syphilis, and let his inhibitions melt away, leaving only the flame of his art. He eased away to the door and made it down the stairs. Then she began sending him letters, hundreds of them, Williams said, but he responded only that he did not want to make love with her. It became a comedy of errors, and it even "flashed across his mind that they might possibly get the act put on at The Palace."

It became especially hilarious when she came out to Rutherford after him. One night a man had called begging the doctor to please come down to see his child who was very sick. Williams walked down the back steps, across to his garage, and got into his car, only to have someone grab him hard from the back with the words, "Villiam Carlos Villiams, I vant you." It was the Baroness. He struggled with her, and then she punched him in the head, Keystone Cops variety. When a policeman on the beat walked by, asking the doctor if he was all right, the Baroness fled into the night. Williams told him to let her alone.

Still, he bought himself a punching bag after that episode and practiced punching it with real relish in his cellar, waiting for her to try something again. And when she attacked again that fall "about six o'clock one evening on Park Avenue," Williams "flattened her with a stiff punch to the mouth," and then had her arrested. As she was taken off to jail, she shouted back at him, "What are you in this town? Napoleon?" Only when she promised to leave him alone was she released. For a while things subsided, and the Baroness turned instead to the memory of her dead husband, writing poem after poem instead to him. But when she came after Williams again, he wrote telling her that she was a "damned stinking old woman," and a "dirty old bitch."[143]

He was comic, flippant, cruel when he talked about the Baroness, but he really did admire her ability to survive and to eat life whole. But he could not, *could not*, bring himself to go to bed with her, even though some of his New York "friends" evidently nudged him in that direction, or dared him outright to do it. In fact, he felt guilty about it, and wondered if indeed he were not simply too middle-class, too safe, too unadventurous. Whatever it was, he had to keep his distance. Later, in 1921, he gave her two hundred dollars to help her get out of New York and return to Europe. But that money was stolen by a go-between. Then Williams gave her another two hundred and she went, living for a while with a German newspaperboy in depression-racked Berlin and, when she began to deteriorate physically, she moved with some Frenchman into a Paris tenement. There, on December 14, 1927, the French boyfriend left her sleeping, turned on all the gas cocks on the kitchen stove, closed the door, and left her to die.

When Williams heard about the death of the Baroness, he wrote to Jane Heap in Paris to find out whether she had died of natural causes or whether she had taken her own life. It did not occur to him at that point that someone had killed her. She was, he told Jane Heap then, a "carnivorous beast as timid as a rabbit." It was a loss to have her gone, but he also had to admit that he felt relieved. Then he admitted how he really felt. "What the hell," he said, "she had a rare gift. I never thought her insane. This is ridiculous, talking this way." But he tried a private improvisation on the Baroness' death after he read Djuna Barnes's note and the Baroness' sensitive letters to Barnes in the February 1928 issue of *transition*. The Baroness' letters, he wrote, were like a thin music, evoking the "dead face in *transition* of the woman, smiling, in the mind." And yet she too was "old and unreasonable like his grandmother." That was on February 28. Six days later he added: "She revolted me, frightened me, beat me finally—out of a necessity which I could not recognize." He could not—as she had taunted him when she reviewed in dadaesque fashion his *Kora in Hell* in *The Little Review* in 1921—get through his own sexual abhorrence of her and so give her himself. For if she was obscene, she also had a purity about her, "a clean flesh of full color & life." And again, on March 11, he came back to her memory, trying to put his finger on his own failure with regard to her. Was he, as his so-called friends insisted, nothing more than a middle-class bourgeois poet, living comfortably on "Rich Road," as the Baroness had once taunted him? Was he nothing more than a respectable doctor and husband and father who might allow himself a few hours of satyr's dancing on a Friday night in New York before driving back home?

What was the truth?

"It can fairly be said," he wrote, trying in that way to objectify himself, hold himself at a distance,

> It can fairly be said that I chose my environment. It can be said that I chose it in order to keep myself from going too far, as a brake to the great

liberalities. No. I have done what seemed closest, most needful, most immediately significant to me. I have worked where it seemed most profitable to me not from the cash viewpoint but from the point of view that I did not want to slight the material means of my writing since I believed that it all goes back to the character center . . . and some were . . . playing with themselves in ways I didn't admire. Let them. I wanted to work. Damned if I'd ask anybody for anything.

The Baroness, then, had been a clandestine faker after all, though there was also, of course, much good in her. She had been "a great field of cultured bounty in spite of her psychosis, her insanity." She had been "courageous" in doing what she wanted "to an insane degree." But he could not, he said again, go to bed with her. What he wanted finally from women was not sex but talk, although he was aware that the fever of sexuality sometimes intruded itself between himself and the woman and had to be gone through to get beyond its insistencies. It was, after all, the "serenity" of morning beyond the "sexual tropics" that he most desired. He had been able to resist the Baroness' advances, finally, but he also knew how mean a boast that sounded even now.[144]

*
* *

By the summer of 1919, Williams knew that the real effectiveness of *Others* had gone long ago. It had become just another little magazine, still managing from time to time to get some good work into print, though its cutting edge had been dulled since 1916. Better therefore to kill it altogether, now, to let it die with dignity than to go gasping on and on in a moribund state, being published whenever Kreymborg could pull enough money together for one more issue. So, when Kreymborg asked Williams to edit two more issues in July and August, Williams decided to give *Others* the coup de grace quickly, in the July issue, and forget any August number.

He did this in an editorial essay he called "Belly Music" at the close of the final number. "I am in the field," he wrote, "against the stupidity of the critics writing in this country today." He singled them out—the influential figures of the moment—like a Jacobin lining them up on the scaffold: John Gould Fletcher for his "polite nonsense," the "sullen backbiting of A.C.H., as if sand had gone to her head," the "vacuities of an [Louis] Untermeyer controversy," the "assininity" of Reedy's *Mirror*, the "ataxic drivel of Sandburg's *Liars*," Amy Lowell's "ginger pop criticism" in *Poetry*. He lashed out at *The Midland, The Pagan, The Lyric*, at Stanley Braithwaite's annual anthologies. Only one newspaper literary supplement had any life at all in it: Geoffrey Parson's Sunday column in the *New York Tribune*. The rest were useless. What in hell were critics mooning about? Loveliness, nature, the young leaves in springtime, H. L. Davis' tepid "Songs" from his *Primapara*? Oh, they were good enough in their own way, Williams admitted, but leaves were also "little engines which make the tree go." The true artist had yet to be taken seriously in this country, for he wrote "to assert himself above every machine and every mechanical conception that seeks to bind him." And H. L. Mencken, with his flippant remarks that every poet had worked out his vein by the time he was Keats's age and should thereafter be killed. What was that kind of talk but "the braying of a superficial jackass"?

The English too: H.D.'s husband, Richard Aldington, defending his wife's classical sonorities at the expense of the harsher discords of modernism. No, Williams insisted, it was not a matter of choosing Villon's Fat Margaret to some "myrrh-tressed Heliodora." It was not a matter of returning to the classics only in their more sonorous visions of beauty and truth, but of remembering the harsher discords the Greeks had also been aware of. His friend Emanuel Carnevali had been wrong to insist that scientific truth and technique had hamstrung poetry. On the contrary, it was imperative to realize what Copernicus and Columbus had discovered. Rather, what made a poet great was not "the weight of loveliness in his meters," but the extent "to which he is aware of his time." And when he looked around at the little magazines for some sign of a razor's edge intelligence, he saw only *The Little Review.* At least that was not a ragbag, at least there Anderson and Heap had a purpose in what they selected and rejected.

"I began when I was twenty," Williams added now, turning to assess himself at thirty-five. "I BEGAN then. *Others* saw its inception when I was thirty, when I had already proved a failure time after time. And yet I sing. And if my voice is cracked at least no one can HEAR singing as I can. . . . There IS a way to come through the loss of youth or first youth and the loss of love and the loss of everything." And that was art, as he had so bitterly learned. There was his voice (cracked), and there was his friend Pound's "discordant shrieking," insisting that American poetry not be equated with dithyrambic paeans about these United States "and the plains and the Sierra Nevadas for their horses' vigor," but rather with a new voice and new forms. Pound, Williams insisted, had the "smell" of that new voice even though the man was writing three thousand miles away from New York in London.

But who was *he,* this wild voice excluded from the most reputable anthologies of the day, who was *he* to lash out against the academic and critical establishment of his day? "Perhaps I am a sullen suburbanite, cowardly and alone," he admitted. "I sit a blinded fool, with withered hands stretched out into the nothingness around me." And yet who else was willing to lead the bayonet charge across the no-man's-land of America? Was Aiken willing to do it? Was Amy Lowell? After all, what were their criticisms but isolated perceptions of certain values, puling testiness, benign igorance? "Where is a man," he demanded, "who has a head for smashing through underbrush" instead of lying belly down as the critics' shrapnel exploded overhead?

There were critics by the dozens who could take potshots at poets experimenting with free verse forms, but where was the critic who could point out what was good and necessary in the new poetry? For free verse, whatever its shortcomings, had been a necessity, Williams insisted, since it was the ONLY form where modern thought and a modern music began to meet, the only form that could carry the new meaning "that is imperatively required today." In time the philosophers and theologians and other abstract thinkers would follow the artists' leads in discovering the meaning of the modernist experiment, but the artist would have to be the one to first discover the imaginative forms that could contain that new meaning. Now, in 1919, what Williams wanted was a poetry that could discuss the desolate present he saw everywhere around him. He did not, for God's sake, want a poetry about the latest aircraft (as Pound too had said), but a poetry that could fix "the distraught mind that must find its release in building planes." What was it, after all, about the modern American mind that made it think it could find peace or safety or refuge in fighter aircraft, in the chimerical conquest of space and time? (It was exactly the question another American poet was asking at the same time: Hart Crane.)

Williams had looked to the intellectuals of the day for answers, but he had found them also wanting. Only John Dewey, whose essays Williams was reading in *The Dial*, might be of help, but Dewey had effectively shut the door against him when he'd said that he was interested only in his own field of specialization, only in philosophy and not in the artist. Now that kind of attitude was as bad, Williams insisted, as the attitude of the professor who was ignorant of the excellent work other professors were doing right "across the quadrangle" from him. He was calling, then, on Dewey especially to force or shame his associates on *The Dial* into making some intelligent decisions about modern American poetry. Especially now that he was in the act of torpedoing *Others*, Williams needed *The Dial* to offer an adequate forum to the new poetry that it might say what it had to say. He ended by admitting his own inadequacies as a spokesman for the American poet. He knew he did not have enough information, that he could be too elliptical, even too vague at times. He also knew he was not always fair in his judgments, favoring some and damning others. After all, he was a poet and a full-time physician. But the "cooler" brains with their "wider fund of information," on the other hand, had not been found to lead the charge, and so Williams had tried to do what he could under the circumstances, to emphasize at least what had to be done, even as *Others* finally went under.[145]

Williams continued his preoccupation with poetic form and the blindness of the critics in two reviews he wrote for the September and October issues of *The Little Review*. In the first, "Four Foreigners," he attacked the war poems of D. H. Lawrence and Richard Aldington because their metrical forms failed to "realize the actuality of life and death" in the trenches. Because he himself had not been in the front lines, he added, he had left the subject of the war to those others who had been there. James Joyce's and Dorothy Richardson's poems, however, which he'd read in the same issue of *Poetry* (July) that carried Lawrence and Aldington, had succeeded in what they were doing because there a world—their world—*had* been realized on the page.[146] And in "More Swill" he compared artists to front-line soldiers and the critics to armchair civilians. Williams would try to dance with the corpse of a critic as long as he could, he said, but he was convinced that there was finally "no transition between critic and artist," that a man might "be one, then the other, but never one within the other." All the criticism in the world, in short, couldn't tell a poet how to write a successful poem.[147]

Williams had opened the final issue of *Others* with special praise for the work of a young poet named Emanuel Carnevali, a twenty-one-year-old Northern Italian who had come to the United States at the beginning of World War I to escape conscription. Carnevali had worked in Chicago and New York in whatever jobs he could find, most of them as a dishwasher in small Italian restaurants, while he wrote in an orotund style in the English language he had adopted for his own. But in 1919 Carnevali's fortunes were already on the downswing, and Williams saw Carnevali as an apt symbol of the stale lie and living death the *Others* movement had become. Hadn't Williams become estranged from Kreymborg by then? And hadn't Maxwell Bodenheim, whose promise a short time before had seemed so great, become the purveyor of stale literary essays? The *Others* vortex was irretrievably gone now, and now Carnevali, already beginning to shake with the encephalitis that was destroying him, was going. Williams had wanted to edit the man's poems, weed them, correct their faulty English and make them flower, but Carnevali had refused. He didn't trust technique.

Well, Williams admitted, Carnevali was right. How doctor up a sick man, "filled with death" and living in a "city of stasis" like New York? And then there was the *Dial* business. Conrad Aiken, *The Dial's* editor, had asked Carnevali for an essay on Papini and had then returned Carnevali's essay as unacceptable. So, when several members of the *Others* group had descended on the *Dial* offices demanding some kind of justice for Carnevali, Carnevali himself had let go, as one member of *The Dial* had phrased it, with a "flood of profane vituperation upon the head of Mr. Clarence Britton of *The Dial* staff." To such an ignominious end had *Others* come by 1919 in that "rubbish heap" of a capital called New

York. Better to kill *Others* off altogether and thus save some vestige of Carnevali's dignity than let it drag its wounded body along, Williams reasoned.[148]

By the end of June Carnevali was back in Chicago working as an associate on the staff of *Poetry*. Williams knew Carnevali for only a short time while he was in New York, and he and Floss had gone up to 40th Street and Tenth Avenue to Carnevali's tenement apartment overlooking the freight yards for a homemade meal of polenta and codfish prepared by Carnevali's wife, Emily, and some talk about literature and life in Northern Italy. Emily took care of the house and the two children and made a few dollars teaching French to two young girls, while Emanuel washed dishes in a scummy restaurant. Williams remembered how the man would devour books in the dingy restaurant kitchen and then, to make up for the time he'd spent reading, attack the dishes with a determination and ferocity Williams had never seen equaled. It was out of that experience that Carnevali would write *A Hurried Man* in the mid-1920s, the one good book he ever managed to write.[149]

Williams apparently met Carnevali at Lola Ridge's apartment in the late spring of 1919, and Carnevali himself remembered that meeting with genuine fondness. "He was a most lovely man," Carnevali would write from a charity hospital bed in Bazzano, Italy—outside Bologna—by which time his tense, athletic body was shaking so violently that Kay Boyle would remember how much of an effort it was for Carnevali to get a single sentence down on paper, much less his memoirs. To Carnevali, Williams was a strange man, a big boy in many ways (despite the fact that he himself was sixteen years younger than Williams), even "naive" and certainly more boyish than those "lovely, earnest, almost-grave children" of his.

So taken was he with Carnevali, that Williams had invited him to come out with his family and stay a few days at 9 Ridge Road. Carnevali remembered going out with Williams in Williams' Ford "over the hills to pick wild flowers with a quantity of earth attached to them," and how Williams had "transplanted them into his back-yard with a hope that they would thrive there." He had noticed how modest Williams really was and how hard it must have been for him to read his own poems in public, which was probably why he did it with a slightly self-mocking "deprecatory twang in his voice." Carnevali loved those poems in spite of what Williams did to them, loved them because they were "full of surprises and white and powerful and true and beautiful." But he remembered another side of Williams too: how his face could become "fierce" and very "unbeautiful from some inner struggle." As for all the talk going around even then of Williams' supposed sexual exploits, Carnevali was convinced that it was all exaggerated, for the man was essentially as "chaste as a virgin, delicately chaste, elusively so, in fact."[150]

For his part, what Williams liked most about Carnevali was his outspokenness, the way he said what was on his mind without worrying whose feelings he might be hurting. For, besides the *Dial* affair, there had also been Carnevali's long speech that night at Lola Ridge's in the spring of 1919 when he'd attacked some of the New York coterie for their preoccupation with technique instead of with the "soul" of poetry. Carnevali had directed his shrill, half-crazed attack against Bodenheim and Kreymborg and Ridge and Williams himself, and Williams himself had loved it. Jesus, this kid, fresh from Italy and Chicago, was good! So he couldn't write poems, so what? At least he was "wide open" and "out-of-doors" and did "not look through the window." The older poets, like himself, did after all seek "the seclusion of a style, of a technique," as Carnevali had claimed, making "replicas of the world we live in and we live in them and not in the world." How he needed this young man now of all times with *Others* gone and nothing to replace the void. "Jesus," he cried, "Jesus save Carnevali for me." But Williams knew it was already too late, and that Carnevali was already slipping away from him.[151]

When Carnevali was offered a place on the staff of *Poetry* in June, he went out to Chicago and left his family behind in New York until such time as he could be settled. But there was trouble already stirring, for Carnevali had forced his wife to admit—actually to confess—to him that she had been unfaithful to him, and now he was doubly eager to get away from her. Emily wrote, pleading with him, but Carnevali first ignored her and then wrote to say that he had a destiny to fulfill as a writer and that she and the children would only be in the way. She should forget him, and perhaps some day she might even be able to forgive him.

Floss, who really cared for Emily and always felt protective toward the wives of temperamental artists, took Emily to stay with her for a month at the farm in Monroe, until Emily could locate work in California and settle there with the children.[152] As for poor Carnevali, the outbursts he'd manifested in New York became aggravated after a short time in Chicago. He was diagnosed as a case of encephalitis (although Williams had always suspected syphilis himself), and as the uncontrolled trembling in Carnevali's whole body became worse and Carnevali became more violent in his actions, he had to be institutionalized. At first he was placed in the psychopathic ward in Chicago's St. Luke's Hospital. But by 1922 he had to be sent back to Italy in his father's custody, where he was placed in a poverty-level charity ward in Bazzano. Both Emily and Carnevali continued writing to Williams, and Williams, like his friends Pound and Harriet Monroe and Robert McAlmon, continued to support Carnevali well into the 1930s. But Carnevali, though he struggled to go on with his writings, grew progressively worse. He died during the Second World War, probably in 1942, in near total poverty, a ward of the state, by choking on a piece of dry bread. It was a pathetic ending, but for a few years Carnevali had made his mark on modernism. It was a legacy of sorts.

*
* *

With the last issue of *Others* behind him, Williams began to wonder when Edmund Brown was going to bring his *Improvisations* out. He had decided finally on calling his book *Kora in Hell*, remembering something he and Pound had once talked about: the descent of Persephone into hell, to return in the flowering springtime. He was going to send Brown some copies of *The Tempers* that had been sitting in his attic for the past six years to let him sell them, he wrote Brown on July 11. So much for business. In the meantime he was on vacation, "surrounded by oval wash basin, double lipped, rococo handled, grooved bellied water pitcher, and piss-pot all white and pink, pink-leaved and stemmed pink poppies, bird's eye maple dresser, beclapboared [sic] walls and ceiling nicely weathered . . . living with wife and children in two rooms near the shore and the weather is fine." Sonny had just walked into his room "with a kitten's face under his chin: both have the same colored grey eyes."[153] It was a pastoral interlude, and he even felt good about Brown for the moment.

But when, that Thanksgiving, Williams had still not received galleys, he wrote to Conrad Aiken at Yarmouth asking him to please find out what the hell was holding Brown up. "I am sorry to have to come bellyaching to you after calling you names in print," he told Aiken, alluding to the "Belly Music" piece, "but I'm up against it and I can think of no one who can help me but yourself."[154] By the time Aiken had written inviting Williams up to his place to talk with Brown himself, Williams had heard from Brown's agent that he would be receiving proof, as he phrased it, "a week ago."[155] Williams read the proof through not once but twice, wanting to make sure there were as few errors as possible—once in December and again in February—and he was still making changes all through April. In spite of all this, the *Improvisations* were not published until September 1920. And by then Williams had already collected enough new poems for another book.

After a series of sorties, attacks, and retreats from his "friends" from *Others*, Williams saw 1919 go out quietly. By then he had called a truce with Bodenheim, who wrote Aiken in mid-December that he'd just had a long talk with Williams out at 9 Ridge Road. *Others* was truly dead, beyond recall, and Kreymborg was blaming Williams for killing it. Some of the staff at *The Dial* were still not talking to the scattered ragtag remnants of the *Others* crowd, who had decided, as Bodenheim phrased it, "to conserve our energy for our creations and remain perpetually aloof from the whole papier-mâché turmoil in which your fellow poets tickled you with tin swords when your back was turned, and grinned" when you turned around. For his part, Williams was still upset with Kreymborg for losing his only copy of his play, *The Apple Tree,* and he could no longer trust the man's smile "which never failed to cover a throng of unannounced designs." The only thing for it was to stay away from one's fellow poets for a while and mingle with outsiders of the sacred art. "We wound up the evening by cursing the day when we first started to write poetry and unconsciously took a short cut into the mercies of diplomatic intrigue." Still, as Bodenheim theatrically phrased it, they knew they were both doomed to be artists and would "probably write a little more of the damn stuff before we die."[156]

Williams himself rounded off the year with a big party for all the old survivors of the past five years. He wrote Viola Jordan to come out on December 28, the Sunday after Christmas, to join "a mob of Tahitians . . . from Brooklyn." He told her about a black patient of his who had served with the U.S. Army in France and had managed to sleep not only with a beautiful French girl but with her mother as well. Lucky man![157] With Marianne Moore he was more restrained. He had been writing "hasty and lewd letters" to the *Others* crowd, he said, "in which you seem so out of place—so in place, like a red berry still hanging to the jaded rose bush—that now I feel chastened." He promised her only tea and sacramental wine to drink, that she might cross the Jersey "meadows with an easy mind."[158] After all, Prohibition would go into effect three weeks later, on January 16, 1920. It was time to drink while you could—even if it was only sacramental wine.

Nineteen twenty saw a curve of depression for Williams, followed by the swirl of a new vortex and new interests at year's end. That May Bodenheim had written Williams that he and his wife were leaving for London and that he no longer held any pleasant memories of Williams. "Like all exuberant megalomaniacs," he added, "you have been ever the first to hurl the charge of self-centeredness at me." It was clear to Bodenheim that Williams preferred Kreymborg's "sweetly optimistic" flatteries, or the shrewd bargainings of a Saphier, or a Carnevali or a Lola Ridge. Well, now Williams could have that whole crowd from *Others* for himself. He was on his way to Europe.[159]

As for Alfred Kreymborg, by that point he was in Los Angeles enjoying himself and sending chatty notes to Williams which attempted to cover over the realization that something had soured in their relationship. How much that friendship had deteriorated Kreymborg really learned only when Williams dedicated *Sour Grapes* to him.

Williams was to say years later that sour grapes after all had the same shape as sweet grapes, meaning that poems with harsh dissonances and unpromising subjects were still after all poems. But the "joke" was a private one between Kreymborg and himself: it was a tart good-by to that *Others* vortex, to the claustrophobia of coteries, to the man who had sold out to Edna St. Vincent Millay. Williams was now on his own.[160]

*
* *

No sooner had Brown published *Kora in Hell* than Williams wrote him quite matter-of-factly that he needed another book of verse and wanted it soon, by the following spring, in fact. He was a damn fool to rush things so, he admitted, but then Brown too was a fool to work with him. The fact was, he confessed, that he wanted the poems he'd collected over the past six years off his chest and away from him so that he might get on to new work. Yes, he expected to have to pay again, but only if Brown moved faster than he had last time.[161] Brown of course still had hundreds of unsold copies of *Al Que Quiere!* to move, as well as the copies of *The Tempers* Williams had sent him, so he did not respond to Williams' new request with any great enthusiasm. It was not until the following February, therefore, that Williams bothered to send the sheaf of poems for his new book with the working title *Picture Poems*.

In the meantime he waited for word on the reception of his *Improvisations*. One person he did not have to wait long to hear from was Ezra Pound, whom Williams had called in print the "best enemy United States verse" had. Pound retorted in kind: "That I sweated like a nigger to break up the clutch of the old. . . . That I tried to enlighten that silly old she-ass, Harriet Monroe. . . . That I sent over French models. . . . That I imported U.S. stuff here." Was this the work of the enemy? He knew Jepson's shortcomings, but he insisted that Jepson had performed a valuable service in waking up Monroe. He struck out too at H.D.—"that refined, charming, and utterly narrow-minded she-bard." He let go a glancing shot at Marianne Moore for her "spinsterly aversion" to "tutto che non me piace." And as for Amy Lowell: her "perfumed cat-piss wd. be putrid even if it had been done by a pueblo indian." But Pound had been sharp enough to pick out of a nation as corrupt as the U.S. (where individual liberties like having a drink were slowly going illegal) the work of Bodenheim and Mina Loy and Sandburg and Frost and even Williams himself. Hell, Williams was no American like poor T. S. Eliot, with the poisoned blood of that vast, stupefied country coursing through his veins. No, Williams was an outsider and belonged, really, because of his "slower mental processes" and late development, to a later generation, whose real impact, therefore, would be felt only as time went on. As for the *Improvisations* themselves: Pound thought them the best work Williams had so far done, and no more incoherent than what Rimbaud had effected in *Un Saison en Enfer*. It was too bad, he added, that "the two halves of what might have made a fairly decent poet should be sequestered and divided by the . . . buttocks of the arse-wide Atlantic.''[162]

One of the New York crowd who survived the transition from *Others* to Williams' new interests in the early 1920s was Lola Ridge, who for a time had edited Kreymborg's magazine. Both Williams and Floss remembered her with fondness as a woman given over completely to the intellectual life and the radical leftist politics of New York. Her concern was with the oppressed masses, and many figures of the Left, like John Reed and his wife and later the Russian poet Mayakovsky, met at her apartment at 7 East 14th Street in the Village. From mid-1919 till mid-1921, and then again from the end of 1924 till the end of 1926, Ridge held parties for the writers and painters and radical thinkers in that New York ambience with an attention that verged for Williams on a religious commitment. It was here in the summer of 1919 that he had first met Emanuel Carnevali and it was here, too, probably in July 1920, that he met a young man fresh from Chicago and the Midwest who was to remain one of his closest friends for the next thirty years: Robert McAlmon. McAlmon was twenty-four at the time and Williams thirty-six, but in spite of their age difference, the two men took an instant liking to one another.

Williams' friend, the painter Marsden Hartley, had brought McAlmon along with him to Ridge's, having found him in one of the studio art classes at Cooper Union, posing in the nude for a dollar an hour for nine hours a day. McAlmon had been living on a garbage scow in New York harbor because the rent was cheaper there, and was waiting to make contact with the New York crowd. Hartley himself, "tortured," as Williams phrased it, by his own homosexuality, had taken McAlmon under his wing and shown him the sights of New York from a trolley car. Suddenly, as McAlmon told the story, Hartley had grabbed McAlmon's hand and begun to smother it with kisses. McAlmon, caught off guard, retracted his hand: so that was what New York was like! Williams himself would later describe how once, having gone to Hartley's apartment at 351 West 15th Street to see him after a particularly grueling session of lectures in one of the New York clinics, he had lain back on Hartley's sofa only to have Hartley make an advance, which he had to cut short. Hartley was an intensely lonely man, Williams remembered, and it was a loneliness intensified by his having to sleep with his head to a thin wall, on the other side of which a young couple could be heard nightly making love.[163] Williams vividly remembered the night he met McAlmon at Ridge's. Hartley had read one of his own poems, "On the Hills of Caledonia," and Marianne Moore had read one of hers: "Those Various Scalpels." Suddenly, he caught McAlmon's hard, steely blue eyes. The man had a tough, wiry build, he remembered, "such a build as might have served for the original of Donatello's youthful Medici in armor in the niche of the Palazzo Vecchio" which Williams had seen ten years before.[164]

McAlmon kept his background purposely blurred, perhaps to make as little as possible of his rather solidly middle-class origin. He had been the last of ten children of a Presbyterian minister and his wife, and had been born in Clifton, Kansas, in March 1896. When his father died in 1917, McAlmon had followed his mother to Los Angeles and enrolled as a desultory student at the fledgling University of Southern California. He joined the army in March 1918, hoping to see some action in Europe, but instead he'd merely been assigned to the air corps and sent for flight training to Rockwell Field in San Diego. He was to tell Williams and others that he'd served with a Canadian regiment during the war, but the mundane truth was that he had spent most of his time editing the air corps's newspaper in San Diego.[165] After the armistice in November, he went back to Los Angeles, picked up his college courses again, and edited a magazine about flying called *The Ace,* for which he wrote some poems, articles, and even editorials. More important, Harriet Monroe published six of his poems on flying in the March 1919 issue of *Poetry.* He also started a correspondence with Emanuel Carnevali, who was by then back in Chicago, and whose work McAlmon had read in *Poetry* with deep admiration. So, when McAlmon finally decided that he'd had enough of Los Angeles (he was already on probation at the university), he boarded a train for Chicago to finally meet Carnevali. What he saw, of course, was a man already sick, confined to St. Luke's psychopathic ward, and given to violent outbursts. Moreover, by 1920 the real force of *Poetry* and the Chicago renaissance were already things of the past. So McAlmon boarded the train again and headed further east for New York and the Village.

It was McAlmon who first broached the subject to Williams of starting a new little magazine with him now that *Others* was finished. Sure there were other little magazines already available, like Thayer's *The Dial* and Matthew Josephson's *Broom,* but McAlmon was interested in something else, something new. Like Carnevali, he too distrusted "literature" and even distrusted people like Lola Ridge for their liberal championing of the oppressed masses without themselves ever having experienced firsthand the lives of the poor. And the more he talked with Williams about the necessity for writing about one's own place in one's own idiom straightforwardly, without obeisance to European models, the more he realized that Williams was his man.

McAlmon was serious about the new venture. He used his own hard-earned money to finance the new magazine—*Contact* it was called—and the money came from what he earned as a model or working that

summer on one of the Long Island estates. He had the sheets mimeographed and got one of his girl friends to collate and staple the pages.
Williams supplied the paper—a cheap foolscap provided by his father-in-
law from his printing business (a ton of it, which was to last Williams
thirty years)—wrote to his friends for contributions, and helped McAlmon write *Contact*'s manifesto—that is, the manifesto's more coherent
passages. In the half year between December 1920 and the summer of '21,
four issues of the magazine appeared, followed by a fifth and final number
two years later in June 1923. Despite its unpropitious beginnings, it
managed to print the current work of Williams, McAlmon, Pound,
Stevens, Marianne Moore, H.D., Kay Boyle, Glenway Wescott, and others.
"We will be American," the initial manifesto read in part, in McAlmon's
half-literate journeyman prose, "because we are of America; racial or
international as the contactual realizations of those whose work we
publish have been these." Or, as Williams added: "For native work in
verse, fiction, criticism or whatever is written we mean to maintain a
place, insisting on that which we have not found insisted upon before, the
essential contact between words and the locality that breeds them, in this
case America."[166]

Besides poems, Williams contributed several comments and essays to
Contact, including his essay in the second number on Matisse's 1907 *The
Blue Nude,* which he reacquainted himself with when he visited the
DeZayas Gallery in New York in December 1920. This essay represented
the kind of thing Williams was after in *Contact.* He wanted to present the
new, the really new, to an American audience. In this case it was French
painting he wanted his countrymen to see. He wanted them to view this
French woman, lying in that French grass, as a creative act, an object of
beauty, her nudity a natural phenomenon and not something to be
viewed in peekaboo fashion, salaciously, in a country where one now had
to drink in the secrecy of one's home or in speakeasies. The heaviness he
was feeling over the torpidity into which American art had once more
settled by the end of 1920 is suggested in a letter he wrote his friend, the
struggling writer Alva Turner, at the end of October, when he mentioned
that he was about to father a new magazine to replace *Others.* "Stupidity
is powerful here as elsewhere," he complained. "It is my own fault. I will
not concede anything to anyone. I will not even work. I do what there is
to do without imagination. . . . I am drowned in triviality, stupidity, my
own heaviness, everything. . . . I have just thrashed my youngest son for
spitting in his nurse's lap. What in God's name is one to do?"[167]

And to Ezra Pound he wrote just after the New Year to tell him that
the first issue of *Contact* was finally out: "I am nearly crazy with paying
attention to halves and quarters (not dollars!)—broken pieces of men that
have me sick trying to patch something up out of the mess." He was still

trying to write but he had to keep from becoming sentimentally involved in what after all were little machine pieces, for he still fell from time to time into the piano strings as he played. He would probably learn to keep his aesthetic distance as a worker of words, but he admitted it was going to take "time—time—time." In the meantime, it was best to accept the "apparition" of this new magazine as "something" and "blot it down as a dog does with dirty feet," or as a poet might stain a clean sheet of paper with type.

How goddamned tired of America he was just now. And how he missed Ezra, missed Europe. "I wish I were in Paris with you tonight," he confessed. "I am a damned fool who sees only the light through a knothole." How he remembered those old talks with Ez in Wyncote and Rutherford, "moments of intense happiness." No, it wasn't happiness, but something else, something that had helped sustain him in the fog of America. God, but the times were pure "bile."[168] What had happened to all that early promise he thought he'd seen for his country? What had it all come to for him at the beginning of the 1920s? A few mimeographed pages stapled together, meant to bring himself into contact with his new world. What a joke!

A few weeks later he wrote in the second issue of *Contact* that from what he could see America had degenerated to "a bastard country where decomposition is the prevalent spectacle," though the contour of that decomposition did not strike him as "particularly dadaesque," as decomposition surely was in Europe, and that therefore simply overlaying dadaism on American subjects would not get to the gist of America's particular pathology. The truth was that Americans understood neither foreign work nor their own except in some vague, blurred fashion, like the flickering of images on the "constantly wavering screen" of the movie houses. First let Americans understand the local culture, the local field of action, and then they might begin to understand what in fact a Picasso or a de Gourmont were holding out to America. Otherwise, here was the danger of borrowing the wrong things, like the wholehearted acceptance of dadaism by the bohemian radical fringes without their understanding what had given rise to dadaism in the first place.[169] Over the next thirty years Williams would return to this subject with increasing insistence, his shrillness becoming more noticeable as his despair over his country's indifference to an indigenous culture became ever more apparent.

For a while, then, in the fall of 1920 and the winter of '21, Williams had someone he could trust to understand what he was after in terms of an American culture. He and McAlmon met often during these months, and Matthew Josephson remembered them together one wintry Sunday afternoon in January, when Josephson and his friend Kenneth Burke joined the two of them for a long walk through the New Jersey countryside. Josephson had interviewed Williams in December for the Newark *Ledger*, and had written Burke about the meeting. He liked Williams, he told Burke, and remarked on his "faun's ears, small, triangular, the most uncanny ears you ever saw. He is very much alive, and is publishing a little magazine of his own named *Contact*." He wanted Burke to meet Williams and so had arranged the Sunday jaunt.

Josephson recalled that meeting with Williams and McAlmon, when Williams told him the story of how he'd first met McAlmon and the story of the Baroness, as they tramped about the New Jersey countryside, heading finally for a tavern in Newark Williams knew about where they served decent bootleg beer. The four of them talked of *Contact* as they walked past landscapes out of the Ashcan School, "through mean streets of the industrial suburbs, past dilapidated factories and warehouses, grimy railway yards, coal bunkers, and mountains of rubble and tin cans; in short, one of the ugliest and most blighted areas in all America." And now, with this Warren Gamaliel Harding fellow about to assume the presidency of the country, Josephson was getting ready to clear the hell out and head for Europe like his compatriots. Burke and Josephson listened to McAlmon—who was making it clear enough that he wasn't too crazy about these eastern aesthetes he was sharing with Williams—as he gave his "tough guy" talk about American culture and his imminent marriage to the daughter of one of England's wealthiest businessmen. McAlimony: that should have been his name.[170]

The surface story of McAlmon's marriage to Annie Winifred Ellerman (Bryher, as she dubbed herself, after one of the Scilly Isles off the coast of Cornwall) reads like something out of the yellow press of the American tabloids of the period. And in fact, the story did hit those papers, which went so far as to hire actors to play the roles of Bryher and McAlmon, so that they might be more easily "photographed" in scenes of newfound domestic bliss, American style. H.D., whose marriage to Aldington had ended in separation, had been taken under Bryher's wing after Aldington's desertion and the birth of H.D.'s only child, Perdita. That had been in the summer of 1919, and Bryher had taken H.D. and Perdita with her to Greece to help nurse H.D. back to some semblance of health and sanity following her multiple losses during the war: her brother killed, her father dead, a first child lost, a husband gone. Then H.D. and Bryher had sailed to the United States, stopping off in New York on September 10, 1920, en route to taking up residence together in Los Angeles. H.D. had written Williams to come into New York and take tea with her at the Belmont Hotel and meet her friend, Bryher, and Williams had brought McAlmon along with him.

Williams disliked Bryher almost at once. He remembered her only as a "small, dark English girl with piercing intense eyes," and then he chose to forget her.[171] He could also see how things stood between the two women. But McAlmon, for all his tough-guy mask, was obviously struck by Bryher, though how struck Williams did not realize at once. On the following day the women left with the baby for the West Coast, to remain there for the next five months. Williams' memory of these events in the *Autobiography* is badly knotted for complex reasons, his own feelings for H.D. and McAlmon among them, but enough of these narrative threads can be untangled to make a coherent story out of what probably happened, though there is still something very Rashomon about just where the truth of the incident lies.

Clearly McAlmon was deeply interested in Bryher, even though he must have known that the proposal of marriage Bryher made to him was on the order of a business deal: marry her and thus afford her legal freedom from her family to let her come and go as she pleased, visit her parents in England from time to time for the sake of appearances, and then let her continue the life she had chosen to live with H.D. In return, McAlmon would have part of her very substantial allowance that he might live in Europe and pursue the avant-garde life he so much wanted. Why McAlmon married Bryher and she him is known finally to them alone, but McAlmon does seem to have been genuinely attracted to Bryher for her intelligence and spirit, and perhaps he hoped against hope that he could make the marriage work in spite of the odds against it. For his own part, he was always tight-lipped about his feelings, preferring to take his considerable losses in silence, and when Williams wrote about the marriage thirty years later in his *Autobiography*, McAlmon broke off his long friendship with him for good.

On the night of February 13, 1921, the Williamses went to the Brevoort in New York for a private dinner in honor of McAlmon's marriage to Bryher. That had been a quick matter before a justice of the peace in the afternoon. But the party was a giddier, sadder thing. Marianne Moore was there, and Marsden Hartley, and McAlmon's sister, Grace, to represent the family, and of course H.D., whose "complicity" in all this Williams would find it hard to forgive. He had wanted to get Bob something very special for his marriage and going away, and he had gone to Roehrs's greenhouses in East Rutherford to get a box of the rarest orchids he could buy. When Hartley saw them he quipped something about the morning headlines reading POETS PAWING ORCHIDS, expecting Williams to catch the sexual innuendo. Next day, St. Valentine's, the McAlmons, together with H.D. and the baby, sailed aboard the White Star liner *Celtic*, one of Byrher's father's line of ships. Sir John Ellerman had of course reserved the bridal suite for his daughter and her American husband. McAlmon was gone.[172]

On the fifteenth, Williams received a postcard in the mail showing a

scene from Edgar Selwyn's *The Mirage*, a comedy playing then at the
New Times Square Theatre on 42d Street. The picture showed several
actors, men and women both, ecstatically fingering coins in a big money
pot. Williams was sure that the card had been signed, obscurely, D.H.,
and he always believed H.D. had sent it to him as a comment on
McAlmon, though she just as violently denied it. McAlmon for his part
believed her, and thought it had been sent by Scofield Thayer of *The Dial*,
who hated McAlmon. Williams of course needed someone to hand the
blame on for what he considered this travesty of a marriage, and he had
come to believe that H.D. had masterminded the whole thing to get
Bryher for herself. What Williams seems not to have noticed, however, is
that the real initials on the card were not even D.H., but a mysterious
A.H.[173]

Just how hard Williams took McAlmon's loss is difficult to gauge, but
some indication can be gleaned from his telling Burke about a week after
the couple sailed that he was still lamenting McAlmon's "sudden
demise." He'd only met Burke the month before on their New Jersey
walk, he reminded him, so that Burke could have no way of knowing how
he'd "been knocked out by Bob's going away." Burke could not replace
that loss, and certainly not Matty Josephson.[174] Williams even developed
a case of pinkeye shortly after McAlmon left which left him generally
miserable and listless, preferring to think that the "hard work in my
profession" had incapacitated him "for anything but drowsiness." But, he
confessed to Amy Lowell at the beginning of March, he wished he "had
the boy back with me and not lost there abroad, to no good purpose I feel
sure." Were there not enough American expatriates already in Europe
with Pound and Eliot over there? "*The Sacred Wood* is full of them and
their air rifles. But perhaps Bob will do better. He will do better only on
condition that he comes back to America soon." Yes, he really was
"heartbroken."[175]

* *

Something was happening to Williams in 1921 that suggested that not
only had the *Others* group faded into history, but that the *Contact* vortex
he had hoped would replace it had fallen prematurely flat with Bob
McAlmon now joining the mass exodus to the other side of the Atlantic.
In 1920 a number of Americans—mostly New Yorkers—had expressed
their deep-felt resentments against the directions in which they saw
America going: puritanism, Prohibition, big business, Babbittry, a corrupt
central administration. These findings had been voiced in an influential
book edited by Harold Stearns and called *Civilization in the United
States*, and it had appeared at a time when many Americans were seeking
a kind of cultural salvation in Europe, especially along the Left Bank of

Paris. The reasons for doing so were many: culture, a greater return for the dollar in a postwar depressed economy, the chance to escape parental and social restrictions, the chance too to live in a more permissive and exotic society. Whatever their reasons, many of Williams' friends and associates had left the city and were in Europe by the middle of 1921.

"New York is very delightful this fall," Williams wrote wryly to Harriet Monroe on November 20, especially now "with all the neurosis in Paris. One walks the streets in quiet enjoyment knowing there is no one of importance to be met at the next corner."[176] McAlmon, he noted ruefully, was still in Europe, but at least his new friend Kenneth Burke was still "in the land of the free." Burke was coming to replace McAlmon as best he could, though for Williams' taste Burke was too much of an intellectual, too much of an analyzer. He even asked Burke, "Do you think me a fool if I say that at present I find you to be the only interesting character writing in America today?" Paul Rosenfeld the music and literary critic was another New Yorker who was "good in his way," but unlike Burke he had no "flare or flaire or insanity to temper his bricklaying."[177] Burke, though the same age as McAlmon, was about as unlike McAlmon in temperament and learning as possible, and it is not surprising that neither Burke nor McAlmon had liked each other when they had met in Williams' company. Williams knew the mutual antagonisms and shrugged: that was their affair. On top of that, when Burke had taken McAlmon up to Malcolm Cowley's apartment to meet him in January, the proceedings had taken on all the gaiety of a funeral, especially since McAlmon had just rapped Cowley in *The Little Review*.[178]

But from Williams' point of view, both McAlmon and Burke had something valuable to teach him. Initially, Burke—who was then twenty-three—had been important because he represented for Williams the kind of criticism he had called for in "Belly Music" and in the *Contact* manifestos: a criticism originating "in the environment that it is intended for." So, when Burke had sent him his essay on "The Armor of Jules Laforgue" at the end of January, Williams had praised it for the same reasons he had praised the Matisse the month before, because Burke had created a *new* Laforgue, a Laforgue Americans could use. "You fairly illustrate what Bob and I mean by contact," he had praised Burke then, for Burke had shown how Laforgue had taken his local surroundings and made of it "THE THING" that was his poetry. And that was what American artists would have to do with their world as well. Burke's Laforgue worked in a way Eliot's version had not simply because Burke had grounded his in a specific environment, while Eliot's floated between three worlds: France, England, and America, at home in none of them.[179]

By late March Williams told Burke that for some time now he had "wanted to have correspondence with someone very dissimilar to myself, the thing to be planned as a dialogue criticizing the universe" of literary matters. Williams did not like literary argument as a rule, in fact he really detested it, especially as neither side was ever convinced and the argument itself was "nearly always a confusion of terms, like a football game." But Burke, he saw, had a mind of his own, and Williams liked the spirit of antagonistic cooperation he sensed in him. "I like your ill-natured jabs at myself," he added, inviting Burke out for a meal in New York.[180] And a week later he told him that God was kind to give "us a few men of sense every generation" like Burke, and kind too "in refusing recognition to them while they live." He liked Burke all the better because the New York critic Floyd Dell, whom Williams had called a "goddamned cuntlapping shitwaggonhound," and "the last syllable of the universal fart," also disliked Burke.[181]

Williams was obviously in one of his sour, sardonic moods when he wrote Burke, his whole world covered with a cloacal pâté. But then, that seemed to be the predominant feeling in New York in 1921. Stuart Davis, the artist who had supplied the frontispiece for *Kora in Hell*, had just begun a magazine called *SHIT*, and it expressed Williams' own world view. "Imagine a temple to SHIT with little booths ranged along the sides," he told Burke, shifting from his discussion of the classical ruins at Samos. But then, he added, what about all those compartments in Penn Station and Grand Central? Weren't they modeled, after all, on the great Roman baths, and what structure was finally more important than a commode? "Someday," he added, "they will dig up these stations and investigate our sad, disused toilets—into which man has slowly disappeared from year to year, teeth and all. It is too sad."[182] So much, then, for the glory that was Greece and Rome. A few days later, on his first spring walk, he'd stepped in dogshit, he told Burke again, with the result that he'd had an almost "irresistible desire to study French literature."[183] As much as he loved French art, the French had managed to devastate and empty his own world. First they'd descended on New York during the war years and, now, sirenlike, they were luring all the young American artists back to Paris and their ultimate destruction.

So, when he saw Stuart Davis' pictures in New York in late April, he complained to Burke that even Davis had become too French. When, when would an American artist be born? At that point he could think of only two services that would help all of mankind. One would be to destroy Freud's influence—"the world has fucked itself with Freud too long"—and the other would be to topple French influence "by some capable Manifesto" written by an American.[184] Unfortunately, *Contact* had failed to do the job. He remembered too what Pound had once warned him and the others: to observe the French, but not wind up imitating them. Instead, the Americans were flocking to the Left Bank like so many lemmings.

Williams tried again to warn his countrymen in an essay he wrote for the Spring issue of *Contact* called "Yours, O Youth." The American critical attitude he wanted established in the younger writers he had to concede, finally, was still very young and even chaotic. But it was no less imperative than it had ever been to make contact with one's local conditions before "rushing into the continental hurly-burly." He was, he admitted, deeply disappointed that Pound had chosen to stay in Europe beyond the initial two years that would have been justified to learn what Europe had to teach them. Instead Pound had been there now for nearly fifteen. It had only "been by paying naked attention first to the thing itself that American plumbing, American shoes, American bridges" had become "notable in the world," he wrote, sounding very much like Emerson and Whitman had three-quarters of a century before. And yet his generation of American artists had been too timid to believe "that in the arts discovery and invention" would "take the same course." Agh! Would even that archetypal American phenomenon, Princess White Deer, finally end up by dancing like some Russian?[185]

Williams knew he was getting shrill. Paris was part of the problem, and the criticism his *Improvisations* had received was another source of irritability, from the Baroness' attack on him in *The Little Review* for his bourgeois sentimentality, sexual inexperience, timidity, male bluster, cruelty, uxoriousness, abstemiousness, stagnation and lack of skill with juggler's balls,[186] to *Poetry's* flippant review of Williams as a kind of jaded Isadora Duncan.[187] That review had so angered McAlmon when he read it in Paris that he shot a letter off at once to Harriet Monroe testifying to the extraordinary newness of Williams' prose poems as they caught the modern consciousness, alternately frightened and reckless, a consciousness Joyce too had captured in *Ulysses*.[188] Only Marianne Moore's review, which had appeared in *Contact* itself, had really pleased Williams. She had decided to counter Williams' flippancy and anger as they'd manifested themselves in the *Improvisations* with her own gentleness. "Perhaps you are right in your adverse view of my sometimes obstreperous objections to decorum," he wrote her. He would have to think about that. But each person had to free himself from the banality that threatened to suffocate him as best he could, and since he knew that he was really "timid or unstable at heart," he had had to try and free himself more violently than someone like herself.[189]

At home of course there was still the daily routine of medicine, the thousands of nameless or faceless patients, local Democratic politics in which he'd immersed himself, his wife in the hospital in May for a neck operation, a seven-year-old boy dancing at the local school, dressed a little uncomfortably in a blue Peter Rabbit outfit, something his younger brother refused to let him ever forget. "Here [in Rutherford] the world of art is nonexistent," Williams confessed to Burke in June. He was on the local school board and had just been up against it "fighting the town in order to get the shitasses to take their hands off the lid long enough for us to get a new high school built." But finally the vote had gone through in his favor. At least here he'd made a dent.

> The net result to me is that I have had to address two large and excited audiences 900 souls to this effect that I have found myself using words like fine instruments to cause an effect. I felt cool, detached, able to feel each word. . . . I am wealthier for having the music. And I won the fight. I couldn't help feeling though all the time: Ah if this energy were only going into art! If only this excitement had some literary matter for its concern. . . .

And then, even as he typed those lines on his office typewriter between patients, he added: "You might know it. The first literary pleasure I have enjoyed in weeks (this letter) has to be interrupted because some bastard of a butcher is bleeding to death, has cut his wrist. Yet I have written these last four lines."[190] Here was America going under, falling into some permanent paralysis, and for the ten thousandth time, his writing would have to wait while he ministered to another of his townspeople. Writing always seemed to have to wait for life, and that fact both angered him and made him feel guilty at his own topsy-turvy system of values. Of course life was more important, of course his patients and wife and kids mattered. God damn it, wasn't that all part of the cost of living in Rutherford!

Floss, too, had had to pay for her husband's impetuousness. He was forever in a hurry, stealing a minute here, a minute there, in order to get back to his writing. That was as true of his driving as it was of everything else, and he often drove like a madman to get someplace. He hated traffic with a passion because it wasted time and he would cut out into oncoming traffic to get around some slow-driving bastard, drive up on sidewalks when snow or other cars clogged the roads, race down winding country roads to get someplace just a little faster. His kids loved going out on the highways with him, feeling him gun the engine down the straightaway.[191] But Floss's neck problems had also been the direct result of Williams' fast driving, when he'd hit a railroad crossing at a clip and sent Floss's head smashing against the tin roof of their Ford, crushing one of her neck vertebrae.[192] For the rest of her life her neck would act up sporadically, and it could not have made an older Williams feel very good to see his wife wearing a cervical collar in her sixties for months at a time, and then to have to remember that it had been his wild-eyed race to save time that had been responsible for this pain too.

From the spring until the fall of '21, Williams did relatively little
writing. He took the family up to the Haslund farm in Wilmington,
Vermont, for August. But he was, as usual, listless, unsettled, waiting
impatiently for Brown to get on with *Sour Grapes,* which already tasted
to him as though it belonged to a long-vanished world. "Of the few books
I have spewed, this is the one in which I have been least interested," he
confessed to Burke in late October, shortly before *Sour Grapes* was finally
published. It was more "composed," he added—using that term ironically
—than any of his other books had been, especially when one considered
the *Improvisations.* If he was publishing this new book, it was simply
because, as he had also told Brown earlier, he had found "a lot of stuff
lying around."[193]

It was "a mood book," Williams would call it thirty-five years later,
"all of it impromptu. When the mood possessed me, I wrote. Whether it
was a tree or a woman or a bird, the mood had to be translated into
form. . . . To me, at that time, a poem was an image, the picture was the
important thing. As far as I could, with the material I had, I was lyrical,
but I was determined to use the material I knew and much of it did not
lend itself to lyricism."[194]

"Here it is spring again / and I still a young man," the opening poem of
Sour Grapes begins: "I am late at my singing." There were poems here
about his profession, about the doctor-artist going out to care for his
patients in the yearly round of blizzards: "The man turns and there
— / his solitary tracks stretched out / upon the world." And "Complaint":

> They call me and I go.
> It is a frozen road
> past midnight, a dust
> of snow caught
> in the rigid wheeltracks.[195]

There were poems to his widowed mother, like "To Waken an Old Lady,"
with its image of sparrows resting on winter weed stalks and shaking the
seed husks to the snow, their piping blending with the winds of early
spring. Or "The Widow's Lament in Springtime," where Williams had his
mother say these words:

> Today my son told me
> that in the meadows,
> at the edge of the heavy woods
> in the distance, he saw
> trees of white flowers.
> I feel that I would like
> to go there
> and fall into those flowers
> and sink into the marsh near them.[196]

He wrote a lighthearted piece praising his wife's new pink slippers with their gay pom-poms, signifying as he thought they did a world of domestic gaiety and industry. And in another he wrote of his children picking blueflags in the meadows along the river:

> *But blueflags are blossoming*
> *in the reeds*
> *which the children pluck*
> *chattering in the reeds*
> *high over their heads*
> *which they part*
> *with bare arms to appear*
> *with fists of flowers*
> *till in the air*
> *there comes the smell*
> *of calamus*
> *from wet, gummy stalks.*[197]

In was the sexual shock of the young children in this unwitting carpe diem ritual, Whitman's calamus invading the air as he—the father —looked on. There were love poems here too, poems to his wife, the poem he'd dedicated to Marion Strobel, poems too like "Queen-Anne's-Lace," about a woman's body become a white field of desire like a field of the weed itself. There was even one poem about his own ambiguous standing with the Greenwich Village people, those "friends" of his, for example, who had winked and told him to stop being so bourgeois and accept the "gift" of syphilis from the Baroness:

> *I have watched*
> *the city from a distance at night*
> *and wondered why I wrote no poem.*
> *Come! yes,*
> *the city is ablaze for you*
> *and you stand and look at it.*
>
> *And they are right. There is*
> *no good in the world except out of*
> *a woman and certain women alone*
> *for certain things. But what if*
> *I arrive like a turtle,*
> *with my house on my back or*
> *a fish ogling from under water?*[198]

No: that would not do. He had to be flamingo-pink for them, steaming with love and stinking like one, to go home to write a bad poem. They had tried the old argument on him: why reject the idea of going to bed with the Baroness until he had at least tried it. An empty decadence that, a wasteland.

"Bill Williams and I write spasmodically," McAlmon wrote Wallace

Stevens from London in December 1921, after McAlmon had managed to meet most of the leading literary lights of London and Paris that year, including Katherine Mansfield and Sylvia Beach, as well as T. S. Eliot and James Joyce, whom he had befriended. But in the meantime there was Bill, back in the States, "upset and churning about in realms of misery, doubt, timid and reckless moments of emotion and ideation," and McAlmon wasn't even sure how to meet Williams' "violent appeal for 'faith' of some sort in the value of life, or of literature." The trouble with Bill, finally, was that he was withering there in Rutherford doing his thing as a small-town doctor when he should have been in Europe with him, especially in Paris, which was at the real center of things.[199]

Almost Williams would have agreed with him. He felt stranded, like someone who had come to a picnic only to learn that it was being held somewhere else . . . yesterday. The Chicago renaissance was dead, and the awakening he'd sensed in New York in 1915 had proved illusory, moribund. At thirty-eight Williams had had to come face to face with the bitter realization of what it had cost to stay at home, to try and grow prize flowers in that volcanic ash. Obviously, Pound and Eliot had been right to clear the hell out and get their culture where they could. And now, many of the younger writers whom he had thought he might be able to work with had caught a whiff of Paris and set sail for the Old World. There was Marianne Moore, of course, but that was strictly a literary friendship. There was no way anyone was going to conscript that woman. And Stevens had retreated to the Insurance Capital of America, Hartford, Connecticut, five years before. One hardly saw him anymore, even when he came down to the city for a day.[200] As for Hart Crane, Williams wasn't interested, or at least so he said. Kreymborg was gone, this time to Italy to set up another little magazine, this one called *Broom*. Bodenheim was gone. Carnevali was in a hospital ward in Chicago. McAlmon was in Europe. Even the crazy Baroness was thinking of going back to Europe.

It was in this nexus of near-despair, then, that Williams determined that there was only one thing left for him to do. Isolated, he would write something *big* and grand about the American experience, all flags flying, banners waving, confetti and ticker tape streaming, neon flashing, even the Statue of Liberty doing the cancan. Williams could at least write *The Great American Novel*.

FIVE

Tracking Through the Fog:
1921—1924

"If there is progress then there is a novel. Without progress there is nothing." Thus Williams began his first novel, an antinovel, really, created out of the kind of despair he was feeling in the fall of '21. It would be a novel about the American experience in an age of expansion and progress, a progress heralded everywhere in the newspapers and the magazines, as in that copy of *Vanity Fair* Floss was reading, curled up there in bed with the boys asleep in the other room, still up when he returned late from the monthly meeting of the Bergen County Mosquito Extermination Commission, the fog so thick outside on this particular September night that he'd almost had to stop the Ford several times. And the words inside him, furious to be spilled on paper or lost forever, that need intensified by the example of Joyce's *Ulysses* before him in the pages of *The Little Review*, the clean taste of that writer's words freed from their past associations or seeming to be freed. "Words are the flesh of yesterday," Williams wrote, frantic with the need to say something about his world, his huge, formless, sprawling, antihistoric world: "Words roll, spin, flare up, rumble, trickle, foam—Slowly they lose momentum."[1] And so the trick he had learned, when the fever was on him, out on Route 17 or Route 3, or waiting at a drawbridge for the river tugs to lumber through or at a railroad crossing waiting for a freight train to clank by, scribbling down an impression, a remembered conversation, a line of poetry, words, on the blank sheets of his prescription pads, to be retyped later, reworked as needed or, when lucky, caught the first time fresh and clean in that moment of lightning insight.

But a novel. Another novel, like the thousands that came off the presses every year to be puffed up in the *Times*, reviewed, and as quickly forgotten? Plot, frankly, was inevitable, predictable, boring. A progression of events. A progress, like the progress of a modern industrial nation, a progress through a grand fog, like the one enveloping his world, enveloping the power house across the way from the room in which he was standing, waiting to deliver yet another in a long progression of children:

The great doors were open to full view of the world. A great amphitheatre of mist lighted from the interior of the power house. In rows sat the great black machines saying vrummmmmmmmmmmmmmm. Stately in the great hall they sat and generated electricity to light the cellar stairs with. To warm the pad on Mrs. Voorman's belly. To cook supper by and iron Abie's pyjamas. Here was democracy. Here is progress.[2]

How to make or even take the necessary words that would fit his world like a glove fitting a hand? The need to write, but to write what? He would imitate Joyce, but "with a difference," he thought. "The difference being greater opacity, less erudition, reduced power of perception. . . . Aside from that simple, rather stupid derivation, forced to a ridiculous extreme. No excuse for this sort of thing."[3] Impossible to write good prose in 1921 and not learn from the Irishman. And, too, there was Pound's taunt about his earlier improvisations, that they were a little Rimbaud, forty years late. It must be new, Williams kept saying over and over, but what in hell was the really new in this poor bastard country that took all its prose styles like its clothes from Europe? America: a country that took the chewed-over pabulum of Europe's cast-off ideas and swallowed them with the frenzy of freshmen getting their first taste of Logic.

Even these words, as he typed them furiously on the pages of yellow foolscap, were borrowed words, after Joyce, and therefore no good, "of no use but a secondary local usefulness like the Madison Square Garden tower copied from Seville."[4] But Joyce's progressions—and Joyce had them, Williams insisted—went all the way from botany to litany, full of categories that included the symbolic. So it was there that Williams could provide a service. He would cut away the symbolic, the litanic, New World purist that he was, and return the attention to the act of writing as the use of hard, discrete words. Words as machines, not as literature. Words like Shaker furniture, like well-made assembly-line Fords, like his own, the way he could make it jump the steep board incline into his garage, throwing the clutch out with his left foot, then pressing with his right foot and grasping the hand brake and stopping before the front end smashed into the old window screens at the other end of the garage. As now. Words were like that: functional, pragmatic, denotative. Not muzzy and soft, but sharp, with edges on them and marked contours to cut through fog with.

And what of Europe with its seething, swarming consciousness —complicated, oh yes, with its dadaism and expressionism dancing around the nothingness of it all. All very beautiful in its way, but of no essential value to American art. "Take their work," he wrote. "I resent it all. I hate every symphony, every opera as much as a Negro should hate *Il Trovatore.* Not perhaps hate it in a purely aesthetic sense but from under. It is an impertinence. Where in God's name is our Alexander to cut, cut, cut, through this knot."[5] America was still only "a mass of pulp, a jelly, a sensitive plate ready to take whatever print you want to put on it,"[6] a country still without its own art, manners, intellect: nothing. Williams had an intelligence as fine as his European contemporaries'; it was a machine as finely tuned as theirs. But that mind had found itself planted in the very hell the United States had become.

Perhaps the answer was to go back to the beginnings: to Columbus discovering *Nuevo Mundo*, his men setting out in the small boats for the islands, their whole beings "filled with the wild joy of release from torment of the mind." Unimportant that they were not the first, that Eric had been there before them, and the parties of Asiatics and Islanders before Eric: what mattered was that here was a new world naked all over again. As it was today—Columbus Day 1921—the schoolchildren lying in the gutters and covering themselves with fallen poplar leaves and looking out on the seasonal transformations that had given them almost overnight their own new world. The new world, a world of change, of revolution: as with Washington making his strategic retreat across New York into the back roads of New Jersey, or Pancho Villa's strategic hit-and-run attacks which had had the U.S. Army scurrying all over Mexico five years before. Revolutions in government, revolutions and strange evolutions in religion, as with the history of Joseph Smith and Brigham Young and the Mormons, a story of repressed sexuality and manifest destiny and of sacred personal visions, the intrinsically insane history of the puritans recapitulated by these latter-day saints in the expansion westward.

Contemporary America: a world of ads for Pisek-designed Personality Modes, "modes that are genuine inspirations of individual styling, created for meeting the personal preferences of a fastidiously fashionable clientèle,"[7] a world of jazz, Follies, flappers, silent movies with honky-tonk piano playing, of modern novels like *Flaming Youth* by Warner Fabian. Black jazz the only true American creation—at least from the European's point of view. And Williams: was he to assume the role of the new Whitman to that Mannahatta across the river, that brash new world?

> There she sat on the bench of the subway car looking idly about, being rushed under the river at great speed to the kitchen of her mother's flat. Malodorous mother. Or wrinkled hard-put-to-it mother. Savior of the movies. After the impact his great heart had expanded so as to include the whole city, every woman young and old there he having impregnated with sons and daughters. For everyone loved him. And he knew how to look into their eyes with both passion and understanding. Each had taken him to her soul of souls where the walls were papered with editorials from the Journal and there he had made herself father to her future child. As they went upstairs he saw her heels were worn—Who will understand the hugeness of my passion?[8]

No poet had come out of America, and no critic, at least no contemporary poet or critic to look at American work from an American point of view.

We were a young nation still, Williams knew, at a disadvantage of ten centuries when compared with Europe. And how much longer could we plead our childhood?

But what of the American renaissance of the 1850s? The thought of an Emerson and a Thoreau? They were all imitation, pure England. The ground of the American experiences rested not with them but further down, with the Indians, with Machu Picchu, with the Eskimos who had learned how to adjust to local conditions and had out of that contact created a culture whose remains still stood. As one found it in a debased but still viable form among the mountain people of Appalachia, where enforced "isolation makes people fiercely individualistic."

It was an idyllic moment, this dwelling on the beauty of mountain people such as two women named Lory and Ma Duncan, listening to what the old earth had to tell her and saying, "If folks wasn't so mad for money they might be here and a preachin' the gospel of beauty."[9] But the vision of the old stock pioneer was not convincing finally. As a poet of detritus Williams could convince. His despair was authentic. But what except at second hand did he know of the southern mountain people? He would have to go deeper than that to find the beauty he was after. With Ben Franklin's Poor Richard's legacy to millions of immigrants Williams did better. There was after all the dream of the penniless foreigner come to the New World to make his millions through industry and hard work, but there was also the cost to the human spirit of pursuing that dream. And what of the fact that for every one who made it there were hundreds who did not? Alongside the myth of the golden paved streets were the hard realities of costs, of ever rising costs to ensure profit margins for the big corporations.

Williams ended his novel with a parable told by one of his anti-Semitic business acquaintances who had made a fortune manufacturing wool shoddy from old rags. Of course, the fellow had said, it was the Jews who really made the big money. He knew one—and Williams must have felt the envy in the man's voice that he hadn't been quick enough himself to do it—who

> took any kind of rags just as they were collected, filth or grease right on them the way they were and teased them up into fluffy stuff which he put through a rolling process and made into sheets of wadding. These sheets were fed mechanically between two layers of silkolene and a girl simply sat there with an electric sewing device which she guided with her hand and drew in the designs you see on those quilts, you know.[10]

And so with the techniques of the novel itself: to take any kind of material, just as Williams had found it—letters, ads, the weather, an image of a Standard Motor Gasoline truck, an image of an old woman looking out a window, suspiciously like the Baroness, local architecture, a debate in the *Times* between Ford Madox Ford and H. G. Wells—and mix them all into the hopper, grease and all, to create a viable mirror of the times: the American novel as shoddy.

That was in the fall of 1921, at the same time that Eliot was undergoing the ordeal that would become—with Pound's editing in early 1922—*The Waste Land*. Years later—thinking back on the impact that poem had had on American letters—Williams would complain how it had almost singlehandedly destroyed the indigenous art that was just then beginning to emerge in the United States. "There was heat in us," he wrote, "a core and a drive that was gathering headway upon the theme of a rediscovery of a primary impetus, the elementary principle of all art, in the local conditions. Our work staggered to a halt for a moment under the blast of Eliot's genius which gave the poem back to the academics. We did not know how to answer him."[11] But Williams wrote that often-quoted passage with a failing memory and with the hindsight that thirty years of the English and American academy had provided to reenforce his judgment, since by 1950 *The Waste Land* had achieved something of the status of a sacred text.

Actually, the first impetus, the original breath of fresh air that *Others* especially had afforded Williams had long soured. It was not *The Waste Land* that had caused such anxiety in Williams but the publication of Eliot's "Love Song of J. Alfred Prufrock," even as Williams wrote his improvisations. The truth is that by 1922 the state of American letters was itself a wasteland, with only a few writers left to man the home fires and the others in Europe editing little magazines or mingling with the Europeans. Eliot had moved into a vacuum with his poem, and his "private bit of grumbling" had touched a universal postwar ennui, Eliot's tone signaling the way thousands of others felt. Hart Crane would respond with the beginnings of *The Bridge* and Williams with poems like "On the Road to the Contagious Hospital," with its own counterimage of the waste fields of his own world in early spring teeming with the promise of a new beginning. But Eliot did not bring local American art to a momentary halt. The disintegration of the older New York group —Kreymborg's group, for easy reference—and the growing factionalism of the younger writers like Kenneth Burke, Malcolm Cowley, Matthew Josephson, Gorham Munson, Harold Loeb, and others kept any viable vortex from forming in New York in the early '20s.

*
* *

Williams' own work staggered, splintered momentarily, before his energies could regroup. Out of the despair of that period, however, he was able to create the extraordinary improvisations that became *The Great American Novel*, followed by new experiments in the forms of the poems he wrote during 1922 which—placed in a radioactive force field with his prose—became one of his strongest books: *Spring and All*. And then, as he moved toward his fortieth birthday, he capped these experiments with his impressionistic history, his intensive imaginative search for the American ground which had been his birthright: *In the American Grain.* These were the triple explosions of his own dynamic vortex, the release of creative energies that exploded like three Roman candles against the American sky in the years between 1921 and 1925. That only a handful of people saw any of these meant of course that the candle had exploded in something approaching an absolute Mallarméan silence. But the impact of these works on figures like Pound, Marianne Moore, Hart Crane, McAlmon, Burke, Munson, and others did have its effect, in this: that a handful of those who mattered did read the work and saw that it was good. When, therefore, Williams won the *Dial* Award and $2,000 in 1926, the newspapers hailed Williams as a poet, and because they said it, Americans in Rutherford and in New York agreed that it must be so. Williams was moving—in the mid-'20s—toward a modicum of fame. Some, including teachers of English—those dispensers of the culture— might even remember that he had written a poem about a red wheel- barrow with white chickens. Meanwhile Williams continued to work.

Just after Christmas 1921, Williams invited Wallace Gould to stay with him at 9 Ridge Road. Like Marsden Hartley, Gould too was from Maine. He was a big hulk of a man—about six three—and one quarter Abnaki Indian, a fact that impressed Williams. Gould had left Maine at Kreymborg's suggestion to pursue a life of poetry in New York City. But in New York, Gould learned that Kreymborg had in the meantime left for new horizons—California, then Paris—leaving Gould stranded. So Wil- liams and Floss took Gould in and he stayed all winter until spring, cooking meals, helping out around the house, teaching young Bill how to play the piano. Williams liked Gould, liked his poems—some of which had appeared in *The Little Review*—and took him with him into the city to the art galleries, to Alfred Stieglitz's place,[12] for example, and went so far as to write Harold Loeb in Rome—who was editing *Broom* from there—to publish Gould's things and send the man some much-needed money.[13] Unlike Maxwell Bodenheim, who had spent a week at 9 Ridge Road after he'd been forced to leave Kreymborg's apartment when Kreymborg moved out, Gould got along well with Floss and the kids. Bodenheim had taken the wrong tack with Floss. She'd served carrots the first night he was staying there and Bodenheim had put his fist down: there would be no more carrots served as long as he was staying at 9 Ridge Road. Floss said nothing, but the very next night she made a point of serving carrots again. Bodenheim caught the message.

Gould was different: he fitted in easily, and Bill Jr. was to remember him with fondness more than half a century later.[14] When Gould finally left that March, with spring in the air, the Williamses scraped together twenty dollars to give him, and he simply headed south, tired of the winters in Maine. He took a train to Washington, D.C., and then just kept walking and hitchhiking until he reached Farmville, Virginia, where his money ran out. There he decided to stay, in the long shadows of Appomattox Court House and the Civil War, writing poetry and doing odd jobs, such as playing the piano in the town's one movie house. Finally he moved in with an elderly southern lady, Mary Jackson, whom he later married.[15]

When Williams heard that Kenneth Burke was doing a piece on him for *The Dial*—a review of *Sour Grapes* in the February issue—he kidded Burke that if Burke slammed the book, Williams' own poems in the same issue with Burke's review would set the balance right.[16] But Burke's review was favorable, and though he didn't care for "the miserable crew" who made up imagism, he did like what Williams had achieved with his apparent formlessness: a physical intimacy with the thing itself. For Burke the *Improvisations* had been a big mistake—"having twenty sentences of chaos to heighten one sentence of cosmos is too much like thanking God for headaches since they enable us to be happy without them"—and *Sour Grapes* had come as the welcome successor to *Al Que Quiere!* The essential Williams, Burke insisted, was a poet of surfaces, a poet of lucidities and concreteness. Williams was not a thinker but a true primitive, with "a complete disinterest in form."[17] Williams bit his lip and thanked Burke for his essay, which had gone at his work "as if it were an interesting problem and not a sign board to be painted."[18] That Burke had missed the point about Williams' search for new forms Williams was willing to overlook. He was not yet ready to trust himself to his new friend in the way he could trust McAlmon.

Despite the fact that he had been feeling generally down on Eliot and on Pound for championing Eliot (rather than himself), Williams responded with characteristic generosity to Pound's *bel esprit* plan meant to aid Eliot. The idea was to get Eliot enough backers to contribute ten pounds each to allow Eliot to leave his job at Lloyds Bank and devote himself to writing for a full year. "The point is," Pound told Williams on March 18, "that Eliot is at the last gasp." The man had already suffered one breakdown which had resulted in his staying at Lausanne during the just-completed winter, and he was in no shape to go back to the bank. Pound himself and Richard Aldington had already pledged their ten pounds. The idea was to continue the plan each year with Eliot first and perhaps Williams second, though Pound was sure that Williams had no intention of setting up in Europe anyway. It was simply a failure of nerve, Pound taunted Williams, that had kept Williams at home: the fear "of destroying some illusions which you think necessary to your illusions." Pound was willing to concede that Williams needed America, that it did give him "contact." But Williams also needed—and needed soon—to get out of Rutherford and over to Europe for anywhere from six months to a year.[19]

"Oh why don't you go get yourself crucified on the Montmartre and will the proceeds to art," Williams shot back at Pound on the twenty-ninth. "I'll come to Paris and pass the hat among the crowd. What the hell do I care about Eliot?" Yes, he admitted, he too wanted to get to Paris, but he wasn't about to trade his own "illusions" about the state of poetry for Pound's. "By unfortunate circumstances I have stumbled on the few particles of truth about writing that I know," he complained, "things which you might have pointed out to me in three words if you had the skill or the understanding." Besides, what Williams himself needed at the moment was not money, but leisure, and how the hell he was going to get that was "difficult to say," but probably "without the least assistance from friends," as the case had always been for him. Still, the siren call of Europe was enchanting. Ah, to be in Paris where he could watch men "walking simply in the sun" and to walk with them. As for Eliot, yes, he would send Pound the fifty dollars he'd asked for, telling him to "stick it up" his "A.S."[20]

For his part, Pound offered Williams his studio apartment in Paris if Williams would only come over for the summer months to get some writing done. Williams looked into the possibilities of coming over for the month of August. It would cost him $107 to travel third class over and the same to get back home, and it would take another $50 in the city. That was for an actual ten days in Paris in the summer of '22. Instead he'd decided to take a sabbatical as soon as he could and come over for at least three months. He would help Eliot for a second year, if necessary, and then Williams couldn't spare any more, since he'd be away from his source of income for a year.[21] By the end of November Williams was looking forward to his proposed visit to Paris with feverish anticipation, his head filled with fantastic notions of the "good life" in gay Paree. "God knows I should like to sit down quietly in contemplation before a few undiseased and naked cunts for a few months—sit down that is until I recuperate from my last ten years' vigil. I should like to come to Europe and fuck my head off (not the head of my cock though)—But that is hardly a reason for leaving the good old U.S.A." And yet there were times when it was "almost insupportable" to stay in the States, even for the sake of art.[22]

McAlmon too had urged Williams to come to Europe for a stay. On February 12, he wrote Williams from the Grand Hotel on the Riviera that the special time they had spent together in the fall of '20 was gone now forever. "*The Dial, The Little Review*, the pros and cons of a Burke, the arguing and discussing about the hows and whyfores and the bigotries of

American life aren't around me," he told Williams. He'd enjoyed the weekend visits to 9 Ridge Road, the meetings in the city, the long walks and good talks. But Europe had something else to offer: "a realization and fairly open minded acceptance of all kinds of human experience." Pound, he knew from the man himself, wanted Williams in Europe. But McAlmon wasn't sure that wouldn't be a mixed blessing. "You would be interested, and also bored," he offered:

> It wouldn't remake you. You need—and this you won't like—Florence, and the youngsters; or you wouldn't be with them. Like Joyce, like myself, and like many a sensible sensitive person you aren't a strong will, and you need a ballast. Joyce is the victim of anybody that has him out for dinner—ready to be dragged from one drink to another. He'd go to hell but for his family. I don't know what you'd do. But Florence bucks you up—dominates and may sometimes oppress you—but she is your rod and staff and you might as well accept that fact.[23]

What Bill and Floss—and the boys—needed was a year away from Rutherford. It would free Williams in some way, McAlmon was sure, and erase some of Williams' romantic ideas about Europe and America, so that Williams might return to his practice after that time, "readier to be a doctor in Rutherford, which is about as able to grant a completeness of life as any place else in the world."[24] Williams listened to Pound and McAlmon and then made plans. Twenty-one months later he would be in Paris. As for *bel esprit*, when Eliot himself got wind of what was happening, he put a quick stop to Pound's altruistic scheme. Eliot wasn't looking for anyone's charity.

Yet Williams—in spite of the fact that many of his own troops had crossed over to the other side of the Atlantic—could sound as tough as Pound about the need to stay at home. "I wish to Lipo Lipi [sic] that you were in New York and not in Rome," he had written in February to Harold Loeb, who was then editing *Broom* from that capital. "What in hell it can mean to anyone that a magazine shall be International is more than I can say. A piece of work is international when it is good but a magazine that attempts to be international must be mediocre—the least common denominator. . . . What in hell can I bless you for?—the good work you might just as well be instigating in some actual locality where you would be IN IT—up to the ass hole. . . . I can't for the life of me see any use in shooting off jism into the atmosphere of Italy."[25] He still missed McAlmon and his aborted plans for *Contact*. But in spite of all that, here at home was where the real work would have to be done.

And yet Williams was anything but blind to the good work coming out of Europe. So, in mid-July he sent Jane Heap a letter praising *The Little Review* for its Picabia number. It had given him "the sense of being arrived, as of any efficient engine in motion." Besides Picabia's work in the French dadaist mode, Williams was ready to concede, "everything else in America, everything new being published seems, beside the present *Little Review*, to be the model of an engine made of wood to represent the power it does not possess."[26] Was he thinking back to the image of his friend Hartley, standing on the platform at Rutherford, as the Erie express roared through, and Hartley saying that everyone secretly wanted that kind of naked power?

*
**

In spite of the local conditions—or perhaps because of them—Williams was himself undergoing a radical transformation in his own poetry. The poems of *Al Que Quiere!* and *Sour Grapes* were behind him; they were even giving him the "willies" now, as he told Jane Heap that summer. So that, even as Burke tried to define Williams' characteristic poetic gesture, Williams was moving beyond those lucidities and linear clarities to a poem like "The Agonized Spires," which Williams himself called "fairly representative . . . of the sort of thing I am working on now."[27] That poem was more like a dadaist collage, a compression of overlapping but sharply discrete images, a conflation of the impressions—intellectual, emotional, perceptual—of New York City from the perspective of a multilevel sensibility. The nearest visual image to the kind of thing Williams was attempting here would have been the kinesthetics of a dadaist film where discrete images followed each other in quick succession without a narrative line or even a subjective eye to hold the images together. Williams was careful to eschew the "I" as observer, preferring instead the photographic lens as receptor. He also broke up the syntax more radically here, and thus the orderly progression of the poem, replacing it with an instantaneous perception of the entire field of the "canvas." He was painting with words, all kinds of words, like Juan Gris, the cubist, painting in wedges of landscape:

> *Crustaceous*
> *wedge*
> *of sweaty kitchens*
> *on rock*
> *overtopping*
> *thrusts of the sea. . . .* [28]

So the poem begins: the city's spires thrusting phalluslike above the sea of energy, of humanity, which New York was and is: a complex organism of coral incrustations, swarming with life, so that the city became an extension of that energy, the spires mirroring all that modern mass movement and the erotic energy the modern city implies. And at night, lights speckling the island, pointed up with the intense silvering of an El Greco in the modern renaissance that New York meant for Williams and for others, a renaissance that included the high drama of the machine (the world of steel and triphammers that Hart Crane too was celebrating in his own "For the Marriage of Faustus and Helen"):

> *Lights*
> *speckle*
> *El Greco*
> *lakes*
> *in renaissance*
> *twilight*
> *with triphammers. . . .*

How to read those lines? Is it "Lights speckle like El Greco lakes with the flickering engine rapidity of triphammers in this renaissance twilight"? Or is it "Lights speckle on the El Greco-like lakes of the Hudson and East rivers, as in that artist's late Renaissance handling of light on dark, with the modern *Mechanique Ballet* sounds of triphammers for accompaniment"? Or something else? Or all of these? Williams had learned—master that he was—how to bend syntax to his own ends to let the images flood over the reader's sensibility simultaneously with their multifoliate possibilities, as in the reading of a scene or a painting. The aggregate of such discrete images, he offered, caught up syntactic and imagistic "irritants," but at the same time this aggregate knitted a kind of peace, corresponding as it did to a deeper psychological reality. In the mind we know such juxtapositions to be valid and even refreshing. We know that machines have their emotional correlatives, where even bridge stanchions—as in a painting by Joseph Stella—can evoke a deep emotional response:

> *certainly*
> *piercing*
> *left ventricles*
> *with long*
> *sunburnt fingers.*[29]

But it was not Stella Williams mentioned, but rather the Spaniard, Juan Gris. The modern problem in painting, as Williams saw it, was not to replace the forms of reality with art's own forms, but to replace the reality of experience with the reality of art. Painting was not an illusion of depths and three-dimensional space—where the grapes were so real birds might peck at them. Painting was, rather, the creating of a new reality based on the perception of "reality." No representation, but a new and separate existence, "enlargement—revivification of values."

Thus, to take J. Alfred Prufrock's refrain, the tenebrous refrain of the woman with soft down on her arms under the gaslight, rejecting Prufrock's watery, pastel desires in advance of their utterance: "No, that is not it. That is not what I meant at all." Take those words and examine them:

> No that is not it
> nothing that I have done

the poem beings. And the reader expects what? A sort of confession? Some universal statement? "Nothing / I have done," the voice continues, to shift then in this violent wrenching into the self-reflexive which obliterates even the "I":

> nothing
> I have done
>
> is made up of
> nothing
> and the diphthong
>
> ae
>
> together with
> the first person
> singular
> indicative
>
> of the auxiliary
> verb
> to have

Looked at this way, "nothing" has lost its abstract immensity to become a word, a pigment on the page, equal to its opposite, "everything," so that

> everything
> I have done
> is the same. . . . [30]

But there were other poems closer to Williams' older lucidities, like the opening one which commented directly on Williams' call for a new world. That was Nuevo Mundo but also the new world of spring: March in New Jersey, death giving way to the stirrings of new life, this wasteland not dead but teeming with promise. As in bringing an infant screaming into life itself:

> By the road to the contagious hospital
> under the surge of the blue
> mottled clouds driven from the
>
> northeast—a cold wind. Beyond, the
> waste of broad, muddy fields
> brown with dried weeds, standing and fallen
>
> patches of standing water
> the scattering of tall trees. . . .

A world to all appearances still leafless, lifeless (that assonance striking in itself), except that already the new plants

>   *enter the new world naked,*
>   *cold, uncertain of all*
>   *save that they enter. All about them*
>   *the cold, familiar wind—*
>
>   *Now the grass, tomorrow*
>   *the stiff curl of wildcarrot leaf*
>
>   *One by one objects are defined—*
>   *It quickens: clarity, outline of leaf. . . .*

A crisp poetic, those last two lines, pointing offhandedly to Williams' way of dealing with images—still lifes nervous with energy, moving from stasis into flux in the act of reading:

>   *But now the stark dignity of*
>   *entrance—Still, the profound change*
>
>   *has come upon them: rooted they*
>   *grip down and begin to awaken.*[31]

"I think often of my earlier work and what it has cost me not to have been clear," Williams candidly admitted in *Spring and All*, thinking back to his improvisations of five years before. "I acknowledge I have moved chaotically about refusing or rejecting most things, seldom accepting values or acknowledging anything." Early he had come to distrust both "acquisitive understanding" and "religious dogmatism," seeking art in their place, and a form that might give him the sense of inclusiveness, a sense of freedom, and an expansion of the spirit. But because he felt he was cursed with an inability to develop and articulate an aesthetic, "to complete the intellectual steps which would make me firm" in the position he knew intuitively to be true, most of this life had "been lived in hell—a hell of repression lit by flashes of inspiration, when a poem such as this or that would appear."[32] Appear. The word suggests what in fact was true of Williams' poetic: that it was only in the heat of actual composition that he could achieve what he knew was satisfying, even if he could not say really how he had come to make that poem out of the prose surrounding it or why he had made most of the thousand machine-calibrated adjustments necessary to the finished poem.

Poetry was neither philosophy nor religion, nor was it a handmaid to these things. In poetry words were set free to dance over the condition of reality. Then the imagination could take the most inert materials and stir them radioactively into life. It could take a word as lifeless as "it" and do to it what prose could not. In a brilliant juxtaposition toward the close of *Spring and All*, Williams wrote:

Imagination is not to avoid reality, nor is it description nor an evocation of objects or situations, it is to say that poetry does not tamper with the world but moves it—It affirms reality most powerfully and therefore,

since reality needs no personal support but exists free from human action,
as proven by science in the indestructability of matter and of force, it
creates a new object . . . [33]

That is an important statement of Williams' belief in poetry as a separate
and equal reality with that other reality we call reality, and he buttresses
his statement with an oblique reference to Einstein's theories, which
were then being popularized in the newspapers and journals. But he is
also playing with the word "it" to refer to the imagination and the world
both, and to neither. And so in the twenty-sixth of the twenty-seven
poems of *Spring and All*, where the crowd at the baseball game, moving in
unison as it shouts its approval or disapproval, suddenly takes on a life of
its own, as "it" undergoes its own protean transformations:

> *It is alive, venomous*
>
> *it smiles grimly*
> *its words cut—*
>
> *The flashy female with her*
> *mother, gets it—*
>
> *The Jew gets it straight—it*
> *is deadly, terrifying—*
>
> *It is the Inquisition, the*
> *Revolution*
>
> *It is beauty itself*
> *that lives*
>
> *day by day in them*
> *idly—*
>
> *This is*
> *the power of their faces*
>
> *It is summer, it is the solstice*
> *the crowd is*
>
> *cheering, the crowd is laughing*
> *in detail*
>
> *permanently, seriously*
> *without thought.*[34]

From stasis into energy back to stasis, the uncoiling of the ouroubouros.
Williams draws our attention to "it" as a word as well as a meaning,
pirouetting thus "with the words which have sprung from the old facts of
history," reunited here in this present passionate meditation on the
collective energy of any baseball crowd swaying flowerlike with its cheers
or boos, as in the Roman arena, as at a public execution. Not, then, an
attainment of poetry reaching toward the condition of music, not the
Mallarméan self-contained self-referential sonnet. Not abstractionism,
but a condition approaching cubism, where the meaning of words has

been lifted into the world of the imagination in new and startling juxtapositions, words rinsed clean of their tired associative meanings and set clashing and clanging like the parts of a machine one against the other.

As in the work of the one artist who had early on shown the way for him: Marianne Moore. For in her poems each word, no matter how unyieldingly prosaic, remained sharp and distinctive, "each" as Williams noted, "unwilling to group with the others except as they move in the one direction"—that is, toward the creation of a poem. In the early '20s, she more than anyone else, Pound included, was the mainstay for Williams' own developing poetic. He would remember her years later—even after they had cooled to each other—as the "rafter holding up the superstructure of our uncompleted building, a caryatid, her red hair plaited and wound twice about the fine skull, . . . one of the main supports of the new order."[35] Certainly by her own example she was one of the figures buttressing the makeshift temple of *Spring and All.*

*
* *

> *A letter from the man who*
> *wants to start a new magazine*
> *made of linen*
>
> *and he owns a typewriter—*
> *July 1, 1922*
> *All this is for eyeglasses*
>
> *to discover.*[36]

Thus a wry Williams in the poem he was to place tenth in *Spring and All.* In the summer of '22 Williams was busy with his poems, parceling them out here and there to *The Little Review, The Dial,* and some of the new magazines that were sprouting up like mushrooms in New York and in Europe, like Harold Loeb's *Broom* and Gorham Munson and Matthew Josephson's *Secession.* The letter from the man with his own typewriter was probably Burke, acting as coeditor of the third number of *Secession,* who had asked Williams to give him something for that number. "Who the hell is Munson?"[37] Williams had asked, and had then given Burke two poems for *Secession* three and four, the latter "The Hothouse Plant," which Williams had dedicated to Charlie Demuth, "one of my longest standing (tour Eiffel) friends."[38]

Williams sent the poems despite his strong personal antipathy for Josephson himself, "whom I heartily dislike and in whom I do not believe for one moment,"[39] as he told Burke in early September. In fact, it had been Williams' finding Josephson's presence in Munson's first letter that had resulted in Williams' simply ignoring Munson's initial request for work, or—as Williams phrased it—had caused his "first failure to erect." Burke, of course, would want to "look into my Jewish ancestry and invoke freudian aid" to explain Williams' simple dislike of Josephson, but the fact was that Williams simply did not care for the man any more than McAlmon had.[40] As for *Secession*, though he'd written Pound in early May asking if he'd met the group, adding, "Do farts secede or are they expelled?"[41] he was willing to help the magazine now that he saw Burke was behind them. So, in September he met with Burke and Munson at Burke's office at *The Dial* at 152 West 13th Street to talk about *Secession*'s future. (Such was the fluid nature of the little magazine in the early '20s that no one thought it incongruous that one should serve as editor for two magazines with different manifestos at the same time.)

When his poem appeared with four of Cummings' in the third issue of *Secession*, Williams was taken by the magazine's new seriousness and was ready—after a month's vacation in Wilmington in the hills of southern Vermont with the Haslunds, Floss's family on her mother's side—for new work, or, as he phrased it, "to drive a cow across the barnyard with my final shove—as they do every day in the mts."[42] He liked Cummings' poems very much and—piqued by curiosity—began reading the man's autobiographical novel about his internment in a French prison, *The Enormous Room*. That novel, as he told Burke, had been "atrociously written in places," and filled with "impossible sentence constructions," but there were also moments of "great intensity" and "through it all . . . a lovely New England Sunday effect *a travers le Montmartyr*."[43]

Yet, though he was writing up a storm now, Williams could not allow himself to think of book publication. None of his books were selling, and he found himself mocking his poor efforts to get his books into circulation in a letter he wrote Edmund Brown in August, while still on vacation at the Haslund farm. There was of course a certain embarrassment in writing Brown, since copies of *Al Que Quiere!*, *Kora in Hell*, and *Sour Grapes*, as well as a hundred copies of *The Tempers*—ten years' work —sat moldering in crates in a Boston warehouse. Useless to ask Brown to think of doing yet another book. And yet Williams in fact knew of the existence of a woman who actually wanted to *buy* a copy of his poems but couldn't find it anywhere. Pity the poor poets, he quipped, "who must send their works to ladies parcel post prepaid. Dried and powdered it might be used as a kind of face powder. Kind of pepper on the meat maybe. Try this work of William Carlos Williams. The very best they say. Why not. They put saltpeter on nigger food when they want them to stick on the job. Cools them down." And later that month he added that even his own (aesthetic) prostate was "boggy."[44]

So when Monroe Wheeler, who had just published a pamphlet of

Marianne Moore's poems in a series called Mannikin, wrote Williams in early August to ask if he was interested in being featured as the second poet in the series, Williams confessed that he was writing very little in terms "of ultimate bulk" and didn't even much care about getting his things into the little magazines. Wheeler wanted to publish Williams, but he'd read in *Contact* magazine that Williams would be asking for fifty bucks a poem from now on. Did those prices still hold? Actually, Williams confessed, that had been just an "empty toot." He had solemnly announced that "nothing could induce [him] to part with a poem for less than the amount stated," and then he had gone and sold "a poem next day for ten dollars." The truth was that it cost him two to three times as much to print his poems as he actually brought in. At the present moment he was not quite ready to do even a small new book, but he was writing "a mass of work" which might "result in a more or less finished state," though they would need either "very light touching here and there" or else "very heavy destroying . . . or deft rescue work."[45]

For one thing, he did not yet have in hand the improvisational prose material he would intersperse between his poems. It was only later —perhaps as late as Christmas 1922—that Williams decided to do an *Al Que Quiere!* and an *Improvisations* in one: poems and prose jostling side by side, the prose "explaining" the poems and the poems defending and enlightening the prose. For in a letter written to Brown the day after Christmas—a lacerated improvisation of its own—Williams, trying to steal a few moments for writing between patients, wrote out of exasperation:

> God damn these sons of bitches of patients to hell and make it hot—Here I just sit down to write a few letters and some fucking bastard of a yid gets a chill and my Olympian moment is shit on—How in Christ's name can a man exist today? Let him shake. I continue. . . . I write to write. Let the result take care of itself. If anything startling results later on why—so much the better. . . . What the reader never knows and never dares to know is what he is at the exact moment that he is.[46]

This, of course, would become the opening of *Spring and All*. For, given the demands on his time, Williams would have to learn to extend his spring indefinitely. Hadn't Ezra told him that he would be sixty before his greatness was recognized? Well, in that case, provide, provide: "I have just learned how to get a hard on at sixty: Have your prostate massaged three to five hours before the event." He ended by raising a paean to his faithful publisher: "You are my soul and always have been. You are the only publisher in existence. . . . Bless you. Dominus Vobiscum."[47]

And yet Brown, by procrastinating, would never publish another word of Williams'. Again, it was Pound who had interceded. "There's a printer here wants me to supervise a series of booklets, prose (in your case perhaps verse, or whatever form your new stuff is in)," he wrote Williams from Paris at the beginning of August.[48] This new prose series would be a limited private edition with a run of about 350, with fifty dollars down to Williams at the beginning and another fifty later. Yeats's sisters' Cuala Press had worked for Yeats to bring out fine, limited editions of Yeats's work, and Pound could promise that at least the printing of his series would be done with care. The printer's name was William Bird, or *L'Oiseau*, as Pound nicknamed him, and the press was to be called the Three Mountains Press, with Pound making the selections.

Pound's letter reached Williams in Vermont, where Williams was, as he wrote, "enjoying a change of climate, fishing, looking at the moon, the stars, smelling the dung, the newmown hay, playing with the children." He had just finished reading *Ulysses* in book form that moment, Tuesday, August 15, and Joyce's prose, he said, had encouraged him "to champion my own particular form of stupidity—or knowledge or intelligence or lacknowledge." Yes, he said, yes, he would dig up some of the prose he'd been doing and send it on when he got back home in September.[49] But the very next day he had "disentombed 50 pages of stuff, all of a batch," the "tail end of a work I at one time had in mind." He had quickly read "his Great American Novel over and saw that the promise of the early pages had fallen off as the piece progressed, but he did not feel that he could improve the thing now by revising. "Haphazard as it is," he added, "it still has something of the nature of the mass that engages my attention here and so had better be printed as it is—or destroyed." Call it THIS, he added, which might then be transposed to SHIT.[50]

Ten days later, having just returned to the Haslund farm after a three-day trip with his family to see Montreal (which trip he would write about in *In the American Grain* a year later), Williams sent a brief note to Pound begging him to let him read the proofs before Bird published his *Great American Novel*. He was anxious to see some errors changed and others remain exactly as they were. The Baroness, he added, was still after him in New York, and he was afraid she might still succeed in killing him. If he did die, he wanted Pound to publish the poems he'd recently been writing in a volume to be called, simply, *Poems*. What he was talking about was the unfinished text of *Spring and All*, none of which had yet appeared in the little magazines except for one piece *The Little Review* was doing in September, that is, unless he acquiesced to the wishes of another expatriate, "a certain Monroe Wheeler who promises to be writing to me from Bonn on Rhein" about "a new magazine he is adding to the garbage heap."[51]

By the end of the month, Pound had read and accepted Williams' 81-page novel, sending off a letter with his own critical comments on the text. "I am overwhelmed by your approval of my NOVEL," Williams told

Pound on September 11. Pound's approval had come at a moment when Williams was feeling unsure of his own worth as a writer, and he still needed the intense, brilliant scrutiny Pound could offer. "I need your critical remarks," Williams told him. "God sometimes I feel myself to be the rottenest sham of the artist. 'Intuition' does me so well that sometimes I think it is nothing but lack of brains. I work and then float off into emptiness—self-critique comes only in flashes, two years apart."[52]

Bird printed Williams' novel, along with Ford Madox Ford's *Women & Men*, Ernest Hemingway's *in our time*, Pound's own *Indiscretions; or, Une revue des deux mondes*, and two other books in the spring of 1923, each in an edition of three hundred which sold for $2.50 a copy. That was an impressive collection of assembled talents for any new publishing venture, though of course the series as such was a financial loss. "The 3 Mts. printing is beautiful as the feet of young damsels on the hills," Pound wrote Williams in early February 1923 as the series went to print. By then Williams had just completed his prose improvisations and arranged his twenty-seven poems within that prose envelope and was looking for someone to publish this new book as well. He asked Pound if Bird might not also be interested in doing *Spring and All*, though of course he would be willing to pay something toward the publishing costs, as he had with every book he'd so far done. "I do NOT advise you to pay for having vol. of poems printed," Pound told him. "You *can't* sell a vol. You can get it published on royalty basis—that's all anyone can do except possibly KIPLING." But as for L'Oiseau doing that volume as well, Pound was skeptical. Bird was putting "so much energy and cash into making 3 Mts. printing the A-1 double X, that I don't know how the press will survive the prose series."[53]

But even as Williams' letter to Pound asking about the possibility of Three Mountains Press doing *Spring and All* was crossing the Atlantic by ship, Williams invited Monroe Wheeler out to 9 Ridge Road for Sunday afternoon, February 4, to have one of Floss's meals. "I have a book of prose and verse—a sort of complemental arrangement of the two forms which I want to have published but can find no one to take me up," he told Wheeler, "no publisher in America—save at my own expense." It was a small book, he told Wheeler, which would come to about sixty printed pages. Could Wheeler's Mannikin series handle that?[54] When Wheeler saw Williams that afternoon, he told him frankly that Mannikin could just not handle a book the size of *Spring and All* but that he wanted instead to feature Williams by printing up ten poems from the new stuff. Williams turned dull, taciturn, dissatisfied with Wheeler's compromise, but the next morning, having thought it over, he wrote him in another manner: "I cannot imagine a greater service at this moment than yours in offering me a *Mannikin* for relief. . . . It may be the one way in which I shall be able to get my book in the end. . . . Just the sheer necessity of selecting the ten has been important."⁵⁵ By mid-March he had decided on the pamphlet's ten poems. Nine of them were to be from his new script; a tenth: "The Hermaphroditic Telephones"—a new poem he wanted included. He wanted the pamphlet to be called *Go-Go* to suggest the sense of breakthrough, of a poetry of rapid transit, like the "Go-Go" of the traffic signals, instead of "Stop-Stop."⁵⁶

Within the week Wheeler had sent Williams galleys of the poems as well as the cover title page, which Williams found "as beautiful in their completion as the chinese cut itself."⁵⁷ But because the poems themselves, without final punctuation, had the feel of being unfinished, Williams was anxious to have each poem end with a period as an aid to the reader. In *Spring and All* this would not be necessary, since the poems would be separated from each other by the prose. But Williams was always a stickler for this kind of detail: the unfinished feel of some of his poems was there by careful attention to the overall design, not because of carelessness or insouciance. Even before Mannikin was out in mid-April, however, Williams and Wheeler were busy with a fifth (and final) issue of *Contact.* Williams had written McAlmon at once, but since he could not be sure where exactly McAlmon would be at any given moment —London, Paris, Florence, or Madrid—or with whom—Pound, Joyce, Hemingway, or even Bill Bird—Williams had decided to go ahead with the shaping of the new issue of *Contact* alone.⁵⁸ Two weeks later he was in the thick of battle. "I am thinking of calling the damned rag '606' I have written the opening paragraphs over so many times. Almost," he wrote in mock despair to Wheeler, "I threw everything away and leaped from the roof (just outside my window) Gord! Why does one wish to get out a new periodical? My family is prostrated—my patients are dying—I have not kissed my mother for three weeks." He would see Wheeler that Friday night—his usual night in the city—at Wheeler's office on East 18th Street—and bring along his "soiled papers." They might even kill someone else besides himself, like that theoretician friend of his, Ken Burke.⁵⁹

One of the happy discoveries Williams made in putting *Contact* 5 together was reading the work of a young poet named Glenway Wescott, Wheeler's close friend. So much was he taken by Westcott's "Men Like Birds" that he wrote Wheeler in mid-April with that contagious enthusiasm of his: "I cannot believe that Wescott realizes what he has written —or indeed I cannot believe that he has written the poem as I read it." If Wescott really did understand what he had written, Williams insisted, then it was "about the best piece of work I have seen from a new hand." It was a "superb rocket," he added, searching for some way to convey what the poem had done for him, "that releases a menagerie that falls—black against sunlight, yet detail . . . ," and then gave up that approach as poor criticism in the impressionistic mode. Wescott had learned everything that he—Williams—might have taught him. "Men Like Birds" was one of the few real "compositions" he'd seen by a "young" working in America at that moment and he wanted to bring out the new issue of *Contact* just to celebrate Wescott's poem. And then—with that other characteristic gesture of his, having thus played out all his cards at once, he complained that he frankly could not "see himself forking out 100 to 150 bucks" to get the guy's poem out. Williams decided on a compromise: he would send Wheeler sixty dollars out of his own pocket to get this one issue of *Contact* published—glossy paper, cover, the best of the five in appearance—and then call it quits. After all, what the hell was the use "of any further effort in a prohibition country" like America anyway?[60]

The truth was that he was hot to get on with the project that had already been consuming him for several months and would consume him for the next year and a half: his impressionistic history of America, which would become *In the American Grain*. He and Floss had already talked over his taking a sabbatical year to research and write that book. He would be forty in September and he needed to cap the ideas he'd been writing about in *Contact*, in *The Great American Novel*, in some of the poems in *Spring and All* like "To Elsie" ("The pure products of America / go crazy") and in pieces like "A Living Coral," and bring them together between the covers of a book. What Joyce had felt in making sure that *Ulysses* would be published on his fortieth birthday Williams was also feeling: the need for a capstone for the first half of his life. His time, he told Wheeler, was very limited now and he had "several very personal literary ventures in hand" that demanded whatever time he had. "I want to go on with the Americana pieces—at least for a couple of months more—And I want to *develop* the matter which the *Contact* would contain rather than popularize it."[61]

To go on with the searching and researching he would need to do to write a convincing personal history of America he would need uninterrupted time away from his practice. This was not, of course, the way he had been writing for the past decade, where a few hours each day over a week would yield lyric after lyric or the improvisational blocks of prose that made up *Kora in Hell* or even *The Great American Novel*. Now he would need time, away from home, away from his professional and family concerns in order to break through to a major statement. To effect this extended period of concentrated effort, he would take a year off from his medical practice—from the late summer of 1923 until the summer of 1924. The first half of that sabbatical would be spent in New York City

with Floss, in a brownstone at 54 East 87th Street, a block down from
Central Park, the apartment to be shared with an old friend of theirs,
Louise Bloecher. On weekends the boys, who were now both in school,
would visit them in New York. Bill was nine, Paul would be seven in
September. Lucy, the black maid who had already worked for the
Williamses for years, would live with them at 9 Ridge Road. Ed was just
down the street; the Hermans were forty miles away in Monroe, and
"Razor" Watkins, who had played football at Colgate and was now the
physical education trainer and football coach at Rutherford High, would
take direct charge of the boys.

The trial period would be from September until Christmas, and if that
worked out well enough, then and then only would Bill and Floss take
their long-deferred trip to Europe. There Williams would enroll for
courses in pediatrics in Vienna—that would be the professional reason
for going abroad—but he would also be able to test his American
background against contemporary Europe, and—of course—write and
write to his heart's content. Albert Hoheb, his cousin on his mother's
side (Carlos Hoheb's son), and Albert's wife, Katherine, had just completed their joint internship at Passaic General and would take over Williams'
practice in his absence. They would have a room at 9 Ridge Road and
work directly out of Williams' office. There were, then, more than
enough guardians for the boys at home.

Williams had begun writing his essays on America in the fall of 1922,
at the same time he was working on *Spring and All.* They were a natural
growth, after all, of his attempt to write his antinovel grounded as it was
on a nonexistent American history. He wanted, needed, now, that history. Characteristically, he began with an essay on his old hero, Columbus,
though he was to continue reworking that piece even after he published
it in *Broom.* By March 1923, Harold Loeb had already published three
of Williams' essays in his then Berlin-based *Broom*—"The Destruction
of Tenochtitlan" in January, followed by "Red Eric" the next month and
"The Discovery of the Indies" in March. Essays on Cortez and Montezuma, Eric the Red, Columbus. By spring, Williams had already completed
several other sketches, including "The Fountain of Eternal Youth" (Ponce
de León) and part of "De Soto and the New World," which Loeb printed in
the fall of '23 once he had enough funds to go on again with the magazine.
Williams was still working on his De Soto chapter in June and therefore
refused to read Cunningham-Graham's standard history of the Spanish
explorer until his own sketch was complete. "I am trying for a certain
slant at the story," he explained to Wheeler, "which is difficult to nail so
that it would be better not to put myself under another influence than the
original documents for the moment." Once he had the thing down on
paper the way he wanted it he promised to go for the Graham book "and

eat him up."[62] It was the original, unvarnished documents, the words of those who had been there, that Williams wanted first. After he had those, he'd listen to what the others had had to say.

In the meantime, even as Williams was steaming ahead on his American essays and enjoying his sabbatical that fall in New York, Robert McAlmon had come to the rescue by taking on the responsibility of publishing *Spring and All* in Dijon in another of those special editions of three hundred. McAlmon had met Bill Bird through Hemingway in 1922 and the two men had joined forces. And though Bird saw himself more as a printer and McAlmon as a publisher, McAlmon was less tidy about such distinctions. When he printed a book, he put his own Contact Editions on the title page and then generously added Bird's Three Mountains Press stamp there as well. In the spring of 1923, hearing from Williams that he was looking for someone to publish his *Spring and All*, McAlmon volunteered to undertake the job at his own expense.

He had the money—part of the allowance Bryher was giving him on a regular basis as stipulated in their marriage contract—and he wanted to help his friend. It was as simple as that. Williams sent him the script and McAlmon had it printed and published in the fall of 1923. McAlmon also published Gertrude Stein's *The Making of Americans* (only to have Stein subsequently ignore him) and Hemingway's *Three Stories and Ten Poems* (and was repaid by Hemingway with a punch in the mouth). Williams was kinder and he genuinely appreciated McAlmon's efforts on his behalf. *Spring and All* was a very important example of both modernist poetics and poetry, more important as a seminal text, for example, than Eliot's *The Sacred Wood*, but unfortunately almost no one saw Williams' book in the original edition. The Paris booksellers weren't interested in limited editions, McAlmon was to explain, and most of the copies that were sent to America were simply confiscated by American customs officials as foreign stuff and therefore probably salacious and destructive of American morals. In effect, *Spring and All* all but disappeared as a cohesive text until its republication nearly ten years after Williams' death. McAlmon shrugged at the loss. He had grown inured to such hypocrisies and injustices. As for Williams, he went on to his next book.

*
**

On June 28, Williams and Floss sent young Bill and Paul off to Razor Watkins' camp at Lake Mattawamkeag in Maine for the summer. With the boys gone Williams hoped to be able to get some work done. Young Bill would spend every spare moment fishing, a sport he would continue all his life, and Paul would soon get himself "a beaut of a shiner from standing too close" to the plate "behind the batter."[63] And Williams for his part would continue with his poems and the American pieces and his visits into the city, especially on Friday nights. He had a particularly delightful evening with Wheeler on Friday, July 20, telling him so the next day: "I had thought conversation was dead, or merely perfunctory. Nothing so delightful as to find there is still an oasis where words do not immediately fall into the sand and die but strike in."[64] And in August, Matty Josephson arranged to have Williams and the painter Charles Sheeler and their wives meet each other over a Dutch treat dinner in a New York speakeasy. Then he invited them all back to his own spartan apartment at 45 King Street in the Village, "each guest bringing his own bottle of wine. We all sat on the floor not out of any Bohemian affectation, but because we had no chairs."[65] Williams thought he remembered Blaise Cendrars as also being there, sitting "among the legs of a piano stool turned upside down," and he even thought Hart Crane might have shown up later, though he wasn't sure. In any event he had already managed to avoid meeting his real New York competition for the past seven years and would wait another five before he finally did meet him (despite his own insistence in 1950 that he'd never met the man).[66]

Williams was still playing a little church league baseball, along with his brother, though he would soon give it up. His son Bill still remembers how his father once ran onto the mound and threatened to punch the opposing pitcher—a big Irishman who played for the local Catholic church team—in the mouth for dusting off his brother at the plate with an inside pitch. That fall, settled in New York, Williams joined the New York Fencing Club to help stay in shape, but fencing too soon fell by the way. Sometime around the end of July, Williams and Floss drove up in their Dodge to see the boys in Maine, and again Williams had to prove he was still in his eternal springtime:

> I still remember those Maine evenings just at dusk for the way we played some game that required a good deal of endurance. The older boys and counselors divided into sides, one side went north beyond the ball field and the other deployed to keep them from filtering through and reaching "home." I ran my guts out after those twelve- and fourteen-year-old kids, down along the lake front, everywhere, and caught them too.[67]

At the end of September, with the boys back in school and the sabbatical begun in earnest, Bill and Floss drove down to Farmville, Virginia, to see how Wally Gould was doing. Williams remembered the dusty roads and the "persimmons . . . just ripening on the roadside bushes as we crossed Appomattox Creek on an improvised bridge." Farmville was "saturated with Civil War tradition," and Williams—his mind preoccupied with the sense of place in American history—was aware that he was on something like sacred ground. Here the epic struggle of the War between the States had played out its final moments. He saw the spot where, "when Grant was standing on the second-floor balcony of the hotel, the round shot landed which had been aimed at him from the near distance." He saw the gatepost where "Lee, sitting astride his horse, his local partisans, broken-hearted, trying to do all they could to comfort him," took a cup of tea from one of the ladies without so much as dismounting.[68] It was a descendant of this old Virginia stock—Miss Mary Jackson—the local high-school principal just retired—who had taken Wally Gould in. At that point, Gould was making his living by a mail order cake business, with the help of young Otie, a nine-year-old black whom the Williamses discovered watching them from a tall tree as they drove up to the old brick farm. Williams took some snapshots of Gould and Miss Mary and even of Otie up in that tree.[69] He and Floss stayed there a week, and Williams walked the old Civil War fields with the intensity of an archaeologist, obsessed with the image of Lee in defeat, as later the image of Washington in defeat would also obsess him. He picked up and pocketed Indian arrowheads and Minié balls in the old gorse fields where Confederate soldiers had once camped, and he tried to get his impressions down with something of the violence with which they had crashed in on him:

> Fried chicken, Virginia ham, persimmons (on the trees) 'possum hunts by moonlight (heard like a quartette: hounds, unearthly cries of the men, horses neighing, an occasional gun-shot—till 1 AM) holly trees, oaks such as God never dreamed, niggers all alive—with their heads on. . . . [70]

It was the violence he felt in the very landscape, symbolized for him by the shots of the coon hunters startling him from sleep, the terror the blacks must have felt trying to run from such men and such dogs. Back in New York City, he wrote an essay on Virginia, using that form self-consciously to examine the very nature of the essay itself. He knew he could write a unified piece with narrative and chronology, but he also knew that the sense of radical dislocation, of the gradual assimilation of perception which the Virginia experience had been to him personally, would thereby be swallowed up. Unity of composition was, after all, a Renaissance matter, not a modern; in fact it was "the shallowest, the cheapest deception of all composition." What Williams was after was the fractured surfaces of a cubist painting. The modern essay should reflect the modern consciousness: it should attempt not unity but "multiplicity, infinite fracture, the intercrossing of opposed forces establishing any number of opposed centres of stillness." As in the intercrossing of the violence of that coon hunt with the tranquil Chinese order of Jefferson's Monticello, which Williams had visited on his way down:

> Oaks and women full of mistletoe and men. Hollow trunks for possums and the future. It clings and slips inside. Hunt for it with hounds and lanterns under the "dying moon" crying rebel yells back and forth along

the black face of the ridge—from sunset to 1 AM: the yelp of the hounds, the shouts, now a horse neighing, now a muffled gunshot. The black women often have the faces of statesmen and curiously perfect breasts— no doubt from the natural lives they lead. Often there will appear some heirloom like the cut-glass jelly stand that Jefferson brought from Paris for his daughter, a branching tree of crystal hung with glass baskets that would be filled with jelly—on occasions. This is the essence of all essays.[71]

That same violent juxtaposition Williams caught as well in a poem like "It Is a Living Coral," written about the same time and probably "inspired" by the same trip south. It is a sharp-witted satire on Congress under either (or both) the Harding or Coolidge administration.[72] Ostensibly a still life of the Capitol and its interior, Williams' focus on the quasi-heroic art of the dome and the statuary hall refracted through a cubist prism deflates the marmoreal pomposity he witnessed there, as the weight of the whole poem is brought to focus finally on the image of the green, bloated corpse of an American soldier, this one a victim of the War of 1812, one more particular in the living aggregate of coral that spelled that damnable myth called unity: *E Pluribus Unum*, From the Many, One:

> *it climbs*
>
> *it runs, it is Geo.*
> *Shoup*
>
> *of Idaho it wears*
> *a beard*
>
> *it fetches naked*
> *Indian*
>
> *women from a river*
>
> *Perry*
>
> *in a rowboat on Lake*
> *Erie*
>
> *changing ships*
> *dead*
>
> *among the wreckage*
> *sickly green*[73]

Settled into his apartment in New York in the early fall of 1923, Williams could take the el or Fifth Avenue bus down to the New York Public Library at 42d Street and go up to the American History Room to read the dusty documents that made up the past he was seeking to recover. "In these studies," he would write later, thinking back on what it had cost him personally to recreate his heritage from the old texts, "I have sought to re-name the things seen, now lost in chaos of borrowed titles, many of them inappropriate, under which the true character lies hid."[74] He read Columbus' journals, the Icelandic sagas in the so-called *Long Island Book*, the letters of Ben Franklin, John Paul Jones's naval dispatches, Hidalgo of Elvas' recollections of Cortez and Montezuma, the fugitive critical pieces of Edgar Allan Poe, the French Jesuit Sebastian Rasles's *Lettres Edifiantes* describing to his superiors his mission among the Abnakis of Maine, Cotton Mather's Puritan sermons, Thomas Morton's recollections of his Cavalier settlement at Merry Mount in the midst of a Puritan theocratic commonwealth. Floss did her share by reading up on the relations between Aaron Burr and Alexander Hamilton and then reporting in detail to her husband what she had read, and that became the basis for Williams' radical revision of Burr in the essay "The Virtue of History," which he wrote—he said—in one sitting. Where another voice had interjected itself into the history—as in John Filson's writing of Daniel Boone's *Autobiography*—Williams tried to recover as well as he knew how something of the authenticity and originality of the figure he was in pursuit of.

"In letters, in journals, reports of happenings I have recognized new contours suggested by old words so that new names were constituted."[75] It was important for Williams that he escape the charge of writing mere subjective history. A history in which he was personally and vitally involved, yes, for hc hoped to learn about himself as a distinctively American writer by feeling the exact contours of the American experience, not as received through a false, numbing tradition, but as something imaginatively experienced. To add weight to his argument, therefore, he would use wherever he could the precise words—caught in the style of the moment out of which they had been uttered—of the figures he was attempting to resurrect: the Spaniards, French, English, Yankees, Indians, blacks, women, and immigrants who together had created the American experience. "Everywhere," he insisted, "I have tried to separate out from the original records some flavor of an actual peculiarity the character-denoting shape which the unique force has given." In every case, Williams had been after the same thing in his sources: "the strange phosphorus of the life, nameless under an old misappellation."[76] It would be up to Williams to name once again the fallen objects and people of his New World Eden, and in thus renaming to come into an authentic possession of his heritage.

There were practical problems. He was up against the clock and he knew it. He did not have the leisure of several years to meditate on the texts; he had before him instead three months. He remembered with unabated irritation how once, when one of the early chapters was swarming in his head—either the De Soto or Ponce de León chapter —how that essay had at once jelled for him on his trip down to the

American History Room. Without ordering a book from the desk, he sat down and began to write furiously, having discovered the fragile phosphorus he was after. Suddenly, he felt someone tapping at his shoulder. It was the library attendant for that room, and he was informing Williams that the room was for reading, not writing, and telling him so in a British accent. Williams whispered to the attendant that he was writing a thesis on American history, but the man knew his orders. Williams would need a book to write in that room, and so—though he wanted to strangle the man—he had to get up and order a book, wait for it, and then dutifully open it before he could go on. By then the frail light of inspiration had flitted up through the high windows of the room and was gone. Williams would remember that incident when he came to write *Paterson*, where the dead authors·flit against the library windows crying to be heard.[77]

All that fall Williams guarded what time he had with something approaching a manic intensity. At the end of September he went with Floss, Monroe Wheeler, and Glenway Wescott to a concert at Carnegie Hall to hear Elly Ney play Bach and Chopin, but when Wheeler suggested that they get together again soon, Williams warned him that "for the moment I am working too hard to want to gad—or even to visit my good friends. . . . The mood is all for priestly quiet."[78] And a few weeks later he had to tell Malcolm Cowley that a play he had been talking to Cowley about writing—for inclusion in *Broom*—had been the talk of a madman. Suddenly the costs were there: "Why man this would mean a practical cancellation of MY ENTIRE PROGRAMME for the next six weeks—a programme that has cost me ten years work to place on a low shelf." He simply could not "sacrifice" the time now: "I must give myself to writing and to that only or I am lost."[79]

He wrote Wescott—for whom he had shown such enthusiasm just a few months before—in early October that he was spending a week at his in-laws' "modest" place in Monroe, New York, and that he would see Wescott (who reminded him in an eerie sort of way of no one so much as H.D.) when the opportunity naturally came. The fact was that he was in hiding and was being "altogether irresponsible for the first time in—my life?" When he regained something like full consciousness, swimming up from his writing, and got back to New York, he'd drop him a line.[80] But he didn't. He had also given Burke his New York phone number, and then asked him not to give it out indiscriminately, explaining that he was in a kind of retirement. He preferred now to keep in touch with the literary world through the little magazines and letters. He discovered a young writer named Ernest Hemingway there, and was much impressed by his *Three Stories and Ten Poems*, which McAlmon had just published. "Hemingway is a star I think," he wrote his friend. "His poems especially are noteworthy but the prose is thrilling. Who is he anyway?"[81] He read McAlmon's *Post-Adolescence*—which McAlmon had published himself

—and found it a falling off after *The Hasty Bunch*, which he'd earlier praised for its setting down of experiences "with no more art than that necessary to make the whole a sound functioning body."[82] As for his own work, he found that Pound was still "shitting" on him in his personal letters,[83] and Marion Strobel—his old friend from that week in Chicago —had just slammed him for being a middle-aged adolescent in her *Poetry* review of his *Go-Go* pamphlet.

It was during the fall of 1923 that Evelyn Scott, a young, brilliant novelist, with whom Williams had had an affair that had lasted for over a year and had only recently ended, vented her anger at Williams in a long, revealing letter to Lola Ridge, who had become her confidante. Williams, she complained, had dismissed not only her own poetry, but Ridge's as well, and now Scott was out for blood. Biased as her letter is, however, Scott's witty portrait of Williams at forty shows us how "Buffalo Bill" could strike other writers who were not used to his enthusiasm, or who disliked his "knee-jerk" gestures. Trying to talk with Williams, Scott recalled, seemed inevitably to end in getting from him "that perfectly inane response of quick emotion which he doesn't understand himself, which makes him look like a wired jumping-jack with broken strings and arms and legs going feebly in all directions at once. Then he would recover and say that marianne's work [Marianne Moore] is good because he cant understand it, or that macalmon [Robert McAlmon] is the best artist he knows, or that women cant write anyway, or that—finally—he himself is a fool and knows it, or that he expects to be considered a great man when he dies and have a monument in rutherford or a plate on his house."

She had recently read Williams' *The Great American Novel* (Kay Boyle had lent it to her) and summed it up with a critical insight that showed both intelligence and a real flair for the comic. Somehow she managed to put her finger on the very weakness in the novel's progression that Williams himself had earlier pointed out to Pound:

> I thought it began magnificently, sort of sweeping down a precipice to destruction, a ford car like a juggernaut, and all the lights of jersey and manhattan making crazy circles upward, standing even overhead as the car rushed past them with a suicidal radiance. Then suddenly juggernaut stands still, has a puncture in the tire or something curfluey with the engine. It wont dash to destruction at all. The great circles of flying buildings, windows, skylines, grain elevators and railway tracks stand still also. Excitement very weak now. Oh yes, where was I? Shouting oyia. Oh, yes, and I'll tell you something about the absurdity of advertising. Oh yes. Stutterings. . . . Always that vacuous termination because he wants to live like a drunkard and unfortunately the day after is in his books as well as the golden moment of most clear-eyed delerium [sic] and it is the day after you end with. . . . Still he deserves more than most, as an artist. . . . [84]

In the summer of '21, Marianne Moore had written a considerate and perceptive essay on *Kora in Hell* for Williams' *Contact*. Williams had of course followed her career very closely, and he had praised her highly in the closing pages of *Spring and All*, copies of which McAlmon had just shipped him. H.D. and Bryher had published her poems in England in a pamphlet called, simply, *Poems*, having done so without her knowledge, though of course she was pleased. In 1924 she would publish her *Observations* in the U.S. with the Dial Press. But in 1923 her poems were virtually inaccessible. (And even Stevens had succumbed to a book when Knopf published *Harmonium* that year.) It was time, then, for Williams to write a real appreciation of her quiet but staggering achievements. "It is a pity not to have a full book of poems by Marianne Moore," he began. "There is of course the London pamphlet and recently the *Mannikin* with its one poem, *Marriage*; also there are the back numbers of the magazines and the two *Others* Anthologies but it is time now that something better were available. I write for the purpose of calling heed to this lack."[85] In reading the classic Americans as he had been doing (including D. H. Lawrence's just published *Studies in Classic American Literature*, though he did not mention this fact), Williams could see that Moore's work was like theirs where theirs was good, when it manifested a cleanness, a clarity, a gentleness, a lack of cement. She got her great pleasure, he saw, "from wiping soiled words or cutting them clean out, removing the aureoles that have been pasted about them or taking them bodily from greasy contexts."[86] She had learned how to make words stand apart, crystal clear. She was a poet of clear, hard edges, like his favorite painter, the Spanish cubist Juan Gris. Even ideas became things in her poems, abstract categories jostling concretely beside apples and bricks. He himself had learned an important technique from her in watching how she eschewed connectives, filler, cement, to fit her images together like some Incan stonemason.

It was a brilliant essay he wrote on Marianne Moore's poetry and poetics, and Williams kept revising it to get the precise contour of his feelings for her achievement down on paper. Then, just as he was finishing it and preparing to send it to *The Dial*, he read in the December issue of that magazine a short, reserved, but favorable appreciation of Moore's work by none other than T. S. Eliot. "Dear Elliot," he wrote, getting the spelling—as he often did with his correspondents—wrong on the first attempt, "I must tell you how pleased and how disappointed I was at seeing your review of Marianne Moore's work in the . . . *Dial*." Williams was polite, deferential even, now that he was actually addressing the author of *The Waste Land*, which had appeared in that same magazine the year before. He praised Eliot's appreciation of Moore (though the review was not really one of Eliot's better efforts) and then confessed that he too had been "working upon the same theme for a month past, the result of which I was planning to offer to *Dial*." He was sure Eliot would understand his disappointment at having been put "out of the running" by Eliot (a Freudian slip?). Now Williams' own thesis was in its final stages of revision and he was sending it on to Eliot for possible inclusion in Eliot's own London-based *Criterion*, especially since, as Williams saw it, "we were both thinking of Miss Moore's work somewhat similarly at the same time." He also mentioned that he was going to Europe shortly and wondered if he might not meet Eliot—as McAlmon had in 1921—"in London or Paris in the spring." Finally, he wondered if Eliot might not be good enough to send along a copy of *The Criterion*, especially as he had never seen one. Then he sent the latest draft of the essay to Eliot just as it was, errors and all. That was on December 9.[87] Two days later he wrote that red-haired caryatid, Moore herself, that he'd written "Elliot" and that the finished version of his essay on her would be shipped off to London in a week's time. Williams hoped Eliot would print the thing, "for your sake—and mine." He was feeling good at the moment, waiting for Flossie to get back to their New York apartment, and wondering if the elation he was feeling had anything to do with "the thirty drops of Nux Vomica" he was taking "three times a day" for his eyes.[88]

As he had promised, a week to the day he'd sent off the essay Williams mailed Eliot the revisions. He had finally finished the thing, "writing it over and over, which is something—to me. Paralleling the phenomena of electricity," he quipped, "the kicks in writing come with the first and final transcriptions only. The rest is just plain transit." He also included his Paris address as in care of Sylvia Beach's bookstore, Shakespeare & Co., 12, rue de l'Odéon, though, if Eliot cared to, he might send him a card acknowledging receipt of the manuscript before he left New York. "Pleasant news I could treasure to make the waves greener on my way over and bad news I could learn in the passage to forget."[89] The next day Williams shot off two closely packed pages of corrections for the copy of the essay he'd already sent on.[90]

But he must have known that Eliot would reject the piece, either out of a sense of having been insulted by what Williams had said about him in his "Prologue" to *Kora in Hell*, or perhaps by something McAlmon had said in Eliot's presence about Williams' strong feelings toward Eliot. Or Eliot might have simply rejected the essay as the work of a strong American contender. For whatever reason, the day after he sent the corrections to Eliot, Williams offered one of his rough copies of the Moore essay to Harriet Monroe at *Poetry*, telling her that he'd first intended it for *The Dial* but that Eliot had beaten them there. Eliot, he added, had the original.[91]

On December 27, in the midst of making final preparations for the trip to Europe—they were leaving on January 9—Williams wrote Moore in a state of despondency from the farm in Monroe. "Billy has a chemical set for Christmas," he told her, and little Bobby (that was Paul's nickname) had a cold. "Dear little mites, it seems impossible to leave them, even for a moment, and we are going to Europe." But then if he'd been a pioneer like his own Daniel Boone "one might have been shot by an Indian a few years ago leaving the children to starve in an isolated cabin." That thought shored him up, at least a bit. On the eve of his departure—with still no word from Eliot—he was particularly sensitive to the drubbing Wallace Stevens' *Harmonium* had just received at the hands of his old enemy John Gould Fletcher in the current *Freeman*. "Perhaps my nerves are ragged over leaving the children," he admitted, but Fletcher had managed to touch "a sensitive spot" in his consciousness for all that. "You know I began with portraits of old women in bed and the rest of it, and it all seemed very important." But now he was writing less frenetically, more quietly, a "more deliberate composition." He had changed in ten years. But Fletcher still seemed to genuinely hate all the younger American writers, rejecting them all as disillusioned. The truth was, however, that if any modern poem seemed disillusioned to Williams, it was Eliot's *The Waste Land*—though maybe there was something of a different tone in the languages Eliot had incorporated into the fabric of the poem, languages that Williams did not pretend to understand and said so. Here he was at forty on sabbatical, feeling "that a vacuum cleaner in under my hair would be a great boon. So he put to sea." He needed to start fresh, now, to begin all over again.[92]

He had decided to keep a diary of his trip, an uncharacteristic gesture on his part, since in effect his letters—sent out to hundreds of literary correspondents—performed something of the same service. But he never kept copies of his letters, and he felt that a diary recording his meetings with the crew that was in Paris or the impressions he might have in seeing Rome or Villefranche or Vienna or Geneva would be worth jotting down to be used for some future project. As it turned out, he was right. Floss and Bill left on the SS *Rochambeau* on a brilliant sunshiny January day, their cabin strewn with flowers from relatives and friends in Rutherford and New York. Two of his friends had taken Williams up to the Columbia University Club the night before sailing and had tried to put him under the table with speakeasy liquor, an experience, he noted in his diary, that would be repeated many times in the coming months.[93]

*
**

It was a nine-day trip across, and Williams spent the time observing a whale and the voracious gulls coming up from under the very prow of the old, slow liner. The ship hit fog and then an incredible winter storm, but it kept lurching on. Here was a crossing literally from the known into the unknown, a passage east into uncertain beginnings, even as he wrote and revised his American essays in his cabin or on deck. He would remember this passage again when he wrote the opening passages of his first real novel, *Voyage to Pagany*, two years later. They made Le Havre on the eighteenth and were met at the train station by Kay Boyle, who was anxious to have them stay with her, but they couldn't. Bob McAlmon was waiting for them in Paris and had reserved a room for them at the Hotel Lutetia. When they got there that evening, Williams ordered a big Chateaubriand and watched the waiter cut it in half and keep half on a shelf—for himself, as it turned out. Williams could not trust his French yet, and so had to watch helplessly as he received his first fleecing.

Floss was enjoying herself immensely, though, and was looking forward to the flurry of faces and places she had already begun to encounter and would encounter now in full swing. For her, the trip would be one long vacation. On Saturday, January 19, they called on Bob McAlmon and then walked over to 12, rue de l'Odéon to meet Sylvia Beach—who was out—and to see if there was any mail. Williams saw there was still nothing from Eliot. He saw his own books displayed there in the bookstore window looking pale and dusty. As for McAlmon, he was heavier; the good life had ballooned him from his customary 115 pounds to somewhere around 150. He seemed older and more world-weary though he had refused to surrender his own western manners. By now he was supporting many artists, both French and American, publishing their works or just paying for their rooms and their food. Still, he wasn't being taken in by any of them, as far as Williams could see.

That afternoon McAlmon took them to see Brancusi in his studio, "a short compact peasant of a man," Williams wrote, "with his long gray hair, like a sheep dog," whose work Williams had already seen and admired in an exhibition in New York. Brancusi had not been expecting them, but he put his work aside to talk to them. "It was a barnlike place filled with blocks of stone, formless wooden hunks and stumps for the most part, work finished and unfinished. I remember especially his 'Socrates': a big hole through the center of the block showing Socrates the talker, his mouth (and mind) wide open expounding his theses. There was the head of Isaac also."[94] Thirty years later Williams would remember that meeting with Brancusi when he wrote—in spite of his crippled condition—one of his strongest appreciations ever for any artist for a retrospective showing of Brancusi's work in New York in 1956.

After that meeting with Brancusi, Williams met Bill Bird—the publisher of his "novel"—in a small bar. "Bill was a tall, sharp-bearded American businessman," Williams wrote, "who looked as though he had been mellowed in Chambertin, gentle, kindly and informal. I fell for him instantly."[95] Williams' publisher was a connoisseur of French wines, and Williams was to enjoy Bird's own collection several months later. Then, that evening, McAlmon had arranged the biggest treat of all: the Williamses were to have dinner with James and Nora Joyce at the Trianon. It turned out to be a delightful evening for Williams. Nora said hardly anything, but Joyce was particularly interested to talk with Floss because he was doing the early history of Dublin for *Finnegans Wake*, when Dublin was a seaport for the Viking invaders. Floss's mother's family were Norwegian, and so Joyce kept asking Floss for Norse words. Williams noticed Joyce's thick eyeglasses (glaucoma) and the way he missed his glass when he poured the white wine until Floss moved the glass to help him. Joyce: with his small compressed head, straight nose, no lips, the Irish accent. Williams ticked them off like a diagnostician examining a case. And McAlmon, raising his glass with the toast, "Here's to sin!" which Joyce refused to join in, so that McAlmon had to take the toast back with a laugh. Then oysters, coffee, and more drinks at the late-night Dingo, Joyce and Nora finding the Williamses "beati innocenti."[96]

That night too, McAlmon, depressed and half drunk, began to reveal to Williams the whole story of his marriage to Bryher, who was then off with H.D. in Switzerland. McAlmon had done very important work as a publisher, teamed up as he was with Bill Bird, and he had published some of the most important books of the modernist period written in English. But Williams could also see what living hard in Paris, or traveling down through the south of France to Spain or Italy or Switzerland, drinking hard and playing hard day after day, was doing to his friend. "No man could go on at that pace forever," he wrote, for McAlmon seemed to know "no limits," either for "physical or for intellectual honesty."[97] How soon then before his friend burned out?

The Williamses naturally did a great deal of sightseeing in Paris: Notre Dame, the Louvre, rue de l'Opéra, the rue de la Paix, the Place Vendôme, the Théâtre des Champs Elysées for Jules Romain's *Dr. Knock*, the Eiffel Tower, the Gare Montparnasse. On Tuesday evening, January 22d, McAlmon threw a big party for the Williamses at the Trianon. Williams sat in the middle, facing the left wall, with Floss on his right and James and Nora Joyce and Ford Madox Ford and his wife directly across from him. It was the first time he had met Ford, and he liked "the lumbering Britisher"[98] at once. Harold Loeb—of the *Broom*—was there and Kitty Cannell, Skip Cannell's ex-wife, was with him. And so was the American composer, George Antheil, whom Pound had championed, who was then working on his *Ballet Mécanique*, which when completed would have a jazz symphony, fourteen grand pianos, a foghorn, and electric alarm bells, and which the Williamses would see performed at Carnegie Hall three years later. Bill Bird too was there, and Mina Loy and her daughter, and Louis Aragon and Marcel Duchamp and Man Ray.

When Williams was called on to make a speech, he felt awkward, especially under the intense, skeptical gaze of the French artists among the group, some of whom had not even been invited. He knew what they were thinking—what could this American possibly signify to the French—and he could not forget Duchamp's cut in Arensberg's studio eight years before. Never again would he allow them to catch him unguarded. A bit flushed with wine, he thanked McAlmon for the party and thanked them all for coming. And then he told them a little parable, about how he had observed among the French that "when a corpse, in its hearse, plain or ornate, was passing in the streets, the women stopped, bowed their heads and that men generally stood at attention with their hats in their hands."[99] That was it. Then he sat down abruptly, feeling like a fool for having insulted them. For a moment there was silence. Then someone asked McAlmon to sing "Bollicky Bill," undoubtedly intended as a response to Williams, and McAlmon sang. Later the French went off with Man Ray, and Williams and McAlmon and the Fords and Joyces went to the Dingo to drink some more. It was three in the morning before Williams got back to his hotel room.

The next morning, suffering from a bad wine hangover, Williams downed six glasses of warm water and went out for a long walk. When he came to the Place François Ier, he was suddenly taken by the French austerity of design he saw in that medieval edifice, "gray stone cleanly cut and put together in complementary masses," unlike anything he'd seen before. That quiet moment of insight into that other France restored his sense of balance and he felt chastened. There was, after all, still much good in France. In the evening, after visiting the Louvre, McAlmon took the Williamses to Brancusi's studio for one of Brancusi's beefsteak dinners. They spoke of the French, Williams making a point of bringing up their tolerance, smarting still from the unfortunate comment he had made the night before. But Brancusi himself let him know that not all French were tolerant, that there was a ridigity among the aristocracy more formidable than anywhere else in the world.

The following day Williams went with McAlmon to Man Ray's studio to have his picture taken. It had been Man Ray's idea and Williams found himself being posed in order to get his "essential" character across on film. Man Ray asked Williams to close his eyes a little, and later, when Williams saw the sentimental effect that had had, he was furious. "I did not want that look on my face," he wrote. "I felt already sufficiently humiliated not to be the hard, 'take it' sort of person all these other characters about me seemed to represent. I felt soft enough, messy enough with my eyes well open."[100] So Man Ray had him twice: once for a photo that Williams hated, and again for the preposterous bill for six prints which came to more than what ten days at the Lutetia cost him. Two years later, Williams would have his cousin, Irving Wellcome, take another photo of him, this time with hair on end, nose aquiline-sharp, the eyes not only opening, but positively glaring with the unrelenting, hard look of an American bald eagle. He was happy with that one.

Although he would later tell his first critical biographer, Vivienne Koch, that he had never met anyone named Valery Larbaud, so that Williams' *Autobiography* remains silent about this French scholar of American literature, Williams noted in his diary that on Saturday, January 26, he went to see "Larbeau" (sic), whom he found "charming." Williams spoke in French, though with some effort, and listened while Larbaud told him how the Spanish had "colonized America on a grand scale. Poe, Whitman (predigeous) [sic], Cotton Mather."[101] In fact, that meeting in Paris on a cold, drizzly afternoon would become the fulcrum on which Williams would balance his *In the American Grain*. It was Adrienne Monnier—the French bookdealer—who had been responsible for the introduction. She had given Williams

> one of my best moments among those days of rushing about and talk-
> ing and seeing, while my bronzed faculties strove to right themselves
> —among the scenes and fashions of this world where all the world comes,
> from time to time, to shed its nerves—after my brutalizing battle of
> twenty years to hear myself above the boilermakers in and about New
> York. . . . I felt myself with ardors not released but beaten back, in this
> center of old-world culture where everyone was tearing his own meat,
> *warily* conscious of a newcomer, but wholly without inquisitiveness.[102]

It was still raining that Saturday afternoon when he took the bus to the small, cloistral inner court and the tiny room that served Larbaud for his study. At first Williams was ill at ease. Why did Larbaud wish to see him? This serious student of America, embarked on a multivolume study of Simón Bolívar, scrutinizing this American, "the brutal thing itself." What were we Americans after all, he thought, and the answer for Williams was devastating:

> Who are we? Degraded whites riding our fears to market where everything
> is by accident and only one thing sure: the fatter we get the duller we
> grow; only a simpering disgust (like a chicken with a broken neck, that
> aims where it cannot peck and pecks only where it cannot aim, which a
> hogplenty everywhere prevents from starving to death) reveals any
> contact with a possible freshness—and that only by inversion.[103]

Larbaud had read Williams' essays on America's beginnings in the *Broom*, and Williams now hammered home the importance of studying America's beginnings, since Americans—whether they were cognizant of the fact or not—had been shaped, generation after generation, by what America as a nation had been from those beginnings. If we did not understand our own roots, our specific origins as Americans, he believed, then as a nation we were "nothing but an unconscious porkyard and oilhole for those, more able, who will fasten themselves upon us."[104] What Williams was coming to learn was the cost of his Puritan heritage —as that word was popularly represented by critics and humorists like H. L. Mencken. The problem with the English, as Williams saw it, was that they had never come into close contact with the natives they had found here. For them, the Indian was a savage, Satan's own inversion of the twelve tribes of Israel in possession of the New World, a force to be repressed, beaten down, exterminated.

The French, on the other hand, had done better by the Indians, allying themselves with them frequently, marrying them, coming into intimate contact with them. The image of the French Jesuit Père Sebastian Rasles working among the Abnakis of Maine, dressing like them, eating with them, going hungry when they went hungry, praising their skills as hunters, warriors, unwilling to pass judgment on them, finally dying with them at the hands of the English: that was the image of the European whom Williams admired. Rasles was the type of the European who had come into intimate contact with the New World, not to rape or despoil it, but instead to marry himself to the new. Against Rasles, Williams juxtaposed Cotton Mather, quoting extensively from Mather's own sermons to show how the English divine had viewed the savages howling in the desert. It was in some ways a romantic view that Williams proposed, but it was also one he believed had actually served to deform his own youth of hellish repressions for some false conception of virtue. In part, then, Williams was writing his book in order to be able to define the malady that had misshaped him and millions of other Americans. He wanted now to diagnose the disease and then—as he was able—exorcise it, cut the cancer out of him. Larbaud, sitting back with the detachment of the outsider, unaffected by the quaintness of the American condition he was watching in this American as Williams worked himself into something like fever pitch, smiled. Ah, these Americans! How quaint. How charming. . . .

Monday morning Williams went down to 12, rue de l'Odéon for the last time to see if a letter from Eliot had come. When he found none, he wrote Eliot that he had expected to hear from him about the Marianne Moore piece and that if he couldn't use it in the *Criterion* to at least return the thing. He apologized for sending the manuscript in the unfinished condition he had and then for sending the corrections which must have looked "terrifying." He was leaving Paris tomorrow with his wife, but he had arranged to have his mail forwarded and he was still "really quite anxious about that article."[105] Eliot apparently never answered, though he may have given instructions to have the article sent back without any comment. In any event, Williams never again wrote to the man who could find no room for him in his *Criterion* and who—over the next twenty-five years and more—became Williams' bête noir, Williams' most celebrated literary antagonist. It was a battle in which Williams was constantly on the offense and in which Eliot, from his established vantage, chose simply to ignore Williams—at least publicly.

That night, preparing to leave Paris next day to go south, the Williamses had dinner with Mina Loy and then went to a party at Ford Madox Ford's place, a garden apartment outside the city. They arrived just in time—as Williams recalled—to see Berenice Abbott, Man Ray's assistant, knocked to the floor by "some English fairy," as Ford called him. Abbott and Ford shrugged the incident off and things returned to "normal." Such things were common in Paris, Williams was learning, but he was even more shocked to see the "English fairy" help the woman to her feet, examine her cut lip, and then continue his drunken dancing with her.[106] Soon after Williams and Floss excused themselves from the party and went back to the hotel. Ten days in Paris: it had been enough.

The Williamses left Paris the next afternoon, taking the train from the Quai d'Orsay to the south of France and toward the already advancing spring. They visited the medieval walled city of Carcassonne, "standing there by virtue of stone, to remain still, dominating the plains, looking to the Pyrenees, empty and sad."[107] They visited the fortress church of St. Nazaire, which was still icy cold, and then—outside—Williams found tiny daisies pressed close to the ground. They were the first harbingers of spring. Then south again to Marseilles and the Hotel Splendide. There they had a splendid bouillabaisse and a bottle of Mersault. Next they traveled east along the French Riviera. Scrub pine and oak, the gray rocks, the Mediterranean appearing and disappearing on their right, past Toulon ("where Napoleon set sail for Egypt") to Cannes, Nice, and on to the old, secluded fishing village of Villefranche, with its narrow streets, irregular steps and gutters running down the middle of the streets. Strings of onions and peppers, cheese, pastry smells, the men in sailor caps, the beacon on the point beyond Beaulieu, the blue sea, mimosas in full bloom, slops dropped past their pension window from above. Even as they arrived at the pink-stuccoed Pension Donat—where they would stay for the month of February—they could see the old fortifications to the left and the casern to the right where the Chasseurs Alpins—the Alpine Light Infantry—were housed, and whose reveille awoke them bright and early each morning.

The Williamses visited Nice from the Villefrance pension, and went with Djuna Barnes and Thelma Wood to the casinos there on February 15

Williams—who disliked betting—cashed only fifty francs and proceeded to lose twenty. Floss won something, but then slipped twenty-five francs to Thelma Wood, who had already lost her own money and then proceeded to lose Floss's.[108] Later that day, Williams discussed Barnes's *Nightwood* with her—a book he liked a great deal. It was here too that Williams read McAlmon's Berlin stories, which he genuinely admired, and he also continued to put in long hours on his own American pieces, especially on cold days. He kept reworking the Columbus piece, even though it had already been published, and then finished up his De Soto chapter. Then he switched to the Boone essay and finished his "Voyage of the *Mayflower*" chapter, sending that off finally to Loeb at the *Broom* on the twenty-fourth. In between he read Joyce's *Portrait of the Artist* and Cummings' *Tulips* and *Chimneys*. He wrote Marianne Moore on the tenth that he and McAlmon were working, each in his own way, and that the two of them wanted her to put together that book of poems he had called for in the essay Eliot had rejected. Contact Editions, he assured her, would publish it.[109] But five days later, McAlmon, restless as ever, gave up work and went on to Nice alone for a few days, unwilling to be with Barnes and Wood, who probably reminded him of H.D. and his own absent wife.

Williams—anxious to help McAlmon where McAlmon would not help himself—also wrote an extended critique of the three books of prose McAlmon had already published, sending the essays in the form of letters off to Ford Madox Ford's *Transatlantic Review*, where they were all eventually published. But by February 21, with Bryher now in Villefranche, it was time to think of moving on to Italy at the beginning of March, without McAlmon. Williams liked McAlmon more than ever, he told Marianne, but he found it painful to be in his presence now that Bryher was around. So, when McAlmon and Bill Bird—who had by then also come down to Villefranche—suggested that the Williamses go with them to Marseilles, Williams simply refused. He and Floss were going on to Italy as planned, and they would see McAlmon and Bird when they got back to Paris sometime in May.

*
**

The Williamses left for Italy on March 3, taking the night train, so that it was dark when they crossed into the new country. At eleven that night they were in Genoa, where they walked about the city and had coffee before taking the midnight train on to Florence. Williams would remember that stopover in his *Voyage to Pagany* as a crossing in darkness into a different terrain, a new interior landscape, into the heart of the old, old upon old, pagan culture of Europe.[110] The warm maternal south, the uninhibited Italians, the dark moist sexuality of it, the heart of this attractive darkness was already beginning to reveal itself again to him. Pound had written Williams that he would not be able to see him in Rapallo and that Williams should look for him in Paris when he returned. So that pressure was removed. Paris was behind Williams now, and so was the Riviera. Before him, as it had been fourteen years before, lay Italy, waiting.

They passed Pisa at four in the morning. Williams, awake and excited, looked out the train window but could see nothing in the dark but shadows. By seven, he could make out a river and grapevines and fields: it was the Arno. "And all the time he was going to Florence," Williams would write in *Voyage to Pagany*, "Dante's city, city of the old bridge, city of 'the David,' of Raphael—and a faint pang of worn beauty struck him. He wanted to say Giotto—Instead he called it: City of the Arno, and the Arno before there was a city, teaching the fields of Proserpine, the fields of the Vernal gods. Botticelli, Donatello—now it was nearer. But he did not care for history. He knew only a river flowing through March in the sun, making, making, inviting the recreators—asking to be recreated."[111] The river—incredibly old and yet as new as the day, throwing up the city of Florence along its banks, an architecture, a formal excellence frozen in time, with its concomitant paintings and frescoes and murals and sculptures. A river: like the Hackensack, the Hudson, the Passaic, with their cities thrown up on their banks as well.

Williams had seen these places earlier with Ed, so that the sights he saw were still familiar to him. At least the architecture was. But the people were different. This was Mussolini's Italy, the third year of the new age, and he noticed young Fascisti soldiers at the train stations kissing their loved ones good-by. But his eye had also caught old derelicts lying in the shadows of the public buildings at Genoa and again here in Florence at the Hotel Helvetia, where they stayed for two days sightseeing. They saw the Ponte Vecchio, the Uffizi, the Pitti Palace, the Boboli Gardens, Santa Croce. March 5 was election day in the city, and Williams noticed clusters of workingmen in Sunday clothes loafing about, a few at the polls, carabinieri and police with guns in hand going about the town. He saw them stop one group dressed up for a carnival—young men and women—to make them show their faces from beneath their masks before letting them proceed.

On the sixth, Bill and Floss took the train south to Rome, passing Cortona and then Orvieto—a marvelous "bare country, savage and untenanted save by drab mountain hamlets and rare names" which he fell in love with.[112] Toward evening they arrived in Rome, seeing the familiar image of St. Peter's in the distance. Floss had a bad cold and Williams took her at once to the Continental Hotel for rest. But the next day they were sightseeing again—the Tiber, the Borghese gardens, Castel

San Angelo, St. Peter's—before taking a room at the Pensione Astoria, via Sicilia. On Sunday morning, they took the train south once again for Naples, and after a long ride, first up over the mountains and then down, they saw Mt. Vesuvius in the distance.

But they were not impressed with Naples. In fact, Williams had come really to see the bay from the hills and then on Monday to examine once more—as he had done with Ed in 1910—the museum in Naples that housed the pieces that had been unearthed from the excavations at Pompeii and Herculaneum. On Tuesday a guide took them through the dead city of Pompeii for two hours, and Williams made a special point of examining the fertility frescoes—the Priapic legend clearing up for him the significance of the images. That evening they stayed at Cava at the Hotel de Londres, where Williams had a long talk with the proprietor about the big soccer game between Cava and Torre del Greco, which had taken place that afternoon.

Next day they went on to Amalfi, then to Sorrento and Paestum, to see—as Williams had seen in 1910—the extraordinary Greek Doric temple to Poseidon from its promontory overlooking the sea. At Amalfi they went into the church of St. Andrew's to see the crypt of the body of St. Andrew. The story was that the body exuded a grease each spring, by which the priests could tell whether or not that year would provide a bountiful harvest. Williams would remember that scene years later in his poem "The Clouds," where the priest he saw saying mass there jigged "on the twin muscles of his buttocks to the whine and groan of a chant and its responses."[113] For Williams, Italy was still very much a pagan country, with only the thinnest overlay of Christianity.

On March 14, Bill and Floss were back in Rome, and now Williams began again to write. But this time it was another set of improvisations, which he called his "Roman Journal." Italy was tormenting him, he would recall later, and he turned to his writing now as to a wife, writing "blindly, instinctively for several hours, a steady flow of incomprehensible words and phrases, until he was exhausted."[114] He wanted to possess somehow the real Rome that he had sensed, wanted to possess it as he had struggled to possess America, to call it by name, a fleeting presence, avoiding—as he said—no word that floated into his consciousness. "There is no writing but a moment that is and dies and is again wearing the body to nothing," he wrote in his journal. To get it down, then, while that moment existed, to cut through the language, the sexual patina, and thus strike clean to the reality of this world:

> I love my senses in the morning. Unclouded by drunkenness, unfucked out—undesirous, still as rock—springing within themselves with strength the fountain of everything if it is the fountain of something —What is the Via Appia? That's what I leave in my bath. Good Christ

what are these sons of bitches about, each with a dead Jew buried in the cellars of their churches. Andrew at Amalfi. Whom do they tell the body is exuding grease? . . . They are the jack-offs in the choir rocking back and forth to the organ. . . . A god walks laughing up the steps, he sees the column they stole *for the church* from Paestum, hears the history, laughs and looks out idly at the sea, smells, is tired and goes to the hotel for dinner where a bastardly waiter passes off a worthless ten lira paper bill on him—It is I—dull as dead Mercury. . . . Who loves to jerk off in his bath when the water is hot and his hands are rich and soapy or to shove her [sic] slippery fingers into her cunt and play. . . . But I know enough not to do it before I write a poem—the poem is the blood coursing full of Madonnas. Sometimes though, after a good free fuck, time is—broken.[115]

Williams had seen Nancy Cunard and her cousin Victor in Ville-franche, and now—in Rome—he went to see her again, alone, in her plush apartment overlooking the Roman Forum, with the wisteria climbing up from the garden to her balcony on the fifth floor.[116] He wrote about her in his journal—in fact Nancy Cunard seems to have been the direct inspiration for his newly-found freedom of sexual expression. He would remember her after that visit with fondness and admiration for what he called her own cleanness of mind, her open sexuality, the white flame of her existence, her tough honesty, her brazening out her own nonconformity, this daughter of a shipping magnate with her devotion to the arts, who would openly take a black lover several years later. He would put up a newspaper photograph of her in his attic study half a dozen years later, and he would invite her and her black manager/lover out to spend the weekend at 9 Ridge Road in 1931. She remained for him always the type of the exceptional woman.

On Saturday, March 15, Williams and Floss visited the Vatican and he became annoyed when he saw the plaster of paris fig leaves the Church authorities had had placed over the genitalia of Michelangelo's figures in the Sistine Chapel. He'd seen too many bodies of all descriptions over the years to see that sort of protection as anything other than coy prurience. Next day the two of them went out by train to visit the Pantheon, only to find it closed for repairs. Instead, they went to the Roman Coliseum, walking all over the steps and arena of the ruined pile. Then it was on to St. Peter's and the Vatican again. Next day it was the Palazzo del Popolo, the Pincio Gardens, and a long walk through the Villa Borghese. So it went, that Friday Nancy Cunard inviting the Williamses to her apartment for lunch to meet Norman Douglas, author of *High Wind Over Jamaica*, a book Williams admired very much. It was during this lunch that the Williamses, with a mixture of nostalgia and guilt, mentioned their misgivings about leaving their two sons in America for so long a period. Douglas' response was that the best thing a parent could do after bringing a child into the world was simply to die, a remark Williams remembered with relish when, twenty-five years later, he came to write about sons and fathers in *Paterson* 4.

He was in the midst of his "Roman Journal" by then, and traces of old Pagany were preoccupying him all the more. Thus he noted in his diary on the eighteenth that while most of the Priapic statues had had their genitalia knocked away centuries before, he was relieved to discover at least one Apollo "with cock and balls intact."[117] And he sent Viola Baxter Jordan a postcard of the Temple of the Vestal Virgins which he'd seen in the Forum, relieved that, except for the wooden roof, he'd found that structure still "intact."[118]

Sunday, March 23d: a "warm rainwashed day," Williams noted in his diary, when he and Floss walked out to the Castel San Angelo and then ate lunch on the Palazzo Lerici. Afterward, as they lay on the grass in the Pincio Gardens, they saw Benito Mussolini, Il Duce himself, pass by on horseback with an escort. Tuesday morning they took the train south down to Frascati for the day and noted that the train and the marketplace were jammed with people. He remembered hyacinths and violets and anemones blooming and belling everywhere. Spring had come to Rome. Time, then, to be heading north once again. He was leaving "this ripe center of everything in a couple of days," he wrote Burke on the twenty-sixth. He was sorry to have to go, but at least he was "carrying away half of antiquity" with him. "I never so fully realized," he added, "how maimed we [Americans] are—and how needlessly we are crippling ourselves." Now, in the new freedom of Rome, he could see just how crippled America was, tied to laws and mores and a Republican administration which had little to do with life itself. He hinted at his "Roman Journal," saying that what he was now writing as a way of clearing the smog of Probibition and its attendant inanities was "unprintable." It was not for him—as he'd already shown—"merely to arrange things prettily." He wanted writing which could include "fucks and booze, and whatever else we can gather of ourselves and a printing press," and then he would christen that writing with "champagne and semen . . . but *not shit.*"[119] What the hell, Europe had opened him up to language, all kinds of language. He would continue that journal whenever the fit was upon him through Venice, through Vienna and Paris, and even back in the States, and he would even try to turn it into a novel. But it was too raw, too much the product of the frustration and anger and helplessness he had experienced in Pagany, and it would remain in manuscript until fifteen years after his death.

Thursday morning, March 27, the Williamses taxied to the Stazione Termini and took second-class seats for the express to Venice via Florence. Next morning they walked first of all to St. Mark's and found its Byzantine forms superb. They were in fact stunned by the church's "perfection of grace and feeling," and even Williams found it difficult to express his admiration for the place.[120] Afterward the couple went out to the Lido and then saw the Ducal Palace with its Tintoretto fresco on the end wall. "The water is blue out of the window from the sky," he noted in his journal, searching for the right word, the right perspective, and being washed under by it all. "But the lamp light in the room is Veronese, great canvases—pigeons and children." "The great Venetians—were great thinkers and great artists—and that is why art is important apart from artists in an absolute sense—because it is the perfect type of all accomplishment—to which every activity, political, scientific approaches. . . ."[121] Yes, but what could he carry out of here and home for home consumption with the Island of San Giorgio and its white pearl floating in the miragelike water of this city where, half a century later, his friend Pound would choose to lie forever?

In the afternoon Williams and Floss went searching the labyrinthian maze of Venice's narrow streets looking for Verrocchio's equestrian statue of Bartolomeo Colleoni (an image of power Williams would evoke when he came to write "Of Asphodel"), and then walked through the adjoining Church of San Zanipole (John and Paul), where Williams found the tombs of the doges and patricians there in the church "the best work in marble" he'd yet seen.[122] But for all his admiration of Venice, two days of seeing the city were enough. He was restless, vaguely uneasy amidst all this splendor. Venice: that impossible white flower, so alien to his own raw world. It was time to move north.

The Williamses left Venice on Sunday morning and crossed into Austria that night, noticing how cold the weather had once again become. Winter had returned. Arriving at their pension in Vienna, Williams rested and then went down alone to the Children's Clinic to speak with a Dr. Wagner about the course of study he would pursue in pediatrics for the next month. He would combine public lectures with private lessons given by Drs. Wagner and Rach, beginning on Wednesday, April 2d and he could feel the old excitement welling up again at the prospect of learning advanced clinical methods combined with the "clear organization of facts" which he so admired in the German mind. His regimen would be simple in outline: classes in the morning while Floss slept in or went shopping—lectures on nervous disorders, mastoids, scarlet fever, diphtheria, and the rest—and then long walks around the city with Floss in the afternoon, followed by an evening at the Burgertheatre and Volksoper. On the eleventh, he heard Bach's *Mattaus Passion* played. It was a "wonderful labyrinth of music," he noted, with "glorious noises, oboe, flutes, voices, boys, orchestra."[123] Soon he was also linked up with two members of the Hungarian avant-garde, Andreas Gaspar and Lajos Kassák, both of whom had read Williams' work (especially the prose pieces he'd done for *Broom*) and liked this American, though they found him incredibly naive when it came to the topic of national and international politics. Williams—for his part—took their measure by noting that neither man had ever heard of James Joyce.

"I have just met a Hungarian modernist painter, Kassak," he wrote Marianne Moore on April 14. "He seems Russian in his beady-eyed, whitebrowed seriousness about things political. He and his friend take me for a boy—and I suppose I am." But it was hard to talk American politics seriously "to a serious Hungarian through a translator who speaks poor English."[124] For his part, Williams just couldn't get excited about what President Calvin Coolidge or the Congress was doing in 1924. Gaspar and Kassák were also coeditors of *MA* ("Today"), an avant-garde magazine published in Vienna, and it was Gaspar who handed Williams a copy of the latest *Secession*. For his part, Williams was surprised to learn that, though the men had yet to hear of Joyce, they were following the work of the relatively minor New York writers: Munson, Cowley, Burke, Josephson, and of course, Williams himself. So these eastern European intellectuals, for all of their intensity and seriousness, were still looking at America through a kind of batlight, Williams realized. "They asked me if any of our men admired the newer Frenchmen, if there had been any exhibits in America!" he told Moore. "I didn't believe such questions possible."[125]

Williams also saw the latest issue of *Poetry* in Vienna, with his old friend Marjorie Allen Seiffert's review of *Spring and All* in its pages, and he wrote her on April 15 that it had come as a relief "to have somebody say something intelligent" about the book. She had helped to clarify his own necessities and had provided him with a way of handling his materials with a firmer control. But, he added slyly, there were other things to look for in a book of poems, "a logic of madness" and "a logic of melody" as well, just as there were Gumpoldskirschner 1917 and good German beer, which in Vienna were art forms in their own right.[126]

On Wednesday evening, the sixteenth, the Williamses had dinner at the Rathaus and then went out to visit Gaspar and Kassák at Gaspar's apartment. There the talk turned to the various movements in modern poetry, with Kassák opting for Gleizes and Williams holding out for his favorite: Juan Gris. Williams was still attending classes, but after two and a half weeks he was cutting corners so that he could get back to his writing. Floss had rented him a nice typewriter from a local shop, but as he sat down to continue with the Rome journal the typewriter began to disintegrate in his hands, the letter *r* dropping out of the machine completely. It had to be taken back and a replacement found and then Williams could get on with his work. On Friday—Good Friday, April 18—Floss celebrated her thirty-fourth birthday, and Williams bought her an Easter plant and some Viennese candy. In the afternoon he banged away at the typewriter while Floss slept. The weather stayed cold, damp, rainy, unusually bad, especially after their Riviera and Roman springs.

As the end of April approached, Williams made preparations to leave Vienna for the loop back to Switzerland and France. It was still raining on April 24, when he returned his typewriter and then went to inquire about return-trip tickets to the U.S. aboard the SS *President Harding*. He also bought tickets for the Spanish Riding School and then hurried to the university for his lectures. In the afternoon he estimated what the trip had so far cost him: $1,000, including the ship fare across. Not bad. Ten dollars a day would get them home and that included the trip back.

In the evening it was the usual at the Rathaus: pork and sauerkraut and Gumpoldskirschner. Next day, he got tickets to see *Die Walküre* and then, the sun having finally come out, he decided to take Floss for a long walk almost to Salmansdorf, where they could see the Alps to the south. They saw cuckoos and skylarks: spring was finally here as well. On Saturday, Williams decided finally to return home on the SS *Zeeland*, a Red Star liner sailing from Cherbourg on June 12. There were seven weeks left. In the afternoon he and Floss took the train out to the Prater and then walked back, lying in the sweet grass with the sound of birds and frogs around them and the willows coming into leaf. Then they went to a summer garden for beer and anshuntz, and then back home where they lay in bed, happy, talking for a long time about their life together. [127]

Williams did not confide the nature of his talk with his wife to his diary. That was for more public events, a way of remembering in later years the important people and places he had seen on his trip to Europe in his forty-first year. But they must have talked about their sons, seven and ten already, how they were growing up, what schools they should go to, the need to send them abroad to Geneva sometime soon, as Williams' parents had sent their two boys abroad a quarter century earlier. As for Bill and Floss themselves, theirs was a good marriage, a bit unorthodox, but nevertheless good. Floss, the plain sister, had known that her awkward, enthusiastic, high-pitched, boyish husband had in him the seeds of greatness, and here she was, the girl from provincial Rutherford, the product of a finishing school over in New York, mixing with this smart international crowd. She enjoyed it, though she let her husband and his friends know when they had overstepped too far, as she had let Bodenheim know who was boss in *her* house. Sometimes she went with Bill to his literary gatherings, but she really didn't care for the people those gatherings magnetized, didn't follow the literary allusions, didn't like the useless flirtations, the infidelities, even—God forbid—the frequent separations and divorces she saw and heard about. Marriage, after all, was for keeps. Sure a man might look after other women, might even get carried away and sleep with another woman, but that was no reason for getting divorced. And here she was, married to a doctor and a baby doctor at that, who came into close physical contact with hundreds, thousands, of women on a professional basis, right there in the office off the kitchen steps. If Bill had slept with other women—and she kept her own counsel—then let him keep it to himself. And besides, she knew that no matter where her husband had been, no matter when he returned from the hospital or seeing patients, she knew it was always back to her and the boys that he returned. One could build a harmony of sorts on that basis. Besides, perhaps for the first time in her life, she was beginning to understand the excitement, the sexual excitement, of the literary and imaginative life her husband had been living intensely for the last ten years. After all, here she was, thank God, away from Rutherford and America for the first time in her life. The world was a bigger place than even she had imagined, and it was good.

Easter Sunday morning they went out to the *Spanische Reitschüle*, the famous Spanish Riding School, "where to music we saw the loveliest horses on earth perform their aristocratic gestures."[128] Williams was astonished at the extraordinary perfection of these horses, bounding four abreast to the sound of the fanfare. It was the outfolding of grace itself, a natural Eastering, which Williams so admired: "the great impossible perfection of the world"—as *Voyage to Pagany* phrased it—"without let or hindrance, 'without fault,' without sin, . . . a parade of horses by grace of the Arabs—inventors of mathematics—and trained in the Spanish mode."[129] That afternoon they went out to Hohe Warte to see the Carpentier–Townley boxing match, only to find that it had been postponed, ostensibly because of the weather, but really—as Williams found out—because only twenty percent of the tickets had been sold. In the evening they went to hear *Die Walküre* with Jeritza in the role of the Sieglinde. Williams found her marvelous.

On Monday the twenty-eighth Williams did some errands, including getting stamps for Sonny, the Williamses' nickname for Bill Jr., who was already becoming an avid stamp collector. Afterward he took Floss out—it was raining again—and bought wine for the Gaspars, who had invited the whole Kassák clan as well for this farewell to the Williamses. It was a simple Hungarian peasant supper at the Gaspars and Williams enjoyed it very much. After dinner one of the men played a "soup song" and Williams read from a copy of *Spring and All*, which Bob McAlmon had sent the Gaspars from Paris. For his part, Kassák gave Williams a long poem of his own to take with him, a poem translated by Emile Malespine into French, which Williams kept as a memento of his stay in Vienna.[130] Next day Williams attended his last lecture at the university—this one given by a prominent dermatologist—and then returned to his hotel and prepared to leave on the following morning. It was still raining on the morning of the thirtieth as they taxied to the Westbohnhoff station with their luggage. Williams got lucky and actually found a seat next to a window, but had trouble with a man he was sure was an Austrian Jew, who insisted on closing the door to the compartment and then smoking a cigar in Williams' face. Without saying a word, Williams opened the ventilator, chilling the entire compartment. Neither man spoke to the other.[131]

In Zurich Williams and Floss stayed at the Globus Hotel Central and went for a walk the following morning to see the lake and watch laborers unloading shipments of brick. Zurich was in bloom: they had caught up with spring once more. They ate lunch at a Jewish restaurant on the Bohuhoffstrasse and watched—in one of Williams' less happy phrases— the "horrible overfed Jewish types."[132] On the following day, Sunday, May 4, they left for Lucerne, thirty miles to the south, for a few days' stay. They rowed out onto Lake Lucerne one day, and another day they took the rack-and-pinion railroad up Mt. Pilatos, where the snow was still deep and slushy on the ground, Williams noting the hyacinths and violets at the lower elevations and the crocuses sticking through the snow at the higher elevations.

From there they traveled south and west to Interlaken, where spring had not yet arrived. They had wanted to see the majestic Jungfrau a dozen miles to the south rising up above the clouds, but they arrived in wet, misty weather. For three days they waited for a glimpse of the mountain —without luck. Then, on Saturday morning, May 10, as they were preparing to leave, they awoke to see the Jungfrau in her naked majesty. The sun had finally broken through, waking Williams from his sleep, and he had turned to wake Floss so that she might get a glimpse of the Virgin shining with the brilliance of new-fallen snow. He would remember that moment with Floss thirty years later, when, fallen from her grace, he would beg her to recall all that they had shared together, including this privileged glimpse of the mountain, virgin pure in the distance, revealing itself to those two: a glimpse of the impossible Romantic Sublime.

Then they made their way to Geneva, past Spiez, past Zweisimmen, past Oberland, with "flowers everywhere, and the pure white mountains in the distance."[133] Williams was anxious to show Floss the school at Lancy outside Geneva where he had come with Ed as a boy more than a quarter of a century before. In a few years he wanted to give his sons the same opportunity his parents had given him of going abroad for a year, and he wanted to see if the old school might still serve. They checked in at the Hôtel des Familles and then took the train out to Lancy, only to find that the old school had been converted into the city hall. But the next day he took Floss and went to find the headmaster of the new school facilities, M. George Brunel, who was waiting for them at the American consulate. There the Williamses made tentative plans for their sons' future.

During their six-day stay in Geneva, Bill and Floss took the steamer out onto Lake Geneva to get a view of Mont Blanc, which Williams (like Shelley and others before him) thought "the greatest mountain view" he'd ever seen.[134] They also went out to Ferney, to see the home of Voltaire, who for Williams—as for Pound—had been a true enlightener, "the divine philosopher." They watched the old men fishing from the bridges, they fed the swans, visited the Triano, ate *patisserie*. The weather remained beautiful, and Williams relived some of the scenes of his boyhood with Floss. "Clean, clear sweet air," he wrote in his diary, for the moment happy. "The swallows are screeching outside the window in droves." Nothing and everything had changed.[135]

Moving on northwest to Dijon, they met Bill Bird at the Hôtel de la Cloche. Williams marveled at the fifteenth-century stonework of the Hôtel de Dieu, with its kitchen and chapel wards with beds built right into the walls. It was, he thought, the "most living sense of the Middle Ages" he'd ever had, and the nuns there reminded him of the nuns he'd seen in a hundred old Gothic paintings.[136] On Monday the Williamses and the Birds took the train to Paris, where they met Bob McAlmon, waiting for them at the Dingo, and all of them were entertained by Clotilde Vail's singing. Williams ran into Joyce on the street, who for some reason—as Williams noted—looked at him as though he'd been caught in the act of committing some unmentionable crime. On Tuesday Williams was interviewed by a woman from the *New York Times* Paris edition at 12, rue de l'Odéon, where he had gone to visit Sylvia Beach and pick up any mail waiting for him.

The following day he took Floss to the Louvre and then dined with George Antheil and Philippe Soupault and his wife at the Restaurant l'Avenue. Williams felt happy "talking to Soupault about Picasso, America, and life in general."[137] So impressed was he with Soupault, in fact, that he would translate the Frenchman's novel, *Last Nights in Paris (Les Dernières Nuits de Paris)* four years later. It was one of the few books he ever allowed himself to translate. Then, as he had when he was in Paris in January, he joined the other Americans and English at the Dingo. At one point he saw Nancy Cunard start to walk in and then turn on her heels, "to everybody's irritation." But, after all, he'd seen enough of Paris to know that that was how things went. Next day, the twenty-second, McAlmon took the Williamses to Clotilde Vail's apartment for lunch and again Williams passed the Joyces in the back of a taxi headed in the other direction. Joyce still looked guilty. It was beginning to be something out of *Ulysses*, these chance passages.

In the evening Bryher showed up with H.D. It was the first time Williams had seen H.D. since she'd left with McAlmon aboard the honeymoon ship in the winter of '21, and though he had much to be angry about, he found to his surprise that he was genuinely happy to see his old friend. That evening Floss and Bill went to the Opéra to hear a Stravinsky concert, and afterward strolled back arm in arm to their hotel. Next morning, though, Williams awoke to find Floss looking very ill. When he examined her, he was troubled to discover a white spot behind her right tonsil that looked suspiciously like diphtheria. That was serious. He kept her in bed and stayed in the room with her throughout the day, leaving only for a quick lunch and then again—at Floss's insistence—in the evening to accompany Clotilde Vail to the Dôme as he'd arranged. Afterward, walking back to the hotel, he was propositioned by a Parisian streetwalker. No, he explained, he was "happily married." Then he thanked her and offered her a cigarette instead. When he got back to his room, Floss was sound asleep.

When he got up next morning, Williams was relieved to see that the diphtheria he'd suspected had turned out to be tonsillitis. In a few days Floss would be back on her feet. When he got back to the States he'd arrange to have his and Floss's tonsils out and be done with it. In the meantime Floss would rest. That evening he left Floss at the hotel and went with McAlmon, Bryher, and H. D. to the Soirée de Paris in his old battered tuxedo, feeling very much out of place in all that showy decadence. He couldn't shake his self-conscious awkwardness, watching the American expatriates trying to outdo the French with their affected ennui and indifference. It was a repeat of that night at the Trianon five months earlier. "My clothes were dull," he would remember, "my manners worse. The drink, as always, meant nothing to me. I was too alert to it, had no intention of going on with it. Among the whole crowd of talents about me not a face was open, not even among my own group." Even McAlmon's face was dead, world-weary. What the hell was wrong with these people? Only for the young girl who had danced her solo part in the ballet, giving everything she had, could he feel anything. Kore, Kore among this crowd of wasteland sophisticates. As for the rest: "From what I know of even those in my group, painfully in detail, the cupidity, the bitchery, the half-screaming hysteria, I wasn't attracted. It was a gelatinous mass, squatting over a treasure; a *Rheingold-musik.*"[138] To hell with them all. If he was alone, so be it. Like that girl, he had work to do.

The next afternoon—Sunday—Williams went out with Bill Bird to see some French flyweight boxing matches in an open courtyard above Montmartre. He noted in particular the restrained violence of French boxing, so different from the rough and tumble of American fighters. There would be no K.O.'s here, and he found it especially comic when one flyweight, hit with a clean left and then a right to the solar plexus, immediately sat down in the middle of the ring to get his wind back. Williams found himself laughing out loud in spite of himself. That evening Kitty Cannell and Harold Loeb called on Williams back at the hotel—where Floss was curled up in bed reading Melville's *Mardi*—and Loeb left Williams a novel in manuscript to read. He spent far into the night reading the novel and then took the *métro* next day out to Loeb's place to talk about the writing, as well as about his own American pieces, which Loeb would publish that fall in *Broom*. It was now that he learned that Eliot had recently shown up in Paris, "appearing at the Dôme and other bars in top hat, cutaway, and striped trousers."[139] That was fine for *fin de siècle* Paris. But for 1924? Williams had missed the elusive Eliot altogether. So be it. The bastard. At least he'd tried.

Williams went with McAlmon to the Luxembourg on the following day, but he could see that his friend was still in a very sour mood. They walked along for stretches without a word passing between them, and Williams probably knew that the presence of Bryher and H.D. in Paris again (after all, they'd all had dinner together at l'Avenue the evening before: Williams, Floss, McAlmon, Bryher, H.D., Loeb, and Kitty Cannell) was having its usual depressing effect on McAlmon. But what was there to say? It had been McAlmon's choice; let him work it out. Suddenly he wheeled on his friend, told him he would catch up with him later, and went on to the Luxembourg alone. At least let him enjoy the impressionists, particularly the Manets and Cézannes and Degas, alone if need be. Afterward Williams went over to the Dôme for a drink. McAlmon was there, but just as sardonic and sullen as ever. To hell with it. Let it go. In the evening he and Floss went to the Trianon for supper and a long talk with the Joyces, this time without McAlmon.

On the following day—Wednesday the twenty-eighth—Bill and Floss taxied over to Nancy Cunard's apartment on the quai d'Orléans and saw the Gaudier-Brzeska "Faun" Pound had so admired in his memoir of the dead artist. Later Williams played four sets of tennis with Loeb and Ernest Hemingway, neither Hemingway nor Williams being willing to give in and neither man able to beat the other. It was Hemingway—sixteen years younger than Williams—who finally called it off, saying something had gone wrong with his knee. Otherwise the two contenders, as Williams well knew, would have gone on playing until nightfall, or until one or the other of them dropped dead. That night Williams spent back at Nancy Cunard's place, talking with Iris Tree, Clive Bell, McAlmon, and Bryher from ten until five in the morning, when he drove down to a local taxi drivers' stand for some fried eggs and to watch the new day begin.

He and Floss slept until noon and then went over to Mina Loy's apartment, where Loy did a sketch first of Williams and then of Floss, which he found good, but "too delicate." Friday morning Williams spent finishing Loeb's novel and then went over to Loeb's place with Floss to talk about the problems he saw in the manuscript. It was l'Avenue again for dinner, this time with Sylvia Beach, Adrienne Monnier, George Antheil, McAlmon, Bryher, and H.D. Williams singled out H.D. in particular to talk about the old days in Philadelphia and Upper Darby, and about Pound and his strange interest in music, both H.D. and Williams recalling how tone deaf Ezra had always seemed to them both. Williams had yet to see his oldest friend.

Next day—Saturday—Williams had a chance to hear George Antheil play his own modern atonal music. It was, he thought, startling but quite good in its own way. Then, in the afternoon, he went back to the Luxembourg, this time to scrutinize the Whistler collection more carefully, and then went to see some more boxing matches at a local stadium in Paris. Sunday evening he and Floss had dinner at Adrienne Monnier's on the rue de l'Odéon, with her own locally praised chicken as the main course. Sylvia Beach was there, and H.D., and McAlmon and Bryher —seven in all—all talking, when suddenly there was a shout from the street below. It was Ezra, at last, announcing his arrival from Rapallo. Williams sprang to the window with the others and shouted down to Pound to come on up, but Pound refused. Thirteen years had passed since he'd last seen Ezra, and if Ezra wouldn't come up, then he was coming down. Williams ran down the wooden stairs and out onto the street and hugged his friend. They looked each other over, laughed, joked, and then Pound gave him his address. Now—with only ten days left before his return home—Williams had finally caught up or been caught up by his real double, his true counterpart, there in Paris on the rue de l'Odéon.

Monday. After saying good-by to H.D. and Bryher, who would be leaving early the next day for a vacation, Williams took Floss to visit the Bois. In the evening the two of them went to Nancy Cunard's for dinner and then joined a group of Americans to see Jean Cocteau's *Juliet and Romeo* at La Cigale. The performance left Williams absolutely cold. Then, the next morning, Williams made his way to Pound's apartment, on the way passing Dorothy Pound without being sure she was the same woman he'd briefly met in London fourteen years before. He said nothing. At Pound's studio apartment they talked about Ezra's trouble with his appendix and then about the theory of music, particularly as Williams had been hearing so much adverse criticism about Pound's attempts at opera while he'd been in Paris. About tone Ezra knew nothing, Williams still believed. But about line, melody, the "musical sentence," time and its compressions and extensions—as with Antheil—about the old music before Bach: there Williams could and would learn a great deal from Pound. Enough to help revolutionize modern American poetry. The two men took a light lunch at a small restaurant nearby and then went back to Pound's apartment for more good talk, where Dorothy Pound now joined them. It *was* the same woman he'd met on the street. They struck up a warm conversation and then, at half past four, Williams went back to the hotel to get Floss and take her back to the Pounds to see Dorothy's paintings, paintings that Floss admired for their gray, linear, cubist planes.

That evening the Williamses went over to the Hemingways' for dinner and Williams examined their infant son. The boy would need to be circumcised—standard medical practice—and Williams told Hemingway he would do it. Then, after dinner, the four of them went to an old theater to see a prizefight up on the stage. But more fascinating for Williams even than the fight was watching Floss get caught up in the ritual bloodletting, as male fist crushed against male body and the rounds went on, until, finally, in an ecstasy of release, his wife was pounding her fists on the back of the spectator in front of her (who turned out to be none other than Ogden Nash) and began shouting "Kill him! Kill the bastard!" What was happening to his good hausfrau? Soon after, Williams left with Floss and went back to the hotel. What was this Parisian thing, this virus, that could so transform American women like H.D. and Nancy Cunard and now his own wife? Hadn't she already told him that she really didn't want to go back to New Jersey, but could have stayed in Paris forever? What was it about the intensity of this world, the purity of that total immersion into the vortex that left the men pallid onlookers, weak ineffectual bystanders, but blew the women into Amazons? Ah, to live like his beloved St. Toulouse-Lautrec in a common brothel or commune surrounded by such women, Floss included, simply that he might paint them with words as he actually saw them, glad simply to be among them, not to judge, but merely to witness and to praise. So a week before they were to leave Pagany behind, Williams thought seriously about making a life of it there in Paris, of taking up his medical practice in one of the quiet suburbs outside the city and becoming an expatriate. After all, wasn't this his real world? The virus had hit him too.

 · Next morning, Wednesday, June 4, Williams went back to the Hemingways' apartment with his surgical kit to examine the baby again and retract its foreskin while the parents, visibly shaken, looked on. Hemingway, Williams would later tell a friend with obvious relish, big tough Hem had nearly fainted at the sight of his son's blood.[140] Afterward Williams had two lunches, the first with Sally Bird after hearing her sing from *Figaro* and *La Bohème* at her teacher's studio, and the second with the Pounds and McAlmon at l'Avenue. In the evening it was another heavy drinking session at Nancy Cunard's, where Williams met Jean Cocteau and the black Prince de Dahomie who conversed with ease and refinement—Williams noted with envy—in both French and English alike. But the drunken hilarity of the evening finally became too much for Williams, who in spite of everything always needed to keep his head clear, and he left, after almost pulling Floss—who was having a great old time—away at one in the morning.

Next afternoon, Pound took ol' Bull Williams to Natalie Barney's for tea to show off "one of the primitives of Ezra's earlier years," as Williams himself soon realized.[141] On the way to Barney's for the meeting, Pound confided to Williams that he was—frankly—worried about Williams' book knowledge being so inferior to his own. Williams for his part understood at once that Ezra was not even being condescending, since that would have raised Williams' hackles at once, but that he was genuinely concerned about the lamentable lacunae in his American cousin's humanistic education. As usual, Williams listened and kept his own judgment, though the extreme civilized decadence of the salon, with its artificial formal garden and laughing doves and Japanese servants, together with the exaggerated delicacy of the lesbians dancing cheek to cheek angered him and left him feeling very uncomfortable, as he had felt that night at the opera. Still, he would do his best to look like an appreciative country bumpkin while Ezra attempted to show him real Kulchur.

Saturday morning the Williamses and the Birds took the 8:30 train out to Rheims for a holiday weekend in the French countryside and to taste some good local French wines. At Rheims they walked about outside the cathedral there but Bill Bird was far more interested in examining the Veuve Cliquot champagne cellars. Afterward the four of them took the train out into the surrounding forest to examine firsthand where the French and German battle lines had been cut into the earth. It seemed now as if no battle had ever been fought there, Williams thought, though just a few years before men by the thousands, by the *thousands*, had died where softly now on this late spring day they walked.

All Sunday morning it rained, clearing sufficiently in the afternoon for them to have lunch at a tiny inn—the Hôtel des Trois Millstones—where thirteen French soldiers had been snuffed out like that by a single incoming German shell as they sat drinking wine and joking there in the hotel garden. Later that day Williams was surprised to see two country girls walking arm in arm, obviously lesbians. Until then Williams had really thought lesbianism was a cosmopolitan affair. Bird, more knowingly, merely smiled. Williams was still learning. Toward evening they returned by train to Paris, passing the still shattered treescapes of Château-Thierry. The sight of all those blasted tree trunks rising grotesquely out of that ravaged earth left them all silent and introspective.

Monday, June 9: the Williamses would be leaving in three days for home. It was time, finally, to say good-by. Williams was not really surprised to learn that Bob McAlmon had left Paris in a taxi without telling anyone why he'd gone. Williams could guess easily enough. He wanted to see Pound now as much as he could anyway. That evening he had supper with the Pounds and the next day Pound took him to visit the painter Fernand Léger at Léger's studio, though Williams unfortunately could find little to excite him in what he saw there. It was hard, Williams noted in his diary, "to sense [Léger's] neat, mechanical drawings of the human figure adapted to fit a canvas," and the painter's theoretical explanations of what he was doing—given in a rapid French—were such that Williams could not follow him closely enough.[142] It was a missed opportunity for Williams to understand one of the great modern French masters of cubism.

On Wednesday morning, while Williams ate breakfast in his hotel room, Mina Loy sketched him in the guise of a wild Indian. Afterward, he took Sylvia Beach and her mother out to lunch, and then took tea with the Birds on the Champs Elysées. Bill Bird was particularly sad that Williams was leaving, for he knew something good was ending, something they would not have again. That evening the Williamses had a final supper with his cousins, Alice Trufly and her sister Marguerite, relics from the Paris of a quarter century before. Then, at ten, Bill and Floss taxied out to see the Pounds for what would be the last time.

Thursday, June 12: departure. Williams was up early. He wanted to see Ezra one last time before leaving Paris, but it was only half past seven when he reached Pound's apartment and Pound was still asleep. As it turned out, it would be another fifteen years before they would see each other again. Sadly, Williams returned to the hotel to pick up Floss and within an hour they were on the express train bound for Cherbourg and the SS *Zeeland*. They caught a glimpse of the cathedral at Bayeux as they sped by, and by midafternoon they were strolling on the docks at Cherbourg. Williams noted a statue of Napoleon facing the English coast in the town square and a fisherman's cart full of sandsharks which, he learned, the French actually ate. He managed to overhear a conversation between an English sailor, looking downcast and shamefaced, and an older Frenchwoman which centered on a very young French girl who stood off to one side. It was one more human drama caught in a flash in the mind's eye, as in a rapid transit cinema. The story, of course, was universal.

Just before six that evening, Bill and Floss boarded a tender that took them out to meet the SS *Zeeland* waiting offshore in deeper water. Now, with Europe drifting off to stern in the wake of the chugging tender, Williams suddenly began to feel very tired. The sabbatical was all but over. He'd done as much of Europe as he could. It would, he knew, take years to map the geographic and psychological terrain he'd just tracked through. It would all need to be assimilated, evaluated, made part of the imagination. But to do that he would need the more familiar perspective of Rutherford and America. In short and in spite of everything, he would need the necessary vantage of the one place he could still call home.

SIX

The Great American Desert:
1924—1929

"As America gets nearer I feel its thrill," Williams confided to his diary four days out of Cherbourg and halfway between two worlds.[1] Between arguments too with a temperance woman about the "virtues" of Prohibition and discussions about Japan's role in the next war, Williams wrote steadily on his Daniel Boone chapter, stressing particularly the sense of that man's relentless contact with the New World wilderness. Ahead of Williams lay his responsibilities, ready to be picked up again: his sons, his medical practice, his role as citizen in an America that was bound to seem insane to outsiders with its prohibitions, its big-business Republican-dominated politics, its puritanical repressions, its grand hoopla and lack of self-knowledge, but also with its generosity and promise and incredible beauty everywhere which few or none actually seemed to be able to see.

"America cannot go on as one monstrous grotesque lie much longer," Williams had written in Vienna after talking with Kassák. But he knew that—incredibly—it could. What, then, was the future of his country, that hog center and granary for the world's population, all belly and no brain?

> Either there will be violent disruption or our natural wealth will be used (frittered away) and we shall become enervated, the best die out and care gradually supplanted by a duller element from under. It must find a level. And this is the social function of the artist and thinkers of all sorts, they frequent the flower, and breed life, keep it at high pitch. You cannot ignore them too long or—death results.

But America, coming into its own as a cultural entity, would by that very fact "attract genius of all sorts to its freedom—fertilizing agents." Yet there would have to be a change, a profound and radical change in America's sense of herself, or she would remain a purely mechanical influence in world affairs—there to be used by Europe and Asia rather than taken seriously, viewed merely as some "world coal and food base, with gradual descent to sordidness, greater banality and supplanting by a readier race from inside or out."[2]

What strategy, then, was one to take in the face of the enemies of a renewed culture for the United States? How use what energies one had when the best—Henry James and Pound and Eliot and others like McAlmon—had already given up on the American experiment and fled to Europe? There was, to be sure, the ongoing flurry of activity in the little magazines coming out of New York: Munson and Burke and Cowley and Hart Crane and Josephson and the others. But there Williams preferred to remain aloof. He did not really believe in their manifestos, and their infighting he considered somewhat precious and self-serving. For now, while he picked up his practice again, reacquainted himself with his sons, and worked to shape his essays into the masterpiece that would become *In the American Grain*, he would keep quiet. At least outwardly, as he told Burke, while within there continued to burn a white-hot core. He had work to do—a great deal of it—and all the *Contact* manifestos in the world would go, he now understood, simply unheeded. He was being practical. The only creed he could subscribe to now in the midst of so much home-grown muddle, especially after what he'd seen in Europe, was simple clarity. "We must all grow clearer," he insisted, and perhaps many individual clarities would create the central blaze necessary for another American renaissance. In the meantime: work alone, quietly, intensely.[3]

When, therefore, at the end of the year, Malcolm Cowley wrote asking Williams to contribute something for his magazine, *Aesthete 1925*, which was being issued as a spoof on H. L. Mencken and Menckenism, Williams sent along something but added that he was frankly not interested in that kind of local infighting. "What's the use of idling over Mencken and Co.," he wrote. "I never heard of Mencken as an influence in American letters save as one who came from behind to inform us that we have a language." In fact, the only person he'd ever heard of who had actually bothered to read Mencken and speak pleasantly of him was one of his "slow paying" customers who'd "had an abortion produced on his wife by some doctor fellow on Madison Ave., I think, who uses an electric method that brings the ovum away intact in one mass: a smart, uptodate, resourceful, cloacal sort of a guy who would be just the one to fall for the sort of intellect that had served to sluice even the beginning American language into the waste tanks." He also told Cowley that he'd followed the exchange in *1924* between Waldo Frank and Cowley and that Frank had showed some surprising energy, though after "scraping away the mud and shit" he thought the judges would probably give the decision to Cowley. As for returning to the whole New York scene, though, he'd had "to hump a bit" to repair his own bank balance after Europe and could not permit the city "and all that that mystical symbol" stood for to occupy much of his thinking.[4] Or, as he told John Herrmann, the novelist, about the same time, what with the "rush of twins dropping, mastoids opening, gops landing (not sailors but the essence of pneumonia) in pans with a little water in the bottom," there was precious time for anything else.[5]

When Williams actually did see a copy of *Aesthete 1925* in early February with its attack on Mencken's *American Mercury*, he was pleased. The *Mercury*'s opening number, published in December 1923, had featured Ernest Boyd's "Aesthete: Model 1924," a barbed arrow directed at the Cowley-Burke-Josephson crowd. Not that Williams cared much, really, about who flung what at whom in New York City anymore, but he could see that Boyd's article had disturbed the strange torpor that had settled over the city now that many of America's best minds were living in Europe. At least *Aesthete 1925* had given rise to some writing that had "succeeded in making SOMETHING live in the poison gas atmosphere of New York." There was a strong acrid odor once again in the New York air, and—as he told Cowley—he'd gotten "a good flavor of COW ley from this AESTHETE." As for the cover which Charles Sheeler had done (showing an abstract of New York's skyscrapers), that was good work by an American. Finally he could smell and hear the "damned slow thunder on-the-horizon COW stench" which was beginning at last "to seep-sound up through" New York itself and out into the surrounding atmosphere. Even shit was a sign of life.[6]

That August of '24 Williams spent a month with his family at the West Haven cottage, and in September—perhaps remembering Floss lying sick in Paris and having just recovered from a bout of tonsillitis himself—Williams had his tonsils removed. He found the operation amusing, he told Burke, "since with the local anesthesia applied, there was no pain to speak of and the sensation of having a pleasant fellow cutting little chunks of flesh out of your own throat was novel." He himself had often performed the same operation on others and he could now better understand what his own patients must have been thinking as he snipped away down their throats. The recovery, on the other hand, had been anything but amusing and his throat—after four days—still "hurt like hell." "Only today have I been without a fever," he complained to Burke. "My knees are still very feeble and my heart beats madly as I lean to pick up a pin."[7]

He also wrote to Sylvia Beach in early October and asked her to "tear that sweet eyed photo of myself" done by Man Ray from her portrait gallery wall in her Paris bookshop and "bury it behind some Encyclopedia." That photograph—which he'd given her just before he left Paris in June—was, he saw clearly now, too typically French, with its languorous sad eyes, and Williams wasn't French. Man Ray, he felt, should be allowed to take pictures only of Marcel Duchamp, "one every year and each sadder than the other," in the French *triste* tradition. He wished also to be remembered to Adrienne Monnier, whose sensuality, he added, astonished him. He remembered especially the squeal she had made once, a sound emanating from her like a pig's throat being cut. "She has left me with a picture of French women carrying the men in their hair." He also remembered "that place in the desert of Haut Savoie" to which Monnier had promised someday to lead him.[8]

As for the American desert, he could still be happy whenever he found a poem or a piece of writing to praise. Admittedly, there weren't many, but one American writer he did admire then was Yvor Winters, who in 1924 was still a young disciple of Williams' and the man who would defend Williams unequivocally in an exchange of letters with Hart Crane two years later. Burke had brought some of Winters' poems in one of the little magazines to Williams' attention, and Williams—who had remembered reading them when they were first published—called them "a breath of fresh air" and the "strongest impression of reality I have had since the [European] journey." He had wanted to write Winters at once, but he'd been so busy trying to reconstruct his practice that he'd let the opportunity slip. Nonetheless, Williams could say that Winters' poems had been the cause of "an event in american letters" since their presence had resulted in "two men in the desert" having "come with such a violent and simultaneously ready rush upon such a tiny spring as Winters' lincs afforded us." Finally after several years of intellectual drought, Williams was beginning "to communicate on some kind of an intellectual basis" with other American writers. That Burke had been able to point out those lines to Williams on his own had given Williams as much pleasure as the lines themselves.[9]

But to Pound he confessed in late December that, if Europe seemed closer for his having spent six months there, it also seemed "infinitely further off: so great has my wish to be there become intensified by the recent trip." To decide then to stay away from Europe and return to his own American place must have seemed ridiculous to Pound. "Either I must be a tragic ass," Williams lamented, "or nothing—or an American. I scarcely know which is worse."[10] But the Rutherford postmark on that letter spoke clearly enough what Williams' own decision had—finally —been.

In early February 1925, Williams was in the thick of his American essays, telling Cowley that he was working as hard as he could to finish them, "which I MUST MUST MUST MUST finish before I can be young again."[11] Soon after he did finish them up, most likely ending with his magnificent chapter on Poe. He had chosen Poe rather than Whitman because of Poe's relentless drive to clear the American field of soft writing (this in his fugitive critical reviews and essays) and because of his clear, sharp, no-nonsense concern with the problem of poetic form. For the first time in his life too Williams had a commerical publisher: Albert and Charles Boni of New York, with offices on 48th Street in New York. It was in fact during a conversation with Charles Boni in those offices that Williams had finally found a title for the book he'd worked on so long. For a title, he'd wanted, as he'd explained to Boni, to give the sense of how all those people he'd written of had made themselves part of the American experience, "to make it clear that they are us, the American make-up, that we are what they have made us by their deeds and so remain in the American. . . ." And Boni had supplied the missing integer: "Grain."[12] That was it: *In the American Grain*. Boni liked the book, asked Williams to add a Lincoln piece, and then the book would go to press. Williams agreed by pounding out a one-page impression of the Great Emancipator as a man/woman conducting the symphony that was America (perhaps the music America made was an extension of the long cry Poe in his despair had himself heard)—and the book was finished.

Williams had high hopes for this one. After all, *In the American Grain* would serve as the testament of his passage into middle life, a summing up of his own preoccupations as an American artist, a placing—in short—of his own writing in the larger context of American history and culture. He hoped that with this book, finally, he would earn the wider audience he both wanted and needed. So, when the book was finally published in November of that year, Williams jealously watched for the advertisements and the reviews. But in spite of some very positive reviews—including one by D. H. Lawrence, which pleased Williams tremendously—Williams was sure Boni had refused to spend any more on advertising than the minimum allotted. Stunned by this turn of events, Williams went into New York several times to complain to Boni or one of his associates until his presence in the office became annoying. He could not convince Boni of the importance of his book, and that ended his association with his new publisher. "In no time at all," Williams remembered bitterly, "the thing was remaindered and I began to pick up copies wherever I could."[13] The book that had cost him so much in terms of money and time, the book that was to have served as his crossing at forty, soon became as inaccessible as everything else he'd ever written. Once again he'd failed to find his audience.

All in all, 1925 was a depressing year for Williams, a holding action in spite of the publication of his book. Pound wrote in April that he thought he might be able to get a pamphlet of Williams' poems published in England, to which Williams answered that he would try and get together some "safe stuff" for him, "a sort of Caroliensis *Palgraves Golden Treasury*—nothing allowed to enter which isn't of purest ray serene, with clean ass, snotless nose and circumcised. Life's like that."[14] But nothing came of Pound's scheme. Williams published a handful of things in '25 and '26 in the little magazines—particularly *The Dial*, where Marianne Moore was now serving as editor—and that was all.

One review he wrote was for H.D.'s *Collected Poems*, which were published that May. For that volume Williams wrote an enthusiastic review for the *New York Evening Post Literary Review*, calling attention to the fact that it was now possible to grasp in a single volume what H.D. had managed to achieve over the past twenty years, writing this at a time when the idea of a collection of his poems seemed more remote than ever. H.D.'s careful use of the Greek model, he wrote, gave the reader the sense of a woman's continuing growth and blossoming despite the fact that life itself was a spectacle of "disorder and emotional stupidity," including what he'd seen of H.D.'s own. Beneath that disorder, however, was the permanence of beauty in these poems.[15] And he told one correspondent that many of H.D.'s poems, such as her long "Helen," really were superb in their kind. Hilda might be a fool, but the woman could write.[16]

On the evening of September 19, Lola Ridge held a reception for Vladimir Mayakovsky, the Russian poet, at her Greenwich Village apartment on East 14th Street, at which Williams was present. Ridge herself was ill that night, and a young poet named Babette Deutsch had taken her place as hostess. After the soirée, Deutsch wrote Ridge that she had liked both the way Mayakovsky had "thundered out his tremendous strophes" as well as the provocative commentary Williams especially had provided.[17] For Williams the Russian's performance had been unforgettable, as Mayakovsky, foot on the coffee table in that small, crowded apartment, half read, half chanted his poems in his native Russian, until they sounded to Williams as if the *Odyssey* itself were being delivered by some "impassioned Greek." Williams remembered that evening at Ridge's, remembered it down to the green and white particolored vest that David Burliuk, Mayakovsky's manager and translator, had worn. Here truly was the figure of the revolutionary poet, bigger than life, bigger even than Carl Sandburg, uttering his songs with true revolutionary fervor and abandonment.[18] Four years later, when he was asked by *The Dial* to review Carl Sandburg's own revolutionary poems in his most recent collection, *Good Morning America*, Williams would write:

> When Mayakovsky, the poet of the Soviets, was here . . . and had taken his foot down from where he had planted it on the table while reading his poem urging Willie, the Havana street cleaner, to join the Third International—he had something to say about Carl Sandburg whom he had met in Chicago, I think, a few days previously.

As Williams remembered it, Mayakovsky had asked Sandburg to say outright what he meant by the common people and "to take his beating for it." But Sandburg was no true revolutionary, Williams insisted, certainly not when measured against a figure like Mayakovsky. Sandburg's strengths, rather, lay in his abilities as a master of language and metrics who had significantly advanced since his earlier deadly catalog poems. He was, in summary, a writer "of excellent hocus."[19] Compared with what Williams would write about Sandburg twenty years later —that the man's brain was dead—what he said here amounted almost to extravagant praise. As for Mayakovsky: even his suicide in 1935 and the growing split between the U.S. and Russia after World War II could not dampen Williams' enthusiasm for him. That single glimpse of the mythic figure in New York would remain for Williams a touchstone of the epic poet.

*
* *

But in spite of this brief encounter, the normal condition for Williams remained isolation and loneliness in his relations with the literary communities both in the U.S. and in Europe. He confessed to Waldo Frank in July, for example, that he had no French connection to speak of, no French writer he could communicate with. Even Valery Larbaud—to whom he had sent a copy of *In the American Grain*—had failed to so much as acknowledge Williams' gesture.[20] So it was with genuine surprise that he opened a letter from a young engineer, a recent graduate of the Yale Sheffield Scientific School then enrolled in a writing course in New York City, to learn that the man had been taking a long and careful look at Williams' poetry and was writing now to tell him how much he liked what he had read. His name was John Riordan, and he was writing specifically to ask Williams what exactly modernism was and who Williams thought his audience was. "I have no audience with whom I am in contact," Williams answered honestly enough. "I have friends who write me from time to time about my work but rarely do they really do it incisively. Thus I am left in a world of unresolved ideas."[21]

But in Riordan Williams sensed someone who might serve as a sounding board, someone who might—as McAlmon had once done —help him focus his own poetics, tell him what it was he seemed to be doing in his search for a modern form. Riordan asked some key questions of Williams, and Williams—hungry for this kind of dialogue—answered as best he could. Had Gertrude Stein influenced Williams? No, Williams answered, except maybe in the past few months, when he had begun to analyze her work, especially the powerful "Melanctha" story from her early *Three Lives*.[22] Riordan wrote back that he personally found Stein redundant and long-winded, that she had the annoying habit of going on and on in the same undifferentiated monotone. Williams agreed, but insisted too that "Melanctha" was golden in spite of it all. Damn it, he answered, such virtues as those of Gertie are so rare that I simply cannot object to anything in her story. It is an emotional qualification I am arguing on but it is valid for all that. . . . You're right though, Gertie is monotonous—yet she uses even that excellently well; it relieves me, her monotony, from this fly-away, skim-the-cream habit which annoys me while it serves me in my own writing and in almost everything American I see. She sinks, sinks, sinks, maybe it's in mud, but she goes to the bottom when she does well.[23]

A month after Riordan intitiated the correspondence, Williams decided to drop in on his new friend while he was in New York. He'd delivered a baby in Rutherford at 3:30, taken Floss with him into New York, dropped her off to do some shopping, gone to see Charles Boni in his midtown Manhattan office by 4:45, and had then driven over to 12 East 37th Street to see Riordan, who was out at the time. Then Williams had gone downstairs again, eaten some fried oysters at Child's restaurant around the corner from Riordan's place ("A lot of swill"), and then tried Riordan's once more before driving downtown to pick up Floss for the trip back home. He would try again, he wrote Riordan. That was his life—a rush from one place to the next—between visits to publishers and housecalls and deliveries. It was, after all, what he'd opted for. "I was born in this town when they had wooden sidewalks and here I am still," he told Riordan. "I've never been convinced that I could get anything interesting to feed on or to see except down under, and down there it's about the same one place as another."[24]

But he liked Riordan, and he wanted him to meet some of the New York crowd, like Burke and Cowley and Josephson, whom he tried to pull together for a supper party in New York on a Friday night in mid-December. That was when he usually got into the city. For his part, Riordan was strong on Burke when he met him that evening, but both he and Williams were soon put off by Burke's praise of T. S. Eliot. For the most part, Williams genuinely liked Burke, he explained to Riordan afterward, because at least the man was serious in his thinking about form and in "his search for a precision such as we all fail to find in each other's work."[25] (Though when Burke tried some "analytical destructive atomization followed by a waxy reconstruction" he could be very annoying.) But to hear Burke actually praise T. S. Eliot had left Williams feeling queasy afterward, unable to sleep with "that waking-at-three AM feeling." Couldn't Burke see that Eliot was the enemy?

Williams was sure that Eliot was already finished, in spite of the realization that Williams could not see himself as stepping beyond him: "Since I cannot compete with him in knowledge of philosophy," he admitted candidly, "nor even technical knowledge of the conned examples of English poetry which he seems to know well—what is left for me but to fall back on words?" Still, if he couldn't yet counter Eliot, he knew that poetry was no more dependent on either philosophy or the English tradition than it was on what Matthew Josephson had unhappily called "spiritual values" and "lyric qualities." Eliot too must surely feel as frustrated about what poetry was and was not as Williams himself was feeling, but he'd be damned if he could see why other poets had to fall into Eliot's verbal trap and "by swilling his words into us arrive in the end at his brand of despair."[26] It was exactly the same sentiment Hart Crane had uttered two years earlier in a private letter, when he'd taken up the American banner after reading *The Waste Land* and had decided to counter Eliot's poem with what he thought would turn out to be his own life-affirming epic in the Whitmanian tradition: *The Bridge.*[27]

No use trying to write free verse to counter Eliot's cultural melange of English literature either. That strategy had already been tried and had failed. The truth was that there was no truly satisfactory philosophy of art, no agreement about what modern writing should be. At least science stayed "on the fact." What was Eliot finally if not "a romantic philosotaster," an insidious throwback and reactionary who had nearly wrecked someone like Burke? The answer, then, was to find a way beyond Eliot's poetic, and beyond Pound's as well. That answer lay not in philosophy, finally, but in sculpting the words themselves, words with hard, concrete, denotative jagged edges. Would even some hypothetical university with the triumvirate of Joyce, Stein, and Eliot give us the poetry we needed? Awesome as that trinity was, Williams insisted, it would not. The answer—whatever it was—lay elsewhere.[28]

Williams' medical practice continued unabated through the fall of '25 and the winter of '26, leaving him precious little time for writing. "I have been drowned in work after a week of vague despair," he told Riordan in January, though he still managed to get into the city on Friday nights.[29] On the twenty-second, he went in to New York to take in some of the art galleries and to have dinner with Burke, Cowley, Josephson, and Sheeler. The New York group had no magazine at the moment, Williams learned, *Broom* having succumbed to the U.S. government's restrictions on mailing "lewd filth" through the mails (a story of Burke's had been the offender: he had dared to speak of a woman's breasts in an erotic context), and *Aesthete 1925* had been a one-shot deal. The New York vortex, never really strong, was once again disintegrating. So Williams wrote Pound on the twenty-fourth that "a few of us who meet occasionally in the city are planning vaguely to set up a club for ourselves," by which he meant a room with heat and chairs so that "possibly a means for getting out some sort of a monthly sheet for purposes of communication may result."[30] To such insubstantiality had the New York vortex reduced itself, and even that shadow soon melted away. In fact, except for the art exhibits in New York—a Tri-National Picture Exhibit, a Brancusi show at the Wildenstein Gallery, paintings of various American cities by Louis Lozowick at the

New Art Circle—about the only thing worth seeing in New York as far as Williams was concerned were the girlie shows, which at least held something of the bawdy vitality of a Quevedo or a Villon.[31] Still, in spite of that, to hell with Eliot and Oswald Spengler's *The Decline of the West* and all the "bellyaching end of the worlders," he told Riordan.[32] American cities still had their own vitality, as Lozowick's photographs of American cities in the current *Herald Tribune* had demonstrated. He himself was at work on a long poem—the first he'd done in months: a poem about the illogical and the vitality of the creative process. It was called "Struggle of Wings."

Only Riordan, therefore, held out any hope for Williams at the moment. "Forget Burke and Josephson—also Cowley." Even Sheeler wasn't "breaking any barriers." If Riordan ever did anything—and as yet he hadn't—it would "be more important than all these," and then Williams added that this prediction, like all predictions, was of course fallible. Burke's insistence on the articulation of a poetics was one thing that troubled Williams. The critical mind was too schematic, too neat, not daring or open enough. "The actual getting of work upon the page is a very complex mechanism that is not included in the mental adjustment to the problem," Williams insisted, adding that articulateness itself was capable of killing the rarest perceptions: "A prying, articulating writer CANNOT articulate until he has made. It is the making that is the articulation."[33] Impossible to write a good poem by *any* formula, no matter how complex.

Five months later he felt even more strongly that Burke's articulations were on the wrong track. Burke, he complained, couldn't "see a damned thing that he hasn't prepared beforehand and he argues from fear of being found out to be wrong. I have been feeling less and less interested in Burke's conception of late." He even preferred arguing with McAlmon to Burke, and McAlmon, he knew, could be a "bastard in his sour lack of appreciation for either praise or argument."[34] On the one side, McAlmon was too unstructured, too indifferent to the way of saying things; on the other, Burke was too schematic, too procrustean. Riordan, however, was altogether different from either and more like Williams himself, with his scientifically trained mind and spirit of tolerance. Still, Burke had staying power, and he would be arguing aesthetics with Williams as forcefully as ever a quarter century down the line, long after Riordan had completely dropped out of the picture.

In June Williams read what Gorham Munson had to say about his writing in *Destinations*, a series of essays on modern poetry, and he wrote Riordan that he'd found Munson's piece on him interesting and even true, even though he felt Munson had completely missed the direction in which he was going. For one thing, Munson had called for a stronger programmatic sense in Williams. Williams, on the other hand, knew now from hard experience that he had built as he had, "block by block," without guideposts or anything "else to stand on" and would have to continue doing just that. He saw himself as the new DeSoto exploring a virgin land step by tentative step. Moreover, Munson had missed "the all-important sensual elements" in Williams' poems in looking too hard for the intellectual underpinnings, just as Burke had. The problem with Burke, Williams confided to Riordan now, was that he thought "too much without having the distinction of being an original philosopher." For himself, Williams had long ago escaped out of philosophy and into art. After all, philosophy wouldn't get Burke any further with the poem than it had gotten Eliot. Munson had even held up Burke's philosophical poems as a corrective to Williams' own poems, but Williams was convinced he'd already gone far beyond anything Burke could teach him in the poetry he was now writing. Well, at least Munson seemed to be genuinely trying to comprehend what it was Williams was after. But Burke: Burke was, finally, still an antagonist, looking out on the blossoming poem as though he were looking "through a slit in a turret."[35]

As for Burke: Williams argued with him for his review of *In the American Grain* in the *Herald Tribune* for March 14, for unduly stressing the subjective nature of Williams' history. "I thought I had salted the original matter with enough historic material to have escaped the bald statement 'Subjective History,' " he offered, though he was willing to concede that he might have miscalculated. But he wished Burke "had sensed a sweep to the book as a whole. Maybe it isn't there but one or two friends have gotten it." There was also the implied ideology of the text, one that he'd hoped his imagistic motifs rather than straightforward articulation had carried. And why hadn't Burke said anything of all that?[36]

In the summer of '26, Riordan put together an essay on precision poetry, which attempted to outline the interrelationships between science and poetry. Williams read the typescript in early August and wrote Riordan that he was feeling depressed about his own poetry, since no one—not himself and not Riordan—had yet penetrated its secret, though Riordan's essay had made a good beginning. Two months later, in October, he came back to the problem:

> As I exist, omnivorous, everything I touch seems incomplete until I can swallow, digest and make it part of myself. I thank you for making this clear to me. . . . I cannot work inside a pattern because I can't find a pattern that will have me. My whole effort—in the light of your observations—is to find a pattern, large enough, flexible enough to include my desires. And if I should find it I'd wither and die.[37]

Riordan's letters kept coming and Williams found himself more and more excited by what he considered the fineness of Riordan's mind until, finally, at the beginning of November, he wrote something that startled the man. "Your letters give me a maddening sense of discovery just glimpsed and then shut off," he began, adding that he supposed "some brilliant ass would deduce from this that I want to fuck you and haven't yet done so," though he was relieved that "that disturbing nightmare" was "fading recently however."[38] What he meant, Williams explained, was that it was time to stop all this linguistic foreplay and teasing and get down to the consummation of the thing. It was time to finish the battle with Riordan, get beyond Riordan's feelings about what he thought the new poetry was, and find some objective basis for the new art they'd both been flirting with for so long.

Riordan however took the metaphor too literally, and Williams found himself having to explain to his startled friend what he'd meant. "You got me wrong, as they say in the Reviews," he told Riordan on the seventeenth. "Read my letter again, I ain't no sodomite, just the opposite. Opportunity does two things, it offers us what we want and takes away what we find we never wanted. It has done the latter for me." What he meant, really (and he was playing with Riordan now), was that the prisoners were "coming into light." Did Riordan understand? He told him to look up an opera by Ludwig Beethoven called *Fidelio,* in which "many prisoners are allowed to emerge from a dark prison into the light to soft music." If he wanted to check the reference out, he could go to the Music Library at the New York Public Library. That could be located at Fifth Avenue and 42d Street. He also wanted to be remembered to Riordan's girl friend, Mavis. Williams pulled back as hard as he could from his awkward declaration of enthusiasm, and then he let the matter drop.[39]

But three days later the question of the creative process was very much on his mind again. It was almost Thanksgiving and the beginning of his busy season again, he complained to Riordan, and he felt he was dying there in Rutherford, "in this god damned atmosphere where, literally, I have not one minute to myself except when I am unconscious in sleep; if I get a minute I have to feel like a thief all the while with the telephone ringing every ten minutes to drive me to madness." At least he didn't have syphilis of the brain, he added, and he knew how hard it was on his family to leave him alone for that mythical uninterrupted hour he pined for. As for Riordan, if he was ever going to write anything of moment, he added, then every word would have to go "into the socket" and squirt "its juice deep there." (That was the image he was after!) Riordan would have to invent something new with words, "Something NEW, New, NEW."[40]

*
* *

Writing to Ken Burke in March 1926, Williams mentioned in passing that he'd just sold a story to the *New Masses* which was starting up again. ("That is they have kept one of my new stories, they say nothing of

paying.")[41] The story *New Masses* took was called "The Five Dollar Guy,"
a piece Williams had written the previous November while on his
medical rounds and which he had then simply filed away until *New
Masses* had written asking for a contribution. It was a story about a
woman friend of his who'd been—he said—propositioned by the owner of
a local oil company. It was a clean piece of writing, especially with its
evocation of a tenement in one of the New Jersey industrial towns, with
its familiar ramshackle Ford rusting in the backyard and with its taste of
authentic New Jersey speech. Williams never saw the galleys of the short
story, but when he saw the thing printed in May he knew at once he was
in trouble. In the heat of getting the story down, he'd failed to change the
names of the people involved, including the name of the oil company.
Someone at *New Masses* should have gone over the story for possible
libelous material, he knew, but that person hadn't, and Williams was left
with a tort on his hand and a $15,000 suit. In 1926 that was three years'
salary!

Williams was desperate, as several pages of notes he typed out to help
steady himself testify.[42] He got a lawyer, but it didn't help him any to look
out his living room window and see the oil man's lawyer sitting in his car
and jotting down notes about Williams' house, property, and his car.
Williams tried to explain that he'd heard the whole story from a woman
pal of his, but she—understandably—signed a statement denying she'd
ever told the doctor any such thing. He knew that all the other oil men
around the area already knew the rumors about the oil man, but of course
they too kept clear of the whole mess. If the case went to a jury, Williams
knew it would take just one rabid middle-class woman looking at the
cover of *New Masses*—that Communist rag—to convict him. He even
had visions of Pound accusing him: "America! ho, ho. Serves you right.
Serve it? Ho, ho. Get it up the pooper for the good you seek." He thought
of Shakespeare before the judge when Shakespeare had been accused of
hunting on royal lands, and the two faces suddenly blended. He had
visions now too of the "amazing procession of vulgarity, of crude vigor"
in the New York environment "pushing out among the stenches of its
own ash heaps, the tin cans of the back lots." He thought back to the
beginnings, to that reverie he'd had just before he left for the university in
September 1902, when he'd made up his mind to go in search of beauty,
to find . . . what? The vulgarity of a Polish kid's dialect as he trundled "a
homemade two wheeled push cart," that dialect seducing his ear, he was
so in love with it. He remembered something Mina Loy had said to him:
that one should be cleaned out every few years and start fresh; otherwise
life would lose its zest. He thought too of John Brown after Harpers Ferry:
how dear life had seemed to him just then when he was about to lose it.
What was American democracy after all but an inchoate mass—like
Whitman's verse? He had come back to America from Paris to work here

in Rutherford among his townspeople . . . for what? To be shafted finally
by his own.

But what hurt him even more was what this sudden turn of events had
done to Floss. She'd been angry, of course. How many times had she told
him to make sure he changed names and places if he was going to publish
something? But she stuck by him now, willing to see the thing through
with her husband. "The loss may be crushing and the bitterness of it may
be that it is not we ourselves who suffer the most but someone dearest to
us, some woman." And images of his own past began floating now to the
surface, guilty images like the memory of some woman's red garters. In
the midst of these thoughts one of his patients, a young boy, had died at
Passaic General of spinal meningitis. He thought of that and of his
younger son saying to him, "You're the bestest father in the world." And
Ezra: if it was Ezra who was standing where he now was, why he'd be
shitting his pants! Better to write some "quiet cottage romance of love"
for these hypocrites he'd once called his townspeople, who went to see
movies every week that were more salacious in intent than anything he'd
ever published. Thank God he had Floss and her courage, though the
heart went out of him when he would hear her trying to hide her nervous
cough from him: a telltale sign that even that fountain of strength
was—after all—vulnerable.

In the end, the case never reached a jury. Instead, Williams agreed to
pay $5,000 damages out of court and promised never to print the story
again. When he won the prestigious *Dial* award that same year, the entire
$2,000 went toward paying off the fine. For the rest, he would "hump"
even harder at his practice for another year (more writing time lost
forever). But he was more careful from that time on. He didn't want to get
burned again. "You know that I was nicked for several thousand dollars
because of my story in *The New Masses?*" he wrote Riordan in August
summarizing what had happened. "It was a beastly piece of business all
through. The story had some actual names in it which I had neglected to
remove and *The Masses* never sent me proof. It has been a serious setback
to me but fortunately it didn't quite break me. Shit. . . . I'm not depressed
but I'm taking no vacation and working like hell to make up the cash."[43]

One way to make money was to write a "popular" novel, and now he
began in earnest to write one, based largely on the diary he'd kept of his
six months in Europe. He'd begun working on it in the summer of '25 as
soon as he'd finished *In the American Grain*. But now, in August 1926, he
worked hard on it, finishing over two hundred pages in a month. "I'm
writing some prose again," he told Sylvia Beach on the eighteenth, "a
kind of novel. Maybe it will be ready next spring. I am writing it straight
ahead without looking back so that I speak of it with some misgivings not
knowing what terrible atrocity I may have perpetrated in the few hundred
pages of manuscript jotted down so far since I have not looked back to see."

He'd almost finished the first draft by then, and he warned her that this book was no *Ulysses* and would contain no modernist experimentation; it was, rather, "a straight account of a man of forty seeing something of Americans in Europe. It is about America you see."[44]

"In self defense I have written a novel in the last six months," he explained to Pound on January 6, 1927. If he could sell it for $3,000, he'd be square again with literature "and ready to do poetry (it gives me a thrill to believe I can do it again)—once more." He toyed with the idea of what he might have done with that $5,000 in his hands again, together with the $2,000 *The Dial* had given him, plus what his house was worth. He might even be able to retire and live on that income the rest of his days. But would he have done that? "I believe not," he answered, at least not yet. After all, it might "be cutting my throat to cut off this fury of running around from house to house that somehow fires me with energy even while it exhausts me." Floss had been reading Hemingway's first novel, *The Sun Also Rises*, but she'd found Maxwell Bodenheim's *Ninth Avenue* had Hemingway beat "by two laps and one lick." He must have wondered how his own first novel would stack up against either of them.[45]

By early April, however, he had serious misgivings about his book. So, when he wrote John Herrmann, whose novel *What Happens* he'd just finished reading in manuscript, he told Herrmann that he'd been so "surprisingly adept at tracking the emotions" that he'd managed to stir up Williams' own raw past. Then he mentioned his own novel: "I wonder if I have been successful in doing what I want to do. My hero is forty and very weak, very weak and very tough, not at the back of the neck though."[46] By early July, with the novel undergoing its final typing, Williams had already written it off as a loss. Riordan for one had given Williams a hard time for trifling with a novel when he should have been getting another book of poems together. But Williams demurred: "Maybe my book is no good," he admitted candidly, but at least it was "not a denial of my best poetic impulses," merely "a slowing of the process or a dilution, at the worst."[47] Riordan had been his correspondent now for nearly two years, and this letter—written in mid-July—was the last letter Williams apparently wrote Riordan. In that time, Williams had finally come to understand that it was not science and logic which had allowed Riordan to penetrate into the deepest recesses of his soul, but—as Williams himself put it—Riordan's Catholicism.

It was that same Catholicism Williams had tried to deal with in his essay on the French Jesuit Père Sebastian Rasles, and that he found in his own apostate spirit-ridden mother. Most scientists, Williams had come to realize, understood poetry even less than philosophers. They were in fact merely sentimental when it came to the topic of poetry. But Riordan had been different: "By your human, Catholic! instinctive and unique power you have been able to get accurately, analytically into me, into the small recesses of my feeling about poetry and build up something . . . which complements my own work. What you say is warm, intimate. It lives as surely as any poem."[48] Now that the novel was finished, poems would follow once more. All in good time. By August he could tell Wallace Stevens that the novel had been launched over New York. Like Lindbergh's *The Spirit of St. Louis* taking off from Roosevelt Field, it had lifted into "the air finely, being piloted by a charming literary agent," though almost at once it had been "lost in foggggggggg."[49] Hopefully, it would land in some publisher's lap.

On Sunday night, April 10, 1927, the Williamses went with their friends Andrew and Madeline Spence to Carnegie Hall for the opening of George Antheil's *Ballet Mécanique*. Williams had heard parts of this in Antheil's studio in Paris in 1924, and he was anxious now to hear the full score of this modernist experiment in atonality. It was quite an evening, and it taxed even Williams' understanding of music. He saw several people get up and leave in protest, particularly "one lantern jawed young gentleman" who stood up and pushed past Williams when Antheil's electric bells began ringing. But, he noticed, most of the people did stay to hear the thing through. After the performance was over, and the Williamses and Spences made their way down into the subway, Williams tried to understand what he had experienced. Had he just come from a Beethoven concert and gone down into the subway, he knew that he would have tried to withstand the assault on his ears of the trains rumbling and screeching into the underground station by holding Beethoven, failingly, in his mind's ear, until that music had vanished. But with his saxophone cadenza, the allegro-andante oscillation of his quartet, and his jazz symphony and atonal experiments, Antheil had managed to master and incorporate all the unrelated noises of modern urban life. So Antheil's music had allowed Williams to go up over the sounds he encountered every day in reality, in effect, and thus find a contrapuntal music for his own modern reality. Not one critic, Williams discovered when he searched the papers the next day, not one music critic in all New York had been able to deal with the musical problem Antheil had laid out before them. What was true of the prominent literary critics, then, was true also of music critics: they too could not grasp the nature of the revolution in sensibility going on—at times quietly, at times noisily—all about them.[50]

On Friday, July 1, Williams drove into New York again to see his old friend Marjorie Allen Seiffert, from the *Others* days. She was taking her annual two weeks' sabbatical from her husband and children and—as she had been doing for several years past—had invited Williams along with some of her other men friends to meet her for dinner in New York when she arrived there from Moline, Illinois. Williams met her that night and discussed her most recent volume of poems, but chided her for not being more daring in her use of the old ballad forms. ("I dare you to write it so that every word left a burn on your flesh," he had written her on June 23. "In this battle [of poetry] only he lives whom they can't kill. And I insist on taking you seriously."[51])

One topic that came up that Friday evening was Lola Ridge, whose gatherings had been of such importance to the New York literary scene in the early and mid-'20s. Now Williams had heard that Ridge was separated from her husband and was ill and in need of funds. Seiffert had given him fifty dollars to send her, and he was adding his own contribution. It was a delicate situation, and Williams handled it delicately when he wrote to Ridge. "I think I have a special privilege to ask you to lay aside delicate feelings in these matters for once," he wrote her on July 5, "and to take freely what is freely given since I love and value highly the poetry you have given us all." He didn't want her to think of the money he was sending as charity, but rather as if he were holding out a bag of apples for her to help herself. She was a poet with a new book of poems out, *Red Flag,* and he felt that she could accept these proferred apples because her poems had earned them for her.[52]

*
* *

Back in 1924 Bill and Floss had decided that their boys should have a year abroad, as Williams and his brother had had back in 1898, when young Bill was finished with grade school. The pattern was to be repeated: Floss would stay in Geneva—at the Hôtel des Familles—and the boys, who would be thirteen and eleven, would go to school at nearby Lancy. Williams' family would be gone, then, for nearly a year. He would take the ship over with them, stay with them for several weeks, and then return home alone at the end of September. Neighbors whispered nonsense that the Williamses must be going through a trial separation, but the real reasons were simpler: to give the boys a year abroad (Paul particularly had seemed to drift through grade school), and to give Williams the chance to get some serious writing done. His mother was living with him now, had in fact been living with the family since Bill and Floss had left for Paris in January 1924, and Lucy would also be there to take care of the doctor. He'd have two women to watch over him, and Elena, now that Floss was gone, was eager to set herself up as reigning female presence at 9 Ridge Road.

Before leaving, Floss and the boys spent a week in August up at the Monroe farm with the Hermans while Williams worked at his practice. He was already beginning to miss his wife fiercely, and she'd only been gone a few days. He wrote her about another of those Christian Science cases, which had always mystified him, from his grandmother on. A nine-year-old boy over in Lyndhurst was dead, he complained, because the parents had refused to let him or another doctor examine the child. "It is now a coroner's case," he said, adding that someone "should be lynched." His new second-floor office over on Main Street in Passaic above the bank was keeping him on the jump, but he'd needed to establish residency there if he was going to stay on the staff of Passaic General. He'd also fumigated the office at 9 Ridge Road and had almost suffocated Lucy and himself in the process.[53] In another letter he talked about the massing of Russian and British troops in Northern India. He was also having trouble with his new glasses, which he had finally—at forty-two—begun wearing, and they had lasted only one day because the doctor had prescribed the wrong lenses. Another specialist in Newark had then correctly diagnosed Williams' eye trouble as hypersensitiveness to light, which he himself had suspected all along. With his new glasses on, he'd taken the others and hurled them out the window into the bushes as he drove home. He talked about his patients familiarly with Floss. A big, fat dark girl in her mid-twenties had come into his office the day before to complain about her second husband, a big slob of a dumbbell. "They have been married seven months. He has only fucked her once when she went after him and made him do it. . . . I'd rather sleep with a nigger or a dog, she says. They at least are natural. But he lies besides her and masturbates!" Practice had been active. He'd had four calls to make in Passaic and another four in Rutherford, and he'd had ten people waiting in his home office the night before. He'd found an old poem of his he'd written last winter and had just sent it off to *transition* ("Now the snow / lies on the ground . . ."). He'd just received his royalty statement from the Boni brothers for *In the American Grain* for the first half of 1927: a grand total of thirteen copies sold in six months. Five dollars. He wished Floss was back with him: "I'd ride you well if you were. It's fun to say so too." He missed his sons and was crazy to be on the ship going over with them.[54]

Williams' eye must have been watching the newspapers for more than talk about the buildup of Russian and British troops in India that August, because he—like thousands of other intellectuals in the States and abroad—was waiting to see whether or not someone—the President or the governor of Massachusetts—would stay the execution of two Italian anarchists convicted of murder during a holdup in Massachusetts: Nicola Sacco and Bartolomeo Vanzetti. "There were several features of the case that stirred the intellectuals profoundly," Malcolm Cowley wrote years later:

> First of all there was the situation of two men tried unjustly and sentenced to death, the old story of innocence endangered. There was the

fact that these men were radicals and had been arrested during the Palmer Raid, when the intellectuals had also been threatened. There was the high smugness of the Massachusetts officials, some of whom turned themselves into caricatures of everything that artists hate in the bourgeoisie. There were the international echoes of the case. . . . Then overshadowing all other issues, there were the personalities of two men who had spent seven years between life and death, seven years of being threatened, praised, lied about and continually tortured with hope. . . . These two . . . managed in their different fashions to remain skeptical and human. . . . It is no wonder that they aroused a blind hatred and a fanatical loyalty.[55]

But on the evening of August 23, with five hundred police and national guard surrounding the Charlestown Prison in Boston, the two men finally died in the electric chair. Williams was outraged and turned his anger against the people themselves, who, after all, had been the ones who had lost. "Take it out in vile whiskey," he wrote.

> take it out
> in lifting your skirts to show your silken
> crotches; it is this that is intended.
> You are it. Your pleas will always be denied.
> You too will always go up with the two guys,
> scapegoats to save the Republic and
> especially the State of Massachusetts. The
> Governor says so and you ain't supposed
> to ask for details. . . .

The invective cut right at the heart of his "townspeople" again, "nature's nobleman" who knew deep down there was nothing to be afraid of from the police, who knew the government was—after all—there to serve him, who knew, "when a cop steps up and grabs / you at night you just laugh and think it's / a hell of a good joke."[56] Williams may have tried to publish his poem at once and failed, or he may have written it merely to try to deal with his sense of outrage. He may even have written it before the execution itself, trying to cope with a sense of mounting tension that two men whom he believed improperly tried were about to die. In any event, he did not publish the poem until 1941, nearly fifteen years after Sacco and Vanzetti had died.

In early September, the Williams family took the SS *Arabic* from New York to Antwerp, taking the same route Williams had taken back in 1909 on his way to Leipzig. From there they went down by train through Basle, Lausanne, and Chillon to Geneva. "There is no chance of my seeing you this visit," he wrote Pound on the sixteenth from the Hôtel des Familles in Geneva. Pound was at the moment once again in an Italian hospital for surgery and it would be impossible for Williams to get down to see him. He promised to land in Genoa instead of Antwerp in the spring of '28 and get his orders from the Maestro on what to read and write for the next ten years. The boys were already at school, and he and Floss were staying in Geneva until the eighteenth before going up to Paris, though they did not expect to go over to the American side on this trip. They were, however, expecting to see McAlmon and Bill and Sally Bird again. Williams had no new work to show Pound, but he would leave a carbon copy of his just-finished novel, *Voyage to Pagany*, with McAlmon. If Pound wanted to see it, all he would have to do would be to drop Williams a line in care of Sylvia Beach's place and he'd send it on at once. He mentioned the pieces he'd written for *transition* (Paris) on Antheil and James Joyce, and told him he was looking forward to the next issue of Pound's magazine, *Exile*.[57] But when Williams left Paris for home a week later, there was still no letter from Pound.

As it turned out, the Williamses arrived in Paris the same week that the American Legion was in the city to celebrate the tenth anniversary of the first American troops bivouacking there during the First World War. There were few rooms anywhere, and the place the Williamses did find was too uncomfortable. McAlmon, however, managed to get them a place at his own Hôtel Istria. But the climate in Paris had changed in the three years since Williams had been there, and he couldn't help sensing the growing anti-American feeling among the Parisians, who did not particularly care for these rich, noisy American ex-soldiers with their hoopla and barbarous tastes.

But the highlight of the week for Williams was an audience with Gertrude Stein at her apartment at 27, rue de Fleurus, with its Picassos from that painter's blue period hovering above Stein's chair as she spoke with Williams. It was an awkward meeting at best. Pound had been there not long before and had managed to break one of her treasured antique chairs with that sprawl of his Williams remembered so well. Stein made several pointed comments about Pound's manners to Williams, and that led to some comments about Pound's writing. It was a tactical error on her part, so that when she asked Williams what he thought she ought to do with the huge collection of manuscripts she had written over the years, Williams suggested she keep the best and then burn the rest. There was an awkward, deafening silence, and then Stein's repartee: "No doubt. But then writing is not, of course, your *métier*." The meeting was over.[58]

On Saturday, September 24, Williams put Floss on the train for Geneva, and then left for Cherbourg, as he had in 1924, this time accompanied by Sylvia Beach and her sister Holly, who would travel with Williams on the SS *Pennland* back to the States. Sylvia, he wrote Floss that same evening aboard ship, had had a talk with McAlmon about his heavy drinking, telling him that it had begun, finally, to affect his writing. She had also filled Williams in on McAlmon's divorce from Bryher the year before. McAlmon himself, for personal reasons, had been reticent about those subjects, both in Paris and when he'd visited the

Williamses in New York earlier that spring on his way back from Los Angeles to Paris to forget the whole sorry mess. Already McAlmon's brief star had begun to sink.[59]

Now, out to sea, Williams on the other hand was already beginning to plan how he would use the year to advance his writing and his name. He would write something every day, he wrote Floss, keeping five or six things going at once. He was lonely and he wrote every few hours to Floss at first, unwilling to believe that they'd actually agreed to a year-long separation.[60] At least, he wrote, they had taken this bold step and had thus "broken the staleness of the boys' education." He read and wrote out in the deck chairs, watching the sea rise and fall. He took his meals with Holly Beach and enjoyed her companionship. But he hadn't expected to find the American Legion boys on board, returning on the same ship as himself. Of course they were still raising almighty hell. Each night, hundreds of ex-doughboys paraded up and down the corridors of the ship, drinking whiskey and champagne and beer and singing "Mademoiselle of gay Paree" while Williams tried to finish a book Riordan had put him onto: Alfred North Whitehead's *Science and the Modern World.*

The trip home also afforded him a period of personal reassessment. Halfway across he wrote Floss: "I was really an unhappy, disappointed child—in general—during my early years."[61] Thus a saddened, lonely Williams, made happy by his wife, who had seen through him and made him good. Whatever he'd done to lessen himself in her eyes had merely served to bring him back, finally, stronger than ever to her. But as he got nearer home, his attention turned to his work. He'd been anxious to make the separation worthwhile. First, there'd been a ten-page reply to Laura Riding for her attack on Poe (and by extension on himself, for his "Romantic" view of a second-rate hack writer). That out of the way, he'd begun his next book of poems, which he was thinking of calling *Sacred and Profane* (but which became instead part of a prose/poetry improvisation called *The Descent of Winter*). The poem he'd written that very day was for Floss and it was called "Portrait of My Friend." He gave a copy of that to Holly as a gift.[62]

Saturday, October 1, 7:45 AM: Williams, staring long at the sea, had come to realize that for all its activity it did not change. It simply annihilated time. There were three dead Legionnaires in the hold now. As for the others, they were rowdier than hell and threatening to do something drastic. On top of that there'd been a series of robberies on board, and the Legionnaires had threatened to kill the person who'd done it if they could find him.

Sunday, October 2, 11:30 AM: Williams could see the red Nantucket Lighthouse offshore, the first sign that they were nearing America. He had watched a Legionnaire named "Nevada" standing up on a table in the smoking room and singing his heart out to the boys who would soon scatter to the four corners of the United States. That same day Williams wrote out a medical certificate for Holly Beach's five Siamese cats to get them through customs. They were, he certified, all "in excellent condition."[63]

October 6—to Sylvia Beach: "It was a real pleasure to travel with your sister—and the cats. . . . Holly and I sat together at table and talked and drank together. We discussed goofer feathers and she taught me to understand the Beach family kitten talk. It was a lot of fun. In return I recited poems into her ear while we were dancing and also read her a few things I had written on the trip. But how can a mere lonely literary man compete with a woman of the world? I had forgotten all my best poems."[64] He wanted to thank Sylvia for all her kindnesses while he was in Paris. He was anxious to get the manuscript of his *Voyage to Pagany* back from Elliot Paul, one of the editors at *transition*. Paul should get it back to Floss, who, in turn, would give Paul a copy of the essay Williams had just written attacking Laura Riding. He thanked Sylvia for the copies of Gogol's *Dead Souls* and Joyce's *Dubliners*, which—along with White-head—he'd read on the trip back.

Home now, Williams would write something every day. He would keep a journal, pouring into that whatever came: poems, prose improvisations, germs for essays, short stories, novels, letters, confessions, fantasies.[65] "I want to write all over the page any way I please," he wrote to himself on October 10, "hit or miss, good or bad."[66] And on the twenty-third: "I will make a big, serious portrait of my time."[67] The hero of his American portrait would be a little Polish girl, born in Garfield in his absence, and he fantasized the life he had enkindled in her: ". . . the thought of her illegitimate conception fills me with joy, I conceived her, I begat her—under the powdery light, in the falling leaves."[68] He was fathering a new world, creating it from the loins of his imagination. Pischak—Passaic—Paterson. The year before he'd written an eighty-five-line poem called "Paterson," for which he'd received the *Dial* Award. (This early poem was his first attempt at the epic he had already begun to envision, though he certainly did not think then of writing a poem that would eventually grow longer than his prose excursus on America, *In the American Grain*. In 1926 eighty-five lines was about as long as he could coax his imagist muse into flying for him.) But now Williams picked the American theme up again, attempting to launch into something on the grand scale, the impetus of *Ulysses* still fresh in his mind. If one could recreate Dublin, why not another provincial city: like Paterson? "All that I am doing (dated) will go in it," he wrote, because he would be the locus where many lines intersected: "Poems. Talk of poetry. Sequently IS it . . . .Paterson is really—part of it."[69] America: "And Coolidge said let there be imitation brass filigree fire tenders."[70] He thought of Russia, ten years after the October Revolution of 1917. Might not America too be revolutionized in the imagination? Might he not recreate Paterson in his mind and thus come into possession of his world?

> We have little now but
> we have that. We are convalescents. Very
> feeble. Our hands shake. We need a
> transfusion. No one will give it to us,
> they are afraid of infection. I do not
> blame them. We have paid heavily. But we
> have gotten—touch. The eyes and the ears
> down on it. Close.[71]

What was the United States in 1927 after all but "a soviet state decayed away in a misconception of richness," her people so many cottontailed rabbits, preoccupied with buying and selling Florida real estate, office workers in cotton pants riding in hot cars through hot tunnels to get to their hot offices . . . to sell asphalt. They did not even come into close contact with the things by which they made their livelihoods. Most of them couldn't even name the parts of the things they handled. He remembered "Nevada," drunk, rolling on top of the table in the *SS Pennland*'s smoking room, singing his drunken cowboy songs to uncomprehending faces. Thus far had local cultures in the States decayed.[72]

And what of himself as singer of his own place, he who had been baptized fifteen years before in the filthy Passaic:

> O river of my heart polluted
> and defamed I have compared you
> to that other lying in
> the red November grass
> beginning to be cleaned now
> from factory pollution
>
> Though at night a watchman
> must still prowl lest some paid hand
> open the waste sluices—
>
> That river will be clean
> before ever you will be. . . . [73]

He thought of literature, made his own list of what seemed living for him, what dead. Dante was dead for him, Chinese and Italian poetry in translation also. But the *Iliad*, Shakespeare, Dostoevski, Villon: these were still living and worth using. And as for America? Someone had to be found to record what was alive in his own American culture, someone who could

> summarize these things
> in the interest of local

> *government or how*
> *a spotted dog goes up a gutter—*
>
> *and in chalk crudely*
> *upon the railroad bridge support*
> *a woman rampant*
> *brandishing two rolling pins.*[74]

He worked hard, both at his medical practice and at his writing, trying to force his sexual energies into his writing. And yet it was also becoming clear to others that Williams was—for all practical purposes—a bachelor alone and lonely there at 9 Ridge Road. His neighbors knew it, his patients soon learned about it. For, away from wife and kids, he experimented now with alcohol and tobacco in an attempt to fragment and break up the rigidity of his own personality, confiding this too to his journal, especially as winter began to make itself felt. Part of his entry for November 24—which did not find its way into the published excerpts —ran this way:

> The necessity for and use of alcohol . . . to excess on occasion . . . the fragmentation of the too stiff personal[ity] which is contracting. . . . Shakespeare drunk in the gutter that he might create—purity. Loosen it, crack it. . . . The desire for a change of women and one woman. . . . But then "the world" finds out about him and his wife finds out and then hell is. She is all tongue. . . . Unless you do what Wallace Gould is doing go back to the Greek for stuff—but the living modern must first be invented. . . . Marriages tend to become incest. A wife is nine tenths a sister or a mother—without adulteries on both parts. Love is unknown in its essence. . . . [75]

He remembered something Stevens had said to him years before: that "the use of a woman to a man is the use of any woman to any man. . . . She gives him stuff in his blood that stands him up. A woman is water. She tightens a man inside." He knew he wanted, from time to time, to play, though he knew that play was "dangerous, rare, [and] abandoned," because it "came out of a woman."[76] He knew what that play might cost his marriage, so that he countered his sexual instincts by keeping serious and by working hard and seldom seeking out society, since when he was with others he often found he had "little to say" that was "intelligible."

The truth was that he had just narrowly escaped one sexual encounter and he was still shaky over it. "Imagine dearest," he wrote Floss on November 22:

> And if I weren't half full of Mr. Conklin's crazy "Burgundy" I couldn't tell you. That [and here he inked out the woman's name beyond recall and substituted an interesting amalgam] Dolores Marie Veronica Magdalena actually or at any rate did come into my office today and ask me to screw

her. She couldn't be got out. Imagine. How I didn't do it I don't know, except by thinking like hell of you. The wild thoughts that go through the head at such times are like mad eagles: Do it. To hell with everything. You're a fool. What of it. It doesn't mean a thing, do it anyway. Jesus! And all the time the body is trembling like a leaf, like sick meat with desire. She begged for it [and] couldn't be got out. A young woman—dripping with desire unsatisfied. No argument could move her, just edging her to the door. I didn't even want to mention it, somehow it seems unworthy of a man to do so but—God damn it I want with all my soul to keep myself spotless for you and I've got to tell you. Even if it mars me—as I do not believe it will. I was crazy to fuck her, just to tear in and do it. But thank God I got her out without doing it and without making a scene. . . . [77]

Now, with his wife separated from him by the ocean, he began to make notes for a new novel which would have her at its core. He'd written of Floss in *Voyage to Pagany*, but he didn't think many people would be interested in a travelogue about a middle-class American couple as they moved about Europe. So he had kept himself in his novel—fairly intact, despite his own demurrers—but had splintered his wife into several women, including two lovers and a sister, marriage being, as he'd said, nine-tenths incest anyway. The book he'd written he already knew—even before he published it—to be "soft, romantic and tentative because unimaginative."[78] Now, however, separated by three thousand miles, he would write about Floss, but Floss as one of all the women he knew, blending her with what he'd learned about all kinds of women, women like Djuna Barnes—whose excerpts from *Nightwood* in *transition* he was just then rereading, and Joyce's Molly, and the women who came into his office every day, as well as Floss in her life and in her letters. It was the first stirrings toward what would eventually become —when it was finally published ten years later—his *White Mule*. A name for his tough, dependable wife, but also the name for a down-home liquor with enough kick in it to knock your head off. As for style? Not the cheapness of a Zane Grey certainly, nor "the English-provincial archaic language" of Djuna, and not the plain novel style of Sherwood Anderson and Ben Hecht and Bodenheim, a style false as the newspapers themselves "which lose everything among the news."[79] He was moving away, now, from his earlier irritability in print—the wild-man iconoclast lamenting in print about the impossibility of locating a ground on which to build one's edifice. The problem in the past had been—in part—that he had known too much to become America's democratic singer. Had he not already balked at Sandburg's later work as too soft, too phony, really? No use, as Pound had long since pointed out, pretending to know less than one knew. But, then, had he at least "added some dignity, cogency, potency, interest, exhilaration, reason" for living in a place like New Jersey? Or, no, not New Jersey and Rutherford—"this microscopic banality, this suburb, this vacancy"—but rather this condition of being in a place called America where the imaginative mind just happened to find itself.[80]

Nor would satire do for him either. That too was a cheap substitute for coming into authentic contact with one's place. Williams had gone to a Christmas Ball sponsored by the local police and had watched them closely to see what—if anything—they might offer in terms of the local scene. How often he'd seen them, worked with them, delivered their wives' children, heard the local scandal from and about them. He knew as well as any priest or cop on the beat what was going on around Rutherford and its environs, knew too who was involved "and would tell it for truth's sake." And yet he dared not because he was not one of those in power—as his brush with that lawyer over his libelous story had taught him—"and would be annihilated, literally," if he should dare to speak. He remembered Jackson the cop saying, "If there's anything in the world I like it's puppies and babies." What to make of that? The temptation there, he knew, was to become a Dickens or a Gilbert and Sullivan, to do the funny papers in another medium.[81] How many stitches had he sewn up trying to put together black and white flesh sliced open like a ripe watermelon? There was the time the big Irish cop had patted his gun and warned him and another doctor not to hurt either his wife or the baby they were trying desperately to bring into the world. Or there was the time he'd had to be escorted home across the cemetery by one of his Italian small-time mafiosi patients because a relative up from Newark had liked the look of *il dottore's* Ford.

What he was after in his writing, though, was not the broad comedy of the situation, but the difficult "dignity of the theme," the poor with their life-sustaining Rabelaisian philosophy, a correlative for the dignity of the Old World in the New. As in this image, perhaps, evoking Brueghel's *Hunters in the Snow:*

> *and hunters still return*
> *even through the city*
> *with their guns slung*
> *openly from the shoulder*
> *emptyhanded howbeit*
> *for the most part*
> > *but aloof*
> *as if from and truly from*
> *another older world. . . .* [82]

No wonder, then, he tried his hand at a fable about "Skunk Mencken." For even H. L. Mencken—who'd made his name and his money attacking the American Booboisie—was part of the river which remembered everything. Mencken was, in this telling, a skunk who hated all the other animals and so had come upon a poor sleeping horse (the people) prepared to tell it why it would have to be obliterated. When he turned to spray the poor animal with its venom, however, he realized with horror that his only weapon—bitter satire—was gone. Not venom, then, but dignity, and contact with one's debased world.[83]

"Wherein is Moscow's dignity/more than Passaic's dignity?" he wrote at this time, enclosing the poem as a Christmas gift in his letter to Floss. A few Russian artists had managed to get their city down in paint better: that was all. But the potential for a new dignity was as much here in New Jersey as it had been in Russia. After all, as with the Arno, the Seine, the Thames, the Liffey and the Volga,

> The river is the same
> the bridges are the same
> there is the same to be discovered
> of the sun—
>
> Look how cold, steelgrey
> run the waters of the Passaic.
> The Church-of-the Polaks'
> bulbous towers
>
> kiss the sky just so sternly
> so dreamily
> as in Warsaw, as in Moscow—
> Violet smoke rises
>
> from the mill chimneys—Only
> the men are different who see it
> draw it down in their minds
> or might be different.[84]

Another fruit of these same meditations was an updated version of Whitman's "Democratic Vistas" which Williams called "A Democratic Party Poem" and which he tried (unsuccessfully) to get printed for the 1928 Democratic campaign, which ran Al Smith against Herbert Hoover. In the fall of '28 Williams would urge his friends to vote for Al Smith, being, as some would remember half a century later, "always a good Democrat." "The strongest feature of the Russian Soviets is their local character," he began programmatically, contrasting them to the individual states of America:

> The first characteristic of the United States is that
> of so many decayed Soviets
>
> The old strength of Europe is its traditional localism
> fixed by a variety of languages
>
> The loss of China has been that of the conglomerate
>
> States' rights precede all other political virtues
>
> The Renaissance was the flowering of rival cities

> *It is inevitable that in all things one must always*
> *know more than the rest of the world*
>
> *And what he knows is bred of some place. . . .* [85]

But the local Democratic Party was hardly ready to accept such radical Jeffersonian sentiments as these in 1928. It was hard enough having a liberal, anti-Prohibition candidate—and a Catholic to boot—without making any connections between some Bolshevik Russia and the good ol' U.S. as a series of "decayed Soviets." Better some local fund raisers and a few good beer parties and let it go at that.

Christmas 1927: It would be the first time Williams had ever spent Christmas apart from his own family, and now the reality of the separation became almost unbearable. "I am attached unfailingly to you," he confessed to Floss on December 20—one of the shortest days of the year—"and yet I am without the comfort of your presence. . . . Last night I thought I saw you. I don't know when it was or whether I was awake or asleep."[86] He spent Christmas Day alone—by choice—so that he might think about Floss and Bill and Paul. Floss was handling the boys and the separation superbly, and it was clear to him that she could take care of them in almost any emergency. So, when little Paul had contacted diphtheria in October, Floss had taken her son out of the school at Coppet—against all regulations—and had had him admitted to the Municipal Hospital in Geneva and put under the care of the best pediatrician she could locate there. Williams had done what he could via cabling the school doctors at Coppet, insisting that they give his son "an initial dose of 50,000 units of antitoxin if it was a laryngeal case," only to be told that European doctors did things differently, did not believe in administering such massive doses, and would handle the boy their way. At first Paul even seemed to get better. Then he had a serious reaction to the "horse serum" they fed him and it was Floss who nursed him back to health again. She was the woman, she was there.[87]

And he was here. So now, on Christmas Day, Williams drove out of Rutherford by himself to spend the day with the lonely animals at the Bronx Zoo. It was the day his father had died, nine years before, and he remembered how he'd tried—fumblingly—to ease his father's pain, and how he'd had to leave to bring another human being into life, only to find his father dead on his return. The Jersey streets were quiet, deserted, but out across the meadows he spotted a man—about thirty—hitchhiking, and gave him a lift. The guy was a drifter, had spent Christmas Eve in some flophouse over in Paterson, and wanted to see New York, though how he was going to do that without so much as a dime was beyond them both. Williams offered him a cigarette, and then, as he dropped him off at the ferryboat at Weehawken, opened his wallet and counted his money.

What the hell. It was Christmas. Twenty-two dollars. He kept half and slipped the other half to the drifter, much to the man's astonishment, telling him to have a meal on him. Later, in the stone gray shadows of the Bronx Zoo's deserted cafeteria, Williams sat alone and ate his Christmas dinner. This one was for his family.[88]

Practice in the winter of '28 was—as usual—hectic. He wrote Floss about the babies he'd been able to help, and about others—like the Walton baby—who had died after he'd operated on it for a double mastoid: "Eight months old. . . . I woke with a start this morning at 4 AM, wide awake in a flash and my mind began milling over the case."[89] He hurt like hell whenever he lost one; could never learn the detachment from his patients that might have saved him so much personal pain. Another of his Rutherford patients had come to see him "with a beautiful dose of clapp." "I got the blues!" he told her. "I ought to take it as lightheartedly as the coons. But I can't. I am more responsible than they." And yet, were not they—in their flesh—in fact "the vicarious atonement" for the repressions that racked and twisted white Americans like himself?[90] He was even dabbling in stocks now. He bought $5,000 worth of oil shares in Atlantic Refining and watched it tumble down to 95 from the 106 he had bought it at, and then slowly climb up to 109. He was hoping to be able to pay for his family's passage home on the *De Grasse* with those shares, for it was "said to be the finest cabin boat on the transatlantic service."[91] He wondered too who this British doctor was Floss had told him she'd met over there, though he tried to act only mildly curious.[92]

He would write a story about that relationship later on, a story he called "Hands Across the Sea," trying to understand the incident from his wife's point of view. The man was Scottish, a physician who had served in Mesopotamia with the British Army from 1914 to 1918 and had thus become an expert in working with large sanitary problems—malaria, yellow fever, cattle pest control. In the fall of 1927 he was with the Sanitary Committee of the League of Nations with headquarters in Geneva, and he was staying at the same hotel as Floss. He was frequently away on medical business—to Italy, Brazil, Egypt, wherever the League saw fit to send him—but he always sought out Floss on his return. Floss was attracted to him because he reminded her of Bill, except that he was unattached and looking for a woman who would be there for him when he returned from his medical missions. There was a young widow half-waiting for the doctor back home in Scotland but he was not excited by the prospect. His real interest, though he was circumspect, was Floss, and Floss evidently piqued Williams' curiosity by mentioning this interesting figure in her weekly letters home. It remained a friendship probably because of Floss's strong will and her devotion to her husband, but also because Bill and Paul—though they liked the guy and liked to listen to him play his bagpipes in his room—didn't want any guy around who wasn't their father. For his part, Williams tried to get down on paper the tenuous, lyrical quality of that relationship, even something of the inherent sadness of it since—had the roles been reversed, had it been Williams and a woman—probably the outcome would have been different. And Williams had a need, really a desperate need apparently, to know that his wife was there for him and him only, no matter how cavalierly he might talk about the possibility of open marriages. After all, he tried to convince himself, after all, Floss had him.

By January, he had found a publisher for his novel: Macaulay of New York. He wanted to send his friend John Herrmann a copy of the thing—to reciprocate for Herrmann's having sent him a copy of his novel the year before. But the script he'd lent Elliot Paul in Paris for *transition* had "gone the way of all American flesh in Paris," as he'd feared it would: it had been "raped, fucked, buggered." In short, it had been lost. He'd heard that McAlmon might be coming back to the States, but had to confess that he was not feeling particularly close to him at the present; McAlmon had stayed away from America too long.[93] He was also writing to Winters, telling him that now was the time to get away from free verse—it didn't exist—and invent a new measure.[94] (But Winters, as it turned out, was about to throw over his experiments in modernism altogether, and would soon be attacking Williams and Crane, Pound and Yeats and Eliot with the same fervor with which he had once embraced them. Winters had at last seen the error of his past ways.)

Williams also did a statement for the final issue of *The Little Review*, which Margaret Anderson and Jane Heap would bring out in Paris in May 1929.[95] It was a statement Williams hoped would make America "wipe its ass on silk,"[96] for he attacked the entire academy there for what it had done to divorce knowledge from a specific locus, leaving it floating in the abstract. Both Pound and Eliot had given up their place at a terrible cost, he believed, since all cultures were necessarily rooted in a specific place (just as much, he might have added, as those French wines which belonged to one soil and one weather only). The only universal, as Dewey had insisted—and Emerson and Whitman before Dewey—the only universal was "the local as savages, artists and . . . peasants know." This was Williams' manifesto—an extension of what he'd insisted upon in *Contact* and in that political poem of his. What he himself wanted was a construction that, rightly or wrongly, would have its roots profoundly in "the senseless world of modern American writing." His own writing, he maintained, would be "the offshoot of an unerudite locality." At least his poems would not smack—like others he could name—of the classroom, but would be written "in the stress of wanting to stay alive." Eliot, he believed, had already begun to slip imperceptibly from power. In fact, Eliot's *Criterion* was nothing more than a piece of neoscholasticism, as even the American critic Morley Callaghan had admitted in print. By divorcing himself from his roots, then, Eliot had committed a kind of slow cultural suicide. Whatever its shortcomings, New York in the late '20s was at least a place. And out of its ambience Williams still believed would come—eventually—a poetry to rival Europe's.[97]

In March Williams received a letter from a young man living in New York named Louis Zukofsky, who had earlier written to Ezra Pound and had been referred by him to Williams out in Rutherford. Pound had stressed Williams' "human value" to Zukofsky, and when Williams heard that, he told Zukofsky that what the bastard probably meant was that Williams was a nice guy who couldn't write.[98] Zukofsky was twenty-three at the time and was finishing a master's degree in English and Pound had asked him to help him edit *The Exile*. Now Zukofsky was calling on Williams. A few days later, Williams wrote to Zukofsky again, telling him to meet him in New York at the Park Central Hotel, Room 2550, at 5:30 on Sunday afternoon, April 1. Someone was going to do a caricature of him for *The Dial* and he wanted Zukofsky there to rescue him.[99] (The artist turned out to be Eva Herrman, whose caricature of Williams appeared in the November *Dial* along with Pound's essay on Williams, "Dr. Williams' Position.")

Zukofsky was there as planned, and the two men went out for a bite at a local restaurant. They talked poetry, and the younger man—in a pattern that would be repeated many times—gave the older man a single poem of his to read. Williams was impressed by what Zukofsky had given him and wrote the following day, congratulating Zukofsky on doing some "actual word stuff." Pound was to be congratulated for discovering this young man, twenty years Williams' junior. Here was still "another nail in the *Dial* coffin."[100] Williams saw Zukofsky as yet "another wave of the movement," as he told him on Easter Sunday. No matter how much he—Williams—and artists like him might be ignored, Williams congratulated himself, "by doing straightforward work we do somehow reach the right people." He wanted to invite E. E. Cummings out to 9 Ridge Road to meet Zukofsky, but Cummings was just then enjoying some success as "a popular playwright" with the off-Broadway production of *Him*.[101] Instead, Williams had Lucy cook up a special meal for Zukofsky himself when he came out to Rutherford on Friday night, April 20, to see Williams in his own surroundings for the first time.

As for Cummings, Williams invited him out for a Sunday afternoon two weeks later, though when he hadn't shown up by 1 PM, Williams went out looking for him, only to find Cummings meandering up the far end of "a deserted Park Avenue stopping at every store window." Williams' mother made them a chicken dinner and was interested in talking to Cummings not because he was a poet, but because his father had been a Unitarian minister. And Williams himself would remember

Cummings playing with the new litter of Smoky, his Persian cat, on the dining room table and looking faraway and dreamy. Such were the strategies of self-preservation when these two contenders for the laurel found themselves in the same room.[102] "I left him alone most of the time," he confided to Zukofsky. After all, Cummings, for all his years in New York, was still at heart "a real New Englander."[103]

In early April Pound wrote Williams telling him that he was going to devote an entire issue of *The Exile* to Williams' new work as soon as Williams could get a sheaf together. Williams was pleased; he'd been feeling a general despondency lately, with little of his good stuff finding a publisher, and Pound's offer had managed to rescue him "from an oozy hell." Williams also praised the one poem of Zukofsky's he'd seen to date, and added that the fellow seemed "worthwhile personally."[104] He had Zukofsky out again the Sunday after he'd seen Cummings, along with another couple—Nathan Asche and his wife—and when Zukofsky left, he gave him a big piece of the journal he'd been keeping since the previous fall for Zukofsky to read through and edit for the fourth number of *Exile*. This fragment became, finally, with Zukofsky's editing, *The Descent of Winter* when Pound published it from Paris in the fall.

Williams saw Charlie Demuth's still unfinished poster *The Great Figure* sometime in early May at Steiglitz's Intimate Gallery on Park and 59th Street in New York. Demuth's painting (which has since become famous) had been based on a poem of Williams' of the same name, the one beginning, "Among the rain / and lights / I saw the figure 5 / in gold. . . ." Williams was pleased with Demuth's poster and wrote to tell his old friend that he thought it "the most distinguished American painting" he'd seen in years, based on criteria of "color, composition, clarity, thought, emotional force, ingenuity." Still, he wanted to pass on a few suggestions. Demuth, he felt, should stress in the painting what he had stressed in writing that poem sitting on a sidewalk in downtown New York years before: first, the figure 5 itself, detached from the great fire truck that had carried it blaring down the cobblestoned city street, and then the overlapping planes, contours cutting cleanly into each other, the whole design providing a unity of emotional expression. He might almost have been describing one of Marianne Moore's early poems if he hadn't been describing one of his own.[105]

In between his visit from Cummings and his second visit from Zukofsky, Williams drove into New York to see Eugene O'Neill's *Strange Interlude*, the only play—besides *Him*—Williams thought worth seeing in the spring of '28. He liked what O'Neill had done, and wrote Margaret Anderson in Paris that it was

very satisfying to me to realize that relying on the god damned commercial stage O'Neill could never have succeeded. It is by a steady cultivation of his faults that he has finally, preserving his lunge, forced a way up through the dead crust of that vile piece of shit the New York professional production. Good Christ when will we be a republic and hack a way for ourselves through the magic ring of excrement with which we are surrounded. Answer: Never.[106]

He'd found Cummings' play at least as good as O'Neill's—and livelier, though in a wider sense both plays were quintessentially American products. In fact, Williams had just told Zukofsky that O'Neill was "so god damned rotten" he was actually good. O'Neill couldn't handle a situation, write dialogue, or delineate character, but his very biases, deformities, and amputations had allowed him to drive his theme—that "thin rigid point"—home to his audiences. What O'Neill understood —and most American playwrights did not—was that on the stage abnormal people become normal. And so his characters had to wear figurative masks and be deformed that the audience might see just how much those figures were like the audience itself. Paradoxically, it was the "normal" person who looked sick on the stage, he insisted. "It would be a way to show sickness" just to let the average person get up there on the stage and be him or her self. It was Williams the pathologist at work now: "The great theoretically fuckable American girl on the stage all stripped and powdered is so grotesquely sick that no one can see it."[107] That was a hard way of looking at that recent American phenomenon, the American beauty pageant, but Williams had hit the mark.

*
**

By January, Williams had also made up his mind that it was time for another book of poems. After all, excepting *Spring and All,* which was a mixture of improvisations and poems and which almost no one in America had seen anyway, it had been seven years now since he'd had a volume to show. He tried Edmund Brown again, telling him in April that he was exploring the possibility of getting his poems together—the ones he'd written since *Al Que Quiere!*—though he knew that that would be no easy task.[108] When Brown expressed some interest, Williams told him what he had in mind: a limited edition this time, "done on finest linen paper with type of special choosing and the size and binding . . . unique."[109] He wanted a first-rate printer and realized with a sinking heart that he might even have to go to France to get what he wanted. That was in July 1928, and since Williams was flirting with the idea as much as anything, he let it drop for the time being. In the meantime, with the "Journal" off his hands since April, Williams went ahead with a spurt of poems in late April and May which he entitled "Della Primavera Trasportata al Morale." It included such poems as "The Sea Elephant,"

"The Botticellian Trees," "The House," "The Trees," "The Neurasthenic," "The Babies," and a poem for Floss which revealed a different message from the one he'd written her six months earlier. (Had not Joyce told him that it would be a strange year for him if he ever actually sent his family away for a year?). "Christ I have / lied to you about small / things," Williams wrote now. He'd lied about such "small" things as his

> whoring
> adulteries, what, what,
> what . . .
> Love me while I am
> not disgusting like that
> while I am still warm
> and a liar and a poet
> and a sometimes devoted
> lover who
>   loves you
> and will lie to you
> always.[110]

And Floss, for her part, back in Geneva from her Easter trip with the boys to Venice and Milan and Lugano, was writing at about the same time: "When one lives as I do it's torture to be away from my darling and I'll never do it again. . . . To hell with what other people think of it." Floss's letters, written every two or three days, were filled with news about the boys, about the school and the teachers there, about the nice friends she'd made, about her trips here and there. She was even thinking of having young Bill—who had made up his mind, he'd said, to become a doctor like his father—spend another year at the school, he was doing so well there, though she was quick to add that as for herself she never wanted to be separated from her "Bunny" again. She could sense her husband's fatigue and restlessness coming through in his letters to her now, and she wanted him to know how very much she missed him. In the face of his own growing misgivings about the year apart she comforted him. "It is very hard to be away from you," she told her husband frankly in early May,

> but I will *not* say that it has not been a good thing. I *know* it has—and we will be by far the most united—congenial—understanding married couple of our acquaintance—as we have always been anyway. Those who can't understand are those who have no faith—no belief in each other and I, in speaking for myself, have all the faith and respect & admiration & love possible for you—intensified many times by your absence.

Oh, she wasn't fooling herself. Separation was by no means the ideal situation. But at least it gave one time to look at one's own imperfections and then to try "to improve for one's own sake as well as for the sake of the darlingest husband in the world."[111] She urged him, as she had so often done before, to keep writing since she knew how important that was to his whole life. And she was eager to be with him again, to see him in some "nice little place with nothing more pressing than your own feverish desire to get the magic words down on paper." She was being a good wife, she was keeping the expenses down as much as possible (except where the boys were concerned), and she wanted her baby to remember her "love and sympathy and understanding." It would only be two months more before they were all together again and, as that time became shorter, she let her husband know that she was ready and eager to make love to him again.

And Williams? He did what he could. He kept busy. He wrote as often as he could—poems, prose, journal entries—went to the theater or the symphony hall (just as Floss was doing), worked hard at his medical practice, saw his friends, suffered anxieties whenever he forgot himself at a party over in New York or in some more intimate place. And the letters to his sons—who wrote back or sent drawings whenever Floss could get them to spend the time—and the letters to his Flossie kept coming, acting as a stopgap measure of sorts against the agonizing loneliness. Thus this Sunday morning meditation for June 3: Williams was enclosing some photographs of the garden so Floss could see how the irises had blossomed. Lucy was going off "with her sheik for the day—to Coney Island." He himself was going to drive into the city and see his friend Zukofsky in his fourth-floor apartment up on East 111th Street. He liked Zukofsky; he was cultured, quiet, smart, and Williams wished he could find a decent job in New York for him. The only thing that seemed open for him was teaching high school English in New York—and that was sure to kill a man of Zuk's sensibilities.

Williams had been out to dinner at his friend and colleague Dr. Hughes's, and they had spent the evening watching an amateur movie of another doctor removing a twenty-five-pound fibroid from a woman's belly while they drank bootleg cocktails. He hated swilling Prohibition stuff: no telling what the hell was in it. Sociability and self-respect might demand drinking those cocktails, but he no longer felt as inclined to perform that stupid "patriotic duty." He had finally found a tom for Smoky, but when he'd put the tom in the kitchen with her, she'd scared the poor thing half to death. The threatened male "suitor" had even smashed a pitcher of lemonade Elena had just made all over the kitchen floor in a frantic effort to clear out of there. He was sending along an essay on Voltaire's Ferney which they'd visited together back in '24. He was still (mildly) interested in learning the name of that nice doctor Floss was seeing in Geneva. The Presbyterians were at it again, making a god-awful racket across the street with their Sunday morning hymn singing.[112]

Three days later he wrote her the latest news: still another Christian

Scientist was dead after some first-class neglect. He'd been out till 1:30 in the morning to see a production of *Volpone* and if it hadn't been the voice of one of his old friends and a longtime patient on the other end of the receiver when the phone rang at 3:00 AM he would never have gone out. He'd also gone to visit Dr. Calhoun, his old family doctor—the one who'd diagnosed him for heart strain thirty years before—who had just had a stroke which had "affected, O strange provision of Providence, his speech." It was only a matter of time now.[113] And again, on the nineteenth, he wrote to tell Floss that he had just that minute finished correcting the galley proofs of *Voyage to Pagany*. He particularly liked the strange ending he'd given the book which helped compensate for his long-windedness. He'd also decided he was going to dedicate this latest child of his to none other than Ezra himself.[114]

"It is said to be not a novel," he apologized to Sylvia Beach. "No one likes it. Mother, however, likes it. I dunno, I dunno. But please do not fall into the usual confusion, should you read the corrected and revised script, of imagining that the hero is myself. That is where most go astray. . . . Had I meant it to be myself I should have said so." The *Voyage* was, after all, "a kind of shallow dream in which I sometimes act a part, that is all." He hoped that—looked at from that vantage—the thing would not turn out to be too stale.[115] And when he wrote again three weeks later, including a check to help out George Antheil, who had fallen on hard times, he added that he thought the novel would please her in its revised form:

> At least it should please you better than the script you saw of it—if you had the time to read that document. I have had many misgivings about this venture but at least I feel that I have done the best I can and I know now that in my desire to be simple and explicit I have not sold myself to the hounds. It has been an illuminating experience all through. Hardly a friend but has found fault with the work.[116]

In any event, *Voyage to Pagany* was behind him now, and he was already thinking ahead to his next novel. In fact, the idea was already there "in my thick bean, making a yolk of itself against my bony skull. I am now eating oystershells hoping to harden the mass." This new novel would take place "very much in America this time" and the whole approach would be new—at least for him. Joyce's example was there, of course, but in the sense that he knew he wanted to do less than what Joyce had attempted in *Ulysses*. As for Joyce's *Work in Progress* (i.e., the work that would be later called *Finnegans Wake*), it looked to Williams to be an unfortunate overextension of only one of the themes Joyce had dealt with in *Ulysses*: the dream mode. The trouble with Joyce's new work was that it left "too much that was magnificent in *Ulysses* undeveloped" and now Joyce would have to develop those themes once he finished this new book he was working on. As for himself, what *he* needed was "a very explicit, limpid, flaringly truthful development of the meaning as contrasted with the all important words—from Joyce."[117] After all, though he did not spell this out to Beach, that was the strategy he had chosen for the opening passage of his new novel: *White Mule.* As for Joyce, what Williams could not have known then was that Joyce would be obsessed with his *Work in Progress* for the next—and last—ten years of his life, and that there would be no other book.

*
* *

Louis Zukofsky spent the Fourth of July at 9 Ridge Road with Williams and two of Ed's daughters, talking about his own poetry and his just-completed M.A. thesis on Henry Adams. Then afterward he and Williams set off some "jigging" fireworks. "I like Louis," Williams told Pound on the twelfth. "He has distinction. He knows and is not puffed up, offensive, perverted by what he has absorbed." He'd seen Cummings too, he added, having invited him out to Rutherford after he'd seen his play at the Provincetown Playhouse. Cummings, he said, was "a very fine machine busting himself up over nothing as usual," and one of the few in and around New York who had anything of that old "gentlemanly" charm that refused to engage in gossip or backbiting. What bothered him about Cummings, though, was that he was letting himself go too much; he was afraid Cummings might degenerate into "a graceful drunken mind lost in fucking."[118]

But the poet who was really on his mind was the man Williams never intended to invite out to see him, though he only lived in Brooklyn: Hart Crane. "They say that Hart Crane is—this or that—a crude homo," he wrote Pound. And Marianne Moore for one—who had completely revised Crane's "The Wine Menagerie" before letting it be published in *The Dial* (for which she'd in turn been attacked by Crane's friends) had confided privately to Williams that she hated Crane's poetry and thought of it as "fake-knowledge." Yet, if Marianne hated it, there were others, Williams was learning, who thought Crane was God Himself, "which naturally offends anyone, like myself, who pretends to the same distinction." The New York boys—Burke and Munson and Josephson—were already calling Crane the "best poet in [the] U.S." Williams himself wasn't so sure, but he knew one thing: he was going to give Crane as wide a berth as he could. So far—in spite of Crane's frequent invitations to get together —he'd been able to steer clear.[119]

When Pound answered Williams' letter on July 27, he commented on the "peculiar sterility" he found whenever he read the New York group—"the Cranes, Ivors, Munsons, Gorhams, Burkes, [sic] etc."—as in the American number they'd done for *transition,* where their work was placed side by side with the French avant-garde writers', and which had for the most part suffered by the comparison.[120] "As it stands," Williams wrote back to Pound on August 11, "Crane is supposed to be the man that puts me on the shelf." But the younger poet, he found, was "just as thickheaded as I am myself and quite as helplessly verbose at times," and with this added stricture: that Crane came "up into clarity far less often" than he himself did. What was needed, Williams reiterated, was for someone to give Pound a half million "to do literature with," and then the "Josephsons and Burkeses and Cranes and all of them" would soon enough dwindle into obscurity.[121]

Coincidentally, Crane himself wrote to Williams three weeks later in mid-September from his Willow Street address in Brooklyn, asking Williams "why in paradise we don't once in a while get together. Especially since I'm told that you frequently get over to Manhattan." After all, there were many things Crane wanted to talk about, especially with a man like Williams.[122] Williams wrote back, still managing to avoid making a specific meeting. "I promised Hart Crane two months ago to let him know when I should be free to see him," he admitted to Zukofsky that December. And then—irritated—he added: "Why all this blather?"[123] It would take another year—until December 1929—for the two contenders to meet in Crane's apartment, and that meeting—in retrospect—would turn out to have something of the tremors of an apocalypse for both men.

But in January, looking at the stanchions going up for the George Washington Bridge—Williams' American hero and his own bridge—Williams was disturbed by visions of the American epic that Hart Crane was even then completing. He had read sections of the poem in magazines like *The Dial* and *The Little Review*, and even Eliot—who had refused to publish *him*—had published a section of Crane's poem in his August *Criterion*.[124] New York City: its white buildings glimmering pearllike in the distance over the Jersey meadows, over the Hudson River. It should have been Williams' domain, the New World city meant to equal Eliot's London and Pound's Paris. But now that city was going over to a younger man, a "crude homo" like Hart Crane.

As for his own writing? Oh, it was excellent in patches, but hadn't it reflected—at least since the nonreception of *In the American Grain*—a series of depressions, with his best new work still in manuscript and with only the publication of a failed novel and a translation (at best borrowed glory) to show the world? And no new book of poems in seven years. For Williams the '20s were beginning to seem like so much recognition withheld. And now . . . the star of Crane ascending in the heavens over New York City. That upstart.

It was out of that complex of anxieties, then, that Williams composed his poem "The Flower." No, he admitted there, he could not "do" New York as Crane had done, for even that city was, finally, but one petal of his own complex flower world. Another petal went only eight short blocks from 9 Ridge Road to 131 West Passaic Avenue, to the house—with all its associations—"in which I happen to have been born." Yet another petal in this asymmetric pattern stretched all the way across the country to San Diego, "where / a number of young men, New Yorkers most / of them, are kicking up the dust." And, at the core of his flower lay "a naked woman" (naturally), "about 38, just / out of bed" who had put him "straight about the city" by telling him what his gay friend Marsden Hartley had told him years before: that what all artists finally wanted was raw power, the power to construct a bridge like the George Washington . . . or like Crane's. Yet no one, of course, was going to simply give him that power merely because he wanted or needed it. It was a time of confusion for Williams, a time of lost bearings, of inadequacy, of powerlessness. For years, he confessed now,

> I've been tormented by
> that miracle, the buildings all lit up—
>
> unable to say anything much to the point
> though it is the major sight
>
> of this region. But foolish to rhapsodize over
> strings of light, the blaze of power
>
> in which I have not the least part. . . .

Rhapsody! As with Crane's godlike rhapsody over the string of lyrics uniting his vision of the Brooklyn Bridge transcended by the power of language:

> Again the traffic lights that skim thy swift
> Unfractioned idiom, immaculate sigh of stars,
> Beading thy path.

"The Flower," then, was Williams' countercry, a cry of impotency, as he composed his lines out of the despair of knowing that the prize was going to the younger man. His own poem was neither "romance" nor "allegory," he said, having eschewed those forms of the symbolic . . . only to be left with a terrifying void and a crushing sense of helplessness. If he only had time, time from his ministering to the sick, time to write:

> I plan one thing—that I could press
> buttons to do the curing of or caring for
>
> the sick that I do laboriously now by hand
> for cash, to have the time
>
> when I am fresh, in the morning, when
> my mind is clear and burning—to write.[125]

To write: indefinite, timeless, optative, like his plan, the plan of a suburban doctor whose life was inextricably enmeshed with a thousand lives, a plan by its very nature impossible, especially for a man for whom human contact, human touch, was life itself. And yet the comedy of it all, as Williams knew, jotting down a Harpo Marx scenario for himself: "Is the doctor in? (It used to ring.) What is it? (Out of the bedroom window.) My child has swallowed a mouse.—Tell him to swallow a cat then. Bam! . . . This is Mrs. Gladis, will you come down this morning. I've got two or three children sick. Trrrrrrring. Can you make a call this morning. I guess the half of the house is dying again."[126] To have, get, *steal*, the time to write.

No, in the summer of '28, Zukofsky was more interesting to Williams than Crane—and also less threatening. The day after Louis was out for the fireworks, Williams wrote him to say that he was finally beginning to "hear" what Zukofsky was attempting in his poems. He'd been looking for the wrong things in Zukofsky: for images rather than sound patterns. "Eyes have always stood first in the poet's equipment," he told him, thinking of his own practice. But Zukofsky was "mostly ear," imbued with the beginnings of newer rhythms which had not yet been fully articulated.[127] Zukofsky's "Lenin," for one thing, had Williams looking hard at his own practice in contradistinction to the younger man's. "It may be that I am too literal in my search for objective clarities of image," he was willing to admit. And Zukofsky might be "completely right in forcing abstract conceptions into the sound pattern." But if that was so, Williams wondered if his own practice of focusing on the sharp contours of images, what he called, disparagingly, his "picayune imagistic mannerisms," only held together by the loosest of linguistic threads what would otherwise simply "fall apart."[128] Zukofsky's essay on Henry Adams interested him, on the other hand, for the same reason—presumably—that he thought someone might be interested in his own essays on Poe and Boone and the others: "as an introduction to the life of an American of extra-ordinary significance," and because it was "the work of another American."[129] Zukofsky, young as he was, was at least on the right track.

When, in October, Zukofsky showed Williams the beginning of his epic poem, *A*, whose arabesques would consume Zukofsky's attention for the next forty years, Williams wrote that he had had a hard time of it getting his mind around that poem to see what it was Zukofsky had attempted. He wasn't all that sure what it was Zukofsky had done, but he knew that the instinct of the poem was right and that the mind would "come lumbering after." It was like a woman, that poem, he explained. An emanation came off it the way an odor came off a woman, especially when she was in heat:

Some women are delicious to smell, like buckwheat and some—reek! Jesus! I can hardly sit in the office with them. Though I can imagine some men will be attracted by that which repels me. It is acrid, fulminous. And should they get hot, hot where it counts. Boy! I look toward the wall for the chemical fire extinguisher. But when a sweet one comes in my virtue exists like a small flower on a loose piece of earth above a precipice.

Zukofsky's poem, he added, belonged to the latter category.[130]

* * *

In mid-July Williams was also waiting with mounting excitement for the return of his wife and sons after a ten months' separation. "My family arrives in three days—after a year's absence, nearly," he wrote Pound on the twelfth. "You may imagine that I'll be worth little to the world in general for a month or six weeks now."[131] He rented a touring car from his local Rutherford garage, complete with driver—a big bull of a woman—to drive him into New York bright and early on Monday the sixteenth.[132] Floss had written to ask Bill if they could drive home through the just-completed Holland Tunnel and Williams was eager to do things up big: to be there waiting with flowers and chauffeur and all as Floss and the boys made their way down the gangplank of the SS *Rochambeau*. The night before their return, Williams had had his last big fling as a bachelor, taking Grace Hellwig, a neighbor and a nurse, out to a party until nearly 3:00 AM, returning her, as he protested, as virginal as he'd found her.[133] Another of his neighbors was a customs officer with the N.Y. Port Authority, who had promised Williams he would have no difficulty getting the Doc past the barriers to greet his family as they came down the gangplank.[134] But there was—naturally—a mixup, and Williams was nearly frantic as he saw his son Bill descend, looking for his father and unable to find him amid the general bustle and confusion. Finally, Williams' customs friend showed up and got Williams through the lines and then he ran to greet his family. Floss, knowing Bill and knowing red tape, had figured something like what had happened would happen and so was not particularly worried. Now they could pick up where they'd left off; once again, the family was back together.

The Williamses spent the next two weeks reordering priorities at 9 Ridge Road, getting adjusted to one another and enjoying each other's company through long talks. For the moment, writing went by the board, becoming—as Williams said—"very hypothetical in importance and probability of existence."[135] On Monday morning, July 30, they drove up to the Hermans' farm in Monroe for a month's vacation. For his part, Williams was happy. He could relax now with his family, play tennis, work in the garden. He went swimming with the boys at a nearby lake, paddling out with them to a small island about a quarter mile from shore, where the boys found four turtle eggs in the sand. They were the first, he realized, he'd ever seen.[136] And how big the boys were getting now, as he enjoyed them to the full! "Bill is almost fifteen," he wrote Marianne Moore at her office at *The Dial.* "He is thoughtful, able and considerate; he has learned to speak rather good French. . . . He is said to have been a month old when he was born. Paul's state is different. When asked by Floss if he would lie to her his reply was: 'I've already done it.' "[137]

Williams had also begun working on a new book shortly before he'd gone on vacation, a book he was tentatively calling *On the Humanization of Knowledge.* He was writing it for the Francis Bacon Award sponsored by *Forum Magazine* and he expected to have it ready to submit by the April 1929 deadline. He kidded Zukofsky that this book would allow him to compete "with the rest of the intellectual lights of the world,"[138] but the impetus for writing it came rather from his need as a father and as an educator—and pediatrician—to say something about the nature of real learning. He had dealt and would continue to deal with the question in his *White Mule* novel, as he had dealt with it on another level in *In the American Grain:* the way in which human consciousness came in contact with its world. Each child was a Columbus of sorts, he felt, floating across the uncharted ocean of the mother's womb to find itself in a beautiful but alien *Nuevo Mundo.* But it was true too that from the start the new consciousness was subjected to the shock of misinformation, lies, myths incapable of sustaining the mind, as well as the extraordinary bombardment of language upon the ear, of image upon the eye. His foray into epistemology was—in effect—another version of the Adamic myth. The importance of naming things correctly, of seeing what was there and of possessing one's birthright with as little interference as possible from the special interest groups—the law, the church, the school, the economic structures: that was what he was, finally, after.

Williams continued to work on his "book" in his "spare" moments, but especially during his summer vacations, until early 1930. What resulted was a sheaf that was never meant to be a systematic treatise on epistemology, something he was by disposition incapable of achieving anyway, since for him systems were always false, suspect, procrustean, life-denying. Better, he thought, to capture the momentary traces of illumination as they shone amidst the hesitancies, false starts, and syntactical coughs that for him more accurately caught the processes of living thought itself. That way of proceeding, at least by way of initial draft, was infinitely preferable to a more logical unfolding of something called cause and effect, where "conclusions" were reached before the words themselves ever touched the paper, only to disappear like snowflakes into a river, or words into the void.

Even here, however, Williams' unsystematic tracings did contain within their own unfolding something of the locus, the all-important place of contact, from which they had first sprung. One such locus was the irritant that Bill had done poorly in his French class at Rutherford

High despite his having spent a year speaking French in a Swiss school. That a child might *know* a subject, as with his own son, and yet still do poorly because he could not learn the subject the way a schoolteacher in Rutherford insisted it be learned—while other students, catering to the game plan as laid out by the teacher (quizzes, word lists, etc.), reaped the higher grades—infuriated Williams. Here, he believed, was a local symptom of a larger pathology, the "medieval" tyranny of insisting on something called the classical learning—another of those misappellations Williams inveighed against.

Against these larger pressures Williams placed his own hero: William Shakespeare. This Shakespeare was a figure molded very much after Williams' myth of himself: the figure of the unlearned "natural" brought into high relief against the classical scholar, Francis Bacon. Williams' Shakespeare was remarkable not because he had created a system or an ideology—he had not—but because he had encompassed a living thought so dense that it had become a kind of action. Out of his imagination Shakespeare had created a world of solidities, of figures moving so skillfully through time that a whole army of scholars had—in focusing on a specific image or symbol or theme—committed errors similar to trying to capture the life of a movie by focusing on a single frame. That, of course, was to create endless distortions, new and inferior fictions. But his Shakespeare had escaped the scholiasts (just as he believed the critics had failed as yet to measure his own work adequately). Shakespeare was—finally—a figure of the artist par excellence: a force, an anomaly, a man outside the new learning, a man without a history, like Ulysses a man with no name, a person realized most fully in the act of creating other figures and most fully defined—perhaps—in the complex rhetoric of *Hamlet*. And this Shakespeare had become for Williams a presence, a ghost, a standard by which Williams might measure the best in modern writing.

It was in art rather than in science that Williams had located for himself the cutting edge of modernist thought, and the names of those presences who had preoccupied him throughout the '20s rose up and fell as he pursued the track of his thought: Picasso, Gertrude Stein, Juan Gris, Cézanne, McAlmon, John Dewey. He praised the French painters especially—from the impressionists to the cubists—for their pioneering investigations into the nature and world of form and design, for making it new, as Joyce and Stein had worked with language to make it new. Words, hard-edged words, as things rather than as ideas, he insisted, remembering his meeting with Gertrude Stein the year before. "Stein had stressed, as Braque did, paint, words," he wrote. And so the real significance of that famous motto of hers, printed circlewise, without beginning or end: *A rose is a rose is a rose.* What did that mean? That a rose was of course a rose. But it meant too that the words making up that apparent tautology were themselves words, capable of infinite substitutions, words standing for all words, and "subject to arrangement for effect," so that the words could operate *as* words, and thus leave the rose alone to be what it too was: "a rose."

To escape what he considered the scholasticism of his own day —embodied in those twin immensities science and philosophy— Williams had opted for a strategy of randomness, striking at the problem of form from a perspective of apparent formlessness, lines of force—as in his poetry—intersecting at loci of varying intensities, and thus, as with experience, coming in contact with moments of clarity when the core of the matter stood naked and revealed, like language, like a woman. "All my life [I have been after] one thing," he wrote, "to break through to a more comprehensive basis away from rule," his work taking its "form" not from tradition but from perceiving the design in the life itself as it unfolded in all its uncertainties and uniqueness. And whoever could help him find the shape in life he was in the process of living would also come to understand the texture of the historical moment of which he was the living product. He was ready to welcome anyone who could help him define what he himself was, what he was even then becoming.[139]

Meanwhile, there was the long weariness of trying to cope with the arrogance and stupidity of the New York critics. Williams went into New York on a Tuesday afternoon in late July to have tea with Isabel Paterson of the *Herald Tribune*, to complain to her that—unlike Paris—there was no place in New York where one could meet anymore, the dirt and the heat of the city in midsummer militating against anything like civilization. Isabel Paterson had asked to interview Williams and Williams found Burton Rascoe with her when he arrived in the city. Paterson began—as Williams remembered it—by lighting into Pound's and Antheil's musical pretensions, but Williams would have none of that. He argued for the necessity for experimentation in modernist music, using the argument he'd already made in his own essay on George Antheil. But Paterson seemed to be there not so much to learn something as to have her own preconceived notions confirmed by Williams. The interview foundered and soon after Williams excused himself.[140]

In September Williams picked up a copy of *The Bookman* and read Rebecca West's essay on James Joyce, an essay he found so condescending and reactionary, damning Joyce with faint praises as it did, that he wrote at once to the editors demanding an opportunity to answer her "High Church" attack, as he called it in a letter to Marianne Moore.[141] They wrote back, apologizing that they simply would have no room for Williams' rebuttal. Nothing daunted, Williams worked at his reply all during October, infuriated at West's cleverness in hiding her real condemnation of Joyce in "fine words." So, when Sylvia Beach wrote Williams, asking for an essay on Joyce for a book she was publishing with Adrienne Monnier on Joyce's *Work in Progress,* Williams told her that he'd just written twenty-eight pages and that she was not to go to press without his essay, which he promised to send as soon as possible. "It is an important work for me," he wrote, and Beach's project would prove "the spur to make me go on and complete the construction." Williams had also learned that his publishers had written to Joyce asking them for a blurb for Williams' *Voyage to Pagany,* and Joyce had had to beg off because of the trouble he was having with his eyes. Now he told Beach to tell Joyce that he was sorry that his publishers had bothered him.[142] He knew that the *Voyage*—the book he would later call his weakest effort—looked anemic beside *Ulysses.* And Williams was honest enough to know there wasn't a word Joyce could have said for the book, as he admitted to Zukofsky. Nobody could be harder on Williams if necessary than Williams himself. As a novel, the book had failed. The New York critics had been "timorous but respectful," merely because of Williams' growing reputation as a writer.[143] And when Pound's essay appeared in *The Dial* in November, Williams saw that Pound had chosen—kindly—to deal with Williams' overall development as an artist over the past fifteen years rather than focus only on the novel, which—even though dedicated to him—Pound had seen was undistinguished. To his credit, though, Pound could also place the *Voyage* in its larger context, focusing, as he did, on the texture of Williams' writing, on the energy and density of Williams' mind when it committed itself to paper.

"Nothing will ever be said of better understanding regarding my work than your article in *The Dial,*" Williams wrote Pound on November 6. "I must thank you for your great interest and discriminating defense of my position."[144] Pound had done what Williams had insisted was the critic's function: he had clarified for Williams the direction his own future would have to take. He saw now—with touching honesty—that his dreams of having arrived at a position by forty-five—his age then —had been premature, and that he would have to work like hell to arrive at that still illusory position of prominence. Now, therefore, he was taking steps to bracket off more time for himself for the future, including becoming a specialist in pediatrics so that he could cut out the "hellish drag" of evening office hours by early 1929.

When Williams was at his in-laws' in August of '28, he took along Philippe Soupault's novel *Les Dernières Nuits de Paris* to read, as well as Gide's *Si le grain ne meurt,* Dos Passos' *Orient Express, The Education of Henry Adams* (at Zukofsky's suggestion), and Pavlov's *Conditioned Reflexes.*[145] He liked Soupault—whom he'd met in Paris in '24—and now he decided to have himself and his mother translate Soupault's novel into

English, in part to keep his mother occupied. But by November, Matthew Josephson, who had just taken on the job of book editor for Macaulay's, learned through his wife that Williams was translating Soupault and wrote giving him a contract for the translation. Williams took the job on, but now he found the translation turning from a diversion into a chore. It finally ate up most of his winter, as he realized too late, without giving him the time he needed to let the French idioms soften up inside him and become as fluid and idiomatic as he would have liked. The result was a slightly wooden version of Soupault's novel.

When Williams wrote to Sylvia Beach the following April to congratulate her and Adrienne Monnier on publishing Valery Larbaud's translation of *Ulysses* into French, he added that he himself had just completed "the immensely slighter task" of translating Soupault's novel. "It was a winter's task what with the influenza epidemic of January and the rest of the work," he added, but in spite of that he had still had to meet an April 1 deadline. At the same time that he was doing the translation, however, he had also managed to write *January: A Novelette,* a fifty-page improvisation, which he was sending Sylvia Beach who in turn should then pass it on to Emile Jolas or Robert Sage, the editors of *transition.* He'd written it, he explained, at the height of the epidemic "to quiet me late at night so that I could go to sleep." He and Floss had liked the flow of the improvisation, but he wondered if anyone else would.[146]

January belongs to the same impetus that had generated *Kora in Hell, Spring and All, Rome, The Descent of Winter:* the need—in the absence of a recognizable formal imperative—to keep on writing. What shaped the pages as they collected was a sense of form or at least of texture analogous to the formation of crystals. Form here was not a kind of container, a bowl. Williams rejected that classical notion in his opening paragraph: "Before, you could eat ice-cream out of it; after, you wouldn't spit in it." The flu epidemic had struck around Christmas, and all through January, Williams—who was always busy at that time of the year with his practice anyway—now found himself continually on the go. House calls came in at all hours of the night, while patients waited in the office at 9 Ridge Road or at his Passaic office. On top of that there was his readjustment to Floss. Flareups, suspicions, angers, two strong wills clashing, confessions or half confessions. So there it was: the fact of death and the concomitant tang of life, so that the extraneous civilities and mild hypocrisies of life in a small suburban town fell away of their own dead weight. What the flu epidemic had done was create a stress, paring off "the inanity by force of speed and a sharpness, a closeness of observation, of attention" flaring through, as in wartime: which was what a town became when an epidemic struck. Now was the time to get down on paper the fitful traces of the living actual, pulling the car over to the curb and digging for pen or pencil and prescription pad to get the phrasing down exactly as he'd heard it. What he wanted was the precise trajectory of life, of language, as it actually existed:

> The rush that simplifies life, complicates it. There is no time to stop the car to write when only the writing that comes of an intense simplification would be actual. January. January. Now actually the sun returns. Ezra Pound is already looking backward. And we, as if unborn, stare at the impossible cluttered with the temporary, the circumscribed. The composed. The inadequate. While the real, by leaves, by a table, on which lies a ten cent bottle of Aspirin tablets stands sufficiently. Under the cheap crochet table cover—the table is of stained wood. . . . An electric lamp, lit, is in the center, a cloth covered cord running from it to the floor.—This is banality.[147]

And to Floss—as to others—this explanation, embedded within the context of the writing, the need to write, the NEED to write:

> You think I take no interest in you? It is not so. I avoid your eye merely to avoid interruption. Gladly, were I able, would I serve you and listen to you talk of your sore toe. But, unless I apply myself to the minute—my life escapes me. You must pardon me. I love you as I hope you will notice by all that I have done to make you comfortable. Talk is the most precious thing in the world. I know that and I will find a way to secure it for you also but my interest in writing is so violent an acid that with the other work, I must pare my life to the point of silence—though I hope surliness may never intervene—in order to get to the paper.[148]

To hell with Pound, for his quip that the *Improvisations* were a little Rimbaud forty years late. In them, in the radical disjunctures possible in such writing, the continual shifting of categories, forcing the attention down on the words themselves as words, in this lay the excellence of the strategy. On the blank sheets, as on a canvas, he pasted letters, a random conversation, bits picked up from magazines as dissimilar as the *Ladies' Home Journal* and *transition,* a telephone conversation from a patient whose child had swallowed something (a mouse?), his thoughts about Juan Gris's cubist paintings while he waited for the drawbridge to let a tug chug through before it lowered again: all these lifted into the design of the painting, of the novelette. And then, almost as suddenly, the realization that every phone call was not professional, that friends were getting through again, that the epidemic was subsiding. And thus, time to wind down the writing now that the fever of it, the trance state, was over. To have tasted the actual, to have caught it on paper, so that it might live, knowing that the actual would in time destroy much of the work of S. and P.—Stevens and Pound—so that someone, picking up his novelette years later, might still sense the living presence of a white-hot imagination moving through a moment that would otherwise have been lost to oblivion.

*
* *

By mid-1928, it was clear—especially to Williams—that *The Dial* was about to founder. There was a mad scramble for new backers, policy meetings, all of it. But it was no use. That magazine too was on its way out, like *The Little Review* itself. It was just as well, Williams thought. *The Dial* had served its time—the moment of the '20s—and was now "about as dead as a last year's birds nest."[149] He'd talked with Marianne Moore about her role as editor there, he told Pound, and, though he had the highest personal respect for her, he knew she would fail to get a better, more forward-looking policy established for the magazine. Long ago it had become lukewarm, Laodocian, halfhearted. Better to let it die, and let another magazine somewhere else take its place. "The little magazine is something I have always fostered," Williams would write in his *Autobiography*, "for without it, I myself would have been early silenced. To me it is one magazine, not several. . . . When it is in any way successful it is because it fills a need in someone's mind to keep going. When it dies, someone else takes it up in some other part of the country—quite by accident—out of a desire to get the writing down on paper."[150] So be it. There would be others.

As the '20s waned, the literary avant-garde—such as it had been —began shifting out of New York, and this time southward. A young man named Charles Henri Ford was about to launch a new little magazine out of Mississippi called *Blues* and had written Williams asking him to be contributing editor. "An outlet at last," he wrote Zukofsky in late December 1928. There was always hope in another "brand new, gritty clean magazine."[151] But already there was a sense of the retrospect in *Blues:* that these new magazines were coming after the real pioneers, the generation of 1914. Williams was now—at forty-five—already one of the grizzled veterans of that earlier generation. Besides, there was a danger too in looking back which he'd sensed already in Pound's efforts in getting another little magazine under way. For when Pound—using the young Zukofsky as his American disciple—tried to get a small press set up somewhere in New York in 1928, Williams was so angry he could hardly bring himself to even talk about the subject with Pound. Did Pound have any idea what the hell he was talking about in looking for a small modern press in New York run by artisans working in the Old World mold? Williams would have none of it. Pound had been away from America too long to know what was really going on in Williams' city.

But that was Pound, perhaps the strongest voice in the modern revolution of remaking modern American poetry, and Williams would never forget that. What troubled him, rather, was that the younger poets should still be publishing poems as though no revolution had ever occurred. He used *Blues* now as a handy forum to hammer his caveats: "It makes me sick to see kids playing around with trite forms, trite rhythms, trite images; prettifying the page, filling books with perfect sonnets, perfect drawings, dainty bits of blah." He had thought that the revolution —and his own practice—would have taught poets at least to "speak plainly in verse," to at least use prose rhythms and a recognizable syntax and idiom.[152] After all, a poem was a mechanism, a machine, like a Model T, and the parts of a poem got old just as an engine or transmission or clutch would, so that it was necessary to invent new mechanisms of expression. He warned the young to avoid Eliot, whose poetics had led him inevitably to his Anglo-Catholicism and his reactionary politics. Instead, Williams told them to turn to the American masters—to Henry Adams (thanks to Louis Zukofsky's treatment of him), to Pound ("Read about everything that Ezra Pound has written, no need to agree with him—but read him anyway"), and to Mina Loy, Djuna Barnes, McAlmon, and those first brilliant short stories Hemingway had written half a dozen years before when modernism was still alive.[153]

In the May 1929 issue of *Blues* he went even further. There was a thing, an impulse, in men, he said, that kept them on the tightrope's edge, but which meant flirting with death itself. In a poet it meant following his own bent, turning inward (as his hero Boone had) to escape the restrictions of society, of the code, that one might do the thing one had to do. Out of this relentless contact with the ground of one's own being and one's own place would come all that was most excellent in the poems a man wrote. This was what had made Eliot his enemy, for Eliot had denied his own earlier instincts and had decided to play it safe and follow what Williams called, with horror, "the academic thing." For, next to "the rascality of our legislative and judicial bodies, the university, the true home of learning," was the "worst scandal of our day." The image of Eliot pontificating about what was and was not the canon of received tradition, what was and was not poetry, was too much for this older revolutionary.

Eliot had already removed himself from the field of action to enter the sacred wood. And now Williams wanted to warn the young that the academic forces would hurt rather than help them in the actual writing of poetry. For poetry was, he insisted, not a matter of erudition, not a matter of religion, philosophy, or even of science. Rather, it took its shape from the age through which it moved, reflecting the essential spirit of that age in "word, line and image." It did follow rules, he knew—it was not formless—but it did *not* follow previously established literary dicta. Instead, it made the rules itself as these were discovered or invented in the heat of genuine composition. The poet was, after all, the true man of action, like the old kings and the Viking plunderers, like Henry Ford, or even like Gerald Chapman, a contemporary American outlaw in the Old West tradition, who had had a genius for flouting the American legal system and its attendant hypocrisies. For Williams, Chapman was the nonconformist who had paid for his revolutionary ways with his life, praise him![154]

Richard Johns was yet another young man who was about to launch yet another little magazine. This one would be published out of Boston and would be called *Pagany*, in honor of Williams' *Voyage to Pagany*. Johns had written Williams asking him if he would serve in an editorial capacity, especially as he saw the magazine as continuing the policies Williams had adumbrated in his writings during the '20s, and Williams had answered that he would do whatever he could to help Johns, but that he begged off being listed as an editor for the present. He was willing to write a manifesto, but he had to have a clearer idea of what Johns was after before he committed himself to the masthead. That *Pagany* would be "A Native Quarterly" gave Williams a lead.[155] Clearly American writers still had to focus their energies on constructing a more recognizable ground before they could write as Americans.[156] That was the trouble—he was already finding—with *Blues*, which, for all its promise, might just turn out to be another "loose end." *Pagany*, he hoped, would "begin low" and "fasten to the native shale or sandstone or what have you. . . . Perhaps things like *Blues* can never make headway until that underground work has first been done. It may be that Europe can permit itself a fling once or twice in a century because that underground work *has* been done." Whatever Johns decided to do, however, Williams warned him to avoid the international eclecticism that had finally undermined *The Dial*.

He told Johns too that *Pagany* as a name for his venture disturbed him. He'd meant Europe by that appellation, not America, though there was of course a deeper sense in which America too was pagan. But there'd be hell to pay when some readers realized that that was what Johns might intend. Besides, didn't *Pagany* sound a little too "Washington Squarish"? And what would a reformed Yvor Winters say when he saw the magazine and Williams' name tied to it? Winters was "already ill" over Williams' "lack of godliness or ecclesiastical organization or evil nature or general cussedness." Oh, to hell with all stodgy well-meaning readers anyway![157]

By the end of August 1929, Williams had read through the first batch of scripts for the first issue of *Pagany*. He found them interesting, readable, and even salable, and then suggested which stories Johns should print and which he should leave out. He himself had written a perceptive essay on Gertrude Stein's achievement for *Pagany* while on vacation that month at the Haslund farm in Vermont. And two weeks later, warming to his role as editor, he wrote Zukofsky, suggesting he send his long poem "The" to Johns, who even paid for contributions. But he also warned Zukofsky not to spill the beans just yet about the new magazine to Pound for fear Pound would try to "father-mother-bugger" (that "new Trinity") Johns's magazine.[158]

Williams, in fact, had just written Pound to give him an up-to-date report on the little magazine in America without once mentioning *Pagany*. *Blues*, he told Pound on September 11, though still "very young," was already buried by its own "aptness." And then he added, in his own *Finnegans Wake* voice: "Nothing accurates does in these here Used Shirts of Amerorrhea. And there ain't no such thing as so much difference in personalities or Its as *Blues* would have us stink. We do, but not so attar as all thatch. But *Blues* is all that is. Henri [Ford] is appealing to me a an [sic] introduction to the first bound volume." *The Dial* was already dead: "dealt and found Freudian," and "fucked out of all indentations that might have received a gentleman however inclined."[159]

But if Williams as one of the older veterans was telling the young what to write, read, and avoid, at least one young man returned the favor in print. Kenneth Rexroth—who was then twenty-four—had written from San Diego for the Fall '29 number of *Blues* that what was needed was a strong spokesman for modernism who could effectively counter the "neoclassic-neothomist-neodostoyefsky philosophy" of that reformed archconservative Yvor Winters. *Transition* had not shown itself equal to the task, nor had *Blues* itself, and Williams' attacks and manifestos had only seemed to make matters worse. They were hardly, he wrote with evident irony, "likely to become proverbial for their Aristotelian lucidity," though they were in themselves neither confusing nor confused.[160] The bottom line remained, however: Williams had not yet been able to defend modernism against the traditional formulas of a classicist like Winters.

But Williams was not offended by what Rexroth had said. He liked the boy, he told Henri Ford, and thought his open letter had been well written. Rexroth had been "quite right in jumping me for my lack of lucidity and my statements which do not help."[161] Well, there was only one answer: find a way to do better. The problem of course was time. He needed critics who would support the new and fight for it, and he had been forced to make statements and half statements that he had hoped others who had the time would then flesh out. But only his enemies—it seemed—had the time, and their efforts were all against him. The modernist experiment was definitely on the wane.

Another sign that the promise of the early '20s was sputtering was McAlmon's sailing to New York from France on September 28, in the hope of interesting one of the New York publishers in his latest novel,

Family Panorama. During the decade McAlmon himself had published a large number of British and American writers, among them Williams, Loy, H.D., Joyce, Pound, Stein, Barnes, Herrmann, Ford Madox Ford, and Hemingway. But he was divorced now, and without the money to continue his avant-garde publishing ventures. After an abortive stay at the Hotel Statler in New York—twenty-five floors up in a pushbutton room that made him feel claustrophobic—McAlmon signed out and got a room down in the Village at the Hotel Lafayette at University Place and 9th Street which felt closer to his rooms in Paris. He went to see several publishers, though his best hope had been with Maxwell Perkins at Scribner's, who was Hemingway's and F. Scott Fitzgerald's publisher. Hemingway had written to Perkins urging him to give McAlmon a chance—much as McAlmon had helped Hemingway—but McAlmon made some true but unfortunate remarks about Hemingway's personality while he was having dinner with Perkins. Then Fitzgerald had written Perkins not to trust a rat like McAlmon and to steer clear of him, and Perkins (who'd only been half-enthusiastic about McAlmon in the first place) took Fitzgerald's advice. McAlmon was too outspoken, too much his own man, and Williams was really worried about him this time. It was a crossroads moment for McAlmon. If he could interest an American publisher in his book, he could continue to work, to improve. If not, he would continue his self-determined drift toward oblivion.

Williams saw McAlmon several times in New York: once at the Sheelers' when McAlmon first arrived, then at his room at the Lafayette, and then on Sunday, October 27, three days after Black Thursday, when the bottom fell out of the Wall Street stock market with reverberations that would shake the world. That Sunday Williams and Floss took Berenice Abbott (the photographer) and McAlmon out into the Jersey hill country of Sussex fifty miles west of Rutherford, to enjoy the fall scenery and visit "a fine country inn with a bar in the basement." The four of them stood there drinking shots of apple brandy at Prohibition prices —fifty cents a glass—"while we talked with the old barman or played the gambling machine—at one cent a shot—for cigars." After twenty tries, he told Sylvia Beach, "Berenice Abbott and he had each won a five cent cigar, turning it into one ten cent one for myself." He had brought McAlmon up into the Jersey countryside hoping "he would like it and would consider spending a few weeks in that retreat polishing his manuscript."[162]

He knew of McAlmon's "unfortunate reputation in N.Y.," that he was admired for his "flashes of keen writing," but feared for "what the NY crowd calls his snobbery." And what he was most afraid of now was that McAlmon would run out of patience and bolt before he'd secured a contract. Just before Christmas, in fact, Williams' fears were confirmed:

McAlmon had been turned down by Perkins at Scribner's and by several others. "I have reason to believe that it has hurt him severely this time," he told Zukofsky on the twenty-second. And here was Hemingway becoming "the modern Playboy" of the Western World, even though —like Pound—he was convinced that McAlmon was finally the better writer.[163] He could see his friend, his younger double, already beginning to drift out toward the darkness, just as McAlmon had left New York for Mexico to find whatever it was he thought he would find there.

Williams would remember this crucial moment in McAlmon's life twenty years later, by which time McAlmon was selling trusses for his brother's firm in El Paso and drinking himself to an early death. "When a man like McAlmon goes down, others go with him," he would write. "In fact, to a greater or lesser degree, the whole front of good writing collapses. . . . When, often at the very moment of success, some prominent support is cut away, nothing for years may get published. Loose ends are left dangling, men are lost, promises that needed culture, needed protection and wit and courage to back them simply die. One book, here and there, gets a preliminary hearing and remains isolated, while the overwhelming flood of insensitive drivel floods the market."[164] Without naming him, Williams was thinking of Perkins' "betrayal."

In mid-November, Williams planned to drive up to Andover with Floss for a Sunday afternoon talk at Burke's place with Burke and Cowley and some of the old New York crowd. One of his Polish patients had just dropped off a case of home-brewed beer—"made by his Ma-in-law in her kitchen (usual temp. 110 by stove all summer and through the winter —the kitchen, not the beer")—and Williams was going to bring up a couple of flasks of the stuff and talk with Cowley, who could be quite interesting ("I like his account of the savage tribes of young men who cock suckingly inhabit all the large cities of the Up Stuck States of the Umpty Stump"). As for what had happened with the national economy, he noted that Wall Street had "been plucked and the sound of the cracking remains with it still." He had some stocks, but he had decided not to panic. "I aint a gonna sell em, not ef I has to use em instid uv corn cobs in the old cannery," by which he meant that at least they could be used as a substitute for toilet paper.[165] He was of course whistling in the dark, like thousands of other Americans.

Three weeks later, on Saturday evening, December 7, with the long winter coming on, Williams finally saw Hart Crane at Crane's Willow Street apartment in Brooklyn. Crane was having a party to celebrate the imminent publication of that long poem he'd been working on for seven years, and Harry and Caresse Crosby were about to publish it in a deluxe edition from their Black Sun Press when they returned to Paris. Crane was throwing this party for them on the eve of their departure from New

York. The Williamses were there, along with Malcolm and Peggy Cowley, E. E. Cummings, and Walker Evans, who'd done the photographs for the Black Sun edition of *The Bridge*. It was quite a party, and it didn't break up until dawn of the following day. If Williams had had one eye on Hart Crane that evening, he had kept his other eye on Harry Crosby as a potential publisher for his own *January,* and he may have broached the subject that evening. Crosby may even have shown some interest before the drinking became too heavy. But it didn't much matter in the long run, for three days later Crosby was dead, having blown his lover's brains out in a suicide pact before he turned the gun on himself. Crane had been out to dinner with Caresse Crosby and Harry's mother and another woman and had expected to meet Crosby at the theater afterward as prearranged. Instead, the police found Crosby and Josephine Bigelow lying mannequin-like, fully clothed, in bed at a friend's studio at the Hotel des Artistes on West 67th Street. That, of course, was the kind of news that sold papers, and the tryst suicide was smeared over the tabloids for weeks.

Williams was first shocked and then infuriated by the news. For years he had hated the papers anyway for serving death up daily along with one's orange juice and toast. Now he wrote his response to the tabloid version of that double suicide. There had been a death and the papers had played up the sex of the thing—eros and death—that cheap tingling sensation of two lovers found in bed (though clothed). What the papers had stressed in their headlines was that Crosby was a poet, one of those free livers who'd been to Paris, though they'd been unable to locate just where his poems were. Well, that was the inviolable secret of the poet with his impossibly clean mind, regardless of what appearances might show to the contrary. Let yesterday's newspaper float off with the December winds. Who would ever know the clean moments of inspiration—all evidence to the contrary—the impossible moments of whiteness, the sudden gravity of

> *snow trees*
> *flashing*
>
> *upon the mind*
> *from a clean*
> *world.*[166]

So Williams wrote in his poem "The Death of See," reducing Crosby to the cipher C, much as Stevens had reduced his own Crispin poet to the same cipher half a dozen years before. But in so doing, Williams had paradoxically expanded Crosby to include the poet as seer, as visionary, seeing what the newspapers for all their words and "facts" would never see. Thus Crosby and Crane and Williams, in spite of all their differences: all members of what Crane would soon call the visionary company, transformed by the sudden white light of inspiration. Such a hope, held out, might sustain one in spite of the crushing banality that seemed to be winning out everywhere by decade's end in the great American desert. It might even sustain one in spite of the long winter of Depression which had already snuffed out Crosby and was beginning now to blanket Williams.

SEVEN

Depression: 1930–1933

*B*y early 1930, Williams had retreated to his attic. His sons were getting bigger now, demanded more space if less time, his mother was living with them as a permanent fixture, and Williams—beginning to smell (as Stevens would put it) the faint tobaccoey scent of autumn in the air—needed to locate a place where he might be able to write whenever he could find the time. It was ironic that he should have undertaken this retreat at a time when his poetic output had definitely declined, but he may have been trying to "goose himself," as he himself would have phrased it, back into a proper frame for writing. He was also seeing a young woman named Myra Marini, a budding writer from one of the neighboring towns and one of his patients, and he may have wanted to be left alone to sort out his own problems.[1] As with thousands of others, his stocks had turned into so much toilet paper, just as he'd feared. And if he still had his practice, any dreams he might have had of retiring or semi-retiring in order to write more had now to be scuttled. For the next fifteen years he would have to work harder and longer, and though he refused to raise his fees, he made matters worse for himself by often refusing to send bills to patients who were finding it harder than he was to make ends meet in Depression New Jersey. Instead, they paid him back by barter or merely by their presence, their stories, their language, which—once out in his car again after a house call, or between office visits—he would transfer in a white heat to his prescription pads.

So, in the late fall of '29, he began to tack up insulation boards along his rafters, pushing the accumulated white elephants into all the eaves, hauling a small wood stove and an old desk and typewriter after him, so that the place began to look as much like a New England "country store" as anything else. He worked on his room in spare moments over the next ten months, "finishing" it finally in September 1930. He used it all year round—warming his feet by a small stove in winter, or sweltering in his underwear in the heat of summer—until his sons were out of high school and gone: Bill Jr. to Williams College in the fall of '32, and Paul to Penn—Williams' own alma mater—in '35. When he abandoned that retreat it was, finally, because he had found the isolation itself—which he'd thought he wanted—too distracting. His need for contact had by then resurfaced.

At one time there were pictures and photos and postcards and news clippings and children's drawings over all four walls of that rectangualar tent with its east/west axis. Some of those mementos are still there. A chart of the stock market begun in January 1928, when Williams bought oil stock, and continuing unbroken until September 1932, when Bill Jr. left for college. As a symbol of what had happened on Wall Street in those years, that chart must have depressed Williams. But as pure design, jagged edges descending, ascending, it could take its place behind his chair along with other designs. Like a news photo of the sun in eclipse and the words: The Black Sun Press. Or a picture of his father's ancestral locus, Careen Hill, St. Thomas, dated June 20, 1931: the summer solstice. A news photo of Nancy Cunard in New York with John Banting, a white painter, and Taylor Gordon, a black artist. There are clippings of the Mooney case, of Diego Rivera, of Ben Shahn, a throwaway for an exhibit of Berenice Abbott's photos at the Julien Levy Gallery at 602 Madison Avenue, an ad for Gertrude Stein's operas and plays (1933), a black and white reproduction of Juan Gris, a photo of the economist A. R. Orage, Picasso's *Harlequin* in black and white, Matisse's *Ballet Dancer*, a painting by Karl van Mander of Shakespeare and Ben Jonson which Williams was convinced had been painted from the life (it was his secret image of the self-effacing Shakespeare with whom he identified).

And there were postcards, too. One of El Greco's *Cardinal* sent by Louis Zukofsky and dated September 23, 1930, to celebrate the "official" opening of Williams' study, with these words: "Bill His Attic." And another, with a picture of Rapallo—*"Passeggiata a mare"*—sent by Louis from Monaco August 30, 1933, with the words: "Ez and Basil [Bunting] & Tibor [Serly] and me under the palm trees, home in 2 weeks." And one too from Pound—another view of Rapallo—20 Maggio 1932, asking about *Contact* 2: "HAZ your bloomin peereeyodicule EVER been printed? an nif so, why dont you send it to me?" And, facing these, half a dozen children's drawings of Williams' poem "The Trees," most likely done by a Rutherford grade-school class in the early '30s, when Dr. Williams, Rutherford poet, visited them.

From the east window of his retreat, he could see the sun rising over the meadows, flooding the attic with the yellow light of promise. From the west window, he could see the Presbyterian church across Ridge Road, and then—at an angle—the stores running down Park Avenue. One of them was the local candy store, with its sign surrounded by lights reading SODA. That too could be made to yield a cubist design, the sign framed from the poet's perspective by the darkened windowpane, the pane too become part of the design. It was the poet's tower in Rutherford, the attic that symbolized desire:

> *the unused tent*
> *of*
>
> *bare beams*
> *beyond which*
>
> *directly wait*
> *the night*
>
> *and day—*
> *Here*
>
> *from the street*
> *by*
>
> ** * **
> ** S **
> ** O **
> ** D **
> ** A **
> ** * **
>
> *ringed with*
> *running lights*
>
> *the darkened*
> *pane*
>
> *exactly*
> *down the center*
>
> *is*
> *transfixed*[2]

One thing Williams had hoped to do was to get out a "collect definitive"[3] of his poetry in his new studio. He was already forty-six, and he knew that his poems were scattered in those elusive little magazines all over the earth or waiting impatiently in his files. Nine years after Brown had brought out his *Sour Grapes*, Williams was no closer to a regular publisher. McAlmon was out of the picture by then, as was Bill Bird, who'd turned his business over to Nancy Cunard in 1926, who had then renamed it The Hours Press. Williams was in contact with Nancy, but that was about another book. So it was back to Brown again. In early March he wrote Brown about the copyright question for his poems, which he would have to settle if he was to do a collected poems.[4] Brown wrote back at once. There were problems about turning over the copyright, especially with so many of Williams' books still in the warehouse after all this time.[5] Williams wrote back suggesting that perhaps he could buy all the books on Brown's shelves if by doing that he could get the copyright.

How many could there be? Why, he only had a dozen copies in all of *The Tempers*.[6]

Brown counted and wrote back. There were still 1,025 books on his shelves: 500 *Koras*, 175 *Al Que Quieres!*, 350 *Sour Grapes*. Brown hardly knew *what*—under the circumstances—to suggest . . . and didn't. Obviously Williams couldn't buy a thousand books.[7] It took him five weeks to answer, and when he did, he was both angry and frustrated. "If you're going to hold me up on the copyrights the thing can wait indefinitely as far as I am concerned," he told Brown on May 11. Brown, he said, was "acting rather shabbily, under the circumstances," but Williams would just have to wait until their contract expired.[8] A week later Brown explained that the real problem was that the Four Seas Company had thought of doing Williams' collected sometime in the future themselves, but they might consider taking $500 outright for the copyright.[9] That did it for Williams. Brown and company could go to hell as far as he was concerned. If he couldn't do a complete collected, then he would do a collected of the poems he'd written since *Sour Grapes* (1921), the last book he'd done with the Four Seas Company. The book he had in mind would become his *Collected Poems, 1921–1931*, though it took until 1934 to get it published by his friend Louis Zukofsky.

When Williams received his copy of the first number of *Pagany* in early January, he had mixed feelings. He congratulated Johns on publishing what was in itself "a splendid gesture." The format was "first rate," and if the contents were "mediocre," still, they were justly representative of the state of American letters in 1930.[10] Williams could see that, even with his manifesto, there was no sharp policy favoring either the right or the left. He had stressed once again the very thing he'd emphasized in editing *Contact* ten years before. By 1930, it was clear, aesthetics were rapidly giving way to social and political concerns, but Williams was too radical, really, to swing all the way in that direction. For the moment he was willing to settle for a magazine that represented the state of writing actually being done in the United States and let it go at that, though pressures especially from the left would soon make such a laissez-faire position harder than ever to hold on to. Williams' own short manifesto for *Pagany*'s first issue had been written under the pressure of medical work in late November, at a time when the economy was clearly in a state of collapse. He had watched the age of unlimited progress, the age of optimism, tumble, to be replaced by what he called now "bizarre derivations," including suicide as the final economic solution. Williams still distrusted science as he did philosophy, distrusted isms and ideology as he did religion. What then could the mind turn to now for rehabilitation? Let it turn to the imagination for solace, he offered, to the word, to "a meaning hardly distinguishable from that of place, in whose great, virtuous and at present little realized potency we hereby manifest our belief."[11]

That was just what his essay on Gertrude Stein, which he'd written for the first *Pagany*, and which Zukofsky had carefully edited, had celebrated: the revolution of the word which Stein had almost single-handedly enacted. It was an important, brilliant essay, this piece of Williams', and it pleased Stein herself when she read it, so that their earlier tiff in her apartment on the rue de Fleurus was now forgotten. Gertrude Stein, Williams had stressed, had returned to the words, words as words and not as a carrier for scientific, philosophical, or religious lumber. He compared her to something Sterne had touched on in his *Tristram Shandy* a century and a half earlier: a feeling for the words themselves, "a curious immediate quality quite apart from their meaning, much as in music different notes are dropped . . . into repeated chords one at a time," the way one heard music as one listened to a piece by Bach. For the modernist, each word had "a quality of its own, but not conjoined to carry the burden science . . . and every . . . figment of law and order have been laying upon them in the past." Words were rather like a swarm of matter in motion, "as a crowd of people might look at Coney Island as seen from a plane."

In pure writing, words transcended their connotations and their semantic logic. Nor was there progress in pure writing, but rather one sustained act of attention over all the words. If Stein was repetitive (she was), that too was an extension of her argument set forth in "Melanctha." To be truly democratic, to be truly local—in the sense of being attached with integrity to one's actual experience—Stein had had to "ascend to a plane of almost abstract design to keep alive." But—and this was equally important—if there was an overriding sense of design it was just as important that what "actually impinges on the senses . . . be rendered as it appears, by use of which, only, and under which, untouched, the significance has to be disclosed." That, in fact, was a key axiom for Williams' own poetic, both in lyrics and in the long poem *Paterson*, which was still a dozen years and more away. Things themselves would render, realize, the larger design while maintaining their own integrity. Williams ended by bringing up the dilemma that all American expatriates had had to face. Stein might fly to Paris to forget the fact that she was an American, but she had taken the United States with her, "the unmitigated stupidity, the drab tediousness of all democracy, the overwhelming number of the offensively ignorant, the dull nerve." All of this was there locked in Stein's mind, to be resolved as best she—or Williams—could resolve it. And to resolve the difficulties meant not changing one's reality or fleeing from it. For Pound and Eliot and James and Stein—in spite of everything—remained Americans. And the only way to come to terms with that reality lay in a comprehensive reorganization of one's materials according to one's deepest formal necessities. Not religion, then, not economics, not philosophy, but words. The most fundamental revolution of all.[12]

Louis Grudin—then an editor at Covici-Friede in New York—was one person who took exception to Williams' general attack on science and philosophy in the Stein article. "Don't fret about my excessively simple reactions to Philosophy and Science to say nothing of Religion," Williams wrote back to Grudin on January 11. "I know nothing of any of them but reserve the right to consider them as subdivisions of interest which one may take or leave as he listeth." Everyone always thought of his own discipline or profession as the most important, Williams knew, but from the artist's point of view science was no more important than—or only equally as important as—a tree or a piece of dress goods. And it was no different with philosophy or religion. All of these were only so many categories—all except art itself. If therefore Eliot used philosophy or religion in a poem, that did not make the poem good, even if the religion or philosophy itself was good. The problem was that "a lot of well intentioned asses, like T. S. Eliot and a whole breed of science worshippers," wanted to set up their disciplines as though they were fetishes, and then measure their art by that religious or philosophic content. For Williams, such measures were just "plain shit." "We talk about our enslavement to machines," he added, probably thinking of *The Bridge.* "Poor shitasses we, as if our enslavement to machines were anything more than the superficial evidence of our five hundred year long enslavement to science itself." After all, a poem was not an envelope for something else; it was a machine that ran according to its own inner necessities and which could use philosophy or religion or nature indiscriminately for its fuel.[13]

Again, Grudin objected—from a philosophical point of view. But Williams would not be trapped. No use objecting to his argument, Williams wrote back. For in the most important sense Williams' letter to Grudin had been "absolute and perfect, like a tree or a stone," a sheet of paper of a certain size with certain markings on it: an artifact, a thing. There was no gist, no center, to his letter. Analyze it, philosophize about it, sketch it, abstract from it, it remained—finally—what it was—words on a page. Williams had wanted to say something about Stein's work and he had done so. If others—using philosophy or one of the sciences—also wanted to say something about her work, he wished them well. Amen.[14]

Pound was still looking to set up a press somewhere in the States and still trying to enlist Williams' help. But Williams, without a publisher of his own, was skeptical. Sylvia Beach had refused to help Pound with her Paris press: she had enough to do getting out the Joyce material. McAlmon of course was through. Nancy Cunard was a possiblity and the

Black Sun Press another, though people like Nancy and Caresse Crosby, Williams realized, were millionaire dilettantes with time and money to burn. In spite of himself, Williams began mocking Ezra's efforts to find a press on the American side of the Atlantic, telling Zukofsky that when they found their fine press they should put it "in a window on Fifth Ave. and have ezra work it from 9 to 5 in billiardcloth green overalls."[15] But Williams, too, bitterly felt the lack of money and resources for the writing he knew still needed to be done.

Then, in the winter of 1930, Nancy Cunard offered to publish Zukofsky's "The," at the same time offering to publish something of Williams'. Once again Zukofsky offered to edit whatever Williams was ready to print, and Williams sent him the "Primavera Trasportata a la Morale" sequence he'd done in the spring of '28. "Mark up the script ad lib," he told Zukofsky in mid-February. "Delete poems, sections of poems, lines, words, the whole works or nothing as it may happen to suit your fancy or conscience."[16] Floss had liked the sequence, even though Williams was afraid she might balk at some of the more confessional pieces. But Zukofsky thought it too fat and told him to pare it hard. Williams thanked him and promised to "cut out the crap."[17] On March 2 he sent the "Primavera"—trimmed now to the thirty pages Pound had requested—to Pound for Nancy Cunard, taking the opportunity to mention his novelette *January,* which had just been turned down by Kreymborg's *American Caravan.*[18] Williams knew, of course, that Pound would demur: Nancy could do one book, not two. Let it be the "Primavera," then, Williams answered, though the novelette was very close to his heart. It had caught something he'd been "trying for half my life" to capture. *Transition* was doing a piece of it, but he still wanted the thing published as a whole. Ah well, someone would do it.[19]

At the end of April Williams was still waiting to hear definitely from Pound about his "Primavera." Richard Aldington in the meantime was publishing a piece of it in his *Imagist Anthology* for 1930 (which appeared in May), but when Williams saw the "cocksucking mistakes" Aldington had allowed into the text he let out a long groan. *Four Grapes* for *Sour Grapes, Tempera* for *The Tempers,* and *In the American Grave!*[20] Now, more than ever, he needed his new poem printed by someone who knew what he was doing. Then, to make matters worse, Williams heard at the end of May that the Hours Press scheme was off.

All that effort and so little to show for it. Time then to turn to other schemes. That spring Johns had talked to Williams about Williams' novel *White Mule.* Johns promised to print a chapter in each number of *Pagany* if Williams would write them. Williams had been stalled in the writing —in fact, all that spring he was experiencing a writer's block, unable to push forward, creatively and even psychologically exhausted. That condition lasted all through the summer until late in the fall, when Williams finally broke through the ice that had held him locked and began steaming through not only with the chapters for *White Mule* but with a dozen short stories as well. What had caused the blockage was not clear, not even to Williams, who could only complain to Zukofsky in May that he'd "never been so hellishly distraught in my life as during the recent past—I can't even tell you precisely why this has been so."[21]

The reasons were complex, and Williams was not accustomed to taking time out to examine what might be troubling him. First of all, though, there'd been personal difficulties that winter and spring. On Monday afternoon, January 20, Elena—then in her early eighties—had dressed up in her new fur coat and high heels and had insisted on walking to a local reading club meeting despite the streets' having been transformed into a solid sheet of ice. Williams had tried to make her take a cab if she had to go out, but no one—not even her son—was going to tell her what to do. And, besides, she had such pretty feet. On her way home she had slipped, fallen, and broken her left hip and elbow. At first, Williams thought his mother would be hospitalized for six weeks, but it was not until June (five months later) that Elena was allowed to come home. She still had twenty years ahead of her, but she would never walk again. Perversely, Elena's son was secretly proud of his mother's vanity, her willingness to brave ice and bruises to show off her new coat and shoes.

Then, two months later, on March 26, Paul Herman died of a self-inflicted gunshot wound at his home in Monroe. The death was ruled accidental, and Williams thought it best to leave it at that, but he was haunted by the specter of young Paul's death which had happened in the same way fifteen years before. Floss of course had been devastated, "torn apart by it all," and Williams himself could hardly bring himself to think about what had happened.[22] He tried to forget it all by working harder than ever ministering to his patients, as though somehow that might compensate for the irretrievable loss of this man whom he had loved so much. Williams would also compensate as he could by creating a sympathetic living portrait of Paul Herman in his *White Mule* trilogy over the next twenty-two years, a trilogy as much about his father-in-law as about his own wife.

Although Williams seems to have mentioned it to no one—not to Zukofsky, not even to Pound—Conrad Aiken and his second wife, Clarissa Lorenz, were married by a justice of the peace in the Williamses' living room at 9 Ridge Road on February 27. Why this spot should have been chosen neither Williams nor Aiken ever made clear. Aiken apparently wanted the ceremony performed quietly and Williams respected his wishes. And when, seven years later, Aiken wrote Williams from Cuernavaca, Mexico, that he now needed Williams to help get him unmarried so that he might marry his "Lorelei Three," Williams complied by going down to the Rutherford Town Hall, getting Aiken a copy of the marriage certificate on file there, and sending it down to Cuernavaca. No wonder, then, that when Aiken published his anthology of American poets in 1944 without including Williams that Williams was upset. Aiken excused himself then by calling it an oversight to be attended to when he revised the text, but when it was revised shortly thereafter, Williams was still missing. Williams shrugged: what in hell could one expect from a crony of Eliot's anyway?

If Williams was in a slump in 1930, however, so were the new spate of little magazines coming out of Depression America. Parker Tyler, coeditor of *Blues*, had written Williams in late April to ask him if he was the one responsible for the stuff *Pagany* was publishing, and Williams had passed that information on to Johns, telling Johns he'd defended him as at least no faker, since the magazine—given the tenor of the times—had to be "a miscellany, a true, even a realistic picture of the rather shabby spectacle America still makes from the writer's viewpoint." It was an unsettled moment in American intellectual circles, Williams knew, and therefore a time of symposiums, of exchanges of opinion, a time for "searching generally for an intelligent viewpoint in those things which concern us." Perhaps in future issues, he suggested to Johns, the magazine would begin to take some more recognizable stand. He had liked Sherry Mangan's strong attack on Eliot and the poem by Zukofsky in *Pagany*.[23] And though he didn't interfere, he let Johns know that he was disturbed by the man's refusal to publish one of McAlmon's stories, a story he said was "as good as anything you are likely to have sent in to you for the next 20 years."[24]

There was also the *Hound & Horn*, and Williams had sent its editor, R. P. Blackmur, one of his poems, "Rain," in the summer of 1929, telling him he was sending it at Burke's suggestion and almost daring the magazine to print it. When Blackmur accepted it at once, Williams softened toward the "Harvard" boys who ran the magazine and apologized for having sent such a disjointed example of his most recent work.[25] There was also *The Miscellany*, which he thought well printed, which also published some of his poems. Norman MacLeod's *Morada*, a few issues of which were published from Albuquerque, New Mexico, and which did publish several things of McAlmon's, was yet another of the "more or less arty magazines appearing in the U.S. of late." But all of these magazines were, "short lived and feeble in their approach, both to a public and to ideas."[26] *Blues* he thought one of the best of the current crop: at least it had some direction and could get heated over an idea. He even tried *Poetry* again, sending them a poem, the first he'd sent them in eight years. But all in all, the intellectual excitement he'd once felt first with *Others* and later with *The Little Review* was missing, even with *Pagany*, even with *Blues*. It was another sign of the times.

In 1929 René Taupin, a young French critic, working in close conjunction with Ezra Pound, published his *L'Influence du symbolisme française sur la poésie américaine (1910–1920)*. In that study he called Williams one of the three best American poets then writing, the other two being Pound and Eliot. Williams, Taupin maintained, had generated an American art by coming into direct and full contact with the place in which he happened to find himself. Taupin had written to Williams to ask him how he'd been influenced by French writers, and Williams had tried to assure him that he had read very little of either the French classics or his French contemporaries. But Taupin, following Pound's lead, was convinced that Rimbaud's *Illuminations* were behind Williams' improvisations. Like Rimbaud, Taupin thought, Williams was a visionary drunk with words, a poet who manifested in his writing a controlled dreamlike quality.

Zukofsky liked much that Taupin had to say and befriended the Frenchman when he came to live in the States in 1930. He also attempted to update what Taupin had said by taking Taupin's argument up through the 1920s and by focusing particularly on Williams. Zukofsky saw Williams now as one of the old masters of something called objectivism. This was an extension of imagism, but more complex in that it it allowed the whole spectrum of emotions as well as the mind into the poem in addition to the world of eye and ear. Critics like Burke and Munson, who had stressed the early imagist phase in Williams, Zukofsky argued, had understood only a part of Williams' aesthetics, an aesthetics that Williams himself had already long left behind. For no one could have predicted the poetry of *Spring and All* by reading either *Al Que Quiere!* or *Sour Grapes*. Long ago Williams had eschewed the sentimental "I" and all "extraneous comparisons, similes, overweening autobiographies of the heart," all nostaligic reflections on the past. Instead Williams had caught the moment of the '20s, had caught America itself, "the shifting, as one hurriedly thinks of it or sees it perhaps as one charges from street car to street car." He said more: that Williams had learned to use the printed page to guide the eye as well as the ear, and that he was no less a poet of essential rhythm than Pound himself.[27]

Williams read the essay in manuscript in early July and felt humbled. He'd done very few poems of the quality of *Spring and All* for the past seven years, and reading what young Zukofsky had written was like traveling through "a country I have always wished to live in and shall never find." When he read the essay he was still in his slump, downcast, unwilling—as he admitted—to even see anyone. But now he would "have to write again—my head is teeming with projects—or never show my face to anyone." And yet there seemed "less and less time for anything." He was "frightened" by the inevitability of the drift in which he found himself, and "powerless to escape." Zukofsky had presented a strong, confident American poet in his essay: Williams as a champion of the new objectivist school, a great modern American master. The contrast, therefore, between that sketch and the depressing reality he felt about himself left Williams feeling merely "pathetic."[28]

But he struggled with the depression he was feeling. So, a week later, he wrote to invite Zukofsky and Taupin out to the house for a drink and some talk (after his Thursday night office hours). Again he reiterated his self-doubts, adding that Zukofsky had written as perceptively as he had because he personally knew what Williams had hoped ideally to get down on the page, projecting "an excellence into my written work which really only exists in my desires." That, on the other hand, was being too hard on himself, and so equally false. What *was* he to think? "Balls!" he added, and let it got at that.[29]

And yet, regardless of whatever depression he himself was feeling, it was time to be getting on. Freud, Williams believed, was part of his problem. There was, after all, all that "cant that the artist is a born weakling, that his works are effects of a neurosis, sublimation, escapes from the brutal contact with life that he, poor chap, horribly fears." So the last word had seemed to be said on the subject. But now, in the June 1930 number of *transition*, Williams had read an essay by an "abler man than Freud," C. G. Jung. In his essay, "Psychology and Poetry," Jung had written that, far from being a weakling, the poet was no less than the leader of the human race. But it was no use waiting for the summative artist to come along, Williams insisted, for there was none. Certainly Eliot, that reactionary, was not the man. All he was doing was toeing the older line. It was time for another revolution in the word, recreating society by recreating the imagination itself. He would devote his own energies in the coming decade to just that revolution.[30]

In August the family went to Monroe again, and then they drove out to Gloucester, Massachusetts, to spend eight days visiting with Richard Johns.[31] By then Williams had broken through his block and had written the first version of a long short story for a writing contest sponsored by Scribner's. The story was "Old Doc Rivers," and he sent the fifteen-thousand-word manuscript off in early September, only to have it returned a month later. He'd written the early version to please the editors at Scribner's, and had been feeling a little queasy about that compromise, so that he felt relieved to have the story back. Now he could slash the thing the way he'd wanted to in the first place and so "get it into shape to lead off a book of short stories as originally intended." This time he would "aim to please no one" except himself.[32]

And now, with his attic room finished in September and his manuscript returned, he found himself writing, not poems—he was at a standstill there—but short story after short story. The finished room helped. When he'd driven in the last nail he was going to drive, Floss came upstairs with "a glass vase full of verbenas as the sign and signature to it all." It was a great room, he exulted, "long and rather low and full of light (dust also for the moment). I am there now at 5 PM after a swim in the nearby pool with my kids. What a place this is, what a place this is for writing. I want to be able to write sitting, standing, lying down and perhaps standing on my head—surely often kneeling."[33]

For once the Depression seemed to be helping him. With less money, there were fewer calls. He found himself with more free time on his hands and tried to use it wisely. Mercifully, the attic did isolate him from distractions. And here he was, writing his stories. "Suddenly for no reason at all I've found myself interested and as a consequence I've written six of them as fast as I can write," he wrote Johns." "I know Ezra would pass out if he could see some of them." Except for "Old Doc Rivers," he was using a form of about ten pages which he called "a sort of self determined classic." He'd also sketched out the idea for five or six others the year before, so that what he now had amounted to a book. If he could only find a full-time stenographer! Oh, Mrs. Johns, his typist, was good. No doubt about it, but since she worked for love as much as anything else, there was no way he could push her. And now she was sick. No matter, no matter. He was actually enjoying watching himself create his stories after a long dry spell. He had tried to rework the "Old Doc Rivers" thing steadily and dutifully, but the inspiration just wasn't there and he'd nearly killed himself in the process. For some reason the story kept collapsing into so many dry fragments. But then he'd been able to do some other stories and now, in October and November, it was "a perfect diarrhoea."[34] Moreover, the short stories had given him the confidence to go on with *White Mule,* and those chapters were also being cranked out one after the other. The dam had broken.

As for "Old Doc Rivers," the problem there went deeper than form, or touched on formal considerations at the level where form intersects with the question of self-identity. For in that long short story Williams was attempting nothing less than to define himself and his own position in relation to his community. To do that, he had had to distance himself from the events of the story, get them out of the house, as he put it. Like his creator, Rivers was a complex figure, one of those old-time doctors in the generation before Williams; when a place like Rutherford was still very much a river town, as Williams was fond of remembering about his own town when people began to put on airs. Doc Rivers had been one of the pioneers when doctors still rode horse-driven rubber-tired surreys and there were still old farms and halfway houses down in the cedar swamps and meadows out by Route 3. He belonged, in many ways, with those magnificent failures with their own absolute humanitarian values that populate Williams' *In the American Grain,* except that dope had made of

Rivers a grotesque, a larger-than-life figure, an idol, a witch doctor, a miserable scapegoat whom people kept calling in to perform the miraculous when all else failed.

The incessant pressure of caring for the sick and dying at all hours of the day and night—of being called on to handle caesareans, ectopic pregnancies, hysterectomies, gastro-enterostomies, gall bladder resections, cyst removals, appendectomies, to treat fistulas, empyema, hydrocele, malaria, typhoid fever, endocarditis, rheumatism. The wearing down, the need for drugs to keep the hands steady, the final addiction, the human cost to Rivers himself. Williams too had learned over the years what it was like to be held in awe as the doctor whose every word was to be followed without deviation. He too had had patients beg him not to let a loved one die. How often he had awakened in the night from a nightmare, some child there on the operating table before him dead of mastoiditis or peritonitis or gastro-enteritis, and thinking: if I had tried it this way, or that way, perhaps the patient would be alive now. How often for self-protection he had assumed a professional stance when he was hurting within, trying to find the right words for a bereaved parent, daughter or son, wife or husband.

And Rivers, escaping to the old Frenchman's for good talk and good liquor and playing cards in the greenhouse while the snow whirled outside. Like Williams, driving into the city to seek out writers and artists and the cultivated—men and women—before he turned back, still exhausted, toward Rutherford and Passaic, to the patients who were his life even as they bled him. He knew the rumors circulating about him, that he was a gay blade and a poet, a bohemian of sorts yet respected as one of the best physicians in the area. A strange man who refused to raise his prices when everyone else was doing just that. He wanted to serve these people simply because they were there to be served, especially the poorer ones: the immigrant classes and the black community. But who could understand Rivers . . . or Williams? "It would take a continental understanding," Williams wrote, "reinforced as it is by centuries of culture—to comprehend and to accept the complexities and contradictions of a nature such as Rivers." And yet there were patients, especially his women, who would have followed Williams anywhere. He was more than a doctor. He was their pal, often their confessor, an ally who could be counted on and trusted to help them in any way he could.

Like Rivers, Williams had had to make some very difficult decisions as a doctor, for which nothing in his background had prepared him. As when a woman had had twins and then found herself pregnant again four months later, very likely with twins again and a husband in the service. Williams had had to weigh the life of the living children against the unborn and had decided in favor of providing for the living by giving the woman an abortifacient, in spite of her religious qualms. And there were families—more than one—who had begged Williams, pleaded with him, in fact, to allow one of their own with a terminal disease to die. And when, reluctantly, he had followed their wishes and allowed the patient to die, they had thereafter excluded him from their house. They had their scapegoat now and at least *they* could sleep at night.

In many ways, then, Williams was like his Jesuit hero, Father Rasles, a confessor, a psychiatrist, an adviser, a man of contact whose very presence could, taken by itself, make a patient feel better. He was one of the best physicians around, and he gave himself to whoever needed him without thought of the cost. They in turn comforted him, believed in him, provided him with the continuing living matrix of their language. They refreshed him even as they spent him. By refracting his impressions of Rivers through the fictional hearsay of others, through the young doctor who knew him peripherally, through the old records at "St. Michael's" Hospital, through interviews with people who knew Rivers (the older doctors, the woman whom he had lived with, the boy who'd stayed with Rivers), Williams caught something of the very life of this fictional doctor, and—by extension—was able to write an extraordinarily perceptive autobiographical fragment. It turned out to be an assessment of the doctor himself as he approached fifty. Not until he wrote *Paterson* in his sixties would he again capture himself so perceptively. And then he would raise himself to the stature of an epic grotesque, some troubled and fantastic shape "in some gigantic fever dream."

*
**

In the fall of 1930 Zukofsky had gone west to California to teach for a year, not having found suitable employment in New York. McAlmon, on the other hand, who'd gone west in early 1930, was back in New York by the beginning of 1931, before returning to a Paris which, if it existed, existed only in his imagination. On the evening of January 5, 1931, Williams drove over to Brooklyn with Floss to have supper with McAlmon and Basil Bunting and his wife. One of the topics that came up was Pound's Artemis cult as he'd presented it in the last of his *XXX Cantos*, just published, and Williams found himself defending Pound's classical ideal of beauty. McAlmon and Bunting had "flayed" him for that misplaced reverence, he told Zukofsky on the tenth, by insisting that "the Greeks never in the least realized or thought of" such a thing as Classical Beauty. Williams had countered by evoking the Greek temple to Poseidon at Paestum which he'd seen with Ed in 1910 and again with Floss in '24, standing alone there on a hill overlooking the sea in "its awe inspiring present condition." Oh, McAlmon and Bunting had been willing to admit that the Greeks "had a sense of neatness and balance" and all that, but they'd drawn the line when it came to "all this hildadoolittlehermes stuff" and Pound's Artemis cult. McAlmon, with his cold, steely-blue eyes, had cut through the tangled web simply: "The Greeks were plain dirty and aimed for the hole—and that's that." Williams, for all of his own preoccupations with the quotidian, the detritic, with red wheelbarrows and gay wallpaper and broken slivers of green glass in backyard coal piles, knew that he was still—when measured against McAlmon—a hopeless romantic, "a hangover from other years," with "an adolescent tendency to grovel to unearthliness —call it beauty, call it what you will."[35] With time, however, he thought he would get over all that, though—fortunately—he never did.

In February, Williams got down to his extended meditation on Pound's *XXX Cantos*. "The goddamn thing almost tore my heart out," he wrote Zukofsky on the twenty-third, after an especially harrowing week trying to fathom what it was exactly his friend had been assembling for the past fifteen years. Williams had read through all thirty cantos again carefully, writing his impressions wherever and whenever he could, as they imploded in on his consciousness, "scribbling what I had to say on street corners—the backs of letters—prescription blanks—and transcribing at 1 AM holding my eyes open (one at a time) with my right hand while I typed with my left." Just the day before he had finished his typed draft, which had run to twenty-eight pages of impressions, signing the last sheet and dating it in pencil.[36]

He sent the essay to the *Symposium*, which had him cut the draft to ten pages: one-third its original length. Williams complied, exhausted with his effort to come to terms, as he said, with "a closed mind which clings to its power—about which the intelligence beats seeking entrance." Pound, he knew, "had had the discernment to descry and the mind to grasp that the difficulties in which humanity finds itself need no phenomenal insight for their solution." The man was essentially a rationalist, Williams knew, believing that human intelligence could work where "a complicated mystery of approach" led only to passivity, as with Eliot. Like Williams, Pound was less interested in the word as symbol and more interested in its concrete reality. As for Pound's language, he had deformed the natural order of speech at times, but his intention had always very definitely been to create a modern speech while somehow saving the excellences and even the forms of the old. The prose and poetry of the *Cantos*, then, were part of a continuum, and the real work of the poem, its real seriousness, came in a close study of how Pound had organized the words on the page and constituted his lines. That, precisely, was where the real revolution in the language of the poem had come. The Greek and Latin and French tags, Williams explained, were really no problem. Where Pound wanted the reader to know what he'd said, he usually provided a gloss a few lines further on in the text. Moreover, there were things he didn't care for in the *Cantos:* those Anglo-Saxon kennings, or the way Pound kept turning American speech into broad dialect or parody. And now (thanks to some friends) he even had his doubts about Pound's Artemis cult. But all in all, Pound had managed to lift the language itself to new heights. And that was no small achievement.[37]

Pound read the longer draft Williams sent him and thanked him for his "nobl effusion," grateful too that someone had comprehended what it was he was "drivin'" at." He knew there were still some rough lines in the text, that some of the *Cantos* were still stiff, but he'd chosen to "leave the mass in the rough than quit in the middle." He would figure out which details would stay and which would go after the whole thing had been put "down on paper in someorother bloodydamn form." For Williams the *Cantos* would remain a primary text, where they would continue to ferment and shape his own practice, both in the '30s, when they remained one of the few examples Williams thought worth following, and later when he was groping toward an epic form for his own *Paterson.*[38]

On March 20, Williams gave a talk at a fortnightly forum conducted by two New York booksellers, David Moss and Martin Kamin. They had approached McAlmon in New York the previous fall, hoping to once again revive McAlmon's Contact Editions under their management, with McAlmon holding the title of editor. But McAlmon had soon lost interest in that venture. Now, with McAlmon in Paris again, they tried Williams. It began by their inviting Williams to give a talk on "The Logic of Modern Letters," in which Williams reviewed some of the directions modern literature had taken—with references to Stein, Joyce, and Pound—and then read some examples from Stevens, Marianne Moore, and himself displaying the new work. Williams gave that talk before a small audience (which included Floss) in Moss and Kamin's bookstore on the ground floor of the Hotel George Washington at Lexington and 23d Street, a nice room, Williams said, "full of big wooden columns."[39] He'd been nervous for days before giving that talk—one reason he always hated doing that sort of thing—and he confessed to Richard Johns that he thought the talk had gone off "like a wet cracker" and that the poems he'd chosen as examples hadn't worked.[40] But at least Marianne Moore's poems had been well received, as he told her on the twenty-second: "At the close I read five of your poems . . . ,from the handclapping at the end my judgment is that you won the 'tourney.' And I have Florence for a witness—a lady of icy veracity in the expression of her opinions."[41]

Williams wrote to Zukofsky on April 2 to tell him how much he'd appreciated Zukofsky's own essay on Pound's *Cantos* which Eliot had published in *The Criterion*, and suggested that a book of essays on the

Cantos might be in order. Then he gave Zukofsky some news. He'd been into the Metropolitan Museum the day before to see the new French impressionist paintings the museum had acquired. "Instead," he added, "I chiefly admired a portrait head by El Greco and his View of Toledo. After that most things look dull." He had gone into the American Wing again to compare their work with the Europeans and had to admit it was "pretty poor" stuff. Why, there were "six or eight living men" in the States who had done better work than what was on exhibit in the museum. And though he didn't mention them by name, Sheeler, Demuth, Hartley, and Ben Shahn would have been four of them. But his real anger went out to the American art patrons with their misinformed sense of the new in American art: "Isn't it a shitting crime that a big stone heap like that [by which he meant the museum itself] should sit on life and keep it under. God damn them to hell, the lousy cancerous bastards with their stolen fortunes and dust bins of heads."

As for the French impressionists and cubists, looked at against figures like El Greco and Brueghel, they seemed more uneven now "and by no means as powerful as we used to imagine."[42] Juan Gris had been his man, and he had made it a habit of measuring contemporary works against this Spanish artist who had worked with Picasso and Braque in Paris until his death a few years before. "That man was my perfect artist," he'd told Charles Henri Ford five months earlier. "He embodied all the personal faults with which I am so familiar myself. I felt a deep grief at his passing—yet I never knew him."[43] But the impressionists and even the cubists were historical phenomena now, like his own earlier work. It was time to consider the larger, more inclusive sweep of tradition and meet those masters as well on their own ground.

And yet he could still get excited by the appearance of a friend's work in one of the avant-garde magazines, like Charlie Demuth's illustrations in the April issue of *Pagany*, work that had lifted his sagging spirits up again, "like a skyscraper." He knew the lefters—the *New Masses* crowd, which saw Williams as some sort of literary fascist, or even the *Blues* crowd, who were disappointed that Williams had given his support to *Pagany*—would be muttering their disapproval once again at the presence of reactionary art which failed to carry sufficient social impact. But even they had had to make unacceptable sacrifices as artists "by the necessity (perhaps) for making a new start."[44] There was such a thing as jettisoning too much of the past. Williams for one was not going to throw over all he'd learned in the revolution of 1914.

But the "lefters" were not the only ones giving Williams advice. Kenneth Rexroth, who had roasted Williams in the pages of *Blues* eighteen months before, had stopped by at 9 Ridge Road on Sunday afternoon, May 3, after having hitchhiked cross-country from California.

Williams liked him, he told Johns, though he found him "somewhat bitten by the prevalent Anglo-Catholicism drift." "Though that was no more a fault," he added, "than anything else which serves as a temporary belief." What did make Williams smile, however, was the young man's inclination "to find some fault with me over my pagan inclinations which all these spiritualists—if one may call them that—find limiting." Left or right, Williams was apolitical enough to be disconcerted by what he called "the amorphous critical bitcheries of today."[45]

Two months later it was Zukofsky who was coming home from California. Williams was happy to have his friend back near him again and told him he wanted to see René Taupin again soon, apologizing for his earlier roughness toward the young Frenchman for things Taupin himself had actually never said. What these were Williams did not spell out in his letter to Zukofsky, but it was probably for making statements about French influence on his work which Williams would not accept. "I want to see Taupin soon," he repeated to Zukofsky. "I feel that I have not taken the time to value him, I regret my resentment against that which he probably didn't say. But he'll have to take his chances with the rest of us in this neglecting barrel bottom." After all, none of them were exactly household words in America.

Another thing he wanted to see Zukofsky about was the new *Collected Poems, 1921–1931* he'd put together that spring. He went into the city to take Zukofsky out to dinner (and had to allay poor Zukofsky's feeling of embarrassment when Williams picked up the tab for both of them) and to talk about the book. "It represents work done over a ten year period and should not be too rigorously pared," he explained to Zukofsky, without going into the enormous roadblock Brown had put in the way of his doing a *Collected*.[46] Williams was looking for a good New York publisher and suggested that Zukofsky—as his unofficial agent—first try Aiken, who still owed him a favor. He also mentioned that Nancy Cunard and Henry Crowder, her "black assistant and boyfriend," had come out to visit him and Floss in Rutherford a few days before. Williams had been impressed with Crowder's knowledge of jazz, and of course he was always glad to see Nancy.[47]

Cunard was getting together an anthology of writing, paintings, and photographs by black and white writers, and she wanted Williams to contribute something to it. This would finally be printed as *The Negro Anthology*, published entirely at Cunard's expense in 1934, and it would contain Williams' "The Colored Girls of Passenack, Old and New," which he wrote especially for her that summer of '31. The story itself was a product of the moment, a romantic evocation of the extraordinary vitality and carriage of the black women he had known in and around Rutherford and Hackensack and Paterson. In it he remembered Georgie Anderson, the maid in his parents' house when he was a boy of twelve, who could peg a stone into the top of the big chestnut two houses down. She had been the first young woman he'd ever seen naked—through a peephole, while she took a sponge bath in her attic room. And later, when he was just starting out as a doctor in Rutherford, Mable Watts, with the body of Goya's *Maja Desnuda*, had offered herself to him and been lightly, embarrassingly, refused. For years he had taken care of her and her two children—one of whom he was sure had been strangled by her boyfriend—and had followed her story with interest and compassion. He remembered too the black maid he'd met back in early '28, when Floss was away with the boys:

> A magnificent bronze figure stood before me. She said not a word but stood there till I told her who I was, then she let me in, turned her back and walked into the kitchen. But the force of her—something; her mental alertness coupled with her erectness, muscular power, youth, seriousness —her actuality—made me want to create a new race on the spot.

They always remained half-mythic, Amazonian presences to Williams, these black women. Forbidden fruit, "tremendous furnaces of emotional power . . . unmatched in any white," except—he added—in those rare "devotional females who make up 'society,' and whose decadent fervors are so little understood." It was a way of encoding his own admiration for Nancy Cunard (Nancy, remembered that March day in Rome), who had dared to rebel against so many of society's taboos, one of those figures, like Doc Rivers and Boone and the more daring of the street leaders he'd known as a boy, who were willing to fling respectability and its attendant hypocrisies to the wind—and to pay the price.[48] No wonder, then, that at the heart of the epic he would write he would recall the tall black woman, taller than himself, recall too Mable and Georgie and all the other black women he'd admired, conflated into the image of the beautiful black Kore, nameless, living in a hell called Paterson, New Jersey.

*
* *

"Mrs. Williams and I are bound for Canada this time for a two week boat trip up along the Gaspé coast," he wrote to an admirer of his on July 29. "They say it's cold up there. In any case it's hot enough here to make one wish for Greenland." He was up in his attic at the moment, wearing pajama pants and Chinese straw sandals and sweating bullets. Still, it wasn't all that bad, "if one feels inclined to work—or has the time for it."[49] Bill Jr. had sailed for San Francisco via the Panama Canal as a bellhop on a steamer on June 27, and a few days later Paul had gone up to Camp Enajerog in Vermont. At first the Williamses had considered spending some time on Nantucket Island, but Floss had come up instead with the idea of a cruise along the North Shore, starting from Montreal, going up the St. Lawrence River as far as St. Anthony's in Newfoundland, and then looping back.[50]

The Williamses started out from Rutherford on Sunday morning, August 9, Williams driving north in heavy rain with every intention of stopping at Lake George to meet the young man he might soon be editing a magazine with: Nathanael "Pep" West. West was spending his summer vacation in a cabin outside Warrensburg with another young writer named Julian Shapiro, Shapiro writing short stories while West wrote the novel that would become *Miss Lonelyhearts*. But Williams was having enough trouble that day just keeping the car on the road with the heavy squalls, and so he drove through, expecting to see West back in New York City in the fall.[51] The Williamses spent several days in and around Montreal and then boarded the steamer SS *Voyageur* of the Clark Steamship Company on Tuesday evening, the eleventh. Before starting off, Williams sent Zukofsky a postcard of the Château de Ramezay in Montreal and asked Zuk if he'd received the sheaf of poems he'd sent him by registered mail. It was to be an extraordinary trip for both Bill and Floss, with the coldness, the desolation, the sense of a new world being seen for the first time, and these two weeks were to find many echoes in Williams' later writing, as in his short story "In Northern Waters," as well as in the fourth part of *Paterson*.

"It's been great going along the 'North Shore' as they speak of it here," he wrote his son Bill on Saturday morning, August 15, four days out from Montreal. All along the shore they'd seen little fishing villages, one looking pretty much like the next: a cluster of white frame houses with a church and a Hudson's Bay Company store at the center. These people made their livelihood trapping and fishing for cod, and the steamer they were on had passed beach after beach "of red and very coarse sand full of cod fish heads in various stages of decomposition—but pleasant for all that." It had been a good year for cod fishing, he told his fisherman son, and these were also the waters for some of the world's finest salmon fishing, except that nearly all of the two hundred rivers that flowed into the St. Lawrence had been leased to American fishing clubs, whose monopoly was so tight that the natives here were in danger of being arrested if they tried to fish their own waters for salmon, even if the take was only for their own consumption. Still, he'd met and talked with some of the natives—Frenchmen, Indians, and French Indians—and he could see they were too smart to be taken in by outsiders. They would keep their own counsel and do what they had to do.

At Seven Islands Williams and the other passengers had visited an Indian reservation. It was no more, he was shocked to find, "than one end of the white town which had been fenced in by barbed wire." The reservation itself had been nearly deserted. He'd seen some wooden square houses, an Indian tent, and three old women squatting on the ground close together. There was a fourteen-year-old Indian girl there who spoke excellent French, and with his own cranky French patois he learned from her that all the ablebodied men, women, and children had gone "into the woods," where they would stay through the winter, returning the following June with their pelts and furs.[52] It was a depressing visit for Williams, this seeing at first hand what had happened to these native Americans, and he would see again—years later—a similar story with the western tribes on his trips west to Utah, Texas, and Mexico.

There were other images too: the faces of the parents of a child who had just been lost over the stern of a skiff at Forteau. The savage look of the huge wolflike huskies in the wintry outdoor pens of Dr. Grenfell's mission hospital at St. Anthony's on the northern tip of Newfoundland, lapping up the scummy remains of thousands of cod livers flung to them by rough fishermen. They visited Greenly Island, where, just three years before, the first east-west transatlantic fliers had been grounded. The German Junker *Bremen* had been in the lead then and had lost its bearings after having taken off from the west of Ireland bound for the New World. Finally, it had come down in a blinding fog onto this deserted island, the only flat stretch of land for miles around. How alien this world seemed. Still, Williams had sworn he would swim in these northern waters and had taken off—alone—for the north end of the island. There he found only puffins and water so cold he could hardly believe it. Nevertheless, he did manage to dip beneath the surface . . . and to gash his stomach on the shelly bottom before he scrambled for shore. At least he'd come into intimate contact with the primitive elements of that place.[53]

From Newfoundland Williams sent a postcard to Dick Johns, joking about the intimacy of the cod fish aroma pervading everything: "Here we are," he'd written, "can't keep away from that old cod fish smell."[54] But the sight of cod fish heads bobbing by the hundreds in the waters provoked a more serious meditation on the nature of sacrifice and death in a world as alien as anything he'd seen before. "Miscellaneous weed / strands, stems, debris—/ firmament / to fishes," he wrote, thinking especially of Labrador, of a Belle Isle more otherworldly and indifferent than any Hart Crane had ever dreamed of in that sea poem sequence of his, *Voyages*. Here was an arctic sea

> where the yellow feet
> of gulls dabble
>
> oars whip
> ships churn to bubbles—
> at night wildly
>
> agitate phospores-
> cent midges—but by day
> flaccid

moons in whose
discs sometimes a red cross
lives—four

fathom—the bottom skids
a mottle of green
sands backward—

amorphous waver-
ing rocks—three fathom
the vitreous

body through which—
small scudding fish deep
down—and

now a lulling lift
and fall—
red stars—a severed cod-

head between two
green stones—lifting
falling[55]

Fourteen years later, Kenneth Burke would write Williams about the symbolism of that poem. The cod head sounded suspiciously like "the Godhead," he would tell Williams. After all, Williams had seen only a fish head and then had turned it into a cod head. But Williams objected. He'd seen hundreds of those disembodied cod heads bobbing in the waters off Labrador, and he knew they were cod heads because they were the "only thing being caught at that place." Besides, he'd "seen many of the assistant fisherman cutting up the fish preparatory to laying the flesh out on prepared boards to be sun-dried." As for the red cross image in the poem, that was no Christian symbol but something actually observed on the cod fish, "just like the ordinary 'plus' mark in arithmetic figured on the back of the large jelly-fish or stingeree."[56]

And yet, Burke's instincts were right. Williams might strip the words of their symbolic weight, but he knew that words like cod head / God head and the red cross and the sea journey all had resonances in any audience he might be reaching for. The act of stripping these words was Williams' way of saying that—after all—the sea was finally not our home, that Crane's vision of Belle Isle and of the Atlantic, seen from the Brooklyn Bridge with its devious, insistent pull toward eternity, was a lie. The bobbing cod head, rising, falling, lulling the observer, was merely dead. To hell with the image of the Orphic poet singing in the cold straits, as Crane had it. It took only a moment's baptism in those northern waters to be divested of the myth of one's potential divinity.

The Williamses were back in Montreal by August 25, after which they drove down to their cottage at West Haven on the Connecticut Shore for a few days' swim in more hospitable waters before returning home on the thirty-first. Williams found a letter waiting for him at the cottage from

Rexroth, asking if he had a manuscript of 150 pages which Rexroth might publish. Well, he had had one which he'd let Chatto & Windus (London) play with for a while before they'd turned it down, and now Williams sent it on to Rexroth. He called it *WRITING(S)*, and it consisted of *The Great American Novel* and *Spring and All*—neither of which could any longer be obtained anywhere—as well as his *January*. Together, the three would make a nice prose package.[57] Rexroth looked these over, but nothing came of the venture. Back home Williams found the copy of his *Collected Poems* he'd sent Zukofsky ready for him, edited and marked up, and Williams—as usual—accepted most of Zukofsky's suggestions, before sending the script on to Brandt and Brandt in New York. At the same time, Zukofsky had thrown out the suggestion of letting his friend George Oppen publish *WRITING(S)*, and Williams went along with that idea as well. But that too fell through, though Oppen did publish *January* and some of Williams' scattered prose pieces written over the past decade. There were many nibbles for his work, he was learning, but few bites.

*
* *

Back at the end of April, Williams had gone into New York to have dinner with Moss and Kamin and Kamin's wife. They were a "queer trio," he told Zukofsky the following day, and it was clear that they had some big plans that included Williams. Martin Kamin he found "the most civilized, the most cultured, the most irresponsible, as he is the most charming of the three." David Moss he found "futilely eccentric," but at the same time the one most insistent on getting down to business. He was a "vegetarian" and seemed to know a great deal about "recent books and writers." Sally Kamin, Williams saw, was the real glue that held the trio together. He liked them. They were not, at least, "bastards," though he did think them a bit naive about the realities of the literary world. McAlmon had refused to go into any deal with them as far as a magazine, but at least he'd sent on all the Contact books he had been able to scare up when he'd reached Paris. The problem there, however, was that like a "damned fool" he'd sent "all the books in a big case in one lot" and the U.S. Customs officials—who didn't like seeing French books with plain brown wrappers getting into the hands of Americans—had "held everything up indefinitely awaiting Consular invoices."[58] Williams had reason to be concerned, for most of the books eventually "disappeared."

But it was not until the end of September that plans for a new quarterly—to be called *Contact* like the magazine Williams and McAlmon had put together ten years before—finally jelled. Nathanael West, whose *The Dream Life of Balso Snell* Moss and Kamin had published earlier that year, would be Williams' first assistant, though Williams had still not met him. In the meantime, Williams met first with Zukofsky at Gary's Restaurant on Thursday evening, October 1, to get his ideas about the venture, and then drove in again the following night to see Moss and Kamin and finally meet West. West, then twenty-eight, was enthusiastic about the new magazine, seeing it as the continuation of the little magazines of the 1910s and '20s. He was even spending long hours at the New York Public Library on 42d Street working on an extensive bibliography of the little magazine since its beginnings. He had two girls and "an earnest young man" going through the card indexes at the library and expected to have the list ready for publication by the beginning of November.[59]

Williams had to admire West for taking on the heavy scut work of getting the new magazine together, especially since he saw himself as something of an elder statesman who'd already served his journeyman apprenticeship years before and so was not willing to do it again at forty-eight. He saw West for only a moment that first evening before Floss called him on the telephone to tell him to get back home to get ready to deliver a child. But he liked West: a tall, dark Jewish guy who reminded him of a half uncle of his whom he'd admired (was it Godwin?) who'd "died of cerebral syphilis contracted in the West Indies from a nigger when he was fourteen or so." It had made all the difference in the world to make this family connection, though of course he couldn't tell West what he'd been thinking. He found West "a very curious type, straight (I think) and capable of discriminating enthusiasm." The fact was, as would become clear over the next few months, that Williams was not overly enthusiastic about doing another magazine.[60] It seemed a young man's prerogative and, like McAlmon, he wasn't really sure the dividends would repay the immense effort involved in getting a little good work out to a pitiably small audience.

"I'm not coming in today," he wrote Zukofsky on October 9. He had the quarterly to edit and a hundred odds and ends around the house to attend to, like dragging a load of shingles into his cellar and painting the roof and getting his mother's tropical plants in from his garden with a frost expected any day now. Besides, his son Bill had just been elected captain of Rutherford High's soccer team and he'd promised to see him play. He was also active again in local politics, trying once more to get his "political poem" published and trying to get more Democrats into office in this traditionally Republican town.[61] He won *Poetry*'s Guarantor's Prize that month for his "Botticellian Trees" (that was a hundred dollars in his pocket), but at the moment he was writing little poetry.

Instead, the magazine began eating up his time—just as he'd feared. "*Contact* is to appear again," he wrote John Herrmann at the end of October, only this time it would be a quarterly. He was the editor and figured the position would last a year "or until they get fresh and begin to tell me what I can and cannot do." He'd been reading Herrmann's novel in mansucript, *What Happens,* and thought it better, for example, than Sherwood Anderson's fiction because Anderson had not really made "contact" with the life of his characters. "I don't want just raw stuff or pornographic stuff or stream of consciousness stuff," he added, "but I do want a contact without literary *side.*" Hemingway's first stories—the things McAlmon and Bird had brought out—had had the feel for the kind of thing he was looking for. But that was before Hem had gone in for "telling arrangement" and "feeling." If Hemingway had something to give him like his early stuff, then Williams would look it over. But he wasn't looking for names and he couldn't pay.[62] As for Hemingway, by 1931 he had already moved into the mainstream of American publishing while Williams—fifteen years his senior—was still looking for his first steady American publisher. After all this time, Williams was still in the front ranks of the avant-garde, but this time he was there with a whole new flock of younger writers like George Oppen, Charles Reznikoff, Carl Rakosi, Basil Bunting, Kenneth Rexroth, and of course Louis Zukofsky.

Not that that bothered Williams. At least nobody could tell him what to write. And Williams still basically believed in the little magazine as a way of featuring some one or two writers of importance. In October, it was Reznikoff, a poet and a lawyer in his mid-thirties, with a long poem that used some contemporary "legal chronicle stuff" which Williams found so good he was willing to stay with the magazine just to make sure that material got published.[63] Then it was Erskine Caldwell and Julian Shapiro in the winter of '32. Williams wanted a plain magazine without "stunts or decorations" but well printed, that was all. But he kept coming up against Moss and Kamin's interference about what would go into the thing. So one moment he was enthusiastic, thinking the magazine was going to jell, and then he was sure *Contact* would not last beyond the first number. At such times he was sure he'd gotten involved in the wrong enterprise.

At the same time, he tried to keep the fact that he was editing *Contact* away from Pound. He didn't tell Pound because he didn't want him interfering yet;[64] he didn't tell McAlmon, who was now drifting somewhere in Munich; he didn't tell Burke until January; and he was surprised when Johns wrote him in late November asking if the rumors were true about his editing another magazine, and what about *Pagany*? "Who in hell told you I was editing a quarterly?" he wrote Johns on the twenty-fourth. Well, the truth was he was, but he didn't see it as being in competition with *Pagany*. No, *Contact* was more or less a special case. He'd been busy writing the *White Mule* chapters and would have them to Johns as quickly as Johns could use them. No worry there. But no editor could reasonably expect Williams to confine all his energies to any one magazine. Not that Williams himself had any work of his own "in the first issue of this new bleat." Oh, he knew he'd probably been a fool to take the magazine on, but there it was. On top of which, he added self-pityingly, he was so "damnably weary these days with medicine all day that I fall asleep before I can pick the grapes of the evening."[65] Meanwhile the magazine continued to take shape. In early December it was the cover design and the general makeup Williams and West had to look after.

In late November, meanwhile, Pound had written Williams asking for news about the American scene. One thing on his mind was getting Zukofsky over to Europe for some Kulchur and he asked ol' Bull now what he thought. Williams answered, mimicking Pound's minestrone version of an American backwoods dialect: "Aw can't see that Zuke needs Urup just now," he wrote on December 8, "not at pussonal sacrifice on his friend's part leastwise. . . . Now his place just now is here facing the harbor and the whited Statue of Miss Liberty—which his cubicle in Brooklyn faces very pleasantly." As for himself: he still had a book of poems—his *Collected, 1921–1931*—going the rounds of the New York publishers, "a nice book too, big and fat and willing to go to bed with almost anyone for a price. But I don't want no cheap guys. I want a regular publisher what knows how to do it, you get me, with a limousine, flowers, a swell feed and, you know. . . . I ain't no Lesbian, I don't care for violets."

He filled in with other news. His oldest son would be going to college in the fall, "if he makes it and I don't get caught by the depression. So far, although I am badly in the hole on stocks I bought, I can still hold my head up, tho' not very high." His "other brat," a sophomore at Rutherford High, had played right end on the squad's second-string football team. Floss at forty was "well and getting buxom." Finally, he had seen what Pound had written about him in the June–July number of the *New Review*, printed in Paris, about Zukofsky's lone notice of Taupin's pioneering essay on Williams's importance as a writer. He especially appreciated Pound's comment that his poetry was looking stronger and stronger, especially in the face of the work of other poets whose logical constructs and superficial sequences had steadily paled beside Williams' more complex poetic strategies. For that kind of incisive comment Williams could still feel thankful and even embarrassed.[66]

Pound wrote again just before Christmas, this time to inform Williams that Eliot had been appointed professor of poetry at Harvard and that he wanted Williams to make Eliot feel at home after his long years away from America. But Williams went wild. "Pussonally," he wrote Pound on December 30, "Eliot can go to hell before I welcome him to these shores. But since your letter is so damned decent, not to say generous, I'll ignore the prof rather than tell him what I think of him. If I must get culchuh I'll take it from some one else. For I'm sure he will pizen a generation by his mere sickly presence—even in New England."[67] After all, even without Eliot, Harvard was bad enough. But Williams wrote Johns in even stronger language that same day that Pound had wanted him—Williams, the man Eliot had not even deigned to answer back in 1923—to give Eliot—the enemy—a "sweet welcome." Ha: "Sweet Thames run softly till I end my song," he crowed. Why the hell should he? "For of all the beshitten—he is the beshattest. But we must be generous and decorous—and everything but phosphorous—or sulphurous. We must lick his shit—and like it—for the sake of good manners." He'd be damned if he would. America neither needed Eliot nor wanted him.[68] And even five weeks later Williams had still not cooled down: "Let 'im come," he told Pound. "But I ain't a gonna greet him with no hozannhas. . . . I ain't never gonna talk to him ef I kin help it."[69] The truth was, as he told Johns in January, that he resented Eliot's intrusion into American literary matters, for he disliked and distrusted the man's mind and all it stood for. Whether Eliot heard any of this fulminous talk of Williams' is uncertain, but once here Eliot kept his own silence, only once referring to Williams in a lecture given at Harvard as a poet "of some local interest, perhaps."[70] Ironically, that contemptuous dismissal did more than mountains of invective to keep Williams' hatred of Eliot at white-heat pitch for the next twenty years.

At the end of December, Williams received an advance copy of his *A Novelette and Other Prose (1921–1931)*, which George Oppen had had printed in Toulon, France, under the imprint of To Press. It was a swell book, he told Zukofsky, though he'd been surprised to learn that "To" was a noun. But once you thought about a name like that, Williams added, it stayed with you. What he'd had in mind, Zukofsky told him, was the idea of drinking to someone's health: this book to the health of Williams, as another would be to the health of Reznikoff or Oppen or himself. One thing about Zukofsky: he could make those little words work every bit as hard as Williams himself. Three weeks later, when a staff correspondent from the *Herald Tribune* interviewed Williams on a Sunday afternoon, Williams was still kidding about the publisher's name. Perhaps "To" was, after all, the dative of the noun, though of which noun he didn't know. As for *January* itself, it was "supposed to portray the wreck that occurs in a physician's life by the tempo of modern times." He'd used his own life, he explained, and the excitement caused by the flu epidemic of '29. He'd also written about his wife, "and of course, no one ever writes about his wife, so that makes it remarkable." What he did not add was that he'd also written about other women besides his wife, which had been part of the problem Bill and Floss had had to face in being thrown violently together again after a year's separation. But that was a matter for his improvisations and poems, not for the newspapers. The old chestnut came up again in this interview too: about Dr. Williams' being a physican *and* a poet. But Williams told his interviewer that he did not find that particularly unusual. Chekhov had been a doctor. And Oliver Wendell Holmes. And Keats. It was, he explained, a natural reaction to turn from the materialism of medicine to the imaginative world of literature.[71]

Williams had also found a publisher for his collection of short stories, which he had decided to call *The Knife of the Times and Other Stories.* A man named Angel Flores who ran the Dragon Press out of Ithaca, New York, published the book in an edition of five hundred copies. It contained eleven stories, beginning with an extraordinarily fine and understated story of a lesbian relationship between two middle-class women of his acquaintance—the "knife" of the times being, therefore, the repression of sexuality and passion in the lives of many Americans—and ended with a revised version of his minor masterpiece, "Old Doc Rivers." Half of the stories had been published in little magazines or anthologies, but half no one had yet seen. Incredibly, Flores had moved with lightning speed in getting the book out. Williams had sent the manuscript volume to him in January and four weeks later Flores had sent him proofs and was telling Williams to expect bound copies in two weeks. "This is too like lightning for comfort," he confessed to Johns. "It's left me frightened lest the stories turn out to be bad. I've read them again but haven't the least idea whether there is any worth in them. Hell, sometimes I wish I had never written a word—or else nothing but incomprehensible jargon. There is too intimate a contact between one's intimate mind and an antagonistic public in all that might be worth while." "Posthumous praise," he added, was the "only acceptable sort."[72] Williams had listened to his patients for years confess their deepest secrets to him as he examined them. He had listened with sympathy and compassion, while they spoke of broken promises and of fears never even uttered to their spouses, and Williams had nodded, refusing, as Father Rasles had refused, to judge them. And now he had breathed life into them again, including himself and even Floss.

Flores kept his word. The book was published in early March in an attractive format. But then that was the end of it. Flores did nothing to sell the books, and three years later one of Williams' colleagues—who'd been down to a convention at Atlantic City in the summer of '35—found a pile of them in a box on the boardwalk selling for fifteen cents each. And though he and Flores had not exchanged words since early 1933, Williams was astounded at the news and asked his friend to pick up as many of the remainders as he could get when he was down in Atlantic City next time. A few weeks later Williams had them packed in a crate, sitting in his study. Ah, sweet fame.[73]

That same January, too, Williams was busy getting the first issue of *Contact* finished and out. He read through the January issue of *Pagany* carefully, trying to determine for himself how *Contact* would differ from the more established magazine which also carried his name on its masthead. First of all, he knew, *Contact* would be smaller than *Pagany*, so that its audience would necessarily be smaller, more narrowly focused. As he had with *Blues* and the first *Contact*, he meant to bear down more heavily on the significance of the word and would stress his own preoccupations in the "Comments" section, which would appear in each number. *Pagany*, he told Johns, had been the result "of effective good taste in selecting material the hidebound minds of present day publishers have muffed."[74] But what he really implied was that *Pagany*, by failing to formulate a strong manifesto, had remained unfocused, its light scattered and diffuse. Williams and Nathanael West, on the other hand, had both been thinking in terms of a possible continuity with the classic little magazines of the past which were now all dead, going back to Steiglitz's groundbreaking *Camera Work* of 1902, and then those later pioneers like *Papyrus*, *The Egoist*, *Poetry*, *The Little Review* (which had featured Joyce's *Ulysses*), *Others*, *Broom*, *Contact I*, *The Dial*, and *transition*. In the first number of their new *Contact* they published Cummings, Zukofsky, Reznikoff, Parker Tyler of *Blues*, S. J. Perelman, Ben Hecht, and an essay by Diego Rivera on Mickey Mouse. Not bad for a first number. And yet it was one delay after another in getting the magazine out, until Williams told one writer that "*Contact* is delayed" might "almost be used on coins instead of *E Pluribus Unum*."[75]

But by mid-February the first issue—such as it was—was out. In his first "Comment," Williams replied self-consciously to the criticism he half expected from the left. What was Williams doing bringing out another literary quarterly in the middle of the Depression? "Put to its full use," he answered bravely, "writing has nothing to convey, either pungently or crassly." He already knew the kind of argument that could be used against him: "People are in distress the world over, writing will not relieve them (or make them worse off). Why not take the money there is for a magazine like this and give it away—as food—to the bums, for instance, living in packing cases over near the East River these winter nights?" But what value did money have in itself, Williams retorted. Hell, there was "food enough rotting now in the world, even within sight of the place where these men are hanging out, to feed them every day in the year." Money had nothing to do with the depression of the human spirit, he insisted, but bad writing—the misuses of the human imagination —had. For that was what kept people under. Theories and propaganda were beside the point for the serious writer. What mattered was the "one thing, the word that is possessing him at the moment he writes." Good writing was its own reason for being.[76]

But being an editor meant writing letter after letter to contributors and would-be contributors, Williams was learning, and he was impatient with that sort of thing. He was expending so much energy on the contributions of others in the winter of '32 that his own writing was beginning to suffer. He wrote to Johns asking for something of Erskine Caldwell's, and then wrote Julian Shapiro—West's friend—to say that he wanted to print a short story of his but couldn't unless Shapiro called it something else besides "Once in a Sedan and Twice Standing up." That title, Williams remarked soberly, seemed provocative and even misleading, as if *Contact* were stressing the pornographic.[77] But Shapiro refused and sent his story to *Pagany* instead. When Williams wrote Shapiro again, he was at Passaic General waiting to deliver a baby who was taking its own good time coming into the world. He'd just read Shapiro's story in *Pagany* and was writing to ask him to send him a new one for *Contact*. This time, he promised, he would print it just as it was.[78] Then, still waiting for the baby, he dashed another letter off to Johns to say how much he'd liked what Shapiro had done; "Once in a Sedan" was a story "full of fresh observation, acute thought, courage."[79] Williams also solicited other stories, only to have West as coeditor turn them down. And he himself had to turn down work with rejection letters like: "You have a quality worth attention, I shan't attempt definition just now. . . . I dread something banal in the next line and it ain't there. Curious. Almost bad at times. I suppose it's your honesty that rescues you."[80] Sometimes writing rejection letters became a game of verbal shuttlecocks. But he could also tear into a writer he felt was too naive in his vision. "Our life is putrescent about us," he wrote one writer just starting out. "We've got to live in it. We're not kids any longer. . . . I don't care how young you are, you've got to live in it as well as I. Your intelligence doesn't have to be mellow—sophisticated—what you will: but it must at least realize what we are up against. Let's at least probe our immediate hells to the bottom."[81]

On top of all that work, there was Williams' general disappointment in the first issue. He told Johns he dreaded his seeing the magazine, promising to do better next time, when he would let Kamin know exactly where he stood.[82] He even confessed to Zukofsky that he considered the first number "the cheapest sort of a subterfuge for good faith in carrying out an agreement,"[83] and that he even felt "disgraced" by it.[84] When he wrote to Shapiro at the end of March asking once more for a story, he was still apologizing for the first number, adding that Pep West had assured him that things would be better in the future.[85] A few days later Shapiro relented and sent a short story called "The Fire at the Catholic Church," which Williams published, just as it was, in the second issue.

Editorial sessions between Williams and West usually took place at the Sutton Hotel in New York, where West worked behind the main desk. The two men would go over a pile of manuscripts in West's room at the Sutton and then decide together, finally, which pieces were to be used and which rejected. The second number, published in May, contained work by West (a section of *Miss Lonelyhearts*), Reznikoff, Nancy Cunard, Marsden Hartley, McAlmon, Caldwell and Williams himself, who contributed "The Cod Head" and another poem from his Canadian experience, "The Canada Lily." His "Comment" once again stressed the importance of good writing, but it also dwelt on the sudden death of Hart Crane at thirty-three, who, Williams had just learned, had either jumped or fallen from the stern of the SS *Orizaba* ninety miles east of Key West, before disappearing into shark-infested waters.[86]

"This primitive and actual America must sober us," Williams wrote. If Americans could not find a virtue in the reality of their lives lived here, they would find it nowhere else. The answer would certainly never be found by using "profound (and borrowed) symbolism." He was clearly thinking of Crane's attempts at a symbolist synthesis in *The Bridge*, a poetic approach that for Williams had been wrong from the start. Americans had to learn to rely instead on the *fact* of a Boston or a Chicago rather than on the dream of the new Heavenly Jerusalem, even if they did no more with such facts than learn to record them accurately in all their apparent desolation (as a photographer like Walker Evans was even then doing). Williams was not talking about the regionalism of a Frost or a Sandburg, but rather about the realization of the local: "the objective intimacy of our hand to mouth, eye to brain existence." Hart Crane had shown that it was possible to sound "like" the classics, Williams noted with an objectivity bordering on cruelty, by using syntactic inversions and high-sounding clichés, fuzzy and inaccurate observation and pigheadedness in the face of the facts. But what was most difficult to achieve was a comprehension not of regional dialect but of the true vulgate, the vernacular as one heard it spoken about one every day, and then to seek the musical forms that inhered fragilely, gossamerlike, in that language. It was of the first importance for the modern artist to learn from the thing itself what its own most profound implications were.

And though Williams did not elaborate, the truth was that Crane's spectacular death had made him more of a threat to American poetry than he would have been had he still been alive. A strong contender for the laurels had died, leaving Williams more vulnerable than ever: "Certainly Hart Crane bumped himself off with no thought of improving or marring his condition," Williams closed his comments by finally naming his contender. "Maybe he didn't suicide at all, maybe he was drunk and just rolled off the ship into the sea—unless he has left some record explaining the act and with which I am unfamiliar. . . . If his work shapes up well after there has been time to evaluate it, so much the better." *Ave atque vale.* Let it go at that.[87]

A month later he tried again to exorcise his obsession with Crane, this time in the pages of *Contempo*. There he managed to praise the extraordinary music he'd heard in Crane, especially in his *White Buildings* volume—"the sound of continual surf" in the poems, "the alternate peak and back rush of waves in them." But the words, the necessary hard-edged words, had escaped Crane, as if somehow he'd spent his short maturity trying to please "someone in charge of a New York Sunday Book Supplement." Crane had tried too hard to be "cosmic," Williams had come to realize, when he should have been more honest in seeing how really low his life had become, especially toward the end. He also hated Crane's sentimentality, the vatic poet in the pulpit, as in the rhapsodic close of the "Atlantis," which sang the benzine-rinsed vision of the Brooklyn Bridge transformed. "I cannot grow rhapsodic with him," Williams wrote, with this "evangel of the post-war, the replier to the romantic apostle of *The Waste Land.*" In fact, Crane's use of language had been "a direct step backward to the bad poetry of any age but especially to that triumphant regression [French symbolism] which followed Whitman and imitated . . . the Frenchman [Mallarmé] and came to a head in T. S. Eliot excellently." Where he did like Crane was in a clean, simple poem like "Indiana," though he knew as well as anyone else that such poetry was not Crane's real strength. He also knew that the agony of Crane's incredible life as the roaring boy drinking himself into oblivion and cruising after sailors in the Red Hook district of Brooklyn, the agony of his desolation and abandonment and early death, had thrown "a white glare over his best work—in the manner of the light in Van Gogh's painting." The truth was that Williams could not forgive Crane his death.[88]

*
**

Yet Crane was only part of the larger picture of American poetry for Williams. Once Williams had put together the stories that made up his first collection and had them out in search of a publisher, he had turned his attention back to poetry once more. But it had been a fallow period for him. A poem here and there, but nothing like the effort he had expended to create *Spring and All*. It had been his assembling of his *Collected Poems, 1921–1931* that had finally stirred his interest in the poem again. Hadn't he hoped to use *Contact*, really, to get good writing—prose and poetry—before a small but discerning audience? But from the start he'd felt hamstrung by the magazine's backers. In December 1931, for example, he had written a long and detailed "Open Letter" about the state of contemporary poetry, sparked by something Kay Boyle had asked him.

He'd first thought of using this letter as a manifesto of sorts for the first issue of *Contact*, but space limitations and his desire to get younger and less-known writers before the public—like West and Reznikoff and Zukofsky—had won out over his personal need to get the letter printed.

That letter had been an important summary on Williams' part, a summary that dealt with the progress of modern poetry from its beginnings up through 1930. "There is no workable poetic form extant among us today," Williams had begun. There were forerunners like Joyce and Stein, but the direction of poetry did not mean returning to these figures or to any other, for that matter. Frankly, Williams did not believe in the continuity of history or in an uninterrupted great tradition, though he did think that the present moment was as capable of producing a classic as any age in the past had been. For himself, he'd done almost no poetry of late while he studied the problem of form. Instead, he was working with prose, which was also capable of throwing up its jewels to be later "cleaned and grouped" and applied to the problem of the poem. He was also closely listening to the speech patterns of his patients and friends and neighbors (as his short stories clearly demonstrate) and "watching for patches of metrical coherence." In short, he was trying to snatch a living music out of the air.

His own preoccupation was with words, as Juan Gris's had been with paint. And all the socialism and communism and other isms would never convince him that poetry's first allegiance was to anything other than words, words related "to the immediacy of my life." He rejected the vers librists and other "disintegrationists," insisting that poetry had to be measured, though that new measure had yet to appear. Pound, he thought, had come closest to providing the artist with the most viable pattern in his *Cantos*. It was "a medieval inspiration," granted, "patterned on a substitution of medieval simulacra for a possible, not yet extant modern and living material" which could provide at least a sort of "precomposition." What Williams seems to have meant by that was that one could extract Pound's musical patterns—themselves tied to the Anglo-Saxon, the Provençal, the early Italian and Spanish, the Greek and Latin—and wed them to contemporary speech patterns by observing the laws of quantity informing the old poetry.

He talked of the shortcomings and strengths of Robinson Jeffers, E. A. Robinson, Wallace Stevens, Yvor Winters, Robert Frost—none of whom had provided the necessary mastery—insisting that the new poetry was not a matter, finally, of theory, but of the actual making of poems. The poetic line would have to be rethought, for as it existed, it twisted and falsified speech as one actually heard it spoken in Williams' experience. Instead, it was "in the newness of a live speech that the new line" would be found to exist. Actual speech was the first necessity, "the fountain of the line into which the pollutions of a poetic manner and inverted phrasing should never again be permitted to drain."[89]

He continued his meditation in a letter to Pound six months later. When he considered the "more or less downrightness" of what Homer had achieved in the *Iliad* and them compared that with "the inexplicitness of modern verse" with its "increasingly difficult music," he at least understood the direction the modern revolution in poetry had taken: toward a more sophisticated quantitative music that would incorporate the subtleties of the spoken language, together with a further accuracy in presenting the image. It had been, then, the lack of focus (as, presumably, in Crane and Mallarmé and even Eliot) that had driven him as an artist to "the edge of insanity."[90]

Finally, he summed up his thoughts about the state of the art in an open letter to Ford Madox Ford written in mid-September, a letter that also praised the pioneering work Pound had done in the *XXX Cantos*. He began with a meditation on Depression America and the need—now more than ever—for an American art. "One hopes," he began, "that America will one day quit disfiguring the landscape of its vastly charming easts and wests and norths and souths and begin to learn (if they have not lost the art forever) once again to enjoy it. When they do they will find the work of our Ezra somewhere up ahead of them—waiting on the hill."

A disfigured new world landscape: he was not speaking in figures. He meant

> the actual blasphemy which has overtaken my own New Jersey for instance and consists in the chaos of factory towns and their squalid suburbs. This chaos and this squalor are pure stupidity and they breed blindness, arrested minds and a furious desperation of the spirit. . . . One of these days all necessary factory work will be done in one twentieth of the mutually cancelling machine menageries we have today—these will be decently arranged in reasonably healthful localities with properly appointed cottages around them and the horror of a past age will become apparent.

Not that he had any utopian illusions that factory hands in 1982 would be gathering of a Sunday afternoon to "go into polite ecstacies over the *Cantos*." But, like Pound, Williams believed in the profound importance of the writer in shaping a culture. And "unless a people is cultured enough to express themselves fully, in all colors and shapes of their living moods," Williams believed that they would be "unfit to have intercourse with their neighbors and unable to make head or tail of their own lives." Pound had realized this even more than himself, Williams was willing to grant. He had molded his *Cantos* and made them "fit for modern bruising and fit to catch in a modern way the delicate invisible waves modern explorations have given us for the refinement of our existences." It was a form that was both tough and delicate, "indestructible and infinitely alive to the most frail 'waves,'" so that the *Cantos* had come to signify for Williams nothing less than "a bulwark against this destructive America which I detest." There were difficulties in the *Cantos*, but those were more a defensive ploy to keep the oxen from destroying the artist while he went about his necessary work of inventing new forms, of getting said what had to be said as well as he could. Americans could do worse, he insisted, than to give this American expatriate a penthouse in New York City—an ivory tower overlooking the new world—and let him go about his work.[91]

Even as Williams was summing up the state of American poetry, Gorham Munson, now editing *The New English Weekly* from London, wrote to ask Williams about his opinions on Anglo-American literary relationships. With Eliot recently at Harvard—the man who as editor had refused to publish Williams in the influential *Criterion*—and with Williams virtually unknown in England, Munson should have suspected that Williams would do his wild man revolutionary act. Which is exactly what Williams did, writing a heavily satirical caricature of the American man of letters summarizing modern British literature in the 1930s. He began, naturally, by dismissing the "blinding stupidity" of "our Mr. Eliot's religistic [sic] attitudes," praised Shakespeare—that "uneducated actor-author"—and next praised his Grandmother Wellcome, explaining that he was—through her—"rather English at heart." Virginia "Wolf" [sic] he did not understand at all; she seemed "more like some creature from Hans Christian Andersen's fairy tales than a human being." He had once written to D. H. Lawrence thanking him for his review of *In the American Grain* and congratulating him "on his un-English breadth of spirit—for which he snubbed me." He dismissed Wyndham Lewis: "New York laughs at his puny inventions." And as for Rebecca West. He'd once answered her criticism of Joyce's *Anna Livia Plurabelle*, only to find that "a month later she recanted everything she had said in the first article and praised Joyce as the genius he is—using every point I had made against her in my defense of him." That, he said, hadn't been "nice." What he did enjoy, on the other hand, was the "crisp prose" the British were capable of, as in their medical texts. But for the most part Williams believed that Americans would have to develop their own vernacular without second thoughts about where England was going. The American poet was on his own.[92]

Munson published Williams' response in the July 21 issue of the *Weekly* and Williams soon forgot about it. But ten weeks later, in the October 6 issue of the same magazine, Williams read an article by the English critic Austin Warren, called "Some Periodicals of the American Intelligentsia." Warren began by attacking Williams' letter for being

"heavily humorous" and "pretentiously and presumably ironically ignorant." The good doctor, Warren wrote, was a primary example of what
Matthew Arnold had once called the French critic who had dared to speak
about English literature: *sangrenus*—guilty of impudently absurd literary
judgments. Warren then went on to discuss the New York critics under
several headings: first, those who criticized only those writers who also
lived in New York, a cozy little arrangement; secondly, the professor-
critics who wrote for the *Sewanee Review* and who utilized the literary
tradition to evaluate the present; next, the uncritical modernism of H. L.
Mencken and the *American Mercury*; then the new leftists writing for
The New Republic, including Malcolm Cowley, Matthew Josephson, and
Edmund Wilson; then the "anti-literary" school of Richard Johns's
Pagany; and—finally—Williams' own *Contact,* to which Williams had
contributed "poems, sketches and rather inarticulate editorials." But,
though critics as responsible as Munson and Burke had praised Williams
in print, Warren was inclined to attribute this to a sense of loyalty to a
leader of the old avant-garde who had "never graduated out of the little
magazines." Williams' importance was, finally, something personal rather than literary. This American cousin at least made a nice contrast to a
more refined British taste, for there was in his writing something
distinctively American, i.e., "something energetic, breezy, uncouth."[93]

   "And did you see the roasting I got in *The New English Review* by
someone signing himself Professor Austin Warren?" Williams asked
Zukofsky on the seventeenth. "Do you know of any such person? I
answered his attack at once."[94] To Johns he was even stronger in his
feelings: "If that's the best our 'Professors' can do they'd better go back to
the old fashioned corn cob for wiping themselves when they feel inspired.
I answered the guy instanter as far as I personally was concerned in his
screed but whether or not they'll print what I had to say I don't know."[95]
Williams' rejoinder did, however, appear in the form of a letter to the
editor, published on November 10. He had lashed out at Warren's general
impropriety in attacking as he had, and then went on to attack Warren's
separate points. As for the little magazines: one did not "graduate" out of
them. One either wrote well or one didn't. That was the only standard
that mattered. Secondly, there *was* an American language as distinct
from the English: "I stand squarely on the existence and practicability of
an American language—among others *like* English which are not English
—and a complete independence from English literature in each case, i.e.,
that of Joyce and our present-day American writers for example." For
Williams, it was the English moderns who were writing in a foreign
language as far as he was concerned. As for the writers in *Contact:* they
wrote as they wrote to express their specific reality. Take it or leave it.
End the battle of the books.[96]

Williams had attended to the French connection earlier in the year, but they too had fared little better than the British. Both, as far as he was concerned, were no nearer relations to American literature than cousins. With René Taupin returning to France in February 1932, Williams had written Zukofsky to tell Taupin for him how much he'd appreciated what Taupin had done for American letters, even if Williams could not agree with all he'd written. Taupin was "a bitter pill for us to swallow sometimes," Williams admitted, because he made Americans "look a rather negative lot." But then, he added, most tonics *were* bitter. The problem with Taupin was this: that he too often appeared "to be no more than a Frenchman looking for that which is French—a sort of French scout in the pay (one might almost say) of France to organize her literary colonizations. This leaves out of his consideration everything (almost) not french in our work. . . ."[97] And four days earlier, Williams had written to the editor of an undergraduate leaflet written in French that the French poets had had no influence on him whatever: "I have never read one modern French poem that I can remember having seen, though I must say I have stumbled on bits of poems." On the other hand, he'd been deeply influenced by French painting and by the French spirit, "which, through my mother, is partly my own."[98] That was the extent of the connection there: not Mallarmé, not Baudelaire, not even—*pace* Pound —Rimbaud, though Villon, of course, had long been one of his favorites, and so too that ribald French physician Rabelais.

At the beginning of June 1932, Williams also wrote to Marianne Moore to praise her for some poems he'd read of hers in a magazine called *New Poetry*. "Your words," he wrote, "have an immediate quality which only comes when the intelligence matches the acuteness of the sensual perception to which you add an aimed heat of the emotions, without which there can never be anything but blur." Her poetry was the very antithesis, in other words, of what he'd said about Crane. He also brought her up to date on the news. McAlmon was floating around in Majorca now and had written Williams to get him to ask Moore for something for *Contact*. Bill Williams, Jr., had graduated from high school and Williams had just driven him up to Williams College in Williamstown, Massachusetts, to look that campus over. The boy had hated Latin in high school and so would have to make up a special exam before he could be admitted to Williams, but his parents were sanguine he would make it. As for young Paul, he'd just finished his sophomore year at Rutherford and wanted to play baseball in the worst way, even though he still couldn't hit the ball. Williams himself was finally wearing glasses and his hair was beginning to vanish. "That's an odd thing," he added, "to find oneself growing toward fifty. Not that I mind it in the least. But I don't like not being able to see dust flecks quite so distinctly as formerly." That was hard, especially on an imagist. Even Pound, in spite of all the tennis he played, was getting thick around the waist. Still, there were compensations.[99]

He and Floss took no vacation that summer. Instead, Williams had the roof porch over the north wing of the house ringed with teak railing so that he could walk outdoors from what he called the vantage of his own Alps. It was a local version of the sublime. He felt as though he were on the deck of a steamer up there, with the house sailing through the trees.[100] Bill Jr. passed his exam on the twenty-third of June and entered Williams in September in the class of '36, the so-called Depression class.[101] The Williamses made short trips up to Monroe and to West Haven, but otherwise Williams stayed close to home, tied down with the problem of making enough for his son's tuition and getting out the third issue of *Contact.*

The second issue—the May issue—had not actually come out until mid-June, and by then it was time to push on with the next. By then, however, Williams and West were both feeling down on the magazine. The delays were "disheartening," Williams wrote his old acquaintance Bob Brown in early June, and "the work uninspiring." It seemed odd that "only the shitty pays."[102] And now Kamin was stepping in again to tell West and Williams that he wanted the third number to feature American Communist writers. Williams thought about that one for a few days, and then told Kamin to hold off until the winter on that issue. By the end of September, Williams and West had chosen the manuscripts that were to go in the third number and then turned them over to their backers. But a month later, neither man knew where they stood. Williams only hoped that the third issue would appear sooner or later. And by then he realized finally that there would be no fourth.

He and West had worked hard to make the magazine worthwhile, but they could no longer go on. After what they considered "repeated and senseless delays over the printing of the 3rd issue," they'd "decided to send all manuscripts back (without explanation) and call it a day."[103] Finally, *Contact* 3 made its appearance in early November, with work by Williams, West, McAlmon, Shapiro, Farrell, Herrmann, Rakosi, and even Yvor Winters. For his "Comment" this time, Williams chose to attack both the new right and the new left. After all, it had been the political disagreement with Moss and Kamin that had really signaled the death of the magazine. For the right Williams chose Eliot and the academics, with their heresy that poetry "increases in virtue as it is removed from contact with a vulgar world." Williams saw this heresy as being fostered by the American universities themselves, pointing to Eliot's appointment at Harvard as a sign of the times. But he also pointed to the heresy of the Communists. "Never, may it be said, has there ever been great poetry that was not born out of a communist intelligence," he wanted to make clear—as he did here and would reiterate in his poem, "The Pink Church," written fifteen years later. For the Communist intelligence was essentially democratic and rebellious, particularly against the old schism "that would have the spirit a lopsided affair of high and low." In Williams' myth of the Communist he evoked "the unchristian sweep of Shakespeare, the cantless, unsectarian bitterness of Dante against his time," the figure and example of St. Francis. For the true Communist spirit was such that it would not speak to please anyone, not even the Communist Party. Poetry was still the one solid element on which one's life could rely, creating as it did "a world in fact come to an arrest of self realization." No wonder, then, that with this (heretical) view of communism Williams was never going to get a fourth (Communist) number of *Contact* out.[104]

Besides, *Contact* had done its real job by getting Pep West the recognition he so much deserved. It had always been that way with Williams: the little magazine existed to get new talent before some sort of public, some one or two names. Having done that, it could then die. Besides, Williams had tired of the whole thing. He would never again take on another editorship, he wrote Marsden Hartley in mid-December. "People who have money to put up for such ventures are too slippery for me and my time is too limited." He kept his word.[105]

At year's end, then, Williams was more depressed than ever. (Even West would soon leave for California and that contact would soon be broken, though Williams would continue to pay tribute to his young friend long after West had died with his wife in the crackup of their station wagon in 1940. Williams would review West's novels—two of them—posthumously in 1950, and would remember West in the elegiac section of *Paterson* 4, when West had still been at the Hotel Sutton struggling to get his first novel finished.) Furthermore, Williams' own book of poems, after all this time, was still without a publisher. The New York publishers rejected it, and Angel Flores—who had published Williams' short stories and now had the poetry script—refused even to answer Williams' letters. Finally, Williams had written to Julian Shapiro, whose first novel, *The Water Wheel*, Williams had read and which Flores was about to publish, asking if he—Shapiro—had anything to do with poisoning Flores toward Williams. Shapiro was shocked by the suggestion and asked Williams what the hell he meant by that accusation.[106] Then Williams backed off a bit, asking Shapiro to intercede for him to get the manuscript Flores had been holding onto for so long. Finally, Flores returned the poems in February 1933, saying he couldn't do anything with them and anyway didn't care for Williams' hangdog attitude. For his part, Williams merely dismissed Flores. It was a bad time for Williams, and he could show that he too had teeth when backed up against the wall.

Even George Antheil had turned Williams down. In the summer of '32, the two men had discussed the possibility of Williams' doing the libretto for an opera on an American theme, and though Williams did not actually get far with it, he had at least outlined an American opera on the subject of George Washington. Washington was, of course, another of his heroes in the American grain and would come—over the next several years—to more and more resemble Williams himself. But in early '33, Williams was complaining of Antheil's "perfidy," of having begged off, leaving Williams with a partial libretto and no composer. [107]

And now, at the end of 1932, Burke was writing him, asking Williams for a prose manuscript, something different, to be published by some new photostatic process. "I have the book you want lying here in my strong box just screaming to get out," Williams wrote Burke on January 6. It had been "waiting to piss itself forth on the woild for twenty moons or more." What Williams was sending Burke was *The Embodiment of Knowledge,* begun in the summer of '28 and recently left moldering. Now here was a chance to get the thing into print after all. "It is a series of writings," he explained, "very random in general arrangement but with one burning theme running through the whole with many historical and other examples—such as french painting as a whole—the character of Shakespeare and the precise value of his work—the education of the American male—and all the agglomerate bellyaches I have suffered for the past ten years—to the one end that there is no knowledge . . . but my own." If Burke published it, however, he would have to publish it exactly as it stood.[108]

Burke read the manuscript and then wrote Williams that he was unconvinced by the logic of Williams' arguments. Hell, Williams answered, he hadn't meant to *convince.* "I thought what you were after was something to print which would amuse, puzzle, entice people suffering from the depression," Williams wrote Burke on the twenty-sixth. "I didn't expect you to be convinced. . . . I have to go on and want to go on living for a few years more perhaps. . . . I have gradually made enough notes, here and there, to keep me busy clearing them up and developing them for a long time after I retire—if ever. I should dread an old age divorced from the thoughts and actions of my more vigorous years." Burke had spotted John Dewey's influence in the *Embodiment* as a weakness, but Williams rejoined strongly that if all he'd done was merely follow Dewey in his manuscript he would "vomit and quit—any time."[109] Still, Burke wrote to say he couldn't use *The Embodiment.*

Well, then, Williams wrote back on February 11, there were now seventeen chapters of the *White Mule,* a project that had become—since the previous fall—a real source of consolation for him. It was the one thing he felt he was doing right. And if Burke didn't want that, then there was "a full size book of poems—all my unpublished (in book form) poems that have been collecting for the last ten years—and more."[110] Burke wrote back that he was interested in the novel, but the fact was, as Williams told Zukofsky, that the *White Mule* was still only one-fifth finished and it was "not a thing which can be unrolled like toilet paper."

Practice too in the winter of '33 was "plumb shot to hell." The phone was uncomfortably idle, and when it rang, it was to say that a patient couldn't afford to pay him yet. So Williams found himself with more time to write, but in no mood to do so.[111] His friend Bob Brown had bought a house at Atlantic Highlands on the south Jersey shore, and Williams had written him that nothing would give him more pleasure than to plan a nonliterary beer bash on Brown's lawn in the late spring to inaugurate the end of Prohibition and the new Era of Beer. Williams himself would "bear" the costs.[112] For, if they never had a great deal of money, they had not wanted, either, during the Depression years. They had enough to get their sons through good private schools and enough for some modest investments. So Williams wanted to throw a wild beer party for his friends, now, with the insanity of Prohibition behind them. Having that midwinter's dream in front of him would somehow get him through his present despondency, his failure to get published, the tedium of case histories and nurses' notes at the hospital. On top of all that, Floss was not feeling well and he missed Bill. As for Paul, the kid kept stealing his cigarettes. There was also another outbreak of influenza in December and January which kept Williams working day and night and out of New York almost altogether. He even missed city life with all its heats and humors. The one bright moment in that otherwise miserable winter occurred when Franklin Delano Roosevelt—the "good President," as Williams called him—took office at the beginning of March, returning a Democrat to the White House for the first time in a dozen years.[113]

When Pound asked Williams in March for a sheaf of poems for the *Active Anthology* he was assembling for Faber & Faber—"active" in the sense that the writers he was assembling were still active, still developing —Williams sent him twenty-one typewritten pages via Zukofsky, who gave them a final check before sending them on to Pound. Williams had chosen his selection from his still unpublished *Collected*, with the explanation that he found the group "excellently representative" and wanted it published just as he had submitted it. There were fifteen poems included, among them pieces from *Spring and All*, "The Cod Head," and a recent one: "Sea-Trout and Butterfish." As for a comment about himself, Williams—exasperated with his repeated failure to find a publisher—told Pound to say that he had in hand "a volume of verse which I have been in the process of making for the past ten years, that it is the best collection of verse in America today and that I can't find a publisher—while, at the same time, every Sunday literary supplement has pages of book titles representing the poetry of my contemporaries." For over a year he had had "the best agent in New York fairly comb the city for me" without luck. What Williams personally took this failure to get published to mean was that his conception of poetry was not that of his contemporaries, and tried to leave it at that.[114]

A week later he wrote to Burke again to say that he'd finally managed to "dress the carcasses" of the *White Mule* fragment and the *Collected Poems* for him and would be sending them on in a few days. He was sorry that the *White Mule* manuscript was as rough looking as it was—he was sending the original—and he feared that the poems would offend Burke's taste. But at the moment that collection was the best he could offer.[115] At the same time, he was working hard to get a clean copy of both the poems and the novel off to another New York agent: Maxim Lieber.[116] Two weeks later, on April 3, he wrote Burke again to clarify what he was doing; "No doubt the messy scripts have reached you by this time." He'd sent clean scripts to Lieber, explaining that he'd thought it best, finally, "to let him handle the whole matter of disposing of these things for me if possible."[117] And then, after another two weeks, Williams wrote Burke again to say that Lieber would be coming as his agent to see Burke about his doing the scripts, "as a first step in his selling campaign." Williams hoped Burke would do them both and that that would be the end of the matter.[118]

Burke held onto the scripts, but nothing came of it. "I seldom succeed in finding a publisher," Williams told a friend in mid-July, still looking for someone to do either the poems or the *White Mule*. He had even become philosophical about his bad luck. "Occasionally a book" of his would get "into print." As for most books that appeared week after week in places like the Sunday *Times:* those would eliminate themselves. He was sure that good work would continue to surface and the rest of it merely sink. He was as sure of that as he was "that scientific discoveries into the depths of physics and chemistry will not be lost." What mattered was that one remain "at the advancing edge of art: that's the American tradition."[119] But by October, having just turned fifty and still without a publisher, he could complain that he was fed up with all concerted efforts and united fronts on the part of artists to help each other. "Why should I at my age waste any more time seeking for others that which I have never been able to find for myself," he finally complained. "I can't find a publisher. All the mags turn me down. . . . There is no real desire for united effort. Never has been. We shit away every chance we have by putting out little piddling magazines here and there." The truth was that, as far as Williams was concerned, there wasn't "enough good writing in the entire U.S. to keep one good magazine going for a year." In fact he could now admit that both he and Pep West had been "positively nauseated by the crap that came into the *Contact* office."[120]

And then, having descended that far, Williams suddenly had his publisher. Carl Rakosi's Objectivist Press, with offices on West 36th Street in New York, as successor to Zukofsky's To Press, agreed in October to do the *Collected Poems* in an edition of five hundred copies. George Oppen was "the angel" behind this venture, as Williams acknowledged, for the Objectivists were a small, dedicated "organization of writers who are publishing their own work and that of other writers whose work they think ought to be read." Williams had needed someone to publish his poems; he had tried the commercial houses and, even with an agent, had failed miserably. Now the younger men like Zukofsky and Oppen and Rakosi had come to the rescue. And, in spite of what he'd said about the community of artists, Williams preferred to think of this project as a community venture. Each volume put out by the Objectivists would be introduced by someone known in the field. And so, for his *Collected*, Williams asked Stevens to do the introduction, at the same time asking Burke to do the introduction to Charles Reznikoff's prose work, *Testimony*, portions of which Williams had published in *Contact*. Again it was Louis Zukofsky who went over Williams' protean script, making the final cuts and arrangements. The same day that Williams wrote Zukofsky about his own script, he wrote to Burke about Reznikoff, since Reznikoff—Williams explained—was too "diffident" to ask Burke himself to do the introduction. "It would be of great help," he explained, "to our budding Press if you'd take on the job."[121] Burke replied at once that he would do the introduction, and Stevens, to Williams' relief, also consented to try his hand at an introduction, telling Williams to omit it if he didn't care for it.

By early December, when Williams had the galleys for the book of poems in front of him, he had also received Steven's introduction. And now he confessed to Burke that it had not been what he had expected. In fact he'd been rather surprised by it. Still, he thought he detected a "general appeal in it. It may sell the book yet—especially if the right Sunday Supplement guy sees it and falls for it."[122] But the more he scrutinized Stevens' words, the stranger they seemed. "It's funny, disturbing, what you will," he told his friend Wilson.[123] Moreover, it was very brief. But what Williams was especially uneasy about was Stevens' breaking Williams' poems into two polarities: a sentimental poetic mode, and a tough, antipoetic mode. "What Williams gives," Stevens had written, ". . . is not sentiment but the reaction from sentiment, or, rather, a little sentiment, very little, together with acute reaction." As far as he could see, Williams was a thorough romantic, the ivory tower poet who found life tolerable only because, from the top, he had "such an exceptional view of the public dump and the advertising signs of Snider's Catsup, Ivory Soap and Chevrolet Cars." Bill Williams was the image of Lessing's Laocoön: "the realist struggling to escape from the serpents of the unreal."[124]

Williams would keep coming back to this introduction, regarding it with the passage of the years as both misinformed and a left-handed salute. The antipoetic might exist in Stevens' mind as part of his own poetic, Williams was ready to concede, but it had no part in Williams' world. For him there was only the poem with a form large enough to allow all sorts of material into it, democratically, and not by a series of antitheses. "It's all one to me," Williams insisted twenty years later in an interview, "the anti-poetic is not something to enhance the poetic—[the poem is] all one piece. I didn't agree with Stevens that it was a conscious means I was using. I have never been satisfied that the anti-poetic had any validity or even existed."[125]

As for the *Collected Poems* themselves, Williams felt pleased by it, seeing it now in print. "By moments it flares up before me as a real entity," he told Burke in December, "then it falls apart again as so many printed pages."[126] But to Zukofsky he was more positive:

> The book looks to be well printed. The most curious effect I received was from the beginning of the Primavera. . . . The whole book has a definite shape now, to me, seems to come up to the attention as a whole—appears to be a creation. That is the test of a book: Is it a book at all or just so many pages of printed matter. More and more one realizes that the creation of a book is a sudden miracle which happens, just like that, at the moment it is assembled—or it doesn't happen.[127]

Williams had had to put up two hundred dollars of his own to help meet the expenses of publishing his *Collected*. It had been a joint venture, he knew, but he still felt uneasy about backing his own book while a fellow Objectivist—Basil Bunting—was having a difficult time of it merely making ends meet. To make matters worse, Williams had found it impossible to send Bunting any additional money for rent, part of the reason being that he'd used his spare cash to pay for his own book. "It's dog eat dog in the end I suppose," he told Zukofsky, "any way you look at it."[128] The advance copy of the book arrived at 9 Ridge Road by special delivery on Sunday morning, January 21, 1934, and the others arrived the following Tuesday morning. Williams wrote at once to thank Zukofsky, saying that he found the book "perfect in format and the cover distinguished."[129] Finally, after so many disappointments, Williams had his book of poems out at last. It had been his first to be published in the United States in thirteen years.

*
**

Music. By May 1933, Williams had given up on Antheil and was now interested in a young composer friend of Zukofsky's, Tibor Serly. He invited Zukofsky out to the house for dinner with Serly on Monday evening, May 8, to talk about music. Then, in between Williams' office hours next door, they discussed the feasibility of Williams' completing the libretto and Serly the music for an opera based on Washington's life. Serly seemed interested and Williams went ahead again with the libretto. Nine days later, Williams drove into the city to the New School for Social Research to hear three of his early poems—"Canthara," "Love Song," and "K.McB"—written for tenor and chamber music by a young composer named Irwin Heilner. The evening, unfortunately, did not go particularly well. George Rasley of the Metropolitan Opera had not been allowed sufficient time to smooth out some of the rough spots in playing Heilner's musical compositions, and Heilner himself was depressed about the performance. But after the performance Williams himself walked down to the pit to tell Heilner not to worry. It was a damned shame, he felt, not to give a composer enough time to adequately present his work to the public, especially where new work was concerned.[130] But, then, that had been the story of his own life. Perhaps, though, Williams had learned something about wedding word to music that night. One thing was certain: he didn't want to make a fiasco of his libretto as he felt Pound had with his *Villon* back in 1924. He thanked Heilner and was gone.

But Williams had his problems with the libretto, problems that would end only several years later, with Williams and Serly finally throwing up their hands in disgust at each other. In fact, Williams would be so upset that he would even stay away from Zukofsky for several years, trying to rinse the bad taste of the opera fiasco out of his mouth for good. In the meantime, however, Williams struggled dutifully with the form of the libretto, getting nowhere. "I have labored at it until my eyes are almost hanging out," he complained to Zukofsky on June 20, "but nothing gets on paper—or nothing that is of interest. . . . It is heartbreaking to toil at something and feel one's interest grow less and less the more he works—panic finally."[131] But he kept at it, reading American history, writing, finally to amuse himself. He called it, in despair, a kind of "jerking off."

Work on the libretto came to a fumbling halt in July when Louis Zukofsky finally got his chance to see Pound and Europe with Serly. Williams told him to see the catacombs and the Eiffel Tower and to give his regards to ol' "Idaho Ezra." "Ask him for me," he told Zukofsky, "if he still drops his voice at the end of a poem when he is reading it so that nobody can hear the last three lines."[132] So Williams went on to other things until Serly and Zukofsky returned to the States in mid-September, when Williams again outlined his plans for the libretto with his composer. "After my keen disappointment with Antheil I lost interest in the project for a while," he wrote his Bill Jr., at the beginning of October. "But after seeing Serly last week on his return from Europe things begin once more to look bright."[133] Six weeks later he wrote Bob Brown that the "Geo. Washington opera has come to life again. Serly has had a success with Stowkowsky [sic] in Philadelphia which was all he needed to put him in the limelight. And now he is yelling for my libretto."[134]

There was another session with Serly around Thanksgiving, and then Williams got down to work in December outlining the actual scenes for the first of the opera's three acts. It would be a dream sequence in which the idea of a new nation was interwoven with the reality of all Washington had been through by the time of his inauguration as the country's first president. It would be a dream of a new world felt as much in the very music as in the words themselves. Therefore, it would have to be an inner music that Serly would somehow have to enflesh for an audience to hear, a music strong enough to carry the hopes and dreams and emotions —the whole inner life—of the man who had sacrificed all that finally for a new nation which in turn would quickly turn him into a statue, a coin, a stamp, without ever realizing the emotional furnace Williams believed Washington had in life been. "The Pap of our Country's coming along fine—in a general way," he wrote Burke in December. "There has to be so much strategy employed though that the actual weaving together of the words and music seems to be almost incidental."[135] The full import of what he said there would not become obvious to him until, two years later and still trying to please Serly with a workable operatic strategy, he would let the words fall how they would and almost forget whatever tenuous, haunting music he thought he might have heard when first he'd fathered the father of his country's dream.

In late June 1933, Williams drove his mother up to the cottage at New Haven and then saw Paul off again to Camp Enajerog in Vermont for the summer. With the house quiet once more and practice—as usual during the summer—light, Williams had normally taken this moment as a signal to begin writing, as much as if "someone shot off a pistol."[136] But this year he was waiting for something to happen. In the meantime he was reading: reading several lives of Washington, and reading H. L. Mencken's *American Language* straight through. He hadn't read Mencken's study when it had first appeared in 1923, nor later, in its revised form. He didn't even like Mencken. But now, having picked the book up, he found himself poring through it carefully, surprised that it should so rivet his attention. It was, he had to admit, the "best thing" Mencken had ever done; in fact, the man "should have stuck to scholarship" and not gone off on his half-assed interpretations of American culture which had so infuriated Williams.[137] Williams finished the book, finally, toward the end of July, and he wrote Gorham Munson that he could finally tolerate Mencken for the first time in his life "because of his views of our new language." He even wanted to review the book for *The New English Weekly*.[138]

So, when he and Floss and the boys went up to Monroe to spend a few weeks with Nana Herman at the old farm in mid-August and early September, Williams took along Mencken's book with him to review. For a few days the weather held and Williams and his sons spent the time chopping down two apple trees in blighted fruit, "putting the wood suitable for heating purposes in one pile, the leafy branches in another, greater one for the flame." Then the three of them began to lay out the spot where the apple trees had been to make a lawn tennis court. But they'd no sooner cleared the ground than it began raining steadily for days, until Williams began to think that the tennis court might soon be transformed into a mud bath of sorts. Driven indoors, he tried his hand in desultory fashion at the Mencken review, finally managing to finish it after a month of false starts.[139] Then he sent it on to Mencken, who thanked him personally by letter in early November, at the same time explaining that he was even then busy on yet another revised and expanded fourth edition and that he would be calling on Williams' help with that in about a year's time.[140] Williams decided to wait on his own review until the new edition appeared and then review that.

He fared worse with *White Mule*, which he'd hoped to "goose" back into action up in Monroe. The trouble was that, after three and a half years, *Pagany* had just gone under for good. Johns had tried valiantly to keep his magazine going, but with the recent death of his father and his funds therefore now gone, together with the added misfortune of having had a briefcase full of manuscripts for *Pagany* stolen from his open Packard when he'd run into a drugstore for a pack of cigarettes, Johns had finally called it quits. When that had happened, Williams had found himself unable to push forward with his novel. After all, *Pagany* had given him the incentive to go on with the book in the first place, and now that incentive was gone. "Poor ol' *White Mule*," he wrote Johns on August 23 from Monroe. "I wish I could go on with it. Not a word have I written on it since *Pagany* busted. I have ideas of course but there seems no chance of getting published so I just stall along taking things as they come—and go."[141] He was not feeling particularly enthusiastic that summer about his own future. But at least Floss was feeling well again and his boys, Bill, nineteen, and Paul, almost seventeen, were growing into young men who were finally beginning, as he delicately phrased it to Zukofsky, "to discover the world of easy culture and the all embracing twat." And if his own work was at the moment stalled, he was at least glad to see Pound still knocking out those *Cantos*. He'd just read the

XXXIVth in *Poetry* and was impressed with his old friend's "easy long lines without strain—almost a revolution in itself." He'd seen nothing better anywhere, including his own stuff.[142]

He had managed to finish one thing, however. The *Paterson* poem, so long deferred, had been tickling him again, and in July he had typed out what he labeled a prose "poem" done on a large canvas, eleven pages long, called "Life Along the Passaic River." He sent it in its unfinished state to Morton Dauwin Zabel, the editor of *Poetry*, on the twenty-ninth, explaining later to Zukofsky that—though it looked like prose—he considered it a poem "in five line sentences (more or less) about the low-life of these parts."[143] In mid-July he'd driven over to the new Third Street Bridge between Passaic and Wallington to meditate on the Passaic—his river —once more. James Joyce was in his ear again, as well as a hundred local conversations entered into and overheard, the miasmic spirit rising from those polluted waters:

> There's a sound of work going on there, and a jet of water spouts from a pipe at the foundation level below the factory onto the river's narrow mud bank which it has channeled making a way for itself into the brown water of the two hundred foot wide stream. The boy is drifting with the current but paddling a little also toward a couple of kids in bathing suits and a young man in his shirt sleeves, lying on what looks to be grass but is probably weeds across the river at the edge of an empty lot where they dumped ashes some years ago, watching him. These youngsters who make boats out of barrel hoops and a piece of old duck, wherever they find it, live by the river these hot summer days. It's a godsend to them.[144]

Poetry didn't publish Williams' prose poem—it was too unorthodox, one suspects, for a magazine Williams had long suspected of becoming middle-aged and sclerotic—but it did publish a group of Williams' poems in the opening pages of their October number under the heading "That's the American Style." There were eight poems by Williams in all, dealing with small life observed closely, and ending with "A Foot-Note" addressed to ideologues in general and to the new breed of frenetic American Communists in particular, like those he'd felt sure had finally been responsible for swamping *Contact* the year before:

> *Walk on the delicate parts*
> *of necessary mechanisms*
> *and you will pretty soon have*
> *neither food, clothing, nor*
> *even Communism itself,*
> *Comrades. Read good poetry!*[145]

Williams was never a Communist, finally, because he distrusted all orthodoxies, all ideologies. He was far too radical. "I won't follow causes," he told Marianne Moore the following year. The reason was that he simply could not, since it was "so much more important to me that I *am*. . . . Things have no names for me and places have no significance. As a reward for this anonymity I feel as much a part of things as trees and stones. Heaven seems frankly impossible. I am damned as I succeed. I have no particular hope save to repair, to rescue, to complete."[146]

In the summer of '33 he found himself once again becoming involved with another little magazine. This time it was "a couple of kids," Fred and Betty Miller, who lived with their children in an apartment over in Brooklyn. And though Fred Miller was out of work—he was a tool designer by trade—he and his wife were still going to launch a new leftist, proletarian magazine and wanted Williams' name on the editorial staff. They wanted to call their magazine *Blast*, and though Williams disliked the name because it recalled Wyndham Lewis' vorticist magazine of the same name, the Millers kept it. Williams tried to explain to them that he would never again take on the editorship of another little magazine after the trouble he'd had with *Contact* and his leftist backers, but they assured him that they themselves would put up the twenty-five dollars each issue would cost. (This in spite of the fact that the Millers were so poor he'd even caught Fred Miller once roasting Japanese beetles in a kerosene lantern in order to eat and still put out his magazine.) They would also do all the editorial work. All they wanted from Williams were some more of those stories they'd read of his in *The Knife of the Times*. One a month for the life of the magazine, and a manifesto now and then.

Well, here was a new chance. *Pagany*, after all, had gone bad, he decided, "because Dick Johns did all the selecting himself and had had a leaning for the fairy stuff. It got to be awful sometimes." Williams liked Johns and was grateful for the break Johns had given him, which he would try to repay by dedicating *White Mule* to him when it was finally published. But Williams was also sure Johns had wasted "a magnificent chance by printing such bad stuff." Maybe *Blast* would be different.[147] The magazine ran from September 1933 until November 1934, beginning as a bimonthly before sputtering out after fourteen months with a total of five issues. For each number Williams sent the Millers a new story, several of which were to become small classics: "Jean Beicke," "The Use of Force," "The Dawn of Another Day," "The Girl with a Pimply Face," and "A Night in June." They were all stories of working-class families he knew in and around Passaic, though he was very careful now to alter names and places to protect himself. And those stories revealed more eloquently than any propaganda could what the economic situation in America had done to thousands of lower-class American families, and how those families had somehow managed to survive—when they were not washed under by death itself—with vestiges and even whole pieces of their humanity intact.

Sometime, probably in August, Williams also wrote what was intended as a comment for the first issue of *Blast,* though that statement was not finally used. In it, Williams waved his fists at the Communists even as he wrote for a young Communist sympathizer. He was still interested in one thing and one thing only: to write as well and as honestly as he knew how, and not in the pay of any ideology. He did not believe the artist should have to subordinate his training and skill as an artist to any party ends; in fact, most proletarian writing he'd read had been merely ineffective (and therefore of no real use to the party) simply because it had been bad writing. It was a mistake to write down to any audience, to assume a superior stance as though one had to educate the working class, he felt. It was "all very well for Romain Rolland [the French Communist] to say all writing which does not lead to action" was "so much garbage," but Williams disagreed. There were different kinds of action, and, besides, the artist had finally to follow his own lead. Williams was sure intelligent Communists would get a better portrait of a decadent society from a decadent like Proust, for example, than they would ever get from a pariah like Louis Aragon. Did people think the Communists themselves such fools "that they do not know integrity?" It was still, then, a matter of good writing, of sensitivity to the forms of narrative or of poetry that mattered. Attend to those essentials with the heart open to the human dilemma and the rest, one could only hope, would follow.[148]

*
**

Autumn and the early autumn of one's life. In itself a kind of renewal, the late promise of gentian and chrysanthemum, the smell of burning leaves on the streets of Rutherford, and Williams and his wife watching their younger son playing first string defensive right end on the Rutherford High football team. Williams wrote Bill, now a sophomore at Williams taking a premedical course and playing on the soccer team there, that his kid brother was doing damn well on the team. He'd played the whole game against East Rutherford until the last minute, when the coach had let someone else have a chance. And, though they'd lost 6–0, that was as much because of some bad calls on the part of the referees as anything else. Paul had held his end well. The following week he could write Bill that Paul had played all the way through again and had "cleaned up Cliffside properly." He was putting in a stone path to the garage now that the weather had cooled a bit and he had employed two brothers —professional gardeners—to finish the tennis court they'd begun that summer up in Monroe before the rains had started. Nana Williams was taking lessons in walking from a Swedish masseur and he was still hopeful that she'd be up and walking in a couple of weeks (though she wasn't). He talked frankly about surgery now that his oldest son had shown an interest in medicine. "I enjoyed the carpentry of it," he said, thinking back to thirty years before, "the purely mechanical planning and execution" of an operation. But for him the decision had finally been made to "practice medicine in a small town and write!" He talked about Dusty, their cat, and their new pooch, Mike. Paul was already going steady with a local girl, though Bill, as the more serious of the two brothers, was also shyer and more concerned with his studies.[149] And while Williams sometimes wondered when some girl would land his older son, he knew all too well his own intense shynesses as a young medical student and kept his own counsel. He would try to let his sons live their own lives and not meddle as his own dear mother had meddled.

At Thanksgiving time, Bill and Floss drove up to Williams College to see their son for a three-day visit. Williams had welcomed the break from his medical routine, and he felt refreshed again once he found himself on the road heading home. They left Saturday afternoon, November 25, in the middle of an unexpected ice storm, and made it as far as Pittsfield, Massachusetts, less than thirty miles away, where they decided to stay over at the Hotel Wendell for the night. As they were driving down Pittsfield's Main Street, Floss had pointed out the window of their car at the sign "of a prominent Real Estate Man" there in the city who had once proposed to her. (Williams may or may not have remembered back to the summer of 1911 when, hearing from Floss about a young man who was paying her a great deal of attention, he had rushed up to see her the following Saturday and find out what was going on.) But all that had happened nearly a quarter century before. And now here he was—at fifty— in a hotel room with that same woman, reading his son's theme papers and explaining in fatherly fashion—at 11:30 that night—that, though he never wanted to meddle in his boys' lives and hoped he never would, he wanted Bill "to understand how very much I should appreciate knowing you better and having a mature confidence develop between us more and more as we go along." Perhaps, perhaps on paper something might develop. He and Mother would drive on down to Charlie Sheeler's place in Ridgefield, Connecticut, in the morning to see his old friend (who had lost his wife six months before) before returning home. Well, there was still the old Ford flivver he'd given Bill for him to drive down and see his parents when he had a chance. And there would be Christmas and the winter vacation and Easter. And President Roosevelt might even someday sit in a box at the grand opening of his opera on *The First President*, which, in spite of depressions of all sorts, he was hell-bent to get working on again.[150]

EIGHT

An Index to the Times:
1934—1937

Money. As much on Williams' mind as everyone else's as the Depression settled into a condition of life, a winter's nightmare, with always the promise of spring giving way before the long shadows of ice. By the beginnings of '34, Williams like Pound had been pretty much sold on the Social Credit theories of the English economist Major Douglas. Of all the theories available to him at that moment with which to combat the economic abuses eating out the very fabric of his society, Williams was ready to advocate Douglas', with its emphasis on a decentralization of credit. The experiment of American democracy, if it had not already failed, had at the very least responded poorly in combating big business interests and the monopolies, which Williams was convinced were riddled with corruption and gangsterism.

That left three forces actively engaged in attacking the economic abuses of his day: fascism, communism, and Social Credit. Now, for all his dislike of certain Englishmen, he felt more comfortable with Social Credit because it insisted on maintaining individual liberties even as it sought to reform a society's economic system. Williams distrusted fascism in all its forms because it kept insisting on destroying an individual's civil liberties for the larger good of the state. But he also distrusted communism, which was, at bottom, just another dictatorship, this time a dictatorship of the proletariat. When he spoke to American Communists about the revolution and the viability of Douglas' ideas, however, they swept Douglas under the table as merely constituting one moment in the larger revolution that would come as soon as the people realized they were only dupes of a small privileged class. But that specter also frightened Williams, not for himself, since with *his* income and practice he was sure he would survive any such revolution. But he was afraid thousands would be destroyed in the inevitable bloody aftermath of that tidal sweep. He wanted change, he insisted in an article published in mid-January 1934 in Gorham Munson's Social Credit biweekly, the *New*

Democracy, but he also wanted to come out on the other side of the revolution still being his own man.[1]

In the meantime, while he hoped for the revolution that would break the ice blockage of the Depression, he was also hoping perversely for some sort of personal windfall. So, when Bob Brown broached the idea to him and Floss of becoming speculators in an oil well, in a scheme called the New Llano Oil Project, Williams decided to give it a try—cautiously. Since it was Floss who handled the finances, kept the books, paid the bills, and tried to figure how they were going to get two boys through college, Williams talked the project over at length with her, and then wrote Brown on January 12 that his twenty percent investment in the well—for drilling equipment—would be forthcoming, in installments of $200 a month, which was all they could afford. In spite of which Williams stalled as long as he could. It wasn't easy doling out even that sum in 1934, especially when his patients, many of them out of work and all of them having their own difficulties making ends meet, could not afford to pay him. Finally, however, he sent his first check (for $150) to Brown on February 16, instinctively knowing that he was kissing the money good-by forever. Two months later he even admitted fatalistically to Brown that he didn't expect to make anything on the oil scheme: "I never have made money and never expect to. Just invincible pessimism. Even if we do 'hit oil' it probably won't be more than a teacupful."[2]

And then there was Paul, taller than his brother or his father—like Uncle Ed—already halfway through his last year at Rutherford High, easygoing, likable, but without the intense seriousness of his older brother. And also without his grades. It was time for Williams père to see what he could do about getting his younger boy into college somewhere. So, on Sunday, January 21, when he drove Bill back to Williams College for his fourth semester, he took Paul along to see the legendary headmaster of Deerfield Academy, Frank Boyden. They left Williamstown early Monday morning and took the Mohawk Trail east out of the Berkshires through snow-covered fields in bright winter sunshine. "I never expected to go over it in January," he wrote Bill two days later, "but then things are always happening which were unlooked for. There was deep snow along the sides of the road and a few animals' tracks in it." They arrived in Deerfield at eleven thirty to find Boyden in chapel and had to wait until noon. Then Boyden took them aside and spoke with Paul. Williams explained that Paul had expressed a preference for his own alma mater, the University of Penn, and he was willing to send Paul to a school like Deerfield for a year if that would help his chances of getting into college. Boyden's advice was to enter Paul at Penn in spite of his grades, as soon as his mid-term exams at Rutherford were over.

The following Sunday Williams wrote Bill again. He was worried about Bill's grade in philosophy, and hoped that he'd been at least able to bring that E of his up to a D. He enclosed, as he often did for his family, a prescription, this one for Bill's head cold. It was a new formula, since Williams conscientiously kept abreast of what was happening in the field of medicine as in poetry, this formula "the result of some new tests made among college students at the U. of Wisconsin." He was sending along a copy of his *Collected Poems* in a day or two and would also send up a copy of a thesis he'd just written "on *The Cultural Background*, of America, that is."[3] Nine days later he wrote to congratulate his son on passing his exams, before telling him about what he now called *"The American Background* essay." And since Bill, like Paul, had expressed an interest in writing, he wanted to show Bill how one did a ten-thousand-word essay for a publisher:

> Boy! have I been working at my "theme." I made a very approximate outline at the start and then proceeded to write and how I have written. The first draught comes to 42 pages, somewhat over the 10,000 words they want. But that's what I planned to have happen. When I start writing I forget the original plan almost entirely, it's a trick, loosens your mind—frees you, permits originality of expression, lets you get excited and allows you to follow new leads wherever they may take you—within the larger scope of the whole scheme, of course. Then comes the revising and the adaptation of the outline to the newly discovered material. That's how I write.

He still had another revision to do, and then he would give "the mess" to Mrs. Johns to type out clean for him. Then there would be a final revision.[4] Bill and Paul would listen attentively to such instructions in the art of writing and try to carry them out, Bill at Williams and later at Cornell Medical in New York City, and Paul at the University of Pennsylvania (which he entered in the fall of '35 after a year at Mercersburg, by way of preparation.) But their father's overwhelming genius in the field would finally preclude their following after him. Bill Jr. would excel even over his father in the practice of medicine, forty years' progress in the field itself helping him there, but the writing would remain at most an avocation, an interest only—as Williams would come to realize about his sons when he dealt explicitly with fathers and sons in the fourth book of *Paterson*, that autobiographical epic of his, fifteen years later. As for Paul, he would marry a potential writer, but stick to business himself.

*
**

Williams had been chosen by Waldo Frank, Dorothy Norman, and Paul Rosenfeld to write the essay on "The American Background" for a book on *America and Alfred Stieglitz* which the Literary Guild was publishing. The book contained essays by Frank, Norman, and Rosenfeld as well as by Hartley, Demuth, Gertrude Stein, and Sherwood Anderson. Williams' own essay—one of the strongest he wrote in this decade—dealt with America's abortive contribution to world culture and the difficulty of an indigenous, local culture to make itself felt. From the mid-nineteenth century on, he argued here, America had had to confront a far more developed European culture which had swept into the New World, particularly through the eastern coastal cities of the United States, presenting its superior products to a fledgling America. Williams reviewed the glacially slow growth of America toward a conscious sense of its national heritage, a consciousness that had made itself felt only during the American Revolution or afterward in the minds of certain pioneers who insisted against overwhelming odds on facing not east but west. The real contribution of figures like Boone, Crockett, and Houston, then, had been this: that they had made some kind of contact with the intrinsic elements of an as yet unrealized material of which America was made. Williams saw Washington—who was at that point very much on his mind—as the great emblem here: the blameless leader caught between the raw new he'd witnessed sporadically at Valley Forge and elsewhere, and the graciousness of an imposed cultural design. Thomas Jefferson, too, with his home at Monticello, represented good taste blended with a distinctive understanding of what the local could offer. But they were only two against the overwhelming mass of Americans who had chosen to maintain a cultural dependence on England, the country from which they had fought to gain their political independence. By 1934, Williams had also accepted Pound's Usura thesis and his portrait of Andrew Jackson as the man who had seen the threat to public moneys coming from private groups. It would turn out to be the cancer that would nearly kill American culture.

The problem here too, then, was money, for increased wealth had been the chief cause of cultural stagnation, drying up the roots of local communities like the Shakers with their model farms and utilitarian designs at Lebanon and Hancock along the New York–New England borders, or finally undermining those local master builders who had constructed the great Yankee trading ships of the nineteenth century. A few writers had tried to maintain a distinctive American culture against the predominant English strain, Poe, Whitman, and Melville among them. Emerson, Williams was willing to admit, was a genius, but his vision and his poetry itself had been circumscribed "by a slightly hackneyed gentility," so that his real native vigor had managed to surface only at moments, in a paragraph of prose here or a line of poetry there. But for all his talk of the American poet, Emerson had neglected his own ground for a vision borrowed in large part from Carlyle and the German transcendentalists. It would therefore remain for Williams to fulfill the promise of Emerson in his own essays on American art. Williams also praised Emily Dickinson's authenticity, so much greater, finally, than Emerson's own, though American women had been sadly circumscribed by the repressive, genteel culture of nineteenth-century America. The pure act of the American woman responding to her world was—Williams sadly suggested—dramatized by the young woman who had just jumped from a broker's yacht off Coney Island only to be found floating face down in the Atlantic two days later.

It was still a pork barrel America, Williams concluded in his parody of the American dream:

> We have an excellent and highly endowed hospital in the metropolis for dogs and an attractive canine cemetery in the suburbs. There are capital yachts and private vessels for transoceanic travel, airplanes, and flying heroes, deluxe cars, princely estates in the West where liberal barbecues are the fashion, and in the East as well, museums, collections and the patronage of swanky Old Masters, horses, racing—Palm Beach and the abandon of an occasional war for profit: even expensive universities for the propagation of something that passes for the arts.[5]

That same month—January—he wrote a two-page blurb for a Harvard undergraduate named James Laughlin (he called him "Loughlin" in a letter to Zukofsky) who was also an advocate of Social Credit. He did not know the young man, but he'd answered his request for something for the *Harvard Advocate* by sending off a piece he called "The Element of Time," in which he advised the young to be revolutionaries, to keep "ripping down the scaffolding from the Grace of God" and to "try and keep profs from ripping your pants off."[6] It was part of the same antiacademic feeling he'd expressed in the Stieglitz piece when he slammed "the extraordinary dullness and sloth of the official preceptors [of the nation] as represented . . . by the heads of the cultural departments, the English Departments in the lead, in the American universities."[7]

In his feelings about the American academics too he was in agreement with Ezra Pound, even though they were about to initiate an exchange of opinions in the pages of *New Democracy*. He wrote Pound on February 16 to say he was following Pound's essays in that publication and to let him know that he was fully allied to him "on the score of a general orientation of knowledge and the bitching it gets at the hands of those who should know better."[8] Two weeks later, in the March 1 issue of *New Democracy*, Pound's "Commentary on W. C. Williams" appeared. Hell, Pound wrote there, anybody knew there were superficial differences between communism, fascism, and Social Credit. Even *Daily Mail* reporters and members of ex-President Hoover's cabinet knew that much. But what Pound was looking for was not the differences but the unity among these three factions. Benito Mussolini, *il Duce*, for example, "working from a

position opposite Douglas's [had] managed to jerk Italy into the ECO-
NOMIC vanguard of Europe." Pound spoke knowingly of the Swope Plan,
which "would have imposed a *de facto* tyranny on one million economic-
sucklings." He was therefore calling for a system of stamp scrip for the
United States. Jackson had abolished the national debt, and now here was
this Franklin Roosevelt starting a new one, "for which there is absolutely
no necessity." Williams, Pounds suggested, had merely flirted with some
very important economic realities.[9]

Williams responded to Gorham Munson at once—on March 5—
though his reply was not published until April 15. "If ol' Ezra had paid the
least attention to what I had written he would have noticed that I had
taken a realistic attitude toward Douglasism," he wrote. "That, in the
way of pure observation, as typified in the processes of natural science, I
had merely set down a phase of the situation as it occurred to me." He
went over his ground again on the differences he saw between Douglasism and communism, and then maintained the central importance of
economics to good government, of which Douglasism was one—but only
one—possible answer. The trouble with Pound, Williams argued, was his
"clogged idealism." The poor man actually thought that most people
took the trouble to think consecutively about something as abstract as
economic theory. But who in hell did he think he was reaching with his
"cryptographic" shorthand anyway? As far as he personally was concerned, Williams would take "the comic strip method of lucid blocks"
and "pictures" as a way of getting an idea across any day. England could
keep its present parliamentarian form of government and still follow the
Douglas formula if it wished to, but in America things were different.
Why, the American Communist Party, poor deluded radicals, didn't even
have the sense to work out an intelligent attack to be achieved by stages;
no, it had to be revolution emerging out of the shambles of bloody street
fighting. But what he wanted was a bloodless revolution. He had no
illusions about the meaning of human suffering and death; he'd seen too
much of it in his profession. Maybe Pound's Italian *fascismo* was the
answer, he was willing to concede as a point of argument, but he still
needed the facts to be persuaded that it was. And he didn't want
communism and Social Credit combined. That would be like trying to
mix oil and water, for what made them essentially different was the
step-by-step intelligent progress of the latter, and the Armageddon
bloodbath tactics of the former.[10]

In March 1934 Williams began publishing chapters of his *White Mule*
in *The Magazine,* a monthly (and then, as money gave out, a bimonthly)
published out of Beverly Hills, California. Between then and May of the
following year *The Magazine* published nine more chapters of the
novel—for which they also paid—and they thus gave Williams the
incentive to complete the book he'd begun in *Pagany.* So that hurdle was

passed. In March Williams also took Floss into New York to see the Municipal Art Show at the new RCA building and then stopped in at Macy's department store to see how his *Collected Poems*, two months out by then, was selling. When he learned that the mere half-dozen copies they'd had on display had already been sold, he wrote at once to Zukofsky to get busy and send Macy's some more. He was also reading Gertrude Stein's *Autobiography of Alice B. Toklas* and had just learned that she was coming to the States for a paid lecture series, beginning at Princeton.[11] He wondered aloud to John Herrmann and his wife, Josephine Herbst, about Pep West, now out in California trying to make a living. A strange one for sure, he wrote: "I can't see why he hasn't at least sent me a picture post card during his travels. What the hell, he's probably embarrassed or something."[12] He read Zukofsky and Taupin's essay on Apollinaire that same month and found it hard going, though he could see "that the difficulty is essential to a correct exposition of the text. It is unusual in America," he added, "for a magazine to give place to a thesis of this sort." After all, it didn't really "pay," though it was finally more important than most of the stuff he saw published.[13]

For years Williams had been searching for a new order in the social as well as in the poetic sphere. He believed that attention to what made a society work could also throw light on the construction of a poem, and vice versa, since a government of the words, that is, an ordering of the imagination, was at the heart of both. So, when he wrote a review in April of George Oppen's *Discrete Series* published by his Objectivist Press, Williams called his review—significantly—"The New Poetical Economy." In that review he made an important analogy between the two orders of society and poetry, both stripped to their working essentials in a well-run economy:

> An imaginable new social order would require a skeleton of severe discipline for its realization and maintenance. Thus by a sharp restriction to essentials, the seriousness of a new order is brought to realization. Poetry might turn this condition to its own ends. Only by being an object sharply defined and without redundancy will its form project whatever meaning is required of it. It could well be, at the same time, first and last a poem facing as it must the dialectic necessities of its day. . . . [Oppen's] poems seek an irreducible minimum in the means for the achievement of their objective, no loose bolts or beams sticking out unattached at one end or put there to hold up a rococo cupid or a concrete saint, nor either to be a frame for a portrait of mother or a deceased wife.

**
***

Williams wished to avoid the inessentials, the nostalgias, sentiments, and propagandistic values of poetry. He was wary of the new "social school of criticism," which found it useful to tag this poem proletarian and that one fascistic. That sort of evaluation, he warned, was as narrow and as self-defeating as the earlier religious or philosophic evaluations of an Eliot or a Winters. Look first, he said, for the "craftsmanlike economy of means," and then for the "meaning."[14]

By April Williams had learned that Fred and Betty Miller, though they were still struggling to keep *Blast* alive, did not have enough money even for rent. So, on May 1, he drove to their apartment, took them and their daughter and their few belongings, and then drove them up to his unheated summer cottage at West Haven to give them a place to stay for the summer. He probably had the Millers in mind when he wrote the editor of *A Year Magazine* that same month condemning the boring trivia and brainless matter he saw every day published in the paying magazines, while the real work of the despised little magazines went unrewarded. At least the little magazines had this effect on the paying magazines, though: it forced them to accept a better grade of work than they would otherwise have done. No, the "radical magazine" was not a series of failures, always dying, as one smart critic had said, but rather, as Williams saw it, "one continuous success, impossible to kill." Damn the paying magazines with their "shrewdly whittled codes" and peekaboo sex. Most Americans, he had learned, were still "infantile in their reactions to sex." That was still "a burning topic with us: fully three quarters of the scripts that come into the small magazine offices have sex for their theme; and they are terrible in their unenlightenment." He doubted that Americans would ever achieve "the French viewpoint or deftness" with regard to this topic. It was a case of sexual pathology, the old Puritan bugaboo again: the pathetic "dirty mindedness of the pay magazine editors with their lists of censored words" actually forcing human sexuality "underground into the frankly sex toilet-paper rags." The underlying problem here again was economics and the failure of America, as compared, say, to Europe, to get real information disseminated to the people. Pound, too, had been arguing the same point about the exorbitant cost of publishing in America. The result was that no literary saturation was possible in this country, and so most Americans were simply kept ignorant of the world around them. Williams was clearly thinking of his own fiction—of *White Mule* and "Jean Beicke" and "The Use of Force"—when he said that most contemporary realism coming out of America which he read looked "pretty sick" next to Emile Zola's accomplishment. And though he believed that "realistic observation" should be related to "an equally real schematic whole"—the juncture of fact and the imagination—even straight external realism was important, for Americans knew "far less, radically, than we should about our localities and ourselves."[15]

*
* *

Tibor Serly and Williams had scheduled a meeting at Serly's New York apartment for May 15 to go over the roughed-out version of the opera, and

Williams invited Zukofsky along. Serly had insisted that the opera would be more satisfying if it had a death in the last act and some sort of reference to modern times. With a sinking feeling in his gut, Williams had said he would follow Serly's suggestions and that had made Serly happy. Williams knew that Mad Ted (or the Mighty Atom, as he also called the diminutive Serly) would "razz things around to suit himself anyway" before he was through, which was fine with Williams, so long as they could finally agree on some sort of structural center for the opera. On top of that, however, he was feeling low, despondent, older than ever this spring: "There's little life in me these days. I suppose the time of year and my time of year have much to do with it." But he'd at least finish "this bloody opera thing, that at least," during the coming year. He was tired of being stuck in the middle of the thing.[16]

Williams tried to follow the temperamental Serly's suggestions, compromising again and again to fit the formal needs of an opera, to which he was—except as observer—still a stranger. But, though he could not yet admit it to himself, he and Serly simply did not mix well. Serly had one conception of the opera, Williams another. By early June Zukofsky too was thoroughly embroiled in the confusion of the proceedings.

Now it was the lullaby in the opening scene. Williams was trying for a lyric that would contrast Martha Washington's attempt to please her husband even as Washington's own preoccupations were elsewhere. How to get across that contrapuntal inner music? the dream quality that he wanted to suffuse the whole first scene? Zukofsky had written a version for Williams, but Williams had found it too complicated. Now he pushed through with his own lyric, managing to send the completed first act off to Serly in early July before he took off with his family for a work vacation up at Monroe, where he finally finished the tennis court and wrote a "detailed synopsis" of the rest of the libretto.[17]

But Serly was still dissatisfied with what Williams had written. "We haven't hit the dynamic intensity requisite yet," he wrote Zukofsky two weeks later.[18] Still, he felt he was finally in touch with that dynamism; now all he needed were the facts, the actual situation, to flesh out that intensity. A few days later, on Friday night, September 21, Serly and Zukofsky came out to 9 Ridge Road for yet another session with Williams. Once again Williams patiently explained to Serly that he understood better now what it was Serly wanted. For his part, Serly suggested that his friend John Klenner get involved in the project. After all, perhaps what Williams really needed was a better sense of how to turn history into high drama. So, on the following Friday, Williams drove into the city to Klenner's apartment for a session with Serly and Zukofsky . . . and Klenner.

"After mooning about for the past week," he told Zukofsky on October 3, "the perfect scene sequence for the second and third acts quite simply appeared to me, embodied in the sky." Here, finally, was what would have to be done: "The second act must be three scenes instead of two. The ballet [in the second act, enacted at Valley Forge] has grown too large in our eyes. In the composition as planned it is one of the scenes only and must remain so. . . . The ballet is a combination of deprivation, the cold and a dream. *Then*, as it ends in an icy, darkening atmosphere, suddenly the scene is projected into a blinding light of summer noon." That dreamlike juxtaposition might just do the trick. As for the inauguration scene in the final act, Williams saw that as a *maestoso:* "Not precisely pomp and ceremony but full of the dignity of office. A national consciousness as of power established. Then a final scene at Mt. Vernon —the disturbance of uncertainty and strength struggling to maintain or undo the work."[19] That closing scene would focus on the dream of a whole life already becoming unwound even during Washington's actual tenure as president. Like death itself, it would give the opera its tragic overtones and speak to a Depression audience about the need to keep Washington's founding dream of a democracy from slipping into oblivion.

They all met again at the end of the month, and for a moment Williams felt better. Serly, Williams thought, had come to see finally what Williams was after, something finally clarified for Williams by his "contact with his practical friends of the stage." Williams was still willing to stay in the background for the present, and to feed himself out to Serly "only so fast as he wants me." He was even pleased to have Klenner in on it, and Zuk and Serly with himself; he even considered it "a very healthy sign that the thing has come from several men rather than one man."[20] It was yet another manifestation of Williams' old dream of a community of artists supporting one another.

But by mid-November Williams was once again ready to throw in the towel on the collaboration. The trouble with Serly—as far as Williams was concerned—was that he really did *not* understand that Williams was not trying to set Washington's life to music. That had never been his intention so far as he was concerned. What he—Williams—*thought* he and the others had been trying to do was to work "on a composition (principally) by myself utilizing certain carefully selected scenes for *an effect*." And who the hell was Serly to suggest to the author of *In the American Grain* that he read up on Washington's life? He had read, he defended himself, and read exhaustively. How would Serly have felt, Williams wondered, if he had told him to go over and ask Irving Berlin how to write music? This was the main problem: to "cut down a thousand possible scenes, to make it all fit into an hour and a half of playing time—and at the same time to make the dream sequence effective." He'd worked on the libretto now for over two years, but if Serly did not make the effort to discover *why* Williams had worked so hard on it, *why* it was so important to him as a subject, then they were all sunk.

The truth was that for Williams this opera was his own Lucifer's song, his own cry of independence from the father, from a superior though foreign culture that he—the new father of his country—was after: he, Williams. "The opera has tremendous possibilities," he was certain, and it was a "real opera in spite of all those European sons of bitches who haven't yet learned how to sit on a toilet seat."[21] What he was attempting, so far failingly, was nothing less than an American opera in an American mode, a modernist declaration of independence against the whole sacrosanct tradition of European opera, a swerving into a new mode that would be authentic, he hoped, but which he was sure would be damned. Serly made another appointment to see Williams in the city on Tuesday night November 27, but this time Williams begged off. He'd been too worn out to drive into New York, he explained to Zukofsky, having been up with a patient since two thirty that morning. He'd reworked the first act once again, but for the moment he was just not writing.[22] What he didn't say was that he was still angry at Serly's cavalier remark. So now it was Serly who tried to ameliorate Williams. He sent him a postcard on December 9 to say he'd just looked over the revised first act after Zukofsky and Klenner had blue-penciled it and that it looked fine. Now he would send it on to his composer friend Stokowski.[23] Another year was nearly over and the libretto seemed as problematic as ever. For the moment, Williams turned back to his patients, glad to do something "productive."

*
**

But if the dream of the opera preoccupied him for a good part of 1934, Williams was also busy with his fiction and his poems. In April of that year he finished two important poems: "The Catholic Bells" and "An Early Martyr," the latter about his friend John Coffey, who more and more was beginning to look like a true Communist as opposed to the strident leftists who talked and talked and left Williams cold. "The Catholic Bells" too was really about a Communist utopia, ringing out over Rutherford for everyone, with perfect Franciscan equality (he would expand on this poem, rework its impetus in "The Pink Church," but he would not equal the power and joy of this first effort, which served as a kind of democratic answer to Hart Crane's late visionary poem "The Broken Tower"):

> Tho' I'm no Catholic
> I listen hard when the bells
> in the yellow-brick tower
> of their new church

ring down the leaves
ring in the frost upon them
and the death of the flowers
ring out the grackle

toward the south, the sky
darkened by them, ring in
the new baby of Mr. and Mrs.
Krantz which cannot

for the fat of its cheeks
open well its eyes, ring out
the parrot under its hood
jealous of the child

ring in Sunday morning
and old age which adds as it
takes away. Let them ring
only ring! over the oil

painting of a young priest
on the church wall advertising
last week's Novena to St.
Anthony, ring for the lame

young man in black with
gaunt cheeks and wearing a
Derby hat, who is hurrying
to 11 o'clock Mass (the

grapes still hanging to
the vine along the nearby
Concordia Halle like broken
teeth in the head of an

old man) Let them ring
for the eyes and ring for
the hands and ring for
the children of my friend

who no longer hears
them ring but with a smile
and in a low voice speaks
of the decisions of her

daughter and the proposals
and betrayals of her
husband's friends. O bells
ring for the ringing!

the beginning and the end
of the ringing! Ring ring
ring ring ring ring ring!
Catholic bells—!

In May he told Morton Dauwin Zabel, the editor at *Poetry*, that he was trying to finish up a long poem on the death of D. H. Lawrence. Four years after Lawrence's death he still felt strongly about the man.[24] A month later he'd sent the poem to get it away from him, afraid that, if he still had it around him, he would "rip it open from end to end" once again.[25] What he probably feared was that he'd fallen into the strings of sentimentality in constructing the elegy, letting his emotions interfere with his critical faculties. His intuitions were right, but there was little he could do; four years had not softened the private impact that most un-English of Englishmen had had on him.

Williams wrote Bill Jr. on June 6 to say that he would be coming up to Williams College with Floss and perhaps the Brat—by whom he meant Paul—on Friday evening the fifteenth to bring Bill home. He and Floss had been to a "big Democratic rally at the Swiss Chalet" the night before. "It was hot as hell," he wrote,

> so that Mother & I could lie on the grass in the floodlights by the little lake and watch the two tame swans paddle by as the lovers flipped them cigarette butts and one of the girls could say "Here come the chickens." Love seems still to be working from what we saw back of the grape arbor.

There were loudspeakers blaring out speeches for local Democratic hopefuls and there was also some "raw entertainment." Most of the people had come out to see and hear Joe Penner, the radio comedian ("Wanna buy a duck?"), who was just then all the craze (and young Paul's favorite), but Penner had failed to show. Instead, there was plenty of drunken dancing and kegs of beer at ten cents a glass, "a whole battery of kegs in a semicircle under the stars and bombs bursting in air. There were colored boys carrying signs on sticks, 10th Ward and so on next to girls in evening clothes and other girls, smaller, with their mamas and no escort wiggling their little asses lonesomely while they looked right and left to see the effect." He and Floss had come home early, the roadway through which they drove "arched over with lattice frames bearing scores of electric bulbs at one end of the display bearing the name Harry A. Moore and at the other William J. Ely." It was a scene that, with very few changes, might have been enacted any time since Andy Jackson, and Williams understood its raw vigor and cherished it. Somehow, it was all deep in the American Grain.[26]

But a month later he told Fred and Betty Miller in a more somber mood that a new revolution in America would not last more than a week before the various special interests moved in to carve up the country. The problem with the American Communists was that they still had no idea of what they were really up against in this country. They were too naive. "They are only thinking in 'big terms' whereas the history of the country and the local dynamite that is embedded in it will blast them to hell and gone before they have had time to wipe their asses after the first shit."

He'd seen enough of Irish cops and Italian construction workers, Polish-American machinists and German-Americans with hunting rifles among his patients to know what he was talking about. What the Communist intellectuals ought to do—and his letter was addressed to one—was study "anatomy and physiology, not to speak of psychology, for a year or two. Or even cooking." In other words, let them do something pragmatic, in the American tradition, and then talk about the revolution. You didn't "make a cake by reading a book (Marx) either."[27]

By July he was writing Bob Brown every few days, growing ever more nervous about his oil investment. He wanted to know how the drilling was going down in New Orleans and debated over whether or not to sink an additional $500 into the damned scheme. The prospectors had written to say they needed additional funds for the casing at Fogman's well —Williams' well—because they'd come up dry at the depth where they thought they were going to strike oil. He thought about it: perhaps in August, when he was back home. But he was worried. By then he'd already lost a total of $500 without so much as that teaspoon of oil. Should he throw good money after bad?[28]

The family was back home from Monroe on Sunday night, August 5. But a few days later Floss was complaining of severe abdominal pains, something that had been bothering her for several months. Williams wrote Brown on the thirteenth to say that he'd had to take his wife to Passaic General that day for "a look into her pelvis to find what is bothering her."[29] Three days later, at eight in the morning, Floss was wheeled into the operating room for what Williams called an "abdominal clean up."[30] She was in good condition following the surgery, Williams told Zukofsky, but it would be a while before she was back on her feet. Now, with Williams himself forced to handle the budget, he was afraid to send the New Llano people any more money. As for Floss, she recovered only slowly. It was six days before she was eating again, and it was October before she was really feeling better. She spent a month away, recuperating, in September and October and—with Bill back at Williams and Paul at Mercersburg—that left Williams "holding the fort with my gimpy mother, a day servant and—the [coal] furnace."[31] But that did not deter the New Llano people. Letters requesting additional funds continued to come in: would Williams be interested in a second well —Alexander—while they went on with Fogman? No, he answered, he needed a new overcoat. By mid-October, he was even beginning to treat the whole scheme as a bad joke: "Chapter X. In this chapter the hero makes himself into a serpent and goes down a drill hole looking for erl. Or what?"[32] And five weeks later: "What happened to that last 45 feet? C'mon, give us the latest."[33]

Practice too—like the oil business—was almost at a standstill. By

January 1935 he could tell Bob Brown quite bluntly that there would be no more money for the oil scheme. Furthermore, he was not going to take his sons out of Williams and Mercersburg to have them support Brown's experimental "Commonwealth" College. If Fogman ever came in, fine. But there would be no more money.[34] In April, Brown wrote to say he now thought he and Williams had been taken in by the oil scheme. Williams agreed philosophically: "It would be a curiosity in my experience if we had not."[35] Yet he could still feel exasperated and angry with the whole scheme, which was becoming more of a myth with the passage of time. "What in hell is it this time," he asked Brown in early May, "some nigger shit down the hole . . . or lawyers?"[36] That was it. Williams had drawn a blank, a big zero. Better to forget the whole thing. Only once did he ever bring up the subject to Brown again: four years later, in December 1939, when he mentioned in passing that five hundred Brown had lost for him.

When George Vaughan, a counsellor-at-law, wrote from Fayetteville, Arkansas, in July of '35 to get a modern poet's view on contemporary morals and what Vaughan called the "definite drift to lower ideals" in America, Williams surprised him by saying that he was aware of no such drift but "only a shuffling off of worn out restrictions which have bound us and which can bind us no longer." There was as much "plain honesty" in the people he knew as there had "probably ever been in the world": that is, "not much except under certain strict local conditions." Even the American Revolution, a time of avowed idealism, had in fact been "riddled with every imaginable form of dishonesty and disloyalty." As for changes in sexual mores: yes, here there had been a profound change, and one for the better. He thought of his own sons and thought of how he admired "their clean minds, their candor, their lack of false shame in matters of sex." He also knew that there were serious abuses of sexual freedom as there always had been, but that, he insisted, was because "a candid outlet for sexual expression" had been "blocked by the old morality."

But the root problem facing the world today—one that went deeper even than morality—was the economic situation. "It is so overwhelmingly important and pervasive," he insisted, "that I cannot begin to discuss it even were I able to do so authoritatively which I am not." The root evil as he saw it was the absence of "a more equable distribution of purchasing power in the world" together with the "lack of general enlightenment as to what causes the present condition." So-called democracies might call communism an atrocity, but that didn't stop them from trading with Communist countries for their goods. And as for the Church: it was itself "the chief barrier" to spiritual enlightenment and one of the world's most vicious influences, since it had "come under the control of the economic vandals" and dared "not speak the truth."

Perhaps one of the strongest signs of health in American men and women had been their reluctance to follow the stupidity of Prohibition. Science had shown the world how to arrive at material plenty, and nothing—no economic or political system—should be allowed to prevent people from "ordering the vast resources of the world . . . to treat our brother man as a brother and not an economic rival." He saluted the great spiritual awakening he saw in America in spite of Depression and the rest of it.[37]

But in another mood he could write—as he did to Zukofsky in late November—about the sheer monotony of modern existence. He'd been looking through a recent copy of *National Geographic* and remembered some pictures of islands in the West Indies. No wonder salesgirls at Macy's and coeds were addicted to popular fiction. Anything to get away from the boring quotidian of life in Depression America: "To let the mind wander on what old-time mariners knew and had witnessed is close to delirium these days." Americans were suffocating; they were too "closed in, choked, beshitted as we have never been in the past." At least in the old days, Williams sighed, giving in for once to nostalgia, "if one did not live long, he had a chance for a wild death after one beautiful 'ride.' There are adventurers today but the mind can't go along with them, it can't, it's just so much syphilis which is too easy to get close to home anyway."[38] And two weeks earlier he had confessed to Pound that at fifty-one he was feeling "less and less" "the cuntish call." Perhaps, he mused, "the conservation [of energy] is essential."[39]

Yet good writing, he knew, was still the ability to perform at will, "of releasing what we know." He complained to Ronald Lane Latimer, the editor of the Alcestis Press and someone interested in publishing Williams' autobiography (or his letters), that he was having trouble at the moment getting it up. Williams felt like many men his age before a willing virgin, he explained: unmoved, though he knew he must still have the potency. "It's a sort of pity, a sort of lack of interest—a good deal a matter of resentment that it hadn't been so easy formerly when it would have meant infinitely more." That was how he felt now about his own life: he simply wasn't interested in writing it up just now. All he was really interested in doing was getting his meaning over as impersonally as possible, to see his work flourish, and to be left alone. For years he had dreamed of a communal life shared with other artists (Kreymborg, Pound, McAlmon, West, Zukofsky), of being important too to his friends and neighbors. But that early dream of a true brotherhood of writers, which he would have liked to write about, had "almost evaporated forever." Even if the "Revolution" *he* had dreamed of were achieved tomorrow, it couldn't help him now. Too many of his friends had already been injured by the inevitable passage of events. Better to let the autobiography alone for the present and come back to it when he felt more inclined.[40]

*
**

In mid-December 1934, Mencken again wrote to Williams—as he had promised the year before he would—asking Williams to write him about what he saw as the relation between modern American poetry and the emergence of an American language. He mentioned that he was now deep into the revisions for the fourth edition, and was trying to assimilate some of the immense material that had accumulated on the American language since the publication of the third edition of *The American Language* eleven years before. Williams wrote back that he would send something as soon as he could, finally telling him that he only wished scholars in the American universities would heed the pioneering work Mencken had done in establishing the reality of the American language. (In *Paterson*, ten years later, he would still lament that there were no scholars of the language whom the poet could turn to for help.) "I do my best to jar my sons into the realization of the cultural superiority of their native tongue over book English," he added, "but even they feel a certain shame in resorting to colloquialisms in word and phrase when they have to do a 'composition.' Their letters, though, are lively when they write me. They'd better be."[41]

The very next day Williams found time to type out three pages of rough draft notes, single space, which he called "Note: The American Language and the New Poetry." Surprisingly, in those few pages he managed to touch base with an extraordinary array of interrelationships between measure, language, and form. The impetus for modern poetry, he began, had been essentially linguistic. It had been a matter of pacing and of discovering what—after all—poetry itself was. This was the deepest and most far-reaching revolution of all, because a country's poems were—finally—its real repository for the language and the key to a people's linguistic character. The poet played a central role in the development of the language (and in measuring the heartbeat of a people) because the act of composition forced the poet to analyze "why one word has to follow another" without distorting the delicate contours of rhythm and sense. This was no easy process, and the new arrangements of words on the page could too frequently degenerate into parody, a kind of folksy dialect, as with James Russell Lowell, Whitcomb Riley, and Paul Laurence Dunbar.

What finally determined the line a poet had to use was usage, the language as actually spoken in a given place.. The line of a similar language—in this case British English—was no longer sufficiently accurate to catch the speech rhythms of someone living in New Jersey or California. As for forms—ranging from lines like blank verse to sonnets, sestinas, couplets—they belonged to special cultures and almost never made acceptable forms for an emerging vernacular. Each new language, therefore, was compelled to create its own special forms. This was why

Milton and Shakespeare as examples were to be avoided: "The Shake-spearean line"—the blank verse line—killed "everything in it today, bastardizing every meaning." The modern poet also had to be careful to avoid easy inversions—those demanded by an adherence to a precon-ceived form—and had to avoid poetic words and the hundreds of insidious clichés that kept cropping up in any language as a substitute for fresh thought.

Free verse too had been wrong, though at least its primary impulse —to preserve the language—had been on the right track. So Whitman had been the great forerunner there, even though "his grandiose sentences and inflated periods were alinguistic very often." On the other hand, the insistent commonness of the image—like Orrick Johns's "blue under-shirts on a line"—and the use of conversational words in poetry had been stabs in the right direction, since language was, at bottom, word of mouth between two people. Williams—as technician—saw the problems of making a new verse in terms of "pause (robbato) as characteristic of the speech," variations in the alignment of emphasis, and the choice of words. It was essential, he stressed, that poets take the search for a new line seriously and that they listen long and hard to the speech patterns about them, not cracker-barrel vulgate but the pace and pauses and risings and fallings of speech heard every day around them.

This would not be easy and—to make matters more difficult—there were influences working against a distinctively American poetry (or for that matter, a distinctive poetry belonging to any place, wherever that might be—whether Ireland, Scotland, or elsewhere), influences that were "more pervasive, subtle and vicious . . . than would be readily believed." Part of the problem, too, lay with the general reader. "All sorts of asses love poetry," Williams knew. "It confirms them in the assininity of their deepest beliefs." For a smoothly lying meter which passed for poetry would always carry such a reader nostalgically back to the lobotomized tranquillity he or she craved. That was why a people in the process of change would always need a new poetry consonant with their moment, a poetry that ensured an unswerving accuracy between word and meaning. As for classics, they were to be admired for having caught the truth of a civilization in its own forms, born out of the stresses of that civilization. But to follow their example, it was imperative that the American poet not follow the classic forms but invent his own. In that way only would Americans ever have a chance of creating work comparable to those earlier models.[42]

Despite their inherent value, Mencken chose neither to use these notes nor even to acknowledge the help he'd received from Williams when the Fourth Edition was published in mid-1936. Nevertheless, Williams went ahead and reviewed the book favorably for the *North*

American Review, though he made a point of saying that he still preferred the Third over the Fourth, feeling that the "often unsupported surmises" and "ill-assorted jumble" of the Third had added a certain zest, a jagged edge he missed in the more polished contours of the Fourth. "Perhaps H. L. Mencken's new edition . . . will help us to adulthood in ways even he did not image would be the case," Williams concluded, invoking, as his mother had before him, St. Stupidity to pray for his countrymen.[43]

*
**

A few weeks later Pound was twitting Williams that he would have defended any place where he happened to find himself. Williams agreed: "No doubt if my cocky ancestors had been driven by penury to Tasmania I'd be sticking up for that spot in the sun also—perhaps." He'd never had any illusions about America or New Jersey or New York, finally, since all places—as he'd told Marianne Moore six months before—meant nothing to him in the long run. But he'd also "found by trial" that he worked best where he'd found himself—"in spite of the drawbacks." As for Pound: why, he'd never been "a lover of the flora and fauna of any place" and still "couldn't tell the difference between lilies-of-the-valley and burdock."[44] On the other hand, Williams had just finished Pound's eleven new *Cantos*—the American Cantos, XXXI–XLI—and had to admit he admired them. He had also learned from them. He published his review in Munson's *New Democracy* a few days later and in it he stressed the central theme running through all these new *Cantos* to be Pound's observation that all men were contemporaries, regardless of historical accident, "whose minds . . . have lifted them above the sordidness of a grabbing world." In his new cantos Pound had focused on the American patriots of '75, especially Adams and Jefferson, minds striking out courageously against the imbecility around them, "observing, inventing, adding to the impressive monument to intelligence, feeling and imagination which Pound is building against our times."

Inevitably, Williams pointed to the theme of Usury in these poems, which he defined as "the work of double-crossing intellectual bastards in and out of government and the church" which "rules the world and hides the simple facts from those it torments for a profit." But he also pointed to a more subtle and no less far-reaching complex of evil which he saw in the thirty-ninth *Canto:* "the unfamiliar magnificence of fornication," the use of sexuality, a good in itself, as a "sin" for individual profit, i.e., for unnatural ends, a perversion of love as much against the natural order as usury was. As for the poetry itself, it was superb. Pound had taken "the speech of the men he treats of and, by clipping to essentials, revealed its closest nature," its real meaning. Williams also thanked Pound for teaching him something about the Jackson–Van Buren era as well.[45] Finally, he wrote Pound personally, everything that Pound had been doing in the *Cantos* up till then was beginning to fit together more clearly for him.[46]

Pound, editing *The New English Weekly* in the winter of '35, for his part asked Williams for some new poems at regular intervals so that he could help reacquaint British readers with his work. Williams sent him three poems at the beginning of February with the note that Pound might describe him as "popularly supposed to be an intelligent and discriminating physician in this here daintily balanced suburb."[47] He also mentioned that *White Mule* was now "harnessed up" and had been sent out to look for a New York publisher. He'd finished the novel in mid-November, checked it through, and had had his typist make a fresh copy. It came to twenty-one chapters, 319 pages. The new poems he sent to Pound were "Genesis" (on his grandmother), "Invocation and Conclusion," and "View of a Lake." On February 25, he sent additional material to Pound, at the same time apologizing for his "View" poem, which he'd done much too rapidly. The truth was, he explained, he was really in no shape "just at present to be sending you new stuff every two weeks." He simply could not write the poems as fast as they were being demanded of him. (In 1935 alone he had contributed to over twenty different issues of little magazines.) He no longer had a single poem anywhere around the house or in his office to give to anyone. It also annoyed him to have magazines accept and pay for poems and then not publish them, or delay them, or promise to feature them and then—when someone more popular contributed something—to shuffle his stuff into the back pages. That had happened for instance with his "Elegy for D. H. Lawrence," which *Poetry* had delayed publishing when Yeats had sent them a play.[48]

But when Pound told Williams that he would have to have T. S. Eliot's support in England if he was ever going to have an audience there—via, presumably, Eliot's powerful influence as editor of Faber & Faber —Williams naturally saw red. "Who the hell is Eliot, that shit ass," he shouted in a letter to Pound on March 5. "I don't want to get on in England if it has to be at the cost of getting a 'yes' from that pot of addled ewe's snot. He can't begin to know anything that is of the least importance to me." He was careful, however, not to include Pound in his vituperation, reserving for his "carissimo" only "the most sweet smelling syllables."

When Pound read Williams' three new poems, however, he wrote back to say that they were a sad falling off from the earlier work Williams had done, and that he'd have to do much better than that if he was going to stay afloat as a significant poet. Williams knew that Pound was right, that his poetry couldn't "be what it was and can't in any case be at all without much more thought than I've given it of late."[49] He knew where he wanted to go with the poem—as his letters to Kay Boyle and H. L. Mencken had suggested—and he knew that the images in a poem like "View of a Lake" were nearly random lens shots, chance images thrown off at odd moments and not serious attacks on the structure of the poem:

> *from a*
> *highway below a face*
> *of rock*
>
> *too recently blasted*
> *to be overgrown*
> *with grass or fern:*
>
> *Where a*
> *waste of cinders*
> *slopes down to*
>
> *the railroad and*
> *the lake*
> *stand three children*
>
> *beside the weed-grown*
> *chassis*
> *of a wrecked car—*[50]

But when would he again be able to attack with the full force of his attention and intelligence? A novel, two collections of short stories, critical prose: these had preoccupied him now for years. Where was he at fifty? "I seem to be in a transitional period of a major sort," he suggested, working "piecemeal for unrelated effects in a more acute manner." Even the drive of various editors wanting this or that poem—some made to order—had "debauched" him to a degree.[51]

*
**

One of those who had been after him for something serious was Ronald Lane Latimer, who had first written Williams for a contribution for the *Columbia Review*, had then "disappeared," and had surfaced once again in late '34. In early January '35, he'd asked Williams if he could publish a full *Collected Poems*, but Williams—not sure about this unknown quantity named Latimer—wasn't ready for that yet. In turn Williams mentioned his *Embodiment of Knowledge* manuscript which was still collecting dust, but Latimer wanted to do a book of poems. Williams couldn't even give him a poem much less a book, he complained —"Everything has been snatched out of my hands the moment it's written"—but in fact he did go along with the scheme for a new volume of poems. He was doing this, he suggested, so that discerning minds might discover the new in such a book, rejecting what he called the "slag" and pulling out the important material, "that which related to the

American language and modern times." He was hungry for the feedback he hoped the critics would provide him—and other poets—in suggesting directions for a grammar of modern poetry. "It makes me weary for some instructor at Columbia to come up to me after a reading and ask why I put a certain verse in the form in which I put it," he explained. In fact, *they* should be telling him, not he them. And if the critics and professionals rejected what he was after and placed him far down some table of values, they would do so at their own risk. He was still certain, at least, that he was out somewhere on the thin cutting edge of the American language.[52]

Six weeks later—on April 8—Williams sent off the script for *An Early Martyr* to Latimer, who would publish the book in a highly priced (seven and a half Depression dollars) limited edition of 165 copies, rag paper, fine print. Williams knew the incongruity of having his American poems published in such a format—he had lectured and written on the importance of getting poems out to as many people as cheaply as possible—but he also knew that there was really no choice. People like Latimer weren't knocking down his door with offers to publish him every day. It would have to be a limited edition, then, or none.

Williams dedicated this new book to John Coffey and placed "An Early Martyr" first in the form of a dedication poem. But he might just as well have called the book *Proletarian Portraits*. For the most characteristic pieces were in fact portraits of the times, like "Proletarian Portrait," "Item," "The Raper from Passenack," "Late for Summer Weather," "To a Poor Old Woman," "The Catholic Bells," and "The Yachts." In these poems Williams celebrated the common person, as in the classic stance of

> *A big young bareheaded woman*
> *in an apron*
>
> *Her hair slicked back standing*
> *on the street*
>
> *One stockinged foot toeing*
> *the sidewalk*
>
> *Her shoe in her hand. Looking*
> *intently into it*
>
> *She pulls out the paper insole*
> *to find the nail*
>
> *That has been hurting her. . . .* [53]

Or there was the poor old woman

> *munching a plum on*
> *the street a paper bag*
> *of them in her hand*

> *They taste good to her*
> *They taste good*
> *to her. They taste*
> *good to her*
>
> *You can see it by*
> *the way she gives herself*
> *to the one half*
> *sucked out in her hand*
>
> *Comforted*
> *a solace of ripe plums*
> *seeming to fill the air*
> *They taste good to her. . . .* [54]

Or—finally—yet another woman Williams had seen in the newspapers: an old woman "with a face / like a mashed blood orange" still clutching her old coat and "stumbling for dread / at the young men / who with their gun-butts / shove her / sprawling."[55]

And "The Yachts," that often anthologized, uncharacteristic effort of Williams', which Williams liked though he knew its technique was imitative. He had begun it with Dante's *terza rima* since he was borrowing the scene from the *Inferno* where Dante and Virgil must cut through the arms and hands of the damned floating beneath them who try to sink their small boat. Williams was remembering the magnificent America's Cup yacht races he had seen off Newport, Rhode Island, and the ambivalence he had felt watching all that aristocratic skill while knowing that it was a nation of poor people who in reality supported this small privileged class. In a letter he wrote in late August of that year to Pound, after "The Yachts" had already been printed in the *New Republic*, Williams provided an extraordinary gloss on the sentiments expressed in that poem. The letter was written from Woods Hole, Massachusetts, where Williams had taken Floss and Paul to visit young Bill, who was working in marine biology at the laboratories there for the summer.

Williams had just finished reading Pound's latest book, *Jefferson and/or Mussolini*, and had enjoyed it because Pound had persisted "in finding a local solution pertinent to the present world situation." But Italy was not America, and Williams believed now that the revolution in America was further off than ever. At that moment the trouble with Americans getting anything like justice served to them, as far as Williams was concerned, was "the organized opposition by the wealthy Republicans to everything Roosevelt is trying to do. It's a race: he'll do it his way, putting over the rudiments of an idea, or they'll get the whip hand back and kill the idea." And if the moneyed Republicans did get power, *any* chance of a revolution would be dead. Williams had called it a race: a political race between Democrats and Republicans like those yachts racing for the America's Cup in the summer of '35.[56] One or the other side would win—probably the special interests once again—and the *sansou*, the poor, the disenfranchised, would be cut aside relentlessly as they clawed against the boats struggling simply to stay afloat:

> *Now the waves strike at them but they are too*
> *well made, they slip through, though they take in canvas.*
>
> *Arms with hands grasping seek to clutch at the prows.*
> *Bodies thrown recklessly in the way are cut aside.*
> *It is a sea of faces about them in agony, in despair*
>
> *until the horror of the race dawns staggering the mind,*
> *the whole sea become an entanglement of watery bodies*
> *lost to the world bearing what they cannot hold. Broken,*
>
> *beaten, desolate, reaching from the dead to be taken up*
> *they cry out, failing, failing! their cries rising*
> *in waves still as the skillful yachts pass over.*[57]

But the general sense of having fought for the better part of one's life and then to have failed in the public eye, to find oneself at fifty-two writing poems for the masses in an edition virtually unattainable! Williams reserved, then, the sense of sour grapes for his last three poems. The first of these, "To Be Hungry Is to Be Great," was a poem ostensibly about the availability of onion grass as a tasty appetizer, to be found everywhere in early spring, gratis, under one's feet, if only one had the eyes to see it. In fact, it was an antisentimental, practical poem about the good things all around us that we never noticed until the poet pointed them out to us. The second, "A Poem for Norman Macleod," called the "revolution" an accomplished fact, since the dignity of the revolution, its nobility, had been achieved (even if only ironically) with the ability of Americans finally to come to terms—for the first time—with the hard fact of their Depression surroundings, the place where they had finally awakened to find themselves:

> *The revolution*
> *is accomplished*
> *noble has been*
> *changed to no bull. . . .* [58]

But the last poem in the book spoke most plainly about what it had cost Williams to achieve his revolution of the word. "You'll notice when you see it [*An Early Martyr*] that the last three poems, including the one about you, are in a different mood from the earlier ones," he wrote Macleod in September. "It's a mood I want to cultivate."[59] But when Macleod wrote back suggesting that he saw an order in those last poems, Williams covered himself by rejecting that suggestion. The final poem, he explained, was simply the result of Pound's having accused him that spring of having "pissed" his whole life away. Feeling as vulnerable as he did at the moment, Pound's statement had stuck hard in his crop: a hard, indigestible bolus, so that, for nearly a year Williams refused to write to Pound. That, of course, was a private matter between Pound and himself, but he knew that almost anyone in his fifties might look back on his life and wince. He'd overheard some kids playing ball in the streets and singing the poem's refrain and he had married that taunting repetition to Pound's accusations:

> *Any way you walk*
> *Any way you turn*
> *Any way you stand*
> *Any way you lie*
> *You have pissed your life*
>
> *From an effectual fool*
> *butting his head blindly*
> *against obstacles, become*
> *brilliant—focusing,*
> *performing accurately to*
> *a given end—*
>
> *Any way you walk*
> *Any way you turn*
> *Any way you stand*
> *Any way you lie*
> *You have pissed your life.* . . . [60]

Williams still wasn't "talking" to Pound in the fall of '35, but he did send letters to Dorothy. So it was not until after Christmas that he decided to send a copy of his poems—to Dorothy—with a note to Ezra that he'd dedicated the last poem to him. Let the lovable bastard take that any way he wished.

Williams was also having his troubles with Marianne Moore, who wrote him in October that she had found *An Early Martyr* too self-revelatory, too confessional. But of course, Williams told her, a book like his was a confessional. It was exactly because there were things that he could not say in conversation with someone that he had to write them down for the world to see:

> It would not be fair to a reader for me to hold back knowledge of the matrix from which comes the possible gem. . . . There is a good deal of rebellion still in what I write, rebellion against stereotyped poetic processes—the too meticulous choice among other things. In too much refinement there lurks a sterility that wishes to pass too often for purity when it is anything but that.

(He may have been pointing to the meticulousness of choice in image and diction he found in Stevens, but he was also holding the mirror up to dear Marianne herself.) What was needed instead, he insisted, was a Rabelaisian sanity, the sudden releasing crudeness he'd often seen, for instance, in his own mother. The truth was that he knew he was "made up of hells and heavens which constitute a truer me than my face-to-face appearance could possibly suggest. This, I think, is that which should make a book. And over everything, good and bad, if possible, poetry."

It was this revelation that explained why a patient or a friend or even a relative might "know" a man—Dr. William Carlos Williams of Rutherford, husband, father, respected citizen, physician, writer—and yet never really know the white-hot core of the man himself, creating himself, his innermost identity, revealed on a thousand thousand sheets of paper. There was nothing, no subject, no material, which could ever rightly be denied the artist. Blast one's various decorums to hell! He recalled how, twenty years before, H. D. had attacked him just as Marianne Moore was doing now, when he had just been starting out. Maybe the two women were right, but he didn't think so. Damn it! To hell with all sorts of hagiography and special pleadings! "If the stories of the mythical saints and virgins could be known, understood and tolerated," he told Moore slyly, "dogma might get an enlightening that would be fiery in its purging effects."[61] Looked at in this way, the real early martyr of Williams' book was, of course, Williams himself, who had paid dearly for his revolution. And he was a revolutionary who, in 1935, wasn't so sure he hadn't simply failed in the world's eyes.

*
* *

In late February of that year a then-unknown writer recently arrived in New York from Paris named Henry Miller sent Williams a copy of his novel, *Tropic of Cancer.* Williams loved it, calling it "a whore with her pants off for purity and candor." He and Floss were reading sections of it each night and reviving their "drooping spirits" with it.[62] On March 5 he wrote Pound, asking if he'd ever heard of Miller or his novel. It was a book "would warm the cockles of your heart. I'm not going to say its great but I am going to say its grown up in a way America little understands."[63] Then Miller's friend, Hilaire Hiler, invited Williams to meet Miller at his place on 12th Street in New York in early May and Williams had a great evening, with good talk, good food, good drinks. A few weeks later he reciprocated by having Miller out to his home. Again he wrote Pound that Miller was a great guy, and he saw him at least once more in mid-June. But after those initial passes both men went their separate ways.[64]

After a couple of desultory meetings with Tibor Serly, Klenner, and the Oppens, Williams went down to Philadelphia to see Serly on September 21 when Serly got back from eight months in Europe. But by now both men could sense that the project was hopeless and that the collaboration would never come off. Time, then, Williams decided, to put the poor libretto to bed. He would finish it and then add a long introduction for some ideal composer if one ever came along. Now, having in near despair decided to go it alone, he suddenly felt relieved. The opera had obsessed him even more than he had realized. He had thought that a collaborative effort might be a boon to all of them—to Serly, Zukofsky, Klenner, himself. He had earnestly desired to see the opera become a community effort. But it was not to be. At least now he could look at his libretto—his dream as much as Washington's—more objectively.[65]

"Betty was right," he told Fred Miller on November 6. He *had* been pregnant with the opera and had needed an abortion. He felt rotten about it, but it had after all been the best thing. "Havin' a big family these days is pretty tough. I wanted it bad too, thinkin' it might be a boy. But you know how it is with us women, we get over it. Then bein' I'm still young, I sez, Maybe next year I can try again. . . . I'm not really right even yet but I begin to to to—take an interest in things."[66] By late December he had even managed to get over his postpartum blues about his aborted opera. "The body of the libretto text has very little if any literary merit," he could tell Pound now. "I tried merely to write a practical rack for the music with a continuity that should be understandable—with the help of God!—to a general audience." He knew that every word would need its "necessary" accompanying note in the libretto. But his was "merely a crude engine designed to go up hill for 100 minutes. Iron tires. No exhaust. Runs on bay rum." And, finally and most tellingly: "I wonder if anyone on earth has it in him to write the music requisite."[67]

In his "Introduction for the Composer: An Occasion for Music," he tried to spell out clearly what he had failed time and again to explain to Serly:

> To project the figure of Geo. Washington across the panorama of American History so that it would galvanize us into a realization of what we are today would require a tremendous music. His is the only figure of sufficient depth of character and universality of genius which we as Americans could present for such treatment. . . . It was an imaginary republic he created and defended with a very real army. . . . It was a country he pasted together—a good deal out of shoddy—to represent the thing we still labor to perfect. His labors and our labors are the same, granted differences and varieties in the tensions involved. . . . But it is impossible to know what, precisely, Washington thought and felt. We can only create him in our own image. . . . Music and the imagination are the keys. They open to a common world into which both history and the present can step on an equal footing of basic agreement.

"It was a country he pasted together—a good deal out of shoddy."[68] So, then, Williams had all along been creating himself as much as Washington, since both men had so deeply desired the incredible dream of realizing an imaginary republic with very real effort. For over twenty years, against overwhelming odds, in spite of strategic retreats and repeated defeats, Williams, like his dream father, had pursued an idea and then tried to realize it. He had thought someone else's music—which he could hear but had not the requisite skill to utter—would help him help others to see the dream out of which his country had emerged. He had gesticulated, pointed in that direction and this again and again. But he had failed. Now he would have to try again to realize the dream of the place in which he had found himself. But this time he would be the father of his own country, father of his own imaginary city/republic. He would eventually call it *Paterson:* the father *and* the son.

*
* *

Again, money. "If you can't tell the difference between yourself and a trained economist, if you don't know your function as a poet, incidentally dealing with a messy situation re. money, then go sell your papers on some other corner." Thus Williams to Pound, March 25, 1935. For Williams and Pound, it signaled the beginning of the jagged rift over the issue of money. Williams had already manifested his interest in economics, but he knew he had limits. He did not wish to be sucked into the hellish waters of economics, where he was without any footing whatsoever. Hell, he knew as well as the next person that there was something radically wrong with the economy. He felt that every time he saw one of his patients, every time he checked in at Passaic General, read about it every day in the news. It was the topic of conversation with neighbors, at dinner table, with Floss as he looked over the unpaid bills; it was the burning topic with Democratic Party workers, with the Polytopics Club, with editors at the *New Masses, Blast,* the *New Republic,* the *Partisan Review* & *Anvil, New Democracy.* But he was first and foremost a poet and not an economist, and when Pound started to chide him that he'd missed the boat, read the wrong things, pissed his life away, Williams had slammed back with his letter.

He was beginning to suspect Pound's image of himself as a latter-day Ruskin even as he'd earlier suspected Pound as musical theorist. What was Pound doing? Becoming a social reformer, an economic ameliorist, more and more using the *Cantos* to show how the misuse of money was at the root of all modern evils? So Pound wanted "to make the world better for the artist," did he? "And what in hell is the artist going to do with his world once it has been made better for him?" Williams asked, as Wallace Stevens was also asking at the same time. The artist had to live in the world in which he found himself and not in something specially prepared for him. "It is NOT," Williams insisted, "It is NOT the artist's major function to make the world better for himself as an artist." His function, rather, was to record the world he *did* find. In the meantime, to underscore that he meant business, he was telling Pound in effect to go to hell. He would send him no more of his writings to publish in English magazines, and he wanted Pound to return whatever of his he was holding onto. Nor did he want Pound to serve as a go-between or censor for English ears. "If there's anything I want the *New English Weekly* to see I'll forward it to them direct," he said simply. And as for the teachings of an economist like Orage, "the things that made him go," Orage's essential message: well, Williams doubted it had ever entered Pound's consciousness.[69]

But though Williams might tell Pound to go away, he couldn't do the same for the problems that Pound was trying in his own brilliant, eccentric, and irascible way to confront. So, ten days after writing Pound, Williams drove into New York City to take a look for himself at what was happening at the American Writers' Congress. He kept a low profile there, staying on the fringes, unwilling to get caught up in what he saw as the leftist orientation of the speeches. But he was also interested in finding out what was happening. He attended the public meeting at the Mecca Temple on the afternoon of April 4 and listened closely, though, he had to admit, "without learning much if anything." He found the people there polite and he was impressed by the prevailing tones of "plainness," "frankness," and "good feeling." Of all the speeches he heard, however, the one that most impressed him was Waldo Frank's. He was surprised, he told Zukofsky, because he had simply not expected such a speech from the man. "His learned terminology was putrid," Williams began, always suspicious when people began to employ specialized, mystifying languages for their own interests, "but he did have something to say. The audience was strangely annoyed and pleased. . . . He said, briefly, that the place of the artist in the revolutionary movement was not in the oversimplification of propaganda, the necessities are far more complex than that, but in conditioning the proletarian mind, making it ready for revolution." *That* position Williams could subscribe to.[70]

As for revolutionary verse. Well, there was his own *An Early Martyr* which he had put together. And there was that young, leftist group in England he'd been reading: the "Auden-Spender group." He found them ambitious, but at the same time he thought their work was "filled" with irrelevancies, with much that was not really poetry. Their work still needed "a vigorous washing with some strong soap powder."[71] On the other hand, there was the work of one H. H. Lewis, Missouri dirt farmer and descendant of Kentucky pioneers and now—since 1930—a radicalized American Communist, a man so down and out on his luck that he'd gone over to the possibility of radical solutions. He called Lewis a "fightin' roarin' American of the old brand—howbeit in a new dress," in a letter to his son Bill, adding that he liked the man's sincerity.[72] Lewis had sent Williams some of his cheaply printed pamphlets of poetry. They were poorly written, Williams found, and they used the old sentimentalized, bastardized forms like odes and sonnets and ballads, forms that creaked loudly under Lewis' feet. But for all that they somehow managed to work, since they set out to do what they were meant to do. Lewis had believed that his songs could make a difference, and the outraged conscience of the man had raised his poems to a pitch so intense that they could not be ignored. The French poet Louis Aragon might be a more accomplished Communist poet, but Lewis was the more effective one. Williams could feel the fire breaking from Lewis through the surrounding mass of inert material, as in the simple refrain of "Russia" repeated over and over. It was . . . a something, a power, "bringing the mind to sudden realization."[73]

Williams reviewed Lewis' four pamphlets and then sent the review off to Zabel at *Poetry* in early May. A drastically shortened version prepared by Williams at Zabel's request did finally appear in the January 1936 number. But Williams would have to wait two years—until November 1937—before an expanded essay he wrote in July 1936 was finally published in the *New Masses*. There, finally, Williams was given the space he needed to deal with Lewis. He praised him there first of all for getting his pamphlets out cheaply in a paperback format. After all, who knew better than Williams himself the futility of getting out deluxe editions for the few who could afford them, as Latimer was doing for him at the time he'd written his review. Cheap paperbacks were probably the closest approximation modern society had to getting the poem out by word of mouth, "next to Homeric singing and a universal stage." After all, it was publication that had become the weak link in getting the word out: fine paper, fine type, managerial costs, distribution costs. What was needed were cheap books.[74] They alone would give Americans the true access to the literary renaissance Williams had been fighting for, since economics—Usury—affected style and therefore thought itself, determining as it did what would and would not sell. (Had not Pound himself lamented the difficulty Americans had to find inexpensive copies even of the documents upon which their freedoms rested? As a result, they knew far less about what the American founding fathers had actually taught than the average Russian peasant knew of Lenin.) Maintaining the profit margins of the trade press had resulted in a tyranny of its own, Williams insisted. What was needed now, then, was for the hundreds of Woolworth's five-and-dime stores across the country to serve as the medium in Depression America to get books like the letters of Jefferson and Adams and even Lewis' poems out to the people. Later someone might do the deluxe editions for art's sake. But for now: cheap and wide distribution and availability.

Secondly, Williams wished to point to Lewis as the type of the true American revolutionary in the tradition of the persecuted colonist, like those who had dumped the oppressor's tea into Boston Harbor rather than pay unjust taxes on it. Was not Lewis being most American when he sang of Russia, just as English colonists had once turned to France for help in their own struggle? Williams looked back, now, at his own part in the poetic revolution. The earlier generation—his and Pound's and the others'—had understood the revolutionary impulse in terms of form, as a sweeping away of the vicious practice that had stood in the way of realizing a poetry consonant with their own time. So it was just here that he thought radicals like Lewis had failed in simply rejecting all that his own older generation had worked so hard to achieve in this direction. And it was useless to write impassioned poems of social reform in an outworn suspect language or in old forms that no one could any longer trust. So, in this sense, Lewis' forms had failed him.

But while the poet must never forget his craft, Williams also wanted to warn those who—like the universities—might be inclined from "an eminence of culture" to dismiss Lewis' poems that they were doing so from a position of mere formal atrophy. At the spring of all poetry was a strongly held belief in something, Williams maintained, and this belief itself generated the rhythmic nature of a poet's lines. Perhaps, after all, this new generation—the one after Williams'—was merely stripping itself of much that his own generation had felt it necessary to continue carrying. He would have to think hard about that. He had already learned a great deal from this Missouri dirt farmer: for example, that a poet might use old-fashioned, incredibly flat forms and still manifest a mind seriously engaged in the task of realizing something. Or that the poet *could* use dialect—"the natural ease of the native speaking his own language, as he hears it spoken in its own place and day." Or that even rhyme—which Williams had thrown out in his own revolution—might still be employed with effect in popular poetry—"in songs meant for mass singing in trucks and on marches." Or that there was something in Lewis' preoccupation (as there'd been with Joyce's *Finnegans Wake*) with coining new words like *flag rags, dailybathism, demockratism, dogmattrix, Rusevelt*. Or, finally, that a belief in one's own worth as a singer was essential to the success of a poem.[75]

"It's too far into the distance to pray for a pro-literary Communism," Williams confided to Burke at the same time he was writing his review of Lewis. Even some League of American Writers, such as he'd recently attended, would "probably vote for just another set of shits." Barring that vision of a literary revolution, Williams himself still needed to find "some more simple, some shrewder, inventive method" of getting printed. "Hell, we act like a lot of lost sheep," he complained. "Yet I have no answer. Are we so impotent that we can't do anything but yell for a Lenin or else go pantsless?" There had to be some practical way of getting on without becoming a martyr, and yet he wasn't about to resign himself to his present fate. How was it that any cheap advertiser could get his stuff sold better than Williams could? Were American writers really crazy . . . or just impotent? The old dream of writers working together to help each other was once again about to raise its battered head:

> We should really work, really sweat for each other. If we did that we'd damn soon get attention. But we haven't the least sense of solidarity or loyalty. Every man for himself seems to be the stupid rule. I wish I knew how to get us together on even the most purely selfish front—barring theory or god damned economics which has Pound ball-tied and cock-trapped.[76]

As for the old dream of Pound and Williams working together—those two older revolutionaries—Williams told Pound bluntly in early June to "go to hell. We just wasn't born to work together. I can respect you—even love you which I do—but from henceforth unto the boundaries of senility aufwiedersehen."[77]

*
**

In 1935 an aging, wheezing, heavyset Ford Madox Ford had come to America and set up a small apartment with his wife, Biala, in New York City. And though Williams was never quite sure why, Ford had not forgotten Williams from that time he'd first seen him at the gay party he'd hosted in Paris in the spring of '24. Now, eleven years later, on Tuesday evening, May 7, Ford invited Williams and Floss to Mark Van Doren's larger apartment in New York City for another party. "We, Mother and I, enjoyed one of the best evenings we've had in years last night supping with friends in New York," Williams wrote his older son. "We had the invitation from Ford Madox Ford, a rather well known English writer and one time friend of Joseph Conrad. He's not too young any longer but still a prince. He's also an excellent cook, about the size a cook should be, high and round. His wife is a little Polish Jewess and as delightful a person as you'd ever want to know." Mark Van Doren and his wife were of course there, and others had dropped by after dinner to see the group. Williams had been particularly impressed by one "young man who rapidly became drunk but did not lose his ability to talk and talk well—if thickly—as the hours slid by." He had been taken by the young man's obvious sense of culture and command of an argument and told his own son that it was "one of life's most rewarding gestures when it throws an intelligent man or woman in one's path. If he or she be cultured in the best sense and at the same time, the result is such an evening as we had last night." He hoped his own son would return to New York City to practice medicine since it was "the cosmopolis where everything that happens in America happens first," and Bill Jr. had already spent his time up in the woods.[78] Williams did not mention the name of the drunken, cultivated young man, but chances are that it was none other than Van

Doren's prize pupil at Columbia and a fledgling poet in his own right: John Berryman.

In early August, after he'd looked through the "Revolutionary" number of *Alcestis* magazine, Williams wrote Latimer's assistant, Willard Maas, that it hadn't after all been a very revolutionary number because it had lacked what someone like H. H. Lewis might have added: "something cruder, more broken, more tortured in form than anything any of us put into it." Even his old friend McAlmon could have helped the issue with "his plainness and romantic-unromanticism." There'd been "no smash in the face to the issue."[79] McAlmon was much on Williams' mind then because, after nearly five years away from the States, he was now returning to New York a ruined man, a good writer gone sour. Williams was at Woods Hole at the end of August, but on his return, he went into the city to see his friend on two separate occasions in early September. Nothing had happened to pull McAlmon through. The fire there was finally out. "He is drinking too much as usual," he told Zukofsky, "but time is passing and the aggregate of his drinking begins to show—though he would deny this."[80] McAlmon stayed on in New York all through that fall, and Williams continued to see him, though nothing came of it that Williams could see. He was worried about his friend but helpless to do anything to turn him around. Since Latimer was his only publishing contact at the moment, he wrote pleading with him to consider doing a book of McAlmon's verse. "His work is of a style which has an important aspect today and it has proven already successful in England and among alert readers everywhere," Williams explained, adding that there was also a personal reason for his request: "For years McAlmon in the most generous fashion possible gave all his time, energies and money to forwarding the talents of such people as Hemingway, Stein . . . and any number of others. And what does anyone do for him? Not one God damned thing. And he needs it and deserves it." He and McAlmon were throwing a small party over at Hilaire Hiler's studio on 12th Street between Fifth and Sixth avenues on Friday night. Now he was asking Latimer to come over and talk to McAlmon. Then, if they didn't get on, Latimer could forget the whole thing.[81] Latimer did go to the party and did talk to McAlmon, who was as surly and suspicious of handouts as ever, and—despite Williams' offer to buy ten copies of any book Latimer did out of his own pocket (that would come to $75) —Latimer told Williams he couldn't see his way clear to publish McAlmon. Besides, he was thinking of doing another book of Williams'. At year's end, McAlmon quietly left New York for El Paso, Texas, where he could work as a clerk in his brothers' surgical supply firm. From then on, the drifting would continue, with gathering swiftness, toward oblivion and death.

As for Williams, all during the summer and fall he wrote little, even though in August he had finally given up his second office in Passaic. Instead, he was reading "in wider circles," as he put it, and waiting for the writing itch to return, as he hoped it would.[82] Once again he was feeling generally oppressed and tormented, as he told Zukofsky in mid-October, without quite knowing why he felt as he did. McAlmon's depressed fortunes were probably one reason. But Pound hadn't helped matters by asking Zukofsky if he thought ol' Bull Willyams was still interested in prosody—to which Williams responded by telling Zukofsky to ignore "the son of a bitch" if he brought the subject up again.[83] As for economic issues, they too were still very much alive, thanks in large part to Pound. So, for example, Williams wrote Munson in October to send one of his people out to Rutherford on the twenty-sixth for the monthly meeting of the Polytopics Club to talk about Social Credit and the Goldsborough Bill, a bill dealing with Social Credit which was then being debated in the House of Representatives. Williams had been made president of the Polytopics Club that year, he explained to Munson, which was made up of a group of Republican types, men and women. They were "good guys," "back-bone-of-the-nation type," but solid bone as far as anything new went and not much interested in "crazy theories." Still, they were anything but dumb. The host for the October meeting would be "a well known lawyer of considerable influence in these parts—a possible candidate for Governor on the Democratic ticket (one of our few Democrats) at the next state election." What Williams was looking for, then—and it spoke to his deepest instincts—was a "non-theoretical point of attack" on H.R. 9216. No one could call a bill actually in the House pure crazy theory.[84]

Two days after that meeting, Williams was in New York at a policy meeting of the Social Credit organization. He wrote Dorothy Pound to let Ezra know he was still doing his homework: "There's plenty of activity along Social Credit lines in America today. The general public is at last beginning to be informed but nothing very hopeful for general action has developed as yet."[85] Obviously, the Polytopics group—who stood as a synecdoche for the "informed" American public in Williams' experience —hadn't been stirred to revolutionary fervor by the Goldsborough Bill speech.

And yet for Williams Social Credit really did seem to be a logical answer, in spite of the slowness of his own townspeople to respond. He'd said as much in his review of Pound's *Jefferson and/or Mussolini*, which he'd written in September. The '30s, he noted in that review, were not finally an age of proletarian revolution but rather of "group power," with "great emphasis on the newly discovered significance of economic forces—the most dangerous of which is today credit control." Give the people credit, he insisted, as he would again in *Paterson 4*. The whole world seemed to be going crazy, as if people actually wanted to be "hypnotized and raped." He was afraid of Japanese expansion into China and elsewhere, but he also saw that Japan was an isolated example of delayed expansion. Italy, with designs on Africa, was the other example. Germany, on the other hand, was an example of "thwarted" rather than of delayed expansion. Pound had shown him this, had shown him too that what Mussolini was facing in his country was really very little different from the problems Jefferson had had to face in his own young country: "the thwarting of democracy by the growing plutocracy—as planned by Hamilton." Hamilton: Williams' enemy and dark doppelgänger, whose statue and presence stood overlooking the polluted falls of his Passaic at Paterson. Jefferson, then, was like Mussolini: two men of extraordinary leadership abilities attempting to make their respective governments work. "Instead of Mussolini it might have been Lenin, Hitler, Roosevelt, Horthy, Mustapha Kemal," Williams summed up. They were all "integers of different values."[86] In 1935 Williams was willing to listen to Pound's view of Mussolini as the good leader with a vision. But by 1937, after Mussolini had invaded Abyssinia and especially Republican Spain, Williams could barely mention *il Duce* without spitting. The rift with Pound would by then have become deeper than ever.

*
**

Within a month of *An Early Martyr*'s being published, Latimer asked Williams for another book of poems. Williams agreed, even though he didn't have the poems to make up so much as a slim volume. But, having looked for a publisher for the *Collected* for three years, he was in no mood now to let this publisher slip away. He told Latimer he felt funny being published in an expensive format which no one ever saw, though he also admired the craftsmanship and design that the small fine press could give a poet's work: the feel, the texture of the thing. But he also felt "hedged round," in danger of becoming "precious," a feeling he was afraid would affect everything he did if at last it got into his very marrow. And yet he had no choice. Let Latimer publish the way *he* wanted to publish, or not be published at all. So it was yes, with a promise to get the poems—not yet written—to Latimer by February, two months away.[87] When he wrote Pound after Christmas, he told him to keep it to himself that he didn't have the goods, that he'd stalled for "revision" time, and that he'd have to write a book of poems in four weeks' time![88]

Incredibly, by writing "furiously," Williams did get a book of poems together for Latimer by late January, on schedule just as he had promised. Williams' strategy here was to write four long poems (one of which, "Perpetuum Mobile: The City," had been written earlier and then sent to Zukofsky, who'd penciled it and returned it to Williams, stronger, Williams felt, for Zukofsky's careful editing), add some translations from the Spanish, and include the shorter poems he'd written since collecting the pieces for *An Early Martyr*. He was also working hard at his medical practice, but he was using every other spare moment he could steal to get the poems written. "The blame be upon your head if we get roasted for publishing raw work," he had written Latimer on January 9.[89]

The poems "Adam" and "Eve," of the new book's title, were meditations on his father and his mother. "Perpetuum Mobile: The City" was really about the dream ("a little false") symbolized by New York: a dream of love and fame, the brilliant but illusory cosmopolis, the white flower shimmering in the east from Rutherford. The fourth long poem was "The Crimson Cyclamen," an elegy for Charlie Demuth, who had died that past October of insulin complications, but really from the diabetes that had racked his body for so long and confined him for so many years to a sanatorium for diabetics in Morristown. Of the two poems written to his parents, Williams wrote the "Eve" first. He wrote it quickly, straight through, and though he was put off by the sloppiness of the form, he left it almost unchanged because it reminded him, as he said, of his mother's essential character. "Adam" was—like his father—more structured and controlled, though there was in that poem a blazing core of passion barely restrained by the form itself.

"Eve" was a confession on Williams' part, a confession of likeness, of guilt at having restrained his mother, imprisoned her when, in her last futile effort for freedom after his father—Adam—had died, he had had to hold her in check, decorously:

> When Adam died
> it came out clearly—
> Not what commonly
> might have been supposed but
> a demon, fighting for the fire
> it needed to breathe
> to live again.
> A last chance. You
> kicked blindly before you
> and nearly broke your leg
> against the metal—then sank
> exhausted.
> And that is the horror
> of my guilt—and the sweetness
> even at this late date
> in some kind of acknowledgment.

Now, bedridden, nearly blind with cataracts, communing daily with the dead from her early past, Elena waited, a frail bird, a broken seed husk of her former self, still refusing to give up any of the least vanities that Time had loaned her, until it should forcibly rip them from her grasp. He marveled at that grasp which even yet—in advanced old age—though it could not "hold a knife / to cut the meat" could still, "in a hypnotic ecstasy,"

> *so wrench a hand held out*
> *to you that our bones*
> *crack under the unwonted pressure.*[90]

With "Adam" Williams attempted once more to come to terms with his father, now seventeen years dead. He remembered the Englishman in Latin America, unwavering in his small duties:

> *God's handyman*
> *going quietly into hell's mouth*
> *for a paper of reference—*
> *fetching water to posterity*
> *a British passport*
> *always in his pocket—*
> *muleback over Costa Rica*
> *eating pâtés of black ants. . . .*

And how like his father he was in some respects, he who also felt that "darker whispering / that death invents especially / for northern men / whom the tropics / have come to hold." Work, duty, an unswerving allegiance to the one final home waiting for him as it had waited for his father before him, that strange, secret exultation in the face of despair and extinction:

> *Staring Him in the eye*
> *coldly*
> *and with patience—*
> *without a murmur, silently*
> *a desperate, unvarying silence*
> *to the unhurried last.*[91]

He was kinder on himself, more muted, in his elegy to Demuth. Charlie Demuth, born the same year as himself, one of his oldest friends, as old a friend as Ezra himself, Demuth the young artist attending Drexel Institute, met over a dish of prunes at Mrs. Chapin's boardinghouse, Demuth in his studio on the third floor of that tenement on Washington Square South, Demuth who'd painted *The Great Figure*, Demuth wasting away to nothing in Dr. Allen's sanatorium for diabetics in Morristown until he could get insulin treatments, Demuth dead. Over the years, Williams had driven down to Morristown from time to time to pick up his friend from the sanatorium and take him back to Rutherford for the day, though he would always have to get him back the same night. Poor Charlie Demuth, whose flower paintings graced the walls of 9 Ridge Road and to whom Williams had dedicated *Spring and All* and written "The Pot of Flowers" in that volume, a poem based on one of the watercolors Demuth had given the Williamses. All his life Demuth had painted flowers, and now, in fitting tribute, Williams would paint his own flowers for Charlie. Now, with Charlie's watercolor very much in mind, Williams repainted the opening of his earlier poem, changing "Pink confused with white" to "White suffused with red" in this elegy. It would be a sign of continuity beneath the stark changes the years had brought.

It was an extraordinary elegy, this poem, standing as it did outside the whole circle of traditional associations connected with the elegy—or at least seeming to. One reads it and is struck first of all with its being one long description of the stages through which the crimson cyclamen passes, a house plant observed by Williams in the winter months of 1935/36. And yet, despite the relentlessness with which Williams focused on the plant before him—

> an abstraction
> playfully following
> centripetal
> devices, as of pure thought—
> the edge tying by
> convergent, crazy rays
> with the center—
> where the dips
> cupping down to the
> upright stem—

one gradually becomes aware that what is being treated here is the whole of the artist's life in this meditation on the flower—Williams' own life as well as Demuth's. There is the world of thought and there is the world of passion, the passion of flowers—the flame-red crimson cyclamens, each a painting or a poem, part of a vast design, as—conversely—each flower was an artist in Williams' community of artists with poor Demuth being the

> highest
> the soonest to wither
> blacken
> and fall upon itself
> formless.

Rising and falling, each flower holding its perfect shape a moment before thought moved on to another passion, another part of the grand design, over a lifetime, longer or shorter, the day itself passing into a horizon of colors at sunset, all meeting, sunset and crimson cyclamens in the west window, like all paintings and all poems, open now for a moment to reveal a design as, Williams meeting Dante here,

> flower touches flower
> all round
> at the petal tips
> merging into one flower. . . . [92]

Call it Williams' version of the visionary company, the philosopher's heaven.

One other poem at least deserves to be mentioned from *Adam & Eve & the City*, the poem that is ostensibly about workmen (perhaps Greek Americans) laying down a roof but which is really about, as Williams himself said, "my struggle with verse." This is the poem, "Fine Work with Pitch and Copper." The title itself gives the tension: Williams' poems will be fine, delicate, carefully sculpted, sharply executed forms dealing with common workmen's materials like tar and copper strips. Workmen and materials rest separately, apart, distinct from each other, and yet all form part of a larger design. It is difficult not to see Keats's "Ode on a Grecian Urn" operating behind this vividly realized "still life," everything at rest—the workmen are finishing their lunch break and are about to get back to work—yet shimmering with expectancy and a life of its own. But whereas Keats's meditation is upon the paradox of young men still in still pursuit of young maidens and a procession that will forever be approaching without ever arriving, Williams' workman prepares to return to work, "still chewing" (that "still" chiming with Keats's stillness, that "chewing" chiming rather with Whitman's more democratic image of people), even as he

> picks up a copper strip
> and runs his eye along it. . . . [93]

So too, the artist, running his eye down each line of the poem to make sure each is at the right angle with its predecessor and successor. After all, the artist must continue, even when creating proletarian portraits, to see his material first of all *as* material.

For in 1936 Williams was worried about the Communist response to his poems, that is, that the left might not give him credit for his own poetic revolution, his own unideological celebration of the working classes. "They will not see straight," he told Latimer on January 26. "They are the ones that for the next few years (as for the last few) will be the major obstacle for excellence to hurdle."[94] The left would soon be responding to Williams, but not for his poems. In the meantime, with this second volume of poems in the printer's hands, Latimer was already asking Williams for yet a third volume of poems. Williams was worried. He'd sold literally a handful of *An Early Martyr* and a second volume was being set up to sell at five dollars a copy, in another edition of 165 copies. "Nobody can afford to buy these expensive books," he wrote Latimer on the thirty-first.[95] Let things wait a while; he was in no great hurry to get up another volume, though he did allow Latimer to toy with the idea of a *Complete Collected Poems*.

By late April Williams had galleys in his hand, but this time he was disappointed by Latimer's workmanship. The Spanish was particularly bad, the Vermont Yankee printer being ignorant of the efficacy of the tilde, for example. "In the Adam poem there is a line of Spanish," Williams wrote Latimer on the twenty-sixth, referring to *"desde que avia cinco años."* The printer had printed *anos* instead, so that the line read, as Williams pointed out,

> Since he had five ass-holes

instead of reading, "Since he was five years old." "Now, my dear and good friend," Williams explained, "that can't be allowed to stand even in a semi-ignorant country such as this. . . . My mother, whose native language is Spanish, would never forgive me."[96]

Williams took the galleys with him on the train up to Hanover, New Hampshire, a few days later, where he would speak at Dartmouth College. He was merely going to sign the sheets for the edition on the ride up, but he'd found at least six serious errors in addition to the Spanish guffaw, four of them "of the grossest sort" in the elegy to Demuth. Before he'd even talk about another volume with Latimer, therefore, he wanted corrections made, even if he had to foot the bill for the changes himself.[97] Besides, what the hell was going on with this mysterious figure who called himself Latimer, but who had also used at least two other aliases with Williams? Since Latimer was also printing Stevens at the same time he was doing Williams, Williams wrote to Stevens to say that the new galleys had upset him and to warn Stevens that there might be something lurking in the woodpile.

"Dear Sherlock Holmes," Stevens wrote back, "I agree that there is something wrong in the woodpile." But whatever Latimer was personally meant nothing to Stevens as long as Stevens wasn't directly involved. He was still going to send the man his own *Owl's Clover* script in a few days. "It is very easy to say of a man of this sort that he is a slopover. His letters are full of little nursery turns, but the books that he has published up to now certainly show discipline, whether it is his or his printer's." So, now that they knew about the woodpile, he and Williams were "no worse off than going along with almost anybody else."[98] Latimer himself did the honorable thing, delaying publication and having the sheets corrected at his own expense. In the meantime Latimer had asked Williams to finish the *Paterson* book he'd been talking about as well as the *Collected*, but Williams had already made up his mind by then not to go with Latimer—at least not yet. As for the *Paterson* script he'd mentioned to Latimer earlier: he had to admit now that the thing did not yet exist as anything more than desire. "When I said I had the next script ready I was not speaking the truth," Williams finally admitted to Latimer himself in early February. "I meant merely that I have enough material for another book among the notes of the long poem, *Paterson*, which it has been my ambition to finish for several years." But he couldn't show Latimer a sheaf of "rough and random sketches" yet. He would need time for this project, and just then medical practice was busy. His plan was this: not to finish the entire poem—that would be, rather, "the work of my final years—if any—but to make a sketch of the whole in about fifty pages and let you do what you please with it. All the essential elements will be there."[99] But by September, when copies of *Adam & Eve & the City* arrived at 9 Ridge Road, Williams was no closer to finishing *Paterson* or to compiling a *Complete Collected.* Latimer was ready for a script, but now Williams told him he would have to wait. "I'm writing little now and do not care to be bound down just now. Forget it for a year."[100] The fact that Latimer had sold a total of eight copies of the first book in the year since its publication may have helped Williams to make his decision.

Even as Williams was sending his script to Latimer in January, he received an invitation from the chairman of the Extension Division at Hunter College to lecture on three Thursday evenings from 8:00 to 9:40 on the topic "Contemporary Trends in Poetry as Illustrated in the Work of the Living British & American Poets." That was six hours of lecturing for sixty dollars (minus deductions), and the other poets scheduled to lecture would be Babette Deutsch, Padraic Colum, and Horace Gregory. Williams was tempted to try his hand at this sort of thing, but he finally decided against it, giving them Zukofsky's name instead. "It would only send me into a stew for the next three months," he explained to Zukofsky, "and this is my rest period—or composition period. I want to be at liberty to do what I please this spring. Eight years of that God damned opera and the fiddling and the fussing that went with it just about had me ready for the psychopathic ward."[101] He still had not completely forgiven Zukofsky for his part in that affair.

The next day Zukofsky wrote Williams again, this time to warn him to be careful how he answered a questionnaire that the editors of the *Partisan Review & Anvil* had just sent him. Williams' response was unusually testy, probably because he knew Zukofsky was right and that he'd already been trapped into making statements that the magazine would probably use against him. "I thought the questions were asked in good faith," he told Zukofsky on January 29. "So I answered them that way. If they don't care to publish my replies it makes no difference to me. Please don't try to protect me."[102] But two days later he admitted that Zukofsky's diagnosis of the questions had been the correct one. He may already have suspected that he was in for it.

The question the *Partisan Review* editors had asked Williams—along with other writers and intellectuals—was part of a symposium they were publishing on Marxism called "What Is Americanism: Marxism and the American Tradition." Most of the answers suggested either that Marxism was essentially in the American grain or that America should be educated to Marxism, so that Williams' response struck the only discordant or heretical note in the whole leftist symphony. "The essential democracy upon which an attempt was made to found the U.S. has been the central shaft about which all the other movements and trends of thought have revolved—without changing it in any way." It was this bedrock belief in democracy, Williams insisted, that had defeated

> the more radical thought of each era, such as that of Tom Paine, Gene Debs, Bill Haywood, making their movements and thought seem foreign to the environment. It is this same democracy of feeling which will defeat Marxism in America and all other attempts at regimentation of thought and action. It will also defeat fascism—though it may have to pass through that. . . . American tradition is completely opposed to Marxism. America is progressing through difficult mechanistic readjustments which it is confident it can take care of. But Marxism is a static philosophy of a hundred years ago which has not yet kept up—as the democratic spirit has—through the stresses of an actual trial.

America already had the theory it needed to survive and so would smile and suffer when the crisis—looming already on the horizon—finally came. As far as revolutionary literature was concerned, Williams finished, most Americans merely tolerated it, knowing deep down that it was "definitely in conflict with our deep-seated ideals."[103]

Williams' response was published in the April issue of the magazine. In the following month's issue the editors were calling for "Sanctions Against Williams" in their correspondence section, making it absolutely clear that most of the *Partisan Review*'s correspondents had taken vigorous exception to Williams' downgrading of Marxism, at the same time insisting that the editorial staff itself was also "utterly opposed to the direction of thought shown in Mr. Williams' contribution." To show the kind of letters that had poured into their offices attacking Williams, they chose one from a Charles Forrest, who wrote: "If the American masses have so far, as he claims, not taken to revolutionary literature, they are even less aware of Mr. Williams' particular brand of poetry. In fact, the whole school of modernist writing of which Mr. Williams is such a shining light has made no dent on the American consciousness."[104] *That* should get the bastard. All *he* thought he'd done, Williams told McAlmon in May, was to answer the *PR*'s questionnaire, and now he found they wanted sanctions against him, which amounted to being placed on their list of those to be shot in the coming revolution. He would run a skirmish with that magazine which would last well into the '40s, attacking and in turn being attacked, in general being made by careful editing of his letters to look the fool.

Ironically, at the same time that Zukofsky was warning Williams about the *Partisan Review*, he also asked him to write an essay on "The Writers of the American Revolution" for the American Federation of Writers, another leftist group. "So I got to work for the Party after all," he chided Zukofsky on February 7. "Well, the project interests me—greatly, only it's quite a job you're handing me."[105] Four days later, writing to John Herrmann, who was then helping organize labor unions as well as writing, Williams enclosed a check to pay for Herrmann's winter coal bill, mentioning in passing that he was writing a chapter "for some Party journal."[106] Williams was swamped with medical work that winter, but he finally managed to get twenty pages finished at ten thirty on the evening of March 16 and then drove over to get Mrs. Johns out of bed for her to type the script the next day. It had been one hell of a job, he told Zukofsky, but it was done and would be in the mails by the morning of the nineteenth.[107]

Williams' essay was a good overview of the writers of the American Revolution, and its twenty pages included a discussion of a large number of American writers of the 1760s and 1770s, beginning with James Otis and his speech against the Writs of Assistance in 1761 (the beginning of the resistance against England) and going on to include Patrick Henry, John Dickinson, Sam Adams, Tom Paine, Philip Freneau, Jonathan Odell, the Connecticut Wits, Washington, Jefferson, and ending—brilliantly—with Baron von Steuben's *Regulations for the Order and Discipline of the Troops of the United States*, the book that had actually turned provincial soldiers into the match of England's grenadiers, as the British learned at Monmouth. Williams ended the essay with the "Creed" of the American officers adapted at Verplanck's Point in 1782, a manifesto that included these sentiments:

> We believe that Baron Steuben has made us soldiers. And that he is capable of forming the whole world into a solid column, and displaying it from the center. We believe in General Knox and his artillery. And we believe in our bayonets. Amen!

Williams began his essay with the figure of Otis, criminal lawyer, Harvard graduate, brilliant legalist, intellectual. But he ended with the straightforward, virile prose of the nameless men who had actually carried out the abstraction called independence into a plan for action. It was an example of the kind of prose Williams admired: a prose with muscle behind it.[108]

But a week after Zukofsky received the essay, he had to tell Williams that the magazine for which it had been meant would not be published. Williams was not surprised. "I think I can already smell the garlic," he told Zukofsky on the twenty-seventh. What did it matter anyway? There were Zuk's corrections and suggestions which he personally found useful, and there were the early spring flowers, "surpassing in the rapidity of their development all human or understandable records of achievement. We are a sluggard race."[109] The essay went into his files and stayed there for another eighteen years, and when it finally came out again, Williams had even forgotten when or for whom he had written it.

If Williams turned down the Hunter invitation, he did accept another invitation to read and talk about poetry at Barnard College's literary society on the evening of February 24. It was the first time he had ever done such a thing, he told Latimer three days later, and he had done it at a "great cost to myself in time and physical energy."[110] He sent Zukofsky some notes he had written that night for the Barnard talk and explained that he hadn't told him about the thing earlier only because he didn't want anyone he knew around, though René Taupin and his wife, Mimi, had found out he was reading and were sitting there in the small audience when he appeared. Facing those undergraduates, he had read "them poems for an hour which they swallowed like so many pills."[111] Two months later, on April 28, he repeated his performance, this time at Dartmouth. He preferred to play the rebel in the classroom, Eliot's Harvard antithesis, and worked up a paper on "the anti-sonnet theory." But his anti-traditionalist, anti-old-forms stance was heatedly disputed by the young English professor in charge of overseeing Williams' stay. On his return, Williams recounted the give-and-take he'd had with that professor to Zukofsky: "He thought I overstressed the necessity for a new and significant form. . . . I agree[d], that if one wishes to cross the ocean there is no need to design a new sort of boat at each crossing, especially one with three ends to it. But does that hold good in crossing a continent with a 200-inch mirror on board?"[112] And yet there was still a need for a new poetry consonant with one's time. He attacked Eliot in his talk (naturally) and cited Mencken in defense of the American language. There was little new here; his own position had been drawn up years before, and when it came to the question of the new poetry he could be as hard-nosed and as unbending in his views as any veteran New York City Communist Party member.

Communications with Pound were also becoming more and more strained. So, for example, in early February Pound ranted on about "our little brown brothers in Japan" and the "glorious sunrise of the cock," and then asked Williams what he as a physician thought the effect of circumcision over so long a period had had on the character of the Jewish people.[113] Williams even tried to answer the question seriously. As far as he could see, there'd been no alteration in character. The truth was that doctors were "clipping the Irish, the Scotch, the Scandinavian and the colored today almost as much as the Jews." Besides the biggest problem was not circumcision, but rather not being psychologically castrated by one's wife or by the law. The greater fear in any event was the fear Williams felt whenever divorce was seriously broached. That was a real "clipping," not a little skin off one's penis. "I'm sure I could get along with or without a foreskin," Williams added, "but one grows weary of the calamitous, faked up consequences of a simple, salutary, hygienic and possibly genius provoking exercise of the whole psyche." And then he added, "Ain't you gettin' yours?"[114]

In March, when Pound asked Williams if he thought there was enough good material for a book of essays among his uncollected magazine material, Williams told him that he thought there was and that it should be called *The Last Gentleman*. He added too that Eliot's *Murder in the Cathedral* was now playing in New York but that he hadn't "been to see his harking back yet."[115] When he wrote again two weeks later it was to say that there were cherry blossoms outside his office window even "though the steam radiator at my right knee is comfortably hot." He also mentioned that he'd recently met one of Pound's correspondents, a young poet named Mary Barnard who had just arrived in New York from Portland, Oregon, and whose verse he liked very much.[116]

Mary Barnard was one of many young poets whom Williams showed an interest in. He'd been in correspondence with her since the beginning of '35, when she'd introduced herself to Williams by letter at Pound's prior urging. Williams had liked Barnard's poems and had told her then that "in general there are only two things to say about any poem, Yes and No. I say yes in your case."[117] He was particularly impressed with her precise use of sapphics and thought that the form might be suited to women. There was, he suggested, "an order which becomes passion in a woman, something which Sappho has typified," something the direct opposite of Whitman's *Song of Myself*, which seemed to be typical of a male voice, though possibly at its worst. On the other hand, he warned her to avoid a too-exaggerated delicacy in her writing.[118]

Barnard questioned him on that last point and Williams tried to clarify what he had meant. What was he to tell a young woman from Portland about a poetry of experience? "I don't ask anyone to be indelicate," he explained. "That isn't it. But when a person has little actual experience of bodily contacts, . . . when we can't get to the world hard enough or fast enough—and yet we must write—then we are likely to draw out a fund of material and make it do—and do too often—over and over—and it gets hard to keep from getting brittle." What example could he give? "Emily Dickinson (I swore I wasn't going to use her name) succeeded by hammering her form obstinately into some kind of homespun irregularity that made it do—but even at her best—it is too far gone to heaven —too much the wish for what it might have been—to be an example for many." For him the problem was that he preferred the toughness of a

Sappho "who got knocked around" to Emily Dickinson or—for that matter—Marianne Moore herself. The woman up against hard times, who had brushed against life, usually possessed a deeper sense of virtue than the woman whose virtue and fineness and delicacy were held so long that they finally soured. Barnard, he sensed in her poems, was still possessed of "a virginity" he distrusted. But don't, he warned her, "for the luv of Pete, ever act on what I say without waiting a year, at least, to pass first."[119]

When Mary Barnard wrote again, a year had passed and she was now living in an apartment at 148 West 11th Street. "I get to New York almost not at all or if I go it is for so special a purpose, such as a visit to Bill's medical school [Bill Jr. had just been accepted at Cornell Medical in the city] or a look at [Marsden] Hartley's pictures, that I see no one," he wrote Zukofsky on April 16.[120] He was still avoiding Zuk, for the next night he dropped by Mary Barnard's apartment and took her to Ticino's for what turned out to be a disappointing Italian meal. Williams filled her in on the literary gossip and left her apartment with a sheaf of her latest poems to look over. When he left, she sat down and wrote to her parents: "Dr. Williams just clasped my hand, told me I was good, and took his departure." She had waited, shaking, for the arrival of the "venerable" poet. Then, at Ticino's, she noticed how much he enjoyed food—lots of it—though he had been disappointed by the meal itself. Afterward they had gone back to her place and he had become enthusiastic over her poems, saying he would try to get Latimer to do one of his exquisite limited editions for her. He was not as good-looking as the picture she'd seen of him (probably the 1926 photo) but his enthusiasm was overwhelming. He spoke rapidly and rather nervously. He told her he was bitter about his lack of success in publishing. She reminded him, he said, of Marianne Moore, whose mother (he confided) was a dragon. He wanted her to meet Zukofsky, Marianne, and Latimer. As for his other New York contacts, most of them were drunken bums.[121]

The following Friday evening, Mary Barnard went to "Farrugio's apartment" at 62 Montague Street in Brooklyn Heights (overlooking lower Manhattan) for a party thrown by Ronald Lane Latimer. There she met Marianne Moore, the critic Ruth Lechlitner, Latimer, and saw Williams again. It was the first time Williams himself had seen Marianne Moore in several years and Barnard found that Moore kept up an incessant barrage of words because—as Williams told Barnard later—she "was frightened and was trying to build up a barrier of words to hide behind." Moore left early and Williams withdrew to sign the colophon sheets for *Adam & Eve & the City*. Interestingly, Moore had advised Barnard "not to pay any attention to what Dr. Williams told [her]—as to content. As for technical advice, he might be very good." But a little while later in the evening, Marianne Moore came over to her again to say that she herself was "a menace, and I oughtn't to pay any attention to her either."[122]

Sixteen months earlier, when Latimer asked Williams to describe Moore for him, Williams had painted a revealing cameo:

> She's a Bryn Mawr girl. Father—indefinite! maybe skipped, maybe dead—never mentioned: probable source of genius. Mother a terrific pain in the neck to whom Marianne pathologically devoted. A brother (Yale?) chaplain in U.S. Navy. Adored by Marianne. Tennis devotee. Shit ass as far as I'm concerned. Likes his sister despises literary guys she might have married among. Marianne a stick of a woman, fence rail with a magnificent head of red hair (to the ground I imagine) fine eyes. Once bemoaned that God had given her no body at all to work with. Nothing feminine about her but the nervous movements, the brain, the eyes, the searching speech. A great personality lost because of devotion to—what the hell. Straight as an arrow in every way—wanting to be able to flex.[123]

The Sunday following the party, Williams sent Mary Barnard back her script, mentioning that Marianne had been in an extraordinary mood: "through the curtain of words the frailty of her body made an affecting silhouette."[124] He was still half in love with Marianne's self-effacing brilliance. Then, in mid-May, he visited Marianne—as he had been promising for years to do—telling her afterward that, while she still bewildered him with her writing, it seemed "less a mystery and more an accomplishment now." If she was intricate in her verse forms, it was only "to disguise a great lucidity."[125]

He was to see Marianne again at year's end, when the two of them shared the podium at the Brooklyn Institute of Arts and Letters on Friday evening, December 4. Amy Bonner had organized the symposium for *Poetry* and had invited Williams back in August to lecture and read from his poems. And, in spite of the silent feud he'd carried on with *Poetry*'s editor Harriet Monroe over the years, he still wished her well and accepted the invitation, though he didn't want to "shadow box" with Marianne. He would read and make some extempore comments, and he even promised not to say "damn" in Marianne's presence.[126]

That evening, with Marsden Hartley and Marianne Moore's friend and protégé, Elizabeth Bishop, in the microscopic audience—as Williams called it—Williams spoke of the new language he had spent years trying to get down on paper, a language still not "broken to poetic form," but which was still insisting on its own as-yet-unrealized forms. Poetry, Williams suggested, was "getting up the heat with—or by the use of—words," expanding the vulgate, the dialect, until, by a kind of rapid motion—the pace indigenous to New York—the words became rhythmic. He also read the fragments of his "Patterson," as he then spelled it, which he'd included in *Adam & Eve & the City* as a bit of speech overheard:

> *I bought a new*
> *bathing suit*
>
> *Just pants*
> *and a brassiere—*
>
> *I haven't shown*
> *it*
>
> *to my mother*
> *yet*

Of such would the new poetry, he said, be composed. It was the understanding of this pace and this rhythm that would make "poetic form natural and suitable" to the American language. But to catch that rhythm would not be easy.[127] There had only been thirty people in an auditorium that sat three hundred, Williams told Zukofsky afterward. But they'd all managed to have a good time, except that Floss had had to tell him afterward that he'd not only said damn but had sworn and cursed far too much. He'd forgotten to wear evening dress, he admitted, and so felt he had had to let loose verbally to make up for that. Marianne, he added, had been beautiful: "I found myself drifting off into the trance which only beauty creates, more than once. Floss agrees. There is a quality there which is unspeakably elevating—through all her frail pretenses of being this or that by God, she IS. The modern Andromeda —with her graying red hair all coiled about her brows."[128]

For her part, Marianne Moore wrote to Williams to say that she and Elizabeth Bishop were very much interested in Williams' anti-sonnet theory, and Williams wrote her expounding on that. And though he had earlier written to say that it was not necessary to see Marianne often since he knew her in her poems, now, just before Christmas, he wrote her that he wished it were possible for the two of them and some others "to have a place, a location, to which we could resort, singly or otherwise, and to which others could follow us as dogs follow each other. . . . Being exiles might we not at least, as exiles, consort more easily together? We seem needlessly isolated and we suffer dully, supinely."[129] But, for complex reasons, that isolation—that necessary separation even from friends—was the price Williams knew as well as anyone the artist paid in order to create.

*
**

In late May of '36 Gorham Munson wrote Williams to tell him that a team of Social Credit speakers were going down to Charlottesville, Virginia, in July to talk before a conference sponsored by the Institute of Public Affairs and that he was inviting Williams to speak as an artist in defense of Social Credit. Williams accepted at once and had twenty pages of a first draft written a week later. "I have used up half my supply of prescription blanks stopping on the street to pull out my pad and write at your tyrannous bidding," he told Munson on June 1.[130] He continued to work on the drafts, revising and expanding the talk right up till the last minute. Finally, on Thursday, July 9, in the middle of a heat wave, with the temperatures hovering around an intensely uncomfortable 106°, he and Floss headed south, stopping over that first night at his boyhood friend Jim Hyslop's farm outside the nation's capital. On Friday, with the temperature at 101°, they took the Sky Line Drive overlooking the Shenandoah Valley amidst fields of bugloss and blue flowers, stopping once again at Jefferson's Monticello—"an amazing house, like none other in the world, beautifully situated"—and then found the house they were being hosted at: a Miss Mary Fishburn's of Ivy Depot, "one of the old families who live in summer in a shack (with all the conveniences) seven miles out of town."

On Saturday Williams gave his talk in one of the lecture rooms at the University of Virginia, though the room, he complained, had been hot as hell. "I did my bit," he told his son, "not entirely to my satisfaction but anyhow, I did it."[131] His talk was called "The Attack on Credit Monopoly from a Cultural Viewpoint," and though it was somewhat dense, Williams basically tried to stress the importance of retaining "the long fought for principles of representative democratic government." He used Pound again—what Pound had told him about Martin Van Buren and the growing power of the banks, and also Pound's Confucian ethic of striking at the root to kill an evil. Alexander Hamilton was the real enemy, Williams maintained, especially of the individual's economic independence from big business. He talked of the continuing need for the rugged individual, for figures of the stature of Lenin and Mussolini and his English grandmother. He called himself a rebel in the Jeffersonian mode, perhaps thinking of the presences hovering about that sweltering room.

Like so many other Americans, he felt like the victim of a twisted economy. "For the past thirty years I have never been able to get one first-rate poem published in a commercial magazine," he confessed to his audience. "I have never been able to get a single book of poems, no matter how small, published except by paying or partly paying for it myself." But what was he going to do about it? If he was being assaulted from the right by the big credit monopolies, he was also aware of the attack from the left in the form of a proletarian revolution. He knew from firsthand experience that there were tens of millions in his country who were without the bare essentials, but he was also afraid that a Communist revolution would sweep away individual liberties along with it. Forced to it, he would himself side with labor and the people if the revolution came, but he also believed that the bloodbath afterward would be far different and far more violent than anything the left had dreamed it would be.[132]

His talk over, he and Floss were "regally entertained" by some of the Virginians. He found them "charming people and better equipped to think than most of us up here. A little slow, perhaps, but they don't over-shoot the mark."[133] Then they left for home, not missing the opportunity to see the Wilderness battle sites and then to visit Mount Vernon, where Washington had lived and died.

By the fall of '36, Williams' *White Mule* had been making the rounds of the New York publishers for over two years. Three different agents had tried to get the thing published without any success. So, when the script came back to him, rejected by the *Short Story* people, Williams was close to resigning in despair. "No, White Mule didn't," he told John Herrmann in June. "The ass at *Short Story* didn't have a hole in it. Poor Mule just came home and has gone to sleep again awaiting better times. He's a fine nag. Never kicks. Just saves his steam till he can find something worth putting it into."[134] The answer came from a completely unexpected corner. Young Jim Laughlin, scion of the Pittsburgh steel family, who was still doing undergraduate work at Harvard, had been reading Williams' *White Mule* as it appeared in *The Magazine*. Now he was beginning a publishing venture to be called New Directions, so named after a column he'd done for *The New Democracy*, and he had been in touch with Pound since 1933. A few years earlier he'd written Williams asking for something for the *Harvard Advocate*, and Williams had been upset to learn that the young man had broken his back in a skiing accident in the winter of '36.

Now, in September, sufficiently recovered from that accident of the previous January, Laughlin wrote Williams to say that he wanted to meet Williams personally. But Williams hedged. "There seems no possibility of our meeting and talking," he told Laughlin on the twenty-second, in what was to be a classic miscalculation on his part. "It won't happen either. We're too far apart in years and neither of us would be able to beat down the bushes enough."[135] Laughlin had hoped to talk over his plans for New Directions face to face with Williams. But now he did so by letter. He wanted to publish Williams and he wanted to begin with *White Mule*, which he would pay for, sharing whatever profits accrued from the book with Williams. For a writer who had several times been willing to pay for at least part of the printing cost to have his novel published, this was almost too good to be true.[136] A week later—on Election Day—Williams wrote Julian Shapiro (who'd changed his name by then at Pep West's urging to John Sanford) to say that a young man named Laughlin was going to publish his novel. He felt guilty about letting Laughlin do the book, "as if caught taking advantage of the young," but he hadn't asked him to do the thing, and perhaps Laughlin could "afford the loss."[137] A few days later he mentioned his good luck to Pound as well. "It sure was a bolt out of the blue of almost despair," he wrote. Laughlin's "impetus has set me polishing (that is, rewriting) the last chapters to make this a definite Book. It is to be Book I and ends with proper regard for an ending. I'm going to like this book. It's put ten years on my life."

It was a moment, then, for hope. He was even doing some more poems. And he was thinking again about "that magnum opus I've always wanted to do: the poem *Paterson*," which he'd been sounding himself out on for years, looking for the proper form. Moreover, *The American Caravan* had just published his libretto and Serly was still at least a remote possibility to do the music. And now he'd just learned that the 1939 World's Fair to be held in Flushing was to have as its theme the sesquicentennial of Washington's inauguration in New York as the country's first president. Which was just what his libretto was all about! On top of that, his brother Ed's architectural firm had just been awarded the contract for the new administrative building to be built for the fair. He himself had been present at the ceremonies held in the Empire State Building where Ed had signed the contracts, though the klieg lights and movie cameras and reporters had made Williams a little nervous. Moreover, Ed had promised to talk to the government press agent about his brother's libretto. Perhaps Franklin Roosevelt would see his opera after all. In the end, as usual, however, all that fanfare came to nothing.[138]

The pervasive sense of disappointment carried over into Williams' next letter to Pound in early December, when Williams dared Pound to come over to the U.S. and try his own hand "at battling some of these currents of liquid shit. . . . Take *Time, Fortune,* the new (?) *Life, Coronet* and all the rest of them who are running the publishing game today and see how much chance you'd have to get hold of a Linotype." Pound would land in the same place that Maxwell Bodenheim and some others had wound up: in the mud. Sure the government through its WPA projects gave money to the artists "to decorate the walls of this or that place," but that didn't mean they were allowed to say anything of value.[139] He must have been thinking of the recent incident of the Orozco murals at Rockefeller Center. The entire mural had been completely effaced when Orozco painted in a portrait of Lenin in a scene depicting the progress of man. When he refused to alter or generalize the portrait, a squad of New York City police officers had escorted Orozco and his crew off the premises of the Center and the mural was obliterated. So much for the artist. Idealized images of American aspiration: fine. But anything suggesting an adverse commentary on the American scene was out of the question. It was one reason why Williams—except for one brief flirtation —stayed clear of the WPA projects.

When he'd tried to suggest his own plan for a Department of Arts and

Letters to one government official the previous year, he had gotten exactly nowhere. "I asked that they give us a periodical in which to pour our helpful work," he explained to Pound, and had received no answer. "I asked for an annual Bulletin. No Answer. I suggested subsidies by the government to publishers to assist such publishers in printing books they would LIKE to print but couldn't afford, as they protest, to print—in paper covers. . . . No answer. It would have worked."[140]

So Williams ended 1936 with a poem that accurately reflected his own inner and outer darkness. "These," he wrote, thinking very much of Stevens' *Ideas of Order*,

> *are the desolate, dark weeks*
> *when nature in its barrenness*
> *equals the stupidity of man.*
>
> *The year plunges into night*
> *and the heart plunges*
> *lower than night*
>
> *to an empty, windswept place*
> *without sun, stars or moon*
> *but a peculiar light as of thought*
>
> *that spins a dark fire—*
> *whirling upon itself until,*
> *in the cold, it kindles*
>
> *to make a man aware of nothing*
> *that he knows, not loneliness*
> *itself. . . .* [141]

Even in the desolation of the present moment, the descent into the darkness of winter and the depths of the Depression, there was still the dark flame of the imagination to see by. Call it a light of sorts.

*
**

The cycle continued: winter and the business of medicine. "I run around through six townships and four boroughs chasing the little twos and threes until I stink of all the international odors from garlic to *bouquet de cochon*. And in between I write poems for rest, relief and relaxation. My three Rs."[142] Williams didn't get into New York much anymore—not as much as he used to, when it had been two and three times a week. He was still working on that old Quevedo translation with his mother, meanwhile taking down what she told him about herself and her girlhood. By writing her biography, or a fragment of that life, he thought, he might endow her with a second life even as the first ebbed inevitably away.[143] Mrs. Johns was even then transcribing his mother's early letters to him as well as the notes he'd taken of their conversations. The poems he was writing now he was dissatisfied with; he called them dirty water dripping from a broken pipe. "I am not proud of my recent quality," he confessed to Zukofsky, "but I let it go on rather than fix the leak." It was beginning to look like "the final break-up" of his gift, he thought, except that there were here and there momentary flashes of insight. Perhaps it was just a transitional phase he was going through, he thought. "I'm not trying to guide it but weakwilled let it dribble, all sorts of trash, sometimes even in complicated rhyme."[144]

Williams was seeing more of Ford Madox Ford in New York that winter of '37 and was also giving Louis Zukofsky's long *A* fragment a close reading. He also suggested to Zukofsky what he'd suggested to Riordan ten years before: that they collaborate on a book about modern prosody with emphasis on the loosely formulated objectivist banner they'd been working under since at least 1930. They would begin with Aristotle, brazenly supporting their own theories, the two men writing alternate chapters and René Taupin providing the introduction. But the book did not materialize.[145]

That winter and spring there was also bad news coming out of Spain, of Franco's Loyalists fighting against the Republicans, of aid coming from workers and intellectuals in England and America, but also from Mussolini and Hitler as well, who were supplying Franco with new weapons and aircraft as a staging ground for the larger conflict that was certainly coming in Europe. It was a bloody civil war, as the despatches and reports from the jagged fronts made painfully clear, but even so few were prepared for the news of Guernica. Shortly before five on the afternoon of April 26, Heinkel IIIs piloted by Germans suddenly and unexpectedly appeared over this small, undefended Basque market town at a time when the streets were filled with townspeople and peasants who had come in from the surrounding countryside. The German squadrons dropped their high explosives directly into the crowd, sending arms and limbs and heads a hundred feet into the air in a surrealistic dance that left hundreds of civilians dead and dying. After they departed, other squadrons of Junkers 52s repeated the grisly performance. Guernica had had no military or strategic importance; its only value was that it had stood as a sort of unofficial capital for the Basque, a sign of their independent spirit and democratic ideals.

Now it lay smoldering, a sign of things to come: of civilian bombings of London, Dresden, Nagasaki. Picasso responded with his extraordinary mural in blacks and grays and whites, fragments of heads of women and children, of bulls and horses, lit by the cold light of modern technology, in the colors of contemporary news photos and film clips. That mural would become a talisman for Williams of human grief transformed into the dignity of art, and he himself would write a number of poems about the war as well as translate Spanish revolutionary ballads over the next two years in an attempt to come to terms with the slaughter of democracy he was witnessing in his beloved Spain. In 1940, after the defeat of France, he would recall his own feelings about Guernica and his shock in seeing that most Americans at the time had shrugged the whole incident off and had gone about business as usual.

"I myself was chairman in Bergen County, N. J., of a committee for medical aid to Spanish democracy," he wrote, "while the Storch Squadron went out with their planes on Easter while the women and children were in the streets—people with whom they had not the slightest quarrel—and blasted them to butchers' meat in the holy Basque city of Guernica to see how effective the planes and bombs would be." He had done what he could, had gone to a meeting at "the 8th St. school in Hackensack and warned and begged for a few dollars to send—not guns or ammunition—but bandages, old clothes, surgical instruments—and to their everlasting shame not a single physician in the whole country, Friedian of Edgewater who had already gone to Spain excepted, so much as turned a hair, though I sent a personal card to every one of them." Looking back at that experience, he could only conclude that he had come "of a criminal generation." It had shocked him to see members of his profession "lying down by disease and watching the patient make counterpoint by her screams to pious mutterings."[146]

Williams continued his work as chairman of the Bergen County Medical Board to Aid Spanish Democracy until the cause itself went down to defeat, and he continued to contribute as he could to the survivors of the Abraham Lincoln Brigade for several years after that. In early '38, as Franco's forces moved in on the remaining pockets of Republican resistance, Williams wrote a strongly worded statement for the League of American Writers: "If Italian history could look down on Mussolini today it would vomit! Think of the century-long struggles for freedom waged by Florence, by Milan, by Venice . . . and then think of the decay of freedom rotting its way into Spain today. . . . Without Mussolini there could not be Franco, it is the same rot eating in."[147]

On the evening of January 25, 1938, listening to the bad news over the radio about the collapse of yet another Republican stronghold, Williams lashed out against Mussolini again, calling him a "prize shit" who had forgotten his "simple peasant virtues." Williams was frustrated. "I don't know what to say or to do," he told McAlmon. "I can't understand, though I should of course, the stupidity of American indifference. But it's in everything. I don't belong here after all."[148] And in April he wrote Pound bluntly: "I detest your bastardly Italy today. You complain of the English and their Chamberlain and with good reason, but if you can tell me who is licking whose ass right now . . . explain."[149] And three weeks later, he wrote Pound again that he was all wrong about Spain, and that he

had allowed himself to be duped either by Mussolini or by his lieuten-
ants. As for Hemingway, who was then in Republican Spain, Williams
refused to see him as anything more than a footnote to the real issues
going on there. The trouble with Pound himself, Williams told him, was
that he was willing

> to crush out the resistance of a people against the elements of an
> economic setup which you yourself oppose—only you want to paste your
> own label on their goods. It happens to be not your particular shade of
> pink so you approve the destruction. . . . It is you, not Hemingway, in this
> case who is playing directly into the hands of the International Bankers.[150]

So the argument went on. By mid-May Williams was becoming
exasperated. "You are so completely wrong in what you say of the
Spanish situation that you have to build up a myth to support yourself
that you only get inside information . . . , never realizing that many
thoroughly trained men and women of all nationalities are spending their
lives in Spain to discover what it is all about." In the meantime, there was
Ezra writing from his room in Rapallo as though he had Mussolini's ear.
But what could either of them do, either Pound in Italy or Williams in
America? "I glance at the papers to see where the troops are today or to
try to discover what, under the news, the prize bastards of the world who
rule it are cooking up." And what humanitarian concessions were Franco
or Mussolini or Hitler willing to make now that the Republicans were
willing to compromise? He ended ominously: "I have my troubles
defending you in America these days but I still do it."[151] By February 1939,
with the Republican army in defeat, thousands daily seeking asylum in
France, and Franco's forces about to enter the Spanish capital, Williams
had stopped talking to Pound altogether. "I refuse to write him or answer
his letters," he told Jim Laughlin, "while he stands up for the son of a
bitch [Mussolini] who sends his son to bomb civilians 'just for the fun of
it.' "[152] Pound for his part couldn't figure out what Williams was so riled
about.

The Depression, Guernica, the Scottsboro Trial, Nazi strong-arm
policy against the Jews, shouts from the left, from the right. As the '30s
rolled toward their own denouement, reality and surrealism seemed more
and more to converge. In May and again in June of 1937, Williams went to
Pavel Tchelitchew's studio apartment on East 57th Street to visit the
Russian surrealist and to look at his drawings and the large unfinished
murals he was then working on. His first impression of the work—"a
drawing of a running foot with a big hind foot"—had left Williams only
with a sense of "desperate beauty."[153] Williams' introduction to Tchelitchew had been through Charles Henri Ford, for whose book of surrealist
poems, *The Garden of Disorder,* Williams had written an introduction in

the spring of '37. Ford had included a poem about Tchelitchew in his book, and Williams had been piqued to go and see the artist for himself.

The late afternoon visit in June to Tchelitchew's apartment resulted in Williams' writing an essay which appeared later that year in *Life and Letters Today*. That day the two men talked about the French and Spanish moderns, especially of Salvador Dali, whom Tchelitchew described as a crab eating the world with his eyes. Before them, there in that studio, was the unfinished seven-by-nine-foot canvas of *Phenomena*. Williams was especially struck by how the whole canvas teemed with human monsters:

> Figures of all sorts filled it, of all sizes spreading out upon a background of mountain, classical ruin, and Mexican adobe house, with sea and sky going off toward the top and back. . . . To the left, the signature, a man with one enormous foot, the back of Diego Rivera it may be, painting the wall of a house. Siamese twins, women with six breasts, acephalic monsters, three-legged children, double-headed monsters, sexual freaks, dwarfs, giants, achrondoplastic midgets, mongolian idiots and the starved, bloated, misshapen by idea and social accident—of all the walks of life. In the foreground was a surf with a girl in a pink bathing suit.[154]

What most pleased Tchelitchew was that Williams, as a physician, had recognized that in fact every monster in the picture had been taken from life. For Tchelitchew had taken his subjects from life itself and had held them up as his mirror in which others could see themselves. To heighten the grotesqueness, the artist had suffused all his creatures in the soft colors of the rainbow to make them more "beautiful."

Yes, that was the way it was with people. Four years before Williams had reviewed Pep West's *Miss Lonelyhearts* and been struck by the truth of what West had revealed there about the poor monsters who mirrored our own flawed humanity. Those letters that poured into the newspaper offices of a hundred Miss Lonelyhearts every day, from "the girl without a nose, [or] the simpleminded child . . . raped on the roof of a tenement": it was "a terrific commentary on our daily lack of depth in thought of others." Should such lives, like the "worst of our war wounded," quadriplegics, brain-damaged, merely be hidden from the rest of us? After all, Williams saw them daily, especially in the poorer sections of the cities, or out in the more remote rural areas. Actually, artists like West and Tchelitchew had done society a service, elevating the observer by their art, even as they plunged him toward the condition of hell in which, truly, he stood. At least those men had dared to go beside us, like Virgil escorting Dante through hell, "to make it possible for us at the very least to look and understand."[155]

Williams would remember the lesson he had learned from West and Tchelitchew when he came to write his own *Paterson*, his own mirror held up to the mind, and peopled it as well with dwarfs and hydrocephalics . . . and himself, the monstrous poet dreaming the grotesque dream of the poem. So, too, as he read Ford's surrealistic poems on a Saturday night in early June 1937, stretched out on his stuffed couch in his living room, the poems seemed to form "an accompaniment to the radio jazz and other various, half-preaching, half-sacrilegious sounds" all around him. "With the windows open and the mind stretched out attempting to regain some sort of quiet and cool," Williams—at fifty-three—thought now of how "in every man there must finally occur a fusion between his dream which he dreamed when he was young and the phenomenal world of his later years." And it seemed especially important to dream that dream of one's youth when the world seemed to have gone out of control and was racing toward disaster.[156]

On June 10, 1937, New Directions released *White Mule,* and the New York press—to Williams' surprise—took to it at once.[157] Alfred Kazin reviewed the novel for the *Times* ten days after it was released, praising it for its new texture, its new world of sound which reminded him of no one so much as Joyce. Williams too had caught in his prose the accent of real speech, with its "rough, gravely ironic rhythm," deeper and more meaningful than "the violent accuracy of naturalism." On the twenty-sixth, Philip Rahv also praised the novel in the pages of *The Nation,* as did Rothman in the *Saturday Review.* And two weeks later Fred Miller wrote a strong (though biased) review for the *New Republic.* "The New York press was crazy about it," Williams recalled years later. "All the reviews were favorable and I thought I was *made.* All the lady reviewers were flocking to me."

But Laughlin had sailed to New Zealand to manage a ski team just before he released *White Mule.* He had bound only five hundred copies for June distribution, and Williams learned to his horror that those had been sold out at once because of the publicity. Frantic, he drove up to Norfolk in western Connecticut to see Laughlin's father and see what could be done. But the old man merely looked at him and said, "Well, what are you going to do about it?" Disconsolate, Williams got back in his car and headed for home. There were no more books to be had and that was that. Actually, Laughlin had printed a total of eleven hundred copies, and the remaining six hundred copies were bound up by late September. For a small press like New Directions that must have seemed fast enough. But for Williams the wait between late June and late September, especially after the reviews, seemed like a new version of hell. Within a few weeks, the world of book publishing being what it is, there were other novels clamoring for their own attention. All Williams' myopic vision could see was that—once more—he had lost his chance at greatness.[158]

During the second half of August, the Williamses took a two-week vacation on the southernmost tip of the New Jersey seashore, on what Williams said amounted "to virtually a sandbar six miles out to sea."[159] Bill and Floss were beginning to feel the burden of both their ailing mothers on them and they needed to get away with their sons while they still had them at home.[160] He described the seashore to his mother, writing in exaggerated dark ink so that she might be able to read his letter with her failing eyes. There were no trees here, he said, only bayberry bushes and a house sticking up here and there. At 110th Street there was a nunnery, "where some unknown order of Sisters come to spend two weeks' vacation every year. They go bathing too, in old fashioned gowns. . . . This is funny today when girls wear their one piece tight up into the crotch and even fat old ladies go about in the most amazing negligee." They were staying in one half of a two-family house, two blocks from the water. Paul had even found himself a Russian princess to dance with, and he was teaching her the latest American steps while she taught him the Russian ballet. It was all very primitive with the sand and waves and the seabirds on the blazing white sand, a respite before returning to the world waiting for them all back there.[161]

But whatever had been dogging Williams before his vacation was waiting for him when he returned. "I've been vague and indifferent," he told Laughlin in mid-September. "I don't precisely know why. The wars in Europe and elsewhere, everything together, age, decay—I don't know what the hell. Floss says I look fine. Maybe I'm resting—like a worm in silk."[162] And a month earlier he'd written McAlmon that his private life amounted to almost nothing now. He still did foolish things from time to time and he still worried about Floss finding out, but he was preoccupied with "so much to think about," though with what he was preoccupied he did not say.[163]

In the fall of '37 he was preparing a new book of short stories, *Life Along the Passaic River*, for New Directions, and he warned Laughlin to go over the scripts carefully for possible libel, lest "some smart kike . . . make a fifty fifty deal with one of my protagonists."[164] After eleven years the "Five Dollar Guy" episode was still very much on his mind, and he didn't want lawyers or the local police harrassing him for something he'd written. There were nineteen stories this time, nearly all of them written in the previous five years, stories of the poor, the oppressed, the outcasts, the victims of the times. Again Williams had caught the life, the toughness, but also the inner resiliency and generosity of these people: streetwise kids, nurses, factory workers, mothers bringing new, questionable life howling into a world continually on the verge of some unspeakable catastrophe.

When Williams got back from his vacation, he also found a letter waiting for him from the revived *Partisan Review* asking him for a poem.

He wrote the editors on September 8, promising to send one along shortly. When he did, however, they rejected it, at the same time asking for another one. Williams, a bit put out that they should ask for a poem and then reject it, nevertheless sent along another, this one "The Defective Record." But they didn't like that one either and asked him to send along better work than that. Williams sent a postcard this time, with the comment, "Your patience will make the flowers bloom," and the editors thought Williams had meant they were going to get something else. Then, in the November 16 issue of the *New Masses*—whose editors were sharply critical of the *Partisan Review*'s softer leftist stand—there appeared a note to the effect that Williams had told *New Masses* that the *Partisan Review* had no contribution of his, nor was he going to send them any.

Dwight Macdonald as editor of *Partisan Review* wrote Williams asking him to explain himself, and Williams responded. "You know, of course, that I have no reason for liking the *Partisan Review*," he said. "I have, at the same time, no partisan interest in the *New Masses*. I had occasion to appear as a writer, for a special reason, in the *New Masses* and it looked as though I might appear also in the *Partisan Review*. As my contribution to the *New Masses* [his essay on H. H. Lewis] was of longer standing and of more importance to me than the other and since I found the *New Masses* violently opposed to you on political grounds, so much so that they refused to print me if I remained a contributor to *Partisan Review*, I made my choice in their favor." Williams asked only that if *PR* was going to make political hay out of the affair that they at least give him the courtesy of printing his letter in full. They did, along with the whole exchange of letters, in the Ripostes section of their January '38 number, with the title "The Temptation of Dr. Williams." They also added a note to the effect that the Communist Party was out to destroy *PR* both by an open denunciation in the Party press and by a whispering campaign of slander, which had involved duping a poet of no less stature than Dr. Williams.[165] Williams himself shrugged the matter off. He'd tried to get Lewis before a wider audience for two years, and if it meant a kick from this or that magazine, he could take it. There were a lot of bastards out there anyway. Moreover, he thought it "both cheap and misleading for the *Partisan Review* to assume such an injured tone and such a face of honesty and openness in their recent comments upon me." After all, they hadn't even mentioned that just a year before they'd called for sanctions against the same man they were now accusing of going over to the other side.[166]

At the same time this affair was gathering force, James Laughlin wrote Williams a touching letter uncommon between editors and their writers. Williams had told Laughlin in November of '37 that he was thinking of getting a *Complete Collected* out and mentioned Latimer's intense interest in doing that book. After all, New Directions would have done two books of Williams' in less than a year. Now, on November 29, Laughlin wrote back:

> I have been a long time in answering your last letter because every time I think about the subject such a flood of emotions starts rolling around in my head that I can't make any sense. Your thinking that you want somebody else is a crisis in my life. I had thought I was doing all right in what I had taken up, in what was probably to be my life work, and now, if you doubt me, I don't know.
>
> You are the cornerstone of New Directions and if you left me I think I wouldn't be able to go on with it. I have built my plans around you. You are my symbol of everything that is good in writing, and if you go over to the enemy I just won't know where the hell I'm at.[167]

Latimer was hardly the enemy, but Laughlin's letter had a profound impact on Williams, though he tried to play his own emotions down. "It isn't that I need money now," Williams answered on December 4, "that's not the point. My sole thought was that sometime or other in the near future I ought to try to make some sort of connection which would enable me to get some sort of returns for my writing. I agree that my chances were slim but I felt that I had to try. I am convinced that my best chances now lie with you, looked at quite coldly."[168] He was giving Laughlin the poems to do, but he was doing something more. He was throwing in his lot with this young man who was bright, rich, and so intensely interested in avant-garde writing, and he would hope for the best. Williams was already in his mid-fifties and beginning to wonder if he would ever get an economic return for a lifetime's investment in the imagination. He wasn't sure young Laughlin could understand all that he felt, all he'd already been through, but he preferred to trust the man instinctively. It would be a hard row to hoe, the next twenty-five years, and there would be violent ups and downs, but in the long run it would be Laughlin more than any other person who would become Williams' guardian, the man to look over his name and work. "All my life I've been hoping to get a regular publisher who would put my stuff out in a more or less uniform style," he wrote a disappointed Latimer on December 17. "Things seem to be shaping up at present in favor of James Laughlin and his New Directions Press." At last Williams had his publisher.[169]

NINE

Clearing the Field:
1938—1942

*F*or Williams, then, it was to be a time of summing up and a time for beginning again. The *Complete Collected Poems*—all the poems he'd published since the beginning (except for that first frail volume, that unwanted child from 1909 which he still couldn't bear to show to anyone) were now to appear under one cover. Laughlin would get the permissions from Brown for the early work and arrange the poems by books with dates and some changes, like putting the longer poems in a separate section at the back of the book and ending with "The Wanderer." It was a generous book, over three hundred pages, and Laughlin thought that it might even get Williams the Pulitzer, though it didn't. Finally, at fifty-five, Williams would have his collected, and people who wanted to see what it was he'd done over a quarter century would have their first chance to do so.

Now, too, he could get on with the new poems he'd been after to do, poems incorporating the new speech rhythms he'd said he heard in those around him, the speech he'd already caught so well in his short stories. Now, too, he might finally get on with the long poem, *Paterson*, he'd wanted to write since the mid-'20s and before. But the time of summing up and of making the promised advance, of crossing over into his own long-delayed majority as a poet with a major form, was now threatened by a political situation that might destroy him along with the rest of the world and turn his major pronunciamento into ashes even before it could be uttered. On the one hand, as he told several people, '38 and '39 "felt" very much as 1913 had: a time of extraordinary promise and flowering, a new beginning for modern poetry in general and American poetry in particular. He felt this especially in the summer of '39, that most ominous of times, when the Hitler-Stalin nonaggression pact signed on August 23 led to Hitler's invasion of Poland on September 1 and thus the beginning of World War II. Williams was convinced that "the bastards" who ran the world had planned it that way, that just when new advances in economics and literature and art had seemed possible, the whole thing had been blown to hell. With two sons of draft age, it meant a temporary halt to his own interior revolution. And with the world moving toward general conflagration, his own priorities—as gigantic and all-consuming as they were—would have to take second place to the pressure of a terrible reality crashing in on him. The ominous storm clouds of Hitler and Mussolini, of Jewish internment and German troops racing through Poland, would have to be heeded first before any question of major form could be answered.

In the winter of '38, Williams was working on an essay on Spanish literature, with its focus on Federico García Lorca, the Spanish poet who had been executed by a Fascist squad in 1936. García Lorca was especially important to Williams because he represented the poet who had remained in contact with the people and with an indigenous Spanish culture as opposed to the European tradition. The subject meant a great deal to him, especially at that moment, when the Spanish Loyalist cause, in which he believed so fervently, was already facing incredible odds, especially with Italian and German military aid arrayed against it and England attempting to keep a sort of neutrality. "So the world degenerates and I'm doing an essay on the development and significance of Spanish poetry," he wrote Burke on December 29, 1937. "What a subject! and how much more important to us than the blight of English literature under which our cocks have all but rotted away into each others' ass holes."[1] In other words, America's turning to England in matters of literary taste, Williams insisted, had led to an incestuous, sterile relationship. The Spanish, on the other hand, could—perceived rightly—inject new life into American literature. García Lorca, Williams noted, was the true romantic, in touch with the traditions of his people, the singer whose songs were on the lips of thousands of illiterate Spanish peasants. He remembered when he had been in Spain almost thirty years before, how he'd come into a bar in Toledo at night and listened to the shepherds there singing the old ballads of the Spanish poets until he was aware he'd made them self-conscious and had then got up and left them alone. They had seemed to him an example of a unified culture.[2]

In March he came back to the question of Spanish poetry again in an essay called "Against the Weather." Here he returned to the *Poema del Cid* and Padre Juan Ruiz's *Libro de Buen Amor*, a poem he thought superior in some ways even to Dante's *Divine Comedy*. He was looking at the Spanish tradition to see what light it could shed on his own practice, to try to learn why certain works of art had managed to live beyond their time. He was convinced that it was the sensual and not the abstract that mattered, the emphasis being on a poetry grounded in the here and now, which—paradoxically—made a work of art timeless. This was why so much writing going on all about him by propagandists for the left and the right would be obsolete—dead—in a very short time. After all, the artist was a man of action working in a field of action. He was not, definitely not, the man of ideas. What, then, was there about the *Divine Comedy*, in spite of its "narrow" psychology and theological framework, that allowed that work to live? In Ruiz's *Book of Love* Williams had found a glowing at the center, the old reprobate priest celebrating earthly love, refusing to judge or condemn, interested only in celebrating the light, so that the poem seemed to radiate with the grace of Paradise itself.

With Dante, however, Williams had had to search deeper, to find a more complex life-giving disorder which transcended the poem's scholastic synthesis. That synthesis had long ago come under fire, just as Marxism and fascism and neo-Thomism and any other ism would in time. And yet, in spite of that creaking theological scaffolding, the poem had survived. Why? Because the formal patterns of the *Comedy* had allowed the irrational to enter into the very fabric of the poem in spite of themselves. Dante had found a way to let Pan or the devil rub elbows with all those triads (aba bcb cdc) which represented the Trinity and orthodoxy.

Williams turned next to the American search for liberty which had been the hallmark of the Revolution. That liberty had been achieved by the joining of forces for a common end, a concerted resistance against the weather—that is, the dominant forces of the time. Americans had learned to employ open formations, flexible columns of war against the precise closed formations of the British regulars. These were guerrilla tactics, similar to those China was using against her Japanese invaders at the very moment Williams was writing his essay. He recalled Chamberlain, making his choice not to support Spanish democracy, not to support "the best of English tradition fighting for its life in Spain" but to support instead "the British Empire under Tory rule." It was a choice, Williams insisted, that "no artist could make without sacrificing his status as an artist." And so England had found itself in the position of being responsible for the deaths of Spanish children while at home it censored "the terrors of Disney's *Snow White*" for its own children.

So too with Eliot and his *Murder in the Cathedral*, which had proved so successful in London and New York. "Murder can't be murder," Williams said. "It has to be some special sort of murder *in the cathedral* —whose momentum is lost, at the full, except to the instructed few." Williams was leery of such symbolism, such mystery. Death was, after all—whether in a cathedral or in the streets of Guernica—merely death. He lashed out against the way churches acted as monopolies over a person's personal religious experience, and then went after the Catholic Church for having sold out, as he said, at the Council of Nicea. "The writing shows it—the secrecy and all the rest of it when compared with the directness and clarity of the first century." He praised Leo XIII for his encyclical *De Rerum Novarum* with its prolabor stance, which had warned the peasants what would happen—and what had happened—if they were to continue to be exploited by a system that had the church's tacit support. And yet the Church through the Curia had continued to exploit the people. It was no different in the U.S., where "the Bishop Mannings of America" exploited the people to pay for huge heaps of stone called churches and cathedrals.

From the Catholic Church Williams turned to Hitler's suppression of the Jews. What was a Jew, after all? A man, just like any other, "an oriental somewhat characterized by certain manners and physiologic peculiarities perhaps, but no different from any others in that," in spite of all the lying garbage the Nazis were broadcasting. But what did trouble Williams—that fierce individualist—was Zionism "as party to a tribal-religious cult," and in that sense it was a force just like any other force, including fascism, to which it was—necessarily—opposed. Nor did Williams much care for the new breed of Socialist poets, whose poems he thought were pathetic and ineffectual, though he'd back in whatever way he could these young compatriots whom he'd seen roughed up "from policeman's fists and clubs." In short, Williams distrusted all special interest groups—one reason he never joined even the American Medical Association—because he believed that consolidated power had by its very nature a corrupting influence.[3]

When his essay was published the following year in Dorothy Norman's *Twice a Year*, he was slammed for what were taken as his anti-Catholic and anti-Semitic remarks. True, they had not been intended as such, though there were of course confusions in Williams' thought (as he himself admitted) as he tried to come to terms with the most burning issues of his time. But of all of them, the Jewish question was the most sensitive as it was the most complex issue. Back in the early '20s, Williams had told Louis Untermeyer about his Jewish heritage and about his gentle grandfather, Solomon Hoheb. But by 1937 the family situation had changed drastically. His brother Ed had never forgiven him for making his Jewishness public. Ed had never believed it anyway, nor had many of his relatives. "What do you suppose I have to stand with my Jewish blood in my veins?" Williams snapped at Fred Miller, who was having enough problems with his own Lithuanian heritage. "Do you think it's easy to tell my kids about it and to face the dread it arouses in my brother and cousins. I blasted it out to anybody who wanted to know about it years ago." But now anti-Semitism was a life-and-death subject.[4]

He had been intensely interested in the issue of anti-Semitism as he saw it practiced in subtle and not-so-subtle ways in his own hometown and environs. His story "A Face of Stone," written in 1935, for example, had dealt with the education of a doctor—presumably himself —confronted by a young European Jewish family. It had begun baldly:

"He was one of these fresh Jewish types you want to kill at sight, the presuming poor whose looks change the minute cash is mentioned." The doctor there had sized up the couple with their sick infant even before they had spoken and had decided not to like them. But as the narrator unfolded the story, it became clear that he had made the wrong assumptions about these people, not even guessing the woman's age or nationality correctly, even though the story's doctor prided himself on his diagnostic abilities. By degrees he had learned the truth about the woman, that she'd contacted rickets in German-occupied Poland because of severe malnutrition, that her entire family had been wiped out over there, that this baby was all she had and that she was understandably jealous for it. And, finally, the truth of the situation began to reveal itself; the sudden realization of the young husband's "half shameful love for the woman and at the same time the extent of her reliance on him." He had been, Williams wrote, touched by the encounter, touched too when for the first time the young woman had looked at this tough American doctor and smiled.[5]

"You'd be surprised how many people looked askance at it before [Laughlin] printed it," Williams told Mary Barnard in early March 1937, "—and how many people have praised it since." There was "just enough of the sour truth in that story to frighten the life out of those who think they must be afraid to offend the Jews or this one or that one for fear lest someone should think this or that or the other. While they miss the whole point of the thing as being a story."[6] And despite accusations to the contrary (especially by several recent critics) Williams was no anti-Semite. He worked all his life closely with Jewish writers, from Kreymborg and Bodenheim and Mina Loy to Zukofsky and West and Moss and Kamin and Sol Funaroff and later with Shapiro and Ignatow and Sidney Salt and Ginsberg and Levertov and any number of others. He was, unquestionably, a product of his times and he did use the old comic-strip vulgarisms, allowing such words as *kike, nigger, wop, Jap, frog, Polack* and the rest of it to infiltrate his speech and his letters. Nor did he always escape the popular racial myths of his time.

So, in a letter to his son Bill, he could joke about the Japanese and the black American teams at the 1936 Olympics in Berlin held under Hitler's watchful eye. "What we're all curious about, naturally," he wrote in mid-July, thinking of Japanese expansionism in China and the Pacific, "is what the Japs are going to do at the Olympics. They have been in Europe a month training like mad, so it is said. They have put all their national energy into it as though the outcome meant the survival or elimination of their race from the biological struggle for existence." He saw that the Americans were having a good time there and not taking the games too seriously, but he was most interested "in the performances of our niggers. They may get so scared [under the pressure of uniformed Nazi officers whose disdain for blacks was scarcely hidden] that they'll jump clean out of the stadium. I'd love to be there just to watch them for if anybody's going to bust a gut it'll be those boys.'"7 It would be interesting to know what Williams thought, for example, of Jesse Owen's sterling perform-ance in those Olympics. But the attitude Williams displayed here clearly suggests the reductive image of the black one saw every day in the movies and in the comics: eyes rolling in terror or feet just shuffling along. And yet Williams was one of the very few doctors around Rutherford who would treat black patients, as he did by the hundreds, from the beginning of his practice right up till the end, delighting in their speech and actions and reserving his highest praise for them as more honest and more dependable than the run of his white patients.[8]

The same was true of his image of the Italian-American community which he also served well, families from the Guinea Hill district and elsewhere whose children he delivered by the hundreds. He had to learn tolerance and understanding and mutual dependence with all of these people, and he was continually being surprised to see qualities in them he had not expected; an Old World charm, an extraordinary generosity, a softness and an acceptance in spite of ignorance, poverty, and suspicion.[9] And so with the Polish-Americans and the Irish families he served, and the Swedes, and Germans, and Russians, and English and old Dutch families scattered here and there. He served them as best he could, imperfectly perhaps, jealous of his time away from writing, but never stinting and often performing those extra services very rarely found today with doctors: stoking up a furnace that had gone out in the apartment of an old woman he was treating for a cold, taking the time with another woman to explain to her that her son—away at war—was probably fine, helping another woman to get away from her mother-in-law when it began to affect her health, talking firmly with the parents of a child who had been beaten by the father at a time when all doctors considered such a course of action an impropriety, or just making extra visits to a house to make sure a patient was mending. You felt good just hearing him come in the door, some of those patients would remember. Such charity might indeed cover a multitude of imperfections.

Too much had been at stake for Williams to take Pound's criticisms about his staying in America lightly. That comment of Pound's that Williams had "pissed" it all away still lashed across his consciousness, and now—in March of '38—he lashed back:

> What the hell have you done that I haven't done? I've stayed here, haven't I, and I've continued to exist. I haven't died and I haven't been licked. In spite of a tough schedule I've gone on keeping my mind on the job of doing the work there is to do without a day of missing my turn. Maybe I haven't piled up a bin of superior work but I've hit right into the center of the target first and last, piling up *some* work and keeping it right under their

noses. I've interpreted what I could find out of the best about me, I've talked and hammered at individuals, I've read their stuff and passed judgment on it. I've met a hell of a lot more of all kinds of people than you'll even get your eyes on and I've known them inside and outside in ways you'll never know. I've fought it out on an obscure front but I haven't wasted any time.

It was a declaration of independence of sorts from Pound, a refusal to admit that what he—Williams—had done had been a waste. He was not claiming for himself that his life as a physician caring for others had made him a humanitarian. He'd cared for others, he said, as much for what others could teach him as for anything else, throwing everything he'd learned from his experiences into the hopper for his writing. He had had to do it his way. "By merely existing here," he insisted, "I've been able to make myself a rallying point for others. . . . All right for you, all right for Eliot to do the things you're doing." What was a lifetime, after all? With luck, you made a step forward here or there and that was all. The thing was to prepare yourself for that step as he was now doing.[10]

"Paterson: Episode 17" had been one such tentative step toward his major poem. Williams published that episode as such (though there is no evidence that the antecedent sixteen episodes were ever written) in 1937, using it again for the very core of his epic *Paterson* ten years later. Perhaps in the summer of '36 Williams had looked out from the west window of his attic study across Ridge Road toward Park to see a beautiful young black maid with "spotless cap / and crossed white straps / over the dark rippled cloth" sitting at her ease on the lawn of the Presbyterian church as she indolently beat a rug. The sight of those erotic "long fingers spread out among the clear grass prongs" seems to have sensibly moved Williams to a near despair of longing, at least as he reworked the vision at his typewriter, merging this particular black woman with the image of another black woman he had—apparently—been called on to care for after she'd been gang raped, first by the boys from Newark and then by another gang from Paterson. Whatever the precise historical details, the woman became now an image of Kore, the maiden, Beautiful Thing, the play of her hand across the rug she was beating reminding him of "the best of famous lines / in the few excellent poems / woven to make you / gracious."

Balancing opposites: Beautiful Thing at rest, indolent, rhythmic, and then the "opposite" pressure of lust and violence awakening "the fury" as Williams reenacted in his imagination the forcible rape of the woman, lashing out at what the male could not understand, and feared, and wanted therefore to destroy:

> and they maled
> And femaled you jealously

> *Beautiful Thing*
> *as if to discover when and*
> *by what miracle*
> *there should escape what?*

The song is as much a confession of guilt on Williams' part for too often wanting to tear into the women around him whom he genuinely loved and cared for and yet by whom he was driven to distraction. His black Kore owed much to his memories of Mable Watts, the seductive patient from his early days as a doctor, a woman who had had as much sexual success with white men as with black. "She worked hard all the time and kept herself immaculate on the street, her aprons were like snow, her dresses, usually black, were well cut." She too, like Beautiful Thing, had worn her hair up in a convoluted fashion topped by "a maid's cap, pure white and crisply starched."[11] Beautiful Thing, living right there in his world, despised, invisible, desired, radiant, like so many of the black women to whom he was attracted. No Artemis, no European goddess, she nevertheless represented for Williams the black plush, the New World beauty, the radiant stain that would illuminate the dirty white sheets of his *Paterson*.

In the early spring of '38 Williams tried again to get *Paterson* under way with a poem called "Morning." For that poem he returned to one of his old haunts for inspiration: the streets of Guinea Hill on a cold, blustery March morning with the icy promise of spring and renewal in the air. He was after a verbal transcription of what he saw about him, digging like the old Italian woman in the poem for something of value among the detritus of an open lot:

> *And with a stick,*
> *scratching within the littered field—*
> *old plaster, bits of brick—to find what*
> *coming? In God's name! Washed out, worn*
> *out, scavengered and rescavengered—*

Out of these dead fields he was listening for the agonizing cry of the spirit of the place in which he had chosen to live his life, a spirit incarnated in that old hag stumbling about, poking into junk, like that other hag/goddess his English grandmother whom he'd called on to guide him twenty-five years before in "The Wanderer":

> *Spirit of place rise from these ashes*
> *repeating secretly an obscure refrain:*
>
> *This is my house and here I live.*
> *Here I was born and this is my office—*
>
> *—passionately leans examining, stirring*
> *with a stick, a child following.*
> *Roots, salads? Medicinal, stomachic?*

of what sort? Abortifacient? To be dug,
split, submitted to the sun, brewed
cooled in a teacup and applied?[12]

The whole poem was filled with an ironic promise of resurrection, springtime, renewal . . . all of which went nowhere finally. What he had written in the end was a poem of crisis, a poem urged into being by the need to be moving forward without actually being able to move forward. And so he was still blocked, as he had been in writing his rambling essay "Against the Weather," wanting to say something and unable to do so. The blockage continued all through that summer and into the fall, when he confessed to Norman Holmes Pearson that he had not been able to write "anything to speak of for a year" because the necessary poison was lacking. "A man has to have a fever to write," he told him, "and I've not had a fever." He feared at last that his inspiration might be drying up. The "easy part" of his life's work was behind him; the hard part still lay before him, and he feared now he might not be equal to the task.[13]

He had become a severer critic of his own work than he'd ever been before, and he came down harder than ever on the poetry he saw being printed now in the little magazines. "I look at some of the continuing writers in the various magazines, not to mention *Poetry*, and I'm glad I'm not among them," he told Mary Barnard on October 6. "Why continue that way? If there's nothing to add to what has been done then why for the love of God do anything?" He was unusually hard on the poems she showed him now, but he was even harder on his own. "I want to write more colloquially," he explained, "more after the pattern of speech, maybe I want to discover singable patterns." One thing he didn't want to do, however, and that was merely to copy his own earlier style. "I don't want to write pictures. . . . I don't want dilutions. . . . I especially don't want to say anything that I don't very particularly mean and mean as I'd mean it if they asked me if I wanted to have my hand cut off and I'd say, No—or Yes." Poems were too serious a business for that.[14]

Why write at all, then? Why add to the veritable flood of new books and magazines that continually crashed in a stream of words over his head, waterlogging his brain as though he were some monstrous hydrocephalic? In early November he caught sight of the coffinlike catchall box sitting in his front hall and overflowing with hundreds of little magazines and books of new poetry, "a steadily mounting stream and none of them so much as looked at." And what did all that energy amount to? Where, in all that flood, was the enkindling word, the new, the truly distinctive? Where could he turn to in all those books for relief? "My own books dismay me," he told Pearson. "I wonder why I too have been so mad as to add to the horrible pile." He attributed it to a change of life, to the weather: "I go about forgetting to cork the cleaning fluid bottle. I strike my dwindling thighs against miraculously obstructing chairs. . . . Inside I possess the heart of a fly . . . I am not even ashamed to speak of these things. Meanwhile four or five books must be written at once.''[15]

And all the while he kept looking at what the other artists and writers were doing, looking for leads for his own new work. In February he'd written a review of Muriel Rukeyser's *US1* for the *New Republic,* noting how she had managed to pull such diverse materials into the fabric of her poem as "the notes of a congressional investigation, an X-ray report and the testimony of a physician under cross-examination" with some of the skill Pound had used in his *Cantos,* Williams' own touchstone in such matters. By attention to the proper language for including such recalcitrant materials, Rukeyser had in fact furthered the social revolution which was the subject and passion of her poem.[16]

Then, in October, in the same magazine, Williams reviewed Walker Evans' photographs of Depression America. Like Williams himself, Evans had wanted to make his audience see the world under its very feet. "Of only one thing, relative to a work of art, can we be sure," Williams underlined. "It was bred of a place. It comes from an application of the senses to that place, a music, and that place can be the middle of the African jungle, the Mexican plateau, a Parisian whorehouse, a room where Oxford chippies sip tea together or a down-hill street in a Pennsylvania small town. It is the particularization of the universal that is important." What the artist was able to do—and it is what Williams himself wanted so badly to do—was to lift his world from its parochial setting, to realize his anonymous, debased world so that Americans —little Americans, working-class Americans, mechanics and nurses and farmers and teachers and janitors and shopkeepers and millworkers —could see the inherent dignity and worth of their world. "What the artist does applies to everything," Williams summed up, "everyday, everywhere to quicken and elucidate, to fortify and enlarge his life about him and make it eloquent—to make it scream, as Evans does at times, or gurgle, laugh and speak masterfully when the occasion offers.''[17]

And all during this time Williams was painting his own portraits of Depression America, composing a book of objectivist details of his environs in an attempt to get the *Paterson* thing finally under way. He worked on his American scene poem all through most of 1938 and the winter of '39, and the final sheaf—the sheaf he sent off to James Laughlin in March 1939—was eighty-seven pages long and composed of a potpourri, a lyrical minestrone of local details, glimpses of Paterson, Rutherford, even of Republican Spain, as well as love lyrics and experiments in rhyme. Some of these Williams would finally add to *The Complete Collected Poems* at the last minute and others were eventually parceled out for publication in the little magazines and a pamphlet Williams published in '41 called *The Broken Span.* But the sheaf as such, which Williams labeled defensively "Detail and Parody for the Poem Patterson," was never published.[18]

Nevertheless, he spoke about the poems to several people, making it clear how important he thought these pre-*Paterson* fragments were to him in spite of his failure to achieve the form he was desperately seeking. "I've begun to think about poetic form again," he told Louis Zukofsky on December 11. "So much has to be thought out and written out there before we can have any solid criticism and consequently well-grounded work here." Part of the problem, as he saw it, was that there were "so many terribly limited minds posing as critics" in America. For him both Edmund Wilson and Yvor Winters were two such examples of the parochial critic, and he also gesticulated in the direction of the "polite literature surrounding such places as Harvard, Princeton and the New York Sunday Supplements," which would have included F. O. Matthiessen, R. P. Blackmur, and the critics writing for the *New York Times.* He was willing to believe that these critics were for the most part "people of good will," but they simply did not know enough about modern American poetry. "I say this coolly and considerately but it is true," Williams insisted. "I have been amazed, of late, to begin to suspect what isn't known. Even dear ol' Ezra is badly lacking in his adjustments." He himself had been doing some very short pieces of prose, short short stories to keep his poetic lines fluid. And as for poetry: he'd been jotting down "many short notes, almost completed lyrics, with an intention to have them be true lyrics—if it can be done in our present day language."[19]

In late February of '39, he told Laughlin about his sheaf of poems, which he'd written "blind all last fall, five in a day sometimes." Floss had read them and found them "impressive" in the aggregate, though Williams himself was still disturbed by them. And now that he'd had them away from him for a short while, he had already begun to wonder if they weren't anything more than "the droppings of starlings among the ruins," or even the ruins themselves.[20] Ten days later he sent the sheaf off to Jim Higgins, Laughlin's associate at New Directions, with a note of explanation: "They are not, in some ways, like anything I have written before but rather plainer, simpler, more crudely cut. Look 'em over. I too have to escape from my own modes. I offer them as one man's digression from the early or recent work of WCW."[21]

The sheaf was, as Williams knew only too well, uneven. Some of the poems worked and worked well, but others, risking the use of the present-day language—New Jersey speech—came off as incredibly flat. The inflections of the language as heard had been carefully observed and rendered, but the poems were flat because the language itself could be so unrelievedly flat. Williams caught the ironies both intended and unintended in the language, caught too the echoing puns in the words heard over and over each day, and he would expect his readers to listen carefully to what he was presenting them until the design of the poem flashed by fits and starts upon them. By the time he came to write *Paterson* in the early '40s, he would know—thanks in part to Joyce—how to make a language inherently less musical than Joyce's resonate. But now, in 1939, he found himself slipping as often as he scored a hit. Formally, he tried everything on again, even attempting rhymes once more, something he had avoided since the early days. Those rhymes were an act of desperation, a self-conscious use of the device used with a percussiveness and obviousness that were both awkward and journeymanlike. But this was hardly a time for feeling ashamed.

Quite simply, Williams would either remake himself, or slide into inevitable oblivion. At fifty-five he knew he was out to break new ground, to discover a form he could use, and no resource could simply be avoided or overlooked. He would have to sift through it all once more. When Laughlin, wincing at the rhymes, asked him about them, Williams shot back that he had used them because he had *had* to use them and so get that chiming device either in or out of his system. And though in *Spring and All* he had said that poets should spit on rhyme, now he explained that there was nothing intrinsically wrong with the device, that it was a tool like any other, neutral in itself. In any event, he added, all of the poems were finger exercises "before going into the heavy work" of *Paterson,* which he hoped would be next in line.[22]

Williams himself knew what the shortcomings of the "Parody" sheaf were, knew too that it could not substitute for the hard work that still lay ahead of finding a major form. And no one knew better than he that no number of discrete details could ever equal more than the sum of their parts. By the summer of '39, therefore, he could refer obliquely in a letter to Robert McAlmon to the "Parody" as that "wad of more or less inconsequential poems" he'd written over the past year. And in the same letter, as a necessary corollary, he confessed that he was "crazy to finish the long poem I started years ago: *Paterson.*" He really wanted to *do* that one, "really go to work on the ground and dig up a Paterson that would be a true Inferno." But he was still terrified, still afraid to make the long leap, afraid too that, that poem finished, the very life he had identified with it—his own—would also be finished. After that, in other words, he would have only his own death to wait for. Clearly the example of the *Cantos* was very much on his mind when he added that the reason he didn't get on with *Paterson* was because he was a doctor, unable "to free myself as Pound has freed himself from the importunities of daily existence."[23]

Still, much of what was good about the "Parody," that halfway house, lay in the very gift his townspeople and patients had given him. It was, strictly speaking, a return on his investment in those people who had drained years of his life from him with their own insistencies and needs. There were lines like these (of a mother calling the doctor on the telephone about her baby):

> *Her milk don't seem to . . .*
> *She's always hungry but . . .*
> *She seems to gain all right,*
> *I don't know.*

Or these lines, perhaps heard at one of the local Democratic conventions:

> *It's about time*
> *the Republicans stopped*
> *using Lincoln*
> *as their figurehead.*
>
> *To me*
> *that's disgusting*
> *because he was anything*
> *but what they are.*

And this, among the mass of manuscripts surrounding this vortex of activity, probably written in late January '39:

> *Doc, I bin lookin' for you*
> *I owe you two bucks.*
> *How you doin'?*
> *Fine!*
> *When I get it*
> *I'll bring it up to you.*

"This is the sort of thing," Williams wrote to himself on the same page, which "in its essential poetic nature, it's [sic] rhythmic make up (analyzed) [of which] the poetry I want to write is made. The reason I haven't gone on with *Paterson* is that I am not able to—as yet, if ever I shall be. It must be made up of such *speech* (analyzed)."[24]

What Williams effected in those six short lines (reduced to five in the version that appeared in *The Complete Collected* in '38) was nothing less than a complete dramatic episode. The irony, one notes, is that the patient has *already* "brought it up," and can now hold on to the two bucks for another indefinite stretch. A further irony is that, being "fine" now, this particular debt has taken its place in the list of the patient's priorities somewhere near the bottom. But in another sense, Williams has already been repaid with these words which he kept bringing up himself out of his own consciousness, trying to analyze them out into the poetry he wanted so badly.

Among the rhymed poems was a "Defiance to Cupid," written in a variation of a four-beat alternating rhyming sequence, the lines forming a jagged, wrenched pattern:

> *Not in this grave*
> *will I lie*
> *more than a summer*
> *holiday!*

> *Dig it deep, no*
> *matter, I*
> *will break that sleep*
> *and run away.*

And another, called "River Rhyme," was a jazz variation on four alexandrines with alternating rhymes:

> *The rumpled river*
> *takes its course*
> *lashed by rain*

> *This is that now*
> *that tortures*
> *skeletons of weeds*

> *and muddy waters*
> *eat their*
> *banks the drain*

> *of swamps a bulk*
> *that writhes and fat-*
> *tens as it speeds.*

Yet Williams remained self-conscious about his rhyming, as even here the halting rhythms and forcible wrenching of rhymes suggest. Nine years later he would throw the issue of rhyme over the side once and for all in a poem with a lovely and comically vindictive title, "When Structure Fails Rhyme Attempts to Come to the Rescue." Even so, the "Parody" reflects Williams' uncomfortable stance with his own flirtation with rhyme. In a poem called "Figueras Castle," dealing with the collapse of Republican Spain, a poem published in October 1939 in a little magazine called *Matrix*, Williams the fierce democrat lamented the imprisonment of Spanish Loyalists who had failed to turn over what was left of their government's jewels to the French consulate when they had fled across the Pyrenees into France to escape Franco's victorious forces. The original version had read:

> *Nine truckloads of jewels*
> *while the people starved*
> *Nine truckloads*
> *in the mud*

> *And the people's enemies*
> *coming fast. Stick 'em*
> *in your pockets*
> *the General said,*

> *They're yours, by God, and*
> *check them in for the*
> *people at the Consulate*
> *in Perpignan.*
>
> *But some of them didn't*
> *bother—like those who had*
> *stolen them first*
> *and were not*
>
> *arrested for it as these were*
> *in their need. Rhyme that*
> *up right for us, yes!*
> *Williams, ol' Keed.*

The rhyme there—of *need* and *Keed*—cuts back on itself with a vengeance, a self-mockery mocking any rhetorical device's ability to answer adequately to the reality and tragedy of the fall of a people who had fought long and hard and had still been defeated. But this issue of rhyme's inability to answer to the jarring dissonance of modern life was a private affair with Williams. So, when he published the poem, while he kept the swipe at *Burnt Norton* (1936) in the poem's opening, where the nine truckloads of jewels in the mud recall Eliot's "Garlic and sapphires in the mud / Clot the bedded axletree," Williams did change the final stanza of the poem into a refrain of lamentation, underlining the sense of necessity:

> *and were not*
>
> *arrested for it as these were*
> *in their need, not held*
> *for it as these were*
> *in their dire need.*

But even as Williams was working on his new poems, the *Complete Collected* was published in early November in an edition of fifteen hundred copies. By Christmas 1938 the book had received more notice than had ever come to Williams before, as he himself told McAlmon, though he was hard enough on himself to add that nobody seemed to like it very much. When Babette Deutsch reviewed it for *The Nation*, she praised Williams' vitality and ability to portray American subjects, though she did point out that what the poetry lacked was a central, all-informing myth. And in early December, a reporter named Jackson came out to 9 Ridge Road to interview Williams for *Time* magazine. When that review was published at Christmas, together with the Sheeler photo, Jackson had praised Williams' work, placing him high, but praising Laura Riding even higher. "All I know of her," Williams told McAlmon on the twenty-sixth, "is that, personally, she's a prize bitch. That doesn't alter her value as an artist."[25] Most of the critics seemed eager to place Williams in some kind of hierarchy now that his *Collected* had been assembled, so that, given Williams' own uncertainties, one of them was bound to get picked off by Williams in return. It was Philip Horton, Hart Crane's biographer, whose review had appeared in the *New Republic* on December 21, whom Williams chose to go after. Horton had argued that, while Williams could not be called an important poet, he should not be dismissed as being on the other hand only an insignificant poet. Williams' style was, finally, too bare, too like an exercise "in spiritual hygiene," eliminating as it did not only the visionary plateau (such as Hart Crane had manifested in abundance), but even more common staples like humor and pathos as well. Stevens, Horton added, had already suggested this in speaking of the radical bifurcation in Williams between his sentimental, romantic side and his "anti-poetic" side. What remained, then, was merely "a public record of a private conflict that happens also to be common to most poets."[26]

When Williams saw himself compared to Crane and Stevens in such a dismissive tone, he shot off a letter to Malcolm Cowley as editor of the *New Republic* meant for Horton's ear. "Sorry to inform you I went vulgar and told Cowley to tell the puke to go wipe his nose," Williams wrote Laughlin on Christmas Eve.[27] The letter itself appeared in the January 11 number of the *New Republic* without a response from Horton and read in part: "I'm not important but I'm not insignificant. Boy! that's pretty cagey shootin'. . . . I guess a fella has to write a biography before he gets that good! . . . If he hadn't had Stevens to teach him how to look crookedly he wouldn't have had anything at all to say. Tell him to go wipe his nose."[28]

Williams' response may have cleared the critical air to some degree, for when Horace Gregory reviewed the collection in early February for the *New York Herald Tribune,* he mentioned the painful futility of attempting to determine Williams' "importance" and focused instead on the poems as poems. They derived, Gregory saw, from "the very center of spoken language," a language that was flexible and austere. More importantly, he saw the *Collected Poems* as a sort of halfway house, promising not a summation, not an end, but rather a new beginning which Williams was even then preparing for. But Gregory was the only critic perceptive enough in 1939 to glimpse how matters really stood.[29] R. P. Blackmur, for example, reviewing Williams along with five other poets in the *Partisan Review* that winter, followed Horton's lead by summing up Williams' style as a highly idiosyncratic mode that had failed again and again in the hands of his disciples, by whom he meant—among others—Zukofsky and Oppen. The reason Williams' style couldn't be imitated, Blackmur maintained, was because it was "a remarkable, but sterile, sport," devoid of any tragic dimension and without the deeper significations of human experience that other poets of his generation had offered.[30] And in July, when Mason Wade reviewed the book for the Sunday *New York Times Book Review* on page 2, he summed up Williams' achievement as "just below the first." As for the *Collected,* from the vantage of 1939 he thought it might serve as an epitaph for the modernist phase of poetry that had witnessed the widening gap between poet and audience. And this, in spite of Williams' long struggle to close, not widen that gap. So the critics had taken his measure against Pound, Eliot, Frost, Stevens, Moore, and the rest and had placed him "just short of being one of the best." Better to shrug it off and get on with the book that would push him over the top, his own "magnum opus," *Paterson.*[31]

*
**

But if most of the critics were only coolly favorable to Williams on the eve of World War II, there was at least Les Amis de William Carlos Williams, the group that Ford Madox Ford had formed in early '39 as a kind of automatic reflex action back to an earlier time when such groups had been fashionable. Ford had formed it to do honor to one of the great unsung poets of America, though Williams was never really sure why ol' Ford had singled him out for the honor other than as an excuse to get a party of the New York bunch going once a month. As for Williams, though he shied away from this sort of limelight adulation, calling the group privately the "Williams for Senator Club," he was willing to bear with the monthly meetings for the sake of his own friendship with Ford. There were five such meetings, each held on the first Tuesday of the month, from February through June of '39, the last of which turned out in reality to be nothing more than a wild bash at 9 Ridge Road, after which, with Ford having already sailed for France, Williams called an immediate halt to the meetings. The charter members of the Friends made an impressive list: Sherwood Anderson, Archibald MacLeish, Marianne Moore, Ezra Pound, Waldo Frank, Alfred Stieglitz, Charles Sheeler, James Laughlin, and even young Charles Olson, who drove down from Harvard with dutiful regularity to attend every meeting. Paul Leake was the secretary of the group, and there were others like Zukofsky who attended the meetings as well.[32]

The first meeting was a Dutch treat supper party held at Ticino's Restaurant in the Village, at which Ford introduced Williams and then Williams spoke and read some of his poetry before everybody settled into some serious drinking. The second and third meetings followed the format of the first. But after the third meeting, Williams decided it was time to let somone else take the podium and read his own things, and he chose E. E. Cummings to lead off at the May meeting, which would be held at the Daylight Gallery on West 13th Street. Williams wrote

Cummings on April 13 to tell him that he himself had come up with Cummings' name, and threatened to read Cummings' poems for him if Cummings wouldn't. As an added incentive he added that "the English poets Auden and Isherwood (do they have first names?)" had "applied . . . en masse to be admitted to the society" and so might also be there. Even Pound might be there, for he was rumored to be even then on a ship headed for the U.S., though Williams hadn't heard from the man himself for months.[33]

Cummings apparently did not show up, however, for whatever reason. The Friends went to the gallery as planned and viewed the pictures there, and Tom Horan, a member of the group, got into an argument with Williams about the efficacy of the sonnet form until Williams cut him short.[34] Then, at the meeting itself, Louis Zukofsky read from Williams' *Collected* until Williams—urged by members of the society to read his own work—took the book from Louis and tried to end the business by reading some of the newer stuff which was at that point very much on his mind. He ended the evening by reading one of his recent short stories, though it did not go over very well. The fact was, as Williams told Zukofsky the next day, his "little Angelina [had] shit in the pan. Boy! was I surprised at how full of shit that small story was." He had decided there and then not to allow himself to read from his own work again. In the future he would do what his medical confreres did: draw up an abstract of the case and "select revealing poems or prose and lay out an ordered half hour or so of palaver." Let them diagnose the particular malady from the specimens he would offer and let that be an end of it. The truth was, as he told Horan the same day, that the meetings were getting him down. Being a figurehead had many disadvantages, not the least of which was that one got "slapped in the face by every wave we head into." He had consented to the meetings only for Ford's sake, because he admired and respected the old man.[35]

On Thursday, May 25, Williams went into New York City to say good-by to Ford and Biala. They were leaving for southern France on the thirtieth and Williams knew with his trained medical eye that Ford would soon be dead. Nevertheless, Ford himself, wheezing and over-weight, was still optimistic. He was taking a villa on the French coast near Le Havre and invited the Williamses to sail over for the month of August.

After Ford left, Williams held a final shindig at his place before calling an end to the Friends. That party was held on June 6 and lasted from early evening until well after midnight. There was no reading this time, just some good talk and food and drinks. The weather was splendid, and the party began out in Williams' backyard and ended indoors. Frances Stelloff of the Gotham Book Mart was there, and Jim Higgins, and Marsden

Hartley, who spent the evening playing with Williams' six-week-old Scotty pup. But one man who missed it, though he'd spent the previous night at 9 Ridge Road, was Ezra Pound. Williams of course had hoped Pound would stay around for the meeting of the Friends, but since it was the Friends of Williams and not the Friends of Pound, he was gone by the time Williams' guests arrived.

Pound was like that, Williams had come to learn a long time ago. One could be with the man for months, years at a time, and never know what he was doing or what he was thinking. And so with Pound's mysterious visit to the States in the spring of '39, his first trip home in more than a quarter of a century, when the "confidant" of Mussolini had taken ship to America to talk some sense into Roosevelt and the Congress before another war broke out. Communications between Pound and Williams had come to a virtual standstill by then, since Williams had found it impossible to talk with the man who had supported Mussolini's presence in Spain. "Ezra has been giving me a more than unusually severe pain in the ass over his pro-fascist sympathies recently," he had told McAlmon in late December 1938. War was coming, as he knew and so many others knew, though where it would break out or exactly when no one could say.[36]

He wrote a review of Pound's *Culture* for the *New Republic* in early February 1939, trying hard to separate Pound's politics from his very real contributions to modernist writing. When Pound wrote about art or even music, for example, Williams could feel a sudden welcome clearing of the mind of all sorts of rubbish. The crippling delay of the universities —themselves infected by the special interests (Usura)—was in part to blame. For they had created a blockage in knowledge, and so Pound had had to "find a way to the gist of learning before we are crippled by age and cannot make use of it." But the problem with Pound's conclusions about culture, as Williams diagnosed it, was this: that they had led the man—almost by despair—to accept totalitarianism, and that had been the failure of Pound's book: that by its tests a bastard like Mussolini could be represented as a great man. Williams himself was heartsick. His friend was a brave man who had taken the gamble "of making a bloody fool of himself" and had, tragically, lost that gamble.[37]

And yet the critics were even then flocking to Pound and Eliot, often at the expense of derogating native poets like himself who were "seeking to rescue and build up a present world of the spirit which is the great garland of the artist in his supreme unselfishness." After all, the personal sacrifices in terms of fame and money to underwrite this vision had been enormous, as he very well knew. By early April he told Laughlin that if Pound did come to the U.S. as he had threatened he personally would hardly be able to shake hands with the man.[38] Then, eight days later he wrote Cummings that Pound was rumored to have sailed for America. In fact, the *Herald Tribune* had already called him by telephone at home to ask him if he knew anything about Pound's plans. But Williams knew nothing, apparently not even that Cummings himself was to meet Pound at the dock when he arrived in New York on the Italian liner *Rex* on April 21.

If Ezra was coming over, Williams told Zukofsky on the nineteenth, then—as Laughlin had remarked—it really must mean war. As for himself, he had no intention of seeing Pound until he'd been invited to. "Let him run for the Senate on the new Fascist slate" for all he cared.[39] The general anxiety he was feeling about the state of world affairs had been underscored a week earlier when he wrote Sylvia Beach in Paris that the old Europe he'd known must surely be gone in a short time if it had not already disappeared. For him his image of Europe and the experiences he'd had fifteen years before were all in the past. "Either I'll be dead before they [the European experiences] can happen [again] or the whole of Europe will become tasteless after they get through with their high explosives and gas."[40] He could not know then just how close to the terrible truth he had come.

The day after Pound's arrival, Williams wrote Laughlin that he'd heard nothing from Pound. He'd read the papers that morning and had learned of Cummings' meeting Pound, but that was all he knew. Perhaps, since Cummings was to be the guest of honor at the May meeting of the Friends of Williams, Pound would also show up. In the meantime, he was taking Floss and heading for Virginia for a well-earned week's vacation.[41] Whether or not Williams knew it, Pound had also headed south for Washington with his own inimitable cloak-and-dagger secrecy. Much of what Pound did there is shrouded in mystery, but he did attend a session of Congress and he did talk—as he reveals in the *Pisan Cantos*—with Senators Borah of Idaho (Pound's native state) and Bankhead. After all, his grandfather had been an Idaho congressman. He also talked with Secretary of Agriculture Henry A. Wallace. But he did not get to see Roosevelt and he did not avert World War II.

In the meantime, in spring rain, Williams and Floss drove down through New Jersey into Delaware. They had lunch at a restaurant in Dover and watched the Mennonites in their distinctive garb walking about the streets of the city in the cold rain. Then, driving south to Cape Charles, they met the spring once more, with roses and great garlands of wisteria in bloom. It rained too to their delight on the ferry crossing at Norfolk, Virginia, and Williams was much taken by a "marvelous old colored waiter" who took care of them at the hotel they stayed at in Norfolk. Rested, they drove down to Newport News, and Williams recounted the naval battle of the *Monitor* and *Merrimack* to Floss, and then they drove on to Yorktown where Cornwallis had surrendered. At Jamestown they saw cardinal grosbeaks and ate shad roe at Tappahannock on the Rappahannock. They saw the colonial reconstructions then under way at Williamsburg and Jamestown, and then they drove on to Washington.[42] There Williams went to see his old friend from the *Others* days, Skipwith Cannell, who'd assumed two new identities as David Ruth (author) and Horace Holley (government employee). Cannell, who had a small-time government job, had found Pound wandering blindly around the administration buildings in Washington. Finally, Cannell's friend Dorsey Hyde had Pound paged so that Cannell could invite Pound to Sunday dinner on April 30. It was there, that Sunday afternoon, that Williams again saw his old friend for the first time in fifteen years. Williams was fifty-five, Pound fifty-three. Williams' old friend reminded him of Henry VIII of England, wrapped as he was "in sweaters and shirts and coats until I thought him a man mountain."[43] And, despite Williams' resentments, he found himself hugging his old friend, followed by a very brief talk with Pound about the serious state of world affairs, a talk that Williams found somewhat incoherent and cloaked in the greatest secrecy.

Williams did not see Pound again for another five weeks, until Monday, June 5, when he stayed the night at 9 Ridge Road before returning to New York. With Williams, Floss, and young Paul—home from Penn—all sitting around the great man in an informal semicircle in the living room, Pound wrapped himself in some blankets and then, as Williams recalled, "spread himself on the divan all evening and discoursed to the family in his usual indistinct syllables." Actually, Williams had to admit to McAlmon, he didn't sound half bad, *if* you could bring yourself to believe what he was saying. But Williams, diagnosing his friend, found that Pound had "acquired a habit of avoiding the question at issue when . . . pressed for a direct answer."[44] So, when he asked Pound point-blank about Hitler's air attacks on Guernica three years earlier, Pound mumbled something incoherently and sidestepped the issue completely. For his part, Williams was convinced that Pound had slipped badly and was "sunk" unless he could somehow "shake the fog of fascism out of his brain during the next few years," and that Williams doubted Pound was at this point capable of doing:

> The logicality of fascist rationalization is soon going to kill him. You can't argue away wanton slaughter of innocent women and children by the neoscholasticism of a controlled economy program. To hell with Hitler who lauds the work of his airmen in Spain and so to hell with Pound too if he can't stand up and face his questioners on this point.[45]

Instead, Pound seemed to have taken the attitude of being interested not in such questionable means but only in the outcome of the major issues, whatever those were. To Williams Pound had come to substitute pontification for dialectic. "I hope he wears the right glasses," he told one correspondent, "or he may in the near future trip over the hem of his skirt. He's an old friend and an able poet, perhaps the best of us all, but his youthful faults are creeping up on him fast and—you can't avoid issues forever by ignoring them or attempting to change the topic of conversation. Even the lion finally gets a horn through the guts."[46] Pound gave a reading at Harvard in Sever Hall, and James Laughlin, as his friend and publisher, escorted him around Cambridge. Then, on June 12, Pound was at Hamilton College—his old alma mater—to receive an honorary degree, though at the dinner following the commencement he found himself embroiled in a bitter clash with the commentator H. V. Kaltenborn, who, like Pound, had also been honored at the commencement. And then, as quickly as he had come, Pound left the U.S. in mid-June to return to Italy and *il Duce,* his mission to talk some sense into America having proved a failure.

As for his own feelings about the coming war, Williams told the *New Republic*—in response to a questionnaire they published on June 28 —that, though he did not favor sending American troops to fight either in Europe or Asia, he was all for supporting the democratic powers. He thought neutrality by that point frankly impossible, since in fact such a policy would favor Japan if they ever struck against Russia's eastern flank. He still wanted peace, but not if it meant a victory for fascism. Better now to "cement an outspoken military alliance with . . . England, France and Russia," so that the Axis powers would know where America stood. "Better," he reasoned, "to show our strength once for all and be licked if we must than to wait and be beaten later as we surely should be by a coalition of Germany, Italy and Japan once England and France had been disposed of."[47]

In the summer of '39 the political situation, especially on the left, was rapidly becoming confused and fragmentary, as Trotskyite attacked Stalinist and the *New Masses* went after the *Partisan Review.* On July 11, for example, less than two months after Williams had signed up as a member of the Committee for Cultural Freedom, he wrote the editor of *The New Leader* resigning from that group. Despite their name, Williams had just learned that the committee had been formed by one splinter group of the left to attack other splinter groups of the left. "Though I'm no Communist as you know I couldn't stand for that so I resigned from their God damned committee," he wrote Robert McAlmon a week later. The result was that he had found himself immediately "attacked right and left in the usual little picky party papers."[48] Now they would probably begin classing him as some sort of "Red," which was ironic, especially since just a short while ago one faction of the left had been calling for sanctions against him for his nonleftist position. What angered him even more was that, when he tried to explain his own position in a letter to the editor of *The New Leader*, the editor had refused to publish it. Then he had tried another magazine, and they too had refused to publish his defense. He was not getting "fair play."[49]

Finally, Williams promised himself not to sign any more manifestos and pronouncements, only to find his own impetuousness getting the better of him. So, in the Fall number of the *Partisan Review*, his name appeared on a pronouncement that the magazine's editor, his old enemy Dwight Macdonald, had prepared. This time it was a league, the League for Cultural Freedom and Socialism, calling for American neutrality in the rapidly escalating conflict in Europe. The pronouncement was signed not only by Williams but by such figures as James Farrell, Kay Boyle, Kenneth Rexroth, Delmore Schwartz, Gorham Munson, Katherine Anne Porter, Weldon Kees, and James Laughlin. It was a particularly dark moment for American intellectuals and especially for the American Communist Party, for on August 23, Germany and Russia—those two seeming antipodes in any Hegelian schema: Fascist, Communist—had signed a nonaggression pact which opened the way for Hitler's storm troopers and panzer divisions to invade Poland nine days later without having to worry about a Russian flank attack. Suddenly World War II was upon Europe, as America went uneasily on its way, business as usual, trying to avoid hearing the shouts in the street.[50]

Even in Williams the impulse to retreat from the unleashed fury of Hitler's armies was strong. If possible, he still wanted neutrality; he was eager to get on with his own work of writing and caring for the sick and wanted to stay out of the tar-baby mess of politics. He was even sorry now that he'd signed that Macdonald letter which Macdonald had printed in the *Partisan Review*. Williams was signing "no more nothins," he told Norman Macleod in early November. He was through; in fact the only reason he'd signed the damned thing in the first place was because his friend Jim Laughlin had urged him to do so. As for himself, he was under attack again, he felt, for writing objectivist poems, pieces of photographic realism, when he was "supposed" to be giving his energies to the left in the cause of a suffering humanity. Like Stevens, he winced under the charge. "I need bucking up to keep on the ball against the very real danger of being put down as an unfeeling beast who never knew his arse from his elbow—when it came to real passions," he complained. But he also knew that his first obligation as an artist was to avoid falling into the strings of the instrument he was playing and to remember always that he was "impelled and compelled by a very definite temporal genius and need." He was still an artist of the avant-garde and not a propagandist or polemicist. He could not be, could not afford to be, all things to all men.[51]

That fall, too, he had other problems on his mind, problems closer to home: such as finally getting an oil heater for the house. From his boyhood on he'd stoked a coal furnace at 131 West Passaic, and then two coal furnaces at 9 Ridge Road—one to heat the house and the other for the office. He was also trying to get his son Bill placed at the Cornell Medical facility at Bellevue and was asking colleagues for advice. His son was the very salt of the earth, he wrote one doctor, but "too damned reserved to put himself forward." At the same time, he didn't want to meddle in his son's affairs and even had to admit that the boy was still something of a mystery to him.[52] As for Paul, though he'd expressed a desire to be a writer and though Sculley Bradley had taken him under his wing at Penn (as much for the father's sake as for Paul's), both father and son knew that Paul's talents lay in the direction of business, of buying and selling quality goods.[53]

Perhaps Williams' general sense of expectation and anxiety in the weeks leading up to September 1, 1939, can best be seen in an unpublished introduction to a book of poems by Skipwith Cannell (David Ruth) which Williams wrote in late July. When Williams saw Skip Cannell in Washington in April 1939, he was seeing a man who had virtually disappeared from sight after 1918 to reemerge with a new identity twenty years later. Cannell had sent a long manuscript poem to Williams unsolicited, under the name David Ruth, and only when Williams wrote back saying how much he'd enjoyed the poem did Ruth reveal that he was his old friend Skip Cannell, from the *Others* days. It was a poem of epic dimensions that Cannell had sent, a poem dealing with the world of senators and congressmen and lobbyists and corruption and bureaucratic red tape, in short the world that Cannell had himself witnessed. It was a newspaper epic, and Williams was stunned by the possibilities, as he had been with Rukeyser earlier, and to a lesser degree with the poet Sidney Salt.

Daily Williams glanced through the papers or turned on the radio for the latest news, to learn what had happened and what might happen next, hearing always the same noise, the same packaged information: murder and more murder in the hearts of men. "We sit waiting, listening to the radio as if we also expected to hear something, possibly a music such as this cutting in through the noise," he wrote, thinking of poetry's ability to discern a pattern and to bring relief to the troubled imagination. For if poems were "seldom moving factors in a world of events," still, they did "sometimes signal far-reaching changes of thought in the general mind." Ruth, he said, had been shocked out of his early lyrics and into a profound silence by what he'd seen in the two years he'd spent on the western front. And as if that world hadn't been enough of a hell to him, what he saw after the war had been even worse. What the surrealists had registered in painting and poetry, Williams said, Ruth had experienced in his own flesh. And now, as he and others were even then beginning to articulate clearly the nature of their modern hell, they were being plunged ever more deeply into the next war and a new hell.

"Only today," Williams lamented, "after the great war is the world, for a moment perhaps before the next stupefying blow aimed at it by its enemies, beginning to come alive in its more remote and sensitive members. . . . We have lived for two decades withdrawn from the fine edges and facets of living." But now Williams could sense a new creative stirring, and Ruth was part of that general awakening. If Ruth had failed in part in his poem, it was because he had not assimilated the hundreds of strands of information, had not arrived at a form that could hold the modern world. Nevertheless, reading his poem was a lot like reading an "inside" newspaper of the news, news that really gave the news and did not "servilely suppress it as inevitably happens." Every day, Williams insisted, Americans were being robbed by the government's usury as it devised ever new ways "to drain our money out of our very fingers by new thievery of taxes." What the real news would be, Williams suggested, was to see how the poet would try to dig underneath that corruption to try and liberate society.

Williams had heard the argument that the modern epic was impossible because the newspapers had replaced the village bard who had once sung of high and public deeds before the community. But he disagreed with that assessment. After all, an epic was, finally, the inner truth of events, and therefore of necessity a poem since there was no full truth otherwise, no truth that touched the mind and heart and emotions of people like the poem could. In fact, Williams argued, the newspapers were "the precise incentive to epic poetry, the poetry of events," since newspapers had learned to lie systematically, to distort the truth, leaving the truth to be told by the poem. The very nature of newspaper reporting was such that it had to aim low enough to be understood by very large numbers of people. This meant that characters became cutouts: flat, two-dimensional, uncomplicated. A page of newsprint was therefore "based on a deliberate seduction of language" with "everything sacrificed to a punch effect" and rounded off with the same "tinkered phrases" to leave the reader thinking he had learned something when in fact he had not.

The language of a modern epic, Williams suggested, would have to be careful not to talk down to the average man, yet it had to reach down to where the people were. It had to use their language, the shared dialect, and not "some fanciful elevation" where the people were in danger of being excluded. Pound's *Cantos*, Williams could now see, seemed to fit his model for the epic, at least abstractly. They were the "algebraic equivalent" of the kind of thing he was after. And yet they were also "too perversely individual," too much the record of one very extraordinary mind "to achieve the universal understanding required" for the new epic. On the other hand, Hart Crane's *The Bridge* (which Williams mentioned only by indirection) was, finally, an unworkable "lyric-epic singsong."

What was needed, then, was a "concise sharpshooting epic style. Machine gun style. Facts, facts, facts, tearing into us to blast away our stinking flesh of news. Bullets. Nobody but the poet knows how the news stinks today of its own rottenness."[54] And yet his own eighty careless lyrics written the fall before had not fit the bill, though they were as much like verbal bullets as anything with their staccato rhythms tearing into the times. Twentieth-century form had to embody "something of the astro-physical, chemical, sociological makeup of its day," Williams had said earlier that year. It had to be a synthesis of its time "in passionately communicable form." The academic critics, those "braying jackasses," kept writing articles "proving" that it was impossible to write real poetry in his time because there were no significant forms.[55] And so it would be Williams' burden—and his glory—to achieve a form that in its apparent flatness and randomness and pluralism, in its apparent confusions and circularity of detritic flow, most closely approximated the condition of America in his own time. But that synthesis was still several years off. In the meantime, Williams would have to suffer the critics' incessant braying.

Three weeks after landing in France, Ford Madox Ford was dead. His death hit Williams hard, harder than he at first realized, though when he told McAlmon about his feelings, McAlmon wrote back from Paris that he could feel nothing for Ford, whom he'd always thought of as a big blusterer and a second-rate writer who'd tailed along in Joseph Conrad's shadow. For his own part, it would take Williams four months to remember Ford in a poem, partly because—though he did it well—he deeply mistrusted occasional verse. But toward the end of October, he finally wrote "To Ford Madox Ford in Heaven."

He addressed that poem to the man who had managed to turn his beloved Provence—to which at the last he had returned—into a heaven by his description of it. And Ford himself had been a heavenly man, if not a saintly one. Heavenly because he had been—like Williams himself —filthy and corrupt and loved to "eat and drink and whore" and to laugh at himself as he fed himself out to time's hungers. Nor did Williams try to transform Ford into something he had not been. Ford had been, in Williams' eyes, a notorious prevaricator, slovenly, a wheezer, indelicate, all of it "a carelessness, the part of a man / that is homeless here on earth." Then Williams ended the poem by addressing Provence itself, the real Provence, knowing that

> *the fat assed Ford will never*
> *again strain the chairs of your cafés*
> *pull and pare for his dish your sacred garlic,*
> *grunt and sweat and lick*
> *his lips. Gross as the world he has left to*
> *us he has become*
> *a part of that of which you were the known*
> *part, Provence, he loved so well.*[56]

Fat-assed Ford. Williams had come a long way since his elegy for Lawrence four years earlier. Ford's Provence itself had had to be remembered from Williams' visit there fifteen years before. With the Germans turning their attention toward France now that Poland had been raped, Williams was writing an elegy not only for a man but for a whole world in danger now of disappearing forever.

*
* *

Williams had begun *In the Money,* his sequel to *White Mule,* in the conversations he held with James Laughlin in August 1938, when he and Floss spent two memorable weeks together at Laughlin's home in Norfolk, Connecticut. That was a golden moment for Williams, an interlude he would remember for the rest of his life, a time when he could plan the *Collected Poems,* plan his novel, plan for years of writing with his newly found publisher. He began *In the Money* then, and finished it now in the bleak winter of '40, when the world was "contracting to its last narrowness" and he himself felt "bound in iron."[57] The winter of '40 was his busy time as a physician, caring especially for influenza cases, a time of concern for what was happening in Europe and in the Far East, with Japan continuing its invasion of China and the Pacific islands, and Hitler turning his attention to the conquest of Norway and Denmark. Russia too was in the war by then, having sent troops into Poland to set ·up a buffer against the Nazis and then into Finland, where, in January, they were temporarily bogged down by fierce Finnish resistance.

"All we know is that only a few years ago we were too smug in our beliefs touching the ultimate triumph of man's coming humanity to man," Williams wrote Harvey Breit on January 25. "We know now, hit or miss, that love is far more remote a power than we suspected." The young poet Kenneth Patchen had been writing poems about the mystical power of love and now Williams found himself rejecting that answer in the face of a deteriorating world situation. "We were too glib, too sanguine," Williams lamented, "too languid in what we thought and said and too doctrinaire in our praise and service." Instead of a Patchen, then, he suggested a Savonarola as a more fitting emblem of the times.[58] And yet, when another young poet named Randall Jarrell attacked Patchen in the *Partisan Review* that May, Williams—as much out of an allegiance for

Laughlin, Patchen's publisher, as for Patchen himself—wrote a letter to the editor telling him to muzzle his "professional literary sophomores."[59] (Ironically, Williams could not know at that point how important a role Jarrell would have in determining the role Williams' own poetry was to have for the next twenty years.)

"The world's in a parlous state," he wrote Mary Barnard. "I don't know what we as poets can do about it either. Perhaps we should have gone to bed together or something, at least we might have bettered the general state of poetry a little by it and so in sum have benefited the world also minimally."[60] Mary Barnard was working then in the Poetry Collection of the Lockwood Library at Buffalo, where Williams, at the suggestion of the director, Charles Abbott, was beginning to deposit large amounts of his manuscripts and letters. So 1940 was also a time of looking back: the poet at fifty-seven rummaging through the bales of "junk" he'd collected in his attic over a lifetime's writing, wondering what personal letters from Pound and Zukofsky and Moore and Stevens and hundreds of others could possibly mean to anyone else. The same day he wrote to Barnard, he also wrote his friend Charles Keppel to say he was having "some grave regrets" about the way he'd acted in the past, though he also knew he was powerless to do anything about it now.[61] As for Floss, he wrote Keppel twelve days later, she was as "hard and useful as the handle of a spade." He was reading poems to her then, though she had told him it wasn't technique *she* looked for but rather the revelation "of rare spirits, unhappy souls or happy ones," a revelation she could find only in good poetry. And even as he typed he could catch her out of the corner of his eye sitting across from him: that "little bitch, . . . tapping her feet to every letter" he pounded out, as they drank Scotch and soda together to keep warm. He admired her, he had to admit, and realized now that he couldn't do without her presence, though he knew too that he could not say even now that he really understood her.[62] She had been worth discovering, though, this woman who had always done everything she could to make life worth living.

On April 2, he wrote Floss himself to tell her how he felt about her. She had been away for a few days and he was already—as usual—missing her. "You know," he told the woman he'd lived with for nearly thirty years, "I've been thinking for days of this business of growing old. Like everything else in life it sneaks up on you. . . . You're in it up to the neck before you've learned its lesson unless you're clever." He was feeling his age lately as she had been feeling hers. No doubt about it: they were getting older, though it was no use dwelling on that. Better to "stop thinking" about it and just go on "from moment to moment." He thought of the captain in one of Jack London's stories watching an earthquake passively, stoically, and the story too of a young man during the Great War who had continued to play poker all through a bombing. He told Floss not to be worried by the time of confusion through which they were all passing. Bill was doing fine in medicine, and Paul he was sure would settle down soon. It was just that their younger son was going through "an amorphous state of mind," unsure yet of what he was going to do with his life. As for Floss and himself: they had finally gotten used to each other. It had been a "hard time breaking down" their "diverse resistances" because they were both headstrong people. And yet he felt closer to her now than he had ever felt. That amounted, he confessed, to "a typical declaration of love on my part. I'm a hell of a declarer of love. I'd rather act it than say it." And, he added, with the knowledge of experience, "no doubt, I don't even act it at times."[63]

By February 26 he had finished the first draft of *In the Money:* twenty-seven chapters and over five hundred typewritten pages. He spent the next four months revising the novel and then sent the finished script to Laughlin in June. By August it was on press, and on October 29 Williams spent the day at the Gotham Book Mart in New York signing copies of *In the Money* and meeting well-wishers. This sequel to *White Mule* took Floss up through her second year and showed the Stechers coming into money. Most of the book was filled with sharp details and cameos like the earlier volume, and Williams carefully drew in the foreshadowing for the dark catastrophes that would be developed in the third volume. But for the most part, Williams did not think the sequel had come up to the writing of the earlier volume. At least, however, the book was behind him, most of it having been written in one curve covering nine months, a far shorter time than the three years and more *White Mule* had taken him.

Williams was also doing readings. On October 26, 1939, he'd read at the YMHA in New York at the invitation of Norman Macleod. That reading had gone over well and he'd enjoyed the evening. On February 18, 1940, he read for an informal group called the Quaintance Club at the Rutherford Methodist Church across the street from the house where he'd been born. And though he'd known many of these people all his life, when he read to them they could still make him feel as if he'd come from the moon. He'd assumed the mask of the "Hometown Boy Makes Good" for them, and yet he couldn't help noticing how the men had, almost in spite of themselves, been "leaning forward in their folding sunday-school chairs LISTENING with their mouths opened, fascinated," at what it was he had revealed to them.[64]

But at his joint reading with W. H. Auden at Cooper Union on April 12, things went differently, for there the young Englishman (age thirty-two) stole the entire show, as Williams reluctantly and bitterly admitted. He would recall that evening vividly, for it came to represent for him a reenactment of the old Eliot nightmare: Williams' American values rejected by his own countrymen in favor of the English import. "Remember at Cooper Union when the young Englishman read his verse to that supposedly tough bunch," Williams wrote in an improvisational piece called *Man Orchid* nearly six years later. There'd been a couple of American poets up there on the stage to share the podium, he remembered—his old friend and enemy Kreymborg, and also Malcolm Cowley —"not too hot but hitting along" an American line. And then Auden "with his smooth Oxford accent got up and smiled at those lunks and said, I hope you'll pardon my accent, I can't help it! And they almost drowned in their own slobber they were so tickled to grant him any small favor that lay to their eager hands. Their faltering hands! And he read them his verses, and very good sweet verses they were and—they raised the roof with their gracious huzzas."[65]

Even in the notes he took down right after he'd read that evening, which have the quiet sense of one prizefighter sizing up another for his weaknesses and strengths, Williams' own sense of failure came through: "Auden's success before the audience as contrasted with the rest of us was the feature of the evening," he admitted to himself at the time, reluctantly. And yet he had managed to find Auden's Achilles' heel in that encounter:

> Listen as I would I could not find that he has traveled the world without perceiving a new measure such as I seek. What he . . . did in his best poems . . . was to give an able exposition of new materials upon the old accepted basis. . . . Peter Munroe Jack, in introducing me, missed the point entirely! I was a physician, a fact finder, truthful and downright. Fair enough, but he appeared to have no inkling of what my purpose is toward verse. And how, if at all, I have succeeded and where and to what extent.

What was needed by such an audience as the large one—perhaps a thousand—that had crowded into Cooper Union (for the most part to hear Auden) was an aristocracy of taste which could see that anything was suitable material for poetry, even as Rembrandt had chosen to paint his *Side of Beef*. So Williams had chosen to write of workmen manning a pump by a seawall and watching a woman floating on a rubber raft in the bay, or a woman looking for a nail in her shoe, or a poem about a piece of green glass, or about wallpaper. Auden, on the other hand, was a success because his audience already knew the word games he was playing. He had stuck to "the old excellences," and his audience had felt comforted, familiar with his cadences and his language. But Williams had been searching for a new measure, though he had to admit to himself that he had not found it yet. He knew that measure would have to be a *"visual division of the parts of a poem into units,"* a new form that would give an "instinctive satisfaction," as in the work of Villon or Whitman, new forms challenging the forms of the past, just as jazz had confronted the musical patterns of the past and had answered them with its own distinctive forms.

In March Williams read Conrad Aiken's "Spain, 1927" in *Poetry* as well as the same writer's critical comments in the *New Republic* in which he'd railed against the new wave of poetry with its antipoetic bent. Was Aiken pointing obliquely at Williams' influence on some of the younger poets? Probably. At least Williams was convinced that he was. But what the hell was the antipoetic anyway? If something could be included into the matrix of the poem, it was poetic, not antipoetic. Stevens' old term was just a smoke screen. And, besides, what was there in Aiken's own poem that was actually new? Nothing, Williams decided. Placed against Picasso's vast black and white mural of Guernica with its agony and exploding bodies, Aiken's poetic forms merely left an old-fashioned "camphorish taste in the mouth." And Yvor Winters' solution —"to trim the form to an externally conventional pattern"—was even worse, since fixed patterns fixed meaning, creating a radical stasis, a death, in the poem itself.[66]

As Williams became a regular on the college lecture circuit from the late 1930s on, his insistence on measure—on new patterns and forms —would become his single clarion call, until with time this issue took on the dimensions of a myth with him. So it was on his speaking tour the week of May 12–17, 1940, when he visited Penn State, then the University of Buffalo, then Dartmouth, and finally Middlebury, before stopping off in Cambridge to visit his son Paul. Williams taught the same formal message at each: that the new poetry, especially the new American poetry, would have to be "consonant—*con-sonant*—with our age and the range of our physical understanding. It must sound with our age and sound new and vigorously."[67] Alchemist of the word that he was, he was looking for a new formula that would allow others to see the nature and bondings of words in as radical a light as Einstein's theories had forced them to see the nature of reality in a way none could have suspected just a few generations earlier. It was the imagination itself which had invented a new world and had discovered new spatial and temporal dimensions within that world. And if the imagination could do that with nature it could certainly do that with words. Radical transformations in the nature of language and poetry were indeed possible, transformations beyond the wildest guesses of an Eliot or even a Pound.

Weren't the scientists even at that very moment transmuting quicksilver into gold, as alchemists for centuries had dreamed of doing? It had been done by physicists at Columbia in the fall of 1940, he told an incredulous Nicholas Calas, by "bombarding the atoms in a cyclotron (a small one would cost $60,000 to produce microscopic amounts of gold)."[68] Nevertheless, it had been done, and the value of that transformation for the imagination went far beyond the value of the gold itself. By careful attention to what Einstein had suggested years before, two scientists in the field had worked out some of the practical ramifications of his imaginative hypotheses. The implications were plain for the artist: a new measure and a new, distinctively new, poetry were possible.

In December Williams underlined what he was after: that "there should be a definite effort on the part of a modern poet to formulate his verse into strict patterns, strict metrical patterns, but NEW patterns, not old ones." He called for a new invention, "taking over what we have learned from everybody including Gertrude Stein." Stupid as Pound had become in Williams' eyes, he was still a very important model to follow, especially for his work with the *Cantos*. Economics was secondary, finally, as was even science itself, to the major work of the poem, Williams reasoned. For it was by a people's literature that they would be judged in the end. Finally, all other disciplines were there as reservoirs of potential metaphors for the human imagination which provided "the most fascinating field of activity possible to man."[69] And Williams could say this at a time when he himself was still blocked and unable to get on with his epic. When he felt, as he told Calas at the end of 1940, "very much undeveloped as to what is next waiting to be done."[70]

It was during his reading and talk at Penn State on Sunday evening, May 12, that Williams first met Theodore Roethke, then a thirty-year-old instructor at the college. The big, burly Roethke treated Williams and Floss to one of his famous steaks and plied them with drinks until Williams, who was still capable of extreme uneasiness reading to a college audience, was feeling very much at home. Seventeen years later he would recall that night when he had undergone his "baptism of fire," a "farm boy without any formal education," as he put it, who for the first quarter of an hour was amazed to find himself uttering words over which he did not even think he had control.[71]

The following day—Monday the thirteenth—Bill and Floss drove north to Buffalo in their '36 Ford and then headed east to find the 150-acre sprawling estate of the Abbotts at Gratwick Highlands in Linwood. That was sixty miles east of Buffalo, as it turned out, and it impressed Williams then and later how Abbott would drive back and forth to Buffalo from the farm as though he were merely going down the road. When the Williamses finally reached the estate, with its dilapidated central house (which had once kept twenty servants busy) and the outlying buildings, they found Wyndham Lewis already ensconced in the book-filled, converted back porch of the Abbotts' home. But Lewis was not ready to give that room up for anybody, and so Abbott took his new guests over to his in-laws' cottage next door—the home of Bill and Harriet Gratwick, who would in time become, like the Abbotts, close friends of the Williamses. This was, then, the first time Williams had ever met Lewis, that old intimate of Joyce and Eliot and Ezra. The man who had rendered those three and so many other famous writers in paint as well as in words had himself been reduced now to doing official portraits. He had in fact come to the United States in the fall of '39 to stay with the Abbotts and to paint the portrait of Buffalo University's chancellor, Samuel Capen. In November he had left Buffalo to go to New York, but he had come back up to Gratwick Highlands for a few days now in May to finish a drawing of the Abbotts' son, Neil, and enjoy the Abbotts' hospitality once again.

That first evening, after dinner, Williams went with Abbott and Lewis "for a moonlight walk about the place just after sundown. We wandered . . . down sheep paths and across a tennis enclosure, pushing aside a section of iron grille-work to enter the abandoned formal garden of the old estate, through masonry arches unbelievably romantic in their semi-decay." So taken was Williams with this "luxury of [bird] sound and rustic profusion" that he could scarcely answer Lewis when Lewis addressed him.[72] In this extraordinary setting Lewis' questions seemed relatively unimportant, and anyway Williams had never really forgiven the man for his caricature of Ezra in *Time and Western Man*. For the elegant decay, the sad romantic sublime of that garden, had caught Williams up. It would come to stand as his private symbol—the more so as he grew older—of surcease and easeful death. Having discovered that garden, he wanted no intrusion from Lewis, or for that matter from anyone else.

With Paterson and the Passaic Falls also very much on his mind just then, Williams drove up with Floss and Abbott to witness for the first time the spectacular crash of water at Niagara Falls. It was an image that was to remain vividly in his mind when—two years later—he came to write of his own falls:

> Rolling in, top up,
> under, thrust and recoil, a great clatter:
> lifted as air, boated, multicolored, a
> wash of seas—
> from mathematics to particulars—
>
> divided as the dew,
> floating mists, to be rained down and
> regathered into a river. . . .[73]

Force and quiet—the clatter of the falls and the cloistered garden —Whitman's yawp and Keats's silences: these were the two opposed impulses (systole, diastole) that had driven Williams and would continue to drive him for the rest of his life.

On June 5, three weeks after Williams had found his dark Eden,

Hitler's armies invaded France and, despite the so-called impregnability of the Maginot Line, marched into Paris on the fourteenth, a mere nine days after crossing the border. On the tenth Mussolini had also declared war on France, though it was the German armies who—in an incredible blitzkrieg—were actually sweeping across the country. By the twenty-fifth, the French government was forced to sue for peace. Williams, listening to the nightmarish news of the fall of France on the radio, lamented that same evening to Charles Keppel that stupidity was running roughshod all over Europe.[74] It had been quite as Archibald MacLeish had been predicting: that by a tremendous effort the very sphere of the world had at last been cracked open like an egg, only to reveal the profound vacancy at the heart of western civilization.[75] So the countries were falling one after the other throughout Europe. Now only Britain remained in the west and—to the east—Russia. And soon Hitler would turn his demonic wrath against both of them. Williams tried to comfort himself by reading the Greek tragedies in translation—Gilbert Murray's at this point, though he found them too soft and passionately wished he could have read those stark, tough tragedies in the original.[76] In a more seriocomic vein, he noted too the 1940 Republican Party convention and wondered if Wendell Willkie might possibly be elected president over FDR. On June 20, Williams had tried to do something about the insane march of events by reading at a large anti-Nazi rally held in New York, though he privately wondered how much good that gesture had really done, or how much good any gesture might do as night descended over the world.

As for Pound, Williams found it painful even to address him now. "We're old friends," he told Pound on April 6, 1940, and—after nearly forty years—they would probably remain so. But Williams told him quite bluntly that he was "slipping badly" in his "mentality" as well as in the force of his attacks. He was also getting tired of having to defend Pound's tirades for the sake of their old friendship and he was sick of Pound's trying to tell him that his whole initiative hadn't been anti-Semitic when Williams was sure it was. "Tell somebody else such things but don't try it on me," he told Pound straight out, at least if he valued "the least vestige of what we used to treasure between us."[77]

And yet his allegiance to Pound's work with the *Cantos* remained unaffected, even when—in mid-September—Williams received a copy of Pound's new Chinese cantos, which he could not bring himself to care for. Nevertheless, in the use of the language of the day, Williams told Laughlin on September 25, Pound and, after him, Cummings were the two most distinguished poets of his time. Pound's lines continued to live, even when he used such "unpromising" material as a long catalog of Chinese kings, princes, and other rulers.[78]

In mid-August, just as Williams and Floss were getting ready to take a two-week vacation together, Floss became seriously ill. On the morning of the fourteenth she suddenly went deaf in her left ear, and Williams raced her at once to an ear specialist, Dr. Ehrenfeld, who thought it a nerve affair. Floss decided to go on with the vacation anyway, but on the morning of the seventeenth, Williams noticed that she was having trouble balancing herself. He wrote his son Bill, speaking now as doctor to doctor, to tell him he thought Floss was suffering either from a "hydrops of the labyrinth or an embolus." Ehrenfeld had sent Floss to bed and Williams had decided to take his vacation at home.[79] He had already disconnected the phone in order to hide from his "insistent patients" (as he confided to Rexroth) and he would work in the yard and "read and write" to his "heart's content."[80] A nurse was called in to watch Floss, their maid Lucy would come by to look in regularly, and even his mother was away at Ed's place in Connecticut for two weeks.

But the radio and movie news were filled with scenes of Hitler's armies moving over Crete and Yugoslavia, the Netherlands and France. And now, in August and September, there were daily reports of the German Luftwaffe's bombing of England, first the southern ports and then London itself. Williams saw those Pathé film clips along with millions of other Americans and was struck momentarily with the terror of the spectacle, so that he found himself writing about it in order to sort out his own feelings about what he was witnessing. He called the essay "The Poet in Time of Confusion" and he diagnosed the pathology of a diseased imagination like Hitler's reveling in the confusion he was creating, behind which—pathetically—he might hide, to reveal his "unfleshed desires" surrealistically, in larger-than-life fashion there on the screen like some black and white nightmare. But the artist was able to see behind that phantasmagoria, that sick dream, to the sickness that lay at the heart of the dream. And that was why, he realized, the artist was dangerous to a government like Hitler's or Mussolini's, for the artist's "superlatively efficient eyes" could see the truth and had therefore either to be heeded or be put out by the aggressor. Williams saw too, more clearly than he had ever seen before, that Hitler's solution to the so-called Jewish question was a lie, a grotesque misrepresentation of a people who had acted historically as a catalyzer to bring "every race to its apex of political productivity." Like the artist, therefore, the Jew had proven dangerous to the totalitarian state and so, like the artist, he would have to be destroyed if the feverish lie of fascism was to be maintained.[81]

And yet, paradoxically, war did have this tonic effect: it could focus a nation's energies and break up sterile power combinations that had maintained their prominence beyond any real usefulness. Take for example the German bombing of London in 1940. The fiery destruction of whole slum districts where disease and squalor had existed uncontended for generations was a good thing. For years committees had talked and talked about doing away with those fire and health hazards and done nothing. And now, phoenixlike, the energies released by war had led to the demolition of those very sink holes. Of course the artist had already foretold all that had happened or would yet happen. In a very real sense, the pictures of death and destruction and the final apocalypse had already been imagined years before by the surrealists, who had "foretold and so sapped the war of all intellectual strength" before the war had even begun. Thus Williams wrote in November in an essay that he had intended for a surrealist magazine called *Midas* which Nicholas Calas had wanted to bring out but finally could not.

Williams could also see that art would once again be asked to serve as a handmaid for the war effort, as earlier it had been asked to serve the cause of World War I and later the Marxists or social humanitarians. But Williams had no patience with art as propaganda. Art was no effete aesthetic game, damn it, and it did not need to be coddled or put aside like some plaything until the war was over. In fact, if anything, now was the moment for the artist to "give way to a triple fury of activity." Now, under the stress of the times, overwhelming changes in the basic design of things might be achieved by the imagination in a matter of a few hours rather than years, just as London had been altered forever by fire. It was the moment for the revolution Williams had been so long waiting for. Forget the tired call back to a simple nature, away from it all, forget neorealism or even pastoralism. There were far greater mountains to discover in the depths of the imagination. After all, the so-called normal was merely a ruse, a surface, a palpable lie. Time now, in the wake of the monstrous death in Europe, to welcome the luminous monsters and phosphorescent energies of the unconscious that until now had slumbered.

Never again should the tragedy of Williams' beloved Spain be repeated, the image of which Picasso had rendered permanent in his imagining of a country with arms uplifted until they had been lopped off "as the great niggardly peoples of the earth stood by." And just as French artists had fled to America at the beginning of World War I, so now they were fleeing once again the destruction of their own country. Now, however, an older Williams no longer felt it necessary to defer to them as once he had deferred to Duchamp. In the trial by fire that Hitler had brought, the French had simply withered like leaves in a bonfire. Now, therefore, *as equals*, French and American revolutionaries together might do something, might announce a new cure for cancer or raise the status of women. Surely they could note whatever pushed an advance in art, geography, painting, astrophysics, or chemistry, though it would still be the poem that would finally focus the world and give it order.[82]

In the meantime, Williams was shoring up what cultural fragments he could against his own and the world's ruin. In the spring of 1940 he had translated several of Ivan Goll's "Landless John" poems from the French, and then, in the fall, he turned to Nicholas Calas' surrealist poems, trying to turn their tortured, introspective syntax and language into an American idiom.[83] He met with certain of the other young Frenchmen that fall who were trying to assemble *Midas*, among them Tanguy and Seligman, though he preferred—as one of the older men—to officer the assault of the new avant-garde himself rather than leave it in the hands of the inexperienced young. And at the beginning of November he wrote Professor Pedro Salinas at Johns Hopkins for an expert's advice on translating the dense, elliptical slang of Quevedo's *El Perro y la Calentura*, the novella he was finally finishing in collaboration with his mother. Williams confessed to Salinas that the slang there had been so impenetrable that not even the huge Spanish dictionaries he had consulted at the New York Public Library had been able to shed any light on the matter. Salinas for his part wrote to tell Williams to forget it, that the Spanish slang of the sixteenth-century text had been irretrievably lost. But Williams could not give it up. There was something appealing about Quevedo's idiom because it was in fact the equivalent of the street talk of any big city. And the phrasing was so modern that it reminded him of Gertrude Stein herself. He could taste those words and he wanted to possess them for himself.[84] In a similar vein Williams had sent a letter to Laughlin two months earlier that Fred Miller had sent to him. That letter, he told Laughlin, had been written "by a jazzaroo who is down south working his way from hot joint to hot joint trying to pick up a living throwing dice." It was so hot it had made even "Henry Miller's stuff look like the anemic ravings of a convent girl." How he would have liked to do a collaboration with a man who could spill words like that![85] *That* American idiom was worth saving a whole civilization for.

In December, as 1940 ended in wintry bleakness, Williams was still hoping for a quick end to the war. For a while it had looked as if it might be over in the spring of '41, but now, with the deployment of German submarine wolf packs in the shipping lanes between England and America, he wasn't so sure. He saluted the stiff resistance the Greek guerrillas were still putting up against the Germans. That was "something to be proud of—live or die."[86] But ten days later he told Laughlin that the whole world was nuts and that he couldn't even "keep up with the mere reading" he felt he should do in order to understand what was happening. On top of that, he was still getting letters from Pound in Rapallo and Rome which riled him to no end. They had degenerated by now into mere insults, "the mewings of an 8th grade teacher." His own perceptions, he suggested to Laughlin, had overtaken Pound's twenty years before, though he had to admit that Pound's was still the greater poetic accomplishment. But the turtle was still in the race, and if he could do the work he wanted to get done, there would be "another measuring" between Pound and himself.[87] For that measuring, *Paterson* and his later poems would have to hold the key.

There was one last piece of bad news before the year went out. McAlmon—who had been in Paris when the Germans took over in June—had finally been allowed to leave for the U.S. in October, without his money and with most of his manuscripts lost or stolen. He had written Williams on December 19 from a room in New York City that he had tuberculosis and that in general he was physically worn down. He was going, he'd decided, into St. John's sanatorium outside El Paso for three months of rest and recuperation.[88] But it would be six months before he was actually released. Williams could not help but remember McAlmon's young promise of twenty years before, remember too his work in Paris as an editor in the early twenties. It was here in this man, then, that Williams saw the real fall of France, the final, irretrievable loss of all that promise when he and McAlmon and Pound were still young men in search of a world that their imagination could reveal to them. And now Pound was a victim of his own self-absorptions, and McAlmon was waiting for the death that in time would most assuredly overtake him.

*
**

1941: With the New Year Laughlin brought out a slim pamphlet of Williams' poems in his Poet of the Month Series. It was sixteen pages long and Williams called it *The Broken Span*, much of it a selection of work already published in the *Collected Poems* but containing in addition fifteen "details" from "For the Poem Patterson," with two *t*'s. He prefaced the details with lines that tentatively linked them as parts of a long love poem:

> *A man like a city and a woman like a flower—*
> *who are in love. Two women. Three women. Innumerable*
> *women, each like a flower. But only one man—like a city.*

By 1941, then, as Williams would tell Edith Heal sixteen years later, the idea for *Paterson* "was there, expressed in the . . . lines that are used word for word, though spaced somewhat differently, in the first few pages of *Paterson* 1."[89] Most of the details had been lifted from the "Parody," but Williams was beginning to find a way to hold his discrete fragments together. What he called on was his unashamed love of women and the dialectic generated by his intensely erotic desire to possess his world as a man might possess a woman. "A woman's eyes / a woman's / thighs and a man's / straight look," he had written in his "St. Valentine." Such love had the power to stand up to the very death of cities, rotting like so many "pig-sties."

He was also writing his play *Many Loves*, that winter and spring, taking some of the one-acters he had written for a local Rutherford drama group in 1939 and combining them with a framing device written in verse. That frame employed a director, a homosexual backer, and an actress in an interplay of tensions that Williams would use again in *Paterson* 4, as he played with the idea of the virgin language and an etiolated, narcissistic homoerotic tradition. What he was after in *Many Loves* in each of the three one-acters incorporated into the play was a sympathetic portrait of the woman and the failure of communication between the sexes. He worked with the themes of infidelity and lesbianism in the plays, as well as with the problem of presenting a viable verse form written in the American idiom. Moreover, he employed a Pirandello-like frame to link each of his discrete scenes. Like T. S. Eliot, Williams presented scenes that echoed the Greek tragedies but without so much as allowing anything like a classical allusion to disrupt the scenes that had been culled from his own experiences as a physician.

He also gave several lectures that winter and spring. On February 5 he lectured at Harvard on the topic "The Basis of Poetic Form," at Theodore Spencer's invitation, and there he attacked the language of university discourse as static, reactionary, and anemic. At the same time, Williams also stressed the need to incorporate into the poetry of his time the American vernacular, the language as it was actually used in homes and factories, garages and shipyards.[90] This too would become one of the major themes he would employ in the dialectic of *Paterson*. Having attacked the academy, he was not surprised to find more than the weather chilly during his stay at Harvard. The English faculty were hardly in a mood to cheer this iconoclast on.

Two months later, on Wednesday evening, April 16, Williams spoke again on the same topic at the First Inter-America Writers' Conference in the theater at the University of Puerto Rico. This time he studded his talk with references to Spanish literature and to the salutary influence that literature had had on the American language. It was a strong speech Williams gave before his international audience as he held up two sides of his heritage for a more equitable hearing. He even compared Lope de Vega's example with his beloved Shakespeare. North American poets could learn much from their compatriots south of the border, he insisted. For example, Americans might try to incorporate the shorter four-stressed line of the Spanish as a substitute for the blank verse line of Shakespeare, something Williams himself was doing at that very moment in the verse passages of his *Many Loves*, and something that —coincidentally—Yeats had employed in his last plays a few years before, though Yeats's prior example had been Anglo-Saxon rather than Spanish.

"In many ways," Williams explained to his audience, thinking obviously of his own work with Quevedo,

sixteenth and seventeenth century Spain and Spaniards are nearer to us in
the United States today than, perhaps, England ever was. It is a point
worth at least taking under consideration. We in the United States are
climactically as by latitude and weather much nearer Spain than England,
as also in the volatility of our spirits, in racial mixture—much more like
Gothic and Moorish Spain.[91]

It was a way of paying tribute to his parents, both to his English father
who had spent most of his life in Central and South America as well as in
the islands, and to his mother, that marvelous hybrid creature of French,
Jewish, and Spanish descent, whose whole life had been shaped by this
island where she had been born and where her son was now addressing an
international audience of scholars and artists. For the first time in his life,
Williams had returned to his mother's ancestral home.

The conference went well all in all, and Williams' speech, together
with the round-table discussion the following day had also gone well.[92]
There was even a page one photograph in the Friday edition of San Juan's
El Mundo of Williams standing next to another speaker, Dr. Jorge Mañach
of the Philosophy Department at the University of Havana, and the
heading, *"Distinguidos escritores que nos visitan."* Then on Saturday
Williams and Floss drove up into the mountains to see more of the island
before flying home again next morning. All in all he'd found the people
there very friendly and he was enjoying his first trip to the islands
immensely: "flowers, birds . . . , mango trees, palms with coconuts high
up, hibiscus. . . . Little lizards everywhere—almost under your feet."[93]
He had had a chance to meet and talk with young writers and he wrote at
once to *Poetry* and several other magazines in the States giving the
editors their names and suggesting they pursue his leads.[94]

There had been some grumblings, of course, even in this island
paradise. For when Williams arrived at the conference, he found that the
local Communists were circulating a manifesto denouncing Archibald
MacLeish—then Librarian of Congress—for his article "The Irresponsibles" and claiming that the whole conference was a put-up affair by the
U.S. government. The manifesto, Williams learned when he read the
Spanish, was "in reality a translation from *New Masses* of an article
perhaps by [Samuel] Putnam." As far as that went, Williams had no
quarrel, since he himself had disliked the self-righteous and backward-
looking tendency of MacLeish's essay anyway. But what did anger
Williams was a story he was convinced Putnam had had circulated in the
San Juan papers that Williams himself had never wanted to attend the
conference and had consented to go finally "only from sentimental
reasons, thinking of my mother." But Putnam was wrong, Williams
insisted, for Williams had had his "enthusiastic reply in the mails"
saying he'd go "half an hour after receipt of the first letter." To say—as

Putnam had—that the whole conference "was a conspiracy of MacLeish and others"—presumably the government—and that it had been "Fascistic in nature and subversive to liberalism in intent" was "pure shit." In fact the conference had done a great deal of good, and if Putnam wanted to hunt out Fascists he would have done better turning to the Rotarians and Lions Club members whom he knew around Rutherford, local businessmen he'd talked to who had voiced their own contempt of the whole conference. At least, Williams believed, the conference had extended a hand to his long-neglected Latin American cousins.[95]

When Williams and Floss had flown down to the islands, it was the first time they'd ever been airborne, and the prospect had so unsettled Williams that he'd actually written Louis Zukofsky and Horace Gregory asking both of them if they would act as his literary executors in the event his plane went down somewhere over the Caribbean. The reality of the trip, however, had turned out to be a marvelous room at the Condado Hotel in San Juan, with "bright sunshine" and "hot summer weather," a cool breeze and a room overlooking the deep blue waters with the sound of ocean surf surging softly below. Still, the image that stayed longest with Williams after the trip was over was the strangeness of the flight down. It had all seemed so unreal, this flying through air with the mountains and then the water and then the island appearing below, and he kept thinking of Hart Crane's earlier poetic flights to the Caribbean and then of the poet's diced bones tossing somewhere in the currents off the Key West islands. The flight had stirred in him a profound return to his own beginnings, reenacting as it had that image of the wanderer, the lost prince of his early aborted romance flying as in a dream over the ocean to his real home. He would recall that dream-flight south nine years later in his *Autobiography*, when he had floated "over a sea of lights to Philadelphia, another light sea, Washington, Richmond, then with a full moon coming up over a livid cloud-shelf to the east to palm trees at dawn and the Miami airport." From there he and Floss had gone by clipper seaplane to the islands in broad daylight, where he could watch the play of shadow puffs over the turquoise sea ten thousand feet below. "That flight," he would write, "had for us the surprising reality of all dreams of flying, leaping, sometimes to music, which both Floss and I had known in sleep during infancy and childhood—now realized." For the first time he was seeing places that had remained vague images in his mind, the places from which all those visitors had come to see his parents and to which they had returned, all distant memories that his father and mother had conveyed confusedly to him. Suddenly, he was seeing those old sepia photographs transformed into the living reality of the places themselves. He was astonished.

The seaplane touched down at San Pedro, Cuba, then at Port au Prince,

Haiti, then at Ciudad Trujillo in the Dominican Republic before finally landing at San Juan, Puerto Rico. Ciudad Trujillo: the former Puerto Plata, whence his father's foster father, the itinerant photographer George Wellcome, had come. And Port au Prince, where his namesake Carlos Hoheb had practiced medicine and sired nine children before being forced to flee in the 1880s during one of Haiti's interminable revolutions. The return there—like the expulsion—had been rough going, for the clipper plane had been thrown fifty feet back into the air when it had hit the water. Later, as the Williamses walked up the narrow boardwalk, they found themselves blocked by a high fence and palace guards so that Haiti's newest president could take off with his blond secretary and his retinue by "special plane to Washington" to "negotiate a loan."[96]

The expulsion, the gates forbidding access, Carlos of the "amorous disposition": it was a mythic reenactment of the expulsion from the Garden, a scene Williams had evoked six years before in his "Adam" and "Eve" poems. But what that first hard contact with the water had taught him was the impossibility of ever going back home again. Which was why, in *Paterson* 1, a book about origins, Williams recalled "the land-locked / bay back of Port au Prince" not for its turquoise and deep blue shades of water, but rather as "blue vitriol / streaked with paler streams, shabby as loose / hair, badly dyed—like chemical waste / mixed in, eating out the shores." By then he was thinking of all that human greed had done not only to his own filthy Passaic, but to these Edenic Columbian islands as well. Williams' description was in fact an oblique evocation of his Grandmother Wellcome, the image of the woman, of the landscape, eaten out by the cancer of all sorts of special interests until his own muse, his own complex generative source, had been permanently crippled, scarred, deformed.

In the spring of '41 Bill Jr. was interning in the orthopedic center of the Jersey City Obstetrical Center, while his younger brother was finishing up his M.B.A. at Harvard and getting ready to marry a girl from Ohio named Virginia Carnes as soon as he graduated in June. Jinny, as she was called, looked as pretty as Barbara Stanwyck, Williams had told Charles Keppel in January when his son had become engaged, and he only hoped the two of them could hold on to one another.[97] He wondered now and then when Bill would bring home a girl, but as yet his older boy seemed preoccupied only with his medical work. Paul, on the other hand, had always been the more outgoing, easygoing of the two: captain of the varsity swim team at Penn in his last year, popular with his fraternity brothers, given to doing crazy things like fishing in the Botanical Garden Pond in his tuxedo at five in the morning after an all-night college dance, and then actually catching a two-pound catfish. (This was the same garden, incidentally, into which Williams himself had sneaked thirty-five years earlier so that he might see his beloved Shakespeare.) He'd really been pretty much on his own ever since he'd gone away to college. But now, incredibly, Williams had a son—age twenty-four—who was about to get married to his college sweetheart and then move to Massilon, Ohio, to be closer to his wife's family.

There was also, of course, the ringside world of writers and critics to deal with, even when—as all that year—Williams found it difficult to do any poetry himself. "I want to write verse," he told Louis Untermeyer in mid-March, "but I can't do what I've done in the past. I want to let go—but there's too great a weight back there holding me rigid and indifferent." And yet he knew that that was becoming a pose in part. "When a man wants to write he writes," he wrote. "It'll be the same with me."[98] He was still angry with young Randall Jarrell and wrote Malcolm Cowley at the end of February congratulating him for taking a poke at "that shit." But Williams also went after Conrad Aiken, who had recently published a sonnet (!) sequence: "Jarrell on one side and Aiken on the other, one as bad as the other, without a whisper of comprehension of what the problem [of the poem] is about." Sure they could write a felicitous phrase or manifest a sharp wit, and those were certainly "possible components of good verse and criticism." But what good was half a machine, "a gas engine on a trestle and without a drive shaft, or chassis or wheels or anything?" As far as he was concerned, Jarrell was "a class-room cutie" without an idea in his head, and all Aiken had ever done was "paste together the things . . . clipped from his milder contemporaries."[99]

One of those "milder contemporaries" was Eliot, of course, and Williams was still following him, waiting for him to manifest signs of life. The day after he returned home from the Puerto Rico conference, Williams sat down at his typewriter to answer—at least for himself —Edmund Wilson's preface to his poetry supplement in the most recent issue of the *New Republic*, which Williams had found waiting for him. In an essay called "American Writing: 1941," Edmund Wilson had written that there were "unmistakable signs of the revival of an interest in literature for its own sake—that is, as a department of activity which has its own aims, techniques and rights." Writers were beginning once again to see the world for themselves rather than through a series of prior texts. That was of course exactly what Williams himself was feeling, as he groped now for a new form.[100]

Wilson had chosen to concentrate on the poetry of Elizabeth Bishop, Rolph Humphries, and Randall Jarrell, and even Williams was willing to concede privately that Jarrell had handled the conventional line—as Stevens had before him—with professional ability. But what was needed now was a line that revealed a concern with its "own, innate and particular formal necessities." This was of paramount importance, Williams felt, for it could determine a whole culture's final value. Suppose England should collapse under the pressure of Hitler's attacks in the next year or two? What would that have meant in terms of England's poetry? Would the poems reveal that England had collapsed first from within, that it had already become a bastard culture incapable of surviving this new hurricane onslaught brought on by Hitler? To hell with what those poems said in terms of something called meaning. The real question to ask was: had they remained awake to the language and the spirit about them? If not, that culture—like Athens and Rome earlier—was already a mere fossil, an empty shell. Williams thought again of his flight. It had not so much mattered where the plane had taken him, he argued, as that he had actually been in a machine that had made vivid to him the *fact* of flight. A poem was like that too: a machine that made vivid the *fact* of flight.[101]

Williams also wrote a letter to *Poetry* magazine praising David Daiches for his attack on an earlier essay in the same magazine supporting the new classicism of Hulme and Eliot, an essay that had called for a return to the medieval synthesis. Daiches had called such a retreat untenable and had supported the strength of modern literature in spite of all its uncertainties and plurality of possible frameworks.[102] And when, in May, the *Partisan Review* published Eliot's *Dry Salvages*, Williams wrote Macdonald again in a strained fashion noticing that the *PR* was "giving a lot of space to Eliot for some mystical reason" and asking if Eliot actually had "any relation to verse of late."[103] By this point Williams' hatred of Eliot had assumed mythic and seriocomic proportions.

Much as he wanted to remain out of Europe's war, Williams could not escape the implications of the nightly bombings of England. He was deeply touched by the bravery and determination of these people to fight on—alone if need be—against what seemed overwhelming odds. France had fallen in three weeks, but England was still holding on after a year of intense sufferings and privations. On the other hand, if the U.S. entered the war against Germany or Japan, what would happen to his own sons? Besides, what in hell had the English ever done for him to expect him to bail them out now except—in the spectre of Eliot—reject his own proffered handshake and also treat his poor grandmother in such beastly fashion?

In June of 1941, therefore, he found himself writing a strange poem called "An Exultation," celebrating the German bombings of London for being agents of just retribution for England's own abominable conduct, its arrogance in treating subject peoples all over the world as colonials, servants, and second-rate citizens. He was willing to see in Germany the apocalyptic scourge of God, a nation itself rotten to the core but still capable of working "a cleansing mystery" upon the English. He remembered Pound's early Hell cantos which had lashed out at England's economic interests in the Great War, a war that had caused the death of the flower of that nation's manhood. He still remembered his poor grandmother, thrown out of her house by the Godwins for having become pregnant by whoever that first Williams was. And so he had carried in himself his grandmother's lifelong resentments against the English. And though he was proud of his English heritage, he had only contempt for a figure like Eliot, who represented for him that part of the English character which had first to be cleansed by an economic force that was in reality a spiritual hurricane. Williams, who was usually so careful not to fall into the piano when he wrote a poem, had really let himself go this time. Of course the *Partisan Review*, realizing that Williams had put his foot into it again, was only too happy to print that poem along with Williams' incoherent accompanying explanation.[104]

A month earlier Williams had written to David McDowell, the editor of *Hika*, at Kenyon College, that it was important for America to stay out of the European mess. "We have always been Europe's cow," he insisted: "We are rich in material resources and poor in culture. . . . *They* are civilized. We are barbarians—and shall always be so to them. When the war is over we shall be blamed for it *all*, as we were after the last one." Europe was merely working out its own "cataclysmic fate," which was a typically European thing for it to do. It had done it dozens of times in the past and would probably do it again. It was all a matter of determining who would be the new leaders. They loved it—all of them. But Americans had to be careful not to be taken in by European claims and counterclaims. Language for a European was an ideological tool, a means of winning, while for Americans it was "still a barrel of apples." If a U.S. expeditionary force were ever sent to Europe, Williams suggested, it would be better to send it over to fight all of Europe and not just one side or the other. In the coming dialectic it would not be America as an ally of this country or that, but America against European civilization itself. But of course to send such an army against Europe was pure insanity. And even though Americans were, after all, transplanted Europeans themselves, it was better to stay out of the embroilment altogether.[105]

On Saturday, August 23, Williams and Floss arrived at the Bread Loaf Writers' Conference in the Green Mountains of Vermont, where Williams delivered a talk that same evening. Again, his speech stressed the need for a new measure and therefore a new reality which would be able to resist the daily lies of the papers and the radio to which millions were each day subjected.[106] He did not stay at the conference long, apologizing to Louis Untermeyer that he definitely had to be back home for his medical practice by Monday. But the real reason he was anxious to say his say and then clear out was the dark presence of Robert Frost, who refused to attend Williams' lecture even though he was conspicuously present at Bread Loaf, sitting in his cabin only half a mile away.

Williams had first met Frost at Williams College in the mid-1930s during one of his visits with Floss to see Bill Jr. As it turned out, Frost was giving a reading of his poetry that same weekend and Williams sat out in the audience listening with his wife and son. During his reading Frost interjected some "slurring remarks" about the "New York poets" which Floss still vividly remembered twenty years after the event, and she nudged her husband, urging him to go up after the reading and introduce himself. When Frost learned that one of his New York poets had actually heard what he'd said up there in the relative isolation of western Massachusetts, he was nonplussed: "My God, Williams, how did you get here?" Williams said something, then turned and left.

But next morning, as the Williamses were having breakfast at the Williams Inn, where they usually stayed on their visits to the college, Frost made a point of coming over to their table and apologizing for what he'd said about the New York poets. The apology seemed to go on and on, and finally Floss noticed that the head waitress was pacing back and forth trying to close up the dining room for the next meal. As she and Bill were leaving, Floss remembered, Mrs. Frost walked up to her husband and scolded him for keeping the family waiting for over an hour. As far as Floss was concerned, the great Frost had turned out to be merely "obstinate and a spoiled brat."[107]

Williams saw Frost again several years later—on March 26, 1939—at a friend's house in Montclair, New Jersey, on the occasion of Frost's sixty-fourth birthday. Then the two men had seemed to hit it off well enough. Frost had even confessed that the main reason he'd avoided Bill Williams for the past twenty-five years had been Ezra Pound's remark to him back in 1914 in London that, when Frost got back to the States, he should look up Williams. He was, Pound had told him, the only artist in the whole country Frost could associate with and still remain clean. That had been enough to keep Frost away for good! Now, however, face to face, Frost and Williams even seemed to like each other, each promising to send the other his books of poems as they were published.[108] But Williams was beginning to measure up too much like one of those heavyweight contenders Frost so much distrusted, and so now—in the summer of '41—he made it a point not only to stay away from Williams' reading but to tell his students to do the same.

One of those he warned away was Charles Eaton, who had been invited to the conference that summer by Frost himself. Williams was no real poet, he told Eaton. All he really wrote were snippets of poems, things like "The Red Wheelbarrow." And, puritan that he was, he warned Eaton that there were stories circulating that Williams was some kind of Lothario. In spite of the warning, Eaton did go to the Little Theatre for Williams' talk and found himself instinctively liking the man. Williams was not physically imposing in the way Frost could be, he thought, but he did find him charming, "very generous with his time and enthusiasms," outgoing, and genuinely interested in what others had to say in a way Frost was definitely not. What particularly struck Eaton was that, though his own poetry was so different from Williams', Williams could still take the time to read and to praise it.[109]

Williams did after all have a strong mothering instinct, especially for beginners who could be so easily crushed by the established critics and poets. So, a month after the Bread Loaf nonincident, he was consoling Ted Roethke, whose first book had been slapped down by R. P. Blackmur. "Weep not, Signor, over the lapses and tortuosities of Blackmur's disappointed mind," Williams wrote. "He is some sort of prince of the book, a latter day collegian." In fact, Williams had himself recently sent Blackmur "a contemptuous letter" for Blackmur's support of second-rate "versifiers" then appearing in Poetry magazine. Williams offered his own advice to Roethke now, telling him to "write more and more fully out of the less known side of your nature if you are to be noticed." It was advice Roethke would brilliantly follow in his next book.[110]

At the end of the year the MacLeish question which had surfaced at the Puerto Rican conference surfaced once again, this time in the pages of the Partisan Review, when Dwight Macdonald asked Williams and others to defend or question his own attack on Van Wyck Brooks for supporting and expanding what MacLeish had written in "The Irresponsibles." Would not Goebbels himself, Macdonald wrote, have applauded MacLeish and Van Wyck Brooks's attack on a "degenerate" modern art? Primary literature—that is, viable avant-garde literature—had of necessity to follow the biological rather than the ideological grain as a "force of regeneration" conducive to race survival.[111] Williams answered Macdonald's letter in late November. Yes, he said, he'd read Brooks's essay, but he'd found it so ridiculous as not to merit serious attention. The problem with Brooks was that he wanted to make literature "safe" for democracy instead of reading what the young were writing. Better to ignore some critics, like this "ignorant sap," bewildered by a "world running away in new and brilliant colors under his nose."[112] A pity, then, that that same world was about to explode, and that the young would soon be carrying rifles rather than pens.

Pound too was still sending an occasional letter from Rome, where he was now broadcasting his own versions of Roosevelt's fireside chats, and Williams would answer or refuse to answer Pound's letters as he saw fit.

But on the morning of July 30, Floss had come running in breathlessly from the local bank to tell her husband that one of the tellers had been listening on his shortwave set to Ezra Pound over Radio Rome the night before and had heard Pound's voice crackling something about "As my friend Doc Williams of New Jersey would say." That was enough! Pound had gone absolutely gaga, had become merely "a mouthpiece for the disreputable Mussolini." Williams went upstairs and began writing an essay to sort out his own feelings for the man. He's seen Marianne Moore a few weeks before at Paul Rosenfeld's apartment in the city and had told her Pound had become a "stupid ass," another Shaw trying to rewrite Shakespeare's *Coriolanus.* Pound was one of those adolescent geniuses who had gone stark raving mad early on. And if he was one of the greatest poets of modern time he was still a spoiled brat. Williams recalled the story Ford had told him about the time Pound had visited him in Provence, garlanded as a tennis champion. He had dressed that way seriously, Ford thought, without irony, to show where he placed himself on the tennis courts. And Williams couldn't help remembering Pound as a young man, unable to carry a tune but convinced he could set himself up as a musician. And he remembered too what Charlotte Herman had once told him—that though Pound couldn't even play the piano *passably,* he didn't mind improvising whole compositions. "Everything touching those great basic understandings upon which the century was turning," Williams could now say in this declaration of his own independence, "the newer comprehensions of physics, chemistry and especially biology . . . were a closed book" to Pound. In short, what Pound lacked was a "knowledge of man, pure and simple." And then, as if to make restitution for his own attacks on the English, Williams added: "Where in Pound's work will you find the faintest inkling of the great force among the English themselves, as a people, that would some day be stirred to such phenomenal resistance in the name of freedom and the dignity of the human spirit" as the world was then witnessing in the air over England.

Pound had all along been out of step with the times. Yes, he had attacked the British special interests, but he'd never understood the British people. And when he'd fled to Paris in 1920 to wage a literary war on the English, he had gone for sustenance to the decayed salons of Remy de Gourmont and Mallarmé even while Céline's extraordinary French world was bursting all about him. And what did Pound know of modern French painting, of Picasso, Braque, Matisse? Had not Picasso and later Stein both dismissed him? And why, when he'd gone to Italy in '24, hadn't Pound been able to see that Mussolini's coup had nipped Italian socialism in the bud? But the unforgivable sin, the final blow had come when Pound had compared the terrible defeat of the Spanish Republicans to "the draining of some obscure swamp in the African jungle." Pound did not like the way his world had gone, and so he'd blamed Freud, blamed the Jews. Better to kill the world than have it rot away, he thought he heard Pound saying. Even his *Cantos* were filled not with the living but with the dead. The trouble was that Pound lacked even the necessary humanity to see all this. Williams published his diatribe in *Decision* in September, under the title, "Ezra Pound: Lord Ga-Ga!" It was a very palpable hit at the man who had set himself up as an insane Lord Haw Haw, already flirting with treason. No doubt about it. Williams was angry with the fool for having mentioned his name over the radio, especially when two FBI agents showed up at his house a short time later with a few questions about his connection with Ezra. Better now to cut oneself clean from that kind of craziness.[113]

"Have had two rather sad letters from Ezra," Williams wrote Laughlin at the beginning of September. "He seems to be in a state of aphasia, doesn't remember that there's a war going on and can't understand why the newspaper from Tokyo doesn't come through."[114] Williams had received both of Pound's letters on the twenty-sixth of August, he told Zukofsky the same day, amazed that poor Ezra actually believed that the Germans—who had attacked Russia on June 22—would be able to finish that campaign by the end of August and that the trans-Siberian railway would soon be delivering his Japanese papers once again. "This," he added, was "something to amaze," and it made him feel uneasy that he'd hit his old friend as hard as he had in *Decision*. At bottom, poor Ez was simply and profoundly out of touch with what the hell was happening in the world.[115]

But the real break with Pound came on November 26, when Williams wrote Pound a blasting letter damning him up and down for his "brutal and sufficiently stupid reference to meat lying around on the steppes" —Pound's heavy-handed pun on the heavy casualties suffered by Russian civilians as Hitler's armies moved on to Moscow. As for meat, Williams retorted, Pound would find "far more of it solidly encased" in his own head. Who did Pound think he was? Did he think that just because he was broadcasting from the Eternal City that gave him some sort of intellectual advantage? And what the hell did Pound really know of Jersey farmers or Chinese peasants anyway? Did he really think Aristotle, Adams, or Confucius—part of Pound's community in the *Cantos*—would have supported his stupid tirades? Come on, he jibed at Pound, whom was he really backing? Was it Moussie or that other bastard, Hitler?[116]

Pound never received that letter. It had been detained by U.S. Examiner 4952 and was returned to Williams nine months later. It was just as well, for less than two weeks after Williams sent his letter off to Pound, Pearl Harbor had become history and the war that Williams—like so many other Americans—had dreaded was now a reality. Once again, as he had in 1917, he would have to examine young men for the draft, would see them—along with his own sons—go off to war, knowing that many of them would never return or, returning, be maimed in one way or another by what they had witnessed. As for Pound, Williams would not hear from him again until 1946, when, broken by what he had had to endure at the hands of, first, Italian partisans and then U.S. Army personnel who had kept him in a gorilla cage at a U.S. Detention Center in Pisa, Pound would write from a prison hospital in Washington, D.C., that he was sure now his "main spring" had been finally "busted."

*
* *

War the Destroyer. At a party at Charles and Musya Sheeler's home in Irvington, New York, in late October '41, Williams had met the photographer Barbara Morgan, who had just published her book on Martha Graham and the dance. She and Graham and Williams spoke about Williams' poems about the Spanish Loyalists, and Williams asked Morgan if she could create a photograph using Martha Graham to symbolize the destructiveness of war, for which Williams would then compose a poem. What the two women finally decided on was a bomb exploding above the figure of Graham, who was dressed in a long black robe, in a gesture of stooped, rhythmic terror. "I shot with a strobe light at 1/10,000 second exposure for a spastic effect in a composition in which I slanted the shadows to dehumanize facial features and imply Death," Morgan remembered years later.[117] When Williams drove up to Scarsdale to get the photo from her in early 1942, he was delighted, and wrote the poem "War, the Destroyer!" which he dedicated to Martha Graham.

Though the poem and picture had originally been intended to be used in a text on the Spanish Civil War, they now came to represent the larger global conflagration of World War II. What was there left to do, Williams wrote, now that the war he had wished to avoid was upon him, upon his world? Nothing for it but to dance, at a time when writing, music, and even prayer had proven ineffective. Nothing for it but to "leap and twist/ whirl and prance," and fasten terror on a dress or in the air "to incite and impel," and dance, dance your fool head off, dance with the blood

> *displayed flagrantly*
> *in its place*
> *beside the face.*[118]

Bill Jr. signed up almost at once. On February 18, 1942, he was commissioned a medical officer in the Naval Reserves, and within a few weeks he had been shipped off to the Pacific with an outfit of Navy Seabees. For Williams and for Floss—as for millions of others—the agony of separation was about to begin. The U.S. was into the war up to its neck now and Williams at once put aside his own misgivings. For months at a time he was not even sure where his older son was, except somewhere in the vast Pacific area on some island or atoll. His letters—at least one and sometimes as many as two or three a week—were mailed to San Francisco to be forwarded by the Navy. Williams and Floss even tried guessing where their son might be by reading up on the articles about the Pacific Islands that appeared in the *National Geographic*. But they both knew they were whistling in the dark. Paul was married now and his wife, Jinny, was expecting her first in August, and he found himself deferred because of the defense job he had with Republic Steel in Canton, Ohio. But he too would eventually be called up, to serve as ensign on the *Alden*, an old destroyer patrolling the Allied shipping lanes in the North Atlantic.

As for Williams, war or no war, the great birth pangs he had been experiencing for several years were still with him. *Paterson* had still to be born, if only he could find a great enough, inclusive enough form for his monster child. He tried reading other long poems that winter of '42: a "bad translation of *Faust*," followed by Chaucer's *Troilus and Criseyde* to get the taste of the Faust translation rinsed out of his mouth.[119] He noticed now for the first time how much Joyce had stolen from Goethe for his own *Ulysses*, and wondered what he in turn might be able to plunder from Chaucer's novellike long poem about a cosmopolitan love triangle: modern love in the city.

He was also lecturing again. On February 10 he was at Vassar, where he spoke before a group of four hundred women on "The Structural Approach to an Understanding of Form in Modern Verse." He told his audience he was aware of his reputation as a maverick, even as an "unsafe" influence on their minds, as some of the critics would have it, because of his unrelenting attacks on the academy, on English professors, on the tradition. He knew he'd been accused of many "sins," including a lack of traditional form and even of intellectual content. He knew all that, but he was still insisting on change, on a revolution in poetry. All the more important was it now, he insisted, to create new forms if Americans were to live, if they were to "have anything *to return to* after the international adventure of war."[120]

He liked his lecture at Vassar and felt pleased with himself, though he confessed to Charles Abbott afterward that he still preferred talking to men, "finding it always rather difficult to take the girls seriously enough except on the one topic!" And yet he'd found them intelligent in their responses to his talk, even more so than most men would have been.[121] He'd also been bemused by the opening remarks of the professor at Vassar who had introduced him, and he committed her remark to paper, thinking to use it in *Paterson:*

> *I don't know that*
> *we should admit you to these halls after*
> *that article I read of yours last week!*[122]

He thought of letting that comment stand as part of the deep antagonism he knew existed between himself and the academy, but he let it go, finally, for something stronger.

Williams called it "the academic shuffle," the "old respectability gag," and it troubled him that even the old avant-garde magazines like *Poetry* had by then gone over to the universities. "You know what I mean," he wrote Harvey Breit in mid-March, "the Rob't Penn Warrens . . . who go to Oxford to find out about Turkey Hollow." He suspected these "conscious shits," this new breed of academics, "who know everything and must keep everything in perfect order"—he was thinking of Eliot's followers this time—those who wanted others to think they actually knew something and that the "church and its INTENTIONS are indispensable and right." There were also neosurrealists and neomystics like Patchen, whose poems made Patchen sound like God or at least that haranguer John the Baptist. Sure you had to give the subconscious its play, Williams was willing to admit, "but not carte blanche to spill everything that comes out of it." Every poet had to let go from time to time to see what was down there, as he had in his improvisations, but he also knew that everything that spilled out wasn't "equally valuable and significant." What was needed was a balance: unbridled madness and formal discipline.

He saw two armed fields between the poets: Eliot and his school, "the hard students of literary knowledge," a knowledge that Williams himself deeply respected. And, on the other side, he saw the "dirt men, the laborers who try to keep alive the *geist*, the undisciplined power of the unimaginable poem." And that, really, was where he was, trying to create a radical new form, knowing that even then the university men were "shitting" on him with their "clean asses, so sweet in their shitting." What was necessary, of course, was a synthesis, a coming together of these forces in some one figure "at some propitious moment in history," as Shakespeare—that essentially ignorant man—had achieved a summation of the English Renaissance. And though he himself was still blocked, he could appreciate whatever signs of the new poetry he found in others.[123]

So, for example, he wrote Carl Rakosi in late February that he'd been looking for just such poems as Rakosi had recently done: accurate observations "of things that cry out to be observed in the terms in which they exist and are important to us—unexpectedly, their exotic (American) beauty, their respect for the canons of art (difficultly realized) in an intimate and new association, . . . their finding their materials in the luxuriant (but mostly ignored) world of form and sound at our feet, their consciousness of the tradition of writing without apology or excuse." But most of all, he admired the "dawning sense of the line! clamoring to be reincarnated in a new image expansive enough for the uses of a cultured, a FULL—not an amputated, cut to horrible configurations of historical establishments—MAN."[124] In fact those lines described accurately Williams' own desires for his as yet unborn Dr. Paterson: a poet large enough to include all men and women, who might be a city in himself/herself, thriving, teeming, debased, magnificent, deformed, grotesque, real.

Get it all in there, all of it, revealing the self without trying, including one's "bad habits, perversions, amputations, falsehoods." It meant not simply spreading one's inner organs out to be displayed on some enamel dish, but showing one's very life thrashing about wildly.[125] He desperately wanted to begin his poem at last, without any more delay, for it would be the major undertaking that should lift him from the second ranks into the top . . . if he succeeded. He had kept delaying *Paterson* for some distant summative phase of his life, mulling over for years the form it should finally take. But now he was approaching sixty, and he would have the *Cantos* to contend with, as well as *The Waste Land* and *The Bridge* and even Zuk's *A*. He knew what he was after, really, and had known for a long time now. "I've been tearing my head apart for years to get at a mode of modern verse suitable for a long poem which would be simple as speech itself and subtle as the subtlest brain could desire on the basis of measure," he'd told Laughlin in June '41. *That* had been the greatest problem in American poetry since Whitman, and the failure to contend with that problem had made almost "all long poems crap" to him because their obvious artificiality had not been able to hold his interest after the first few pages.[126] At one point or another he'd taken every strong contender's measure. Fine. Like Poe before him, he had cleared the field then. Now it was up to him finally to *make* his long poem, his impossible poem *Paterson*. And soon, before it would really be too late.

Mother,
Hélène (Elena) Hoheb Williams
(c. 1895).

WCW's father,
William George Williams
(1898).

William Carlos Williams, age two (1885).

Rutherford Star Athletic Club (1900). *Middle row:* Williams is second from left, brother Ed is second from right. BOTTOM LEFT: The Williams family (c. 1899). BOTTOM RIGHT: Williams as intern at Child's Hospital Infant Asylum (1908).

TOP RIGHT The Hermans about the time Williams first met them (1907). *From left:* Paul, Gurlie, Florence, Charlotte, and young Paul.

ABOVE Charlotte Herman (c. 1908).

RIGHT Later (1928) portrait of Floss by unknown artist.

The *Others* group at 9 Ridge Road, April 1916.

ABOVE *Back row from left:* Jean Crotti, Marcel Duchamp, Walter Arensberg, Man Ray, R. A. Sanborn, Maxwell Bodenheim. *Front row from left:* Alanson Hartpence, Alfred Kreymborg, William Carlos Williams, Skipwith Cannell.

ABOVE *From left:* Helen Slade, Mary Caroline Davis, Yvonne Crotti, Floss Williams, Kitty Cannell, Mrs. Davis (Kitty Cannell's mother), Gertrude Kreymborg, Mrs. Walter Arensberg. (*Photo: courtesy State University of New York at Buffalo*).

RIGHT Portrait of Williams by Charles Sheeler for the Dial Award (1926).

BOTTOM RIGHT Portrait by Man Ray in Paris (1924).

BELOW Robert McAlmon (1924).

Bill Jr., Williams, Paul,
and neighbor's boy (1932).

Williams at Passaic
General Hospital (1936).

In his second-floor study (c. 1947).

Williams and Ezra Pound at their
last meeting, photographed
by Richard Avcdon (July 1958).

Williams and Floss (March 1961).

The Yaddo group (July 1950). *Back row:* Willson Osborne, Theodore Roethke, Robel Paris, Harvey Shapiro, Elaine Gottlieb, Beryl Levy, Cid Corman, Simmons Persons, Gladys Farnell, Hans Sahl, Clifford Wright, Richard Eberhart. *Front row:* Ben Weber, Nicholas Calas, Jessamyn West, Eugenie Gershoy, William Carlos Williams, Floss Williams, Mitsu Yashima, Charles Schucker, Elizabeth Ames, John Dillon Husband. (*Photo by George S. Bolster, courtesy Yaddo*).

TEN

Dragging the River for Giants: 1942–1946

As usual with Williams, the impetus that actually got him started again on *Paterson* was a woman. It happened on Palm Sunday evening, March 29, 1942, when an unexpected windfall in the figure of a dark, wiry, diminutive, and bedraggled young woman landed at Williams' office door in the middle of a cold spring storm and asked if the doctor could please examine her sick boy. She had no money, she was a single parent living over in a cheap flat in New York, she had some poems with her, perhaps Dr. Williams would be interested? Her name was Marcia Nardi, and Williams could see almost at once that under that soaked-through pint-sized body was a person "in frightened need, in desperate need."[1] He examined her son, free of charge, and when Nardi left, she left behind a sheaf of poems.

Busy with his practice, Williams did not at first answer Nardi, perhaps not knowing how to get in touch with her, though she did know Harvey Breit and Williams could have asked him for her address.[2] Besides, Easter was almost on him and he had other things on his mind. First of all, there was his older son, who was then in Port Hueneme, California, en route to the Fiji Islands (though all Williams knew was that his son was somewhere west of him, perhaps in Hawaii). Now, near midnight of Holy Thursday, with a full moon floating in the clear heavens outside his east window, Williams sat down to write his son a letter. "Easter doesn't seem to mean much this year," he wrote Bill, "but for all that it's Easter which means, call it what we may, the return of the sun—and the moon." He wanted to remind him that the flower shops in Rutherford were "flooded with wires from Hawaii and Australia ordering corsages for Ma, Sis and the girl friends," though he wanted Bill to understand that he wasn't throwing out any hints about Bill's sending flowers to his mother. He already had the '36 Ford up on blocks with the wheels off because of wartime gas and rubber rationing, though Frick at the Hart Battery had suggested he keep the battery in to run the engine a few minutes every couple of weeks to keep the rods from rusting and the cylinders from gumming up. He was going to a cocktail party in New York the next day "to keep up my artistic life," though he didn't much feel like going with his son away at war.[3]

Williams spent part of that Easter Sunday—mercifully uninterrupted by patients[4]—writing an essay on Tchelitchew's paintings and meditating on the secret core at the heart of every artist. How could we understand any artist's work, he wrote, unless we knew what the wellsprings of the artist were, "the underlying purity from which ALL a man's work emerges." Lacking that luminous insight into the core of the imagination, we ended not with the purity and tranquillity of a Raphael, "his luminous quality of the sphere," but rather with something like the "opacity and confusion of Ingres' scene in the harem." From the monstrous seed would grow the monstrous tree, he wrote, perhaps remembering the parable of the mustard seed. And no one could ever have determined ahead of time "the tree of the artist's life . . . growing out of the upturned end of his left great toe, what difference?" The world, he had come to realize after inhabiting it for sixty years, was indeed monstrous, and only a monstrous art like Tchelitchew's surrealistic nightmares could truly reveal that monstrous nature. And so it would be with him. His own *Paterson*, like Tchelitchew's painting, would be made of all that anyone would wish to hide, "of himself, of his times," revealed there on the canvas or on those dirty sheets in all its disgraceful, shocking reality, hitting to the core of a man's profoundest secret about himself, that "eel-like presence hiding there" in the paint or the words for its own dark survival. . . . [5]

Williams received his first letter from Marcia Nardi on April 10, five days after Easter. It was a neurotic, self-defensive scrawl abjectly demanding Williams' forgiveness for troubling him with the poems she'd left with him and asking him to please return them. Williams replied at once, telling her he'd now had a chance to read through them and that they contained "some of the best writing by a woman (or by anyone else) I have seen in years." He wanted to hold on to them until he could get copies made of them for further study.[6] In the meantime, their monstrous reality had triggered something in him. It took him another month to write again, and when he did, he apologized, citing the pressures of wartime medical practice as the reason. "One pressing duty dovetailed into another all day yesterday," he wrote, telling her he hadn't even been able to read her letter when it had arrived, "and in the end I lost a baby I was most anxious to save."

But it wasn't even Nardi's poems he wanted to talk about; it was rather her extraordinary letters, letters he knew then he would transplant into the very fabric of his autobiographical *Paterson*. At last he'd found—or was about to realize that he'd found—the exact monstrous female voice to complement his own monstrous hydrocephalic self. "Your letters show you to have one of the best minds I have ever encountered," he wrote to her on May 13. "I say nothing of its reach which I have had no opportunity to measure but its truth and strength. Your words as I read them have a vigor and a cleanliness to them which constitutes for me real beauty. I sincerely and deeply admire you.'"[7]

By then the blockage Williams had been experiencing had finally been dynamited and he had flung himself at last into the poem. Amidst the flotsam and jetsam of false starts on the falls, he had written a poem celebrating the turnabout, the breakthrough, the crossing into life, the "Catastrophic Birth," carefully dating it: April 22, 1942. That poem remembered the incredible destruction of Mt. Pelée back in 1902, a violence that had shattered a whole world, only to give birth to a new beginning. And against that eruption Williams evoked the image of "the big she-Wop" whom he had delivered of six children in six straight years. In time the great change, the revolution he had been predicting, would come regardless of what the offical prognosticators said:

> The laboratory announces officially
> that there is no need to worry. The
> cone is subsiding, smoke rises as
> a funnel into the blue unnatural sky—
> The change impends! A change stutters
> in the rocks. We believe nothing can change.
>
> The fracture will come, the death dealing
> chemistry cannot be long held back.
> The dreaded eruption blocks out the valley,
> the careful prognosticator as well as
> the idlers. The revelation is complete.
> Peace is reborn above the cinders . . . [8]

"Catastrophic Birth" was, then, one of the pieces thrown out by the volcanic fury of Williams' early attempts to find the form of *Paterson*. He called his long effort the "Prelude" to *Paterson* itself, in an attempt to bracket the awesome imaginative forces he was finally unleashing. He had tried to come at *Paterson*'s major form in many ways, among them by taking his 1927 "Paterson" and expanding its eighty-five lines into a book-length poem. But that approach had failed. He had tried using dramatic characters like Doc and Willie, thinking perhaps of Yeats's interior dialogue between two characters named Hic and Ille (which Pound had changed to Hic and Willie). And several times that spring Williams had driven or would drive over to Paterson to stand on the iron bridge that crossed the chasm of the Great Falls and think. There, with people strolling by, he could stare down at the old man in the river, that granite outcropping in the middle of the falls that formed the grizzled features of an old man's head. Silent himself, that shape continued to endure the roar of the river, that unceasing flow of language, cascading over his head in all seasons. It was Williams' secret image of himself: the monstrous, hydrocephalic poet, a water-head obsessed with the down-pouring of words and the dream of an impossible poem from which he would awaken only in death. Here then were the delineaments of one of his giants, the water curling "about him," as Williams wrote now, in mid-1942, "forming the outline / of his back. He lies on his right side, / his head near the thunder / of the water filling his dreams."[9]

"I've been over riding around Paterson again," one of his patients, Helen Fall, remembered him as telling her about this time. "I've got it in my head that Paterson is to be a person, representative of beginnings, but it's not a city—that city of Paterson will represent something else. I know how I want to work it out, and I just was over this afternoon, soaking up the feeling of Paterson."[10] He was also reading the local histories of the region, like Barber and Howe's mid-nineteenth century *Historical Collections of the State of New Jersey*, as well as Nelson's history, stealing what he could. One thing he stole was the story of the hydrocephalic Peter the Dwarf, whom General Washington had visited—among other natural oddities of the region—during the Revolutionary War. The poor, crippled dwarf who'd stayed home in Paterson to contemplate the falls was another image of Williams himself, who'd also stayed at home to write his crippled, monstrous poem, hobbling on its limping feet, while the other dogs—Pound and Eliot—had run far and wide sniffing at the trees, barking their profundities to each other.

Another mass of material that Williams had found ready for his own designs was a file of historical transcriptions copied over the years by a local historian, Herbert Fisher of Bloomfield. Fisher's was, essentially, a compilation extracted from Barber and Howe, Nelson and Shiner's *History of Paterson and Its Environs* in three volumes (1920), and a curious little monograph originally published by Charles Pitman Long-well in 1901 called *A Little Story of Old Paterson*. This last was Williams' secret text, and he stole whole sections from it, turning its archaic prose into a seriocomic nostalgic pastoral of old Paterson, in part to show that no one, not even the artist, could ever go back home again. This file, together with additional information that he simply lifted from his close friend, typist, and neighbor, Kitty Hoagland—who had been collecting data for her own history of Paterson and environs during the early '40s—constituted the bulk of the historical strata that found its way into Williams' epic of a city that was also a man.

Unlike either Pound or—later—Charles Olson, Williams logged relatively little time in libraries, either in Paterson or at the New York Public Library. He could do that kind of research if pressed to it, as he and Floss had done back in the early '20s when he did the background for *In the American Grain*, or later, when he was researching the life of Washington. But now he was principally concerned with measuring and sifting, with finding a form. The image, then, of the poet in the library in the third book of *Paterson*, who listens to the distant sound of the falls while surrounded with the life-in-death presences of a thousand books, was less a literal condition of the making of *Paterson* and more a mythic reenactment of the descent into the underworld where the poet reads from the Book of the Dead, watching the tragic implications of the living core of the imagination turning inevitably into a Book of inert Lead.

Williams knew instinctively he would need historical material to broaden the base of his poem, otherwise he would be in danger of failing as Keats had failed before him with *Hyperion*, where Keats's giants had remained static, frozen, unable to stir into life.[11] Epic lines in and of themselves were not enough for the modern epic, for the language—at least Williams' language—could not be supported on so slender a base. He wanted to write so the poem would—as he wrote—"hold water." He wanted to delineate finally the beautiful thing and reveal to the world the flesh of the giant Ymir, an image of himself as "cosmic" poet. After all, "beauty" was "the quest and how will you find beauty when it is locked in the mind?" By May 1942 he had collected close to a hundred pages of fragments, much of it repetitious, with figures like Noah Faitout, Sam Patch (who had dived several times from the falls and lived to talk about it), Billy Sunday, and Edgar Allen Poe, as well as a sermon by a preacher delivered near the lake on Garret Mountain, some park scenes, some old sermons delivered by black ministers, and some lyrics. And all of this, he noted on one manuscript sheet, he was writing for his sons, as a final explanation of the man their father *really* was.[12] In short, he would create his own complex identity by writing his true autobiography: *Paterson*. "I'm doing the introduction to the long poem I have had in mind for twenty years or more," he wrote to Ted Roethke, now one of his literary sons, on May 20. "The prelude looks as if it alone would take me a year or two: just another way of pretending to work when the very smell of discipline and drill nauseate me." And yet he had to work, had to push himself, since otherwise he would remain insufferably blocked. It was either "bring the objective through to completion" or continue to suffer from mental "hemorrhoids" from "straining so hard."[13]

"The details, the minute features carefully drawn, the yellow and the red rose, the multiple phase and identities," he wrote to himself now. These would come in the "body of the book," when he came to write that, if he ever did. In the meantime, he would evoke in this "Prelude" the ghost of the whole, "the mind, the adumbration and partial advances: small discrete features like their roses."[14] He was shaping these tentative new beginnings toward a fuller understanding of his life's work, he explained to Byron Vazakas on the thirtieth, "persistently hitting along, steadily to a definitely envisioned construction." And yet he was aware just how close he was to simply falling over the poem's edge, wordless, a failed poet whose voice would soon be lost in the roar of the times, *unless* he could bring his life's work in poetry "through to some finished work of major proportions."[15]

And when, two weeks later, he sent Whit Burnet at *Story* some of his flower poems, he added this note, which had more to do with *Paterson* than with the flower poems themselves: "Unless every age claims the world for its own and makes it so by its own efforts in its own day and unless the mark of this effort and success is left upon all forms of that age including those formal expressions which we call art, no one can be said to have lived in any age at any time."[16] The same day he wrote those lines, he also sent a note to Marcia Nardi asking her to meet him on Tuesday the sixteenth at six thirty at a second-floor restaurant on the corner of 40th Street and Sixth Avenue. He'd been mulling over her poems, as he'd told Laughlin a few days before, and had to admit that she'd gotten under his guard. As a group they were "as close to honest work as I've seen in a decade," he insisted, and though personally the woman was "bedraggled to the point of a Salvation Army reject," she had "the guts of a Kelly." Moreover, unless he and Laughlin did something for her, he was afraid the "damned thing" would die.[17] Twice she had written Williams, asking to see him, and now he did. What he wanted to tell her at dinner the night of the sixteenth was that he was sending a batch of her poems off to New Directions, that he wanted her to reshape certain others, and then he would send them off as well.

He was—as usual—as good as his word. The following day he sent the poems off to Laughlin and—when Laughlin had made his selection for the *New Directions Annual*—Williams also supplied a note introducing Nardi's work. "Marcia Nardi," he wrote in his introduction to Nardi's poems for New Directions, "was a woman in her early thirties, the kind of woman "you remember who disappointed her shocked parents by insisting on art school rather than college—and came to grief because of it." She was the woman "who refused to give in following her first defeat and came to the city with determination," expecting to live in the world of letters by her wit and wound up finding herself "working on tables in a cheap restaurant." She was the "woman who taught herself French because of an admiration for Gide and Corbière." The woman who wore "glasses and is terrified by the police on the slightest provocation. The one who wanting love, with or without, finds herself embarrassed by her own courtesy breaking her brain on the hard stone of necessity." Williams had found, mixed in with some very bad writing, a line or two lines running which he was convinced were "as fine as anything that anyone, man or woman, writing today can boast of," better than the work of any of the so-called professionals. Admittedly they were only lines, not whole poems, rising from the rubble of this woman's life, but it was a life that revealed the radiant gist of a fine mind "and an emotional force of exceptional power." She was a difficult poet, as Williams had seen, but the woman was rare in her ability to coin lines like these:

> *The mind and flesh embrace each other,*
> *Words yearning like breasts within a brain of stone—*
> *Thought's fine perceptions thickening to press*
> *A cageless mirrored body to her own. . . .*

or these lines, from "Poem":

> *Not that I hoped the kind sense would reclaim*
> *A heart in exile,*
> *But flame at least conceals*
> *The nature of its fuel,*

that fuel being nothing more than "the rotting beams" of some New York tenement. That fuel being some "boss's glance" on the "Nylon hose" of the secretaries in his office, that fuel being "willing choir boys" whipped by some figure standing in for the ultimate Father authority.[18] They were angry poems, painful and passionate and at times maddeningly inarticulate, but for all that authentic utterances of the woman poet in a male-dominated world. Williams was crazy about her.

At the same time, Williams was also trying to write a review of some of Anaïs Nin's prose pieces, trying again and again to get the exact right tone in dealing with Nin's own more complex and astringent attitudes toward men. Here too, in Nin, as in Nardi, Williams had another test case of the tragic cleavage between the sexes that would figure so centrally in his *Paterson*: the tragedy of voice crying across the chasm to voice, while each missed the other's meaning.[19]

Now too he wanted to clear the decks so that he might spend the summer finishing the preamble to *Paterson*, and that meant getting all letters and literary requests finished and out of the way. He told Louis Zukofsky he hoped to have the "Introduction," as he was calling it by mid-June, "in reasonable condition" by August.[20] What protean changes that "Introduction" underwent in June and July cannot be recovered, but on the Fourth of July Williams surfaced from the falls long enough to try this pattern: the paragraph he'd sent *Story* a month earlier, the section he'd written about the Paterson strike for "The Wanderer" thirty years earlier, his 1926 version of "Paterson," letters he'd been getting from one David Lyle of Paterson since the end of '38, the narrative of a black minister published in 1859 describing a religious conversion, three letters Kitty Hoagland had just given him which her part-time black maid, sixteen-year-old Gladys Enals, had left behind when she disappeared (with some of Kitty's clothes), and—finally—parts of his Paterson poems, "Morning" and "Beautiful Thing."[21]

When Williams read the letters to Gladys, he was struck by the magnificent rawness and rightness of the language as an American artifact, as distinctively local as black jazz itself, and one of these he lifted right into the core of his epic—"Hi, Kid. I know your just *about* to shot me"—which Gladys' friend Dolly had written her only four days before Pearl Harbor. Such a letter held—if anything held—the gist of the language Williams had been searching for: the radiant stain in the test tube, a marvelous example of why the American language could never be confused with its English cousin. If his Beautiful Thing should ever speak, he realized, these letters would contain her authentic cadences, ready to be translated into his own poetry. "I did crack you know yourself I been going full force on the (jug) will we went out (going to Newark) was raining, car slapped on brakes, car turned around a few times, rocked a bit and stopped facing the other way, from which we was going. Pal, believe me for the next few days. Honey, I couldn't even pick up a half filled bucket of hot water for fear of scalding myself."[22]

The David Lyle reference in Williams' glorious Fourth note summoned up a complex of relationships for Williams, and indeed at one point he had seriously considered making Lyle the real hero of *Paterson*. David Lyle was an ex-Gloucester man, a hulk of a man, a Maximus figure in himself. He was an old radio operator who had settled in Paterson with his wife, Mary, in the late 1930s to devote all his prodigious energies to one extraordinary project. By dint of hard work he had turned himself into a one-man information station, reading and digesting everything he could get his hands on in an attempt to discover in that aphasic river of random words just what were the central energies and patterns of the times. Blake-like, he moved into the tonnage of news media pitchblende in order to extract what Williams had called the radiant gist, the luminous center. Like a computer, Lyle would discover or invent certain words and phrases, including homonyms, antonyms, synonyms, and even doubtful puns that his antennae found embedded in that journalistic matrix. Here, then, and by accident, Williams had discovered another man who might help him define the logic of his own "newspaper epic" to himself. Lyle mailed off his missives—sometimes five or eight or ten pages long, single-spaced and glossed—to artists, musicians, poets, politicians, engineers, in short, to whatever names he found in the news. It was as though he had managed to freeze the very radio waves themselves and make their energies visible in ink as they flowed through the thousands of names and places and especially verbs that were in the air at any given moment. Like Williams, Lyle had wanted to share the news, hoping for some kind of luminous synthesis of the energy toward which all things seemed to tend, as though drawn there by a magnet.

As things had happened, Williams had first heard from Lyle at the very moment when—as he'd told Norman Holmes Pearson—he was feeling overwhelmed by the steady stream of books and little magazines that were constantly flooding into the coffinlike catchall in his front hall. Most people, annoyed by the size and density of Lyle's letters, merely deposited them in the wastebasket and went about their business. But Williams sensed something: that, like himself, Lyle had felt the crash of words tumbling over his head and had done something about it. Perhaps just there—in the prose effluvia—Williams had found the hint for the major form he was searching for: a jumble of words, a fluid prose, from which and out of which the poem, the lyric voice, could emerge and return, firmly rooted in its surroundings.

Still, it took Williams a long time to discover just what to do with Lyle's example. In March of '39, half a year after Lyle's first letter had reached him, Williams sent Laughlin one of Lyle's letters, asking him to publish it for its own sake and telling him the author was some "wild man in Paterson."[23] When Laughlin wrote back saying he couldn't even understand what the hell the letter said, Williams in turn answered that he was thinking of meeting the guy and getting him to explain at least the sequence of ideas in it. But there the matter rested, except that Lyle kept sending his letters and Williams wrote him from time to time. Then, on July 12, having decided by then to use Nardi's letters as the female voice to be played as a contrapuntal music against the male voice of Lyle's letters, Williams also decided it was time to drive over to 12th Street in Paterson and finally meet the man. Lyle was a "strange character," Williams told Laughlin the following day, but he did fit

> marvelously into my material both personally and symbolically (tho I hate that word; it robs all actuality from the meaning). . . . I've never known anyone with such a background of reading in the fields he affects, with names, page numbers right there tic tic tic right on the button. Quite a thrill to find anything like that around these parts. . . . A wonderful guy, good to look at, six foot three. . . . Blond. Has read everything on God's earth, including poetry, Whitehead and so many others I am dizzy.

And yet, having met the man, Williams knew at once he would have to "throw him, somehow." He knew now "how those British generals in Libya must have felt facing Rommel."[24]

About the same time, Williams went through part of one of those ubiquitous prescription pads of his and jotted down some notes for an essay on Lyle. "All literature is made of froth," he wrote. "But we, poor fools, think that the best of literature is on the tops of New York's counters." In fact, the best literature came not out of runaway growths like New York but small cities like Paterson. Athens had been a small city, smaller than Hoboken, so that everyone could be in on the conversation. Rome, on the other hand, had deteriorated as it had grown. Good writing demanded getting the best minds together; had not Shakespeare been a product of good conversation and his plays a kind of froth of a first-rate mind? And while Thoreau had lived in his "compulsory bean patch" in Walden, he could speak well of other cultures because he had had the benefit of intimately knowing the Concord ambience. What America needed now was the company of "physicians, poets, soldiers, geographers and oil splitters" to arrive—as Lyle had—at "a codification of the language, an unBabeling of our constipated vocabulary so that we may understand each other and rush on to good writing." Lyle, he wrote, was the very "gist" of what he was looking for, a man whose correspondence was "ubiquitous" and who had made a Walden of his own Paterson. Here was a man, then, who had bent his whole life on "drawing a pattern, the correlations of knowledge . . . to show us its uselessness and to sharpen our wits."[25]

Now Williams began referring to himself as Noah, the man who —with a helping hand—had managed to survive the flood of words and texts that had threatened to drown him. And Lyle he took to calling Faitout: the man who could do everything. But if he was to "throw" Lyle, he would have to demote him to the role of assisting Williams, and so by 1944 Williams had arrogated for *himself* the name Noah Faitout Paterson. He decided finally to keep Lyle's letters out of *Paterson*, though he did use their strategy of random prose selections and their multiple puns to point toward the poem's major themes. There might be many women in *Paterson*, but Williams was going to make sure there was only one man. He continued to receive letters from Lyle at least into the early '50s, but by then he no longer needed Lyle as he had needed him earlier to work out the shape of *Paterson*, and then he simply put aside Lyle's letters unread.

By mid-July of 1942, then, Williams had decided on doing only an "Introduction" which would summarize the poem and leave *Paterson* itself for the major work of the next twenty years. And when he wrote Nardi to tell her that *New Directions* would publish some of her poems in its *Annual*, he also added that he would eventually be using some of her marvelous letters in his own long poem.[26] On July 15, he told Nicholas Calas he was trying to shape the poem he'd wanted to do for twenty years, but found himself still shying away from it because he wasn't strong enough yet to do it. *Paterson* was to be a "study in poetic form," and it would use the city closest to him and to his desires, treating that

city as a married man among many women. It had been very rough going
so far, and it had cost him dearly in time and anxiety, but Lyle had been of
tremendous help. In fact it had been "as if what I have been thinking all
these years" had been a "clairvoyance, a prediction and affirmation and
that suddenly this THING"—David Lyle—had "come up out of the
ground."[27]

Williams kept after the intractable mass of materials he'd collected,
trying to form it into a poem, but by the end of July his energies were
already beginning to flag. He simply had not been able to drag up out of
that verbal bog the requisite giants, the major form he had wanted. In a
letter to Kenneth Rexroth on July 31, he lamented what he took to be the
failure of Zukofsky's own epic attempts in *A*. "I don't know what to say
sometimes," he explained. "I like him, . . . and I sometimes like what he
writes but somehow it just ain't writing. It's something else. Maybe it's
painting. Maybe it's sculpture—but by God it ain't writin'. And then
again he'll do something that is very much writing, a few superb
passages—then it goes off again." He could have been talking about his
own efforts at that point and probably was, for he turned at once to talk of
his own "long 'thing,'" admitting he was doing no better than Zuk.
Already the long effort was beginning to depress him. He knew that it
might still "turn out to be the best I ever shook out of my balls," but it
might also be "worse than Citrate of Magnesia." He simply did not
know.[28]

When he wrote a week later to McAlmon out in Phoenix, Arizona, he
described what he was doing with *Paterson* as a book of prose mixed in
with verse, "an account, a psychologic-social panorama of a city treated
as if it were a man, the man Paterson." He told McAlmon too how "hot"
he was to work, but that something in him kept shying away from the
enormous task confronting him. In spite of that, however, he had
managed to compile "a hundred pages or so," so that the poem should
have by all rights been "nearly finished now."[29] But of course it wasn't
and he knew it. The peak of inspiration he had experienced for about ten
weeks was definitely over, and he told Bill Jr. as much at the end of
August: "For myself, I go down and up as I feel well or ill, as the news
[about the war] goes and as my occasional scribbling dictates. As you
know when I am working on a 'masterpiece' I am always absorbed and so
reasonably happy. When I can't write that's a sign that I'm sunk." At the
moment he was sunk.[30]

By mid-September he had to admit to Bill that something terrible had
come over him, that he could no longer "write as easily as I used to—not,
that is to say, as confidently." He found himself going over and over the
same heavy ground with *Paterson*, trying to discover some shape there
until he was sick and tired of the mess of papers in front of him.[31] The

multiple drafts of the poem—he would revise the thing nearly one hundred times before he was finally satisfied—show how frustrated he was as his first serious spring offensive bogged down by late summer.

By December he told Laughlin that the poem he'd promised was to be ready by fall had failed to materialize. He'd been too "optimistic" in saying that *Paterson* would be ready for the Spring '43 list. And now he could legitimately complain about the heavy medical work that had to be done, especially with so many younger doctors serving in the armed forces. In fact, as far as he could make out, he could salvage only nine good pages out of the hundred he had written.[32] A week later he was blaming the debacle on his eyes, complaining that he couldn't even read, much less write. And on December 21—the bleakest time of the year for him—all he could do was promise that when the "Introduction" was finally finished it would "summarize many a half start and fragment I've left in my trail"—that is, if he didn't die first.[33]

In mid-August of '42 Williams and Floss had taken the train out to Canton, Ohio, to visit Paul and Jinny and their first grandchild: Paul Jr., who'd been born on August 3. Floss stayed on to help the young couple, but Williams allowed himself only four days for the trip both out and back, since there were so few doctors to cover for him. "It was marvelous to travel on a railroad train again, soldiers, sailors and everything," he wrote Zuk on September 15. "Sat up all night in a coach, around the Horseshoe Curve, through Pittsburgh at night with the blast furnaces sending up infernal flames and sulphurous fumes, orange and brown. It's a hell of a world all right." He was busy, he admitted, but he felt pressed to do the work that came his way, knowing that younger men were putting their very lives on the line every day. He was anxious to do his part. Just that day, for example, he had crawled under his office looking for scrap iron for government defense. It was one "hell of a dirty place to look for old pieces of iron pipe, old wire, anything at all," and on top of that he'd gotten "a throat full of muck" shaking up all that dust. But what was a little dirt to what the "kids" were getting? He even took "a masochistic pleasure" in whatever he could force himself to do for them.[34]

The "kids" were much on his mind, especially during the first year of the war, and he wrote a short essay that September for the editors at *View* magazine called "Advice to the Young Poet." There he stressed the importance of releasing the dragon chained within every artist. He wanted especially to warn the young to avoid the academies, because those immensities had a way of killing the necessary dragons of the young with their "defensive, protecting knowledge." For the most part, professors were no better than so many clerks waiting for a master to tell them how to think and what to do, and at their worst they were capable of doing real harm. Take their knowledge, he counseled, but avoid them, for within each artist there lie "imprisoned the infinitely multiplex quarry" which only a "channel of words" could release: sensuous words whose presence would be verified by the way they moved "instinctively," with a life of their own and not part of some dead literary tradition, where the writer was like "a seal trained to say papa."[35]

As for culture in wartime America, he was reading F. W. Foerster's *Europe and the German Question* to try to understand better why the war had happened in the first place, and he was also reading (and enjoying) Lawrence Durrell's *The Black Book*.[36] In mid-September, he and Floss went to see a performance of Irving Berlin's *This Is the Army*, which proved to be a disappointment. He'd seen as good, he was sure, when he was in the Mask and Wig back in his college days.[37] Harvey Breit came up with the idea of doing a feature on Williams and Stevens—the poet as lawyer, the poet as physician—for *Harper's*, and did so in December, with photos and all. But he had to do it without much help from Stevens, who told Williams he didn't much care for that sort of thing. Williams for his part had very much wanted to appear together with one of the few poets he deeply admired, though he could understand Stevens' reticence and desire for privacy.[38]

As for Marcia Nardi, though he had told Laughlin in July that she was "a very rare spirit in a woman," a "woman in a very special and . . . valuable sense" with a small but significant vein of valuable ore in her, he was finally beginning to wear down under her insistent cries for help, compounded by accusations she now began hurling at Williams out of her own self-loathing.[39] She even began to ask for money to help her see her way through some hard times. Pressed for time at the hospital, Williams asked Floss to send Nardi a money order for ten dollars wrapped in a blank piece of paper so that it wouldn't be stolen. When Nardi saw the blank paper, however, she took it as a personal affront. Obviously Williams was too busy to help her and a mere ten dollars was in any event a pittance. A few days later she left the city, bus-bound for upstate New York to work as a laborer for the summer. She'd read an ad in the New York papers promising pickers good money and free transportation upstate, only to learn once she'd reached her destination that she'd been swindled and stranded. Meantime, in this pathetic comedy of errors, Williams had mailed her a second money order—this one for fifteen dollars—on the very day she'd left New York without leaving a forwarding address.

Nardi's janitor found that one, forged his own name to it, and cashed it, though Williams did not discover what had happened until the end of the year. As for Nardi, he didn't hear from her until early October. She wrote then to say that she was now up in Woodstock and then went on and on about the grueling work, the swindle, and Williams' betrayal. Williams wrote back at once, explaining what he'd done, adding that he'd even been trying to find her work in New York before she left. But it was clear from the tone of Nardi's letter and his response that he knew he had trouble on his hands with this woman and that from now on he was going to keep as much distance between himself and her as he could. He was still very busy with practice, he told her (it was his favorite ploy for begging off), but he wanted to do what he could within his limited powers. When he could digest her long letter he'd write again.[40]

*
**

It took him ten weeks, apparently, to digest the letter, for it wasn't until December 16 that he wrote, enclosing yet another money order for her. He was still trying to find work for her and had written to several of his friends—including Marianne Moore—asking for help. But he also wanted Nardi to know that people were just not going to drop everything and answer her long letters in kind and detail. Other people had difficulties too, he told her, and "long accounts explaining this that or the other simply concern no one but yourself."[41] Nardi's response to that letter was her own very long letter which Williams read with dismay, until he saw that it was just what he would need for *Paterson*. In the published poem the letter, edited by Williams, would take up eight full pages of small type at the close of Book 2:

> My attitude toward woman's wretched position in society and my ideas about all the changes necessary there were interesting to you, weren't they, in so far as they made for *literature*? . . . And you saw in one of my first letters to you (the one you had wanted to make use of, then, in the Introduction to your Paterson) an indication that my thoughts were to be taken seriously, because that too could be turned by you into literature, as something disconnected from life.[42]

How accurate the woman was, Williams saw. How very close she had come to the deep truth of the matter! How many other men and women, including Floss, had made similar accusations over the years, either to him or about him? And now he felt the need to let the woman in him have her say. At the same time, however, his sharp diagnostician's eye saw that Nardi's letter would serve to recapitulate nearly all the major themes with which his autobiographical poem had been concerned: the woman as victim, complaining, accusing, crying out in pain; the divorce between the two sexes and the danger that the woman would turn to other women for solace; the woman as the energy and the flower of a man's life; the poem itself as a confession of inadequacy; the socioeconomic ills that had created so many of the tensions between men and women, making of the man a false nurturer and forcing the woman into an unnatural dependency on the man. Nardi's letter even contained many of the image clusters Williams had already employed in the poem. In fact that letter had turned out to be, as Williams would explain years later, a found object paralleling Eliot's infamous use of footnotes at the end of *The Waste Land.* Moreover, the letter would serve too as a prose coda to a poem, insisting on language's inability—even at its most lyrical—to eradicate the all-pervasive facts of blockage and divorce in modern love. Williams meant that letter to send the whole poem into a tailspin at its halfway point, though he also hoped this prose coda, this tail, would not end up wagging the dog of the whole poem. But all of this would be later, after Nardi had disappeared and he could think more clearly about what a treasure he'd found in her letters. For the present, with Nardi once again breathing down his neck, Williams had to fall back on the stratagem of simply refusing to answer the woman's letters.

But Nardi persisted into the winter of '43, alternately demanding or begging for civilized discourse and trying to shame Williams into seeing her again.[43] Finally, on February 17, 1943, he had to send her a curt note to the effect that he'd tried to find her work without success and that he was now advising her to go to the Federal Employment Bureau. As far as he was concerned, that was the end of the matter between them. Good-by.[44] Nardi took the hint and did such a good job of disappearing that when Williams went looking for her in '45 to get permission to quote her letter in the first part of *Paterson,* he could no longer locate "the bitch." He looked everywhere but he and Laughlin had—finally—to use the letter without finding her. Similarly, in 1947, when *Paterson* 2 went to press, he tried again to locate her, asking around Greenwich Village if anyone knew where she'd gone. But no one had seen her for years, and some thought the woman might even be dead.

She hadn't died, though, and when she finally surfaced in March 1949, she sent Williams a note from Woodstock chiding him for not sending her copies of *Paterson* 1 and 2 in which her letters had appeared and suggesting that he send her a money order at once for two hundred dollars. Thus the second phase of the Williams / Nardi correspondence began, though by that time Williams no longer had any use for the letters. Williams had had to submerge Nardi's stridencies so that the voices of other women might take their rightful place in Williams' autobiographical poem. Besides, by then Nardi's pained cry had already exacted its heavy toll on *Paterson,* heavier even than Williams had bargained for.

By November 1942, when the Allies began moving decisively against Rommel in Africa, Williams began to feel a little better about the progress of the war. "If only we do not fumble the ball," he told Zukofsky on the seventh, "if only our Congress can forget its innate stupidity and catch fire. . . . I sometimes think that there is no longer a possibility of spontaneous and generous action left in the human soul—outside of Russia." The English, he thought, possessed "a plodding sort of virtue." They were an island people who were too self-defensive, too self-protective in their instincts.[45] But the Russians and Chinese: they were the real hope of the world, they were people who plunged into life with an extraordinary profusion of energy, as the Chinese were doing in their continuing struggle against Japan, and as the Russians were similarly doing in their magnificent fight against the Germans at Stalingrad. In the meantime Williams was having his own skirmish (part of a protracted war in itself) with the *Partisan Review* and its editor. He complained to Calas in mid-November that the people at *PR* simply did not understand what literature was really about. They saw only the ideas in literature and not its force, its intrinsic life, its breath and bile. As if to bear his contention out, *PR* published Eliot's essay "The Music of Poetry" in its December issue. And what was that, really, but old hat, the very thing Williams had already been preaching for thirty years, with its talk about "the inadvisability of persisting in dawdling with past forms" and "the importance of *place.*" Williams was convinced that this time Eliot was stealing from him, no more acknowledging what Williams had given him than he'd acknowledged all the cribbing he'd done to stucco up his own poems. "You'd think a professional bastard of the sort would make some attempt to give credit where it is due," he told Laughlin on December 9, though he didn't really expect it from someone like Eliot.[46] But when, the very next day, Williams got a copy of Eliot's essay and a card from Macdonald at *PR* with the words "live and learn" written on it, he shot back at once that Eliot's gesture in "The Music of Poetry" was not one of reconciliation with Williams but rather of arrogance. "I have never had the slightest assistance from T. S. Eliot in my career," he insisted. "And now you, who should know better, go to the pains of remarking that now that he is 'on my side' I should salute him. I'd like to salute him by the good kick in the ass he deserves and you along with him." Eliot was still the "sum of the stupid academic type," Williams insisted, ready to steal whatever he could if he thought he wasn't being watched. He was not creative and he had never been so. Let him, Williams rounded off, let him read his contemporaries more and "make more apt references to living work" than he had so far done.[47]

A week later Williams sent his friend Cummings a poem for Christmas in which he thanked him for the profound help of his example, saying he'd been "a very guide" to him in ways no one had even suspected, because he'd thrown the language outdoors into the fresh air at a great cost to himself. The circle of revolutionaries of the generation of 1914, Williams added, who had not been seriously damaged by intellectual sclerosis of one form or another (as Pound and Eliot had) was getting smaller with the passing years. Better then to celebrate one's having come through while one could still manage it.[48]

Almost from the beginning of America's entry into the war, Williams had matched his own progress on his American epic with the progress of Allied troop movements, especially in Europe. When he spoke of *Paterson* it was in terms of pushes, assaults, retreats (strategic and otherwise), of being bogged down, mired, overrun, of making advances and break-throughs.[49] He read the newspapers daily, following the maps of troop deployments, the island hopping in the Pacific, and assessed the relative strengths of the nations engaged in the conflict, including the American character as it was showing itself under fire. He was, after all, writing an epic that future generations speaking other tongues might examine for evidence of what had been particularly distinctive about the American people at the precise moment when they were crossing their own Rubicon to emerge out of the phoenix flames of the world holocaust as the single most powerful nation on earth. In a sense, then, Williams' position would parallel that of Virgil, whose epic *Aeneid* would recount the time when Rome had passed over from a republic to an empire and what it had cost the country to undergo that change.

Williams did not, of course, himself make such a grand parallel, though he did wonder aloud what would remain intact of his America when the boys returned home from the war. Much of what he had collected, much of what he himself felt was most characteristic in the American experience was already shifting rapidly under his feet, includ-ing the anxiety he now felt that in America the poet's voice no longer mattered, and that the last vestiges of Jeffersonian and even Jacksonian democracy—which even the American left had accepted in the '30s as a viable tradition—were fast giving way under the pressures of wartime industry to larger conglomerates. The result was that the new economic order was leaving behind thousands of American factory and mill towns like Paterson, stranded and empty, their living cores sucked out and their shells left to bleach as the flood of capitalism surged south and then away from American soil altogether. And yet there were all those people, all those blue-collar workers who had settled these industrial towns in search of something called the American dream, who had raised families and mortgaged their small homes and spent their life's blood daily at those silk mills and locomotive factories fighting for a living wage, being ignored, repulsed, in some cases beaten down by mounted police—the very sons of these workers—even as the factories themselves began to close down to relocate where cheaper labor could be found. Ironically, it was these same workers and their sons who were now fighting in Tunisia, Sicily, Anzio, Guadalcanal, Iwo Jima and whose daughters—farmers' daughters, Rosie the Riveters—were supplying the labor force to build

B-17s and B-19s, battleships and Victory ships, Sherman tanks and antipersonnel mines and 50-millimeter machine guns. And yet much of that picture was little more than an enormous blur, a surge of incredible energy.

America: the breadbasket for the world, as Williams had said twenty years earlier. What he needed instead was a specific diagnosis, a particular understanding of his own place—and of himself—so that out of that unflinching diagnosis of his culture he might speak to all people. There were, after all, no ideas that did not arise from attention to the things under one's nose. If he could accurately say who he was, if he could create a viable, complex identity for himself as he moved through his own time and place—Rutherford, Paterson, New York, now, in the early 1940s—he would have his social panoramic personal epic, call it what he would. He would have *Paterson*. He might even come, finally, to possess himself.

*
**

But 1943 brought Williams no relief. He simply could not get the long poem going again. For all practical purposes, it remained a huge locomotive sitting on the tracks without a drive shaft, and it was beginning both to anger and to embarrass Williams that he was so badly stalled. He kicked the thing, tried lighting fires under it, even tried "goosing" it, but all to no avail. There it sat, unbudging, refusing to go forward or even to disappear. Nothing for it, then, Williams realized, but to move on to something else while the deeper recesses of the mind mulled over the problem. The something else he decided on in the meantime would be another book of poems, this one bringing together the poems he'd written since the *Collected* had appeared in 1938. After all, he would be sixty in September, and it was time to show others (and himself) that he still had the right stuff. Putting together a new book of poems, he hoped, would also serve as "finger-practicing" in getting on with *Paterson*. He mentioned the idea for the new book first of all to Laughlin at the end of '42, explaining defensively that he wasn't forgetting *Paterson*, no sir, but Fate had been heavy on him.[50] He also blamed the war, with justification, since he was being called on day and night to help out, with the shortage of doctors worse than ever. The more *Paterson* became impossible to write, the more it loomed as the most important thing he'd ever attempted. Williams was trying to follow his own leads, not to get across anything so banal as a "message," but to get to the form, which would reveal the real meaning of the poem.

When Laughlin wrote Williams in mid-January to say that wartime paper shortages had not left him sufficient paper to do Williams' new book of poems, Williams believed him and began looking elsewhere. And though Laughlin had once promised to do all of Williams' poems, the book Williams had described to Laughlin had seemed so ill-defined, so much a mishmash, a potpourri, a prose and poetry minestrone, that it was natural for Laughlin to want to hold on to what paper he did have for his other writers. What Williams had told Laughlin he wanted was to bring together "a whole mass of scattered things," some already published and others discovered in going through his files. He wanted some early improvisations in this new book, "at least half the things from *The Broken Span*, the complete short verse scene from the 2nd Act of *Many Loves*," what was still left unpublished from the "Parody" sheaf, and some other things to bring him after five years once more up to date. What Williams hoped for from such a collection would be to show "in retrospect" what it was he had "always been trying to do." In short, it would reveal his range in a way no chapbook like *The Broken Span* had been able to do.[51]

Laughlin must have sensed that Williams was whistling in the dark, trying to avoid the difficult work of *Paterson* (which New Directions had had to reschedule for 1944) with this ready-made. One of the giants who had loomed up unexpectedly to threaten Williams' major poem had been Wallace Stevens, whose superb *Parts of a World* Knopf had published in September 1942. Stevens, of course, had always been the real contender Williams worried about (as Stevens had just as assuredly been watching out for Williams) and Stevens' own poetry had been growing steadily in power and self-assuredness ever since the publication in 1937 of *The Man with the Blue Guitar*. Williams had reviewed that book, praising its strengths while finding fault with Stevens' insistence on sticking with traditional forms, especially the blank verse line, while he—Williams —was deep in the travail of looking for new verse forms. The trouble with using the old line, Williams had quipped, was that Stevens thought he had to keep sounding important when he used it.[52]

Williams might—by 1943—disparage Eliot and Pound, rise beyond Hart Crane, ignore Frost, or patronize Marianne Moore, but he instinctively sensed that Stevens was a different matter. If Stevens could get away with calling his book *Parts of a World*, he told Laughlin, then he would outflank him with this new book he wanted to publish which would be "definitely *Parts of a Greater World*—a looser, wider world where 'order' is a servant not a master." After all, he contended, order was something "discovered after the fact" and "not a little piss pot for us all to urinate into—and call ourselves satisfied." And as for *Paterson*: hell, he'd show "the universities and their cripples" an order such as they had never dreamed, an "international infiltration into the dry mass . . . of knowledge and culture" which passed for Order. His poem—when it was finally done—would be a "keg-cracking assault upon the cults and the kind of thought that destroyed Pound and made what it has made of

Eliot."[53] And (unlike Stevens' poetry) it would bring the benefits of culture to the masses, to his poor, debased people as well, and not just speak for an ivory tower elite.

All through February and March of '43 he worked on his new collection, collaborating heavily with his old friend Zukofsky. The two men had cleared the air between them candidly at the beginning of February, when Zukofsky, with diffidence, his heart in his mouth, had finally asked his old friend what had come between them. What had come between them had been the George Washington libretto fiasco, which had soured Williams, though that was hardly Zukofsky's fault, except that he'd known Serly and been caught in the crossfire. But there was also a growing difference of perception between Williams and Zukofsky as to what was and was not a poem. By the late '30s, Williams confessed, he had begun "to feel restless" with Zukofsky's objectivism, as he had ten years or more before that felt restless when Pound (or, for that matter, Ken Burke) had tried to make him a disciple. Whenever Williams felt pressed, he instinctively felt the need to break away. And when Zukofsky had begun to symbolize for him a certain kind of critical restraint, Williams had bolted. He respected Louis' "meticulousness"—that was for him Zukofsky himself—but Williams had found that that kind of confinement had cut across his own irritable search for a new, more open mode of writing poetry.[54]

Now, however, Williams was seeking his friend out again, this time on a new footing. This new book of poems, he thought, would embody the "contemporary forms" he and Zukofsky had been searching for. On the first day of spring he told Zukofsky he was sending him the "damned book," asking him to "slash it unmercifully."[55] He knew the script was too overweight, too repetitious, and—despite their differences in writing poems—Williams knew he could rely on Zukofsky for a close, intelligent reading. Williams sent the manuscript itself six days later, adding defensively that he didn't expect Zukofsky to make a book out of what he'd "slung together assways," but he did believe that somewhere in that wad of paper he was sending existed a book containing the "language."[56]

What Zukofsky found when he opened Williams' package in his Brooklyn apartment that March was a sheaf of poetry and prose that Williams had entitled *THE (lang) WEDGE* and then, thinking better of it, had called simply, *The Language*. (He would finally settle on *The Wedge* for his title.) When Williams sent Zukofsky the poems, he was leaving with Floss to visit Paul and Jinny and the baby in Ohio for the second time in seven months. But the script was still very much on Williams' mind, as the postcard he sent Zukofsky on the thirty-first made clear. On one side was a photo of the Republic Iron and Steel Company defense mills in Massilon where Paul was working and on the verso Williams had quipped that here was "the great American rolling mill" itself, which could roll one "out flat hot or cold, to desired thinness."[57] Zukofsky, of course, understood that he was acting as another such great American rolling mill, industriously thinning down Williams' typescript at that moment from 115 pages to 82. What Zukofsky did was to remove every piece of prose as well as a number of questionable poems, including —even—the title poem itself. By April 6 he had finished the job and sent the sheaf back to Williams, adding a two-page letter advising Williams not "to accept the detailed criticism" unless it "verifies your own misgivings, doubts, etc."[58]

Williams followed nearly all of Zukofsky's suggestions. At last the script was beginning to feel more like a book—thanks to his friend—so that Williams felt "a slight choking from the cumulative effect—almost as much from your arrangements of the individual pieces as from their separate virtues."[59] The book had not yet reached its final shape, but Zukofsky's editing had been so critical that he dedicated the book to him. A month later Williams had finally decided to take out all the prose—he would not recapitulate *Spring & All* or *The Descent of Winter* in *The Wedge*—had added some other poems he'd found, and then sent the revised manuscript out to the New York publishers.[60] Almost at once Simon & Schuster turned it down—like Laughlin—because they said they were short of paper. He'd be damned, though, if that was going to stop him. He was going to send the manuscript "to every God damned publisher in the country" before he was through. Somebody somewhere had to have paper. To be a sixty-year-old poet and not have enough power to get a book out when so many others were appearing every day: that hurt. "The older I get," he complained, "the more it stings me not to be in power, some sort of power, enough power to get done what I want done. It riles me to have to go on practicing Medicine with only a year left, a month or a week left perhaps before I'm deaf, blind, paralyzed or whatever it may be."[61]

He decided to write Frances Steloff at the Gotham Book Mart now for advice on how to find a publisher in New York, but got nowhere. He tried Duell, Sloan & Pearce in June, only to be turned down a month later. Then he decided to hold onto the sheaf for a while and let it ferment before sending it out again. In the meantime he picked up the *Paterson* again but found himself too depressed by the war to get on with the poem, which by then had become—as he told Mary Barnard—"a Mt. Everest for me to surmount."[62] The problem was that late in May, Paul too had decided—like his brother—to enlist in the Navy, even though his defense job had given him a deferment. Paul's commission and induction came through in early August in New York, and he was able to spend a few hours with his parents at 9 Ridge Road before heading out to Cornell for training in the operation of a destroyer. Bill Jr.—in the meantime—was mercifully out of the theater of action in the South Pacific, always managing to arrive·at some place other than where the war at that moment was raging. He took care of appendectomies and jungle fever cases and fished and sent home short pieces describing South Sea island life, several of which Williams had printed in the local paper. Then in June Williams was shocked to read in *Coronet* that Ezra Pound would probably be hanged for treason after the war. Whatever his differences with Ezra, that solution seemed excessive to Williams, particularly if the government was willing to let "a Hamilton Fish, a Lindbergh, and some others live."[63]

In May, with the Allies in Sicily and the Germans on the retreat in Russia, Williams was sanguine enough to think the war would be over before Paul ever saw action. But by July, with the Italian campaign bogged down, Williams was less sure. "The war goes on and more and more of our youth become involved," he wrote Burke on July 12, a year to the day he'd seen David Lyle and thought he finally had *Paterson* in the bag.[64] Paper was scarcer than ever and yet it was the soldiers themselves who most needed such poems as he had written. A month later he was even more depressed. He had the goods this time, he told Burke, but could find no one to print them. And now, as summer began to fade, he knew medicine would begin to eat up more and more of his time. Ah, to be out of the struggle altogether, to dream, to take on a job as a "houseman in a whorehouse" when he got old and dream of women as Toulouse-Lautrec had before him.[65] Williams even sent a letter to the *New Republic* which they published in late August under the title "Paper Shortage, Poets, and Postal Rates," in which he lamented his inability to get the word out to the troops. But even that public notice brought no publishers his way.[66]

Then, in mid-September, four months after he'd begun actively searching for a publisher, two young printers approached him saying they'd be willing to publish *The Wedge*. It was a small private affair called the Cummington Press which worked out of an old school up in the foothills of the Berkshires in Cummington, Massachusetts, and they had enough paper to do a limited edition of 380 copies. They thought they could get the book printed on their hand press and out by the spring of '44. Williams was delighted and sent Zukofsky the script one more time for a final checkup. He had his book.

The "Introduction" to *The Wedge* came out of a talk Williams gave at the New York Public Library a month later on the evening of October 26. As luck would have it, he gave his talk during the height of a tremendous rainstorm to about one hundred bedraggled, soaked, and uncomfortable listeners, most of them strangers, who had braved the weather for the occasion. He began his talk by remarking what he knew everyone was thinking about: the war. It was on everybody's mind, he said, knowing it was "the first and only thing in the world today." But, he insisted, poetry too had its own importance. It was not an escape from action, but rather action in a "different sector of the field." Since the poet was constantly searching for his own complex designs, he was in a sense in his own continuous state of war, driving hard toward his own ends. So with Williams, who was after a strategy, a machine, a formal invention, and not some high thought or synthesis or sentimental evasion. He too was fighting his own war, a war against the entrenched interests of the "various English Departments of the academies," and if what he was creating was only a prototype, a kind of pre-art, then so be it. Let the new poems he was going to read that night serve as a wedge to drive open consciousness. He had had in mind when he first thought of his title, *The lang (WEDGE)*, the image of the tongue opening the vaginal cleft to fire the woman, but he had backed off from that image and settled instead for the wedge as a military metaphor, with his poems forming the advance columns moving against the reactionary and entrenched powers of the establishment. "When a man makes a poem," he insisted,

> makes it, mind you, he takes words as he finds them interrelated about him and composes them—without distortion which would mar their exact significances—into an intense expression of his perceptions and ardors that they may constitute a revelation in the speech that he uses. It isn't what he says that counts as a work of art, it's what he makes, with such intensity of perception that it lives with an intrinsic movement of its own to verify its authenticity.[67]

The tongue, then, to make love with and to mouth words, words flaming into a life of their own in Williams' intensely felt erotics of the imagination.

To hell with the critics and the other intellectuals who sat on their pedestals and dictated what poetry or—for that matter—national policy should be. Liberals like John Dewey and Max Eastman and the *Partisan Review* crowd would never understand the masses, for their arrogance effectively divided them from the people they insisted on treating as so many counters. Look at what had happened to Pound for separating himself from the mainstream. His misleading talk about economics and the international Jewish conspiracy had led to his being indicted, finally, for treason that August. And Williams had not been surprised, as he told Burke in July, since Pound in 1943 was a "logical development" of the Pound he'd known for forty years.[68] Williams had just written an essay attacking a rigid adherence to *any* logical position as leading inevitably to an insanity of its own. He had called it "A Fault of Learning" and had directed it against Dewey and Eastman, and would have mentioned "Pound and his end products" except that it hadn't fit. Pound had always patronized him, however subtly, Williams had confided to Laughlin in August, and he could almost feel justified now that Pound's arrogance and rigidities had ended in his being charged with treason. He'd warned Pound for years to be careful about what he said, and now the man was in deep trouble.

Williams sent his essay to the *Partisan Review* and received a letter from Delmore Schwartz—who had just taken over for Macdonald—that he was going to print Williams' communication with a reply from someone and would he mind? Of course not, Williams answered, though he didn't sound any too sure, remembering the earlier sanctions the magazine had called for against him. "I told him I would be delighted and hadn't the least compunction in saying whoever attacked me should be given free rein," he told Burke at once. All he'd wanted to do, really, was to bring the subject into the light, and now he suggested that Burke might send *PR* a rebuttal of their attack, if it "amused" him.[69]

And, as he had feared, when the September/October issue appeared, Williams' essay was followed by a condescending dismissal that blatantly misread nearly everything Williams had written. Williams had made the point that intellectuals could be intolerant, especially when they felt their integrity was being assaulted by people who they felt were intellectually inferior to them. When their position became too rigid—as when Eastman had refused to cooperate with the Russians because of the Stalinist purges—they were actually capable of leading the United States into making policy decisions that could destroy the nation. It was just such a rigidity of political purpose which had caused the Spanish Nationalists to bomb Guernica in '37. On the other hand, because leaders like Washington and Lincoln had not been rigid intellectuals, they had actually been factors toward a greater order than a logical adherence to their positions would have dictated. Certain intellectuals, however, actually did "violence to the body politic by their insistence, in vacuo, that is, on a basis of pure thought, on some principle, some blockade which must be leveled before action will be permitted to proceed beyond it." All such persons could see was the strategy of a stiff, unyielding frontal attack, when it might very well be the oblique attack, the flank assault, that was needed. Williams himself of course had been practicing just such a strategy for decades now. Alter the names of Dewey and Eastman to Pound and Eliot, recall the rigidities of Eliot's call for a new Christian society or Pound's call for Social Credit as the only alternative to Usury, change Washington's name to Williams, and one was out of politics and right back in the middle of the poem, working in that field of action.[70]

The *Partisan Review* response to Williams' "anti-intellectualism" was urbane, ironic, and patronizing, and shrugged its shoulders at a mind that could ever allow itself to justify the Soviet purges because they had eliminated a potential fifth column inside Russia. (Williams did come close to saying just this.) And it clucked its tongue at Williams' accusing the venerable John Dewey of having been in league with those who had ordered the bombing of Guernica (something Williams did not say, and would not, especially of a man whom he deeply respected). There was the suggestion too in *PR*'s response that Williams would do better to leave politics to the big boys who knew how to handle ideas and get on with his poems. What after all did the Rutherford doctor know of the complexities of figures like Bukharin, Pyatakov, Tukachevsky?

Williams did not do well in that exchange, and in November he called a truce with another intellectual whom he deeply respected for the range of his mind: Edward Dahlberg, whose *Shall These Bones Live?* he had recently read with deep interest. Dahlberg's letters were to find their way into the beginning and end of *Paterson,* serving as they did for Williams to suggest a sophisticated, cosmopolitan, wide-ranging voice in *Paterson* which his own "Dr. Paterson" would lack. But now, in late 1943, Williams needed to get away from Dahlberg's overpowering presence. On November 5 he wrote Dahlberg—although he did not send the letter—to say that he no longer wanted to pursue the correspondence any further at the time. Dahlberg had just attacked Williams' life as a physician for interfering with his life as an artist, but Williams was ready for that one. "One isn't always creating," he wrote, "certainly I am a very limited person as far as my imaginative life is concerned. There are days and weeks and months often when there is just nothing there that could possibly interest anyone but myself and my immediate associates in the family." He called these his breeding periods when his mind was happy to chew its cud and be left alone until it was ready to deliver and Williams could write. These were the periods when Williams was happy to have medicine to practice for the "homely human contacts of it," which were in fact his reason for writing. Medicine allowed him to discover all sorts of amazing people around him, "disguised by their own shapes and manners." He needed them, but what he did not need, at least for the time being, was a Dahlberg.[71]

In late October Williams sent Zukofsky a letter congratulating him and his wife, Celia, on the birth of their son, Paul. And in early December Williams wrote to Bill that he and Floss were watching their own grandson, Paul, while Paul and Jinny were away for a few days. Williams doted more over his grandson than he had ever doted over his own sons. "He's just tripped over his own feet," Williams wrote, and then proceeded to give an account of how the kid had knocked a cup of prune juice all over Floss's pale blue gown. Yet in spite of it all, the baby was really "marvelous, the best and sweetest little speck of love one would wish for." Williams himself was busy with practice, especially with an influenza and an intestinal virus making the rounds, on top of which there'd been night calls and three maternity cases that week alone. And here it was, nine thirty on a Sunday morning and the office bell was already ringing. But he wasn't complaining, adding, "I'd do twice as much and charge nothing for it with pleasure if it would do you guys any good." Paul was to report for duty on Thursday and Jinny would take an apartment nearby with the baby. Aunt Charlotte and cousin Eyvind were busy with their Christmas card business. Eyvind was an excellent artist, and Williams had recently commissioned him to paint a full-length mural of the New York area around the Williamsburg Bridge. Now that mural hung on the wall of the landing leading to the second floor of the Williams' home. It would be the second Christmas that Bill would be away from home and Williams felt down about that. Merry Christmas, he wrote, though it sounded hollow in his ears. And yet it wasn't a completely empty greeting: "There it is and such as we are there's a real meaning attached to it no matter how remote or removed the attachments which prompt it have become."[72]

A week before Christmas Williams was confined to bed with a bad cold and spent the time reading Melville's journeyman novel *Pierre*. That novel made him feel queasy at so much bad writing and reminded him of his own long apprenticeship. He finished E. M. Forster's *The Longest Journey*, which had made him aware of what an Englishman could still achieve. "England," he told Laughlin, was apparently still "capable of making love operative."[73] But two days after Christmas the problem of *Paterson* had surfaced once again. "I am burned up to do it," he told Laughlin, though he still didn't know *how* to do it. "I write and destroy, write and destroy. It's all shaped up in outline and intent, the body of the thinking is finished but the technique, the manner and the method are unresolvable to date." Still the form had eluded him. He was facing a stalemate nearly a year and a half after the first push, looking for the flank attack that would get his forces moving once again:

> The main thing is that I'm in the war effort to the hilt—actually, physically and mentally. In other words the form of the poem stems also from that. It is one, inescapable, intrinsic but—there is not time. I am conscious of the surrealists, of the back to the home shit-house mentality, the Church of England apostasy, the stepped-on, dragging his dead latter half Pound mentality—with the good and the new and the empty and the false all fighting a battle in my veins: unresolved.

He felt like one of his women patients trying to come to term, trying to push the poem out of himself in some "perfect form," involving as it would have to all he had learned about the poem. He had thought he might be able to do it, though now he had to admit that he might simply not be a strong enough poet for the necessary deed. At times—as now—he was almost devastated by his own fears. Perhaps with the new year.[74]

*
**

By early '44 Williams had—as the drafts will show—nearly all the materials he would use for *Paterson* 1, as well as much of what would make up the next three books of the poem. He had already described a tentative ordering of the whole poem in a lyric written in late '42 and published the following year as "Paterson: The Falls," and he had even arranged certain blocks of the material in ways that would approximate the published version.[75] But Williams knew the stuff he had was still too "constipated," without flow, without inner grace or necessity. "I couldn't get the right lead," he told Charles Abbott in early February, "and so have been stuck but now, at last, I see my way clear and time alone will stop me."[76] As if time alone weren't a troubling enough condition for the most sanguine of poets. He was still working on the "Introduction," as he thought, thus keeping the poem itself at a distance. It was a way of holding his monstrous child from coming, finally, to term, where the world could make fun of its large head and lame, spindly feet. And he was to remain tentative about the shape of his child even after it had been delivered.

He knew Laughlin was still waiting for the poem and he tried shaking himself into doing the thing, but it was useless. In the meantime he consoled himself by writing shorter pieces and keeping up with his medical practice. He was reading Horace Gregory's *The Shield of Achilles* for its wide-ranging criticism in a distinctively American vein as well as Herbert Read's *The Politics of the Unpolitical.* He wrote McAlmon about the literary debt he felt he still owed Pound, despite his Fascist politics, commenting that many others also owed him much (and should remember that debt when the time came). On the other hand he was furious with those American patriots who really thought they could win the war single-handedly without the support of the Russian army.[77]

Then, in late February, Bill Jr. was back home after being away for twenty months. He had sailed from New Caledonia to the States and was being transferred now to Camp Bainbridge in Maryland. At the same time Paul had returned from a tour of sea duty in the North Atlantic and was waiting to leave for Key West for training in submarine detection at the Navy's Fleet Sound School there. For a brief moment, then, at the beginning of March, the Williamses were all together again before the sons had to disperse once more. Bill—who had just turned thirty—was now engaged to a Navy nurse stationed at Pearl Harbor, and Paul's wife, Jinny, was expecting her second child in August. Bill looked essentially the same, Williams wrote Zukofsky on the fifteenth, though he was beginning to bald a little and he had obviously been sobered by the war. What his son had missed most in the Pacific was good music, and for the two weeks he was back at 9 Ridge Road he had kept all the radios in the house tuned to different stations, soaking up all the classical music he could. But if Bill Jr. had missed most of the action in the Pacific, being left isolated on one island or another, Paul had been hurled almost at once into a more violent world. One month out of school and he had found himself working on a destroyer, sailing toward North Africa as he zig-zagged through a winter storm in the choppy Atlantic constantly on the lookout for German U-boats moving singly or in wolf packs. "He says the porpoises at first gave him heart failure," Williams wrote, since they would approach the destroyer "in exactly the manner of a torpedo," only to dive at the last moment under the hull and up the other side. "What a world these young men are seeing," he summed up. "The dark alleys of Casablanca while on guard duty expecting to be shot in the back by some Arab at any moment. Or the foul Melanesians washing, bathing in the same muddy water they take home to drink."[78]

"Imagine what minds this war is building up in those of the young who will survive it," he wrote Fred Miller the same day. Against this new world dawning the old seemed more irrelevant than ever; it was static, it was a museum piece. He hardly ever got into New York anymore, he added, since "the surviving surrealists, the god damned Trotskyites," and all those other "spavined theorists" looked more and more like "boxes of sardines" on a shelf sliding onto the floor during an earthquake.[79] He had no use for them at all. And on April 4, he expanded on his feelings about the French avant-garde in a letter to that one-time patron of the old New York avant-garde, Walter Arensberg: "The French are swarming in New York as they did in 1917–1918 and some of the old ones still among them. Many of them seem to be men and women of importance but I can't for the life of me bring myself to go look at them. They seem unrelated to anything I want to do." He knew that these men and women would dismiss his either seeing or not seeing them as unimportant, but it no longer mattered to him as it had mattered to him so desperately in that New York ambience of twenty-five years before. He had already caught in his sons' eyes and in the eyes of other men and women caught up in the war a newer, wider sense of reality which pointed to a new order of things. And of that dawning reality the old French exiles in New York seemed simply unaware. The axis of the vortex had once again shifted.[80]

*
**

At the beginning of spring Williams sent Louis Zukofsky a seven-page dialogue between Washington and Lafayette which he called *Under the Stars*. Williams set that dialogue between the commander in chief of the

American army and his younger staff member on the night following Washington's strategic victory at Monmouth, New Jersey, as both men lay on an army blanket under the stars. Since it had been the Washington libretto that had driven the wedge between these two leaders of the avant-garde, it was entirely appropriate that Williams should make his peace now with his friend by asking him to look over and correct the confessional dialogue he was sending. And when Zukofsky read Washington's words to the younger man who had remained faithful to him —"What I need was what you've given me, better than sleep, peace of mind again. . . . Some instinct kept you at my side. I needed your support"—Zukofsky understood at once that Williams—in Washington's voice—was addressing these words to him. In the delicate editorial minuet that followed in which Zukofsky edited out or toned down Washington's strong declaration of affection for Lafayette, changes that Williams accepted without arguing, Williams for his part understood that Zuk had tacitly accepted his apologies for having cooled toward him for the past seven years. Now all that was behind them.[81] "Were we to lock up historical fact with keen enough present day associations and really write the stuff with some distinction we might open some eyes," he told Laughlin on March 22, talking about the first draft of *Under the Stars*. Zukofsky for one had not been blind.[82]

On the other hand, Williams was still skirmishing with the *Partisan Review* crowd, smoldering at the innuendoes he was sure were being directed by them against him. (And now even *View* was turning out to be another enemy.) He was still looking for an American critic who was not spellbound by every word that the sacred Eliot and his allies uttered. The latest offense had been Eliot's "Notes Towards a Definition of Culture," which the *Partisan Review* had published in early May 1944, much to Williams' disgust. Granted much of what Eliot had said there was good. Even Williams could see that: like the idea that a societal culture was an organic part of the place where a people actually lived their lives. Hadn't Eliot said too that the "greatest achievements of the imagination, religious and artistic," were those that had "the firmest roots"? Had he not even admitted to the growing autonomy of New York as a culture center for English-speaking people? And had he not stressed the need for a balance between the city and the surrounding countryside, thus pointing to the role the provinces played in the life of a city's culture? These were of course ideas that Williams himself had insisted on in his own poetry for thirty years and which were even then playing a central role in *Paterson*. Excessive concentration only on the city, Eliot had said, always had a bad effect on the provinces, but it also had a bad effect on the intellectual life of the city itself. This urban tendency had been fortunately "counteracted" in England to some degree "by the attachment to the land for which the English are still distinguished," Eliot had noted, but in

America he thought the case had been different. There, since "the upper strata of modern society" were for the most part city dwellers, "the divorce between culture and agriculture" was more evident, to the extent, in fact, that the farmer had become in literature and conversation pretty much a comic figure. The future boded even worse as cities like New York and London continued to expand beyond any possibility of forming cohesive centers and became megalopolises. And once those "centers" lost contact with their surrounding populations, they would be cut off from the very source that had always nourished them. At that point the idea of a viable culture—which needed a place in which to grow—would become frankly impossible.

Eliot was right, Williams wrote Gregory in early May, but Eliot was also "strangely blind" in a "peculiarly British sense to universal values as they appear in work whose feelings he does not accept." And—as far as Williams could see—all America still constituted for Eliot a blind spot. What Williams needed now, more than ever, was a critic with Eliot's formal literary training who would reveal to others what was worth saving in his own American culture. Williams knew that culture was maimed, imperfect, and incomplete. But at least he did not praise the idea of local cultures out of one side of his mouth even as he dismissed a burgeoning American culture out of the other. In the final estimate, then, Eliot, the man who a dozen years before had dismissed him as of "some local interest, perhaps," was still a "son of a bitch."

Williams had already written a two-page response to Eliot for the *Partisan Review* stressing the need to acknowledge the provinces and not "impound" (the pun was Williams') culture at the heads, including the universities. Otherwise a blockage resulted, leading to a widespread popular distrust of learning itself. But Williams' reply could not hope to stand up against Eliot's essay. Which was why he needed a critic like Horace Gregory. In a letter written May 5, Williams stressed the need for a continual intercourse between city and province, male and female, direction and generativity. Only by testing the local could the general be tested for its universality, he argued:

> The flow must originate from the local to the general as a river to the sea and then back to the local from the sea in rain. . . . It is the poet, locally situated, and only the poet who is the active agent in their interchange. It is the poet who lives locally . . . who is the agent and the maker of all culture. . . . But if the head, the intellect, on which he rightfully calls for direction, contemns him, fails to leave a friendly channel open for him but blocks him off—then dynamite is the only thing that will open that channel again.

Williams still distrusted Eliot for playing possum, for putting on a mask of mock seriousness that hid his lack of real earnestness. He did not really seem to care about American culture after all. The man was tedious, tired, a fraud.[83]

The central question for Williams in mid-1944 was still one of new forms reflecting that new reality he sensed in the younger generation of Americans. The country was still forming itself and so could not allow itself to go back to the empty forms and husks of other countries. Now was the time for the American poet, flanked by the American critic, to "move into the field of action and go into combat there on the new ground." This would mean closely examining what Poe and Whitman had done earlier to clear the field for American writers to follow. Yvor Winters, having denied there was even such a thing as a formal difference between English and American poetry, had returned—after some creditable early experiments in the 1920s—to the conventional stanza, making poems that Williams found tightly constructed but completely sterile.[84] Williams had just gone to see his friend Martha Graham perform in New York and—though he admired her for her work in American dance—he found her latest piece of work, an American theme set in Salem, Massachusetts, flat and uninteresting from a formal point of view. Her second piece, "Deaths and Entrances," had, on the other hand, been an impressive lyrical evocation of the three Brontë sisters. Unfortunately, what had made that piece impressive was not its form but rather its "borrowed distinction," the inherent pathos of the three English sisters' lives. That was not good enough for his purposes; what he wanted was the authority that came not from a borrowed meaning but rather from a mastery of form itself.

He knew he was gesturing toward a form conspicuous mostly by its very absence, but he hoped Gregory could understand what he was after. Call it a substratum, an underground bass, a dumb fellow feeling he was sure Poe and Whitman had also felt. Nevertheless, he had known the music, that major American form, in its "neglects, its gait, its passionate approaches." But for someone like Eliot none of this even existed, really, since for him there was England, now and forever, and then there were the mere English provinces, like America. Williams knew too the exotic loveliness of Pound's elitist, Fascist culture, "disappointed and inhuman," as well as Winter's static, medieval world. But against all of these he was willing to bet on his own culture, unformed and ugly as it still was. For at least that was still very much alive, waiting only to be released from its mass of pitchblende to become radium, shining in the dark. It was time now for a "public outlet," time for a magazine to do for Americans what Eliot's *Criterion* had done for the British: take a conscious position toward our culture—"from Eddie Cantor to the shadow of H.D., newspapers, anything"—to discover what was the radiant gist of American culture as it derived from "our history and our psyche." And though the whole effort might lead only to "one or two small pebbles of certainty," or even to less than that, it was still worth a try digging into that ground.[85]

The image of extracting a residue of radium out of a mass of seemingly inert pitchblende was very much on Williams' mind in the spring of '44. It would serve as one of the most widespread and profound metaphors throughout *Paterson*, and it was most immediately Williams' having gone to see M.G.M.'s *Madame Curie* with Greer Garson and Walter Pidgeon in March or April 1944 that provided him with his radiant image. Writing to Cummings on April 10, he praised Cummings' new book of poems as less than some of his other books of poems, explaining that he meant by this a compliment. "You know what Mme. Curie did to the tubs of pitchblende in the movie, she boiled it all down to about as much as a drop of aromatic piss in the bottom of the pot after the summer vacation when, in the hotel, the chamber maid forgot to empty the pot after the young people from the city had slept there one night."[86] In that image, then, he had the image of process, of transformation, of unstable elements moving toward inert lead or toward its biological equivalent, waste stool or generative semen.

Out of all this flurry of critical and imaginative activity, then, something was coming to a head. Coincidentally, in the same May issue of the *Partisan Review* that had contained the Eliot irritant, Williams had spotted a poem by Byron Vazakas, who had written to him earlier. Now Williams wrote Vazakas to praise him for his poem, which he saw made no pretensions to being anything but good work. Placed where he'd found it, however, it had served as its own irritant against the *PR* crowd, against intellectuals like Sidney Hook and Mary McCarthy, John Dewey and Philip Rahv. It was time, Williams suggested, for Vazakas to get a book of poems like that one together and he asked Vazakas to send him a sheaf of poems as soon as possible.[87] What Vazakas sent two days later was a group of poems that—when Williams could finally give it his attention several months later—came to symbolize for Williams the gist of the new form he had been searching so long for: the wedding of a long prose line to a sharply defined jagged-edged stanza, each independent, yet each complementing the other. That nuclear fracturing of line and meaning would have enormous consequences for *Paterson*.

In early June, with the heartening news of D-Day and the successful invasion of France, Williams was once again back at work on *Paterson*, trying to get the "Introduction" into better shape and finished by the end of that summer. Early Monday morning, June 26, Floss and Williams drove up to the shack at West Haven in the '36 Ford for three weeks of sun and ocean. Williams had brought along his typewriter this time, to work on *Paterson* and to review a "key" to *Finnegans Wake*, both of which he also brought along. He found the late Joyce's immensely difficult book a good way to clear his mind, especially "before attempting composition on one's own part," since it left the mind drained of any preconceived ideas and only a "feeling for the sound of words paramount" in one's head. In spite of that, he still could not get on with the poem. Instead, he kept going over and over the notes he'd compiled two years before on *Paterson*, "gradually arranging and rearranging the stray bits with the more solid sections" until he thought he might be approaching the order he was looking for to begin writing his "final first draft."

Then on Wednesday, June 28, he took the train alone out of New Haven up to Northampton, Massachusetts, waving in the direction of Stevens' house as he passed through Hartford. In Northampton, however, the woman at the desk of the Hotel Wiggens told him that the Cummington bus wouldn't be leaving for another four hours, so he decided instead to hire a taxi driven by a very nice young woman in a black dress to make the sixteen-mile trip out to the press. At Cummington he met Harry Duncan and Ed Williams for the first time—the two young men who ran the Cummington Press there and who were printing *The Wedge*.

When he toured the print shop the next morning in summer sunshine, he saw Wolff, the printer who was putting *The Wedge* together at the rate of three pages—both sides—per day (that is, when the excitable printer didn't throw a tantrum and throw the plates on the floor in disgust). Williams visited the eighteenth-century birthplace of the American poet William Cullen Bryant nearby, remarking to Stevens a month later that Bryant's home had seemed "completely off the earth" up there in the foothills of the Berkshires.[88] Then, early Friday morning, Williams hopped a bus for Pittsfield and from there took another one up to the Bennington campus, where Ted Roethke and Kenneth Burke—both on the faculty there—were waiting for him. It was like old times, and he enjoyed meeting the Bennington students, as he told Roethke when he'd finally made it back down to New Haven, once again by bus. Even the bus ride had been an unexpected pleasure. So much of his traveling for thirty years now had been done driving alone in a car that he'd "nearly forgot what Chaucer found on his way to Canterbury, that people are delightful when on a journey, footloose and therefore voluble."[89] At Bennington he'd read from his unfinished *Paterson*, trying to explain what it was he was searching for by reading from the manuscript itself. He regretted only that he hadn't been more "practical" with those kids, that he hadn't been able to point specifically to this or that, but had had to define his profound absences by gesturing, by trying to shape out of thin air the very thing he was still after.

The time spent at West Haven that June and early July provided Williams with a surcease from the heavy demands of his profession and he reveled in it. He found himself now only "twenty feet from Heaven —the salt water with the sun over it (last night full moon) plenty of work for my hands cleaning up the place, chopping wood." He had even been able to locate some meat and butter in spite of wartime shortages so that he and Floss could have a few superb meals. For the first time in two years, he told Vazakas, he could finally think clearly: "The practice of medicine has been a cruel chore since the beginning of the war. I have to go on with it as soon as I am rested. But at the moment I am using the opportunity given me . . . to work at some verse, . . . at the poem *Paterson*."[90]

When he returned home on July 15 he was rested and even satisfied for the moment with his "maneuvering" of the inert mass of *Paterson* which he'd managed to plot in more detail.[91] Three weeks later, on August 5, Jinny gave birth to her second, a daughter, Suzanne, who weighed in at a slight four pounds, seven ounces. She would need help with two small children. So, a month later, with Paul on destroyer duty once again somewhere in the North Atlantic, the Williamses had a bedroom on the second floor at 9 Ridge Road altered so that Jinny could move in with their grandchildren. With Elena in a nursing home now, there was room for Paul's young family. "We have a one month old girl on the premises together with the two year old boy now," Williams wrote Zukofsky on September 11. "It is as it is, we enjoy the children—and Jinny also but it takes energy."[92] And once again medical work was so incredibly demanding on Williams that he called his existence now a purgatory. Moreover, the long hot summer had sapped him of all desire to get on with the poem. "Haven't been able to do much more with *Paterson* though I did what amounted to a year's work on the thing during my vacation," he wrote bravely. And now with the "Yanks" forcing their way into Paris Williams was about ready for "the final push" to put the poem over. If he could just find a place to break through he would "Patton" *Paterson* right into Jim Laughlin's hands at last.[93]

· Then, in the first few days of September, Vazakas sent Williams a copy of the current *Poetry* with two of Vazakas' poems in it. Vazakas' new poetic line was not measured as Williams wanted it, but he could see that Vazakas was after something instinctively. Most poets did not even know that a new invention in the line was of first importance, he realized, and so were content to keep using the old over and over. At least he and Vazakas had made a first step. "Perhaps the Hebrew and Leger (in French) may be along the same track. But we don't stem from that. We stem from Whitman. Poor Whitman never did get started on the mechanics of the line. . . . He knew instinctively that he had barely scratched the surface . . . as a technical artisan but was not quite able to deduce how the new character of the LINE was the major factor in his 'democratic vistas.' " For it was in the line itself that democracy spoke, just there, in the bold breaking with the English tradition.[94]

The next day, as he worked again on *Paterson,* Williams wrote out these lines:

> *Only of late, late! begun to know, to*
> *know clearly (as through clear ice) whence*
> *I draw my breath or how to employ it*
> *clearly—if not well. . . .* [95]

How close these lines came to the kind of jagged vernacular he'd been reading in Vazakas' new poems, with lines like these:

> *In the outer office, the wind moans by*
> *steel window sash, echoing the terror*
> *of my being here. No other hand*
> *constructed this; no brain conceived*
>
> *So monstrous a detachment. I want nothing*
> *in this place. . . .*

On October 9 Vazakas sent Williams a typescript of his *Transfigured Night,* to which Williams responded two weeks later that Vazakas' poetry seemed "to occur in the prose as if hidden there."[96] That was it! That was what he wanted so badly for himself. But by mid-October Williams was suffering from general exhaustion, a "neurasthenia perhaps," he thought, which sapped him of all creative energy and even the desire to read. *The Wedge* had appeared in late September finally, but he'd waited so long for the book that its publication now seemed to him anticlimactic. "I feel better tonight than I did this afternoon," he told Zukofsky on September 23. For that afternoon he'd been ready "to go to the hospital or the sewer" and hadn't really much cared which.[97]

As for the war, he was beginning to suspect that that old whore, economics, was as much behind this one as it had been behind the First World War. He wanted the war over now and he didn't feel like squabbling over whether the Chinese who fought the Japanese were supporters of Chiang Kai-shek or Mao Tse-tung. "Everyone is talking of our bad strategic position in China," he wrote Malcolm Cowley at the *New Republic* in mid-September. He knew that Madame Chiang's sable coats—her ostentatious flaunting of wealth—were a symbol of the division between the Communists and the Nationalists and made American support of Chiang suspect in the eyes of the left. But why not let China divide herself into two defense zones, one under the Communists and one under Chiang? Thus, Williams reasoned, the government could divide military operations between the two forces and Russia could then come in and tell Japan to leave Communist-run China while the U.S. and Britain could support Chiang's fight against a common enemy.[98] Get the war over and done with!

He read Rexroth's *The Phoenix and the Tortoise* in early November and enjoyed it, though it was still *Transfigured Night* that continued to hold his attention, revealing as it did for him a quality he found very rare in American literature. Americans as a whole were "too brash, too pushing," he told Vazakas on the fifth. But Vazakas had reminded him of an older indigenous courtesy, such as he'd found in Chaucer and Charles Lamb. It was "a metropolitan feeling which we have only on a very low plane, the cheap Man-about-town attitude that the newspapers and the *New Yorker* sometimes feature." Only one or two Americans had cultivated this cosmopolitan style, including one man "who greatly influenced Stevens in his early days—but he's dead and gone." But, if Vazakas had his faults, if he was not entirely an urban poet, still one did not get in him, as Pound had said of Williams himself years before, "the SWeeP of the PEErairies in your underwear as so many of our pushing poets affect from Carl Sandburg onward." Instead Williams had discovered in Vazakas a "gentleness," a mellowed perception "of our more sophisticated traditional world." Here, in other words, was an American poet sensitive to an American urban culture to which Eliot and the New York intellectuals seemed peculiarly blind. "Who knows anything of the old days of our cities," he asked, cities like Boston, New York, Philadelphia, and New Orleans as cultures affecting contemporary America: "something apart, old families—not English or French but American —strange family ways." Wally Gould had had a touch of this special feeling for the past: the man with Abnaki Indian blood in his veins, a man who had known the world of Maine before settling in Farmville, Virginia, where the sounds and smells of the old antebellum South had survived down to the present. But Gould was gone now, taking with him something of that special knowledge of the phosphorescent presences that for a short time at least had inhabited American places.[99]

He picked up the American city theme again in a letter to Marianne Moore two days later. He'd been reading over Rexroth's poems and Vazakas', comparing the two side by side, he told her, and he had come to the conclusion that Rexroth was like a general contractor when it came to the use of words: there were certain predetermined designs meant for certain kinds of constructions. But Vazakas, while "retaining regularity," had also allowed room for "improvisation." Like jazz, Vazakas' line was "an American mode which has possibilities." Beyond that, however, was a "metropolitan softness of tone, a social poetry that Chaucer had long ago to such perfection."[100] He was thinking of *Troilus and Criseyde*, and of the way especially Chaucer's modern heroine had signed herself in her letters to Troilus after she'd gone over to the Greeks, in a few short hours to be bedded down with the enemy. *La Vôtre C*, she had written, signaling in that formal signature the final separation and divorce that had already occurred. Williams would have Marcia Nardi—the Cress of his own poem—sign off her long, rambling, deranged eight-page letter in exactly the same way.

Williams also began sending Vazakas an extended commentary on his *Transfigured Night* on November 5, a commentary that would finally become—with changes—his "Introduction" to Vazakas' poems when they were published by Macmillan in '46. What Williams stressed in his commentary was the inventiveness of Vazakas' four-line stanzas, where each initial line jutted out to the left so that the stanzas had the shapes of Oklahoma with its panhandle, or the shape of a "toy cannon." Here was a measure, a definite regularity of form that resembled a musical bar, though it existed independently of syntax, sentence, paragraph, or clause. It was a design, a musical sentence, where grammatical meaning was not tied to stanzaic form but could flow over into new stanzas as needed. Einstein's theory of relativity was somewhere in Williams' consciousness as he worked with the ramifications of the theory he saw working in Vazakas, for he saw enfleshed there one kind of relative measure, more fluid—he felt—than anything he thought he himself had done even in *The Wedge*, as he went back over that book now with a fresh eye. What Vazakas had in fact achieved was one viable substitute for the standard blank verse line which had dominated English poetry for so long.

"What an unimaginable pleasure it would be to read or to hear lines that remain unpredictable," Williams summed up. To think of line following line, each holding "the ear in suspense," each a surprise, and yet the whole consort of lines remaining orderly, retaining "a perfect order, a meter to reassure us." By order he meant a pattern discovered in the world, from things as they were, like "the newspaper that takes things as it finds them—mutilated and deformed"[101] and presents those things unchanged. There were patterns there—as David Lyle had taught him— there in the river of newsprint, and those patterns would have to hit the modern reader the way love did: obliquely, at a slant, its realization striking the alert mind on its own terms—or not at all. It was the poet's task to challenge events, to stare hard at the welter of things until their inner radiance and significances exploded in upon him and made him see the thing before him with new eyes: new words rinsed of their borrowed and hackneyed connotations. It was a matter of an idea of order and the possibility of new discovery; of tedious, ongoing exploration and the sudden revelation for which medical diagnosis could provide an example. A hardheaded formal invention—the cold eye searching—and the necessity of sensual, nurturing, regenerative stimulation. Those were the necessary male and female counterparts of the creative act.

He was so grateful for the example of a Vazakas at a time when he was radically blocked with the making of *Paterson* that he could call him "the best poet in our language," at least for the moment. Of course Williams qualified such extravagant praise at once. Who the hell was he, after all, to make such claims for anybody? His own tastes could change tomorrow. Yet "the God damned stupid pholosophic poets" thought they could "reach" poetry through philosophy, he told Vazakas, though none of them had the "sheer poetic flair," the necessary "language," to carry out the task of creating the new poetry. Tate did not have it, nor Blackmur, nor Auden. Not even Eliot, "good" though he was. Realizing that he'd let himself go too far in his enthusiasms again, Williams began to pull back. Anyone reading his letter would no doubt wonder who "this marvel is that I'm writing about." Well, the marvel was—finally—Man himself, and his ability to use the imagination to work his way out of whatever impasse he found himself in, as Vazakas had done with some of his poems.[102]

Williams reinforced his aversions for the university poets in a letter to Theodore Roethke written in the midst of his dialogue with Vazakas. When Allen Tate at the *Sewanee Review* turned down some of Roethke's experimental greenhouse poems as being all image without a sufficient intellectual frame, Williams sardonically welcomed him to the club of rejected poets, of which he himself was the foremost. "Serves you right," he chided Roethke, "fer trying to play around with them Taters. Couldn't you just feel how proud, righteous and uppity they are? Po' chil'un like us ain't for them people from the big house. Now don't you never go where they are again. You hear?" He admitted that modern poetry needed a modern concept at its core and that images alone—no matter how finely realized—were not enough to make a poem. But he insisted too that a poem needed the sensuous component to flesh out the intellectual. Otherwise it would become merely "bone dry." The problem with Tate and Blackmur and the others was that they'd swallowed Eliot's theories of impersonality completely, so that poetry, "like the owl," would no longer have any "serviceable ass hole," no way of digesting experience and making that its own. The only way for Roethke "to beat those philosophic punks" was not to try their own cerebral game but to drive his own "sensuality to an extreme," though Williams was also aware that the administration at that "female seminary" he was teaching in —Bennington—might take umbrage at such a tack. The sensuous, then, and—equally important—"a definite intellectual concept about which to correlate" those sensuous images. It was exactly what Williams was doing in *Paterson*.[103]

In naming Tate and Eliot and the others, however, Williams had avoided confronting the one poet who was still his most worthy American contender: Wallace Stevens. It was, after all, Stevens whose urbanity and sophistication with the traditional blank verse line (with all the accumulated weight of Shakespeare, Milton, Wordsworth, Shelley, Ten-

nyson, and others behind it) stood behind Williams' own evident anxieties. Always in public and in their exchanges there was the utmost
cordiality and deference between these two giants while each jockeyed for
position and watched the other. In July, for example, Williams had
written Stevens that it was beginning to look as though they were
themselves becoming the "elder group" who formed both a "critique and
a *vade mecum* of an art that is slowly acquiring reality here in our God
forsaken territory," and that their task was to make the way ready for the
later "assembler" who would actually make "the history."[104] Vazakas,
finally, was merely the intermediary for Williams. Here was a younger
poet who—like Stevens—had hailed from Reading, Pennsylvania, and
who even knew Stevens personally.[105] What Williams was doing in this
exchange of letters in late '44, then, was acknowledging Stevens' real
strength—the one thing he had to such consummate perfection and
which Williams felt he lacked in himself—a sophisticated, urbane voice.
He would need that himself to hold his complex city poem together.
Williams knew he had that voice in him as a distinct possibility, but for
years now the New York crowd had dismissed him as a wild man or—as
Stevens had done—as Carlos the wild Spaniard. He'd been patronized by
Blackmur, Winters, Jarrell, Tate, and the *Partisan Review* and dismissed
by most of the other critics because he had not fit the acceptable
university molds. And the more they ignored him, naturally, the more his
own stridencies had increased.

He knew what his own characteristic voice signature had been: a
breathlessness, a jagged, hurried, clipped voice in the higher registers,
urging the reader to see what was under his or her eyes. He had the speech
of his own people—the common people of his own region—Rutherford,
Paterson, the provincial voice, down to perfection. He had the neurasthenic voice down as well, and the voice of the backcountry, rural hill
people with their broken brains and hidden lives existing within fifty
miles of the foremost intellectual capital of the United States. He even
had the brilliant, bitter, accusatory cadences of an Edward Dahlberg to
draw on. But what he still needed was the voice of authority to hold the
others together, a voice like Stevens', say, in *Notes Toward a Supreme
Fiction*. With this difference: that his voice would be less a disembodied
fiction and closer to the precise cadences of his own time. Not, *not* a
voice that insisted by its mode of imitation on evoking the English
literary tradition, but rather a voice that in its cadences, in the way it
unfolded on the page, was clearly of his own time.

At the end of '44, waiting for the final breakthrough, Williams was
finding signs everywhere that he was not alone in his search for new
forms. He even discovered signs in—of all places—*Life* magazine. So, as
he browsed through a long, patriotic poem by Russell Davenport called

"America" in the November 24 issue of *Life,* he found in a section of the poem called "His Teacher Speaks," an "extension, a loosening up" of Vazakas' own invention. How had this happened, Williams wondered? Had Davenport read Vazakas, or was it simply a coincidence? He thought of writing to Davenport and asking him, though he changed his mind almost at once. No, as Lyle had suggested, the new was something in the air, for the antennae of the race to discover. So here was another poet who had "thoroughly worked out" what he himself was doing in *Paterson,* though in his correspondence with Vazakas he had never once mentioned the poem that had been constantly on his mind. After all, that was his own "dirty little secret," as he would call it in *Paterson.*[106]

Where exactly that new conversational tone—authoritative, urbane, assured—entered *Paterson* was part of Williams' own secret, worked out in the silence of his study, but one can hear it in such stanzas as these, added at this time to the fabric of the poem, the first lines shuttled to the right instead of to the left:

> *I remember*
> *a* Geographic *picture, the 9 women*
> *of some African chief semi-naked*
> *astraddle a log, an official log to*
> *be presumed, heads left:*
>
> *Foremost*
> *froze the young and latest,*
> *erect, a proud queen, conscious of her power,*
> *mud-caked, her monumental hair*
> *slanted above the brows—violently frowning.*[107]

Whether anyone else saw what Williams saw so clearly at the close of '44 was beside the point. Enough that Williams had seen it and was convinced that now was the moment for the major breakthrough he saw being mirrored in the Russian advance all along the eastern front and in Patton's tank columns spearheading the American advance from the west. But as that advance ground down with the approach of winter, so too work on *Paterson* came once more to a halt. Williams watched breathlessly now as the war reached its final crisis. Just before Christmas the dreaded German counteroffensive that had been threatening for months began, centering on a place called Bastogne in an action that came to be called the Battle of the Bulge. Until this moment, Williams wrote Zukofsky three days before Christmas, the world had viewed the American soldier as little more than "a sort of specialized mechanic" equipped with all sorts of mass-produced gear and machinery, cranked out in much the same way as American tanks and planes and victory ships.

But now the GI was "being terribly tested" as a man and Williams was sure that the American soldier's performance was "affecting every last human being in our country." The country itself was waiting, waiting "not so much as to see ourselves tested by a desperate Germany, a dangerous individual" equipped with V-1 and V-2 rockets and germ warfare and some even more horrendous weapons being rumored about, who might "annihilate not one man or ten or twenty thousand helpless (mentally) soldiers but us, you and me, now." That was the crisis, and Americans would never be the same after it was over, "win or lose." For Williams believed America could still lose the war. He paralleled the national crisis with his own crisis, his own deep need to make his national statement. "It really takes a lifetime not only to do anything worthwhile," he concluded with his sixty-second winter settling in, "but even to find what we want in others." One was "so unsure, so tentative." And, besides, "any decent intelligence" was—really—"humble at core, too humble to want to make too brash an assertion in a fluid world." In the long run, one might be able to make some small "positive statement." That was surely enough for any one lifetime.[108]

*
* *

New Year's Day 1945: the feast of Janus, a looking back and a looking forward. Writing to Horace Gregory that day, Williams noted the present tragedies in Europe and the dawning of a new future: "Were it not for the tragic news from the war front (contrasted with the intellectual front and many another), we might look at the approaching last years of our lives . . . with real anticipation." He was eager now to finish the long-stalled "Introduction" of *Paterson*, but he was also afraid, he admitted, to "become involved" with a task that would surely exhaust him as it had in the past. On New Year's Eve he'd finally realized he would have to begin writing his poem all over again, that the tinkering and rearranging he'd been doing since '42 was merely a Band-Aid measure when what was needed was major surgery:

> Much that I have collected is antique now. The old approach is outdated, and I shall have to work like a fiend to make myself new again. But there is no escape. Either I make myself or I am done. . . . THAT is what has stopped me. I must go on or quit once and for all. Here's hoping. Your confidence and favorable words help me . . . for the final onslaught.[109]

Then for the next two weeks Williams found himself immersed in his medical work: babies to deliver and kids with colds, mumps, appendicitis, meningitis, so that he could work on the *Paterson* only in spare moments. He managed to finish the introduction to Vazakas' book of poems and the preface too to Rexroth's *Phoenix and the Turtle*.[110] He even found time to get over into New York on Wednesday night, January

24, to see *The Fighting Lady*, a sixty-minute Technicolor film about life on a U.S. aircraft carrier that had seen action in the Marianas and in Guam. Watching downed Navy pilots in the Pacific had made him think of his own sons and he remarked to Vazakas that if it was realism American audiences were after, that was the film to see. Let Americans have that film in the back of their heads, he commented, when they wanted to see what the war was costing.[111]

By the end of the month, however, he wrote Laughlin to say that the "Introduction" was now nearing completion, that there would eventually be four parts, that each part would run to about seventy-five pages in typescript, and that he could expect to get one part for each of the next four years.[112] Now—after delaying the first part for nearly three years—he was pushing Laughlin to know how quickly he would move to get the thing out. What Williams probably had at this point was the seventy-one-page typescript called "Paterson: the Introduction," which contained the much revised plan, a "Preface," and a recognizable version of "The Delineaments of the Giants." Williams had rifled several earlier versions to come up with his latest version, which included Nardi's letters as well as letters from Alva Turner and Edward Dahlberg. Sam Patch, the semimythical figure who had dived from high places, was here in this version, as well as poor Mrs. Cummings, who had leapt or fallen to her death at the Great Falls in the early nineteenth century. So were the Sisters of St. Anne (whose convent in Lodi, New Jersey, Williams had visited in the spring of '42), and so were those images of waste farina clogging his office sink and the thawing water dripping off his roof and the cleft in the rock at the Great Falls.[113] "If only I could get to it when I *want* to and feel in the mood I'd have the first part . . . ready for the typist in a day," he complained to Laughlin on February 3.[114] As it was, Kitty Hoagland was already at work on the script, preparing it for publication. On the fourth, he wrote again to Laughlin: he would send the script by St. Patrick's Day, March 17, the beginning of spring. Six weeks.

The exchange between Kitty and Williams carried on in the script itself had its light moments. "WCW: "fileing (like a file)." KH: "I ain't that dumb. & Its filing not fileing, but I'm using your spelling." But such lightness was offset by Williams' anxieties. Now that the poem was being prepared for the publisher, was it really "there among the words"? Or was it merely gravel for the critics to peck at? If it was, they could cut their miserable hearts out; he'd done what he could.[115] But at least Floss and Kitty were "curiously impressed" by what he'd done "and agreed that I should have my pants kicked—a good sign." Horace Gregory was still an important support for Williams, for he was one of the few critics he could still trust in a world where most scholarship had the rancid stench of "meat set out by a trapper to decoy a coyote." He'd seen Gregory at a party in New York on Friday night, February 2, and had found himself calmed by the man's lack of shrillness and self-importance, so that he had come home once again composed and ready to work. Gregory had also suggested that Williams avoid footnotes in *Paterson*, an idea Williams had been toying with, and the suggestion had steadied him so that he found himself "docilely" doing what Gregory had suggested with the "absolute assurance that it is the correct answer." Wasn't that one of the functions of the critic: to stir up, make clearer the artist's work to the artist? Surely the artist and the critics were not like buck rams in heat, battering ego against ego. Rather it was for the critic to support, extoll, commend.[116]

Through most of February and halfway through March, as the Allied armies broke through the last German resistance in a dozen places and prepared to cross the Rhine, Williams worked steadily on the major breakthrough that had occurred in his own poem. He wrote to virtually no one, letting letters and requests pile up while he forged ahead with the poem. Finally, on March 9, he wrote Laughlin—who was on a skiing holiday in Utah at the time—that when he got back to New York on the twentieth *Paterson* would be waiting for him. "Look it over and for the love of Joyce's Jesus"—he'd been reading *Stephen Hero* just then—"do let me know within a reasonable time just what you plan for it."[117] He was still working on the revisions, still unsatisfied, as he cut the script from seventy-five pages to sixty, before sending it off on the eighteenth, just one day after his own target date. When he wrote to Charles Abbott four days later he was hoping he hadn't slipped up his "footing" with the poem he'd finally sent, though he knew even mountain goats were capable of great falls.[118]

But Laughlin was evidently pleased and accepted the poem at once, promising to bring it out in a handsome format by the fall of 1945. On the twenty-eighth Williams asked him to use the typeface he'd seen in the Winter issue of the *Partisan Review* in the printing they'd done of Robert Penn Warren's "Billie Potts" for the poetry passages and to use a newsprint type for the prose sections, such as that used in the *New York Times*. He made a few small changes over the next few months—a deletion here, an addition there—like the postscript to *Paterson*, which he took from John Addington Symonds' *Studies of the Greek Poets* about deformed verse being suited to a deformed morality. When he read that passage in the summer of 1945 he could see that that certainly described what he'd been after all along.

But for the moment, at least, *Paterson* was out of the way. And almost at once he began work on a play that had been haunting him since the summer of '42, when he'd dreamed his own death while in a hotel with a woman. That dream had left him drained, with a sort of nameless guilt at having to leave Floss to sort out the aftermath of their thirty-year dream of love together some day when he was permanently out of the picture. He needed to write out that psychodrama in the form of a play in an effort to come to terms with his own feelings, to apologize for his momentary crazinesses in having slept with other women. But he needed to defend his actions as well and, hopefully, make Floss understand why he had sometimes acted as he had. As in *Paterson*, the problem of divorce surfaced in the play as well. That play had fantasy elements in it: the dead doctor returning in the night to his kitchen, as he had come home so often at all hours from house calls or from the hospital, to be confronted there by Floss. The whole night scene was illuminated by the single cold light of the opened refrigerator, with husband and wife blending surrealistically with the shadows cast by that strange, domestic light.

In that play—*A Dream of Love*—which Williams kept reworking, he had his double slowly convince his wife of the amoral dynamics of infidelity, the mutual nervousness, the buildup, the sexual act coming almost as an afterthought in the excitement generated by literature, until even she could applaud her husband and the woman as they sank into the bed together. But applause had turned at once to staccato machine-gun fire, and the doctor's wife had found herself back in her house, alone, her husband most assuredly gone now, but she herself able finally to cope with the fact of his death and its surrounding scandal. In '42, Williams had accurately called his dream a modern tragedy of the spirit, though by '45 he had come to resent his guilt and had tried to turn his own death into something like a comedy of manners with an upbeat denouement.[119] He really tried hard to convince Floss by his play to come over to his way of seeing marriage and fidelity, but he was to fail, so that he wound up finally providing a second ending years later in which he allowed her to speak for herself.[120] The tragedy was not in the sexual encounters he'd had, finally, but in the dawning realization that he would never be able to eradicate the hurt he'd done her nor the hurt he himself felt in having hurt her. All he could finally do with the problem, which would continue to nag him in his last years, was to try and leave it alone and go on with his all-consuming work.

In April of '45 Williams was also trying to become a convert to black jazz, at Fred Miller's promptings. So on April 1—Easter Sunday—he borrowed Jinny's Emerson phonograph and let the sounds of half a dozen jazz records he'd just bought bounce off the walls of the house. "It's a bit of an acquired taste you'll have to acknowledge what with Bach's Matthew Passion filling the afternoon radio program in competition but I did enjoy Ugly Child and That Da Da Thing."[121]

In April, too, Williams—like millions of other Americans—was shocked and saddened by the news he heard over the radio even as the war in Europe drew to a victorious close. The man who had taken them through the Depression and seen them through the war, the man who had raised the hopes of some and struck dismay in others with his policies was now gone. On April 12 the world learned that Franklin Delano Roosevelt, just beginning his fourth term as President of the U.S., the man Pound would curse as "that ambulating dunghill," had died of a cerebral hemorrhage in Warm Springs, Georgia. Williams, hearing the news, found himself weeping for his lost leader. He wrote a poem about that moment which was published the following spring in the *Harvard Wake*, a poem that clearly had in mind Auden's tribute to another lost leader, Yeats:

> *Suddenly his virtues became universal*
> *We felt the force of his mind*
> *on all fronts, penetrant*
> *to the core of our beings*
> *Our ears struck us speechless*
> *while shameless tears sprang to our eyes*
> *through which we saw*
> *all mankind weeping.*[122]

That same night he and Floss went into New York to see a production of Tennessee Williams' *The Glass Menagerie*, though the pleasure Williams felt was muted by the daily costs of the war, shouted by newsboys hawking the late edition all over the city. Three weeks later, on Saturday, May 5, Williams was in Washington, D.C., making a recording for the Library of Congress at the invitation of Robert Penn Warren. He did three 78 RPMs—five sides of verse (forty-nine poems from 1909 up till the present) and one side of prose: his short story "A Night in June." But even in Washington reciting his poems he had not eluded the war, for he learned on his return home that the son of his old friend Ben Hecht was being buried by Rabbi Silverman of East Rutherford at Arlington National Cemetery even as he made his recordings at the Library.[123] In May he read a life of F. Scott Fitzgerald as well as Richard Chase's *The Sense of the Present* and of course Symond's study of Greek poetry. Then, in mid-May the war ended in Europe, though that simply meant transferring American soldiers and supplies to the Far East for what promised to be a protracted conflict there. And though there was the respite of the shore and water at West Haven that summer, so that the water lapping against those sands came to resemble ancient Cos or Lesbos for Williams, he could not shake the reality that once again—at the end of July, in fact—both his sons left for the Pacific and the war.[124]

In late July Laughlin wrote to warn Williams not to expect much in the way of understanding from the critics when *Paterson* was finally published. For his part, Williams answered on the twenty-fourth that in spite of Laughlin's "doleful predictions," he thought the book might at least pay for itself.[125] But Laughlin had come too near the truth and the following day Williams wrote Macleod that, while he had tried to answer the academic critics in the poem itself, he'd just been warned that the poem was too "formless" to be accepted. Only he knew the years he'd spent searching for an acceptable form and he'd be damned if he was going to "organize" his masterpiece now "into some neo-classic *recognizable* context." He knew the poem was still a little wild by contemporary standards, but he was also convinced that he'd got hold of something "worth holding" onto. The philosopher-critics were still trying "to label the arts," but sooner or later they were going to burn their fingers playing with something as radioactive as poetry: "Somewhere, in some piece of art resides a radioactive force beyond anything but their copying in their static spheres. I fight with Blackmur, I feel resentments against them all, and all I can do (growing old) is to compose. It is the only recourse, the only intellectual recourse for an artist, to make, to make, to make and to go on making—never to reply *in kind* to their strictures." And then, recalling the image of Madame Curie returning in the night to her womblike alembics to find a radiance glowing in one of her retorts (it was Williams' retort to the critics as well), Williams added that he was sure he too had discovered forms with their own luminous cores. He too had had to work by batlight without help from the so-called experts, "in a sort of night, in a sort of dumb philosophic stupor," where, within, he knew there burned "a fiery light, too fiery for logical statement."[126]

How the mind leapt to the truth! For that image of a fiery atomic light confirming the discovery of new unstable elements in the table took on a horrifying new dimension in the late summer of '45. The prologue began for Williams on July 29, when one of the thousands of American bombers that were headed westward over New York City and New Jersey for California and eventually Japan exploded into the side of the Empire State Building. Laughlin was in his New Directions office on Sixth Avenue a few blocks south of the impact point when the crash occurred and was so shaken by the event that he tried to tame it by writing a poem called "Above the City." He sent Williams a copy of the poem asking his advice, and on August 7—Hiroshima plus one—Williams answered that he liked the poem, but that as far as explosions went the one over Japan had been for him absolutely "mind quelling," touching deeper even than the imagination seemed to be able to follow.[127]

That image of what a bomb could do would grow like a cancer in Williams' imagination over the years. Once one accepted the fact of the bomb and the fact of man's capacity for destruction, there were no limits to the terror, as his late poetic meditations on love and death would explain. For the moment, however, this new power merely numbed him with its sheer reality. In a matter of hours, the war in the Pacific which had dragged on for more years than he wished to remember was suddenly over—or at least that phase of it which had needed hundreds of planes to carry out the civilian bombings of a Guernica, a London, a Berlin. Something new, a single bomber unleashing a single bomb with enough energy to level a city larger than his own Paterson had radically altered man's dependence on the classic strategies of war. At last even Armageddon appeared within man's reach. Still, when Williams first learned about the bomb, he was more immediately concerned that Laughlin had—after repeated delays—finally located a printer for *Paterson*. He felt he had had to be "Job's personal god to withstand the delays of the present time." And then, thinking of what had just happened to a Japanese city, he wondered if he wasn't "being small about this relative to world affairs."[128]

A week later the war was over. When the news hit Rutherford on the night of August 14, Williams was home alone with Jinny and her children, who were fast asleep upstairs. The two of them were just sitting down to a late supper of Spanish rice in the dining room when suddenly they began to hear automobile horns all up and down Park Avenue and Ridge Road. "I got up from the table," he wrote Floss (away on a short vacation), "went to the radio and got the news. By then the cars were driving by one after the other, more and more with every minute and all tooting their horns to the limit. Jinny and I had a glass of sherry to toast with by which time you couldn't hear yourself think for the noise, horns, bells, tin cans, whistles, and even a steam whistle of some sort with paper streamers, kids and sleigh bells, even sleigh bells." But the war had been too long and protracted an affair for him. Too much had happened, too much suffering, too much death, for him to get caught up in the spirit of victory now. He told Jinny to go to the movies and that he would watch the kids. That night he finished Shakespeare's *Antony and Cleopatra* and then read another play. When Jinny returned, she talked about the short documentary they'd shown at the movies, explaining the atomic bomb "to the public in an elementary sort of way." Upstairs he found little Suzie awake in her bed, quietly staring out into the darkness.[129]

Almost at once, Williams—like millions of other parents—began to write to congressmen, military officials, political connections, demanding that the boys be brought home by Christmas. Paul and Bill had linked up at least for a short while on Bill's ship, and Williams wrote Bill that he was doing whatever he could to get them both home and to help check "the autocratic ways of Army and Navy," which would have liked nothing better than to maintain their huge base of power even in peacetime. Williams had taken blind old Elena out for a ride on Friday afternoon along the new road that had been built during the war across the meadows "to the place where it joined up with the old road this side of the Hackensack Bridge."[130] That place had brought back strong memories of Bill and Bill's boyhood friends so that Williams had felt the need to turn the car around and go home again. The meadows as he had known them, as his sons had known them, like so many outer and inner landscapes, had been changed forever. Some wild sunflowers were once again in bloom along the road out past Berry's Creek where it cut in through the skeletons of the old cedar swamp, vestiges of a time before the Mosquito Extermination Control Board of which he had been a member had raised the level of the water, thus killing off all those majestic old trees. Now the new highways had killed off the rest of the woods as well, so that all that remained were the foxtails along the meadow roads. Those new highways were a sign of the times, Williams knew, a sign of New Jersey's importance as an industrial link between New York and the rest of the nation. Soon Berry's Creek and the Hackensack, like the Passaic, would merely be sluices for draining off industrial wastes, virtually nameless to truckers or passengers racing over Route 17 or Route 3 or—in a few years—the New Jersey Turnpike. The meadows would become a place to dump concrete, car engines, garbage, even an occasional body—dismembered or whole—filling up slowly with detritus until the land began—after Williams' death—to disgorge its ill-digested wastes, vomiting back cancer-producing agents. By 1945 the cancer eating at Paterson was already spreading out toward Rutherford. That too Williams would have to take into account as he finished his poem about his place.

The press Laughlin found for *Paterson* in August was the Van Vechten Press located in Metuchen, New Jersey, and the printer there, working swiftly, had the "Introduction" ready by the first week in September. But now, with the galleys of the poem he had so long struggled with finally before him, Williams was repelled by its grotesqueness and recalcitrance. "I wish I had the guts to say to burn the whole *Paterson* script," he told Laughlin on the seventh. But he couldn't bring himself to do that. Instead, he began slashing the thing "unmercifully" in a frantic effort to save it, in a few days cutting out whole sections he had once pored over for years.[131] He must have felt the poem was worth saving, though, for it had cost him too many agonies and even a few moments of elation not to have had something of the gist he had been looking for. And he knew that the changes he was making in the text would mean at least another six months' delay in publication, but that didn't matter now.

A week after his initial revulsions, however, Williams could at last face his poem "rationally," though he was still not convinced that he'd "really caught anything" in what he was now calling *Paterson* 1. He had slashed away nearly a fourth of his poem by then to get rid of "the worst of the mess" before sending the poor galleys back to Laughlin. And he told

Miller on the fourteenth that he would send him a copy of the revised galleys when they were ready, meaning he didn't want anyone seeing the thing now. As for slashing, that had been necessary to loosen the thing up. He'd been at the poem "too long, cutting and adding," until it had gotten "tight, pebbly, cracked, rubbly—full of dried shit." It had become constipated, a poem without flow. He could still see possibilities with the thing, though at that moment they all seemed "unrealized."[132] For years he'd worked and reworked the form of his epic, he told Miller a week later, "deciding what in hell to write in the first place, what to include, what form to have it in and what, especially, to exclude." Now at last he had all four books "down on paper with their sequence and titles mapped and written in": "The Delineaments of the Giants," "Sunday in the Park," "The Library," "The River" (as it coursed to the sea). He even thought he could finish the other three books "in a matter of months" if only he could work at the poem "consecutively."[133] But for now his *Paterson* lay in shambles like Hiroshima or Nagasaki, looking, as he told Laughlin, "as tho' an atomic bomb had hit it before it was born."[134]

"When I saw the galleys I almost vomited," he wrote Kenneth Rexroth on the twenty-first. "I was heartbroken, the mess looked so foul. I slashed right and left, reedited bits here and there, pulled things together as best I was able and—the Lord only knows what the final result will be." If he could have done more than that he would have, but it was too late. Too much, he lamented, too much had "slipped away in my efforts to compress and pare the significances to the very bone. I know perfectly well that most readers will be bewildered and baffled, not knowing what [sic] I should have called the thing *Paterson*"—that is, if it was "even a poem." His only hope was that, here and there, one or another reader would "realize what I have been up against in taking the crude mass which I determined to attack and make it into SOMETHING, anything. What in hell I went through to even find any kind of form that would do will go unappreciated and unperceived. I started with a blank mind and a blank piece of paper—together with a mass of local knowledge to build into the imagination." He was glad to be able to write to Rexroth about the poem, to think that Rexroth would even consider himself one of Williams' disciples. It was good that September to have a "pal," he felt that lonely, especially now, when his major form—the poem that would proclaim or dismiss his majority status—was about to enter the world cold, naked, uncertain, but alive. There was "heavy work" to be done for American poetry still by those who—like Williams and Rexroth—could see where "the difficulties and the opportunities lie." He thought for a moment of Yvor Winters there in California with Rexroth, and of how, twenty years earlier, Winters too had considered himself Williams' disciple and had written those marvelously chiseled imagist poems before turning formalist and turning on his old master with a vengeance.

Winters too had "looked like really an aid at first," but time had shown him to be "an ass," especially now that he was going over the modernists with his big elephant guns, trying to knock them all off—Yeats, Eliot, Hopkins, Crane, himself—one by one or all together.[135]

On Wednesday, September 12, Williams took his "sensation-starved" daughter-in-law, Jinny, and the Hoaglands (Kitty and Clayton) into Greenwich Village to Joe Gould's place to help that village character —who was writing his personal history of the whole world—celebrate his birthday.[136] Two weeks later, on the thirtieth—a Sunday—Vivienne Koch came out to 9 Ridge Road to spend the afternoon interviewing Williams for some large project which she tried to keep under wraps but which Williams had already guessed was to be a critical biography that Jim Laughlin wanted for *New Directions*. It would take Koch nearly five years before that study was published and it would be the only full-length study Williams would see written about himself in his lifetime. But early on he dissociated himself from it and could hardly bring himself to read it even when it was published in 1950. The ambivalence he felt toward the project and toward Vivienne Koch apparently stemmed from the time of that initial interview and is apparent in a poem Williams wrote at the time which he titled "The Visit."

Williams' own sense of inadequacy, his harsh personal judgment against himself—especially at a time when his major effort seemed to be crumbling through his hands—and yet at the same time his determination that no one—*no one*—should lightly dismiss his work, together with his vision of a fuller poetic which would net a larger piece of modernity's complex reality all jostled for space in Williams' poetic dialogue with his inquisitor/interviewer. If it was only Vivienne Koch who sat across from him in his living room—a woman he personally cared for a great deal —what he kept seeing over her shoulder were the delineaments of that giant: the Critic as Final Judge. Naive poets like himself, he wrote, thus disarming the Critic from the start, could be as deceptively simple as a sunny day. He was like one of those gulls on the Hudson or the East River or the Passaic who continually dipped into "the featureless surface" of the river after fish they could see down there . . . and fish they kept bringing up. Williams too had winged, pivoted, and dipped into the flux of his own river, his own time, too often, returning again and again with poems, to doubt that he knew his own aim. He knew that most critics in 1945 considered his poems raw, unfinished, pre-art stuff, seeing Williams, therefore, as a mere spadeworker in the field of art. All right, then, let it be:

> *Say I am less an artist*
> *than a spadeworker but one*
> *who has no aversion to taking*

> *his spade to the head*
> *of any who would derogate*
> *his performance in the craft.*

The interview over, Williams got up like Stevens' speaker in "So-And-So Reclining on Her Couch" saying good-by to Mrs. Pappadopoulos, to say good-by to his own interviewer, with a subtle eye on the "view" she had afforded him even as she was busy watching him:

> *You were kind to be at such*
> *pains with me and—thanks*
> *for the view.*[137]

The following weekend Williams drove up once again to Cummington with Floss and Charlotte to see Williams and Duncan at the Cummington Press, this time to talk about Williams' next book of poems, which he'd already begun. (Charlotte had spent the war years with her son, Eyvind, in a small apartment over in New York City, running a sort of art boutique, while Eyvind painted and designed greeting cards. It was not an easy time for Charlotte, but she was tough and a fighter and had long ago learned to fend for herself. Unlike Floss, for example, who never learned to drive a car, Charlotte was already a veteran behind the wheel of a car and could spell her brother-in-law on long trips.) The new book would be called *The Clouds, Aigeltinger, Russia, &.* when it was finally published in the summer of '48 in another limited edition of 310 copies. So the visit in early October was merely a preliminary, more to establish the boundaries of the undertaking and the nature of the miscellany, meant to give Williams a sense of direction for his poems. On October 9 he wrote Bonnie Golightly, who operated the Washington Square Bookstore, asking for a copy of Pound's recent translation of Confucius' *The Wobbling Pivot*, a title Williams was sure had "dirty implications."[138] He had just sent Koch up to the Poetry Room at Buffalo to examine Pound's early letters to him, and within a few weeks he was writing an essay for *PM Magazine* as part of a symposium on "The Case For and Against Ezra Pound." Pound himself had been in U.S. custody at the Disciplinary Training Center in Pisa, Italy, ever since the end of April, when Italian partisans had turned him over at gunpoint to the U.S. Army command in Genoa.[139] All that summer Pound had been kept in a steel gorilla cage, at first without even protection against the rain and chill while an arc light was kept on him all through the night. Later he was allowed a tent and even a small table, typewriter and paper on which to write his *Pisan Cantos*. But in the fall he had been flown to the U.S. to prepare to stand trial on charges of treason against his country. Williams' essay, written at a time when Pound's fate was being decided in Washington, D.C., is a strange, ambivalent statement, acknowledging Pound's errors at the same time that it is a plea to let the poor bastard live. And Williams' anger with his friend for his arrogance and stupidity in getting himself into this position pervaded the piece he wrote now. "Ezra Pound the consummate poet," he argued, "taken as any sort of menace to America when compared with some of the vicious minds at large among us in, say for instance, the newspaper game, as well as other rackets which have the public ear, is sheer childishness."

Pound was not a "dangerous man," Williams insisted, and his own guess was that the man's "infantile mental pattern" would finally yield up some pretty "dull stuff" when the wartime broadcasts were examined, though he was quick to add that he himself had not heard the actual broadcasts Pound had made from Rome, other than that single sentence about himself which Floss had heard from the bank teller several years before. Williams could still remember that visit from the FBI men, could still remember his own fear, his own helplessness before them, and he still blamed Pound for implicating him in his stupid broadcasts. He was aware that some FBI agent would undoubtedly monitor the essay he was now writing once it was published, but he still felt compelled to defend his friend. "When they lock the man up," he ended, "I hope they will give him access to books, with paper enough for him to go on making trans- lations for us from the classics such as we have never seen except at his hands in our language." In other words, Williams wanted the U.S. authorities to know Pound was no threat to them and that he might even do some good if they let him live. Knowing this about Pound, he added that "it would be the greatest miscarriage of justice, human justice, to shoot him."[140]

And yet he still could not bring himself to write to Pound. It would take another three weeks to do that, and much longer to go down to Washington and actually see the man. But three days after Christmas, having heard from Viola Jordan once again that she'd heard from Pound, Williams couldn't refrain from adding his disappointment that the son of a bitch actually seemed to "be getting out of it"—out of being hanged —"by pretending madness." And wasn't that the modern way of doing things! "Why in hell" didn't he just "come clean" instead, Williams went on, "acknowledge his guilt and take it in the neck." Maybe "we could turn the Jews over to him and let him run the country," the anti-Semitic bastard! And yet it was Louis Zukofsky, himself a Jew, Williams had to acknowledge, who had written "the finest defense" of Ezra he'd seen by anyone. What was one to do?[141]

*
**

Sometime in early November—perhaps the seventh or eighth—Williams finally got into New York with Floss to hear Bunk Johnson and his New

Orleans band play classical jazz at the Stuyvesant Casino on Second Avenue and East 9th Street. Fred Miller had been after him to go hear Bunk for weeks and he was even to have gone into New York to hear him on Friday night, September 28, but had had to cancel out because of a patient. When he did see the band, finally, he was so taken by the experience that he urged Laughlin to be sure and go and then went back himself a second time the Friday after Thanksgiving. This time he took Jinny and went with Fred and Betty Miller to tap out the music, dance a few dances with Jinny and Betty, and drink some beer. He would write a jazz piece shortly after called "Ol' Bunk's Band," trying to capture something of the jagged tempo of black jazz in his own lines:

> There are men! the gaunt unfore-
>   sold, the vocal,
> blatant, Stand up, stand up! the
>   slap of a bass-string.
> Pick, ping! The horn, the
>   hollow horn
> long drawn out, a hound deep
>   tone. . . . [142]

That night Williams met another man, Bucklin Moon, who would come to serve as his doppelgänger in an improvisation he would begin a few weeks later with Fred Miller. Moon was thirty-four at the time and an editor at Doubleday who had already written one novel, *The Darker Brother* (which Miller had heard about but not read), and had also edited an anthology of fiction about the American black. Moon had taken a friend of his, Ed Fenton, to hear Bunk Johnson at the Casino, but an argument had erupted at his table when another editor, already half smashed, had loomed over the table and accused Moon of stealing Fenton away from him. Moon, to avoid a scene, got up from his chair and began to head for the door. It was then that Miller spotted him walking across the dance floor and invited him over to join him and Williams and the others for a drink.

Recalling that night, Moon remembered talk of jazz—especially New Orleans jazz—and literature as he drank beer.[143] And for her part Betty Miller remembered how Moon had begun "with easy speech and there was talk at first of an interracial magazine but Moon soon took to stammering." Williams she had always known as "a warm congenial person," but there were times when he "would become the coldly analytical surgeon . . . and the effect it had on those around him at such a time was quite devastating. So, squeezed between Williams and Fred, and getting a message for help from my husband, I batted around the subject of jazz and its impact on our lives and time with Williams. . . . I spoke of the poetry of jazz, the natural . . . outpouring of the soul, of how this was truly an outgrowth of our newly welded society. . . . I advocated the theory that if our . . . society was to stabilize, . . . all of the artists together . . . should strive to give meaning to the American Man's evolution into something desirable. . . . Williams just listened. Not just politely either, listening for him was serious."[144]

Two days after that meeting, Fred Miller wrote that he wasn't interested in pursuing the idea of the interracial magazine Williams had broached to Moon. But Moon himself stayed fresh in both their minds. Williams and the Millers had all been under the impression that Moon was a "light-skinned negro" who was trying to pass for a white. After all, he'd written *The Darker Brother* using a black persona, and he knew a hell of a lot about black jazz, including writing a fine piece on it for the Sunday *New York Times Magazine* in late '46. "Would you ever think that Bucklin Moon was a Negro, if you passed him—as a stranger—in the street?" Miller asked in his letter:

> He looks whiter than a lot of whites. . . . A good point Betty brought up: a stuttering or stammering Negro is a pretty rare bird indeed: your darker brother is articulate enough, when he isn't too frightened to talk.[145]

It was an error on Miller's part—and Williams'—but it would bear fruit. Ten days later, on December 4, Miller threw out the idea to Williams of the two of them doing an improvisational novel together. After all, Williams had suggested the idea a number of times since '42. A book "a la Auden–Isherwood," Miller called it now. Here was the idea: No plot. Williams would write the first chapter, then send it to Miller to write the second chapter, then back to Williams and so on, "until one of us has a brain blowout. . . . The end product may be, may not be great litrachoor, but it would be a lot of fun doing it. . . . Everything would go . . . at the same time remaining true to the logic of the book. . . . Who knows? We might even hit upon a *new* satiric form!"[146]

Williams picked up the hint at once. Why not make Moon the hero of their new novel, Williams wrote back on the eleventh. "I don't know a damned thing about him so that ought to give me a good start."[147] As for the size of segments or chapters: forget them. Just write until there was no more jet of inspiration, then pass the ball on to the other guy. And to get that ball rolling, he sent Miller three pages of jazz improvisation which began:

> Is it perchance a crime—a time, a chore, a bore, a job? he kept saying, he remembered that. Not a musician. He wasn't a musician—but he wished he had been born a musician instead of a writer. Musicians do not stutter. But he ate music, music wrinkled his belly—if you can wrinkle an inflated football. Anyhow it felt like that so that's what he wrote (without changing a word—that was his creed and always after midnight, you couldn't be earlier in the morning than that).[148]

Williams called the improvisation, tentatively, *Man Orchid*, for the plant that looked like an oversized scrotum and that lived on air, words, ideas, that sort of thing. Moon's stutter would become a half-comic, half-serious metaphor for the bifurcated psyche stretched between two worlds, the way Williams himself sometimes felt. There was white, classic America and there was black America, two cultures living in uneasy coexistence. So with William *Carlos* Williams, who had styled himself Evans Dionysius Evans twenty years before and now tried on a black / white persona. Williams' thesis—and he had taken the idea in part from listening to Fred Miller talk about American literature and black jazz—was this: just as Bunk Johnson and classical New Orleans jazz had been supplanted after World War I by the sweet jazz of the white musicians altering and muffling the classical forms, so Eliot's *The Waste Land* had run roughshod over an indigenous American poetry just when Williams was convinced it had been about to flower. Auden's presence in America in the early 1940s and the wide reception American audiences had accorded him had only exacerbated the situation, and so now Williams had his mouthpiece take a shot at him too.[149]

Williams was also furious with Conrad Aiken in late 1945 for having left him out of the revised and expanded edition of his *Modern Library Anthology of American Poetry*. What Williams wanted now was his own anthology—a *Private Anthology of American Poetry*—which would omit *The Waste Land*, that bane on American poetry, once and for all and treat it with a kind of benign neglect. To hell with the Tates and Eliots and *Partisan Review* pupils who were monopolizing the field in the mid-'40s, he'd told Miller in early '45.[150] Now was the time to search out and crystallize "the rare qualities . . . in modern American writing" with an anthology "of singing American poems."[151]

When Miller began to bog down with the improvisation in February 1946, Williams tried to get it rolling again by inviting a third writer into the collaboration, Lydia Carlin, a patient of Williams' who had had both her children delivered by him and was also an ardent admirer of his work. And though she and Miller were never to meet, their work came to rest side by side in the *Man Orchid* improvisation. During the summer of '43 the Carlins had rented the shack at 201 Ocean Avenue from the Williamses and Lydia Carlin had told Williams then about what it felt like to find herself as a little girl fresh from England in a settlement in Florida.[152] Her experiences of American blacks seemed to fit in with what Williams was doing and he asked her now to write it up, which she did, Williams interleaving her two chapters between Miller's. But by the end of May, Miller told Williams that what had stumped him was making Moon their hero. He had to admit that he simply did not know the "colored intellectual" well enough to write convincingly about him. He couldn't do jazz "faking" or improvising with that kind of figure and so he'd frozen.[153] Williams wrote back almost at once with another page of improvisations to stir up Miller. Let Miller do the woman, then, like the girl he'd once told Williams about who'd worked with him in his drafting office: "Make it hot and let her run side by side (in the novel only) with Moon. She the white, impossible queen."[154] But Miller had lost all heart in the project. To regard the black as an object of aesthetic interest was still to regard him as an object, Miller argued lamely, and to do that was to deny him his humanity.

Six months later, Miller sent one more installment: what was to become the final "chapter" of the novel. In it Miller described a literary party in the Red Hook district of Brooklyn—Hart Crane's old haunts —and in this installment a white hero got gloriously smashed and then tried to find his way home. It was Miller writing about what he knew best: himself. Williams was delighted with what Miller had done. "Really you did let go finally that time," he told Miller, "and I'm proud of you."[155] And though nothing more was ever added to the "novel," the two men periodically referred to it over the next ten years. The effort had failed, but in the process of its being written it had released a good deal of humor and imagination and a keen insight into the particular anxieties troubling Williams at the very moment when he was making his crossing into majority status.

In the fall of '45 Williams was seeing more of Kenneth Burke as well, now that Burke was back at his farm in Andover. On Friday, November 9, Williams and Floss had driven down to see the Burkes. They walked out through Burke's apple orchards and the next day Williams remembered "the beginnings of many valuable conversations" between himself and Burke beginning to stick "their heads up as we passed them by yesterday." That night, back home, he had awakened with "a half-sentence on my metaphorical lips, 'the limitations of form.' It seemed to mean something of importance."[156] And this in turn had led to a poem, "At Kenneth Burke's Place," which Williams found himself rewriting several times over the next two months as he tried to articulate for himself what the significance of his encounter with Burke had been. With Burke too as with Miller he'd discussed his *Private Anthology* and his insistence that the "Esoteric" should have no place in it, but only "the earth under our feet," as he had also stressed in *Spring and All*. But that too—the earth under our feet—even that had its own private language, as esoteric as any other. What made it different was, as Williams suggested, the life that clung to its skin, like the green apples on Burke's farm: the reality of "the small green apple / still fast here and there / to the leafless brush of unpruned / twigs sprouting from old knees / and elbows upon the tree." To take one of these local green apples and to bite into it, into this reality, was to experience once more "a taste long lost and regretted" which had now at last, like good talk between these two men, been "brought to life again."[157]

In the November issue of the *Sewanee Review* Williams had read
Wallace Stevens' poem "Description Without Place" and, apparently
taking Stevens' talk about the "seeming of the Spaniard, a style of
life, / The invention of a nation in a phrase" as being personally addressed
to him—as it probably was—answered Stevens with his own poem,
which he called, pointedly, "A Place (Any Place) to Transcend All
Places." Williams chose New York City as the place, beginning with its
skyscrapers and gigantic energies, and then shifting downward to the
city's dank but necessary roots in the complex sewer system that spread
for hundreds of miles beneath the city's streets and sidewalks. Any place
imagined, Williams insisted, had still to be rooted in a real place.
Otherwise a culture became too stylized, too unrelated to anything, a
sterile sport, a manner worn too obviously, as the Baroness had worn her
manner too obviously (Williams slyly insinuated, remembering how she
had scared the hell out of Stevens so that he had refused to go below
Fourteenth Street for years). New York, for all its obscenity and abstraction, was still finally a place, and as a place it could still nourish one's
roots, still nourish a poetic.[158]

That same month—on the twenty-ninth—Williams gave a lecture at
Briarcliff Junior College (at Norman Macleod's invitation) on the topic,
"Verse as Evidence of Thought." He also wrote an essay on Cummings'
poetry and another on Karl Shapiro's long *Essay on Rime*.[159] He was
incredibly busy again and looking for some brief respite from it all.
"Someday! Someday!" he wrote Burke in late November,

> no babies will be being born, no one will have a cold, no one will have
> miscarriages—there will be no committee meetings or clinical
> conferences—or cocktails or Anaïs Nin or Shapiro writing about *Rime* or
> rime on the windows or sumack or talks to be given at Briarcliff or printers
> or even Shakespeare to tempt us and torment us. There will be only
> philosophers and bombs.

He quoted a story about one of his expectant mothers, to whom he'd
confided in one of his more sardonic moments that he and she and the
baby and everyone would all probably be "blown to higrade manure"
before her baby was even born, leaving only "a few Esquimaux" behind to
carry on the human race. Maybe those barbarians could do better than
Christianity had done, she'd answered, and Williams had noted the past
tense of her statement. For many people, Christianity had already slipped
into past history.[160]

Williams had had an unexpected wire from Bill Jr. from Seattle of all
places telling him to expect a call (which never came), so that Williams
now suspected that Bill was probably on a transport headed for Tokyo.
Paul, on the other hand, had made it all the way to Tokyo, where an
aircraft carrier had picked him up. By Christmas he was home, though

Bill—being single—would have to wait a few more months for his discharge to come through. Williams talked in his letter to Bill Jr. about the growing importance of penicillin, that new miracle drug, especially in treating the bacterial complications of virus infections, like the "vicious virus infection of the respiratory tract" that was making the rounds at that very moment. He had taken his grandson Paul down to the Hackensack River with Jinny and Suzanne and then, for a special treat, he had taken the three of them over to "a marvelous old-car dump" with "hundreds of junked cars." Young Paul had been beside himself as Williams "paraded him up one alley and down another, old cars on all sides."[161]

When the new proofs for the revised *Paterson* reached Williams in early December, he was still dissatisfied. This time he sent them on to Miller as he'd promised, and he complained to Burke about the failure of the poem under what were to prove rather grotesque conditions. Burke had driven over to Williams' home on Sunday morning, December 9, and together the two men had gone to the office of Williams' colleague, Dr. DeBell, to have a "bull" (i.e., a *taurus palatinus*) removed from Burke's palate. Then, just as DeBell cut into the growth, Williams began to tear apart his *Paterson*. He had failed, he said, and the poem had failed to be realized. He was finished! Through! Poor Burke could do little but listen and wince while Williams carried on, knowing that for this once at least Burke would not be able to demolish him with his sharp-edged tongue. Burke was furious, but unable to argue. A week later he wrote Williams that he had been disgusted with Williams' bad self-advertising. At least Williams might have believed in his own poem.[162]

In January, when Williams had page proofs and could stand back far enough from the poem, he felt much better about it. He was even eager to see it in print, though now he had to wait until a binder could be found for the book. In early May he finally received an advance copy and liked the poem enough to think it might even sell all one thousand copies. He was ready to get on with *Paterson* 2 at once. Finally, after so many years of dreaming and then writing, the event he'd sweated blood for was a reality: a slim volume in white dust cover: *Paterson* 1. Williams had a piece of his giant. Now all he had to do was wait for the critical hounds to begin their baying and decry the formless hoax they would think he had perpetrated against them.

ELEVEN

Intimations of Mortality:
1946—1948

A new world was about to dawn and Williams could sense it rising in all its naked splendor from the ashes of the old nest of Europe. He could sense that new birth in the stirrings everywhere in the world around him, in people's faces, in the recovering economy, in the poetry at that moment being written, in the fact of the New World cities still standing while much of England and Germany and France and Japan lay in burnt embers. His sons had been among the lucky ones, for both had somehow managed to come home again with bodies intact while millions of others—soldiers and civilians—had been shot, burned, bombed, drowned, and maimed. By mid-January 1946 Paul had found a good job in management at Abraham and Straus's department store in Brooklyn and soon he was able to move Jinny and the children out of 9 Ridge Road to give "Floss a break," as Williams put it.[1] Then in February Bill too was back home, doing residency pediatrics at New York Hospital, still single after saying good-by to the nurse he had been seeing, and still concerned foremost with his professional duties. At last the war was over and—except for the troublesome case of his friend Pound —Williams could get on once more with his poetry, including the rest of *Paterson.*

The first book of *Paterson* had been a search for a new form, yes, but even more it had had to come to terms with the other masters in the field of poetry. He had had to contend with Pound and Eliot—those exiles who had fled the new center to find refuge in the "certainties" of Europe. They had gone off to be closer to the vortex of imaginative energies—first to London and then to Paris and then—more problematically—Fascist Italy for Pound. But now the first phase in the modern revolution of the poem which had seen Europe in the ascendancy was over. It lay in ashes like the place from which it had arisen. Now the second phase of the revolution in the word was beginning to make itself felt, and this time it was America that would take the lead.

Williams had already had to deal with his American contenders. He'd dealt with Frost indirectly, setting up his own urban landscape to counter Frost's New Hampshire pastoral, his own language countering Frost's New England nasals and twangs with his own flatnesses. He had had to counter Hart Crane's transcendental leaps, his neo-Elizabethan sonorities alternating with a street slang and colloquialism that outvied Cummings' typographical graffiti. And then, more subtly, he had had to find a counterweight to Stevens' cosmopolitan urbanities, a voice that could contain all the other voices of Paterson and New York as Chaucer's language had contained the world of *Troilus and Criseyde.* But the anxiety such a confrontation had afforded him was—for better or worse —now behind him. He had paid his dues to the masters de-lining the giants in "The Delineaments of the Giants" with his own lines. Now it was up to him to find the "present-day replicas" for his poem not only in his contemporary landscapes but in discovering the new measure in harmony with the language he heard every day but rarely saw in the poems he read.

No wonder, then, he was obsessed with discovering a new poetry in postwar America. He would have to find it—and now—before he could get on with the new parts of *Paterson.* And though he was still hard put to it to point out where in his own poems one could find the new measure, he could sense its presence in the poetry of younger Americans. "The writing of poems is bettering about us of late in a rapidly accelerating degree," he told Vazakas in April.[2] He'd found it, of course, in Vazakas himself, but also in a long poem like Parker Tyler's *The Granite Butterfly*, as well as in some of the poems in Zukofsky's new collection, *ANEW*. Hell, what could the English show the Americans now? Eliot was finished, his diminuendos falling away in the old fixed forms. And Auden: hadn't he come to America hoping to remake himself with the radioactive vitalities of the American language?

As for the French: Mallarmé was good, but only as a halfway house, finally, because he'd been unable to go beyond the "Idea of the Sonnet." He had suggested seeing the poetic line of the sonnet as a single word, but Williams wanted to go beyond that: to see the line not as a unit, not even as a single word, but as a structural invention itself, something completely "fluent." As for the French surrealists: they had "let almost everything go, structurally, in the expectation, perhaps, that when you reach bottom you reach elementary lines." The trouble with the surrealists, however, was that they were so self-absorbed with "dredging up their precious guts" that they had forgotten the question of form, of a new measuring. The only exception he could find to this generalization among the French was Paul Eluard, whose flexible prose cadences—experimental yet still in the French tradition—he would praise to Laughlin a few months later. "It's amazing how the god damned frogs keep to the major line in all their apparent disorientedness," he wrote then. "It puts so much that others do in the shade, makes it cheap, old-fashioned—shucks away so much that is inessential in so much that is done about us. . . . Even my own work seems stale to me after Eluard."[3]

When asked by doubters to actually point to this new measure and new line he was talking about, Williams had turned to lines like these in Tyler's *The Granite Butterfly:*

> Point of the nose
> Long, classic, virile, out
> From the face
> > Nostrils pyramidal
> Flatulent, openings almost
> Level with the bottom
> > > line. . . .

Or the jazzlike cadences, "variations of metric all in one pattern," of

> Slow as the first long look of love
> Slow as the last look
> Slow as the music of a sigh
> Slow as the moment after goodbye
> Slow as the meaning of a dream
> Slow, slow as the dream is quick. . . .

Williams found it too in Zuk's own "No. 42," included in *ANEW*, the one poem—he wrote—that could serve as a keystone for the entire collection. In that poem he had found lines demonstrating the fluidity of modern consciousness, expanding and contracting "physically before the pressure and the speeds of thought":

> You three:—my wife,
> > And the one, whom like Dante,
> > I call the chief of my friends,
>
> And the one who still writes to me—
> > This morning we are in the mess of history,
> > That low crime, and like the devil in the book of Job
>
> Having come back from going to and fro in the earth
> > I will give the world all my hushed sources
> > In this poem. . . .

But where was the new in Williams himself? An older man had come up to him after a talk he'd given in New York in early February to ask Williams to point out where he could find the new in his own work. "It was a fair question," he told Parker Tyler,

> but one I shall have to postpone answering indefinitely. I always think of Mendelejeff's table of atomic weights in this connection. Years before an element was discovered, the element helium, for instance, its presence

had been predicated by a blank in the table of atomic weights. It may be that I am no genius in the use of the new measure I find inevitable; it may be that as a poet I have not had the genius to do the things I set up as essential if our verse is to blossom.[4]

But someone, he knew, someone would one day soon come up with the new line. He had been satisfied that he'd caught something of that elusive animal in *Paterson* 1. But now, a year later, he wasn't so sure. The search for the new measure, he knew, had motivated and colored nearly all of his own critical opinions—his essays, lectures, readings, reviews—for years and would continue to dominate his thinking for a long time yet. It was, really, his one great theme: the scientist—Mendelejeff, Curie—gesticulating into the thin air at something out there to be discovered and invented. If he could write just three lines in that new measure, three lines the day before he died, to prove that a new American poetry really was possible, then he could die feeling his whole life had been justified. Three lines. In another year he would have them, in the step-down triads of "The descent beckons" passage, lines he would point to by which he could measure the work of his old age. Three lines: a pattern, repeated over and over again.[5]

In politics too Williams saw the opportunities for a new revolution. Fascism had been beaten and the Russian revolution was entering its thirtieth year. The two Allies—America and Russia—had managed together to defeat Nazi Germany and Williams was still hopeful in 1946 that they might remain friends in spite of old differences, even as he read about the Army hearings in Washington and watched as the Cold War was already beginning to solidify and freeze the differences between those two nations. In March he'd written a hundred-line poem called "Russia," a poem he liked well enough to think of calling his next book of poems by that title. The Russian people after all had been his greatest hope during the darkest days of the Second World War, and he had praised the courage and determination of these people, who at great personal sacrifice had first turned the German advances at Stalingrad. Williams meant "Russia" as a gesture of fraternal friendship to all the Russians, a hand extended in friendship like those he'd seen the GIs extend to Russian soldiers in Pathé film clips of Berlin and other Allied joinings in the spring of '45. Williams took the broad stand of a Walt Whitman, appealing to the Russian people to look into the great democratic heart of America to see that millions of Americans like himself wanted an end to war and a chance to live —finally—in peace and friendship.

In his poem Williams evoked that meeting in 1925 with Mayakovsky when the Russian poet—one foot on the coffee table in front of him—had half sung, half said his poem about Havana Willie, the words flowing in a torrent of Russian which sounded to Williams for all the world like "the outpourings of the Odyssey." Poor dead Mayakovsky: a suicide, a victim of the revolution: "I have a little paper-bound / volume of his in my attic," Williams wrote, "inscribed by him / in his scrawling hand to our mutual / friendship." Now Williams extended that friendship to include all of the Russian brothers and sisters to "come with me into / my dream and let us be lovers, / connoisseurs, idlers—Come with me / in the spirit of Walt Whitman's earliest / poem, let us loaf at our ease—a moment / at the edge of destruction."[6] And as for the Stalinist purges then going on in Russia? If Stalin was guilty of murder, then of course he would have to be slapped down. But what was really behind the antagonism growing between Russia and the U.S.? Was it a question of two opposing ideologies . . . or was it a bald economic power play between the leaders of the new superpowers all over again?

Yet who was going to listen to *him* talk about such things? "It has become a minor fashion to speak of me, when I am spoken of at all, as a good enough poet but not much of a thinker," he complained that August to Fred Miller. Take those adulators of Eliot at the *Partisan Review* who still dismissed him as "pretty much of a boob where world thought is under consideration." He'd heard all that before, beginning thirty years before with ol' Ezra, whose stance toward Williams was still one of dismissal and condescension, even now that he was behind bars in an institution for the criminally insane.[7]

It was only after Laughlin had been to see Pound in late December of '45 and only after Dorothy Pound had written Williams personally the following month that Williams finally wrote to Pound.[8] He'd told Horace Gregory on February 1 that he hadn't been able to write to Pound until then "either from cowardice or—disgust with him."[9] But on February 4, he finally did write to his old friend, after first composing his letter on a prescription pad. "That you're crazy I don't for one moment believe," he began. "You're not that good an American, and if you're shot what the hell difference does that make in your case: all it means is that you go down into the future intact—your argument undamaged—not too many years left for either of us anyway."[10] Yet he ended his note by saying he was ready to do whatever he could for him. In the letters that followed over the next several months at the rate of about one a week, Pound began quietly enough, though he was soon insulting Williams all over again, this time for the sorry time lag which he thought had stifled his provincial friend's mind. What was the last good book Williams had read? What was he doing now for Wyndham Lewis or for the memory of Ford Madox Ford? What did he really know about economics? What the hell did he know even about history except for the local conditions of a place like Paterson?[11]

By midsummer, it was getting harder and harder for Williams to continue writing Pound. So he complained to Miller on July 15, for example, that Pound had just written to inform him "that none other than I was holding up the works as far as progress in literature was concerned." That was Pound's right to say if he wanted to, Williams was willing to admit, but to say it to "a so-called friend without supporting the argument . . . or even attempting to answer his prior arguments sent me off like a bomb. I cursed him out to my heart's content. Then Floss made me soften it by writing another letter both [sent] in the same envelope. My final diagnosis of that guy is that he's got a blank spot in his thinking which he has exploited all his life as profundity."[12]

And sixteen days later he wrote Pound himself that he was angry with him for his "egocentric irrelevances" and "assumptions of knowledge which I know you well enough to know you do not have." The problem between them now was that their lives had grown too far apart during the years when Pound had stayed abroad, and so all they kept doing now was "talking at cross purposes to no good end." Williams didn't enjoy lashing out at Pound. In fact, knowing the man was a caged animal made Williams relent, ashamed that he'd lost his temper with him.[13] Pound answered stubbornly, defending Mussolini and his own economic position, and ended by telling Williams that if he wanted to die in his "dung of a 25 year TIME LAG" there was nothing that could save him.[14] So once again Williams found himself slamming Pound, this time asking if he needed a toothbrush in his prison to clean his mouth out so that he could speak properly.[15] By the end of 1946, Williams had once again stopped writing Pound completely.

So much for Pound and the right. On the left it was still the *Partisan Review*. Williams had read an essay by Philip Rahv in the August number of *PR* which he saw as one of those fence-straddling pieces that tried to support liberalism by condemning Stalin's national polices. For Williams such a position was untenable because it was too intellectually rigid, too abstract, too "bloodless at heart," and failed to take into account the deep-seated problems the war-ravaged Russians were then facing. The problem with American intellectuals, Williams suggested, was that he could find no love of the Russian people themselves in anything they wrote.[16] It was—though he did not say so—another parallel with those Puritan Americans he'd written of in *In the American Grain* who had also feared to come into physical contact with the local inhabitants themselves. Better to offer salvation or at least a solution while keeping one's hygienic distance.

So in March he'd written "Russia." In May it was another hundred-liner about Russia, this time a poem for voices entitled "Choral: The Pink Church." This poem was meant as a celebration of the new social order that was about to dawn, as he hoped it would, now that the

Russians had had a chance to consolidate their gains. And though this new dawn would have to be announced, as his poem said, "Covertly. / Subdued," Williams felt it was really coming. "It is truly a dawn or the beginning of a dawn for me," he'd told Zukofsky in March.[17] Once he'd thought Pound would be "the dawn" not only for him but for others, like Louis Zukofsky, though Pound had finally let himself "be led astray by baser ambitions than those he so beautifully embodied" in his extraordinary translations.[18] Well, Pound's time was past now. He was merely a shadow of himself, eclipsed by the new dawn, the new in poetry as well as in politics: "Poe, Whitman, Baudelaire / the saints / of this calendar," so his "Choral" had sung.

To hell with this or that partisan revolution, small-minded and restrictive, Williams wrote in his choral. Praise rather to all true revolutionaries of whatever color, praise to the self-reliant ones, praise to the heretics, to all those who had refused to become handservants to the old, refused to become mere "liveried bastards." Even John Milton, that "unrhymer," could be counted among Williams' new calendar of saints at the dawn of the new age, for he too had broken with the established tradition to the point of supporting the execution of the king. Hadn't Milton as a young radical (so Williams believed) also broken with the old metrical traditions with his new verse lines in the *Samson Agonistes*? And then there was that other heretic saint of his: Michael Servetus— Miguel Serveto—Spanish theologian and physician, Williams' personal patron saint from his old Unitarian Sunday school days, a man who'd been burned at the stake for heresy, having managed in his short life not only to alienate the right—the Catholic Church in Spain—but the left as well, in the figures of the Swiss Protestant reformers.

Let all philosophers and philosophy departments do their worst, "wondering at the nature / of the stuff / poured into / the urinals / of custom." Beyond them all, beyond the *Sewanee Review*, beyond even the *Partisan Review*, a rosy-fingered pink dawn was rising to replace that other dawn which had risen two thousand years before over Galilee. It was the beginning of that post-Christian era he sensed in people. It was his own version of Yeats's "Second Coming." But here the voices of Williams' grotesques, the maimed, the "aberrant, / drunks, prostitutes, / Surrealists," as well, yea, as "the fool / the mentally deranged / the suicide" sang *in discordia concors*. It was a vision at least as problematic as Yeats's own, but it was also far more optimistic, as in some Bosch comedy.[19]

"Choral" was not one of Williams' stronger efforts, though it should be remembered that he was writing a musical piece, meant to be set to music and sung by a chorus. Celia Thaew—Louis Zukofsky's wife—did in fact orchestrate the piece, and poem and setting were printed together that fall in the special Williams issue of the *Briarcliff Quarterly*. True to his own ingrained rebel streak, Williams had first insisted on trying his heretical poem out with the *Partisan Review*, thinking he would prove something to himself when they rejected the thing—as they did. Next he sent it to John Crowe Ransom at the *Kenyon Review*, who returned it on the grounds that he preferred Williams "in a different mood."[20] Then Williams gave it to Macleod at the *Briarcliff Quarterly*. "To have that performed adequately would shake the world as far as I'm concerned," he confided to Zukofsky in late July.[21] But—really—he knew better. After all, he was only a poet—an American poet—and therefore not to be taken seriously. Wasn't that the "modern technique" for handling poets: to call them crazy or insane—as with Pound—and thus intellectually and socially castrate them? Ironically, it would be this same strange poem that the press and the FBI would point to in the fall of '52 as evidence that Williams was a "pinko." If they had trouble reading the thing as a poem, at least it could serve as a document.

*
**

So deep was the need to remake himself as he moved into the radiant new dawn of the postwar era that in May Williams decided that from this time on his name would be, simply, William Williams. But that was going too far, Floss said, and she wrote Laughlin within a few weeks to say that "Bill's name *stays* William Carlos Williams."[22] Thus she saved her husband from a kind of ultimate blandness, his Adamic impulse to name, rename, having momentarily gone haywire. The deeper reason why Williams had considered changing his name was, of course, that he was trying to remake himself and begin again with a new poetic—at age sixty-two. At bottom it was another symptom of Williams' need to break down to their constituents the kinds of poems identified with his name. He wanted to split decisively with the past, including even his earlier self, now, while he still had the time.

For already the first chill reminders of his own mortality had come home to roost when, that same month, the physician, the "cutter," as he called himself, suddenly found himself at the other end of the knife. It was the first time in his life he'd ever been a "cuttee," as he jokingly called it in a letter to Louis Zukofsky a few days after he underwent a herniotomy at Passaic General Hospital.[23] He certainly wasn't "looking forward to the experience with any real pleasure," he'd told Bonnie Golightly, though the masochist in him did see imaginative possibilities in the experience.[24] So, at 8:00 AM Wednesday morning, May 1, he was wheeled into an operating room in the same hospital where he himself had served for the past thirty-five years.

The operation, however, was not successful, and Williams mended only slowly and incompletely, so that it had to be done all over again in December—only this time at New York Hospital, where his son Bill, interning there, could look in on him each day. But now, lying here in the predawn the day after his operation, he suddenly felt the terror of growing old, the powerlessness, the inability to be up and around. Somewhere outside, as he wrote in his poem "The Injury," a coal-fed locomotive was rounding a bend. He could hear its soft chugging, the power of it out in that wide world beyond, while he himself lay helpless in a hospital bed. He may have recalled poor Marsden Hartley, dead these last three years, standing on the railroad platform there in Rutherford back in the '20s, saying that all people wanted the power of those big locomotives. But what Williams heard now instead was

> the white-throat
> calling in the
> poplars before dawn, his
> faint flute-call,
> triple tongued, piercing
> the shingled curtain
> of the new leaves;
> drowned out by
> car wheels. . . .

A high-pitched long wail, the screech of the railroad cars about their business, obliterating everything else, including his own voice, mocking Williams, who from here on in would have to learn to take his own curves more slowly. Slowly: "the only way left now / for you."[25]

To Zukofsky, however, he was braver. He'd had a lot of fun lying there in bed, reading Zuk's poems, the Irish poems of Leslie Durkin, and a thirty-five-cent paperback life of Billy the Kid: the iconoclast par excellence whom this other Billy "the Kid" could identify with.[26] "Hope I haven't busted out any sutures these last few days," he wrote from his hospital bed a week after the operation. He'd been spending the time talking and joking with the nurses and replotting his entire life "with the greatest satisfaction" to himself.[27] By May 11 he was home again, though he still felt shaky on his feet. He joked with Roethke that they'd "amputated" his "right ball—or might have if they had slipped," and told him he liked Roethke's new poems—which would appear in *The Lost Child*—very much.[28] They too were signs of that new dawn in American poetry.

In March Williams had also begun work on the third part of his Stecher trilogy as well. Bonnie Golightly had been responsible for that, he told her, because of the way she had praised the first two parts which Laughlin had brought out under one cover a year earlier with the title, *First Act.* "Something about your admiration . . . touched me," he wrote her in early April, so that he found himself becoming really "excited about going on with the story—and did." Six years had already passed since the second part had been written, and now he was suddenly conceiving the last part—"the whole book at a sweep," title and all (*The Build-Up*)—and had then written the first chapter, sixteen pages, without stopping. "That's what the right sort of admiration" could do for him, he told her, adding that he could not work well without it.[29] But that was all he would do with the novel for six more years. In late October he told her that, though her praises had made him "break into song . . . like Sinatra," he'd had to put the novel to bed until he finished the *Paterson* poem first.[30]

As for *Paterson 1*, he was waiting for the initial response to come in in the summer of '46. Ken Burke was one of the first to congratulate him on his achievement, telling him in July that the old blood was still flowing in Williams' veins. Burke's generous response triggered something in Williams, and he told Burke he was excited about getting on with *Paterson 2*. "I don't know how you could have said anything about the poem I'd rather have heard than what you did say," he wrote Burke. "Nostalgia, constipation, achievement, the flower pressed perhaps between the pages of a book but still retaining a suggestion of the color and even (if you put your nose to the press) a faint odor through the dryness."[31] He also thanked Parker Tyler for his early appreciation of the poem, which would be published that fall in the *Briarcliff Quarterly*.[32] And in August he saw Isaac Rosenfeld's short but favorable review in *The Nation*—the first to be published. Rosenfeld had proven "a tremendous help" to him, he told Laughlin, his words forming "a graph, you might say, of my own mind picked up by a neutral and laid out for me in my own terms." A week later he learned—to his astonishment—that Randall Jarrell of all people was doing a long (and favorable) review of his poem for *Partisan Review*! Williams had already taken several potshots at Jarrell in print, calling him several unsavory things, so that he was astonished to learn that Jarrell had decided to praise his poem.[33]

Jarrell's was high praise indeed. He began by calling *Paterson* quite simply "the best thing" Williams had ever written. Here indeed was a "language so close to the world that the world can be represented and understood in it." Jarrell praised the way Williams had juxtaposed the lyric and the homely actual. He praised it too for its thematic strategies, repeated over and over, developed, transformed, echoed "for ironic or grotesque effects in thoroughly incongruous contexts." And he ended by noting that if Williams could keep the level of the next three books up to the level of the first, he would have written "the best very long poem that any American has written."[34] Williams could not have asked for higher praise than that. It was by far the best review the poem was to receive, and even Robert Lowell would point to it as the keynote critical act of attention for *Paterson* that it was. For a while, at least, Williams and Jarrell stood reconciled, feeling even somewhat friendly toward each other, so that Laughlin was convinced that Jarrell would be the man to write the introduction to Williams' *Selected Poems* when that was ready.

Something strange was going on. For the long war he'd waged with the *Partisan Review*, the *Sewanee Review*, and others was suddenly over, or at least the more virulent phase of those hostilities. So, for example, with Allen Tate at the *Sewanee Review*, whom Williams wrote at the end of June, enclosing his essay on Zukofsky's *ANEW*, with the comment that though he and Tate did not have much in common, he thought Tate might still enjoy his essay on Zukofsky's work.[35] When Tate—Eliot's and Hart Crane's old friend—wrote back a month later, it was to say that he'd resigned from the magazine in April and was working at Holt Publishers but that he would definitely have printed the essay otherwise. And when at the same time he asked Williams for a five-year truce, Williams was surprised but glad to accept. Tate asked Williams to look him up when he came into New York on one of his trips, but the two men would get to know each other instead a year later in—of all places—Salt Lake City.[36]

Williams and Floss spent the second week in June at Gratwick Highlands with his friends the Abbotts and Gratwicks. It was the first time in seven years they'd been there, but now that the war was over and gasoline was available once again, Williams could recuperate from his operation in that lovely pastoral setting. Williams loved that place like few others. "It is like nothing I have ever seen in this country," he wrote Kitty Hoagland on the tenth:

> A real farm where a brother and sister both married and with children live on a decayed farm—but carry on their lives effectively. The brother [Bill Gratwick] is a horticulturalist. . . . We are living with the sister [Theresa], who is married to my friend Abbott. The farm is situated nearly sixty miles east of Buffalo which is their nearest city and to which they commute, by car or bus, for work, for music lessons, etc. as though it were Passaic. Too much for me. . . .

He and Floss had an apartment "over the garage near the barn and overlooking the garden and pen for some young ducks, a big gander and two Guinea hens." There were books everywhere, he noted, some eighteen thousand by Abbott's count, enough to actually terrify Williams. But the "most spectacular thing about the place" was the yellow tree peonies blooming everywhere, a specialty of Bill Gratwick's.[37] Before Williams left the farm he'd done three more flower poems, including one called "The Yellow Tree Peony."[38]

Back home in Rutherford, the afterglow of that pastoral interlude disappeared when Williams learned that an old friend and former patient of his—Eleanor Musgrove—had been shot to death by her third husband.

That death, the meanness and pathos of it as rudely closing the small life that woman—like so many others—had lived, disturbed him deeply. In her he saw still another example of what happened to the "beautiful things" of the world. Here was the gist of the joke about the farmer's daughter, like so many of her sisters the victim of neglect, bullying, abuse, and—finally—abandonment. He had seen too much evidence of emotional starvation, physical abuse, and the rest of it to doubt the likeness here.

So when another patient—a mutual friend—returned Williams' books to him, copies of books Williams had given the dead woman over the years, Williams was touched to find one of his old letters—written ten years earlier—still there inside one of his books.[39] In early July, he sent the books and the letter to Abbott for the Lockwood Library in memory of the woman. And soon after he sat down and wrote a first draft of a long short story which he would call "The Farmers' Daughters," sending a carbon to Fred Miller on August 3. What he was trying to write, he told Miller, was another "hot short story such as once made me write for BLAST," though—with the murder trial still coming up—he knew he couldn't risk publishing the thing yet.[40] As it turned out, it would take him another ten years before he could finally find the form he needed to tell the story through his own eyes as well as through the woman's eyes, tell it without falling into the piano, and yet tell it so that the inherent dignity of that outwardly-seeming tawdry life could stand clear.

The Fourth of July weekend the Williamses spent at Greenport, on the eastern end of Long Island, with some old friends who'd moved there from New Jersey. It was a chance to enjoy an old-fashioned clambake and the ocean, which they both loved so much. In early August, instead of going up to West Haven, they took rooms at the Viewcrest, an old farmhouse with four Greek pillars just off the Mohawk Trail up in Charlemont, in western Massachusetts.[41] On the tenth, a week into their stay, Williams wrote Kitty Hoagland that he and Floss were having a good rest "on the brow of this hill overlooking the winding green valley of the Deerfield River." It was a Saturday evening and, as he sat in his room "looking east over a plowed field," he could see lightning flashing across the whole valley in a driving rain. Two young women—Ruth Borklund and Helen Grieder—had decided to leave the Passaic National Bank and start an inn here in the mountains, Williams explained, and through their hard work had made a successful go of the old farm. There was only one male on the premises, Emil Grieder, the eighty-three-year-old father of one of the women, "a charming old Swiss who says almost nothing but smokes his ½ cigar a day after dinner and smiles appreciatively at the women with whom he finds himself surrounded." That was Williams' dream for himself for his own old age, though he did not say so in the letter. He liked to watch the old man puttering about in sleeve garters, "stiff collar, vest and tie," trying to keep District, a mangy cat "with ragged ears and a broken front leg that has healed crooked," out of the house. Up the hill was "an extremely able and intelligent" farmer named Horace Warfield who had befriended the women, and Williams and Floss had taken long walks through Warfield's woods, "discovering the marvels of ferns and small native orchids" about the place. Williams listened to the way the New Englanders spoke, laughing out of a deep admiration for the language he heard here, a language as "superb" and as "rich" as their natures were "wholesome." Even a review of *Paterson* he'd read in one of the Newark papers attacking his poem as incomprehensible had merely left him laughing. "Let 'em flounder" with the thing, he confided. After all, that was part of his intention. He had wanted to "lay down a meridian" to divide the incompetent critics from the ones who could at least see something, so let the bastards break themselves over his poem. That was their problem.[42]

Williams managed to finish an eight-page draft of an essay he was writing for an Australian editor, Flexmore Hudson, on the real differences between himself and Pound when it came to the question of the sources of literary creation. He was thinking, obviously, of what had led him to write *Paterson* and Pound to write the *Cantos*. Pound's reliance on literary allusions as an end in themselves sprang from his insisting that minds begat minds, that, in Joyce's terms, Hamlet had been "out to seek his own father—his spiritual father." For Pound and Eliot and the others, the mind was "a sort of bird bred of air without female or in fact nest of any sort. It leaps ages and places and if it is not perpetuated by fission it at least emerged whole," full-grown, out of the shoulder of the masters. Such men were, finally, the "translators," bringing down the "riches of the ages" to one's own time either by direct translation—as Pound had made Cavalcanti and the Provençal poets and the Anglo-Saxon singers part of American poetry—or by carrying the forms of the past—sonnets, ballads, the blank verse line—over into their own work by extension. In either case, their work had been bred "androgynetically from the classics which father every thought."

But for Williams, of course, a literary source every bit as important as the burden of the past was the flux of the present moment determined at least in part by the "hurly-burly of political encounters." What had set him off writing in this direction had been Arthur Schlesinger, Jr.'s, *The Age of Jackson*, which he'd just read. Schlesinger's comments on literature and the intellectual life in a broad-based democracy had convinced him once again that a new poetic *could* be generated, could be invented "direct from the turmoil . . . or the quietude . . . directly from the form society itself takes in its struggles." First clear the field of the old forms that had accreted over the centuries, as Andrew Jackson had himself done when he took office, and then begin to recreate. For it was one's present that gave birth to the artist and not, primarily, the tradition. In turn the artist took the raw material that was generated "in the political social and economic maelstrom" on which he rode and shaped it. Sure, a poet could live for a period on "a gathered hoard of skills," but that hoard would have to give out eventually, as it had with Pound. And if the poet was to continue to produce new work, if he was not to dry up, then he would have to maintain close attachments to the world that had supplied him with roots. To think that one could cut oneself "off from that supplying female," the language as it was actually spoken, was to dry up, "as Pound did in the end, heading straight for literary sterility." Life was lived, finally, "out of manure heaps" (as he'd also warned Stevens in his poem the year before), those day-to-day stresses that would produce the fragrant flower of the poem.[43]

Now, in postwar America, it was Pound devalued and Williams' stock rising. On Friday afternoon, October 4, Williams made it up on the dais for the University of Buffalo's Centenary Convocation ceremonies to receive his first academic honor: an LL.D. The invitation had come soon after Williams' visit to Gratwick Highlands in June, and though he had asked Abbott to see if that honorary Doctor of Laws couldn't be changed to a Doctor of Letters (it couldn't, they were only giving Doctor of Laws degrees), Williams was "knocked out" by the invitation. He was scheduled for six maternity cases at the hospital in as many days—"at least one of them I myself delivered (by the grace of God and with her mother's legs around my neck) a quarter of a century ago"—and he found it almost impossible to "abandon" these women now, even though he knew the doctor he would be entrusting them to was more skilled than he was.[44]

Finally, Williams decided to race up to Buffalo and then race back home. He and Floss and Bill Jr. took a Pullman sleeper for the overnight run up to Buffalo on Thursday night, went through the ceremonies on Friday and returned that night on the same sleeper, arriving home on Saturday morning. Even so, in the day and a half he'd been gone, "two of the gals had delivered" and another was "in active labor."[45]

"It's strange to be sixty-three and to think of the honors that have recently come my way," he wrote Charles Sheeler a week later as he sat in his office correcting galleys for the *Briarcliff Quarterly* number that would feature him in November:

> It's pleasant but that's about all. I appreciate what is being done and yet, aside from the effects it seems to have on those about me, it seems to have very little meaning for me. Why should it, of course? . . . Many a man has lived and died and could have lived and died twice over having succeeded in his achievements that are a thousand times more important than anything I ever accomplished. . . . At Buffalo on the platform and after-

ward I enjoyed seeing some of the big boys who received honors along with me. I was impressed by their records. For the most part they have been names in newspapers and periodicals for me; it is somewhat startling to realize that they are no more than extremely fallible men and women who, as a matter of fact, hold the world in their hands. . . . The sense of the importance of the artists as a direct influence on men, men who actually carry the world in their hands, awoke in me on that platform.

It was Williams' version of Shelley's mot that poets were the "unacknowledged legislators of the world," and being up there *within* the symbolic and actual vortex of energies had made a difference. One man in particular who had impressed Williams was Vannevar Bush of the Carnegie Institution, "the head of the atomic bomb project," whose energies had helped unleash that terrible energy over Japan a short year before. Up there on the platform he'd told Bush how impressed he'd been by the "sheer accomplishments" of those around him, and Bush had graciously replied that there other kinds of energy as well, such as what it took to create a book. Williams had answered then that had he had the opportunity to know the important men of his time, "as the men of past ages, living in city groups such as Florence, Paris, London," had once lived, that his books would have been all the better. He had had a taste—the merest taste—of the possibilities of an American culture, where living mind might fertilize living mind "by daily conversation and other intimacies."[46] Apparently he saw no irony in the exchange.

But America was not a city-state, after all. It was more like a loose confederation of widely separated centers, and Williams stressed this when he answered R. P. Blackmur's questionnaire about ways in which the American government might support the little magazine and what it represented in this country. Williams' answer took three thickly packed pages together with two additional pages of postscripts. He wanted to see only those little magazines supported that had "the broadest possible basis in the arts—like the old *Seven Arts* or that wonder of the early twenties . . . *The Soil.*" He also added *The Dial* as a model, though he excluded *Poetry*, one magazine he still distrusted. But there were other magazines, of course, that he disliked even more, in spite of their recent softening tone toward him: the *Kenyon Review*, the *Sewanee Review*, the *Partisan Review*, "each with some sort of ax to grind," each with its scholarly editor with his own "prejudices and predilections." What he wanted in place of these magazines were "centers of interests": one out of New York and another in Boston, of course, but also other city centers in Washington, Minneapolis, New Orleans, Augusta, and Chapel Hill.[47]

*
**

On December 13—Friday, as he wryly noted—Williams underwent another operation at New York Hospital to correct the work of the first one. This time Williams knew the surgeon had done his job right, exploring the man/city Paterson and all his "broadways, boulevards and Main Streets . . . not to mention [his] subways and Holland Tubes."[48] They'd "found a big femoral hernial sack," he wrote the nurses at Passaic General, and were going to send it "to the Museum of Natural History for future generations to ponder over." He was being spoiled by the nurses here, "especially the young and beautiful ones—with red hair: or so you are to believe," though he could also see how hard the New York staff—nurses, interns, and all—were worked.[49] Bill Jr. stopped in several times each day to look in on his father while on his own rounds, and Floss had come in to New York whenever she could "to sit quietly and talk" with her husband, which Williams found very soothing. What particularly pleased him, though, was the magnificent view from his bed, sixteen stories above the pavement "overlooking the East River and Welfare Island" in that early winter landscape, with "at night the lights of planes about La Guardia Field in the distance." But it was the river itself, he added, which was his "chief joy." He found himself peering down at it hour after hour; he even thought he could spend the rest of his life in "a little apartment somewhere in this part of the city with the view of that river always at hand."[50] The image of the East River would continue to haunt him, until finally in *Paterson* 4 it would enter the poem itself before it too was swallowed by the Atlantic Ocean and death. And in the manuscripts for that poem written three years later, Williams would house his marvelous *fin de siècle* decadent old lesbian in a penthouse apartment fifteen blocks below New York Hospital on Sutton Place, high over the East River, where, as her nurse masseuse Phyllis so delicately put it, the old bitch could watch the gulls crapping all over the rocks rising out of the river.[51]

Williams was also reading in the hospital, as usual, this time a controversial book Louis Ginsberg (Allen Ginsberg's father) had put him onto called *The Function of the Orgasm: The Discovery of the Orgone*, by Wilhelm Reich, a book he found fundamentally sound in its approach regarding the biological release that occurred in orgasm, and another book which he dismissed as "a psychological phenomenon on the pathological side": Yvor Winters' study of Edwin Arlington Robinson, which New Directions had just published. When he'd finished it, Williams sent it on to Burke from the hospital, telling him to read it as a clinical case study in the pathology of a failed poet (meaning Winters) and then to throw the thing away.[52] He was home again on December 22 and began at once to assemble his notes for *Paterson* 2 and 3, thinking to write them together in one burst of activity. He thought he might even have them both ready before summer. The fourth book, he could see now, would need particular attention, since it would have to deal in a special way with the sense of

ending, especially as the ending of *Paterson* would obviously come to
include his own.

*
* *

In spite of Jarrell's high praise for *Paterson* 1, Williams knew that he
would have to remake the succeeding books in a new mode. This was
critical, for the kinds of verbal and prosodic excellences that a critic like
Jarrell could tabulate were not, finally, sufficient to delineate what it was
Williams was after in the new books of *Paterson*. Jarrell could praise those
elements that an intelligent reader trained in close textual analysis might
be expected to locate with his critical radar. They were excellences,
granted, but they belonged to an established poetic: sharp, incongruous
juxtapositions, ironic understatement, image clusters and leitmotifs
developed on musical lines. But now Williams wanted something more:
the formal means to write an epic that would not be "a diminution from
the Attic or the Renaissance," but something that would present his
readers with the very moods of people as they were lived in his own
moment: something "real, trenchant, to the point and inclusive of the
whole world of our feeling and our minds."[53] Now he would have to show
the discovery of "a new metrical pattern among the speech characters of
the day . . . comparable to but not derived from the characters of past
speech. *For each speech*"—and the stress was Williams'—"*must have
somewhere in it that quality corresponding to the potential greatness of
the environment which engendered it.*"[54] For *Paterson* 2, then, he would
need an idiom discovered in the distinctive locale of Paterson itself.

Much of the material that would go into this book he already had. He
had, for example, those letters from Marcia Nardi which would make up
one-fifth of *Paterson* 2. And he also had those historical documents he'd
gleaned from *The Prospector* newspaper and other local sources, sources
that gave him the story of the Dalzell shooting on Garrett Mountain back
in 1880, the story of the mysterious black animal chased by two cops in
1878, the history of Paterson's downfall caught in the economic scheme
of Alexander Hamilton and his kind with the formation of the tax-free
Society for Useful Manufactories (SUM), a scheme that had turned over
the Passaic River in perpetuity to a handful of Federalist entrepreneurs.
He'd already done an early version of the poor minister's long and ineffectual Franciscan Sermon on the Mount. It was Joyce's Jesuit in *A Portrait of
the Artist as a Young Man* transposed now to this New World Protestant
preaching ineffectually on Garrett Mountain to a few bored captive
children. Williams had even done several versions of the "Wops on the
Rock" scene, Italian-Americans out for a Sunday picnic on the mountain,
marking one of his versions for the entrance of Silenus—that old satyr
from the ancient pre-tragedies—into the world of pastoral Paterson.

During January and February 1947, Williams sifted through the work he'd already composed for *Paterson* 2, including some newer pieces which, in the flux of random words that had floated past him, he'd snagged as being of some possible "interest." So, an essay on "Dynamic Posture" in the Summer '46 number of the *Journal of the American Medical Association* was lifted into the new poem, to serve as an ironic foil to the theme of walking, of foot following foot outward, leaving the track of the new measure. It was one way of walking across the field of the poem. Again, in January '47, a mimeographed throwaway by Alfredo and Clara Studer, attacking the U.S.'s Federal Reserve System, and another throwaway on "Tom Edison on the Money Subject." Then, in February, as Williams fully engaged himself in the ordeal of composition, he took one of Fred Miller's letters about the A-bomb and inserted that too into his poem as another found object. Miller had been complaining about the Senate's attempts to block David Lilienthal's confirmation as chairman of the Atomic Energy Commission, a blockage that would have—in Miller's view—turned the bomb over to a few powerful industrialists, and Williams realized that Miller's letter had touched on several key themes in his own poem: blockage, special interests, energy, Hamilton, and SUM.

Now too Williams turned to Kenneth Burke as he struggled to come to terms with the formal implications of his epic, what he praised Grover I. Jacoby for when—in an editorial in the magazine *Variegation*—Grover had spoken of "the mysteries lying at the metrical core."[55] It was precisely that Williams himself was after: his Kore in hell, the metrical core of his poem. Williams had hoped to enlist Auden in his search for the new poetry, and Auden's friendly manner at a party given by Bonnie Golightly had given Williams the incentive to invite him out to 9 Ridge Road, along with several other "masters," for three days of informal talks about "technical matters relating to modern poetry." For literary models Williams had suggested the choruses of Milton's *Samson Agonistes*, Pound's *Cantos*, Eliot's early quatrain poems, and André Breton's *Young Cherry Trees Secured against Hares*, an experimental book of poems Williams had recently reviewed for *View*. Together Williams had hoped that he and Auden and the others could look at some representative modern poems with the detachment and passion of scientists, and thus clear the field of some linguistic blockage before Williams began work again on *Paterson*. But Auden, essentially a shy man, was probably unnerved by such a procedure and did not bother to answer Williams' invitation.[56]

Williams also wanted to seek out Pound's advice. The problem there, of course, was that he wasn't talking to the man at that point, so that he found himself arguing with Pound's position in a letter he wrote now to himself. Perhaps he was merely "excusing himself," he wrote, "for I do not seem to have succeeded so far in making studies of what I *think* can be done. I write about it in all my so-called criticism, but have not, in my own work, made some practical tests. I just go on writing, which isn't what I want to do." And as for Pound? He was the great translator, especially of the Provençal, making available to English a new musical sensitivity. It was in the later Chinese Cantos, though, where he had worked with ideograms for which he had provided no verbal equivalent, that Pound had gone astray, Williams believed. For Pound had then replaced his earlier emphasis on the sound a poem made with something else: philosophy, economics, a Confucian ethic. But Chinese classical poetry had never really sounded for westerners, Williams insisted, either for Pound or for his readers.[57]

So Williams turned instead to Kenneth Burke, even though he knew from long experience that Burke's participation in such a dialogue would be more problematic, leaving the field of composition more frequently to engage in more abstract and theoretical rhetorical procedures. The correspondence with Burke had begun with a discussion of Reich's *Theory of the Orgasm*, which Burke had read only in the excerpts he'd seen in the *New Republic* and which Williams for his part had only skimmed. No matter. Williams had read enough to see that Reich had managed to unravel several "knots of old confusion" about human sexuality that had baffled him for years. What was more important, though, was that Reich had given Williams the chance to attack Freud's theory of art as rooted in the sublimation of the sexual drive. Reich, Williams could see, was "in no sense an off-shoot from Freud like Jung or Adler but remained Freud's staunch defender to the end." And yet he too had come out against Freud's theory of aesthetic sublimation which held that the artist, "unable to satisfy his sexual impetus *diverts* it into music." This for Williams had always been "the bunk," and Reich had confirmed his own belief that art was more than a neurosis. All Reich had done, after all, was to reason from observed, clinical data, and you couldn't go far wrong "in following a man's discoveries from his objective findings, step by step, to his conclusions in the field."[58] Which was exactly what Williams would ask his own readers to do when, in the opening of *Paterson* 2, he began to metaphorically walk across the open fields on Garrett Mountain, leaving his tracks there for others to follow, step by step, as best they could.

Burke was after other game, though, attacking Reich for confusing biological pathology with politics. Williams backed off from the argument at that point, because that argument was of no practical use for him in what he was personally after. Within a few days he was chafing once again under the weight of Burke's logical constructions, preferring instead to dismiss all logic in what was at heart an illogical world. Trying to argue with a rhetorician of Burke's stature, he quipped, was like "fiddling with the keys of a piano" when all *he* could play was the violin. Burke had an unfair advantage over him, he complained, as he retreated now into an intellectual know-nothingism. He knew what he wanted—the poem —and Burke was merely getting in the way. For when it came to the field of the poem itself, he warned Burke, he had so developed his own resources that he did not think he would be overtaken by *any* critic. That was why he had wanted to work with a poet like Auden in the first place: to "avoid all the amateurishness of the usual poetry magazines, cut out the empty 'criticism' that such magazines deal in (especially *Poetry*), completely sidetrack metaphysics, philosophy, and all such side issues and get down . . . to the skillful making of poems." In that way "reams of incompetencies" might be "wiped out in a day and some sort of basis for a true criticism of poems as technical constructions" could be reached.[59]

What Williams wanted instead was some meta-field where poetry and philosophy might merge. Logic was small potatoes in the field he was looking for, and "meaning" was beside the point. What *was* important was how ideas were embodied in the very fabric of the poem itself, in the way a poem said itself. For only there could poetry be said to live. "Without invention," he would say in *Paterson*, "nothing is well spaced, / unless the mind changes. . . ." But now Burke picked up the cudgels, asking Williams what in hell he meant by separating out philosophy from poetry. Williams, seeing where Burke's argument was heading, made a strategic retreat from that position as well, perhaps thinking of Washington moving off New York to win at Monmouth. Oh, philosophy was all right, he told Burke on January 31, as long as it kept its hands off "the difficult art of getting said in verse" what could only be said *in verse*, the first thing to evaporate when the philosophers dissected the poem trying to isolate the poem's "meaning." And yet, though he wanted Burke to keep hands off, he could also acknowledge the possibility of a dance of sorts where the philosopher's language might move contrapuntally against the poet's, neither partner seeking to upstage what the other wanted to say, each respecting and observing the boundaries of the other's space.[60]

On February 5, Williams began another letter to Burke on the question of form. Of course a poem had a meaning, he wrote, but in a living poem that meaning lay "in the structure" or at least was "*in*structed by the fact of the poem itself as a structure. . . . It is, in a poem, something as it is in music—tho' not just music (vide Swinburne's failures). . . ." And there Williams stopped writing, turning the page over, and used the verso as his title page for *Paterson* 2.[61] Williams had complained to Zukofsky a few days earlier that he was having trouble beginning the poem.[62] Now, a sufficient pitch of desire kindled, he began to walk across his pages, composing, *in*structing his thoughts (concretely) upon the body of his female, Garrett Mountain, stroke after stroke.

The night before he had written the original Mr. Paterson, David Lyle, asking after Lyle's wife, Mary, then lying near death of cancer in a hospital bed in Paterson General. "I'm almost afraid to ask you, but —How is Mary?" he wrote apologetically, realizing that the death of Mary was in one sense the death of Paterson's wife, and therefore of the woman in *Paterson*. "Would she want to see me," he asked now. "It's late, my trained imagination doesn't help me in any way." He had thought of the two of them and of their plight every day, but he'd "shrunk from calling on the phone or even sending a letter." Yet, having experienced two operations himself in the past eight months, he had come to "think hard of the fate of others, that even after they have been treated to the best of all abilities" they had to realize that they had "not been basically cured."[63] That was the lesson he had learned long ago. The only consolation he and Lyle could share was that in Mary's death, the spirit, the imagination, might be set free. Lyle, standing over his dying wife, would exorcise the cancer in Mary's throat, as Lyle and Mary believed, so that the doctors would be astonished to find the cancer gone when Mary died. Williams' "trained" imagination could not accept such an occurrence but instead sought to respond to her death by writing a song that would conquer that death. He would call the song *Paterson* 3.[64]

Just as the impetus for *Paterson* 2 and 3 was coming to a head, he was elected president of the Medical Board at Passaic General. "I tried to get out of it," he told Laughlin in early February, "but nobody would listen to me. The more excited I get over Part II the more I am in despair knowing the work involved. I feel isolated and browbeaten—but I am thrilled with what I have mapped out. A good sign I suppose."[65] It *was* a good sign, and two days later he had made a major breakthrough in getting the scheme of the poem down on paper.[66] By the nineteenth he was "stripped down for action and enjoying" himself, at moments frightened by the poem before him, and at other moments elated.[67] Now, like a plant forcing every other thing aside, he immersed himself in writing, "neglecting Flossie and nearly everything else," he admitted, "including reading, but my practice of Medicine—unremunerative as I seem bent on making that."[68] The poem actually had him "sleepless" so that he had "to believe the Guy up THERE is working on it." By then—March 6—he had compiled a full version of the poem and had only to cut it back "to workable limits."[69] In little more than a month he had managed to assemble a ninety-page manuscript from materials he'd gathered over the years, together with the writing he did now. He would have to retype the entire poem himself and try to determine whether the thing was good or merely "a redundant heap of garbage."[70] He had the outlines and many of the details completed, and he even had his new measure: a line with a triple measure based on a modulated and sophisticated use of the caesura based in turn on the classical notion of quantity. He had even composed one passage that, in retrospect, would stand as a real milestone for him, though he did not realize this at the time. It was the "descent" passage using a step-down triple measure, such as he would use over and over again in the early '50s, and in part the passage looked and sounded like this:

> The descent beckons
>   as the ascent beckoned
>   Memory is a kind
> of accomplishment
>   a sort of renewal
>   even
> an initiation, since the spaces it opens are new
> places
>   inhabited by hordes
>   heretofore unrealized,
>   of new kinds—
>   since their movements are towards new objectives
> (even though formerly they were abandoned). . . . [71]

"For myself," he wrote Burke on March 17, with all but the scaling down of *Paterson* 2 behind him, "I reject almost all poetry as at present written, including my own. I see tendencies, nodes of activity, here and there but no clear synthesis. I am trying in *Paterson* to work out the problems of a new prosody—but I am doing it by writing poetry rather than by 'logic' which might castrate me." He meant to think with the poem and not with a preconceived master plan, going where the poem led him.[72] That was why Burke had so badly miscalculated when, in late February, he'd sent Williams an outline and summary of the *Aeneid* to suggest how Virgil might have proceeded. Williams had laughed at that, for he could not bring himself to believe that anyone could compose in the fashion Burke had ascribed to Virgil. Afterward, sure, the poet might fool around inside the poem like a "squirrel in a box of birdseed" looking for something. But not while the heat of composition was upon him.

No, Williams decided, that was not how Virgil had worked. What he had probably done was just what Williams himself had done. Virgil—like Williams—had been "an alert and intelligent citizen of his times and besides a gifted poet" who had seen the need and the pleasure in the act of creating his epic. It was a complex pleasure he must have felt to make a poem with history in it—"sensual, sociological, historical." And he might have "indulged in a bit of logical philandering," but that was all. No, the poet had to avoid prior patterns at all costs. No use following a map for this *Paterson*, no matter how well intentioned. It was dangerous to follow the critic while the poet was walking across the field of the poem. If he followed Burke's—or any critic's—advice in the making of the poem, he would "inevitably be of little use to the very philosopher himself as a field of investigation" once he'd "completed his maneuvers."[73]

*
**

In *Paterson* 2, the male poet—Williams' double—walks along the back of his female giant, stroking the despised ground under his feet into a counterresponse. As he walks he listens, trying to hear what the woman struggles to articulate beneath all the other voices, all talking at cross purposes, all divorced from each other. Williams' need is to present with unrelenting accuracy and the prosaic flatnesses all about him the unrelieved quotidian bleakness everywhere in this modern "pastoral." It is a working-class Sunday in the park, and Williams has made "the aesthetic shock occasioned by the rise of the masses on the artist" felt in the very drabness of the language. To capture a scene known in one form or another to millions of working-class Americans looking for some momentary respite by escaping to the illusory Edens of crowded public parks with their gravel paths and chlorine-treated pools, where families stake out eight hours of squatters' rights beneath some maple or chokecherry or viburnum, where twelve- and fourteen-year-old boys watch young couples lying on army-surplus blankets from their hiding places in the bushes: this was Williams' business in his epic. Theodore Dreiser and James Farrell had done this kind of American scene in their prose fiction, but it was Williams who would bring it into his poem in this pathetic diminuendo of *Paradise Lost*. But he would do so with a distinctively modern music, the slightly elevated diction echoing an old music, a dying cadence not without its own dignity:

> At last he comes to the idlers' favorite
> haunts, the picturesque summit, where
> the blue-stone (rust-red where exposed)
> has been faulted at various levels
>   (ferns rife among the stones)
> into rough terraces and partly closed in
> dens of sweet grass, the ground gently sloping.
>
> Loiterers in groups straggle
> over the bare rock-table—scratched by their
> boot-nails more than the glacier scratched
> them—walking indifferent through
> each other's privacy . [74]

And here on Garrett Mountain, with each slight rise in our expectations as we follow Dr. Paterson through the old fields, there is a descent, a fall, as—time after time—people rise for a moment from the dream of their lives only to fall back into their insulated selves. It is a world we purposely avoid staring at, as we walk past this Adam and Eve piteously and pathetically attempting to communicate with each other and failing. So with Williams himself, seeing his own parents in that primal scene, seeing too his own life with Floss, stealing time again and again away from being with her, from their boys, from his friends, even his patients when he could, that he might write, and write well—at what cost to all of them.

To pursue what? Like Stevens, the "core of gaiety," Kore, the female of his imagination, the perfect woman. So here, at the center of *Paterson* 2: a mythic scene older than literature itself, older than Theocritus, repeated here atop this ancient, obsidian upthrust. The revelation of the woman beyond naming in the act of dancing:

> *Here a young man, perhaps sixteen,*
> *is sitting with his back to the rock among*
> *some ferns playing a guitar, dead pan*

Dead pan, this young Italian-American, one of Williams' immigrants in the New World, the figure of Pan, the goat-footed demigod of the old pre-tragic, ribald one-act plays, older than Greek tragedy itself, caught momentarily as in a frieze. And then, out of that stasis: a movement, a whirring of wings, an annunciation, as Mary—in her traditional black dress—brings to this scene a language of her own, a local dialect, a variant of English in a world where the English, like the fellow in English tweed grooming his collie, are conspicuously silent, and where the voices we hear belong to young black girls, or to an Italian woman or a Scandinavian preacher. It is the language in its raw, virulent local idiom.

And now, as Mary begins to dance, the language too catches fire, the dance of the language moving with its own grace in time to the gaiety of the woman's steps:

>   *but Mary*
> *is up! Come on! Wassa ma'? You got*
> *broken leg?*
>   *It is this air!*
>   *the air of the Midi*
> *and the old cultures intoxicates them:*
> *present!*
>   *—lifts one arm holding the cymbals*
> *of her thoughts, cocks her old head*
> *and dances! raising her skirts:*
>   *La la la la!*
> *What a bunch of bums! Afraid somebody see*
> *you?*
>   *Blah!*
>   *Excrementi!*
>   *—she spits.*
> *Look a' me, Grandma! Everybody too damn*
> *lazy.*[75]

"Look a' me, Grandma!" Williams has Mary say, though it is a private joke as well, Williams invoking his own first muse, his Grandmother

Wellcome, who had taught him the language. And the gesture, identical with the dance everywhere, as in the image of the goddess older than the others—Shiva, her head too cocked, hand held high with cymbals (symbols), dancing, though she does not know it, with the poet who has discovered her here and dances her into the heart of his poem. It is the divine pagan pattern, "the old, the very old, old upon old," so old that it can serve as one of the cores of gaiety for Williams' New World epic. Against this backdrop, Eliot's and Leavis' and Blackmur's six-hundred-year-old English tradition falls away into insignificance. It is an older music Williams is after, one imaginatively con-sonant with the cave dwellers of Altamira and—conversely—a newer music—realized only by coming in contact with the female of his own world, the real world under his feet. His world transfigured momentarily on his holy mountain.

*
* *

With the heavy work of *Paterson* 2 behind him, Williams could come downstairs again to touch bases with his world. The journals and magazines had been collecting again—"so many books from this one and that with letters sometimes asking me to comment on them that I just can't move," he complained—and he and Floss had been forced to carry piles of them up into the attic unread "to remain in a pile somewhere about until I'm dead." He'd been keeping up with Pound's *Pisan Cantos* as they appeared one by one in the little magazines, but he had not really been much impressed. There were of course "good passages here and there" as in everything Pound wrote, but these seemed "woefully repetitious," without any "new departure anywhere or any new lead in construction or enlightenment"; in fact it was "pretty sad stuff." Pound still remained devalued.

On the other hand, there was "a mass of stuff" in the little magazines, original poetry and some first-rate translations which, taken together, were "breathtaking." There was, for example, a young black writer from Chicago named Paul Bland who'd sent Williams a short novel which Williams had found "excellently written and a hot story." But against the "shrewd boys" like Steinbeck and Hemingway, Williams could see, young writers like Bland didn't stand a chance—at least in the commercial market. No, the market was split between the "brass-knuckle" gang on the one hand, and the "university, world-weary boys" like Eliot and Jarrell and St. John Perse on the other. And somewhere in the middle were amateurs like himself, destined to pull in at most a few hundred dollars a year for good work while Hemingway had made 125,000 Depression dollars for *For Whom the Bell Tolls* alone. And as for the future? Williams could see his own grandchildren—as he'd seen his own sons—have their "marvelous aptitudes" blasted to hell by some "sterile bitch of a schoolteacher" for the "next miraculous twenty years or more." Lies and shit were still everywhere around him, as now in the newspapers Americans were being forced to choose between one abstraction called "Russia" and another called—grandly—"Democracy." And these were the same newspapers that had saluted the Russian people just two years before as America's ally![76] Nothing, he told Macleod, "nothing could be more false—or more vicious in preventing the truth from even coming up to be seen, much less acted on."

He was certainly aware that Stalinist Russia was forcing a "mental succotash" on its people, but the deep freeze that America was settling into with regard to all things Russian in the period following the war frightened him.[77] He'd just read some of the neorealist fiction by the younger generation of Italians—many of them on the left—and had found them free in a way that Russian—and American—writers were not. Would that he, in America, could "smash the hell out of where I am" as some of these Italians had, though he knew all too well that the only possible avenues open to him for doing anything effective were caring for the sick and writing.[78] He wanted to escape the special interest groups surrounding him on all sides, to escape the non-news he heard every day in the newspapers and the best-sellers. Wasn't that why those forms were so popular, he wrote in a short essay at this time called "Revelation": that they merely reiterated the kinds of things people had already heard a thousand and a thousand times and so—for all their deathly grimness —had become palatable, even safe? Rather than being released to develop according to their own inner grain, Americans were being weighted down, frightened—as their Puritan forebears had been before them—by rumors of so many external dangers that they had had to close up on themselves like so many clams "in order to be able to survive under the new order." Williams was convinced that the Cold War was, finally, an impoverished imaginative construction, one more witch hunt, and he hated what he saw it doing and what it would do, not only to his generation, but to the young generation just then beginning to grow up. He could smell big money and special interests—Usury—all over again.

He wanted a slackening of the reins, not a tightening, so that the child might grow in his or her mold and the woman be allowed to escape "the domination of childbearing" that she might have the time to free up her mind. Such a freeing could uncover hidden revelations about the self and so "restore values and meanings to our starved lives." Williams' basic affinity with Dewey's liberal philosophy—his dissatisfaction with all forms of oppression, like procrustean educational practices, the recidivism of many of his colleagues in the medical profession who had steadfastly refused to allow women a choice in the use of contraceptives, his own refusal to turn the other way when he saw evidences of wife beating and child abuse—all this had come through untouched, despite his political differences with Dewey. In '47, these were still avant-garde ideas in his part of the world, as avant-garde as his search for a new measure.[79]

Williams set the end of May as his deadline for getting *Paterson* 2 to Laughlin and, though he was having his "troubles holding up under the schedule that makes it possible to write at all—convinced at the moment that my right arm is becoming rapidly paralyzed," and afraid that in his present frame of mind he was going "to vaccinate somebody right smack on the ass hole"—he did manage to finish on time.[80] Besides, he had to finish now, since he'd just accepted an invitation to give a paper on the "new poetry" at a week-long conference to be held in Salt Lake City in July and he would need to keep June as free as possible to write his paper.[81] Allen Tate would be there, and though they had a five-year truce in effect between them, Williams was sure that was nothing more than a thaw in the cold war between himself and the university boys. He found himself studying Saintsbury's tomelike *Manual of English Prosody* now to be ready to answer—as he could—whatever objections the academic community assembled in Salt Lake City might bring against his talk of a new measure. He did not, as he told Burke, want "to be caught with my pants too far down on technical matters."[82]

He earned the five hundred dollars they gave him for his part in the conference many times over as he prepared his talk. He told Miller at the end of May that he was going to call it "Our Formal Heritage from Walt Whitman," though he finally settled on the title "An Approach to the Poem." One of the key texts he would use would be one Louis Zukofsky had suggested to him as representative of Whitman's free verse, "Respondez," the text of which Williams included in his talk. He was still revising that talk on the eve of his departure, even as he and Floss and Charlotte, an old veteran at driving cross-country, started out in the overhauled '41 Buick on Saturday morning, June 28, bound for the West. It was only the second time Williams had ever been west of the Mississippi (and the first time for Floss), and they were both looking forward to the prospect of experiencing that world for themselves. That Saturday they drove up to Gratwick Highlands to see Charles Abbott and the Gratwicks, staying over until Monday morning, June 30. Then, after saying good-by, they began the trip west in earnest, nosing the Buick down through Pennsylvania, across Ohio, Indiana, Illinois, Iowa, then through Nebraska and Utah, covering four hundred miles a day. Finally, they reached Salt Lake City, parched and dusty, on Saturday evening, July 5, so that Williams had one day to rest up before the conference began the following Monday morning. That long six-day drive had given Williams his first chance to see a whole new area of his America for the first time, and the small western towns cropping out of those primitive, overwhelming landscapes had impressed him so much that even New York seemed "pretty dim compared to those strange places and creatures." For an easterner that was saying something. The desert especially had touched something deep within him. It was "something not to be imagined," he would write, and he was glad to be able to "soak that away" in his "coco" as he drove across its dwarfing landscapes—mile after mile after mile—under a blazing sun.[83]

The conference itself ran for two weeks, from Monday the seventh until Friday afternoon, the eighteenth. Like the other featured speakers, Williams' task was to give one formal lecture and then to act as literary adviser to some of the 110 students "of all ages who paid their good money to hear us." And, along with Tate and Ray West, Mark Shorer and Walter Van Tilburg Clark, Brewster Ghiselin and Eric Bentley and Carolyn Gordon, all his "teaching pals," as he called them, he and Floss stayed at one of the empty sorority houses on the campus.[84] He noted with secret pleasure that he was the only non-university person there, "which put me on my mettle," as he phrased it, to make up in emphasis what he lacked in knowledge. And despite his well-known anti-university stance, he was secretly glad too when the others accepted him.[85]

The thing that had really brought him west in July, however, was the promise of public exposure that such a literary forum seemed to promise. He'd been in the advance guard of modernism now for thirty years, and he wanted his poems given a hearing by the academy and the formulators of the New Criticism. And what he told the Salt Lake City group was this: that unless they found forms fitted to their own times, they would remain derivative writers, a voiceless people. Walt Whitman, he told them, was their only lead as Americans. If they looked at the opening lines of "Song of Myself," they would find there Whitman's declaration of independence from the British tradition of the iamb, "the cry of a man breaking through the barriers of constraint IN ORDER TO BE ABLE TO SAY *exactly* what was in his mind." It was not Whitman's language he wanted to point to, however, for that was merely some kind of "universal Esperanto" long out of date. No, it was rather in his "formal imperative" that Whitman had had "to rebegin a literature, disengaging its formal elements from past fixations." He offered them Whitman's "Respondez" as an example of the kind of relative measure he was looking for, lines disciplined by their parallel syntax, yet capable of expanding and contracting at will:

> Let the old propositions be postponed!
> Let faces and theories be turn'd inside out! let meanings be freely criminal, as well as results!

> *Let there be no suggestion above the suggestion of drudgery!*
> *Let none be pointed toward his destination! (Say! do you know your*
> *destination?)*

Once a form had reached its perfection, as the blank verse had in Shakespeare's handling of it, there was no alternative but to break that line down again into its constitutive elements and then begin again to build toward some other form. The poetic forms of the past belonged to the past, the river of history had receded, leaving behind old poems in all their perfection "like complex shells upon a shore," shelly rimes, Shelley rhymes, as he would pun in *Paterson* 3. White-hot men had "lived in those poems as surely as fish lived in the shells we find among the fossils of the past," he added, but those men were no longer there. Still, Whitman had shown the way out, a voice crying in the desert. Now it was up to Williams and others to locate and define the "new element" that Whitman had pointed to in breaking down the linguistic pitchblende of his own day.[86]

The other precursor who was very much on Williams' mind that summer was—of all people—Robert Bridges, whose "Testament of Beauty" Williams had earlier discovered. Williams was fascinated with Bridges' experiments with a quantitative verse coupled to Hopkins' modified sprung rhythm. And those rhythms kept haunting Williams' ear even as he drove south and east after the conference was over to view the imposing ruins of the Cliff Dwellings at Mesa Verde. Settled in his hotel room in Cortez, Colorado, Williams copied out the opening lines of Bridges' poem, filling in the spaces between the lines with lines of his own, equivalents, he hoped, for the quantitative music he'd heard in Bridges. He called his poem "The Testament of Perpetual Change," thus underscoring the fierce need he felt to locate his own music in his own America:

> *Mortal Prudence, handmaid of divine Providence*
> *hath inscrutable reckoning with Fate and Fortune:*
> *We sail a changeful sea through halcyon days and storm,*
> *and when the ship laboreth, our steadfast purpose*
> *trembles like as a compass in a binnacle.*

Thus Bridges. And Williams:

> *Walgreen carries Culture to the West:*
> *At Cortez, Colorado the Indian prices*
> *a bottle of cheap perfume, furtively—*
> *but doesn't buy, while under my hotel window*
> *a Radiance Rose spreads its shell. . . .* [87]

There were other sights he remembered on the trip home, including several Indian women, one in the shadow of the Sangre de Cristo mountains,

> *walking*
> *erect, the*
> *desert animating*
> *the blood to walk*
> *erect by choice*
> *through*
> *the pale green*
> *of the starveling*
> *sage. . . .* [88]

And the other, farther east,

> *a half-breed Cherokee*
> *tried to thumb a ride*
> *out of Tulsa, standing there*
> *with a bunch of wildflowers*
> *in her left hand*
> *pressed close*
> *just below the belly. . . .* [89]

From the Hotel La Fonda in Taos, New Mexico, Williams wrote Laughlin on Monday night, July 21, that he and Floss had driven out to Pueblo to shop for gifts for their grandchildren and to see Kit Carson's house—typical American tourists seeing a place for the first time. But with his artist's eye he'd spotted a very beautiful and primitive nine-paneled red, black, and white wooden screen in the east transept of the little church at Rancho de Taos. It was the kind of authentic local work he was always looking out for, like Shaker furniture or American primitive paintings. Then, in the afternoon, he and Floss had driven out to see D. H. Lawrence's widow, Frieda. For Williams it was an act of homage to the dead Englishman whose work had meant so much to him, and whose review of *In the American Grain* twenty years before had led Williams to write Lawrence, though Lawrence had never written back. Now, as he sat talking with Frieda and her daughter, Williams casually mentioned the elegy he'd written ten years before to the memory of her husband. She was sorry, she told him, but she'd never seen it. Williams promised to "dig up" a book that contained the poem and to send it on.[90] And, thus, quietly, awkwardly, ended the meeting that would bring him as close as he would ever come to Lawrence's presence.

Next day the Williamses met up with Bob McAlmon in Taos and together they drove down as far as Santa Fe, talking over the old times in New York and Paris and about how McAlmon's writing was going. But Williams' eye was too sharp not to see that his old friend was deep in a tailspin. He was pale with tuberculosis, drinking too much, and still eking out an erratic living at his brothers' medical supply firm. Nor was he doing much writing. The old Paris days and the days of *Contact* and the old associations with Joyce and Stein and Pound and Eliot and Hemingway and the others—the days of being geniuses together—were over for McAlmon. Williams could feel it in the air, the faint scent of mortality in this man a dozen years his junior, though he kept his own counsel. And then there was the trip back home and McAlmon's face a shadow receding into the distance. They drove on through the heat of the Texas Panhandle on Route 66, on through Oklahoma City and Tulsa and St. Louis. By nightfall on the twenty-seventh, the old Buick pulled up the short incline of the driveway at 9 Ridge Road. The trip west was history.

Home again, Williams began seeing his patients once more and trying to sort out his mail. Babette Deutsch, the poet-critic, had written to ask Williams about his intentions in *Paterson*. She was eager to see something of Paterson's history of labor violence, but Williams wrote to tell her not to look for that kind of thing. He was after something else in his epic, and he was not interested in repeating what he'd already done thirty-five years before in "The Strike" section of "The Wanderer." Besides, the history of the people who made up Paterson had already been written in all those short stories he'd published since the early '30s. As for the social unrest that had marked that city since the nineteenth century, yes, that was inextricably woven into the very fabric of his poem as it was in the people themselves: the unrest and "economic distress occasioned by human greed and blindness—aided, as always, by the church, all churches in the broadest sense." Yet he reminded her that he was not a Marxist and that she should not expect to find a Marxist resolution to the problems presented in *Paterson*.[91]

He took off early Friday, August 8, and picked up his mother and her nurse, Mrs. Taylor, at the nursing home nearby and then drove up to West Haven to spend the day and get some swimming in. The following day he took Floss in to New York to see their team, the Giants, play Chicago. It was a bad game, he had to admit, and his Giants had stunk. "The only thing that saved the game from any point of view except a Chicago point of view," he told Bill, was Johnny Mize's homer. That man seemed "to pack a really terrific wallop which not he himself seems to understand." The following morning—Sunday—he took his two grandchildren for a ride up Garrett Mountain to go blackberrying, but it was so foggy he could see nothing. As for his pediatrics, he wondered aloud what it was about his role as a doctor that had people confessing to him all the time with their "psychiatric stuff, . . . infidelities, late syphilis and Freudian obsessions." But there it was, and he did what he could to listen.[92]

Williams had also found Robert Lowell's review of *Paterson* 1 in the current issue of the *Sewanee Review* on his return home and had written Lowell on August 6 to thank him. Lowell had written that there was "no living English or American poet" who had "written anything better or more important," and yet *Paterson* had caused "no stir either in the little magazines or in the commercial press." Taking his cue from Jarrell, Lowell also praised the poem's complex musical organization, especially for having somehow managed to use short imagist lyrics to tie a long poem together. Next to *Paterson*, Lowell realized, almost the whole range of modern poetry looked "a little secondhand." And if there was any defect, Lowell noted apologetically in a footnote, it was only that "human beings exist almost entirely in the prose passages."[93] Williams took note of that observation, and took care to correct it, especially in *Paterson* 4.

Eight months earlier Williams had agreed with Roethke that Lowell was both "turgid" and "dull."[94] But he changed his mind now as the correspondence between himself and Lowell began to flourish. In September Lowell invited Williams to come down to Washington in October to do another recording for the Library of Congress and Williams in the meantime busied himself reading Lowell's own American poems in *Lord Weary's Castle*. He was especially struck by Lowell's ability "to mention local place names"—names like Nantucket and Woods Hole, 'Sconset and Madaket, Black Rock and Martha's Vineyard—"without that jumping out of context which so often occurs to make a work false sounding." Williams had learned himself how hard it was to "treat of American things and name them specifically without a sense of bathos." Stephen Vincent Benét, for example, writing of John Brown and Harpers Ferry, had not escaped that bathos. And even Thoreau, Henry Adams, and Henry James had not always escaped that charge when talking of American places. For Lowell had managed to handle the American scene in lines like these:

> When the whale's viscera go and the roll
> Of its corruption overruns this world
> Beyond tree-swept Nantucket and Woods Hole
> And Martha's Vineyard, Sailor, will your sword
> Whistle and fall and sink into the fat?

Perhaps, Williams suggested, it was because Lowell had "anchored" his "data in ground common to Europe and to Christianity—if that has to be."[95] But Williams too had escaped a similar bathos in his own *Paterson*, partly by refusing to name his American places—and then only where the documents themselves required his doing so—but more because he rigorously eschewed any nostalgic layering in the names he did evoke. Beyond that, Paterson and its environs did not lend themselves to a very wide range of emotional resonances, as New York or Boston or Nantucket or New Orleans might have. There was, really, very little in the way of a natural emotional groundswell in the evocation of a "swillhole" like Paterson.

The fall was a quiet time for Williams after the fury of creativity that had marked February and March and June, and once again he waited impatiently for another part of *Paterson* to appear. He was invited to read his Salt Lake City address before a distinguished group of professors at the annual English Institute meetings held at Columbia University and he read it straight through without deviation or expansion on Wednesday night, September 10, in Columbia's airless, heated Faculty Club. He had been nervous enough before he started, but by the time he finished, seventy minutes later, he was sweating and eyeing some of the professors there who were making it clear by the way they glared at him that they had not been well pleased. "Fuck 'em," he thought; as far as he was concerned, he'd just given the "best talk of the whole two-week session," and if they couldn't see that, they could all go to hell.[96]

On the first Saturday in October, Williams, Floss, and Charlotte drove up to Cummington, Massachusetts, to enjoy the fall foliage and give Williams another chance to talk with Duncan and Williams about the printing of *The Clouds*. Then, on Friday, the seventeenth, he drove with Floss down to Silver Spring, Maryland, to stay at Jim Hyslop's farm there, the Cameronia, before driving into Washington next morning to meet Lowell at the Library of Congress for his recording.[97] And being in Washington meant, of course, being very near "the author of *Jefferson and/or Mussolini*." For Pound was still at St. Elizabeth's, as he had been, in fact, for nearly two years. And in all that time Williams had avoided going to see him. The truth was that Williams had been afraid to see his old friend. Eight years had passed since that summer of '39 when Pound, bundled in sweaters and traveling incognito, had tried to talk sense into Roosevelt and the Congress. Whenever he thought of Pound now he thought of the crazed face of the beast in Cocteau's surrealist film *Beauty and the Beast*. There'd been enough madness in his own family, especially with Godwin, and scenes—ugly scenes—when his own father had cried out that some power of evil was loose in the Williams house—to scare Williams away from those unknown places in the mind that he could not bring himself to explore for very long.

But now he was in Washington for the first time since Pound had been sent to St. Elizabeth's and he could not in conscience any longer avoid going to see him. He had not told Pound that he would be in Washington, thus leaving the option open of not seeing him. But, after leaving the NBC studios—where the recording had finally been made—Williams hailed a taxi for the twenty-minute ride out to the hospital. It took him a few minutes to orient himself and to find Pound among those gray buildings, but he finally saw him "sitting out on the lawn of the hospital with his wife reading to him and seemed no crazier than he has always been," as he told Fred Miller.[98] When he saw Williams walking toward him, Pound had jumped out of his beach chair, grabbed Williams' hand, and embraced his friend. In spite of all that had happened between them, Pound and Williams were still glad to see each other. "We talked at random for an hour that day," Williams remembered. "He looked so much as I had always found him, the same beard and restless twitching of the hands, . . . the same bantering smile, screwing up his eyes, the half-coughing laugh and short, swift words, no sentence structure worth mentioning." And then, as though time had stood still, Pound evoked the old issues once more: economics and the bastards in the government and the Jews. It was a tape played over and over in Pound's obsessed mind. And so Williams and Dorothy listened as Pound lectured with his "halting jabs and ripostes of conversations" about the special interest groups who really ran all the major powers, his special invective being reserved for that bastard Roosevelt, who'd been responsible for his being where he was.

An hour later, Williams was back in a cab, headed for his Washington hotel room. The ice had been broken, then, and over the next several years he made it a point of stopping in to see Pound whenever he was in Washington. He never did get over the surrealistic presence of the other inmates at the mental hospital, though, and he remembered too vividly the image of one inmate he'd seen as he looked up at one of the buildings while trying to find his way out of that modern hell. Several stories off the ground he could see a man clinging stark naked to a plate-glass window, like some "great sea slug against the inside of a glass aquarium," his genitals pressed "hard against the cold . . . glass, plastered there in that posture of despair." He wondered how in hell Pound could keep any semblance of sanity month after month surrounded by those grotesques.

Two weeks later with Floss in New York he saw a play about madness—Robinson Jeffers' *Medea*—and found he could at least cope with that artifice. (He had praise for Judith Anderson in her role, but disliked John Gielgud in his.) He had gone to hear how another American poet had dealt with the problem of verse drama, but he'd found the lines "very undistinguished." When would "someone invent a new and satisfying line" for the stage, he asked Lowell, or had Shakespeare "ruined us forever?"[99] A copy of the Washington recording reached him on November 7, and he was dismayed to hear the same buzzing on the records he'd heard that Saturday in the NBC studios. He knew the buzzing would be recorded, he told Lowell, but he figured that "the wooden-faced ass behind the glass" in charge of the recording would tell him what to do. What was that technician, after all, but one more example of "the familiar indifferent artisan of the present day" who shrugged his shoulders and said "to hell with the company" who was paying him. "You wouldn't get that in Russia or Palestine or even, perhaps, in France," he added, "but for older cultural reasons." He only hoped that Elizabeth Bishop, who had recorded the same day with him, had been able to escape the same fate.[100]

Williams had invited Lowell to stay at 9 Ridge Road on Friday and Saturday, November 14 and 15, and Lowell spent that time talking with Williams and reading through the page proofs of *Paterson* 2 twice, pronouncing the poem, as Williams told Laughlin, "the best long poem ever written by an American not excluding Eliot," though Williams suspected that Lowell had added that last for his benefit, knowing as he had to of Williams' long-standing antipathy for Eliot.[101] They talked also of the "Gloucester Man," David Lyle, "son of the fishing-boat captain, who has made Paterson his physical and philosophical centrum," who was still sending Williams long letters, which he in turn was still inspecting for possible leads into the last part of *Paterson.*[102]

Williams found Lowell a "nice guy," modest and agreeable, though he seemed—at thirty—to be "awfully young" to a veteran of the generation of 1914 like Williams.[103] And as for Lowell, he too would remember that weekend (though it was years later when he himself was older), capturing Williams in essence though his facts would be wrong. He would remember Williams "in collegiate black slacks, gabardine coat, / and loafers polished like rosewood on yachts," talking with his "stone-deaf" mother with her hair like the "burnt-out ash of lush Puerto Rican grass" and her "black, blind, bituminous eye inquisitorial." And Lowell would remember Williams confessing to him that "the old bitch is over a hundred, I'll kick off tomorrow," and, characteristically, "I am sixty-seven, and more / attractive to girls than when I was seventeen." It was a composite picture Lowell drew, and—since this was the only time Lowell stayed at 9 Ridge Road—he would have to be recalling this particular visit. But Williams had just turned sixty-four, he had not yet had one, much less "three autumn strokes," and he would not know his mother's true age until after she was dead. Still, Lowell caught the dress, caught too the tough, loving speech, the crack about sex, the warmth of the man. The rest was unimportant.[104]

Williams also wrote an eight-hundred-word essay on the "Woman as Operator" to accompany Romare Bearden's painting *Women with an Oracle*. It was part of a collaboration of eleven artists and eleven writers, all dealing with women. What he tried to touch on in that brief but important meditation was the sense of what made woman woman. He knew, for example, that a man's sexuality could no more swallow her than the mind could lose its depth to reason in the man who was thought. For the essential *she* continued "down into the mid-brain below the possibility of his deepest masculine approaches." This was why painters and poets like himself were fascinated with the woman in her primary colors, and why "casual pictures representing women in the contemporary scene" were so unsatisfying, like women in *Life* or *Time* or *Esquire*, or women in ads and travel pictures. They baffled the imagination because such women were, finally, androgynes: female men and male women. In *Paterson* 4 Williams would come back to this problem of the woman playing the male role and the male the woman's role.[105]

He did a review of Frost's *A Masque of Mercy* for *Poetry* and could bring himself to praise it only halfheartedly, remembering Frost's conspicuous absence at the Bread Loaf Conference back in 1941. Frost, he said, had shown that artists could still ransack the Bible "for pithy statement" if they pursued it "diligently enough under the right circumstances." But as for poetry itself, he personally preferred "a richer verse than Mr. Frost prefers, richer in verbal resources and metric than I find in this Masque." There was a minimal beyond which even he would not go.[106]

When, in mid-November, Bruce Berlind, an undergraduate at Princeton, wrote to invite Williams to Princeton's literary "Club" for December 3, Williams wrote back testily that he was not a free agent and so could not get down for the set-to. And then he added: "Perhaps some day when Princeton U. as an official body consents to cast honor upon my name by lifting me to a seat beside Edna Saint Vincent Millay—to the tune of a thousand bucks or so for an hour's dissertation—you and I and the rest of the boys can go down to the tavern and really let our hair dangle a while after hours."[107] But something more than old, half-stifled animosities against Frost and Millay was troubling Williams, something he himself could not define, a malaise, a sense of frustration. "The pace is too fast for me in the present set-up of events, public and private," he had complained to Miller in late October:

> I don't quite understand why I feel so pressed, there seems to be, on the surface, nothing more than I have always handled somehow in the past, more or less successfully, but these days I'm going about in circles. . . . The great art of today is to ignore. It has gradually developed through the last two centuries until now it is a crushing force: nothing. We are buried, drowned in nothing at all. Nothing is the great force of our day.[108]

It was Williams' own version of an encroaching nihilism, the waste deserts filling up the tracks of his past, the leaden flood, *Le Néant*, a palatable nothing drowning out the self and pulling his whole world under with it.

*
**

His depression deepened with the snows that came early and stayed late that winter of '48, covering the roads and filling up the streets, the passes, even before the previous snows could be removed. He must have known something was wrong with himself when even the photograph of a pretty blonde in a one-piece bathing suit on the cover of *Life* left him indifferent. "When I look at the LIFEs, the LOOKs—a grinning blonde with her ass over the edge of an iron pipe in gay sunshine, against the bluest of blue water . . . I want to puke: not at her but at my own bitter indifference— bred of too much knowledge." Thus to Bonnie Golightly on January 12 in a vein similar to the Bearden essay two months earlier.[109] A week later he was complaining about the weather to Laughlin and McAlmon. He could not remember a snow-clogged winter like this one. "We're really getting it this year," he told McAlmon in El Paso on the nineteenth, "down to 3 degrees last night and probably hitting zero tonight. Lots of fun."[110] And the day before he'd complained to Abbott up in Buffalo that there was snow everywhere, on top of which some bastard had parked his light truck in Williams' driveway so that he couldn't get out for emergency calls.[111] "Do you think the people from Buffalo (they are people, aren't they? not muskrats who live under the ice and snow) will ever come out again after these days?" he asked Mary Barnard a week later. And as he looked out the window he could see another blizzard still shrieking and blowing.[112]

That was on Saturday, January 24. Three days later he was down with an intestinal virus, "puking and shitting along with the rest." On top of which he was having his own problems with the Board of Directors at Passaic General.[113] As president of that board and as representative of the Medical Board, he was being inundated with professional responsibilities even as he wished—hope against hope—to retreat into his study and work on his long poem. His son, Bill, had decided finally to work with his father and gradually take over his practice to let him retire and get some well-earned leisure to write when he wanted. But that would not become a reality until that summer, when Bill finished his New York residency and passed the New Jersey examinations making him eligible to practice in Rutherford. Edgar Williams had taken on the job of planning the renovations for the office, which would now have to accommodate both men. So Williams pined for the summer and the promise of surcease. He was tired and he knew it. He would be sixty-five that fall, and he still had a great deal to do.

Then, in mid-February, what Williams had feared would happen happened. He'd been at the hospital all day and night until one in the morning, working with patients. When, finally, he came out into the hospital parking lot, he saw that the clouds had moved off and that the night had turned cold and clear. He backed his Buick out of his parking space, nosed it into the curb, straightened the front wheels, and began rolling downhill for home. There was a three-foot wall of settled snow on his left side and he began to skim his fender off the wall for the fun of it until, suddenly, his front left wheel plowed into the bank. He was stuck good and there was no one around to help him out. He tried rocking the car, back and forth, back and forth, but he only managed to get the wheel in deeper than ever. He looked at his watch: one thirty in the morning and the hospital quiet. He got out, walked back up to the hospital garage, and borrowed the only shovel he could find at that hour: a coal shovel with the handle broken half off. Then he walked back and began fiercely to shovel himself out, at one point becoming so frustrated that he tried to kick the packed snow away and cut his shin badly. Then he lost his temper and began to push himself, even after he could feel the sharp pains begin shooting up through his chest. Finally he stopped and leaned against the car to rest. How peaceful the snow looked then in that black night. How easy it would be to just drop down now, to be found by somebody the next morning, peaceful and cold and dead.[114]

Instead he finished digging himself out, returned the shovel to the garage and drove home, with the pains still branching through his chest. Next morning he got up, ate breakfast, and had his heart attack. He called in a cardiac specialist, Dr. Gold, who diagnosed the chest pains as "a small anterior thrombosis" and ordered Williams upstairs to bed at once for the next six weeks. Williams was to get one ounce of brandy three times a day, and in the following weeks he would go through Palestine prune brandy, Greek brandy, domestic brandy, even expensive French brandies. When Gold was examining him, he had winked and asked Gold about having sexual intercourse, with Floss standing there. He was smiling broadly, but Gold—poker-faced—told him to put "a little nitro-glycerine" under his tongue and to go right ahead with whatever he had in mind.

Still, Williams followed Gold's orders as well as he could for a man with as much nervous energy as he possessed. Indeed, he'd been looking for just such an enforced pause, a mini-sabbatical of sorts, away from medical duties for once, when he could read all day in bed to his heart's content and even do some writing, though the typewriter and even the bathroom remained off limits. In fact, as he told Burke later, he spent much of those first few weeks wondering "whether the cobweb above me contained a live or dead spider," telling Floss and Lucy that the cobweb was to stay there until he could get up and inspect it for himself. When he could finally get at it with a broom handle, he discovered that he'd been contemplating "a dead mosquito, a Tut-an-kamen of his world."[115]

By the end of February, propped up in his army bed and armed with a red fifteen-cent notebook, Williams was busy outlining his projects. He made notes for *Paterson* 3 and 4, wrote some pages for his projected autobiography for Marion Strobel at *Poetry*, and began the long lecture he would give in Seattle in mid-July at the University of Washington, thanks to Ted Roethke's invitation. But he needed his typewriter to compose seriously and for that he would simply have to wait. In the meantime he read constantly, confiding to Zukofsky on March 9 that he hadn't "read so much in so short a time since I got fuzz on my belly."[116] He read Chapman's translation of the *Iliad* and took deep pleasure in Chapman's lines. Then he read Edmund Wilson's *Axel's Castle*, that classic study of symbolism and modernism, a book he would rely on extensively for the Washington lecture. He also read a collection of Frank O'Connor's short stories, Auden's new poems, Louis Untermeyer's anthology of British and American poets, Carlo Levi's *Christ Stopped at Eboli*, some more Chaucer, Freud's *The Interpretation of Dreams*, and a book that would find its way into *Paterson* 3: George Santayana's *The Last Puritan*.[117]

By Wednesday, March 3, he felt safe enough to joke about his close brush with death, writing Robert Lowell that day that he was still flat on his back after his attack of "angina (not vagina) pectoris."[118] That same day he also wrote the nurses in the pediatrics ward at Passaic General —his "girls"—to thank them for the lovely "shower" of gifts they'd sent him. Really, he joked, he didn't know how to thank them (or did he?) for the electric razor and the pajamas. Now there was only the baby to account for. ("She's a honey—if I only knew who her mother is, bless 'er 'eart.") The razor had been a particularly apt gift, he said, because his son Paul had lost his, leaving it on the subway train when he'd taken it in to A&S to get it adjusted. It was an apt gift, too, because it had given him a very close shave, like the "close shave" he'd had "with this old pump of mine last month." And that very morning the community nurse who was taking care of him had complimented him on his new tan pajamas, telling him how they matched his brown eyes. Boy, could *she* rub his back! "And you ought to see her get on the back rung of my hospital bed (from the Red Cross), lean over me, grab the mattress on both sides and yank it up toward the head of the bed! Wow! She's got umpf, she has. She learned it in the army!" He couldn't get into the bathroom yet to play with his new water toys, but did he look handsome sitting there on his beautiful commode! He told them he was reading Freud's *The Interpretation of Dreams* and recommended it to them, but *only* after they got married. Boy, was that book giving him dreams as he lay there doing nothing in bed: "Such dreams! Such lovely dirty dreams." ("You know how it is with some guys, especially doctors," Marie Leone would remember thirty years later. "They tell you a 'dirty' joke and you want to vomit? Well, it was never like that with Uncle Billy. There was always good fun in him, that twinkle in his eye. He really cared."[119])

He continued the banter with his "girls" a week later, when he sent his "Tweet Lil' Nursies" a poem he'd come across called "Song of the Queen Bee," about the indiscriminate and lovely lasciviousness of the queen bee who mated "with whatever drone she encounters." He prescribed that poem for them, telling them to read it over to themselves each evening before they went to bed and then they'd "have pleasant dreams for yourselves all about the big! world!" It was a kind of substitute, really, for the heavy doses of Freud he himself had been taking with the same end in view. He was doing all right, he told them, though in fact he was still so weak he couldn't get out of bed. Maybe they'd give him "the green flag" to stand up sometime that week. He was having a grand time doing nothing, though he could also see how "economically unsound" too much of a good thing could be. He was already beginning to get restless, forgetting that it was his heart which, at sixty-four, had given out.[120]

The day before he'd written Fred Miller in his best Jimmy Cagney imitation: "They got me, kid, they got me!! Right tru the pump. But I fooled 'em, I didn't croak. So what, huh? Now dey got to do it again. And dis time I'll beat 'em to de punch." Already they were letting him sit in a chair for a few minutes.[121] On the sixteenth, having just finished reading Eric Bentley's book on George Bernard Shaw, Williams wrote to tell him how much he had admired the book's humanity. It was not a pompous treatment of the artist, as he found so many books by American scholars, but instead the best treatise on contemporary manners he'd ever read. He ended his letter by confessing that for a while after his heart attack he thought he was finished for good, but now his "rugged constitution" was reasserting itself and he hoped to be up and around in a few weeks.[122] By the following Sunday, the twenty-first, he was feeling strong enough to walk downstairs and have dinner with the others, while the canary sang to see him again.

On Easter Tuesday, March 30, Williams wrote to Charles Reznikoff, one of his associates from the objectivist days. Nineteen years before, Reznikoff had sent him two sections of his *By the Waters of Manhattan: An Annual*, but he'd simply put it on his shelf without so much as opening it. Now, during his illness, he'd taken the poem down and read it through. To his surprise, both he and Floss had been thrilled by it and now—after all these years—he was acknowledging the pleasure that book had given him. Williams knew it had been a long time since Reznikoff had published anything, and now he asked him point-blank why he didn't go back to his writing. "Why do you not start again now?" Williams pleaded. "This book has so much in it that marks you as a first rate artist that it is shameful of you not to have persisted." Begin again, he added, it was still not too late. The letter so moved Reznikoff that he did in fact begin again, and he would point to Williams' letter—coming as it did at this moment—as the incentive that had triggered his return to poetry.[124]

Roethke's *The Lost Son* volume reached Williams at the end of April and Williams wrote to congratulate him, saying that, though he found the music often conventional there, the thought showed "a curious decay that is a just comment on our world." Roethke, he said, reminded him of Baudelaire in that both presented the "unflinching stare at corruption and disease" as being finally nothing more than a subject like any other to be explored. He particularly singled out "My Papa's Waltz," adding that if a poet could raise that quality of childhood trauma into adulthood consciousness and sustain it, "savagely but with impeccable perfection of surface," it would be something. Roethke too paid close attention to Williams' advice.[125]

Having survived the heart attack, Williams tried now to dismiss his illness, acting as though it had been nothing, a minor setback at most. But Floss knew better. By the end of March she'd taken over most of the nursing duties, preparing his meals, watching over him, even writing to Pound and Lowell and Laughlin to let her husband alone, that in spite of what he told them, he was still a sick man. Then, on Wednesday afternoon, March 31, she had Bill Jr. drive his father and herself down to Atlantic City for a ten-day early spring vacation. They stayed at the Chalfonte-Haddon, one of the stately old hotels that faced right on the boardwalk and the ocean. And though Williams did some work on his "Field of Action" paper for the University of Washington, trying to work out to his own satisfaction some of the ramifications of the new measure, he also managed to enjoy himself. "Almost two months now and I'm still not working," he told Zukofsky a week after his arrival. "Just made up my mind this morning while taking my salt 'tub' in this luxurious hotel that until the small wound on my right shin I got kicking snow away from the front of my stalled car in February finally looks normal again I shan't be cured. It still looks an angry red." Atlantic City, after all, was "just the place for wounded veterans" like himself, and he was feeling much better. He even wished he could give a little of what he was enjoying to "stupid ol' Ezra," still locked up in that prison of his, little as he might in some ways deserve it.[126]

Just before he'd left for the Jersey shore, Williams had received advance word that he'd just won the National Institute of Arts and Letters' Russell Loines Award for Poetry, along with Allen Tate. That award meant some long-delayed recognition, a medal, a formal reception with an introduction by Marianne Moore, and a check for $1,000. But he was glad just now that he was away from home when the news hit the papers on April 3. He knew the phone would be constantly ringing with well-wishers, and he didn't know if he could handle that right now. "Not that I want to do my dear townspeople out of a thrill but what in hell do they really know or care about my spiritual metabolism—bless 'em," he told Abbott.[127] That had been his second honor since the beginning of the year. The first had come after some preliminary feelers by Lowell in late January to see if Williams might not be persuaded to accept the position of Consultant in Poetry at the Library of Congress in the fall, after Lowell closed out his term. Williams thought hard about what the position would entail: leaving his medical practice for a year and living in Washington. On the other hand, there was the public recognition of the thing. And though he had serious qualms about doing it, he finally wrote Lowell on January 29 accepting. He'd done that, of course, before his heart attack, and he would later in the year find himself using his illness as an excuse for not accepting the consultantship, at least for the present.

Allen Tate wrote to Williams at once congratulating him on sharing the Russell Loines Award with himself, and Williams answered from Atlantic City that he was glad he'd had the chance to get to meet Tate at the Salt Lake City Conference. "Had it not been for that," he added, "think how our lips would have curled at each other as we glared back and forth behind Mr. [William Rose] Benét in furious rivalry on that famous evening to come. All we need do now is grin and think of the pretty flowers of Alta!"[128] Back home from Atlantic City, one of the first things Williams did was to read through Tate's collected poems, telling Tate on the twenty-fifth that, though it took a great effort to "like" Tate's poems, the mind finally did open and could appreciate them. "You and I are at opposite poles of the tradition," he added, so that in the sense of a circle of poets they were really "close together." He also wanted to know when he would get his money, since he wanted to split early from the celebration and get some rest.[129]

Then, on the twenty-seventh, he rushed off a frantic note to Tate asking what he should wear for the afternoon ceremonies on May 21 at the Institute's West 56th Street auditorium. Tate replied next day that what the poet should wear to be absolutely correct was the following: "faded vine-leaves as a fillet around the brow; a breech-clout tied at the navel with sea weed; the staff of Hermes, a caduceus, in the left hand, and, in the right, a bunch of sour grapes which we munch in order to set the teeth of our posterity on edge. But since this correct costume would be hard to find on short notice, I expect to wear a light grey Business Suit, the pants of which are too short."[130] Williams too chose a business suit over the other option for the occasion. He was feeling better by then, had even been allowed to drive the car again, telling Abbott on May 8 that he'd just driven Lucy, their maid, home. It was the first time he'd been behind the wheel of his Buick in three months, and he crowed then that he'd be all right soon enough if he could just learn to behave. He was also seeing patients again, though on a somewhat reduced scale.[131]

Marianne Moore introduced him that Friday afternoon at the Institute's auditorium, telling the distinguished audience there assembled that Williams had always detested falsity and that, if he was still incorrigible (in other words, if he was still the wild man of American letters), it was as "an incorrigible expert of beauty." He was both deadly earnest and seriously humorous; he was also "our Audubon of locality and American behavior."[132] Then Williams made a little jump up onto the platform beside Marianne and gesticulated to the large Blashfield painting of the female figure Academia behind him, holding Pegasus' bridle in her left arm, and said, "Never in my life did I expect to appear under the aegis, the image even, of Academia, bearing, as you see, upon her left hand and forearm a bridle fitted with what to me looks suspiciously like a snaffle-bit!" Even here, the slightly battered revolutionary could not avoid joking about the academy's desire to curb the poet, even as he welcomed the chance to be one with them.[133]

*
* *

By the middle of May Williams had created a "ponderous" essay for the Seattle Conference and was trying now to cut it back. He wanted Burke's help with the thing and so, on the last Sunday of the month, he had Bill drive him down to the farm at Andover to hear his friend's impressions. Burke, who'd already read it through, made a few comments, then passed it back, a sign that Williams interpreted to mean it had passed Burke's general muster.[134] Armed with his talk, Williams was ready for the trip west. A trip by car—such as he'd done the summer before—was now out of the question. And a plane flight—though the faster way there—would mean high altitudes and possible medical complications. Better then to take the train out and back. This time, however, Floss would not be traveling with him, because the entire office and house would have to be rearranged to accommodate Bill Jr.'s practice at 9 Ridge Road. It would mean an army of carpenters, plumbers, painters, and plasterers swarming over the house from July until—as it turned out—the end of September, and Floss would have to oversee all that activity.

Bill Jr. and Floss drove up with Williams to Gratwick Highlands, beginning by easy stages on the morning of Friday, July 9. They spent an idyllic five days together there, Bill himself fishing every spare moment he could find and Williams and Floss taking walks together around the decayed estate and enjoying the company of the Abbotts and the Gratwicks. Then, alone and feeling a bit frightened "as if going to war," Williams, armed with a suitcase full of clothes, his talk, and a pint of Hennessy Three Star brandy for his heart, boarded the train for the trip west. That was Wednesday evening, July 14. He took the northern route out, on the Chicago, Milwaukee, St. Paul & Pacific, stopping over in Chicago for a few hours to have lunch with his old friend Marion Strobel and talk over old times as well as discuss plans for his projected autobiography before continuing on his way west.

Almost at once he began to miss Floss terribly, writing to her all the way out and all the while he was in Seattle. On Friday morning he looked out the train window to see that he was now in Lennox, in the southeast corner of South Dakota, in the heart of prairie country: "just endless miles of rolling country and green broken only by a few mounds & ridges, an occasional poor looking farm & a town." The evening before a conductor had asked him to help another passenger who'd swallowed glass in his dinner. Then that evening—the sixteenth—he met two sisters from Seattle and a professor named Lipsky who taught economic history at Berkeley. As they talked, the question of Harry Truman's bid for the presidency in the '48 election had come up and then "tentatively and then enthusiastically we all showed ourselves to be all out" for the man.[135]

All Friday afternoon he watched the extraordinary landscape rolling by his window: the pines, the aspen, the saxifrage everywhere. It was an "eye-opener," that trip out, he would tell Libby Burke—Kenneth's wife—when it was all over. He would not soon forget how much of that world "this beast man has devastated. The brainlessness of the entrepreneur was never so forcibly jammed down my gullet." It was shades of the Puritans and of Hamilton all over again, for the modern-day entrepreneur was no different from his forerunners; he simply had "better lawyers." All the schemers had left in many places were "the barren mountains, the sea the sky and—lots of weather."[136] Then, just at sunset, near ten in the evening, he saw the awesome sight of Butte, Montana, its copper smelters flaring out against the darkness like some modern city of the damned. Still, Williams was struck by the strangely beautiful sight, Butte's single main street "like a flight of giant steps ascending the mountain side, brightly lit, as if some temple site to the deity," the overwhelming grandeur of "the smelters flaming about the mines high upon both sides."[137] Tenochtitlán, Montezuma, Chapultepec, Grasshopper Hill.

The sight seemed to dizzy him, and then he realized with a shock that he really was dizzy. What was happening to him? He became frightened, disoriented, until he suddenly realized he was riding at 6,000 feet, approaching the Continental Divide. So that was it! He got up, fumbled in his suitcase until he found the Hennessy's under his pajamas, lurched to the men's room at the end of the car, opened the bottle, pulled a paper cup out of the dispenser, and shakily poured himself a drink. Once they began the descent over the mountains, he felt better.

The barrenness and wildness of the landscape with its primitive music touched a responsive chord deep within him, especially where the train crossed the Columbia River. On Saturday morning they were still high up, though gradually coming down through the Cascade Mountains, through heavy fir and spruce forests and—far below them—a small stream. That morning he also saw Mt. Rainier, alone and majestic, "the whole white mass of it" suddenly coming into view, "cloudless on a clear blue sky to the west." At breakfast he tried to engage a heavyset woman of fifty in a conversation, telling her about the extraordinary view of Rainier he'd just had, but she just stared at him. Better to watch out the window, then, at young deer bounding through the trees, or at the foxgloves in bloom.[138]

By midmorning he was in Seattle. He'd been met at the terminal by Ted Roethke and another member of the English Department, who drove him to the girls' dorm where he would be staying. He had his own room, with a double-decker bed and a toilet and bath right across the hall, and the men had already made him feel at home. Out his window, down below on the grass, he could see "two vigorous looking queens sunbathing." He was happy. He had dinner with Roethke and a Mrs. Leslie at the woman's apartment that evening. Once again it was one of Roethke's famous beefsteaks along with champagne and brandy. They spoke about the climate, about Seattle's high suicide rate, about the local flora, then called it a night. Williams was back at his dorm room by half past twelve.

But he found it impossible to sleep with the radiator going in the room and he was up before seven Sunday morning. One subject that had come up during his talks with Roethke and which had deeply troubled Williams was the Communist "witch hunt" going on at the university, as the press and the legislature searched out any suspected "Commies" on the faculty. "What are we headed for, my dear," he asked Floss, "another war?" Roethke had been right: Russia was at fault, but so were his own countrymen for their own "narrowness and smallness of mind."[139]

The Seattle Conference began on Monday the nineteenth and Williams proceeded at once to enjoy it. He saw a good deal of Roethke, and he came to like Granville Hicks and Charles Perrin as well as the other guests at the conference. It meant a week of "teaching" for him, a daily lecture or reading of an hour before an audience ranging from 100 to 150, followed in the evening by a seminar with from fifteen to twenty students for another hour or so. He gave his primary address—"The Poem as a Field of Action"—first thing off on Monday. It was a sprawling, open-ended affair, the fruit of half a year's meditation on the state of the contemporary English and American poem. He used Auden as a symbol of the failure of the British to find "a new way of writing," even though—like Auden—they had tried to find a way out of their difficulties by turning to the United States. Auden had failed just because he had succeeded so well in writing poems in the old tradition. But all he was really doing was closing that mode out without finding a suitable replacement, so that all he could do was replay the same old patterns with consummate skill. The significant advance, however, Williams told his audience, would come out of the provinces, out of America, which was still grappling with the "mobile phase, the changing phase, the productive phase" of the English language. It was the same message he'd been at now for nearly ten years, and Roethke himself would have remembered it from that time at Penn State back in 1940. But by '48 it had become a central rallying cry to which the younger writers—those born in the 1920s, like Creeley and Ginsberg, Levertov and Snyder, O'Hara and Tomlinson—were about to begin to take seriously as a formulation for their own poetry.

On Tuesday afternoon, Williams made a brief appearance on a local radio program called "The Ann Sterling Show," where—crowded in among ads for Bon Ami, Rockwood's Chocolate Bits, the Seattle First National Bank, and a plea from the Silver Shower to help get radios over to Germany so that the people there might hear the "truth" about peace-loving Americans—Ann Sterling asked Williams a few questions about poetry. Next day Williams sent the transcript of the show to Kitty Hoagland along with a note. Seattle, he wrote with heavy irony, was a "fine place for a young man or woman to grow up in." Besides the main attraction of a real witch hunt, there were other amusements. The week before, for example, a young man from a good family had stolen a new Lincoln, "picked up a girl at a road house, raped her, murdered her —cutting off one breast in the process," before the police had caught him. And two weeks before that another young man had beaten up his wife, then "thrown her and their small daughter over a cliff killing the former but not the latter." All in all, he added, it was "a vigorous man's world. Very bracing." *Paterson* stuff.[140]

He had dinner that night at the home of a Dr. Rogers, "an institution man at the T.B. Sanatorium" in Seattle. And—in spite of the beautiful, husky Scandinavian blonde who came into his room to make up his bed each day—he had been glad to be invited to a real home for a meal.[141] He enjoyed his seminars, except for some overly earnest faces staring at him which made him uncomfortable. He noticed too that it was not his lecturing the people wanted to hear, but Williams the poet reading from his own poems. Even Granville Hicks had announced during the conference that this audience would never forget him, and Williams could even feel his "old stage presence" returning by week's end. On Thursday he spent the entire hour reading all of *Paterson* 2 and was surprised at how strong he'd felt during that performance. That evening Roethke came by his room to say good-by, taking a pint of bourbon and the rest of Williams' Hennessy Three Star brandy with him when he left.[142]

Friday night, with the conference officially over, Williams and the other guests celebrated, though there was one sour note when the college authorities became overly watchful of one of the guests who had gotten "lit to the gills" and had then to be protected from them by Williams and some of the others.[143] Williams spent all day Saturday out on Puget Sound with members of the university conference. It had been a lyrical close to the Seattle stay, especially the view of Mt. Rainier "bathed in evening sunlight," surrounded as he was by several young women he'd met at the conference and to whom he'd taken a real liking.[144] Sunday morning he was homeward bound on the same train that had taken him west the week before. He kept busy working on *The Build-Up* and jotting down notes for "a small simple treatise for women on how to write modern poems."[145] He'd been pleased and surprised to find the students on the West Coast radical "in the old American way," and been impressed particularly by the intelligence of the younger generation of women, eager and serious to write and looking for advice.[146] The treatise never materialized, though, since Williams still had *Paterson* to attend to.

Back home on the evening of the twenty-seventh, he unpacked and began to get his correspondence once more in order. He'd come home to a house and office in shambles, and he found himself disoriented. The old desk that had sat in his office and on which he had written so many of his poems and stories and essays and letters for the past thirty-five years had had to be moved up to the second floor now. Bill Jr. had moved it up there for his father on Sunday morning so that his father could get back to his typing. With the conference finally over, Williams was ready to "bang *Paterson* III out" that summer and fall, though he soon found himself too confused with the reality of the new order of things and the final realization too that he would soon be sixty-five and unable after that time to practice at the hospital.[147]

At the end of August, Williams' new book of poems, *The Clouds*, came off the combined presses of the Wells College Press and the Cummington Press. It was another limited edition, this time numbering 310, of which Williams signed sixty. It was a sixty-four-page book containing sixty-one poems, many of them quite short, and nearly all written during the mid-1940s. And it was a solid book, a miscellany bracketed by two oblique elegies, opening with "Aigeltinger" and closing with the four-part symphonic "The Clouds." Written in the autumn of his life, the image of November which seemed everywhere here matched the book's elegiac mode. It seemed a natural pairing for a poet of sixty-five, even if it wasn't characteristic of a man who had always insisted on beginning again.

*
* *

The Aigeltinger poem which opened the volume formed a kind of Horatio Alger story in reverse. Aigeltinger: a memory from those student days at Horace Mann High at the turn of the century when Williams and his brother, as he told Zukofsky, would take the "Chambers St. ferry, then

the Ninth Ave L for 116th St." At about Desbrosses Street Aigeltinger
and the other New Yorkers would join him for the daily ride uptown.
Aigeltinger was the mathematical genius who seemed to be able to take
any algebra problem Williams or any of the other boys had and figure it
"in his head in about thirty seconds." Later Aigeltinger had gone on to
Columbia, played football, graduated, and become a successful engineer
in New York—until heavy drinking ruined everything. Eventually Williams had lost track of his friend until one day years later a neighbor in
Rutherford had mentioned that he'd soon have to go into the city to find a
certain "Aigeltinger" to help his company solve "a particularly tough
piece of figuring." Aigeltinger was the only man who could do it and
among the engineers in the New York area the man had become a
byword. They'd have to find the poor guy, probably in the back of some
saloon, take him to a hotel, sober him up, give him the problem to solve,
pay him—and then abandon him to drift back off into the submarine
world of drink.[148]

It was enough to make a person weep, that story, and Williams
addressed his poem to the boy who had "stuck" in his "conk" like some
luminous irritant "for nearly half a century." Profundity, he noted
bitterly, remembering how the critics and academics had dismissed
Williams himself for not being profound enough. Well, here was profundity and more in Aigeltinger. And what did Americans do with the rare gift
of true profundity? The same thing they did with women or with any
other rare gift: raped it, as they had raped his black Kore, dragging her in
her white dress from some bar to be gang-banged first by the boys from
Newark and then by the boys from Paterson, before they too abandoned
her:

> They say I'm not profound
> But where is profundity, Aigeltinger
> mathematical genius
> dragged drunk from some cheap bar to serve
> their petty purposes?
>
> Aigeltinger, you were profound

Aigeltinger: it was one more American success story to add to all the
rest.[149]

"The Clouds," the title poem which also closed the volume, was the
longest piece in the book and certainly one of the most sustained poems
Williams had written outside *Paterson* in the 1940s. Its musical form
may have been undertaken as a direct response to Eliot's *Four Quartets*.
In that sense it was Williams' agnostic answer to Eliot's religious and
even "mystical" synthesis about ultimate meaning. It took Williams a
long time to finish this poem, for he began it in 1942, when "Little
Gidding" appeared, and finished it only in early '45, revising it heavily as

he shifted from its initial center in a meditation on his father's death nearly a quarter of a century before, moving instead to a meditation on the unknowability of death itself. "It is the opposite of piety" he was after in "The Clouds," he told Burke in late '46: "the unknowability of knowledge and the professional asses who trade on that basic fact —pontifically proclaiming this or that." Eliot, he said, had been a "prime mental shit" for having "used" poetry for his own religious ends.[150]

As Williams approached his mid-sixties, he had told Floss he was afraid he too might die of cancer as his father had. He was convinced, for example, that when they opened him in the hospital for his second herniotomy they would find cancer, though they had not.[151] Ill himself, he could only smile sardonically when—in his later years—someone would come to him and beg or even demand that a loved one be made whole again. For what could this wounded physician, after all, tell them, what cure could he really offer them? "They come to me white-faced in fear of their lives," an early draft reads,

> but I have seen my father die
> after a long illness and I laugh at them.
> I loved my father.
>
> Where has he gone? Up over the clouds,
> more, so far as I can say, than into that hole
> they dug, so foreign to him. That is, I satisfy my
> mind so and say nothing.[152]

For twenty-five years he had been troubled at his inability to save his own father, of the botch he'd made of that last day. "Had one patient this evening," he'd written Zukofsky back in February 1943, "a ponderous, 65 year old Englishman." That had almost been his father's age when he died, and this man too had at first frightened him, in the way his own father had. He too was a "big, big fisted, slow speaking, red faced, H dropping Englishman from Birmingham—the town where my father was born." Like his father, this fellow also had that air of being master of the world, as though it were all "really his and he was destined to be tolerant of it." He'd been a guard on an armored truck, one of those "absolutely trustworthy" souls, the very "ribs of the Empire." What was one to do with such magnificence, Williams asked, but "to fuck it. I can now understand why Englishmen are buggers by nature, there's absolutely nothing else to do but take out a 3 ft tool and shove it up the man's ass. It would be like a crown on one's head to have been connected with so much empire."[153] He must have been half remembering, half suppressing the enema tube he'd forced up his poor father's emaciated rectum that Christmas Eve, knowing he'd hurt him badly at the last even as he sought to comfort him. And then his father had disappeared, cloudlike, over the horizon, gone.

And where do our loved ones go? Into the ground or up into the heavens, to ride the clouds there? By the time Williams finished "The Clouds," his father had all but disappeared from the poem . In his place there was a meditation on the half-fanciful forms the clouds seem to make, as Hamlet before him had seen as he sought shapes in the heavens above. When Williams wrote his poem there was a war going on and thousands of men and women were dying all over the world, disappearing like so many tattered cloud puffs. And in the heavens: the "horses of the dawn" charging "from north to south," half-formed, their flanks "still caught among low, blocking forms," still tied to this earth with its "mud / livid with decay and life!" The "soul" seemed caught too like the black flag before "the sepulcher of the empty bank," whipping against the staff head in its futile struggle to be free. Why was it the poor human brain struggled, "unwilling to own the obtrusive body," trying instead to

> crawl from it like a crab and
> because it succeeds, at times, in doffing that,
> by its wiles of drugs or other "ecstasies," thinks
> at last that it is quite free. . . .

And yet, how else to think of our lost ones except as statuesque dead riding high the horses of the dawn, forever "undirtied by the putridity we fasten upon them," as they moved on and on "into the no-knowledge of their nameless destiny"?

Williams framed the second movement of the poem with the old *ubi sunt* motif. Where were all the good minds, he asked, minds who knew better than to try to ask anything of "the soul's flight" but who instead "kept their heads and died" when their time came? He named Villon and Erasmus and Shakespeare and Aristotle and Aristophanes (that other who'd also written about clouds), and Socrates—"Plato's better half"— and especially Toulouse-Lautrec, "the / deformed who lived in a brothel and painted / the beauty of whores." Here were the real truth tellers "of whom we are the sole heirs / beneath the clouds." In the third movement —a scherzo—Williams thought back to that priest he'd seen at St. Andrew's in Amalfi in 1924, "riding / the clouds of his belief." He remembered how that "holy man," jiggling "upon his buttocks to the litany / chanted, in response by two kneeling altar boys," had been caught "half off the earth / in his ecstasy," turning to wink at Williams. So much then for the metaphysical.

What, then, remained? "With each, dies a piece of the old life, which he carries, / a precious burden beyond," the last movement of "The Clouds" begins. So it is the old life that we the living treasure and nothing more. And yet, and yet: what if the dead do somehow live on, contrary to all our expectations? Williams simply did not know, and so the poem could do nothing but circle at its close back to its beginnings: with the clouds, "the disordered heavens, ragged, ripped by the winds / or dormant," made up of a calligraphy of sorts, a writing on the sky in a world constantly changing, "in which the poet foretells his own death," forms forming and dissolving, "convoluted, lunging upon / a pismire, a conflagration, a. . . ." Thus Williams dissolved his own meditation, in mid-sentence, open-ended, halting on the indefinite article, the extended dots forming a signature for the "no-knowledge" of his "nameless destiny."[154] Till the very end of his own life Williams would never come any closer than this to a certitude of what followed that final breath. . . .

TWELVE

A Dawning Awareness:
1948—1951

When T. S. Eliot delivered his famous second lecture on Milton at the Frick Museum in New York in May 1947, Williams had tried to make a public point of it by *not* showing up. It wasn't as though he didn't know about it and so had missed seeing Eliot; he knew well enough, for he wrote Bonnie Golightly at the end of April that New York was becoming "a lair of anthologists, radio-commentators and other vipers—not to mention the lecturer at the Frick Gallery, May 12."[1] What Eliot said on that occasion—or what Williams thought Eliot said—was that Milton's influence on the younger generation of writers was not, after all, as pernicious as he'd earlier suggested, and that there was now enough distance between Milton's time and the present moment that the young could study Milton's craft to their own benefit. But from where Williams stood, Eliot's was the advice of a man who had sold out to the academy, for Eliot was in effect calling a halt to the modernist revolution in the arts. The period of experimentation was now over, the Possum had argued, and the period of the '50s and '60s should see writers consolidating the gains made for them by the generation of 1914. "We cannot," he summed up,

> We cannot, in literature, any more than in the rest of life, live in a perpetual state of revolution. If every generation of poets made it their task to bring poetic diction up to date with the spoken language, poetry would fail in one of its most important obligations. For poetry should help, not only to refine the language of the time, but to prevent if from changing too rapidly: a development of language at too great a speed would be a development in the sense of a progressive deterioration, and that is our danger to-day.

For the next half century Eliot hoped to see poetry take the "right course," and that would mean a further elaboration of language patterns already established. In this search, then, Milton's "extended verse structure" could be useful, especially in helping the young "avoid the danger of a *servitude* to colloquial speech and to current jargon."[2]

570

Eliot might as well have aimed his remarks directly at Williams (and perhaps that was what he was doing). For here was Williams, at that very moment searching for a new measure that would carry the weight of the real language, of New World colloquial speech, as he heard it around him every day but almost never in poems. The search for an adequate poetry had only barely begun, Williams had been shouting up and down the land, and here was Eliot, intoning that it was time for an end to the revolution in which both had taken part for the past twenty-five years. It was not only wrongheaded advice Eliot was giving, then, it was dishonest.

Even Pound, who had championed Eliot years before (at Williams' expense), sent Williams one of his gnomic postcards with the words "Perverter of the young," after he'd read Eliot's essay on Milton. As for Williams, he was so angry with Eliot he wrote an essay answering it in the only place he could get a hearing: a small printed leaflet called *Four Pages* established in Galveston, Texas, by Dallam Simpson, a disciple of Pound's. "That Mr. T. S. Eliot is an idiot I see no reason to insist," he began. No, Eliot was clever enough; after all, he'd "wheedled himself into the good graces of the Church of England" and the British Empire and even into Harvard and you had to have intelligence to do that. But about Milton Eliot was wrong, for Milton had perverted "the language in order to adhere to certain orthodoxies of classic form" which stood in the way of modern poetry's getting on with its work. In fact Eliot was himself another Milton: an insidious barrier to the younger writers just then coming into their own. Rather let the young go on looking for a new means of expression, Williams insisted, "an enlargement of mood and style in our days which Mr. Eliot has never sighted." Besides, weren't Americans self-conscious enough of their cultural dependency without having an Eliot telling them "to go with our chins upon our chests before the Milton of our day"? Williams' essay was an important corrective to Eliot's, but published out of Galveston few ever saw it.[3]

When his blast at Eliot was published in early '48, Williams confided to Laughlin that he still knew Eliot was a good poet, but he was sick of critics and teachers treating him "as though he possessed the universal genius of a St. Anthony."[4] And two months later he even admitted that the *Four Quartets* were really "about the only poems . . . that are truly inventive (Pound not writing much) today."[5] So when, in November of '48, he had another chance to hear Eliot read at the Library of Congress, he went down to Washington by train, leaving Bill in charge of his office and taking Floss with him to confront his bête noire face to face for the first—and only—time in his life.[6]

All the things Williams had promised to do to Eliot for the past twenty-five years—including kicking the man in his metaphorical balls —did not, at the moment of truth, come to pass when he actually stood before the great man that Friday evening, November 19. It was Robert Lowell who made the introductions—at Pound's instigation—and Williams was rather taken with Eliot's suavity and evident command of the situation. Williams would remember that meeting later, remember how Eliot had said something about "the good characters" in his work, adding that he hoped Williams would give the world some more.[7] And that was that, as Eliot turned to meet another well-wisher in the crowded reception hall. It was said simply and courteously enough, and then the moment passed. After all, the reading was for Eliot's benefit, not Williams', and Williams once again became merely another observer. And yet how marmoreal, how stonelike and discomforting the formal proceedings had been. Williams underscored the fact the next morning when he sent Bob McAlmon a picture postcard of the Capitol's Statuary Hall with the comment: "Today Riviera sunshine—but in spite of liking Eliot, now I have met him, the party last night closely resembled the reverse of this card."[8] Once again Eliot had returned in Williams' imagination to the condition of marble presence.

A week later his opinion of Eliot was once more about what it had been for the past quarter century, minus the old angers. The man was, he told Robert Lowell, basically "dull at some central point in his perceptions." He was like the lion "in the Assyrian wall decorations, the blue and yellow ceramics of sculptured tiles," the one with "a spear through his spine . . . paralyzed from the haunches down." He'd seen the same dull look "in insects that have been stuck to the surface on which they have been crushed by their own gummy secretions while the front half strains to get away."[9] Perhaps that was what a mystical appearance came down to, and what he might expect to "find in heaven with Eliot at the head." In a postscript added three days later he realized that Lowell, coming from a later generation of poets, might appreciate Eliot and even Pound for that matter in a way he himself would never be able to. But for Williams himself there had been too much infighting, too much maiming of the only world of ideas he'd ever loved by those two contenders for him to open his arms to them now. To do so would have meant betraying so much that he had fought for for too long.[10] In fact, earlier that year Williams had put down on paper—in an early draft of *Paterson 3*—his deepest feelings about the Eliot/Pound tradition. Such men were moths, he'd said, translators of the dead, fluttering against the high, closed windows of the library of tradition, as they vainly sought a way out into the real world beyond.[11]

Most important for his own future, though, was Williams'-reaching retirement age on September 17: Constitution Day. And on that day he sent Zukofsky a poem he'd just written called "Turkey in the Straw," an early version of the poem he would later call, simply: "I kissed her as she pissed," *she* being Flossie.[12] It was a comic piece, and what he had in mind was "a contrast between a residual sensuality and the romantic dreams of youth," both of which, he realized, were seldom brought together in the same poem.[13] In that poem he juxtaposed the high romanticism of his early love poem to Floss—"Your thighs are apple trees / whose blossoms touch the sky!"—with the changeup to the faster: "On my 65th birthday / I tussled her breasts." He knew *this* woman better than he knew any other, had been married to her now for over thirty-five years. Let him celebrate his wife in all moods! Three weeks later Celia Thaew—Zukofsky's wife—set the piece to music, though Floss continued to have lingering doubts about her husband's sanity.[14] "Turkey in the Straw" was finally cut from the revised version of the *Collected Later Poems*. "I got such a sharp barking at by Floss when the music Celia wrote for my BEAUTIFUL song came back that I've never had it played for me," Williams wrote Zukofsky. "Not serious on Flossie's part, just a momentary flash of anger, that I had, actually 'kissed her while she pissed' I guess. 'Aren't you ever going to grow up?' is the way she phrased it."

Now that he was sixty-five and could no longer practice obstetrics at the hospital or even serve on a hospital committee, Williams should have felt relieved. How many times had he complained in the past about the time his patients had demanded of him and how they'd kept him from writing! Now he might finally be free of those responsibilities and —moreover—Bill would be joining him in his office in a few weeks. But the truth was that he still craved his daily contact with people, and it took him a long time to adjust to his newfound freedom. Moreover, he had reached sixty-five without a pension and with no large cash reserves. He had never meant to get rich as a doctor and he had let too many of his patients off free, so that now the pressure of what to do with a substantial part of his income suddenly gone pressed against his consciousness like a pinched nerve. He had somehow hoped to live off royalties and advances, money from lectures and prizes, but after a lifetime of steady writing he was lucky if he could count on more than a few hundred a year from that source. In two years' time he would turn bitterly against Laughlin (that "rich scion" of a steel magnate) until he became unreasoning. Why should Eliot and Hemingway and Steinbeck do so well and he—the true revolutionary—not be paid fairly for his work! And he'd already had one heart attack.

But work on he did. Even as medical work eased up, he took on more lecture assignments. He gave four Thursday night lectures in October and November for the YMHA on 92d Street dealing with the new measure, the first of which he called "A Few Hints Toward the Enjoyment of the Modern Poem." He also kept abreast of the new, befriending another new poet from New York whose work he'd come to admire. This was David

Ignatow, whose first book of poems Williams reviewed for the *New York Times*. In October he also reviewed a critical biography of Edwin Arlington Robinson by Professor Emery Neff of Columbia for *The Nation*. He gave a reading to a packed audience of students and faculty at CCNY in mid-October and then spent two days reading and lecturing at Bard College on the Hudson River in early November.

He was also back at work on *Paterson* by early November, expecting to finish the third book by Christmas. But by the end of the month he had once again run into difficulties with his epic. On the thirtieth he told McAlmon that all he could do with the poem at the moment was "grunt and sweat and pound the keys and kick my mind and soul in the ass, tickle them under the crupper and even bang them in the balls—but they ain't what they uster be."[15] And—the same day to Bonnie Golightly—he became the woman in labor, getting "slight pains in the ovaries" over *Paterson*.[16] A week later he confessed to Abbott how weary he was becoming. "I used to throw the energy around as if it were in fact a waterfall," he lamented, thinking of his wizened loins. But now he was ruined for the day if he typed "for three or four hours at a stretch."[17]

His relationship with Pound was one thing very much on Williams' mind that fall as he worked on *Paterson* 3. Pound the pedagogue, Pound the master, sending along those interminable and unasked-for reading lists in a continuing effort to educate his country cousin from Rutherford. And though Williams kept telling Pound to leave him alone, to let him get on with his work, he secretly took Pound's suggestions seriously —though he'd be damned if he'd tell Pound that. So, for example, when in the summer of '47 Pound had told Williams to read George Crabbe's eighteenth-century anti-pastoral, *The Village*, to see how another poet —and physician—had treated small-town provincial life in a long poem, Williams ordered the book from Bonnie Golightly. He read it straight through and then wrote to tell her that it had been "surprisingly good—largely because of its clamping of the eyes and mind down on the subject and SEEING it as it existed."[18] Pound, however, he told nothing. And when Pound suggested Williams read Gesell, Williams asked David Lyle what he should read by that economist.

On the other hand, when Pound told Williams in the late summer of '48 to take a look at what Antonin Artaud had done in developing a modern theater technique, Williams shot back that what he'd read of Artaud's hadn't been worth his time. To which Pound responded: "Fer gor zake / don't so eggzaggerate / I never told you to read it. / let erlone REread it. I didn't / say it *wuz*!! henjoyable readin. / I sd / the guy had done some honest / work divilupping his theatre technique." Enough on Artaud anyway. Bull Williams needed a more basic reading list than that anyhow. For starters: "re read *all* the Gk tragedies in Loeb.—plus Frobenius, plus / Gesell plus Brooks Adams / ef you ain't read him all.— / Then

Golding 'Ovid' is in Everyman lib. / & nif you want a readin / list ask papa. . . ."[19] That letter—dated October 13—found its way into the third section of *Paterson* 3—the leaden flood section—between a passage of freely flowing detritic verbal fragments and a ninety-year-old artesian well chart of Paterson, which showed that deep drilling for potable water was out of the question in *Paterson.* Or, better, that the water found at such depths as Pound had gone to in the *Cantos,* for instance, was "altogether unfit for ordinary use," a counterthrust Ezra did not miss. "Just because they ain't no water fit to drink in that spot (or you ain't found none) don't mean there ain't no fresh water to be had NOWHERE," he retorted when he found his letter of the thirteenth enshrined in *Paterson* 3, only to find this retort in its turn embedded in the middle of *Paterson* 4 two years later.[20] But if Williams shrugged off Pound's high-handed pedagogic manner, telling Laughlin on October 19 that Pound was "lecturing" him (still!) on his lack of reading, he added that he'd probably have to satisfy his friend and read what he suggested.[21] And in the next few years that was exactly what Williams did, as he turned once again—with a renewed seriousness—to the old masters.

After all, Williams had finally realized, Pound could still write and write well. When the *Pisan Cantos* were published as a group in August 1948, Williams did a review of them for Thomas Cole's *Imagi,* another new little magazine, remarking in his review that—while some passages of the *Cantos* left him cold—there were others where the words lay fertile between the thighs of the sentences. As for Pound's general theory about usury, about the way special interest groups could destroy the fabric of an entire society, Williams had seen too much to doubt the essential truth of that insight. He ended his short piece by evoking his friend's plight once again: "Pound's loyalty, humanity (conspicuously revealed by the devotion he inspires in other men who devote themselves to him), kindness and good sense, would strike like lightning into us. So we proceed to legally slaughter him (in the face of the lice and swine we let live) that we may escape the implications of his genius. We might better acquire stronger stomachs against his peccadilloes."[22]

What was it Williams had finally found new and important in the *Pisan Cantos?* For one thing, passages like the following, embedded in the 78th Canto, a dialogue heard by Pound at the outdoor latrine of that prison hellhole at Pisa, its criminal population composed mostly of blacks, those expendable scapegoats of American society thus condemned to be hanged for large and small crimes from the scaffold built near Pound's own cage:

> *The touch of sadism in the back of his neck*
> *tinting justice, 'Steele that is one awful name.'*
>   *sd/ the cheerful reflective nigger*
> *Blood and Slaughter to help him*

> *dialogue repartee at the drain hole*
> *Straight as the bar of a ducking stool 'got his pride'*
> *get to the states you can buy it*
> > *Don't try that here*
> *the bearded owl making catcalls. . . .*

Among those offscourings which now included himself, Pound had caught something of the dialect phase of the American language once again, could run his tongue against the inaccuracies of his cracker-barrel Yankee and Uncle Remus imitations, having been for too long a period surrounded by the cadences of Italian and German. Williams ticked off passages like these rather than Pound's more lyric passages to show where he felt the real advances in the *Cantos* had been made.

In late November 1948, Williams heard privately from Lowell that Pound had been voted the Bollingen Prize for the *Pisan Cantos*, as the best book of poems published by an American that year. But this was the problem: the Bollingen was a new, government-sponsored award granted by the Fellows in Poetry of the Library of Congress. And since Pound was then in Washington, incarcerated there on charges of treason against the same government that would now be honoring him with its first Bollingen Prize, Williams, like the committee that had actually voted for Pound, knew that there'd be hell to pay on Capitol Hill and in the American press. But no other book of poems had even come close to Pound's *Pisan Cantos*, and there the matter stood. In spite of heated differences, the Fellows had voted Pound the prize. On November 27, Williams wrote Lowell in Washington to ask how Pound had responded to the news of the award and the $1,000 that went with it. He had seen Pound for a second time on his trip to Washington the week before to hear Eliot, and he'd been pleased to find ol' Ez "particularly clear and coherent."

And yet he still had qualms about the violence with which Pound pursued the question of the credit conspiracy. "He is 'sure' that all the rest of us are babies," Williams wrote, for Pound still believed he was in on some great secret about what was really going on in the world:

> He speaks particularly of some Italian, who was murdered "by the British Secret Service." . . . Then there was Henriot, who was killed or committed suicide. His . . . insistence is that as soon as anyone cracks the 'Secret' cabal and its nefarious machinations—he is murdered. Just, let us say, as our ex-ambassador to the Court of St. James, Winant, was "murdered" by one of his maids, a plant in his household by the British Secret Service—because he knew too much. Now, is that insanity or is it not? We believe it is but then there was Machiavelli, Metternich, to say nothing of Hitler, Stalin, Churchill and (according to Ez), F.D.R., all criminals who would stop at nothing. And at the bottom we find the wealthy Chews. A horrible misgiving comes over us that history may (more or less) prove that Ez was SANE!

Williams was struggling to "reconstruct Ezra's 'mind' or mindlessness, his sense or nonsense." But of one thing Williams was sure: usury was indeed "a public crime of such overwhelming proportions" that it alone might make the difference between happiness in the world—an earthly Paradise—and "our present disastrous disunity—bred of economic fears."[23] Thus in *Paterson* 3 and 4 Williams would point to the underlying cancer of special interest groups which had destroyed and then abandoned American cities like Paterson by the hundreds. So Williams would point to Hamilton and SUM—and later to the Englishman Catholine Lambert, who had tried to break the unions in Paterson in the early years of the twentieth century—as specific examples of greed that had hurt his own city and himself. But he still refused to buy into Pound's anti-Semitism. So, for example, he'd written Kenneth Rexroth in May that "ol' Ez could be a bastard" when he spoke about the Jews and that he for one had no use for the man when he went on ranting that way. He remembered once with satisfaction how Basil Bunting had put Pound in his place for his anti-Semitism "in as scathing a letter as I imagine Ezra ever got. He called him proper for his bigotry."[24]

The news that Pound had indeed won the Bollingen became public on Sunday, February 20, 1949, and Williams was glad he'd been at a social function at Princeton, talking with Kenneth Burke and John Berryman, when a reporter had called 9 Ridge Road to find out what Williams' feelings were about a traitor and anti-Semite receiving a government prize.[25] As Williams knew it would, the awarding of the Bollingen to Pound did, of course, stir up a controversy that would have reverberations for years. The issues involved were complex, but among them were the justice or lack of it in giving Pound the award *in spite of* the flawed surface of the *Cantos* because they were, finally, the best poems produced by an American in 1948. But the fact also remained that a government-sponsored group had offered a government prize to a person still charged with wartime treason against that same government. And then there were also Pound's harsh remarks against the Jews, coming at a time when America had incontrovertible evidence of what had actually happened to some six million of their people in concentration camps even as Pound was broadcasting over Radio Rome.

Williams had never been able to stomach Pound's talk about the "Chews," and he had already broken several times with him for his arrogance and political insensitivity. But—his own Jewish heritage notwithstanding—William's temper flared when Pound's name was mentioned in the May issue of his old enemy the *Partisan Review* in what Williams considered unfair and unjustifiable contexts. The first instance was in a series of replies to an editorial by William Barrett that had appeared in the previous issue of *PR* dealing with Pound and the

Bollingen. The replies had come from three members of the committee of Fellows that had awarded the Bollingen to Pound—Auden, Karl Shapiro, and Allen Tate—as well as from several others, among them George Orwell and Irving Howe. At issue here was not Pound's alleged treasonous behavior (after all he had never been tried on those charges), but rather his anti-Semitism.

The second essay, which Williams read closely, was Sidney Hook's "Reflections on the Jewish Question," an attack on Sartre's just-published book, *Anti-Semite and Jew*. And while Hook went ostensibly after Sartre, he was equally concerned with the intellectual giants of Europe and America who by their writing and example had helped "poison the little minds" of millions of others. "The sensibilities of the Ezra Pounds are finer than those of the Himmlers, the stomachs of the Célines are weaker than those of the Streichers," Hook wrote, "but is the objective meaning of their statements about the Jews so fundamentally different?"[26] To this Williams objected strongly. Pound might be crazy, he had certainly been out of touch, the economic problem had indeed become myopic with him, but to liken him to a Himmler was absurd—and dangerous. Besides, Williams argued, Hook's line of reasoning amounted to special pleading. In literature, there was neither Semitism nor anti-Semitism, but rather "a democracy of talent," and it made no more sense to him for a literary committee member who was Jewish to vote against Pound for his alleged anti-Semitism than it would have been to vote against him for his being anti-Catholic or anti-American or anti-Russian.

Williams' point was this: *all* sectarianisms in America were suspect to him. He himself had always been in favor of a secular humanism, and so he saw both pro-Semitism and anti-Semitism as being sectarian and therefore counter to the democratic impulse he felt basic to the American experiment. The tribal aspects of Jews were therefore like the tribal aspects of any group—Irish, German, or black—though Williams could also see that the Jews especially had had to pull together "simply to survive," as the late war had made too painfully clear. He remembered for example the picketing of the anti-Semitic pianist Gieseking at Carnegie Hall in the winter of '48 by various Jewish groups, including a large number of Jewish ex-GIs who had witnessed at first hand the shocking evidence of Hitler's "final solution" to the Jewish question. But, Williams argued, might not those same groups have made the musician work for their own cause by espousing not a dividing sectarianism but a greater democratic humanism, including even Gieseking in "a wider philosophic, historic, and pyschologic alertness"? And so with Pound: why not simply take his art—flawed though it was—and make it work for a more humane poetry for both Jew and non-Jew alike?

Williams reworked his reply, polishing his arguments, and then sent it off to Kurt Mertig, chairman of the Citizens' Protective League, to see if he couldn't get it printed somewhere. But no one seemed interested, and so Williams' direct response to the Bollingen Prize controversy was consigned to his files.[27] He also sent Allen Tate a letter in early July agreeing with what Tate had said in response to those who had attacked him for voting to give Pound the prize. And in September he wrote Tate again saying he would support Hayden Carruth's program to have the full story about the Bollingen affair published in *Poetry* magazine to offset the controversy about it which Robert Hillyer had stirred up in the *Saturday Review of Literature*.[28] Hillyer's attack on the Bollingen Committee's decision had reached such proportions that by early October Congress forbade the Library of Congress from offering any more such awards. Williams was furious with the "lily-livered legislators"—as he called them in a letter to Bill Bird—for buckling to pressure and "squelching" those much-needed prizes.[29] And he was saddened too by what Hillyer had done. Hillyer was, after all, a pretty sad specimen, Williams told a friend the following April. He'd had a real opportunity to do good work and to teach, but something in his own mind had thwarted him, turning him away from productivity. But what made the man "tragic" in Williams' estimate was his steadfast refusal to admit that he'd been wrong in his all-out attack on Pound.

Williams had not been a Fellow of the Library when the Bollingen Award was made, but he had already been elected to that position beginning in January 1950. He had had to turn down the Consultantship in Poetry for 1949–50, finally, ostensibly for health reasons but really because he couldn't see living alone in a rented room in Washington and reporting for work each day from nine to five—and all for $5,700. But as much as he wanted to be a Fellow, he was even willing to resign from that group as well because Eliot had also been made one and Williams had "no intention of working with Eliot on an American job."[30] It was Tate who finally persuaded him, and then only after several letters, not to resign. Williams reasoned that there were, after all, as he told Tate in August, "worse sons of bitches than T.S.E.," though it would be "hard to find them." In fact there was one in Congress—Senator Jacob Javits—who had apparently taken Williams' name "in vain," saying that the Pound "forces" had been strengthened by the inclusion of Williams among the Fellows. Williams was even ready to let Eliot go for the moment "and transfer the fight" to the senator from New York.[31]

And as for the *Pisan Cantos*, which had been the reason for so much fuss? Oh, they were by no means "all gold," he agreed with Louis Zukofsky at the beginning of March. But there was "a music that *perhaps saves all of it*"—all, that is, except for those crazy printed Chinese characters which he couldn't even pronounce, much less understand. "When I first looked at the *Cantos* and began to read I had to quit," he said. They were so dull he'd kept falling asleep over them. In fact he'd complained to Pound then that he couldn't seem to get past page 18. To which Pound had replied: "Wall, you never could read more than 18 pages of anything since I knew you." Williams had to admit that Pound was probably right.[32] He knew Pound still thought of himself as an exiled leader, knew too that even in prison the man could be awesome, and so, when young Tom Cole planned to visit Pound in June, he asked Williams how he should act. Williams answered that even he had been nervous the first time he'd gone to see his friend at St. Liz's. So if Pound asked Cole what he thought about his *Cantos* he was to say that he'd read them as carefully as he could but that there still remained difficulties. Cole should also not bring up the subject of FDR or the American Constitution. And he should remember that Pound was, after all, "really a very reasonable and charming person." He was definitely a traitor, Williams believed, but he was *not* "malicious."[33]

*
* *

By January 1949, as Williams moved ahead with *Paterson* 3, he could taste for the first time since his sabbatical twenty-five years earlier the leisure to write when his mind was "hot." Within a few months Bill Jr. had taken over fully half of his father's medical practice and was fast gaining a reputation for being the best qualified pediatrician in the immediate area. He was living back home again, but this time paying room and board to help with expenses. Ideally, Williams should have felt relieved, glad that his last years might be filled with the time and leisure to write. But he was worried, worried because he had not put aside sufficiently for his old age. So, as he should have begun to live in that imaginary garden he had often talked about, and which he had more than once seen at Gratwick Highlands, he allowed his time to be taken over more and more with lectures and meetings of the National Institute of Arts and Letters, the Fellows of the Library of Congress, and with readings—mostly done for nothing. Nor would he relinquish his medical practice altogether, though Bill more and more helped him when he was fatigued or when it was necessary for him to be out of town.

Much of *Paterson* 3 Williams had assembled over the years, and now he intensely reworked certain passages, such as the "Beautiful Thing" passage—Episode 17—which he'd composed ten years earlier. By January 5 he was already in what he called "the stage just before the semi-final stage." It was down on paper now and needed only to be ordered and then pruned. It was still too big "for its pants" and he was afraid that it might end up twice the size of the previous book.[34] So he kept circling the poem, then jabbing at it, then wrestling, until by mid-February he told Burke that, though the giant had had him on its hip for a while, he'd finally managed to throw it and come up once more for air.[35] Then, on Wednesday night, the twenty-third, he wrote Zukofsky that he'd just finished the thing an hour before. He was even thinking of plunging directly into *Paterson* 4 though the prospect of finding a form to end his poem still frightened him:

> When I go into the composition stage I go a little nuts and have to count on irritability, bad dreams, horrible moments of depression, for what? A few moments of heavenly exhileration [sic] when I think I'm king of the world. But with age these flights are not as convincing as formerly. They are, though, as much fun as ever if I can take the exhaustion they entail. So maybe I'll start IV. . . . At least I can START. Once the thing is emplaced, divided into its 3 component parts and very roughly laid out maybe I'll be able to rest until fall.[36]

But he could not yet go on with the poem and he knew it. Instead, he turned back to *Paterson* 3 to readjust its parts, tinker, revise. Only in mid-March was the poem really finished, and then he wanted it away from him as quickly as possible. Things moved swiftly. By the middle of May Laughlin had sent the prepared script to Van Vechten; by early August Williams had read and corrected the galleys, leaving them intact except for two small cuts. In November he had advance copies of *Paterson* 3 in his hands, in time for the National Book Awards committee to decide to give Williams its first annual Gold Medal for Poetry in early 1950.

Paterson 3 contains the very core of Williams' epic, if one can speak of a poem as radically decentered and as horizontal as this one as having a core. For the secret heart of the matter was revealed here, as Williams recapitulated in his poem Pound's enactment in the *Pisan Cantos* of the goddess's presence in his tent at that Disciplinary Training Center at Pisa. "There came new subtlety of eyes into my tent," Pound had written in *Canto LXXXI,*

> whether of spirit or hypostasis,
> but what the blindfold hides
> or at carneval
>
> nor any pair showed anger
> Saw but the eyes and stance between the eyes,
> color, diastasis,
> careless or unaware it had not the
> whole tent's room. . . .

And at the core of *Paterson* 3, Williams' counter vision, not of Aphrodite, but rather of a nameless black woman, Kore the maiden, mauled, disfigured, raped—*ecce femina!*—this radiant gist illuminating the apparently inert mass of the world of Paterson. Here was the woman lying in an inversion or negative of Manet's *Odalisque* or Goya's *Maja Desnu-*

da, lying there on the stained white sheets of the page in a basement hell
somewhere in his debased city:

> *—the small window with two panes,*
> *my eye level of the ground, the furnace odor .*

>   *Persephone*
> *gone to hell, that hell could not keep with*
> *the advancing season of pity.*

> *—for I was overcome*
> *by amazement and could do nothing but admire*
> *and lean to care for you in your quietness—*

> *who looked at me, smiling, and we remained*
> *thus looking, each at the other . in silence .*

> *You lethargic, waiting upon me, waiting for*
> *the fire and I*
> *   attendant upon you, shaken by your beauty*

> *Shaken by your beauty .*

>   *Shaken.*[37]

Kore: one of the many grim jokes and riddles propounded in *Paterson*. But
the gist of this joke—this riddle—is central to getting all the riddles.
Kore: Curie: Core: Cure: Care: Cor—ner: Caw Caw. These and other
linguistic sparks strike from the central figure of Kore, the radiant gist,
the magnetic core organizing the detritic "randomness" of *Paterson*.

All his life, as he worked his way up from under, Williams had been
rejected, dismissed, laughed at, patronized—like most revolutionaries.
No wonder, then, that his goddess should also have come to assume
something of his own features, having been discovered by this poet in the
place more than one person had called Hell. Like her, he would sing in
spite of hell, her radiance unquenchable, finally, "a fire / a destroying
fire," an "attack" on the status quo, on religious orthodoxy, the academies, a corrupting economic system. It was a fire that the big boys wanted
put out because it upset all their poetic theories, entrenched since
Saintsbury's time at least, and they were at least as jealous of their powers
as the boys from Newark and Paterson had been of theirs, willing to bust
the nose of that black girl because they had feared her beauty:

> *They see*
> *to it, not by intellection but*
> *by sub-intellection (to want to be*

> *blind as a pretext for*
> *saying, We're so proud of you!*

> *A wonderful gift. How do*
> *you find the time for it in*

> *your busy life: It must be a great*
> *thing to have such a pastime. . . .* [38]

Williams was only eighteen when fire destroyed nearly all of old Paterson, and what was left of the city the swollen, frenzied Passaic had swept away a month later when the spring thaws came. Then, to heap insult on injury, a freak cyclone had swept down on Paterson in the summer of 1903, and that destructive element Williams had also added to the triad that makes up *Paterson* 3: first wind, then fire, then water, that leaden flood. In the complex joke of *Paterson* these become radical metonyms for the "elements" of language itself. For no matter how revolutionary the search for a redeeming language should be, that search must lead—finally—either to failure or discovery. And even discovery leads inevitably to the incorporation of that breakthrough into a larger tradition of previous discoveries by earlier, equally authentic poets. So the flow of the river—the timebound tradition, the timebound epic—is inevitably seaward, leadward, from the mass of unrefined pitchblende to the release of energy to a subsequent disintegration, as unstable radium moves by an inevitable process toward the stability of lead. Or, to recall another complex pun Williams used in *Paterson:* as we the reader digest *Paterson,* the imagination is illuminated by the unstable processive activity of encountering the living gist of the matter. And active there in the apparently inert text of several hundred pages of poetry and prose is the meat, the nutrition, while the rest becomes waste, leaden matter. In effect then, the whole poem is really only Paterson the giant's enormous leaden stool.

So even *Paterson* becomes another "Book of Lead"—a Book of the Dead—like all those other books in the library: a "ruin left/by the conflagration" of a "white-hot man become/a book, the emptiness of/a cavern resounding." Neither past nor future is real, Williams' poem says. Only the present moment exists, and it has been Williams' intent to write the poem of earth, to realize himself in his own present, to find a meaning in his world and then "lay it, white,/beside the sliding water," the detritic flux, the massive verbal aphasia we call modern experience. The aim of *Paterson,* he has told us, has been to make a "replica" of life itself as distorted as those "images of arms and knees/hung on nails" in the chapel of San Rocco "on the sandstone crest above the old/copper mines," hung there in thanksgiving for diseases "cured" and sins confessed and so forgiven. *Paterson:* itself a complex, multifaceted confession and cry of anguish, a three-hundred-page "joke," distorted, debased, limping on grotesque feet like the poor city and the poor self who had come to identify with that city: the city/the man. An interpenetration both ways.

The debased city: Williams had had another taste of the city on a

Sunday afternoon in late winter, even as he finished *Paterson* 3. He and Floss had driven down to Newark to wait for the train that would take them down to Princeton to see Burke, who was then finishing his *Rhetoric* at the Institute for Advanced Studies. It was a warm day—in fact the winter had been incredibly mild, as if to make up for the one before—and Williams and Floss had decided to take a short stroll around "the lowdown district of Newark." In less than an hour they had run into "5 Sunday afternoon bums," and Williams' heart had gone out to them. The sight had hurt him deeply, leaving him with an overwhelming sense of impotence. "I can't have anything to do with tramps," he told Zukofsky:

> I can't take it. What in hell is one to do? Become a bum oneself? I can't see any other answer. Anything else is a complicated lie. These men in their 40s or so, big broken-nosed wrecks either ought to be taken out and shot or be sheltered and fed and loved. God damn it. It distresses me more and more as I get older. I feel dirty and cowardly. I can only avoid looking at them.

Of all those he saw, only two young blacks still seemed to have any life in them. At least they were young, and Williams noticed how one of them had preened himself in the window of an empty showcase, "using it as a mirror to arrange his fedora." But if it was hard looking at the men, it was hell itself to look at women derelicts. A few weeks earlier, at the beginning of February, he'd spotted one of those women as he'd driven out of the Hell Mouth of the Lincoln Tunnel into midtown New York. She'd been "standing on the corner of 40th Street just near where the cars from Jersey disgorge from the tube," he remembered. "It was horrible—a sick, deathly sick piece of female filth and rags—practically falling apart." There was nothing he could do about it but look as he drove on. Somehow, he summed up, somehow "we don't connect the right things together."[39] But that image would haunt him, that image of another victimized, nameless woman, to surface as he wrote *Paterson* 4 in the summer of '50. *Voi ch'entrate*, Williams would write, calling on Dante's admonition to all who would enter the hell of New York, thus abandoning all hope, as that other voice—Hart Crane's—had cried out twenty years before in "The Tunnel." Abandon all hope, here, "where the tunnel / under the river starts," Williams wrote:

> . the traffic is engulfed and disappears .
> to emerge . never
>
> A voice calling in the hubbub (Why else
> are there newspapers, by the cart-load?) blaring
> the news no wit shall evade, no rhyme
> cover. Necessity gripping the words . scouting
> evasion, that love is begrimed, befouled. . . . [40]

In March Williams' fourteen-page chapbook, *The Pink Church*, was published by Richard Wirtz Emerson and Frederick Eckman in a limited edition of four hundred copies at the Golden Goose Press in Columbus, Ohio. What Williams wanted to point up in this small collection was the direction his poetry had taken since 1946—its range and diversity. But though Williams was pleased with that effort, he knew that his real chance for getting his work out and read in an edition the college kids could afford "without borrowing or going broke" was the *Selected Poems*, which James Laughlin brought out that same month in a run of 3,600 copies. For $1.50 one could now get a cleanly designed hardback that contained 86 poems in its 128 pages of text, poems Williams had written between 1912 and the late '40s, complete with an introduction by Randall Jarrell. Williams had made the selection himself the year before, though he was not in this case his own best editor. And though the selection was adequate, it did not indicate Williams' full strengths as a poet; moreover Jarrell was right to complain about New Directions' choice to keep *Paterson* out of the *Selected* altogether.

And since the only poem Jarrell had indicated he liked was *Paterson* (and only the first part of that), there were problems from the start. Williams sensed something was off when, after having the Jarrells out to 9 Ridge Road for dinner in early '47, Jarrell had virtually ceased communicating with Williams. Moreover, by the time he got around to writing the introduction—which caused him no small anxiety—Jarrell was feeling far less sanguine about Williams than he had been when he wrote praising *Paterson* 1. Most of Williams' poems he thought of as being more in the vein of notes toward complete poems rather than poems themselves: "winning machine-parts minus their machine." Writing that introduction, therefore, had made him feel "rather like Little Lord Fauntleroy introducing Henry Wadsworth Longfellow into Heaven," and Williams—noting Jarrell's waverings—had several times confided to Laughlin that perhaps he should have done his own introduction or had someone else do it.[41] But Laughlin's instinct was to go with an introduction by a recognized poet and critic.

When Williams finally had a chance to see the introduction, he wrote Jarrell to say how pleased he was with that effort, though secretly he chafed at Jarrell's giving with his right hand what his left hand kept taking away. Jarrell's review of the first four books of *Paterson* in 1951 dispelled forever any doubts Williams might still have had about Jarrell's being disillusioned with the direction the poem had taken after the first book. And the Introduction here served as a halfway house between the praise of *Paterson* 1 (1946) and the disenchantment of Jarrell's essay five years later. In his introduction, Jarrell worked a strategy of syntactic balances that kept verging on a kind of aesthetic schizophrenia. If

Williams was neither intelligent, nor a master craftsman, nor a major poet—none of which Jarrell accused Williams of being—he was at least "American" and "outspoken, good-hearted, and generous," fresh, sympathetic, enthusiastic, spontaneous, open, impulsive, emotional, observant. It might have been a transmuted Boy Scout oath Jarrell was giving, and his unfortunate evocation of Yvor Winters as Williams' "most valuable advocate" must have reinforced Williams' mistrust of anything Jarrell had to say by way of praise. What Jarrell said he said well and wittily, if with a certain labored urbanity, but with a condescension that finally reduced Williams' total output of fully realized poems to something approaching Winters' "half dozen" number. That he closed his introduction by noting how "honest, exact, and original" the poems were, filled with "generosity and sympathy," did not negate the sense one was left with that one was dealing here with a circumscribed and minor talent. In 1949, on the other hand, there were few enough critics willing to give him even as much credit as Jarrell had given him.[42] What did become troublesome was how Jarrell's overview came to narrow the entrance to the one volume most American readers of Williams were to pick up for the next thirty years. It was an irony that would hardly have escaped Williams.

*
**

In late March of that year, Williams heard again from Marcia Nardi—the Cress of his *Paterson*—after a six-year silence. She was living up in Woodstock, New York now, and she wanted copies of *Paterson* 1 and 2 and some money, say two hundred, right away. Williams didn't *have* two hundred dollars, and, besides, that wasn't the answer to her problems anyway. He told her he would get in touch with Laughlin to see if he could give her some sort of advance on some poems. He also enclosed a money order for twenty dollars.[43] In early June Nardi sent Williams a sheaf of five poems, several of which she'd already sent to Laughlin. Williams was still impressed by the woman's talent. "She's got stuff and I have written telling her so," he wrote Laughlin on June 8. She had "more depth of feeling than any of the females, bar none, and a sense of words and intrinsic merit that is outstanding. I go for her all over again."[44] Six days later he wrote Laughlin again, pleading with him "to give her a book (a baby)."[45] When he had not heard by the twentieth, he wrote yet again, telling Laughlin that if Laughlin did not "make some sort of advance to her" then he would. The difference was that with Laughlin "it could be in the form of a business arrangement" while with Williams "it would have to be a gift outright." And he was anxious to give the woman some dignity.[46] Laughlin in turn wrote Williams telling him that he just could not see his way clear to doing a book of Nardi's poems, but that he was sending her an advance of fifteen dollars for her poetry. Perhaps in the fall he could manage a chapbook of sorts.[47]

In the meantime, Williams asked Nardi to send him a sheaf of her poems for a possible volume, which she did. He was surprised at how she'd managed under adverse conditions to continue to develop, and on July 16 he wrote her to say how very much he admired her new work: "Really, Marcia, I may be unbalanced one way or the other by my prejudices, but I have interrupted my reading of your poems to say as candidly as possible that I think you're wonderful." He was going to write Norman Holmes Pearson, asking him to help her with a grant, if possible, and he was sending along some of her poems to a new magazine published out of Rome called *Botteghe Oscure*.[48] (On the twenty-second, he also sent along—with reservations—some free medical advice she'd wanted about a duodenal disorder she'd been complaining about.) True to his word, Williams wrote to Pearson in late August, asking him to help Nardi if he could, and two months later he was able to tell her that Pearson had managed to get her a grant for $250. That December, Williams and Nardi also appeared together in Laughlin's *New Directions* 11. Nardi's newer work, Williams told her, was "the best you have ever written and, for they strike completely through my guard, they appear to me among the best poems of our day." They were "so much better than what is being accepted as good that I feel ashamed for my sex, to say the least, which generally monopolizes the scene." These were really poems, "warm, defenseless and well made," poems where the very form was "intrinsic, as it must be and especially for the female of our wits—for we are all male and female in varying degrees but a woman has her part of it strongest."[49]

Having begun again, Nardi would continue to ask Williams for help. A year later, in the fall of 1950, she wrote to him about the failure of love in her own life. She was writing Dr. Williams now as she had eight years earlier, she explained, out of the same desperate loneliness she had felt then. It was a long letter and in it she lamented that she and Williams had never become emotionally involved. She had never wanted any man the way she had wanted him and—not having had him had made her loneliness even more desperate. But there it was, there was her vulnerability for Dr. Paterson to see. Williams, for his part, immediately sent Nardi's letter to his lawyer, James Murray, for safekeeping. Marcia Nardi was unstable, Williams explained, and he didn't want any trouble from her in the future. "The woman and I remain friends, as you see," he explained to Murray, "though I early foresaw what was happening and cut our correspondence as of that early date off short." He was convinced she was "really a genius of sorts" and he wanted to do all he could short of becoming "emotionally involved which I refuse to do."[50] And six years later, perhaps thinking back to this moment, he would write in the fifth book of *Paterson:* "Paterson has grown older / the dog of his thoughts / has shrunk / to no more than 'a passionate letter' / to a woman, a woman he had neglected / to put to bed in the past. / And went on / living and writing."[51]

Nardi also asked him to find her another grant, and he promised to see what he could find for her, reminding her again that everyone needed "close friends . . . to whom to 'confess' at times with a sure feeling that we shall be given unfailing sympathy and unquestioning support in our emotional agonies. I am that sort of friend to you." And yet he warned her that "the battle itself we must undergo entirely alone."[52] When she wrote again in January 1951, asking for more help, Williams was in the midst of his *Autobiography*—a book that was at that moment threatening to swamp him—and he was in no mood to listen, though his letter showed remarkable restraint under the circumstances.[53] Nardi, perhaps frightened, returned to her silence until early August, when she asked Williams to meet her in New York, as she had nearly ten years earlier. The answer came back sharply and belatedly. Williams had suffered a stroke in March and was feeling generally depressed. "You had no reason to expect that I would run off to New York to meet you last Thursday even if I could," Williams told her. "You assume much too much. Therefore you have no occasion to be disappointed." He softened then a bit, explaining that he couldn't get around much anymore, and he had no idea what the future would bring now that he'd been knocked under by his stroke.[54] But in October he went ahead and wrote a letter of recommendation for her to Yaddo (she was turned down), and suggested that she also write to John Ciardi for help. Nardi tried those angles and then asked for more help.

Finally, in January 1952, Williams told her to just stop writing for a while and to take on any kind of job—just "plain ordinary work" —whatever might feed her.[55] When she wrote him again in late August complaining that she needed more help, it was Floss who answered. Her husband had been hit by a serious stroke just two weeks before and she was in no mood for the likes of Marcia Nardi. Dr. Williams was "critically ill," she warned the woman, and could "under no circumstances write or give you any assistance. With all good wishes."[56] That ended the correspondence for four years. There was one final letter, and that came in October 1956, when Nardi told Williams that Black Sparrow Press had just published her first book of poems. She was also asking him for a Guggenheim recommendation. By all means, a crippled Williams wrote back. "You are one of the hardiest women and one of the most gifted and generous women I know, I am happy at your success." With his left hand he scrawled out his first name. It was the last letter he ever wrote to his Cress.[57]

*
**

The lecture circuit also had its costs. On Saturday evening, May 7, 1949, Williams was in Washington, D.C., to do a reading for some outfit that John Berryman from his own experience had warned him might not pay up. And they didn't. Chalk that one up. From then on it would be money on the line for Bill Williams. The following Monday night—May 9, at 8:15—he did a reading for Vivienne Koch at NYU at Washington Square. He'd seen his old friend Fred Miller somewhere out there in the audience, and then realized that Miller was trying frantically to clear the hell out of the place, probably to escape meeting some woman. Williams himself hadn't cared much for his reading; he didn't think of himself as a particularly strong reader, and his high-pitched voice had given out before the reading was over. He'd done too many readings to feel intimidated by the podium, and he'd written Fred Miller on April 26, when he invited him to come on over, that the audience could "hoot or piss over the edge of the rostrum" for all he cared.[58] Now, after the reading he wrote Miller again: "Why the hell . . . should one confess to such a public?" Wasn't reading one's own poems a lot like pulling "back your foreskin (if you have one) in public"? Besides, there were some poems so personal he wouldn't read them to anybody. As it was, he knew he'd surprised Miller by reading one or two of his more confessional pieces, but he'd done that without realizing what he was doing—had just picked them up and read them—and then it had been too late. To make matters worse, the ceiling in the room had been "too low, the place was overcrowded" and he'd felt as though he were "talking into a felt mattress." But he did it after all for art, he noted sardonically, for people who year after year insisted on the spurious and who kept putting their money on other things.[59] "When I think of what might be done with money toward literature," he complained to Charles Abbott in July, "I mean money and I mean literature, a nausea comes into my breast at the failure of present day man to evaluate his world and himself such that knowledge of a cancer in my guts could not, I think, make me feel worse." Pound would have understood that sentiment perfectly.[60]

For over three years Williams had been trying—unsuccessfully—to get his play, A Dream of Love, performed somewhere in New York. Agent after agent had looked it over, indicating that the play—with some minor adjustments—showed promise and actability, but no theater group had taken it on until the summer of '49. It was a young off-Broadway group who finally performed the play, a company called We Present, and they put it on at the Hudson Guild Playhouse, a basement theater located at 436 West 27th Street. For Williams A Dream of Love was a subtle play, a confessional, a "pulling back of his foreskin," and it needed professionals to handle the complex of angers, confusions, and defenses surrounding the dialogue of the problematics of fidelity in a modern marriage. But what he had instead were some "nice professional kids—as innocent as day" and some others who had been "horribly miscast."[61] He refused to attend any of the rehearsals, though he did talk with some of the actors, but he was right there at the back of the theater on opening night—July 19—in what was unfortunately the middle of the worst heat wave New York had experienced in years. "Generally speaking the play went off very well," he told Abbott next day, though—without air conditioning—the basement theater had soon become "hellishly hot." It had been ninety-seven degrees at the back of that small unventilated room, into which 130 persons had wedged themselves. Williams had noticed too that the actors, as they became more and more uncomfortable under their clothes and greasepaint, had been more intent on getting through their lines than on dwelling on the "psychological nuances" of the play. That too was probably just as well, he acknowledged now, since he didn't want some of his friends in the front rows understanding everything that was going on in the play. After all, that was *his* life unfolding up on that stage and, in some sense, theirs as well.

On the other hand, several luminaries had been there, including the ever faithful Marianne Moore and the playwright William Saroyan. Williams had met Saroyan the previous December at a cocktail party, and when Saroyan had asked him how his play was coming, Williams had looked hard at him from behind his glasses and asked him what he —Saroyan—was personally doing about it. Now Saroyan responded by showing up that night and reviewing the play warmly in the Sunday *New York Times* for July 31. As for Moore, she had been wonderful, Williams noted, "blaming her infantilism relative to *amour* for many things." But clearly she was intelligent enough to be uncomfortable with the psychodrama Williams had presented for all the world to see and had masked it with her own brand of naiveté. Williams had planned to attend the first two or three performances of the play, but after opening night he could see "how very difficult it must inevitably be for a playwright such as myself to get a play performed, a difficult play, as he had conceived it," and he decided to stay away.[62] The underlying truth probably was that he'd hit too palpably close to the heart in revealing himself as he had. It was too much like a final judgment. By the end of the second week, with the heat still baking the subterranean reaches of the city, the play had closed and Williams was already 350 miles away, relaxing with Floss at Gratwick Highlands.

No sooner was *A Dream of Love* behind him than the idea for "a possible libretto for an opera" began to obsess him. It had its genesis at Gratwick Highlands that July, at the Toby, the restored gardener's cottage on the estate, where Bill and Harriet Gratwick lived year round. Harriet Gratwick had close connections with the Eastman School of Music in Rochester, and Williams was given to believe that help would be forthcoming from that source in getting music for this new libretto of his.

The theme this time would be the Cold War itself and the American penchant for witch hunts, and he would superimpose the Salem Witch Trials of 1692 upon the Washington Army hearings of 1946. Hadn't he confided to Bill Bird back in February how hopeless the times were? "The Commies will soon murder us all," he wrote,"—the poor bastards —before the guy standing back of them carves a hunk of round steak off their buttocks for a barbecue grill on his own." Why, he half expected to look out his front window some day soon and see the murdering bastards marching up Park Avenue toward his house "led by the ghost of Hughey Long [sic] and burning the place right and left."[63]

He worked sporadically at the libretto, and could tell Abbott at the end of October that he'd "ground out of my brain, mostly during my sleep, a series of three scenes, with attendant characters, to make up a PLAY upon the general theme of the Witchcraft trials." Already he had composed "a very simple array of sequences, very novel and, perhaps, extremely dramatic in character." But—he noted—the idea could also be "very easily copied," and so he was saying no more for the moment until he'd found out about copyright. Besides, he was already running into one unforeseen trouble: he'd wanted to make the libretto lyrical, but instead it was turning out to be about "as lyric as *Macbeth*." Maybe, after all, there was more prose in the thing than verse, and maybe it would finally turn out closer to "*The Tempest* or *Midsummer Night's Dream* (lacking of course the genius)." The other problem was that he'd planned to do *Paterson* 4 that winter and he would have to get that obsession out of his system first.

Finally, he told Abbott to get hold of the October 24 issue of the *New Republic* and to read the "Books in Review" section. He would "find there a juxtaposition which gives, without the key of course, the matter of my play—a theme which we, the Toby and I, hit upon last summer long before we knew anything of those books."[64] What Williams had read in the *New Republic* was a long review by James R. Newman which had skillfully juxtaposed Marion Starkey's *The Devil in Massachusetts*—a study of the Salem witch trials—and Merle Miller's *The Sure Thing*, a novel set in Washington, D.C., in 1946. The novel was about a young State Department economist who had joined the Communist Party for a few months in the late '30s, and who, eight years later, was systematically destroyed by a combination of the FBI, a politician up for reelection, the yellow press, and the refusal—through fear and intimidation—of even his closest friends to come to his support.

Williams' libretto itself had turned into his nightmarish drama, *Tituba's Children*, and when he finished it the following year he set the contemporary scenes not in 1946, but even closer to his own moment: 1950. The witch hunts were far from over in Washington—indeed Senator Joe McCarthy's heyday still lay in the future. But the terrible irony of Williams' play was how life would conform to art once again as Williams himself became a target of suspicion and the object of an official witch hunt, with his own FBI file and all. And before that hunt was over, he would lie broken himself, the vicious innuendoes of the attack upon him contributing—as he and Floss believed—to the prolonged effects of the stroke of August '52, which was the one (*peine dure et forte*) which would leave him permanently crippled. But in December 1949 his spirits were still high, and he could kid the Abbotts and the Gratwicks that he was "much intrigued to discover that one of ye judges at the final trials was a Saltonstal of Haverill," Harriet Gratwick herself being a Salton-stall. Williams had only praise for that earlier Saltonstal, however, who, "rather than face the ordeal of condemning men and women whom he felt certain were innocent," instead "resigned and—laudably took to drink in so big a way that it made quite a stink." Williams himself would not get off that lightly.[65]

*
**

"Decided this morning with fog outside the bedroom window that I might as well believe in a future life," Williams had written Louis Zukofsky the day he went to meet T. S. Eliot in Washington. "Why not if it makes the mind lively?" For years he'd watched his old mother, first in his own home, and then, when that became impossible, at the local rest home run by a "marvelous" couple, the Taylors. Williams was still fascinated by his mother, had spent years listening to her and copying down her lively conversation. More and more, however, he could see her drifting as the years passed, her mind turned ever more frequently toward the invisible world of spirits. She had always been a medium, as far back at least as he could remember, frequently in contact with the dead or the living dead. And he remembered how, as a boy, he'd been frightened —both he and his brother—when, caught up in a trance, she would speak in a strange voice, failing to recognize either her husband or her children. As Williams grew older, he had had to learn to talk about his mother's "visitations" with an easy familiarity and a sense of humor. So, for example, in the same letter to Zukofsky in which he momentarily opted for a future life, he added—characteristically—this note:

> Me Ma is wonderful on the subject, the only difficulty being that all her *revenants* are such nasty bastards. I don't know why she has to pick such skunks. She says they want to "hurt people" but she can't say why. Poor soul, being unable to see or hear or walk she has invented the most marvelous assembly of witches and whore-masters to entertain her. The other day it was an endless column of Mexican cavalry riding bareback "to show us how they ride." There's a war on between Mexico and the U.S., you know. She tells you all about it.

Earlier, he had told Zukofsky that his critical prose had the same clean, sweet-smelling quality as his own mother's near-raving lucidities: "Mother said to me yesterday, 'I have been philosophizing all afternoon' (she sits alone there in her room for months and years at a time—and was very clear in her statements then,) '. . . and I have come to the conclusion that life is worth nothing at all.'" It was a "serious if demented statement, . . . the total dedication of absolute statement."[66]

"The Horse Show," written in late 1948, transforms one of Williams' talks with his mother into a poem of extraordinary delicacy and poignancy. Williams, already in his mid-sixties, and his mother, past ninety: the son trying to know the mother before she will have slipped away forever:

> Constantly near you, I never in my entire
> sixty-four years knew you so well as yesterday
> or half so well. We talked. You were never
> so lucid, so disengaged from all exigencies
> of place and time. We talked of ourselves,
> intimately, a thing never heard of between us.
> How long have we waited? almost a hundred years.

In the world of this poem, the son has come to tell the mother about a horse show, though he must add that he has not been able to get away to see it. Folded within the poem, however, there is talk of a man the son has read about in the papers who had dug himself out of a mountain slide in Switzerland to come back as it were from the dead. It is the theme of the afterlife again, the very thing that had haunted Williams' earlier meditation on his father. His mother insists quietly that the world of the spirits *does* exist, that it is "the same as our own," and that the presences really *do* come to visit: "I talk to them just as I / am talking to you. I see them plainly." And yet, Williams knows, his mother is locked into herself by lameness, deafness, blindness, so that all she "can do is to try to live over again / what I knew when your brother and you / were children." Williams might try to limit the validity of his mother's experiences, what he called her "visions," but he also respected them. In a sense deeper than he was able to admit to himself, he stood in quiet awe of these visitors who had quite as much substance as himself in his mother's shadow world: bitches, midges, her whole bin of blooded hallucinations.[67]

Then, in the spring of '49, when it looked as if his mother was finally going to die, he found himself composing a twenty-page poem in two parts which he called "Two Pendants: for the Ears." The first part juxtaposed a nightmare with the quiet of Easter Sunday morning at 9 Ridge Road. It was another image of the phoenix, of the terrible wound followed by a resurrection of sorts. In the nightmare that opens the poem, a tiger, seriously wounded, lies on a low parapet. It is dark, and—in that strange logic which dreams possess—the tiger lies in the "open plaza

/ before the post-office," the same one two blocks from Williams' home in Rutherford that his brother had designed years before. Out there in the dark the trainer also lies, also "horribly wounded" in the encounter with the beast. The dreamer—Williams the physician—has been called to help the trainer lying there, even as he sees that everyone around him is huddled and "terrified." Stepping into the dark alone to help the wounded trainer, he notices that the beast has suddenly stopped breathing, "as though the better / for him to listen and I could feel / him watching me." Suddenly realizing that he is "unarmed" and "helpless," he turns back to ask if anyone has "notified the police." . . . And then he wakes up. It is an admission of failure on Williams' part to do anything against the beast that waits in the dark for all of us. Williams, wounded physician that he was, who had watched one parent die and now watched the other, knew all too painfully his own human limitations.

He juxtaposed this dream with the familiar surroundings of his own home. From his bathroom window overlooking the back of his house, Williams could make out (in the second section of this poem) the early signs of spring—"the yellow of the flowers" and the "short and brilliantly stabbing grass." His son Bill has been out on a call and has returned to catch a few hours of sleep on the couch in the living room: a familiar presence. Williams can hear the church bells ringing the faithful to church, and his mind turns toward thoughts of young women—many of whom he himself had delivered—coming to him with their own first pregnancies. They are women whom he loves . . . and *can* help. He thinks too of his countrymen—realizing even as he uses that word that there is (in 1949) an inherent bathos about the term he had used so unironically thirty years before. How is it, he asks, that his people have let themselves "be so cheated—your incomes / taken away and . . . chromium / in your guts (rat poison)." Nor will "the ideals / preserved for us / by primitive peoples" save his own society—his "Paterson"—from its maladies. Familiar faces, familiar things, familiar concerns: a relief from the pressure of his Easter morning nightmare. To top it all off, he reads to Floss and Bill Jr. after breakfast from Dudley Fitts's new translation of *Plato's Inscription for a Statue of Pan*, with its pastoral world of water nymphs and dryads. And yet, for all the pastoral's antiquity, it "seems less / out of place than the present, all the / present for all that it is present," his fruit trees and battered old watering can—and all they signify—seen out the dining room window, reminding him of old continuities with that lovely, remote past. Truly, as the title of the first part tells us, *"The particulars of morning are more to be desired / than night's vague images."*

The second "pendant" presents a visit from Williams to his mother, for, "Now it is spring / Elena is dying." He talks with her, talks with the

Taylors who are caring for her, about an array of topics, ranging from the mango and the guava (Caribbean childhood memories) to a fashionable grocery list (the appetite for life) to a newspaper piece about a small St. Anne's statue which "wept at a kiss / from a child," remarking of this last that he hopes "it doesn't turn / out to be something funny." Watching his mother weave in and out of her inner spiritualist world—her own vague images of night—so that often she does not see her son standing there in front of her, Williams' own mind turns once again to the question of death and resurrection:

> *Then after three days:*
> *I'm glad to see you up and doing,*
> *Said she to me brightly.*
>
> *I told you she wasn't going to*
> *die, that was just a remission,*
> *I think you call it, said*
> *the 3 day beard in a soiled*
> *undershirt.*

Why this record, Williams asks, this record of his mother? To make pendants, decorations, for his mother's deaf ears: "To make the language / record it, facet to facet," and to give too "the unshaven, / the rumblings of a / catastrophic past, a delicate / defeat—vivid simulations of / the mystery." It is all a son, whether as physician or poet, can do.[68]

On Friday morning, October 7, Williams sent a note to Laughlin about business matters, and then added: "Me Ma to be 93 the day before Christmas, O Phoenix."[69] That very night, however, the phoenix underwent the final terrible transformation. She looked like some "Mediterranean Queen in her coffin," Williams told McAlmon a week later.[70] And to Louis Zukofsky:

> She curious little thing that she was simply went to sleep. Whether or not I could have "saved" her by giving penicillin the week before is something I have debated in my mind ever since her death. So that, in effect, I "killed" her. In her coffin her features were astounding, an Egyptian princess.[71]

The queen, the princess, gone, Williams—who had spent endless hours trying to pry the secret of his mother's life from her, to "know" her before it was too late—was to go on learning more about her. "When we, my brother and I, opened her big trunk in the attic," he told a friend of his, "we found among other things three coin-shaped, bright red cases large enough to hold, say, a silver dollar." Each of these, he explained, contained medals "she had won by her painting and drawing in Paris, at the School for Industrial Design, in 1877, '78 and '79." And in all the intervening years she had kept those medals secret. Why, he asked, why did we hide ourselves from one another? It made no sense. It was one of the "cardinal sins that we do not break bounds one way or another and come out of our prehistoric caves."[72]

Two months after his mother's death, Williams told Selden Rodman of another secret he'd recently uncovered. Further excavations into his mother's trunk had unearthed her old Mass book which she had specifically bequeathed to her older son. Inside the missal Williams had discovered a letter written in 1880 by a Frenchman proposing marriage. She must have refused, he said, for she married William George two years later. And while she'd never in all this time once mentioned that proposal, she'd left that letter there for her son to find after her death. Why? Vanity? A confession?[73] But the biggest surprise was to come only in 1956, when a friend—at Williams' request—managed to uncover Elena Hoheb's baptismal records down in Mayagüez. When Williams looked at the date he saw with shocked amusement that his mother had been born not in 1856 as her husband and sons had always believed, but in 1847. His ninety-two-year-old mother, it turned out, was actually four years older than her husband and had almost lived to see her 102d birthday.

There were several other domestic events to close out 1949. On Saturday evening, November 19, Bill Jr. married Daphne Spence, the daughter of close friends and neighbors of the Williamses, and the couple flew down to Bermuda for their honeymoon, whence, as Williams wryly noted the following Monday night, Bill had "wired that the skies there are blue." Then, on December 20, Floss's bed-ridden mother, Nannie Herman, also died. She too had long ago passed into Williams' fictional world, of course, in the robust and elbow-sharp figure of Gurlie Stecher, fully and disagreeably drawn over the years, first in *White Mule*, next in *In the Money*, and then finally in *The Build-Up*. Grasping, hardheaded, seeking a narrow, monetary version of success in the New World, Gurlie had early come to stand for Williams as a symbol of all the negative values inherent in the Horatio Alger story. And though Williams freely admitted that Gurlie Stecher was, after all, a fictional construct only loosely modeled on his mother-in-law, Floss felt vaguely uneasy whenever Williams worked on her mother in his trilogy. Pa Herman he loved, but he never came to terms with Ma Herman. And now, after years in a nursing home with a broken hip—like Elena—she too was gone, just before Christmas, so that the season itself, as Williams mentioned to Laughlin, had been "thrown into a strange light" by the double loss. And that was all—except in his fiction—he had to say about this second death.[74]

In late October Williams had gone into New York with Jinny to hear Cummings read and was amazed at the size of the crowds his old friend had been able to attract. "It is an experience to listen for the cadence and not, even in the sonnets, to walk over the open grid of an iambic pentameter—with hot air coming up and the subway rumbling under," he told Cummings after the performance. The man was still breaking new ground prosodically and had even managed to make the sonnet "unnecessary."[75] In mid-December he wrote to congratulate Wallace Stevens on his preface to the Gromaire catalog for the retrospective of that painter then in progress in New York. It was, he said, "one of the most impressive pieces of writing" he'd ever come across and he was making a special trip into the city to see the exhibit for himself. He wrote Stevens again a week later to tell him to look out for Winters' open letter in the December issue of *Poetry*—"The Poet and the University" —because it had lumped the lawyer and the doctor together to say that poets, even good poets like Stevens and himself—would have been "better off and possibly would have written better poems had we had the advantages of a university entourage." It was one master winking and poking an elbow into the ribs of another.[76]

On Christmas Day Williams wrote his own catalog note for a showing of seven portraits of Dora Maar by Picasso done during the Occupation in Paris. He used a war metaphor to describe Picasso's attack on the subject of the human face, a subject that had been fascinating him for several years. What was a "face" after all, he asked, if not a battleground for the artist? "Slash it with sharp instruments, rub ashes into the wound to make a keloid; daub it with clays, paint it with berry juices." It was something—the face—that could terrify because it reminded us of our own death. He may have stopped to look up at the death mask a sea-man admirer of his, Red Ruud, had brought back from Malaya and which held such a prominent place in his living room, the lidless eyes staring out on the void. Why did we always try to deform or reorganize the face, "by hair, by shaving, by every possible means?" Was it to transform it into a work of art and thus distance it from the fact of death? And so with Picasso. He had made his progressive attacks on the face, de-composing it, killing it, so that something else, something deeper, might rise from it, "upon which the whole world hangs breathless."[77]His own mother's face must have been vividly before him as he wrote these lines, and even more so the face of his mother-in-law, whom he'd waked only two days before. It was almost as though he was straining after something he called the possible transcendence of spirit, though that phrase would have embarrassed his modernist sensibilities. One thing was certain, however. He was now without either parent and, as far as he could see, that—as he told Roethke a few weeks later—certainly made him next.[78]

*
**

Facing the threshold of his own terminus now, when the father must inevitably give way to the son, when the beloved river should finally lose itself in the sea of blood, the sea of eternity, Williams turned once again to his own spiritual father in *Paterson*: Walt Whitman. Protest as Williams might, Whitman's song of death and the sweet word uttered by that primordial mother, the sea, lisping "the low and delicious word death, / And again death, death, death, death, / Hissing melodious," was very much on Williams' mind as he worked on the end of *Paterson*. One way to distance the father, of course, was to deal with him as abstract pattern, as bumbling measurer. Thus, in two letters written in early January to Robert Lawrence Beum, editor of the *Golden Goose*, Williams' lifelong preoccupation with Whitman's abiding presence once again surfaced.

What Williams stressed in those letters to Beum was the need for American poetry to move decisively away from a prosody of stress and toward a "prosody of the measurement of time," (i.e., toward the qualitative sonorities of a Robert Bridges as demonstrated in *A Testament of Beauty* and away from what he called the vulgarities of Hopkins' "constipated" sprung rhythms). Whitman, Williams was still insisting, "knew nothing of structure. . . . In *Paterson* IV that will come up—but as he grew older he went gaga, thinking a lot of loose talk meant democracy." What this son of Whitman wanted to show was that the democratic experiment had sifted ineradicably into the very texture of the American language, in its looseness, its receptivity, its pliability in the hands of generations of New World immigrants. Now it was up to the "new" poem, the poem Williams was after, to "lift the consciousness of a culture, a group, from the level, the barest levels, the levels of the newspaper (that unintentional parody of the modern epic), to the subtlest levels of consciousness."

"Whitman saw it," an early draft of *Paterson* 4—written during this same month—tells us. "The classic is / the past, columns regularly carved and / arranged, the new is like the waves / of the sea—as they plunged fawning at his / feet on the New Jersey shore." And this, among the same papers:

> No my own man stood upon my own beach
> and listened with his eyes and his
> whole sense. Whitman listened and looked
> and terminated an era and still we
> cannot sense it. The falls pours down
> its torrent, it has deafened me. . . .

"The greatest moment in the history / of the american poem was when / Walt Whitman stood looking to sea / from the shelving sands," Williams wrote in what was at one point to be the terminus of *Paterson* 4—or very near it:

> and the waves
> called to him and

> *he answered, drilling his voice to*
> *their advance*
> > *driving the words above*
> *the returning clatter of stone*
> *with courage, labor and abandon*
> *the word, the word, the word. . . .*

He knew that in 1950 there were English professors at Princeton who were reading his poems to undergraduates as an example of a poet without an ear for cadence. "They go on in niggardly fashion seeing that the beauties of English are being ravaged by a lot of barbarians of whom I am one of the crassest. Fuck 'em." For the syntactical cadences he was searching for were *"discoverable in prose* but used as metric" and *they* were "the true sources" of Williams' verse. America was not "poverty stricken in the area of the New Language." In fact it was "the richest in opportunity and, strangely enough, in accomplishment, in the making of poems, the richest area on earth." Let him demonstrate what could be done, he told Beum, and then let there be another measure between himself and that turncoat Yvor Winters, or even himself and Eliot, who had "vitiated the good and emphasized the stereotype and the dead."[79]

In an essay dated January 13—but not published in his lifetime—Williams extended his argument about the new measure to include Pound. If Whitman "had started" the search for a new and comprehensive American poem "in a crude way," Pound, having come of age (like Williams) in the new century, had begun early working to extend the possibilities of the "new" language. But Pound (unlike Williams) had early migrated to the "old," that is, to the European tradition with its European models. Nevertheless, once the English saw that Pound had meant what he said when he insisted on the new—"a new sense of time, a time, an efficiency timely to the age"—even the English, who had at first welcomed him, had wound up by rejecting him. This drift back to the old—repeated over and over again in all the successful journals of the day, in the newspapers, in politics and finance—this deathlike stasis, was in itself, Williams had come to see, a moral evil. The search for the new: in that direction lay Pound's—and Williams'—real contribution to poetry and their real virtue. For it was *all in the effort,* as *Paterson* 4 would say, all in the effort to give us a language and a measure for discourse consonant with our own moment—to make us *see*—that real virtue lay:

In the work of the poem, the joining of phrases, the trimming away of connectives, the joining of stone to stone, as a Greek column was joined, as the Incans joined their great wall—there is virtue. [Pound] calls it virtue, excellence—and continues to say that virtue is timely. It pays off in life, in behavior, in poems—as it would pay off in many another thing, if we could learn from our poets.[80]

Whitman, Pound, death, and the sea: it was Williams' complex enactment of his own death and the nature of a subsequent resurrection in the last book of *Paterson* as he'd contemplated it until then. He was focusing his attention on the sea of death and the whole romantic tradition—the two identified in Williams' mind with the terrifying ability of language and the symbols of that language to swallow up all distinctiveness, including Williams' own forty-year cry for distinctiveness and individuation. For no revolution in sensibility, no delayed spring-time, no prolonged meandering of the river, could keep the poet forever from reaching the sea. It was the call of those presences hovering about him: the call of Whitman, and—more subtly—of Keats and of the Joyce of the close of *Finnegans Wake,* as well as, now, the half-effaced presence of Eliot and Yeats and Hart Crane. It was the siren call to merge, to become one with the sea (which for Williams was one with the European tradition), to become faceless, like Dora Maar, like that corpse floating in the East River in *Paterson* 4. It was a call that would (finally) wash even Williams under. Only the assertion of the last pages of *Paterson,* and the dawning awareness that he had—for the moment—survived his own imaginative death, would make plausible his return—like Odysseus' —from the sea, to turn inland—as Poe and Boone had before him— inland, toward Camden, toward his elusive and early father: Whitman.

"We say Emerson," Williams commented wryly in his early drafts for *Paterson* 4, and then we "turn to some other source / of inspiration, to England to France. To / Cervantes to Cavalcanti." Or we say "Whitman," and "turn / to Pope or Donne. We turn perhaps to chemistry / not knowing it is the sea," by which we meant—and he meant—the bomb, meant death:

> *Thalassa, the sea. It*
> *is to the sea of abstract chemistry we turn. We say*
> *there are some bright young men in Chicago and*
> *Berkeley with their cyclotrons and their*
> *atomic piles—we have some good men also in*
> *Boston. . . .*

Thalassa: the sea. Whatever the sea was to other civilizations—Williams began this early draft of *Paterson* 4—for Americans the sea toward which they had always tended had been western Europe and its knowledge. Against that tug, a handful of imaginative thinkers—figures like Emer-son, Whitman, and Williams himself—had placed the opposing figure of the woman who symbolized "the struggle and privation / for remote victories, to come."[81]

Remote victories! To hell with them: Williams could no longer afford to wait for remote victories. He was sixty-six, already on a reduced income, and tired of the few hundred he managed to make each year from readings, royalties, the rest. On top of that a belated recognition was finally coming to him. He was a bona fide Fellow of the Library of Congress now, and attended his first meeting of the Fellows that January in Washington. Moreover, on the nineteenth of that month he received word that at the annual meeting of the National Institute of Arts and Letters he'd been elected a member of the Department of Literature, and he wrote William Rose Benét on his return from Washington that he was accepting and was waiting now for the "usual suit of light armour" he'd heard went with the honor. On the fifteenth Harvey Breit's interview with Williams had appeared in the Sunday *New York Times Magazine*, and at the end of the month he learned that he was to receive the National Book Awards' first Gold Medal for Poetry for *Paterson* at a ceremony to be held that March. On top of all that, Vivienne Koch's critical study appeared at almost the same moment. No wonder he told Zukofsky that something had "let loose the furies of communication" upon him, so that he found himself deluged with letters. There were so many, in fact, that he had been forced to put *Paterson* 4 on the shelf to attend to his admirers.[82]

Fame, even belated fame, he was about to learn, could be exhausting. On January 25 *Time* magazine sent a man out to interview Williams about *Paterson*. Then three days later a photographer for the same magazine came out to get some "candid shots" of the Rutherford physician. The doctor-poet had to be in white coat (Williams almost never wore a white coat, preferring instead a sports jacket or even shirt sleeves, but the photographer insisted on the white coat for the sake of "realism") and he had to be "shot examining children," so that he had to borrow one of his son's patients in the office for the occasion.[83] Now if only someone would make it possible for him to "quit cold" and let him write his heart out "unobstructed by the necessity to make a living."[84] He was even stronger in voicing his indifference to these new honors in a letter he wrote Roethke at the end of February. All such honors, he said, were merely nine-tenths "shit," and meant nothing. Had they really wanted to honor him they would have gotten behind his work and given that a shove. As it was, they only wanted to honor themselves.[85]

And what, then, about Jim Laughlin? What was *he* doing to make things easier for his star poet? The problem of fame compounded by the need for money made Williams more susceptible now to an offer from David McDowell, an editor at New Directions who had left Laughlin over a difference of opinion and had gone over to Random House. Now McDowell held out the carrot of some "big" money to Williams: $5,000 for three books of prose to be published between 1950 and 1952. These would be the collected short stories (already completed), an autobiography, already begun for *Poetry*, and then *The Build-Up*, for which Williams had by then completed the first four chapters. Laughlin could continue to do *Paterson* and the other poems. So, as the carrot dangled closer to him, Williams' suppressed dissatisfactions with Laughlin erupted. The "opening gun" in the battle was fired by Williams, when he wrote Laughlin on February 9 what was on his mind. "I'm glad to have you speak well of David McDowell," he wrote. "I liked him a lot and was particularly moved by his enthusiasms for pushing my work. That's what I need. I think I'll have a talk with him now that he's with Random House for I tell you frankly I'm not satisfied to let things run on the way they've been going." As for Laughlin: had he not himself said that Williams would never make any cash—any *real* cash—through him, though Lauglin would help to make him famous. And that had been fine with Williams . . . until now.[86]

Laughlin, caught completely off guard, answered at once. "Yours of the 9th to hand," he wrote, "and what a magnificent kick in the teeth that is." He was hurt and reeling and he said so:

> A hundred times when other publishers have told me what faithless bastards writers are I have held you up as an example of loyalty. I feel exactly like Gretchen's brother in Faust. . . . Oh Bill, when you do a thing like this to me I feel like quitting. If you of all people don't understand what New Directions is about and don't want to back me up, then what is the use of my going on with it?[87]

But the breach had begun. Ironically, the same day Laughlin was writing to Williams, Williams was writing to Tom Cole, lamenting the sorry need for contemporary patrons of the arts. He had just heard, for example, from Zukofsky of a local millionairess who had refused to contribute three hundred dollars so that young Paul Zukofsky—already a musical genius "who at the age of 5 years" had "mastered some of the most agile requirements of a Bach fugue"—could get the musical training he needed and deserved. Williams himself was so frustrated at such economic abuses that he wanted "to rush naked into the street yelling SHIT SHIT SHIT" at the top of his lungs, just as his young grandson, Paul, had done.[88] He complained to McDowell himself a few days later that New Directions had not been able to keep his books in print. Why, hadn't Paul told him that no salesman from New Directions ever came to his Brooklyn Abraham and Straus store to sell his books?[89]

That was the beginning of a difference of opinion that would grow more heated in the following months, until Williams finally put his dealings with Laughlin in the hands of a Fifth Avenue lawyer named James Murray, a specialist in contract laws between artists and publishers. Just before that happened, however, Laughlin had written Williams at the end of April offering him $250 per month as an advance against royalties for the rest of his life. That was in 1950 an attractive enough offer, and Williams thought hard about it for two weeks before deciding against it and going over to Random House. The mediation of a lawyer strained relations between Laughlin and Williams almost to the breaking point, though Williams and Laughlin finally reached an agreement that Laughlin would do *Paterson* and probably any other books of poetry Williams might write. That state of drawn battle lines would last for ten years, until June 1960, though—after his initial anger had blown over—Williams made his peace with Laughlin, dedicating both "The Pink Church" and—at year's end—the *Collected Later Poems* to the man who had been his publisher for the past fourteen years. Now, with the problem of fame and the disruption with Laughlin to contend with, sustained work on *Paterson* 4 stopped for five months, not to be resumed until Williams could get away for several uninterrupted weeks of work at Yaddo. But by then the poem's opening section had suffered a sea change from a meditation on Whitman on the Jersey shore to an anti-pastoral Fellini-like landscape set on New York's fashionable East Side.

*
* *

The corollary to Williams' renewed search for the father was, of course, his search for the son. The early drafts of *Paterson* 4 stress this too: Williams's paternity—his half-expressed, half-repressed desire to see his own sons carry on his work—and his complex relation with Floss, whom he calls Olympia in the drafts. For thirty years he'd shown an "interest" in his sons' experiments in writing, especially Bill's. But it was in the field of medicine that this son was to follow him, in time overtaking his father in training and expertise, though it was literally out of his father's house that he was to establish and build his own practice. But to find someone to continue the literary tradition from which he himself had sprung—the tradition of Whitman and Pound—Williams would have to look elsewhere for a son. And now, in *Paterson* 4, the inevitability of passing on his own work, his own concerns, had come to the foreground of his consciousness.

First his own son, his oldest, his namesake: thirty-six at the time Williams wrote *Paterson* 4, a veteran of World War II, a doctor whose wife was expecting their first child even as Williams was closing his epic. "You were not more than 12, my son," Williams began the second section of *Paterson* 4, "14 perhaps, the high school age / when we went, together . . . to a lecture . . . on atomic / fission." In memory, then, Williams recalled a moment from the late twenties when he had taken his son—on the threshold of deciding the future direction of his life—into New York to hear a lecture by a professor at Cornell Medical, because his son had expressed an "interest" in the subject. It is a complex chiming Williams gives us here—this solarium, this tower, chiming with that other New

York tower overlooking the East River where an aging lesbian tries (and fails) to make love to a nurse from the backwoods of New Jersey young enough to be her daughter. And his son, so "pale and young . . . among those pigs, myself / among them! who surpassed him / only in experience, that drug." Odysseus and Telemachus, the father yearning after his young son, who sits there, erect, like his father, listening attentively to a lecture on the new measuring possible with the elements, needing only time to come into his own.

As with, for example, Charles Olson, Robert Creeley, and Allen Ginsberg—all of them unknown in 1950, and each of them looking to Williams as to a father, for support, having also expressed an "interest." Olson as older son had written Williams on January 12 to congratulate him on the fire passage of *Paterson 3*—"It's the FIRE section still keeps me / right with it boy, is it good i / keep readin it, brother bill."[90] And then, on February 11, Creeley had written from his snowbound farmhouse in New Hampshire to tell Williams he was starting a little magazine and did the doctor have anything he might care to give him?[91] (The most important thing Williams gave him, as it turned out, was an introduction to Olson in April, that fortuitous fusion releasing a brilliance still not adequately charted in the American literary consciousness.) But—though he liked Creeley—Williams was not to see a representative sampling of Creeley's poetry for years to come, since it was the short fiction Creeley felt comfortable with in the early '50s. So, no son there, at least not at that juncture.

And then, on March 30, a letter from a local Paterson boy who had been secretly trying to make himself over into Williams' mode until the fiery presences of Blake and Whitman had intervened, a twenty-three-year-old unknown named Allen Ginsberg. "Dear Doctor," his letter began, "In spite of the grey secrecy of time and my own self-shuttering doubts in these youthful rainy days, I would like to make my presence in Paterson known to you, and I hope you will welcome this from me, an unknown young poet, to you, an unknown old poet, who live in the same rusty county of the world." The letter was almost too good to be true: a splendid, wildly comic, neurotic missive from someone actually living in Paterson:

> I envision for myself some kind of new speech—different at least from what I have been writing down—in that it has to be clear statement of fact about misery (and not misery itself), and splendor if there is any out of the subjective wanderings through Paterson. This place is as I say my natural habitat by memory, and I am not following in your traces to be poetic: though I know you will be pleased to realize that at least one actual citizen of your community has inherited your experience in this struggle to love and know his own world-city, through your work, which is an accomplishment you almost cannot have hoped to achieve.

Bless the young, bless their brashness, their own self-importance, their necessary egoism, the comedy, the pathos of it all. Ginsberg enclosed a sheaf of nine poems, a mixed bag which included an early and dense lyric in the mode of Crane, Robinson, and Tate, an "Ode to the Setting Sun," another to Judgment, and a mad song "to be sung by Groucho Marx to a Bop background." He ended by telling Williams that he'd seen him a few days earlier at his reading at the Guggenheim Museum: "I ran backstage to accost you, but changed my mind, after waving at you, and ran off again." That letter, of course, found its way into the fabric of *Paterson* 4 as did part of another letter which Ginsberg wrote ten weeks later on June 6, telling Williams that he was now working on the *New Jersey Labor Herald, AFL* in Newark, and asking Williams if he knew the black section of Paterson around Mill and River streets which, he said, was "really at the heart of what is to be known." Ginsberg's wanderings around Paterson, and Williams' early wanderings around that city forty years before: a chiming, a resonance which was to haunt Williams when he began to flesh out the fifth part of *Paterson* several years later. But for now he had his theme and his figure of crossing in Ginsberg, Pater's son.[92]

The reading Ginsberg had referred to in his first letter was the one Williams had made at the Guggenheim on Tuesday evening, March 28. And early the following morning he had told another of his sons—an Anglo-Indian studying in the States named Srinivas Rayaprol—that that reading had not gone well. Floss had liked some of it and not liked other parts, for she was "a silent person and does not want to hurt my feelings. But she loves me and wants to correct me when I need it, so her position is difficult." And besides, there was something perverse about reading private poetry in public, something he could never imagine Homer, for example, doing. Ours, he said, was a sad world "where we all go about in masks, or better than that, with our faces bent over a newspaper reading it on the subway or in our private houses. If only we could break into that world—not to exploit it but to share and enjoy it, quietly—without intrusion or the sense of intruding."[93] But then there was the ever present bomb, not only the fact of the atomic bomb and the threat of a new war with the Russians, but the imaginative *idea* of the bomb which had preceded its actuality: the idea of an instrument that could bring instantaneous nuclear holocaust upon his world in moments. "So we're going to lose 50,000,000 of us in the first 20 minutes of the next war," he'd written to Tom Cole in February. "Then why doesn't somebody have some sense and quit taking it all seriously?"[94] Still, knowing that —knowing the worst death had to offer—a man or a woman might turn back to the poem once again, to the poem and to the life it contained.

For the poem, Williams told Henry Wells, a New York scholar-critic, on April 12, in what amounted to a continuation of his meditation begun with Rayaprol, the poem was "the assertion that we are alive as ourselves—as much of the environment as it can grasp: exactly as Hellas lived in the *Iliad*." It was an assertion, admittedly "with broken means," of a new and total culture, "the lifting of an environment to expression." So the poem was, really, a "social instrument" whether or not a society accepted that poem, since it embraced, quite simply "everything we are."[95]

But in fact Whitman had also given Williams his theme: old age and death, as those early drafts of Whitman facing the sea listening for "the word" make clear. For the only word the sea had sung to Whitman had been death. And his own death was very much on his mind that spring. He and Floss had gone into New York in mid-April to view a Haitian art exhibit at the invitation of Selden Rodman and then all three had gone to see Charlie Chaplin in *City Lights*. Williams had laughed so hard at Chaplin's antics that tears had streamed uncontrollably down his face.[96] Yet, even as he sat laughing in that movie house in New York, he told Zukofsky, a close friend of his, a man his own age, had died "just sitting in a chair talking with friends." And what had that death amounted to? What had it changed? No one had even been "moved by this death to think of death. Consequently they cannot act in *any* general way against death as a factor in our lives, cannot take any action to even change any opinion they have on the general concept of their lives. . . . We speak of—glibly—death and the poem not realizing what we are talking about, neither is apprehended—but both . . . are the same nature."[97] And that meditation would find its way into the closing pages of *Paterson* 4, in the figure of the poet attracted and simultaneously repulsed by the sea, by the woman, by the presences waiting there for all of us:

> *Thalassa*
> *immaculata: our home, our nostalgic*
> *mother in whom the dead, enwombed again*
> *cry out to us to return. . . .* [98]

"I am sitting at the center of a vortex that doesn't vortex," he complained to Beum in early July. "Everything seems to be heading up to some disaster that we poets mistake for seriousness—while we wait with folded hands, just waiting for THAT without realizing that we might be making something else: of the same sort." By then the threat of war with Russia had become a real war with North Korea. For Williams that meant death and more death for young Americans, even as he preoccupied himself with the poem, the sea, and his own inevitable closure. It was indeed something else: of the same sort.[99]

*
**

When Williams had put *Paterson* 4 aside, it was also to get at other more pressing work. Besides his medical practice, he had had to locate all his short stories and get them to his typist for Random House. Then he had had to collect and rearrange forty years of poetry for New Directions for what he thought would be the last *Complete Collected.* That would take two volumes. Then there was also a small book to prepare for the Cummington Press people: another limited edition, this one of "Two Pendants: For the Ears," though that project finally fell through. On top of all this, he had been invited to spend three weeks on the West Coast that fall teaching the theory of the short story at three colleges. Now, therefore, he began in March to assemble a long, rambling essay which he called "A Beginning on the Short Story," giving that to Oscar Baron's Alicat Bookshop Press in Yonkers, New York, to get printed in time for his trip west. He also asked Baron to publish Fred Miller's short story "Gutbucket and Gossamer," which had come out of the *Man Orchid* collaboration and which Williams wanted to get published now for his friend. He told Baron himself that it was the work of someone he both admired and pitied, and that the story was "a delicate piece of work made of coarse, strictly contemporary materials of the crudest kind" such as Williams himself loved.[100] Baron obviously agreed and published Miller's story even as he prepared Williams' script for publication.

Williams was also giving frequent readings of his own poetry in New York, such as the one at the Guggenheim in late March, though he didn't feel very good about them. He could still feel a resistance to his work, he told Selden Rodman in late April, "the same old resistance to what I have to say. It is all uphill and it tires me." He didn't want their praise and applause, knowing full well that "if it weren't cheap they wouldn't give it to me." What he *did* want to do was "to move them, to MOVE them! But they don't move. It's like moving anything, you've got to get it rocking first, then lift it onto your knees, then heave it. But the only thing they'll rock to is the old religious swing. And that they can have."[101]

But they were also rocking by the thousands to Dylan Thomas, who had recently been on his first U.S. tour. Williams had found it impossible to go and hear Thomas while he'd been in the States, he said, because Thomas' poetry was the direct antithesis of what Williams was trying to do and he could not bring himself to support the Welshman. "Just the dreamy look that comes into the eyes of our partial writers and so-called competent critics" had sickened him. He was sure he would have liked Thomas had he been able to get him alone, but not with all those hangers-on drooling over him. He knew what they were thinking: that Williams was jealous of Thomas' success with American audiences, a popular success that had so far eluded him.

"They look at me out of the corners of their eyes as much as to say,

Well, Williams, there's no one in this country who can read like that. So that if you speak slightingly of him we can only come to one conclusion: you'd read that way if you could, but since you haven't the voice or the manner or even his wonderful poems to give us—you try to belittle him." But that was not the case at all. The truth was both simpler and more complex: that American poems were entirely different from Dylan Thomas' Welsh-influenced poems, which were by their nature "more authoritarian, more Druidic, more romantic," and even—alas—"more colorful." But, he insisted, Americans could not and must not write in that vein. Better, then, to stay away from Thomas altogether. Only after Thomas' death from alcoholic abuse in 1953 was Williams able to approach the man's work calmly and critically.[102]

Fame. The kudos continued that June, when Williams received two Doctor of Letters degrees, the first from Rutgers on Saturday, June 10, and the second from Bard the following Saturday. "What the hell must I be?" he joked with David Ignatow. "But I suppose one of the virtues of a good horse is to accept the bridle gracefully."[103] The day he received his degree from Rutgers, he and Floss drove out to Hightstown, New Jersey, with Selden Rodman to see Ben Shahn, who presented Williams with a large painting of a factory building and tracks which he had entitled *Homage to Paterson*. Williams was surprised by the man he saw in Shahn. He had expected to see someone completely immersed in the world of painting, but instead he found someone who reminded him of an Old Testament prophet.[104] Williams accepted the painting gratefully, even though personally he found the picture too bare to give it his unqualified appreciation. Nevertheless, by November he had had it framed and put up in his front hall, where visitors could see it as they walked in. Yet, after nearly half a year of looking at it, he still thought it a bit featureless: "I'd like to have seen a big figure of a mill-worker applied all over the surface of it with the windows showing through."[105] That, of course, would have suggested the figure of the man/city so important to his own idea of the poem. As it was, he could still like it for its colored windows.

On Sunday, June 18, Williams was interviewed by a local radio announcer, John Gerber, who came out to 9 Ridge Road that rainy afternoon to tape Williams' response to some questions, most of them about "the problems of being a doctor and being a poet." Williams remembered his past and talked about Pound, reiterating what he'd said many times by then, that the man should be freed now because he was too valuable to be kept imprisoned. He also spoke up for socialized medicine—"I don't like the person who takes the poor guy and soaks his wife two hundred and fifty dollars for a Caesarian section and then twenty-five dollars for a circumcision, when he hasn't even enough to eat." He laughingly confessed to being so radical that he and Floss had once joined a co-op and were almost shot by the neighbors for it. He talked about his poems—about "Ol Bunk's Band," and "Portrait of a Lady," and "This Is Just to Say," and was glad to be spared the reading of "Tract," which he now found hackneyed. Finally, he turned to the need for continued experimentation, for the need to be an iconoclast. After all, he noted, human life had existed a mere 700,000 years—"a very brief thing"—and there was so much yet to know about human behavior. Break the tradition, the old stultifying icons, he insisted, since "the secret spirit of that ritual can exist not only in that form, but once that form is broken, the spirit . . . can take again a form which will be more contemporary." He was speaking of the ageless spirit existing once again in the new poem. Rarely had Williams allowed his Emersonian bias to reveal itself so nakedly.[106]

In mid-July Williams was finally able to get back to some sustained and uninterrupted work on *Paterson* 4. That was during the two weeks —from July 15 until August 2—that he spent at the writers' colony at Yaddo up in Saratoga Springs, New York, where special arrangements had been made so that Floss could be with him. He found the working conditions at Yaddo ideal (as guest of honor he was given the tower room in the mansion for his studio), and he even discovered that there were people who actually treated the artist as though he were important, so that in a single week of uninterrupted work—writing from nine till four—he'd been able to block out the entire first part of *Paterson* 4: that pastoral idyl, that *ménage à trois* consisting of Phyllis, Corydon, and a younger Dr. Paterson. "Everyone closely confines himself," he wrote Kitty Hoagland on the twenty-sixth:

> writer, painter or composer, and slaves his head off. I too work every day consuming reams of paper trying to complete a first draft of *Paterson* IV before I leave. . . . I won't finish but without this period of concentration I don't know how I should have been able to complete the task for another year.

Floss, he said, was "the only lost soul in the place." She had wandered back and forth over the large wooded estate, "a bit chewed up by deer flies but on the whole contented."[107] They'd even managed one trip up to Vermont to see young Paul at summer camp. Moreover, Ted Roethke and Richard Eberhart and Harvey Shapiro were also at Yaddo that July, as well as a man he hadn't seen in years: Nicholas Calas, working then on a detailed study of Hieronymus Bosch's medievel triptych, *Garden of Earthly Delights*. (That painting, as it happened, would figure prominently in the design of Williams' poem written in 1953: "Of Asphodel, That Greeny Flower.")

"This has been a rewarding experience for me," he wrote Kenneth Burke on Monday, July 31, with two weeks of work behind him, "inasmuch as I have never, you might say, in my life had any leisure for writing." He had simply called a halt to his practice,

> hopped in my car, drove up here and immediately plunged into my work. At first I thought I was dying! My back ached from sitting in one spot for hours at a time, my ass hole bulged, my eyes began to drop from their sockets and my stomach felt as though it had swallowed a decayed rat. Age, sez I to myself, has at last got me. I'm through. All the fakery I practice now that it has the full light of day upon it is being revealed to me for all the shoddy that it really consists of. . . . But, after finding that mornings are the best time for me, and not trying to push myself too hard after noon, I have done very well, in my opinion. At least I have destroyed a lot of paper.[108]

Caught up in the matrix of *Paterson* 4, Williams' eye saw a potentially new significance in much that passed before it that summer. So, for example, an advertisement in the June 1950 issue of *Money* (an offshoot of the old *New Democracy* weekly) was lifted and then inserted into the second part of *Paterson* 4 as a kind of sardonic joke at the expense of amateur economists (Pound among them) whose panaceas—however correct or well-intentioned—simply fell on a multitude of deaf ears. As such, the inclusion of this ad served as a belated good-by to Williams' own Social Credit days of the '30s. He also spotted Melvin Tolson's "Libretto for the Republic of Liberia"—followed by Allen Tate's "Preface"—in the July issue of *Poetry*—and incorporated Tolson's refrain, "Selah!" by way of praising Tolson's "cultured intelligence turning back to praise a native intelligence, negro to negro—no white." As such the passage chimed with Corydon's attraction for Phyllis, as well as with Paterson's praise for his son:

> *and to Tolson and to his ode*
> *and to Liberia and to Allen Tate*
> *(Give him credit)*
> *and to the South generally*
>   Selah![109]

And again, leafing through his *Journal of the American Medical Association* for July 29, Williams cut out an article on cases of infectious *Salmonella*, inserting it into the poem to reinforce the theme of literature as waste, as end product, like Sir Thopas' telling the poet Chaucer that "Thy drasty ryming is not / worth a toord." (Thus placed, it would serve as a sharp counterfoil to the image of Madame Curie, pregnant in belly as well as mind, the breakdown of inert material that made up *Paterson*'s surface giving way to a luminous revelation, the radiant gist, the gist of Williams' fantastic, complex solutions to the love riddle he called his poem.)

*
**

As for the first part of *Paterson* 4. Why Williams chose the form of a drama—even a closet drama—compounded with the stylized form of the idyl—even the anti-pastoral idyl reminiscent of those experimental one-act plays of the '10s and early '20s written by figures like Stevens, Kreymborg, Millay, and Williams himself—is not entirely clear. But the first drafts for the first section of *Paterson* 4, written in a startlingly confessional mode in the first few days after Williams settled into Yaddo, reveal much of what Williams felt it was necessary to confess—though he would confess it obliquely—about himself as husband, father, lover. He had already "confessed" his indiscretions to Floss in his play, *A Dream of Love*, the allegory of his own life and his life's impetus made bare for all to see. But the need to work with that side of him came to obsess him once again in the cloistral surroundings of Yaddo.

Assignations, affairs, an aging lame lesbian saying, "It could be a poem—Paterson or Un Rendezvous avec la belle vièrge." Much of *Paterson*, Williams has made us feel, concerns a waiting for something which may or may not materialize, but which for the most part never appears. It is a waiting especially for Kore, the beautiful virgin, the impossible Perfect Woman. On Tuesday, July 18, barely settled in at his writing table, Williams recalled an incident he remembered as having occurred in the spring of his forty-sixth year: 1929. The assignation and the cost of that game: "How much has the adored—not the adorable— not the Blessed Virgin—conceded me? How much have I given her? And what? To most it would be, how little have I paid? How much will I pay?" He fantasized of virgins coming into his office to be deflowered, "virgins mostly undesirable, on their knees—meanwhile working to live, as all must, some abler than others. Pleading with staring eyes." He remembered one time in particular when he had waited for a woman to come to his office and he had stared at "a starling, with one leg, picking among the cinders in his neighbor's driveway."

And nine miles to the east: New York, that symbol of unrestrained phallic energy, the sexual and creative impetus registered in those rising towers, the newer ones, rising "higher than the others," and thinking: "I suppose to some it seems the force of the American mind thrusting itself into the sky. To me, *ersatz*. The proper symbol [of New York], if you wish a symbol, is a bed." And then, at his typewriter, fantasies of his Black Kore again, the maid who had "desired him," the exquisite one in "the most immaculate starched whiteness, a flashing smile, the body of Goya's *Maja Desnuda*." He remembered too those three men who had also desired him, one "openly," one "willing to accept something else," and one content with self-created innuendos, though, Williams added, he himself had "loved better, other things."

What Williams was remembering or inventing—or both—was a

flirtation with a young nurse, whose speech he got down to perfection in Phyllis—"I've always played with boys. My Dad's trying to get me a horse. I had a cousin I loved when I was a child. I used to bite him. . . . And a brother but he died when he was a baby. Do you know Doc Crotch . . . ? He wanted to marry me. His wife wouldn't give him any children." Thus Phyllis, even as Paterson fumbles for her lovely, taut breasts, simultaneously attracted and repulsed by the coarse, rather dull-witted beauty before him. And all of it, with its pathetic layering of eroticism, in turn relayed to the old, lame lesbian while Phyllis rubs her down, indifferent, unaware of this other woman's pitiful but very real erotic intentions.

Williams remembered a sign he'd seen somewhere advertising KOO-PER'S KLEEN KOKE, flashing on and off against the Passaic, as he drove off into some lonely place—a swamp road—with the young nurse, his mind all the while on his wife, on Floss, on Olympia—Jupiter/Paterson's consort—she seeming to know that her husband was up to something, but unwilling to confront him directly. And the guilt of it and the obsession to "tear into" the woman, into women in spite of that guilt:

> Not to turn home he stopped at a telephone booth to call a woman. Her husband answered. He hooked back the receiver. Excuse it please, no one on the line now. These are things his recent memory dandled before his eyes—before his mind. He felt . . . old (I am old—for this) saddened, burning with desire—and doubt, thinking of all the past—caught, inhumanly possessed, exhaustless.

Sixteen years he had been married when those events—real or fictional, more real than fictional—had occurred. Sixteen years. And his wife, waiting for him at such and such a place as they had earlier arranged, telling him—for the first time (so that he could remember it vividly twenty years after the event here in Yaddo with Floss walking the verdant pastures of that pastoral estate)—"that for the first year of their married life she hated him."[110]

Williams had already enacted this incident or one like it in a poem with the ironic title "Eternity," published in *The Wedge*, and dating back to the early 1940s, when he was still calling himself "Noah" instead of "Paterson." In that poem there is an assignation: a dark street, the click of high heels, a bare head, "pearl earrings/and a cloak":

> *the boy friend was expecting me*
> *it was hard to*
> *get away*
>
> *Where are you supposed to be?*
> *Night, greater than*
> *the cataract*
>
> *surged in the cisterns of Noah's*
> *chest, enormous night. . . .*

Two hundred miles through night landscapes, filling the gas tank "once near midnight," a turn to the left off the road, a stop, with a short, impassioned interlude while "the stars performed / their stated miracles," and then the wind rising at 3 AM and the long ride back with a pause under a "street lamp to make / some notes," the engine still idling, and, finally, home to "Olympia, her face drawn but relieved" and saying nothing. "Breakfast / at seven."[111]

Paterson 4 is one of Williams' most daring experiments though no critic has been able to say much more about it than that it fails, or, at the very least, that it is a falling off from *Paterson* 1. "What I miss, said your mother, is the poetry, the pure poem of the first parts," Dr. Paterson says to his son at the opening of the fourth book's second movement, and critics have taken this without the sense of irony Williams intended. But *Paterson* 4, Williams had written back in September 1949 by way of a blurb for the book jacket of *Paterson* 3, would "show the perverse confusions that come of a failure to untangle and make it [i.e., the language] our own as both man and woman are carried helplessly toward the sea (of blood) which, by their failure of speech, awaits them. The poet alone in this world holds the key to their final rescue." If the poem seemed to be falling apart as it neared its conclusion, veering away from the classical sense of ending, of summation, of satisfactory crescendo, that was because James Joyce, for one, had made the older notion of romantic closure untenable.

The ending of *The Bridge*, for example, had been intolerable for Williams, especially when one considered Hart Crane's own run to the sea: that jump over the side of the SS *Orizaba* into shark-infested waters twenty years before. Williams had actually contemplated Crane's death in an early draft of *Paterson* 4, shaken by the hard realization that the sea was *not* our home, any more than it was the home of that waterlogged corpse called Phlebas that floats in Eliot's *The Waste Land* or the home of that other body, torn by sea gulls and drifting in the East River in *Paterson* 4. The failed poet, drifting into oblivion, glimpsed at the beginning of *Paterson* as the lump caught in the logs at the Great Falls, glimpsed again in the figure of Sam Patch and Mrs. Cumming, man and woman, drowned, resurfaces once more at the other end of Williams' epic. "Poet / of the sea," Williams' draft reads, in a mode of address recalling Eliot and Eliot's son, Hart Crane:

> *O voluble speaker the*
> *shark tooth waves insensate to*
> *the feast, our no brains—and*
> *snails make lairs of our skulls.*
>
> *O shark, attended by squids to blind*
> *us, shark that rends with madness*
> *whose teeth are shining knives*
> *in rows to rip us into atomies. . . .*

The best defense of *Paterson* 4—to which no one seems to have listened—is contained in a series of letters Williams wrote in the first weeks after the poem was published. To Marianne Moore, for example —whose sensibilities were offended by the presence of a lesbian moving around in Williams' text, and who thought Williams' intention to find a redeeming language had been woefully sidetracked—Williams answered brilliantly that if the close of *Paterson* contained its own failure, that was because the very *grounds* of the search had implied a failure (indeed the whole American experience as he had lived through it had demonstrated over and over a tendency, a proclivity, toward failure). "If the vaunted purpose of my poem seems to fall apart at the end," he was willing to concede to Moore, "it's rather frequent that one has to admit an essential failure." In fact, what better strategy to assert the need for a redeeming language—a language that would reveal ourselves to ourselves—but "by stating our failure to achieve it"?

At least he had not been willing to end his poem by melting "myself into the great universal sea (of love) with all its shapes and colors," like Whitman, Eliot, and Crane. On the other hand—and this was his brilliant strategy—he had succeeded in actually presenting "a living language" even as he spoke of the tremendous difficulties inherent in achieving such a language. The force of the poem, then, would depend on the reader's returning to the seemingly transparent fabric of the text to hear a speech consonant with one's day: "The poem, as opposed to what was accomplished in the story, came to life at moments," Williams asserted gingerly (to assert more forcefully would be to explain the whole gist of his joke, and that would not be giving his readers the "credit" his poetics insisted upon), "even when my failure was most vocal and went above that to a different sort of achievement."[112]

Where was this language caught, then, this language consonant with Williams' own world? It was here, for example, in this exchange between Corydon, the aging, world-weary cosmopolitan lesbian, and her provincial young nurse masseuse from the environs of Paterson:

> *What sort of people do you come from, Phyllis?*
> *My father's a drunk.*
> *That's more humility than the situation demands.*
> *Never be ashamed of your origins.*
> *I'm not. It's just the truth.*
>
> *The truth! Virtue, my dear, if one had it!*
> *is only interesting in the aggregate, as you will*
> *discover . or perhaps you have already found it*
> *so. That's our Christian teaching: not denial*
> *but forgiveness, the Prodigal Daughter. Have you*
> *ever been to bed with a man?*

> *Have you?*
>
> *Good shot! With this body! I think I'm more*
> *horse than woman. Did you ever see such skin as*
> *mine? Speckled like a Guinea hen .*
> *Only their speckles are white.*[113]

It is there, an authentic speech, but in other places as well, as in the image of Paterson, surviving, finally, to swim into shore like Odysseus before him or like Rip Van Winkle awaking from his twenty-year sleep: the dream of the whole poem now ending, except that *Paterson*'s whole bent works directly against Eliot's Prufrock, as Williams' poet immerses himself in the sea, and then turns back inland:

> *When he came out, lifting his knees*
> *through the waves she went to him frisking*
> *her rump awkwardly .*
> *Wiping his face with his hand he turned*
> *to look back to the waves, then*
> *knocking at his ears, walked up*
> *to stretch out flat on his back in*
> *the hot sand . there were some*
> *girls, far down the beach, playing ball.*[114]

Out of the pitchblende of the language in its virulent, unstable condition: an amazing range of voices that Williams' American predecessors and siblings had either rejected or were deaf to, a language so transparent that most people had passed over it in search of something else called "meaning."

If the first part of *Paterson* 4 is an idyl, it is also an allegory of the poet caught between two phases of the language, what Williams in *Paterson* 1 had called the "wild" and the cultured, and in *Paterson* 3 "the locus / where two women meet / One from the backwoods / a touch of the savage / and of T.B. . . . / The other—wanting, / from an old culture / . . . . the same dish / different ways."[115] Phyllis and Corydon represent another aspect of Williams' sterile androgynetic mode—male to male/female to female—ending necessarily for the poet in defeat. Two halves of the language process: Phyllis representing the language in its raw, virulent stage—that language Williams had jotted down daily for half a century on whatever paper was at hand as he heard it fresh from the mouths of his patients, from those citizens of his own specific locus. And Corydon, representing the inevitable perversion of the language as any specific phase of a culture solidifies and degenerates into stasis, but especially when that language loses contact with its own local origins and becomes more general and flavorless the more it becomes "cosmopolitan" and "international." Williams had, of course, lamented the loss of a distinctive American culture for years. He had seen what happened to local cultures—to Shaker art or primitive American painting—when American city markets were deluged by European ideas and fashions. Then the local was merely obliterated, inundated, washed under. In like manner the direction of the American language was from the clean rural headwaters of the Passaic moving toward the incredible urban pollution of Newark Bay, with its gas tanks and raw sewage, its oil spills and brine, merging at last with the North Atlantic. Or again, the language was like a process, a gradual revelation of the radiant stain of a new element, a new phase. But its very instability kept moving toward the stability of lead, of death.

There were, then, perversions and perversions: the filthy Passaic and the perversion of characters in *Paterson* 4. "With the approach to the city," Williams tried to explain to Edith Heal in 1956, "international character began to enter the innocent river and pervert it; sexual perversions, such things that every metropolis when you get to know it houses."[116] Or nearly every human being, as they too moved from innocence to knowledge. The poem called for perversity and—willy-nilly —he would draw his characters accordingly. Take Corydon. "I don't mind telling you," he told Robert Lowell in July 1951, "that I started writing of her in a satiric mood—but she won me quite over. I ended by feeling admiration for her and real regret at her defeat."[117] She had a "hard part to play," he explained in defending her presence to Marianne Moore, "and to my mind plays it rather well." In terms of the allegory—or the "story," as he called it—Corydon represented the "great world" as opposed to "the more or less primitive world" of his provincial female Paterson: "She is informed, no sluggard, uses her talents as she can." Moreover, the poem demanded her world against which the other could test itself. That last was a telling observation, for much of *Paterson*'s power lies just there, in a poetics of detritus—the poet's overt admission of failure, as when the river in *Paterson* 3, past flood, recedes, leaving

> *a sort of muck, a detritus,*
> *in this case—a pustular scum, a decay, a choking*
> *lifelessness—that leaves the soil clogged after it,*
> *that glues the sandy bottom and blackens stones. . . .* [118]

"It happens that I knew in my personal experience of an instance which contained all the elements that I needed," Williams told Marianne Moore in a follow-up letter to the one he'd written on the nineteenth. What he'd been looking for was "an image to typify the impact of 'Paterson' in his young female phase with a world beyond his own, limited in the primitive, provincial environment." He had found that image in the person of a "prominent figure in the New York and international world." (She was the sister of a financier, various drafts make clear, and one of the nurses from Paterson—who had struck out for bigger things in New York City—had told him this story years before, back in '28 or '29. The woman lived in a penthouse over on Sutton Place, and was old, ugly, and lame. And—"Phyllis" had told Williams—she had made advances toward her young, inexperienced nurse/masseuse.) "In writing out the passage, this woman, who was at first a mere symbol, came to life for herself and I forgave her. I even realized that she has as much reason for being as the cruder counterfoil that the young nurse provided."[119] He even came to love "the old bitch," he told Babette Deutsch, for Corydon could praise Phyllis even while she despised her mental vacancy. Williams felt good about his idyl, felt it was "technically and feelingly . . . far advanced over anything else in the whole of *Paterson*." (In fact, he told Marianne Moore that the language of *Paterson* 4 was even "more sensuous, more convenient to the line," than had been the case in the highly touted first book.) If anything, it was the figure of the little Paterson nurse—whoever she might have been, and she may well have figured in the prototype of that "upcountry" girl in "Eternity" —who had not been sufficiently realized. When he'd sketched her first off in the drafts, the "nudes" for Phyllis had been done "rather raw at first," so that you "could almost smell her." But in moving from draft to finished poem he'd left his memories of her behind to move instead into a more Stevensian allegorical world of language.[120]

If Corydon is a symbol of the language in its degenerate, *fin-de-siècle* condition, however, she is also a familiar, compound presence. For it is Phyllis/Paterson/Williams—the raw, indigenous phase of the language, promising but as yet unfulfilled (a virgin)—confronting a heavily encrusted, symbol-laden, tradition-bound, and perverted phase of the language in the figure of Corydon. It is here that the New World hussy Williams had praised thirty years before literally rubs up against the Old World hag, without benefit of the poet. It is an allegory—this entire first part—of Williams' preoccupation with the American language, the virulent upriver formative phase clashing with the polluted downriver phase. And we ought not be surprised to find Williams' own version of Eliot's familiar compound ghost in Corydon. For if the ghost that haunts "Little Gidding" is made up of Yeats, Dante, Mallarmé, Swift, and half a dozen others, so Corydon's poem is a pastiche of Yeats, Eliot himself (witness the language of "He is the city of cheap hotels and private / entrances . of taxis at the door" and "At the / sanitary lunch hour packed woman to / woman"), and of course Hart Crane ("directed missiles / in the greased shafts of the tall buildings / They stand torpid in cages, in violent motion / unmoved"). Thus Corydon's poem suggests the modern direction of American poetry, with its strong tug toward Europe—toward which it had inevitably tended—once it had abandoned American cities for London, Paris, and Rapallo. This unfortunate cosmopolitanism had

occurred either by taking over the English tradition altogether—as with
Eliot—or by aligning oneself with a symbolist aesthetic, as Crane had
done. But, Williams insisted, the American poet would have to commit
himself first of all to his own place and to the unpromising young virgin,
Phyllis, and "give her a baby," a resolution that—for Williams' alter ego,
Dr. Paterson—remained frustratingly problematical. After all, real writing for Williams was, as he'd told Josie Herbst three years earlier, "at its
best a marriage, a real marriage between the sense and the words so that
everything is brought to life, a true reproduction, a good fuck, if you want
to say it and one that takes."[121] It meant getting your ideal virgin with
child, as Dr. Paterson would finally manage to do in *Paterson 5*.

*
* *

By the time Williams left Yaddo the morning of August 2 to drive across
New York State to Gratwick Highlands for a two weeks' rest with the
Abbotts and Gratwicks, he'd finished the first part of *Paterson* 4 and was
well along with the last two sections. He knew how the poem would end:
in the only way he knew it could, with a turning inland away from the
"ocean of savage lusts" where the "wounded shark," frenzied, gnashed at
its own tail, destroying itself by feeding on its own substance.[122] But his
would be no turning inward as with so many writers to feed on the self
and call it the return to the Father, a melding into the sea, whatever.
Instead, he would force himself to waken from the dream of the whole
poem and move on to yet new beginnings, to new inventions and new
poems. Not closure, then, but promise, the promise of "the seed that
floats to shore, one word, one tiny, even microscopic word" which alone
could save him. The seed, then: the beginnings of a new evolution, the
basic radiant element, like those scattered dots all through *Paterson*,
bombarding the pitchblende of that inert mass and pointing toward the
release of some new radiant energy.

Korea of course was very much on Williams' mind, as he watched
Congress assume the role of policing the world. When hostilities had
begun in June Williams had had to admit that he'd felt almost relieved
after the rumors of war that had daily bombarded the newspapers for the
past two years. Still, he didn't like the sounds of so many hawks in his
country, as they sent the latest generation of young men off to die in a
land war that might very soon be bringing millions of Chinese down the
Korean peninsula. America had too soon forgotten what World War II had
cost the world. He thought of pictures he'd seen of Dachau, Belsen,
Auschwitz, and of what that war had done to the European Jews, and he
told a friend that America should first lose "as great a proportion of our
adult population (by enemy blastings of our principal cities) as the Jews
lost in Europe during the last war" before Americans committed them-

selves to some "patriotic" course of action that might lead to World War III and nuclear devastation. The problem with most Americans, he realized, was that they were "slovenly idiots" when it came to "hard thinking." That was in mid-July, just before he had left for Yaddo. And, on August 4, he wrote Ted Roethke—whom he'd just left—to say that he was looking forward to November, when he'd again be out on the West Coast—that is, if the war did not prevent him, as he was afraid now it might.[123]

But at Gratwick Highlands he could at least find some respite from events out in the world and live for the two weeks, as he told McDowell, like a "real country man."[124] When they'd arrived at the estate on the evening of the second, Williams had heard Harriet Gratwick's choral group practicing his own "Rogation Sunday Hymn," which "a man from Rochester School of Music had composed for next Sunday's garden concert. . . . It sounded very well though they were only rehearsing, that is singing parts of it over and over—and without orchestra which it will have on Sunday." Thus he wrote early on the fourth to his daughter-in-law, Daphne, eight months pregnant with her first. He kidded her, suggesting that—if she had a girl—she call it Tabitha, Tabby, the name of a cat he'd found in a booklet on Yaddo. He and Floss were staying in the upstairs of the garage, in what had once been the carriage house before cars had changed all that. They each had their own bedroom, so that his snoring wouldn't keep Floss up half the night. They had had their breakfast both mornings "on the little second floor back porch overlooking the garden and the low hills in the distance," with geese and a bantam rooster to salute them from time to time. It was overcast and cold this morning, he said, but he'd been treated to a rare sight: "goldfinches, robins, a cat bird, a Baltimore oriole, a pewee, wren, sparrows," a female cardinal, and then—a streak of red and another of blue—a male cardinal being chased by an indigo bunting! "The Metropolitan opera," he added, "could not have done better for us."[125]

At the farm, Williams retyped the first part of *Paterson* 4 so that it could be put in the hands of his typist as soon as he was back home. And then he worked with the last two parts, though not with the intensity he'd found at Yaddo. On August 3 he wrote a "song" for the second part on a single sheet of paper which revealed one of the central clues to his epic. "Money: Joke," the first line read, and the last: "Credit: the gist." It was an equation, really, one he'd promised his writers in the prologue to the poem years before. Expanded, that equation read: Credit is to money what gist is to a joke.[126] That was what Williams had meant by asking his readers if they were "getting it" in *Paterson*, though the sexual pun was unquestionably there as well. Do you get it, he asked? Do you get the joke? Can you see how the gist of the thing illuminates the *Kore*-ner where you are? So Madame Curie, movie queen, returning to her movie-set laboratory in the dark, had discovered a womb-shaped alembic glowing with the radiant seed, the unstable, virulent element: radium. It was that which had promised a cure for cancer, though it was that too, sadly, which had led to the atomic bomb.

And credit—"give him credit," the poem echoes and reechoes. It was credit that could dynamite the blockage created by special interest groups, from the financiers to the church. Williams compressed all those villains into the figure of the greedy evangelist, Billy Sunday, whom he remembered had been called into Paterson in 1913 to break the back of the long, drawn-out strike by preaching God to the workers and reminding them of their religious duty to return to work. That Billy Sunday had preached at the Hotel Hamilton (ironically recalling the father of all those special interest groups that had crippled Paterson from its inception as a city), and that he'd received $27,000 for his services from the United Factory Owner's Association, did not escape Williams:

> —getting his 27 Grand in the hotel room
> after the last supper (at the Hamilton)
> on the eve of quitting town, exhausted
> in his efforts to split (a split
> personality) . the plate
>   What an arm![127]

The joke was a complex one, reverberating, "splitting" half a dozen ways at once. For the last supper recalls Christ in the upper room with his apostles, on the eve of his final sacrifice, breaking the bread—his body—to be shared by all. So Billy Sunday, "evangel / and ex-rightfielder," splits into three in his efforts to split the plate—the collection plate, the communion plate, the baseball plate—though he is unable to split the X-ray plate with his words, which are a perversion of the Word he pretends to work for. We get the joke, and we realize, too, that the joke has been at *our* expense. We remember those other evangelists in *Paterson*, especially the ineffective and comic figure of Klause Ehrens preaching on Garrett Mountain—juxtaposed to Alexander Hamilton—telling the people to get rid of their money if they would be happy as he is happy. And we see this other evangelist, merging with the sons of Hamilton, in the act of "quitting town," having raped Paterson once again. "Come to / Jesus and be . All together now, / give it everything you got!" intones the preacher, but this time the line from the old revivalist hymn, "Brighten / the corner where you / are!" reveals no fructifying split, no Kore in *cor*-ner, no radiant gist, no light.

On August 29, Williams told Laughlin that *Paterson* 4 could "*begin* to go to the printer at once." The first part was "polished to the last degree," "a completely studied poem of 22 pages" unlike anything else he'd done in *Paterson*, "though it fits there, I hope, perfectly."[128] As for the last sections of the poem, Williams had had them, essentially, as early as 1944. There was, for example, a long section taken from Charles Pitman Longwell's prose memoir *A Little Story of Old Paterson*, which Williams had reset as poetry, to give a sense of Paterson's colonial history, though the effect of these passages—which run (interspersed with other materials) for six pages—is of another false pastoral, of the impossibility of ever recapturing the past. Williams edited these passages on old Paterson so that they would begin and end with the falls which Ginsberg's second letter (also embedded in the poem) tells us are "really at the heart of what is to be known." But one might not notice that these six pages are bracketed at their start by a birth and at their close by a death. In fact, by two births and two deaths.

"Here's to the baby, / may it thrive!" Williams had written in September in the midst of working on these pages, celebrating baby, labia, and the "peak / from which the seed was hurled!" That baby was Emily Barrett Williams, Bill Jr. and Daphne's first, born on the eighth of that month, and named for Williams' English grandmother, his first muse. A granddaughter, then, but a symbol too of generativity, of beginning again. And then, a page later in *Paterson*, that baby was joined with Allen Ginsberg, the young, half-promising poet, to suggest another beginning. And against these: two deaths. The first Williams picked from the local Paterson papers for September 17, 1950 (Williams' sixty-seventh birthday), which recorded the murder of a six-month-old girl by her father, who'd fractured her skull with the wooden tray of her high chair and then buried her under a rock on Garrett Mountain. The second death recorded another Paterson murder just one hundred years before: the death of the Van Winkles by John Johnson of Liverpool, subsequently hanged for that crime in holiday fashion before a crowd of spectators on the same mountain where the baby would be buried and where the poet had walked.

As his poem ended, Williams saw himself as both victim and murderer. It was the poet sacrificing himself, spending himself for his people, his readers, for his sons, as the father necessarily gave way to the son, even as his townspeople looked on uncomprehendingly: "I guess it's all right / but what the hell does it mean?" What *did* it all mean? Here was a hanging, a death, but—in the tightening of the hangman's rope—a metamorphosis, as rope became umbilical cord and the baby—come now to term—prepared to make its "final somersault," just prior to being born or born dead. In the end, then, a new beginning. John Johnson: John son of John: the voice of one crying in the wilderness, giving way, inevitably, to other voices rising out of that same locus.

There were other "interests" too as Williams moved toward the conclusion of his epic. With the tide coming in at the end of the poem, he recalled one of those who had preceded him: Pep West, "an old friend, now gone," killed in 1940 in a car crash. Laughlin had just sent Williams a copy of the reissue of *The Day of the Locust* and Williams did a six-hundred-word review of that novel for *Tomorrow Magazine* in early September. Reading West's novel—set in Hollywood in the '20s —Williams had come across a passage about a woman who had come to a hotel clerk for help in paying her bill, and he remembered a story similar to this one that West had told him nearly twenty years before. That was when West was working the desk at the Sutton Hotel in New York in the early '30s, a time when the two of them had edited those three issues of *Contact*. West had told him how once he'd found a beautiful young woman in his room, naked and asleep and how astonished he'd been, so that he'd simply lain down naked beside her and then likewise fallen asleep, both of them waking together, refreshed. A death of sorts and a resurrection, that. Now, as Paterson prepared to fall asleep at the end of his poem, exhausted from his efforts to lay his meaning, white, across the sheets of his epic, Williams recalled that privileged moment with Kore which his dead friend had shared with him years before.[129]

By the end of September, Williams had mailed out the second part of *Paterson* 4. But he would be leaving for the West Coast for five weeks of readings and lectures on October 19 and he didn't know if he could get the final section of the poem to Laughlin before then. Time was running short and, besides, he'd promised to review Edward Dahlberg's *The Flea of Sodom*.[130] On top of that, he also had to write a two-thousand-word essay-review of Ford Madox Ford's *Parade's End* for the *Sewanee Review*, and then finish the talks he would give at the University of Washington, Reed College, and the University of Oregon.[131]

Then, on October 9—ten days before Williams was to leave for Washington—Laughlin asked Williams to please get the last part of *Paterson* 4 to the printer *before* he left for the West Coast. Williams had not planned to rush that, for he knew the postpartum blues would gnaw at him once his major poem was finally away from him. Still, he promised Laughlin to try and get the thing off if he possibly could, finally leaving it with his lawyer for Laughlin to pick up just three days before he left. Now, in October, even the world news conspired with Williams' tragic sense of the inevitable run to the sea, a sea of blood, that massive death wish which was sending American troops of the Eighth Army even then across the 38th Parallel into North Korea to support ROK army units. "Turn back I warn you / (October 10, 1950) / from the shark, that snaps / at his own trailing guts, / makes a sunset / of the green water," he wrote into the final pages of his poem.[132] He'd begun *Paterson* with German troops marching into Czechoslovakia and Poland and had worried for four years that his own boys would become sacrifices in that sea of blood which would claim some fifty million people worldwide. And now, in the poem's closing pages, the possibility of an all-out war with China and Russia which might claim that many again (in the first few days) seemed closer than ever. It was the great return all over again: the irresistible siren call of death and the bomb, towering in its awesome terror like a giant umbrella pine over New York: "I warn you, the sea is *not* our home."

Between October 10 and 13, Williams managed to type out several pages of notes on Dahlberg's *The Flea of Sodom*, just as he had promised. And though these notes were focused on Dahlberg's novel, they clearly touched on Williams' own preoccupations as he put the final touches on the poem that had obsessed him for so long. Dahlberg, he said—and we can substitute Williams' own "Dr. Paterson" for Dahlberg here—

> despises the suave language that is used for the blather of our slickness. He wants us to be aware of the difficulties; he is making a thing, a replica, as the maimed make a replica of a lost limb to hang in a chapel where they go for relief and comfort. Only Dahlberg is making a replica for the whole man, the whole man beset by panaceas called economics, politics of whatever color, whatever fabric. . . . He speaks of a fable, of an image, of the need for myth. If we only knew how sadly the myth of man himself is neglected. We are images of despair, all our politics is an image of despair. . . . [But] the imagination, the rekindling imagination, is a foible, it is a fluid, as true as the fluid that generates the child itself.[133]

One small seed floating in off that sea of blood, he may have thought. One small seed at the end of his poem. Amidst a public hanging (the death of the poet) and the threat of World War III (the death of America): a hope, a small, desperate hope in a new generation. *Paterson* had ended by spiraling all the way back to its beginnings, the seed that had floated in with wrack and scum at the close of the poem reverberating with the multiple packed seed of the "Preface," "rolling up out of chaos," now, "a nine months' wonder," to begin, yes, to begin all over again.

*
**

Paterson behind him, Williams packed and left with Floss for the West Coast. Flying, of course, would have been the easiest and fastest way out in 1950, but since Floss had not been able to travel with her husband on the '48 trip, they had decided to fly from Newark to Chicago, and from there take the Great Northern to Seattle. "We want the feel of creeping over its surface, such as the choo choo gives," he told Richard Emerson in early October. To see that part of the world north and west of the Mississippi again, to feel it as Williams had vicariously felt the surface of the sea when he'd read Thor Heyerdahl's *Kon Tiki:* that was what he wanted once again. He told Emerson to read that book, adding that he knew it wasn't any literary masterpiece, "but who the hell" wanted to read "literature" all the time anyway?[134]

They flew out of Newark on Thursday evening, October 19, and were seated comfortably aboard the *Empire Builder* the next afternoon when it pulled out of Union Station in Chicago heading west. Floss began a journal, but almost at once abandoned it. Writing was not her métier, and, besides, there was too much to see without having to waste the time writing. Williams' duties would include a series of readings, lectures, and consultations with student writers, and—despite the promising young students he would meet and the influence he would be exerting—he found the lecture circuit suddenly exhausting. He was at the Universty of Washington, Seattle, from Monday the twenty-third until the following Sunday, when he and Floss took the train south for the 160-mile trip to Reed College in Portland. There was another week of the same there. And then another trip south to Eugene and the University of Oregon for another week-long round of the same.

This time, the University of Washington put Williams and Floss up at the Hotel Edmond Meany. From his fifteenth-story window he could look down over the campus below him and see the splendid panorama of the Cascades in the distance. In fact that first week went better than he'd thought it would. He'd written Oscar Baron his first morning there asking him to pray for him because he was going to be sacrificed that evening at eight, when he would give his keynote talk on the creative process to three hundred people jammed into a hall.[135] He was nervous and tired at first and—as he confessed to Laughlin—not at all sure of his own abilities. He only hoped he wouldn't stink *too* much. But in fact they loved him. Then, on Wednesday, he was asked to give an impromptu public lecture on the modern novel, and he managed somehow to get through that (and well), though he couldn't for the love of him remember the following day *what* he'd told his audience.

Thursday morning he was up early, as usual, looking over a pale turquoise sky while Floss slept soundly. At half past seven he was writing to Dave McDowell, describing what it felt like to be on the lecture circuit at sixty-seven. He'd been taking a beating up till then, he felt. He'd been disgusted with himself after his Monday night talk, but the talk on Tuesday afternoon on the short story had gone better. As for the impromptu session on the novel, Floss herself—a tough woman to please—had told him that, aside from too many "God damns" strewn liberally through the talk, it had gone well. For the rest of it, he was happy to be west again, among these mountains and among these friendly faces. He was even excited by all those displaced easterners in Seattle and by the flowers that were still in full bloom in this "lovely small city warmed the

year around by the Japanese current."[136] That afternoon he simply read
his poetry to Ted Roethke's class and enjoyed himself. It was a two-hour
session and he began by reading the "Beautiful Thing" passage and then
talking about his poems in general. Beyond that he had to read four
unpublished novels plus a large number of short stories and poems, all by
creative writing students, some of whom genuinely impressed him.

Then it was on to Reed College, where Gary Snyder and Phil Whalen
were among the students in his audience. He was impressed with Reed
College and with some of "the hot kids" he'd talked to and he told
McDowell they might be worth scouting. He liked the English Department faculty there as well, and singled out Donald MacRae, Lloyd
Reynolds, and Frank Jones, as well as Stanley Moore of the Philosophy
Department—"all good guys." He taught, lectured, read manuscripts,
and even managed to get a good hangover after one particularly good
party. Then, that Sunday, November 5, he was in Eugene to do it all over
again. On Thursday afternoon, with the sessions nearly all behind him,
he wrote Laughlin his impressions of those three weeks. All that
speechmaking, he said, had had him in a continual state of feverishness,
and he was glad now that the hectic part of his trip was over. The lecture
tour had after all been worth it and he'd enjoyed the students, especially
the coeds, though he'd been somewhat disturbed by a strange apathy he'd
felt among them. "They don't come alive emotionally and intellectually
as our [eastern] kids do," he said, though he was willing to blame it on the
"inevitable time lag due to the slowness of the cultural drift." Yet,
paradoxically, he'd seen work among a handful of these students that he
found fresher than anything he'd seen recently back home, fresh work
"not yet . . . corrupted by the dry rot of our pseudo sophistication."[137]

That same evening, his chores at the University of Oregon finished, he
and Floss boarded a sleeper for San Francisco, five hundred miles to the
south. When they reached the city next afternoon, they found it crowded
with people preparing for the big football game to be played on Saturday.
They took a room at the Hotel Huntington on Nob Hill and had dinner at
the Rexroths' Saturday night—a fine chicken dinner which Rexroth had
prepared himself, followed by an evening of good talk. On Monday Eyvind
Earle picked the Williamses up at the train station in Los Angeles and
took them out to stay at his home in the suburbs in Van Nuys for a
five-day visit with his mother, Floss's sister, Charlotte. Williams got in a
reading of his poetry to a large audience at UCLA that Wednesday
afternoon and attended a party in his honor given by the bookdealer, Bob
Wetterau, at Flax's bookstore on the sixteenth, where Anaïs Nin, Man
Ray, and Donald Paquette had gone to hear him. He even recited some of
his poems into a tape recorder for Eyvind. Then, on Saturday evening
—November 18—Eyvind drove them down to the railroad station to take

the *Sunset Limited*'s sleeper for the trip east to El Paso, Texas, where they would see Bob McAlmon for what was to be the last time. At dawn on Sunday Williams awoke to see the sign for Tucson, Arizona, out his train window. Already the West Coast whirlwind was subsiding into memory.

Pre-Vichy France: Paris, Montparnasse, Pont d'Avignon. When the Sunset Limited rolled into the station at El Paso that Sunday afternoon, Williams could see his old friend pacing up and down the platform, already old-looking at fifty-five, his blotched, weathered face squinting up at Williams in recognition. And looking down at McAlmon what Williams saw was failure, could feel it deep within himself, having tasted it so often, in spite of the victory procession he'd just completed through the western states. So here was the man whom Pound himself had told Williams that past January was a better prose writer than Hemingway himself. Hemingway: the writer who had made it, made it big, followed everywhere by photographers, still posing stripped to the waist to show off his arms and chest, though Williams' trained eye could see fat where others thought they saw muscle. Nearly twenty years had passed since Hemingway had punched McAlmon in the mouth for some imaginary slight. And now, the man himself, the artist reduced to selling trusses in a godforsaken out-of-the-way desert province. McAlmon was no longer writing, had written virtually nothing since the war, though he still had plans to begin soon. But in fact he'd been reduced to selling off most of his signed first editions from the 1920s for the money those relics could bring him now. Handshakes and laughter all around on the platform, the sparrows fluttering amidst the waiting crocodiles in the fountain there in the public square of El Paso, an evening walk over the metal grid bridge into Mexico for tequila and quail and a burlesque show. And McAlmon's tubercular hack and splotchy face—the death's head of the failed artist— coming toward Williams from out of the winter shadows with a sidelong glance of brotherly recognition.

The Williamses spent three days in El Paso, except for one night when Williams and Floss and McAlmon and McAlmon's two brothers and their wives—seven in all—strolled across the international boundary into Mexico to see the sights and enjoy a quail dinner in Juárez. There had been Spanish music in the square and the usual chatter and then, halfway across the bridge, Williams had been startled by a form he saw wedged into the iron girders, "safe perhaps from both sides," he remembered, but "incredibly compressed into a shapeless obstruction." It was one of the local Indians, he realized, a despised people, caught between two worlds, but at least here unmolested. In that shapeless mass he would see yet another image of himself, another dark double which would haunt his consciousness like fire for months.

On Wednesday afternoon, the twenty-second, Williams waited with

Floss once again in the train station at El Paso for the express that would take them to New Orleans for Thanksgiving. Now, as he waited, Williams scribbled two messages on the backs of two identical picture postcards, nondescript views of the metal bridge over which he'd walked and where he'd seen that formless shape in the darkness. One of the notes was in pure *turista* idiom: "Over this bridge lies tequila—at 5¢ a shot and T bone steaks at 75¢ with soup and coffee thrown in. I shall miss them all." That one he sent to Louis Zukofsky.[138] The second was addressed to Bob McAlmon, and this touched a deeper chord, reverberating with significances it would take Williams himself months to understand. "It's been a wonderful experience being here and seeing you again," he wrote, thinking back to all that had forever been lost. "This bridge symbolizes some not soon to be forgotten hour. Stick it out, keed. Things may change for the better."[139]

New Orleans was cold, but Williams enjoyed seeing John Husband again, a professor from Tulane University whom he'd met at Yaddo that July and to whom he'd taken an instant liking. The Husbands and the Williamses took in the sights, saw Bourbon Street, dined well. Then, on Saturday, Bill and Floss took the plane from New Orleans and headed for Newark. Williams' natural nervousness in planes was not made any easier when—at a stopover in Atlanta—he heard over the intercom that a terrific storm was blowing over the New York City area. Then, as the plane approached Washington, D.C., he learned that the flight was being rerouted there because of the storm. As soon as he could, he called Bill, who told him not to head up yet but to stay in Washington for the night and take the train Sunday morning. He had Paul and Jinny and their kids with him because the power lines were down all over the area and 9 Ridge Road, at least, with its underground cables, had been spared that. When they did reach Rutherford at four o'clock Sunday afternoon, Williams found both his sons straddling a large maple tree that had fallen onto the office roof, trying to saw and chop the tree away. Thus ended the great western trip. Williams was once more back home.[140]

*
**

But no sooner was Williams home than it was the New York circuit again, since both his collected short stories, *Make Light of It,* from Random House and his *Collected Later Poems* from New Directions—both in editions close to five thousand—were published on November 30, as if vying with one another for attention. He had to do several radio broadcasts in early December, as well as television interviews like the Mary Margaret McBride hour and "Luncheon at Sardi's," and he was already worn down with the trip he'd just completed.[141] On top of that there was bleak news about the Korean "police action." Here he was, as he had been in '38, on the verge of a major breakthrough, as he felt, for hadn't those crowds at UCLA outnumbered even the crowds who had come to see Dylan Thomas a year earlier? And here were his collected works and *Paterson* to show to the public. Then why, *why!*, another war just now? "Nobody minds dying," he told Macleod, "but for God's sake not for sheer wrongheadedness, for stupidty. Make a poem out of that. . . . Maybe it'll happen tomorrow, the war will be on and, for the moment, we'll feel virtuous, quieted by a singleness of purpose to save our skins." And nothing would have been accomplished. And yet there was the specter of the bomb looming over him and all that he loved and he was afraid that a mistake, a miscalculation now would mean "the end of us all."[142]

Nothing for it, again, but to work like hell while there was still time. For he still had a twelve-hundred-page manuscript—his *Autobiography* —to write in the next three months. The contract had called for delivery of that script on March 1, 1951, and Williams was going to do his damnedest to get it there on schedule. All through December he wrote in a generous, broad longhand, unusual for a man who had always typed, but he tried the new way on the advice of a friend. After all, he was writing about what he knew best: himself. Write, write, as fast as he could, leaving gaps and pockets where his memory would fail him, but push on at the rate of nearly thirty pages a day.

Now he burrowed into his study, writing letters or making appearances only when necessary. He began to see himself as a prisoner, chained to his desk, periodically sending out page counts to friends. Six hundred and twelve pages longhand by December 30; 750 by January 4; 934 by January 11; 1,119 by January 20; 1,249 by the twenty-sixth. Kitty was making the first triple-space draft from his own longhand version, and he praised her ability to "decipher almost anything I misspell."[143] "Come hell and/or highwater," he'd have the equivalent of four hundred printed pages in Random House's hands by March 1, "on the dot or die in the attempt," and—ha ha—he didn't feel like dying.[144] He told John Berryman on January 9 that his time at the moment was "mortgaged as are the days of a man waiting out a condemnation to death—except I hope not to die in process of composing my autobiography. . . . For I have to be my own prison to keep out the cold of events: Cervantes, Bunyan, 'or iron bars a cage,' Ezra Pound. Lucky guys to be so protectively housed during the months of composition."[145]

But as busy as he was, he still had time to spend an afternoon with the composer Ben Weber, whom he'd met at Yaddo, to talk over the possibility of Weber's doing the music for Williams' libretto, and another afternoon with Brendan Gill for a proposed "Profile" for *The New Yorker* (which did not appear).[146] He attended the meeting of the National Institute of Arts and Letters in early February. He read his poems in New York at a benefit performance for Kenneth Patchen, bedridden and crippled by then for several years. He had lunch with Auden on March 16 and could honestly praise his *Nones*, which he thought stronger than much of Auden's earlier work. He agreed to present that year's Russell Loines Award to John Crowe Ransom in May, when his own book should be done. He even took the train up to Wellesley on February 20 to give a reading, returning to New York at three in the morning to get back to his book.[147] Again, he gave another reading at the New School in mid-March and yet another for Norman Holmes Pearson and Louis Martz at Yale on Tuesday afternoon, March 20. He had all-day sessions with McDowell going over and correcting the typescript of the *Autobiography*. On top of all that, Floss was in bed the second half of February and the first half of March with an intestinal virus that Williams seemed powerless to arrest and which left them both in an unrelieved siege of mental depression. As for the book itself: it was dragging him with it, this spontaneous, unstudied failure.[148] Still, he was obsessed to push on with it and get it finally away from himself. He was even down to revising the last fifty pages of the thing when it happened. It was Wednesday, March 28. And having pushed himself as hard as he could for as long as he could, his body finally turned on him. *Ping!* Later he would remember something Paul had told him once about being on destroyer patrol on the old *Alden*, out in the North Atlantic during the war, how he used to lie there at night in his bunk before he fell asleep, and how he could hear large fish colliding against the ship's hull. Then there would be a small *ping* reverberating through the drumlike interior of the ship. Now, suddenly, Williams heard that *ping* coming from somewhere inside his own head just before he collapsed. He had just had his first stroke in the midst of a fury of work. Like that. *Ping.* Like that.[149]

THIRTEEN

Hunting Down the Unicorn:
1951—1956

Bard College: Friday night, March 30, 1951. Amidst thunder and the loud patter of rain on the tin roof of the gymnasium—the only building on campus large enough to hold the event—Wallace Stevens read his short address to the crowd who had assembled there to witness this august presence. He made no effort to make himself heard beyond the first few rows of faces he could see there straining to hear what he said, but it made no difference now: it was the fact of his presence that mattered. He was there to receive an honorary degree from the college, as Williams had the year before, and Williams was to have been there as part of the celebration to talk about the Modern Poem. Now, however, Williams lay in a hospital bed in the intensive care unit at Passaic General Hospital, capable of no more than a weak stutter. He had insisted on talking to Ted Weiss at Bard from his hospital phone himself, to try to articulate in a broken voice just what—in medical terms—had happened to him that would make it impossible now for him to be there to greet Stevens. Hemorrhage . . . cerebral accident . . . eyes unfocused . . . pronounced slurring . . . listed as critical . . . stroke. So Stevens had somehow managed to do it . . . to outlast Williams, though he was four years Williams' senior. And here he was, the strong contender, receiving a standing ovation while the outer weather tapping on the metal roof for once conspired with the inner and the applause rolled on and on. Alone, the portly poet turned away from the lectern, caught Ted Weiss's eye, and said, as he left the room, "Well, we didn't need the old man after all, did we?"[1]

For a brief moment, the veteran contender's massive edifice had left the front door opened, but he obviously must have felt something like remorse, for he did genuinely care too much about Williams to let the remark stand. Having survived the wake, and astonished to find such pleasure in the act of survival, he wrote Williams on April 23, after he'd at last heard that Williams would not suffer too much damage after his "recent collision with Nature." Williams, he wrote, had worked too hard all his life to get to the top to be deprived now of a leisurely old age. No, not old age. He caught himself at once. "As the older of the two of us, I resent those words more than you do. If a man is as young as he feels you are, no doubt, actually twenty-five and I am say twenty-eight." He wished he could come by to see Williams when he was in New York, but his time always seemed to be taken up with errands to run—shoes, socks, etc.—so that there was "rarely time to meet people."[2] Stevens' poetry, of course, had already told Williams that.

Now Williams wrote Stevens as soon as he felt strong enough to do so. It was the first letter he had typed since his stroke and he told Stevens he was happy, no, thrilled, to be able to be writing at all, and especially to a friend he had known now for forty years. The stroke, he admitted, had caught him completely by surprise, "for though I know I am far from invulnerable I didn't expect THAT! . . . It seems to have resulted from trying to write a book in three months while carrying on a practice of medicine. Just couldn't bring it off. I almost had the book finished at that." He was already back at work on the *Autobiography*, checking the first two parts and putting the finishing touches on the third and last. As for old age, he agreed with Stevens. Either of them might "croak at any moment," but they weren't old. And though his medical practice was virtually behind him now, he was looking forward not to the end, but to a whole "new way of life." He wanted the time to "hobnob" with his few rare friends, among whom he wanted to include Stevens.[3] But what he could not know then was that—at least this side of Dante's heaven of the philosophers—the two were not to meet again.

Considering the seriousness of what had happened to him, Williams' recovery was amazingly rapid. It was as if Williams—having suffered whatever he had to suffer—wanted to get back to business as usual as quickly as he could. But he also realized that he could just as easily have been dead now, and so he began to look at this poststroke period as a time of grace, as the space between lightning stroke and thunder clap.[4] He would use it for his art. At the beginning of '51, the Alpha Chapter of Phi Beta Kappa at Harvard had invited him to be their poet of the year and deliver a "fifteen-minute poem" for the group's commencement exercises on June 18. Until the time of the stroke he'd done nothing about actually composing his poem, other than that he knew that his bridge —the one at El Paso—would somehow figure in it. But now, in the hospital, unable to write, he had time to think about his life and about his poem.

By early May he had sent the third part of the *Autobiography* to his typist, Mrs. Pettengill, and had written his foreword, telling McDowell that he hoped he would not object to his saying there that the *Autobiography* would *not* talk about the women he had been to bed with "or anything about them," and he was warning his readers not to look for that side of his life in his book. Such encounters and intimacies, he argued, had really not had anything to do with him as a writer. Besides, the *Autobiography* was a public document, unlike *Paterson*, where he had talked—confessed—about the problem of intimacy. Then he and Floss were dropped off at the summer home of a colleague of Williams', Dr. Sullivan, up in Schuylerville, New York, outside of Saratoga, for a two weeks' rest. For the moment Williams was free of his Random House commitments and so free to tackle his poem for Harvard. And since he was unable to drive and now found himself isolated in a still-wintry Saratoga, where spring was a cold, raw, and drizzly affair, Williams spent most of his time mildly depressed, just sleeping and thinking or reading Rouse's translation of the *Iliad* and trying to shape his poem. At first, try as he might, nothing happened. But finally, "after a good deal of labor," he managed to midwife the thing into life, "forcing" himself, as he told one person, "to put the words down." He was back home on Monday, May 21, and by Friday he had "finished the first, faulty but complete draft: 17 pages."[5] By the end of the month he had a clean and corrected copy ready for his stenographer. It had taken him five weeks of close work to produce one fifteen-minute poem, and though he still had mixed feelings about what he'd written, Harvard had ordered a poem "sight unseen," and now, like it or not, "they were going to get it."[6]

What Harvard was getting was "The Desert Music," and Williams had written it quite simply to prove to himself that—in spite of very strong intimations of his own mortality—he was still a poet. It was a highly self-conscious piece of work, this poem: words in search of a form consonant with Williams' dramatic sense of his own radical deformation. He'd created a desert music for a desert time, the poet afoot in a wasteland of his own with a poem moving out of embryonic formlessness toward the assertion that Williams could still write a poem. So the shadowy presence of his old friend McAlmon, wandering toward his own desert oblivion, stood behind the poem, a figure embodying Williams' own fears that he too might be swallowed up, his ability to create cut off permanently, without warning, before he'd had the chance to say what it was he'd felt compelled to say.

To create: the verb-centeredness of that act. And to *imitate* reality, not merely copy it. It was a pervading concern of Williams', particularly in the months when he'd worked on the *Autobiography* at top speed, when he found himself day after day writing at that level: not reenacting his life, not driving toward its intimate center as he had in *Paterson*, but simply copying the surface of his life over. One could keep busy that way, as the memory selected out thousands of discrete events without revealing the essential figure of the man himself. He had engaged only part of himself in the act of writing his life, so that now "The Desert Music" became a necessary and welcome counterresponse to the finger exercises of the *Autobiography*. In "The Desert Music" he would try once again to touch the self. The poem would need another dimension, then, other than what prose had been able to give him if he was to imitate the descent into hell once more. A descent with its necessary sense of disintegration, its formlessness moving once again toward its opposite, form, like a fetus moving toward the form of the child.

Writing to Ken Burke in late January, Williams had told him how only recently he had come to understand the *real* "significance of Aristotle's use of the word 'imitation.'" It was the central word for the creating artist; in fact it had become for Williams a "new" word, fraught with new significance for him:

> The imagination has to imitate nature, not to copy it—as the famous speech in *Hamlet* has led us to believe. There is a world of difference there. The whole dynamic of the art approach is involved, to imitate invokes the verb, to copy invokes nothing but imbecility. It is the very essence of the difference between realism and cubism with everything in favor of the latter.[7]

The *Autobiography* was, after all, only a mode of realism: page on page of narrative, most of it "true," and much of it somehow missing the revelation he was after. But in "The Desert Music" he used a cubist strategy, with the poem's dislocated, shattered forms bringing his images into high relief. Thus the poem's sharp edges and dissociated voices, its crazy quilt of forms ranging from sprawled prose to tight quatrains to heighten the "realistic" narrative of the poem grinding against those self-consciously sharp patterns revealing the man's deepest anxieties.

Like *Paterson*, "The Desert Music" provided a narrative thread and a journey.[8] This time it was a journey between worlds, and the poem began literally in a no-man's land: the international boundary between two countries—the U.S. (English-speaking, masculine, assertive, manipulative) and Mexico (Spanish-speaking, feminine, passive, generative, exploited). It was a mirror of the split, then, in Williams himself between his dead father and his recently dead mother, and recollections of Williams' journey to Potosí forty years before—"You see, we do not all live like *los negros*, gringo"—stirred in Williams, his entry into Juárez at nightfall triggering the split—and regression—into that side of his psyche which he identified with his female half.

He went even further, personifying the debased female—his artist double—in the figure of a stripteaser from the States, whom he'd watched in one of the local Mexican spots, gyrating one more time to her honky-tonk music. Here once more was the eternal feminine: his old muse, battered and badly used, but still dancing, still giving the poet courage. What struck Williams was how closely this brassy, tired music fit the woman's performance. So here, then, just here was the deeper music he'd searched for and which he now reenacted in his turn, fitting her music to his poem:

> *There is a fascination*
> *seeing her shake*
> *the beaded sequins from*
> *a string about her hips*
>
> *She gyrates but it's*
> *not what you think,*
> *one does not laugh*
> *to watch her belly.*

In *The Bridge*—the poem Williams had had to confront in order to write *Paterson* 1—Hart Crane had reduced his own Indian/American muse at one point to the level of a burlesque queen. Now, twenty years later, in a complex crossing with this dead poet, Williams responded to Crane's high romantic figure with his own low romantic, using a countermusic and a rhythm he clearly saw as being more in tune with the truth of such matters. Williams' bridge across the Rio Grande would answer Crane's vision of hell in *The Bridge*, as his stripped, jerky quatrains countered Crane's own Eliotic quatrains with their complex, artificial Elizabethan music. "Her eyes," Crane had written,

> *Her eyes exist in swivellings of her teats,*
> *Pearls whip her hips, a drench of whirling strands.*
> *Her silly snake rings begin to mount, surmount*
> *Each other—turquoise fakes on tinselled hands.*

Williams' music was by far the flatter, like his dancer, "heavy on her feet," yawning her way through her accustomed moves, cold eyes watching, aware that she was "part of another tune." As Williams watched her he could see that she too knew her customers, knew her audience, and could hold the "same / opinion" of them that they held of her. "What," the poem asks,

> *What in the form of an old whore in*
> *a cheap Mexican joint in Juárez, her bare*
> *can waggling crazily can be*
> *so refreshing to me, raise to my ear*
> *so sweet a tune, built of such slime?*

The answer comes as he crosses back over the bridge, after having come in contact with the people of that place by literally touching them, as his hero in *In the American Grain* had touched the Abnaki Indians in Maine. Once more, then, he must confront the deathlike figure asleep on the bridge, who is not after all dead but instead promises "a birth of awful promise." For now Williams sees that that shapeless mass has become "a

child in the womb prepared to imitate life." The force of that infinitive
—*to imitate*—should not escape our attention, for it was with the verb
that Williams had promised to enact the poem. The shapeless figure is, of
course, an extension of Williams' own crippled condition, both physically
and artistically, except that he could be protected against the fact of his
own encroaching annihilation by a "music" that acted like a "mucus."
That punning echo suggests that the act of writing the poem could itself
act like a film, an amniotic fluid, to protect the crippled poet, ironically,
from returning to preconsciousness. Poetry, then, could be "a benumbing
ink," staining and coloring the mind, and giving Williams a way of coping
with the terrible reality of what had happened to him. So "The Desert
Music" is in a sense an action painting, like Jackson Pollock's paintings
concerned with the process of their own enactment. It is a poem built out
of the need to locate the moment of life-sustaining inspiration: the recall
of a distant music remembered on the other side of the bridge when he
was still in his prestroke, prelapsarian condition.

Out of his fears about creative impotence following the shock of his
first stroke, out of the need to assert that, in spite of his accident, he was
still a poet, Williams managed to create his fifteen-minute poem for that
Harvard audience. But facing them, facing those who were synonymous
for him with the academy and more especially with the camp of Eliot (one
of Harvard's most famous sons), Williams had a crippling anxiety as well
to deal with. Especially now that he'd been hit in mind and eye and
tongue. What would it be like to be up there on that platform in
Cambridge performing his poem before the curious or indifferent or
openly hostile shadows surrounding him? Williams: that old trouper
from the States, made more comic than ever by his stroke. The day after
his reading he'd told Zukofsky that the atmosphere at Harvard had been
just what he'd expected: "semi-ecclesiastic, a hall hallowed by tradition,"
and that his own poem had been "low" church in comparison to such
high church surroundings.[9]

What was all this "nauseating prattle" about platonic love in the face
of a sordid reality everywhere about him? Williams the revolutionary
would give his audience a new kind of music, performing his own
rebellious strip in church, singing about—of all things—a whore in a
cheap Mexican joint in his own rendition of the American West. And if
the academicians there shook their heads or gritted their teeth or
dismissed this American naif: no matter. The feeling was mutual.
Williams still believed the universities were "rank / with" the old music
of Eliot and Eliot's disciples, the New Critics. Like his stripper, he was
"part of another tune," knew his customers and knew their worth,
and—though he might be "heavy" on his feet—he would keep on
dancing.

Self-lacerating, self-contemptuous, determined to survive, Williams would dance for them, maintaining in their very faces that, in spite of indifference, in spite of neglect, in spite of his brain's self-betrayal, he was still a poet:

> I am a poet! I
> am. I am. I am a poet, I reaffirmed, ashamed.

"The Desert Music" had been written to allow Williams to make that statement. And yet, with that poem and that reaffirmation made, it would cost him another year before he could bring himself to compose another poem. In the meantime he had demonstrated to himself that he still could write a poem, still "keep his pecker up." It was not without its own pathos, his effort. *I / am:* that line break reinforcing the sense of the poet in the act of doing that which constituted Williams' deepest sense of self. *I / am:* creation and affirmation at the poem's close simultaneously realized. *I am.*

*
**

Williams' first "cerebral accident" had come as a total surprise, knocking him backwards and robbing him of his ability to write and to speak. But by the time he gave his reading at Harvard ten weeks later, he'd willed himself back into some semblance of normality. "I have been ill," he wrote Professor Louis Martz of Yale at the end of May, to thank him for the piece he'd written on Williams' poetry for *Poetry New York.* It was the second time he'd been knocked out, he explained, the first being his heart attack three years earlier. But at least he'd come out of his setback "with a clearer head." He knew now that he had no more time to waste in bringing his work into some sort of summary, to make the direction of that work "clear." He did not want to return to medicine again if he could help it. Instead, he wanted to spend whatever time remained to him reading, thinking, and creating so as to complete his "task as a poet."[10]

Moreover, there were still so many commitments to be met: odds and ends, reviews, galleys to correct, speeches to make, readings. On May 25 he made the presentation speech at the American Academy for John Crowe Ransom, that year's recipient of the Russell Loines Award for Poetry, the award he himself had won in '48.[11] In early June he finished an eleven-page review of Carl Sandburg's *Complete Poems* for *Poetry* magazine, insisting that Sandburg had "petered out" as a poet at least ten years earlier. He dismissed the massive volume under review—except for a handful of lyrics buried in the "Cornhuskers"—as "a dunelike mass . . . formless as a drift of desert and engulfing the occasional shrub or tree," and populated by "a drift of people" who lay "piled up filling his pages." In short, Sandburg's own desert music amounted to nothing more than a wasteland. Approaching seventy, Williams could no longer afford to mince words; it was time now for a strict accounting of his contemporaries.[12]

Just before going up to Cambridge to read "The Desert Music," Williams had finished the galleys for the *Autobiography* and sent them off to McDowell. The book that had nearly cost him his life—as he'd told Marianne Moore in June—and which would soon cost him the friendship of Robert McAlmon and others had already become for him "a magnificent blurr."[13] He spent an afternoon in late June with Burke discussing the implications of a poetry of imitation in his Harvard poem and then spent a week with Floss at his brother's farm in southern Connecticut recuperating. Now, his desk once again cleared, Williams began thinking about finishing *The Build-Up*, which he'd promised Random House for early 1952. He was, as he put it, eager "to rape all those virgin chapters" still unwritten.[14] Despite his stroke, he was preparing once more to get his "pecker up."

But the intensive phase of writing his novel would come in August, after a long rest at West Haven with Floss and their seven-year-old granddaughter, Suzy. In the meantime he wanted to read the classics to get his bearings straight again, to see his own frenetic poetic moment in a larger context. He was also hungry for the "good old salt water" at their shorefront cottage where he'd been coming practically all his life, to listen once again to the sound of waves lapping the shore here much as they had lapped the Aegean in Homer's time with their "good obscure noise," a noise that, unlike language, needed "no explanation."[15] Facing the old sea wall and the Long Island Sound in this protected inlet, he could absorb the sun and the sea and read Homer to his heart's content. Back in April and May, he'd read through Rouse's prose translation of the *Iliad*. And now, in July, by what seemed to him a stroke of good fortune, he learned that the attractive young woman in the cottage next to his was the wife of a classics professor who had brought his working library with him to the shore: Livio Stecchini of the University of Chicago. Williams borrowed Stecchini's copy of the *Odyssey*—also in the Rouse translation —because Pound himself had helped Rouse with that translation years before. For hours Williams and Stecchini walked the old sea wall discussing the classics and the economic decline of the ancient world "in this most inconspicuous place . . . in the world."[16] Homer, after all, had the ability to make "the modern disturbances of the poets" look more "like flies instead of elephants." He needed that longer perspective now.[17]

Stecchini, Williams noted with the eye of the diagnostician, was "a dark-skinned, balding man, but tall and very sure of himself." He had difficulty cutting through Stecchini's "strong foreign accent" (for the man's native tongue was Italian), but he marveled at just how "remarkably well-informed" and "thoroughly well-read" he was. Stecchini had published one book on the Greek system of money and now he gave Williams a "4-page synopsis of his next project: a treatise on the transformation of Greece from a matriarchal to a patriarchal society." All of this deeply impressed Williams. He had not had much luck finding "unrestrainedly straight-thinking" among academics, but his anti-academic stance had been eroding in the past few years as he came to know specific individuals better. Now it was Stecchini.[18] In fact, when one of Norman Holmes Pearson's students, an undergraduate named Donald Cheney, drove out from Yale to interview Williams for the *Yale Literary Magazine*, Williams spent half the time discussing a poem Stecchini had written called "Space and Being," which "explained Plato" by focusing on a man and woman making love in a hotel room. That, Williams added, was one way of getting Plato's abstractions across to undergraduates.

There were short forays out from the cottage as well. So, on one such trip, Williams and Floss drove over to Old Lyme, Connecticut, to see Louis Zukofsky and his wife, Celia, and just missed running into Edward Dahlberg, for which small favor Williams was grateful since Dahlberg —as Louis told him—was in one of his particularly obnoxious moods.[19] On another day Williams lunched with Pearson and Martz in New Haven, and yet another afternoon was spent at Pearson's spacious shorefront home. But the major public event for Williams was his reading at the Bread Loaf Writers Conference on July 25. Williams knew Frost would be at Bread Loaf again, and he could hardly forget that Frost had snubbed him ten years earlier when he'd lectured there. And that Frost was still on his mind was evident from what he told Cheney during his West Haven interview. In spite of what had happened, he liked Frost, whom he read as a poet who had managed marvelously to give voice to a whole region. But he also read the man as a reactionary with "no grasp of the crucial issues" facing his world, such as "the Jewish question, or India or the bomb," all of which had helped shape modern verse and were therefore part of the modern poet's responsibility.[20] And at Bread Loaf itself, though he liked the instructors and thought them "a good sort" who had paid attention to what he had to say, he couldn't help noticing that Frost was once again conspicuously absent at both his talk and his poetry reading, though he was convinced the old bastard had been off skulking somewhere on the grounds or hiding in his cabin. So be it. He had more important things to think about.

In early August, back from the Connecticut shore, Williams began the work of completing his novel, devoting mornings to the task except when other duties called him away or his eyes, noticeably affected by his stroke, began to wobble on him again. Besides, he really didn't want to do *The Build-Up* anyway. It had been more than twenty years now since he'd first begun the Stecher trilogy, and so much had happened in the intervening years that it was as though someone else had written it. The *Autobiography* had nearly killed him, and would it be worth while dying over a novel he was unenthusiastic about? All he could think of was the weight of the 350 pages and the precious eight months he would lose to get the thing done, and he could see the whale of his death rising out of his unconscious, "rolling over and flipping its flukes" and threatening to take him with it when it should sound once more.[21] So irritable was he, in fact, that when Alfred Eisenstadt and his assistants came out to 9 Ridge Road to photograph him for *Life* magazine in mid-August, all he could think of afterward was not the honor but the two days they'd taken out of his writing schedule, so that now he'd "have to go like hell, do at least 8 pages a day for the next two days to make up for it."[22]

Seven weeks into the novel he let go his frustrations in a letter to Pearson. The first two books—ten years' work—had taken Floss up through her first two years. Properly speaking, she should have been the focus for all three volumes. But *The Build-Up* was turning out to be a kind of *Portrait of the Artist as a Young Man*. Sure he wanted to see the book done, at least the way he saw it shining in his mind, but it was such "an awful chore" and "so slow in the making." He was laboring "to reconstruct" his "own early years" this time, "to make it move again" and it was "so hard to reanimate it; it takes all my strength just as if I were physically trying to make those dead arms awaken and lift themselves—and all their trivial maneuvres." The problem was, as it had always been, to take the drab stuff of his actual life and "make the hidden significances come alive and be profound." Moreover, the experience of writing his *Autobiography* was still too close to him not to influence his novel, and what he found himself doing now was rewriting with greater candor the real nature of his courtship and early marriage. He had already written the myth of his life in terms of the American success story—how a local boy from Rutherford had made good against a hostile world. Now he was struggling to raise his "circumambient world of trivia," to blow life into the dust of that small-town world where he and Floss had grown up and at the same time confess to anyone who would listen how that life had been in its own unfolding an American tragedy, shaped as much by loss and promises cut short as by anything else. It was his last chance to set the record of his starting out straight.[23]

The *Autobiography* had been another matter. Its colors, he'd said, were pastels, rather than harsh primaries, written throughout in "cool, factual, . . . short easy sentences." Whatever shocks there might have been "to the sensibilities of the gentle reader" he'd carefully "filed down to take out all the hooks."[24] Fear of libel had organized his memory as much as anything (in spite of which there were several who by year's end were seriously considering suing him for defamation of character anyway). But in *The Build-Up* the transparent mask of a fiction allowed him to confess to the facts of his strange courtship and for once get those nagging, insistent early ghosts off his chest. In December it would be forty years he and Floss had been married and it was time finally to reconstruct that marriage's strained beginnings. Like Joyce recreating himself in young Stephen Dedalus, Williams reanimated himself into the awkward young doctor and wild-eyed poet who had been given Joe Stecher's daughter in marriage. Williams was unsparing in his honesty as he peered into the glass of history back to the strange figure he had been, but he still allowed his father-in-law and mother-in-law to dominate the book as they had been meant to do. For what he was finally after was a diagnostician's report of the emptiness of the American dream. Joe Stecher: the immigrant who'd made it in America, at the cost of burying his only son, disowning his elder daughter, and seeing his younger daughter leave his house to marry a young poet who had gotten her pregnant without even having enough money for the down payment on a house. In the final scene of the novel, Williams had drawn Joe and Gurlie looking for a mountain site for their American dream house, a veritable Old World castle constructed on a reduced scale, alone with each other, their world already in shambles in spite of their having "made it." Williams had loved his father-in-law, still loved the memory of him, but he also knew that the man had conformed with uncanny accuracy to the pattern of his earlier American heroes, to the final loneliness of Columbus and Washington, Boone and Poe, except that his "success" had turned out to be his final failure. *The Build-Up*, finally, did not come up to the level of imaginative writing of either *White Mule* or *In the Money* except in isolated passages, for the impetus and the conditions for that kind of sequel belonged to the Depression '30s and not the '50s. Yet, in spite of that, old memories did enflame and enkindle some extraordinary moments in a book written under what were for Williams trying circumstances.

At the end of August Williams received advance copies of the *Autobiography*, which for complex reasons he'd kept from showing Floss until then. But now, as she read through it, she found typographical errors on nearly every page and, even worse, factual inaccuracies everywhere. The "magnificent blurr" had degenerated to a mess, and Williams began to deeply regret that he'd ever consented to do the thing in the first place. On top of that, though the lawyers at Random House had been careful to check the manuscript for libel, so that one chapter dealing with friends he'd known years earlier had had to be excised, Williams thought it wise to make a special trip to New York to see his lawyer, James Murray, about the further possibility of libel. He did not want a recurrence of the mess surrounding "The Five Dollar Guy." He could no longer afford that sort of thing.[25]

Still, the publication of the *Autobiography* was an event and, to celebrate, Kitty Hoagland had arranged a party with the Rutherford Chamber of Commerce at the Elks Club in honor of Williams' sixty-eighth birthday, September 17, the day his book was officially released. The party was for the most part a local affair, though, as Williams' publisher, McDowell was invited. Always uneasy at such gatherings, Williams wrote McDowell the following day half apologizing for the "atmosphere" from which he had sprung. And when *The Build-Up* hit Rutherford, he added, he was going to make damn sure he was "in Florida or Los Angeles." Not that his townspeople would be sore at him for doing them in yet another book, he explained. It was just that they'd be all "worked up" again over their local celebrity and he felt that one Chamber of Commerce affair "was enough" for one lifetime.[26]

At the same time Williams was being lionized in Rutherford, he was also sitting for his portrait by a painter named Emmanuel Romano, a friend of McDowell's. But after several sittings in late September and October (since Romano's first attempt had to be aborted), Williams began to grow restless. As much as he liked Romano and wished the man well, he chafed at not being able to get on with his novel. Moreover, Romano had had his own reasons for doing the portrait, one of them being to get Williams to write some sort of statement about his paintings for a one-man showing in New York in December, and Williams' first attempt at a statement, like Romano's first attempt, had been rejected.

The portrait itself showed Williams indoors and seated, wearing a sports jacket, his right arm across his lap, his head resting on his left hand. The face was angular, almost fractured in a style recalling Cézanne, and it was striking how much Williams had come in these later years to resemble his mother. But if there was a feminine quality to the features, there was also the unmistakable look of masculine impatience in the eyes and in the set of the mouth, as if Williams had found it uncomfortable to be sitting there idle when there was work to be done. "No time for any-/ thing but his painting," he would write in 1959 in a poem called, significantly, "Self-Portrait."[27]

"The only thing disturbing me" about doing Williams' portrait, Romano had entered into his own diary on September 27, "was the reflection of the light in his eyeglasses. Something maddening—the light was so strong I could not see Williams' face." Strip Williams of those glasses and the hard light they caught and thus strip him of his "boyish enthusiasm" and suddenly Williams had become his own age, a man nearing seventy, his mother's "silky independence" and her dark Caribbean features revealing themselves there.[28]

But as Romano watched Williams, Williams was also watching Romano. And what fascinated Williams was the artistic process revealing itself five feet away from him, in this artist totally absorbed in realizing an elusive presence. After all, Williams knew from his own work, the "artist is always and forever painting only one thing: a self portrait." He did not mean a narcissism, a portrayal of one's own guts, but rather the artist's own "imaginary image" manifested in word or paint in terms of the object before him and the materials and techniques he had to work with. The tragedy was that it was the world of the imagination, Williams insisted, that was the more real world, more real than any world the rest of humanity agreed to call the real world.

Finally, then, Williams was able to say what he wanted to say about Romano's work and say it with absolute sincerity. If Romano was no great artist, he was nevertheless a real one, consumed with the need to make a statement on canvas as Williams had been equally consumed to make one on paper. The "truly real" was in the artist's imagination, thronging in on his "inward view," and the artist had no time for anything but his painting: "to show his gift," to show not himself but the praise that was in him. And the artist showed that praise, Williams explained, by his meticulous concern for his craft and by his mastery of the new techniques "which the artists of the immediate past" had taught him. And if that meant Cézanne and Picasso for Romano, it meant Whitman and Pound for Williams.[29]

Williams came back to the painters again in his speech at the Dinner Meeting of the National Institute of Arts and Letters held on December 18. He'd been asked to address the writers and artists of the Institute on the subject of contemporary trends in arts and letters, and he'd prepared a ten-page talk for the occasion called "The American Spirit in Art." He stressed the role America itself had played in the development of the visual arts, making the argument that the most recent phase of American painting, particularly abstract expressionism, might well be more deeply anchored to the deepest wellsprings of the American tradition than was readily apparent. It wasn't so much that the abstractionists were willful obscurantists, he argued, so much as it was a problem that other artists had yet to catch up with the deepest impulses of modern art. The same thing was true, he pointed out, about the charges of willful obscurantism brought against the modern poem. Religious obscurantism or mysticism —like Eliot's or Merton's (though he named neither here)—was for a pragmatist like himself "beyond solution." But what might appear difficult in someone like a Robert Motherwell *was* capable of being understood and appreciated and might even be shown in time to have been "inevitable," a necessary step in the development of painting from Cézanne to the present. Cézanne had begun the modern revolution by insisting that it was not subject matter or content that was of utmost importance, but rather technique, and that artist had made color itself carry much of his argument. Modern art was a strategy of laying pigment to canvas (or of placing words on the page). From Cézanne through analytic and synthetic cubism to Matisse and on through Motherwell there had been a continuity, an emphasis on making "a picture or a poem of *anything*." Subject matter for all these artists was secondary: a successful painting or poem could be about anything—a side of beef, the backside of a Parisian prostitute, a plum. What really mattered was the artist's ability to shape, to structure, to inform his canvas or his lines. So Williams called now on his audience to celebrate the phenomenon of a Motherwell, to be "glad that someone has turned up among us to work out that (thankless) historical process." It was not the only process, of course, but in time Motherwell's work—like Williams' own—would come to "constitute a criticism" of his time and prove, eventually, to have enlarged the very possibilities of art itself. So it had been with Whitman, who had rejected the old line, what Williams called the self-delighting "medieval masterbeat," opening up the poem instead to the possibilities of a new measure. Not a new subjectivism, for that would have been worse than the old tyrannies of the iamb, but rather a new accent and a new measure. Emerson had called for a national literature as long ago as 1837 in his address to the Harvard divinity students, and here was Williams at the end of 1951 again insisting that the National Institute heed what was truly distinctive in the American art experiment.[30]

Williams had hardly read through the opening lines of his speech, however, when the catcalls and boos began. "I damned near DIED reading my ten pages to the wolves," he would complain to Kenneth Burke a month later. He'd been nervous enough as it was, he admitted, and he'd even refused to have a cocktail in order to be as fresh as possible for his delivery:

> I didn't eat what was on my plate, but as the pressure mounted my old heart began to torment itself until it was a painful lump in my chest. I had to grit my teeth and grind out the words from a parched throat. They wanted to kill me. That Irishman, Hackett, former editor of the *New Republic*, I think, was the only one who defended me at least vocally. It was a standoff otherwise; half the guys went away scowling, the other grinning. I felt better as soon as I had finished reading.[31]

At least Williams had learned something about such august gatherings, he told Louis Zukofsky on January 6. True, it had been good to meet the men and women who made up the National Institute, "to dine with them and take part in their discussions," but it still came down to the individuals who made up such assemblies. But his reception at their hands during his address had made of Williams both "a wiser and sadder man," and he had had to "round out" his own concept of the state of American art as against theirs. "If I survive," he added, "I may have learned something at the end of another year."[32] But six years later he still remembered that night with unabated disgust. In a letter to Dahlberg in February 1958, Williams admitted that, while he was not familiar with everything that the young American expressionists had been "putting on canvas" then, he had merely asked his audience to "WAIT AND SEE, meanwhile be generous, give them a chance to express themselves." But when the booing began, he had become "furious and continued talking furiously. A month following the talk there were those in the influential organization who did not talk to me—so that following my stroke [this was the big one in mid-August of '52] I do not go to the meetings any more. Trala trala."[33]

Williams had worked hard to recover from his stroke of March. By the end of the year, the *Autobiography* had been published and reviewed, the first draft of *The Build-Up* was finished, and he'd even managed a small reading tour in early December with stops at Harvard, Brown, and finally the University of Buffalo once more, though this time he was caught in a snowstorm. And if he was writing no poems at this time (he did only "The Desert Music" in '51), he'd still managed to keep himself busy. But in spite of all that, there were things happening to him that frightened him. So, writing to Charles Abbott on September 27, he had had to stop typing when his eyes had suddenly blurred on him and lie down for twenty minutes. And the next day, when he resumed his letter to Abbott, he confessed that, driving home that day from Passaic General, he'd begun to panic when he realized with a shock that he could not judge the distance between himself and the cars moving around him. A month later, at the end of October, he told Dave McDowell that just a few days earlier he'd been sick, his head "whirling round like a carousel" until he was sure he "was going to be laid up again with something serious." But that too, like his other symptoms, passed for the moment.[34]

A few weeks before Christmas, Paul and Jinny and the kids (Paul, nine, and Suzy, seven) moved into the house again with Floss and Williams until they could find a new home for themselves. And though he was glad to have his son and family with him, their presence inevitably "complicated" things for Williams. In fact he complained that it took all his strength to cope with young Paul, and he was relieved when his rambunctious grandson returned to school in Massachusetts in early January. Problems had already surfaced in Paul's and Jinny's marriage, but what troubled Williams most of all was the "unhappiness of my grandchildren." He pitied the young as much as he pitied their parents. He would do what he could for the kids, but he had to admit to Zukofsky that

idered changing the last line to "in spite of lightning," as he
ered once more the stroke that had crippled him and which
ready to act up again.[37] Memory and the imagination. Could not
like all great art—somehow annihilate time "as far as poor
may," as—for example—Titian's *Man in a Red Cap* which he'd
red at the Frick Museum had annihilated time, his statement in
t as fresh now for Williams as it had been for Titian's contempo-

April, the general unsteadiness Williams had been experiencing on
since his stroke had indeed intensified. He was seeing double for
retches at a time now. No sooner had he finished *The Build-Up*
e collapsed from what he diagnosed as "a nervous ailment,
ly psychic in origin but nevertheless effective in laying me low."
attacks, he complained to Tom Cole in May, were "becoming
ad habit, a disastrous weakness," and though he seemed to keep
ring, he had no hopes of ever really pulling through. It was just a
r of time now till the end.[39] He even told McDowell that he'd felt on
than one occasion as though he were "about to cash in" his chips,
most wished he had. If only he could *see* normally again. For with
e trouble came a depression that sapped Williams of all desire to
[40] The truth was that he couldn't write then—as he confessed to
od—because he couldn't shift his eyes properly, or even focus
[41]

spite of his illness, however, he was still determined to honor his
nitments. On May 14, he flew with Floss out to Indiana to take part
symposium at Hanover. "We all seek for ourselves the richest
rds from life that we can obtain," he told the students and faculty
. For most Americans this was represented, he knew, "by a Cadil-
But there were other goods, other values: an old ancestry, religion,
ing, sculpture, the poem. Communists too, he said, in spite of all
brutal concepts, were really only after a piece of the pie. But they so
d the artist, feared what he might say in showing them up, that they
"cut themselves off from what he might add." For only the artist, he
d, sought his reward from life itself and what he could make of life
of his art. Still, if Soviet Russia kept its artists under its thumb—and
id—America did the same out "of fear of the onslaughts of our
uage upon the secret rigidities of the past—which we fear to attack ir
r to renew ourselves." It was the same revolutionary message he
n offering for years, except that now it had a new urgency becaus
Cold War climate he could feel all around him. Nowhere did tha
nate make itself felt more than when he mentioned during on
s that even Shakespeare had made mistakes, was, after all, h
rest of us. At that point, one student stood up in the au

he felt helpless to do anything. "To say that
added. Everyone needed love, but sometimes
frankly not available.[35]

*
* *

All through January and February of '52,
Build-Up, after having finished the first draft
On January 12 he wrote to Marianne Moo
winning the Yale-sponsored Bollingen. He had
he'd given at the University of Pennsylvania th
her that her name had come up in the discuss
who had been down there forty years before
and—though he hadn't known her then—Ma
February he drove down to Newark with Floss t
the Hechts. Now too, for the first time in his life,
winter vacation. At first he'd thought of taking F
Florida for a few weeks, but Floss thought that
and even dangerous, especially with the fits of di
having, so instead they decided to turn over their
and go into New York for two weeks, staying at th
Madison and 50th. At first Williams had demurre
Floss assured him they really could afford th
Williams decided to do the city up big. From
nineteenth floor they could descend in comfort to
movies, the various museums, St. Patrick's, even
State Building. Williams enjoyed it all and decided
book of *Paterson*, which he'd been mulling over f
This would be Floss's poem, he'd already decided,
tion on the woman, the counterpoise of the ma
Paterson. So it was here, on Saturday, March 1, that
menu while they waited for dinner at the hotel and b
lines of his new poem. Still tired in spite of his rest
aware of his mortality, of his own defeats, he felt the
sort of summative statement, a confession of love fo
across from him before it should be too late. Let r
honored, memory and the inner spaces of the mind
defeats. It would be the theme he'd signaled in the "
Paterson 2. And now the lines came to him in the tria
earlier passage, as he wrote out with his right hand:

> *Of asphodel that greeny flower*
> > *wet with morning dew.*
> > > *I have laid u*
> *that in spite of all defeats. . . .*

he felt helpless to do anything. "To say that they need love is idle," he added. Everyone needed love, but sometimes love was simply and quite frankly not available.[35]

*
**

All through January and February of '52, Williams worked on *The Build-Up*, after having finished the first draft a week before Christmas. On January 12 he wrote to Marianne Moore congratulating her on winning the Yale-sponsored Bollingen. He had just returned from a talk he'd given at the University of Pennsylvania the night before and he told her that her name had come up in the discussion about the Penn group who had been down there forty years before: Pound, H.D., himself, and—though he hadn't known her then—Marianne herself.[36] In early February he drove down to Newark with Floss to spend an evening with the Hechts. Now too, for the first time in his life, he was anxious to take a winter vacation. At first he'd thought of taking Floss and driving down to Florida for a few weeks, but Floss thought that might be too strenuous and even dangerous, especially with the fits of dizziness her husband was having, so instead they decided to turn over their home to Paul and Jinny and go into New York for two weeks, staying at the New Weston Hotel at Madison and 50th. At first Williams had demurred at the expense, until Floss assured him they really could afford the vacation, and then Williams decided to do the city up big. From their room on the nineteenth floor they could descend in comfort to go to the theater, the movies, the various museums, St. Patrick's, even the top of the Empire State Building. Williams enjoyed it all and decided now to begin the fifth book of *Paterson*, which he'd been mulling over for the past two years. This would be Floss's poem, he'd already decided, an extended meditation on the woman, the counterpoise of the male sensibility of Dr. Paterson. So it was here, on Saturday, March 1, that Williams picked up a menu while they waited for dinner at the hotel and began writing the first lines of his new poem. Still tired in spite of his rest and more than ever aware of his mortality, of his own defeats, he felt the need to make some sort of summative statement, a confession of love for this woman sitting across from him before it should be too late. Let memory for once be honored, memory and the inner spaces of the mind, impervious to all defeats. It would be the theme he'd signaled in the "descent" passage of *Paterson 2*. And now the lines came to him in the triadic patterns of that earlier passage, as he wrote out with his right hand:

> *Of asphodel that greeny flower*
> *wet with morning dew.*
> *I have laid up a memory*
> *that in spite of all defeats. . . .*

He considered changing the last line to "in spite of lightning," as he remembered once more the stroke that had crippled him and which seemed ready to act up again.[37] Memory and the imagination. Could not these—like all great art—somehow annihilate time "as far as poor mortals may," as—for example—Titian's *Man in a Red Cap* which he'd so admired at the Frick Museum had annihilated time, his statement in pigment as fresh now for Williams as it had been for Titian's contemporaries?[38]

By April, the general unsteadiness Williams had been experiencing on and off since his stroke had indeed intensified. He was seeing double for long stretches at a time now. No sooner had he finished *The Build-Up* than he collapsed from what he diagnosed as "a nervous ailment, probably psychic in origin but nevertheless effective in laying me low." These attacks, he complained to Tom Cole in May, were "becoming a . . . bad habit, a disastrous weakness," and though he seemed to keep recovering, he had no hopes of ever really pulling through. It was just a matter of time now till the end.[39] He even told McDowell that he'd felt on more than one occasion as though he were "about to cash in" his chips, and almost wished he had. If only he could *see* normally again. For with his eye trouble came a depression that sapped Williams of all desire to work.[40] The truth was that he couldn't write then—as he confessed to Macleod—because he couldn't shift his eyes properly, or even focus them.[41]

In spite of his illness, however, he was still determined to honor his commitments. On May 14, he flew with Floss out to Indiana to take part in a symposium at Hanover. "We all seek for ourselves the richest rewards from life that we can obtain," he told the students and faculty there. For most Americans this was represented, he knew, "by a Cadillac." But there were other goods, other values: an old ancestry, religion, painting, sculpture, the poem. Communists too, he said, in spite of all their brutal concepts, were really only after a piece of the pie. But they so feared the artist, feared what he might say in showing them up, that they had "cut themselves off from what he might add." For only the artist, he added, sought his reward from life itself and what he could make of life out of his art. Still, if Soviet Russia kept its artists under its thumb—and it did—America did the same out "of fear of the onslaughts of our language upon the secret rigidities of the past—which we fear to attack in order to renew ourselves." It was the same revolutionary message he'd been offering for years, except that now it had a new urgency because of the Cold War climate he could feel all around him. Nowhere did that new climate make itself felt more than when he mentioned during one of his talks that even Shakespeare had made mistakes, was, after all, human like the rest of us. At that point, one student stood up in the audience and accused Dr. Williams of attacking the very foundations of free western civilization. Williams, astounded, stood frozen for a moment in his place. What in hell was going on here? Six months later he would have good cause to remember this incident.[42]

Before flying to Indiana, Williams had had several meetings with Conrad Aiken about the Consultantship in Poetry he would be taking over from him in September. He looked "pretty shaky," Aiken remembered, and depressed ("a moral tail-spin"), but Floss had told him that she thought the job would "blow a little confidence back into" her husband. Williams was taking "impotence pretty hard," Aiken noted, but then he saw too that everyone would come to such impotence sooner or later. The Williamses also looked at Aiken's apartment when they were in Washington and decided to rent it rather than go apartment hunting. Everything seemed ready for the fall.[43]

In June Williams drove up to Brandeis with Floss for another reading and then went into Boston to see Merrill Moore, the poet and psychoanalyst, about his nervous condition. Moore, a great admirer of Williams', took a special interest in the case, writing to Floss and Williams for several years afterward to keep himself abreast of what was happening to Williams. On June 20, he suggested to Floss that Williams stay away from situations and people who put an emotional strain on him. "The more he learns to vegetate peacefully," he summed up, "the longer he will have to vegetate." And to Williams that same day he wrote with patronizing solicitude: "You are going to take lots of reinforcement and perhaps a firm hand before you learn to 'act your age.' "[44]

More than ever, Williams continued to write letters to poets and young struggling writers.[45] Allen Ginsberg was one, and he asked Marianne Moore in late May to see Ginsberg personally because Ginsberg warranted the attention. Williams was "instinctively drawn to him" for his "clean, rigorously unrelenting mind that would do outstanding work if only the man can survive."[46] He had been thinking of young writers like Ginsberg when he told Tom Cole the year before not to worry about what Cole had called the "Suck Eggs Mule crowd" (that epithet referring to the poets who would in a few years' time come to be called the Beats). Williams knew these young Beats had already begun to claim him as a father of sorts, though he was sure they were following "their own relaxed impulses" more than they were following his own example. He himself admired their "relaxation" and advised Cole not to get "tightened up over their shows." After all, neither Ez nor Williams himself nor anyone else had yet shown the new generation much of anything new upon which they could build. "Let the boys and girls let down their hair and splash around a bit." For God's sake, he ended, Americans' spirits had already been "so cramped by precedents that we revere in spite of ourselves that it is still far better to let go than to stiffen with indignation before a lot of kittens gamboling harmlessly on the back lawn."[47]

In mid-July Williams drove up to Gratwick Highlands with Floss to see the Abbotts and Gratwicks for six weeks of rest and recuperation at the Toby. He'd been through "one hell of an illness" with his "nervous instability," he told McDowell at the end of June, and by then the nervous disorder had been nagging at him for three months. "I hope you are spared it forever and a day," he wrote:

> It saps your marrow, it really does. It's a terrific drain too on the forbearance of a devoted wife and friends. And God knows you need your friends. I need mine, all of them. A man fears everything in the world and out of it, in heaven and in hell. I tell you the poets are not dreamers; they know what they are and what they are talking about is a living hell.[48]

Now, having made themselves at home in their old apartment over the garage, in those old chauffeur's rooms decorated with prints and photographs, the Williamses prepared to enjoy their pastoral retreat, listening to the songbirds and watching the geese eat up the garden below them.

They had a month of it nearly, with long walks around the old buildings and extensive gardens with those yellow tree peonies Williams loved so much and the live music rehearsals from the summer orchestra over from the Rochester School of Music playing on the grounds. By August, Floss observed that the "old life" seemed to be stirring once again in her husband. He was correcting galleys on the novel and had even written a poem, "The Orchestra," in those step-down lines he'd used in his first draft of *Paterson* 5, a poem continuing the meditation begun there and capturing the "cacophony of bird calls / lifting the sun almighty / into his sphere," blending now with the sounds of the orchestra at Gratwick Highlands, and all of these conspiring in Williams' poem to tell Floss how much he loved her. "Now is the time" he wrote,

> in spite of the "wrong note"
>   I love you. My heart is
> innocent.
>   And this the first
>   (and last) day of the world
>
> The birds twitter now anew
>   but a design
>   surmounts their twittering.
> It is a design of a man
>   that makes them twitter.
>   It is a design.[49]

The wrong note. At seventy how could he make amends to his beloved? To want to sing of love, and always to be singing in the wrong note. . . . In mid-August, as Williams and Floss were preparing to return home to Rutherford, it hit him with all the force of a killer hurricane, such as the one that had knocked that maple against his garage. Another stroke![50] At first he'd tried to shrug it off. After all, he was away from home and he didn't want to burden his hosts with his carcass. He kept joking about it, even as Floss began packing. And then suddenly, as Floss would recall ten years later, "you could hardly understand him." Then Williams simply collapsed and had to be put to bed at once, with a physician and nurse in attendance. This time too Williams lost the use of his upper right side as well as his speech and the use of his eyes. He was sure he'd really bought it this time, but as the weeks passed at Gratwick Highlands and August gave way to September, he began to use the fact of his cerebral accident as the basis for what would be his last play, dictating his ideas and some of the dialogue to Floss, who had once again become his nurse, sharing that job with a local nurse whom Williams—even in his illness—had soon come to admire. Before long she had become yet another image of Kore, discovered in the midst of this new hell of impotence, and something of the sexual energy he'd felt as a physician toward some of his patients he began to experience now as a patient grateful to the ministrations of both Floss and this other woman: Demeter and Persephone. Here was another Phyllis, another Kore, discovered in an old farmhouse, and the very title he chose for his play pointed to the role of the woman in aiding his recovery, for *The Cure* was in the Kore.

The Cure is less a finished play than it is a psychodrama, an allegory of Williams' own questionable recovery, since he must have known that he would never actually be "cured" again. In the play, a young man named Prospero (the connection with Shakespeare's protagonist from his last play, *The Tempest*, is not accidental), who is both a poet (he tells the police that his name is John Keats) and an outlaw, survives a motorcycle crash that kills his partner and leaves him with a mangled leg. The accident occurs at a farmhouse outside Buffalo when the motorcycle literally slams into the side of the house, so that the play begins in darkness and confusion, in the midst of a death. Williams, of course, was reenacting something of the confusion and embarrassment attendant upon his own sudden stroke, and the image of the ambulance attendants lugging off a dead man in the dark with lights flickering offstage acts out one possible conclusion to the stroke he'd suffered. Halfway through the first act, however, the young married couple whose home has been visited by this nighttime disaster hear groans from their cellar: it is the dead man's partner, thrown through a trapdoor into the cellar and knocked unconscious. Williams has reenacted, once again, the theme of death and resurrection.

Connie Mitchell (whose maiden name is Laboard, a French homonym meaning the edge, as in the edge of a pit—as in hell—but suggesting as well a bordel, or brothel), is a registered nurse who, six months into her marriage to George, is playing housewife while she waits to have a baby. Now, with this grotesque yet fascinating turn of events, she sees her chance to "play" at nurse once again, as she nurses young Prospero back to health. Prospero is of course Williams' autobiographical creation, college educated (Princeton), a poet, but an outsider too, with a Sicilian mother (for which read Puerto Rican) and an Irish father (for which read English). As Prospero becomes stronger and his mangled leg mends, the return of the life force is signaled by his desire to sleep with this woman who has so expertly restored him to health (and that mangled leg mending should remind us not only of the restored phallus, but of goat-footed Pan as well). But Connie, who is by this time pregnant by George (another of Williams' near-nonentity husbands), refuses Prospero, who knocks her unconscious and then flees, thus leaving her much as Connie had first found him.

Within this rather flat drama, however, there is the theme of judgment, of a judgment played out against Williams himself in the figure of the bad boy who had already impregnated several other women. There is, first of all, the stereotypic figure of the state trooper on the scene to make a report, and one senses that something of the FBI investigation that was about to be made into Williams' past is enacted here in this authority figure who keeps missing the point of what is really going on around him. But there is another figure who judges Prospero in a more damaging fashion: Prospero's "bearded father." Once again, Williams' father's ghost—distant, disapproving—moves onto the stage like Hamlet's father, to warn the nurse that his son is a married man who has already served time for impregnating another woman. "Can you imagine that that good-for-nothing writes poetry?" this visitor asks, looking at the son who has nearly bankrupted him of his money and his name. "You're a woman and women are this sort of man's special bait," he warns Connie as he leaves. "I wish I had more influence with the good Lord to damn him to hell into eternity." Those are the father's last words as he sneers at his son and then lets himself out. It is a haunting scene, especially when we remember the dream Williams kept having when his own father had died: of his father walking away from him, then turning his head back toward his son to say, "You know all those poems you've been writing. Well, they're no good."

"I went to Gratwick's in '52 to bring Dad home on the Lackawanna," Bill Jr. recalled. "We took a sleeper one evening at a whistle stop near the Abbott place, arriving in Hoboken about 4 AM, where the Rutherford Volunteer Ambulance met us."[51] It was at this time too that Merrill Moore wrote to Floss to explain the "vascular accident" which Williams had had. He told her the extent and severity of Williams' illness: that he'd suffered another stroke, and that still others were bound to follow, until finally one would hit him from which he would never again get up. In the meantime, however, Williams should keep himself occupied. There was, after all, the job in Washington waiting for him, where he could take it easy.[52]

But as if the stroke had not been enough, there was more trouble in store for Williams. Ironically, a week before Williams was hit with this second stroke, the press had run the announcement that that September Williams would undertake his duties in Washington as Consultant. It was then the height of the red-baiting fever in the country, however, and Williams—projected thus into the limelight and already singled out three years before for supporting Ezra Pound—became at once a prime target of the patriotic witch hunters whom Williams had so feared. It was a time when the papers were filled with accusations and counteraccusations by national figures like Senator Joseph McCarthy and Richard M. Nixon, and the Cold War had gone into a new deep freeze with new denunciations of Stalin and the trials of Alger Hiss and the Rosenbergs. But in a hundred local places as well attacks were being circulated, and one of these was launched directly at Williams from Roanoke, Virginia, by a certain Mrs. Virginia Kent Cummins, editor of a rather pale little magazine called *The Lyric.* For years she had been attacking the countless enemies of good, old-fashioned poetry with its consolations of rhyme and meter and high thoughts. In fact, since 1948 she'd managed to attack as either obscene or obscure (they amounted almost to the same thing anyway) most of the major living poets writing in English in America, including Pound, Eliot, Marianne Moore, Auden, Cummings, and —finally—Williams.

Without ever even hearing of *The Lyric,* Williams had already been denounced in its pages for *The Clouds* (that atheistic poem), "Russia" (treasonous), and even for being a Fellow of the Library of Congress, that insidious group which had honored that traitor Pound. But now, in October '52, she had a separate open letter inserted into copies of that month's *The Lyric.* It was a letter attacking Williams for signing leftist or Communist-organized statements during the late thirties and early forties. Subsequent history had shown some of these organizations to be Communist fronts. Ergo: Williams by signing had shown himself to be a Communist sympathizer. Williams had signed some of these statements, it is true, but that was a time when thousands of American intellectuals and artists were being asked to support this or that cause and, having signed, Williams had forgotten about them. For the fact was that, while Williams saw himself as an American Democrat and a liberal and a virulent anti-Fascist, he was at heart apolitical, a loner who would, if the cause was worth it—a cause such as supplying Spanish Loyalists with medical supplies or working to get a new school in Rutherford—gladly lend his time, money, and name.

As for Russia, he had had great hopes for that country until Stalin's brutalities and postwar strategies had destroyed his hopes for the Russian people, and then he had lamented the failure of one of the great political revolutions of modern times. But even in "The Pink Church" and "Russia"—the two poems specifically cited by the newspapers as "treasonous"—he was lamenting, finally, the failure of Russia to live up to his own early dream for her. Two years earlier he'd explained his feelings about "Russia" in a letter to Selden Rodman. "The Russia piece," he wrote then, "ends on the note of empire in an ironic sense, bitterly. Russia whose avowed intent has been to free the world from capitalism (for which we tentatively praised her) has turned out to be an empire seeker of the most reactionary sort. It will be her downfall BUT in the meantime we shall all of us suffer." The Russians too, like many Americans, had lived to see themselves deceived by their own leaders.[53]

Mrs. Cummins' open letter in the meantime had come to the attention of the *Washington Times Herald*, where their story was noticed by some Library of Congress underling, as Williams came to believe. It also came to the attention of someone on Fulton Lewis Jr.'s staff and Lewis, unswervingly devoted to ferreting out the nation's enemies, published a piece in the *Seattle Post-Intelligencer* on November 24, reciting some of the charges Mrs. Cummins had made six weeks earlier and adding—in the inimitable prose style of that moment—that the "House Committee on un-American Activities index on William Carlos Williams contains 50 cards, listing his association with some of the smelly outfits that have been peddling Moscow propaganda in the U.S. for 25 years." That the major newspapers, such as the *New York Times*, carried no stories or releases about Williams suggests that even at the moment when such tactics were the order of the day the more responsible journalists were still able to distinguish between what was newsworthy and what were red-baiting rhetorical ploys. Nevertheless, these reports had their numbing effect on Williams' appointment to the Library of Congress. Before the accusations about Williams had been published, however, Floss had written to Merrill Moore to ask if her husband could still undertake the Washington job in spite of his stroke. On September 17 Moore answered that he'd talked to Aiken and had learned that a four-hour day would be sufficient for Williams to do what had to be done: that meant two hours in the morning and two in the afternoon. As for Williams' mania for confessing about his past to Floss, something he'd been doing for the past few weeks to clear his conscience, Moore tried to persuade Floss that most of his talk would be "nonsense" but necessary for Williams' sense of recovery.[54] Williams, of course, was in no condition to assume the Consultantship in September, so he was given a three-month delay, the intention being that he would begin his duties on December 15. By then Williams was able to use the fingers of his right hand again and to speak haltingly with effort. He was even able to write again, though at first he had a great deal of trouble seeing what he was typing.

Then, as they were getting ready to leave for Washington, Floss received a special delivery letter from Verner Clapp, acting in the absence of the chief librarian, Luther Evans, who was then in Europe on UNESCO business. Clapp, who was also chairman of the Library of Congress Loyalty Board, had written directly to Mrs. Williams, his letter explained, out of a "humane concern" for her husband's health. He was sorry to have to inform her that the Library was now obliged to await a "full investigation" by the Civil Service Commission and the FBI before Dr. Williams could begin his official duties, as he had not been cleared by the "preliminary" investigation.[55] As Floss studied the language of the letter, it became evident that something was horribly wrong. No one—not Clapp, not Evans, not the Library itself—was going to stand by her husband, though they'd offered him the Consultantship not once but twice. Her husband was in no condition to talk coherently with Clapp over the phone, so she called Washington herself for an explanation. When she finally reached Clapp she could tell his voice was at once icy and distant. What were these derogatory reports Clapp had mentioned in his letter? Well, Clapp answered, Dr. Williams sure had gotten around a lot. Floss asked him what he'd meant by that. Hadn't her husband been in Germany and Austria once? Yes, but that was back in 1910 and 1924. What about it? Well, he answered, just that: Dr. Williams sure had gotten around. This conversation was getting nowhere, she thought. Better to go down to Washington and see what was really going on.

On Monday morning, December 8, Floss and Williams were met in Clapp's office at the Library of Congress by Clapp and other members of his staff. Coldly and formally, Clapp explained the nature of the government's "loyalty processes" to them. If, Clapp stressed, Williams was still not cleared after the full Civil Service Commission report had been received and subsequently evaluated, then a full hearing would be afforded Dr. Williams by the Library's own Loyalty Board, of which he himself—he reminded them—was chairman. In these exacerbated times, neither Clapp nor Evans was presumably willing to do more than that for Williams. Floss was confused. She had been ready to explain that her husband had been in Leipzig in 1910 to study pediatrics, and had gone to Austria in 1924 for advanced work in the same specialty. But now Clapp said that there were more serious charges, for Williams had appeared in both the *New Masses* and the *Partisan Review* in the 1930s when those magazines were "subversive organs." Furthermore, her husband had signed certain petitions for Communist front groups. Moreover, he'd written a pro-Communist poem called "Russia." What infuriated Floss more than anything, however, was the mixed look of terror and delight she thought she saw in Clapp's eyes and the way he kept shaking his fist in her husband's face. "I came away *convinced,*" Floss told Aiken later, that Clapp was "either terribly antagonistic to Bill or terribly scared of something."[56]

Williams himself was shaking with rage and confusion, but he managed to control himself. When Clapp was finished, Williams rose unsteadily and thanked Clapp as civilly as he could manage for the conference and then left, though he could not conceal, as one eyewitness noted with remarkable understatement, that Williams "seemed . . . understandably annoyed and non-plussed." When Williams and Floss returned to their hotel room, Floss wrote at once to Norman Holmes Pearson, who had served in the U.S. Counter Intelligence Service during World War II and so knew many influential people in Washington, asking him as a friend what she should do. Only now were they even learning what some of the allegations that had been made against him actually were. In her letter to Pearson, for example, Floss mentioned that Bill was being hunted down for signing petitions and that the FBI was using "The Pink Church" "as evidence of his Red leanings—quoting lines here and there to make it seem what it isn't."[57] A week later she wrote again to Pearson, mentioning an article in the American Legion paper to the effect that Williams had actually ridiculed Shakespeare when he was at Hanover in May.[58] It was Karl Shapiro at *Poetry* who first alerted the Williamses to *The Lyric* affair, and Floss had to tell him on the sixteenth that her husband hadn't even seen those accusations when Shapiro's letter had arrived. "If Bill were well—he'd be glad to fight," she told him, "but we are in daily fear that he may have another stroke if he gets tense and upset."[59]

So now the "witch hunt" was on, she told Shapiro and Betty Eberhart in two separate letters on the sixteenth. "They are out to get Bill—as a communist sympathizer." It was "terrifying [to see] to what lengths people will go to destroy an innocent person."[60] For Floss the attack on her husband brought back nightmares too of the attacks on her father for his German sympathies before the outbreak of hostilities in 1917. On January 16, 1953, Mrs. Francis Biddle wrote Conrad Aiken about what she knew of the sorry Library of Congress affair. One member had asked Williams if he had signed a letter urging cooperation with Russia in 1937. And another wanted to know if Williams had ever suggested that the Committee on Un-American Activities should be abolished. "Williams," she noted, "just shook his head and said, 'I signed a lot of letters, with other writers. I don't remember.' " When Francis Biddle explained to the Williamses that there would be no salary forthcoming from the government until Williams had been "cleared" and that that procedure might well take a year to complete, Williams told him weakly that he was afraid a fight like that now might simply kill him. Would Biddle think him "yellow" if he just resigned and tried to forget the whole affair? For his part Biddle thought *all* the Fellows should resign in protest. As for Mrs. Biddle, she was frankly worried now about "the current wave of pussy footing" she saw everywhere in Washington.[61]

Williams had no choice as far as he could see but to get in touch with his own lawyer, James Murray, who then wrote Clapp on December 22 to inform the Library that his client had been ready to assume his duties on the fifteenth of December and that he was waiving his right to neither his job nor his salary, which he had yet to be paid. At first no one in Washington answered Murray's letter. Christmas and New Year's came and went, as Williams' health degenerated and he slumped into a deeper and deeper depression. On January 1, still unsure of what was happening, Williams wrote a love letter to his wife to tell her again all she had always meant to him before it should be too late. "I do not feel well," he wrote,

> and I despair of ever again feeling well. But when I think of having another stroke which will leave me bedridden, perhaps blind, it is too much to think of. You, of all people, should know what that means. I might not even be able to communicate as I am doing now. And when I see you growing tired, as you confessed to me that you were already growing tired, desperate—allow for all the exaggeration and false emphasis that you know to be me. Tear this paper up and throw it away as the record of a man who, in spite of everything, loved you and my children to the end. . . . You will know how to take care of yourself whatever happens to me, you have all my love. I've been a fool for reasons that are not clear to even me but, believe me, I truly love [you] and believe with all my heart that you love me. Nothing can change that.[62]

A week later he wrote Tom Cole that the sky itself had caved in for him when he'd had his stroke in August, "and then the newspapers with their story" that he was "a communist sympathizer blocked me from my job in Washington, and completed the wreck." Now he was trying to make as brave a comeback as he could. He was working with his left hand only and he begged Cole to forgive him for his errors in typing. In December he had written several poems out of his despair and one in particular which he wanted Cole to know about, a poem he'd written "For Eleanora and Bill Monahan." He'd dedicated it to "The Mother of God" and was particularly interested to know what Cole as a Catholic thought about it. "What right has Williams," he asked, "a non-believer, to write such a poem? But there it is and I would like you to read it," especially since he'd written it "under the greatest difficulties."[63] "That which we have suffered / was for us / to suffer," he wrote, and now,

> *in the winter of the year,*
> *the birds who know how*
> *to escape suffering*
> *by flight*
> *are gone. Man alone*
> *is that creature who*
> *cannot escape suffering*
> *by flight*

He confessed to being half man and half woman, a man brought to the point of dissolution, as Pound had been in that Disciplinary Center in Pisa in 1945. Like ivy clinging tenaciously to a piece of crumbled wall, he wrote, so now he clung to his wife, knowing that if she should leave him both of them would go under. He was an old man in desperate need, he realized, and he said so, crying out of that need to Mary, Diana the Virgin, his wife, to "the female principle of the world."[64]

Eleanora Monahan had been one of Williams' patients since the early 1940s when she and her husband, Bill, and their small child had moved to Rutherford. She and Bill still remember that night in August 1943 as though it were yesterday, when she had started from sleep at three in the morning, ready to give birth to her second child and finding blood soaked through all the sheets. Bill Monahan had called Dr. Williams at once, and when, a few minutes later, he'd raced across town in his Ford to their home at 241 Washington Avenue he tried to tell Eleanora once again what he'd warned her of earlier: that hers was a low placental pregnancy, extremely rare and extremely painful for the mother, a pregnancy that ended inevitably in the death of the baby. By the rarest of coincidences, one of his patients, a nurse, a woman he dearly loved, had just terminated another such pregnancy and—though he'd done everything he could to save it—he'd finally lost the child. Now he wanted Eleanora to try and understand the gravity of the situation before them.

But Eleanora had refused to accept what Williams was telling her. "I've waited too long for this baby," she told him through clenched teeth and matted hair, "and I've prayed too hard to the Blessed Virgin to lose it now. I'm *having* this baby." Williams couldn't understand that kind of faith but he could admire and love the woman who, in all that white-faced pain, doubled up on the bloodstained sheets of her bed (as his Kore would be in *Paterson*), could still hold on as Eleanora Monahan was holding on. He called Passaic General at once and had them dispatch an ambulance to Washington Avenue to pick up Eleanora and himself. And then, all through the night at the hospital, he and the nurses worked to save that baby. Somehow, unbelievably, they did. It was a little girl, brought screaming into the world, whom the Monahans would call Ann, after the mother of the Virgin. For Williams, Eleanora would become another private symbol for the courage he had seen here and elsewhere in women which allowed them in the face of insurmountable difficulties to come through.[65]

No Catholic himself, as he'd said in 1936, Williams nevertheless moved now—in the winter of '53—towards something very much like the prayer forms of his mother's Catholic youth.[66] Now he too, having touched the bottom of his own personal hell, cried out, unembarrassed, to the "Mother of God," begging the woman—and all women through her—to forgive him for his many transgressions against her, against them. It had not been easy for him to come to the Virgin, he admitted, but now he had been forced "painfully / across sands / that have scored our / feet." He knew, for he had been one of them, that there were "men / who as they live / fling caution to the / wind" and that there were women who "praise them / and love them for it." But there were other women, like his wife, especially, whom he'd hurt by his amorous recklessness, and now he was begging forgiveness, even as he was willing to forgive those—like Clapp and Evans and Cummins and the FBI—who had hurt, and, in other cases, even abandoned him.

"It's not going so good with me recently," he told Fred Miller on January 9. "What with [the] injury to my right flipper and the trouble they have cooked up for me over the Library of Congress job I'm in a bad way." And then he caught himself up short: "Forget it. Many men have been in tighter spots than this—but men who are temperamentally better equipped to stand it perhaps." As far as his mind was concerned, he'd been through hell.[67] All he could do now to assuage his pain was sing, and that was why he had written the poem to the Monahans, and another "To a Dog Injured in the Street" as well as "The Host" and "The Yellow Flower," all painfully worked out in the loneliness of his room typing with his one good hand.

He remembered René Char's poems written during the German occupation of France when he was fighting with the French Resistance. Char had seen deaths, tortures, betrayals, had seen people "disappear," breakdowns, deportations of Jews and others to nameless destinations, and yet in all that pain he had been able to "speak only of / sedgy rivers, / of daffodils and tulips / whose roots they water. . . ." And now, the sequel of brakes and a thud and then a dog lying in the street "yelping with pain," so that Williams had been brought to himself "with a start— / as at the explosion / of a bomb, a bomb that has laid / all the world waste." Nothing for it but to create beauty and so blot out that poor beast's pain as well as his own, with whatever "invention and courage" he might be able to summon.[68]

He thought too of Michelangelo in old age escaping self-torture by articulating his pain in the sculptures of his *Slaves*, so that he had seemed to make the marble itself bloom. From that Williams too might learn a lesson, he wrote in "The Yellow Flower" in January, that if all around him he saw ruin for "myself / and all that I hold / dear," then he could also see that his eyes and lips and tongue might also free him from that pain, transferring that pain to the poem, "the tortured body of my flower," an "unearthly flower" for him to order and assuage his pain.[69]

And he would need all the help he could get. The Bollingen committee for that year tried to help Williams by awarding him (along with Archibald MacLeish) the Bollingen Prize, news that reached him now in January. But that news was more than offset by the letter Luther Evans wrote him on the thirteenth and which arrived in the mail on the morning of the fifteenth.[70] Evans himself made it tersely clear that he was annoyed by the letter Williams' lawyer had sent his office three weeks before. He was calling off the loyalty investigation against Williams at once and canceling his appointment as Consultant. He wanted it understood, however, that he was not terminating the appointment because of any doubts his office had as to Williams' loyalty but because he understood that Williams was really in very delicate health and also because Williams had acted in a most irregular way by using James Murray as an intermediary. "After full consideration," Evans wrote, "I have determined that the condition no longer exists which at an earlier date made your appointment appear desirable and profitable." Now, therefore, he was revoking the appointment altogether.

The day after he received that stunning letter, Williams wrote to Zukofsky to say that, "as towards the end of I PALLIACHI [sic], the comedy is played out. My appointment to serve as consultant in poetry at the Library has been revoked." So be it. All he wanted now was to recover the money he had already spent for the apartment in Washington, though that fight would have to wait until such time as he could "recover a reasonable use" of his faculties.[71] For his part, Murray answered Evans at once for his client, demanding to know on what grounds Evans had set himself up as an "expert" concerning Williams' health, insisting that Williams could not now "permit the FBI investigation to lapse" without first clearing Williams' name. But now there was a legal catch: the FBI countered by saying that, since Williams' official status had been terminated with Evans' revocation of the Consultantship, they were no longer in a position to investigate Williams under the guidelines established for the Federal Employees Loyalty Program.

To their credit, the Fellows came to the defense of Williams once they had been made aware of what Evans had done. Thus Leonie Adams and Cleanth Brooks had a long session with Evans on February 8 to see what kind of order could be made out of a scandalous mess. The talk must have had some effect, for eight days later Evans softened a bit, telling Adams—as Williams' intermediary—that he would look "favorably" on the testimony of a "qualified" physician willing to state that Williams was capable of fulfilling his duties as Consultant, though under no circumstances would Williams be allowed to serve beyond the original termination date of September 14, 1953. And he would look favorably on that physician's report *only* if Williams was willing to waive any talk of having "rights" to the Library position. If Williams agreed to these stipulations, then Evans would allow the loyalty investigation to continue so that it might hopefully be brought to an expeditious close, at which time the Library's own Loyalty Board would evaluate the FBI's findings and—if he was cleared by both groups—Williams could then fill out whatever time remained of his original contract.

Like a Puritan elder in the American grain Evans had stood firm, unyielding, virtuous, even as Williams, sickened by the whole ordeal, capitulated to his demands. Williams did procure a physician's certificate and he wrote Evans to say that he was waiving all rights to the position. But by this point Williams' depression over the hell he found himself in had become so deep that he began to fear for his own sanity. "Writing has become a painful process for me," he wrote Byron Vazakas on February 6, "not physically but mentally painful." He did not wish to go into detail just then because it took him so long to write with his left hand; the method was arduous and not at all conducive to fluency.[72] The following day Floss wrote Laughlin that her husband was so deeply depressed by events that the family was trying to decide whether or not Williams would have to undergo shock treatments to bring him around.[73] And yet, on the tenth, Williams could still write to Abbott from his personal hell that the selections from the classical Greek of Theocritus that Harriet Gratwick had read him while he lay in bed at Gratwick Highlands recovering from his stroke were still haunting his ear. He was trying to do a translation at that very moment of Theocritus' first Idyl, to bring it over intact into the American idiom with his step-down lines, and needed ten lines of the original script in front of him to hear once again how the original had sounded. He wanted to get Theocritus' easy, urbane music into his own lines.[74]

But he would have to work on that in other surroundings. By mid-February his depression had become so severe that his doctor—Roy Black—urged Floss that he be admitted to the private mental hospital facilities at Hillside Hospital in Floral Park, Queens.[75] Reluctantly, Floss agreed. Both she and her husband distrusted mental health facilities. For all of their forward-looking ideas, they were still of an earlier generation who attached a certain social stigma to such places. But Floss was in charge now, and if the hospital stay could help her husband, then so be it. On Friday evening, February 21, Paul—accompanied by his mother and heavily burdened with his own domestic disintegrations—drove his father to the hospital. Floss gave her husband a packet of envelopes already addressed to her to use in writing to her, tried to make him comfortable, and then left with Paul. When the heavy doors closed, Williams felt more isolated than he had ever felt before in his life. The only contact he would be allowed were the letters he wrote his wife and those she in turn wrote him. Otherwise, he was virtually a prisoner in a strange and alien world. It had taken him two years to see Pound at St. Elizabeth's because madness so terrified him. And now here he was, in a world not very different from his friend's. Williams had suddenly discovered hell.

At first he felt almost as if he were in Dachau or Auschwitz, surrounded as he was almost completely by Jewish patients and Jewish doctors. He wrote Floss that he felt like a stranger in a strange world, but he very quickly made several friendships with both the patients and the doctors which would last until his death. Moreover, though he had a deep distrust of psychiatry, he gave high marks to the doctors assigned to his care, following their suggestions as fully as he was capable. So, for example, when he learned a year later that Robert Lowell had been admitted to Payne-Whitney in New York City for psychiatric observation, he wrote to cheer him up and to tell him that he himself had traveled a similar road. "You will no doubt be at least entertained by your companions at the institution," he told Lowell at the end of June 1954. "I was when I was in a similar place over a year ago. Some of them have remained my friends after I came home. Swell guys. All are of the opinion that it is better on the outside but all, including myself, agree that we were lucky to have such a place to go to when we needed it."[76]

No one of course can know all that Williams went through during this bleak period, when he felt like a wounded unicorn attacked by hounds calling for his death. But it seems certain that the eight months he endured from his stroke until his release from the mental hospital were exactly what he himself called them: "a living hell." Still, he was determined to pull through this too as best he could. At first he was about as much of a nonperson as he had ever in his life felt. He had no freedoms to speak of, no typewriter, not even ground privileges, which meant that he was always attended by a nurse whenever he took his exercise. He was allowed use of the telephone only once a week for a short call to his wife. He was allowed to see absolutely no one from the outside except Floss.

To offset this claustrophobic sense of isolation, he wrote each and every day—and sometimes twice a day—to Floss with his shaking, nearly useless right hand, hoping to coax it back into life again, then folding those letters into the envelopes she had prepared for him. He was worried about her, he told her, worried about who would take care of her after he was gone. As for the Washington job which had cost him so much: he simply wanted to forget the whole sordid thing. He was concerned too about Paul and Paul's family, concerns he would have talked to Floss about if only he were with her instead of in this institutional prison. But the overriding theme of his letters was his unembarrassed love for Floss and his utter dependence on the woman he had been married to for over forty years. And what he wrote her in these letters was built of the same material that was making up the long poem he was writing for her especially, the *Paterson 5*, which would eventually become "Asphodel." "I've got to get well for your dear sake," he told her his third day there.[77] And, again: "I really feel as if I had just been married and this to an experienced woman but nonetheless pure. I love you completely." Until now, he confessed, he had never loved anyone except himself, but this forced separation from her had taught him his lesson.[78] And four weeks later he wrote, "It is the proof of our love that we have gone through veritable hell to obtain it." In "Asphodel" this would become:

> I cannot say
>   that I have gone to hell
>   for your love
> but often
>   found myself there
>   in your pursuit.[79]

What he also learned about himself as he met with his psychiatrist during the weeks he spent at Hillside that late winter and early spring was that he had a deep-seated need to confess as he had been doing obliquely for years and more candidly since his stroke in August, so that he had actually frightened his wife with his disclosures. No one, understandably, besides Floss ever heard this psychic unburdening and Floss apparently never uttered a word of what her husband revealed to her even to her own sons. She was always an intensely private person, reticent by nature, and in large part unsuspecting. But apparently Williams felt it necessary now, in the face of imminent death, to treat his wife as his confessor. As the names of women he had known intimately were revealed, Floss began to cave in under the accumulated weight until something went dead.

Williams had always loved his wife deeply and she would always be his first flower. But he always loved women, many women, and sometimes he had acted passionately on those impulses, even right there in his hometown. He had always returned afterward to Floss—he would have found it unthinkable after the first flurry of passion not to return to her—but over the years there had been those interludes. Surely she had in some sense already known? Apparently she had not. And now, here she was, with a husband permanently disabled and drifting toward inevitable death.

Williams for his part had always had the need to confess, hating lying as he did, and he did not want to die with the burden of his (hopefully innocuous) deceptions still on his troubled mind. After all, he had already left clues about his sexual history everywhere for Floss to read in his poems and novels and plays, and Robert Lowell would be more on the mark than he knew when he called "Asphodel" a poem of "simple confession" several years later. Williams even blamed his poems now for helping to bring on his present condition, believing that they had been "a dangerous thing . . . to fool with." But that feeling, apparently, passed.[80] As for the faces he found himself surrounded with: he needed them, needed them desperately, for such small favors as talking to him and helping to dress him and even showing him how to get his food from his plate to his mouth. In a short time he was talking to Floss about his newfound pals. And as for Floss: he would wait all week for the one hour when she would be allowed to come out to see him, or for the few minutes when he could speak with her on the phone. He needed her, and he would need her even more as his remaining years rolled past him. For her sake now he was willing to stay where he was until his psychosis—or the worst effects of it—had been resolved.

For there were times during the eight weeks he spent at Hillside when he felt as though he were on a manic rollercoaster, touching depression as well as the heights of elation. He felt something of his old enthusiasm for poetry, for example, when he discussed that subject with some of the other inmates. "I feel like Coleridge or Rimbaud or any other nutty poet you can name," he told Floss, except that feeling like that wasn't "nutty."[81] He was even asked to read some of his poems before a gathering of inmates in the hospital auditorium, and did so to his immense satisfaction. Even his right hand had begun to respond to orthopedic physiotherapy as he exercised it each day for hours by squeezing a small sponge-rubber ball and forcing himself to write with that hand. And though he could not completely shake the feeling that his eyes and brain were covered with cotton gauze, he was responding to psychoanalysis by the beginning of March, analyzing his depression as something that had "probably been stewing in my bones since childhood."[82] He only hoped he wasn't too old to shake that depression now. Three weeks into his stay and he was even back at work on his translation of Theocritus. It was ideal therapy for him, recreating that ancient pastoral world, so redolent of Keats's world of the odes, a world free of the bomb and the world that had spawned it, a world of radiant, still images and elevated, unhurried rhythms where shepherds conversed with each other courteously in a recognizable New York idiom, such as he could hear around him:

> No, shepherd,
>> nothing doing;
>>> it's not for us
>> to be heard during the noon hush.
>> We dread Pan,
>>> who for a fact
>> is stretched out somewhere,
>>> dog tired from the chase. . . . [83]

Although he was receiving "electric current for . . . stimulation," a treatment that he allowed, Williams finally refused to let the authorities administer shock treatments.[84] He preferred physiotherapy instead —what he called beginning "at the beginning" and building up from there. That was his real "meat" and not the other, more radical measures. He knew, for example, that it was his inability to use his right hand and the ensuing feelings of creative and sexual impotence that had largely accounted for his becoming so depressed. But he also understood that the cure for his depression rested in his regaining the use of his hand or at least compensating for that loss. If he was limited by the stroke, if he would never be able to drive again, for example, what of it? There was still much to do. There would still be young women patients who would come to him as their mothers had before them, and he would diagnose them and prescribe medicines for them and give them injections with his good left hand. And some of those patients would remember how Dr. Williams had been able to give them injections with his left hand more gently than other doctors using both hands. And then there was the marvelous realization that the stroke had not impaired his creativity but had instead released a new way of writing, more autumnal, more Keatsian.

Now, with the advent of another spring and the birds crying from somewhere outside, he was more restless than ever to be out of the hospital and home. He would have to see a New Jersey psychiatrist once he was out of there, at least for the next few months to appease the doctors, and that he agreed to. On March 21, midway through his stay, he was transferred to a small cottage on the hospital grounds which he shared with several other patients. It was a kind of halfway house to the outside world. A week later he even felt independent and adventurous enough to request permission to go to the local Catholic church for Palm Sunday services with one of his roommates, Stanley Levin. The request had been, he frankly confessed to Floss, an excuse "to get off the grounds of the hospital," though some deeper needs were also being addressed, however obscurely, some need to touch the old faith of his dead mother once again, as he had in his poem to the Monahans. They must have made quite a duo—this ex-Unitarian and his Jewish roommate—two inmates from the local mental hospital, bundled up against the cold and shuffling off at an awkward gait to Sunday mass.

As it turned out, they arrived there late and—because the church was packed for the palm service—Williams and Levin had to stand at the back of the church. Williams even tried to look reverent, or at least—as he told Floss that afternoon—"impressed," but standing there in his weakened condition soon became too much for him. So, when the ushers began distributing handfuls of palm to all the faithful as they sang their hymns remembering the triumphal entry of the King of Kings into Jerusalem, Williams watched nervously. He could see the usher approaching him with a sheaf of palms and people taking the blessed branches, and then he had his left hand out to take the proffered gift, and then—the suspense too much for him—he bolted for the back door, followed by poor Stanley Levin, who could see that he was about to be deserted. "It was a disgraceful performance," he confessed to Floss, and—to make matters worse—he "hadn't even contributed to the pot!" He had "made the attempt" in his extremity at something like piety, but the upshot of it all was that he still felt "no better for it."[85]

But something of the strange, quasi-religious twilight Williams was moving through during this period found its way into the very moving and puzzling pastoral that replaced the Theocritan meditation, a new poem called "The Mental Hospital Garden." Two days before his Palm Sunday venture, Williams had watched two lovers, oblivious of his or anyone else's presence, walking "nonchalantly" between the hospital buildings. It was characteristic of the officials there, he explained to Floss, to allow "the sexes pretty much to mingle," though he was quick to add, pathetically, that he himself had not been tempted.[86] What he caught in his garden poem was a world light-years removed from the scene he'd described seven years before in the "Sunday in the Park" section of *Paterson*. There sexuality had been something furtive, cruel, or unrealized. Now, however, he caught the sense of sexual innocence layered with a quasi-Franciscan piety. Now even the hospital lawn and shrubs of spring became for him a second Eden, a prelapsarian world such as he was building in "Asphodel" and would build in *Paterson* 5.

But "The Mental Hospital Garden" was something more: a study of a mind coming slowly to the staggering realization that what he had previously done under what he'd assumed was a condition of "bawdy" innocence—flirtations, affairs, infidelities—was indeed something else altogether now that one's deeper motives began floating up into the light. It was a poem, then, about the fall from innocence into a new knowledge of one's past, especially, as here, the knowledge of one's sexual fantasies and acts. Looking at these pairs of lovers walking about in their unself-conscious innocence and ignorance, touching one another intimately, Williams became aware—even as he tried to escape the implications of that awareness—that he was looking at a replay of his own former condition. "I too took my marriage seriously, too seriously," he told Floss in the same letter in which he talked of local lovers strolling about the grounds, "but I slipped, for reasons I still only partly understand." Now, however, all of that was in the past. He was "cured," finally, in mind as in heart.[87]

It was the old idealist in Williams speaking, the same who as a young man had demanded absolute perfection from himself in his life and in his work. At the same time he was calling on himself for a renewed commitment to his wife. And if they came to depend totally on each other in these last years as Floss took on more of the burdens—she growing with a new strength even as her husband grew weaker—why, that was part of their new understanding and acceptance of each other. "You have forgiven me / making me new again," Williams would say hopefully in "Asphodel." And that understanding would soon become the new reality.

Eight weeks to the day after he'd been admitted, Williams was back home. It was April 18: significantly, it was also Floss's sixty-second birthday. Slowly now Williams began to pick up the pieces once more. So, six days after he was home, he could write to Cid Corman that he was

> a little the worse for wear but still functioning. I hear you dropped in last week to inquire how I was getting on. . . . I'm not really in circulation again but it feels good to be typing with BOTH hands which has encouraged me no end. Can it be that with time I'll be able to make the grade again? . . . Best from behind the 8 ball.[88]

The use of that right hand was to be intermittent, however, and within a year he'd lost virtually all use of it. It was faster and more efficient to use the forefinger of his left hand, he found, and to let that dart over the keys, right hand be damned. And, in spite of all his good intentions, Williams had already rejected the notion that psychiatry could help him less than two weeks after returning home, though he continued to see a psychiatrist in Newark, as he had promised he would. "I am giving myself up to the mercies of the psychiatrists," he told one correspondent on April 29:

> Have you ever been in the hands of a psychiatrist? My advice is, stay away. They reverse the usual medical process to which the whole profession has accustomed itself since the beginning of time, they present to the patient not a sympathetic ear but a cold front. It isn't pleasant. I am going through a depressed phase following a stroke last August and undergoing a course in their specialty. I might as well be experiencing treatment by a frog! I don't like it. Oh, for the kind heart of an old-fashioned country doctor! Poets have always been among the unfortunates of the world. At that they are much loved—and quoted. The world must be a sad place granted this . . . be so.[89]

In the meantime, Floss herself had been going through her own personal hell. She tried to keep the fact that her husband was undergoing psychiatric care a secret because of the stigma she associated with it. That her husband was at the same time being investigated by the government, by forces whom Senator Joe McCarthy, unshaven, arrogant, brilliantly insidious, had come to represent, did not make matters any easier. On top of all that was the spate of personal confessions Williams had burdened her with, some real, some imagined, in an effort to clear the slate once and for all. When she wrote to Richard Eberhart on April 9, for example, she simply told him that Williams was "away" but was expected back home in another week. He was coming along fine now, she told him, and even "the Library mess" was clearing up. Just that day she'd received a letter from Murray saying that Evans was going to order the reopening of her husband's case for the FBI. Moreover, her husband was almost his old self again and was still anxious to go to Washington to prove a point—"if and when." She herself, on the other hand, was hoping that he'd have enough sense to stay away from Washington. What had also cheered her was the way McDowell and Random House had come to Williams' defense "at no small expense to them."[90] Floss herself had attended a "rump" session of the Library Fellows in New York to discuss what was to be done about the Consultantship in Poetry, which was now—for the first time in its history—vacant. That session included, besides Floss, Conrad Aiken, Robert Penn Warren, Cleanth Brooks, Leonie Adams, and Louise Bogan, all of whom were looking for a "happy termination of an unfortunate business." Then, on April 24—six days after Williams returned home—Evans wrote James Murray that his client had once again been "appointed" to the Consultantship in Poetry effective May 15, or (and here was the catch) "as soon thereafter as loyalty and security procedures are successfully completed."

The FBI report on Williams' loyalty status, however, did not officially reach Evans for another two months, that is, until June 26. Now it remained only for the Library's Loyalty Board to evaluate that report. But now Evans himself was on his way out as Librarian, preparatory to assuming his new duties as Director General for UNESCO, duties that would begin July 5. Surely Evans might have moved swiftly at this point to evaluate the FBI's routine investigative report so that Williams could make at least one visit to his office before Washington closed down for the summer months. It would have been a minor triumphal entry into the capital—minus palm branches—and might have assuaged some of the stigma Williams had unjustly suffered. And it would have been a gesture of goodwill, however inadequate, on the part of the federal bureaucracy. But Evans chose to do nothing, leaving his office vacant and Williams with nothing more than a paper appointment.

A footnote to the Library affair occurred fourteen months later, in October '54, when Evans' replacement, L. Quincy Mumford, officially assumed his duties as Librarian. The McCarthy fever was history by then, and more and more stories about the nightmare that had dominated the American imagination for several years were beginning to break. One of those stories broke the same month that Mumford assumed his office, when a British newspaper noted that the last poet who had been appointed Consultant in Poetry had "failed to receive security clearance." When the American news service picked up that story, Mumford felt obliged to write Williams directly explaining that the story was not true, simply because the FBI report had never been evaluated by the Library. It had not after all been a question of Williams' security status, Mumford tried to explain now, but simply a matter of what the role of a Chair in Poetry sponsored by the American government ought to be and how it ought to be financed. When Williams received that letter in the mail two days later, he wrote Mumford at once, asking permission to publish the letter. Mumford called him on the eleventh to grant him the permission he had requested. The next day—Columbus Day—Mumford's letter appeared in the *New York Times*. Williams was—now that it no longer mattered—"vindicated."

*
* *

Like Ovid and Horace and other "disgraced" poets before him, Williams had to learn now to cultivate his own garden. "I am getting slowly better but it is an awfully slow process," he told Tom Cole three weeks after returning home. "This morning I had an invitation . . . to go to Salzburg next year to teach, it broke my heart to turn it down which I did after a nostalgic two hours of futile pondering. Well, in this world you cannot have everything as I am fast finding out."[91] And to Richard Eberhart he wrote three days later that, though he was not yet cured, he was feeling much better:

> When the old bean goes wrong it apparently takes time to put it to rights again. Meanwhile I've done quite a bit of writing, prose and verse. . . . I am very limited as to what I can do, but as long as I can do something I must be content.[92]

Paradoxically, what Williams had managed to do over the past year, in spite of his stroke and depression, was to write some very fine poems in a completely new mode, all using the step-down line with its variable measure which he had discovered in writing the descent passage in *Paterson* 2 in early '47. By the fall of '53 McDowell could point out to him that he had actually written eleven long pieces, which—if he included the earlier "Desert Music" and the piece of "Asphodel" he had already finished—were enough for a new volume of poetry. Since it was McDowell who had thought of the idea for a new book of poems, Williams gave the manuscript to Random House rather than to Laughlin, though he also assured Laughlin at the same time that he was still going to give him *Paterson* 5—as he'd promised—when he finally got around to it. When Random House published the volume in March 1954, in an edition of 2,500 copies, Williams called it—fittingly—*The Desert Music*.

What these new poems revealed when taken together was a sense of pain mixed with tranquillity, the poet's refusal—as he phrased it—to allow his poems "to fall into the machine," that is, to let his own feelings take over the artist's duty—in all seasons—to write a finely crafted and controlled poem. Char had taught him, as Keats had earlier, not to become "too intimately involved" with the self, but to keep a distance, via symbols, so that one's vision never became "blurred." As for rhythm, Williams placed his emphasis now on the easy and the colloquial, on the fiction of a man speaking at length and unhurriedly, a quality that Floss for one applauded in her husband. There was another emphasis as well here: the sense in these poems of a man no longer talking only to himself or to a generalized or idealized audience, but rather addressing another person, his wife, his son, his two daughters-in-law, his friends, the Virgin, a dog struck by a car and dying on the street outside.

The theme of most of these late poems, as Robert Creeley shrewdly observed in his review of the volume, was love: the intense, quasi-confessional, altruistic love of an old man for the things of his world.[93] All of these qualities came together in the marvelous close of the poem Williams addressed to his sons' wives—Daphne and Virginia—begun after breakfast one morning in late July or early August of '52, when he and Floss were vacationing at the Gratwicks'. There is the smell of boxwood rising in the summer heat as the poet watches from the upper balcony of the Toby the Gratwick's pet goose waddling in the mud below him. Over the years that goose had become a symbol for the poet himself, of course: comic, inconsequential, and penned in (as his unicorn would also be penned in in *Paterson* 5) to keep goose—and poet—from eating up the garden:

> *Staying here in the country*
> > *on an old farm*
> > > *we eat our breakfasts*
> *on a balcony under an elm.*
> > *The shrubs below us*
> > > *are neglected. And*
> *there, penned in,*
> > *or he would eat the garden,*
> > > *lives a pet goose who*
> *tilts his head*
> > *sidewise*
> > > *and looks up at us,*

> *a very quiet old fellow*
> 　　　*who writes no poems.*
> 　　　　　*Fine mornings we sit there*
> *while birds*
> 　　　*come and go.*
> 　　　　*A pair of robins*
> *is building a nest*
> 　　　*for the second time*
> 　　　　　*this season. Men*
> *against their reason*
> 　　　*speak of love, sometimes,*
> 　　　　　*when they are old. It is*
> *all they can do*
> 　　　*or watch a heavy goose*
> 　　　　*who waddles, slopping noisily*
> 　　　　*in the mud of his pool.*[94]

By late summer of 1953 Williams was well on his way to recovery, though he still had his nerves to contend with. He told Fred Miller at the end of August that he still felt as though his head were "half or deeply wrapped in cotton," though that was still an improvement from what he'd experienced in the spring.[95] And a few days later he joked half-frenetically about his condition in a letter to Louis Zukofsky describing the loss and relocation of a "piece of sponge rubber I keep in my pocket or near it upon which to exercise my fingers." That momentary loss, given his present condition, had taken on the dimensions of "a major tragedy" in itself, so that from the nature of that crisis he was sure Zukofsky could guess at the "state of my mind—and soul." That he had been able to find "the offending article again" unassisted had not changed the case, "except philosophically," since the damage to his equilibrium had already been done.[96]

Six weeks later, in a letter to Robert Creeley, he reviewed the events of the past year. There'd been the stroke, he said, the worst part of that being his "mental derangement," a condition he candidly called an "unadulterated hell." His right hand—which had seemed to be improving in April and May—was dead once more, and his eyes were still giving him a good deal of trouble. But with what the psychoanalysts had been able to do—and with the passage of time—he was feeling so much better now that he was about to make his first public appearance in over a year that very evening: as a guest on a CBS television talk show, "Author Meets Critic." He wrote Creeley about his having "had to undergo an examination as a 'red,' which"—he added vehemently—"I am not and have never been." The "stink" down in Washington had finally done him "out of a job" and thrown him "for a loss." But at least he had his new poems for the trouble, with their "new line stressing the importance of measure." (Just a week before, in fact, he'd sent Cid Corman his considered statement on measure with his discussion of the variable foot, a topic that would occupy him increasingly for the next several years and which would become as much of a nuisance in some ways as Stevens' earlier talk of the "anti-poetic."[97]) Williams ended his letter to Creeley by mentioning his "faithful Flossie," without whom, he frankly admitted, he could not have gone on. It was she who had made his new poems "possible."[98]

* *
*

Flossie: Williams' constant companion in his old age, his flower, his wife of forty years when Williams turned his attention to her in one of the most notable pieces of his last years: "Of Asphodel, That Greeny Flower."[99] This thirty-page poem which Williams began, thinking that he was beginning a fifth book of *Paterson*, was to occupy him for the better part of two years, the period of his most severe incapacitation and mental depression, when he was convinced that he had finally been defeated by the time bomb that had exploded in his own brain. No wonder then that "Asphodel" reads like a summary confession, a confession of personal fault, it is true, but a determined confession as well that, in spite of what others might legally call infidelities, his love for his wife had remained something special, apart, intact. It is also an apologetic apologia, at once proud defense and defensive appeal for Floss's understanding and forgiveness for her husband's past faults, that he might come to "die at peace in his bed." And yet, for all its sense of confessional intimacy, for all its prolixity, its sense of rambling, nostalgic reminiscence, Williams has created a complex and highly organized design around a handful of symbols that, like the odor of his flower, penetrate "into all crevices" to yield up the poem's deeper significance. As with Jackson Pollock's or Robert Motherwell's abstractions, both of whom Williams admired, the canvas of the poem reveals within its apparent randomness a design of mathematical purity and a calculus of persuasions.

    "Asphodel" forms a coda to the long and difficult love affair between Williams and his wife. It is a highly selective recounting not only of Floss's felt presence on Williams, but an unveiling of Williams' persistent erotic impulse seen through the muted wavelike layering of his last years. In fact, "Asphodel" is Williams' attempt to make Floss finally understand the nature of the impulses that had all his life driven him and even— perhaps—finally broken him. In *A Dream of Love* Williams' alter ego had died of a sudden heart attack in a New York hotel room in the arms of another woman, and his ghost had come back home to explain why what had happened had happened. He does not attempt in the play to justify himself nor to beg pardon for what happened, but rather to let the hotel scene, reenacted in a surrealistic dream sequence, affirm itself. By "Asphodel" Williams had become less insistent, less strident in his defense, but he still hoped to be able to explain to Floss that—given his own nature (and indeed the unalterable condition of man)—his past flirtations and loves *could* be comprehended, if only Floss would let her own imagination and love for her husband "mount" to a finer perception of the power of eros over humans.

In this poem Williams keeps weaving back and forth between memory —the memory of the race as well as the memory of his own past—and the present time in which the poem is set. But even the present—the public events drifting across Williams' consciousness in '52 and '53—float in a larger timelessness, where the threatening news about the Cold War, with its daily deaths and destructions, is contained within the larger patterns of mythic recurrence. So the swift lightning flash of the electric chair that silenced Julius and Ethel Rosenberg in June 1953, the wanton destruction of art by the forces of death—in this case the burning of priceless Goyas by Juan Perón's goons at the Jockey Club in Buenos Aires—the dismal presence of witch hunters during the McCarthy Senate investigations, and the incessant pressure of instant nuclear Armageddon which Williams had feared since Hiroshima and Nagasaki are all bracketed, not by our receding distance from these events, but by Williams' measuring of these increasingly minor irritants against a world of lightbearers. "Asphodel" is Williams' closest approximation to the apocalyptic genre, and his pantheon is filled with such life-giving presences as Cézanne and Melville, Darwin and Spenser, Villon and Chaucer, St. Anthony and Confucius, Homer and those nameless painters who had decorated the caves of Altamira with bison and fertile women six thousand years earlier.

"Asphodel" also weaves into its fabric a heavy incidence of personal memory. And here Williams' emphasis has shifted from the first four books of *Paterson*, where he kept moving about his modern wasteland in search of the light that would sustain him *within* that wasteland. There the light was small, vulnerable, a radium discovered in a womblike alembic in a dark workroom or in a cellar in Paterson. But here that tentative light has blossomed like a mushrooming atomic explosion until it has entered every dark crevice. Now Williams opts for a strategy of open space and timelessness—the eighth day of creation, with the garden of Eden finally blossoming everywhere. In *Paterson* Williams had given us the sense that he himself was discovering a tentative beauty in the local conditions along with us, aware at each moment of the enormous failures evident in his world and in himself. But in "Asphodel," as in the last book of *Paterson*, it is the wounded artist-lover who is in control. This is Williams' world, and he is our teacher as he is Floss's, garnering now the difficult fruits of his epic journey of seven decades. It is Odysseus in old age returned to tell his tale to Penelope.

Like its namesake, "Asphodel" is both "green and wooden," for it portrays the poet and his eternal bride under the simultaneous aspects of old age and youth, past and present, each layer of time presented in its spatial discreteness and isolation, yet the whole forming a timeless surface of light. The poem itself, Williams suggests obliquely, is like the "free interchange / of light" over the surface of an ocean—momentary flashes lighting up the surface of unfathomable depths—which Williams further likens to his omnipresent mythic garden. And the multifoliate mass of flowers he evokes all draw their sustenance and significance from the single strong stem of the major pattern, the magnetic core that is Kore, that—here—is Floss. In the timeless moment of the poem it is in this simple flower that Williams finds his central, exfoliating, expanding symbol. The asphodel, the flower of the dead, looking "like a buttercup / upon its branching stem," an unexceptional flower which now in his pain and sense of deprivation Williams remembers was "forebodingly" among the pressed flowers in the book he'd kept as a child.

In the *Autobiography* Williams recalled how, while at school in Switzerland back in 1897, he had collected the "green-flowered asphodel," which, he says, had even then "made a tremendous impression" on him. That same flower, he would later learn, grew not only in the Old World and—cutting across time and space—in Homer's hell, but in his own Jersey meadows as well. Here then was a symbol of the confluence of tradition with his own local world. That flower is, in fact, the central symbol linking Floss, whom Williams pictures in "Asphodel" as watering her flowers—like Kore—in the dead of winter, with his own epic journey to the underworld to see his dead father, discovered in the modern hell of the New York subway, thus recalling Aeneas' visit to his father Anchises amidst the asphodel-covered fields of hell. Unlike the more exotic rose of Dante, Eliot, and Yeats, Williams has chosen a more humble flower which might realistically flourish in the modern hell that his public and private worlds had become. His is a flower *without* odor, that reminder of mortality, since sweetness inevitably gives way in time to rankness. Instead Williams' flower has a "moral odor" released by the imagination, as the poet, offering this last flower to his wife, had hoped to be revived by Floss's forgiveness and acceptance. Without forcing, the asphodel expands outwardly until it includes all other flowers, until it contains even its opposites: the sea, the mushrooming bomb, and death itself. And then, having spread out to the limits of darkness, the poem condenses back on itself in the concluding image of the "Coda," with the poet's marriage once again to Kore. Once again, the tail of time circles around to the serpent's mouth as Williams' wedding day is "begun again" in the rejuvenated imagination, and the attendant difficulties of a long life lived together by two people become as mere specks in amber as Floss herself is transfigured into the still unravished bride, inviolate as art itself.

Recalling his talk with Stecchini on the *Iliad* as they'd stood on that sea wall, of how Helen's "public fault" had "bred" pain and death, sending many men "to their graves," even as men were still dying in Korea as he wrote his poem, Williams offered a new song, bred also by his own "public fault," but which he hoped would end not in psychic death but in acceptance. How many men had gone to their deaths in silence, without ever revealing to their wives the secret of their lives, even as the Rosenbergs had died "incommunicado"? But silence could be no answer for him, neither Floss's silence nor his own. It was imperative that she understand who this man was whom she had lived with for over forty years. No, the pattern of the *Iliad* could not serve for what Williams had to say. Not furtive eros and the silence of death, but rather love and forgiveness. Death was no resolution for Williams, some final moving into an eternal silence where, hopefully, one took one's deepest secrets with one. Death was nothing so grand but merely a bastard biological fact, a final negation. What Williams was after instead was a celebration of the forces of love and the imagination—to conquer whatever the poet should have to confess. Nor was the silence of the dead an answer, and the forgiveness we might more easily grant them then was worse than useless. It was the mind, he insisted, "that must be cured/short of death's/intervention" so that the imagination itself, which might grant that forgiveness, could blossom again into a garden.

There was already too much talk of the bomb, of all manner of suppressions and forced confessions in our lives, Williams stressed. It was not these images of crude force we had to emulate, but the delicate flower, "in that/frail as it is/after winter's harshness/it comes again/to delect us." Here was "a new measure" which Williams had discovered in his journey to love: his belief in his wife's unfailing generosity and faithfulness toward him. It was this meditation on her, begun during that midwinter vacation in February 1952 in New York City, when they were for once away from everything but each other, which had literally generated his poem. But if the poem tells us that Floss had forgiven Williams whatever was between them, that was not in itself enough. Williams also needed to explain why he had sometimes acted as he had, and so, step by step, he would take Floss in her turn on a journey through their love.

In the second and third movements of his poem, Williams moves back in memory over some important signposts along his forty years of married life. Time falls away, surges forward, falls away again. He recalls a conversation with one of the many young writers he knew, about the importance of Cézanne in the revolution of modern art, but the young man's interest is at the moment all for the "abstractions of Hindu painting." He knows a few of Williams' anthologized imagist poems, early pieces like "Between Walls" and "On Gay Wallpaper," both essentially flower poems and both owing something of their verbal design to the painterly strategies of Cézanne (though the young man fails to make that connection). We are made aware here of the erratic and problematic nature of fame, of the misreading or indifference of the young toward the older masters, and there is a particular poignancy in Williams' closing remark that he "was grateful to him / for his interest." But it is as nothing beside the "interest" his wife has taken in him, day in and day out, all these years.

In the next step of his journey into his past, Williams recalls two epiphanies of Kore. The first is the splendid unveiling of the majestic Jungfrau (the Virgin), a sight he had shared with Floss thirty years before, during his "sabbattical" in 1924. They had waited for four days through heavy rains that May to get a glimpse of that mountain, and then finally, as they were about to leave Switzerland, they'd seen it, majestic in its virgin whiteness, "covered with new-fallen snow." In *A Voyage to Pagany*, Williams' alter ego, Dev Evans, had felt it necessary to shake himself loose from the hypnotic splendor of that image of the romantic sublime, but now Williams allows it to become a "pinnacle" in his memory.[100]

Williams' second epiphany of the Virgin is even earlier, going back to his short holiday in Spain in 1910, when he was engaged to Floss but separated from her. In the *Autobiography* he remembered the encounter this way:

> I broke away [from the Alhambra] to the bare yellow hills back of the town, to be alone, to shake my shoulders from such impossibilities of past glory. There . . . on the way down . . . I was picked up by a gipsy girl, twelve or fourteen years old, with whom I talked innocently while she guided me out of the village paths where I had been lost. I told her how beautiful she was—though pretty grimy. She told me how beautiful I was. With that we bowed and said good-bye.[101]

The remembrance of an innocence long since gone and yet, in the memory, a presence of the Virgin kept fresh into old age. What was merely anecdote in the *Autobiography*, however, becomes in "Asphodel" mythic encounter, with the young artist coming down by a "new path," and "guided by a young girl / on my way." Innocence and virginity, then, have their own special beauty, Williams suggests here. But, like silence, they will not take us far. For even innocence, kept beyond its appropriate time, sours and becomes rank. So, when Williams tells Flossie early on in the poem "that the lily-of-the-valley / is a flower makes many ill / who whiff it," he is recalling what he'd written thirty-five years before in *Kora in Hell*, something he'd picked up from Shakespeare: "Ah well, chastity is a lily of the valley that only a fool would mock. There is no whiter nor no sweeter flower—but once past, the rankest stink comes from the soothest petals."[102] Floss may have married a wide-eyed innocent boy-doctor, but Williams—for his own survival—had had to grow into the world of experience.

Williams parallels several other voyages of discovery to his own: Darwin's voyage on the *Beagle*—which gave us a new measure of man in time—and Columbus' voyage—which gave us a new measure of man in space. But there is also Williams' lifelong search for a "new measure," for a language with which to speak in the accents of his own voice about his world. Williams' personal voyage was as crucial as those others, he tells Floss, since "men die miserably every day / for lack / of what is found" in "despised poems." His measure, his relative foot, had in time become an expanding flower in an expanding universe. It had to be, so that when the bomb—symbol of every form of suppression—roared, as it had roared for Williams in 1952 and '53, the poem might be able to outdistance it. Then the "news" of the poet's voice could outdistance the "public print" showing the dazed, confused faces of public officials out of control: "a mark of the times" and the *Times*.

The third movement brings Floss, as it were, into the very temple of the Eleusinian mysteries. Williams' central lesson has three steps of mounting difficulty and importance, he warns Floss, telling her that if he speaks in "figures"—in symbols—she must try to understand that such figures are everywhere, like the very dresses she wears, and that "we could not meet / otherwise." The first step has two figures, and the first one he shows her is the equestrian statue of that condottiere—that captain of war—mounted on Colleoni's magnificent horse which they'd gone to see together in Venice in 1924. (There is also a pun here on "cullions"—testicles—as well). And the comic figure of that "thickset little man / on top / in armor / presenting a naked sword" is meant to represent the figure of phallic force. Williams' second figure recalls "the horse rampant / roused by the mare in / the Venus and Adonis." The first figure, then, gives us the sexual drive in man, the second that same drive in innocent beasts. It is a twinning of the phallic drive in man and horse, of man astride horse, suggesting the man/horse and—by extension—the man/goat: Pan.

Williams' second step in his education of Floss recalls a moment from the early 1920s, when he had waited "at a station / with a friend," the figure of the dead artist Marsden Hartley. In that recollection, a fast freight had thundered past the station in Rutherford, forcing Williams and Hartley to turn away from the blast. "That's what we'd all like to be,

Bill," Hartley had said, and Williams had smiled, "knowing how deeply
/ he meant it." In his *Autobiography*, Williams had recalled Hartley's
loneliness, living by himself in a small Greenwich Village apartment, had
recalled Hartley's homosexual advances and his own rejection of those
advances.[103] Here in the poem, however, the train incident comments on
the pathetic aspects of the human condition, of a man's clumsy sexual
drives and advances, as often the by-product of his loneliness and
personal inadequacies as much as a manifestation of male bluster, but
made small against the overwhelming force of the train, the symbol
here—like the bomb—of the power of the imagination itself.

The third and final figure that Williams presents to Floss is the most
extended, the most particularized, and the most complex single image of
the entire poem. It conflates the earlier images of man, beast, and
machine, and brings us up to the most recent past: "yesterday." Sitting in
a subway car as it races under the streets of New York, Williams watches
a black man sitting across from him, a man about forty with a black beard
"parted in the middle" who is wearing an old "double-breasted black
coat," brown hat, reddish-brown trousers, brown socks, and polished but
worn shoes. The long description begins with the "worn knobbed
stick / between his knees / suitable / to keep off dogs," and ends with the
"worn leather zipper case / bulging with its contents / lay[ing] between
his ankles / on the floor."

"For some reason / which I could not fathom," Williams notes with
brilliant understatement, "I was unable / to keep my eyes off him." Nor
can we, for what we have here is another of Williams' familiar compound
ghosts, a counterpart of Hart Crane's nightmare vision of Poe's severed
head hanging from the straps in the demoniacal subway passage of "The
Tunnel." For what Williams sees as he looks at this man thirty years his
junior sitting across from him is the presence of his father come back
from the dead. But it is his father as origin, as dark progenitor, at one with
the figure of the unicorn/satyr—that "great one-horned beast" of *Paterson 5*—the beast/artist lured by the Virgin. It is his father as Pan, still
alive and living in the twentieth century, though confined by the forces of
repression to live in this hell. The knobbed stick and the case "bulging
with its contents" between his father's legs is, we suddenly realize, the
huge phallus we have seen in a hundred representations of the satyr.

So this Black Pan is akin to that Great God Pan whom D. H. Lawrence
had celebrated years before, discovered as his was in our modern mecha-
nized hell. In his 1926 essay, Lawrence had celebrated the father of all
"fauns and nymphs, satyrs and dryads and naiads," also possessed of a
"black face," and "careful never to utter one word of the mystery," as he
stands over against "the mechanical conquered universe of modern
humanity."[104] But if the goat-footed god has come on hard times, dressed

in browns and black like Old Nick with a dirty undershirt showing through, his eyes remain "intelligent," "wide-open/but evasive, mild." Assumptions about human sexuality in America are like assumptions about the black man: a figure misunderstood, feared, mistrusted but—for Williams—profoundly admired. The god, Lawrence had said, was careful never to utter a word of the mystery. Just so, when Williams tries to question this mysterious stranger, the train stops and the figure disappears, taking with him forever the secret of the sources of human creativity. We have been allowed a glimpse of the mystery but without fully comprehending it.

The transition from the subway to Floss watering her flowers in winter is the transition from Pan to Persephone, Kora in Hell, the image of the possessed virgin/bride so central to Williams' poetics. It is she—his muse—who stands over all his flowers, including his own poems, pouring "at their roots/the reviving water" while he stands "lean-cheeked" among them. Now, against these simple flowers with their drooping heads Williams juxtaposes those "heads" of government who fill up *Time* and *Life* and the daily newspapers, heads, he has long since learned, filled with cupidity and following "the Pied Piper/of Hamlin" [sic]—a figure like Senator Joe McCarthy himself—to their ruin. Not death, then, but love. And "what power has love," Williams asks, "but forgiveness." Now, then, with Floss's forgiveness assured, he brings her, with the gesture of the lover, a bouquet of flowers, another in a long list of flower poems, with this "last flower," "Asphodel" among them.

In the final scene of his poem, the light, which has outdistanced the heat of the poet's hellish encounter with the bomb and with death, is made to stop. In the vibrant limbo of the recreated memory, Williams twists the poem all the way back to its light source in Kore, back to December 12, 1912, his wedding day, when he waited, trembling in anticipation for his young virgin/bride. Now, in the reinvigorated imagination, the scentless asphodel which is the actual poem is made to give off a fresh odor as from his wedding day, an odor that has "begun again to penetrate/into all crevices/of my world." *Begin again:* the signature of Williams, early and late. It is "light," and the "imagination/and love" have wiped out time, cutting across half a century with the rapidity of nuclear fission, with the speed and ease of light-time, so that time and death have been annihilated "by grace of the imagination." What remains in the timeless ambience of the poem, then, are the figures of the artist and his muse revived by the imagination. It is the marriage of the Virgin to the great one-horned beast: Kore coming to meet Pan.

When, several years later, Williams read from his "Asphodel" to three thousand women at Wellesley College outside Boston, Robert Lowell was in that audience. "The poet appeared," Lowell recalled, "one whole side partly paralyzed, his voice just audible, and here and there a word misread. No one stirred. In the silence he read his great poem, 'Of Asphodel, That Greeny Flower,' a triumph of simple confession —somehow he delivered to us what was impossible, something that was both poetry and beyond poetry."[105] Williams too would recall that moment in *I Wanted to Write a Poem:* "At Wellesley . . . they practically carried me off on their shoulders. I was speechless. You could hear a pin drop. A million girls were there . . . at least it looked that way. . . . Floss had asked me to read the Coda to 'Asphodel' . . . I thought I didn't have time . . . but they stood on their heels and yelled . . . the girls . . . my god I was breathless, but I said do you really want more and they said yes so I read what Floss knew they would like. They were so adorable." And then, by way of unregenerate afterthought, the old man would add "I could have raped them all."[106]

*
* *

That last, of course, was Williams' "public" voice, and not the voice to which he himself was listening most intently during these years. The voice he *was* listening to, and the voice that struck paydirt for him, was a matter of a complex crossing with Keats, especially the Keats of the *Hyperion* fragments and the odes. Why this should have been so is difficult to say with any exactness, for Williams himself probably did not understand why. What *he* thought he was "capturing" was the voice of the classics—the stately rhythms and sharp straightforward idiom of the Greeks as he thought they must sound should they be discovered walking the streets of his Paterson. But there was something more, a kinship Williams had felt with Keats for over half a century, the plight of the romantic poet who would have spoken as the gods speak if only he had had the power to render their speech in the accents of his own debased language. *Hyperion* is in part the portrait of the dying of the ephebe into the life of the major poet, and Keats had aborted it at the very moment that his poet was undergoing that transformation.

And so with Williams, opting for the step-down line as his "classic" signature as he surfaced from the realization of his mortality, the new rhythm providing a stately, slow saraband to echo Keats's Miltonic and Dantesque phase with a difference. The crossing with Keats is there too in the nature of Williams' late iconography, in the stasis of his late images, frozen for eternity in the realized artifact, as in Williams' translation from Theocritus' first idyl, with its images limned on a "two-eared bowl / of ivy-wood," a girl and two young men, an ancient fisherman, and a small boy preoccupied with "plaiting a pretty / cage of locust stalks and asphodel." The images of "Asphodel" too belong to the same strain: sharply realized but without Williams' earlier breathlessness and jagged line cuttings.

Williams published his step-down poems in two volumes eighteen months apart—*The Desert Music* in March 1954 and *Journey to Love* in October 1955. But there is really no significant differentiation between the two books in his use of the triadic form. Williams had begun to employ the step-down line out of a felt need in early 1952, and by the spring of '55 he was—with two exceptions—finished with it. It is this three-year period, then, that in retrospect takes the shape of a single poetic rhythm, after which Williams once again began to remake his art. And it is Keats who stands as the major presence behind these poems because Williams was reenacting his own dialogue with death in much the same terms that Keats had done in his late odes. So the presence of death is felt almost everywhere in Williams' step-down meditative verses, regardless of what the ostensible subject happens to be, as we feel its pressure too in Keats's late poems. Even Williams' Theocritan idyl ends with the goatherd's cajoling Thyrsis to sing a song for him, since

> *you cannot,*
> > *you may be sure,*
> *take your song,*
> > *which drives all things out of mind,*
> > *with you to the other world.*

In "The Host" it was "the poor animals / who suffer and die / that we may live." And in "Deep Religious Faith," Williams blamed the poets for having forgotten their "job / of invention" so that their imaginations had "fallen asleep / in a poppy-cup." Or again, in the close to "The Sparrow," that beautiful late elegy to the memory of his father:

> *Practical to the end,*
> > *it is the poem*
> > > *of his existence*
> *that triumphed*
> > *finally;*
> > > *a wisp of feathers*
> *flattened to the pavement,*
> > *wings spread symmetrically*
> > > *as if in flight,*
> *the head gone,*
> > *the black escutcheon of the breast*
> > > *undecipherable,*
> *an effigy of a sparrow,*
> > *a dried wafer only,*
> > > *left to say*
> *and it says it*
> > *without offense,*
> > > *beautifully;*
> *This was I,*
> > *a sparrow.*
> > > *I did my best;*
> *farewell.*[107]

Just before Christmas 1953 Williams had written Tom Cole on the death of Cole's father that death came "to such as he as a blessing," as part of the natural life process. "It is hard only in the slowness and pain," Williams added, otherwise there was really very little to say about it. As for the rites of death: they seemed trivial after the fact of death itself. In that same letter he also commented on Dylan Thomas' recent death in New York: "His wild metaphors somewhat repelled me but I have to say that it is the tradition of the greatest poetry and I salute his memory for them." Thomas too must have seen his own end approaching, Williams had come to see in reading through the poems again, and he admired the Welshman's courage in welcoming that end.[108] Pearson, writing to a friend at the same time, had also mentioned Williams' brooding on death and his refusal to talk any more with a psychiatrist.[109] But that brooding over death had been going on at least since Williams' first stroke. "We have a carved East Indian mask that was given to us by a sailor friend of one of my sons," Williams had written in the spring of '51:

> We have it hanging in our front room. It's partly covered by a curtain at one of our front windows. I saw it last night while I was sitting listening to some music. It came to life, complacent before death, complete peace. It was a lesson to me—and no dogma to soften its blow. It had the peace before violent death that is in the *Iliad*, and the consciousness . . . before it that is in the heroes of Greek legend. . . . [110]

Another death mask that had fascinated him was a photograph he'd seen in the newspapers and magazines of the Tolland Man, the recently exhumed corpse of an adult male who had been hanged and then thrown into a northern European bog a thousand years before only to be unearthed in the early '50s, the face incredibly preserved by the tanning qualities of the bog. Williams was struck especially by that face with its rictus—its frozen smile—and its large nose. In fact he might almost have been looking at himself in death. But so what?

> > > > > > > > *. . . what if*
> > > *the image of his frightened executioners*
> > > > *is not recorded?*
> > > > > > > *Do we not know*
> > > *their features*
> > > > > *as if*
> > > > > > > *it had occurred*
> > > *today?*
> > > > > *We can still see in his smile*
> > > > > > *their grimaces.*[111]

Besides his major undertaking—his thirty-page "Asphodel" which had taken him nearly two years to complete, Williams allowed fifteen new poems, all in the step-down line, into *Journey to Love*. Some of these were quite short and to the point, a sentence or two winding like a helix down the page, as in the image of "Sergeant So-and-So / at the road / in Belleau Wood" during the First World War, saying "Come on! / Do you want to live / forever?" Others, on the other hand, like "The Sparrow," ran on for several pages. All of them, however, had their philosophical quotient, their wisdom, or a certain touching piquancy about them. And in nearly every case their occasion, or their subject, suggested Williams' penned-in, circumscribed condition during the years 1952 to 1955. A memory, a photo in a magazine, a color photograph of a Swiss canton on a commercial calendar, a Japanese print of a sparrow, a black woman glimpsed on the street outside his window carrying a bunch of marigolds like an emissary from another world, a bum screaming in the Port Authority Bus Terminal, his son's face glimpsed in a mirror with a look on it of despair as his marriage began to fall apart: these were the moments Williams used now to generate his poems.

For, though Williams was on the road to "recovery" by the end of '53, so that even Floss could relax a little by then, he would never really be completely well or "cured" again. Denise Levertov had suggested that he take lessons in public reading at the Reading Improvement Center on East 46th Street to help minimize the damage done to his speech by his second stroke, and that fall he did attend several sessions which in fact did help his delivery. He began again now to give readings and lectures, though he also had to refuse more offers than he wanted to, for he knew too well that lightning could strike again at any time. On January 28, 1954, for example, the day after he read at the YMHA, Floss wrote to Fred Miller that Bill was "coming along fine." Never had he read better, she remarked, because he had finally learned to read slowly. That trick alone had "made his reading 100% more effective."[112]

In early February Williams told Corman that he'd "been recently working on a new statement (it is all I think of recently touching verse)" which he planned to learn by heart so that he could recite it "to a group of N.Y.U. professors at one of their faculty club dinners." He was also studying Gerard Manley Hopkins' sprung rhythm again to see what light Hopkins could throw on the "essential relativity of the modern foot." The point he wanted to make, he cautioned, would "be very simple" and its broad implications "missed" unless the listeners were "aware of the history of prosody." The elusive presence of the measure: it might almost have been Stevens meditating on the nature of the imagination.[113] So in early January Williams had confided to Denise Levertov that poetry was "an elusive thing," the poem "made up not of the things of which it speaks directly but of things . . . which it cannot identify and yet yearns to know." He mentioned this to her, he said, because he could see that she as a woman had "brushed the raiments of an unknown host" in one of her poems. And then, as if he had revealed something of the mystery, he became embarrassed and told her to forget what he had written. As if she could have.[114]

And to Tom Cole at the beginning of April, he wrote: "My own work has had only one objective: to bring order out of chaos." What he wanted was not free verse—that contradiction in terms—but a line that might retain a certain freedom, a certain elasticity, "while retaining the formality of classic arrangement." The Greeks—in spite of misunderstanding by their Renaissance formulators—had always had a "living, vibrant quality" in their lines which was only now beginning to be revived in the verse of his own moment. "Einstein," he explained, "with what he has taught us of the relative measure, implying a variable, is at the heart of it." So the old verse was doomed. And even Dylan Thomas, "with the brilliance of his elaboration of the metaphor" would not escape "the general condemnation of the old verse" when the time of radical judgment came.[115]

Then, for a brief moment in early March, Williams was sure his own "time" had finally come. It wasn't lightning, this time, but it was something that nevertheless nearly killed him. "Last Wednesday I came as near seeing the angels as from the descriptions of the event from the lips of my darling wife I shall ever get," he confided to Robert Lowell. "I was unconscious 17 or 18 hours. I have to report that I didn't see nothin! It was almost the end of me. That I am still alive and able to write this letter is due entirely to the combined efforts of Flossie and my son Bill's efforts—together with those professional aids which we were able to summon."[116] That brought a few more worried letters from Floss to Merrill Moore, who assured her that the worst of the attack was over. It was less severe than a cerebral hemorrhage, he explained, and probably more like an acute disturbance in her husband's circulation. There was nothing for it but for her to follow her physician's instructions.[117]

Still, it was the kind of accident that kept Williams fearfully and even exhaustingly close to Floss. Others would remember the look that would come into Williams' eyes if, while they were at a gathering of some sort, Floss suddenly got up to leave his side. Then his hand would reach out to her pathetically until she could reassure him of her presence. The man who had put eleven cars through their paces, often pulling out to the left (or right) to pass some sonofabitch who was driving too slow, racing down state highways to get where he had to go, the man who had composed thousands of lines while driving alone on his rounds, that man now had to learn to decipher bus schedules and ride the New York subways. Now a simple trip over to Brooklyn—something Paul did every day—to see Louis Zukofsky was a matter of a month's detailed planning. It meant a bus from Rutherford across the meadows to the Port Authority Terminal in Manhattan to be met there by the anxious Zukofskys, and then the subway to their apartment in Brooklyn. By 1954, he told Louis, it had actually become easier for him to get to the West Coast than it was to make that journey alone over to Brooklyn.

The occasion for Williams' journey over to Brooklyn on Friday afternoon, October 1, even resulted in "The Drunk and the Sailor," a poem that tells us something of Williams' unsteady state of mind and his fragile nervous condition during this period. As he waited at the busy 40th Street terminal for the Zukofskys to escort him, he was suddenly shaken by an old drunk—a derelict about Williams' own age—screaming at a young sailor. Williams had sized up the situation at once: the young man, he saw, could have "flattened" the silly screaming bastard with one shot. The "screeches / that sprang" how?—*sforzando*, Louis's wife, Celia, suggested—"from that stubble beard / would have distinguished / an operatic tenor," Williams wrote. And

> the shock of it—
> my heart leaped in my chest
> so that I saw red
> wanted
> to strangle the guy
> The fury of love
> is no less.[118]

Here it was, then, a cry of sorts from outside, only this was no scrawny chorister's but rather another of the thousand petty furies that had come to dominate Williams' last years. He could only liken it to the fury (in a telling metaphor) of continually striking the wrong key on one's typewriter, a practice that would become more and more pronounced as his illness progressed. Williams had indeed become the wounded unicorn, penned up in his room or garden, with a rare excursion out on his tethered golden chain.

One of the few extended trips he did make in 1954 was to Washington, D.C., at the end of April to review for *Art News* the Garbisch Collection of American Primitives then on display at the National Gallery. He had not come down to see the "prize ape recently active there"—by whom he meant Joe McCarthy—but rather to enjoy the paintings and to remember "a quiet, old-fashioned city" which was the only fit home for such a collection of primitives.[119] The amazing thing was how Williams caught in the very style of his writing something of the style of these American primitives, with the eye indifferent to any but the most elementary perspective and the attention riveted on the details making up the world of these paintings. It was as though he were rehearsing here the very syntax, attention to eccentric detail, and oblique autobiography that would mark his painterly translations from Brueghel five years later. Describing one canvas, *The Plantation*, he wrote:

Apparently it is near the sea, for a full-rigged ship occupies the foreground. Above rises a hill. The theme is formally treated and not without some skill by the artist. The perspective is elementary. Clusters of grapes larger than the ship's sails come in from the right meeting two trees, one on each side, that reach the sky framing the plantation house, with its garden, in the center distance toward the picture's upper edge. Birds are flying about, and down the hill nearer the foreground, linked by paths, are the farm buildings and at the water's edge a warehouse.

One picture in particular struck him because it seemed to be talking directly to him and Floss. It was a picture of two *Sisters in Red* and the younger one especially struck him. She was "holding a flower basket, . . . a blond with wavy hair, wore an alert, a daring expression of complete self-assurance, the mark of a typical second-child complex," so that "I fell in love with her—and with my wife all over again for she too was a second child." What he saw in these 109 paintings as a group, and which had sent him back for a moment into some primitive New World Eden, "was a beginning world, a rebeginning world, and a hopeful one" such as he in old age so sorely wanted for himself. "The men, women, and children who made it up were ignorant of the forces that governed it and what they had to face. They wanted to see themselves and be recorded against a surrounding wilderness of which they themselves were the only recognizable aspect. They were lonely." Perhaps, though, the first painting he remembered seeing—which he mentioned and then left behind, as if the memory were too terrible—was the image of "a cat with a bird in his mouth—a cat with a terrifying enormous head." And though he did not say so, the giant cat's head dominating that scene looked suspiciously like Joe McCarthy himself.[120]

During his three-day stay in Washington, Williams went out to St. Elizabeth's—probably on the afternoon of the twenty-seventh—to see Pound unannounced. As it happened, Tom Cole and a friend, Audrey McGaffin, had already signed in to see Pound and so witnessed that occasion. Williams was still not feeling well, Cole recalled, and Pound was obviously in control of the meeting. "During the visit we sat in an alcove off the ward corridor with a wide window onto the grounds of the hospital. A screen was set across the entrance to keep other patients from wandering in from the corridor where they paced up and down during our visit." Williams "was quiet and receptive and seemed just happy to be there." Then, that evening, Cole treated Audrey McGaffin and the Williamses to a seafood dinner at the old Hogate's on the Potomac River. Williams, who loved seafood, ordered raw oysters and broiled finnan haddie, which he ate with obvious relish. "He was always aware and involved himself in just about any news of the world," Cole observed, whether that news were good or bad, "as if it were his personal problem and he responsible for its solution."[121] "Give your . . . wife my greetings and smack your kids on the ass for me, hard!" he wrote Harvey Breit that same month. Smack them hard, he said, "to remind them of what the world is preparing for them—so that they may be prepared for it when it comes."[122]

It was a time of summing up, too, of going through a life's work with Jack Thirlwall, professor of English at CCNY, Williams' own diminished Boswell, of talking for hours into a tape recorder, about his past, his poetry, influences, whatever. A time too of going up into the attic to see what was still lying around up there in boxes and file cabinets from his literary and personal past. "Jack Thirlwall has just left, Sat. afternoon, 5 P.M.," he wrote Norman Holmes Pearson. "We have been in my attic since 2 going through my papers, old junk that (in some cases) I have not looked at in years. I hasten to tell you that we found (without disturbing it) a large quantity of the original manuscripts of *Paterson* 1,2,3, & 4! It contains all my scribbled notes on the margins of pages, rejected first draughts, etc. . . ."[123] Thus to Pearson for the American Collection at Yale, "the active buyer now," as he'd explained to Charles Abbott, as his old papers took on an increasing monetary value. (How many he'd thrown out over the years, never realizing that he would become an aging monument!) He liked Thirlwall, was impressed with his industry, with the sheer doggedness he showed in gathering his letters preparatory to writing a proposed biography. Now, as his own energies slowed to a trickle of their former waterfall, Williams wondered how any man could spend several years of his life to get out the *Selected Letters* of another man, or spend week after week in libraries ferreting out his lost poems in those elusive little magazines which seemed so quickly to vanish, like last year's snow. He wrote to various old and new acquaintances, asking them to help Thirlwall in any way they could, but when he found out that Thirlwall was attempting to contact McAlmon, from whom he was estranged now, he wrote him sternly: "If you have any respect for me at all please lay off writing to Bob McAlmon or indeed anyone concerning my relationship with him." These were, he insisted, "closed incidents." The loss of McAlmon's friendship was still too close to him for Williams to be able to treat it as literary history.[124]

A deeper problem with Thirlwall as biographer would surface only later on, when Thirlwall finally had to admit to Williams that, as much as he loved working with the poet, he was tortured when it came time to do the actual writing. Then the page remained frustratingly blank and unyielding in its typewriter. Williams tried to coax him into writing, as he had coaxed so many others, but, when he saw a draft of the introduction to the *Selected Letters*, he had to tell Thirlwall to get rid of it and try again, or let the letters speak for themselves. By the late '50s, after half a dozen years working with him, Williams knew that Thirlwall's energies and even interest had finally flagged. Besides, other critics had been suggested as biographers superior to Thirlwall (as indeed they were), and it was they who should be called on to do the significant work on Williams. Hugh Kenner was one name frequently mentioned. So, when Thirlwall found out about this behind-the-scenes jockeying, as he saw it, he told Williams he felt betrayed. After all, he'd been there first. He'd wanted assurances early on, including a contract of sorts for first shot at the biography, and he got it—a five years' headstart. But Floss grew more and more unhappy with Thirlwall, wondering what had happened to this letter or that manuscript, and then became deeply upset, especially with the "unauthorized" publication of certain of her husband's writings. Finally—shortly after Williams' death—she saw to it that the Thirlwall connection was completely broken. It was a pathetic ending to a good friendship. But for the last decade of Williams' life, it was Thirlwall who was there, not only to record, but to serve as companion, adviser, even a chauffeur of sorts to drive Williams to New York or accompany him to Indiana. To his credit, Thirlwall did get a collection of letters out, did uncover a large number of Williams' lost poems, and did get Williams' ideas on a wide range of subjects down on tape for others to study. He did what he could as well as he could, though it eventually cost him the very thing he had wanted to do from the start: the biography of William Carlos Williams.

All through the mid-1950s, Williams continued to mull over the question of measure and to read—that is, have Floss read to him—the work of other poets, especially the young. So he discussed the variable foot at length with Richard Eberhart and Cid Corman in a series of letters, and read Olson's early *Maximus* poems in August 1954, writing something on those poems for Jonathan Williams, though it was not a finished-enough essay for his own purposes. He also told Creeley that those *Maximus* pieces were by far the best work he'd yet seen of Olson's. "He seems to require space in which to expand," Williams told his young friend,

> and a reader also needs space to move around in to get the feeling of what he is after. . . . At least the unity which he has achieved, a unity of place, a unity of story, the narrative coherence effected rescues Olson from diffuseness and gives him a chance to develop [a] long, rhythmic structure without our losing track of him—or he of what he is saying. I was much moved by the poem especially I suppose because of its local theme which is always near my heart.[125]

And that same afternoon he wrote Zukofsky—with Creeley and Olson and Louis himself very much in his mind—to say that, in spite of everything, he felt blessed that he'd been able "to spend a lifetime in pursuit of a style in both prose and verse which if we never achieve it has enlivened many otherwise dull hours for us."[126]

And to Denise Levertov that same month: a letter on the woman as poet, especially the brave figure of Sappho at the beginning of that tradition. She "must have been a powerful wench," he wrote, "to stand what would have torn a woman apart otherwise. The tensions she must have withstood without yielding have made her poems forever memorable."[127] He thought much about Sappho now, the female artist, so much so that he would soon go to great pains to translate at least one of her poems into the American idiom. It would be one more way of saluting the feminine in himself to which he had been brought in his extremity. "When you are past 70," he'd heard a friend of his tell him during a walk in Rutherford, "you don't care so much what happens you know it can't last much longer and that's a great comfort." He related that anecdote to Fred Miller in mid-May of that year. And yet in another vein he could still advise Miller to keep his pecker up, as his own father "used to say."[128] To keep one's pecker up, alert for images of Sappho and the woman he kept seeing in the dark wood, among the tangled bine stems, the woman he'd seen in one guise or another all his life, to keep him warm now and his imagination fresh, as Abishag had comforted Old King David. So, when someone asked him what kept him at his writing, he answered that it was the look in a woman's eyes he'd seen at a poetry reading, sitting there in the third row and watching him with a special radiance. That was what it was all about, he said, for just that look. Let them keep the rest.

He spent July at West Haven again with Floss, who had broken her ankle and had been off her feet for several months. It was another sign of their growing frailty. "Here in the country by the sea—your letter was forwarded to me," he wrote Ken Burke, though when he read over what he'd written he quipped that he was beginning to sound more and more like Edna St. Vincent Millay, and that made him feel as though he were losing his manhood "even more rapidly that I suspect."[129] At the shore he wrote an essay on Whitman for a collection to celebrate the hundredth anniversary of the first publication of *Leaves of Grass*, and the sea must have reminded him again of Whitman's meditations along the Jersey shore on the other side of the Sound: the greatest moment in American literature, Williams had called it four years before.[130]

In November Williams underwent another Rutherford celebration when he was made the town's leading citizen for 1954. The dinner included speeches, photographs, and the presence of four hundred Rutherfordians who turned out to help celebrate the occasion. That month too the book Williams had written many years before, the translation of Quevedo's *El Perro y la Calentura (The Dog and the Fever)*—the book Pound had "abandoned" fifty years before and which Williams had labored over with his bedridden mother—was published by the Shoe String Press through the efforts of Norman Holmes Pearson in an edition of one thousand. At the same time, Williams' *Selected Essays* was published by McDowell at Random House in a run three times that size. When Eberhart reviewed the *Essays* for the *Saturday Review of Literature* later that same month, lamenting that Williams had avoided dealing with religious questions over an entire lifetime, Williams wrote to tell him that he found that omission strange, especially since he was continually thinking about the "other world," even if he was "disinclined . . . to talk of it." He chalked that disinclination up "to the damned rot spoken of it [the spiritual] in the pulpit and among other devotional writers." More importantly, he lacked the framework to talk about the subject with intelligence, though that didn't stop him from wondering what was waiting for him after death, if anything.[131]

*
* *

By 1955 Williams felt strong enough to make extended trips once again. He and Floss flew down to Florida in mid-March of that year for a two weeks' vacation, and then Williams undertook two extended reading tours, one in April and a second, longer one in May. "I'm beginning to take a chance with myself again and schedule myself for a lecture or a reading once in a while which I have not been able to do for the last three years," he told Winfield Scott on April 20. In fact just that day he had returned from a week-long loop which had taken him by plane to the Art Center in Chicago, the Writers' Workshop in Iowa City, and then back home.[132] Then, beginning May 7, he began a three weeks' reading tour of the West Coast, one even more ambitious than the tour he'd done five years earlier. The trip began at Washington University in St. Louis—for which he received $500—and then he and Floss made trips to the University of Washington, Seattle (May 13–14), where they stayed with Roethke this time, then San Francisco State, Berkeley, San José, Santa Barbara, UCLA, and, finally, Riverside on May 31. For each reading Williams received $150. From there they flew on to Santa Fe, New Mexico, to visit with Winfield Townley Scott and his wife.[133] On June 5, four weeks after they had begun, the Williamses were back home. Williams knew that that tour had been quite an undertaking, but he also knew that to function as a reader before large and enthusiastic audiences—though it cost a great deal of preparation—was probably keeping him alive.[134]

In mid-June, the staff at Passaic General presented him with a new electric typewriter which could respond to his slightest touch, and though at first he complained that the machine was so sensitive that it seemed to jump out at him, he soon learned to master it. A few weeks later, at Pearson's urging, he wrote several letters dealing with his early memories of Pound's and H.D.'s families from the Philadelphia days.[135] He also did a radio broadcast about Rutherford for the "This Is America" series which was aired on Radio Free Europe.[136]

But, even as he regained a belated and circumscribed sense of independence, he also stopped writing poems. The truth was that he had grown tired of the step-down line with its slow, measured cadences, for the situation that had given rise to that mode had passed now, and Williams was interested once again in making his poetry new. What he began to fear in early '55—after filling two books with the same step-down line—was that he was beginning to parody himself. It was not until the end of '55, then, that he began once again to experiment with the poem, this time in a number of styles. In the meantime, as he told Cid Corman on July 4, he was concerned instead with concentrating on "a prose defense of the variable foot," adding that he felt then that he might never do another poem.[137] So involved did he become with that defense of his new measure that, reading some of Ken Burke's poems in the blank verse mode a few weeks later, he had to admit that the very "counting of the five regular" stresses had actually made him want to grind his teeth. After all, he added, a poem was "a construction and not what the poet has to say."[138] Something was happening to Williams, for the same man who had written "Asphodel" and "The Sparrow" and those other poems of extraordinary sentiment could tell one correspondent in early February that, as far as he was concerned now, "sentiment [had] no valid part in poetry" and that a poem was only "a construction made . . . to snare an effect which is on the page like music."[139] He was—incredibly —returning in advanced old age to the avant-garde poetics he had championed in the 1920s.

Even before the younger poets had begun to use his step-down innovations in the line for their own uses, then, the old master had moved beyond those to new constructs. The conditions that had given rise to that step-down form—his illness, his need to command a poetry that could reflect his meditative, philosophical mood—all that had changed as he felt strength returning. In fact, it was seeing his poems in *Journey to Love* in print in the fall of '55 that had finally ended that phase for him altogether. The poems he had written in the step-down line seemed "forced" to him now, as he told Cid Corman in November, at least in "the way I have spread the lines on the page to make my point on the meter." They were too "overdone, artificial, archaic—smacking of Spencer [sic] and his final Alexandrine." Once again it was a brilliant, harsh analysis of his own past work.[140] True, those lines *had* escaped the pitfall of the blank verse line. But they had done so by moving instead toward the longer, more stately hexameter. Long before him, however, Swinburne and Hopkins, both students of Keats, had employed the alexandrine strategy. And now Williams—this latter-day student of Keats—had followed a similar strategy, transmuting the cadences of the odes into the "variable" measure of "Asphodel." Williams had wanted to break up the reading of his lines into units that could be understood *only* on "the basis of the HEARD speech," while at the same time his American idiom would follow the contours of "a recognizable and regular pattern."[141] That pattern had been based on the concept of elapsed time and had allowed for rests, grace notes, expansions and contractions. That had been achieved so successfully in the poems of the early 1950s that others would be able to use what he had invented. Granted. Now it was time for Williams himself to move on.

At the end of July Williams invited Tom Cole to spend a week at 9 Ridge Road to help him read over *Kora in Hell*—long out of print—and prepare a selection of that book for Lawrence Ferlinghetti's City Lights Editions. Cole did work over the text and he did make suggestions, although Ferlinghetti finally decided in favor of publishing the entire work. But what Cole remembered most vividly about that stay was how hot Rutherford had been during that week and how for the first few nights the house had been tormented with the cries of a diseased kitten coming through the screen windows. Williams himself was convinced the poor thing had been dropped off near his house by some bastard who wanted an easy way to get rid of it. And it did not help that his neighbor was feeding the animal so that it refused now to leave the vicinity. Finally, Williams had had enough. He walked across the street to the druggist to get a bottle of chloroform and then asked Cole to lure the kitten into the yard for him. Then, taking the kitten from Cole with his good left hand, he dropped it into a clean garbage can, poured in the chloroform and quickly shoved the lid back on top. Then they both stood there holding the lid down while the cat screamed and spat and scratched futilely against the tin sides of its prison, while Cole tried to avoid Williams' guilty eyes. Neither said a word. Finally, the clawing and the hissing stopped altogether. When they looked inside, they knew the kitten was dead. Then Cole helped Williams bury the carcass under a large spreading bush on the slope facing the side street. The job had to be done, he knew, but that hadn't made it any easier either for the young ex-Marine or for the veteran physician. It was one more death to think about.[142]

In September, Williams listened to the World Series on the radio while he wrote two pieces: an essay on Brancusi for the Guggenheim gallery —one of the strongest pieces of art criticism he wrote during the entire decade, and then an appreciation for *Poetry* of Wallace Stevens, who had succumbed to cancer on August 2. Williams had written Pearson for help on any details he could provide him with about Stevens, whom he had not seen now for years, and his essay was an attempt to break down part of the edifice Stevens had spent so many years creating for himself. He wanted people to remember the early Stevens, before the man had acquired a highly self-conscious conscience; he wanted them to remember the poet of the "hibiscus," the poet of the "Jar in Tennessee" and

"Bantams in Pine Woods," the poet who had dared to applaud the Baroness Elsa von Freytag-Loringhoven and had then fled from the Village for years when that specter had decided to pursue him as she'd once pursued Williams himself. Well, the man was gone now, and Williams knew he could not have much longer himself. He had wanted to know Stevens more intimately, but Stevens himself had insisted on keeping his distance. And now it was too late. Stevens too had disappeared into the clouds. Like Pearson, whose letter he quoted in his essay, Williams too knew he would miss that grand plump-bellied presence.[143]

In November Williams and Floss took the *Phoebe Snow* up to Buffalo for a reading at the university there and to spend a few days with the Abbotts at the farm. Taking the train was, Williams confessed, somewhat of a "comedown" after two months of flying all over the West Coast, especially for Floss. He was working once again—and had been working for several months—on prose, this time "The Farmers' Daughters" once again, trying to get the intricacies of that story to come right by writing and rewriting the point of view. He picked up his unfinished play, *The Cure*, and tried to get that moving again, and he was also translating some more of René Char's poems from the French and trying to analyze the verse forms of another French poet whose lines had fascinated him: Henri Michaux.

He also kept abreast of as many of the little magazines and avant-garde publications as he could, which meant waiting for Floss to read to him, often for two and three hours at a stretch. There was Robert Creeley's *The Black Mountain Review*, Jonathan Williams' *Jargon Books*, Cid Corman's *Origin*, Gilbert Sorrentino's *Neon*. And—despite his crippling illnesses during these last years—he managed to keep up vigorous correspondences with Denise Levertov, Charles Olson, Allen Ginsberg, Robert Creeley, Jonathan Williams, Paul Roche, Tom Cole, Ted Roethke, "Cal" Lowell, Richard Eberhart, Winfield Scott, David Ignatow, Gil Sorrentino, Mary Barnard, Charles Tomlinson, Cid Corman, Richard Wilbur, Stevens, Cummings, Marianne Moore, Edward Dahlberg, Zukofsky, Burke, and Pound among others.[144] He also kept up with what was happening among new writers in Europe (especially France), Latin America, Canada, and the Far East—writers like Irving Layton, René Char and Henri Michaux, Alí Chumacero and Alvaro Figuerdo, Nicanor Parra and Osamu Dazai. And he encouraged translators as well: Corman, with his *Aenied* fragments and Horatian odes, the Englishman Peter Whigham with his Catullus, Mary Barnard with her Sappho, Harold Norse with his renderings of Giuseppi Belli's Roman sonnets, Robert Lowell for his *Imitations*, especially the Villon and Baudelaire, and Rafael Wang, with whom he collaborated in bringing Li Po—Pound's old favorite—over into an American idiom.

But by the beginning of 1956 *Paterson* was once again stirring in his brain. Toward the end of January he could tell Eberhart that he was finally getting tired of the prose he'd been doing almost exclusively for the past nine months. Now he was ready to get back to the poem, to the *Paterson* sequel, which would take "him out of himself and into a 'real' world of the imagination, looking down" over the world of Paterson below him.[145] And while that poem began fermenting in his imagination, Williams got on with the task of living. In late January, for example, he gave a reading at Columbia. Then, on the evening of February 1, he and Floss hopped a bus and went into New York to see Marcel Marceau, the French mime, at the City Center. "Alone on that enormous stage in his pierrot's suit, with chalked face and a red flower in his fool's cap, without a word spoken and only a minimum of tinny music he held that audience and me spellbound," he wrote. What had fascinated him most had been Marceau's uncanny ability of giving the impression of walking across the stage without in fact moving from the same spot.[146] But then Williams had performed something of the same trick in his own poems, especially *Paterson* 2.

On Valentine's Day Williams gave a reading in Newark at—of all places—the Lauter Piano Company. At the same time he and Floss had young Paul, now thirteen, and Suzy, eleven, staying with them while Paul and Jinny took a short winter vacation in Florida. Williams enjoyed having the kids with him once again, believing that their presence gave him a chance to renew his own youth once more. Perhaps it did. He was also writing a short note on objectivism for the *Princeton Encyclopedia of Poetry and Poetics*. That same month—on February 2—Robert McAlmon, his body racked by drink and tuberculosis, died of pneumonia in Desert Hot Springs, California, virtually alone and forgotten. He had never forgiven Williams for telling the truth about him.[147]

*   *
*

March 12: another spring was coming, like a cry from outside himself. For a week Williams had watched three fox sparrows in his backyard pecking and scratching the cold ground for their food. "I think they are all males," he wrote Thirlwall that day, "handsome birds, bigger than sparrows, ordinary English sparrows, with rufus red tail feathers like the hermit thrush."[148] Penned in, more circumscribed by illness than ever, he'd watched those birds—those harbingers of spring—more closely than he'd ever had time to in the past. From his rear window he noted the way they attacked the ground, "both feet together, vigorously, then back up into the patch where they have been scratching to search for grubs or worms or whatever they can find." All day and into the early darkness he had seen them, hearing their song for the first time that year. It was a "very musical series of mild chirping notes, very sweet indeed, which has surprised me with its musical quality. It was particularly welcome to me as the first birdsong of the spring season."

That same morning he'd awakened at dawn, those fox sparrows very much on his mind. And then he'd sat down to his electric typewriter to begin work. Already he'd been "pecking" at *Paterson* 5 "for a month or two," he told Thirlwall, but now he began the poem in earnest: "I got out my machine and began to make a few notes. It was thrilling to me," and by the time Floss came into his room he was actually feeling "hilarious" with the excitement of creation. Outside it was overcast, bitterly cold, and snow was expected, but already he could taste his seventy-second spring:

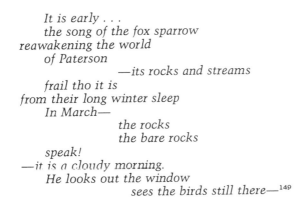

> It is early . . .
>   the song of the fox sparrow
> reawakening the world
>   of Paterson
>   —its rocks and streams
>   frail tho it is
> from their long winter sleep
>   In March—
>   the rocks
>   the bare rocks
>   speak!
> —it is a cloudy morning.
>   He looks out the window
>   sees the birds still there—[149]

After breakfast, he'd gone out for the papers in a thin overcoat and been stopped by a neighbor—"a well-meaning Italian guy"—who had decided that this was the opportune moment to raise the old ghost of Williams' lost appointment as Consultant in Poetry at the Library of Congress three years before. He'd had to listen to the man offer his unwelcome "condolences" and promise to back the Doc if this government thing should ever come to a showdown. Behind his would-be benefactor he could see another man, a patient of his, also listening, "a man of German descent—I took care of his old grandmother until she died, his grandfather too, his father also, and delivered him and most of his brothers and sisters." The man just stared, his mouth open. Williams was beginning to feel chilled now, and he crossed the street back to his house. But the "Wop" was still following him, and Williams had to assure the man that he really was not a "red" and that he really did think he could get by without his help. He'd already managed somehow for the past three years. By the time he'd made it inside, he was shaking with cold and agitation and had to lie down again on his unmade bed to warm himself and collect his strength. He hadn't even bothered to read the papers he'd just bought other than to glance at the headlines. For it was not those external pressures—the insane events moving out there beyond his window—that were working on him now, but his new poem, moving to its own stately measure. In a few minutes he was up again and sitting at his typewriter, eager to touch that other world so vividly there to his imagination. Again the forefinger of his left hand began pecking at the keys like those fox sparrows he'd been watching as they too pecked for food: peck, peck, and a peck. Suddenly, he realized, he'd been given a new spring in advanced old age. Once more the labor of *Paterson* was upon him. That scrawny cry from somewhere outside had struck some hidden chord in him and the chorus was about to begin. Stevens would have understood.

FOURTEEN

The Whore/Virgin and the Wounded One-Horned Beast: 1956—1958

Time now to deal with the woman. After a lifetime's pursuit, to let her reveal herself there at the core of the imagination, queen, mother, virgin, whore. Not any one woman, not even Floss, but the ineluctable mystery of Woman. Thus far *Paterson* had been a search for love, a search therefore for a fuller understanding of the self by seeking out the other and all that one was not oneself. It had been a lifelong search, Ulysses' voyage, Dr. Paterson wandering Garrett Mountain or the back streets of his debased city, a search for that most elusive of presences, a phosphorescence, a pale light growing stronger and stronger, brightening the corner of Williams' imagination. All his life he had sought her, in contact with thousands of women day after day, in contact with his wife, with other women. Dissect the face, peer into the microscope, order her a hundred ways, fragment her, reconstruct her, but somehow she would always escape. Creeley for one, in his review of *The Desert Music*, had remarked that Williams was indeed a love poet and Williams had written him to say that somehow, after a lifetime's pursuit, he had still to come down strongly enough on that theme.

How many times had Floss complained that her husband had the unhappy trait of falling in love with every woman he met? Brendan Gill, working up a portrait for *The New Yorker*, had wondered if he was seeing the same world Williams was when, in the early '50s, just before that first stroke, Williams had taken him on his rounds. He remembered seeing Williams talking with some plain-looking woman in a house dress, her hair up in pink curlers, holding a baby with a soiled diaper as she let the doctor out. Then, as Williams got into his car, Gill, sitting across from him, had noticed how he'd scrambled for a prescription pad to get down some trenchant phrase he'd just heard from the woman, words he wanted to get hot with the living odor still on them. What a beautiful woman, Williams had said as he started to pull away from the curb, and Gill had wondered if in fact he had been looking at the same woman Williams had. But of course he had not.[1]

"Suppose all women were delightful, the ugly, the short, the fat, the intellectual, the stupid, even the old—and making a virtue of their inequalities, each for each, made themselves available to men, some man, any man—without greed. What a world it would be—for women!" Thus Williams in—of all places—the *Kenyon Review*, 1946:

> Take for instance the fat: If she were not too self-conscious, did not regret that she were [not] lissome and quick afoot but gave herself, full-belly, to the sport! What a game it would make! All would then be, in the best sense, beautiful—entertaining to the mind as to the eye but especially to that part of a man which we call so mistakenly the intellect. It is rather the whole man, the man himself, alert. He would be analyzed by their deportment and enriched in the very libraries of his conscience. He would be free, freed to the full completion of his desires.[2]

Recovering from his first stroke that summer of '51, Williams had written the Foreword to his just completed *Autobiography*. With death staring him in the eye, he had felt compelled to write what amounted to a short defense of his life, though one that he knew Floss would scrutinize carefully, as a wife would. What then to say and what to leave unsaid? Well, what about the women, the hundreds and hundreds of women he had known, feeling a love for them that was Franciscan in some instances and Panlike in others, though he really did care about them all. "I do not intend to tell the particulars of the women I have been to bed with, or anything about them," he'd decided, in writing about his life. Better not to, since that would only cause more problems than it was worth, and he'd already been burned by one lawsuit. Besides, the bedroom encounter had always been something of an afterthought for him, an intense sexual irritant to be gone through to get on with the serious business of getting to know the woman as woman. Sometimes, in the mounting fever of talking with a woman, he had been overcome with desire, a desire sometimes returned with interest by the women. So be it. He'd done "foolish" things in his past, slapping women on the rump, goosing them as they climbed the narrow stairs to his attic study, touching them as he'd touched his patients in sickness and in health because contact had always been everything to him. Over the years he'd delivered over three thousand babies and examined thousands of women for everything from appendicitis to vaginal infection to cancer. And yet there'd been a purity about the way he handled the body, a respect for the patients he worked with.

"I am extremely sexual in my desires," he'd written in his Foreword. "I carry them everywhere and at all times. I think that from that arises the drive which empowers us all. Given that drive, a man does with it what his mind directs. In the manner in which he directs that power lies his secret. We always try to hide the secret of our lives from the general stare. What I believe to be the hidden core of my life will not easily be deciphered, even when I tell, as here, the outer circumstances." And, true to his word, in spite of a four-hundred page book, Williams had kept the core of his inner life hidden from the general stare.[3]

Instead, the real news about himself had been told in his poems and stories and plays, but told aslant, in a lifetime's writing trying to understand who in fact he was, as if he or anybody else could know! So *Paterson* 5—the book of the Woman—had quietly insisted on being written at least as early as January 1950, even as Williams began thinking of *Paterson* 4 and the original close of his poem. The ending of his epic had caused him no little anxiety, and it did not take him long into the actual writing of the fourth book to realize that yet another book would be needed to even begin to deal adequately with the Woman. After all, *he* contained that woman within himself and he said as much by creating Phyllis, the figure of Paterson in his young female role. And yet Williams knew that he contained Corydon as well within him, that lame lesbian, that failed poet.

Williams had come in old age to accept the woman as equal, as complementary, as his necessary counterpart if the self was ever to be whole again. Time now, then, to reveal the hidden core of his life, the hidden Kore: the woman who had always sat at the center of his imagination, waiting patiently for him to acknowledge her. Over a lifetime he had written two hundred flower poems, equating the woman with the flower and himself with the insistent bee, stumbling from one to the next, pollinating each and in turn being laden down with riches from that contact. Time then to reveal to those who had eyes to see something of the inner mysteries—Eleusinian or otherwise—of his own imagination, to reveal the Whore/Virgin, nameless under an old misappellation, keeping her son's paternity to herself and able—out of that daring act of love—to have a world believe that no less than God had been the child's father. Praise for the woman who, out of her imagination and silence had been able to generate such a far-reaching myth!

Time too to put the old anxieties behind one, the jabbing, stumbling probes of the poet's egobeak slashing frenetically through the matted underbrush in search of the beautiful thing. To hell with the hounds of one's thoughts—with other strong poets, ignorant critics, baffled townspeople. They would never in this world bring down the fabled Unicorn, the poet with the erotic imagination, his phallic pen protruding wonderfully, grotesquely, from his head. Now let him celebrate in a quieter fashion the final downfall of the poet, caught at last by the woman, killed finally, only to rise again in the eternal world of art. Yeats had summoned a golden bird and Eliot a rose to stand for the artist become his own artifact. Now Williams was choosing the Unicorn, sacrificed but living still—and forever—in his love poems.

The most important battle to be won, finally, would be "the eternal hassle between a man and a woman. That [would] be some battle, as it always has been," and only "genius" could resolve that one. "What the hell," he added, "can we do with them, or without them?" There it was, the age-old dilemma for Williams to reconcile as he could.[4]

*
**

"On Sunday I went with Floss . . . to see her parents forty miles back in the country," Williams had written to Louis Zukofsky back in the spring of '29:

> It brought all the old delight in the delicacy, profusion and color of nature back to me. What can we ever do to equal that? The hills on which the grass has not yet grown too long were blue with short stemmed violets and yellow with cinquefoil; the woods were full of singing birds, of all colors, blue, scarlet and black. I saw a grouse, a rabbit, a woodchuck. I love it . . . and wonder at myself for being where I am—neither in the city nor, really, out of it. Oh well, the country is there, if I should live to be old and choose not to kill myself with debauchery as I sometimes think I may. . . . In any case the violets are still there.[5]

Violets still grew on country backroads, still grew at 9 Ridge Road, and grew still in those Unicorn tapestries at The Cloisters in New York City Williams loved so much, still as fresh as ever, though it had been nearly five hundred years since French craftspeople had woven those threads into those huge designs. Those woven flowers had become increasingly central to Williams in his old age, for they were the fragile yet enduring connective between the world around him and his world within. For it was there and there only that any idea of the city could really last. The walled city of those tapestries, with its slender towers and men in silk stockings and women in velvet gowns still lived on, at least here in a world of art that, by its excellence, had survived. Here then was the world of Keats's "Ode on a Grecian Urn" in Williams' meditation on art and life, with a difference.

Like any city caught in the processes of time, Paterson would go on changing, as indeed it—like any living organism—would have to, changing even beyond the poet's flagging ability to catch the unstable radioactive traces of its life on paper. Obsessed though he had been with the idea of his modern provincial city—that place through which he had moved for seventy years—Williams knew that it, like life itself, finally had its own direction apart from any poet. As surely as Sappho's Lesbos or Catallus' Rome or Villon's Paris or Shakespeare's London or even Joyce's Dublin was still there and yet not there, so even his own American city, a city he had caught in one of its most unstable and characteristic downward phases, was already—by the mid-'50s—demographically and topologically unlike the Paterson of *Paterson*. It had moved beyond the

Paterson of the 1913 silk mill strikes and beyond the decaying city of the Depression; it had even moved beyond the fragmented and hectic energies that characterized the city during and shortly after the war years. Not that it had changed for the better; no, it had merely continued to change. Time, then, before it was altogether too late, to celebrate the continuity of the city—made up of a man *and* a woman—which he'd managed to catch in the interstices of his poetic lines and raise it to the level where all those other heavenly cities existed that had been fortunate enough to be transformed by the human imagination.

By 1956, then, *Paterson* had become a symbol for the particular place in which the artist had been privileged to walk. Now, however, Williams was willing to let his city go. Let that depressed industrial locus be obliterated once more, as it had already been razed by fire and flood in 1902. Let it go up in flames with one of those atomic bombs that daily threatened annihilation, hanging over the poor, depressed city's head ever since Hiroshima and the Cold War. Paterson could be obliterated now because of Williams' care over it. Yes, Paterson had, inevitably, become *Paterson*. "The artist is the most important individual known to the world," Williams had said in 1951, even then shocking his audience:

> He is not an accessory, not a decoration, not a plaything. His work is supremely necessary, proved by the urgency with which we insist on preserving it. Man will not let it die. The very inner casings of Egyptian sarcophagae, made of paper sheets, are ungummed in the improbable hope that a shred of papyrus found there may contain even a few words from a poem by Sappho. If England is destroyed by Russian bombs it will hardly be a matter of importance to history so long as the works of Shakespeare be not lost.[6]

Paterson 5, then, would celebrate the only Paterson that would—in the long run—matter: the city of the imagination.

For *Paterson*'s early readers one problem that confronted them was how to account for the fifth part of an epic that Williams had repeatedly told them would have only four parts. From 1943, when Williams published a poem outlining *Paterson*'s four parts, until 1951, when he brought that epic to a close with the publication of *Paterson* 4, everyone (including for most of that period Williams himself) had come to believe in the inevitable quaternity of *Paterson*: a Trinity, with the inclusion of the dissonance of Pan. And yet *Paterson* 5 had come along to upset all those earlier expectations. In his statement published by New Directions along with *Paterson* 5, Williams stressed the point that too much had happened since *Paterson* 4 for that ending to serve as the closure for all that he now saw. Accordingly, the poem would have to be opened up to allow for the poet's new sense of his world. And yet those early readers were right to sense that something more profoundly radical had happened to Williams' conception of the poem than the mere passage of seven years. Something else would have to account for the great divide between the first four books of *Paterson* and this afterthought, this latecomer, coda, footnote, extension, call it what one might.

Increasingly, Williams' world became identified with his second-floor study and the fenced-in area of his backyard garden, where he and Floss could tend to their flowers each day from spring to late fall. It was here, then, that his crippled body moved toward its inevitable dissolution, moved toward that twilight world of old age where men and women become more and more indistinguishable from each other. Penned in by that garden at 9 Ridge Road, however, with the noose of time closing in on him, Williams fought desperately to keep alive the world of his imagination, the one escape still open to a man for whom the consolations of religion or the preoccupations of politics seemed closed. No wonder, then, that at some point—perhaps even as he gazed at the Unicorn tapestries on one of his several trips from Rutherford via the George Washington Bridge to The Cloisters in uptown Manhattan—when a friend or a neighbor would drive him in—Williams suddenly realized that the figure of the tamed Unicorn, at rest there inside that wooden fence in the last of the tapestries, was none other than Williams himself.

A whole world of allegory had grown up around the Unicorn tapestries, and Williams was at pains to break that symbolic world down, to decreate it, to make his readers see instead the particulars of a place: a French landscape peopled by fifteenth-century kings and huntsmen and women. "If the art which puts these figures down / were to be inverted to facts again . . . ," Williams had written in an early draft for the poem.[7] It is an impulse familiar to readers of the late poems of Wallace Stevens, of the Stevens, for example, of a piece like "Large Red Man Reading," where the dead return to be warmed as best they can by phrases uttered from the book of life, phrases such as "the pans above the stove, the pots on the table, the tulips among them." Those returning presences, Stevens says, "would have wept to step barefoot into reality." Moreover, remembering the monastic silences of Yaddo, where Williams had written much of *Paterson* 4, remembering too The Cloisters themselves, Williams set out to demythologize, secularize and return to their earthbound origins much that had been lifted to the level of religion.

There was the tale from the old bestiaries, for example, about the Unicorn that could be tamed only by a virgin, how it had finally been killed by hunters but had risen from the dead. It was a theme for secular and divine love, as here in these tapestries, where the narrative of the hunt, of the capture, death, and rebirth of the divine beast had been enacted in cartoon fashion across these seven tapestries, moving "from frame to frame without perspective / touching each other on the canvas

/ [to] make up the picture." And the religious allegory seems clear: Christ the Unicorn, whose unique horn possesses healing powers, is tamed by the Virgin, ensnared by love, pierced by the evil of men, dies . . . and rises, chained by the flimsiest and most delicate of halters to the tree of life, rendered here as the pomegranate tree.

In Williams' retelling of the myth, however, the Unicorn in search of the Virgin becomes the artist's imagination in pursuit of the Woman. And the corollary to that pursuit is the unabashed, naked pursuit of the poem in search of the virgin language which must of necessity be whored, mauled, and finally possessed. It was a pattern the poet had reenacted again and again throughout his life, driven to it by the hounds of his thoughts, though each "conquest"—as Hart Crane also knew—brought him that much closer to his own death. In the reenactment of the poetic act, it was the erotic energy—the male in pursuit of the female of it—that generated a force field embracing a whole world of particulars, from "the sweet white rocket, / on its branching stem" to the King himself, "in a velvet bonnet, puce, / slanted above the eyes, his legs / . . . in striped hose, green and brown." If the earlier books of *Paterson* had focused on the anachronistic mystery of the "convent of the Little Sisters of / St. Ann" out by the "rhubarb farm," if they had gathered into its democratic field "the sink with the waste farina" or a "grasshopper of red basalt" or an old bottle "mauled / by the flames," here Williams—transposed to a new dimension, to a world where art alone had survived—could survey with a newly earned leisure Paterson as the redeemed city located along the River of Heaven, that river which also ran through the Unicorn tapestries.

The River of Heaven: the phrase first appears among Williams' drafts on a sheet dated January 15, 1950, at the time Williams was seriously getting down to the business of composing *Paterson* 4. However that book was going to end—and it would end with murder and death—Williams knew that it would be out of character with the earliest books of *Paterson* to transpose his autobiographical epic this early into a timeless dimension. The poet as a latter-day Troilus peering down over the ramparts of heaven at the patch-quilt city in the distant, philosophical haze: this would demand another reading, another book. That future fifth book would contain—Williams noted modestly to himself—"Everything left over that wasn't done or said," a book whose unfolding would be unfrenetic, "at ease." In 1950, *Paterson*'s river was still recognizably the Passaic, and it still had to urge its weary, Liffy-like way out past Newark Bay to merge at last with the chilling North Atlantic. The story of the River of Heaven would, in the meantime, have to wait upon future events.

When, therefore, two years later, Williams began again to think of

Paterson 5, he thought he would make Allen Ginsberg "the center" of the poem, as he told Ginsberg himself on February 27, 1952.[8] So the clue to Williams' early conception of *Paterson* 5 was already there in Book 4, in the letter from Ginsberg, dated June 6, 1950, which Williams had incorporated. "I have been walking the streets and discovering the bars—especially around the great Mill and River streets," Ginsberg had written. "Do you know this part of Paterson? I have seen so many things—negroes, gypsies, an incoherent bartender in a taproom overhanging the river, filled with gas, ready to explode, the window facing the river painted over so that people can't see it." And then, a sentence pointing to the heart of the matter: "I wonder if you have seen River Street most of all, because that is really at the heart of what is to be known."[9]

River Street and the River of Heaven: "I have been thinking a lot of your son recently," Williams wrote Louis Ginsberg on Valentine's Day, '52, on the eve of his departure for his New York vacation, "and shall want to get in touch with him before long." Williams was still "hog-tied" with revisions on *The Build-Up* at that point and would see no one until after the beginning of March. But that bar, that run-down bar with its black satyrs dancing about and the painted window facing the river was very much on his mind. What he wanted young Allen to do was to take him to that spot. "I don't know what the joint is like or whether we'd be welcome there," he added, "but if it's something to experience and to see I'd like to see it for I want to make it the central locale for a poem which I have in mind—a sort of extension of Paterson."[10]

Young Ginsberg had recently sent Williams some more verse, including an eight-line poem called "Metaphysics," which had insisted that the world before us was "the one and only / firmament" and that the poet was therefore already "living in Eternity." Ergo: "The ways of this world / are the ways of Heaven."[11] It was Williams' own early theme precisely. For *Paterson* 5, therefore, he would use Ginsberg's short poem as a headnote "as some shit uses a quotation from some helpless Greek—in Greek—to precede his poem" (the reference undoubtedly glancing at Eliot's headnotes from Herakleitos in the *Four Quartets*). Williams wrote to tell Allen that he wanted to see more of his poems, and so, in early March, probably on the ninth, he went out to see the Ginsbergs, presenting Allen with a copy of *Paterson* 4, the poem in which his "son" already figured so prominently. He also took away a sheaf of the young poet's recent work, which came to some "80 or more poems."[12] This sheaf, pared and cut back by more than half, would become the nucleus of *Empty Mirror*, Ginsberg's early poems, for which Williams wrote an introduction soon after reading the poems through. And in that introduction (which would not be published until 1961) Williams spoke of finding in these early poems a new line "measured by the passage of time, without accent, monotonous, useless—unless you are drawn as Dante was to see the truth, undressed, and to sway to a beat that is far removed from the beat of dancing feet but rather finds in the shuffling of human beings in all the stages of their day . . . the mystical measure of their passions."[13] It was a description of a measure that tallied nicely with the measure of Williams' own "Asphodel" and *Paterson* 5. So Dante's initial tercet, englished by Williams at the start of his introduction to Ginsberg as

> *In the middle of the journey of our life (I came to)*
> *myself in a dark wood (where) the*
> *straight way was lost*

becomes, with a little shifting of the typewriter tab, a close approximation of Williams' own staggered tercets, as in

> *Of asphodel, that greeny flower,*
> *like a buttercup*
> *upon its branching stem. . . .*

On March 11, with Ginsberg's sheaf freshly in mind, Williams wrote to Robert Lowell about this unknown young poet from Paterson "who is coming to personify the place for me." The direction of *Paterson* 5 was still tentative at that point, but Williams knew that the new poem would embody "everything I've learned of 'the line' to date." He even had some kind words for Eliot in writing Lowell, kinder than was usual with him, acknowledging that Eliot and Pound were "both top men in the craft." But, he added, he himself would have to go on beyond them: "I must make the new meter out of whole cloth,"—and the voice here had a new urgency, since Williams saw what he was not ready to disclose even to Lowell—"I've got to know the necessity back of it." It was not a matter of fame for Williams, not even of the acquisition of a personal distinction. He himself would be content to let the "unknown" new measure shine through his own work "like a sunrise," like a radiant gist. For he wanted to see the "overpowering mastery" of the new line "inundate the whole scene" and "penetrate to that last jungle" like some new light, some new energy source. And that line, that measure, he was still insisting, could "be detected in the remote province of a Paterson as well as elsewhere." *There* was his measure, and there too his great theme.[14]

Asphodel, the flower (poem) that grows in hell in hell's despite: *that* would provide the primary theme for the extension of *Paterson*. It would be a constant, "all of a piece and all the same," but with variations. Against the asphodel would be the countertheme, played in a "different melody," the theme Ginsberg had given him: the struggling city, that "hole in the wall on River Street." Then, to tie the new part into "the first 4 parts of the poem," he would use all the earlier themes in *Paterson*, returning, finally, to the asphodel theme "as a fugue as in Mozart's *Jupiter.*" Memory, then, and a concomitant world of art: these would provide the new dimension of *Paterson* 5. Nor would there by any prose in the new book; instead, he would use a relatively uniform line throughout—"a triple line (all the same line really) on three levels across the page. Unchanging."[15]

What Williams was *actually* describing was of course "Asphodel," the hole in the wall transformed into the larger problem of the atomic bomb, and Floss—the woman—replacing Williams' earlier concern with Ginsberg and his poetic sons. It would take Williams himself a long time to realize that he wasn't writing *Paterson* 5 yet, so that, when the opening lines of "Asphodel" appeared in *Poetry* in October 1952, they appeared under the title, "Paterson, Book V: The River of Heaven." A year later, however, when another section of "Asphodel" appeared in *Perspective* under the more tentative "Work in Progress (*Paterson* V)," Williams inked out that title in his own copy and gave it its final title.

When he gave "Asphodel" to Random House in 1954, he wrote Laughlin that his first *Paterson* 5, promised to him four years before, had turned into something else. At the same time, however, he told Laughlin that he would keep his original promise and send him *Paterson* 5 when—if ever—it was written. That poem would do, he added, "with the world after I am dead."[16] It had been the second volume of Williams' poetry Laughlin had lost to Random House in as many years, and Laughlin was understandably upset. What he wanted to know—*now* —was when *Paterson* 5 would be ready. Give him another two years, Williams told him, and then, if he did it, it would be Laughlin's.

*
* *

The material for the new poem continued slowly to grow. There was the gathering of the letters during the five-year period when Williams was most centrally engaged in the making of *Paterson* 5: 1952 to 1957. The first letter one finds in *Paterson* 5 is from the novelist Josephine Herbst—"Josie"—written in May 1952, congratulating Williams on the publication of his *Autobiography* and thanking him for his memories of her seventeenth-century sandstone farmhouse in Erwinna, Pennsylvania, just across from the New Jersey border, a place Williams and Floss had visited regularly for many years. For the particular theme that Williams had discovered in Herbst's letter is contained in her incisive comment that "a place is made of memories as well as the world around it."[17]

"The old stones of the house were a superb background for nasturtiums," Williams had recalled in his *Autobiography,* and Herbst's letter generously evokes a whole world of flowers—"forgetmenot, wild columbine, white and purple violets, white narcissus, wild anemones and yards and yards of delicate wild windflowers," her catalog of flowers chiming nicely with that other world of flowers evoked in thread at The Cloisters which finds its way into the long list of flowers at the end of *Paterson 5*.

The second letter in *Paterson 5* was sent by Allen Ginsberg (now author of *Howl* and part of the beat movement) from San Francisco in late May 1956. It became, ironically, a subtle and complex transformation of Williams' original countertheme of the hole in the wall on River Street in another melody: Dr. Paterson's son in a more ironic, ambivalent, disappointed, and even nostalgic voice now that he too had grown older. And though the son of *Paterson 4* was making another appearance here in Book 5, he was no longer at the center of the new poem. Instead, Ginsberg's letter reads like a kind of *Pater, Ave atque Vale,* for that "big sad poppa," Dr. Paterson, "who needs compassion." Ginsberg was writing Williams now to thank him for doing the introduction to *Howl*, which Williams had read in March 1956 when he began *Paterson 5* in earnest. "Your foreword is personal and compassionate and you got the point of what has happened," Ginsberg told him, "though there was also a strength and gaiety" in the poem beyond what that big sad poppa had emphasized. And by '56, Ginsberg wanted his "father" to know, there were other sons of Williams' out there in San Francisco having a grand old time with him. Robert Creeley, with whom Williams had corresponded since 1951, was there, as well as "various other extremely interesting zen buddhists . . . , all good poets, whom you met and influenced around Reed years ago, 1950?" (He meant of course figures like Gary Snyder and Phil Whalen, who had both been struck by what Williams had had to say during his visit to that school in the fall of 1950.)

Ginsberg was leaving San Francisco in a few weeks headed for the North Pole on a military sea transport ("if the FBI doesn't get me first,") to help "refurbish the DEW (defense radar arctic paranoia installactions)," where he would "see icebergs and write great white polar rhapsodies." But, he insisted, he was not, NOT forgetting Paterson. When he'd done his cosmic Whitman thing, he'd "be back to splash in the Passaic again only with a body so naked and happy City Hall will have to call out the Riot Squad."

And then, in a pointed reference to *Paterson*, Ginsberg waved away the travail of Williams' twenty-year struggle to articulate his own world. "There is no struggle to speak to the city, out of the stones etc.," Ginsberg assured him with all his thirty years of experience. "Truth is not hard to find." Moreover, *Paterson* was not only "a task like Milton going down to hell," a theme Williams had stressed in both introductions written for Ginsberg; it was "a flower to the mind too."

A flower to the mind: "IF YOU DON'T HAVE ANY TIME FOR ANYTHING ELSE PLEASE READ THE ENCLOSED *SUNFLOWER*

SUTRA." With these words Ginsberg had closed his letter, but that command—so reminiscent of Marcia Nardi's pleas at the close of *Paterson* 2 to take the time to study her long, rambling letter—compels the reader of *Paterson* 5 to pick up his *Howl and Other Poems* and read his Whitmanian sutra for the sunflower, symbol of the modern industrial landscape (the real city is San Francisco but no matter). Whatever the success of *Howl,* however—and Williams genuinely admired the poem (though it did go, he thought, a bit soft in the middle)—Ginsberg had clearly taken off on a track of his own. That was, of course, as things had to be, as any son would have had to do. The poet, like death, has no peer, Williams says in *Paterson* 5, and in the earlier manuscript version we find Williams noting that the poet has no *père*—no father—that he does not soon abandon. It is a resolution that splits through the very title of the epic, dividing it like the scar down Ahab's face: Pater/son.

But the sons kept coming anyway. In January 1956, for example, Gilbert Sorrentino sent Williams a four-page sketch he'd done four years before about another border town like Juárez, Sorrentino's whores chiming with the old troopers and Mexican girls in *The Desert Music.* He did not really expect Williams to answer, but Williams did with enthusiastic praise and in September 1957 decided to print the whole second half of Sorrentino's sketch in the first part of *Paterson* 5, almost back-to-back with Ginsberg's letter.[18]

There were hundreds of young writers during the '50s asking Williams for all sorts of literary and personal advice, happy just to have an acute and sometimes sympathetic ear. And though they frequently did not know it, they in turn became consumed in Williams' own creative process and stood a good chance of winding up somewhere inside *Paterson* 5. At one point, for example, Williams thought of including a letter from another of his sons, the choices being either John Pearce, a young pre-med student at the University of Washington, Seattle, or Cid Corman, editor of *Origin* and a friend of Charles Olson and Robert Creeley. Pearce seems to have been the earlier choice, and Williams' direction here would have been to move toward a radical sense of regeneration, the young man of twenty discussing love, life, and literature with the old poet approaching death. Pearce, the raw neophyte, almost sophomoric in his intensities, a nervous network of constant and uncertain changes, and Williams—half a century and more older—the artist who had "achieved" most of what it was he would achieve in the one lifetime allotted him. "You recommend 'Birdman of Alcatras' [sic] in your letter," Pearce noted at one point in his letter. "The only part that I really understood was Stroud as a young man. How can I understand those things so far from my experience,—growing old in prison? The young man meant a lot to me though. . . ."[19]

But this letter may have struck Williams as too raw for *Paterson* 5; it was too close to the letters that had circulated throughout the earlier books of *Paterson*. Williams' second (and more refined) choice, then, devolved on Cid Corman, with whom he had been corresponding since 1950. Writing from Matera, Italy, in August 1956, Corman centered his interest on the question of mimesis in poetry. For the voice of this son was older, more controlled, the poet hard at work on his craft, willing to quarrel with the master about the inexactness of such terms as "imitation," "realization," and the unacceptable passivity of the poet as "recorder." A poem should not *re*present at all, Corman insisted; rather, it should *pre*sent, make present. To dance, that is, to create a poem, was a specific "I-function": "It is not nature that dances, but we, each one of us, that 'dances' it into 'being.' A poem is a presentation, or an introduction, if you will, into being. Of being."[20] It is clear that Corman engaged Williams' critical mind in a way that not even Olson or Ginsberg did, and one can see how this letter would have chimed with many of Williams' central concerns with technique in *Paterson* 5—the dance, the presentation of a present world.

But at the very last minute in the final draft of *Paterson* 5 (January 1958) one of those gratuitous occurrences took place that finally focused the poem as Williams had wanted it, perhaps unconsciously, from the beginning. By a simple substitution of a letter from Edward Dahlberg for Corman's letter, placed in exactly the same position and with no other changes in the surrounding text, Williams moved the poem away from the subject of the transmission of the craft to one's sons to the more fundamental issue of the Woman: the hidden core of his poem finally revealing herself.

In a long newsy letter from Palma de Mallorca about the good life he was living there, Dahlberg related a story about a highly intelligent woman writer "who had come to America and there had a child by a wretched scribbler. Poor and forsaken she had returned to Copenhagen, where she earned her niggard indigence doing reviews for the Politiken . . . trying to support a wonderful boy, sturdy, loving, and very masculine." A woman (and an artist), trying to support herself and her son born out of wedlock, harassed by the police at every step for nonpayment of taxes: it is a portrait of incredible courage and of fierce dignity, and it struck a sensitive chord with Williams.[21]

That woman of Dahlberg's—nameless—chimed with so many women Williams had known over a lifetime. She chimed with Marcia Nardi and the black women in *Paterson* 3 and the Jackson Whites—Elsie among them. She chimed perfectly with the figure of Kazuko as well, the pregnant, unwed narrator of Osamu Dazai's *The Setting Sun*, a novel Laughlin had sent Williams in October 1956, as soon as it had come off the press at New Direction. Williams had been stunned by the beautifully and sensitively registered portrait of the woman and had written to Laughlin on the twenty-eighth that Dazai's rendition of "the female plight" left "nothing to be said." "Until woman makes free with her sex for the one purpose for which she is made we are both of us, man and woman, powerless in the world. Mary [the Virgin] had to have her baby, who was a bastard. Until that has sickered down in the consciousness with an acknowledgment of the dignity, even the glory, of the occurrence, we don't know nuthin."[22] So Dahlberg had unwittingly given Williams a modern-day presentation of the central icon of *Paterson* 5: the icon of the Virgin holding the Baby, whose father is surely not the old man standing behind the two of them. In Williams' recreation of Peter Brueghel's *The Adoration of the Kings* (1564), the nativity scene has been demythologized and thus returned to a "present" reality. What Brueghel has given us, Williams says, is simply (and gloriously) a pretty peasant girl holding a baby—naked—upon her lap, serene, at peace, while all about the mother and child the scene bustles with life. It is a realistic portrait both artists give us rather than a mere sermon in paint. Here too, as with the woman and child in Dahlberg's letter, there are "savagely armed men" magnetized to that core, soldiers, police officers, themselves too much the realists to be taken in by all this talk about a virgin birth, as they whisper to each other "with averted faces" about "the potbellied graybeard (center) / the butt of their comments." "Poor Joseph," as the old Italian joke goes.

Writing to Dahlberg in July 1958, with the book already complete, Williams explained the central theme of *Paterson* 5 to the man whose letter had unknowingly helped to reinforce his theme by simply entering as a found object into the grid of energies that made up the poem. Since the whole theme of *Paterson* was both single and dual—a man and many women, as well as the poet who contains both within him—the woman had been left dangling at the close of *Paterson* 4 with the murder of the father. "Woman," Williams told Dahlberg, "is *not* implied in a man's fate but calls for a resolution of her own," one he hoped *Paterson* 5 would provide. And the final reconciliation of the various aspects of the woman had found its resolution in the figure of the Virgin Mother, "that whore, that glorious whore adored by the ages, rightly adored by the ages into perpetuity."[23] Mary was to be honored, then, not because of her infinite inaccessibility or because of her perpetual chastity, but because she had given herself to her lover freely and fully, to some soldier, perhaps, as his own grandmother had also done in his mythology of her lost history.

The significance of this gesture of giving oneself with dignity not only holds certain theological implications (to understate the case), but also some aesthetic ones as well, which had been dear to Williams' own poetics for many years. Essentially, what was at issue here was that the icon, the symbol, the word, the logos, be returned to the fully human, and the symbolist or neo-symbolist poetic—with or without its Christian underpinnings—which underlies the practice of an Eliot or a Hart Crane (as well as a Baudelaire and even a Mallarmé) should be deprived of its logocentric, symbol-making connective. It was a poetic that should then return the world to men and women. What Williams marveled at as obstetrician was how well Mary had maintained her secret, making out of it—as his own sacred grandmother had perhaps done as well—a glorious fiction, serene and dignified. The Virgin and the Whore: the woman as artist, generator of myths who is herself generated by myth. It was another—and central—identity of all women into the one Woman who sat at the center of Williams' imagination.

*
**

Beside this letter, the other prose passages in *Paterson* 5 take on a secondary cast, containing important but ancillary themes. Themes, that is, that also find their resolution in the figure of the Woman. So the opening of the second section of *Paterson* 5, which begins with a quotation from a letter written to Williams by one A. P., Arnold Post, classics professor at Haverford, editor of the Loeb Classical Library, the man who had taught T. S. Eliot Sanskrit at Harvard forty years earlier. When the Williamses visited Gratwick Highlands in October 1956, Williams and Abbott had discussed the problem of rendering Sappho into the American idiom. Williams had decided to translate Sappho's "Peer of the Gods."

What he had seen by way of English translations of Sappho left him cold. There were, for example, Merivale's rhymed quatrains in three iambic tetrameters and a final dimeter:

> *Blest as the immortal gods is he,*
> *The youth whose eyes may look on thee,*
> *Whose ears thy tongue's sweet melody*
> *   May still devour.*
>
> *Thou smilest too?—sweet smile, whose charm*
> *Has struck my soul with wild alarm,*
> *And, when I see thee, bids disarm*
> *   Each vital power.*

But how, he complained, could anyone "insist on translating that magnificent poem which even the ancients themselves treasured as the work of a god into silly rhyme"? No, what was needed here was a translation that would eschew rhyme, inversion, the "poetic" phrase. But, since Williams knew no Greek, he would need to spend at least "an afternoon" with someone who knew the language well, who could "familiarize" him with the original "and go over that poem so that I may absorb [it] into my soul to do with it what I want to do with it." He asked Abbott to drop Post a line asking if he would be willing to talk with Williams about Sappho, and this Abbott did.[24]

"When Sappho was sweating for a woman, she put it down," Williams told Thirlwall, thinking obviously of the very poem he was translating. "The suppressions of my youth drove me to free and frank expressions," he added, though he knew too that one could "go too far in the other direction." What mattered, finally, whether you were Sappho or Ginsberg or Kerouac or Corso, was the poem itself, "the organization of the thing." There were young beat poets whose "life-styles" included drugs, homosexuality, and lesbianism, poets who made his own freedoms pale into a kind of puritanism.[25] But that was all beside the point, for what mattered was only the poem itself. Capture the sound of Sappho's lyric dance across the page, capture that, and you could capture—though it be for a tenuous gossamer instant—that lovely woman's passionate, living presence.

Here in her lines was the presence of a sensuous reality, undimmed by the passage of twenty-five hundred years, still fresh, still able to move the reader, as when the words had first been passionately uttered. *If*, that is, that presence could be blooded once again, *if* the American idiom could be made to trace out the essence of the Greek. Williams did finally write to Post, but the professor's response—the gist of which Williams placed at the head of the second movement of *Paterson* 5—must have chilled him, for he never did get around to spending that afternoon with Post.

Congratulating Cid Corman in April 1955 for his translations from Horace, Williams praised him for bringing back to life "an ancient mode, which the translators have done to death, brought it to life again with a bang so that it speaks to us in a way we can understand." What a good translation of the classics could accomplish was "to show how our present modes differ from the past by showing what in the present is *equivalent*, not the same, with what existed then. To attempt to adopt the ancient mode by word-for-word rendition of the old mode is to acknowledge defeat before you start." That was to court failure, to "lose the whole thing," to render "a lifeless imitation of a lively invention."[26]

Consider, then, this version of the opening lines of Sappho's lyric:

> *Peer of Gods he seemeth to me, the blissful*
> *Man who sits and gazes at thee before him,*
> *Close beside thee sits, and in silence hears thee*
> *Silverly speaking . . .* [27]

with its high quotient of filler and the tintinnabulation of alliterations in the phrasing, "in silence hears thee / Silverly speaking." Compare this translation with the normal syntax, jagged rhythms, and recognizable idiom of Williams' lines:

> *Peer of the gods is that man, who*
> *face to face, sits listening*
> *to your sweet speech and lovely*
>   *laughter.*
>
> *It is this that rouses a tumult*
> *in my breast.*[28]

"It may be that women are different from men in that they may have to strip themselves barer than men do," Williams had written Denise Levertov on March 21, 1956. "The history of Sappho seems to indicate it—nothing held back, absolutely nothing, complete incontinence, but the cost is exorbitant."[29] Sappho, of course, had been in Williams' consciousness for many years, for she was the Woman as Poet par excellence. She was already in *Paterson* 3, and she haunts the early drafts of *Paterson* 5 as well. "She was half a man / small and dark," he writes there, "Sappho was half a man anyhow—and she / could WRITE—her tail in her mouth / deny it who may: the virgin turned / whore: an identity."[30] We were all, to one degree or the other, Williams had insisted for years, both male and female, and acknowledging this was to experience a sense of wholeness, of amity within oneself. For there was, finally, a basic complementation between the sexes, an interpenetration both ways. And no poet who was "not in essence a woman as well as a man" could know anything of "the deictic divisions of the words" or—finally—"amount to anything" as a poet.[31] "A trembling hunts / me down," Sappho is made to utter in this lover's recreation. And the words create an identity between that woman and the dying Unicorn of *Paterson*, pursued by the demon hounds of his—and her—unyielding, insistent passions.

Living with those crystalline syllables of Sappho's had the added bonus of effecting for the poet a genuine counterresponse, for Williams' act of translation resulted in one of the most finely realized lyrics to be found anywhere in *Paterson*. "There is a woman in our town / walks rapidly," it begins, sandwiched triptych-fashion between a letter from Pound dispatched from St. Liz's—an American version of Bedlam—on the left and an excerpt from Mezz Mezzrow's *Really the Blues* on the right. Now the woman detaches herself, for we are at the very core, the very center of *Paterson* 5 (and "this is a fiction, pay attention") gathering to herself the energy of the detached, unencumbered verb, to WALK alone through the streets of Paterson's mind, as Paterson himself had earlier walked the streets of his city and stroked the bare rocks of Gea, the feminine principle, Garrett Mountain. The woman in this lyric, moreover, is a fully realized person—a lesbian (and so Sappho's sister), both man and woman—whose presence on the streets of Paterson astonishes the poet and stops him in his tracks to admire her, before she disappears, vanishing once again into the milling, nondescript crowd of sentences that make up Williams' city. It has been, then, for once something: a visitation by a vibrant, living, unchanging presence across the centuries: Sappho alive and well, in Paterson.

One such visitation had actually occurred to Williams on Rutherford's Park Avenue on the morning of August 9, 1955 (thus accurately can such annunciations be located in time and space). He had gone down the street for the morning paper, he wrote Floss a few hours later by way of manual and mental exercise, and he'd seen a tall young woman, "wearing a smoothly fitting plain black dress." Drawn to her, he'd followed as quickly as his legs would carry him, but the woman was obviously on her way to work and in a hurry:

> She was outstanding in appearance in the nearly empty street of that hour of the morning from her finely shaped long legs with slender ankles to her dark hair and erect posture. She was ahead of me going in the same direction as I was and going faster than I. I wanted to see the features of her face to see if I recognized her.

An old man of seventy-one, the wounded unicorn, still after the impossible Virgin, hopelessly trying to overtake her:

> I saw her turn off from the street and disappear into a newspaper store down the block, the same store in fact to which I myself was going. I hurried my step as much as I could, hoping to overtake and recognize her there but before I could accomplish my purpose she re-emerged from the store and hesitating a moment at the curb, crossed the street and was gone—to my keen regret. Ho hum![32]

How many times Kore had appeared in Rutherford and Paterson over a lifetime even Williams could not have said, but always—characteristically—she remained one step ahead, elusive, and finally nameless.

In Pound's last of many appearances in *Paterson*, Williams was using his friend's letter—dated November 13, 1956—as a way of saying farewell to several of *Paterson*'s earlier "interests," now that the "(self) direction" of the poem had decidedly shifted. Pound, as ever, was still insisting on the central importance of economics in the scheme of things, and Williams had paid back that interest with a subtle vengeance in *Paterson* 4. The correspondence between the two men from the mid-1930s on leaves one with the sense that we are frequently reading two unrelated monologues. For, as Williams more than once complained, Pound had the annoying habit of leaving Williams' questions unanswered, talking at Williams and going on with his own half of the conversation, usually suggesting that Williams read this or that book, which more often than not turned out to be some dreary economic treatise. Just two weeks before the letter that found its way into *Paterson*, however, Williams had written Pound that he'd had enough talk about economics. "What I want out of you is not economics but the poem," he told Pound. "Maybe you'll say it's often or can be the same thing but not out of you and it's you I'm interested in."[33]

Interest: the pun is unavoidable. In a poem dated June 30, 1956—just four months before this letter was written—Williams had concluded his "To My Friend Ezra Pound" with a similar pun: "As a writer of poems/you show yourself to be inept not to say/usurious."[34] It was a rather odd kind of complaint to a friend, even where that friendship was made up of the grittiness that had existed for years between Pound and Williams, a friendship that had survived years of silence, various incarcerations, surveillance by the FBI, and a divergence in politics that can be described only as radical. But what Williams was acknowledging in his poem to Pound was that he owed a very heavy debt to his poetic and even economic theories. Now, however, it was time to put those old interests and directions to bed.

One way to do this was to let Pound ramble on in *Paterson* until the reader found himself dismissing this shrill and—unfortunately —ineffectual voice. It is hardly a voice òf great wisdom, the Pound who could go on as here in these words: "The hardest thing to discover is WHY someone else, apparently not an ape or a Roosevelt cannot understand something as simple as 2 plus 2 makes four. . . . Wars are made to make debt, and the late one started by the ambulating dunghill FDR . . . has been amply successful."[35] Pound was incorrigible, Williams was convinced, and it prompted his own exasperated response a week later. "Dear Assen Poop," he began, "Don't speak of apes and Roosevelt to me—you know as much of the IMPLEMENTATION of what you THINK you are proposing as one of the Wops I used to take care of on Guinea Hill." Hadn't he—Williams—gone through his own Major Douglas period in the '30s trying to make some sense of Pound's economic issues? When it came to economics, Williams had come to believe, Pound was simply fetishistic, muddy, stupid, and full of obfuscations.[36] Still, in Pound's poems, his best poems, the man had done "supremely beautiful" work. And therein lay Williams' real interest in the Pound.[37]

"Money: joke," Williams had written in *Paterson* 4. After all, money was, finally, an imaginative construct, and the human imagination could wipe out the value of currency with the mere stroke of the pen, or by placing those who opposed the monetary powers in the penitentiary, as "when/gold and pound [Pound] were devalued." Significantly, when at the end of February 1958 Williams wrote Pound to say that he intended to include Pound's letter in *Paterson* 5, Pound at first said no. After thirteen years in that pen in Washington and the number of moves to get him freed which had all ended in failure, Pound could sense that he was finally going to be released. Now, therefore, he was particularly reluctant to let Williams publish his sentiments attacking Roosevelt and the U.S.'s economic policies. "There is still a good deal of weight on my protruded and aged neck," he answered Williams on January 27, 1958. "I dunno that I can afford to be quoted at this time. especially as you indicate the expressed emotion has not been Wordsworth'd in tranquility." There was an alternative, however. Quote the letter, but then "straighten the passage by quoting from McNair Wilson's 'Mind of Napoleon' starting at p. 104."[38]

Williams wrote at once to Laughlin (on March 2), saying that Pound had not given permission and that the passage should be removed from the text. Besides, he explained to Laughlin, he had "only included it for purely literary reasons, to relieve monotony," and "it would have been misinterpreted anyhow."[39] But Laughlin wrote to Pound and a compromise was reached, which consisted in a slight revision of the text "mostly by cutting any names which might cause Pound problems." "Pound wanted his letter revised," Williams wrote Zukofsky on March 5, "something I had not foreseen, much to my amusement. What could I do? When the final text is in, momently, we should have something which will resist attacks from every quarter." The letter stayed.[40]

*
**

One man Williams seems to have gotten nowhere with was John Wingate (standing in for Mike Wallace), who interviewed Williams on a host of topics, ranging from politics to the American idiom, on the national CBS television program "Nitebeat," on Wednesday night, September 4, 1957. Wingate's questions were provocative, teasing, even entrapping, as the portion of the transcript that appeared in the *New York Post* for Friday, October 18—and which Williams used in *Paterson* 5—will show at a glance. Even the caption, "Mike Wallace Asks William Carlos Williams Is Poetry A Dead Duck," suggests the kind of high comedy and cavalier dismissal with which the American poet is normally greeted in his own country.

"Mr. Williams," an unused portion of the published transcript runs, "the critics of poetry these days are other poets themselves. Isn't this because nobody but poets understands poetry anymore?"

Williams: "I acknowledge that the difficulty of the poet's writing is a barrier to the public. Definitely. But I say he is forced to it in the modern world—to reflect the complexity of his thinking. . . . When I see a poet who's perfectly clear, I have to laugh."

Question: "Why?"

Williams: "He isn't SAYING anything."

Question: "You mean that you're 'saying' something when it's too obscure to be understood?"

Williams: "No. No. Not put that way."

But it was put that way, time after time. The transcript reads less like a dialogue where one person can learn from another and more like the journalist's opportunity to play cat-and-mouse with that despised, ineffectual creature called the American poet.

But that was not the worst of it. "Did you hear anything of a television appearance I made a couple of weeks ago: stirred up quite a bit of trouble for me," he wrote Fred Miller in late September. "They tricked me into making some damaging statements against the Jews and Senator Kennedy. I fell for it and now have to pacify my friends." He was on the defensive here and knew it, as his tone made clear. "Too damned bad about those thin-skinned bastards," he added. "But maybe I'm more prejudiced than I realize but I don't think so."[41]

Bill and Eleanora Monahan, watching Williams that evening on "Nitebeat," had sent him a telegram which had arrived just as he was going on the air. He'd been so nervous about his appearance that he'd slipped the telegram—unopened—into the inside pocket of his business suit jacket, where it had remained, forgotten, until he'd put his suit back on eight days later to attend a testimonial for a friend of his. The following day, Friday the thirteenth, he thanked the Monahans for their singular thoughtfulness and explained to them what had happened that night when he'd faced John Wingate. "I had to go straight ahead with my answers," he wrote, "which in the pressure of events were not always expressed in as well chosen words as I could have wished." As for his supposed anti-Catholic, anti-Jewish remarks, he had this to say: "You know that I am an unbeliever. I live by human love, male and female. . . . Nothing is more serious to me than to be unfaithful to a friend—but I have had to go ahead. Catholic and Jew are equal as I have faced the world, the pagan and even savages which the Church has so brutally slighted are equally sympathetic to me."[42] And, since part of the furor had been caused by his continuing friendship with Pound, whose name had become synonymous for some with words like anti-Semite and traitor, Williams knew that sooner or later he would have to pay for that friendship. It hadn't helped him with that job in Washington, he felt, but there it was. In the clash between his own principles and his defense of a man he'd known and even loved for over fifty years he was bound to get mauled.

Yet, embarrassing as the incident had been for Williams, he still managed to come out ahead in his discussion on the American idiom and the new poetic line. Wingate—or Wallace, or whoever formulated the questions—seems to have been out to "catch" Williams by asking

Williams to pass judgment on a poem by Cummings, whom he called, patronizingly, "another great American poet." It was Cummings' poem about a falling cat which begins "(im)c-a-t(mo)b,i;-l:e." Well, *was* it a poem? Williams publicly admitted that he had to reject that effort as a poem (which may explain in part why Cummings soon after the publication of *Paterson* 5 cooled to Williams), to which Wingate—brief in hand—then responded by quoting from Williams' own "Two Pendants for the Ears." The lines Wingate quoted sounded, he said, "just like a fashionable grocery list."

Well, Williams responded, it *was* a fashionable grocery list. But the lines had been ordered on the page to form a jagged pattern, a kind of rhythmic improvisation—like jazz. Practically, then, it was a grocery list, but beyond that common-sense level there was another level of meaning, a second sense in the very lay of the syllables. He might have explained that that fashionable list of groceries served as a metonym for the unconquerable will of that old woman, his mother, to go on living, as her appetite would have indicated, but would this interviewer have caught the poem's meaning?[43]

When the partial transcript of the interview appeared in the *New York Post* on October 18, Williams was already well into the final version of *Paterson* 5, but he must have seen at once that this exchange, with its mode of inquisitorial catechesis, caught something of the countermelody he needed to anchor his poem. Its placement at the close of the second part of the book was easy. It merely followed Williams' previously published "Tribute to the Painters" (from *Journey to Love*), where it now served as the flat note preceding the final lyrical section of the poem. But, if one's memory was long enough, one could see that the interview also served a function analogous to that provided by the inclusion of a quotation from John Addington Symonds at the close of *Paterson* 1 on the relation of crabbed verses to distorted subjects. (Both sections —incidentally—were afterthoughts, added late.) For both prose passages stand as vindications of Williams' own poetic practice. Limping feet across a jagged pattern: call it the dance of the priapic satyr, that other crippled one-horned beast.

*
**

One analogue for the jagged patterns that distinguish Williams' poetic lines—in fact the central analogue—is black jazz. And the proximity of a passage from Mezz Mezzrow's and Bernard Wolfe's *Really the Blues* (1946) to the "Nitebeat" interview reinforces the analogy of black jazz and Williams' variable foot as two of the unique contributions to American music and American poetry in our century. Listening to recordings of Bessie Smith's renditions of the blues, Mezzrow recalled how he was absorbed by "the patterns of true harmony in the piano background, full of little runs that crawled up and down my spine like mice." So Williams, responding to a poem Fred Miller had sent him in the summer of '56, told Miller to watch "the timing within the lines, ignoring the grammatical divisions *but* organizing the measure to make a musical sequence." The pace itself could be varied as much as was needed to give the poem "a jagged surface."[44]

Interestingly, however, it is in the lines immediately following the passage quoted in *Paterson* 5 that the clearest link between Mezzrow and Williams as musician and word man is made: "What knocked me out most on those records was the slurring and division of words to fit the musical pattern, the way the words were put to work for the music." Like Williams listening to his patients, Mezzrow was intent on capturing Bessie Smith's "unique phrasing," of getting "the words down exactly as she sang them." When Mezzrow's sister, acting as stenographer, began " 'correcting' Bessie's grammar, straightening out her words and putting them in 'good' English," Mezzrow recognized a danger that Williams likewise inveighed against—the proper (and deadening) guidelines of the academy for correctness against the exact contours of the idiom as it existed on the tongues of "a hundred million Americans."

In his synopsis of the American idiom in 1960, Williams defined it as "the language we speak in the United States." It was a language "completely free from all influences which can be summed up as having to do with 'the Establishment,' " though American scholars had succeeded in driving the idiom into "a secondary place," and even of having denied—as Eliot had done as late as the mid-'50s—that there really was any such thing as an American idiom as distinct from a mere dialect variation of the mother tongue.[45] But to Williams' fine ear the timing —the pace, the measure, the phrasing—*had* perceptibly shifted in the intervening centuries since the first English settlements in the New World. And that had made the crucial difference. It was this shift in timing that Williams hoped would be made self-evident in the very lay of his syllables, variations in time like Bessie Smith's infinite variations on the line as she delivered herself of a song.

*
**

On June 11, 1957, fresh from a three-week trip with Floss down the Mississippi on the *Delta Queen*, a stern-paddle steamboat, Williams wrote Laughlin to say that he hadn't "yet started to work up my *Paterson* 5" (he meant here the final version), though "the basic plan" had "been laid out long since."[46] Three months later, however, he wrote saying he was glad that Laughlin was ready for the poem now because he too was ready to finish it, though, reduced to typing with the forefinger of his left hand, it would still be "another 3 or 4 months until I can turn it over." It was patience he was asking for from Laughlin and from himself, invoking his mother's frequently uttered exordium: *"Petit à petit l'oiseau fait son nid"*—"Little by little the bird builds its nest."[47]

Even so, it was not until mid-October that he actually undertook the final draft of *Paterson* 5 in earnest. And, as usual with Williams when he was working a poem into its finished form, he was anxious, fretting, unsure of his own powers. "I've begun on the final version of *Paterson* 5 in a far from confident mood," he told Norman Holmes Pearson on October 16. "But I have to go on even though what I have to say may be bathos, I can't quit now. Every line creates new problems. Am I growing wordy, can't I say it in fewer words and if I do will it be clear what I intend—and in short have I still the genius or have I grown too old to continue?"[48]

All through the second half of October Williams kept at the poem, arranging the prose sections (which would make up fully one-third of the published text), and shaping his lines, selecting these, rejecting those. Then, on October 29, he informed Laughlin that he'd "finished" the poem that very day. But, since he and Floss would soon be off to California (where he had volunteered to submit to an intensive three-day battery of questions at Berkeley, led by a team of professors of psychology and philosophy, and would then have a two-week stay at Charlotte's home in the Los Angeles suburbs), he was leaving the manuscript with his son Bill until his return. At his age, he half-joked, one had to provide against "all contingencies," death among them.[49] Even on his trip, however, he continued thinking about the poem, for on Thanksgiving Day he was still not satisfied with it, telling Laughlin defensively that it had "not yet been completed," and that there was a "final revision . . . still coming up." "I still believe in it, of course," he added, "but you never can be sure. Heaven help the poor woikin goil."[50]

On December 4, two days after he'd returned home, Williams signed and dated his now "finished" manuscript, and then sent it out to be typed. There was a bit of sparring between Williams and Laughlin about terms—Williams insisting on $1,000 in advance, a run of three thousand copies, and an advertising budget of another $1,000. Laughlin was hesitant, wishing to see the manuscript before committing himself. But no sooner had he seen the poem, which reached him right after Christmas, than he sent an enthusiastic letter to Williams, accepting his terms. Then, and then only, would Williams show the poem to Floss, archetype of all the women in *Paterson* 5. On the last day of the year, Williams tried to steady his left hand long enough to sprawl his dedication across the finished version of the script: "To my darling wife."[51] Flossie was pleased.

The poem finished now, Williams could afford to detach himself from that field, to scan it Troilus-like from a distance. What made the fifth book "'necessary'"—Williams made several critical explanations for the appearance of *Paterson* 5 over the course of 1958, this one offered to Babette Deutsch—what made it necessary was the realization "that merely coming 'home' could not be the end of it unless you say what 'home' is." Maybe home was "merely woman and all I have ever wanted was to achieve her, the sexual act!" It was no use trying to place the raison d'être for the poem on some abstract, philosophical plane, for he was more than ever convinced—as the close of *Paterson* 5 would demonstrate—"that man can know nothing. Poetry is my answer, for the poem, dealing exclusively with sensation, knows what cannot be known."[52]

Williams returned to this theme when he told Cid Corman in August: "I use the word 'measure' in the original sense to 'mete,' as the English used it at the beginning," meaning here that he was using it in its sense of a measuring *out*, which implied—obviously—a standard against which to measure. In every language, he offered, a foot was a measure, "loosely stated a pace as in the dance, the Greek or any other kind of ritualistic dance." It followed, then, "that a poem is a kind of dance." What "all our most complex philosophies (and mathematics) have come finally to mean to us is that we cannot begin to go beyond the evidence of our senses. We can know nothing. The sole exception is that we can measure, therefore the pertinence of the dance." The Greeks, he was sure, had known this and had "made of it their sole verity." To know nothing . . . but the dance.

In time Americans had come to break with the blank verse tradition as no longer operative in their own sense of what time was. Amidst a world of grave uncertainties involving their very sense of themselves as a people, their sureties had been dramatically circumscribed to the relative certitudes of mathematics. The variable foot itself—unsatisfactory as Corman and others might find it as a working instrument—had to be "conceived as solid" for there was "nothing else left for us. A fixed foot is merely unacceptable in the present state of our minds because there is no ground for it to tread." Thus Williams in 1958, himself in a decidedly "post Einsteinian world," while most poets continued to measure as though Euclid still dominated the scene.[53]

In mid-May of '58, returning the slightly corrected galleys to Robert MacGregor at New Directions, Williams decided to include a defense for the fifth part of a poem that had supposedly closed with *Paterson* 4. Since 1951 and the publication of the original ending of *Paterson*, he wrote, he had been made to realize that there could be no closure "to such a story as I have envisioned with the terms which I had laid down for myself." He had had, therefore, to take "the world of *Paterson* into a new dimension if I wanted to give it imaginative validity." So, while there *was* a new dimension in the poem, he still hoped that his readers could make out "a unity directly continuous" with the earlier parts. It was this statement that New Directions disseminated as the rationale for the new poem. For despite the fact that critics argued fiercely for and against the inclusion of the fifth part, Williams himself had considered just such an extension for nearly a decade by the time that poem appeared.[54]

"I hope you will not be disappointed with *Paterson* 5," Williams wrote *Paterson*'s aristocrat, Dahlberg, on July 7, in the same letter in which he spoke of the overriding theme of the woman. "It was very necessary for me to have it appear for the rescue of my peace of mind. Too much had been left unsaid and the world had gone on. . . . The purely physical aspects of the story, the descent of the river to the sea, was completed. But I in my own person had not died but continued to live and go on thinking. The mind, my own mind persisted." He had also to admit, however, that he'd sent page proofs of the poem to several friends (Fred Miller got one of them), only to find that they had all expressed dissatisfaction with the poem, advising him "to abandon the thing or give it some tangential name." But he had refused. *Paterson* 5 belonged, and as its father, Williams had a right to name the child.[55]

Yet, despite his insistencies, Williams himself had his doubts about the poem and about himself. "I'm certain you will not find me the man I was when you left," he wrote Cid Corman in early March 1959. He admitted that he often felt confused now, that he "dreamt too much sleeping and waking and though you expect that in a poet it seems excessive in my case." Moreover, he found all his poetic theories fading fast now, and he was no longer producing poems in the quantities he had. It was in this state of general depression that he called *Paterson* 5 a partial failure: "I had to say what I wanted but the result is [that] the text turned out rather forbidding." He had not, he thought, dwelt long or hard enough on the impression the poem "would make on the reader who justifiably wants his poetry without defects in the medium."[56] By "defects in the medium" he meant the amount of seemingly raw prose material that had found its way into the poem. If anything, however, those prose passages had kept the whole poem hard, jagged, balanced against the tendency toward revery and nostalgia to which the passages on the Unicorn set against the millefleurs background, if left to themselves, seemed prone. Virgil wishing to have his *Aeneid* burned as he lay dying, Pound summing up fifty years' labor on the *Cantos* as a botch, Williams apologizing for *Paterson* 5: there are times when others must save the poet from himself.

Paterson 5: that six-year poem in search of the imagination's own City of God. The escape clause, the hole at the bottom of the pit, deeper than the idea of death itself. Here, then, in this poem Williams has finally brought himself to look coldly at his own death. For there, among the "sweating horses / and gored hounds / yelping with pain," the hunters in the tapestry are finally bringing in his corpse in the shape of the dead Unicorn, strung "across the saddlebow / among the oak trees." Yet even this scene Williams can watch serenely now, as he focuses his attention almost at once on "the lady / through the rough woods / outside the palace walls." Hell, he'd explained to Thirlwall in early 1955, was merely an imaginative construct after all, to be altered or rethought as necessary by the intellectual imagination itself, "the dominant force in the world today" and a human being's "most valuable possession with which to face the world."[57] Here, then, it is: the eighth day of creation, a return outside time to another kind of beginning, to a lovely world where beautiful young men and women move about in a stately saraband among horses and hounds and rabbits and birds. There is a beautiful Virgin (no doubt experienced in the ways of love) and there is a Unicorn prancing about or resting at ease. In the background, no doubt to the east, a city rises beckoning. A murder has taken place and they have brought the poor beast's body in for the young couple as a very special wedding present. "A present, a 'present' / world," Williams has instructed his poem. At the very end of his life he had once more managed to begin again.

FIFTEEN

Lightning Stroke and Thunder Clap:
1956—1963

*L*ike a cry coming from outside. Not Foxsparrow or Thrush nor even the Perfect Woman, but Floss sitting across from him in their living room reading from the manuscript poem in front of her:

I saw the best minds of my generation destroyed by madness, starving hysterical naked,

dragging themselves through the negro streets at dawn looking for an angry fix,

angelheaded hipsters burning for the ancient heavenly connection to the starry dynamo in the machinery of night,

who poverty and tetters and hollow-eyed and high sat up smoking in the supernatural darkness of cold-water flats floating across the tops of cities contemplating jazz. . . .

Young Ginsberg's *Howl*, a cry of anguish from a new generation of poets, for whom Williams was already—in ways he had not foreseen —becoming a father. He'd been asked by Ginsberg and Ferlinghetti to write an introduction to the poem for City Lights, and now, in March 1956, even as he began *Paterson* 5, he listened to his wife read the poem for him. Who would have thought Ginsberg would ever have survived long enough to write a poem like this, that poor, lost son who, soon after being released from the Columbia Psychiatric Institute, had written Williams to say he was a poet from Paterson?

Williams listened, impressed by the craziness, the sheer energy of the poem. Yes, it sagged a bit in the middle; it might be tightened up here or there. But here was a poet who had gone through a hell such as he himself had recently gone through. He had gone there too "in his own body," through the experiences he'd described in his poem. And not only had he survived, like one of those who had managed to survive Dachau or Auschwitz (except that it was America he was describing), but he had managed to find a fellow—his fellow inmate Carl Solomon—whom he could love. "Say what you will, he proves to us, in spite of the most

722

debasing experiences that life can offer a man, the spirit of love survives
to ennoble our lives if we have the wit and the courage and the faith—and
the art! to persist."[1] To himself, Williams expressed some doubts about
the quality of work Ginsberg and his friends were producing. But he was
willing to wait and see what would come of it. He knew that just then
there was an awful lot of "nutty experimentation," but that would soon
"evaporate," taking with it so much that was still stodgy in American
poetry, and then there would be "a great dawn" bursting over America. So
he told Louis Zukofsky that Easter Sunday.[2]

At least what the beats were doing was better than what Eliot had
done. "I despise writers that pretend to be so deep in their knowledge of
the mysteries of life that they go beyond the understanding of their
friends. Usually you find them using a foreign language such as Greek."
Thus to the Canadian poet Irving Layton on March 19, thinking of Ol'
Possum, even as Williams was writing the introduction to *Howl*.[3] After
all, what did we really know beyond the world we walked through other
than our breath, a measure, a dance? Warren Allen Smith, book review
editor for *The Humanist*, had written Williams that same week to ask
him if he thought of himself as a humanist. And if he was, was he a
theistic humanist or a secular humanist? No use dealing with the
question in that way, Williams answered on the twenty-fifth. Atheism,
he wrote, was "laughable as a positive belief." Death awaited every man,
and that seemed to be the end of the matter. And while he knew that
there was no use sounding "positive" about that conclusion, as a doctor
he did know that "since all data in the case are withheld from me I find
myself absolutely unconcerned." All his life he had lived "side by side
with men who believe in the miracles of Christ," and though they were
his friends he never thought of discussing his beliefs with them or they
with him.

The truth was that the brain was so "complex" a "mechanism" that
man had always been intrigued by its workings, though any sort of
certitude was out of the question. "I was bred a Unitarian," he underlined, "but whether I transect the cone of my preferences nearer or farther
from the light has become as I grow older indifferent to me." He did not
know if there was a God, though he did find himself—like Pound
—attracted as an artist by the concept of polytheism. "Being forced back
from any knowledge except the report of the senses," he concluded, "a
humanistic naturalism is all that is left to me lit by the lightnings which
play about the minds of saints and sinners." Thus, having opted rationally for a pragmatic naturalism, he threw out the possibility that it was the
Light after all which he wanted to celebrate. If there were contradictions
in what he said, he'd nevertheless said what he had to say; let someone
else unscramble it.[4]

Even as he approached the mouth of the sea, then, his senses kept coming up on a dead end with the large questions. He wanted certitude as much as anyone, but he had early despaired of ever achieving it and so had immersed himself instead into the random flow of experience, to let whatever patterns there were in his life gather as they would. In the meantime he was experiencing—in the years 1955 through 1958—his last springtime, the time between a partial recovery from one stroke and the inevitable onslaught of the next: that interval between lightning stroke and thunder clap. Thus, without explaining why, he'd sent Louis Zukofsky a postcard in mid-March 1956 with the lines: "Once more ye laurels and once more ye myrtles ever seer," a slight misquoting of *Lycidas*, which had signaled Milton's engagement once again with the act of the poem.[5] Actually, Williams was signaling the beginning of *Paterson* 5 and, beyond that, a period of retooling the poetic line as he moved from the step-down lines of "Asphodel" to the short jagged tercets of the "Pictures from Brueghel" sequence. And that retooling, which lasted for the nearly three years Williams spent writing and publishing *Paterson* 5, would take him through a medley of forms ranging from the very short line and stanza to the very long, proselike blocks of his "The High Bridge above the Tagus River at Toledo."

If we unscramble the seventy pages of poetry that make up his last collection, *Pictures from Brueghel* (1962), and approach the making of those poems chronologically, we will better understand the poetic "logic" of Williams' variable foot and the direction in which that untiring sculptor of the word was tending in his final phase: the recapitulation of the whole direction of his poetry from the 1910s up through the late '40s. So he reexamined his strategies with tercet and quatrain, long line and short, to see what he could rework in order to get the taste of the step-down line out of his mouth. Like Brancusi, like Brueghel, he would continue to work at his craft until the last stroke hit or until he became incapable any longer of handling a pencil or wrestling with his new electric typewriter which snarled and spit back at him whenever his left forefinger tried to dance across the keys. He never did fully subdue that machine, and he was glad to have Floss there to read over his letters and poems to tell him if he'd hit enough of the right keys. He was circumscribed by a world of newspapers and magazines (many of which he now left unopened for weeks at a time), as well as by a world of prints and paintings, an occasional ride on a subway, a walk on Park Avenue, a rehearsal of one of his plays, gossip, a postcard. Penned in by his own deformities, the wounded unicorn would now make contact with the greater world beyond his living room through friends who would come to spell Floss and read to him or take him for a ride or to a reading—St. John's in Jamaica, Wagner College on Staten Island, CCNY, NYU, Fairleigh Dickinson, The Cloisters. One woman would remember taking him out for a ride on the New Jersey highways and another car weaving in front of them. She could see that Dr. Williams wanted badly to say something, to articulate what was on his mind. "What is it?" she asked him solicitously. "Go ahead and say it." And Williams, stammering to get the words out, saying: "SH . . . sh . . . sh . . . shit!"[6]

Now too the young kept coming out to see him at 9 Ridge Road, until he could no longer handle their intensities. There was Ginsberg and Corso and Kerouac and Orlovsky, Denise Levertov and Robert Creeley, Tom Cole and Cid Corman, Gael Turnbull and Charles Tomlinson. But there was also Jack Thirlwall and Dave McDowell, James Laughlin and Louis Zukofsky, Walter Sutton and Edith Heal, Stanley Koehler and Hugh Kenner, and even Pound. They were coming to Williams as to an old master, to pay their respects or to glean what information they could about that presence fast becoming venerable. But Williams' tenacious contact with his world still lay, as it always had, in the execution of the poem, the placing of each letter and word on the page.

On the one side were poems with long, proselike cadences, as if Williams had tried to collapse his step-down lines into one, or to imitate Ginsberg's line in *Howl* in a quieter mode, as in the dreamlike scene he evoked as he recalled his visit to Spain forty-five years before:

> *A young man, alone, on the high bridge over the Tagus which*
> * was too narrow to allow the sheep driven by the lean,*
> * enormous dogs whose hind legs worked slowly on cogs*
> *to pass easily . . .*
> *Pressed against the parapet either side by the crowding sheep,*
> * the relentless pressure of the dogs communicated*
> * itself to him also*
> *above the waters in the gorge below. . . .*[7]

That one was written in '56, but then—at the other end of the line spectrum—so were his "Calypsos," one fruit of Williams' visit to Puerto Rico in April of that same year. These were poems that caught in their short circular rhythms the calypso music Williams had heard in the islands:

> *Well God is*
> *love*
> *so love me*
>
> *God*
> *is love so*
> *love me God*
>
> *is*
> *love so love*
> *me well*[8]

And between these: poems like "To My Friend Ezra Pound" and "Sappho, Be Comforted," "The Turtle" and "The Gift"—those last two reverting to the step-down line, and "The Gift," based on Giotto's *Adoration of the*

Magi, a doubling of the poem Williams had written based on Brueghel's rendition of the same religious topic.

By the time he'd completed *Paterson* 5, however, Williams was using a sharp, jagged tercet or—less frequently—a quatrain without benefit of any punctuation beyond an initial capital. What he achieved with this form was a sense of speed where line breaks kept cutting against syntax. The result was a fine tension between the "meaning" of a line and the presence of the line as a formal entity with as much solidity as pigment squeezed out onto a canvas. He had learned that lesson repeatedly from the painters—Cézanne, Juan Gris, Jackson Pollock, Robert Motherwell—all of whom directed the observer to see the very planes and blobs of color on their canvases apart from any "meaning'" those forms or colors might have.

Beyond this was a renewed cinematographic sense in Williams. Several times in essays and letters he had remarked that he preferred seeing the coming attractions of a film over seeing the film itself because narrative had become for him an intrusion, lessening the impact of scene set against scene, image against image. Present the curve of a moment, catch that and let the reader imagine the rest. Williams had of course been capable of doing that sort of thing as far back as the early '20s, but now in these late poems he provided a new emotional complex which included the reaction of the observer brought into the field of the poem itself. Now too Williams experimented with bringing his metaphors and similes into the same foreground as the subject of his poems, so that both sides of a verbal equation remained balanced and present in the reader's mind. No false depths, then, no false perspectives in these late poems. Williams had found a verbal equivalent for cubism: flat surfaces with sharp edges tightly fitted together, where all parts of speech from verbs and nouns to lowly prepositions and even more lowly articles all equally demanded the reader's attention. A work of art, he'd told Josephine Herbst in late 1947, was "all surface, believe it or not. We think it is depth but it is not. It is surface. But that surface must bespeak depth. It is words Gertrude Stein kept insisting."[9] Now, ten years later, Williams had found a new way to realize on paper that persistent conviction.

All his life he had studied the cadences of prose, reading newspapers and journals and magazines and letters not only for their information, but for something beyond that: their intrinsic cadences, cadences dictated by the American idiom. He summed it up as best he could in an essay called "Measure," which he worked on in the mid-1950s. There was, he said, an idiom, a language, that surrounded us in the same way that algae in the sea were bathed "by the same light that penetrates all the gardens we know." Like Pound's in his late *Cantos*, Williams' metaphors now strove toward a neoplatonic vision of language. He saw the living language as surrounding and sustaining and upholding human beings; like light itself it was everywhere present and transparent. It was almost as if he had been speaking not of words but of the Word. He had listened to the prose matrix for fifty years to see what he could bring over from it into his lines. And now, after a period of lineal expansion in his step-down lines, it was time for a new spareness, a time to make each word count, to trim wherever possible without losing the sense of employing "the fullest vocabulary of speech terms to maintain a sensible effect" at the same time "concentrating what I have to say so that an alert mind is encouraged to take the leaps necessary to bridge the gaps in the sense left to save time."

But he was not interested in "mere eccentricity"—the kinds of typographical wizardry his friend Cummings had practiced over a life-time of writing poems. Always, Williams insisted, it had to be "possible to reconstruct the sense from the scheme, the grid of the words supplied," though this must follow and not precede the reader's "interest" in the subject and the lay of the lines so that the reader would *want* to make the effort. The curve of that reader participation would be a sense of "awakening" in the initial encounter with the poem, "followed by a complete rest in which to enjoy his sensations." Finally, the passage through the poem's arc had to "come instantly in an epigram to a climax." A word, a phrase, enough to make the whole poem explode in on the reader with a sense of revelation.[10]

"Chloe," written at the same time as Williams' "loosely assembled essay on poetic measure," brilliantly incarnates the poetic strategies of this last phase, and its trajectory and open-ended closure deserve to be presented in full:

> *The calves of*
> *the young girls legs*
> *when well made*
>
> *knees*
> *lithely built*
> *in their summer clothes*
>
> *show them*
> *predisposed toward flight*
> *or the dance*
>
> *the magenta flower*
> *of the*
> *moth-mullen balanced*
>
> *idly*
> *tilting her weight*
> *from one foot*
>
> *to the other*
> *shifting*
> *to avoid looking at me*

on my way to
mail a letter
smiling to a friend[11]

We begin almost as if we were to have a dispassionate lecture on the anatomy of young girls' legs (or is it, then, the young girl's legs?). There are legs—and knees—"predisposed" toward flight, elusive, caught in the act of shifting away from the speaker in order to avoid looking at him, so that he, to cover that moment of awkward, vulnerable self-recognition —with its potential or actual rejection (as one would turn instinctively from a scarecrow)—in the same moment turns his own attention to a third party who enters the picture only in the poem's last line.

And the flower: "the magenta flower / of the / moth-mullen balanced / idly / tilting her weight"—fully realized and presented, a metaphor for the stance of the young girl, who like the flower also balances "idly / tilting her weight," (though, like the poet, she shifts too "from one foot / to the other"). Structurally, then, the flower jostles for the same foreground that the girl herself occupies. There is no perspective here, no sense in which flower gives way to girl or girl to flower, for both are caught up and sustained through the curve or wave of the poem's syntactic unfolding. From start to finish, then: one complex syntactic unit, made up of discrete planes. One complex, shifting, forward-riding sentence. It is a far cry—this poem—from the radiant stasis of "Asphodel." When, in 1960, Walter Sutton interviewed Williams, Williams was as preoccupied with the shorter, sparer lines of his last poems as seven years earlier he had been with the line of "Asphodel." The Whitmanian line, he said then, was just "too long for the modern poet," in spite of what someone like Ginsberg had done with it. What the times demanded now, he thought, was a new terseness, a new sharpness, and though he himself still hadn't been able to nail the damn thing down, he was closer, convinced that the last poems he'd written were superior to his earlier work. Oh, he could still teach the young a thing or two. When he told Sutton all this, he had already composed over fifteen hundred pages of poetry and was within months of writing his very last poem. And yet, after a lifetime of pursuit, the poem still eluded him, much as that woman he'd followed down Park Street had managed to elude him as he hobbled after her, foot following foot outward, until she'd disappeared forever.[12]

*
**

There were prizes and awards and other forms of recognition as well in these last years: the Levinson Prize in '54, the Oscar Blumenthal Award in '55, and a $5,000 fellowship from the American Academy of Poets in February 1957. Williams was thankful but not much impressed by such belated public signs of honor. "They gave me a swell reception . . . when the award was officially presented," he noted wryly to Fred Miller about the Academy award. "Fifty people were invited to an apartment on Central Park South and ninety came to see the caged poet!"[13] And the following month Williams was finally elected to the Academy itself. That was at the Ambassador Hotel, and Nelson Rockefeller was there to welcome Williams and present Richard Wilbur with an award from the Academy.

And there were trips, too, once again, now that Williams had all the time in the world. In April 1956 he flew down with Floss for a ten-day visit to read at the University of Puerto Rico, to revisit places he'd seen sixteen years earlier. He left on the evening of the third and next day gave a reading to an audience of about 150. It was still wintry when he'd left the airport in Newark and he found "the sudden change in temperature . . . staggering." He remembered, as he prepared to give his reading on the evening of the fourth, how a tree toad had begun to pipe, so that he'd felt an urge "to stop and listen to him with his *coquoc quille* rather than talk to a world of humans."[14] He spent three days in San Juan and then flew to the other end of the island to Mayagüez to see if he could not finally locate the house where his mother had been born and to learn finally just *when* she had been born. He barely escaped an official welcome by the mayor of the city, read there for a small group, and managed to find in the city hall records the license his mother had received so many years before which had allowed her at fifteen to drive a carriage. Then, having touched the soil of his mother's origins, he flew on to Charlotte Amalie on the island of St. Thomas to touch base with the place where his father had grown up in the 1860s and '70s. Williams and Floss walked the streets of that town, noticing the colonial architecture and going over the Moravian School there where William George had been sent as a boy.

A week after his return home, Williams was at Cornell University to present his poetry and talk with students and faculty. He read to a large crowd assembled in one of the large lecture rooms (Olin M) but confessed to the student who interviewed him, Barbara Loebenstein, that he felt nervous before large crowds now and had just vowed to himself never to do it again (though of course he did).[15] He also spent some time up at the cottage in West Haven again, but for the most part, as he told Zukofsky, he and Floss stayed close to home, enjoying "our own back yard hobbling between the flowers as we were able and believe me I mean hobbling."[16] He and Floss took the *Phoebe Snow* express up to Gratwick Highlands for a week's vacation in late September, where Williams could contemplate that ruined garden he loved so much and have some good conversations with the Abbotts and Gratwicks. Then it was home again. At the end of October he read "Asphodel" to a crowd of students at CCNY and then, on the thirtieth, read once again, this time at Arnold Constable's in Hackensack.

In November he wrote Kenneth Rexroth in San Francisco that the beats—"that crew in your city that surrounds The City Lights press" had "been very active recently." Ginsberg had done a good book with his *Howl*, though the new manuscript—the early poems of Ginsberg's—he did not like so well.[17] And a month later he wrote Cid Corman, then teaching in southern Italy, that there was "a young gang kicking up the dust out San Francisco way that will bear watching. They are more or less led by Allen Ginsberg for whom I wrote an introduction for a paper cover book. The title is *HOWL*, it's a good poem—the gang has been going around San Francisco reading to audiences up to 400 people FOR Free!"[18]

In early January 1957 Williams had a chance to see his wandering son once more when Ginsberg came east with his friends before departing for Tangiers. Allen asked his father, Louis, to drive him and Gregory Corso and Peter Orlovsky and Jack Kerouac out to 9 Ridge Road so they could spend the afternoon there reading their poems and talking to Williams. Ginsberg had even written earlier, asking Williams to read some of Kerouac's stuff, but Williams had told him he wasn't interested. Now, however, actually meeting this young French-Canadian with his powerful fists and broad shoulders and his two blackened eyes, Williams was taken by him. Kerouac had gotten those shiners, he explained, when he'd left a New York apartment rather hurriedly, i.e., when the husband of the woman he was visiting had unexpectedly walked in on them. Necessity had forced Kerouac to exit out the bedroom window, smashing his head against the backyard fence when he landed two stories down. Williams liked that story.

"They were dressed as bums," he told Fred Miller that September. In fact, he said, "they were bums, they hung around most of the afternoon into the evening until Louis Ginsberg . . . called for them in a car. [They were] reading their own poetry and prose and drinking cheap wine (all they wanted) until Floss dug out some of our own good stuff and gave it to them." Williams also took a liking to Corso and Floss spent the time talking with Kerouac in the kitchen.[19] Later Ginsberg would write a poem about that visit, remembering the master pointing out his living room window and telling Ginsberg there were "Lotsa bastards out there." Ginsberg would also add then what he could not bring himself to say to Williams personally, that he had lied to him, "told you I was never a fairy / when I was—didn't want to / shock yr palsied hand. . . ."[20] Twenty-six months after that January visit, Williams would write Cid Corman that he still heard a great deal from Ginsberg "about the Zen Budists [sic]" though their practices had not—as far as he could tell—much improved their poetry. In fact, he suspected that they were probably "maruanna [sic] users."[21] What was particularly comic about that last surmise was that he remembered how they'd smoked some funny-smelling stuff in his house when they'd visited him. And when, in '59 or early '60, Alfred Aronowitz interviewed Williams at 9 Ridge Road, discussing Kerouac's prose, Ginsberg's *Howl*, and the homosexual practices of the younger writers, Williams told Aronowitz that he'd held back from discussing "the sexual business" in *Howl*, but had praised—and could still praise—that poem's "vigor and forthrightness."[22] But in 1957 he was more unqualified in his enthusiasms. The West Coast had come "into quite a reawakening of all the arts," he wrote Roethke shortly after Ginsberg's visit. "I think you have heard of Allen Ginsberg and his gang, Karuak [he still couldn't get the name right] and Corso. What does it mean? At least we live in an age when anything goes and I for one welcome it." It was, after all, another sign of burgeoning life in American poetry.[23]

The following day he wrote to Denise Levertov, who was then living in Mexico, in the small coastal village of Barra de Navidad, north of Manzanillo. She had just written Williams about Robert Creeley's surprise visit to see her and her husband, Mitch Goodman, at Christmas and Williams, who'd finally met Creeley just before that, told her he was glad the local people who'd seen Creeley, one-eyed and bearded, walking toward her place on the beach hadn't shot him. "He sent me a couple of poems recently, short lyrics on an enormous page which after all were very good . but so few on such a big page!" Maybe, though, that was "the way to do it to give full dignity to the art." Whatever, he personally liked the man.[24] When he wrote Levertov two weeks later, it was to tell her what he thought of Ginsberg. Sometimes, he admitted, he had his doubts about the "authenticity" of some of Allen's "recent activities and also about his poetic abilities." How much of it, after all, was bold posturing to shock the bourgeoisie? Still, he'd known him for years now and knew the "gruelling time" the young man had been through, so that, having "survived and triumphed to any extent," Williams wanted "to greet him triumphantly as far as I am able." Even so, what would matter in the long run, for Ginsberg as for himself, was the poem, how one made the poem, dividing the lines on the page to make a distinctive music.[25] Besides, as he would tell Robert Lowell in April, the so-called "wild eyed radicals" who were upsetting the newspapers and the American people were really not "so wild as they think themselves."[26] Williams had seen it all years before, with the Greenwich Village bohemians and the dadaists and surrealists, and even Ginsberg could not lay claim—as he and Stevens and Crane could—to having been chased by an authentic baroness.

In May of '57 Williams and Floss took their three-week riverboat cruise down the Mississippi River on the *Delta Queen*. They'd flown out as far as Cincinnati, armed with spring wear and Mark Twain's *Life on the Mississippi*, which Floss read to Williams during the long, lazy afternoons floating down the river. The cruise photographer snapped some photos of Williams—aged seventy-three—as a fetching lady-in-waiting (one of several) carrying the "Delta Queen's" trailing skirts: some big burly cigar-chomper, perhaps some insurance salesman from Akron or Milwaukee. But that was the public, good-guy figure of Williams enjoying his retirement. The more private Williams revealed himself in a comment he made to Thirlwall three weeks after the trip, when he said that the leisurely rhythms of the *Delta Queen* and of Mark Twain's less pressured America told everyone who boarded that old, creaking stern-wheeler to slow down or go to hell, put themselves at ease as, all day, each day, they slid quietly past tree-lined shores.[27] Oh, he knew as well as the next man that, the international situation being what it was, he might well "be blown to eternity" by the jet planes he could even then—as he wrote to Pearson—hear storming high above his head in Rutherford.[28] But there were other rhythms besides the cry of the moment to heed as well, and the river had once again—thankfully—reminded him of them.

A week after they returned home, the Williamses headed up to Brandeis on the New Haven Railroad for the college's annual Spring Festival of Poetry and Music. Williams was the featured poet that year and he read them a poem—"The Birth"—he had especially prepared for the event. He and Floss stayed with Robert Lowell and Elizabeth Hardwick and their daughter and the public occasion went smoothly, except for one snag, when Richard Eberhart introduced Williams as "the Buffalo Bill of American poets." Williams let the remark go at the time; after all, Eberhart had said it in good will, as a token of his own admiration for a friend and a master. But three months later Williams told Eberhart that the comment still rankled him. "Maybe that's what you think of me, and maybe that's what I am," he told him, "but there are many connotations to the epithet which should be explained before it is accepted." After all, "the old boy," Buffalo Bill, had hardly been a writer, and besides Williams had been writing for too many years now "to be classed as a cow-hand." Better to leave that name "to such a naive poet as Carl Sandburg," he added, though he meant "no offense to Carl, by the way."[29]

That summer Williams wrote a piece for the *American Scholar* called "Faiths for a Complex World," and in it he touched on something that had given direction to his life for the past forty years. "My life is a constant watching of the field," he wrote; in fact, watching had been his "daily business." Like David Lyle, he had scanned "every newspaper, every journal, every letter, for hints as to what is going on in the world of events." He knew he could not catch everything, that there might well be "a genius in France or China or Finland" whom he had missed, and he knew his own limitations. Still, he had striven all his life to discover the gist of the new, and—though it might be suppressed at any given moment—his belief was that eventually such writing would surface to the light. If he once caught "the rumor of such things, every ounce of loyalty" in his bones compelled him "to enter the campaign to bring it to light." He had tried to adhere to that principle all his life, regardless of how much trouble it had cost him personally, and he would continue to do so until he could no longer work. For fifty years his own models had been selfless scientists like Herbert Clark—in pursuit of the *Anopheles* mosquito and the *Aedes aegypti*—who had worked long and hard to find a cure for malaria, a disease that had killed more people than all wars combined. So too with Williams, spending his life "to discover and track down that particular demon" who had been "outwitting him." As a doctor, Williams had had constantly to size people up. He was a master diagnostician and he was seldom wrong in his assessments of others: "A big dollar sign shows me at once to beware. Even the clothes a man puts on his back, his habits of speech, a snatch of conversation heard in a public conveyance or at a board meeting or country club, should be enough to alert us to what particular circle of hell he comes from."

Once, his son Bill remembered, a man had come out to talk with his parents about their finances and investments. Seated and comfortable, the man had asked Williams for his financial portfolio. His *what?* Financial portfolio. Williams got up, told Floss he had a patient to see, and left her to deal with the adviser as best she could. That was the last time Williams ever tried that kind of advice. He was after all, a poet, an artist, the Unicorn, and therefore someone with royal blood, a member of the only aristocracy that mattered: the aristocracy of talent. Let others worry about money:

> If a man is of the royal blood, an artist . . . he will be above all this. He can't afford to be caught at it. That is why men with whom you want to be associated keep themselves mostly silent, frequent mostly the family circle and groups of intimates. They do not give themselves away; the best of them are enigmas to their fellows, covertly open in their dealings with other men. They have nothing to sell.

Such men were his real treasure . . . and of course the woman, too, like the one he'd seen just yesterday at a reading. He felt proud to have been able to evoke the look he'd seen—or thought he'd seen—in her eyes. It was not vanity either—he was too old for that—nor a memory since, he added with perhaps a touch of bitterness, love had never been as sweet as that. Nor did he feel sorry for himself, since he was ready to lie down in his bed "and die as uncomplaining as any man, as my father did under similar circumstances." He was proud to have his own father as his model as he moved closer to his own death now. But it was the woman who'd kept him going, "the gentleness and tenderness and insight and loyalty of women and what they see, I am sure, in most masculine looks which should disgust them."[30]

And yet he knew that there was a dark underside to the human heart, something tied up, for example, with the way Americans had actually lived their lives in this New World Eden. So, after Floss had finished reading him Frederick Manfred's western, *Riders of Judgment*, Williams wrote Manfred to congratulate him on adding "one more chapter to the epic of our west to counteract some of the bunk that is every day filling our television scripts to the point when no adult can bear to look at them any more. Cruelty and the inevitability of cruelty is the mark of such a story [as] *Billy the Kid*," and it fed something in the human heart which could not be denied. "Morals have no part in it. Therefore I was happy to see your hero killed. He had to be. Sentimentality was kept out of the story, thank goodness." In fiction we could accept another man's tragic fate with gladness, and the inevitability of an outlaw's end even had a certain gaiety about it. Better to face one's end thus than to "skunk off," Williams added.[31]

Thus he could remonstrate with Eberhart at the same time: that Eberhart's poems were "too hopeless, too resigned in the face of an overwhelming fate without protest" for Williams to enjoy them much. Williams had "always objected to the use of the godhead as a figure in a poem" as being either redundant or tautological. But even more, he disliked a poet's crying out to God with some petition or appeal. That, he said, was "pure stupidity, . . . no better than entirely to quit the job of an artist." It was a refusal to attempt to create, to find a way out for oneself. After all, he did not believe that Eberhart was really as disgusted with life as his poem had led Williams to believe. Read *Howl*, he advised him, to see "how this Jew [had raised] his voice" against the postwar holocaust in which he had found himself.[32] (And Eberhart did just that, reviewing the book for the *New York Times*, to which Ginsberg replied with a thirty-page letter outlining his own aesthetic principles in that poem.)

In early October, Williams sent Gilbert Sorrentino a copy of the "only serious poem" he'd written in months: "a triumphant lament for the great Finnish composer Sibelius who has just died." The poem was "Tapiola," written in a measure Williams told Sorrentino was similar to his earlier step-down measure, though the lines were not so divided. But if the poem was ostensibly about Sibelius, it was more profoundly about the act of composition and the power of music—and of words—to keep off "the devil of emptiness." "You stayed up half the night," Williams wrote, remembering his own need to write at all hours of the day and night, in an

> attic room under the eaves, composing
> secretly, setting it down, period after period,
> as the wind whistled. Lightning flashed! The roof

> creaked about your ears threatening to give
> way! But you had a composition to finish that could
> not wait. The storm entered your mind where all
> good things are secured, written down, for love's
> sake. . . . [33]

The Williamses spent the last three weeks of November 1957 in California. Williams had been invited out—expenses paid—to spend three days at Berkeley's Institute of Personality Assessment and Behavior being psychoanalyzed—grilled and cross-questioned—by the institute's staff in an effort to learn what made the artist function. It was a free-for-all, Williams remembered, "when all manner of impertinent questions were asked" and all kinds of tests administered. He tried to take the proceedings lightly, to joke about it all, even as he followed the staff's orders. How many times a night did he urinate? Could he create an instant play with some dolls someone had handed him? He especially remembered one poker-faced woman analyst whom he'd tried teasing to see if she would laugh, and—that having failed—had then tried to please her, all to no avail. He found her gaze particularly unsettling and could not remember her expression changing even once during the whole time he was there. What came of it all—for he was one of five artists thus being tested—he never did find out, though he hoped someone had gotten some good out of the experiment. Certainly he hadn't.[34] For the rest of the period, he and Floss stayed with Charlotte at Eyvind Earle's home in Sepulveda. Williams also got a chance to see Rexroth again when he passed through San Francisco.

When Williams arrived back home on December 2, he found Robert Lowell's manuscript for *Life Studies* waiting for him, and Floss read the poems to her husband straight through in a single sitting. Williams was deeply impressed by that experience and told Lowell he was sure the man had advanced himself "as an artist and a man in the world." He was proud Lowell had chosen him thus to share in this "early view" of what would surely be the man's mature style. What particularly pleased him now was how Lowell had broken free of his dependence on traditional rhyme schemes and metrical forms in these new poems; that overriding sense of self-reliance had opened "a new field" for Lowell. He "needed that break," Williams emphasized, for "rhyme would not contain [Lowell] any longer." The man had too much to say to be limited by the forms of other cultures and other people.[35]

Eleven days later, Williams began yet another literary friendship, this one with a young English poet named Charles Tomlinson about whom Hugh Kenner had written him. "God be praised!" he wrote Tomlinson, "for to meet an Englishman to whom my name is not anathema is almost to be classed by me as an event. Not that I give a damn except as it

signalizes the advent of someone who may turn out to be a friend."
Tomlinson had just published a poem dedicated to Williams in *Spectrum*,
the magazine of the University of California at Santa Barbara where
Kenner taught, and Tomlinson had used Williams' step-down lines to
signal his own sense of debt to Williams. "It makes me feel that my
divisions are valid and not mere eccentricities," Williams told him, "and
that they may be susceptible of proliferation. There is no room for rancor
in any serious study of English verse, your attitude shows a lighthearted
spirit which is tremendously encouraging to me." He did not have many
friends among American and British scholars, but he was thankful for the
"small clan" of which Kenner was one and now Tomlinson another, a
clan that made "for penetration in the attack when our front must be
consolidated at all costs."[36]

Williams was glad to have Kenner on his side, he told Tomlinson in
mid-January. The poetic values he had spent his lifetime defending had
been gathering steady support, though the fight to determine whether or
not those values would win through was far from decided even then. The
intelligence, as manifested in the critical essays Williams had just read in
Kenner's *Gnomon*, would now have to be given its chance to see what it
could do for Williams and his followers. Nor was he even then sure that
his kind of poetry would win out in "the academy as it is encountered at
Oxford & Cambridge." But that was no reason for not going ahead and
continuing the fight in his own country. Let the British follow or not as
they might, he had work still to do and very little time left in which to do
it. Even Pound, he had come to see, had not taken "the necessary changes
in our poetic construction half seriously enough," sidetracked as he had
been by economics.[37]

In early 1958, as Williams put the finishing touches on *Paterson* 5, he
began to feel a profound letdown. That, plus his health, which was
beginning again to falter, now led him into what he described as one of his
"shit caked sloughs."[38] He did not like what he was witnessing all about
him in the world. There was, for example, the increased anti-intellectual
and neobarbarian front of the younger poets which, he felt, would not
bode well for the future of the craft, though he could still praise
the craft demonstrated by Olson and Creeley, Lowell and Levertov and
Tomlinson. As for politics, which he could view now only as a spectator,
that too was in its own slough of despond. Eisenhower was for him merely
a nonentity who made sure he was in bed by nine-thirty each night and
saw that he got enough exercise on the golf links, and when Ferlinghetti
wrote calling for the president's impeachment, Williams—old Democrat
that he was—was delighted. "This is one of the days when one really
doubts the possibility of a liberal political philosophy for the U.S. or the
world," he complained to Lowell in January:

The idea of capitalism and a priestly Christianity has dominated our world for too long a time. When I look at the faces of the drivers of our oversized and really inconvenient cars and how all who . . . resemble [each other] have the money for them, I see how much they [all] resemble each other. There is no liberality of mind among the lot of them.

Was Pound so very off the mark, then, with his harping on the effects of usury and greed on the very life's blood of modern society? And as for the rest of us? We'd all "go on looking at our television shows and when good, applauding them . . . all the while knowing that the sons-of-bitches among us still hold the upper hand."[39]

It was there, the sickness he felt all about him, plainly there in the face of a black man he saw in April in a subway car as he was coming back from visiting the Zukofskys over in Brooklyn. Once again Williams caught the essential human condition in the worried face of this man sitting across from him in the flickering, uncertain light of the underground:

> *a huge Negro*
> *a dirty collar*
> *about his*
>
> *enormous neck*
> *appeared to be*
> *choking*
>
> *him*
> *I did not know*
> *whether or not*
>
> *he saw me though*
> *he was sitting*
> *directly*
>
> *before me how*
> *shall we*
> *escape this modern*
>
> *age*
> *and learn*
> *to breathe again*[40]

It was amazing, he told Zukofsky in January, before his visit, how he dreaded the subway, and yet there was good reason to do so, "when you consider the circumstances, those we meet on the tubes seem to have the faces of the damned."[41] In this he was one with Hart Crane and Eliot and LeRoi Jones. *Abandon all hope.* . . . The same month in which he wrote his poem, he also wrote Cid Corman in Japan to praise him for his ability to recognize that all people were the same, all "one under the skin," and all possessed of "a universal love of life" that made Williams, in spite of everything, want to go on living. And yet what he missed in his own countrymen was that sense of breathing easily, that sense he had up till then identified with his countrymen, a people traditionally anxious to be up and about and doing. But now, in the late 1950s, for whatever complex reasons, Americans had "lost so much that formerly inspired them." Even so, as a last resort, he was willing to admit the possibility that all his grumbling about the contemporary scene might be "nothing more than the result of a hard winter and old age."[42]

February: Still in the midst of that hard winter, Williams had walked outdoors on the night of the tenth to watch the aurora borealis, as he had so often done in the past, as Stevens too had so often done. It was quite a sight, Williams had to admit, and it forced man's "puny sputniks and missiles," first hurled into the heavens by the Russians the previous fall, to "return to size."[43] Even poets were vulnerable against that vast, dark backdrop. So, when he heard that Lowell had entered McLean's in Boston for psychiatric care, Williams wrote him a word of consolation. And other sons and daughters clamoring. Now it was Raphael Wang, who had called earlier to ask Williams if he would be interested in doing some translations from the Chinese with him, who came out now to read to Williams from the Chinese of Li Po and others. "You were very kind . . . to read to me the wonderful old language which no one has been competent even faintly to reproduce," he wrote Wang on February 25. "To my mind it is futile as Pound has done to reproduce the ideaographs [sic] which are so beautiful in themselves. They can mean nothing to an English speaking reader. The sound of the ancient language is lacking. . . . It is an ancient poetry whose very feeling is too far away from us to be captured by us."[44] And yet Williams was soon collaborating on some thirty-seven translations and adaptations from the Chinese of Meng Hao-chuan, Li Po, Wang Wei, Li Yu, Tu Fu and others (though Wang did not publish these until 1966, three years after Williams' death, when they appeared under the title "The Cassia Tree" in New Directions 19.)

"In the international of the intelligence," he'd told Tomlinson in January, he knew that the artist was "often blocked" by a "lack of knowledge of a foreign language." Take himself, for example: "What would I do without my very faulty knowledge of French?! I know no Greek at all and a very scanty knowledge of German and Spanish."[45] And yet he had translated from the French, the Spanish, even the Greek and the Chinese as best he could. When he heard from Mary Barnard at the beginning of March after a long silence, she included a copy of her translations of Sappho. Williams wrote her saying he'd wished he'd known of those translations six months earlier when he'd been "forced to attempt a translation" of an important poem of Sappho's for Paterson 5. Now he only hoped she would like his own "rendering."[46] He wrote her again two weeks later to tell her how much he'd enjoyed her translations. Sappho's fragments could, after all this time, still fill the air about them.

That woman, he told Barnard, had been important for him personally because she'd provided "the modern understanding of womanhood as a variant of the male impetus which cannot show off at its maximum without the full female complement." This impetus, he added, was due women in strict justice and not as a favor, which was really how he'd always felt about them. The problem was that women themselves were "not vocal enough in their own support" and so needed someone like Sappho "to teach them how much" they needed her, which might explain why—in a male-dominated world—so much of her work had been allowed to be lost. "The brain and sentiments of a woman are triumphant in so many of the situations that concern us in our life together in the world that I am thrilled when it has to do with her champion." It was one reason he'd written *Paterson* 5.[47]

The Williamses spent a week at the end of March and the beginning of April once again at Gratwick Highlands, traveling as usual via the *Phoebe Snow* express. Williams was still waiting impatiently for spring to arrive, craving the warm weather again, and he told Eberhart the day before he left for Buffalo that if spring didn't break soon he wouldn't "care very much whether they do or do not bury me—except as Hamlet says of the body of Polonius . . . that they will whiff me on the stairs if they wait too long."[48] The week at the farm was a good one, except that, as Floss told Abbott after they'd returned home, while her husband genuinely enjoyed people, he was restless away from his typewriter. She also added that it had been a shock to her when she'd arrived back in Rutherford to see that the identity of her town really was "gone forever." What had made her realize this was the huge sign she'd seen on her return proclaiming that Virginia Dare Shops—symbols of the larger conglomerates—would soon be opening in her town. It was yet another dubious sign of progress.[49]

*
**

By May, Williams knew it was just a matter of weeks before the authorities would release Pound and let him return to Italy. For several years, Pound had solicited the help of figures like Eliot, Hemingway, Frost, Lowell, and Williams himself to help get him released from St. Elizabeth's. Williams had done what he could to help his friend, though he had had to explain to him that the Library of Congress affair had hurt his own effectiveness with the government, no matter how unjustly. There wasn't much someone suspected of being a "subversive" could do for another "subversive." Then, in September 1956 William Faulkner, who had been chosen a few months' before to head the government-backed American Writers' Group, met with President Eisenhower to talk over ways in which the image of the ugly American might be changed. On the fifteenth, Faulkner wrote to Williams—among other prominent figures—to say that he'd been asked to "organize American writers to see what we can do to give a true picture of our country to other people" and wanted to know what Williams' personal ideas might be on furthering that project.[50]

Williams answered Faulkner on the twenty-fourth, telling him to quote to the president the *"Times'* excellent editorial of the literary section, quoting in turn Earnest [sic] Hemingway on Ezra Pound. And say if the President wants to advance the cause of cultural advancement in the U.S. to see to it that Ezra Pound is released." Sure one could pay tribute to Pound, but what Williams really wanted to do was to "get him the hell out of St. Elizabeth's, have him given a passport and allow him to return to Italy where he is justly valued as a poet." He knew Pound had "made bad mistakes in the war continuing to broadcast for that sod Mousolini [sic]" after America had declared war on Italy. But he also believed Pound had paid for those mistakes "in full" and that "continued confinement" would constitute "cruel and unusual punishment."[51]

Williams' views were taken into consideration and tabulated, along with the views of other writers on other issues, by the committee, which then wrote to the other writers to ask how they felt about freeing Pound. Some were for it, they answered, some against, many with reservations on both sides of the question, although John Berryman was particularly adamant in wanting Pound released. On the nineteenth of November a letter was sent to Williams along with the other writers living in and around New York on Faulkner's list calling for a meeting of the group at Harvey Breit's home on the twenty-ninth. There they would discuss the subject of cultural exchange, the relaxation of government controls on censorship, and—at the very bottom of the list (though it had received strong support)—the freeing of Pound.

A week after Thanksgiving, Williams was one of fourteen writers who met at Breit's home. Among the others present were Donald Hall, Horace Gregory, Robert Hillyer, Saul Bellow, Edna Ferber, John Steinbeck, Donald Klopfer of Random House, two representatives of the United States Information Service, and Faulkner himself in the chair. Almost at once—though he had not told Pound what he was planning to do —Williams turned the discussion to the subject of Pound's imprisonment. Since Hillyer, who had so strongly denounced Pound when he'd received the Bollingen Award, was in no hurry to see Pound freed, and since Saul Bellow was particularly upset about Pound's anti-Semitism, the question of Pound quickly—and perhaps inevitably—degenerated into a heated argument.

But Williams was at Breit's home for one reason: to do what he could to get his difficult friend out of prison. Pound, Williams argued, had been unjustly punished, for he had already spent eleven years in an American prison without a trial; it was a disgrace for his government to "mistreat" such a distinguished poet. But young Bellow came back with the argument that Pound was an anti-Semite who deserved to be punished for his wartime collaboration and Hillyer at once came to Bellow's defense. Williams, however, refused out of his own fierce loyalties to give up Pound's defense and Bellow, after storming back and forth around Breit's living room, finally lost his temper altogether and left the house. At the moment nothing was resolved. When the committee met in Washington after the New Year, however, Faulkner—in spite of opposition—felt strongly enough about Pound's continued imprisonment to vote to have him freed as soon as possible. But somehow even Faulkner's decision was not enough to move the committee and soon after, for a number of reasons, Faulkner resigned from the committee. In the shuffle that followed, nothing more was done about Pound's release, and it would be another eighteen months before Pound was finally freed.[52]

Now, finally, in June 1958, Pound—in his seventy-third year—was being allowed to return to Rapallo. The Williamses offered their home as a convenient resting place prior to Pound's setting sail for Europe, and Pound, together with his wife and three others, stayed at 9 Ridge Road from the evening of the twenty-eighth until the morning of the thirtieth, before driving into New York City for embarkation to Genoa. "We have been deluged with newspapers and *Life*," Floss wrote Abbott the day she was expecting Pound, though she had said no to all of them. Only Richard Avedon, a photographer friend of James Laughlin's, was allowed to come out from New York on the twenty-ninth to photograph the "event," with Williams seated and Pound hovering—still—over his friend.[53]

It was Floss who recalled that stay for Abbott: the five visitors, Pound "jittery as an eel" and Dorothy "terribly nervous"; the young couple, Pound's attorney, Dan Horton, and his wife—Horton a "big 6 ft. 4 in. chap—(a good bodyguard)"; and the fifth a young woman named Marcella Spann, who was collaborating with Pound on an anthology, *Confucius to Cummings*. "When I asked why they had stopped at E.E.—I was told —there are no poets since E.E.—Ho Hum!" Ezra, Floss thought, was "definitely a mental case," and Bill had found it difficult to even talk to his friend in his insufferable peacock role. The morning they'd left, Pound had come down early with a pile of laundry and given it to Floss's maid to do. That had left Floss doing all the cooking in the kitchen in the muggy summer heat. She was happy and relieved when her company finally left.[54]

Williams himself was of two minds about the visit. On the one hand, he still felt loyal to his friend. He was convinced, for example, that Pound had spent thirteen years in an insane asylum for his ideas, that many hated him deeply for those ideas, that he himself had been "deeply involved" in those same ideas and even in Pound's fate, and that there was no hope of ever reconciling those who hated his friend. On the other hand, it infuriated him to see Pound still up to his old college tricks. Hadn't he at once taken over the living room couch where his "adorers" could worship at his feet to their hearts' content? Witnessing this parody of the Last Supper, it was all Williams could do to go out through the kitchen and down the steps to pace back and forth around his garden. It had been nineteen years since Pound had been in Williams' house, and when Pound and his entourage left on Monday morning the thirtieth, both men must have known they would never see each other again. In spite of that the visit had not been a particularly happy one. "Ezra Pound has just spent the night here on his way to the boat which is to take him to Italy," he wrote Corman that same day. That "tortured soul," he said, was still—after all those years of confinement which would have broken a lesser man—"a fury of energy."[55] Nor did it surprise Williams very much when, a week later, he saw Ezra's picture in the *New York Times* disembarking from an Italian liner in Genoa, his old friend's arrogant, unregenerate arm raised in a Fascist salute.

*
* *

That summer Williams continued to write letters—to Tomlinson, Gael Turnbull, Cid Corman, and yet new correspondents, like Tony Weinberger, whom he wrote on September 17, his seventy-fifth birthday. "I am inspired to think that you have remembered me as a poet these years past and as a man that shares your [Jewish] birthright," he wrote. "There have occurred in the past," he added, "several occasions when it would have been easy to misinterpret what I have said publicly"—he was thinking of the interview on "Nitebeat" of the previous year for one thing—and he was "happy" that Weinberger had taken "the more generous way of interpreting my position."[56]

Laughlin had a big party for Williams that same evening at his sister-in-law's home in the fashionable East Seventies. It was a good party and Williams thoroughly enjoyed himself, on top of which the Sheelers had a second party for him at their place on the Hudson near Tarrytown. He did not get home again until Monday the twenty-second, five days later. And when he did, he found his house once again in chaos—as it had been ten years before—because Bill Jr. had had to enlarge the office and was using the dining room for surgery and the living room as a waiting room. A week later, on the twenty-ninth, Gael and Jonnie Turnbull drove out from New York to call on Williams and he took them up into the attic to show him the place where he'd written for years. It was empty now, they could see, except for boxes of yellowing little magazines and old first editions—the junk pile of modernism. Williams talked briefly about the old parties he'd had out at the house, about the girls and all Floss had had to put up with, and he told them he often wondered what Floss really thought of him. But he was old now, just an old man who kept getting in the way. Better to be out of it and gone altogether and let his son take over the house. "I've always felt so lost here," he confessed to them, "this town, I wanted to get out, I couldn't stick it, so I had to write, you see, there wasn't anything else I suppose. And now my life is gone." And Turnbull could for a moment almost feel Williams' death.[57]

Young Bill Monahan had asked his mother if she would ask the doctor to read at his college, St. Peter's, over in Jersey City, a Jesuit institution. Williams said he would be glad to do it, but that he became fatigued easily now and so had stipulations that he would need met: a car to pick him up and a room to rest in before and after the reading.[58] The afternoon of October 10, a Friday, was selected for the reading and the college authorities met both Williams' stipulations handsomely, hiring a limousine to pick up young Bill Monahan and his mother and then getting Williams at his home. They also hired a hotel room for Williams' use on the main boulevard in Jersey City next to the campus. Williams spoke and read his poems—including the one he'd dedicated to the Monahans—in a low voice and, though he soon showed signs of fatigue, seemed to enjoy himself as usual. But that reading turned out to be his last, for the following evening Williams suffered another stroke. It was his first since the big one of August 1952, six years before, and though this one had not been "too bad a shot," as he tried to reassure Jim Laughlin four days later, it had been enough to lay him "low." Once more he had to be confined to his bedroom, this time for several weeks. Once more, too, Floss had become "the man of the family." The truth was that, though he spoke lightly of it, this stroke left his right arm completely useless and made his right foot drag noticeably. He did not lose any more control over his eyes, but his stuttering became more pronounced than ever. And yet he insisted on calling the stroke a minor inconvenience. It meant having to give up all reading and lecturing engagements for good, "including one to read in Baltimore the first week in November at a poetry festival at Johns Hopkins which breaks my heart."[59] He was to read for the Institute of Contemporary Arts in Washington, D.C. on the tenth, but that too had to be scrapped. In short, Dr. Irving Wright at New York Hospital had ordered complete rest for Williams for an indefinite period and no more public appearances on the platform under any circumstances. It was, in fact, the beginning of the end.

He became testy again, confined to the house as he was, and tried to keep busy by inspecting the carpentry work being done in his son's office. But all he seemed to be able to do now, as he'd said, was get in the way. When Kenneth Burke sent him one of his philosophical poems to comment on, Williams answered that he was still flat on his back and in no mood "for poetry at all, God forgive me."[60] And yet, he could still manage to write Zukofsky at the same time to say how impressed he was with Zuk's marvelous quatrains in his long experimental poem, *4 Other Countries*. Floss had been reading Zukofsky's poem to Williams when he had looked over to see how the lines had been arranged on the page. When he saw those sharp, crisp quatrains his mouth had literally fallen open. Until he could imitate what Zukofsky had done in this poem, he wrote, he was "going to stop writing forever."[61] It was form Williams was still after and not the philosophical poem, and he showed all the impatience of the old craftsman who wants to get on with his work and knows that time is running out. "It still goes on getting later and later," he told Zukofsky at the end of November, and he was still trying to write an occasional poem when he could, though now more than ever, with this latest stroke, "the clouds from a befuddled brain have first to be swept away."[62]

At a meeting of the American Academy of Arts and Letters on November 28, Williams was elected a member, and Mark Van Doren wrote at once inviting Williams to the Academy's meeting on the morning of December 5. Williams was delighted with his election, he wrote, but added that his illness prevented him from attending. Two days before Christmas he wrote Laughlin, saying he wished now in old age he had been able to find something more to believe in than "the idea of abstract love" but that—alas—he couldn't.[63] He saw no one anymore, and even Floss wrote Abbott to say that her husband's desire to be left alone was worrying her. "He doesn't want to see people," she said, "except the family. . . . It isn't like him to be that way—and by now he should be making some effort at being social."[64]

Williams had the study next to the southeast corner bedroom now; he slept alone, across from the room he and Floss had for so long shared. His snoring and restlessness had dictated that move, and so first a cot and then later a bed had been put in the study. He did not know why he could not sleep except by fits and wondered half jokingly if it was a case of bad conscience. But even awake he found himself experiencing a depression for which he could not find an adequate cause. The slightest error in conducting his life, he was learning, could become so exaggerated that it became "an obsession" with him. To help him sleep nights he began taking stronger sedatives, though he still retained his old dislike of taking drugs unnecessarily. He tried adjusting his doses of Miltown and later Nembutal to quiet his nerves, only to find that they did little more than blur his vision. He became so irritable at times, in fact, that he even found himself saying no to more and more younger writers who wanted to come out for an afternoon visit to talk with him, not because he didn't want to see them (he did), but because he found their enthusiasm often left him excited, highstrung, and unable to sleep.

And Floss: "The women as they grow older living with men (let's not say a poet, it's too close), have a shifting burden to carry," he'd written Roethke in October, just before his stroke. "I have been grateful for my woman."[65] And to Tomlinson a few weeks earlier: "I'm sorry for my wife whom, you must have understood long since, I worship tho' she will not acknowledge she finds much evidence of it sometimes in my deeds. We get along."[66] In the fall of '56 he'd told Eberhart: "Flossie cooks my oatmeal every morning as usual and kisses me good night and tucks me in as usual before turning off the light—but I go on snoring she tells me, she hears me even through the wall."[67] And to Floss herself he had written in January 1956:

> You are a silent person and not given to sing your own praise. Sometimes I forget that you are a woman and all women like to be praised—with intelligent concern for the facts. That I couldn't get along without you is obvious so it is no compliment. But all the routine things you do for me—even when you spill the oatmeal!—have to be celebrated in some way to be recognized as a deed of love, brought to the level of consciousness or they will be forgotten. . . . What we share makes the game worth while. I want to salute you with open eyes and tell you man to man that I love you more as I grow older and—that includes man to woman as far as I know anything about it. But a man does not really know what a woman wants.

And then he closed by adding, "You're a silent, patient little bitch who knows how to get her own way in the end." It was Williams' loving, "intelligent concern for the facts."[68]

*
**

After several years' delay, Julian Beck and Judith Malina's Living Theatre group finally put on a production of Williams' *Many Loves*, which opened on Tuesday evening, January 13, 1959. The theater itself was a converted department store at 530 Sixth Avenue, on the corner of 14th Street. Beck had first contacted Williams about putting on *Many Loves* as far back as May 1948, but nothing had come of it at that point. But when Williams saw Beck's performance of Gertrude Stein's *Doctor Faustus Lights the Lights* on the evening of December 14, 1951, he wrote Beck the following day to say that he was "walking in a dream, the aftermath of what I saw and heard at your Cherry Lane Theatre last evening—in all that snow. . . . Such a beautiful thing. Such a truly entrancing experience!"[69] Williams had asked Beck to do *Many Loves*, and now finally, after seven years, it was being performed.

Brooks Atkinson saw the opening night performance and wrote in the *New York Times* that Williams' play was "original in form, exhilarating in content and alive with knowledge about human beings," all of which pleased Williams, who finally got in to see a performance on Sunday, January 18. "That was a 'tonic' experience, as Brooks Atkinson wrote and a particularly pleasant one for me to have seen your production of my play last Sunday afternoon," Williams wrote two days later. "Really, I was thrilled. . . . The persistence of your effort in spite of disappointment was phenomenal—and you put it over triumphantly—to the least member of the cast, they worked together to produce not perhaps a finished performance but a performance in which you were all interested and showed your interest in the intelligent reading of the lines."[70]

"On seeing my own play / Many Loves / on the stage for the first time," Williams wrote soon after, realizing what it was he had created,

> I recall
> many a passage
> of the original con-
>
> versations with my
> patients, especially the
> women, myself
>
> the interlocutor
> laying myself bare for them
> all there. . . .

But who would take the trouble to evaluate what he had done? Still, one of the actors, his poem recalls, by learning the lines by heart, had come to him

> his face aglow openmouthed
> a light in his eyes
> Nothing more[71]

The play ran in repertory through November 17, for a total of 216 performances, and was then revived in the spring of '61, again with marked success. It also played in Europe along with Jack Gelber's The Connection and Bertolt Brecht's In the Jungle of Cities, though European audiences could not catch many of the subtleties inherent in the American idiom. (If there was a harsh note in the Living Theatre's production, however, it was in Beck's not remembering to pay Williams his share of the money soon enough, so that Williams—irritated—finally had to write Beck in February 1960 to ask him to make good on his promises of payment.)[72]

Now, too, with Paterson 5 behind him and Many Loves playing off Broadway, Williams undertook what was to be his last sustained poetic utterance: the dozen one-page poems that would make up his "Pictures from Brueghel" sequence. All twelve poems used the same short-lined tercet form, and each of the poems was either seven or eight tercets long. Williams celebrated nine paintings by Brueghel in this sequence and the fragment of a tenth: a portrait of a Dutch peasant which Williams took to be Brueghel's self-portrait. Children's Games, one of his favorite Brueghels, Williams chose to do from three different perspectives, ending his sequence with the ominous picture of children playing the deadly games of adults. For decades now he had admired Brueghel for his realism and "grim / humor," and he had made it a special point to take Floss with him to see the splendid collection of Brueghels in Vienna when they were there in the spring of '24. Now, however, it was a coffee table edition of the painter's works that Williams pored through and which gave him the inspiration to do his own word paintings.

If he chose Brueghel rather than Juan Gris or Picasso in his advanced old age, however, it was to do the old master in a dozen cubist portraits, fracturing Brueghel's surfaces to create new ones. What Williams was after, what he said he was after, was the "living quality of / the man's mind," which had always drawn Williams to this artist who had painted so splendidly his own workaday world. Just as the predominant school of Eliot had tried to absorb or dismiss Williams and had failed, so with Brueghel, Williams believed, whom the Italian Renaissance had tried likewise to absorb. There was the old master's world as he'd seen it, those fields and woods and buildings put down on canvas so that no one would ever "take that / from him," any more than anyone could take what Williams had rendered in fiction and poem from him. And that self-portrait of Brueghel, a portrait whose center pivoted on that monstrous, "bulbous nose." Even here, in this private joke on himself, Williams saw a man much like himself, a man

> unused to
> manual labor unshaved his
>
> blond beard half trimmed
> no time for any-
> thing but his painting[73]

He saw too in Brueghel's paintings the evidence of a mind that had been asked to accept what it could not: the all-pervasive Christian myth of its day. Looking at Brueghel, he thought he could see the man revealing the Virgin, the woman with no name, Kore—call her Mary or whatever —suitably rendered here "as a work of art / for profound worship." For Williams as for his Brueghel, it was still the Woman at the radiant core of these paintings who energized the entire setting, whether surrounded by "the Wise Men in their stolen / splendor" or as the eternal bride of the *Peasant Wedding,* silent among the gabbing women in starched headgear, her "hands folded in her / lap . . . awkwardly silent." And at the center of *The Corn Harvest,* the male of it over against the female, "a young / reaper / enjoying his / noonday rest / completely / relaxed . . . unbuttoned / on his back," a "spot of wine" with his lunch, forming—like the shade tree under which he rested—the "resting center of" the women's workaday world. Once again William's rendered in words Brueghel's dance in the open air, this time subtly modulating the music of the scene into something flatter and more final than the rollicking measure of "The Dance," the poem he'd written fifteen years earlier to celebrate this same painting. Toward the end of this series, he also presented the grim *Parable of the Blind*. Here, his own troubled eye on the composition of the painting—its color and strong diagonals—he caught the horror of the old men's blind faces raised as if to the light they could not see, as each figure followed "the others stick in / hand triumphant to disaster."

But it was with *Children's Games* that Williams chose to end his sequence, using the painting for three "pictures" of the world of children he too had known so intimately. The three formed a coda, a recapitulation, of the game of life itself, here in this schoolyard where children of all ages are busy at their play weddings and christenings or, more grimly amidst the din and clatter, swinging weights "with which / at random / to bash in the / heads about / them." Here too were "games to drag / the other down / blindfold," like the blind man leading the blind, and one child even leaning

> *hollering*
> *into*
> *an empty hogshead.*[74]

That last image would serve as a final summation of Williams' own life, his words reduced to a vanishing sound. Everywhere in these poems there is motion, the random, frenetic activity of life itself, a world concerned, as Williams wryly noted, only "with itself," and the artist—still in love with that world—concerned only "with it." The old master had seen it all, Williams ended, had seen it all and—like himself—

> *with his grim*
> *humor faithfully*
> *recorded*
> *it*[75]

*
**

All that winter and spring Williams continued to feel depressed and sick; clearly now the stroke of October '58 had come to have a debilitating and lasting effect on him. If he was still writing it was only to keep busy, for his mind was not at all "happy."[76] "The worst thing to do with my present life," he wrote Kenneth Burke on New Year's Day 1959, "is that with this most recent stroke, although I can sleep fairly well I am eternally so depressed that I can't live with myself and my slightest error in conducting my life is exaggerated until it becomes an obsession. Everything I do goes wrong and I never seem to learn by experience. . . .

Last night Floss tells me I slept through the New Years racket. God be praised."[77] He was confused by his condition, did not understand what was happening to him; stroke, depression, apparent recovery (at least partially), and then . . . another stroke. But at least he was seeing people again. He told Corman not to expect much when he finally saw him after having been away for several years, and he invited another young man to come out to the house, though he warned him he was not "in the best of health right now."[78] They could at least talk, at least insofar as Williams was able to. And on April 1, he told another correspondent not to expect much from writing, that it was a "tough racket" and that for every one who succeeded after a lifetime's effort there were many others who had failed. "I attended a meeting last night of the National Academy of Arts and Letters [sic] and the wrecks into whose eyes I had to look all evening far outnumbered the men and women of distinction," he noted. It took a lifetime to realize one's distinctive voice and by that time one had made so many enemies that it was hardly worth the effort it had cost. In the end what had been achieved was a style, and back of a style "the man or woman who made it having sweated his heart out for it." And that, really, was all.[79]

He'd even managed to alienate his old friend Cummings, perhaps for his comments on "Nitebeat," perhaps for something else. He confessed to Corman on April 7 that he'd heard how Cummings had rejected his name when it had been proposed for membership in the Academy of Arts and Letters, though he'd managed to be elected anyway. So it came to that, sometimes, in the end.[80] Williams still tried keeping up with the new little magazines that kept cropping up, magazines with a life of one or two issues and no more, like *Jan. 1st 1959: Fidel Castro, A legionnaire,* and *Hearse.* He was also working on the proofs for his *Yes, Mrs. Williams,* which McDowell, Obolensky would issue in mid-June, Williams having once again followed McDowell when the man left Random House to begin his own publishing house. That manuscript had been lying around in various stages of completion since the early '40s and now he wanted to get it away from him before he died. It was not a finished book—too many people (himself, his mother, McDowell) had had their hands on it—but he felt "powerless" to do anything about changing it now. What was done was done.[81]

That winter he'd also found someone who was willing to do the music for his Washington libretto: Benjamin Harris, an energetic "musician, a man of 45 with an impressive musical background" who lived over on 9th Street in Brooklyn.[82] In May he wrote Geffen at the American Academy about Harris' wanting to see her about the score Harris had completed by then for *The First President,* adding that he knew very little personally about the man.[83] In June he mentioned to Denise Levertov that Harris had "written a piano score of the opera in addition to the full orchestral score" and that he was trying to interest the City Center people in putting it on. The man might be crazy, Williams added, but there was no stopping him and he was personally glad to finally have someone interested enough in his libretto to have done the kind of work Harris had done.[84]

In May, by way of a gesture of reconciliation, Williams wrote Cummings to tell him how much he'd liked his "Thanksgiving," a poem on the Hungarian uprising of '56 which Selden Rodman had just that morning read him. Williams had reviewed Cummings' *95 Poems* a few months earlier and was "heartbroken" that he'd missed that poem then. It may have been as a result of Cummings' response to this letter—a response that did not come for several months—that Williams wrote his own "Poem" about the craft of the poem: "I was much moved/to hear/from him if/as yet he does not/concede the point/nor is he /indeed conscious of it/no matter."[85] Since Williams had had his reservations about Charles Norman's biography of Cummings, stressing that nowhere in that biography could he learn why Cummings broke his lines as he did, Williams' poem constituted a subtle joke that continued that argument in the division of his own lines, even as it went to some pains to assure Cummings that—whatever differences the two of them might have about their craft—he still loved the man.[86]

In July Williams heard again from Pound, who wanted to let him know about the true origins of World War II, and how ol' ambulating dunghill Roosevelt had all along known about the attack on Pearl Harbor because U.S. intelligence had managed to crack the Japanese code before the attack had taken place. Pound was busy then reading Samuel Johnson's *Dictionary*. "It's an old story by now," Williams wrote back on the twentieth, "but I'm happy for you that you have your freedom." Better to let the two poets go their own ways "for the few years that are left to us on this earth. . . . I won't say that my verse no longer interests you, it may on occasion, but your own verse is . . . so much your primary interest that it excludes all else, which is natural." He himself could of course no longer read, and asking Floss to read a dictionary—Dr. Johnson's or anyone else's—was out of the question. Poor Floss: with her neck collar on again, looking tired, and her voice going hoarse. "She reads me a novel once in a while—translated from the Mexican or the Japanese (there [are] some good ones like *Snow Mountain*) or even the Russian." And was it true that Ol' Possum's young wife was about to have a baby? More power to him.[87]

"Today or tomorrow I have to go into the N.Y. Hospital for an operation during which it will be determined whether or not I have a malignancy in a form possible of successful operative attack," he wrote Zukofsky on August 12.[88] He did have a malignant tumor of the rectum and a resection was done on that, in one stage, without the necessity for a follow-up colostomy. "It was a rough experience," his son Bill remembered, and though Williams "looked like death warmed over for a week or so post operatively . . . , he had a surgical cure."[89] At one hundred and twenty pounds Williams looked cadaverous, and he knew it. Marie Leone on the staff at Passaic General still remembered Uncle Billy and sent him a get-well card. "I didn't come to our hospital for the job they had to do on me. No one will blame me," he wrote on September 18. "Whatever the result will ultimately be all you need to know is that I love you all [at the hospital] as I have always loved you. And it's a curious thing after one has loved a group for a long time you love every individual in the group as if he or she was your sister! That's nutty! but a fact."[90] But twelve days earlier he'd written more darkly to Fred Miller in Vermont to say he'd "been through a session with the knife" and had been home only a few days. He was still feeling "rocky," though the surgeon—one of the best they had—had "cut the gut" out of him, and done "a clean job" of it as far as he could tell. As for poetry, though a few months before he had thought he was through writing, he could see there was more work to be done in the field. Yet he knew too that for him personally it was "still tough titty." He could still see his way clear into the province of the poem, at least for a "short distance ahead," though he almost despaired now of ever "bringing the critics round" to his "point of view." Not that it mattered in the long run, of course, since it would be the poems themselves he had written which would be "the final criteria." Either they did or did not have "the goods," and there only time would tell.[91]

As for the younger competition, what he saw of their work in the little magazines at least boosted his own badly sagging spirits. "When I see how unenlightened, technically unenlightened, many of our prizewinning poets are," he told Cid Corman in mid-September, "I do not feel discouraged though my time is running out. Once in a while I can still do it." He saw nothing new, for example, in the poems Ginsberg and the other beats were writing now. The truth was that they were really far more conventional than they suspected they were. Except for their business acumen and their ability to stay in the limelight, they couldn't touch a poet like Louis Zukofsky, who was still "miles ahead" of them all when it came to making the poem new.[92]

A week later—on September 22—he wrote Denise Levertov to praise her for some of her new poems and to tell her he'd been ill for the past month. He was "just now beginning to get on" his feet again after an ordeal that he called, simply, "not a pleasant experience." He hoped to recover his appetite in another two to three months and thus put some of the twenty pounds he'd lost back on. He was even "beginning to want to write again," so that with time "the urge, the mysterious urge" might return. He had already written one short poem, about the return to life after the operation, which he called "The World Contracted to a Recognizable Image":

> at the small end of an illness
> there was a picture
> probably Japanese
> which filled my eye
>
> an idiotic picture
> except it was all I recognized
> the wall lived for me in that picture
> I clung to it as to a fly[93]

It was during the summer and late fall of this year that he undertook a series of poems for his grandchildren as a kind of legacy that he might leave them: Paul's two, Suzy (fifteen) and Paul (seventeen), as well as Bill's three: Emily (nine), Erica (five), and Elaine, the baby. Again Williams used the jagged tercets he had used in the Brueghel sequence to capture the sense of energy and even indwelling mystery he saw in his grandchildren. It was as if, having ended the sequence with children at play in a sixteenth-century painting, he now opened his meditation to include his own grandchildren at play about him, as they often did. "A bunch of violets clutched," he wrote of Suzy, perhaps his favorite:

> in your idle
> hand gives him a place
>
> beside you which he cherishes
> his back turned
> from you casually appearing
>
> not to look he yearns after
> you protectively
> hopelessly wanting nothing. . . . [94]

And Emily, "long legs / built / to carry / the small head," enough to show Williams that the dance was her "genius," and "the cleft in / your / chin's curl" a signature that she had the courage to see the dance through.[95] And young Paul, like his own son Bill, spending hour after hour patiently catching blackfish with an art approximating his own, sharing the flesh, but knowing that the "blackfish heft / and shine" was his and his alone, like Williams in the ecstasy of snagging another poem.[96]

*
**

By the beginning of 1960, Williams saw that he had managed, in spite of everything, to write enough new poems since *Journey to Love* and *Paterson* 5 to make up one final volume. This one he would give to Jim Laughlin as a final gift and he wrote to tell him to look for that volume in another year. The young, after all, by their inability to write poems, were forcing him "to keep eternally at it."[97] He did not like what the "so-called 'beatnics'" were doing with the poem, despite his earlier praise of Ginsberg, for he still demanded, as he wrote the Canadian poet Irving Layton in late February, an irreducible "minimal of regularity, not completely breaking down to a formlessness" as the beats seemed to be doing. Not Richard Wilbur, then, but not Ginsberg or Corso either, at least not in their present modes. Layton, by his own "formal improvements," had finally arrived, and now Williams wanted to caution him to watch his step "facing the bastards—on both sides of the New World border."[98]

That same month Williams' introduction to Anthony Bonner's translation of *The Complete Works of François Villon* (Bantam) appeared in paperback, in which Williams obliquely set the fifteenth-century Parisian student against the young of his own day. Villon "must have wandered the city's shabbier dives whenever he felt the urge to go wherever the fancy took him," Williams knew from his own experience, and yet the Frenchman's art, "bred of his literary training, was a restraining influence that protected him," reared as he was "in a tradition of scholarship which kept his head high." Villon, then, was Williams' man, and the essay gave him one of his last opportunities to talk about a poetics that was central to his own practice. "Direct is the word for every word that Villon set down," he wrote. "There was no intermediate field to his address. He was directly concerned in the affairs of his life, took his responsibilities deeply and, as he grew older, bitterly, but saw no reason to seek to avoid them or to confess them."

Coming from the man who had written "Asphodel" and "The Sparrow" half a dozen years earlier, Williams' comments sounded like Stevens' "Farewell to Florida," as he turned in his last years away from the confessional to a new preoccupation with the object under his immediate scrutiny. Directness. Not ideas about the thing but the thing itself. "That directness of a wholly responsible man among his peers entered into the very structure of his verse," Williams noted. "When he used a figure of speech it was not 'as if' but coming from *himself* in one of the 'disguises' that the world forces us to wear. . . . To Villon, any ruse, or indirect approach, even at the excuse of art, savored of the lie." So the old dialogue with Stevens, four years dead, continued in Williams' celebration of one of his own fathers.[99] "As if." Stevens' signature of the conditional masquerading as certitude, ghostly presences in the poem hovering over the void. No. Make it rather of this. Of this:

> *Blocking the sidewalk so*
> *we had to go round*
> *3 carefully coiffured*
> *and perfumed old men*

> *fresh from the barbers*
> *a cartoon by Daumier*
> *reflecting the times were*
> *discussing with a foreign*
> *accent one cupping his*
> *ear not to miss a*
> *syllable the news from*
> *Russia on a view of*
> *the reverse surface of*
> *the moon   .*[100]

In late February the Williamses flew down to Tampa, Florida, for a month to escape the worst rigors of another winter. They rented a bungalow on the beach next to Ken Burke and his wife, with stores nearby to take care of whatever diminished needs they had. Once again, Williams did not bring his typewriter with him. After all, this was to be a month spent relaxing, sightseeing, and taking long walks on the beaches. But, compulsive worker that he was, the enforced rest made him all the more restless and fidgety. He took the newly finished sections of Zukofsky's *A* with him to have Floss read to him on the beach, but that long poem still eluded his grasp, as it had for twenty years past, and he gave it to Ken Burke—that omnivorous reader—to pore over instead.[101]

Burke would remember an incident during this stay in Tampa when he and Williams had strolled slowly down the beach together. It had suddenly made him more aware of what Williams had meant by insisting so long on contact with the things of one's world. "A neighbor's dog decided to accompany us, but was limping," Burke wrote:

> I leaned down, aimlessly hoping to help the dog (which became suddenly frightened, and nearly bit me). Then Williams took the paw in his left hand (the right was now less agile) and started probing for the source of the trouble. It was a gesture at once expert and imaginative, something in which to have perfect confidence, as both the cur and I saw in a flash. Feeling between the toes lightly, quickly, and above all *surely*, he spotted a burr, removed it without the slightest cringe on the dog's part—and the three of us were again on our way along the beach.

Tactus eruditus: the knowing touch. For Burke that incident summed up Williams' kind of poetry: a sheer "physicality imposed upon his poetry by the nature of his work as a physician."[102]

"It was cold in Florida," Williams wrote Zukofsky on his return home in early April, "but we amused ourselves picking up shells. Not too pleasant in the driving wind most of the time, we would have been lost without the Burkes to take us about the waterfront whenever they could find the time for it. The jet and helicopter were marvelous, they whisked us about the cities of our flights like enormous soulless presences which they are bearing us in their bellies, we and our trivial businesses. It will take some time before we waken from the vision." Thus the poet on the inner nature of the businessman's flight from Tampa to Newark.[103]

But at least one very good poem had come out of that stay in Florida: "Tribute to Neruda, the poet collector of seashells." "Now that I am all but blind," he began, "however it came about,/though I can see as well/as anyone—" his imagination had also turned inward on itself as his mother's had in her old age. Her native tongue, he remembered, had been Spanish, like the Chilean poet, Neruda's, collecting seashells "on his/native beaches, until he/had by reputation, the second/largest collection in the world." So now Williams too collected seashells on the Florida coast and listened still in old age to the sea and the sound of the sea in those shells strewing the beaches. "Be patient with him, darling mother," Williams ended his poem, for the

> changeless beauty of
> seashells, like the
> sea itself, gave
> his lines the variable pitch
> which modern verse requires.[104]

The same day he wrote Zukofsky, he wrote in a similar vein to Denise Levertov, telling her to take care of herself and to keep on with her writing. And though he loved her, he advised her not to bother coming out to the "suburbs where you can do nothing to help us find ourselves in this mystifying dilemma in which we all find ourselves. The poet is the only one who has not lost his way. . . ." At least he was back at his typewriter again and soon able to type again.[105] Since he could hardly read, his only contact with the page was to remember where the keys were and work that way. And for a while now he was really terrified that even that little contact had been lost when he forgot where the keys were. But he soon recovered from that scare. Still, now that he could feel his memory also beginning to fail him, he began to think of quitting writing for good.[106]

On Friday, April 8, James Laughlin drove out from New York to talk with Williams. Ostensibly he was there to go over some business matters, including the new book Williams had mentioned in January as still progressing, but in truth something else was on Laughlin's mind. He himself described this meeting with Williams in a slightly disguised short story called "A Visit," how he'd chatted a while with Floss and Bill, and then, the business part of it over, had left to return to New York, only to turn his car around somewhere on the highway and drive back to 9 Ridge Road. Floss met Laughlin at the door and could see how desperately he wanted to speak with his old friend. Bill was upstairs resting, she told him, and then motioned him to go up. He walked upstairs alone, knocked on the door, and then sat on the edge of Williams' bed in the shadows of the drawn curtains to tell him now how sorry he was that there had ever been a falling out and that he wanted, before it was too late, to try to rectify things as much as he could. It had been ten years of strain, of lost opportunities, of anger and stubbornness on Laughlin's part, he was willing to admit, but he wanted a chance now to work with this man who had been so central to his whole dream of a new direction in writing.[107] Both men were so touched by this encounter that five days later Williams wrote Jim Murray to say that the cold war between the two men for which Murray had acted so long as intermediary was over for good.[108] By mid-June, Williams had terminated all of his business connections with McDowell and the McDowell, Obolensky Press. He was determined to go "back to New Directions for the last time, making a clean sweep of it." And to Laughlin he wrote that it felt good to be back with his old publisher for what he knew would be "the last time."[109]

"After weeks of depression WCW has bounced back to a manic state," Jack Thirlwall noted in his private papers on July 9. That new sense of activity, he saw, had been the "result of a visit from Jim Laughlin, who is to publish a volume of new poems, reprinting the short stories and a collection of plays. . . . Bill has split with McDowell and plans to stay with Jim L. until death. Floss came down and mixed us all a Tom Collins and approved the new JL, whom she believes to be a changed character. . . ."[110] Laughlin was in fact changed, and he pushed himself (and Williams and Floss) first of all to get all of Williams' short stories together and publish them the following year under the title of the newer long piece that had appeared in the *Hudson Review* in '57: "The Farmers' Daughters." As for publishing the collected plays, there was no problem. Williams would have to finish *The Cure*, which still had no completed third act. By constantly coaxing and personally editing the fragments that Williams had managed to compile, Laughlin was able to get Williams to "finish" the play, though it still creaked heavily in places. By early '61 galleys would be ready for both volumes, and Laughlin lined up Van Wyck Brooks to do the introduction to the short stories and Jack Thirlwall to do a "Notes" at the back of the volume of plays on Williams as playwright.

What could not be reversed, however, was Williams' continued slide downhill. "I have gone far backward in my personal condition though I still write an occasional poem of questionable merit," he wrote. In fact, as he told one correspondent in mid-April, he was "slowing up to such an extent that I can scarcely write a proper letter any longer."[111] And again, twelve days later, to another correspondent: "I'm getting old, frighteningly old sometimes, parts of the equipment doesn't [sic] seem to work any more," though he still wanted to shake hands with this well-wisher as long as he could lift a hand.[112] And to Abbott on May 12: "My own progress is not so good but I can't complain. Everyone says I LOOK wonderful and the mirror seems to verify it but my feet and the inside of my head give them the lie."[113]

On Wednesday afternoon, May 25, the American Academy of Arts and Letters honored Hilda Doolittle at its annual meeting in New York with the Award of Merit Medal for Poetry. It was the first time a woman had ever received this coveted award, presented only once every five years, and Mark Van Doren as president made the presentation, quoting from H.D.'s "Sea Gods" of forty-five years before. In spite of his health, Williams insisted on making the trip into New York to see his old friend, and John Thirlwall drove him and Floss into the meeting. Thirlwall found a folding chair for Floss and then had to sit on the steps next to her, the place was so crowded. Eberhart was there, and so was Roethke, but Williams was primarily interested in seeing H.D., which he was able to do for only a few minutes at the back door before she left. She had slipped on a rug several years before and had permanently injured her hip, so that she too—like him—walked only with difficulty. "The old gal is a notable figure and a distinguished poet right to the end," he wrote Eberhart two weeks later. "Didn't she make a grand entrance to the platform with her crab's walk brushing all formality aside in her determination to be there?" Having seen her, Williams himself had ducked out the back door, unwilling to face the crowds milling about.[114] It was the last time he would ever see the woman who had meant so much to him a half century and more before. As for H.D., when she came to write about that moment and that award, it would be St. John Perse (who had steadied her as she walked up to the podium) and not Bill Williams whom she would recall in *Helen in Egypt*. She had still not forgiven him for what he'd written in his *Autobiography* about her and Bryher and McAlmon. But Williams himself had been, as he told Ezra that November, "very happy to see her again."[115] As for Floss, she merely noted that she and her husband had been "delighted to see H.D. poor dear" who seemed "as youthful as ever" and her "usual flustered" self.[116] A year later H.D. was dead.

At the end of April Williams had been asked by Louis Zara to write an introduction to a deluxe Ziff-Davis photographic project that would celebrate the timeliness of Whitman's *Leaves of Grass*. For Williams it was a chance to make his final assessment of the variable foot, but he also found himself "reading" Whitman with a new attention to that poet's images. The photographs, he noted, had made "the poem come alive" for Williams as though he were reading it for the first time. What these stills allowed him to do in fact was to rest the eye and "penetrate into the depths of the picture—to turn about in the full ease of Whitman's phrase to stretch 'and play at my ease.' " These photos did not ridicule the people they portrayed as the comic strips did, but gave back to the viewer something of "that dignity that Whitman has proclaimed for us as human beings." And for that Williams was thankful.[117] He thought his essay one of his "best pieces of prose,"[118] though it was in fact loaded with a high quotient of redundancy and was moreover a recapitulation of ideas he'd already emphasized years before, especially the idea of Whitman as rude progenitor of a new measure. (On June 11, for example, he told Tomlinson that "Whitman was a clumsy artist," but "the first to hold the bridge-head.")[119] But the fact that he had been able to sign a contract with Zara for the portfolio had made him inordinately proud. In spite of setback after setback, he could still keep his metaphoric pecker up. "I can't tell you how happy your letter has made me," he told Zara on June 1. "I don't dare attempt it lest you find out what an emotional creature I have become in my old age—at the same time I can still write when I am pushed to it by such a man as you, God bless you."[120] What Williams could not know then was that the book would not appear until 1971, and then only with new photos and a heavily edited version of his introduction.

In late July the Williamses, accompanied by Thirlwall, flew out to the University of Indiana at Bloomington to hear Mary Ellen Solt talk on the variable foot and the American idiom in Williams' work. The professors there, Floss noted afterward, didn't like Bill and not one had turned out to hear Solt or see her husband. But Williams himself had been disappointed by Solt's talk. She was faulty in her thinking, he told Denise Levertov ten weeks later, and besides, her prose had no edge and was not "thought through." And though he had waited a long time for her talk, he'd been shocked when he'd actually heard her deliver her paper. And yet, though she hadn't put her ideas over either effectively or convincingly, he was still sure she was right in her underlying premises about his art. What was still needed, he was coming to understand, was a way of communicating what he knew to be true about his measure.[121]

August and September were taken up by Paul and Jinny's divorce after years of attempting one kind of reconciliation or another. Still, though Williams had seen it coming, the actual divorce had threatened to upset his "microscopic household."[122] Paul moved in once again with his parents at 9 Ridge Road, along with young Suzy, who was just beginning her third year at Rutherford High. Paul Jr.—a six-footer and a good athlete—was about to leave for Bates and would return to his father (who had received custody of both children) at Christmas. Floss herself felt relieved now that the inevitable had happened, but Williams was more depressed than ever that such things had to be.

In August too Williams sent out nearly fifty mimeographed copies of a two-page essay he'd written summing up his ideas on "The American Idiom." Coming as it did shortly after Mary Ellen Solt's talk, it may have been meant to correct whatever misconceptions he thought she might have had. He scattered the copies to people all over the face of the earth, including Pound (for whom he wrote a comment at the bottom: "Ez: you are the first user of the American idiom of our day.")[123] He was therefore disappointed when only three people acknowledged his final "manifesto," two of whom were Tomlinson and Corman.[124]

It was indicative of his general mood at this time that he could congratulate Winfield Townley Scott on deciding to stay in Santa Fe instead of coming back east to be blown to hell.[125] And in June he'd told Corman that he agreed with him "about the noise of our streets and the clutter of cars and of our minds" which forced American writers "to a distorted violence in our verse and plays."[126] And ten days later he complained to Tomlinson that he'd been "heartbroken" at the failure of the garbagemen "to take away the trash from our curb during our trash removal week." Even when they had come finally they'd done "a very slovenly job of it." What troubled him was that, except for the serious artist, no one seemed to care much anymore about the work they performed.[127]

He was still writing a "few horrible poems a month," sometimes aware of what he was doing and sometimes merely drawing a blank.[128] He knew too that it was getting harder and harder to get even the shortest lyric down on the page to his own satisfaction. So for three days and nights in early October, for example, he had worked and reworked his "Jersey Lyric," a poem based on a lithograph called *Jersey Composition* which his young painter friend Henry Niese had sent him to announce an upcoming showing of his work. Finally, after seventy-two hours, Williams had managed nine lines:

> *view of winter trees*
> *before*
> *one tree*
>
> *in the foreground*
> *where*
> *by fresh-fallen*
>
> *snow*
> *lie 6 woodchunks ready*
> *for the fire*[129]

Williams had Robert Lowell out to his house on October 8 to listen to Lowell's translations from Baudelaire and the French classics, which were to go into *Imitations* the following year. It was amazing, Williams told Levertov, how the American idiom had penetrated that man's work. He had kept his own counsel when Lowell was out to the house, but he wanted her to know how good he really thought Lowell was.[130] Four weeks later it was Levertov herself who was out to see Williams and to read from her own new work, especially "The Jacob's Ladder." Williams thought about that poem and decided finally how very much he had liked it, writing her the day after her visit to say how sorry he was that he hadn't been able to catch some of the poem's subtleties when she'd first read him the poem.[131]

In mid-November, he had to consult his doctor about the possibility of yet another operation, this one for the prostate. But this time it was good news. "He shoved his finger up my ass and when he told me I didn't need an operation I literally jumped for joy. . . . The old mind again is my chief tormentor," he told Fred Miller. "When I can escape its torments I am invariably a new man." Now he could get back to writing his poems "when they continue to come to me if they ever do."[132] Then, a few days later, having just escaped the knife, he had another cerebral accident, though this one was comparatively mild. What it did do, of course, was remind Williams—and Floss—that the end was lumbering closer.

There was one bright spot, however. After eight years of Republican rule, John F. Kennedy had been elected to the presidency in early November. Back in '56 Williams had had read to him not once but twice young Kennedy's *Profiles in Courage,* and though he'd made some damaging comments about the senator to John Wingate in '57, he was elated to see that Kennedy had won. It had been a close election, and the "margin of victory" had been "too narrow to be comfortable." But the young senator from Massachusetts had managed to "put the skids under" Richard Nixon, a man whom Williams, thinking back to the McCarthy hearings, found "so despicable that the thought that he might now be the President of the U.S. still" gave Williams "bad dreams."[133]

*
**

1961: With the New Year, a new beginning. Incredibly, despite illness, despite depression, Williams began work on a sixth book of *Paterson* during the first week of the new year. The figure of his old enemy Hamilton was very much on his mind, but so were dandelions and old Hudson River stoneware, the kind of work Charlie Sheeler had taught him to admire. He was taking stronger drugs now, Alertonic for one, and feeling their effect—as of a snake coiling around his brain and eyes and legs—and his typewriter still remained his only touch with the world of the imagination. If he could only free himself, lift his dead right arm, or command his eyes to focus, he had it in him to do his best work ever now. "Dance, dance!" he wrote, the letters of the words forming among other extraneous letters on the blank page before him: "loosen your limbs from that art which holds faster than the drugs which hold you faster —dandelion on my bedroom wall." He managed a few pages, then slid them into his top drawer. There would, after all, be no *Paterson* 6.[134]

Once again, he complained, the winter was killing him, and he was reduced to communicating by keeping one finger of his left hand "wiggling" wormlike on the typewriter. It was a major effort now for him even to get over to Carnegie Hall to hear young Paul Zukofsky in a violin recital on February 12. He kept writing Louis to say he wasn't sure if he could make it in, but he was going to try. Only a snowstorm on the 12th kept him from attending. The more helpless he found himself the more depressed he became. He watched young Kennedy on television assume the office of the presidency, saw the lectern smolder as old Frost began to read his poem and may have cheered inwardly as the thing caught fire. Kennedy's inaugural speech with its promise of a new beginning, he told Pearson, had even given him the heart to want to survive the winter and go on living.[135] But it was almost impossible for him to do anything like sustained work. He tried correcting the galleys of his plays and then, in a fit of despair (like the one Floss remembered he'd had after the stroke of '52) he sent them back to Laughlin for Thirlwall to check over. At the end of February he managed to see one of two performances of his *A Dream of Love* staged by the National Arts Club in New York, but that too required a herculean effort. He still tried doing an occasional prose piece for a friend, but found his body balking him. So, for example, he had to write Robert Lowell apologizing that he was keeping his appreciation of the *Imitations* to a few short paragraphs only because of his "confused mental condition."[136]

It was just a matter of time. "I don't know what is happening to me the last few days," he wrote Laughlin in mid-March, but—before it was too late to do anything—he was asking for that last book of poems he'd mentioned the year before.[137] Laughlin wrote back at once to assure his friend that the book would be done as soon as possible. Ten days later, Williams told Fred Miller that he was having real trouble now remembering where the hell the keys on his typewriter were. If he suddenly stopped writing, he tried to explain, that would be the reason. "Nice to have known you Fred," he finished. "Tough titty!" On top of all that, there was the enactment of Paul's and Jinny's divorce and the radical dislocation that was causing at home. "A poet," he conceded, was "a curious beast to house in a family especially a poet" who was "half crazy to begin with."[138] And six weeks later, again to Miller, he spilled out his fears:

> The thing that frustrates me is that I cannot read more than a few lines before the type blurs and I am lost. It is maddening to be so cut off within myself. If it was not for Floss I could not communicate. . . . Maddening. And yet when someone reads to me I can understand perfectly. . . . Something has happened to me.[139]

And yet he could manage a poem—a very good poem—when the mists momentarily lifted. On April 10, for example, he wrote, at the tail end of his life as a poet, the poem he insisted should come last in his last book of poems: "The Rewaking." The end was upon him, he realized, and yet, by virtue of the imagination, he might push that end back a bit further. "Sooner or later / we must come to the end / of striving," he wrote (the break between the second and third lines reversing the sense of closure), of striving "to re-establish / the image the image of / the rose." That cut two ways: we came to the end of striving by finally re-establishing the rose. Or we finally came to the end of our striving to re-establish the rose because death intervened.

And the rose, laden with significances from Dante's time to his own:

> *but not yet*
> *you say extending the*
> *time indefinitely*
>
> *by*
> *your love until a whole*
> *spring*
>
> *rekindle*
> *the violet to the very*
> *lady's-slipper*
>
> *and so by*
> *your love the very sun*
> *itself is revived*[140]

From summer's rose back to spring's early flowers to the source of spring, the source of life itself: the sun. And the sun revived by nothing less than love, by nothing less than Floss's daily care for him.

But Williams' vein was not yet worked out. Two days later, on April 12, Williams—along with millions of others—heard the electrifying news that a man had successfully entered outer space for the first time and had been returned safely to earth. Yuri Alekseyevich Gagarin, strapped into a Vostok spaceship, had completed one orbit of the earth, reentered the earth's atmosphere, and then parachuted safely back to earth. That flight had signaled yet another new dawn, as Williams knew, as he knew also that what had made that flight into the dark heavens possible had been a new measure. Hundreds of thousands of scientific measurements to end here once again: in the dance of this man above the clouds. In Gagarin he saw, no doubt, not only a brother of Mayakovsky and the Russians who had selflessly defended Stalingrad during the war, but a figure of the poet himself. "He could have / gone on forever," Williams recorded, before he returned to take his place "among the rest of us." And, "from all that division and / subtraction," like Williams still at it measuring his lines, had arisen the dance:

> *toe and heel*
> *heel and toe he felt*
> *as if he had*
> *been dancing. . . .* [141]

Williams sent that poem to Laughlin on April 15 and, as he had all his life, went on to the next poem while the ecstasy of creation was still upon him. This time, however, the letters and the words absolutely refused to cohere on the page. He kept trying over and over, returning each morning to his typewriter while the anxiety mounted, determined to lay his meaning on the new white sheet in front of him. Week followed week, yet he could get nowhere, as Floss could see when she went up to check on him.[142] Page after page, discarded, lay there crumpled on the floor. She could not understand *what* her husband was trying to communicate, nor could Williams any longer tell her what it was he wanted to say. His blurred eyes looked hopelessly up at her, and then he became frenzied. Floss tried to calm him down, to tell him that his poem would come. No use. He signaled for her to leave him alone and feebly pushed her protesting aside; he even threw some things around the room before going back exhausted to his machine. He *would* do it or he would die trying. There was nothing for it, then, but to let him work before demanding that he rest. For six weeks Williams kept at it, Floss downstairs anxiously listening for the familiar click of the typewriter, though the dance of the keys was decidedly more erratic now.

And then it happened. It was Friday, June 2, and he was apparently working on the same poem that had eluded him now for six weeks (though Floss could not tell for sure) when suddenly—there was a lightness, a *ping*, and then Williams fell with a thud to the floor, unconscious. He had had another cerebral hemorrhage and had to be rushed by ambulance to Passaic General once again. "I very much fear this is the end for him—as far as any creative work is concerned," Floss wrote Fred Miller three days later. "I hope I'm wrong—but things don't look good."[143] Yet, incredibly, Williams was back at his typewriter again by the end of June. Floss had been advised, she told Pearson, to let him alone, let him work for an hour, and then divert his interest elsewhere. But in a week all he'd managed to do was to make "several hundred copies of the poem—all the same—all terribly misspelled."[144]

But that was not the worst of it. He worked as he could all through July trying to get his typescript for *Pictures from Brueghel* into some kind of order and then, one evening early in August, he finished up his clean copy of the poems, including his corrections and the new poems he had done that spring, tore up the painfully completed clean copy, hobbled slowly downstairs, and dropped the pieces into the garbage can out back. Floss had been watching her husband's erratic behavior closely and, when she realized what he'd just done, she ran down the back steps, emptied the garbage, and retrieved the poems. "Not that it would have made any important difference to the world's peace," he explained sheepishly to Laughlin on the seventh, by which time Laughlin had the patched-together poems safely in his office, "but at just the time of sending you the final draft of the poems. . . . I thought my mind had finally given up the ghost." He was feeling a little better now, and he was thankful that Floss had been so vigilant. But he wasn't fooled; he knew his condition was extremely precarious.[145] "I should be steadier in my psychiatric stability but that takes time," he wrote Laughlin on the sixteenth. "Maybe it is gone forever." Now, however, that "certain family imbalances" had been removed—by which he meant Paul's family's adjustment to the divorce which had so profoundly disturbed him (though he kept mostly silent about it)—he was still hoping he might "right himself" before he capsized completely.[146]

After the severe spasm of June, Williams' typing became extremely poor, for he now had trouble keeping his memory intact long enough to create coherent sentences. There were still lucid moments and even a few more poems, but for the most part Floss was simply forced to destroy Williams' letters and write them for him herself. She did not want anyone seeing her husband in his present condition. In the meantime, Laughlin went ahead setting up *Pictures from Brueghel*, having decided that he would include both *The Desert Music* and *Journey to Love* in the new volume and bring out all three in a paperback format. Williams was delighted. Thirlwall still came out to see the Williamses, though less frequently now because Williams was tired of dredging up his own past or discussing the meaning of his work with his biographer or with anyone else.[147] And when, at the end of September, Thirlwall was leaving the house and Williams, rather than give him his customary "Au revoir," said simply, "Good-by," Thirlwall felt that something profound had come upon the man. His hunch was confirmed when Williams called him a few days later and told him not to bother about coming out that Saturday to talk. He wanted to watch the New York Yankees and the Cincinnati Reds play ball rather than talk about poetry anyway. He was sure this was going to be the last World Series he would ever see and he didn't want to miss it. That same month Williams wrote Denise Levertov a short note to say: "I can't describe to you what has been happening to me," and she too was struck by something in his words, a something that found its way into her poem "Sept. 61," about how the old masters —Pound and H.D. but especially this man—were all disappearing over the hill forever.

For years Williams had been unable to read or to lecture, but he still found it difficult, after so many years of neglect, to give up readings or personally accepting all the honors that were coming his way while he spent his days pacing his living room or lying down in his study. During the third week of October alone, Floss wrote Laughlin, Harvard, Bryn Mawr, and Haverford had all invited Williams to their campuses to read. "It is all so depressing for Bill—who reacts with unnecessary emotion," she told him. "He knows he can't read—and he should be able to toss it off." But she also knew that to relinquish such contact—such final recognition—was for Williams paramount to relinquishing life itself.[148]

But by mid-November, Williams could no longer even kick against the inevitable. Now, the man who had written eight years before that he would regret more than anything else the time when he could no longer put down "the words / made solely of air / . . . that came to me / out of the air / and insisted / on being written down" finally gave up writing forever.[149] There would be no more flowers, no more poems. Even Floss was puzzled by her husband's firm resolve not to write anymore. "He ought to write," she confided to Thirlwall in early December, "but he won't." Instead he just puttered around the house, inevitably getting in the way.[150]

That same month, Stanley Koehler and a photographer from the *Massachusetts Review* came out to interview Williams and to photograph him in his study dressed in sports jacket, sport shirt, and bowtie —none of which matched. The *Massachusetts Review* gathering, published in the winter of '62, was itself an assemblage of mismatched parts, though its primary function was to give homage to the old revolutionary, and this it did succeed in doing. Koehler was back the following April to interview Williams for the *Paris Review*. But by then Williams, though he could see that Koehler was trying to understand him, soon became impatient with his own inability to make himself understood or even to find the words he needed. Finally Williams simply dragged himself out of the room to let Flossie finish the interview for him as best she could.[151]

"I have been ill for over a year and unable to communicate with you," Williams wrote Tomlinson at the end of January. "I picked up an old copy of the magazine *Poetry* and stumbled on a poem that you had written. It had a familiar ring, called to mind something over which we had been working together. It's a theme familiar to me which we had not worked out by half. Go on developing the theme for there is much good grist still in it." But, in spite of Williams' enthusiasm, Tomlinson was never able to figure out which poem Williams had meant.[152] Five days later Williams wrote to Tom Cole, misdating the letter November, the month he'd given up writing. "I'm almost reduced to silence due to my inability to frame a word which would make sense," he wrote. "So have to rely on Floss to do it for me. Yet I must make the attempt. It's hell." He mentioned his new book of poems, which he was impatiently waiting to arrive, adding that since he'd assembled that he'd been "able to do nothing." There was a note attached to the letter from Floss. For two years the *Ladies' Home Journal* had been after Bill for a poem and he had finally complied by sending "The Dance." Now she had just learned that they had turned it down as not "sufficiently clear" for their readership. Oh well. Cole had recently heard from Pound and Floss couldn't help adding that neither Bill nor she had heard from him now for nearly two years.[153]

Fearing that her husband would not survive the winter, Floss flew down to St. Thomas with him on February 15 for a three-week vacation. It would give him a chance to see once again the island and the town where his father had grown up. But Williams was restless the whole time. "I can't say the trip did him any good!" she told Laughlin the day after they returned. "He was ready to come home the day after we landed there." The only thing on his mind was seeing a copy of *Pictures from Brueghel*.[154]

Thus the months dragged on, spring giving way to summer, summer to fall, as Floss marveled at her husband's patience in the face of his inability to read or write or even talk now. In the special Fiftieth Anniversary number of *Poetry* there appeared the last poem Floss was sure her husband had written. It was a short piece, still explosive and dynamic, about their young Shetland pup, "Stormy":

> *what name could*
> *better*
> *explode from*
>
> *a sleeping pup*
> *but this*
> *leaping*
>
> *to his feet*
> *Stormy!*
> *Stormy! Stormy!*[155]

In mid-September, Floss took her husband for another three-week vacation, once again to the Virgin Islands. But that trip too did little good for him.[156] Her old neck injury was acting up again and she was still forced to wear her orthopedic collar for months at a time. She continued to take care of her husband, though there were days when the time seemed to drag interminably or when her vocal cords were raw from reading to him hour after hour. But it was one of the few pleasures still remaining to him and somehow she managed to carry on. In early November, Laughlin wrote to Williams to tell him that it was beginning to look as though even the English were finally about to sit up and take notice of his poems and fiction. Williams might soon have an English publisher. On the eleventh, Williams managed his last letter to Laughlin, perhaps his last letter to anyone. "If it only showed a corresponding penetration on the part of the [English] critics I'd be made," he managed amidst many verbal and syntactic repetitions and misses on the typewriter he could scarcely guide now even by touch. And then, by way of farewell: "You have been very faithful, it is deeply appreciated. I wish I could write as I could formerly."[157]

Paul Blackburn had called Williams in mid-October, and—like Denise Levertov the year before—was so struck by what he heard on the other end of the receiver that he wrote a poem about it. He called it, simply, "Phone Call to Rutherford":

> *"It would be—*
> > *a mercy if*
> *you did not come to see me . . .*
> *I have dif-fi/ culty*
> > *speak-ing, I*
> *cannot count on it, I*
> *am afraid it would be too em-*
> > *ba*
> > *rass-ing*
> *for me ."*
> > *—Bill, can you still*
> > *answer letters?*
> *"No . my hands*
> *are tongue-tied . You have . . . made*
> *a record in my heart.*
> > *Goodbye."*[158]

Christmas came and went, Floss adding in her Christmas cards to Bill's old friends that he was failing rapidly now and that she herself was not in the best of health. "So be it."[159] Then it was another New Year. It was a brutally cold winter, the winter of '63, and Williams, too weak even to travel south, was sleeping for longer and longer periods at a time. "Bill isn't too well," Floss wrote Byron Vazakas on February 27. "He has had so many strokes. . . . The days—drag . . . I read to him all I can—but my vocal chords [sic] give out . . . But we carry on."[160] March 1 had always signaled the real beginning of the year for Williams, but that too came and went without incident. And then, on the morning of the fourth, when she did not hear Bill moving around by half past eight, Floss went to wake him up. As usual, Stormy followed her to the closed door. Floss opened the door, but this morning Stormy refused to follow her into the room. Instead he lay down and began to whine. Floss walked over to the bed, and looked at the small figure facing the wall. She knew at once that, finally, the end had come.[161] She called Bill to examine his father for the last time and pronounce him dead, just as Williams had done for his father forty-five years before.

*
* *

The previous December 12 had marked the Williamses' fiftieth anniversary. Half a century together, nearly all of that time in that house. And now, as spring began to steal in, Williams had gone. The family waked him in a closed coffin, covered with some of those spring flowers he'd celebrated again and again in his poems. Once, when Floss had asked him what kind of service he would want, he had told her a simple one without "a lot of religious stuff." So now a young Unitarian minister was called in to say something and read Williams' early "Tract," written forty-five years before, with its instructions to his townspeople on how

> to perform a funeral
> for you have it over a troop
> of artists—
> unless one should scour the world
> you have the ground sense necessary. . . . [162]

Many of those townspeople came now to say good-by to their doctor-poet, including some—like the police officer whose patrol car led the funeral procession out to Hillside Cemetery a mile away—who had been brought into the world by the man they were now taking out of it. At the cemetery, where Elena and William George Williams and three Hermans already lay buried, the mourners—including Floss and Bill Jr. and his family and Paul and his second wife, Betty, and his children, waited in the cold rain under a tent for the services to conclude. Halfway through, an old beat-up car carrying some of Williams' sons from New York, caught in the morning traffic, pulled up in time to let these young poets pay their last respects to the man who had taught them so much about the craft: Gilbert Sorrentino and Le Roi Jones and Joel Oppenheimer, among others, dressed in ill-fitting dark suits as a mark of respect and carrying their own spring flowers for Williams' coffin. It was the classic gesture of the pastoral elegy, of poet paying homage to poet.[163] "A magnificent fight he made of it," Pound had cabled at once from Italy, breaking his self-imposed silence. "For you he bore with me sixty years. I shall never find another poet friend like him." Now, that magnificent fight was over.[164]

Marianne Moore had written Floss immediately when she'd heard of Williams' death, but had asked Floss not to try to answer at once but to wait till things were quieter. Floss waited six weeks and then answered. She was spending a few days with Paul and Betty at a place called the Skytop Club in Pennsylvania when she wrote her old friend. She and Bill had had a good life together, she told her, fifty years of it "and all but the last few years when he could no longer read—write or at last not talk—years to treasure—full of companionship—partnership—ups & downs—in fact a *life*."[165]

*
**

Floss outlived her husband by another thirteen years. When she died on the morning of May 19, 1976 at 9 Ridge Road she was eighty-five. A local Presbyterian minister read the service, including at the sons' request the Twenty-third Psalm and "Asphodel." In his last years Williams had talked with Floss over whether or not his body should be buried or cremated. Finally, he'd opted for being buried in the local cemetery, the (slightly) false dream of New York shimmering over the ridge nine miles to the east. Someday Floss would join him. But Floss, at the last, made another choice: to be cremated, her ashes scattered, for reasons known finally only to herself.

*
* *

It had indeed been quite a life: the uphill struggle of an American revolutionary to establish—against the incredible odds of neglect, misinterpretation, dismissal—an American poetic based on a new measure and a primary regard for the living, protean shape of the language as it was actually used. It had been a fight, a magnificent fight, against the academy, against the numbing sclerosis of the universities, against the very scholars of the language (there were none, Williams insisted), against special interests of all kinds, and he had had to create a strategy and sometimes even desperate homemade measures where none had existed before. He had had to fight long and hard, only to be repeatedly dismissed by critics (who should have known better) as a minor, inconsequential poet, a latter-day imagist, a clown, a bumpkin incapable of serious consecutive thought.

Williams had of course heard it all countless times. And yet he kept on writing his way because he knew that he was right, as even Pound had to admit tacitly and as hundreds of other poets would soon become convinced. But Williams was not after personal glory. In fact he despaired of its ever coming his way and felt uncomfortable with it when it finally did come. He disliked being lionized and he had to ask younger poets not to call him father or maestro. He wanted rather to be viewed as one of the gang, as part of a community of disinterested craftsmen, members of a guild, who would have the dedication of scientists in the field passionately searching for answers. He was self-effacing, hardworking to the point of its finally killing him, and generous as few poets have been generous. He was a man of rare honesty, easy on others but extremely hard on himself, a man who had made mistakes, who had faltered or run up blind alleys in his single-minded "selfish" pursuit of his poetry. But he was above all a lover, a lover of people, a lover of his world, a lover of his craft. He wanted a poetry that would speak with an authentic accent directly to his own time, for he was a citizen of his world—which he knew intimately—in ways that few others had come to match. And, in his insistent manner, often alone, he did manage to effect a revolution in the word that is still being felt, a revolution that has affected and will probably continue to affect poetry in America and elsewhere far into the next century.

In midwinter 1956 Williams, then seventy-two, had written Louis Zukofsky to say that he had a picture postcard sitting on his desk

> sent to me by a friend, a woman living in Brasil now, whom I met in the nut house when I was there. It shows four old musicians walking poorly clad in the snow from left to right between—or approaching a village no doubt somewhere in Europe. They are all scrunched together their instruments in their hands trudging along. I mean to keep the card there a long time as a reminder of our probable fate as artists. I know just what is going on in the minds of those white haired musicians.[166]

His was a life devoid of the dramatic tragedy or intense pathos of some other poets, a life lived by choice in the provinces, attending the needs of the people he came up against in Rutherford, Hackensack, Passaic, Carlstadt, Lyndhurst, Garfield, Paterson. But it was a life too that kept in constant contact with the intellectual currents of New York as that city grew from a provincial capital into the leading cultural center of the world. His was, then, a representative life and he was himself a Representative Man as Whitman had been in Emerson's sense of that phrase: a figure who in his actions and his words had raised his particular world to the level of art with a single-mindedness and persistence approaching the heroic. What made it difficult for many Americans, let alone others less centrally concerned, to accept this estimation of Williams was that they could not believe that the major poet could happen here, here in the postlapsarian, gritty yet burgeoning world of America. It was Williams' genius to have seen—seventy years ago—that it could happen here . . . and that it did.

Notes

The following abbreviations for works by William Carlos Williams are used in the Notes:

AQQ   *A Book of Poems: Al Que Quiere!* The Four Seas Company (Boston, 1917).
KH   *Kora in Hell: Improvisations.* The Four Seas Company (Boston, 1920).
SG   *Sour Grapes: A Book of Poems.* The Four Seas Company (Boston, 1921).
GAN   *The Great American Novel.* Three Mountains Press (Paris, 1923).
SA   *Spring and All.* Contact Publishing Company (Paris, 1923).
IAG   *In the American Grain.* Albert & Charles Boni (New York, 1925).
VP   *A Voyage to Pagany.* The Macaulay Company (New York, 1928).
WM   *White Mule.* New Directions (Norfolk, Conn., 1937)
IM   *In the Money.* New Directions (Norfolk, Conn., 1940)
W   *The Wedge.* Cummington Press (Cummington, Mass., 1944)
P   *Paterson.* New Directions (Norfolk, Conn., 1963). Books 1 through 5 appeared respectively in 1946, 1948, 1949, 1951, and 1958.
CLP   *The Collected Later Poems.* New Directions (Norfolk, Conn., 1950).
CEP   *The Collected Earlier Poems.* New Directions (Norfolk, Conn., 1951).
A   *The Autobiography of William Carlos Williams.* Random House (New York, 1951).
Al   *The Autobiography of William Carlos Williams.* Unpublished version, in the Collection of American Literature, Yale University.
BU   *The Build-Up.* Random House (New York, 1952).
SE   *Selected Essays of William Carlos Williams.* Random House (New York, 1954).
SL   *The Selected Letters of William Carlos Williams.* Edited with an introduction by John C. Thirlwall. McDowell, Obolensky (New York, 1957).
IWWP   *I Wanted to Write a Poem: The Autobiography of the Works of a Poet.* Reported and edited by Edith Heal. Beacon Press (Boston, 1958).
YMW   *Yes, Mrs. Williams.* McDowell, Obolensky (New York, 1959).
FD   *The Farmer's Daughters: The Collected Stories of William Carlos Williams.* New Directions (Norfolk, Conn., 1961).
ML   *Many Loves and Other Plays: The Collected Plays of William Carlos Williams.* New Directions (Norfolk, Conn., 1961).
PB   *Pictures from Brueghel and other poems,* including *The Desert Music* and *Journey to Love.* New Directions (Norfolk, Conn., 1962).
I   *Imaginations. (Kora in Hell, Spring and All, The Great American Novel, The Descent of Winter, A Novelette and Other Prose).* Edited with introductions by Webster Schott. New Directions (New York, 1970).

EK   *The Embodiment of Knowledge.* Edited with an introduction by Ron Loewinsohn. New Directions (New York, 1974).

Int   *Interviews with William Carlos Williams.* Edited with an introduction by Linda Welshimer Wagner. New Directions (New York, 1976).

RI   *A Recognizable Image: William Carlos Williams on Art and Artists.* Edited with an introduction and notes by Bram Dijkstra. New Directions (New York, 1978).

Rome   *Rome.* Edited with an introduction by Steven Ross Loevy, *Iowa Review,* 9, 3 (Spring 1978), pp. 1–65.

Diary   WCW's unpublished Diary for January–June 1924, in the possession of the Williams family.

Also the following abbreviations:

ND   *New Directions*

WCWN   *(WCWR* as of Fall 1980*) The William Carlos Williams Newsletter* (now *Review*).

Letters EP   *The Letters of Ezra Pound: 1907–1941.* Edited by D. D. Paige. Harcourt, Brace & World, Inc. (New York, 1950).

Letters WS   *Letters of Wallace Stevens.* Selected and edited by Holly Stevens. Alfred A. Knopf (New York, 1966).

The following abbreviations are used in the Notes for some of the many *dramatis personae* in WCW's life. Where confusion might result, the name itself is given.

CA	Charles Abbott	VBJ	Viola Baxter Jordan	KR	Kenneth Rexroth
BB	Bob Brown	AK	Alfred Kreymborg	TR	Theodore Roethke
EB	Edmund Brown	AL	Amy Lowell	WTS	Winfield Townley
KB	Kenneth Burke	DL	Denise Levertov		Scott
MB	Mary Barnard	HHL	H.H. Lewis	AT	Allen Tate
CC	Cid Corman	JL	James Laughlin	CT	Charles Tomlinson
EEC	E.E. Cummings	RL	Robert Lowell	JT	John Thirlwall
NC	Nicholas Calas	RLL	Ronald Lane	BV	Byron Vazakas
RC	Robert Creeley		Latimer	EW	Edgar Williams
TC	Thomas Cole	DM	David McDowell	FW	Florence Williams
ED	Edward Dahlberg	FM	Fred Miller		(Floss)
HD	Hilda Doolittle	GM	Gorham Munson	HHW	Raquel Hélène Ho-
RE	Richard Eberhart	HM	Harriet Monroe		heb Williams (Elena)
TSE	T.S. Eliot	MM	Marianne Moore	MW	Monroe Wheeler
CHF	Charles Henri Ford	NM	Norman Macleod	WCW	William Carlos
FMF	Ford Madox Ford	RM	Robert McAlmon		Williams
BG	Bonnie Golightly	MN	Marcia Nardi	WEW	William Eric
HG	Horace Gregory	EP	Ezra Pound		Williams
JH	Josephine Herbst	NHP	Norman Holmes	WGW	William George
KH	Kathleen Hoagland		Pearson		Williams
RJ	Richard Johns	JR	John Riordan	LZ	Louis Zukofsky

LETTERS

One of the major problems facing the biographer of Williams today is the gathering of the thousands of still unpublished letters that he wrote and scattered all over the face of the earth. Williams never kept copies of his letters and so, while most of these are now housed in a few major library repositories or are still in the possession of the Williams family, many important letters are to be found in some seventy other library collections and many others are still in private hands. These letters keep showing up like unexpected gifts for the biographer and will no doubt continue to do so for years to come. Some, like WCW's letters to W. H. Auden and Yvor Winters, have been destroyed, others are lost, other collections—for a variety of reasons—are not now available. Many family letters still remain in the family: most of WCW's letters to his wife and his letters to his older son. If WCW's letters to his son Paul still exist, they are not now available. Many of WCW's early letters to his brother, Edgar, are in the Poetry Collection of the State University of Buffalo, though Edgar Williams' family is still in possession of others, at present unavailable to researchers.

In the late 1930s Charles Abbott, curator of the Poetry Room then in the Lockwood Memorial Library on the old Buffalo State University campus, had the foresight to begin collecting manuscripts and working papers by contemporary poets, and WCW generously "unloaded his attic," giving many manuscripts and letters written to him to this collection, designated in the Notes as B. In the early 1950s the American Collection at Yale became, as WCW phrased it, "the active buyer," especially through the industry of Norman Holmes Pearson. This huge collection, which contains so much of what WCW wrote, especially from the mid-1930s until his death twenty-five years later, is designated in the Notes as Y. In the 1960s the Research Center of the University of Texas at Austin purchased several large collections of WCW's letters, including most of the eight-hundred-odd letters WCW wrote to Louis Zukofsky from 1928 until 1962. This third major repository of WCW papers is designated T in the Notes.

The letters to Charles Abbott are in the B Collection, as are those to Robert Beum and Charles Keppel. The letters to Mary Barnard, HD, Josephine Herbst, Viola Baxter Jordan, James Laughlin (copies), H. H. Lewis, Robert McAlmon, Henry Niese, Norman Holmes Pearson, John Sanford, John Thirlwall, Byron Vazakas, and many to Edmund Brown, Ezra Pound, and Louis Zukofsky are in the Y Collection. The letters to Oscar Baron (Barondinsky), Julian Beck, Kay Boyle, Cid Corman, Edward Dahlberg, Charles Henri Ford, John Herrmann, Bonnie Golightly, Dwight Macdonald, David McDowell, Marcia Nardi, Carl Rakosi, Frances Steloff, as well as a large selection to Zukofsky are in the T Collection. The letters to E. E. Cummings, James Laughlin (originals), Amy Lowell, Robert Lowell, Pedro Salinas, and one to T.S. Eliot are at the Houghton Library, Harvard University, a collection designated H in the Notes. (The other Eliot letters are in the possession of Mrs. Valerie Eliot.) The extensive collection of letters written to Kenneth Burke from 1921 until 1959 are in the Pennsylvania State University Library. The letters to Robert Creeley and Babette Deutsch are at Washington University, St. Louis. The letters to Richard Eberhart and David Raphael Wang are at Dartmouth, those to Theodore Roethke at the University of Washington, Seattle. The letters to Kathleen Hoagland, John Riordan, and—in part—those to Fred Miller and Edmund Brown are in the Clifton Wallis Barrett Collection of the Alderman Library of the University of Virginia, a collection designated as ViU in the Notes. The letters to Gorham Munson are at Wesleyan University, those to Nathanael West and Bob Brown at Southern Illinois University at Carbondale. The letters to Gilbert Sorrentino, Emanuel Romano, Richard Johns, and many of those to Fred Miller are at the University of Deleware, designated D in the Notes. The letters to Nicholas Calas, Louis Untermeyer, Bill Bird, and those to Pound written between 1921 and 1923 are at the Lilly Library, Indiana University, designated as L in the Notes. The letters to Waldo Frank and I. L. Salomon are in the University of Pennsylvania Library. Those to Monroe Wheeler, Tony Weinberger, Richard Wirtz Emerson, as well as a group to Louis Zukofsky, are in the McKeldin Library, University of Maryland; those to Marianne Moore are at the Rosenback Foundation in Philadelphia. The letters to Wallace Stevens and Conrad Aiken are at the Huntington, designated Hunt. in the Notes.

The letters to Hart Crane and Allen Ginsberg are at Columbia University; those to David Ignatow at Kent State; those to Kenneth Rexroth at UCLA. The letters to Malcolm Cowley are at the Newberry Library, Chicago; those to Horace Gregory are in the George Arents Research Library for Special Collections at Syracuse University; those to Harvey Breit are at Northwestern University, with a few at Fairleigh Dickinson; those to Rolfe Humphries are at Amherst College; those to Charles Tomlinson are in the Kenneth Spencer Research Library at the University of Kansas; and those to Marjorie Allen Seiffert (Elijah Hay) are at the University of Colorado, Boulder. Those to Irving Layton are at the University of Saskatchewan; those to Charles Olson at the University of Connecticut; those to John Berryman and Frederick Manfred at the University of Minnesota; and those to Selden Rodman at the University of Wyoming. The letters to Walter Arensberg are at the Huntington and at the Francis Bacon Library; those to H. L. Mencken in the Enoch Pratt Free Library (Baltimore); those to Winfield Townley Scott are at Brown University; those concerning the American Academy of Arts and Letters are in their archives. The John Gould Fletcher papers, including the exchange between Fletcher and Amy Lowell, are at the University of Arkansas, Fayetteville.

Princeton University holds the *Broom* collection of papers, as well as WCW's letters to Sylvia Beach, Allen Tate, and R. P. Blackmur. The *Little Review* papers, including WCW's letters to Jane Heap, are housed in the Fromkin Memorial Collection of the University of Wisconsin–Milwaukee. The extensive *Poetry* magazine papers, including WCW's letters to Harriet Monroe, Ronald Lane Latimer, Morton Dauwen Zabel, and Karl Shapiro, are in the Joseph Regenstein Library of the University of Chicago. The *Partisan Review* papers are at Rutgers University, including WCW's letters. The Free Public Library in Rutherford contains several letters, tapes, manuscripts, and photographs, most of them donated by the Williams family itself.

There is, of course, John Thirlwall's edition of WCW's *Selected Letters*, McDowell, Obolensky (New York, 1957), which WCW himself oversaw, and the larger manuscript version of letters containing many more unpublished letters, which is now in the Y Collection. Important letters from WCW to various correspondents have appeared and will continue to appear in the little magazines and quarterlies, as in the selection of letters WCW wrote to Ivan Goll and to Denise Levertov that appeared in two issues of *Stony Brook* magazine (although Denise Levertov graciously provided the author with copies of all letters in her possession for this biography). Other letters have appeared in *Pembroke* (Norman Macleod's letters from WCW), and several letters WCW wrote Norman Holmes Pearson have appeared in successive issues of *WCWN*. There is as yet no satisfactory edition of WCW's letters, and it appears as though it will be a long time yet before such an edition becomes available. Many individuals own important manuscript letters of WCW's. In some cases they are the original recipients of letters from WCW; in other cases letters have come into the possession of individuals through purchases. Such letters are designated Pri. in the Notes. The largest single private collection, of course, belongs to the Williams family.

Ezra Pound's letters to WCW are divided between the B and Y Collections, with several letters still in the Williams family collection. Louis Zukofsky's letters to WCW are divided between the Y and T Collections, with several in other collections. Most of the early letters to WCW—i.e., of those which he chose to save—are at B (i.e., those up through ca. 1940). The later correspondence to WCW, very extensive, for the period ca. 1940–1963, is largely housed in the Y Collection.

MANUSCRIPTS

Most of Williams' extensive manuscripts are housed, like the letters, either in the B or Y Collection, although there are significant exceptions. *Paterson*, for example, is divided–scrambled really–between B and Y, although the early *Detail and Parody for the Poem Patterson* is in H and the crucial 1945 rejected galleys are now at Kent State. Most of the earlier works, i.e., through ca. 1945, are at Buffalo, including the 1927 Journal, from which *The Descent of Winter* was extracted, and *The Wedge*. The manuscript of the *Autobiography* and those for most of the works WCW published from the mid-1940s on are in the Y Collection. But many of WCW's earliest poems, including the original text of *Poems* (1909), edited by William George Williams, and several important early sheafs of poems in the Viola Baxter Jordan Papers are in the Y Collection. The original typescript of *The Great American Novel* passed from Pound's hands to Bill Bird's hands and thence to the Lilly Library. But many library collections have WCW's manuscripts because WCW was generous with these and gave them as gifts, so that they have ended up with the papers of a particular person when they were given to a library. So, for example, WCW gave Louis Zukofsky many such manuscripts for his help in editing; he gave Horace Gregory in 1944 a penciled copy of *The Wedge* that is now at Syracuse and David Ignatow a copy of *Paterson* 3 now at Kent State. In 1940 WCW gave the librarian at Middlebury College the various manuscripts for *In the Money*, the novel he had just completed.

The B Collection has been ably cataloged and published as *The Manuscripts and Letters of William Carlos Williams in the Poetry Collection of the Lockwood Memorial Library, State University of New York at Buffalo: A Descriptive Catalogue*, Neil Baldwin and Steven L. Meyers, with a foreword by Robert Creeley, G.K. Hall & Co. (Boston, 1978). The standard bibliography remains Emily Wallace's *A Bibliography of William Carlos Williams*, Wesleyan University Press (Middletown, Conn. 1968), with addenda provided periodically in the *WCWN*. For an overview of the literature surrounding WCW's critical reception from his beginnings up through the mid-1970s, see my *William Carlos Williams: The Poet and His Critics*, American Library Association (Chicago, 1975).

Chapter One. The Beast in the Enchanted Forest: 1883–1902

1. See *A*, p. 3. Few primary documents written by WCW himself have turned up for these earliest years. There is a dog-eared scrapbook filled with faded postcards, mostly from relatives and friends to WCW's mother, written in French and Spanish and English, in the possession of the family. There are legal documents and certificates. But for the most part we must still rely on WCW's memories of his youth, as we have these in letters, poems, and especially his *Autobiography*. This exists in the published version and in the original, unpublished version. For the most part this document was written rapidly and without checking dates and facts when WCW was in his late sixties.

2. *A*, pp. 3–4.

3. *A*, "The Bagellon House," pp. 6–8. WCW would recall this scene again at the end of *P* 5, written when he was in his early seventies.

4. *Al*, See also *YMW*, passim.

5. *YMW*. Also, see *A*, pp. 23–24.

6. This saying, or a variant of it, appears in several of WCW's letters and again in *P5*.

7. Following all the changes in WCW's "history" of his grandmother would make a picaresque odyssey in itself. WCW's references to his lineage through his grandmother appear in his letters, poems, and in *A*. Early on Emily Wellcome became a central mythic presence for him, the details changing to fit WCW's own needs at any particular time.

8. WGW, always a silent man when it came to his own personal history, remained particularly silent about his own paternity, having solemnly promised his mother to respect that silence.

9. Some of these photographs still remain in possession of the family.

10. Marriage license (Pri.).

11. *A*, pp. 9–10.

12. See the early chapters of *A*. There are also some revealing scenes that WCW wrote into *Al* and then chose to leave out. These suggest his fear and repugnance at the memory of these primal events, so different in tone from his more professional stance of treating them as amusing and harmless hallucinations.

13. *A*, pp. 16–17. See also *Al*.

14. *A*, pp. 167–168.

15. "The Last Words of My English·Grandmother," *CEP*, pp. 443–444.

16. "The Wanderer: A Rococo Study," *CEP*, pp. 3–12.

17. *P5*, p. 238.

18. *A*, passim. The poems too are filled with explicit or oblique references to WCW's father.

19. WCW to LZ, 15 Feb. 1943. (T)

20. *A*, pp. 279–280.

21. *A*, p. 15.

22. *A*, pp. 15–17, passim.

23. *A*, p. 106. The copy of WCW's *Poems*, marked up by WGW, is at Y.

24. Y.

25. *CEP*, pp. 371–374.

26. See *Blues*, No.9 (Fall 1930), 22–23.

27. *A*, p. 14.

28. The facts surrounding HHW's early life have been gleaned from scattered references in *A* and *Al*, *YMW*, *SL*, *CEP*, *CLP*, unpublished letters, and scattered interviews with WCW.

29. A copy of one of HHW's oil paintings, *Portrait of a Niece in Mayagüez*, picturing one of her brother Carlos' children and painted about 1880, appears following p. 130 of *RI*. Another is the portrait of Emily Wellcome which, like the *Portrait of a Niece*, hung for many years in the living room of 9 Ridge Road.

30. WCW learned of this offer of marriage only after his mother's death in 1949, when he discovered the letter of proposal in his mother's old Catholic missal.

31. WCW to BB, 11 May 1930.

32. *YMW*.

33. *A*, pp. 15–16.

34. *Al* and unpublished letters from WGW to WCW (Pri.).

35. *CEP*, pp. 375–378.

36. *A*, p. 27.

37. *I*, p. 83. From *Partisan Review*, IV, 4 (Summer 1939), 41–44.

38 Susan Vreeland appears in *A* and in the early drafts for *P5* (Y).

39. In old age and suffering genuine mental anguish, WCW would remember this scene again in his poem "To A Dog Injured in the Street": "he took a hunting knife / and with a laugh / thrust it / up into the animal's private parts. / I almost fainted." *PB*, p. 87.

40. See *A*, especially "A Look Back," pp. 279–285. Also references to Rutherford in unpublished letters of WCW and FW, as well as a radio script describing the town, delivered in July 1955 for "This Is America" (Y).

41. *A*, p. 281. Also *Al*. Given the circumstances of his memories of her, WCW seems to have felt a strong sexual preadolescent attraction to his fourth-grade teacher, not an uncommon phenomenon in nine-year-old boys.

42. Interview with Dana Ely, March 1979.

43. WGW to HHW, postcard mailed from Geneva, 6 Aug. 1897 (Pri.).

44. See *A*, pp. 28–34, also *Al*, where WCW dwelt longer on the darker side of his school year abroad.

45. See opening of "Asphodel," *PB*, pp. 153–155.

46. *Al*.

47. See early chapters of *A*. Also *Al*.

48. A group photograph of the Rutherford football team, taken about 1900, has penciled in on the verso the names and positions of the team members.

49. See *A*, "Paris," pp. 35–42.

50. *A*, "Back to School," pp. 43–49. Also *I*, passim.

51. See WCW's high-school transcript for the three years he spent at Horace Mann (where WCW's birthdate is incorrectly entered as 17 Sept. 1884). WCW entered Horace Mann officially eight days after his sixteenth birthday: 25 Sept. 1899. His record for the three years was as follows:

1899–1900:

	ENGLISH	LATIN	HISTORY	CHEMISTRY	ALGEBRA	DRAWING	MANUAL TRAINING
Dec. 1	E	C	E	C	B	C	C
Feb. 1	D	B	D	C	C	B	B
April 1	D	D	C	C	C	B	A
May 15	C	D	C	C	C	B	B

1900–1901:

	ENGLISH	FRENCH	PHYSICS	PLANE GEOMETRY	DRAWING	MANUAL TRAINING
Dec. 3	D	C	C	B	C	B
Feb. 1	D	B	C	C	B	B
April 1	C	B	B	C	C	A
May 31	C	B	B	C	C	D

Chapter One. The Beast in the Enchanted Forest: 1883–1902 (cont.)
1901–1902:

	ENGLISH	GERMAN	FRENCH	HISTORY	ALGEBRA	PLANE GEOMETRY	DRAWING	MANUAL TRAINING
Dec. 3*	U	A	U	U	U		U	C
Feb. 1	C	B	C	D	D		D	B
April 1	C	B	C	C		C	C	A
May 31	B	C	C	D		C		A

*Quarter term when WCW was out sick with adolescent heart strain due to physical exertion in running.

52. WCW referred to this incident on a number of occasions: in *A* and in *I*, especially p. 6.

53. Quoted in the June 1950 interview with John Gerber, as edited by Emily M. Wallace (*I*, p. 8). Also in *A*, p. 47 and in *IWWP*, p. 4. In her essay "The Forms of the Emotions . . . the Pointed Trees" (*William Carlos Williams*, ed. Charles Angoff, Fairleigh Dickinson University Press [Rutherford, N.J., 1974], pp. 20–30), Emily Wallace assumes that WCW's poem "Tree," published in *The Dial* (Jan. 1927), was actually composed by WCW about 1893 when he was ten. The "evidence" for this assumption is the "original manuscript" of "Tree" in the Beinecke (Y), a reproduction of which appears between pp. 24–25 of Wallace's essay. This reproduction shows the poem written in ruled prose lines on the left side of the ms. page with a drawing of a tree on the right of the page together with two girls standing by the tree. One, in a sailor blouse, pulls on a leafy branch while the second watches. The name "William Carlos Williams" is printed boldly at the top of the "poem." Wallace's is a humanly appealing story: WCW at forty-three remembering the ready-made he'd constructed at age ten. Rod Townley for one, in his *The Early Poetry of William Carlos Williams*, Cornell University Press [Ithaca, 1975], sees this as "an indispensable document" in understanding WCW's early poetic development; Wallace's discussion, he says, "is so sane, sensitive, and thorough that there is not much need to comment further" (pp. 27–28).

But in fact there is need for further comment, for WCW is not the author of that drawing. It is, in fact, the work of a now anonymous fourth- or fifth-grade student, probably a girl, from the local Rutherford grade school. For in Williams' attic one can still see, though some of these have crumbled badly, another ten drawings of trees with the same poem, "Tree," printed out in ruled lines and "William Carlos Williams" printed neatly across the top. They are all done on the same kind of school-issue yellow drawing paper as the one in the Beinecke. What probably happened is that WCW visited the local school in the early 1930s as a living example of a real poet and then the children were set to copying WCW's poem, oblivious to the niceties of line break. These were later presented to WCW, who thumbtacked them to the walls of his attic study, along with postcards from Pound and Zukofsky. The thumbtack indentation can still be seen in the photo reproduction, and even the girls' dresses are in the style of the '30s rather than the 1890s. We cannot be sure, therefore, as Townley claims, that WCW had "perpetrated something of a hoax" or even that WCW was capable of "writing excellently at ten and execrably at thirty," but only that he was capable of writing execrably at thirty.

54. *I*, pp. 7–8.

55. *A*, p. 48.

Chapter Two. J'ARRIVERAI: The Turtle Too Gets There: 1902–1909

1. "Dr. Williams' Position," originally published in *The Dial* (Nov. 1928). Included in *Literary Essays of Ezra Pound*, New Directions (New York, 1968), p. 389.

2. WCW to HHW, letters in B.

3. 26 Sept. 1902 (B). See *SL*, p. 3, where this letter is dated "ca. Oct., 1902."

4. WCW to CA, *SL*, pp. 195–196.

5. Information culled from *A, I,* and especially private papers of WCW written in 1926 (B).

6. EP to WCW, undated, but about 1950 (Y).

7. *A,* p. 56.

8. *A,* p. 57.

9. *A,* p. 57.

10. *A,* p. 58.

11. EP's anger can be felt in the letters he wrote WCW in October 1920 (*Letters EP*).

12. WCW's record at Penn's School of Medicine was much better than his record at Horace Mann. He graduated 13 June 1906, very near the top of his class.

First Year, 1902–1903:		*Second Year, 1903–1904:*	
Anatomy	74	Anatomy	80
Chemistry	93	Physiology	90
Bacteriology	85	Pathology	81
		Physical Diagnosis	90
		Materia Medica and	
		Pharmacy	68

Third Year, 1904–1905:		*Fourth Year, 1905–1906:*	
Medicine	71	Medicine	76
Surgery	78	Surgery	79
Obstetrics	90	Obstetrics	88.5
Therapeutics	71	Gynecology	89.5
Pathology	74	Hygiene	90
Applied Anatomy	86	Dermatology	78
Ophthalmology	95		

13. WCW to HHW (B). See also *SL.*

14. WCW was in a sense "caught" in the undertow of Unitarian society in Philadelphia because of the prominence of his parents in Rutherford's small Unitarian society. WCW went to the Unitarian services at first because it was expected of him and because it provided a contact of sorts at a time when he felt especially isolated from friends. But the humiliating rejection he experienced with the daughters of the local Unitarian pastor, Rev. Ecob, seems to have been the reason why WCW separated out early from Unitarianism as a social structure, though its ideal of light and reason stayed with him all his life.

15. 1 Nov. 1903 (B).

16. 17 Jan. 1904 (B).

17. *SL,* p. 5.

18. 10 Oct. 1904 (B).

19. Friday, 4 Nov. 1904 (B).

20. *SL,* p. 7.

21. Ca. 15 Nov. 1904 (B).

22. WCW to EW, 22 Nov. 1904 (B).

23. WCW to EW, 16 Nov. 1904 (B).

24. WCW to parents, 29 Nov. 1904 ff. (B).

25. WCW to EW, 4 Dec. 1904 (B).

26. WCW to EW, 12 Jan. 1905 (B). See also *A,* p. 61. It is probable, therefore, that the girl was none other than Dorothy Wilson, the one of "marriageable age" who made her presence felt whenever WCW showed up to paint with John Wilson. Apparently this strategy of showing up a day late convinced the Wilsons that young WCW was indeed a strange young man. WCW probably stopped going to the Wilsons' altogether shortly after this incident.

Chapter Two. J'ARRIVERAI: The Turtle Too Gets There: 1902–1909 (cont.)

27. WCW to EW, 12 Jan. 1905 (B).

28. Unpublished conversation, WCW and JT, 7 Jan. 1956 (Y). The date for the meet is derived from an unpublished letter from WCW to HHW, 19 Feb. 1905.

29. *SL*, p. 8.

30. *SL*, p. 9.

31. *A*, p. 68.

32. 10 Dec. 1905 (B).

33. See WCW to NHP, 11 July 1955 in *WCWN*, II, 2 (Fall 1976), 2–3. WCW misdated the letter here and in *A* as 13 Jan. 1905. But he had not yet met HD then.

34. 6 Feb. 1906 (B).

35. 11 March 1906 (B).

36. WCW to NHP, 11 July 1955, op. cit., p. 2.

37. 18 March 1906 (B).

38. 22 March 1906 (B).

39. WCW to MM, 2 May 1934. *SL*, p. 147.

40. JT has misdated this letter in *SL*, p. 6. He gives the date as 3/30/04; it should be 3/30/06.

41. WCW alludes to this tension in *A*, p. 68, where, even at 67, he was still waffling: "Ezra was wonderfully in love with her [HD] and I thought exaggerated her beauty ridiculously. To me she was just a good guy and I enjoyed, uncomfortably, being with her. . . . 'For God's sake,' I told him, 'I'm not in love with Hilda nor she with me. She's your girl and I know it. Don't be an ass.' " See also *IWWP*, p. 7: "Ezra was the official lover, but Hilda was very coy and invited us both to come and see her. Ezra said to me, 'Are you trying to cut me out?' I said, 'No, I'm not thinking of any woman right now, but I like Hilda very much.' Ezra Pound and I were not rivals, either for the girl or for the poetry." WCW made these curious and disingenuous remarks in May 1956, when he was 72.

42. WCW to JL, 25 June 1938.

43. WCW to EW, 26 April 1906 (B). This is probably the incident WCW was referring to in *A* when he spoke of staying the night at the observatory alone "to my embarrassment on one occasion. I took Hilda to a Mask and Wig tryout and dance one night and even got some dirty looks from Ezra over it" (*A*, p. 68).

44. WCW to EW, 26 April 1906 (B).

45. WCW to EW, 6 May 1906 (B).

46. WCW to HHW, 1 April 1906 (B).

47. WCW to HHW, 27 May 1906 (B).

48. Review of H.D.'s *Collected Poems*, written by WCW in May 1925 (B). See also *A*, pp. 69–70.

49. WCW to HHW, 3 July 1906 (B). In this letter WCW asks his mother to ask his father for a $25 check to pay a Joseph Weil, tailor, 84th Street, for his new white duck suit.

50. CW to HHW, 19 Sept. 1906 (B).

51. Information for the Lake George walking tour culled from postcards sent home to HHW by WCW and EW (Pri.).

52. EW to HHW, Monday, 3 Sept. 1906 (Pri.).

53. Ms. at Y. Ann W. Fisher kindly provided me with a copy of her unpublished monograph, "William Carlos Williams' *Endymion* Poem: 'Philip and Oradie,' " which stresses particularly the autobiographical elements of this blank verse exercise.

54. Mentioned specifically in letters home or to EW.

55. WCW to EW, 28 Oct. 1906 (B).

56. WCW to EW, Election Day, 6 Nov. 1906 (B).

57. Ibid.

58. *SL*, pp. 13–14.

59. *SL*, p. 14.

60. WCW to EW, 15 Nov. 1906 (B).

61. WCW scribbled this comment on a letter from EW postmarked 19 Dec. 1906 (Pri.).

62. HD to WCW, 23 Jan. 1906 (B).

63. EP to WCW, 6 Feb. 1907 (B).

64. WCW to EW, 13 Feb. 1907 (B).

65. WCW to EW, 27 Feb. 1907 (B).

66. See *A*, "French Hospital" and "The Wrath of God," pp. 76–89. Also see letter to EW, 27 Feb. 1907, where WCW mentions the piano at the hospital which he and Krumweide took turns playing.

67. Photographs (Pri.).

68. WCW to EW, late March and early April 1907 (B).

69. Postcard of Flower Astronomical Observatory, 5 April 1907 (Pri.).

70. *A*, p. 85.

71. WCW to EW, 2 Dec. 1907 (B).

72. Information culled from postcards and letters sent to HHW by her sons (Pri.).

73. WGW to WCW, 27 April 1906 (Pri.).

74. WGW to WCW, 1 Oct. 1907 (Pri.).

75. WCW to HHW, 18 Dec. 1909, from Leipzig (B).

76. See *A*, "Dr. Henna," pp. 71–75. There WCW remembered the month but misdated his Mexican trip 1906. But a postcard mailed by WCW from San Luis Potosí is postmarked 6:45 PM, 14 Dic [iembre] 1907 (Pri.).

77. *A*, pp. 73–74.

78. HD to WCW, 12 Feb. 1908 (B).

79. HD to WCW, 7 March 1908 (B).

80. See letter from WCW to EW, 18 March 1908 (B).

81. Interestingly, in this same letter in which WCW told EW that he thought EP had been impressed by his *Endymion* poem he also explained that he and EW both worked best "by ourselves and not in competition." The reason for this was that the Williams boys were already "too highly strung" as it was. A "less nervous fellow" needed "competition to stir him up but we are sufficiently stirred up by our innate love of perfection." WCW may already have felt that his deepest instincts as a poet were to go it alone.

82. WCW to EW, 6 Feb. 1908 (B).

83. Ibid.

84. Undated letter WCW to EW, but internal evidence suggests late Feb. 1908 (B).

85. WCW to AT, 9 July 1949.

86. In 1956 WCW remembered this meeting with Arlo Bates as having taken place earlier, in Nov. 1905 (*A*, pp. 53–54). "It was the weekend of the Harvard–Penn game (which by the way Penn won and I remember I guessed the exact score in a pool and won the money). This was my Keats period. Everything I wrote was bad Keats" (IWWP, p. 4). The reason for following a different chronology is based on the early letters, which point to EW's showing Arlo Bates his brother's poems in the winter of 1908. WCW may also have tried to put more distance on that meeting, perhaps being unwilling to admit even then that at 24 he was still writing execrable Keats.

87. 2 March 1908 (B).

88. WCW reconstructed this meeting with Bates in both *A* and *IWWP*. In the latter he plainly calls this meeting "a turning point in my life." Bates's advice there (p. 4) is given in these words, different from *A*: "You may, I can't tell, develop into a writer, but you have a lot to learn. Maybe in time you'll write some good verse. Go on writing, but don't give up medicine. Writing alone is not an easy occupation for a man to follow."

89. WCW to EW, 2 March 1908 (B).

90. WCW to EW, 18 March 1908 (B).

91. WCW to VBJ, 28 April 1908.

92. Notes in private collection, partially printed as Appendix B in Rod Townley's *The Early Poetry of William Carlos Williams*, Cornell University Press (Ithaca, N.Y.), pp. 186–192. Among the books WCW finished during this period were Darwin's *Origin of Species* and Shakespeare's *The Tempest*. He spent time planting in his backyard and taking long walks along the Passaic River and the edge of Kipp's Woods where, at 10:00 at night on May 10 he was chased by a screech owl who darted at his head, "making two clicking sounds each time. Once it made a sound between neigh of a horse and squeak of a rat." As for poetry, he was concerned at this time with "centrality of address, with vigor of purpose and enthusiastic conviction: to God, to my lady, to my brother, my friend and fellow creature," all subjects that would find their way into WCW's *Poems* (1909) in one form or another.

93. WCW to EW, 22 June 1908 (B).

94. See *A*, "Hell's Kitchen," pp. 93–105.

95. WCW kept records of these children, marking their progress and—more frequently —their small deaths. Reading these records one feels the hopelessness of the situation for the nurses and doctors at the mansion (Pri.).

96. WCW to EW, 22 July 1908 (B).

97. Trip through Sloatsburg to Wingdale, New York, 5–9 Sept. 1908 (Pri.).

98. One of WCW's early favorites was Botticelli. Looking at the mulberry tree in his yard on 8 May 1908, WCW observed, "Mulberry tree not yet in full leaf. Certainly a dainty light tree. Reminds me of Boticceli [sic]." See, for comparison, WCW's "The Botticellian Trees," written more than twenty years afterwards.

99. WCW to EW, 22 Aug. 1908 (B).

100. "Emotion does not continuously pertain except in the briefest ode," WCW reminded himself about this time. "When it does let it mould its form, for it is hot and can but the colder subject of less passion should hold or revert to the regular form to which it is fit." There should be no departure from this rule, he added, except when it is impossible to contain one's passion, a condition that he believed "rarely occurs" (Townley, Appendix B, p. 190). Twenty years later WCW would reject Yvor Winters for holding to just such neoclassical textbook formulae as he had himself uttered here.

101. WCW's early letters to EP, from the beginnings up until early 1920, have yet to be uncovered. But what WCW must have said to EP can be gathered from EP's point-by-point rebuttal to WCW's objections.

102. Letters EP, pp. 3–7.

103. WCW to EW, 21 Oct. 1908 (B).

104. Ibid.

105. WCW to EW, 9 Nov. 1908 (B). WCW was also writing another one-act play, this one containing four characters and set in Fort Carolina, Florida, circa 1600. VBJ would type it out—"my first to be typewritten," WCW would say—and it would be ready for the spring of 1909 (WCW to EW, 19 Nov. 1908). It too would seem to show the central influences on WCW of the Elizabethan (i.e., Shakespearean) and nascent American traditions.

106. Reid Howell to WCW, 18 Jan. 1909, addressed to Child's Hospital (Pri.).

107. See *A*, pp. 106–107, and *IWWP*, pp. 9–10.

108. Poems (B).

109. A, p. 107.

110. WCW to EW, 6 April 1909 (B).

111. This volume now in Y.

112. Rutherford American, XXXIV, 977 (Thursday, 6 May 1909), Supplement, 4. Quoted in Emily Wallace, *A Bibliography of William Carlos Williams*, Wesleyan University Press (Middletown, Conn., 1968).

113. EP to WCW, 21 May 1909 (*Letters EP*, pp. 7–8). So deeply did EP's letter apparently affect WCW that he refused even to talk about this book (*Poems*) for years afterward. WCW even put EP's letter out of mind, for he wrote in *A* that "Ezra was silent, if indeed he ever saw the thing, which I hope he never did" (*A*, p. 107).

Chapter Three. Deaths and Transfigurations: 1909–1914

1. *A*, pp. 102–105.

2. WCW to EW, 18 March 1909 (B).

3. Ibid.

4. Ibid.

5. Interview with Charlotte Herman Earle, April 1979. In a letter from RM to JH in 1954, RM—who was angry with WCW for his *A*—said that he remembered Charlotte telling him once that EW had turned out to be a "tightwad" and that WCW himself "lacked virility" (Josephine Herbst papers, Y).

6. WCW was curiously silent about this central event in his life in *A*, but he spoke of it two years later in *BU* (see especially pp. 257–259).

7. "Always, if you're going to ask a woman to marry you, a cynical old friend had once advised Charlie, do it before noon, because you want to have your wits about you." *BU*, p. 259. In a letter to FW, dated 5 July 1911, WCW writes: "This is our anniversary too." This could mean only that July 5 was the day WCW and FW became engaged (Pri.).

8. *A*, p. 101.

9. WCW describes his own feelings about his engagement to FW in *BU*, pp. 260–264.

10. The year of scientific German taken at Horace Mann eight years earlier hardly constituted a working knowledge of the language.

11. Undated, but definitely early July 1909 (Pri.).

12. 11 July 1909. From Rutherford (Pri.).

13. 21 July 1909 (Pri.).

14. 11 Aug. 1909. *SL*, pp. 15–19.

15. Ibid., pp. 16–17.

16. 9 Aug. 1909 (Pri.). "The first Sunday I almost passed out for loneliness." *A*, p. 109.

17. See *A*, "Leipzig," pp. 109–111. Also unpublished letters from WCW to EW and FW.

18. WCW to FW, Sunday morning, 19 Sept. 1909.

19. 24 Nov. 1909 (Pri.).

20. 24 and 28 Nov. 1909 (Pri.)

21. 16 Jan. 1910 (Pri.)

22. *A*, pp. 111–112.

23. 23 Jan. 1910 (Pri.).

24. *SL*, pp. 20–21.

25. The poem is dedicated to "Ellen whom he is freeing" and begins:

> *Thou priceless nun of a holy mind*
> *Ellen lady of praise and song*
> *Break from thy sleep in the darkness kind!*
> *For me are the iron bars not strong.*

26. 17 January and 7, 9, and 20 Feb. 1910 (Pri.).

27. 17 Jan. 1910 (Pri.).

28. 8 Feb. 1910 (Pri.).

29. WCW to FW, 1 March 1910 (Pri.).

30. Published as "Martin and Katherine" in the group, "Interests of 1926," in *The Little Review*, New York, XII, 1 (Spring–Summer 1926), 10–12.

31. *A*, pp. 113–114.

Chapter Three. Deaths and Transfigurations: 1909–1914 (cont.)

32. *A*, pp. 114–116.
33. WCW to FW, 19 March 1910 from the Hotel Como, Milan (Pri.).
34. WCW to FW, 27 March 1910 from Florence (Pri.).
35. WCW to AT, 13 May 1954.
36. WCW to FW, 12 April 1910 (Pri.).
37. "Wild Anacapri out on its point of rocks meeting the sea—pre-Christian surely, if anything in Europe is that. The girls carrying baskets of new-picked lemons from the cliff stairs. . . . Ed and I climbed down the cliff from which Tiberius used to throw his women when he tired of them to a small, sloping ledge of bright grass twenty feet below the summit, and lay there stretched out side by side in the sun, isolated and happy, high above the sea" (*A*, p. 121).
38. See *A*, p. 121. But in *Al* WCW makes it clearer what this incident really signified for him.
39. WCW to FW, 10 April 1910 (Pri.).
40. WCW to FW from Madrid, Sunday, 15 May 1910 (Pri.).
41. *A*, p. 123.
42. *PB*, p. 53.
43. *A*, p. 124. WCW in *A* has scrambled the sequence of events in Spain, but the letters and the logic of the itinerary—one great loop out from and back to Gibraltar—help clarify what happened and when.
44. *BU*, p. 265.
45. WCW to FW, 9 Aug. 1910 from West Haven (Pri.).
46. *CEP*, p. 38.
47. WCW to FW, 26 Aug. 1910 (Pri.).
48. WCW to FW, 15 Sept. 1910 (Pri.).
49. WCW to FW, 20 Sept. 1910 (Pri.).
50. WCW to VBJ, 21 Nov. 1910.
51. WCW to VBJ, 6 Jan. 1911.
52. WCW to VBJ, 21 Jan. 1911.
53. *A*, p. 129.
54. *I*, p. 11.
55. EP's recollection is contained in a letter he wrote WCW on 11 Sept. 1920. (*Letters EP*, pp. 159–160.)
56. This was a favorite of WCW and he recorded it at least twice, once in his Prologue to *KH* (*I*, pp. 10–11) and again in *A*, pp. 91–92. In both versions WGW, standing in for his son, comes out of the encounter the victor.
57. *A*, pp. 92–93. "If I had ever spoken to Ez of a Herxheimer reaction he would have thought I was talking like a Pennyslvania Dutch farmer. Risks? The practical details meant nothing to Ezra."
58. WCW to FW, 4 July 1911 (Pri.).
59. WCW to FW, 5 July 1911 (Pri.).
60. WCW to FW, 10 July 1911 (Pri.).
61. WCW to FW, 15 July 1911 (Pri.).
62. WCW to FW, 21 July 1911 (Pri.).
63. *P*, p. 121.
64. "Hilda Doolittle sails for Europe Saturday. She sends you her love." WCW to FW, Thursday, 20 July 1911 (Pri.).
65. WCW to NHP, 11 July 1955. *WCWN*, II, 2 (Fall 1976), p.3.
66. WCW to VBJ, 15 Aug. 1911.
67. WCW to FW, 21 Aug. 1911 (Pri.).
68. *P*, p. 172.

69. WCW to FW, 21 Aug. 1911 (Pri.).

70. In *CEP*, p. 35. Originally called "Sicilian Emigrant's Song: In New York Harbour" when it was published in *Poetry* in June 1913.

71. WCW writes to FW about "our team" in a letter of 27 Aug. 1911 (Pri.).

72. 29 Aug. 1911 (Pri.).

73. WCW to VBJ, 15 Oct. 1911, addressed to 174 W. 89th St.

74. That poem—*still* in the Keatsian mode—begins:

> Ye who live in conflict against false love
> And sometimes would be crowned above the pain,
> Hear me! for from an old chanson to gain
> The wherewithal breeds comfort. . . .

(Included in a letter to VBJ of 20 Oct. 1911.)

75. See *A*, p. 130. "And so to our marriage. . . . To me it more resembled a performance of the Mask and Wig Club than anything serious." WCW is speaking of the wedding ceremony here, but he means by extension the entire courtship scene, the latter part of which he says he went through in a kind of sleepwalk.

76. WCW to VBJ, 30 Oct. 1911.

77. WCW to VBJ, 1 Dec. 1911.

78. WCW to VBJ, 10 Dec. 1911.

79. WCW to FW, 26 March 1912 (Pri.).

80. WCW to FW, 23 March 1912 (Pri.).

81. WCW to FW, 18 March 1912 (Pri.).

82. WCW to VBJ, 19 March 1912.

83. *A*, pp. 128–129.

84. WCW to FW, 22, 27, 29 June 1912 (Pri.).

85. EP to WCW, 26 May 1913 (B).

86. In a letter to FW dated 11 July 1912, WCW tells her he is going to be printed in *The Lyric Year*. But by early August Earle had returned WCW's poem (2 Aug. 1912, WCW to FW, Pri.).

87. WCW to FW, 20 Aug. 1912 (Pri.).

88. Published in *Poetry*, II, 3 (June 1913), 114–115.

89. "A Selection from *The Tempers*," *Poetry Review* (Oct. 1912), 481–482.

90. WCW to VBJ, 19 July 1912.

91. Ibid.

92. WCW to VBJ, 30 March 1912.

93. WCW to FW, 3 Oct. 1912 (Pri.).

94. Interview with William Ely, Clara Ely's brother, April 1979.

95. From "Asphodel," *PB*, pp. 181–182.

96. *BU*, p. 307.

97. *A*, pp. 130–131.

98. 5 March 1913, *SL*, pp. 23–24.

99. Ibid.

100. In *A*, p. 134, WCW wrote, "There was at that time a great surge of interest in the arts generally before the First World War. New York was seething with it. Painting took the lead. It came to a head for us in the famous 'Armory Show' of 1913. I went to it and gaped along with the rest at a 'picture' in which an electric bulb kept going on and off; at Duchamp's sculpture (by Mott and Co.') [sic], a magnificent cast-iron urinal, glistening of its white enamel." The discrepancy here is that what WCW remembered occurred at the 1917 and *not* the 1913 New York Show. And Floss, speaking with Edith Heal in 1956, said bluntly, "Bill did not attend the first Armory Show, though he always insisted he did. He went to the second one [in 1917] where he read ["Overture to a Locomotive"] along with

Chapter Three. Deaths and Transfigurations: 1909–1914 (cont.)
Mina Loy and the others. He wasn't himself when he swore he'd been to the first one so I gave up trying to convince him" (*WCWN*, II, 2 [Fall 1976], 11).

101. *A*, p. 138.

102. Quoted in Weaver, pp. 82–83. Original among VBJ papers at Y.

103. Mss. of *P* 4, early version of January 1950 (Y).

104. "Speech Rhythm," Weaver, p. 82."*Vers libre* is finished—Whitman did all that was necessary with it. Verse has nothing to gain here and all to lose."

105. 10 Oct. 1913, *SL*, p. 25.

106. *SL*, p. 26.

107. 14 Oct. 1913, *SL*, p. 26.

108. "The Tempers," *New Freewoman* (Dec. 1913), 227.

109. *Letters EP*, pp. 27–28.

110. *SL*, p. 27.

111. *A*, pp. 131–132. Also see WEW, "The House," in *WCWN*, V, 1 (Spring 1979), 1–5.

112. *BU*, pp. 317–318.

113. *Al*.

114. WCW to VBJ.

115. *BU*, pp. 320–322. Also interview with WEW, April 1979.

*116.*WCW to VBJ.

117. "The Wanderer: A Rococo Study," *CEP*, pp. 3–12. First published in *The Egoist*, London, I, 6 (16 March 1914), 109–111. Whitman's "Crossing Brooklyn Ferry" is one of the key texts standing behind "The Wanderer," but so is also Keats's *Endymion*, though here WCW purposely fractured Keats's language to force his muse—like Whitman's—to cross the Atlantic and come home to America. In 1921 WCW "remade" himself in an essay he called "Sample Prose Piece," recalling that he was only 17 when he wrote "The Wanderer" (instead of the 30 he actually was). There he recalls that he—in the guise of his persona, Evans Dionysius Evans, "was thoroughly disgusted with everything, thoroughly schooled in the dangers from syph, maternity, heartbreak and the clap and wrote a long love poem, about the Passaic River and an old woman, which Orrick Johns, dear Orrick [a New York poet active in the 1920s], called great. . . ." (*Contact*, No.4 [Summer 1921], 10).

Chapter Four. Smashing Windows in Paper Houses: 1914–1921

1. VBJ papers (Y).

2. 29 April 1914 (Y).

3. *CEP*, pp. 129–131.

4. Reprinted in "The Lost Poems of William Carlos Williams," JT, *New Directions* 16 (1957), p. 9.

5. *ND* 16, p. 10.

6. "To the Outer World," *ND* 16, p. 10.

7. "Woman Walking," *ND* 16, p. 12.

8. 7 July 1914 (Y).

9. *CEP*, p. 39.

10. 25 June 1914 (Y).

11. These appeared under the collective title "Root Buds," in *Poetry*, VI, 2 (May 1915), 62–66.

12. 22 May 1914, *SL*, pp. 27–28.

13. This poem ("Pastoral 2") and the following ("Idyl") are from a group of poems, seven typed pages in all, entitled "Pastorals and Self-Portraits" in the VBJ papers (Y). Rod Townley has printed them as Appendix A in *The Early Poetry of William Carlos Williams*, Cornell University Press (Ithaca, 1975). They date from 1914 and 1915.

14. "Idyl," Townley, p. 184.

15. See *BU*, pp. 326–328. "But he was gone, that energetic, that intelligent, that handsome young boy, so admired by all and so loved and planned for by [his mother] and his father. He had been wiped out, had vanished from their lives just at the moment when it seemed as if every promise that a child could show was to be realized."

16. *BU*, pp. 329–333.

17. WCW to EB, 30 April 1917 (Y).

18. "The Drill Sergeant," *ND* 4 (1939), p. 244. In late 1914 or early 1915 WCW had described the very rain in Rutherford as falling from the sky "onto the edged leaves" where the "Bayonettes of the grass" could receive them to "be broken finally / —and your life ends!" It was the vicious thrust of the bayonet that WCW most associated with the horrors of WWI. For the most part, having seen enough suffering in the homes and hospitals around New Jersey, he avoided war stories and the glories of war whenever he could.

19. Reprinted in *ND* 16, p. 13.

20. 15 Jan. 1915 (Y).

21. WCW to HM, 13 April 1915.

22. "The Great Opportunity—New York Letter," in *The Egoist*, III, 9 (Sept. 1916). Reprinted in *SL*, pp. 30–33.

23. Quoted in Alfred Kreymborg, *Troubadour: An American Autobiography*, Liveright (New York, 1925), pp. 204–205.

24. It is characteristic of WCW that he seems to have been the first to support the reading aloud of poems by the poets themselves. Yet when he read his own poems he snarled and spit them out self-consciously until Kreymborg mercifully suggested he read them for WCW.

25. *RI*, pp. 57–59. Bram Dijkstra, the editor, gives the date as not later than 1915, with which date I concur. The handwritten notes that WCW added, and which Dijkstra thinks belong to the early 1920s, were probably added in September 1918, when WCW was thinking of reworking his "Vortex" to include it in the "Prologue" to *KH*.

26. *I*, p. 16.

27. Or so WCW recalled the incident in *A*, pp. 136–137. Duchamp, four years WCW's junior, may have been drunk or just feeling "bitchy" when WCW talked to him on that occasion. Or he may simply have had difficulty communicating with WCW; WCW's French was really quite rusty and Duchamp's English almost nonexistent. The truth seems to be that WCW saw in Duchamp a model of the ironic, detached artist, constantly breaking down the classical expectations of art to make the object new. Duchamp is the secret center behind Williams' *Improvisations* of 1917–1918, which WCW began soon after Duchamp left New York for South America to avoid military conscription by the U.S., Duchamp's talented brother having recently been killed in action in France.

By 1923, when Duchamp was back in New York but had at that point already given up "art," WCW would challenge him in print in an editorial he wrote that spring for *Contact* called "Glorious Weather." One maintained one's central position in the arts only by producing, no *ifs, ands,* or *buts*:

> If the object of writing be to celebrate the triumph
> of sense, and if Marcel Duchamp be the apex of the modern
> sense, and if he continues in New York, silent . . .
>   We say only in view of Marcel's intelligent and devas-
> tating silence, etc., etc., Budapest, Argentina, Sinalon,
> Siberia, West Coast of Africa—if, if, if—etc., that

> there is no comment on pictures but pictures, on music
> but music, poems but poetry:

Chapter Four. Smashing Windows in Paper Houses: 1914–1921 (cont.)

if you do, you do

if you don't you don't

and that's all there is to that.

(See Henry M. Sayre, "Ready-mades and Other Measures: The Poetics of Marcel Duchamp and William Carlos Williams" *Journal of Modern Literature*, 8, i [1980], 3–22.)

28. "The Great Opportunity," *SL*, p. 33.

29. 15 Jan. 1916.

30. 26 Feb. 1916.

31. 11 April 1916.

32. 3 May 1916.

33. 18 Dec. 1916.

34. 26 Oct. 1916.

35. 9 May 1916. *SL*, pp. 34–35.

36. 2 June 1916 (Hunt.).

37. 8 June 1916 (Hunt.). Reproduced in *WCWN*, I, 1 (Fall 1975), p. 16.

38. EP to WCW, undated, but clearly early June 1916 (B).

39. EP to Iris Barry, June 1916 (*Letters EP*, p. 82).

40. AL to WCW, 28 June 1916 (B).

41. WCW to AL, 28 (sic) June 1916.

42. Reprinted in *CEP*, p. 140.

43. *CEP*, p. 154.

44. Retitled "Sympathetic Portrait of a Child" in *CEP*, p. 155.

45. See "Perpetuum Mobile: The City," written late 1935, early 1936, where WCW writes of the city as "A dream / a little false" rising in the east, beckoning, as WCW continued to batter at his "unsatisfactory / brilliance" (*CEP*, pp. 384–390).

46. These photographs now in B collection.

47. 27 April 1916 (Pri.).

48. WCW to HHW, 20 Oct. 1915 (Pri.).

49. 27 April 1916 (Pri.).

50. 26 Aug. 1915 (Pri.).

51. Ferdinand Earle to WCW, 28 Oct. 1915 (Y).

52. "This is a slight stiff dance to a waking baby whose arms have been lying curled back above his head upon the pillow, making a flower—the eyes closed. Dead to the world! Waking is a little hand brushing away dreams. Eyes open. Here's a new world." And again, a little later, this, in another mode: "By this deep snow I know it's springtime, not ring time! . . . The screaming brat's a sheep bleating, the rattling crib-side sheep shaking a bush. . . . Reproduction lets death in, says Joyce. Rot say I. To Phyllis [Floss] this song is!" *KH*, I, pp. 73–74.

53. WCW to EB, 18 July 1916 (Y).

54. WCW to EB, 19 July 1916 (Y).

55. WCW to EB, 22 July 1916 (Y).

56. WCW to EB, 20 Oct. 1916 (ViU).

57. WCW to EB, 31 Oct. 1916 (ViU).

58. *SL*, p. 36.

59. 9 Oct. 1916 (B).

60. 12 Oct. 1916, *SL*, p. 37.

61. AL to WCW, 13 Oct. 1916 (B).

62. 16 Oct. 1916, *SL*, pp. 37–38. An interesting aside to the WCW-AL exchange which gives us an early view of how WCW appeared to his contemporaries at the start of his

"public" career as a poet (age 33) occurs in a series of letters between Amy Lowell and John Gould Fletcher, who was then in England. "I have just had rather an unpleasant passage of arms with William Carlos Williams," Lowell wrote Fletcher in a letter dated 11 Oct. 1916 (but perhaps written two days later than that date). She was sending Fletcher (and H.D.) copies of the two letters WCW had at that point sent her: those of October 4 and October 12. Lowell had taken the first letter, in which WCW had told her to send *Others* some money at once, as "half a joke, and answered accordingly." But WCW's second letter had raised her ire. "You were quite right in suspecting that 'Others' had gone to the wall," she told Fletcher, "and it proves to me more conclusively than anything else could, that art which is not sincere has no chance. It may make a splash for five minutes, but counts for nothing in the long run." Pound, she added, was a liar, but WCW struck her as "sincere," though "evidently terribly bitter over the failure of 'Others,' and utterly bamboozled by Ezra." She was sure that WCW would *not* see her when she came to New York, since he would be "too upset to desire to be just." Time then to bring out the 1917 Imagist anthology just to show "the public at large that we have not gone under in the 'Others' crash." Besides, in five years Lowell was sure nothing more would "be heard of the Ezra group," and that—by implication—included WCW.

On the twenty-fifth Lowell wrote Fletcher again, this time enclosing WCW's letter of October 16. She was not going to answer this one since she considered the episode closed: "I knew that Williams preferred to hide behind vague generalities, to coming to see me and making his charges specific." And now she had "proved" it. A week later Fletcher wrote Lowell to say how sorry he was about the whole *Others* affair. Just before he'd left New York, he explained, Aiken had mentioned the special number of *Others* which WCW was getting up and that WCW wanted Fletcher to send him something, which Fletcher had, forgetting "all the squabbles we had had with that crowd." In any event, *Others* itself was "dead." Why, WCW hadn't even had the courtesy to send Fletcher a copy of the special number. And as for WCW himself, though Fletcher had yet to meet him, he was "inclined to think he has the Ezra trait of considering himself of immense importance to the universe." A southerner himself (from Little Rock, Arkansas), Fletcher lamented WCW's lack of manners and hoped Miss Lowell wouldn't go out of her way "to make him feel more friendly, as he isn't worth it" (31 Oct. 1916). Then, on the following day, Fletcher wrote Aiken in New York to warn him to have nothing to do with *Others*. "They all seem to have been imbued—Williams especially—with the desire to shock the public at any price and to proclaim their own infinite importance in the scheme of things. This is the old Ezra game, and I am too wary to be caught by such tricks. . . . Harriet [Monroe of *Poetry*] and *Others* can perish for aught I care" (1 Nov. 1916). John Gould Fletcher papers, (University of Arkansas Library, Fayetteville, Arkansas).

63. 7 Nov. 1916 (Y).

64. 12 Oct. 1916 (Colorado).

65. Undated, but late November or early December 1916 (Colorado).

66. Letter of 15 Nov. 1916, which Crane pasted into the inside cover of his copy of *KH* in 1920 (Columbia).

67. Letter of 19 April (Columbia). Both Hart Crane and WCW were in and around New York City through most of the 1920s. Each appears in the correspondence of the other (there are, for example, a series of letters between Crane and Yvor Winters in the mid-1920s dealing with WCW's poetry). They knew many of the same people in New York—Gorham Munson, Kenneth Burke, Matthew Josephson, so that it must have been WCW's homophobia as much as anything that kept him from seeing Crane until 1929. (For the Crane-Winters correspondence see Thomas Parkinson's *Hart Crane and Yvor Winters: Their Literary Correspondence*, University of California Press [Berkeley, 1978].)

68. Information on the Polytopics Club comes in large part from an interview with Prof.

Chapter Four. Smashing Windows in Paper Houses: 1914–1921 (cont.)
John Dollar of Fairleigh Dickinson U. and a present member of that group. He is in possession of the club's minutes. Other references to the Polytopics Club are found scattered among WCW's papers at B, in unpublished letters, and in *YMW*.

69. There is a hint of humorous condescension in the minutes for the Polytopics Club. And FW told Edith Heal in 1956 that "there were no literary connections in Rutherford. I asked [Bill] not to read his poetry in Rutherford where he was misunderstood and parodied. I told him to cut it out. . . . They don't know what it's about . . . it's insulting to you and me" (*WCWN*, II, 2 [Fall 1976], 10). A parallel situation existed for Wallace Stevens, who was one man in New York and another in Hartford.

70. Interview with Madeline Spence at her home in Rutherford, April 1980.

71. Copies of these plays are among WCW's papers at B.

72. See "The House," *WCWN*, V, 1 (Spring 1979), 4. Also Polytopics Club minutes for dating.

73. Interview with Madeline Spence. See also "Cars," WEW in *WCWN*, III, 2 (Fall 1977), 4. During "the annual Williams, Spence, Wagner and Dugdale progressive dinner" one New Year's Eve, probably in the late 1920s, an event that began that year at the Spences' (23 Lincoln Avenue) and ended at 9 Ridge Road, Williams decided to drive on the sidewalk "down Park Avenue along the west side of the Presbyterian Church. A member of the local constabulary interrupted the frolic about halfway down the block, but in keeping with the holiday mood, and on recognizing Dad, he advised him to get back on the road and wished him a Happy New Year."

74. AK to WCW, 9 Nov. 1916 (B).

75. AK's reminiscences in *Troubadour*. WCW talks about the play in *A*, pp. 138–129.

76. *A*, pp. 139–140.

77. Reprinted in *The Palm at the End of the Mind*, ed. Holly Stevens, Vintage Books (New York, 1972), pp. 23–24.

78. Fragment of letter, about April 1917, from WCW to Hay (Colorado).

79. "The Great Sex Spiral, A Criticism of Miss [Dora] Marsden's 'Lingual Psychology,'" in two parts, *The Egoist*, IV, 3 (April 1917), 46 and IV, 7 (Aug. 1917), 110–111.

80. *FD*, pp. 33–37.

81. "The Ideal Quarrel," in *The Little Review*, V, 8 (Dec. 1918), 39–40. This prose may have been originally intended for inclusion in *KH*.

82. 26 Jan 1917 (Y).

83. 5 Feb. 1917 (Y).

84. ·14 Feb. 1917 (Y).

85. 20 Feb. 1917 (Y).

86. 21 Feb. 1917. *SL*, p. 40.

87. 23 Feb. 1917 (Y).

88. 15 Nov. 1917 (Y).

89. *CEP*, p. 118.

90. In a letter to Brown, undated but about May 1917 (ViU), WCW made it clear that he was no ideologue trying to create a closer bond of brotherhood through poetry. "Shit!" he told Brown, "I hate brotherhood. I have a brother. I grew up with him. We haven't grown far enough apart yet to be brothers." If men were brothers then they were brothers, pure and simple. Poetry had other work to do: "Being brothers, poetry may convey between us a remark or two upon the weather or upon the state of our health etc. but what the devil has it really to do with making us one thing or another." No, the reason WCW wrote poems about his world was that he was driven to it, "word crazy":

Then again there's the mob who use words like nails or screws or hair pins. . . . The rhythms of everyday speech drive me mad. Not with an artistic dementia due to horror at bourgeoise ignorance but with a feeling of the perfections that mock me from ignorant mouths. Ignorant people use the most idiotic words sometimes with a dignity, a force a depth of feeling that makes them glow and flare. I listen in profound silence and thank my luck that Pop created me—later I try to imitate. I almost always fail. It is a pretty game.

91. CEP, p. 121.

92. CEP, pp. 132–134. "I have one ambition in life. To have nothing to do but love my wife and my family. . . ." WCW to EB, May 1917 (ViU).

93. CEP, pp. 150–151.

94. CEP, p. 148.

95. 12 Feb. 1918 (Y).

96. EB to WCW, 16 Feb. 1918 (Y).

97. WCW to EB, 15 Nov. 1917 (Y).

98. EB to WCW, 15 March 1918 (Y).

99. Reprinted in Emily Wallace, *A Bibliography of William Carlos Williams*, Wesleyan University Press (Middletown, Conn., 1968), pp. 11–12.

100. A, p. 158.

101. A seems to suggest the spring of 1917 and the frustration WCW felt when America finally declared war on Germany that April: "Damn it, the freshness, the newness of a springtime which I had sensed among the others, a reawakening of letters, all that delight which in making a world to match the supremacies of the past could mean was being blotted out by the war. . . . It was Persephone gone into Hades, into hell. Kora was the springtime of the year; my year, my self was being slaughtered" A, p.158.

102. "In many poor and sentimental households it is a custom to have cheap prints in glass frames upon the walls. These are of all sorts and many sizes and may be found in any room from the kitchen to the toilet. The drawing is always of the worst and the colors, not gaudy but almost always of faint indeterminate tints, are infirm. Yet a delicate accuracy exists between these prints and the environment which breeds them" (I, p. 76). WCW made a lifelong habit of examining the art work in the homes of his patients, as if by studying those he might come into closer contact with the secret at the core of these people.

103. I, p. 79.

104. I, p. 74.

105. I, pp. 60–61.

106. I, p. 38.

107. IWWP, p. 27.

108. I, p. 6.

109. I, p. 9.

110. From "March," published in *The Egoist*, Oct. 1916. In CEP, pp. 43–46.

111. "A physician often comes upon delightful objects d'art inauspiciously lighting the days and years of some obscure household in almost any suburban town—anywhere, everywhere on his rounds. All sorts of things which, if he is fortunate, he will share with his friends and acquaintances in praising. My own small town Rutherford is like any other in that." "Effie Deans," RI, p. 129.

112. I, p. 15.

113. I, p. 13.

114. I, p. 14.

115. I, p. 22.

116. See Dickran Tashjian's "Note: *The Little Review* Vers Libre Contest, 1916," WCWN, VI, 1 (Spring 1980), 33.

117. I, p. 23.

118. I, p. 24.

Chapter Four. Smashing Windows in Paper Houses: 1914–1921 (cont.)

119. I, p. 24. See also IWWP, p. 30.

120. 9 Sept. 1918.

121. 17 Dec. 1918 (Y).

122. 4 Oct. 1918.

123. A, p. 140.

124. 19 Nov. 1918.

125. In an interesting juxtaposition in A, WCW mentions that, after Kreymborg confessed that he was going to work with Millay so that the two men no longer got on "so well," he remembers visiting AK's apartment on Bank Street and AK—to hide the fact that he'd just been arguing with his wife, Gertrude, and her mother—jumped up and smacked his head hard against "the low connecting doorway." It was a wonder, WCW added, that the force of that contact didn't kill AK. Thirty years after the event WCW could still rankle at AK's betrayal. He never joined the Poetry Society of America either, perhaps because of AK's public prominence in that group. When he was invited as a guest at the PSA's annual banquet at the Biltmore Hotel in January 1938 he was frankly bored. On the evening of the twentieth, he sat at the head table along with Marianne Moore and tried to look interested: "I discovered while the speakers were at it that if you take a fern frond and lay it face down on an ironed tablecloth then hold the stem between your fingers and gently push the thing slowly forward tip end first that it appears to crawl like a turtle or a centipede or other entertaining creature. . . . Then if you take your fork in your right hand and toss the fern into the air you can make believe you are pitching hay in a field. You can even try to catch the thing on the fork if you feel real interested. . . . Neither Marianne nor I was asked to speak. . . . Floss . . . said she was itching to have me cut through that heavy atmosphere" (WCW to MB, 21 Jan. 1938).

126. "Invitation," from AQQ, reprinted in ND 16, pp. 18–19.

127. A, p. 159.

128. 24 Dec. 1918 (Hunt.).

129. The letter suggests, although ambivalently, the sense of regenerativity as well as of loss in the stirrings WCW says he felt in his "crotch," in the emphasis on Proteus (change) rather than on a sense of an ending ("not Amen!"), as well as in the final comment: "who can say what this may do."

130. In "Three Professional Studies," Little Review, V. 10–11 (Feb.–March 1919), 36–44. The passage was written at the beginning of January 1919.

131. 27 Jan. 1919.

132. 10 Feb. 1919.

133. Little Review, V, 9 (Jan. 1919).

134. WCW to EB, 13 Feb. 1919.

135. 7 Feb. 1919 (ViU).

136. 3 March 1919 (Y).

137. Published as "Notes from a Talk on Poetry" in the July 1919 issue of Poetry, 211–216.

138. In CEP, pp. 192–193.

139. A, pp. 161–162.

140. WCW to HM, 8 April 1919.

141. WCW to Eleanor Musgrove, 16 Oct. 1936 (B).

142. See "Comment: Wallace Stevens," Poetry, LXXXVII, 4 (Jan.1956), 234–239.

143. "Sample Prose Piece: The Three Letters," Contact, 4 (Summer 1921), 10–13.

144. From unpublished portion of WCW's Journal, 1927–1928, to which "The Descent of Winter" likewise belongs (B).

145. "Belly Music," Others, V, 6 (July 1919), 25–32.

146. *Little Review,* VI, 5 (Sept. 1919), 36–39.

147. *Little Review,* VI, 6 (Oct. 1919), 29–30.

148. "Gloria," *Others,* V, 6 (July 1919), 3–4.

149. *A,* pp. 266–269.

150. "Spring," from *The Autobiography of Emanuel Carnevali,* compiled and prefaced by Kay Boyle, Horizon Press (New York, 1967), pp. 137–140.

151. "Gloria," pp. 3–4.

152. Letters from Emily Carnevali to WCW and FW (B).

153. 3 Aug. 1919 (Y).

154. WCW to Conrad Aiken, 21 Nov. 1919.

155. WCW to Conrad Aiken, 11 Dec. 1919.

156. Maxwell Bodenheim to Conrad Aiken, 17 Dec. 1919 (Hunt.). Aiken was then serving as one of the editors at *The Dial.*

157. WCW to VBJ, 23 Dec. 1919, then living in Bogota, New Jersey.

158. WCW to MM, 23 Dec. 1919 (Rosenbach).

159. This letter, simply dated "Friday evening," seems to date from May 1920 because of internal evidence. WCW saw little of Bodenheim after this period, though Bodenheim's name still comes up occasionally in WCW's letters and essays. Bodenheim's literary fortunes slipped badly by the 1930s, when he was reduced to taking whatever New Deal aid he could. When he and his third wife were murdered in their dingy Greenwich Village apartment on 7 Feb. 1954, Floss cut the story out of the *New York Times* to keep as a memory of the old days.

160. Unpublished letters from AK to WCW (B).

161. 22 Sept. 1920 (Y). *KH* was published on September 21.

162. See EP's two letters of 11 September and his follow-up letter of September 12—all really parts of the same long response to WCW's "Prologue"—in *Letters EP,* pp. 156–161.

163. *A,* pp. 170–173. In *Al* WCW adds that, feeling bad for having had to reject Hartley, he had kissed him good-by in the doorway and then left. "A tragic figure," WCW calls him. "I really loved the man, but we didn't always get along together, except at a distance" (*A,* p. 171).

164. *A,* pp. 175–176.

165. RM "was drifting after having done a bit in one of the Canadian regiments" *A,* p. 172. A special word of praise for Sanford J. Smoller's biography of RM, *Adrift Among Geniuses: Robert McAlmon, Writer and Publisher of the Twenties,* Penn State University Press (University Park, 1975). I owe much to Smoller in my own treatment of RM.

166. *Contact,* 1 (Dec. 1920), 1.

167. 27 Oct. 1920. *SL,* pp. 46–47.

168. WCW to EP, 4 Jan. 1921 (L).

169. *Contact,* 2 (Jan.1921), 11–12.

170. Matthew Josephson, *Life Among the Surrealists: A Memoir,* Holt, Rinehart and Winston (New York, 1962), pp. 72–77.

171. *A,* p. 176.

172. *A,* pp. 176–178.

173. This card is now in B collection. RM told WCW's biographer, JT, in 1954 that he thought it was Thayer who had sent it.

174. Undated letter from WCW to KB. Internal evidence points to late February 1921.

175. 6 March 1921. *SL,* pp. 50–51.

176. 20 Nov. 1921.

177. 19 Nov. 1921. *SL,* pp. 54–55.

178. WCW to KB, 26 Jan. 1921.

179. Ibid.

Chapter Four. Smashing Windows in Paper Houses: 1914–1921 (cont.)
  180. 22 March 1921. *SL*, pp. 51–52.
  181. Ca. 27 March 1921.
  182. Ibid.
  183. 31 March 1921.
  184. 27 April 1921.
  185. *Contact*, 3 (Spring 1921), 14–16.
  186. Published in two parts in *The Little Review* with the title, "Thee I call 'Hamlet of Wedding-Ring': Criticism of William Carlos Williams' 'Kora in Hell' and why . . . ," Jan.–March and Autumn 1921 issues.
  187. Helen Birch-Bartlett, "Koral Grisaille," *Poetry* (March 1921), 329–332.
  188. RM's letter was published in the following issue. "Unless from an impulse to say something keenly felt," he insisted, "writing is without justification." The *Improvisations* were, he added, "the most important book of poetry that America" had yet produced ("Concerning 'Kora in Hell,' " *Poetry* [April 1921], 54–59).
  189. 23 March 1921. *SL*, pp. 52–53.
  190. 10 June 1921.
  191. See "Cars," WEW in *WCWN*, III, 2 (Fall 1977), 1–5.
  192. Interview with WEW, April 1979.
  193. 21 Oct. 1921. *SL*, pp. 53–54.
  194. *IWWP*, pp. 34–35.
  195. *CEP*, p. 199.
  196. *CEP*, p. 223.
  197. "Blueflags," *CEP*, p. 225.
  198. "To a Friend Concerning Several Ladies," *CEP*, pp. 216–217.
  199. RM to Wallace Stevens, 2 Dec. 1921 (Hunt.).
  200. For a discussion of Stevens' trips to New York, see Peter A. Brazeau, "A Trip in a Balloon: A Sketch of Stevens' Later Years in New York," in *Wallace Stevens: A Celebration*, ed. Frank Doggett and Robert Buttel, Princeton University Press (Princeton, N.J., 1980), pp. 114–129.

Chapter Five. Tracking Through the Fog: 1921–1924

  1. *GAN* in *I*, p.158.
  2. *I*, p. 163.
  3. *I*, p. 167.
  4. *I*, p. 168.
  5. *I*, p. 174.
  6. *I*, p. 175.
  7. *I*, p. 190.
  8. *I*, pp. 198–199.
  9. *I*, p. 219.
  10. *I*, p. 227.
  11. *A*, p. 146.
  12. WCW to Alfred Stieglitz, 12 Jan. 1922 (Y): "I want to bring with me my friend Wallace Gould, an old friend of [Marsden] Hartley's from his home in Maine, whose work you may remember having seen in the *Little Review*."
  13. 1 Feb. 1922 (Princeton).
  14. Interview with WEW, May 1980.
  15. *A*, pp. 180–183.
  16. 12 Jan. 1922.
  17. "Heaven's First Law," *Dial* (Feb. 1922), 197–200.

18. 3 Feb. 1922.
19. *Letters EP*, pp. 172–174.
20. 29 March 1922 (L).
21. WCW to EP, 13 July 1922 (L).
22. WCW to EP, 22 Nov. 1922 (L).
23. RM to WCW, 12 Feb. 1922 (Pri.).
24. Ibid.
25. WCW to Harold Loeb, 1 Feb. 1922 (Princeton).
26. Letter of 15 July 1922, *Little Review*, IX, 3 (Autumn 1922), 59–60.
27. WCW to Jane Heap, late July 1922.
28. *I*, pp. 124–125.
29. Ibid., p. 125. This is WCW's version of the contemporary interest in machine eroticism, which has its counterpart in the work of Duchamp and Picabia. Among several good discussions of WCW and this phenomenon by Weaver, Tashjian, Dijkstra and others, see especially Peter Schmitt's "Some Versions of Modernist Pastoral: Williams and the Precisionists," in the special Art and Literature number of *Contemporary Literature*, XXI, 3 (Summer 1980), 383–406.
30. *I*, p. 104.
31. *I*, pp. 94–95.
32. *I*, pp. 115–116.
33. *I*, pp. 149–150.
34. *I*, pp. 148–149.
35. *A*, p. 146.
36. *I*, p. 118.
37. WCW to KB, 10 June 1922.
38. WCW to KB, undated, but about July 1922.
39. WCW to KB.
40. Ibid. WCW seems to have taken a dislike to Josephson from the beginning, when he and RM had walked with KB and Josephson across the New Jersey winter landscape in January 1921. A month later WCW wrote KB, "You call me a Whitmanite (Jesus Christus what lightning like penetration) then you want me to admit Josephson to my cellar closet—I am raw and stupid" (late Feb. 1921).
41. WCW to EP, 5 May 1922 (L).
42. WCW to EB, Aug. 1922.
43. 4 Oct. 1922.
44. WCW to EB, Aug. 1922.
45. WCW to MW, 20 Aug. 1922.
46. WCW to EB, 26 Dec. 1922.
47. Ibid.
48. EP to WCW from Paris, 1 Aug. 1922. *Letters EP*, pp. 183–284.
49. WCW to EP, 15 Aug. 1922 (L).
50. WCW to EP, 16 Aug. 1922 (L).
51. WCW to EP, 26 Aug. 1922 (L).
52. WCW to EP, 11 Sept. 1922 (L).
53. EP to WCW, 9 Feb. 1923, from Rapallo. *Letters EP*, p. 185.
54. 2 Feb. 1923.
55. 5 Feb. 1923.
56. 15 March 1923.
57. 21 March 1923.
58. 29 March 1923.
59. 12 April 1923.
60. Undated, but ca. mid-April 1923.

Chapter Five. Tracking Through the Fog: 1921–1924 (cont.)

61. Letter dated "April—toward the end" 1923.

62. WCW to MW, 12 June 1923.

63. *A*, pp. 179–180.

64. WCW to MW, 21 July 1923. WCW included with this letter a new poem written that morning called, "The Down Town Jazz," never published.

65. Matthew Josephson, *Life Among the Surrealists: A Memoir*, Holt, Rinehart and Winston (New York, 1962), pp. 253–254.

66. See *A*, p. 171. WCW also made the error there of thinking he'd accepted an early poem of Crane's for *Contact* 2 (1932), but he'd actually accepted Crane's poem for *Others* back in 1916.

67. *A*, p. 180.

68. *A*, pp. 180–181.

69. (Pri.)

70. Letter dated "Sunday," but probably September 1923. WCW to MW.

71. *I*, p. 322.

72. President Harding died 2 Aug. 1923 in San Francisco, just as the scandals involving his administration were about to break.

73. *CEP*, pp. 325–328.

74. Foreword to *IAG*.

75. Ibid.

76. Ibid.

77. *A*, p. 183.

78. WCW to MW, ca. 27 Sept. 1923.

79. WCW to Malcolm Cowley, dated "Tuesday AM," probably October 1923.

80. WCW to Glenway Wescott, 3 Oct. 1923 (ViU).

81. WCW to KB, dated "Monday," probably Nov. 1923.

82. WCW to RM, undated, probably October or November 1923. *SL*, pp. 56–57.

83. WCW to KB, Nov. 1923.

84. Sophia Smith Collection at Smith College. I am indebted to Elaine Sproat, Lola Ridge's biographer, for this information. See also *A*, p. 171.

85. Thanks to Mrs. Valerie Eliot for providing the author with a copy of the original essay (with corrections), which WCW sent TSE in December 1923.

86. The Marianne Moore essay was published in the May 1925 issue of *The Dial*, LXXVIII, 5 (pp. 393–401). See also *SE*, pp. 121–131 and *I*, pp. 308–318.

87. WCW to TSE, 9 Dec. 1923 (V. Eliot).

88. WCW to MM, "Sunday," i.e. 11 Dec. 1923 (Rosenbach).

89. WCW to TSE, 16 Dec. 1923 (V. Eliot).

90. WCW to TSE, 17 Dec. 1923. In pencil someone, probably TSE himself, has written on the page of corrections, "Please attach to MS," and WCW's Paris address.

91. WCW to HM, 18 Dec. 1923. WCW may also have thought that there would be no conflict in having the Moore essay printed in both an American and a British publication.

92. *SL*, pp. 57–58.

93. This diary is still in possession of the Williams family. WCW used it extensively in composing both *VP* and *A*. "From here out," he wrote at the beginning of Chapter 32 of *A*—"Our Trip Abroad"—"for the sake of what accuracy may be gained thereby, I shall follow the diary for a while" (p. 185). I have silently corrected several errors in dating in *A* made by WCW.

94. *A*, p. 188.

95. *A*, p. 189.

96. The diary makes clear what *A* makes murky at this point, which explains why

Richard Ellmann, in his excellent biography of Joyce, thought Joyce was referring to himself and Nora as *beati innocenti*. Rather, Joyce had used that phrase to describe the Williamses —the latest of the innocents abroad. (See Ellmann, *James Joyce*, Oxford University Press (New York, 1959), p. 576.

97. *A*, p. 191.

98. *A*, p. 194.

99. *A*, p. 195.

100. *A*, p. 199.

101. Diary.

102. *IAG*, p. 105.

103. *IAG*, p. 108.

104. *IAG*, p. 109.

105. WCW to TSE, 28 Jan. 1924 (H).

106. *A*, p. 200.

107. Ibid. For the Villefranche experience (Feb. 1924), see *A*, pp .200–207 and *VP*.

108. Diary. In an unpublished interview with JT (28 July 1956), WCW remembered this event again: "Thelma Wood, the Robin of Djuna Barnes' *Nightwood*, Djuna, Floss and I went to Monte Carlo, where Djuna lost her money and some of Floss's. I had a nervous habit of pulling out the hairs on the back of my hand, and Djuna told me to stop, yet Thelma Wood was still dominating her. . . ." (Y)

109. *SL*, p. 59.

110. See "Night," Ch. XIV of *VP*, pp. 90–94.

111. *VP*, p. 97.

112. *VP*, p. 106.

113. *VP*, p. 123.

114. *VP*, p. 109.

115. *Rome*, p. 14.

116. This meeting took place on Friday, 14 March 1924. In *Rome* WCW wrote, cryptically, "I go—to know that every woman one admires is not to be screwed—but some are a view over the forum from Cunard's window" (p. 16). WCW "overlooked" this meeting completely in *A*, mentioning in general terms the meeting instead with Nancy and Victor Cunard which took place a week later.

117. Diary, 18 March 1924.

118. 20 March 1924 (Y).

119. *SL*, pp. 60–62.

120. Diary, 28 March 1924.

121. *Rome*, p. 20.

122. Diary, 28 March 1924.

123. Diary.

124. *SL*, p. 63. Kassák had been exiled from Hungary after the fall of the Republic of Councils in 1919 and was living in Vienna, publishing *MA* and taking part in the intense ideological debates of the various political émigrés then gathered in the Austrian capital. For a discussion of WCW and Kassák, see Gyula Kodolányi, "Ideas of the New in Modern Poetry: Notes on the Anglo-American Tradition," in *WCWR*, VI, 1 (Spring 1980), 11–22.

125. 14 April 1924, *SL*, p. 64.

126. 15 April 1924 (Colorado).

127. During this month Floss sent her mother-in-law a picture postcard of the Karlskir-che and the comment, "There may be other citys [sic] as fine as Vienna but I have yet to see them. Even Paris is eclipsed by this city for me at least" (Pri.).

128. Diary, 27 April 1924.

129. *VP*, p. 197.

Chapter Five. Tracking Through the Fog: 1921–1924 (cont.)

130. This was *Le Cheval meurt et les oiseaux s'envolent (The Horse Dies and the Birds Fly Away)*, which Kassák wrote in 1922. WCW's copy at B.

131. WCW was as guilty as many Americans of his generation in sometimes making stereotypic judgments. It was one reason he would later write "A Face of Stone"—to examine and hopefully to exorcise this reflex habit in himself. In his diary for 30 April 1924 he wrote: "Got seat next to window by luck. Jew as usual objectionable closing door and smoking but froze him out by letting wind blow in ventilator." In *VP*, this episode became: "A Jew of the usual objectionable type made himself objectionable by closing the door to the compartment and smoking copiously, a vile smell. Dev by the window opened the ventilator, froze out the other, who took to the corridor. Fresh air! For this relief much thanks. He felt irritable and sick. Vienna was going by in the rain" (p. 218).

132. Diary, 3 May 1924.

133. Diary, 10 May 1924.

134. Diary, 13 May 1924.

135. Diary, Saturday, 17 May 1924.

136. Diary, 18 May 1924. In *A* this became, "It [the Hôtel de Dieu] gave me the most lively sense of the reality of the poor that I have ever had" (p. 211).

137. Diary, 21 May 1924.

138. *A*, p. 215.

139. *A*, p. 217. In *VP* Williams' female alter ego says to Dev Evans in Paris: "They have made a virtue of their poverty—and that is what it all is. Your silly profusion . . . defeats us. Dev, you've got to quit fooling—quit your cash job and study it out." To which Dev replies, "Like Eliot?" If WCW showed his resentment to TSE anywhere for not at least answering his letters after WCW had been willing to support the man in the amount of $100, it was just here in this fictional scene (p. 241).

140. In a letter to DM (14 Jan. 1951) WCW wrote, "Do you realize that when I was in Paris in 1924 I retracted Hemingway's oldest boy's foreskin for him while the redoubtable lion hunter almost fainted?" (*SL*, p. 294)

141. Diary, 5 June 1924.

142. *A*, p. 232.

Chapter Six. The Great American Desert: 1924–1929

1. Diary, Monday 16 June 1924.

2. *Rome*, p. 60.

3. 5 Sept. 1924, *SL*, p. 65. Misdated there 6 September.

4. WCW to Malcolm Cowley, 24 Dec. 1924 (Newberry).

5. WCW to John Herrmann, 11 Dec. 1924.

6. WCW to Malcom Cowley, dated "Wednesday." About Feb. 1925 (Newberry).

7. 23 Sept. 1924. WCW had his tonsils removed at Passaic General Hospital on Friday morning, 19 September. Floss, on the other hand, in spite of her tonsilitis in Paris, decided to wait until December 1929 to have hers removed (WCW to LZ, 11 Dec. 1929).

8. WCW to Sylvia Beach, 8 Oct. 1924.

9. WCW to KB, 21 Oct. 1924.

10. WCW to EP, 23 Dec. 1924. *SL*, p. 66.

11. WCW to Malcolm Cowley, Feb. 1925 (Newberry).

12. *A*, p. 236.

13. *A*, p. 236. Had he found his audience, WCW was ready to do a sequel to *IAG*, which would include essays on Thomas Jefferson, Grover Cleveland, and Pancho Villa, the last of whom he had already sketched in *GAN*. "But the bad reception I got," he added, "put an end to all that."

14. WCW to EP, 10 April 1925 (Y).

15. New York Evening Post Literary Review for 23 May 1925. In the original typescript (B) WCW has written at the top of the first sheet, "He wrote his sister's work." What WCW presumably had in mind here was the relationship he would create in *VP* between Dev Evans (a fictive account of himself) and his sister, who would take on the character of WCW's version of H.D. herself. That suggestion raises tantalizing possibilities of the way WCW saw himself—i.e., his female half—actualized in the person of H.D.

16. WCW to Alva Turner, 12 May 1925 (B).

17. Babette Deutsch to Lola Ridge, 21 Sept. 1925. Information provided by Elaine Sproat.

18. See *A*, p. 163.

19. "Good . . . for What?," *Dial*, LXXXVI, 3 (March 1929), 250–251.

20. WCW to Waldo Frank, 3 July 1925. Frank himself was enthusiastic about *IAG* and took the time to tell WCW himself. "You are the first who has valued the Columbus chapter highly or in fact paid any attention to the design in the book at all," WCW wrote Frank on 11 July. See also *IWWP*, p.42: "Waldo Frank was the only person who recognized the technical difficulty and wrote me a letter praising the ending."

21. WCW to JR, 12 Oct. 1925.

22. 5 Nov. 1925. "['Melanctha'] is one of the chief jems [sic] of recent American writing."

23. 16 Dec. 1925.

24. 16 Nov. 1925.

25. WCW to JR, 23 Dec. The gathering took place on December 17.

26. WCW to JR, 23 Dec. 1925.

27. See, for example, Hart Crane's letter to Louis Untermeyer of 19 Jan. 1923, enclosing the last part of "For the Marriage of Faustus and Helen." That poem, Crane suggested, taken in its totality, had been "designed to erect an almost antithetical spiritual attitude to the pessimism of 'The Waste Land,' although the poem was well finished before 'The Waste Land' appeared." (See Richard Allan Davison's "Hart Crane, Louis Untermeyer, and T. S. Eliot: A New Crane Letter," *American Literature* [March 1972], pp. 143–146.)

28. WCW to JR, 23 Dec. 1925. Fragments of a counterresponse, WCW believed, could be found in the "precisionist" poetics he had formulated in late 1923 in his essay on MM's "geometric" poetics and again, the following year, in his portrait of Edgar Allen Poe as a critic of mathematical clarities. It was one reason why WCW was drawn to JR's scientific and analytical bent at this particular moment, when American precisionism in art was at its strongest (as in the work of WCW's friend Charles Sheeler in a painting like *City Interior*).

29. 14 Jan. 1926. WCW's letters for the period reflect the personal cost of trying to write and maintain a medical practice. "My head is figuratively on my knees tonight I am so tired," he wrote Waldo Frank on 11 July 1925. "I have been writing again after several months' slopping about doing foolish things. It is prose this time—but the intense effort necessary for the work tears me to pieces—especially since I must keep up my practice at the same time." The phrase "foolish things" in WCW's vocabulary usually means intimacies of one kind or another, which WCW was at pains to cover until he felt the overwhelming need to "confess" in one form or another and so get those events away from him.

30. WCW to EP, 24 Jan. 1926 (Y).

31. Speaking of Quevedo's bawdy in his letter of 14 January to Riordan, WCW added that, though he wasn't of Quevedo's school, he wanted to take in one of the "girlie" shows in New York City with JR sometime in February, to "see 'em up close." WCW could enjoy machine eroticism (à la Duchamp) as much as anyone and praised JR in this same letter for noticing with admiration "the ladies little asses all in silk and steamengines and things—as they turn 'em over to fry on the other side."

32. WCW to JR, 26 Jan. 1926.

Chapter Six. The Great American Desert: 1924–1929 (cont.)
 33. Ibid.
 34. WCW to JR, 10 June 1926.
 35. WCW to JR, 24 June 1926.
 36. WCW to KB, 15 March 1926.
 37. WCW to JR, 13 Oct. 1926.
 38. WCW to JR, 6 Nov. 1926.
 39. WCW to JR, 17 Nov. 1926.
 40. WCW to JR, 20 Nov. 1926.
 41. WCW to KB, 15 March 1926.
 42. Private notes in B collection, dated 12–16 June 1926.
 43. WCW to JR, dated "Thursday," but ca. August 1926.
 44. WCW to Sylvia Beach, 18 Aug. 1926.
 45. WCW to EP, 6 Jan. 1927 (Y).
 46. WCW to John Herrmann, 10 April 1927.
 47. 19 July 1927.
 48. Ibid.
 49. WCW to Wallace Stevens, 17 Aug. 1927.
 50. Published in transition, No.13, American Number (Summer 1928), 237–240, as "George Antheil and the Cantilene Critics: A Note on the First Performance of Antheil's Music in NYC; April 10, 1927." In I, pp. 351–357. Earlier WCW had written Sylvia Beach to look after the Spences when they were in Paris in September 1926. Madeline Spence, he wrote, was a pianist "much interested in modern music though she is not a radical there in any respect" (18 Aug. 1926).
 51. Colorado.
 52. WCW to Lola Ridge, 5 July 1927 (Smith College).
 53. WCW to FW, "Wednesday," Aug. 1927 (Pri.).
 54. 16 Aug. 1926 (Pri.).
 55. Exile's Return: A Literary Odyssey of the 1920s, Viking Press (New York, 1951), pp. 219–220.
 56. "Impromptu: The Suckers," CEP, pp. 315–317.
 57. WCW to EP on hotel stationery, 16 Sept. 1927 (Y).
 58. A, pp. 253–254.
 59. Nine PM Saturday, 24 Sept. 1927. SL, pp. 71–72.
 60. So he wrote again on Sunday morning, Sunday afternoon, Monday morning, Monday afternoon ("absolutely heartbroken"), Tuesday, Wednesday, Thursday, twice on Friday, twice on Saturday, and again on Sunday before disembarking that evening (SL, pp. 71–91.)
 61. Wednesday, 7:45 AM, 28 September 1927. SL, p. 80.
 62. This copy (at Princeton) is dated 30 September. It is an early version of the poem published in DW under that date.
 63. Princeton.
 64. Princeton.
 65. WCW's Journal is now in B. Part of it remains unpublished and restricted; part was published as "The Descent of Winter" in EP's The Exile, New York, No.4 (Autumn 1928), 30–69. This was reprinted in I, pp. 234–265.
 66. Journal.
 67. I, p. 238.
 68. Journal. The baby was born 15 Sept. 1927—a second child—and weighed in at six pounds, two ounces. WCW spoke of her conception in his Journal for 29 Oct. 1927. "Cash she'll have," he mused. "What will become of her?"
 69. Ibid.
 70. I, p. 240.

71. Journal.

72. *I*, p. 254. Five years earlier WCW had made a similar connection between revolutionary Russia and contemporary postrevolutionary America under the Harding administration. In late March 1922 WCW evidently attended a performance of *Katinka*, a Russian folk ballet put on in New York City by Nikita Balieff's Chauve-Souris (i.e. Bat) Company. On the twenty-ninth he told EP that the Moscow troupe's performance had been "superbly done" and later—probably in late April—wrote a 94-line poem, "When Fresh, It Was Sweet," which *The Dial* published in Dec. 1922. In that poem WCW made reference to the Bat's charity performance on April 9, when Al Jolson and other American vaudeville actors working together raised $11,000 for charity. What especially moved WCW was the unceasingly fresh spirit of the dance surpassing the "mercenary" landlord "who kills the splendour of national character / by his demands for rent, / the filth of / stupidity which has no escape." Beyond that universal impulse toward greed WCW saw in the beautiful young peasant girl Katinka—another of his Koras—"life's exquisite diversity / its tenderness / ardour of spirits" moving gracefully to the rebeginning dance. WCW, deep into his meditation on Columbus at this time, saw the revolutionary spirit of new beginnings enacted once again for a brief moment in his own city. (See Christopher J. MacGowen, "Two New Williams Citations," *WCWR*, VI, 2 (Fall 1980), 27–30.

73. *I*, p. 255.

74. *I*, p. 257.

75. Journal.

76. Ibid.

77. Private coll. He also named his "baby" Veronica Magdalen (Lena) from Garfield, New Jersey, in his Journal for 16 Nov. 1927.

78. Private coll.

79. Journal for 15 Dec. 1927.

80. Ibid.

81. Ibid.

82. *I*, p. 261.

83. Journal for 20 Dec. 1927.

84. WCW to FW, 20 Dec. 1927 (Pri.). "The Men," *CEP*, p. 459.

85. B collection.

86. WCW to FW (Pri.).

87. This drama is contained in a series of letters between Floss and WCW during the fall of 1927 (Pri.). Also, see *A*, pp. 257–258.

88. See *A*, pp. 260–262.

89. WCW to FW, 27 Feb. 1928 (Pri.).

90. WCW to FW, 7 March 1928 (Pri.).

91. WCW to FW, 14 March 1928 (Pri.).

92. WCW to FW, 15 March 1928 (Pri.).

93. WCW to John Herrmann, 30 Jan. 1928.

94. WCW included an excerpt of this letter in his Journal for 11 Jan. 1928. The actual letters WCW sent Yvor Winters were apparently destroyed—burned by Winters himself—along with hundreds of other letters YW had received over a lifetime of literary correspondence.

95. The statement was written in Jan.–Feb. 1928.

96. WCW to John Herrmann, 30 Jan. 1928.

97. "A Tentative Statement," *Little Review*, Paris, XII, 2, Last Issue (May 1929), 95–98.

98. WCW's first letter to LZ is dated 23 March 1928. *SL*, p. 93.

99. WCW to LZ, 28 March 1928. In *A*, WCW calls Eva Herrmann "Hoffman."

100. WCW to LZ, 2 April 1928. *SL*, p. 94.

101. WCW to LZ, 8 April 1928. *SL*, p. 95.

Chapter Six. The Great American Desert: 1924–1929 (cont.)

102. This visit of Cummings' out to Rutherford—apparently the only time he made such a trip—took place 6 May 1928. See *A*, pp. 258–259. Further details are found in WCW's letters to FW at the time and in his Journal.

103. WCW to LZ, 12 May 1928 (T).

104. WCW to EP, 16 April 1928. *SL*, p. 96.

105. WCW to Charles Demuth, 7 May 1928, *SL*, pp. 97–98. The painting was finished that August. For the genesis of WCW's poem, see *A*, p. 172. "Once on a hot July day [probably in 1916] coming back exhausted from the Post Graduate Clinic [in New York], I dropped in as I sometimes did at Marsden's [Marsden Hartley's] studio on [West] Fifteenth Street for a talk. . . . As I approached his number I heard a great clatter of bells and the roar of a fire engine passing the end of the street down Ninth Avenue. I turned just in time to see a golden figure 5 on a red background flash by. The impression was so sudden and forceful that I took a piece of paper out of my pocket and wrote a short poem about it."

106. WCW to Margaret Anderson at *Little Review* office in Paris, 11 May 1928.

107. WCW to LZ, 8 May 1928 (T).

108. WCW to EB, 11 April 1928 (Y).

109. WCW to EB, 18 July 1928 (Y).

110. Journal.

111. FW to WCW, 5 May 1928, from Geneva (Pri.).

112. WCW to FW, 3 June 1928 (B).

113. WCW to FW, 6 June 1928 (Pri.).

114. WCW to FW, 19 June 1928 (Pri.). WCW wrote EP himself six days later to tell him about the dedication.

115. WCW to Sylvia Beach, 2 June 1928.

116. WCW to Sylvia Beach, 24 June 1928.

117. Ibid.

118. WCW to EP, 12 July 1928 (Y).

119. Ibid.

120. EP to WCW (B).

121. *SL*, pp. 103–106.

122. Hart Crane to WCW, 16 Sept. 1928 (B).

123. WCW to LZ, 2 Dec. 1928 (T).

124. This was the "Tunnel" section of *The Bridge*.

125. *CEP*, pp. 236–238.

126. *I*, p. 276. Written Jan. 1929.

127. WCW to LZ, 5 July 1928 (Y).

128. WCW to LZ, 18 July 1928 (Y).

129. WCW to LZ, 12 July 1928 (T).

130. WCW to LZ, 18 Oct. 1928 (T).

131. WCW to EP, 12 July 1928 (B).

132. Interview with WEW.

133. *A*, p. 263.

134. Bill Quinton of Rutherford.

135. WCW to LZ, 22 July 1928 (T).

136. WCW to LZ, 22 Aug. 1928 (Y).

137. WCW to MM, 23 Aug. 1928. *SL*, pp. 106–107.

138. WCW to LZ, 4 Oct. 1928 (Y).

139. WCW's *EK* remained unpublished until 1974, eleven years after his death, when ND brought out an edition, edited by Ron Loewinsohn. The dating suggests that WCW began *EK* in late June 1928, while his family was still in Europe, picked it up sporadically throughout 1929, and added a section on his hero Shakespeare in April 1930, before putting the script—dedicated to his sons—away. In a sense *EK* is a continuation of the Journal he'd kept since leaving Floss and his sons in September 1927.

140. The interview took place on 24 July 1928 and appeared in the Sunday edition of the *Herald Tribune* (Book Section) for August 5. Six days later WCW sent EP a clipping of the interview with the comment, "I was invited up to see this here Isabel Paterson. She lit into you and wanted to larf you and Antheil off the stage. . . . Later I quoted them the gist of my article about Antheil." (*SL*, p. 105.)

141. WCW to MM, 2 Nov. 1928.

142. WCW to Sylvia Beach, 4 Nov. 1928.

143. WCW to LZ, 4 Oct. 1928 (Y).

144. WCW to EP, 6 Nov. 1928. *SL*, pp. 108–109.

145. WCW's response to his reading of these texts (and others like John Donne) appears in the pages of *EK*. So, for example, writing about his own theory of knowledge, he warns himself to go slow: "Anyone acquainted with the grave and beautiful processes of science—even if no more so than to the extent of having read Ivan Pavlov's first one hundred pages on the 'Conditioned Reflexes,' and especially anyone who has known such men as Erdheim—must go slow" (*EK*, p. 75).

146. WCW to Sylvia Beach, 10 April 1929.

147. *I*, p. 275.

148. *I*, p. 280.

149. WCW to LZ, 22 July 1928 (T).

150. *A*, p. 266.

151. WCW to LZ, 28 Dec. 1928 (Y).

152. WCW to LZ, 28 Oct. 1928 (Y).

153. "For a New Magazine," *Blues*, Columbus, Miss., I, 2 (March 1929), 30–32.

154. "A Note on the Art of Poetry," *Blues*, (May 1929), 77–79.

155. WCW to RJ, 12 July 1929.

156. In a letter to Jesse L. Greenstein of 23 Aug. 1929 WCW had this to say about the importance of understanding the place out of which the artist sprang: "That is precisely the artist's problem: to unlock from what he sees before him, wherever he happens to be, the universal. It is only with the local that he can begin and not by slighting that to run off into theories and the great thoughts of antiquity. . . . He begins with what is before him. . . . Does not anyone see that all schools of the past are local in origin?" (B).

157. WCW to RJ, 12 July 1929.

158. WCW to LZ, "Wednesday," mid-September 1929 (Y).

159. WCW to EP, 11 Sept. 1929 (Y).

160. Kenneth Rexroth, "Letter from San Francisco," *Blues* (Fall 1929), 42–43.

161. WCW to CHF, 12 Nov. 1929.

162. WCW to Sylvia Beach, 28 Oct. 1929.

163. WCW to LZ, 22 Dec. 1929 (T).

164. *A*, pp. 265–266.

165. WCW to KB, 14 Nov. 1929.

166. *CEP*, pp. 381–382.

Chapter Seven. Depression: 1930–1933

1. Myra Marini's letters to WCW, most dating from 1930–1931, are at B. FW wrote WCW from Geneva 5 May 1928, "So sorry to hear about the Marini child. What a bitter blow to have to get accustomed to" (Pri.).

2. *CEP*, p. 353.

Chapter Seven. Depression: 1930–1933 (cont.)

3. WCW to LZ, 4 Dec. 1929 (T).

4. WCW to EB, 9 March 1930 (Y).

5. EB to WCW, 11 March 1930 (Y).

6. WCW to EB, 23 March 1930 (Y).

7. EB to WCW, 4 April 1930 (Y).

8. WCW to EB, 11 May 1930 (Y).

9. EB to WCW, 17 May 1930 (Y).

10. WCW to RJ, 6 Jan. 1930.

11. "Manifesto," Pagany, Boston, I, 1 (Winter 1930), 1.

12. "The Work of Gertrude Stein," Pagany, I, 1 (Winter 1930), 41–46.

13. WCW to Louis Grudin, 11 Jan. 1930 (Pri.). Grudin's letters to WCW are in B.

14. WCW to Louis Grudin, 26 Jan. 1930 (Pri.).

15. WCW to LZ, 14 Jan. 1930 (Y).

16. WCW to LZ, 13 Feb. 1930 (T).

17. WCW to LZ, 20 Feb. 1930 (T).

18. WCW to EP, 2 March 1930 (Y).

19. WCW to EP, 13 March 1930. SL, pp. 112–113.

20. WCW to LZ, May 1930 (Y).

21. WCW to LZ, 9 May 1930 (Y).

22. WCW to LZ, 3 April 1930 (Y).

23. WCW to RJ, 1 May 1930. Mangan's essay was called "A Note: On the Somewhat Premature Apotheosis of T.S. Eliot."

24. WCW to RJ, 2 May 1930. RJ rejected it, by his own admission after WCW's death, because he had taken a dislike to RM personally for some slight RM had proferred.

25. See WCW's letters to R. P. Blackmur of 15 July and 22 Aug. 1929.

26. WCW to BB, 11 May 1930. In a letter to one of Morada's editors, Donal McKenzie (18 Jan. 1931), WCW wrote that he didn't care for the magazine's "tri-lingual notion" (English—Spanish—French) since there wasn't enough new good literature in "one language let alone three" (Fairleigh Dickinson).

27. "American Poetry, 1920–1930," Symposium (Jan. 1931), 60–84.

28. WCW to LZ, 2 July 1930 (T).

29. WCW to LZ, 8 July 1930 (T).

30. See WCW's "Caviar and Bread Again: A Warning to the New Writer," Blues (Fall 1930), 46–47. Jung's essay appeared in transition (Paris), Nos. 19–20 (June 1930), 23–45.

31. WCW to LZ, 9 Sept. 1930: "We had a splendid eight days at Gloucester where we all four of us enjoyed the hospitality of Richard Johns and a lady friend. He is a curious phenomenon . . . ,an enthusiast in a quiet persistent way for modern writing" (T).

32. WCW to LZ, 15 Oct. 1930 (T).

33. WCW to LZ, dated "Saturday," most probably 13 Sept. 1930.

34. WCW to RJ, 20 Oct. 1930.

35. WCW to LZ, 10 Jan. 1931 (T).

36. WCW to LZ, 23 Feb. 1931 (Y). Original typescript at B, signed and dated in pencil: "Feb. 22, 1931."

37. "Excerpts from a Critical Sketch: The XXX Cantos of Ezra Pound," Symposium (April 1931), 257–263.

38. EP to WCW, 22 March 1931 (B).

39. Letter from WCW to LZ, 9 March 1931. On March 13, WCW told LZ that he was mulling over the lecture so much that it was beginning to wreck his stomach and that his dreams were getting lurid. Public talks always set WCW up that way.

40. WCW to RJ, 22 March 1931.

41. WCW to MM, 22 March 1931.
42. WCW to LZ, 2 April 1931 (Y).
43. WCW to CHF, 10 Nov. 1930.
44. WCW to RJ, 31 April 1931.
45. WCW to RJ, 6 May 1931.
46. WCW to LZ, dated "Thursday," probably 23 July 1931 (T).
47. WCW to LZ, dated "Sunday," probably 26 July 1931 (Y).
48. "The Colored Girls of Passenack—Old and New," *FD*, pp. 50–57.
49. WCW to Edward P. Jennings, 29 July 1931 (B).
50. On 22 March 1931 WCW told RJ that he'd received a letter from Nantucket that hadn't really told him anything about finding a place for the summer. He thought of driving up and taking the ferry across to see the island for himself, but by early May he had about given up the idea. "Cape May, New Jersey has been suggested to us as a likely resort," he told RJ on May 6, but Floss was by then "casting an eye toward Canada and the Great Lakes region." A blue immigration card was issued to "Williams William" by Canadian Immigration on August 15.
51. Postcard sent to Nathanael West's Warrensburg address by WCW from Canada (Pri.).
52. WCW to WEW, dated "Saturday a.m.," i.e., 15 Aug. 1931 (Pri.).
53. *A*, pp. 274–276.
54. WCW to RJ, postcard from Newfoundland, Aug. 1931.
55. "The Cod Head," *CEP*, pp. 333–334.
56. WCW to KB, 2 Dec. 1945.
57. WCW to KR, 30 or 31 Aug. 1931, from West Haven.
58. WCW to LZ, 29 April 1931 (T).
59. Nathanael West to WCW, 10 Oct. 1931 (B).
60. WCW to LZ, 8 Oct. 1931 (Y).
61. WCW to LZ, 9 Oct. 1931 (T).
62. WCW to John Herrmann, 25 Oct. 1931.
63. WCW to LZ, 25 Oct. 1931 (Y).
64. WCW finally told EP about *Contact* in his letter of 8 Dec. 1931, explaining defensively that it was really Moss and Kamin's magazine and that he was "just the, you know, editor. . . . All I does is to pick out what goes into the magazine." *SL*, pp. 117–118.
65. WCW to RJ, 24 Nov. 1931.
66. WCW to EP, *SL*, pp. 117–118.
67. WCW to EP (Y).
68. WCW to RJ, 30 Dec. 1931.
69. WCW to EP, 3 Feb. 1932 (Y).
70. WCW to RJ, 6 Jan. 1932. In a letter to RJ (22 Jan. 1932) WCW added that he was depressed by "Eliot's coming to blast our generation." Looking back on TSE's Harvard stay, WCW would comment to one correspondent: "For me, without one word of civil greeting (a sign of his really bad breeding, which all so-called scholars show—protectively) he reserves the slogan 'of local interest perhaps.' " WCW to T. C. Wilson, 12 July 1933 (*SL*, pp. 141–142).
71. "Doctor-Author Calls Writing Balance Wheel," *New York Herald Tribune*, Monday, 18 Jan. 1932. Includes Sheeler photograph.
72. WCW to RJ, 19 Feb. 1932. "The Dragon Press . . . stunned me by sending the proofs of my book of short stories to me yesterday. I hadn't known that they were even sure of doing the job."
73. In *A*, WCW says it was only a few months after publication that Flores remaindered the books, but that was a lapse of memory on WCW's part, the result, no doubt, of his lingering resentment of Flores.
74. WCW to RJ, 6 Jan. 1932.

Chapter Seven. Depression: 1930–1933 (cont.)

75. WCW to J. Lawrence Salomon, 27 Jan. 1932.

76. "Comment," *Contact*, New York, I,1 (Feb. 1932), 7–9.

77. WCW to Julian Shapiro, 11 and 15 Jan. 1932 (Pri.).

78. WCW to Julian Shapiro, 15 Feb. 1932 (Pri.).

79. WCW to RJ, 15 Feb. 1932.

80. WCW to J. Lawrence Salomon, 5 Feb. 1932.

81. WCW to T. C. Wilson, 10 March 1932 (Y).

82. WCW to RJ, 6 March 1932.

83. WCW to LZ, 14 March 1932 (Y).

84. WCW to LZ, 17 March 1932 (Y).

85. WCW to LZ, Easter Sunday 1932 (Y).

86. Hart Crane's death occurred at midday, 27 April 1932.

87. "Comment," *Contact*, I, 2 (May 1932), 109–110.

88. "Hart Crane (1899–1932)," *Contempo*, II, 4 (5 July 1932), 1,4. WCW came back to the question of Crane's dramatic death and poetic currency thirteen years later while reviewing Karl Shapiro's *Essay on Rime* for the *Kenyon Review*. He still considered Crane's poetic methodology no more than "an excrescence—no matter what the man himself may have been." Crane had done all he could with his kind of poetry, writing it "right and left, front and back, up and down and round in a circle both ways, crisscross and at varying speeds," but he could go on with it no longer. What really killed Crane, WCW now believed, was not his sexual failures but his inability to create. "That he had the guts to go over the rail in his pyjamas, unable to sleep or even rest, was, to me (though what do I know—more than another?) a failure to find anywhere in his '*rime*' an outlet." That leap into the abyss WCW had just rehearsed in *Paterson* 1 when he wrote his comments on Crane in the fall of 1945. (*SE*, pp. 261–262)

89. *SL*, pp. 129–136. Misdated by JT "1932."

90. WCW to EP, June 1932, *SL*, pp. 125–127.

91. WCW to FMF, 18 Sept. 1932 (B). WCW's letter was reprinted in part in *The Cantos of Ezra Pound: Some Testimonies by Ernest Hemingway, Ford Madox Ford, T. S. Eliot, Hugh Walpole, Archibald MacLeish, James Joyce and Others*, Farrar & Rinehart, (New York, 1933).

92. *New English Weekly* (21 July 1932), 331.

93. *New English Weekly* (6 Oct. 1932), 595–597.

94. WCW to LZ, 17 Oct. 1932 (Y).

95. WCW to RJ, 25 Oct. 1932.

96. *New English Weekly*, (10 Nov. 1932), 90–91.

97. WCW to LZ, 14 Feb. 1932 (Y).

98. WCW to Wayne Andrews, 10 Feb. 1932 for *Demain*, an undergraduate leaflet in French mimeographed at Lawrenceville. *SL*, p.119. WCW began this letter in French but switched over to English after a few lines, explaining that his time was precious and "*mon français est mauvais.*"

99. 2 June 1932, *SL*, pp. 122–124.

100. WCW to LZ, 1 June 1932 (T). Also letter to MM of 2 June 1932.

101. Interview with WEW.

102. WCW to BB, 7 June 1932.

103. WCW to RJ, 25 Oct. 1932.

104. "Comment," *Contact*, I, 3 (Oct. 1932), 131–132.

105. WCW to Marsden Hartley, December 1932. In *SL*, this letter is dated "Fall." WCW, however, broke with *Contact* decisively only in mid-December.

106. WCW to Julian Shapiro, 14 Dec. 1932: "Why hasn't Flores answered my last three letters? I thought maybe you'd planted poison in his ears—or something of the sort" (Pri.).

107. WCW to LZ, late Feb. 1933 (T).

108. WCW to KB, 6 Jan. 1933.

109. WCW To KB, 26 Jan. 1933.

110. WCW to KB, 10 Feb. 1933.

111. WCW to LZ, 10 Feb. 1933 (T). And yet just a month earlier WCW had complained to Julian Shapiro that he'd been unable to answer earlier "for the simple reason that I have been drowned in work for the past three weeks due to the outbreak of flu which we are suffering" (7 Jan. 1933. [Pri.]).

112. WCW to BB, 30 Jan. 1933.

113. WCW to KB, 11 Feb. 1933.

114. WCW to EP, 15 March 1933. *SL*, pp. 138–139.

115. WCW to KB, 21 March 1933.

116. WCW to LZ, 22 March 1933 (T).

117. WCW to KB, 3 April 1933.

118. WCW to KB, 15 April 1933.

119. WCW to T. C. Wilson, 12 July 1933. *SL*, pp. 141–142.

120. WCW to T. C. Wilson, no date, but probably Oct. 1933 (Y).

121. WCW to KB, 9 Oct. 1933.

122. WCW to KB, 6 Dec. 1933.

123. WCW to KB, 22 Dec. 1933.

124. Wallace Stevens' "Preface" is reprinted in his *Opus Posthumous*, ed. and with an introduction by Samuel French Morse (New York, 1969), pp. 254–257. Interestingly, Stevens had attempted his own catalog of American detritus in his early drafts for "The Comedian as the Letter C," and had then decided—wisely—to excise that list:

> The shops of chandlers, tailors, bakers, cooks,
> The Coca Cola-bars, the barber poles,
> The Strand and Harold Lloyd, the lawyers' row,
> The Citizens' Bank, two tea rooms, and a church.
> Crispin is happy in this metropole.

(See Louis L. Martz, " 'From the Journal of Crispin': An Early Version of 'The Comedian as the Letter C,' " in *Wallace Stevens: A Celebration*, ed. Frank Doggett and Robert Buttel, Princeton University Press [Princeton, N.J., 1980], pp. 7–8, *passim*.)

125. *IWWP*, p. 52.

126. WCW to KB, 6 Dec. 1933.

127. WCW to LZ, 6 Dec. 1933 (T).

128. WCW to LZ, 6 Jan. 1934 (Y).

129. WCW to LZ, 23 Jan. 1934 (T).

130. Letters from Heilner to author.

131. WCW to LZ, 25 June 1933 (T).

132. WCW to LZ, 20 July 1933 (T).

133. WCW to WEW, 1 Oct. 1933 (Pri.).

134. WCW to BB, 13 Nov. 1933.

135. WCW to KB, 6 Dec. 1933.

136. WCW to LZ, 25 June 1933.

137. WCW to LZ, 20 July 1933 (T).

138. WCW to GM, 25 July 1933.

139. WCW to LZ, ca. 20 Aug. 1933 (T).

140. "Mencken wrote me a very decent letter about my article. He mentioned that he knew a little about poetry. . . ." (WCW to BB, 13 Nov. 1933).

141. WCW to RJ, 23 Aug. 1933.

142. WCW to LZ, ca. 20 Aug. 1933 (T).

Chapter Seven. Depression: 1930–1933 (cont.)

143. WCW to LZ, 20 Sept. 1933. WCW called his prose piece a "poem" in letters to GM on 25 July and to Morton Dauwin Zabel on 29 July.

144. *FD*, pp. 109–116.

145. *Poetry*, XLIII, 1 (Oct. 1933), 8.

146. WCW to MM, 2 May 1934, *SL*, pp. 147–148.

147. WCW to T. C. Wilson, Oct. 1933 (Y).

148. Published as "Art and Politics: The Editorship of BLAST," in *RI*, pp. 75–81.

149. WCW to WEW, 8 Oct. 1933 (Pri.).

150. WCW to WEW, 11:30 PM, Saturday, 25 Nov. 1933 (Pri.).

Chapter Eight. An Index to the Times: 1934–1937

1. "Social Credit as Anti-Communism," *New Democracy* (15 Jan. 1934).

2. WCW to BB, 12 Jan., 16 Feb., and 16 April 1934.

3. WCW to WEW, 28 Jan. 1934 (Pri.).

4. WCW to WEW, 6 Feb. 1934 (Pri.).

5. "The American Background: America and Alfred Stieglitz," *SE*, pp. 134–161.

6. WCW to LZ, 28 Jan. 1934 (T).

7. "The American Background," *SE*, p. 159.

8. WCW to EP, 16 Feb. 1934 (Y).

9. EP, "Commentary on W. C. Williams," *New Democracy* (1 March 1934).

10. WCW's eight-page letter to GM was apparently forwarded to EP, for the original is now among the EP materials at Y.

11. WCW to LZ, 13 March 1934 (Y).

12. WCW to Josephine Herbst and John Herrmann, 13 March 1934 (Y).

13. WCW to LZ, 28 March 1934 (T).

14. "The New Poetical Economy," *Poetry*, XLIV, 4 (July 1934), 220–225.

15. *SL*, pp. 145–147.

16. WCW to LZ, 10 May 1934 (T).

17. Postcard from WCW to LZ, 9 July 1934 (T).

18. WCW to LZ, 17 Sept. 1934 (Y).

19. WCW to LZ, 3 Oct. 1934 (T).

20. WCW to LZ, 30 Oct. 1934 (T).

21. WCW to LZ, 14 Nov. 1934 (T).

22. WCW to LZ, 26 Nov. 1934 (Y).

23. Tibor Serly to WCW, 9 Dec. 1934 (B).

24. WCW to Morton Dauwin Zabel, 10 May 1934.

25. WCW to Morton Dauwin Zabel, 11 June 1934.

26. WCW to WEW, 6 June 1934 (Pri.).

27. WCW to Fred and Betty Miller, "Friday," July 1934 (D).

28. WCW to BB, 5, 11, 12, 19, and 20 July 1934.

29. WCW to BB, 13 Aug. 1934.

30. WCW to LZ, 16 Aug. 1934 (Y).

31. WCW to Julian Shapiro, "Sunday," Sept. 1934 (Pri.).

32. WCW to BB, 11 Oct. 1934.

33. WCW to BB, 14 Oct. 1934.

34. WCW to BB, 29 Jan. 1935.

35. WCW to BB, 3 April 1935.

36. WCW to BB, 3 May 1935.

37. WCW to George Vaughan, 21 July 1934 (B).

38. WCW to LZ, 26 Nov. 1934 (Y).

39. WCW to EP, 14 Nov. 1934 (Y).

40. WCW To RLL, 26 Nov. 1934.

41. WCW to H. L. Mencken, 16 Dec. 1934.

42. WCW to H. L. Mencken, 17 Dec. 1934. On a Sunday morning in February 1935 WCW expanded on the theme of American poetry and the American language over WOR radio. "The success of a poem that might be called 'American' lies first in its identification with the sensual qualities of the language, which the poet hears in his ears all day long" (A. M. Sullivan, "Dr. William Carlos Williams, Poet and Humanist," in *William Carlos Williams*, ed. Charles Angoff, Fairleigh Dickinson University Press [Rutherford, N.J., 1974], pp. 37–46).

43. "An Incredible Neglect Redefined," *SE*, pp. 170–174.

44. WCW to EP, 14 Jan. 1935 (Y).

45. "Pound's Eleven New 'Cantos,'" *New Democracy*, (15 Jan.–1 Feb. 1935), 10–11. Also in SE, pp. 167–169. In "A 1 Pound Stein" for *The Rocking Horse*, Madison, Wisconsin, II,3 (Spring 1935), 3–5, WCW emphasized what he'd learned from EP's latest Cantos: that in dealing with the administrations of Andrew Jackson and Martin Van Buren, EP had revealed "the illegal use by private interests of the resources of government." Usury would become a major preoccupation with WCW in *Paterson* as it had been and would continue to be for EP in his *Cantos*.

46. WCW to EP, 18 Jan. 1935 (Y).

47. WCW to EP, 1 Feb. 1935 (Y).

48. WCW to EP, 25 Feb. 1935 (Y).

49. WCW to EP, 5 March 1935 (Y).

50. *CEP*, p. 96.

51. WCW to EP, 5 March 1935 (Y).

52. WCW to RLL, 25 Feb. 1935, *SL*, pp. 152–153.

53. "Proletarian Portrait," *CEP*, p. 101.

54. "To a Poor Old Woman," *CEP*, p. 99.

55. "Item," *CEP*, p. 95.

56. WCW to EP from Woods Hole, Massachusetts, Sunday 25 Aug. 1935 (Y). "I think you greatly exaggerate the intelligence of the general populace," WCW warned EP, "if you expect any understanding in relation of action [sic]. I do not exclude myself. The chief bar to action is [the] vastness of [America's] terrain, subtlety of camouflage as to which heads to bash and comparative lack of difficulty nowadays in finding bread & circuses. The movies and the tabloids are cheap and one is fed, by God, and well fed out of the public kitchen—everyone can eat and eat well in America at least."

57. "The Yachts," *CEP*, pp. 106–107. The poem first appeared in the *New Republic* in May 1935.

58. *CEP*, p. 114.

59. WCW to NM, 4 Sept. 1935.

60. "You Have Pissed Your Life," *CEP*, p. 461.

61. WCW to MM, 18 Oct. 1935. *SL*, pp. 155–156.

62. WCW to LZ, 1 March 1935 (T).

63. WCW to EP, 5 March 1935 (Y).

64. In 1944 WCW contributed to a "compendium of Millerana" by writing "To the Dean," praising Henry Miller and—by extension—Lawrence Durrell for his Miller "imitation," *The Black Book*, which WCW read with evident gusto in 1942. "To the Dean" is in *CLP*, p. 255.

65. WCW to LZ, 22 Oct. 1935 (T).

66. WCW to FM, 6 Nov. 1935 (ViU).

67. WCW to EP, 28 Dec. 1935 (Y).

68. *ML*, pp. 303–304.

Chapter Eight. An Index to the Times: 1934–1937 (cont.)

    69. WCW to EP, 25 March 1935 (Y).

    70. WCW to LZ, 7 April 1935. WCW told BB in a letter of 3 May that he'd gone only to the Temple meeting and had not seen the parade.

    71. WCW To RLL, 16 April 1935.

    72. WCW to WEW, 20 July 1936 (Pri.).

    73. "A Twentieth Century American," *Poetry,* XLVII, 4 (Jan. 1936), 227–229.

    74. WCW to RLL, 22 Nov. 1935. In this letter WCW voiced his qualms about being published in limited editions: "For myself, barring a direct exchange of appreciation and criticism among a lively group of friends, I'd rather have what work I've done come out in fine small books than in any other way—but I feel hedged round—would rather not appear at all then to become precious—it affects everything, gets under the skin, into the bone at last—castrates one."

    75. "An American Poet," *New Masses,* XXV, 9 (23 Nov. 1937), 17–18.

    76. WCW to KB, 7 May 1935.

    77. WCW to EP, 5 June 1935 (Y).

    78. WCW to WEW, 8 May 1935 (Pri.).

    79. WCW to Willard Maas, 5 Aug. 1935 (RLL papers).

    80. WCW to LZ, 6 Sept. 1935 (T).

    81. WCW to RLL, 25 Nov. 1935.

    82. WCW to EP, 5 June 1935 (Y).

    83. WCW to LZ, 18 Oct. 1935 (T).

    84. WCW to GM, 11 Oct. 1935.

    85. WCW to Dorothy Pound, 29 Oct. 1935 (Y).

    86. "Jefferson and/or Mussolini," *New Democracy,* (15 Oct. 1935), 61–62.

    87. WCW to RLL, 22 and 25 Nov. 1935.

    88. WCW to EP, 28 Dec. 1935 (Y).

    89. WCW To RLL, 9 Jan. 1936.

    90. *CEP,* pp. 376, 378.

    91. *CEP,* pp. 373–374.

    92. *CEP,* pp. 397–404.

    93. *CEP,* p. 368.

    94. WCW to RLL, 26 Jan. 1936.

    95. WCW to RLL, 31 Jan. 1936.

    96. WCW to RLL, 26 April 1936.

    97. WCW to RLL, 1 and 5 May 1936.

    98. Wallace Stevens to WCW, 13 May 1936. *Letters of Wallace Stevens,* sel. and ed. Holly Stevens, Alfred A. Knopf (New York, 1966), p. 311.

    99. WCW to RLL, 6 Feb. 1936.

    100. WCW to RLL, 13 Sept. 1936.

    101. WCW to LZ, 26 Jan. 1936 (T).

    102. WCW to LZ, 29 Jan. 1936 (Y).

    103. *Partisan Review and Anvil,* III, 3 (April 1936), 13–14. *SL,* pp. 157–158.

    104. "Correspondence," *Partisan Review and Anvil,* III, 4 (May 1936).

    105. WCW to LZ, 7 Feb. 1936 (T).

    106. WCW to John Herrmann, 11 Feb. 1936.

    107. WCW to LZ, 17 March 1936 (T).

    108. "The Writers of the American Revolution," *SE,* pp. 38–54. The date there is erroneously given as 1925 instead of 1936.

    109. WCW to LZ, 27 March 1936 (T).

    110. WCW to RLL, 27 Feb. 1936.

    111. WCW to LZ, 27 Feb. 1936 (Y).

112. WCW to LZ, 5 May 1936 (Y).

113. EP to WCW, 8 Feb. 1936 (B).

114. WCW to EP, 27 Feb. 1936 (Y).

115. WCW to EP, 7 April 1936 (Y).

116. WCW to EP, 22 April 1936 (Y).

117. WCW to MB, 30 Jan. 1936.

118. WCW to MB, 19 March 1936.

119. WCW to MB, 12 April 1936.

120. WCW to LZ, 16 April 1936 (T).

121. MB to her parents, 17 April 1936 (Pri.). MB was 26 at the time. Ticino's was a cellar restaurant on Thompson Street, two blocks below Washington Square South. It was a favorite of WCW's.

122. MB to her parents, 25 April 1936 (Pri.).

123. WCW to RLL, 20 Dec. 1934.

124. WCW to MB, 26 April 1936.

125. WCW to MM, 24 May 1936, *SL*, pp. 159–160.

126. WCW to Amy Bonner, 18 Aug. and 18 Nov. 1936 (*Poetry* papers).

127. "Brooklyn Lecture" (B).

128. WCW to LZ, 7 Dec. 1936 (T).

129. WCW to MM, 23 Dec. 1936, *SL*, p. 165.

130. WCW to GM, 1 June 1936.

131. WCW to WEW, 14 July 1936 (Pri.).

132. "The Attack on Credit Monopoly from a Cultural Viewpoint," *RI*, pp. 97–118.

133. WCW to LZ, 22 July 1936 (T).

134. WCW to John Herrmann, 1 June 1936.

135. WCW to JL, 22 Sept. 1936.

136. WCW to JL, 27 Oct. 1936.

137. WCW to John Sanford (Julian Shapiro), 3 Nov. 1936 (Pri.).

138. WCW to EP, 6 Nov. 1936, *SL*, pp. 162–164.

139. WCW to EP, 8 Dec. 1936 (Y).

140. Ibid.

141. *CEP*, p. 433.

142. WCW to RLL, 4 Jan. 1937. The week before Christmas, FW and WCW had driven in to Harlem to see a black musical, *Bassa Moona.* "It was terrific!" WCW told MM with heavy irony. "Diluted Hawaiian tunes put in the mouths of Harlem Darkies wearing batik costumes whose origin seemed to be the suburbs of Jerico [Jericho, Long Island]. What a sell! A new all time low for us. Keep away" (WCW to MM, 27 Dec. 1936).

143. When Elena wrote MM's mother in early January, she explained that she hoped "everyone would follow the teachings of Jesus," which transcended "all those churches denominations." Then she added that she too did not like modern poetry any more than MM's mother because she preferred to look for "the spiritual and the symbols, the sublime." WCW read over that note, smiled and kept his own counsel. He had obviously wandered since his first book of poems. (8 Jan. 1937. Rosenbach)

144. WCW to LZ, 5 Feb. 1937 (T).

145. WCW to LZ, 25 Feb. 4,7, and 17 March 1937 (T).

146. "Midas," *RI*, p. 165.

147. B Collection.

148. WCW to RM, 25 Jan. 1938.

149. WCW to EP, 6 April 1938 (B).

150. WCW to EP, 29 April 1938 (Y).

151. WCW to EP, 18 May 1938 (Y).

152. WCW to JL, 16 Feb. 1939.

Chapter Eight. An Index to the Times: 1934–1937 (cont.)

153. WCW to CHF, 25 March 1937 (Y).

154. *RI*, pp. 120–121.

155. "Sordid? Good God!," *Contempo*, III, 2 (25 July 1933), 5, 8.

156. "The Tortuous Straightness of Charles Henri Ford," introduction to *The Garden of Disorder and Other Poems* by CHF, frontispiece by Pavel Tchelitchew (London, 1938). The introduction is dated 5 June 1937.

157. When WCW saw copies of the book in late May, he confessed to JL that all he could feel was "a sinking," a fear that *WM* would fail and so let JL down (29 May 1937). Two days later he added, "Certainly I feel as if I were sitting before a severe jury waiting to be decapitated" (31 May 1937).

158. *IWWP*, p. 62. In spite of this turn of events, WCW defended the capitalist JL to the Communist H. H. Lewis: "Laughlin is all right. He has his difficulties his father being a multi-millionaire but Geeze! what would you do if your Dad had twenty or thirty million?" After all, JL tried to see straight and publish some of the books he liked (WCW to HHL, 11 Aug. 1937).

159. WCW to HHW, 20 Aug. 1937 (B). "I'm looking forward to [this vacation]," he told HHL, "as an Arab must look forward to an oasis after three days in a sand-storm" (11 Aug. 1937).

160. HHW had broken her other leg in the spring of that year. See letter to LZ 10 March 1937 (T) and to JL, 11 March 1937: "We shall try to put her up in some sort of a splint this afternoon and keep her here [at 9 Ridge Road], out of the hospital where I can still use her to continue our spanish translation."

161. WCW to HHW, 20 Aug. 1937. HHW spent August with her son Edgar at his farm up in Connecticut.

162. WCW to JL, 13 Sept. 1937.

163. WCW to RM, 11 Aug. 1937.

164. WCW to JL, 8 Nov. 1937.

165. "Ripostes" in *Partisan Review*, IV, 2 (Jan. 1938), 61–62. WCW's letters to the editors of *PR* were reprinted in part in this issue at WCW's insistence. As for *New Masses*, WCW had told HHL back in April that he still felt "very little toward that crowd having had my own difficulties with them many years earlier (1926)." He also told HHL that, though he'd met the editor of *New Masses*—"a person named Freeman"—at a literary conference at Princeton in mid-April, he didn't think that any "new Lenin is likely to carry me around in his pocket" (WCW to HHL, 28 April 1937). It was HHL himself who warned WCW that *New Masses* wouldn't publish WCW's essay on HHL if WCW's work appeared in *PR* (as WCW himself acknowledged in a letter to HHL, 10 Nov. 1937). "Those New Masses transcendentalists make me weary," WCW had written FM earlier. "So God has spoken to them, has He, and told them how to classify licherachure." The only true universal or international was excellent work, and that *always* came first out of a particular region or place. The trouble with the American left, he complained, was that they forgot that fact, forgot too that even the Soviets were plural, and that their excellence derived from a specific locality first (WCW to FM, 11 June 1935 [D]).

166. WCW to Parker Tyler, 29 Dec. 1937 (Y).

167. JL to WCW, 29 Nov. 1937 (Y).

168. WCW to JL, 4 Dec. 1937.

169. WCW to RLL, 17 Dec. 1937.

Chapter Nine. Clearing the Field: 1938–1942

1. WCW to KB, 29 Dec. 1937.

2. "Federico García Lorca," *Kenyon Review*, I, 2 (Spring 1939), 148–158. *SE*, pp. 219–230.

3. "Against the Weather: A Study of the Artist," *Twice a Year*, 2 (Spring–Summer 1939), 53–78. *SE*, pp. 196–218.

4. WCW to FM, 18 June 1937 (D).

5. "A Face of Stone," *Harvard Advocate*, CXXII, 3 (Dec. 1935), 19–23. Repr. in *ND* 1 (1936), pp. 68–77. *FD*, pp. 167–176.

6. WCW to MB, 4 March 1937.

7. WCW to WEW, 20 July 1936 (Pri.).

8. At the very heart of his epic *Paterson* is an encounter with a black woman from that city.

9. See, for example, the story "Ancient Gentility" (*FD*, pp. 273–275), which begins: "In those days I was about the only doctor they would have on Guinea Hill. Nowadays some of the kids I delivered then may be practising medicine in the neighborhood. But in those days I had them all. I got to love those people, they were all right. Italian peasants from the region just south of Naples, most of them, living in small jerry-built houses—doing whatever they could find to do for a living and getting by, somehow."

10. WCW to EP, 17 March 1938 (Y).

11. See "The Colored Girls of Passenack—Old and New," *FD*, pp. 50–57. Passenack is WCW's own portmanteau word for Passaic and Hackensack.

12. *CEP*, pp. 393–396.

13. WCW to NHP, 3 Oct. 1938, *SL*, pp. 172–173.

14. WCW to MB, 6 Oct. 1938 (Y).

15. WCW to NHP, 7 Nov. 1938, *SL*, pp. 173–175.

16. "Muriel Rukeyser's US1," *New Republic*, LXXXXIV, 1214 (9 March 1938), 141–142.

17. "Sermon with a Camera," *New Republic*, LXXXXVI, 1244 (12 Oct. 1938), 282–283. *RI*, pp. 136–139.

18. Typescript now at the Houghton, presented by JL.

19. WCW to LZ, 11 Dec. 1938 (T). WCW was also toying with the idea then of becoming the director for the Literary Project of the New Jersey Works Progress Administration, but he turned that offer down.

20. WCW to JL, 27 Feb. 1939.

21. WCW to Jim Higgins, 8 March 1939 (Pri.).

22. WCW to JL, 20 March 1939.

23. WCW to RM, 18 July 1939 (Y).

24. Ms. in B Collection.

25. WCW to RM, 26 Dec. 1938 (Y).

26. "Anthology of a Mind," *New Republic*, XCVII, 1256 (21 Dec. 1938), 208.

27. WCW to JL, 24 Dec. 1938.

28. "On the Spot," *New Republic*, XCVII, 1258 (11 Jan. 1939), 289. It could not have helped Horton that he was the biographer of Hart Crane—WCW's nemesis.

29. "Fresh, Impudent Poems," *New York Herald Tribune Book Review* (5 Feb. 1939), p. 10.

30. "John Wheelwright and Dr. Williams," *Partisan Review* (Winter 1939), 112–115.

31. Writing to H. H. Lewis at the end of 1938, WCW complained that there was a waiting list of 200 at the Rutherford Public Library for the *Collected* and "not one of them with the decency to back their fellow townsman to the tune of a couple of bucks" (30 Dec. 1938 [Y]).

32. Author's correspondence with Paul Leake (Aug. 1978).

33. WCW to EEC, 13 April 1939.

34. WCW to Tom Horan, 3 May 1939 (Pri.). The "anti-sonnet" streak was still very much on WCW's mind. WCW promised Horan to "take a shot at your prize stressing the sonnet in the sense intended to be no more than a short poem in regular stanza form." WCW's response appears to have been "Three Sonnets," published in *Calendar: An Anthology of 1942 Poetry*, ed. by Norman Macleod. (See *CLP*, pp. 30–31.). The three, which

Chapter Nine. Clearing the Field. 1938–1942 (cont.)

even eschew "regular stanza form," together make a very fine sequence on modern love.

35. WCW to LZ, 3 May 1939 (T).

36. WCW to RM, 26 Dec. 1938.

37. "Penny Wise, Pound Foolish," *New Republic*, LXXXXIX, 1282 (28 June 1939), 229–230.

38. WCW to JL, 5 April 1939.

39. WCW to LZ, 19 April 1939 (T).

40. WCW to Sylvia Beach, 12 April 1939.

41. WCW to JL, 22 April 1939.

42. WCW recalled this idyllic interlude in a letter to FW written the following year, when FW was away and WCW was—as usual—feeling lonely in her absence (25 April 1940 [B]).

43. WCW to RM, 25 May 1939. *SL*, pp. 177–182.

44. WCW to RM, 18 July 1939.

45. WCW to JL, 7 June 1939. *SL*, pp. 183–185.

46. WCW to editor of *Furioso* (Yale), 7 June 1939. *SL*, pp. 182–183.

47. "America and the Next War: III," *New Republic*, LXXXXIX, 1282 (28 June 1939), 209. WCW was no hawk. He had everything in the world to lose—his two sons, both eligible for military conscription—but he saw no way out now except to stand up to the Axis powers. And yet, in October, he signed a petition calling for American neutrality in any European conflict. WCW's confusion was part of the larger confusion shared by many Americans at the time, especially when they remembered back to World War I and the promise that that war would end all wars.

48. WCW to RM, 18 July 1939. See also letter from WCW to James Oneal, editor of *The New Leader* (7 East 15th Street, NYC), resigning from the committee.

49. See WCW's letter to NM of 31 Oct. 1939 (*Pembroke*), trying to explain why he'd resigned from the Committee for Cultural Freedom. Oneal had refused to print WCW's letter explaining the reasons for his resignation. Then WCW had tried to enlist the aid of Babette Deutsch in getting his letter printed in another magazine, all to no avail. "So much hidden bitterness," he wrote NM. "About what? Damned if I know."

50. A month after the pact was signed, FW wrote HHL that she was heartbroken and her husband "crushed" over what Russia had done. And though neither she nor WCW was a Communist, still, they'd both had such high hopes for the Russian revolutionary experiment:

> Our visits to the [1939 Flushing] Worlds Fair were real delights due to our continuous visits to the Soviet Pavilion. And now! . . . I know that Russia in Spain was grand. Russia last fall was the only nation to go on record for decency—but after all why do what they have done to Poland—and tie up with that bastard Hitler!—I'm half German and I say it with plenty of emotion!—All my ideals, all my hopes for a people's world are smashed.
>
> (23 Sept. 1939 [Y])

51. WCW to NM, 6 Nov. 1939 (*Pembroke*).

52. WCW to Dr. Casamajor of the Cornell Medical Service at Bellevue, 6 and 15 Nov. 1939 (B). WEW was then (1939–1940) in his last year at Cornell Medical. For a fictional account of doctor father and doctor son at this time, see WCW's short story "The Insane," (*FD*, pp. 287–290), which ends with father praising son for what he has learned about the humane implications of medicine. "I must say," WCW wrote WEW in Feb. 1940, "from your enumeration of the types of cases handled, that you are getting a splendid background for your future work" (13 Feb. 1940 [Pri.]).

53. After graduation from Penn in June 1939, Paul spent two years at Harvard's School of

Business Administration (1939–1941), though several times Paul thought of quitting and going out to find a job. WCW, more relaxed with his second son, seems to have understood Paul's restlessness and to have been willing to let Paul make whatever career choices he wanted. Both his sons, each in their own way, he told Sylvia Beach in 1939, were "delightful kids" (12 April 1939).

54. All excerpts from WCW's unpublished "Introduction" to Ruth's proposed book of poems (B).

55. WCW to Frances Steloff at the Gotham Book Market, New York City, 15 March 1939.

56. *CLP*, pp. 60–61. WCW wrote JL on 23 Oct. 1939 that he'd just finished his elegy to Ford, in spite of its being "the sort of occasional verse which I somewhat mistrust." WCW remembered Ford again a dozen years later in a review he did of Ford's *Parade's End* for the *Sewanee Review*, a review he wrote in the fall of 1950, as he finished *Paterson* 4 and was in a generally elegiac mood. There he remembered old Ford, fat and wheezing, coming out to Rutherford in July of '38. Ford, that eternally curious Englishman, had asked WCW to drive him out into the New Jersey countryside to look at some of the truck farms. "We spent the afternoon at it," WCW remembered,

> a blistering July day when the sprinkler system was turned on in many of the fields, straight back into the country, about three or four miles, to the farm of Derrick Johnson, who personally showed us around. I was more interested in the sandpipers running through the tilled rows—birds which I hadn't seen up to then other than running on the wet sand of beaches as the water washed up and retreated, uncovering minute food. But on the farm they were nestling, here their eggs were laid and hatched in the heat between the beet rows on the bare ground. But Ford, who was looking around, questioned the farmer closely about the cultivation of the lettuce, carrots, dandelion, leeks, peppers, tomatoes and radishes which he was raising. It was all part of his understanding of the particular—and of what should properly occupy and compel a man's mind.

As such, of course, Ford was WCW's good Englishman, the opposite of that adopted Englishman, T.S. Eliot. (See *SE*, pp. 318–319 and also the closing pages of *P4*, with its evocation of the sea, the sandy beaches, little Derrick the Dutchman, and John Johnson the murderer.)

57. Postcard from WCW to CHF, 25 Jan. 1940.

58. WCW to Harvey Breit (Foka), 25 Jan. 1940. *SL*, pp. 189–190. On Feb.2, WCW wrote Breit frantically, "They say Patchen isn't well, that he has some sort of ailment affecting his back. . . . He is coming to New York. . . . Laughlin wants me to take care of him. Geezus! that's a big order."

59. "Poets and Critics," *Partisan Review*, VII, 3 (May–June 1940), 247–248.

60. WCW to MB, 8 Jan. 1940.

61. WCW to Charles Keppel, 8 Jan. 1940 (B).

62. WCW to Charles Keppel, 20 Jan. 1940 (B).

63. This was the first of two letters WCW wrote his wife that day (B).

64. WCW to Charles Keppel, 18 and 28 Feb. 1940.

65. WCW wrote this in Dec. 1945 when he was collaborating with FM on the *Man Orchid* improvisation. See my "Williams' Black Novel" and the improvisation in the special WCW supplement of the *Massachusetts Review*, XIV, 1 (Winter 1973), 67–117.

66. All references are to WCW's "Notes" for his Cooper Union talk of 12 April 1940, written immediately before and after that evening, as he struggled with the idea of a new measure (Y). See *Poetry* for March 1940 for Aiken's "Spain, 1927." See also Aiken's "Poetry: 1940 Model" in the *New Republic* for 22 April 1940.

Chapter Nine. Clearing the Field. 1938–1942 (cont.)

67. From WCW's "Dartmouth Talk," given 16 May 1940 (Y).

68. WCW to NC, 15 Nov. 1940.

69. WCW to NC, 12 Nov. 1940.

70. WCW to NC, 29 Dec. 1940.

71. WCW to TR, 24 Dec. 1957.

72. *A*, pp. 324–325. WCW says there that it was "a beautiful evening in June," but contemporary evidence points to 13 May 1940 as the date. (See especially WCW's letters to CA.)

73. These lines appear in the early (1942) drafts of *P*.

74. WCW to Charles Keppel, 25 June 1940.

75. WCW to Charles Keppel, 7 July 1940. This is a reference to MacLeish's essay "The Irresponsibles," attacking the avant-garde, and the left especially, as being irresponsible in not dealing more forcefully with the political realities of the moment, especially the growing threat of Nazi Germany.

76. WCW to Charles Keppel, 25 June 1940: "I've been reading one or two of the ancient Grecian tragedies, the *Coëphorae* among the rest." WCW was particularly struck by the stark, mad figure of Clytemnestra. In a letter to TR on 30 June 1940 WCW wrote, "Read what Clytemnestra says after she opens the curtains and shows the crowd what she has done to her husband. That ain't diminutive."

77. WCW to EP, 6 April 1940 (Y).

78. Y Collection.

79. WCW to WEW, 17 Aug. 1940 (Pri.).

80. WCW to KR, 19 Aug. 1940. WCW even took to reading *Walden* while he puttered about his own bean-patch garden that week.

81. "The Poet in Time of Confusion," written September 1940, pub. in the *Columbia Review and Morningside*, XXIII (Autumn 1941), 1–5.

82. The essay was finally printed in the first issue of another new little magazine, *Now* (New York I, 1) in August 1941. See *SE* and *RI*. He called it "Midas: A Proposal for a Magazine," suggesting that his proposals might serve for any number of little magazines, since all the magazines taken together formed part of a continuum anyway. On the so-called Jewish question, see WCW's short story, "Jew," which WCW had written in 1939 as part of *IM*. Rejected there for want of space, WCW published it in a little magazine out of Kenyon College called *Hika* in May 1940. See also WCW's comment to JL after JL had turned down LZ's fragment of *A* for *ND*. "Why in hell does a man have to be so pathetic without wanting to be pathetic," he lamented. "There is, of course, the Nazi answer. But a man of feeling [like LZ] can't just take it [rejection of his work] and smile." It hurt WCW to see his friend hurt, even if he himself had to admit how difficult LZ's long poem was even for the well-intentioned reader like himself (WCW to JL, 27 June 1938). By 1940 WCW realized the absolute depravity underlying the Nazi talk of Jewish inferiority. But, like most of the world, WCW did not yet understand where the Nazi solution was logically tending.

83. WCW met Ivan Goll and his wife at Alfred Stieglitz's gallery in March 1940. He apparently translated six poems by Goll in 1940, three of which were published in 1944 and the other three in 1958. He had his doubts about the quality of his translations, finding Goll's French "simple and direct," but his English renderings "involved and awkward" (2 June 1940, WCW to Goll. *Stonybrook* magazine)

84. Letters from WCW to Pedro Salinas, 1, 18, and 22 Nov. 1940.

85. WCW to JL, 23 Aug. 1940.

86. WCW to NC, 4 Dec. 1940.

87. WCW to JL, 14 DEC. 1940.

88. RM to WCW, 15 Nov. and 19 Dec. 1940 (Y). WCW mentioned the "chilly" atmosphere at Cambridge to JL (7 Feb. 1941). In a lighter vein he wrote EEC on Feb. 10 that

Mrs. Bernard De Voto had told him while he was Harvard that EEC had managed, during his earlier visit to the school, to kick her "and she with child, then splashed ink on her book." That, WCW added, "wasn't nice" (WCW to EEC, 10 Feb. 1940).

89. *IWWP*, p. 72.

90. "The Basis of Poetic Form" (Y).

91. "A Statement as to the Modern Basis of Poetic Form" (Y).

92. WCW to WEW, 18 April 1941, on hotel stationery (Pri.).

93. Ibid.

94. WCW to George Dillon at *Poetry*, 17 April 1941.

95. WCW to RM, 27 June 1941.

96. See *A*, pp. 313–315.

97. WCW to Charles Keppel, 7 Jan. 1941. Paul had met Jinny Carnes while at Penn.

98. WCW to Louis Untermeyer, 14 March 1941.

99. WCW to Malcolm Cowley at the *New Republic*, 23 Feb. 1941. WCW had also used the machine image in a letter to the anthologist Oscar Williams: "We are too inclined to fill the mould in order to complete the work, and fill it and fill it again as if we were making Ford parts" (13 Nov. 1940 [Lilly]). Yvor Winters was a classic example of the kind of mechanistic trap the poet could fall into, WCW told R. P. Blackmur at the same time he wrote Cowley (11 Nov. 1940). "How are you going to give a precise value to each syllable in an art which is in flux? It can't be done. Granted, in principle Winters is completely right, but his theory is purely mechanistic and has very little creative value for anyone. I, too, am looking for what he is looking for but I am looking for it in the *speech* about me."

100. See the *New Republic*, CIV, 16 (21 April 1941).

101. WCW's five-page essay, unpublished, is dated 21 April, the very day he returned from the San Juan Conference (Y).

102. "A Warm Word for Daiches," *Poetry*, LVIII, 2 (May 1941), 112.

103. WCW to Dwight Macdonald, 16 May 1941.

104. "An Exultation," *Partisan Review*, VIII, 4 (July–Aug. 1941), 311–312.

105. "Dr. Williams Cocks a Shook," *Hika*, VIII, 7 (May 1941), 13, 27.

106. "Bread Loaf Talk" (Y).

107. "Further Conversations With Flossie," ed. Edith Heal, *WCWN*, III, 1 (Spring 1977), 2–3.

108. WCW to JL, 26 March 1939.

109. Letter from Charles Eaton to the author.

110. WCW to TR, 26 Sept. 1941. Among the second-rate versifiers: Winters and Aiken, the latter of whom seemed "foot and boot" with R. P. Blackmur himself.

111. "Kulturbolshewismus Is Here," Partisan Review, VIII, 6 (Nov.–Dec. 1941), 442–451. Reprinted in *Memoirs of a Revolutionist*, Farrar, Straus & Giroux (New York, 1957).

112. "On the 'Brooks-MacLeish Thesis,'" *Partisan Review*, IX, 1 (Jan.–Feb. 1942), 39. WCW wrote this letter in November 1941.

113. *Decision*, II, 3 (Sept. 1941), 16–24.

114. WCW to JL, 3 Sept. 1941.

115. WCW to LZ, 26 Aug. 1941 (T). WCW read the Dean of Canterbury's *The Soviet Power* in October and recommended it to LZ: "To let such an enlightenment as Russia represents no matter how failingly be blotted out by the brutality of Nazidom would be the final disgrace." And yet WCW knew that there were those, like the shadowy Englishman Montague Norman, who feared socialism and Russia even more than they feared Hitler's Germany (6 Oct. 1941 [Y]).

116. WCW to EP, 26 Nov. 1941 (Y).

117. Barbara Morgan to the author.

118. *Harper's Bazaar* published the poem in its issue for 1 March 1942. Repr. *ND* 16, pp. 36–37.

Chapter Nine. Clearing the Field. 1938–1942 (cont.)

    119. WCW to JL, 8 Jan. 1942 and 6 Feb. 1942.

    120. Original in Y Collection.

    121. WCW to CA, 13 Feb. 1942.

    122. Early drafts of *P* (B).

    123. WCW to Harvey Breit. *SL*, pp. 193–194. This version has been severely cropped.

    124. WCW to Carl Rakosi, 22 Feb. 1942.

    125. WCW to CHF, 25 Feb. 1942. Published in *View*, II, 2 (May 1942), 19, as "Surrealism and the Moment."

    126. WCW to JL, 16 June 1941.

Chapter Ten. Dragging the River for Giants: 1942–1946

    1. WCW recalled this episode in a letter to NHP, 31 Aug. 1949.

    2. Breit had, according to MN, been a very close friend, though, when WCW met her, she and Breit had had a falling out. It may have been Breit's friendship with WCW that prompted MN to seek out WCW, who already had a reputation for generosity and empathy and befriending the young.

    3. WCW to WEW, 2 April 1942 (Pri.).

    4. As he told Harvey Breit the following day (6 April 1942): "Easter was a grand day for me, not a call in the whole twenty-four hour period. I thought I was in Heaven." WCW had just written recommendations for Breit (as well as for Jim Higgins) for Houghton Mifflin Fellowships (Fairleigh Dickinson). WCW also gave Breit the West Haven cottage for the first two weeks of July 1942.

    5. "Cache Cache," *View*, II, 2 (May 1942), 17–18. *RI*, pp. 124–125.

    6. WCW to MN, 10 April 1942.

    7. WCW to MN, 13 May 1942.

    8. *CLP*, pp. 8–9.

    9. Early draft of *P* (Y).

    10. Courtesy of Oral History Research, Columbia U. Interview of Helen Williamson Fall, conducted by her son, James Edward Fall, 8 May 1977.

    11. WCW mentions *Hyperion* in an early work sheet (B): "But it won't stand alone any more than Hyperion could, too narrow at the base in spite of whatever language I can get into it. Topples over."

    12. These work sheets are collected in B and Y Collections. WCW sent some of these to CA at various times in the 1940s, and then sent others to Yale via NHP. The reconstruction attempted here is the work of ten years' investigation, going between the two major collections. Other pieces of the puzzle are scattered, Osiris-like, in other libraries and in private collections. WCW wrote and rewrote his epic over and over, using fragments from earlier attempts palimpsestlike in his later constructions. What emerges in part is the story told here.

    13. WCW to TR, 20 May 1942.

    14. B Collection. Dated 22–23 May 1942.

    15. WCW to BV, 30 May 1942. WCW, characteristically, called his poetry "a service of desperation" at this juncture, then reversed himself, knowing that it was, after all, somehow "a building of the understanding."

    16. Included in *This Is My Best*, ed. Whit Burnett, Dial Press (New York, 1942), pp. 641–644. The statement is dated by WCW 14 June 1942.

    17. WCW to JL, 9 June 1942. For a week in early June MB had been a guest of the Williamses, "cataloguing my attic," as WCW told JL on June 5, "looking over old and rare letters, [and] pricing first editions" for the Buffalo collection. She too had left WCW a sheaf of poems and a play to look over.

18. Williams' "Introduction" and Marcia Nardi's "A Group of Poems" appeared in the *New Directions Annual* for 1942, pp. 429–436.

19. "I'm doing some pages about Anaïs Nin and her new book" WCW wrote JL on 5 June 1942. And, twelve days later: "I'm having a hell of a time with the Anaïs Nin thing. I've rewritten it four times and am going into the fifth. It requires as much discretion as insight" (WCW to JL, 17 June 1942). The book WCW was reviewing was *Winter of Artifice*, a review published in JL's *New Directions Annual* for 1942, along with a group of poems by MN with an introduction provided by WCW. In *Paterson* 1 "Cress" (i.e., MN) throws WCW's review of Nin back at WCW. (See also the very close of *P2*, where A.N. is Anaïs Nin. WCW had a brief correspondence with Nin in 1941–1942 and again in 1946.)

20. WCW to LZ, 19 June 1942 (T). Also WCW to JL, 23 June 1942.

21. B Collection. On the need for a new form consonant with one's own moment, WCW wrote Harvey Breit twice, on 19 June and again the following day. What was needed, WCW stressed, was a "new creation," not the sonnet with its deadly implications for the new, but the discovery of forms comparable to the old in the language of one's own time. This meant either finding a new form or completely breaking up the habitual expectations of older forms, as Villon for example had done—in WCW's estimation—by taking the ballad form ("a parlor game" by Villon's time) and investing it with a new seriousness.

22. *P3*, pp. 123–124.

23. WCW to JL, 14 March 1939.

24. WCW to JL, 13 July 1942.

25. These notes, in B Collection, are detached, their sense scattered across the prescription pad pages. The reconstruction given here seems to me to make the most sense. The best date for these notes: July 1942.

26. "My long 'Introduction' of which I spoke to you is moving along slowly, the material is so abundant I am having to go slow with its organization. It is in this material I am incorporating your letters. I'll see that you are properly informed of what I'm doing before printing anything" (WCW to MN, 13 July 1942).

27. WCW to NC, 15 July 1942.

28. WCW to KR, 31 July 1942.

29. WCW to RM, 8 Aug. 1942. In *SL*, pp. 215–216, this letter is misdated 1943.

30. WCW to WEW, 30 Aug. 1942 (Pri.). In the previously cited letter to RM too WCW had admitted how heavy a distraction the news bulletins were becoming:

> I wish I could omit the news from my days entirely. I can't help more than I am doing and I do castrate myself by the constant disillusion I feel before the news. . . . Sometimes the thought comes over a man that we may be in a far worse fix than they are telling us and our leaders may be infirm. I know I can't help, but when I see the smug faces of many in the street, I don't know, I don't know.

Dr. Paterson, too, in 1942, sees "a thousand automatons" walking "outside their bodies aimlessly for the most part . . . unroused" (*P*, p. 6).

31. WCW to WEW, 13 Sept. 1942 (Pri.).

32. WCW to JL, 9 Dec. 1942. Work: scattered throughout the early *P* drafts, the names of WCW's patients: Baldaza, Irving, Coulton, Barnes, Butterfield, Carroll, Tuttle, Tarris, Lancaster, Karvonon, Perry, Michal, Gallagher, Daly, Agafolio, Cadarborg, Baker. And medicines: Camirol, Totabex, Vitron, Choleol. Dr. Paterson worrying his epic into life.

33. WCW to JL, 21 Dec. 1942.

34. WCW to LZ, 15 Sept. 1942 (Y). In early July, with Harvey Breit and his friends partying it up at the West Haven cottage, WCW wrote to say that he hadn't been up to joining the crowd now that his older son was swallowed up somewhere in the vast Pacific. And as much as he would have liked to see the girls Breit had up there with him, it was no

Chapter Ten. Dragging the River for Giants: 1942–1946 (cont.)
use trying to hide his depression: "the inside of the kettle is such that it's no use to polish the outside" (WCW to Breit, 8 July 1942 [Fairleigh Dickinson]).

35. *View*, II, 3 (Oct. 1942), 23. WCW sent WEW a copy of this essay, written as much for him as for anyone (WCW to WEW, 13 Sept. 1942 [Pri.]).

36. In April, asked by Frances Steloff for a list of his favorite books, WCW mentioned, among others, Chaucer's *Troilus and Criseyde*, Rimbaud, Cummings' *The Enormous Room*, *The Education of Henry Adams* (thanks to LZ), Brooks Adams' *Civilization and Decay* and Lincoln Steffens' *Autobiography* (both taken from EP's ubiquitous reading lists), Dos Passos' *The Ground We Stand On*, Kenneth Fearing's poems, and H. H. Lewis' *Red Renaissances* (WCW to Steloff, 20 April 1942).

37. WCW to TR, 22 Sept. 1942.

38. On July 18, WCW wrote Breit that he thought he could fix things up with Stevens about the *Harper's* interview and suggested that Walker Evans be used to do the photographs. Then, after talking it over with Breit at 9 Ridge Road, WCW wrote Stevens about the scheme, admitting that he personally wanted very much to appear together with Stevens in *Harper's* (WCW to Wallace Stevens, 23 July 1942). But four days later Stevens wrote Breit (sending WCW a copy of the letter) to the effect that he didn't go along with the idea and was sorry, especially as WCW wanted it so much. Quite simply, Stevens explained, he did not like "personal publicity." He'd already been burned once with an interview he'd given and he didn't want the experience repeated. Instead he offered the name of Edgar Lee Masters, also a lawyer, as a substitute(!) (WS to Breit, 27 July 1942, *Letters of Wallace Stevens*, sel. and ed. Holly Stevens, Alfred A. Knopf [New York, 1966], pp. 412–413).

39. WCW to JL, 21 July 1942.

40. WCW to MN, 6 Oct. 1942.

41. WCW to MN, 16 Dec. 1942.

42. *P2*, pp. 86–92. "Miss X" on p. 89 is MM. The probable date of MN's letter is late December 1942.

43. On Feb. 1943 from her 12th Street apartment, MN wrote, for example:

> I very likely seem deplorably lacking in constraint to you, in self-discipline and self-control, and even in that reticence which is merely a part of good manners. But it's not really that. I'm merely desperate in my constant hankering to lead a peaceful, scholarly, *civilized* existence of some kind; to have, above all things, a life of my mind; and it's impossible, unless someone out of that world from which I myself have always been exiled, comes to my rescue.

WCW, she hoped, would play Perseus to her Andromeda (Y).

44. T Collection.

45. WCW to LZ, 7 Nov. 1942 (T).

46. WCW to JL, 9 Dec. 1942.

47. WCW to Dwight Macdonald, 11 Dec. 1942.

48. WCW to EEC, 18 Dec. 1942.

49. So too with WCW's practice. "This winter [of 1942–43] I expect to be on the front line, fighting the war at home as a suburban doctor. I believe it will be very exhausting" (WCW to NC, 15 Oct. 1942).

50. WCW to JL, 9 Dec. 1942.

51. WCW to JL, 24 Jan. 1943. *SL*, pp. 213–215.

52. *New Republic*, LXXXXLLL, 1198 (17 Nov. 1937), 50.

53. WCW to JL, 24 Jan. 1943.

54. WCW to LZ, 3 Feb. 1943 (T).

55. WCW to LZ, 21 March 1943 (T).

56. WCW to LZ, 27 March 1943 (T).

57. WCW to LZ, postcard, 31 March 1943 (T). Of the American defense plant workers WCW wrote: "A hyper-stimulated people, all look alike, fast eaters, polished like ball bearings—and they do."

58. The letter and revised script of *The Wedge* are in B Collection.

59. WCW to LZ, 9 and 11 April 1943 (T).

60. WCW to LZ, 11 May 1943 (Y).

61. WCW to LZ, 25 May 1943 (T).

62. WCW to MB, 22 May 1943.

63. WCW to CA, 26 May 1943.

64. WCW to KB, 12 July 1943. In late May WCW told MB that he thought the war was approaching a crisis and an end, perhaps hoping it would be so before his younger son was swallowed up in its maw.

65. WCW to KB, 14 Aug. 1943.

66. *New Republic*, CIX. 8, 1499 (23 Aug. 1943), 256. He complained bitterly to HHL at the time that for all the talk of paper shortages, "more paper is wasted for assinine purposes than there is piss in an army latrine" (27 Aug. 1943).

67. Printed as "Author's Introduction (1944)" to *CLP*, pp. 3–5. HG read on the same bill with WCW.

68. WCW to KB, 12 July 1943.

69. WCW to KB, 14 Aug. 1943.

70. "A Fault of Learning: A Communication," *Partisan Review*, X, 5 (Sept.–Oct. 1943), 466–468. The response was titled "The Politics of W. C. Williams."

71. WCW to ED, 5 Nov. 1943 (Pri.). WCW had admired ED's prose for years when he wrote this letter to his testy literary friend.

72. WCW to WEW, 5 Dec. 1943 (Pri.).

73. WCW to JL, 17 Dec. and 15 Nov. 1943. WCW told RM too that *Pierre* made "all the horrible failings of my own beginning period come before my eyes—and make me sick" (WCW to RM, 2 Nov. 1943). But he told LZ that though Melville's book was badly written there was still "a unique seriousness to it—unique for American literature" (24 Oct. 1943 [T]).

74. WCW to JL, 27 Dec. 1943.

75. "Paterson: The Falls," first pub. in *View*, III, 1 (April 1943), 19. *CLP*, pp. 10–11.

76. WCW to CA, 2 Feb. 1944.

77. WCW to RM, 23 Feb. 1944. *SL*, pp. 220–223.

78. WCW to LZ, 15 March 1944 (T).

79. WCW to FM, 15 March 1944 (D).

80. WCW to Walter Arensberg, 4 April 1944 (Francis Bacon Libr.). One of the big issues preoccupying WCW was the same issue preoccupying Stevens at the same moment in his *Esthetique du Mal:* the problem of evil in a post-Christian world of values. What was one to make of the deaths of the young in time of war? "If there's anything to death apart from a simple canceling out then it had better be stated (in a modern acknowledgment, a modern language—which it has never been) at once so we can know just how to evaluate self-seeking." *Self-seeking* was the old Nietzschean problem of the superhero, the figure with extraordinary gifts who claimed special prerogatives and therefore protection from the dangers that confronted the common human being in time of all-out war. EP was one such figure as far as WCW was concerned. For his own part, WCW believed that the natural authority that came with extraordinary gifts had to be used for the good of others. For unless a person made himself or herself "a servant in some sense for humanity, . . . to those about him who need him—he turns out to be a selfish bastard like Pound, like Napoleon" (*SL*, pp. 222–223). That was in February. By year's end he had found his answer. War, he had come to see, had this value: that it purged the human race. One man died that another man might live, not only purged but positively reborn by that sacrifice. This meant looking at humanity

Chapter Ten. Dragging the River for Giants: 1942–1946 (cont.)
in the aggregate, as a totality, for without that "feeling of solidarity we are nothing" (WCW to LZ, 22 Dec. 1944 [T]).

81. "Under the Stars," *The University of Kansas City Review*, XI, 1 (Autumn 1944), 26–28. The edited script is in the B Collection.

82. WCW to JL, 22 March 1944.

83. WCW to HG, 5 May 1944. *SL*, pp.224–226. From the third until the tenth of May WCW bombarded HG with letters dealing with the nature of the local and the problem of forms indigenous to a culture. TSE's *Notes* had sparked the controversy and WCW was eager to enlist HG on his side in the struggle to define and locate an American poetry.

84. WCW to HG, 9 May 1944. *SL*, p. 227.

85. WCW to HG, 10 May 1944. "Horace Gregory as a critic . . . has a quality that is . . . rare—a rallying point for our purposes" (WCW to BV, 6 May 1944).

86. WCW to EEC, 10 April 1944. What WCW said about EEC's latest book of poems refers—as usual—to the distillation process LZ had applied to *The Wedge* the year before.

87. WCW to BV, 6 May 1944.

88. WCW to Wallace Stevens, 24 July 1944. *SL*, pp. 230–231.

89. WCW to TR, 14 July 1944.

90. WCW to BV, 5 July 1944.

91. WCW mentioned his "progress" on *P* to a number of friends, KH, BV, TR, JL, Stevens, and HG among them. To HG he wrote on 11 July, enclosing a copy of the manuscript of *The Wedge* as a gift and the note, "I've worked on *Paterson* steadily aligning the mass of material I had collected for it until now all is in order for the final draught."

92. WCW to LZ, 11 Sept. 1944 (Y). Jinny lived at 9 Ridge Road with the children for eighteen months: from September 1944 until March 1946, when Paul, discharged finally from the Navy, found a house for his family.

93. WCW to JL, 20 Aug. 1944.

94. WCW to BV, 7 Sept. 1944.

95. These lines are dated 8 Sept. 1944 in a draft in the Y Collection.

96. WCW to BV, 23 Oct. 1944.

97. WCW to LZ, 23 Sept. 1944 (T).

98. WCW to Malcolm Cowley, 13 Sept. 1944. See WCW's poem "Threnody," written at this time:

> The Christian coin—
> embossed with a dove and sword—
> is not wasted by war,
> rather it thrives on it
> and should be tossed
> into the sea for the fish
> to eye it as it falls. . . .   (*CLP*, p. 262)

99. WCW to BV, 5 Nov. 1944.

100. WCW to MM, 7 Nov. 1944. *SL*, pp. 231–233.

101. Another flurry of letters, like those to HG in May, this time to BV in November. WCW's introduction to BV's poems, not published until 1946, actually came out of the letters WCW wrote now.

102. WCW to BV, 15 Nov. 1944.

103. WCW to TR, 14 Nov. 1944.

104. WCW to Wallace Stevens, 21 July 1944. *SL*, p.229.

105. BV corresponded with Stevens, WCW, and MM. This correspondence is now housed at Y, although BV was kind enough to send the author copies of the WCW materials while they were still in BV's possession.

106. The closest WCW came to mentioning *P* at this juncture was to say that BV's "book in script" had been "the occasion for my saying a number of things that have been at the heart of my purposes for many years" (WCW to BV, 18 Nov. 1944). WCW wrote BV about Davenport's poem on 24 Nov. 1944.

107. *P*, p.13.

108. WCW to LZ, 22 Dec. 1944 (Y).

109. WCW to HG, 1 Jan. 1945. *SL*, pp. 234–235.

110. WCW to JL, 14 Jan. 1945. WCW also broke with the surrealists and with *View* in mid-January. "You can't elide the wide-open weaknesses of surrealism," he told Calas, "by yelling or attempting to confuse the opposition by a smoke screen" (WCW to NC, 13 Jan. 1945). Also, see letter from WCW to JL, 14 Jan. 1945. By July of '45 WCW was calling surrealism the "science of misnomers" (*SL*, p. 240).

111. WCW to BV, 26 Jan. 1945.

112. WCW to JL, 30 Jan. 1945. WCW had mentioned *P*'s four-part structure to JL in the spring of '44.

113. WCW mentioned the nunnery in a letter to WEW in August of '42: "I was astonished on taking the back road from Hasbrouk Hts to Passaic through Lodi to find the tremendous construction work that has been going on on the old farm across from the Nunnery, you remember the place, where only rhubarb grew last year" (WCW to WEW, 30 Aug. 1942 [Pri.]).

114. WCW to JL, 3 Feb. 1945.

115. WCW to JL, 4 Feb. 1945.

116. WCW to HG, 8 Feb. 1945. *SL*, pp. 235–236.

117. WCW to JL, 9 March 1945.

118. WCW to CA, 22 March 1945. WCW's 78-page typescript was apparently retyped to 60 pages. This "Introduction" became "Book I." It was set in type in the summer of 1945 and the original galleys, dated 1945, are now at Kent State. These are the galleys slashed "unmercifully" by WCW in September, so that the galleys had to be reset and *Paterson* 1 published in 1946 instead of a year earlier.

119. "I dreamed a play one night," WCW wrote LZ on 15 Sept. 1942 "and jotted down the plot, the name and made sketches of one or two scenes." It was in this letter (Y) that WCW called his play "a modern tragedy of the spirit." WCW's preoccupation in 1942 with the murder of Menelaus by his wife assumes—in this light—a new significance.

120. Revised version at Y.

121. WCW to FM, 1 April 1945 (D).

122. "Death by Radio (for F.D.R.)," *CLP*, p. 258.

123. WCW to LZ, 8 May 1945 (Y).

124. FW and WCW spent the first two weeks of July at West Haven.

125. WCW to JL, 24 July 1945.

126. WCW to NM, 25 July 1945. *SL*, pp. 238–240.

127. WCW to JL, 7 Aug. 1945.

128. WCW to BV, 7 Aug. 1945.

129. WCW to FW, 15 Aug. 1945 (B).

130. WCW to WEW, 9 Sept. 1945 (Pri.).

131. WCW to JL, 7 Sept. 1945. The following day he told FM that he was thinking of chucking "the whole mess, just burn it up." The only thing stopping him was that he didn't feel "sure enough" of himself "to do that." He felt at the moment "desperately afraid" (WCW to FM, 8 Sept. 1945 [D]).

132. WCW to FM, 14 Sept. 1945 (ViU).

133. WCW to FM, 21 Sept. 1945 (ViU).

134. WCW to JL, 19 Sept. 1945.

135. WCW to KR, 21 Sept. 1945.

Chapter Ten. Dragging the River for Giants: 1942–1946 (cont.)

136. WCW to LZ, 31 Aug. 1945 (Y).

137. CLP, pp. 234–235.

138. WCW to BG, 9 Oct. 1945.

139. Apparently, though, the evidence here is conflicting. EP said that he turned himself over to the partisans.

140. "The Case For and Against Ezra Pound," PM, New York, VI, 138 (Sunday, 25 Nov. 1945), 16.

141. WCW to VBJ, 28 Dec. 1945.

142. "Ol' Bunk's Band," CLP, p. 236. On Sunday, 25 November, WCW wrote WEW that he'd gone in late Friday night with Jinny to hear Bunk Johnson's band "which has been making a little Bohemian stir in the Greenwich Village sector of late. Ma and I had seen and enjoyed the old colored guys two weeks ago. They are an original troupe that had practically original jazz music in New Orleans forty and fifty years ago—still alive, rescued, rehabilitated and featured now by two men [William Russell and Eugene Williams] who remembered them, searched them out, refitted them. . . . They're good, very good—a nostalgic show that you may want to look at. . . . I even danced a few minutes with Jinny" (WCW to WEW, 25 Nov. 1945 [Pri.]).

143. Letter from Bucklin Moon to author, 11 Sept. 1972. See "A Garland for William Carlos Williams," Massachusetts Review, XIV,1 (Winter 1973), esp. "Williams' Black Novel," pp. 67–75.

144. Betty Miller to author, 21 Oct. 1972.

145. FM to WCW, 25 Nov. 1945 (Y).

146. FM to WCW, 4 Dec. 1945 (Y).

147. WCW to FM, 11 Dec. 1945 (D).

148. The original of the Man Orchid collaboration, pub. in the Massachusetts Review (op. cit.), is in the Y Collection. The original beginning, in pencil, is in the B Collection.

149. A year earlier WCW had written Calas praising him for his sour review of Auden's For the Time Being. He was "fed up," he told Calas, "with the recent attempts of the mystics and the metaphysicists to grab poetry as their possession." He hated the "cheap pomposity and lying announcements of 'certainty' " propounded by Auden and TSE in his Four Quartets (WCW to NC, 22 Dec. 1944).

150. WCW to FM, 29 March 1946 (D).

151. Man Orchid.

152. Letter from Lydia Carlin to author, 13 June 1972.

153. FM to WCW, 26 May 1946 (Y).

154. WCW to FM, 28 May 1946 (ViU).

155. WCW to FM, 21 Dec. 1946 (D). This was a draft of Gutbucket and Gossamer, which WCW was able to get published for FM in a chapbook from the Alicat Bookshop Press in Yonkers, New York.

156. WCW to KB, 9 Nov. 1945.

157. CLP, pp. 256–257.

158. CLP, pp. 113–115. The first draft of this poem is dated 3 Oct. 1945. WCW told BV on 11 Nov. 1945 that the poem had been written as a reply to Wallace Steven's poem, "which I didn't like at all."

159. The Cummings essay, "Lower Case Cummings," appeared in the special Cummings issue of the Harvard Wake, ed. by José García Villa, No. 5 (Spring 1946), pp. 20–23.

160. Undated letter from WCW to KB, but internal evidence points to late November 1945. The "printers" reference was to the Cummington Press, which was to do The Clouds.

161. WCW to WEW, 25 Nov. 1945 (Pri.).

162. KB to WCW, 15 Dec. 1945 (Y).

Chapter Eleven. Intimations of Mortality: 1946–1948

1. WCW to LZ, 13 Jan. 1946. "Paul," WCW wrote, "has found himself a job with Abraham-Straus in Brooklyn! It's what he has always wanted to do, sell things to people, give them what they want at a reasonable price." His son, he pointed out, had the highest IQ "ever found among the store's applicants" (Y).

2. WCW to BV, 12 April 1946.

3. WCW to JL, 26 May 1946.

4. WCW to Parker Tyler, 9 Feb. 1946. *SL*, pp. 242–243.

5. "A New Line Is a New Measure," *New Quarterly of Poetry*, II, 2 (Winter 1947–1948), 8–16.

6. *CLP*, pp. 93–96.

7. WCW to FM, no date, but ca. 7 Aug. 1946 (ViU) when WCW was at View Crest Inn in Charlemont, Massachusetts.

8. WCW wrote JL on 2 Jan. 1946 that he could "understand" JL's continued "enthusiasm" for EP after JL's visit to St. Elizabeth's in late Dec. 1945.

9. WCW to HG, 1 Feb. 1946.

10. WCW to EP, first drafted on a prescription pad, 4 Feb. 1946 (Pri.). That WCW actually sent the letter is clear from another letter he wrote JL the following day. In spite of WCW's telling EP that he didn't believe he was crazy, he confided to HG on Feb. 1 that all artists were "crazy or had better be," and he told JL on Feb. 5 that he was convinced now that EP's "insanity" was "hereditary." The truth is that WCW didn't want his friend shot though he saw good reason to believe he might still be . . . and there was nothing, really, that WCW could do about it.

11. So, for example, in a letter dated 19 April 1946, EP wrote, "If you wanted to fight Eliot you ought to have looked to Wyndham Lewis, or to ole Fordie who knew more than any of us. . . . Eliot going as far as buggy milieu permits. both of you [TSE and WCW] adaptin [to] local necessity—fortunately DIFFERENT locales" (Y). And on August 9: "What is best book you have read in last 7 years? or @ least tell me one good one" (Y).

12. WCW to FM, 15 July 1946 (D).

13. WCW to EP, 31 Aug. 1946 (Y).

14. EP to WCW, 1 Aug. 1946 (Y).

15. WCW to EP, ca. 1 Sept. 1946 (Y). (See EP to WCW, 3 Sept. 1946 [Y])

16. WCW to FM, ca. 7 Aug. 1946 (ViU).

17. WCW to LZ, 31 March 1946 (T). In LZ's poetry WCW sensed "a real renewal, an actual coming out of the heaviness of a war that is more a war than the Churchills will ever know, an actual springtime, actual, not merely left to the plants and the stars."

18. WCW to LZ, 5 April 1946 (T).

19. "Choral: The Pink Church," *CLP*, pp. 159–162.

20. WCW to LZ, 26 July 1946 (T).

21. WCW to LZ, 29 July 1946 (T).

22. FW to JL, 6 June 1946 (Y).

23. WCW to LZ, "Tuesday" [7 May 1946] (T).

24. WCW to BG, 27 April 1946.

25. *CLP*, pp. 242–243.

26. *The Saga of Billy the Kid* by Walter Noble Burns. It was KH, then editing *1000 Years of Irish Poetry*, who introduced WCW to Durkin and to Durkin's poetry. It was during this hospital stay too that WCW wrote the first draft of his review of LZ's *ANEW*.

27. WCW to LZ, 8 May 1946 (T).

28. WCW to TR, 13 May 1946.

29. WCW to BG, 4 April 1946.

Chapter Eleven. Intimations of Mortality: 1946–1948 (cont.)

30. WCW to BG, 29 Oct. 1946.

31. WCW to KB. Undated, but ca. July 1946.

32. WCW to Parker Tyler, 10 July 1946.

33. WCW to JL, 13 and 20 Aug. 1946.

34. Randall Jarrell, "The Poet and His Public," *Partisan Review*, (Sept.–Oct. 1946), 488–500.

35. WCW to AT, 25 June 1946. Earlier that same day WCW had mentioned in a letter to LZ that he was going to write to Tate, whom he detested, though he knew the man only by name and reputation (T).

36. AT to WCW, 21 July 1946 (Y). WCW wrote back five days later to accept the "five years' armistice" (WCW to AT, 26 July 1946).

37. WCW to KH, 10 June 1946. The Williamses spent June 8th to the 14th at the farm.

38. Published in William Gratwick's *My, This Must Have Been a Beautiful Place When It Was Kept Up*, Pavilion (New York, 1965). WCW also wrote his "Two Deliberate Exercises" during his stay at the farm, the first after seeing a dance recital by Agnes Gratwick, the second initiated by two prints hanging on the walls of the Toby, where he and Floss were staying. See *CLP*, pp. 83–84.

39. WCW to Eleanor Musgrove, 16 Oct. 1936 (B).

40. WCW to FM, 3 Aug. 1946 (ViU).

41. FW and WCW each signed their own name in the guest register when they arrived on Sunday, August 4. Their room was on the second floor, facing the valley.

42. WCW to KH, 10 Aug. 1946. The Williamses enjoyed their stay, "walking about in the woods and fields," WCW told LZ a month later, "but the weather was vile, too cold and rainy for full delight. I was glad to get back and to work again" (WCW to LZ, 12 Sept. 1946 [T]). WCW sent Ruth Borklund a copy of *Paterson* 1, inscribed, "With happy memories of View Crest and all those in it" (Pri.).

43. "Letter to an Australian Editor," *Briarcliff Quarterly*, III,11 (Oct. 1946), 205–208. This was the special Williams issue. On the importance of the supplying female, WCW's short story "Country Rain," which he apparently wrote while at View Crest, gives an interesting analogue. Floss and WCW go for a ride in the countryside around Charlemont and WCW stops to look at a rock covered with ferns and dense moss and sees there "the rotten stump of a tree long since decayed" as well as a *"brother* to that tree—coming in fact from the same root and very much alive, as big as a *man's* arm, a good solid arm." Male tree gives birth here to male tree, but both are supported by the sexual tangle of ferns, moss, and rock. In short, by the nurturing mother earth. (*FD*, p. 316. Emphasis mine.)

Ruth and Helen, the old man, Warfield (his name changed here to Tilford), and even District the cat appear in this story. It is a complex doubling of the male-to-male androgynetic mode WCW was thinking so deeply about just then in his "Letter to an Australian Editor," only here WCW focused on the complementary female-to-female mode, wondering why women couldn't make it apart from men if they so wanted to. He knew of course that they could (*FD*, pp. 309–316).

44. WCW to CA, 26 June 1946. *SL*, pp. 244–245.

45. WCW to CA, 5 Oct. 1946.

46. WCW to Charles Sheeler, 12 Oct. 1946. *SL*, pp. 246–248.

47. WCW to R. P. Blackmur, 11 Nov. 1946.

48. WCW to KH, 18 Dec. 1946. WCW's room was in the George F. Baker Pavilion.

49. WCW to Marie Leone, 18 Dec. 1946 (Pri.).

50. WCW to KH, 18 Dec. 1946.

51. Y Collection.

52. WCW to KB, 21 Dec. 1946.

53. "A New Line Is a New Measure," op. cit.

54. Ibid.

55. WCW to Grover I. Jacoby, 9 Feb. 1947 (B).

56. In some notes he wrote for himself and dated 21 to 23 Jan. 1947, WCW wrote: "I'd like to note here that I proposed a conference to Auden (who had encouraged me by giving me his [New York] address: 7 Cornelia St.) that 4 or 5 'masters' should meet here, 9 Ridge Rd., to discuss technical matters relating to poetry." (See "A Study of Ezra Pound's Present Position," ed. Paul Mariani, in the *Massachusetts Review*, XIV,1 (Winter 1973), 122.

57. In a letter to LZ (26 Jan. 1947), WCW mentioned his private paper on EP and spoke of the man's "deterioration" as a poet to have begun when he "imagined himself Kung [Confucius]" and "equated himself with all wisdom." No poet in modern times could afford to take that tack and survive as a poet, as WCW—working then on his democratic epic—well knew (T).

58. WCW to KB, letters of 9 and 10 Jan. 1947.

59. This letter, dated "Tuesday," 3:30 PM, was written on 21 January, the same day WCW began his private notes to himself. In this letter he explained in detail the proposed seminar of five masters he wanted at his home. He told KB now that, even though he classified KB as "a professional philosopher" (meant as a compliment), he had still wanted him to make up part of the group that, by looking at the craft of the poem, would "advance the writing of poems twenty years in our time."

60. WCW to KB, 31 Jan. 1947. As for philosophy or logic, WCW told KB, he knew that the "placed" critics (like Blackmur, Tate, Winters, and the others) considered him as "fooling or rambling or at best uninformed." But WCW was convinced that when it came to the actual writing of poems he left those men far behind. That was because WCW understood his own "natural" field to be the actual construction of poems. There the critics were more "freshmen who because of irrelevant learning think themselves competent to write a poem" (WCW to KB, 7 Feb. 1947).

61. This letter, never sent, is now among the *Paterson* papers at B.

62. WCW to LZ, 27 Jan. 1947 (T): "Laughlin has given me the green light on the next installments of *Paterson* and I'm having trouble working myself free for it."

63. WCW to David Lyle, 4 Feb. 1947 (Pri.).

64. In correspondence with David Lyle's disciple, Ronald Wood. See also Mike Weaver, who mistakenly supposes that Lyle and his wife, Mary, were married only in February 1947 while Mary was dying in the hospital. According to Wood, the Lyles had been married for several years at the time of Mary Lyle's death.

65. WCW to JL, 9 Feb. 1947.

66. WCW to JL, 12 Feb. 1947.

67. WCW to JL, 19 Feb. 1947.

68. WCW to CA, 4 March 1947.

69. WCW to JL, 6 March 1947.

70. WCW to RM, 9 March 1947. *SL*, p. 253.

71. *P* 2, pp. 77–78.

72. WCW to KB, 17 March 1947. *SL*, pp. 257–258.

73. WCW to KB, 25 Feb. 1947. *SL*, pp. 251–253.

74. *P*, p. 56.

75. *P*, p. 57.

76. WCW to RM, 9 March 1947. *SL*, pp. 253–257.

77. WCW to NM, 9 March 1947 (*Pembroke* magazine).

78. WCW to RM, 9 March 1947. *SL*, p. 256.

79. "Revelation," *Yale Poetry Review*, No. 7 (Summer 1947), 11–13. *SE*, pp. 268–271.

80. WCW to FM, 2 May 1947 (ViU).

Chapter Eleven. Intimations of Mortality: 1946–1948 (cont.)

81. "You know I've been really dogging it over the Paterson II, I've been using every available minute not medically occupied in the completing of that book. It's done now, tonight. . . . The book goes to Laughlin next week" (WCW to BG, 28 May 1947).

82. WCW to KB, 20 June 1947.

83. WCW to JL, 7 July 1947. Itinerary established from letters written to JL, CA, RM, BV, and especially HHL (15 Sept. 1947).

84. WCW to BD, 28 July 1947. *SL*, pp. 258–259.

85. WCW to CA, 1 Sept. 1947. *SL*, p. 261. "At Salt Lake Allen Tate, whom I had always despised, and who in turn had always considered me of the lunatic fringe, and I learned mutually to respect, even to like each other. . . . He and Eric Bentley were at Mozart's sonatas whenever they could get off together. . . . Clark, Caroline Gordon, Mark Schorer, all swam with us in a nearby pool evenings, and at Alta we rode in the ski-lift . . . over the snowless ground now blossoming profusely on the slopes between the tall firs: columbine" (*A*, p. 312). JL's wife's family, from Salt Lake City, also hosted the Williamses during their stay.

86. WCW's Salt Lake City address became an English Institute essay that September and was published as part of the *English Institute Essays, 1947* the following year.

87. *CLP*, p. 103. See also "A Study of Ezra Pound's Present Position": "I don't think Bridges' experiments were sufficiently important to warrant going on with them *in that way*." Thus WCW in January 1947. By July he had obviously rethought the matter.

88. "Navajo," *CLP*, pp. 101–102.

89. "Graph," *CLP*, p. 102.

90. WCW to JL, 21 July 1947.

91. WCW to Babette Deutsch, 28 July 1947. *SL*, pp. 258–259.

92. WCW to WEW, 10 Aug. 1947 (Pri.).

93. "Thomas, Bishop, and Williams," *Sewanee Review* (Summer 1947), pp. 493–503.

94. WCW to TR, 23 Dec. 1946.

95. WCW to RL, 26 Sept. 1947. *SL*, pp. 261–262.

96. WCW to RM, 30 Sept. 1947.

97. WCW to RL, 12 Oct. 1947.

98. WCW to FM, 27 Oct. 1947 (ViU). See especially "Ezra Pound at St. Elizabeth's," *A*, pp. 335–344. This first meeting at St. Elizabeth's took place 18 Oct. 1947. Further information among papers in Y Collection, including *Al*. "Naturally Pound will tell you EVERYTHING!" WCW confided to FM on the twenty-seventh. "But look where it has landed him. . . . He'll never find out he's in the nut house. That's part of the times we're in. He'll just ignore it—slick it over with superior brows and say, Kung [Confucius] knew better. Sure he knew better, he kept out."

99. WCW to RL, 4 Nov. 1947.

100. WCW to RL, 8 Nov. 1947.

101. WCW to JL, 28 Nov. 1947.

102. WCW to RL, 18 Nov. 1947.

103. WCW to JH, 18 Nov. 1947.

104. Robert Lowell, "William Carlos Williams," *Selected Poems*, rev. ed., Farrar, Straus and Giroux (New York 1977), p. 179.

105. "Woman as Operator," in *Woman: A Collaboration of Artists and Writers*, Samuel M. Kootz Editions (New York, 1948).

106. "The Steeple's Eye," *Poetry*, LXXII, 1 (April 1948), 38–41.

107. WCW to Bruce Berlind, 20 Nov. 1947 (Pri.).

108. WCW to RM, 27 Oct. 1947.

109. WCW to BG, 12 Jan. 1948.

110. WCW to RM, 19 Jan. 1948.

111. WCW to CA, 18 Jan. 1948.

112. WCW to MB, 24 Jan. 1948. WCW obviously envied Charlotte's leaving New York City with her son, Eyvind, on January 21, heading for Los Angeles and the sun, this time "for good."

113. WCW to RL, 29 Jan. 1948.

114. *Al* plus letters written at the time. The heart attack occurred about February 10 or 11.

115. WCW to KB, 10 May 1948.

116. WCW to LZ, 9 March 1948 (T).

117. Reading list collected from various letters written by WCW at the time.

118. WCW to RL, 3 March 1948.

119. WCW to Marie Leone and the nurses at Passaic General Hospital, 3 March 1948 (Pri.). Telephone interview with Marie Leone, May 1980.

120. WCW to Marie Leone (Pri.).

121. WCW to FM, 8 March 1948 (D). Floss, he added, was "a grand nurse." He referred to his heart attack several times as his "Mayor O'Dwyer attack," O'Dwyer being then mayor of New York City.

122. WCW to Eric Bentley, 16 March 1948 (Pri.).

123. WCW to TR, 22 March 1948.

124. WCW to Charles Reznikoff, 30 March 1948.

125. WCW to TR, 30 April 1948.

126. WCW to LZ, 6 April 1948 (T). WCW also wrote the opening passage of *Paterson* 3 during his Atlantic City stay with its lines:

> *Spent from wandering the useless*
> *streets these months, faces folded against*
> *him like clover at nightfall,*
> *something has brought him back to his own*
> *mind.*

127. WCW to CA, 7 April 1948.

128. WCW to AT, 8 April 1948.

129. WCW to AT, 25 April 1948. AT had represented for WCW—in Philip Rahv's terms—the pale face of the academy. For AT, WCW represented the redskin or wild man of letters. Interestingly—and significantly—RL's first mentor had been AT, though by the late 1940s RL had shifted his allegiance to WCW. For a good introduction to the AT-WCW influence on RL (himself the representative man of poetry during the late 1950s and 1960s), see Steven Gould Axelrod's *Robert Lowell: Life and Art,* Princeton University Press (Princeton, N.J., 1978).

130. WCW to AT, 27 April 1948. AT to WCW, 28 April 1948 (Y).

131. WCW to CA, 8 May 1948.

132. Copy of MM's speech at Y.

133. Copy of WCW's comments at Y. Prof. Harry Levin, who was present, recalled the incident for the author (Sept. 1978).

134. WCW sent KB a 50-page carbon copy of the paper on 13 May 1948.

135. WCW to FW, 16 July 1948 (Pri.).

136. WCW to Libby Burke, 9 Aug. 1948 (Penn St.).

137. *A,* p. 323. WCW also described this scene in a letter to FW the same evening he witnessed it.

138. WCW to FW, noon, 17 July 1948 (Pri.). WCW may well have remembered the image of the Jungfrau he and Floss had seen together in the spring of 1924.

139. WCW to FW, 7:00 AM, 18 July 1948 (B).

140. WCW to KH, 21 July 1948, with transcript of "The Ann Sterling Show" (V).

Chapter Eleven. Intimations of Mortality: 1946–1948 (cont.)

   141. WCW to FW, 21 July 1948 (Pri.).

   142. WCW to FW, 23 July 1948 (Pri.).

   143. A, p. 323.

   144. WCW to CA, 2 Aug. 1948.

   145. WCW to JL, 25 July 1948.

   146. WCW to FW, 23 July 1948 (Pri.).

   147. WCW to JL, 2 Aug. 1948. Even as late as Sept. 22 WCW told AT that he felt "very uncertain of my pins at the time of the Seattle trip." He still wanted to write *Paterson 3* during the winter of '48–'49, but wasn't sure he could do it now: "Perhaps I didn't realize how devastating it would be to undertake to rip my offices apart, rearrange not only them but my life to suit—and take my son in with me. To write on top of that has been nearly impossible" (WCW to AT, 22 Sept. 1948).

   148. WCW to LZ, 15 Sept. 1948 (T).

   149. CLP, pp. 65–66.

   150. WCW to KB, 1 Nov. 1946.

   151. As FW told RM at the time, 25 Nov. 1946 (Y).

   152. B Collection.

   153. WCW to LZ, 3 Feb. 1943 (T).

   154. CLP, pp. 124–128. In an exchange with KB on "The Clouds," WCW wrote that he was *not* talking about heaven in the poem. Heaven was a "bad word," he argued, because it was too inaccurate as a concept. Certainly clouds could never mean heaven for a Christian, even such a non-Christian as himself. For himself he chose to put his own faith in meeting death in "doctors and chicken broth," since as far as he was concerned there was no chance of ever being "cured," whether by philosophy or by Christ. Except, he added, in the case of T. S. Eliot (WCW to KB, no date, but ca. mid-August 1948).

Chapter Twelve. A Dawning Awareness: 1948–1951

   1. WCW to BG, 28 April 1947.

   2. "Milton II," Collected in T. S. Eliot, *On Poetry and Poets*, Noonday Press, (New York, 1961), pp. 165–183.

   3. "With Forced Fingers Rude," *Four Pages*, Galveston, Tex., No.2 (Feb. 1948), 1–4.

   4. WCW to JL, 18 Jan. 1948.

   5. WCW to JL, 14 March 1948.

   6. In early November WCW also met Dame Edith Sitwell in New York. She was "a figure of a woman," he told RL:

> It's as if the 16th century had dredged up a queen for us. I didn't tell her but it was as if I were talking to my grandmother, I knew just what to say to her—just like one of the family. She blinked her small eyes and went at me in just the manner which I knew she would assume it had all happened so often before: the same blinking obstinacy, the same blank wall facing anything new, or at least the pretence of ignorance while covertly watching to see how to defend ones self. Watching for the opening like a fencer. But a cold, hot-cold wall. I could have kissed her. She sent Sir Osbert [her brother] to ask me to a luncheon!

WCW also told Sitwell that she had "come to her best period" of poetry late because she had learned to make her poetry new in a way that Dylan Thomas, with his "pseudo-innovations of internal rhyme" had not. She, being an aristocrat, could afford to "chuck" the English tradition and make it new even while Thomas and Eliot were still trying to defend the corpse of that tradition (WCW to RL, 12 Nov. 1948). What WCW did not understand, New World Shaker artisan that he was, was that Dylan Thomas' "pseudo-innovations of internal rhyme" belonged rather to the old and honorable tradition of Welsh *cynghanedd*. It was one reason he—WCW—failed to understand what Hopkins had attempted to do with English prosody.

7. In a note he made for himself for a reading he gave at the Guggenheim on 28 March 1950, WCW wrote: "As T. S. Eliot said to me the only time I saw him, Williams you've given us some good characters in your work, let's have more of them" (Y).

8. WCW to RM, 20 Nov. 1948.

9. WCW to RL, 27 Nov. 1948.

10. WCW to RL, 30 Nov. 1948.

11. Notes for *P* 3, dated 15–18 May 1948 (Y).

12. WCW to LZ, 17 Sept. 1948 (Maryland).

13. WCW to LZ, 21 Sept. 1948 (Maryland).

14. WCW to LZ, 19 Nov. 1948 (T).

15. WCW to RM, 30 Nov. 1948

16. WCW to BG, 30 Nov. 1948.

17. WCW to CA, 5 Dec. 1948.

18. WCW to BG, 12 Jan. 1948.

19. EP to WCW, 13 Oct. 1948 (Y).

20. EP to WCW, 13 Dec. 1949. *P* 4, p. 183.

21. WCW to JL, 19 Oct. 1948.

22. "The Fistula of the Law," *Imagi*, Allentown, Pa., IV, 4 (Spring 1949), 10–11.

23. WCW to RL, 27 Nov. 1948.

24. WCW to KR, 1 May 1948.

25. WCW to LZ, 23 Feb. 1949 (T).

26. *Partisan Review*, XVI, 5 (May 1949).

27. WCW's 7-page essay, "Semitism/Antisemitism in the Field of Letters," is in B Collection.

28. WCW to AT, 23 Sept. 1949.

29. WCW to Bill Bird, 8 Oct. 1949.

30. WCW to AT, 2 July 1949.

31. WCW to AT, 11 Aug. 1949.

32. WCW to LZ, 1 March 1949 (T).

33. WCW to TC, 17 June 1949 (Pri.).

34. WCW to JL, 5 Jan. 1949.

35. WCW to KB, 15 Feb. 1949.

36. WCW to LZ, 23 Feb. 1949 (T).

37. *P* 3, p. 125. Helen Williamson Fall, then living at 159 Home Avenue (the same street Floss had grown up on) and one of WCW's patients, recalls a parallel example. She had gone to Dr. Williams for a postnatal checkup in the early 1940s and was reclining on the couch in WCW's office, a leather couch with one rolled end in the French Empire style. "I got on the couch," she recalls, "and I assumed the position of a photograph I had seen of [Jacques Louis David's] Madame Récamier." She had placed one arm on the window sill behind her and had rested her other arm

> on the rolled end, and draped myself, and I said, "It's the first time in my life I've ever been able to feel like Madame Récamier," and he said, "Oh?" and he laughed, because I was posing. . . . We talked a little bit about her, and I said, "But I'll bet you she was never in the position I am now." This is while he was doing his examining. And he said,

Chapter Twelve. A Dawning of Awareness: 1948–1951 (cont.)

"Oh, I don't know, knowing her, it's highly possible she was in your condition many times. Who knows?"

(Oral History Research Office, Columbia U., 1977)
  38. *P 3*, pp. 113–114.
  39. WCW to LZ, 23 Feb, 1949 (T).
  40. *P 3*, p. 164.
  41. Randall Jarrell to WCW, n.d., but ca. March 1949: "I feel guilty not to have finished the Selected Poems introduction long ago, it's very hard for me to write (*Paterson*'s being out of consideration is the great difficulty) and I want to do a good job" (Y).
  42. Introduction to *Selected Poems*, New Directions (Norfolk, Conn. 1949).
  43. WCW to MN, 31 March 1949.
  44. WCW to JL, 8 June 1949.
  45. WCW to JL, 14 June 1949.
  46. WCW to JL, 20 June 1949.
  47. JL to WCW, 23 June 1949.
  48. WCW to MN, 16 July 1949.
  49. WCW to MN, Sept. 1949.
  50. WCW to James Murray, 22 Sept. 1950 (Pri.).
  51. *P 5*, p.230.
  52. WCW to MN, 22 Sept. 1949.
  53. WCW to MN, 17 Jan. 1951.
  54. WCW to MN, 8 Aug. 1951.
  55. WCW to MN, 4 Jan. 1952.
  56. FW to MN, 2 Sept. 1952 (T).
  57. WCW to MN, 5 Oct. 1956.
  58. WCW to FM, 26 April 1949 (D).
  59. WCW to FM, 11 May 1949 (ViU).
  60. WCW to CA, 10 July 1949.
  61. WCW to LZ, 16 July 1949 (T).
  62. WCW to CA, 20 July 1949. A few days later WCW wrote AT asking to be remembered to Eric Bentley. "Tell him," he added, "my play went off well enough, well enough that is to show what it might have been if it had been better acted." Even sitting in the front row WCW had missed several key speeches and, considering what he realized he'd revealed about himself, he was glad his friends there with him "didn't hear more" (24 July 1949).
  63. WCW to Bill Bird, 13 Feb. 1949.
  64. WCW to CA, 26 Oct. 1949.
  65. WCW to CA, 2 Dec. 1949.
  66. WCW to LZ, 19 Nov. 1948 (T).
  67. *CLP*, pp. 185–186.
  68. *CLP*, pp. 214–229.
  69. WCW to JL, 7 Oct. 1949.
  70. WCW to RM, 14 Oct. 1949.
  71. WCW to LZ, 23 Oct. 1949 (T).
  72. WCW to Helen Russell, whom WCW had met at the Seattle Conference in the summer of '48 (22 Oct. 1949; *SL* pp. 274–275). The same day WCW wrote Russell he also wrote EEC asking if Cummings remembered his visit out to 9 Ridge Road twenty years before when there were just the three of them: "my mother, yourself, and me here at home."

And now she was gone. "She died a week ago—2 weeks ago—God how time S*T*R*E*A*K*S." (WCW to EEC, 22 Oct. 1949).

73. WCW to Selden Rodman, 9 Dec. 1949. *SL*, p. 277.

74. WCW to JL, 30 Dec. 1949.

75. WCW to EEC, 22 Oct. 1949.

76. WCW to Wallace Stevens, 15 and 22 Dec. 1949. See Yvor Winters, "The Poet and the University: A Reply," *Poetry*, LXXV, 3 (Dec. 1949), 170–178.

77. "Picasso Sticks Out an Invested World," Louis Carré Gallery, NYC. See *RI*, pp. 223–224.

78. WCW to TR, 19 Jan. 1950.

79. WCW to Robert Beum, 5 and 9 Jan. 1950. Poetry from early drafts of *Paterson* 4 at Y. Beum extracted from these letters, publishing excerpts of both in his magazine, *Golden Goose*, but the originals, used here and housed in B Collection, are fuller and more complete.

80. "The Later Pound," ed. Paul Mariani, pub. in the *Massachusetts Review*, XIV, 1 (Winter 1973), 124–129.

81. Early drafts of *P* 4 (Y).

82. WCW to LZ, 27 Jan. 1950 (T). WCW wrote Harvey Breit that he was grateful "for your piece which [David] Ignatow praised highly to me. It was well done, with feeling, warmly; a rare thing in a newspaper" (26 Jan. 1950 [Fairleigh Dickinson]).

83. WCW to CA, 29 Jan. 1950.

84. WCW to Harvey Breit, 26 Jan. 1950 (Fairleigh Dickinson).

85. WCW to TR, 23 Feb. 1950.

86. WCW to JL, 9 Feb. 1950.

87. JL to WCW, 12 Feb. 1950 (Y).

88. WCW to TC, 12 Feb. 1950 (Pri.).

89. WCW to DM, 17 Feb. 1950.

90. Charles Olson to WCW, 12 Jan. 1950 (Y).

91. RC to WCW, 11 Feb. 1950 (Y).

92. Allen Ginsberg to WCW, 30 March and 6 June 1950 (Y). See *P* 4, pp. 173–175 and 194.

93. *SL*, pp. 281–283.

94. WCW to TC, 3 Feb. 1950 (Pri.).

95. WCW to Henry Wells, 12 April 1950. *SL*, pp. 285–286.

96. WCW to BG, 15 April 1950.

97. WCW to LZ, 15 April 1950 (T).

98. *P* 4, p.202.

99. WCW to Robert Beum, 3 July 1950.

100. WCW to Oscar Baron, 25 March 1950.

101. WCW to Selden Rodman, 23 April 1950.

102. WCW to Srinivas Rayaprol, 24 May 1950. *SL*, pp. 287–288. Dylan Thomas' heavy drinking and carrying on had already become legendary in the recountings, and WCW passed on a bit of literary gossip to Harvey Shapiro a few months later to the effect that "Thomas had dedicated himself before he come [sic] to America to the proposition that it was his bounden duty to prove [to] us that ALL British poets were NOT homosexuals" (WCW to Harvey Shapiro, 10 Aug. 1950 [Pri.]).

103. WCW to David Ignatow, 7 June 1950.

104. WCW to Selden Rodman, 9 June 1950.

105. WCW to Selden Rodman, 1 Dec. 1950.

106. Interview with WCW, edited from tapes by Emily M. Wallace in *Int*, pp. 3–26.

107. WCW to KH, 26 July 1950. *SL*, pp. 290–291.

Chapter Twelve. A Dawning of Awareness: 1948–1951 (cont.)

108. WCW to KB, 31 July 1950. Harvey Shapiro, remembering that summer interlude at Yaddo with WCW, wrote in the Sunday literary supplement of the New York Times:

> He seemed to me a young man, though in fact . . . he was 67. But there was a shine to his conversation, a liveliness that made him the center of our gatherings for drinks after the working day, great energy (one hot day he and . . . Flossie scoured the neighboring woods to bring back mushrooms for our dinner). Always proselytizing for his point of view (he saw no other), he once spent the better part of a Yaddo party urging Theodore Roethke to put some social protest into his poetry. A most unlikely notion.

109. *P* 4, p. 183.
110. Drafts for *P* 4 (Y).
111. *CLP*, pp. 36–38.
112. WCW to MM, 19 June 1951, *SL*, pp. 303–304.
113. *P* 4, p. 157.
114. *P* 4, p. 203.
115. *P* 3, p. 110.
116. *IWWP*, p. 79.
117. WCW to RL, July 1951. *SL*, p. 302.
118. *P* 3, p. 140.
119. WCW to MM, 23 June 1951. *SL*, pp. 304–305.
120. WCW to Babette Deutsch, 2 March 1951.
121. WCW to JH, 12 Nov. 1948.
122. WCW to José García Villa, editor of *Harvard Wake*, late July 1950. *SL*, pp. 291–292.
123. WCW to Richard Wirtz Emerson, 14 July 1950. WCW to TR, 4 Aug. 1950. And to Harvey Shapiro he wrote on 10 August: "Then comes the fighting in Korea. How could I have foreseen in planning my happy life which was to blossom into verse when I was forty or forty five at the latest, that it would have to withstand 3 terrible wars? Which as far as I personally have been concerned in my own carcass have meant nothing but which may in the end make everything for which [sic] I am dedicated disappear. All we can say is a half facetious, 'Carry on,' using a British accent and half clowning it" (Pri.).
124. WCW to DM, 9 Aug. 1950.
125. WCW to Daphne Spence Williams, 4 Aug. 1950 (Pri.).
126. "Song," dated 3 Aug. 1950 (Y).
127. *P* 4, p. 173.
128. WCW to JL, 29 Aug. 1950.
129. *P* 4, p. 188.
130. WCW to ED, 15 Sept. 1950: "I will definitely do a piece on the *Flea of Sodom* (which I have not yet finished reading) just as soon as I am able to get at it. At the moment I am (I'm sorry to say) timeless, without time, busted: too much on my tail, I am being driven to the wall or into a run rather by demands upon my energy." Without realizing just how truly he spoke, he added, "It will not be allowed to last overlong."
131. In his review of the tetralogy making up FMF's Tietjens series, WCW paid his old friend the high compliment of being the model of what was best in the British character: "Few could be in the position which Ford himself occupied in English society to know these people. His British are British in a way the American, Henry James, never grasped. They fairly smell of it. The true test is his affection for them, top to bottom, a moral, not a literary attribute, his love of them, his wanting to be their Moses, to lead them out of captivity to their rigid aristocratic ideals—to the ideals of a new aristocracy." Thus WCW chose to remember his old friend (*SE*, pp. 319–320).
132. *P* 4, p. 200.

133. Notes sent to ED, 10–13 Oct. 1950.

134. WCW to Richard Wirtz Emerson, 3 Oct. 1950.

135. WCW to Oscar Baron, 23 Oct. 1950.

136. WCW to DM, 26 Oct. 1950.

137. WCW to JL, 9 Nov. 1950.

138. WCW to LZ, 22 Nov. 1950 (T).

139. WCW to RM, 22 Nov. 1950.

140. WCW to RM, 30 Nov. 1950.

141. DM had been responsible for much of the public activity WCW found himself immersed in on his return home. "Take it easy on the New York stuff," WCW wrote DM the day before he left for Los Angeles. He was not yet "ready to be inflated," for he still had to relieve WEW, "who is carrying two jobs now," and besides WCW had all sorts of "obligations to fulfill relative to my good friends and patients who have relied and depended upon me" (WCW to DM, 17 Nov. 1950).

142. WCW to NM, 29 Nov. 1950 (*Pembroke*).

143. WCW to DM, 4 Jan. 1951.

144. WCW to DM, 11 Jan. 1951.

145. WCW to John Berryman, 9 Jan. 1951.

146. Ben Weber spent Saturday, 13 Jan. 1951, with WCW looking over *Tituba's Children*. Brendan Gill of *The New Yorker* came out to see WCW on 9 Jan. 1951—a Tuesday. "Gill was out here a week or more ago," WCW wrote JL on January 20. "We had a good day together but when a man's on salary you never can tell what he may have to write."

147. "Just eight more days in which to finish my autobiography," WCW wrote Helen Russell on 20 Feb. 1951. "I'll never do it. I am devastated—like a West Coast mountainside after a lumber gang hits it" (Y). And three days later to DM: "Been through a hell of a 24 hrs . . . . Tho't we were all sunk" (WCW to DM, 23 Feb. 1951).

148. WCW to MB, 17 March 1951: "I started with a certain enthusiasm but that has worn pretty thin. I started writing the thing longhand but that has brought on the complication that, writing at the speed I had to affect, I had to find a typist who could interpret what I was putting down. Thus from one thing to another I've been in hot water from the start."

149. WCW to MB, 26 Oct. 1951.

Chapter Thirteen. Hunting Down the Unicorn: 1951–1956

1. Theordore Weiss, "Lunching with Hoon: Wallace Stevens," *The American Poetry Review*, VII, 5 (Sept.–Oct. 1978), 43.

2. Wallace Stevens to WCW, 23 April 1951. *Letters of Wallace Stevens*, sel. and ed. Holly Stevens, Alfred A. Knopf (New York, 1966), pp. 716–717.

3. WCW to Wallace Stevens, 25 April 1951. *SL*, pp. 295–296.

4. Just how close WCW had come to dying then is registered in Floss's rather than WCW's response. Stanley Moss, JL's assistant at New Directions, heard from Floss via telephone on the thirty-first and immediately sent a telegram on to JL, who was skiing at Alta. The telegram read:

> THOUGHT YOU WOULD WANT TO KNOW BILL WILLIAMS
> TAKEN TO PASSAIC GENERAL HOSPITAL ROOM 219
> PASSAIC NEW JERSEY CEREBRAL HEMORRHAGE CONDITION
> CRITICAL NEXT WEEK OR TEN DAYS SHOULD DECIDE.
> STILL HOPE.

A week later Floss wrote a concerned JL that WCW's recovery had been "remarkable" but that he would still need a "long rest" (FW to JL, 7 April 1951 [Y]). And the same day she

Chapter Thirteen. Hunting Down the Unicorn: 1951–1956 (cont.)

assured AT that though her husband was getting along he would have to let up at last "on his four-man schedule." By the fifteenth WCW was able to scrawl a congratulatory note to TC; by May 2, in a very shaky hand, he wrote CHF, "My speech is still affected and my writing is bad but I can at least make myself understood." But within three weeks he was writing and typing with his left hand for long periods of time, though his right hand was still weak and his speech still halting.

5. WCW to David Ignatow, 26 May 1951.

6. WCW to RM, 1 June 1951.

7. WCW to KB, 24 Jan. 1951.

8. "The Desert Music," *PB*, pp. 108–120.

9. WCW to LZ, 19 June 1951 (T).

10. WCW to Louis Martz. *SL*, pp. 298–300.

11. WCW wrote Douglas Stuart Moore, president of the National Institue of Arts and Letters, from Schuylerville on 9 May 1951 to assure him that he would "have no trouble either in standing, walking or speaking upon the platform," and that the presentation speech for Ransom would be in Moore's hands by May 22. The day after the ceremonies WCW told Ignatow he'd been especially glad to see his friends out there in the audience because he was sure there'd been others who would have loved to see him go under (WCW to Ignatow, 26 May 1951).

12. "Carl Sandburg's Complete Poems," *Poetry*, LXXVIII, 6 (Sept. 1951), 345–351. *SE*, pp. 272–279.

13. WCW to DM, 16 June 1951.

14. WCW to DM, 24 June 1951.

15. WCW to KB, 12 July 1951.

16. WCW to LZ, 17 July 1951 (T).

17. WCW to TC, 7 June 1951 (Pri.).

18. WCW to KH, 23 July 1951. *SL*, pp. 306–308. "This morning," WCW wrote NHP on July 20, "we [WCW and Stecchini] stood on top of our sea wall [behind the cottage] right after my breakfast while he discoursed on the effect of the introduction of money into Greek civilization. . . . In those few minutes while I stood fainting on one foot he spoke of the Iliad (an escape for the men to their own company before Troy), Odysseus for all he was coming home to Penelope nevertheless was sleeping with Calypso and Circe and for years!"

19. That was on July 19, when they also saw Kenneth Patchen at Zukofsky's place. In spite of Dahlberg's dark moods, WCW told LZ that he admired ED's writing and would continue to help him in any way he could. The attacks WCW could afford to shrug off (WCW to LZ, 19 June 1951 [T]). Yet WCW intensely disliked the "roughshod discourtesy" which so many intellectuals like ED and EP affected (WCW to LZ, 30 July 1951 [T]).

20. Interview with Donald Cheney. *Yale Literary Magazine*, XIXC,2 (Oct. 1951), 10–13.

21. WCW to DM, 3 Aug. 1951.

22. WCW to DM, 20 Aug. 1951. But WCW was honored by Eisenstadt's attention and wrote into the flyleaf of a presentation copy of one of his books on 17 August the following: "How strange that from staring through a glass of peculiar shape at dictators and kings, generals and statesmen, those who have sought one way or another to rule the world, you have come away so whole a man, so willing still to search. . . . It is as if that miracle of glass . . . had endowed you with its grace of infinite purity, anastigmatic, . . . [making you] fit and even eager to record a poet's fleeting shadow." *RI*, pp. 226–227.

23. WCW to NHP, 20 Sept. 1951.

24. WCW to DM, 8 July 1951.

25. WCW still saw specters of Harlow Shapley, the man who'd sued him for libel a quarter century before. Now Bryher, Charles Henri Ford, McAlmon, Berenice Abbott, and

others considered legal action, though WCW's illness and his promise to rectify matters should the book ever be revised stopped them from doing anything more. About the errors in the book, he told Selden Rodman that they couldn't be helped. With the stroke he had had "to hammer out the sheer text with one finger and couldn't check everything as I should have liked to" (12 July 1951).

26. WCW to DM, 18 Sept. 1951. In another vein WCW wrote to John Wilson, editor of the *Rutherford Republican*, on the seventeenth, thanking the local Chamber of Commerce for their testimonial luncheon. "It is a remarkable thing for a man when his friends gather to wish him well on his birthday. . . . But when it is a physician who has lived among them intimately for two generations the circumstances become extraordinarily affecting. . . . As we grow older and become less active we gradually drift away from those whom we used to see. . . . Suddenly I was confronted by innumerable memories from a sea of well known faces. It was in the end overpowering. . . . I never expected that a hard boiled Chamber of Commerce would have it in it to speak of a poet in that way" (Rutherford Free Library). This letter appeared on page 1 of the newspaper the following day. Public success could make WCW as circumambient as anyone.

27. The portrait of WCW by Romano appears as the frontispiece of *RI*, which also contains two essays on Romano: the first, called "The Portrait: Emanuel Romano" (1951), and the second, "The Broken Vase" (1957). *RI*, pp. 196–209.

28. "Emanuel Romano," introduction by Michael Weaver, *Form*, Cambridge, England, I,2 (1 Sept. 1966), 22, 24–25.

29. "The Portrait," *RI*, pp. 196–205.

30. "The American Spirit in Art," *Proceedings of the American Academy of Arts and Letters and the National Institute of Arts and Letters*, Second Series, No.2 (1952), 51–59. In *RI*, pp. 210–220.

31. WCW to KB, 23 Jan. 1952. *SL*, p. 311.

32. WCW to LZ, 6 Jan. 1952 (T).

33. WCW to ED, 19 Feb. 1958. When ED had urged him to resign from the Institute in the summer of '51, WCW had answered that, if he wasn't "as keen minded and rebellious as I once was, if *Paterson* doesn't measure up to the quality of *In the American Grain*," it wasn't because of the Institute but rather because age had modified his views. That did *not* mean, however, that he had "softened" any "toward the contemptible bastards who run the world we inhabit. I am as much their enemy as ever and will never cease to try to controvert them in my own way" (11 July 1951). His speech on "The American Spirit in Art" delivered that December would indeed do just that, as some members of that group understood quite well.

34. WCW to DM, 27 Sept. and 27 Oct. 1951.

35. WCW to LZ, 6 Jan. 1952 (T).

36. WCW to MM, 12 Jan. 1952.

37. Draft in Y Collection.

38. WCW wrote this on a picture postcard of Titian's painting purchased at the Frick and sent it to LZ, 21 Feb. 1952 (T).

39. WCW to TC, 10 May 1952 (Pri.).

40. WCW to DM, 5 May 1952. *SL*, pp. 313–314.

41. WCW to NM, 29 May 1952 (*Pembroke*). "I'm having a hard time. One result is that I am not writing and have no inclination to write. In briefer words, I can't write. What will come of it I can't say."

42. This talk is published for the first time in *RI*, pp. 227–229.

43. Conrad Aiken to Kempton Taylor, 13 July 1952 (Hunt.). Siegel too had noticed how frail WCW looked. Suddenly WCW had become an old man.

44. Merrill Moore to FW and WCW, 20 June 1952 (B).

Chapter Thirteen. Hunting Down the Unicorn: 1951–1956 (cont.)

45. In the first half of 1952 alone WCW gave support in the form of recommendations to the following writers: Stanley Lawrence Berne, David Lougee, Harold Norse, Kenneth Beaudoin, Eli Siegel, Marcia Nardi (again), and Louis Grudin.

46. WCW to MM, 24 May 1952.

47. WCW to TC, 7 June 1952.

48. WCW to DM, 24 June 1952. SL, pp. 314–315. To Louis Grudin WCW confessed on June 10 that something had gone wrong with him. "I don't mention it to speak of myself," he explained, "I mention it not to lose the opportunity to tell you something before it will perhaps be too late."

49. "The Orchestra," pp. 80–82.

50. See Paris Review interview, conducted by Stanley Koehler in April 1962, pp. 25–26.

51. WEW to author.

52. Merrill Moore to FW, 17 Sept. 1952 (B).

53. WCW to Selden Rodman, 1 Dec. 1950.

54. Merrill Moore to FW, 17 Sept. 1952 (B).

55. Copies of these letters are housed in the Library of Congress. But FW also collected these letters for the record.

56. FW to Conrad Aiken, 14 Jan. 1953 (Hunt.).

57. FW to NHP, 8 Dec. 1952 (Y).

58. FW to NHP, 14 Dec. 1952 (Y).

59. FW to Karl Shapiro, 16 Dec. 1952.

60. FW to Betty Eberhart, 16 Dec. 1952 (Dartmouth).

61. Mrs. Francis Biddle to Conrad Aiken, 16 Jan. 1953 (Hunt.).

62. WCW to FW, 1 Jan. 1953 (Pri.).

63. WCW to TC, 8 Jan. 1953 (Pri.).

64. PB, pp. 83–86.

65. Interview with Bill and Eleanora Monahan, May 1980.

66. In the summer of 1951, by contrast, WCW had told NHP about a conversation he had had with Stecchini on that sea wall at West Haven. Stecchini had rejected the Catholic Church because it was—from his point of view—a throwback belonging to an earlier age in the development of the human race. "It is only while we have to do with the peasant and lower middle class mentalities of recent immigrants that the church can hold them," WCW had reported approvingly to NHP (20 July 1951). But now WCW's need was desperate.

67. WCW to FM, 9 Jan. 1953 (ViU).

68. PB, pp. 86–88.

69. PB, pp. 89–91.

70. WCW to CA, 15 Jan. 1953: "My connection with the Library of Congress has been terminated, by them, as of this morning."

71. WCW to LZ, 16 Jan. 1953 (T).

72. WCW to BV, 6 Feb. 1953.

73. FW to JL, 7 Feb. 1953 (Y).

74. WCW to CA, 10 Feb. 1953. It is instructive to see WCW preoccupied with the music of poetry in a letter with a postscript from Floss speaking about the probability of her husband's receiving shock treatments to bring him out of a deepening depression brought about by an official investigation of undetermined import. Floss was reading Eberhart's and Cole's poems to WCW at this point, as well as a book that Pound had recommended.

75. WCW's letters to FW written during his stay at Hillside Hospital are in the possession of the Williams family. Floss and WCW were both reticent about this painful episode in their lives, and it was rarely mentioned in their letters or conversations, so that even close friends, the author learned, were not aware of all the details. But on 17 Feb. 1953 Floss wrote Tom Cole that her husband was going to "a Hospital for some treatments—to

see if he can't be brought back to his normal self. He is frightfully depressed and generally miserable, so this is an effort to see what can be done—much is promised"

76. WCW to RL, 28 June 1954.

77. WCW to FW, 23 Feb. 1953.

78. WCW to FW, 24 Feb. 1953.

79. WCW to FW, 24 March 1953. *PB*, p. 156.

80. When WCW had begun confessing everything, apparently, to Floss after the stroke of August '52, Floss had become so upset that she had written Merrill Moore to ask for his professional advice. Moore, wisely, had shrugged it off, calling it in WCW's case a "confession mania" and a good thing for WCW to get off his mind. Most of it was probably "nonsense," he assured Floss, "even though it is irritating to you."

81. WCW to FW, 1 March 1953.

82. WCW to FW, 7 March 1953.

83. *PB*, p. 103.

84. WCW to FW, 17 March 1953.

85. WCW to FW, 28 (i.e., 29) March 1953.

86. WCW to FW, 27 March 1953.

87. *PB*, pp. 97–100.

88. WCW to CC, 24 April 1953.

89. WCW to Richard A. Norton of Saybrook, New York, 29 April 1953.

90. FW to RE, 9 April 1953 (Dartmouth).

91. WCW to TC, 11 May 1953 (Pri.).

92. WCW to RE, 14 May 1953. *SL*, pp. 317–318.

93. Robert Creeley, "A Character for Love," *Black Mountain Review*, (Summer 1954), 45–48.

94. *PB*, pp. 78–79.

95. WCW to FM, 24 Aug. 1953 (D).

96. WCW to LZ, 27 Aug. 1953 (T).

97. "On Measure—Statement for Cid Corman," *Origin*, I, 12 (Spring 1954), 194–199. In *SE*, pp. 337–340.

98. WCW to RC, 8 October 1953. For a discussion of Creeley's relationship with WCW, see my "'Fire of a Very Real Order': Creeley and Williams," *Boundary 2*, VI, 3/VII, 1 (Spring/Fall 1978), 173–190.

99. *PB*, pp. 153–182.

100. "In the morning," WCW wrote in *VP*, "he [Dev Evans] was leaving at nine, the Jungfrau showed its white breast. O swan of rock and snow—new fallen, blizzard white. A mountain of snow he saw, the snow white mountain breast, the sun upon it. *Sein de neige!* He woke as from a lethargy. The stupid lethargy into which he was falling, to some kind of feeling at that sight. Snow breast, white and icy: a pang of anguish. . . . Damn Switzerland, it lulls you to sleep" (p. 231).

101. *A*, pp. 122–123.

102. *KH*, p. 59.

103. *A*, pp. 172–173.

104. Reprinted with the title "The Death of Pan," in *The Modern Tradition: Backgrounds of Modern Literature*, ed. Richard Ellmann and Charles Feidelson, Jr., Oxford University Press (New York, 1965), pp. 416–423.

105. Robert Lowell, "William Carlos Williams," *Twentieth Century Views: William Carlos Williams*, (Prentice Hall, Inc., 1966), p. 159. Reprinted from the *Hudson Review*, 14 (Winter 1961–1962), 530–536.

106. *IWWP*, pp. 94–95.

107. *PB*, pp. 129–132.

108. WCW to TC, 20 Dec. 1953 (Pri.).

Chapter Thirteen. Hunting Down the Unicorn: 1951–1956 (cont.)

109. NHP to Mrs. Hannah Josephson of the American Academy, 18 Dec. 1953 (Academy papers).

110. WCW to Frank L. Moore, 21 May 1951. *SL,* p. 297.

111. "The Smiling Dane," *PB,* pp. 148–149. This is the same face that Seamus Heaney has also written of in his book of poems, *North.*

112. FW to FM, 28 Jan. 1954 (D).

113. WCW to CC, 9 Feb. 1954.

114. WCW to DL, 6 Jan. 1954 (Pri.).

115. WCW to TC, 7 April 1954 (Pri.).

116. WCW to RL, 16 March 1954.

117. Merrill Moore to FW, 16 and 24 March 1954 (B).

118. *PB,* pp. 146–147.

119. WCW to KB, 11 May 1954.

120. "Painting in the American Grain," *Art News,* LIII, 4 (June–Aug. 1954), 20–23, 62, 78. In *RI,* pp. 238–245.

121. TC's unpublished reminiscences of WCW.

122. WCW to Harvey Breit, 10 April 1954 (Fairleigh Dickinson).

123. WCW to NHP, 15 May 1954.

124. WCW to JT, 26 June 1954. JT had written Josephine Herbst for information on WCW and RM.

125. WCW to RC, 9 Aug. 1954. WCW's essay on Olson, not published in WCW's lifetime, was printed in *Maps,* 4 the special Charles Olson issue, 1971, pp. 61–65. This was a review of *Maximus* 11–22. Denise Levertov had just sent WCW Olson's book from Mexico and WCW pondered now on Olson's work. WCW could see that Olson was somewhere in the forefront of contemporary poetry, but he also saw him as too fragmented and disconnected like EP, often leaving out too much or including too much that was "inessential." Still, the overall impression WCW had after reading Olson's new poems was that it had been "a thrilling experience." What WCW did *not* like about Olson was the way the man attacked "his friends indiscriminately with his enemies" in the poetry (perhaps a reference to Olson's treatment of Vincent Ferrini). No matter how big a man's ego, WCW believed, a writer had no right to do that. Even Olson, all six feet six of him, was "not God" and not even "Napoleon" (WCW to CC, 20 June 1956).

126. WCW to LZ, 9 Aug. 1954 (T). Zukofsky, Creeley, Olson, Levertov, Williams: an extraordinary vortex in itself.

127. WCW to DL, 23 Aug. 1954 (Pri.).

128. WCW to FM, 15 May 1954 (ViU).

129. WCW to KB, 24 July 1954.

130. "An Essay on *Leaves of Grass,*" in *Leaves of Grass: One Hundred Years After,* ed. Milton Hindus, Stanford University Press (Stanford, Calif., 1955), pp. 21–31.

131. WCW to RE, 28 Nov. 1954.

132. WCW to WTS, 20 April 1955. John Montague, the Irish poet, recalled meeting WCW at the Iowa Writers' Workshop that May: "After a reading where / you had been made / fun of, . . . / you stood on the Old / Capitol steps, . . . / and when I spoke / you put your arm / around me, saying / 'poet, poet!' " (*A Chosen Light,* Macgibbon & Kee [London, 1967], p. 64)

133. WCW was particularly anxious to see Santa Fe. "That country has always fascinated me with its dream of savage well being, Coronado and his Spaniards" (WCW to WTS, 20 April 1955).

134. WCW to RE, 4 May 1955.

135. Published in several issues of *WCWN.*

136. Script at T. It derives from an essay on Rutherford by WCW originally for *Holiday* magazine.

137. WCW to CC, 4 July 1955.

138. WCW to KB, 19 July 1955.

139. WCW to Frederick Manfred, 8 Feb. 1955.

140. WCW to CC, 30 Nov. 1955.

141. WCW to CC, 10 Dec. 1955.

142. Unpublished reminiscences of TC.

143. "Comment: Wallace Stevens," *Poetry*, LXXXVII, 4 (Jan. 1956), 234–239.

144. Although by 1955 the correspondence with MM had petered out. "I never hear from the Moore any more," WCW punned in a letter to KB. "I wonder what, if anything, has happened. She used to send me her books whenever published and I always did the same. . . . Can that be why M.M. is through with me? since she cannot agree with my experiments?" (WCW to KB, 7 Sept. 1955). But surely the estrangement had been a result of WCW's "sex mania," as MM called it, as she'd spotted it in *Paterson* 4. Bill Williams, in old age acting like King David, trying to find a little warmth.

145. WCW to RE, 28 Jan. 1956.

146. WCW to LZ, 2 Feb. 1956 (T).

147. On 7 June 1954, for example, RM had told JH that it wasn't what WCW had written about him in *A* that had soured him, but rather that the man had revealed himself there to be "a petty soul with a 'malign' streak in him, as HD wrote me" (Y). WCW, of course, had shown himself to be anything but that, but he had come too close to the unadorned truth in speaking of RM's past.

148. WCW's long letter to JT (12 March 1956), published in the *Massachusetts Review*, III, 2 (Winter 1962), 294–296.

149. *P* 5, p. 207. Six weeks later WCW wrote a William Wilson that his guess had been right: that no sooner had WCW begun *P* 5 in 1952 than he realized that he was writing a different poem, "Asphodel." At that point he had no idea that he would do Books 2 and 3 or the Coda of that poem. Now, however, "since the first of the year I have begun to write the final *Paterson* 5—it has not progressed far but has already taken more the form of the previous books [of *Paterson*]" (WCW to Wilson, 27 April 1956) (Lilly).

Chapter Fourteen. The Whore/ Virgin and the Wounded One-Horned Beast: 1956–1958

1. Brendan Gill, *Here at the New Yorker*, Random House (New York, 1975), pp. 332–333.

2. "Shapiro Is All Right," a review of Karl Shapiro's *Essay on Rime* (1945). Reprinted in *SE*, pp. 258–262.

3. *A*, pp. xi–xiv.

4. WCW to Fred Manfred, 19 Dec. 1956.

5. WCW to LZ, 15 May 1929 (T).

6. "The American Spirit in Art," *RI*, pp. 212–213.

7. Early drafts for *Paterson* 5 are in Y Collection.

8. WCW to Allen Ginsberg (Y. Originals at Columbia).

9. *Paterson* 4, p. 194.

10. WCW to Louis Ginsberg, 14 Feb. 1952 (Y).

11. Allen Ginsberg, *Empty Mirror*, Totem/Corinth (New York, 1961), p. 17.

12. WCW to Allen Ginsberg, 27 Feb. 1952.

13. *Empty Mirror*, p. vi.

14. WCW to RL, 11 March 1952. *SL*, pp. 311–313.

15. Early drafts of *Paterson* 5, i.e., "Asphodel."

16. WCW to JL, 4 Sept. 1954.

Chapter Fourteen. The Whore/Virgin and the Wounded One-Horned Beast: 1956–1958 (cont.)

17. Y Collection.
18. WCW to Gilbert Sorrentino, 25 Sept. 1957.
19. Early draft of *P5*, 1956 (Y).
20. CC to WCW, 13 agosto 1956 (Y).
21. ED to WCW, 20 Sept. 1957 (Y).
22. WCW to JL, 28 Oct. 1956.
23. Five days later WCW expanded on the theme of the Virgin in a letter to Charles Tomlinson. *Paterson* 5, he explained, carried "the theme out of the physical world of the Paterson environments into the mind, off the earth, unconfined by any one place to a congeries of places. . . . And since a man is the chief hero, a woman carries the burden in this part. She is no virgin, that is emphasized. My whole life has been spent in close association with one woman or another and so I felt it would be a misrepresentation to end the poem without saluting women" (WCW to CT, 12 July 1958.)
24. WCW to CA, 16 Oct. 1956.
25. JT, *ND* 17 (1961), pp. 291–292.
26. WCW to CC, 6 April 1955.
27. Translation by J. Addington Symonds.
28. *P* 5, p. 217.
29. WCW to DL, 21 March 1956 (Pri.).
30. Early draft in Y Collection.
31. WCW to DL, 21 March 1956 (Pri.).
32. WCW to FW, 9 Aug. 1955 (Pri.).
33. WCW to EP, All Saints [1 Nov.] 1956 (Y).
34. *PB*, p. 66.
35. *P* 5, pp. 217–218. EP to WCW, 13 Nov. 1956 (Y).
36. WCW to EP, 21 Nov. 1956. *SL*, pp. 338–339.
37. WCW to EP, 9 Nov. 1956 (Y).
38. EP to WCW (Y).
39. WCW to JL, 2 March 1958.
40. WCW to LZ, 5 March 1958 (T).
41. WCW to FM, 24 Sept. 1957 (ViU).
42. WCW to the Monahans, 13 Sept. 1957 (Pri.).
43. *P* 5, pp. 224–225.
44. Postcard from WCW to FM, postmarked 5 Aug. 195[6] (D).
45. "The American Idiom," published in five different magazines and books during 1960–1961. See *ND* 17 (1961), pp. 250–251.
46. WCW to JL, 11 June 1957.
47. WCW to JL, 20 Sept. 1957.
48. WCW to NHP, 16 Oct. 1957.
49. WCW to JL, 29 Oct. 1957.
50. WCW to JL, 28 Nov. 1957.
51. Y Collection.
52. WCW to JL, 8 Feb. 1958.
53. WCW to CC, 11 Aug. 1958.
54. WCW to Robert MacGregor, 16 May 1958 (Y).
55. WCW to ED, 7 July 1958.
56. WCW to CC, 4 March 1959.
57. WCW to JT, 4 March 1955, *ND* 17, p. 295.

Chapter Fifteen. Lightning Stroke and Thunder Clap: 1956–1963

1. From WCW's introduction to Ginsberg's *Howl and Other Poems*, The Pocket Poets Series, No.4 (1956), pp. 7–8.
2. WCW to LZ, 1 April 1956 (T).
3. WCW to Irving Layton, 19 March 1956.
4. WCW to Warren Allen Smith, 25 March 1956 (Pri.).
5. WCW to LZ, 14 March 1956 (T).
6. Mrs. Helen Armstrong, in a letter to the author.
7. "The High Bridge above the Tagus River at Toledo," *PB*, p. 53.
8. "Calypsos," *PB*, pp. 56–57.
9. WCW to Josephine Herbst, 5 Nov. 1947.
10. "Measure—A Loosely Assembled Essay on Poetic Measure," *Spectrum*, III, 3 (Fall 1959), 131–157. This essay was to have been WCW's summative pronouncement on the subject of poetic measure, but failing health curtailed his completing it and it was left to Hugh Kenner to assemble and edit WCW's extensive and redundant notes. WCW told RE in June 1958 that, though he had only the beginning of his essay done at that point, he'd already made enough "important discoveries" to "shock the professors." If only, he lamented, he still had his "good right to work with—and more than half a brain" (6 June 1958).
11. *PB*, pp. 50–51.
12. "A Visit with William Carlos Williams," *Minnesota Review*, I, 3 (April 1961), 309–324. Reprinted in *Int*, pp. 38–56.
13. WCW to FM, 8 Feb. 1957 (ViU).
14. WCW to WTS, 28 April 1956. Tram Combs did much of the hosting while WCW was in San Juan.
15. Correspondence with Barbara Loebenstein. "Williams Reads Poetry, Explains His Philosophy" and "Poet Emphasizes Need to Express Emotions"—so the headlines in the college newspaper ran.
16. WCW to LZ, 20 Sept. 1956 (T).
17. WCW to KR, 9 Nov. 1956.
18. WCW to CC, 6 Dec. 1956.
19. WCW to FM, 30 Sept. 1957 (D).
20. Allen Ginsberg, "To WCW," in *Indian Journal*. See Ann Charters' description of this visit in *Kerouac: A Biography*, Warner Paperback Library (New York, 1974), pp. 282–283.
21. WCW to CC, 4 March 1959.
22. Unpublished transcript of interview (Pri.).
23. WCW to TR, 22 Jan. 1957.
24. WCW to DL, 23 Jan. 1957 (Pri.).
25. WCW to DL, 11 Feb. 1957 (Pri.).
26. WCW to RL, 20 April 1957.
27. WCW in conversation with JT.
28. WCW to NHP, 27 March 1957.
29. WCW to RL, 11 Sept. 1957. About "The Birth," WCW told JT on 22 June 1957 that he had done "about twenty verses, slaving over the birth of an Italian baby from my own past." This poem appears in the *Massachusetts Review*, III, 2 (Winter 1962), 280–281.
30. *American Scholar*, Washington, XXVI, 4 (Autumn 1957), 453–457.
31. WCW to Frederick Manfred, 4 Aug. 1957. Manfred dedicated this novel to WCW.
32. WCW to RE, 19 Aug. 1957. If WCW had not appealed directly to the Godhead, he had only come down the ladder one rung to appeal to the Woman as Deity in the figure of the Virgin in his poem to the Monahans five years before, though he apparently forgot this now in remonstrating with Eberhart. A month later WCW tried to clarify to RE what he'd meant:

Chapter Fifteen. Lightning Stroke and Thunder Clap: 1956–1963 (cont.)
"Since every important idea in our lives may be ascribed to God I do not in my poems want continually to ascribe them to a primal source. To do so is in my opinion tautological. Merely a preference on my part, of no basic significance" (WCW to RE, 19 Sept. 1957). It was Williams employing Ockham's razor.

   33. PB, p. 67.

   34. JT papers (Y).

   35. WCW to RL, 4 Dec. 1957.

   36. WCW to CT, 15 Dec. 1957.

   37. WCW to CT, 16 Jan. 1958.

   38. WCW to FM, 21 Jan. 1958 (ViU).

   39. WCW to RL, 14 Jan. 1958.

   40. "An Exercise," *PB*, p. 58.

   41. WCW to LZ, 22 Jan. 1958 (T).

   42. WCW to CC, 15 April 1958.

   43. WCW to JT, 11 Feb. 1958.

   44. WCW to Raphael Wang, 25 Feb. 1958 (Dartmouth).

   45. WCW to CT, 16 Jan. 1958.

   46. WCW to MB, 7 March 1958.

   47. WCW to MB, 20 March 1958.

   48. WCW to RE, 26 March 1958. The Williamses were at Gratwick Highlands from 27 March to 3 April 1958.

   49. FW to CA, 7 April 1958 (B).

   50. Y Collection.

   51. WCW to William Faulkner, 24 Sept. 1956. Cited in *Paideuma*, VIII, 2 (Fall 1979).

   52. See Francis J. Bosha's "Faulkner, Pound and the P.P.P. [People-to-People Program]" in *Paideuma*, (op. cit.), 249–256.

   53. FW to CA, 28 June 1958 (B).

   54. FW to CA, 17 July 1958 (B).

   55. WCW to CC, 30 July 1958. There are also some notes JT wrote in Sept. 1960 remembering WCW's reaction to EP's visit (Y).

   56. WCW to Tony Weinberger, 17 Sept. 1958.

   57. "A Visit with WCW: September, 1958," *Int*, pp. 91–96.

   58. See too Charles Angoff's "A Williams Memoir," *Prairie Schooner*, XXXVIII (Winter 1964–1965), 299–305. When Angoff asked WCW to speak at Wagner College on Staten Island in the spring of '58, WCW had made two requests: that a chauffeur pick him up and take him back home, and that someone get him a bottle of good whiskey to keep his circulation up, preferably Wilson's. Angoff, worried because Wagner College was Lutheran-sponsored and officially forbade alcohol on campus, nevertheless got the whiskey for WCW, who took half a tumbler straight before the talk, another right after the talk, and another when Angoff bundled him up for the trip home. It apparently helped.

   59. WCW to LZ, 15 Oct. 1958 (T).

   60. WCW to KB, 24 Oct. 1958.

   61. WCW to LZ, 23 Oct. 1958 (T).

   62. WCW to LZ, 30 Nov. 1958 (T).

   63. WCW to JL, 23 Dec. 1958.

   64. FW to CA, 27 Dec. 1958 (B).

   65. WCW to TR, 1 Oct. 1958.

   66. WCW to CT, 3 Sept. 1958.

   67. WCW to RE, 12 Oct. 1956.

   68. WCW to FW, 3 Jan. 1956 (Pri.).

   69. WCW to Julian Beck, 15 Dec. 1951.

70. WCW to Julian Beck, 20 Jan. 1959.

71. "15 Years Later," *PB*, p. 54.

72. See David A Fedo, "The William Carlos Williams–Julian Beck Correspondence and the Production of *Many Loves*," *WCWN*, III, 2 (Fall 1977), 12–17.

73. *PB*, p. 3.

74. *PB*, p. 12.

75. *PB*, p.14.

76. WCW to FM, 10 March 1956 (V).

77. WCW to KB, 1 Jan. 1959.

78. WCW to CC, 4 March 1959. WCW to Tony Weinberger, 29 March 1959.

79. WCW to Clarence Major, 1 April 1959.

80. WCW to CC, 7 April 1959.

81. WCW to WTS, 11 April 1959.

82. WCW to FM, 10 March 1959 (ViU).

83. WCW to Felicia Geffen, 15, 19 and 25 May 1959 (American Academy papers). WCW himself came to New York on May 20 to be inducted into the American Academy of Arts and Letters, along with Samuel Barber for music, Charles E. Burchfield for art, and Reinhold Niebuhr for theology. WCW's supporters in the Academy had been Conrad Aiken (most strongly), Mark Van Doren, Marianne Moore, Sherwood Anderson, and John Dos Passos. But *not* Cummings.

84. WCW to DL, 26 June 1959 (Pri.).

85. WCW to EEC, 25 May 1959.

86. WCW's comments on Norman's biography of EEC and his review of EEC's poems are in the *Evergreen Review*, II, 7 (Winter 1959), 214–216.

87. WCW to EP, 20 July 1959 (Y). It was the first letter WCW had received from EP in over a year. In June 1959 Tom Cole had sailed for Europe, stopping first in Rutherford to visit with the Williamses. WCW gave Cole Pound's address—the Hotel Grande Italia in Rapallo—and explained that Pound had moved there from his daughter Mary's castle in the mountains. When Cole returned home six weeks later, he stopped off again at the Williamses' to tell them about his visit with EP.

88. WCW to LZ, 12 Aug. 1959 (T). WCW wrote 18 Aug., but LZ has corrected the date on the letter itself.

89. Letter from WEW to author. See also FW to TC, 28 Aug. 1959: "Yes—Bill went to the Hospital—was operated on—and it was cancer.—They believe it is all out—and there is no extension as far as they can tell."

90. WCW to Marie Leone, 18 Sept. 1959 (Pri.).

91. WCW to FM, 6 Sept. 1959 (ViU). "I'm nothing but a wreck now. . . . They cut me up last August but left enough of my guts for me to survive on" (WCW to Irving Layton, 21 Oct. 1959).

92. WCW to CC, 15 Sept. 1959.

93. WCW to DL, 22 Sept. 1959 (Pri.). *PB*, p. 42. See also Emily Dickinson's "I Heard a Fly Buzz."

94. *PB*, p. 21.

95. *PB*, pp. 19–20.

96. *PB*, pp. 22–23.

97. WCW to JL, 4 Jan. 1960. Also WCW to RE, 10 Oct. 1959.

98. WCW to Irving Layton, 19 Feb. 1960. Also, see WCW to Kay Boyle, 30 Sept. 1959: "Once in a while I still write something that pleases me which I fondly believe is an advance on anything I have done in the past but for the most part as Pound used to say, the old is the best of it."

99. "Introduction" to *The Complete Works of François Villon*, trans. by Anthony Bonner, Bantam Books (New York, 1960), pp. ix–xv. WCW praised Layton, for example, for

Chapter Fifteen. Lightning Stroke and Thunder Clap: 1956–1963 (cont.)
the same poetic values he said he had found in Villon: "You have broken away from a too slavish adherence to the stanzaic form at the same time adhering to a minimal of regularity, not completely breaking down to a formlessness as has happened with some of our so-called 'beatnics' " (WCW to Irving Layton, 19 Feb. 1960).

100. "The Gossips," *PB*, p. 41.

101. Floss sent LZ a postcard from Tampa saying her husband would write when they got back home and he could use his typewriter once again. In the meantime KB was reading and critiquing the book (FW to LZ, 9 March 1960 [T]).

102. Kenneth Burke, "William Carlos Williams, 1883–1963," *The New York Review of Books*, Special Issue (20 May 1963), 47.

103. WCW to LZ, 9 April 1960 (T).

104. "Tribute to Neruda, the poet collector of seashells," *Rutgers Review*, Rutgers, I, 2 (Spring 1967), 24–25.

105. WCW to DL, 9 April 1960 (Pri.). Earlier WCW had paid Levertov an important compliment: "The words, the choice of words you use is disturbing to a man. It is linked to something unknown to the male wonderfully well used. As an independent artist you hold the key to the attack." Writing was, after all, a mystery, and when a woman was involved that mystery was deepened. It was "something cryptic which the world solves by calling her a whore" and he was going to read and reread Levertov's poems "until as an old man I have penetrated to where your secret is hid" (WCW to DL, 31 Dec. 1959 [Pri.]).

106. WCW to LZ, 14 April 1960 (T).

107. James Laughlin, "A Visit," *WCWN*, IV, 1 (Spring 1978), 1–9.

108. WCW to James Murray, 13 April 1960 (Pri.) (copy to JL): "I am writing to relieve you of having any further concern with James Laughlin and New Directions."

109. WCW to LZ, June 1960 (T). WCW to JL, 16 June 1960.

110. Y Collection.

111. WCW to Tony Weinberger, 14 April 1960.

112. WCW to Jon Bracker, 26 April 1960 (Lilly).

113. WCW to CA, 12 May 1960.

114. WCW to RE, 9 June 1960.

115. WCW to EP, 26 Nov. 1960 (Y). And for EP's benefit, WCW added in this same letter: "You're not worth it but I forgive you nevertheless for all your shortcomings as a friend."

116. FW to Felicia Geffen, 2 June 1960 (American Academy papers).

117. "Introduction" to *The Illustrated Leaves of Grass*, ed. Howard Chapnick, Grosset (New York 1971). This introduction was heavily edited and lacks the rough vigor and immediacy of WCW's own late prose. See *RI*, pp. 231–232 and Bram Dijkstra's explanatory note, p. 267.

118. WCW to Kay Boyle, 2 June 1960.

119. WCW to CT, 11 June 1960.

120. WCW to Louis Zara, 1 June 1960 (Pri.).

121. WCW to DL, 10 Oct. 1960 (Pri.). Of course WCW was no less hard on himself for having failed to make sufficiently clear the nature of his variable foot. Floss wrote CA on July 30 that "not one prof" had "turned up" to hear her husband, and then added: "Shades of Eliot!" (B).

122. WCW to CC, 15 Sept. 1960. Also FW to CA, 24 Aug. 1960 (B).

123. WCW to EP, 18 Aug. 1960 (Y).

124. The third was Thomas Edward Francis of the Hun School of Princeton, to whom WCW sent a shorter version of "The American Idiom." WCW had told Francis that he would be willing to lecture on the new measure and when Francis took him up on this WCW had to reply, sadly, that he'd "exaggerated" when he'd said he "could write a lecture on the American idiom & the varyable [sic] foot, I can no longer do so." Instead he sent along an early poem from *The Descent of Winter* (1927) to give Francis an example of the kind of measure he had meant. The poem was "Even idiots grow old" (3 Aug. 1960 [Fairleigh Dickinson]).

125. WCW to WTS, 21 Oct. 1960.

126. WCW to CC, 1 June 1960.

127. WCW to CT, 11 June 1960.

128. WCW to WTS, 21 Oct. 1960.

129. PB, p. 33. Also, letters to Henry Neise, 6–9 Nov. 1960.

130. WCW to DL, 10 Oct. 1960 (Pri.).

131. WCW to DL, 6 Nov. 1960 (Pri.). Others who had been out to see WCW in late 1959 and 1960 included Tony Weinberger, Tomlinson, M. L. Rosenthal, and Walter Sutton (in Oct. 1960).

132. WCW to FM, 16 Nov. 1960 (ViU).

133. WCW to WTS, 19 Nov. 1960. "Too narrow to be comfortable": WCW to FM, 16 Nov. 1960 (ViU).

134. The fragment of P 6 is dated Jan.4/61, 1/8/61, and 7/1/61. WCW apparently worked on *Paterson* one last time in early July after being released from the hospital.

135. WCW to NHP, 21 Jan. 1961. WCW had a new doctor now who was trying a new kind of treatment, though WCW was not very hopeful.

136. WCW to RL, 28 Feb. 1961. *Harvard Advocate*, CXLV (Nov. 1962), 12.

137. WCW to JL, 13 March 1961. A few weeks earlier, for example, WCW had written NHP to give him a final disposition on his books, adding that he was failing rapidly now. The following day Floss wrote NHP herself to apologize for her husband's erratic behavior. She didn't know *what* had come over her husband (24 and 25 Feb. 1961).

138. WCW to FM, 22 March 1961 (ViU).

139. WCW to FM, 2 May 1961 (D).

140. PB, p. 70.

141. PB, p. 69.

142. So, for example, writing to RL on 23 May, WCW praised RL's translations from Villon and then added, "I wish I could do as well with the language as I used to but it is quite beyond me of late nevertheless I must try even if it takes me a half hour to complete a sentence." And this postscript from Floss: "Bill is having a tough time. He's very weak—his mind is confused—most of the time—and he can scarcely talk. I'm hoping with better weather he may pick up" (23 May 1961).

143. FW to FM, 5 June 1961 (D). That was the last FM heard from either WCW or FW. Ten months later he wrote Oscar Baron of the Alicat Press for copies of his *Gutbucket and Gossamer*. "I quit writing for some years, but have now caught my second wind," FM wrote halfheartedly from Winston-Salem, North Carolina, after drifting from one place to another around the U.S. "This time I mean to make it, in one way or another. Our mutual friend Bill Williams as you know was the victim of a series of strokes, & when last I heard from him (through Floss his wife) he was incapable of any writing whatsoever, any *new* writing" (FM to Oscar Baron, 19 April 1962 [D]).

144. FW to NHP, 3 July 1961 (Y). The basic account of WCW's June 2 stroke is contained in this letter.

145. WCW to JL, 7 Aug. 1961.

146. WCW to JL, 16 Aug. 1961.

147. During August and September, for example, JT helped WCW by collecting the poems that would make up PB.

148. Floss to JL, 19 Oct. 1961 (Y). A few weeks earlier WCW had been convinced that he once again had cancer, until the doctors assured him otherwise.

Chapter Fifteen. Lightning Stroke and Thunder Clap: 1956–1963 (cont.)

149. "Asphodel," *PB*, p.169. JT's papers: "November 18 [1961]: 'I've given up writing completely,' he told me. I asked Floss about the stuff he was typing in the Spring. 'He never showed it to me—probably threw it away,' she replied" (Y). But this may well have been the *Paterson* 6 fragment.

150. FW to JT, 2 Dec. 1961 (Y).

151. "The Art of Poetry," *Paris Review:* 32 (Summer–Fall 1964), 110–151.

152. WCW to CT, 26 Jan. 1962. Throughout 1961 and early 1962 WCW wrote whenever he could to praise good writing, particularly in the young who—he believed—were carrying his banner forward. So, on 18 March 1961 he wrote Le Roi Jones (Amamu Amiri Baraka), then editor of *Yugen*, thanking him for sending him a copy of the latest issue. He especially liked the piece by Gil Sorrentino which Floss had read to him, "a fresh point of view, fresh as a daisy across so much academic dross." He was also glad to see the names of his friends, "Creeley and Olson among the rest."

153. WCW and FW to TC, 31 Jan. 1962 (Pri.).

154. FW to JL, 8 March 1962 (Y).

155. "Stormy," *Poetry*, CI, 1–2 (Oct.–Nov. 1962), 141.

156. Sept. 15–Oct. 7, 1962. They stayed at the Caribbean Beach Hotel.

157. WCW to JL, 11 Nov. 1962.

158. "Phone Call to Rutherford," in *The Cities*, Grove Press (New York, 1967).

159. So, for example, to LZ, 13 Dec. 1962. "The last time I saw him was about a month before his death," Denise Levertov remembered, "and it was the only time I left 9 Ridge Rd. despondent instead of exhilarated." Letter to author.

160. Y Collection.

161. JT papers (Y).

162. *CEP*, pp. 129–131.

163. FW to Gil Sorrentino, 11 March 1963: "It was good of you and so many others to come to the service for Bill. He said he would O.K. a service but not a lot of religious stuff. Being a unitarian it was easier to arrange. . . . I have done most of my grieving the past few years—watching Bill slowly leave us. . . . He finally just went to sleep—peacefully—in his bed" (D). By the end, she told Tom Cole, it had been a "blessed relief" to see her husband finally go (FW to TC, 13 March 1963 [Pri.]).

164. EP to FW, 5 March 1963 (Y).

165. FW to MM, 22 April 1963 (Rosenbach). That same month WCW finally won his first Pulitzer for *PB*. And the following month he was given the Gold Medal of the National Institute of Arts and Letters. Malcolm Cowley, as president of that august body, read the letter of presentation. WCW even found an English publisher for his work—MacGibbon and Kee—just two days after his death. For the story of WCW's critical reception in the decade following his death, see the chapter, "The Critical Current: Towards Canonization, 1963–1973," in my *William Carlos Williams: The Poet and His Critics*, American Library Association (Chicago, 1975), pp. 185–257.

After WEW's divorce from Daphne Spence in 1976, he settled into the house at 9 Ridge Road with his second wife, Mimi. After all, the office was conveniently right next door, as it had been for the past sixty years. "I will be here in my life time," Dr. Williams, aged 62, told Tom Cole, "the guardian of the trust, Holy Grail, or whatever" (WEW to TC, 7 June 1976 [Pri.]).

166. WCW to LZ, 30 Jan. 1956 (T).

Acknowledgments

I have had a great deal of patient assistance from many libraries and their staffs. At Yale, where I have spent many occasions over the past decade, I want especially to thank Donald Gallup and Anne Whelpley of the Collection of American Literature housed in the Beinecke Rare Book and Manuscript Library. Their many kindnesses toward me have allowed this record to assume the kind of complex detail it has, and I hope our literary friendship will continue far into the future. I also owe a large debt to Karl Gay, then Eric Carpenter, and finally to Robert Bertholf, successive curators of the Poetry Collection at the State University of New York at Buffalo, all of whom have been most helpful. And I want to thank Ellen Dunlap and her staff at the Research Center of the University of Texas at Austin for being so unstintingly generous in providing me with materials from their large Williams collection.

Beyond these three major archives of Williams material I also want to thank the following libraries and their dedicated staffs: the Huntington Library; Rodney Dennis and the Houghton Library of Harvard University; the William Carlos Williams Collection (# 7456), Clifton Waller Barrett Library, University of Virginia Library; Princeton University Library; the Joseph Regenstein Library of the University of Chicago (for the *Poetry* magazine papers); Dartmouth College; the University of Delaware Library, Special Collections; the McKeldin Library of the University of Maryland; the Lilly Library at Indiana University, Bloomington, Ind.; Special Collections, Washington University Libraries, St. Louis; Southern Illinois University at Carbondale; the Newberry Library (Chicago); Pennsylvania State University Libraries; Special Collections Department, Golda Meir Library, University of Wisconsin—Milwaukee (for the *Little Review* papers); Wesleyan University, Special Collections; the University of Washington, Special Collections; Special Collections, Columbia University; Kent State University; Middlebury College; the University of California, Los Angeles; the Berg Collection of English and American Literature; Mrs. Sonia Jacobs of the Special Collections Department, University of Colorado at Boulder; the Kenneth Spencer Research Library of the University of Kansas; the George Arents Research Library for Special Collections at Syracuse University; the Charles Patterson Van Pelt Library of the University of Pennsylvania; the University of Connecticut, Special Collections; the University of Wyoming; the University of Minnesota; Northwestern University; the Enoch Pratt Free Library (Baltimore); the Francis Bacon Library; Special Collections, University of Arkansas, Fayetteville for the John Gould Fletcher papers; the University of Saskatchewan; the Sophia Smith Collection (Women's History Archive), Smith College; Amherst College, Special Collections; the Oral History Research Office, Butler Library, Columbia University; the Rosenbach Foundation; the New Jersey Historical Society; the Passaic County Historical Society at Lambert Castle, Paterson; Rutgers University Library; Fairleigh Dickinson University, Rutherford; the Free Public Library, Rutherford; the Library of Congress; and the archives of the American Academy of Arts and Letters. I also owe a special word of thanks to the seeming indefatigability of the library staff at the University of Massachusetts, Amherst, in procuring for me over the past eleven years literally hundreds of pieces of difficult-to-obtain materials used in the making of this biography. In particular, I want to thank the Interlibrary Loan Co-ordinators, Ute Bargmann and Edla Holm.

This biography was aided at several critical junctures by research grants from the Graduate Research Council of the University of Massachusetts and by released time granted by my department. I very much appreciate the support given this project by Provost Loren Barritz, Deans Jerry Allen and Richard Noland, and my chairmen, Vincent DiMarco and Charles Moran, as well as the English Department's Long-Range Planning Committees. These people are examples of what enlightened leadership can do to foster serious, long-range scholarship. I also want to thank the National Endowment for the Humanities for a very important Independent Research Fellowship which helped see this project through to completion. I am particularly grateful to the American Philosophical Society for two important early grants-in-aid.

Fearing that I have forgotten some who were there during my ten-year odyssey to recover Williams' life, I would like to acknowledge help from the following. First and foremost I want to thank Dr. William Eric Williams, without whose help I could not have approached his father with anything like the detail and openness I hope I have caught here. He and his wife, Mimi, made me their guest at 9 Ridge Road on many occasions and Dr. Williams helped me time and time again with all sorts of details that I might otherwise have despaired of ever learning. He also took the time to read through the manuscript, though to his credit he never once suggested that I change anything to alter my perceptions of his father's life. He is himself an extraordinary individual. Paul Williams was also helpful, especially during the early stages of the writing of this book, and I hope his openness and honesty will likewise be felt in the unfolding of this biography. In a profound sense this is their life as much as it was their parents'.

I also owe a large debt of gratitude to James Laughlin for making so many of Williams' papers accessible to me and especially for his hospitality in allowing me to examine the Williams papers in his possession at his home in Norfolk, Connecticut. I want to thank him for his constant encouragement all during the years I was working on this and other Williams projects, as well as for his single-minded dedication to the memory of his old friend. The following, listed in alphabetical order, were all helpful, in small ways and big, in the conception and writing of this biography, and it is a pleasure now to sound their names here in one long roll call: Caroline C. B. Arcier, Mrs. Herbert E. Armstrong, Neil Baldwin, Mary Barnard, Roy Basler, John Bauer, Eric Bentley, Bruce Berlind, Edith Heal Berrien, Kate . Berryman, Lois Bianchi, Sarah Blackburn, Harold Bloom, James Breslin, Carolyn Burke, Kenneth Burke, George Butterick, Harry James Cargas, Lydia Carlin, Else Albrecht-Carrie, Donald Cheney, Mrs. Ruth Churchill, Thomas Cole, Malcolm Cowley, Robert Creeley, Babette Deutsch, John Dollar, Charlotte Herman Earle, Mr. and Mrs. Eyvind Earle, Charles Eaton, Richard Eberhart, Gladys Eckardt, David Eisendrath, Valerie Eliot, Dana Ely, Mrs. Eleanora von Erffa, James Edward Fall, David Fedo, Ann W. Fisher, Joyce Fried, Emily Goessler, Theodora Graham, Horace Gregory, Louis Grudin, Curtis Harnack, Theodore Harris, Irwin Heilner, Clayton and Kathleen Hoagland, Thomas Horan, Mary Jarrell, Conrad Jordan, Sidney Kahn, Marilyn Kallet, Hugh Kenner, Beatrice Knudsen, Stanley Koehler, Hilton Kramer, Paul Leake, Marie Leone, Denise Levertov, Harry Levin, Yolanda Le Witter, Robert Lima, David McDowell, Norman Macleod, Barry Magid, Frederick Manfred, Jay Martin, Jeffrey Meyers, Barbara Loebenstein Michaels, Betty Miller, J. Hillis Miller, Bill and Eleanora Monahan, John Montague, Bucklin Moon, Barbara Morgan, Steven Oates, Wayne Van Orman, Robert Pack, the late Norman Holmes Pearson, Marjorie Perloff, Omar Pound, Sr. Bernetta Quinn, Mary de Rachevitz, Joseph Riddell, Selden Rodman, John Sanford, Leslie Schreyer, Harvey Shapiro, Suzanne Williams Sinclair, Madeline Spence, Elaine Sproat,

Holly Stevens, Stephen Tapscott, Byron Vazakas, Emily Wallace, Reed Whittemore, Daphne Spence Williams, Emily Dickinson Williams, William Appleman Williams, Patricia C. Willis, and Ronald Wood.

I want to thank too certain friends and colleagues for their unstinting help over the long haul: Richard Meehan and John Johnson, James and Margaret Freeman, Ron Berger, Barry Moser, Jules Chametzsky, James Tate, Madeline DeFrees, David Porter, Laury Magnus, and especially Allen Mandelbaum, for encouragement, for being there again and again. I also want to single out Frederick W. Turner, who particularly helped to shape the American scope and direction of this book by his close and demanding reading of several key chapters. I know I owe a great debt also to many of my students, students like Kurt Heinzelman and David Frail, Bill Lucey and Kathleen Weiss, who over the years bore with me while I worried my way through so many difficult knots in the life of this complex and central poet. I want to thank too the many typists who at one point or another helped see this book through five successive drafts, through visions and revisions, people like Donna Stevens and Caroline Gouin and Nonny Burak and Wanda Bak, but especially Jeanne Los for her truly gargantuan efforts in getting the final, clean fourteen-hundred-page copy prepared. I want too to acknowledge the encouragement of Jonathan Galassi, James Raimes, Adam Horvath, and especially Peggy Tsukahira, who so skillfully saw this project through the press.

But finally I want to thank my wife, Eileen, and our three sons for putting up with my ten-year obsession with another person's life. No one can know without having tried it what a biography like this costs the human spirit in terms of what it takes and what it gives. But my wife by her sympathy and sacrifice has come awfully close. It is to her then that I have dedicated this book.

Index

.